# The Pictorial Book Of Anecdotes And Incidents Of The War Of The Rebellion, Civil, Military, Naval And Domestic

With Famous Words And Deeds Of Woman,
Sanitary And Hospital Scenes,
Prison Experiences

R. M. Devens

Alpha Editions

This Edition Published in 2021

ISBN: 9789354509889

Design and Setting By
**Alpha Editions**
www.alphaedis.com
Email – info@alphaedis.com

As per information held with us this book is in Public Domain.
This book is a reproduction of an important historical work. Alpha Editions uses the best technology to reproduce historical work in the same manner it was first published to preserve its original nature. Any marks or number seen are left intentionally to preserve its true form.

THE PICTORIAL BOOK OF

# ANECDOTES AND INCIDENTS

OF THE

# WAR OF THE REBELLION,

Civil, Military, Naval and Domestic;

EMBRACING THE MOST BRILLIANT AND REMARKABLE ANECDOTICAL EVENTS

OF THE

# GREAT CONFLICT IN THE UNITED STATES:

HEROIC, PATRIOTIC, POLITICAL, ROMANTIC, HUMOROUS AND TRAGICAL,

FROM THE TIME OF THE MEMORABLE TOAST OF

ANDREW JACKSON—"THE FEDERAL UNION; IT MUST BE PRESERVED!"

UTTERED IN 1830, IN PRESENCE OF THE ORIGINAL SECESSION CONSPIRATORS, TO THE ASSASSINATION OF PRESIDENT LINCOLN, AND THE END OF THE WAR.

WITH

FAMOUS WORDS AND DEEDS OF WOMAN,

SANITARY AND HOSPITAL SCENES, PRISON EXPERIENCES, &c.

By FRAZAR KIRKLAND,

AUTHOR OF THE "CYCLOPEDIA OF COMMERCIAL AND BUSINESS ANECDOTES," ETC.

Beautifully Illustrated with over 300 Engravings.

PUBLISHED BY SUBSCRIPTION ONLY.

HARTFORD PUBLISHING CO., HARTFORD, CONN.

NATIONAL PUBLISHING CO., PHILADELPHIA, PA., AND CINCINNATI, O.
J. A. STODDARD & CO., CHICAGO, ILL.
ZEIGLER, McCURDY & CO., ST. LOUIS, MO.

1866.

# PREFACE:

### AND

## PLAN OF THE WORK.

It is safe to assume that no family—no intelligent man, or woman, indeed,—in the sisterhood of States composing our common country, will be willing to forego the possession of some portraiture of the more lively or personal sayings and doings which crowded themselves with such rapidity into each succeeding day of the GREAT FOUR YEARS' WAR: and, to supply that want, in the most fit and attractive form, this volume has been prepared, and is now offered,—in confident assurance of its value and popular reception,—to the AMERICAN PEOPLE.

Not only would it be a difficult task to find that man or woman whose mind has not been thus enlisted to the most intense degree of interest in the great procession of events during the period named, but the attempt would be almost equally futile to discover the family circle or individual upon whom those events have not fallen, either directly or indirectly, with a shock which memory will never efface nor time obliviate. And whilst, of these latter, it may be said the number is well nigh past enumeration, who have spilled their blood, sundered the nearest and dearest ties, endured wearisome and relentless persecution, and been brought to irretrievable penury and desolation; on the other hand, multitudes there are, who now find reason to rejoice, as surviving participants in the grand and triumphant, though bloody and appalling train of events, which, under an overruling Providence, have doomed forever this and all future similar attempts to destroy a Government founded in the blood and prayers of earth's wisest and best, and upon which the hopes of the world are centred.

GREAT COMPANY OF HEROIC MARTYRS! The Nation's acclaim of gratitude hails and blesses you, and the Song of Jubilee which you have put into the hearts of the people—yea, of thrice ten millions!—shall be taken up by coming generations, and in far distant lands now awaking to political consciousness, until every voice shall sing responsive to the Universal Anthem of Manhood Vindicated, Justice Regenerated, and Liberty Enthroned.

To exhibit and commemorate the course of events thus inaugurated in crimeful ambition and sectional heresy, and culminating in a New Birth, and in a larger, stronger, and more enduring Life to the Nation thus sought to be destroyed, the historian has gathered together and woven into thoughtful chapters the documentary materials and official details of the Struggle; the poet's genius has lent its inspiration to the charm of glowing and melodious rhyme; and the pen of romance has indited its most touching story of mingled pathos and horror, of principle tested, and suffering crowned with victory!

All these have their appropriate place,—their peculiar usefulness and adaptation. Future generations, scarcely less than the present, will read with absorbing avidity the historian's volume; the poet's ringing verse will not cease to be the keynote to warm the sympathies and rouse the heart to greater love of patriotism, freedom and justice; and the more gushing sensibilities will find food in the well-wrought tale of heart-trials not simply "founded" on fact, but the delineation of gaunt fact itself, in its relation to individual cases innumerable.

PREFACE.

The character of the present work,—THE BOOK OF ANECDOTES AND INCIDENTS OF THE WAR OF THE REBELLION,—is distinctive alike from that of the sober History, the connected Narrative, and the impassioned Story. Whilst embracing all that is striking and marvellous, touching, witty and pathetic, in the scenes from which the latter have been produced, its object is not to weave together any individual theory, philosophy, or methodical detail of affairs, but to present, in attractive form and classification, a volume of the most *thrilling, racy and wonderful incidents* in the Nation's four years' experience of War, culminating in the assassination of LINCOLN, the Beloved Chief Magistrate, and in the ignominious doom of the Arch-Conspirators!

It may be remarked, in a word, that, equally to the ARMY, the NAVY, and to the CIVILIAN,—one and the same in their glorious consecration to the great cause of National Existence,—are the pages of this work devoted.

Nor is this collection confined to any particular State, Section, Corps, or Department, but embraces them all. The States loyal, and those in rebellion, are here portrayed, in the scenes, incidents and episodes, which transpired in them respectively. The Army of the Potomac, of the Cumberland, of Virginia, of the Southwest, of the James, and every other, of whatever name, is alike and copiously represented. Generals Grant, Sherman, Sheridan, McClellan, Burnside, Hooker, Thomas, Butler, Fremont,—Admirals Farragut, Foote, Porter, Rodgers, Dahlgren, Dupont, and the rest of the great host of Chief Commanders on the Land and on the Sea,—their grand armies, corps, divisions, brigades, fleets, squadrons, etc., and the brave men under their lead,—are here duly commemorated.

The stirring deeds of the Armies and Fleets *en masse*, and of their officers and men individually,—those momentous days and hours, those transcendent acts and movements, the memory of which will live in letters of blood before the eyes and burn like fire in the hearts of those who participated in them; these, sifted like gold, are here spread out in all their varied attractiveness. Thus it is, that the *rank and file*, as well as the superior officers, are made illustrious in these pages, by the valor, skill or achievement, which distinguished them,—and such instances may be said, without any strain of truth, to have characterized every regiment and crew, without exception, in the Grand Army and Navy of the Union!

A glance at the General Contents of this work will furthermore show that they comprise Anecdotes of Scenes and Events relating to several hundred battles, skirmishes and collisions, on land and sea, including every engagement of note during the prolonged Conflict; that the vessels from whose mast-head the gallant ensign waved memorably in the nation's service, have here their annals of fame and honor; and that not a single general officer, of historic fame, in either arm of the country's defence, has been lost sight of, in giving completeness to the volume as a repository of whatever is piquant, racy, marvellous, pathetic, or grand, in the different departments and fields of military operation.

The most famous sayings and doings in political circles, bearing upon Secession in its public and private aspects; camp, picket, spy, scout and battle-field adventures; the brilliant tactics, ruses, strategy, etc., which have made this war so remarkable even in the eyes of European military governments; thrilling feats of bravery among the tarpaulins and blue-jackets; "hard-tack" and mule beef legends; recruiting, conscripting and substituting oddities; female soldiers; the harrowing sights and experiences of the hospital and prison; and all the *inner-life* happenings, humors and drolleries of an army;—these cover the broad pages of this richly filled volume, and, it is believed, render it, above all other works which the war has called forth, the one in especial which, for the spare hours of home reading, every soldier, seaman, citizen and family, will desire to possess.

But, in addition to the above brief summary of contents, it may be claimed for this work that it is, almost exclusively, the one specially planned for a choice and discriminating exhibition of Woman's Career in the Scenes and Events of the War! Perhaps no other fact could give such peculiar value to these pages, or secure for them such ready acceptance on the part of the reading public.

PREFACE. 9

The separate volume, originally contemplated by the editor, to be devoted entirely to that deeply interesting record, has been merged with this, into one, thus adding to its departments a most attractive feature—rich, unique, and surpassing romance in its *resume* of startling facts and strange developments of the Perils, Valor, Amours and Devotedness specially pertaining to that sex, the wheat being carefully sifted from the chaff. The wonderful character of Woman's Career, North and South, during a four years' fratricidal war which reached all classes and penetrated every element and interest of society, and in which she herself was summoned to bear such variety and burden of experience, has no counterpart whatsoever in the history of mankind; a fact which, indeed, could not have been otherwise, when it is considered that never before, in the ages of the world, was such a contest waged, and that at no previous period was woman's social and intellectual equality with the other sex so generally admitted, or her influence so powerful and wide-spread,—thus necessarily bringing her, by a coincidence truly memorable, in active identity with public affairs, in the greatest of human crises!

The part which the sex enacted, under these unparalleled circumstances, is here most amply illustrated,—excluding, of course, much that was of inferior interest, and the record will at least be adjudged a Brilliant, Romantic and Inviting one, on glancing at the Index of subjects comprised in this volume, those relating to Woman being there printed in *Italics*.

Not only in respect to the specialty just remarked upon, but equally with reference to all the other topical divisions of the volume, it may be asserted that no trouble, labor, travel, nor consideration of time or cost, has been allowed to stand in the way of their most complete preparation. Familiar intercourse with officials and privates, attendance at the Departments in Washington, personal observation and correspondence, all the official documents, the teeming issues of the newspaper press, in their vast and prolific range,—of all these, the editor has painstakingly and freely availed himself, during the last five years, in order to produce a work, if not absolutely perfect, yet certainly not excelled, in the quality of readableness, by any Book of the War. Of the many thousand anecdotes which have passed under his inspection, in the immense accumulation of materials named,—common to all and special to none,—the contents of this volume comprise those which were found to have called forth the greatest interest and admiration on the part of the public, and which were thought to most aptly exhibit the lights and shades of the war. This was the aim and object kept in view.

A conscientious care was justly called for, and duly exercised, in excluding those productions concerning the war, to which the pens that gave them birth affixed a retaining claim; and a faithful comparison, in that respect, of what is here brought together, with the contents of other collections, is freely invited. It was nevertheless found inherently impossible, in a vast number of instances, (out of more than seven thousand memorabilia in hand,) owing to the rapid and wide-spread publication in so many issues of the press, interchangeably, of the same anecdotes or performances, to trace out and authenticate their paternity or first source;—a difficulty still further increased by the citation, in frequent cases, of different authorities or sources for the same narration, incident, poem, etc., etc. This lack and confusion of identity, so common, and perhaps unavoidable, in the making up of anecdotical columns, selections of miscellany, poetry, and extracts from current books, for the press, did not, however, interpose any barrier to their use in a work like this. But if, arising from this circumstance, anything has thus unconsciously been appropriated for these pages which encroaches upon any exclusive and verified proprietorship, or upon any repository of avowed and genuine originality, such matter will as readily and cheerfully be eliminated from the text as it was there given a place.

With reference to those passages which involve the heated language of personal colloquy or combat, it seemed not always possible, however much to be desired, to divest them of all their excited, and even irreverent expletives, and at the same time preserve the *animus* of the occurrence as it actually transpired. Nor, indeed, is it a question in ethics, readily to be answered in the affirmative, whether the recital of those ghastly scenes of blood and death, which necessarily constitute the substance of every war and of all war literature, and which are read of with such avidity, can be considered any more congenial to a correct taste and moral sensibility, than the merely verbal attestations, however imprecatory, by which they were accompanied.

As showing the extent and variety of matter contained in this volume, the simple statement will suffice, that the accompanying list of Battles, Engagements, Collisions, etc., etc., consulted in the preparation of these anecdotes, numbers several thousand; —of Generals and Naval Commanders, and of Public Vessels, many hundred;—each list reflecting a multitude of pleasing, spicy, unique, and startling events. Besides these, there is presented a classified outline of the topical contents or special subjects pertaining to each of the Eight Parts, and a most copious Index to the leading anecdotes is placed at the close.

Of the mechanical appearance of this book, the names, enterprise and liberality, of the eminent Publishers, will at once be accepted as vouchers that nothing in the typographical and illustrative art has been omitted by them, to gratify the eye, and to render the publication one in every way deserving universal patronage.

The numerous ILLUSTRATIVE ENGRAVINGS, executed in the highest style of beauty and without regard to cost, by the most skillful artists in the country, which are here presented, constitute a feature of embellishment in no other instance attempted in books of this kind. They are of themselves alone worth the full price of the volume.

# LIST OF ILLUSTRATIONS.

## PLATES, PORTRAITS, AND DESCRIPTIVE EMBELLISHMENTS.

Designed and Engraved Expressly for this Work, by N. Orr & Co., New York.

|  |  | PAGE. |
|---|---|---|
| 1. | LIEUT.-GEN. GRANT AND HIS BRAVE SOLDIERS, | FRONTISPIECE. |
| 2. | EMBLEMATIC TITLE-PAGE,—BATTLE AND CORPS' FLAGS,—PRINTED IN COLORS, | 3 |
| 3. | DEDICATORY VIGNETTE, | 10 |
| 4. | ILLUSTRATIVE PLATE FOR PART I.—THE AMERICAN FLAG TRIUMPHANT! | 21 |
| 5. | ILLUMINATED INITIAL LETTER, | 23 |
| 6. | PORTRAIT OF JOHN C. CALHOUN, | 24 |
| 7. | AFRAID OF THE GIRL'S EYE, | 26 |
| 8. | ACCORDING TO THEIR SYMPATHIES, | 27 |
| 9. | VINDICATION OF THE FLAG ABROAD, | 30 |
| 10. | PORTRAIT OF EDWIN M. STANTON, | 34 |
| 11. | PORTRAIT OF JOSEPH HOLT, | 35 |
| 12. | PORTRAIT OF ABRAHAM LINCOLN, | 38 |
| 13. | HOMAGE TO THE FLAG BY AN EAGLE, | 39 |
| 14. | FRONT-DOOR CONFABULATIONS, | 43 |
| 15. | PORTRAIT OF FERNANDO WOOD, | 47 |
| 16. | PORTRAIT OF C. L. VALLANDIGHAM, | 48 |
| 17. | CAROLINA UNIONIST, | 53 |
| 18. | PORTRAIT OF STEPHEN A. DOUGLAS, | 57 |
| 19. | PORTRAIT OF WILLIAM H SEWARD, | 58 |
| 20. | AND THE BROTHER SHALL DELIVER UP THE BROTHER TO DEATH, | 59 |
| 21. | HARD SHELL BRETHREN, | 65 |
| 22. | PORTRAIT OF GEN. ROBERT ANDERSON, | 68 |
| 23. | PORTRAIT OF LIEUT.-GEN. WINFIELD SCOTT, | 72 |
| 24. | MINUTE MEN OF MASSACHUSETTS, | 73 |
| 25. | PORTRAIT OF COL. R. BARNWELL RHETT, | 74 |
| 26. | PORTRAIT OF JOHN TYLER, | 76 |
| 27. | PORTRAIT OF PRESTON S. BROOKS, | 78 |
| 28. | THE BOY FATHER TO THE MAN, | 80 |
| 29. | PRESIDENTIAL FAVOR FOR EVERYBODY, | 86 |
| 30. | PORTRAIT OF HOWELL COBB, | 89 |
| 31. | WHICH SIDE? | 92 |
| 32. | PORTRAIT OF MRS. LINCOLN, | 93 |
| 33. | ROMANTIC ADVENTURE, | 98 |
| 34. | PORTRAIT OF EDMUND RUFFIN, | 102 |
| 35. | REFUSING TO VOLUNTEER, | 106 |
| 36. | PORTRAIT OF ANDREW JACKSON, | 110 |
| 37. | SWEAR HIM, &c., | 114 |
| 38. | WITNESSING AND DYING FOR THE TRUTH, | 120 |
| 39. | PORTRAIT OF EDWARD EVERETT, | 121 |
| 40. | PORTRAIT OF J. C. BRECKINRIDGE, | 125 |
| 41. | STATING THE EXACT ALTERNATIVE, | 126 |
| 42. | PORTRAIT OF MRS. STEPHEN A. DOUGLAS, | 127 |
| 43. | PORTRAIT OF CHARLES J. FAULKNER, | 130 |

## LIST OF ILLUSTRATIONS.

|  |  | PAGE |
|---|---|---|
| 44. | Interceding for her Father, | 134 |
| 45. | God's Flag, | 140 |
| 46. | Portrait of R. M. T. Hunter, | 141 |
| 47. | Portrait of Gen. Philip Sheridan, | 143 |
| 48. | Length of the War, | 144 |
| 49. | Accommodating Himself to Circumstances, | 152 |
| 50. | ILLUSTRATIVE PLATE FOR PART II.—Ho! for the War, | 155 |
| 51. | Illuminated Initial Letter, | 157 |
| 52. | How does he grow 'em? | 158 |
| 53. | Love and Patriotism, | 162 |
| 54. | Ira's Wife and his Breeches, | 165 |
| 55. | Fate of a Coward, | 168 |
| 56. | Fannnie and Nellie, | 170 |
| 57. | Career of Frank Henderson, | 173 |
| 58. | Portrait of Lieut.-Gen. Ulysses S. Grant, | 177 |
| 59. | Hopeful Tackett, | 178 |
| 60. | Portrait of John Letcher, | 182 |
| 61. | Effect of Crinoline, | 182 |
| 62. | Portrait of "Stonewall" Jackson, | 183 |
| 63. | Portrait of Col. Billy Wilson, | 184 |
| 64. | Quite the Youngest Recruit, | 185 |
| 65. | Drafting Scene, | 186 |
| 66. | Equal to the Emergency, | 193 |
| 67. | Fightin' ober a Bone, | 195 |
| 68. | Bounty Jumper Captured by a Dog, | 200 |
| 69. | Tender in Years, but Patriotic, | 207 |
| 70. | Snaked Away and Drummed In, | 213 |
| 71. | Tenderness of the President, | 217 |
| 72. | ILLUSTRATIVE PLATE FOR PART III.—Bombardment of Fort Sumter, | 219 |
| 73. | Illuminated Initial Letter, | 221 |
| 74. | Rallying around the Flag, | 222 |
| 75. | Portrait of Gen. Geo. H. Thomas, | 222 |
| 76. | Young America, | 228 |
| 77. | Is the Colonel at Home? | 230 |
| 78. | War and Navy Buildings, | 232 |
| 79. | Old Capitol Prison, Washington, | 235 |
| 80. | California Joe, | 236 |
| 81. | Portrait of Gen. Felix K. Zollicoffer, | 238 |
| 82. | Portrait of Gen. John C. Fremont, | 240 |
| 83. | Going in Quest of Satisfaction, | 242 |
| 84. | Portrait of Gen. Humphrey Marshall, | 245 |
| 85. | General Meade's Head-quarters, | 246 |
| 86. | Well Done for a Youth, | 247 |
| 87. | Portrait of Gen. Judson Kilpatrick, | 248 |
| 88. | Good Samaritan, | 250 |
| 89. | Portrait of Gen. Wm. W Averill, | 252 |
| 90. | Too Big Not to be a Soldier, | 258 |
| 91. | Portrait of Judah P. Benjamin, | 259 |
| 92. | Lieut. Davis's Task, | 263 |
| 93. | Portrait of Major Zagonyi, | 267 |
| 94. | Mrs. Brownell, the Heroine, | 268 |
| 95. | Portrait of Gen. Pope, | 270 |
| 96. | Portrait of Gen. Saxton, | 272 |

## LIST OF ILLUSTRATIONS. 13

|   |   | PAGE. |
|---|---|---|
| 97. | Courtesies of Picket Life, | 273 |
| 98. | Portrait of Gen. A. Sidney Johnston, | 276 |
| 99. | Won his Wager, | 279 |
| 100. | Portrait of Gen. Longstreet, | 284 |
| 101. | Uncomfortably Warm Place, | 286 |
| 102. | Head-quarters of Lee, Gettysburg, | 287 |
| 103. | Preferred to Die in the Field, | 292 |
| 104. | Characteristic Pluck, | 296 |
| 105. | Ragged Texans, | 302 |
| 106. | Remember Fort Pillow, | 305 |
| 107. | Use for a Shell, | 306 |
| 108. | Portrait of Gen. Jeff. Thompson, | 307 |
| 109. | Fate of Two Germans, | 310 |
| 110. | Owning Up, | 314 |
| 111. | Portrait of Gen. Philip Kearny, | 318 |
| 112. | Negro Rifleman, | 319 |
| 113. | Portrait of Gen. E. D. Baker, | 320 |
| 114. | Fairfax Court House, | 320 |
| 115. | Portrait of Col. Ellsworth, | 321 |
| 116. | Bull Run Battlefield, | 323 |
| 117. | Neutral Cornfield, | 325 |
| 118. | Portrait of Gen. J. E. Johnston, | 326 |
| 119. | Climbing the Mountains, | 328 |
| 120. | Union Bushwhackers and Rebel Cavalry, | 329 |
| 121. | Portrait of Maj.-Gen. McPherson, | 330 |
| 122. | Portrait of Gen. Barksdale, | 332 |
| 123. | Portrait of Gen. David Hunter, | 334 |
| 124. | Union and Rebel Pickets, | 335 |
| 125. | Portrait of Gen. A. E. Burnside, | 336 |
| 126. | Soldiers Captured by a Boy, | 337 |
| 127. | Portrait of Albert Pike, | 337 |
| 128. | Intrepid Conduct, | 338 |
| 129. | Bob, the Spunky Drummer Boy, | 339 |
| 130. | Portrait of Gen. H. W. Slocum, | 341 |
| 131. | Portrait of Gov. H. A. Wise, | 342 |
| 132. | Capt. Tilden's Lucky Escape, | 342 |
| 133. | As Good as a Captured Gun, | 343 |
| 134. | Portrait of Gen. J. C. Pemberton, | 344 |
| 135. | Portrait of Gen. L. Polk, | 345 |
| 136. | Ahead of his Troops, | 346 |
| 137. | Surrender of Gen. Lee, | 347 |
| 138. | Portrait of Gen. G. A. Custer, | 348 |
| 139. | ILLUSTRATIVE PLATE FOR PART IV.,—Naval Scenes and Exploits, | 350 |
| 140. | Illuminated Initial Letter, | 351 |
| 141. | Raking a Traitor, | 352 |
| 142. | Naval Peacemaker, | 353 |
| 143. | Portrait of Lieut. Worden, | 355 |
| 144. | "Charge! Chester, Charge!" | 356 |
| 145. | Portrait of Admiral Dupont, | 357 |
| 146. | Half-hour's Visit at Island No. 10, | 358 |
| 147. | Light-House at Fort Morgan, | 361 |
| 148. | Portrait of Admiral Porter, | 361 |
| 149. | Before Vicksburg, | 362 |

# LIST OF ILLUSTRATIONS.

| | | PAGE |
|---|---|---|
| 150. | Pleasant Hoax all Round, | 363 |
| 151. | Wreck of the Monitor, | 364 |
| 152. | Portrait of Capt. J. A. Winslow, | 365 |
| 153. | Portrait of Admiral A. H. Foote, | 367 |
| 154. | Blue-Jacket on his Mule, | 368 |
| 155. | Lieut. Cushing's Great Exploit, | 371 |
| 156. | Another Cassabianca, | 374 |
| 157. | Pictorial Humors of the War, | 375 |
| 158. | Portrait of Secretary Welles, | 376 |
| 159. | Portrait of Com. Bailey, | 376 |
| 160. | Portrait of Capt. Semmes, | 379 |
| 161. | Buchanan's Sword Yielded, | 380 |
| 162. | River Devils for Carrying on War, | 383 |
| 163. | The Merrimac, | 387 |
| 164. | Gunboat Fight at Fort Pillow, | 389 |
| 165. | Fleet of Gunboats in the James River, | 390 |
| 166. | Farragut lashed to the Mast, | 391 |
| 167. | Gunboat Kansas, | 394 |
| 168. | Willing to part with his other Leg, | 397 |
| 169. | ILLUSTRATIVE PLATE FOR PART V.,—Varieties of the War, | 399 |
| 170. | Illuminated Initial Letter, | 401 |
| 171. | "Mark Time," | 402 |
| 172. | Portrait of Gen. Sherman, | 402 |
| 173. | Sentry's Encounter with a Regular, | 403 |
| 174. | Halting Effect of the Ardent, | 404 |
| 175. | Portrait of Secretary Chase, | 405 |
| 176. | Col. Owen's Squad Drill, | 407 |
| 177. | Portrait of Gen. McClellan, | 410 |
| 178. | Portrait of Gen. Rosecrans, | 411 |
| 179. | Portrait of Gen. J. C. Davis, | 413 |
| 180. | Encounter between Nelson and Davis, | 414 |
| 181. | Portrait of Gen. Nelson, | 414 |
| 182. | Portrait of Gen. McCook, | 417 |
| 183. | Col. Gazley doing Guard Duty, | 418 |
| 184. | Portrait of J. C. Ely, | 424 |
| 185. | Caught in his own Trap, | 424 |
| 186. | Portrait of Gen. Hardee, | 427 |
| 187. | Gen. Butler's Head-quarters, | 429 |
| 188. | Whar's dat Nigger, | 430 |
| 189. | Belligerent Work, | 433 |
| 190. | Military Etiquette, | 435 |
| 191. | Orders on the Battlefield, | 439 |
| 192. | Portrait of Gen. N. P. Banks, | 440 |
| 193. | ILLUSTRATED PLATE FOR PART VI.,—Colored Soldiers, | 441 |
| 194. | Illuminated Initial Letter, | 443 |
| 195. | Swamp Angel, | 444 |
| 196. | Sanitary Commission, | 444 |
| 197. | Wicked Joke upon a Postmaster, | 446 |
| 198. | Relay House | 447 |
| 199. | Army Kitchen, | 448 |
| 200. | Swearing in a Cook, | 448 |
| 201. | Milking the Cow, | 451 |
| 202. | Sergeant Davis's Tender Beef, | 453 |

## LIST OF ILLUSTRATIONS.                                                    15

|     |                                                                    | PAGE |
|-----|--------------------------------------------------------------------|------|
| 203.| PORTRAIT OF GEN. TERRY,                                            | 456  |
| 204.| PORTRAIT OF GEN. HALLECK,                                          | 457  |
| 205.| PORTRAIT OF GEN. WADSWORTH,                                        | 458  |
| 206.| PEDDLER AND GEN. NELSON,                                           | 459  |
| 207.| PUMPKIN PIE FOR WICKFORD,                                          | 463  |
| 208.| FRESH PORK FOR THE EIGHTH ILLINOIS,                                | 466  |
| 209.| AFFECTING APPEAL TO A COMMISSARY,                                  | 473  |
| 210.| CONFERENCE OF NEWSPAPER CORRESPONDENTS,                            | 476  |
| 211.| PORTRAIT OF GEN. HOOKER,                                           | 477  |
| 212.| TELEGRAPH STATION,                                                 | 477  |
| 213.| LIEUT. ———'S PERFUMED BREATH,                                      | 478  |
| 214.| PROMPT SETTLEMENT OF A CLAIM,                                      | 482  |
| 215.| FIELD CARRIAGES DISPENSED WITH,                                    | 485  |
| 216.| QUESTION IN INFANTRY PRACTICE,                                     | 488  |
| 217.| PORTRAIT OF JOHN H. MORGAN,                                        | 489  |
| 218.| NO BUSINESS WID A GUN,                                             | 490  |
| 219.| PORTRAIT OF GEN. BEAUREGARD,                                       | 491  |
| 220.| WRITING HOME,                                                      | 495  |
| 221.| SIGNALLING,                                                        | 500  |
| 222.| NELLIE, THE BRAVE BATTLE HORSE,                                    | 501  |
| 223.| INDIAN MOUND, CHATTANOOGA,                                         | 503  |
| 224.| FLIGHT FROM THE SHENANDOAH,                                        | 506  |
| 225.| AUNT CHARLOTTE, THE OLD COOK,                                      | 507  |
| 226.| BRIDGE ACROSS PLATTE CREEK,                                        | 509  |
| 227.| INFLATING THE PONTOON,                                             | 510  |
| 228.| FOUR LEGGED MESSENGER PROVED DISLOYAL,                             | 511  |
| 229.| SADDLING TO SUIT THE ROUTE,                                        | 513  |
| 230.| ILLUSTRATIVE PLATE FOR PART VII.,—CHRISTIAN AND SANITARY COMMISSIONS, | 516 |
| 231.| ILLUMINATED INITIAL LETTER,                                        | 517  |
| 232.| PORTRAIT OF MISS BROWNLOW,                                         | 517  |
| 233.| BEAUTIFUL, BUT DEAD,                                               | 518  |
| 234.| THAT IS MY BROTHER,                                                | 519  |
| 235.| TRACTS VERSUS POUND CAKE,                                          | 522  |
| 236.| PORTRAIT OF ALEX. H. STEPHENS,                                     | 523  |
| 237.| ELIZABETH COMSTOCK WITH DYING SOLDIERS,                            | 526  |
| 238.| DALLIANCE AND TREACHERY,                                           | 532  |
| 239.| PORTRAIT OF GOV. MORGAN, N. Y.,                                    | 534  |
| 240.| AMOURS AND FANCIES OF THE CAMP,                                    | 536  |
| 241.| SWEET SEVENTEEN OVERHAULING SECESSIONISTS,                         | 540  |
| 242.| CASTLE THUNDER,                                                    | 541  |
| 243.| EMBALMING-BUILDING BEFORE RICHMOND,                                | 544  |
| 244.| COURT HOUSE AND HOSPITAL,                                          | 546  |
| 245.| SERGEANT'S PROPHECY FULFILLED,                                     | 547  |
| 246.| INCIDENT IN THE BATTLE OF FREDERICKSBURG,                          | 547  |
| 247.| PORTRAIT OF PAULINE CUSHMAN,                                       | 549  |
| 248.| LIBBY PRISON,                                                      | 551  |
| 249.| LOYALTY IN VIRGINIA,                                               | 552  |
| 250.| PORTRAIT OF MRS. GEN. GRANT,                                       | 554  |
| 251.| PORTRAIT OF GEN. TILGHMAN,                                         | 557  |
| 252.| GEN. LANDER AND HIS BIBLE,                                         | 558  |
| 253.| MISTOOK THE GUNS,                                                  | 561  |
| 254.| PORTRAIT OF GEN. R. E. LEE,                                        | 562  |
| 255.| BODIES LAID OUT,                                                   | 563  |

16                        LIST OF ILLUSTRATIONS.

|  |  | PAGE. |
|---|---|---|
| 256. | Head-Quarters of Gen. Burnside, | 565 |
| 257. | Monument at Stone River, | 568 |
| 258. | Proof against Federal Gallantry, | 569 |
| 259. | Old Hannah, | 574 |
| 260. | Familiar Soldier Scenes, (Housekeeping,) | 575 |
| 261. | Burns, the Gettysburg Hero, | 577 |
| 262. | Mose Bryan, | 578 |
| 263. | Soldiers' Graves, | 579 |
| 264. | Military Prison at Salisbury, | 581 |
| 265. | Miss Lee and the Yankee Corporal, | 582 |
| 266. | Portrait of Gen. Lyon, | 586 |
| 267. | Watch kept by a Dog, | 587 |
| 268. | Sherman's Absence of Mind, | 590 |
| 269. | Portrait of Gen. Ben. McCulloch, | 590 |
| 270. | Jerry and Gen. Thomas' Spy Glass, | 591 |
| 271. | Portrait of Gen. Meade, | 594 |
| 272. | Carving his own Head-board, | 595 |
| 273. | Wickedness of Woman, | 597 |
| 274. | Portrait of Bell Boyd, | 599 |
| 275. | Old Ladies Conversing about Gen. Bragg, | 605 |
| 276. | Gen. Butler as a Young Lawyer, | 607 |
| 277. | Railroad Depot, Atlanta, Ga., | 608 |
| 278. | Alas, Poor Soldier! | 609 |
| 279. | Portrait of Gov. Andrew, Mass., | 611 |
| 280. | Enjoying Negro Hospitality, | 613 |
| 281. | Frankie Bragg, | 614 |
| 282. | A Young Woman Shoots a Guerrilla, | 617 |
| 283. | Major B. en route with the Widow, | 624 |
| 284. | Portrait of Gov. Curtin, Pa., | 628 |
| 285. | A Soldier Mustered Out, | 629 |
| 286. | Portrait of Gen. Howard, | 630 |
| 287. | ILLUSTRATIVE PLATE FOR PART VIII.—Early Home and End of Pres. Lincoln, | 632 |
| 288. | Illuminated Initial Letter, | 633 |
| 289. | Portrait of Chas. Sumner, | 636 |
| 290. | Death of the Assassin, | 639 |
| 291. | Portrait of Secretary Fessenden, | 640 |
| 292. | Patience Tried Too Far, | 641 |
| 293. | Portrait of Jeff. Davis, | 642 |
| 294. | Portrait of President Johnson, | 643 |
| 295. | Andrew Johnson's Tailor Shop, | 646 |
| 296. | Portrait of Mrs. Jeff. Davis, | 649 |
| 297. | Jeff.'s Capture by the Yanks, | 650 |
| 298. | Familiar Talk with Mr. Lincoln, | 652 |
| 299. | Jeff. and the Blacksmith, | 656 |
| 300. | Portrait of Geo. N. Sanders, | 657 |
| 301. | Grand Finale—"To whom it may Concern!" | 660 |

# GENERAL CONTENTS.

|  | PAGE. |
|---|---|
| PREFACE, AND PLAN OF THE WORK, | 7 |
| LIST OF PLATES, PORTRAITS, AND DESCRIPTIVE EMBELLISHMENTS, | 11 |

## PART FIRST.

PATRIOTIC, POLITICAL, CIVIL, JUDICIAL, ADMINISTRATIVE, ETC.

Pages 23–154.

MEMORABLE ANNALS AND REMINISCENCES OF MEN AND MEASURES IDENTIFIED WITH THE GREAT STRUGGLE; HEROIC DEVOTION TO THE STAR-SPANGLED BANNER,—VALOROUS DEFENCE OF AND DYING BLESSINGS UPON IT; DARK AND TROUBLOUS EXPERIENCES OF UNIONISTS AND CONSPIRATORS; TESTS AND TRIALS OF LOYALTY, NORTH AND SOUTH; FAMOUS LEGAL AND JUDICIAL INCIDENTS; PECULIAR INSTANCES OF ADMINISTERING AND TAKING THE OATH; ALLEGIANCE UNDER STRESS OF CIRCUMSTANCES; DISPOSAL OF KNOTTY CASES; LOGIC AND LESSONS FOR SECESSIONISTS; AMUSING COLLOQUIES; FLASHES OF RHETORIC; OFFICIAL GRAVITIES, JOKES, RAILLERY, BLUNDERS, RETORTS, BURLESQUES, WITTICISMS; &c., &c.

## PART SECOND.

VOLUNTEERING, DRAFTING, COMMUTING, SUBSTITUTING, DESERTING, ETC.

Pages 157–218.

NOBLE INSTANCES OF RALLYING TO THE RANKS, AND OF ENLISTMENT AMONG THE AGED AND YOUNG; HEARINGS, LUDICROUS AND PERPLEXING, BEFORE THE COMMISSIONERS; RAW RECRUITS AND ECCENTRIC CHARACTERS; APPLICANTS FOR EXEMPTION; RUSES AND QUIBBLES TO ESCAPE DUTY—STRANGE PHENOMENA OF NATIVITY, AGE AND INFIRMITIES; BEWILDERED SURGEONS; LUCKLESS CONSCRIPTS; RARE BROKERAGE AND BOUNTY DEALINGS; FLUSH PURSES; HARDSHIPS AND MISERIES; SIDE-SHAKING GAIETIES, JESTS, PUNS; &c., &c.

CONTENTS.

## PART THIRD.

GREAT CONFLICTS AND ACHIEVEMENTS OF THE ARMY, AND ILLUSTRIOUS EXAMPLES OF INDIVIDUAL HEROISM IN THE RANK AND FILE, ETC.

Pages 221–348.

BRILLIANT BATTLE SCENES; MILITARY CHARACTERISTICS OF THE LEADING GENERALS,—THEIR APPEARANCE, CONVERSATIONS, ORDERS, TACTICS AND BRAVERY, WHEN CONFRONTING THE ENEMY; MARTYRS ON THE GORY FIELD; UNPARALLELED FORTITUDE AND ENDURANCE; COOLNESS AND INTREPIDITY IN DANGER; BOLD MOVEMENTS OF ARTILLERY, CAVALRY, AND INFANTRY; SPLENDID CHARGES; DESPERATE HAND-TO-HAND ENCOUNTERS; EXTRAORDINARY SHARPSHOOTING; MEMORIALS OF YOUTHFUL COURAGE; DEALINGS WITH BUSHWHACKERS AND GUERRILLAS; CELEBRITIES AND ADVENTURES OF CAMP, PICKET, SPY, SCOUT AND STAFF; PERIL, TERROR, PANIC, AND DISASTER; MIRTH-PROVOKING SIGHTS, SCENES, WHIMS, SQUIBS, ODDITIES; &c., &c.

## PART FOURTH.

NAVAL AND COMMERCIAL; SQUADRON, FLEET, STEAMER, GUNBOAT, TRANSPORT AND PRIVATEER; THEIR CRUISES, OFFICERS, PERFORMANCES, ETC.

Pages 351–398.

TERRIBLE ENGAGEMENTS; SUFFERING AND DEATH FOR THE FLAG; HAVOC AND HORRORS OF MODERN BOMBARDMENT; BLOCKADE EXPLOITS; FEATS OF SEAMANSHIP; FURIOUS PERSONAL COMBATS; LONG AND EXCITING CHASES; ESCAPES, RESCUES, PRIZES; THRILLING CATASTROPHES AND TRAGEDIES, CAPTURES, SINKINGS AND SURRENDERS; AWKWARD LANDSMEN, RAW MARINES, JOLLY VETERANS, AND TREACHEROUS PILOTS; JACK AFLOAT AND ASHORE; FREAKS, DROLLERIES, HAPS AND MISHAPS, AMONG THE LOYAL TARPAULINS AND BLUE JACKETS; &c., &c.

## PART FIFTH.

MILITARY ORGANIZATION AND EQUIPMENT, DISCIPLINE AND DRILL, PARADE, REVEILLE, REVIEWS, ORDNANCE, PAROLES, PASSES, FURLOUGHS, COUNTERSIGNS, FUGITIVE HUNTS, ETC.

Pages 401–440.

MUSTERING-IN; SPLENDID SPECIMENS OF SOLDIERLY MOVEMENT; DEXTEROUS HANDLING OF ARMS; EVOLUTIONS, COMICAL AND PIQUANT; QUEER DILEMMAS; UNCOUTH SUBJECTS AND VERDANT VICTIMS, WHITE AND BLACK; GROTESQUE PERFORMANCES; NOVEL TERMS AND PHRASEOLOGY; BIVOUAC SIGHTS; TASKS AND PLEASANTRIES; MISTAKES, JOCULARITIES, FACETIÆ; &c., &c.

## PART SIXTH.

COMMISSARY AND RATIONS, FINANCE AND CURRENCY, THE PRESS, THE MAILS, THE TELEGRAPH, ETC.

Pages 443-514.

UNCLE SAM'S SUPPLIES; SUBSISTENCE UNDER DIFFICULTIES; 'HARD-TACK' AND MULE BEEF LEGENDS; FORAGING RAIDS; DISLOYAL FOWLS AND CONTRABAND DAINTIES; IMPROMPTU CONFISCATIONS IN A SMALL WAY; DIALOGUES WITH THE QUARTERMASTER; SHAMEFUL IMPOSITIONS; SCRIP AND CURRENCY VARIETIES; UNIQUE BANKING OPERATIONS; COLLECTION EXCURSIONS AT THE SOUTH, CHIVALRIC REPUDIATION; TRICKS, ARTIFICE, AND ACCOMPLISHMENTS OF EDITORS, REPORTERS AND CORRESPONDENTS; INCIDENTS OF THE MAIL; TELEGRAPHIC ODDS AND ENDS, MISCELLANIES, NOVELTIES, FINESSE; &c., &c.


## PART SEVENTH.

DOMESTIC, MORAL, WOMANLY, SANITARY, AFFECTIONAL, MATRIMONIAL, ROMANTIC, ETC.

Pages 517-630.

EXHIBITION OF PERSONAL TRAITS,—BENEVOLENCE, GENEROSITY, COURTESY, MAGNANIMITY, &c.; ILLUSTRATIONS OF THE HOME AFFECTIONS AND HOUSEHOLD ATTACHMENTS; FEMALE SOLDIERS; REGIMENTAL PETS; MARRIAGES IN CAMP; NOBLE WORDS AND DEEDS OF LOYAL WOMEN; RANCOR AND CRIMINALITIES OF FEMALE SECESSIONISTS; HOSPITAL PATIENTS; MINISTRATIONS TO THE SICK AND WOUNDED; BOGUS INVALIDS; PARTINGS, REUNIONS, BEREAVEMENTS, AND BURIALS; TOUCHING DEATH-BED SCENES,—LAST WORDS, MEMENTOES, KEEPSAKES AND SOUVENIRS; PRISON CONTACTS, COMPANIONS, AND HORRORS; SAYINGS AND DOINGS OF CHAPLAINS; GENIALITIES, CARRICATURES, PATHOS, FANCIES AND REALITIES; &c., &c.


## PART EIGHTH.

FINAL SCENES AND EVENTS IN THE GREAT DRAMA; ASSASSINATION OF PRESIDENT LINCOLN; IGNOMINIOUS DOOM OF JEFFERSON DAVIS, ETC.

Pages 633-660.

THE MOST STRIKING OCCURRENCES RELATING TO THE ASSASSINATION CONSPIRACY, THE TRAGEDY, THE ACTORS AND THEIR DOOM; REMARKABLE PASSAGES AND CONVERSATIONS IN MR. LINCOLN'S PRESIDENTIAL LIFE,—MEMORIAL INCIDENTS OF HIS DEATH AND OF A NATION'S MOURNING; CAPTURE AND CUSTODY OF JEFFERSON DAVIS,—HIS SAYINGS AND DOINGS, PERSONAL BEARING AMONG HIS CAPTORS, AND IGNOMINIOUS FATE; INTERESTING REMINISCENCES IN THE CAREER OF ANDREW JOHNSON; &c., &c.

## CONTENTS.

| | Page. |
|---|---|
| LIST OF BATTLES, ENGAGEMENTS, COLLISIONS, CAPTURES, SURRENDERS, SURPRISES, ETC., ON LAND AND SEA, DURING THE REBELLION,—CONSULTED IN THE PREPARATION OF THESE ANECDOTES, | 661 |
| LIST OF THE PUBLIC VESSELS EMPLOYED IN THE WAR, AND CONSULTED IN THE PREPARATION OF THESE ANECDOTES, | 681 |
| NAMES OF THE GENERALS AND CHIEF NAVAL OFFICERS, UNDER WHOSE COMMAND, OR IN WHOSE DEPARTMENTS, THE ANECDOTICAL INCIDENTS, ETC., HERE GIVEN OCCURRED, | 685 |
| INDEX TO THE LEADING ANECDOTES, | 691 |

PART I.—AMERICAN EAGLE TRIUMPHANT.

# PART FIRST.

## ANECDOTES OF THE REBELLION—PATRIOTIC, POLITICAL, CIVIL, JUDICIAL, ADMINISTRATIVE, ETC.

MEMORABLE ANNALS AND REMINISCENCES OF MEN AND MEASURES IDENTIFIED WITH THE GREAT STRUGGLE; HEROIC DEVOTION TO THE STAR-SPANGLED BANNER—VALOROUS DEFENCE OF AND DYING BLESSINGS UPON IT; DARK AND TROUBLOUS EXPERIENCES OF UNIONISTS AND CONSPIRATORS; TESTS AND TRIALS OF LOYALTY, NORTH AND SOUTH; FAMOUS LEGAL AND JUDICIAL INCIDENTS; PECULIAR INSTANCES OF ADMINISTERING AND TAKING THE OATH; ALLEGIANCE UNDER STRESS OF CIRCUMSTANCES; DISPOSAL OF KNOTTY CASES; LOGIC AND LESSONS FOR SECESSIONISTS; AMUSING COLLOQUIES; FLASHES OF RHETORIC; OFFICIAL GRAVITIES, JOKES, RAILLERY, PERPLEXITIES, BLUNDERS, RETORTS; BURLESQUES, WITTICISMS, &c., &c.

"Once to every man and nation, comes the moment to decide
In the strife of TRUTH with FALSEHOOD, for the good or evil side."
"Keep step with the music of UNION,
The music our ancestors sung,
When states, like a jubilant chorus,
To beautiful sisterhood sprung."

Can either of you to-day name one single act of wrong, deliberately and purposely done by the government at Washington, of which the South has a right to complain? I challenge an answer.—ALEXANDER H. STEPHENS, *before the Georgia Secessionists' Convention.*

### Andrew Jackson's Famous Union Toast.

On the 13th of April, 1830, there was a remarkable dinner party in the national metropolis. It was the birthday of Thomas Jefferson, and those who attended the party did so avowedly for the purpose of honoring the memory of the author of the DECLARATION OF INDEPENDENCE. Such was the tenor of the invitation. Andrew Jackson, the President of the United States, was there. So was John C. Calhoun, the Vice President. Three of the cabinet ministers, namely, Van Buren, Eaton, and Branch were there; and members of Congress and citizens not a few.

It soon became manifest to the more sagacious ones that this dinner party and the day were to be made the occasion for inaugurating the new doctrine of nullification, and to fix the paternity of it on Mr. Jefferson, the great Apostle of Democracy in America. Many gentlemen present, perceiving the drift of the whole performance, withdrew in disgust before summoned to the table; but the sturdy old President, perfectly informed, remained.

When the dinner was over and the cloth removed, a call was made for the regular toasts. These were twenty-four in number, eighteen of which, it is alleged, were written by Mr. Calhoun. These, in multifarious forms, shadowed forth, now dimly, now clearly, the new doctrine. They were all received and honored in various degrees, when volunteer toasts were announced as in order.

The President was of course first called

upon for a sentiment. His tall form rose majestically, and with that sternness appropriate to the peculiar occasion, he cast that appalling bomb-shell of words into the camp of conspirators, which will forever be a theme for the commendation of the patriot and the historian—"THE FEDERAL UNION: IT MUST BE PRESERVED!" He was followed by the Vice President, who

J. C. Calhoun.

gave as his sentiment—"*The Union: next to our Liberty the most dear: may we all remember that it can only be preserved by respecting the rights of the States, and distributing equally the benefit and burden of the Union!*" Those who before doubted the intentions of Calhoun and his South Carolina friends, and were at a loss to understand the exact meaning of the dinner party to which they were bidden, were no longer embarrassed by ignorance. In that toast was presented the issue—liberty *before* Union—supreme State sovereignty—false complaints of inequality of benefits and burdens—*our rights* as we choose to define them, or *disunion.*

From that hour the vigilant old President watched the South Carolina conspirator, his lieutenant, with the searching eyes of unslumbering suspicion. THE CONTENTS OF THIS BOOK FORM THE SEQUEL TO THAT TOAST.

#### Some Mistake in the Card.

A ball was to be given in Toronto, C. W., in honor of Lord Moncy, and a secessionist from Windsor visited a member of the Cabinet hoping thereby to obtain an invitation to the ball. He presented his card—"Mr. ——, Southern Confederacy." The gentleman took it, examined it curiously, and remarked dryly, "Mr. ——, of the S-o-u-t-h-e-r-n C-o-n-f-e-d-e-r-a-c-y, eh! Well, Sir, our Government is not aware of the existence of such an 'institution.' There must be some mistake, Sir," and the secessionist was courteously bowed out. It would have done honor to that Cabinet had the example of rebuff thus set in the early stage of the rebellion, towards its abettors, been carried out consistently to the end. But, if there were others similarly *bowed out,* there were certainly a much larger number who were *bowed in,* and to whom the doors of provincial favor opened on golden hinges.

#### Not "Jeff," but "Geoffrey" Davis.

Among the "gentlemen" furnished with lodgings for the night, at the Union street station house in ——, was an Irishman. He had a large amount of masonry in his hat—in other words he was unmistakably tipsy. When such persons are brought to the station house the first process is to search them. This process is intended entirely for the benefit of the prisoner, and prevents him from being robbed by other gentlemen or ladies who may be placed in the same cell.

The prisoner is next asked concerning his name, occupation and nativity. These points are recorded, and reported to the mayor next morning. If the prisoner is too drunk to answer questions, the explanation is made when he pays his fine, or goes to jail. The Irishman in question proved to be a character in his way, as the following will show:

"What's your name?" asked the turnkey, as he was brought in.

"My name's Davis, an' it's as good a one as yours any day in the year."

"Very well; What's your first name?"

PATRIOTIC, POLITICAL, CIVIL, JUDICIAL, ETC.     25

The Milesian told it; and the turnkey recorded it on his slate, "Jeff Davis."

Though decidedly drunk, the Irishman was anything but an ignoramus. He looked at the turnkey's memorandum, and saw the name "Jeff Davis."

"What the divil's that?" he sharply asked, with forefinger pointing to the slate.

"Why, it's the name you told me was yours."

"*I* toold you so?"

"Of course you did. Didn't you say your name was Jeff Davis?"

The Irishman looked at him in silence for a moment. Then clenching his fist he brandished it menacingly over the turnkey's hat, saying—

"Av' it warrent for yer gray hairs or yer ignorance, one or the other, I'd mash the nose ov ye till ye couldn't tell it from a turnip."

"And for what?" asked the turnkey, looking up in surprise.

"For writin' down me name like the name of the black hearted Judas ov a Jefferson Davis."

"Didn't you say that was your name?"

"I did not. Overhaul your dictionary ye ould omadhoun. It's ignorance, that's all that ails ye. Rub out that Jefferson. Instead of a J put a G, and then spell out me name Geoffrey Davis. Bedad, if me name was Jefferson I'd change it to Peter, so I would!"

With this remark the speaker disappeared into the cell, whose door the officer was holding open for him. Two minutes afterwards his snoring resounded through the whole building. He didn't mind the degradation of the lock-up, but hadn't quite descended to the level of the patricide whose name he was supposed to wear.

**President Lincoln Treating the Richmond Commissioners to a Little Story.**

After the formal interview between President Lincoln and the three Confederate Commissioners was over—in February, 1865—there was a lengthy general conversation held. It seems that it was during this informal talk that the Confederate embassadors first heard of the passage of the constitutional amendment by the House of Representatives, prohibiting slavery. One of the number remarked that this action might complicate affairs a little with the South, the heavy planters insisting upon maintaining that institution and defending it,—and President Lincoln was asked if he thought he could get around that fact. Old Abe, true as steel to his *forte*, was ready for them with one of his parables or stories, and said:—

There was an old farmer out in Illinois who had made his arrangements to raise a large herd of hogs; he informed his neighbors that he had found a way to raise cheap pork. This excited the curiosity of his neighbors, and they asked him how he was going to do it. The old farmer replied that he should plant a large field of potatoes, and when they had got their growth would turn the hogs in and let them dig and eat, thus saving the expense of digging the potatoes and feeding them.

"But," said his neighbors, "the frost will come before they are fattened, and in all probability the ground will be frozen a foot deep. How do you propose to get around that?"

"Oh," replied the farmer, "they will root somewhere anyway, and may as well root away there, even if it is hard work."

**Reception of the Rebel Commissioners in London by Mr. Bates.**

While the Commissioners from the Rebel States were in England, they were formally introduced to Mr. Bates, the head of the house of Baring Brothers, the great financier, who told them to proceed. They commenced with a most elaborate and glowing description of the resources and wealth of the Rebel States. After a pause:—

*Mr. Bates.* Have you finished?

*Commissioners.* Not quite. (Then a speech from Commissioner No. 2, and a pause.)

*Mr. Bates.* Have you finished?

*Commissioners.* Almost. (Then a speech from Commissioner No. 3, and a pause.)

*Mr. Bates.* Are you through?

*Commissioners.* Yes, sir; you have our case.

*Mr. Bates.* What States did you say composed your Confederacy?

*Commissioners.* Mississippi, South Carolina, Alabama, Georgia, Florida, Texas, and Louisiana.

*Mr. Bates.* And Mr. Jefferson Davis is your President?

*Commissioners.* He is. We are proud of him.

*Mr. Bates.* We know Mr. Davis well by reputation. He is the same gentleman who stumped his State for two years in favor of repudiation, and justified the conduct of Mississippi in the United States Senate. We know the gentleman; and although we have no reason to be proud of him or his antecedents, I think I may safely say, that if you have brought with you to London the necessary funds to pay off, principal and interest, the repudiated millions owing to our people by your States of Alabama, Mississippi, and Florida, there is a reasonable prospect of your raising a small amount in this market! Our Mr. Sturgis will be happy to dine you at 8 o'clock to-morrow evening!

*Exeunt omnes.*

### Afraid of the Girl's Eye.

The house of the celebrated, bold-hearted and out-spoken Parson Brownlow, was, at one time, the only one in Knoxville over which the Stars and Stripes were floating. According to arrangement, two armed secessionists went at six o'clock one morning to summarily haul down said stars and stripes. Miss Brownlow, a brilliant young lady of twenty-three, saw them on the piazza, and stepped out and demanded their business. They replied:

"We have come to take down them Stars and Stripes."

She instantly drew a revolver from her side, and presenting it, said—

"Go on! I'm good for one of you, and I think for both!"

"By *the look of that girl's eye* she'll shoot," one remarked: "I think we'd bet-

Afraid of the Girl's Eye

ter not try it; we'll go back and get more men," said the other.

"Go and get more men," said the noble lady; "get more men and come and take it down, if you dare!"

They returned with a company of ninety armed men, and demanded that the flag should be hauled down. But on discovering that the house was filled with gallant men, armed to their teeth, who would rather die as dearly as possible than see their country's flag dishonored, the secessionists retired, much after the fashion of cur-dogs sideling along with their tails between their hind-legs.

### Dramatic Scene in Mr. Buchanan's Cabinet.

The manner in which John B. Floyd was forced to resign his place as Secretary of War under President Buchanan, which he had used to further the ends of treason, forms a memorable incident in the political history of the rebellion.

In February, 1861, Major Anderson, commanding at Fort Moultrie, Charleston harbor, finding his position endangered, passed his garrison, by a prompt and brilliant movement, over to the stronger fortress of Sumter. Immediately on the reception of this intelligence, Mr. Floyd, Secretary of War, much excited, called upon the President to say that Major Anderson had violated express orders, and thereby seriously compromised him (Floyd), and that unless the Major was at once remanded to Fort Moultrie, he should resign the War Office.

The Cabinet was assembled directly. Mr. Buchanan, explaining the embarrassment of the Secretary of War, remarked that the act of Major Anderson would occasion exasperation in the South; he had told Mr. Floyd that, as the Government was strong, forbearance toward erring brethren might win them back to their allegiance, and that that officer might be ordered back. After an ominous silence, the President inquired how the suggestion struck the Cabinet?

Mr. Stanton, subsequently called to the War Department, but then Attorney General, answered:

"That course, Mr. President, ought certainly to be regarded as most liberal towards 'erring brethren;' but while one member of your Cabinet has fraudulent acceptances for millions of dollars afloat, and while the confidential clerk of another—himself in California teaching rebellion—has just stolen nine hundred thousand dollars from the Indian Trust Fund, the experiment of ordering Major Anderson back to Fort Moultrie would be dangerous. But if you do intend to try it, before it is done, I beg that you will accept my resignation."

"And mine," added the Secretary of State, Mr. Black—

"And mine, also," said the Post-Master General, Mr. Holt—

"And mine, too," followed the Secretary of the Treasury, General Dix.

This, of course, opened the bleared eyes of the President, and the meeting resulted in the acceptance of Mr. Floyd's resignation.

### Treating Them According to their Sympathies.

During one of the raids of John Morgan, an interesting incident occurred at Salem, Indiana. Some of his men proceeded out west of the town to burn the bridges and water-tank on the railroad. On the way out they captured a couple of persons living in the country, one of whom was a Quaker. The Quaker strongly objected to being made a prisoner. Secesh wanted to know if he was not strongly opposed to the South? "Thee is right," said the Quaker, "I am." "Well, did you vote for Lincoln?" "Thee is right; I did vote for Abraham," was the calm reply.

According to their Sympathies.

"Well, what are you?"

"Thee may naturally suppose that I am a Union man. Cannot thee let me go to my home?"

"Yes, yes; go and take care of the old woman," was the welcome answer.

The other prisoner was trotted along with them, but not relishing the summary manner in which the Quaker was disposed of, he said:

"What do you let him go for? He is a black abolitionist. Now, look here; I voted for Breckinridge, and have always been opposed to the war. I am opposed to fighting the South, decidedly."

"You are," said Secesh; "you are what they call around here a Copperhead, an't you?

"Yes, yes," said the Butternut, propitiatingly; "that's what all my neighbors call me, and they know I ain't with them."

"Come here Dave!" hallooed Secesh. "Here's a Butternut. Just come and look at him. Look here, old man, where do you live? We want what horses you have got to spare, and if you have got any greenbacks, just shell 'em out!" and they took all he had.

### Calumnious Charge of Loyalty against John Hawkins.

Holt's drinking saloon was one of the most fashionable in New Orleans. The proprietor, a son of the famous New York hotel keeper of that name, kept fast horses, a fashionable private residence, and received his income by the hundred dollars a day. In an evil hour secession seized upon the land, and Holt was induced to issue shinplasters. His reputation for wealth and business profits made them popular, and inducements were held out for immense issues. Gradually, however, business fell off, and Holt, when General Butler ordered that personal paper money should be redeemed by bank-notes, found it impossible to comply with the proclamation, and this inability was increased by the fact that he had taken the oath of allegiance, and his regular customers refused, therefore, to be comforted at his house. The finale was that Holt was sold out, and his establishment, repainted and restocked, opened under the auspices of one John Hawkins. To give the place the due amount of eclat, Captain Clark, of the Delta, knowing that it was against the law for any one to sell liquor in the city, unless by a person who had taken the oath of allegiance and obtained a license, caused it to be published that at last the citizens were blessed with a 'Union drinking saloon,' and at the same time invited all persons who loved the Stars and Stripes to patronize the new establishment.

This flattering notice fell upon John Hawkins as a thunderbolt; he frantically rushed over to the newspaper office and protested that he was a rebel, and that he relied upon his secession friends for patronage—he declared that he was a ruined man unless something was done to immediately purge his fair fame of any taint of loyalty to his native land. Captain Clark, who fully appreciated the unfortunate publican's feelings, and with the spirit and liberality of a chivalrous editor, offered his columns for an explanation, which offer resulted in the publication of a card by Mr. Hawkins, in which he pronounced the editorial statement that he had taken the oath of allegiance, "a fabrication."

Secession was delighted. John's friends crowded his precincts all day, and drank to John's health, *and at John's expense.* The dawn of the following morning promised a brilliant future; but, alas! Deputy Provost-Marshal, Colonel Stafford, whose business it was to see that public drinking-house keepers *had* taken said oath of allegiance, sent after Mr. Hawkins, and asked him what right he had to keep a shop open without license, and farther inquired if John did not know that he could not get a license unless he took oath to be a good citizen under the national government. That he was permitted to carry on his business *without* taking the oath will be believed by all who do not know the man with whom he had to deal at head-quarters.

### Voting for a Candidate on Principle.

"Gentlemen," said a Virginia planter, trembling with passion, in a conversation between half a dozen persons in the parlor of a New York insurance office, before the Republican nomination had been made, "gentlemen, if you elect Mr. Seward President, we shall break up this Union."

"I think not, Sir," calmly replied the man to whom he seemed more particularly to address himself.

"You'll see, Sir,—you'll see; we will surely do it."

"Then, Sir," said the other, as quietly as before, but looking him steadily in the face, "we shall nominate Mr. Seward. Mr. Seward is not my man, for I am a free trader and an old Democrat. But if Virginia, or any other state or states shall declare that, upon the constitutional election of any citizen of the United States to any office, the Union shall be broken up, then I nominate that man and vote for him on principle."

And all present, with a single exception, uttered a hearty "Ay!"

### Scene in the President's Room the Evening preceding the First Proclamation for Troops.

Hon. George Ashmun, a distinguished politician of Massachusetts, has given an interesting account of an interview which took place between himself and Senator Douglas, and subsequently between the two and President Lincoln, on the night preceding the issue of the first call for troops to put down the rebellion. Mr. Ashmun had gone to Mr. Douglas's house to induce him—he being looked upon as the senatorial leader of the opposition to Mr. Lincoln—to take a public stand in support of the Administration in entering upon the war. Mr. Douglas was at first disinclined to such a step, but yielded to the representations made to him,—his wife, who came into the room during the interview, giving the whole weight of her influence towards the result which was reached. The discussion continued for some time, and resulted in his emphatic declaration that he would go with Mr. Ashmun to the President and offer a cordial and earnest support. Mr. Ashmun's carriage was waiting at the door, and it was almost dark when they started for the President's house. They fortunately found Mr. Lincoln at home and alone, and upon Mr. Ashmun stating the errand on which they had come, the President was most cordial in his welcome, and immediately prepared the way for the conversation which followed, by taking from his drawer and reading to them the draft of the proclamation which he had decided to issue, and which was given to the country the next morning. As soon as the reading was ended, Mr. Douglas rose from his chair and said—

"Mr. President, I cordially concur in every word of that document, except, that instead of a call for 75,000 men, I would make it 200,000. You do not know the dishonest purposes of those men (the rebels) so well as I do."

Mr. Douglas then asked them to look with him at the map which hung at the end of the President's room, where in much detail he pointed out the principal strategic points which should be at once strengthened. Among the most prominent were Fortress Monroe, Washington, Harper's Ferry and Cairo. He enlarged at length, and with his accustomed power of demonstration, upon the firm, warlike footing which ought to be pursued, and found in Mr. Lincoln an earnest and gratified listener; indeed, no two men in the United States parted that night with a more cordial feeling of a united, friendly and patriotic purpose than these two irreconcilable political opponents during the past, Mr. Lincoln and Mr. Douglas.

After leaving, and while on their way homeward, Mr. Ashmun said to Mr. Douglas—

"You have done justice to your own reputation and to the President, and the country must know it. The proclamation will go by telegraph all over the country in the morning, and the account of this interview must go with it. I shall send it, either in my own language or yours. I prefer that you should give your own version."

"Drive to your room at Willard's," said Mr. Douglas at once, "and I will give it shape."

This they did, and Mr. Douglas wrote the following, an exact copy of which was given to the agent of the associated press, and on the next morning it was read all over the North, in company with the President's proclamation, to the great gratification of his friends and the friends of the government. The original draft, in Mr. Douglas's handwriting, is still preserved as cherished evidence that, whoever else may have fallen by the wayside, in the hour of the nation's peril from 'false brethren,' Mr. Douglas was not of them. Below is a copy of the memorable dispatch to the press, Sunday evening, April 14, 1861:—

"Mr. Douglas called on the President this evening and had an interesting conversation on the present condition of the country. The substance of the conversation was that while Mr. D. was unalterably opposed to the administration on all its political issues, he was prepared to sustain the President in the exercise of all his constitutional functions to preserve the Union and maintain the government and defend the federal capital. A firm policy and prompt action was necessary. The capital of our country was in danger, and must be defended at all hazards, and at any expense of men or money. He spoke of the present and future without reference to the past."

### Gallant Vindication of the Flag Abroad.

Captain C. Lee Moses, of Saco, Maine, formerly United States astronomer, etc., was a party to a singular and not unromantic affair of honor, which was fought on the Seine, near Paris, in August, 1861, the particulars of this affair being as follows:

Captain Moses, although a South Carolinian by birth, remained a strong and devoted adherent to the cause of the Union, and during his journey through France made no hesitation in expressing his sympathies and feelings for the United States Government, and his abhorrence of the southern traitors and rebels who were engaged in destroying the most enlightened, best administered and most prosperous Government on the face of the globe.

Vindication of the Flag Abroad.

Hon. F. G. Farquar, of Virginia, meeting the Captain at a hotel in Paris, and knowing his parentage, reproached him in opprobious terms as a renegade from his native State. He charged him with being a traitor to the South, and a man of no honor because he abandoned her when she needed the services of all her sons, particularly her seamen and navigators. He took occasion also in his vituperation, to cast imputations upon the character of Northern ladies, which, as the Captain had married a New England wife, was resented on the spot by a tremendous blow, entirely doubling up the chivalric Virginian, and laying him in ordinary for the balance of the evening.

Farquar was taken charge of by his friends, and when he had gathered his scattered faculties, he sent a challenge to the Captain by the hands of his friend, Mons. Stephani. The challenge received a prompt response, and not twenty-four hours from the first meeting of the combatants, they stood on the banks of the Seine, prepared to take each other's lives. The weapons selected were Derringer pistols, the distance ten paces, the combatants being ordered to wheel and fire at the given signal. Farquar was boastful and coarse in his remarks and manners. The Captain was calm, though determined.

All being ready, Captain Moses handed two letters to his second, one addressed to the American consul at Liverpool, and the other to his wife at Saco, Me., to be delivered in case he fell. He then removed his coat, bandaged back the hair from his eyes, and took his position. The word was then given, and with a simultaneous report of both pistols the combatants fell to the ground. Both were shot through the head. Farquar received a mortal wound, with which he lingered several days, finally dying at a hamlet a few miles from Paris, where he had been removed to avoid the noise of the city. Before dying, he solicited an interview with Captain Moses, made an acknowledgment of his base conduct, and solicited the latter's forgiveness, which was freely granted. The Captain, escaping from the French police, took refuge at Liverpool, where he was concealed by the American shippers of that city and sent on to New York, where he arrived in a very critical condition, the ball of his adversary having passed just under the ear, causing a severe concussion of the brain.

### Solemn Scene at Midnight.

The following from a Knoxville (Tenn.) rebel journal, describing a secret meeting of thirty or forty Unionists, called together by a well known patriot, David Fry, admirably illustrates the 'idolatrous love for the Stars and Stripes,'—according to secession phraseology—and suggests a subject worthy the highest inspiration of the historical painter:

Fry drew forth a United States flag, and spreading it upon a table in the centre of the room, called upon his followers to surround that emblem of the Union, and take with him the oath of allegiance. This was late in the night; and after the whole plot had been fully understood, the loyalists surrounded the table in groups, and, by direction of the leader, placed their left hands upon the folds of the flag, raising aloft their right hands, and swearing to support the Constitution of the United States, to sustain the flag there spread before them, and to do that night whatever might be impressed upon them by their chief. The oath was taken by all except two or three, in solemn earnestness and in silence—the darkness relieved alone by the dim and flickering light of a solitary candle.

The scene was impressive—the occasion was full of moment—and everything conspired to fill the hearts of the loyalists with a fixed determination. That determination they abundantly fulfilled by their deeds.

### "More Brains, Lord!"

Rev. Dr. Sunderland, on accepting the pastorship of an American church in Paris, offered his farewell prayer as Chaplain of the United States Senate, a short time after. On this occasion he made some peculiar home-thrusts at the honorable gentlemen for whom, during four months previous, he had been daily interceding at the Throne of Grace. He uttered the following supplication very audibly:

"We pray Thee, O Lord! to give to the councillors and statesmen of America more brains! More *brains*, Lord! More BRAINS!"

On hearing this very well-timed entreaty, but rather harsh criticism, Mr. Sumner dropped his head upon his breast quite feelingly, Jim Lane rolled his eyes piously, Garrett Davis evinced signs of emotion, and a gentleman in the reporters' gallery uttered an emphatic "Amen!" by way of response.

Many of the honorable secretaries dropped their heads upon their desks to conceal a smile at the Chaplain's supplication, which smile extended to the dimensions of a broad grin, as the "Amen" was heard to proceed from the reporters' gallery. The worthy Sergeant-at-Arms, who was standing in his usual deeply reverential attitude, (with solemn countenance on religious thoughts intent,) turned the white of one of his official eyes in the direction of the self-constituted clerk in the gallery, but he evidently could not discover a countenance which did not exhibit the utmost decorum of expression.

### Literal Interpretation of Northern "Sympathy" by a Rebel General.

When the rebel force appeared in front of Hagerstown, on its Northern raid and invasion, one of the principal citizens of that town undertook a measure to which he looked for the preservation of his property. He farmed about two hundred acres of land. His barns were full of grain, his pastures were dotted with sheep and cattle, and forty well-fed swine were gathered in the rear of his corn cribs. He was emphatically a man of plenty and substance. When the rebels came he walked out to their lines, with a damask linen napkin—(white flag) affixed to his walking cane. The first rebel soldier he encountered he requested to show him to the commanding officer. He was passed under guard to the object of his search.

"General," said he, "I am a warm sympathizer with the South. I heartily wish success to this invasion and your forces. My object in seeking you out is to ask that you and as many of your staff as will accept the invitation will make my house your head-quarters during your stay here. My house is yonder upon that hill"—pointing to a fine old-fashioned mansion, with modern additions, and with a long row of hay-ricks in the background.

"You sympathize with the South, did you say?" queried the General blandly.

"Very earnestly, sir, and always have done so."

The rebel General beckoned to a sergeant who stood near him. "Bring a musket for this man," said he, "and take him into the ranks."

The 'sympathizer' opened wide his eyes, but stood mute with horror. He 'couldn't see it' in that light. He stammered out at last, "Oh, I didn't mean that, General. I don't want to fight. I want to entertain you and your staff while you remain here, and to show you that I am your friend."

The rebel General contemptuously informed him that they interpreted sympathy only in its literal sense. He had claimed to sympathize with them, and they intended to avail themselves of his good will. A string of wagons was at once trotted out, driven to the sympathizer's premises, and in the same afternoon he was stripped of everything. The rebels carried off all his cattle, sheep, hogs, and smaller live stock, removed all his hay and wheat crop, leaving his barns utterly empty. The cavalry horses were turned into his growing oats, and his corn was cut and made excellent fodder for the stock while on the march. The 'sympathizer' was detained until all was done, and was then released with thanks for the sympathy he had so promptly and kindly manifested.

### Ben Butler in Council with the Secession Conspirators.

In December, 1860, after the election of Mr. Lincoln, General Butler, who had supported Breckinridge for President, in preference to either Douglas, Bell, or Lincoln, went to Washington, where he had many and serious conversations with his Southern brethren. According to the interesting account of these interviews given by Parton, those Southern brethren were determined on secession, and asked Butler to go with them. There was room in the South, they said, for such as he. He told them the North would fight against secession, and they laughed at him. He told them, "if the South fights, there is an end of slavery," and they laughed again. They asked him "if he would fight in such a cause," and he replied, "Most certainly."

When the South Carolina 'ambassadors' came to Washington, Butler proposed to the Attorney-General to try them for treason. "You say," said he to the Attorney, "that the Government cannot use its army and navy to coerce South Carolina. Very well. I do not agree with you; but let the proposition be granted. Now, secession is either a right, or it is treason. If it is a right, the sooner we know it the better. If it is treason, then the presenting of the ordinance of secession is an overt act of treason. These men are coming to the White House to present the ordinance to the President. Admit them. Let them present the ordinance. Let the President say to them—'Gentlemen, you go hence in the custody of a Marshal of the United States, as prisoners of state, charged with treason against your country.' Summon a grand jury here in Washington. Indict the commissioners. If any of your officers are backward in acting, you have the appointing power—replace them with men who feel as men should at a time like this. Try the commissioners before the Supreme Court, with all the imposing forms and stately ceremonials which marked the trial of Aaron Burr. I have some reputation at home as a criminal lawyer, and I will stay here to help the District Attorney through the trial without fee or reward. If they are acquitted, you will have done something toward leaving a clear path for the incoming administration. Time will have been gained; but the great advantage will be, that both sides will pause to watch this high and dignified proceeding; the passions of men will cool; the great point at issue will become clear to all parties; the mind of the country will be active, while passion and prejudice are allayed. Meanwhile, if you cannot use our army and navy in Charleston harbor, you can certainly employ them in keeping order here."

This advice was not heeded. The 'commissioners' or 'ambassadors' heard of it.

"Why, you would not hang us?" said Mr. Orr, one of them, to Butler.

"Oh, no," was the reply, "not unless you were found guilty."

He had one last, long interview with the Southern leaders, at which the whole subject was gone over. For three hours he reasoned with them, demonstrating the folly of their course, and warning them of final and disastrous failure. The conversation was friendly, though warm and earnest on both sides. Again he was invited to join them, and was offered a share in their enterprise, and a place in that 'sound and homogeneous government' which they meant to establish. He left no room to doubt that he took sides with his country, and that all he had and all he was should be freely risked in that country's cause. Late at night they separated, to know one another no more except as mortal foes.

### Advice from the "Disbanded Volunteer."

President Lincoln, in the perplexities surrounding him, sent to "A Disbanded Volunteer" for counsel and sympathy. "D. V." describes this interview as follows:—

He (the President) was standin on the front door steps when I arrove at the White House, pullin on his left whiser as his wont when his will is disregarded, and conducted me at wonst to his sanktum. He said he was worried amazingly by the dogged obstanacy of the War Department, upon which I axed if he wanted a piece of an honest man's mind.

"Spit it out, Old Fidelity," ses he, his fetters lighten up with a hole-soled smile.

"Wal," ses I, "wat I hev to say in the fust place is this. It's not so easy to lick anyboddy as it is to lick nobody, is it?"

He remained for a few minits absorbed in deep thort and then shook his hed.

"But," I continued, "It's easier to lick

a considabul than to lick the same boddy when it's twiste as considabul, isn't it?"

After a brief interval for reflexin he conenrd.

"And," ses I resoomin agin, "it's easier—isn't it—to smash horseteal boddies wen we air able, than it is when they air able to raze Cain with us?"

"D. V.," he rejoined, smildin compleasantly. "you borrord that silly gism from a remark of mine in the Missidge, and I am proud to say the logic is correck."

"Ef so," ses I, "why in thunder don't you tell Burnside to go in and win, afore the rebils sets ther arthworkt, and rifle pits and mast batteries a twixt him and Richmond, thicker'n mink traps in a Western Swomp?"

"My noble and esteemabul friend," he responded, wipin his nose with visabul emoshin, "your sentiments does honor to your hed and hart; but I've gin the Seckatry of War discreseunnary powers."

"I'me right glad to larn it," I remarkt sneeringly, "for it's the gineral opinyun that he hesn't enny of his own."

You should have seen the Honabul Abe lay back and shake his honest sides. It dun me good to look at him.

### Hurrahs for Jeff. Davis in the Wrong Place.

One morning, as a returned soldier named Thompson, residing in Washington, was engaged in conversation with some parties at a public house in Peoria, Illinois, an individual entered, and as he passed the soldier, shouted, "Hurrah for Jeff. Davis!" In an instant the soldier turned and asked, "Did you shout for Jeff. Davis?" The individual surveyed Thompson for a moment, and, seeing that he meant mischief, replied that it was not he. "Well," said the soldier, "I believe that you did, and if I was sure of it I would give you cause to remember it." He again declared that he had not done so, when at this juncture one of the men Thompson had been conversing with, and who had always acted with the Democratic party, stepped up, saying to the soldier, "I am a Democrat, but I can't stand that; he did hurrah for Jeff. Davis, and now pitch into him." The veteran hesitated not a moment, and, though by far the smaller of the two, he went at the Jeff. Davis sympathizer and administered a spirited and most thorough drubbing, concluding the performance by compelling him to shout twice, as loud as he was able, for Abe Lincoln. Then, allowing the fellow to get on his feet, he cautioned him never to repeat that operation again in his presence, saying—

"I have fought rebels three years, and had a brother killed by just such men as you are, and whenever a traitor shouts for Jeff. Davis in my hearing I will whip him or kill him."

### Stanton's First Meeting with Cabinet Traitors.

When General Cass—grieved and indignant—left Mr. Buchanan's Cabinet, Mr. Attorney-General Black was transferred to the portfolio of State, and Mr. Stanton, then absent from Washington, was fixed

Stanton.

upon as Attorney-General. The same night he arrived at a late hour, and learned from his family of his appointment. Knowing the character of the bold, bad men, then in the ascendency in the Cabinet, he determined at once to decline; but when, the next day, he announced his resolution at the White House, the entreaties of the distressed and helpless President, and the arguments of Mr. Black, moved him to accept.

At the first meeting of the Cabinet which he attended, the condition of the seceded States and the course to be pursued with the garrison at Fort Sumter, were discussed, Floyd and Thompson dwelling upon "the irritation of the Southern heart," and the folly of "continuing a useless garrison to increase the irritation." No one formally proposed any course of action, but the designs of the conspirators were plain to the new Attorney-General. He went home troubled. He had intended, coming in at so late a day, to remain a quiet member of this discordant council. But it was not in his nature to sit quiet longer under such utterances.

The next meeting was a long and stormy one, Mr. Holt, feebly seconded by the President, urging the immediate reinforcement of Sumter, while Thompson, Floyd and Thomas contended that a quasi-treaty had been made by the officers of the Government with the leaders of the rebellion, to offer no resistance to their violations of law and seizures of Government property. Floyd, especially, blazed with indignation at what he termed the "violation of honor." At last, Mr. Thompson formally moved that an imperative order be issued to Major Anderson to retire from Sumter to Fort Moultrie—abandoning Sumter to the enemy, and proceeding to a post where he must at once surrender. Stanton could sit still no longer, and rising, he said with all the earnestness that could be expressed in his bold and resolute features:

"Mr. President, it is my duty as your legal adviser to say that you have no right to give up the property of the Government, or abandon the soldiers of the United States to its enemies; and the course proposed by the Secretary of the Interior, if followed, *is treason*, and will involve you and all concerned in treason!"

Such language had never before been heard in Buchanan's Cabinet, and the men who had so long ruled and bullied the President were surprised and enraged to be thus rebuked. Floyd and Thompson sprang to their feet with fierce, menacing gestures, seeming about to assault Stanton. Mr. Holt took a step forward to the side

Holt.

of the Attorney-General. The President implored them piteously to take their seats. After a few more bitter words the meeting broke up. That was the last Cabinet meeting on that exciting question in which Floyd participated. Before another was called all Washington was startled with the rumor of those gigantic frauds which soon made his name so infamous. At first he tried to brazen it out with his customary blustering manner, but the next day the Cabinet waited long for his appearance. At last he came; the door opened—his resignation was thrust into the room, and Floyd disappeared from Washington, with a brand of infamy upon him, which only ceased to increase in blackness till the time when he was called to his final account.

*Such was the end of Floyd and the beginning of Stanton.* Stanton and Holt were noble co-laborers in that dark period of the country's political travail, and nobly did they sustain themselves through the four years' conflict.

### Hiding the Flag—Female Artifice.

The Federal commander at Camp Herron, Missouri, having learned that a certain very fine secession flag that waved defiantly from a flagstaff in the village of Manchester, twenty miles distant from the camp, (until the successes of the Union forces caused its supporters to conclude that, for the present, "discretion would be the better part of valor,") was still being very carefully preserved, its possessors boasting that they would soon be enabled to re-hoist it; determined upon its summary capture.

On the 15th of November, 1861, First Lieutenant Bull, of Company C, Ninth Iowa regiment, was directed to take charge of this little expedition, and to detail fifteen good men for the purpose, which detail the Lieutenant made from Company C.

They left camp by the cars at half-past five o'clock in the afternoon, landing at Merrimac, three miles from Manchester, proceeding from thence to Manchester on foot, and surrounded the house of Squire B., who had been foremost in the secession movement of that strong secession town, and was reported to be in possession of the flag in question.

But the 'Squire protested against the imputation, declaring that the flag was not in his possession, and that he knew not of its whereabouts. His lady acknowledged that she had for a time kept it secreted in a box in the garden, but as it was likely to become injured, she took it out, dried it in the sun, when it was taken away by some ladies who lived a *long* distance in the country, whose names she refused to give. Finally, after a thorough but fruitless search of the house, after the Lieutenant had put her husband under arrest, and he was being started off to head-quarters, the lady, probably hoping it would save her husband, acknowledged that it was taken by a Mrs. S., who resided a mile and a half in the country,—not such a terribly long distance, after all. Her husband was then sent to Merrimac, escorted by four soldiers, and the remainder, conducted by the gallant Lieutenant, started to visit the residence of Mrs. S., in search of the flag.

The distance to the lady's residence was soon traveled, the house surrounded, and the flag demanded of Mrs. S., who proved to be a very intelligent lady, and had around her quite an interesting family. The lady replied to the demand, that she would like to see the person who stated that she took the flag from Esquire B—'s; that as to its whereabouts she had nothing to say; that the Lieutenant could search her house, and if he could find any thing that looked *like* a flag, he was welcome to it. Accordingly, a thorough search was made, in which the lady and her daughter aided, but no flag was to be found. The lady then thanked the officer for the gentlemanly manner in which the search had been conducted, and added that she trusted he was satisfied. He replied that he was quite satisfied that she had the flag, and that it would have been far better for her to have yielded it; but as she did not, as unpleasant as the task was, he should arrest her and take her to head-quarters at Pacific City.

Two men were then dispatched for a carriage with which to convey the lady to Merrimac, and from thence the lady was informed that she would be sent by railroad. She accordingly made preparation to go, but after an hour had elapsed in waiting for the carriage, the lady again demanded the name of the informants, and when told that it was Mrs. B., and that Esquire B. was already in custody, she then asked whether any indignity would have been offered to her had the flag been found in her possession. To this the courteous Lieutenant replied:

"Certainly not, Madam; our object with Esquire B. was his arrest and the capture of the flag; but with you, our object was the flag."

"Will you pledge your honor," said she, "that if I surrender the flag I shall not be arrested, nor my family disturbed."

PATRIOTIC, POLITICAL, CIVIL, JUDICIAL, ETC.     37

"You will not be arrested, nor your family disturbed."

"I wish you to understand, Sir, that no fear of arrest or trouble would ever have made me surrender that flag; but 'Squire B.'s family induced me to take that flag to save them from trouble, saying that it should be a sacred trust, known only to ourselves, and I consequently surrender it."

She then went to a bed that had been fruitlessly searched, took from it a quilt, and with the aid of her daughters, proceeded to open the edges of the quilt, and cut the stitches through the body of it, and pulled off the top, when, behold! there lay the mammoth flag next to the cotton, being carefully stitched twice and nearly a half across the quilt. When taken out and spread, it proved to be a magnificent flag, over twenty-one feet in length, and nearly nine feet in width, with fifteen stars to represent the prospective Southern Confederacy.

"Recollect," said the lady to Lieutenant Bull," that you did not' find it yourself, and when you wish detectives you had better employ ladies."

She also added, that she gave up the flag unwillingly. The daughter remarked that she had slept under it, and that she *loved* it, and that fifteen stars were not so terribly disunion—in her estimation—after all.

### An Alabama Planter and the Anti-Slavery Leaders Together.

About the time of the breaking out of the rebellion, John G. Whittier, the Massachusetts anti-slavery Quaker and poet, met with an Alabama planter in Boston, who expressed a desire to converse with him, and an interview took place, during which there was a free interchange of views and opinions concerning the events of the day. The planter frankly acknowledged that there was in the South a strong feeling of hate toward the North and Northern men, and they were determined to fight. He explained how this feeling was fostered by the politicians of the South, and how the feelings of the North were represented there, and stated that almost his sole object in coming to Boston was to ascertain for himself whether the facts were as they had been represented. He was evidently surprised to find the anti-slavery poet "so mild a mannered man," and confessed that, generally, he did not perceive that the feeling of the North toward the South was so bitter and unfriendly as he had been led to expect. He had received nothing but civility and courtesy, and admitted that Southerners generally received the same treatment.

Finally, Whittier, after attending him to some of the places of resort interesting to a stranger, told him that, as he was now here, he might as well see the worst of the anti-slavery phase of Northern fanaticism — as the fashionable phrase was,— and proposed to visit Garrison. The planter consented, and so they turned their steps to the *Liberator* office, where they found Garrison, Wendell Phillips, and Fred. Douglass, and there they enjoyed a "precious season of conversation." Would it not have been a sight worth seeing—that conclave in the Liberator office, with Garrison, Whittier, Phillips, Douglass, and the Alabama planter, in the foreground? The planter went to his home a wiser, and perhaps a sadder man, than he came, for, after hearing all that was said, he protested that all he could do, while mourning for the condition of the country, was to *pray* over it.

### Hoisting the American Flag on Independence Hall by President Lincoln.

On the twenty-second of February, 1861,—the anniversary of Washington's birthday,— the interesting ceremony of raising the glorious flag of the American Union was performed in Philadelphia, opposite Independence Hall, by President Lincoln, then on his way to be inaugurated at Washington.

Just in front of the main entrance to the State House, and but a few feet from the sacred hall of liberty, a large platform had been erected for the President-elect to stand upon before the people, while he raised the starry banner of the republic. The elevation, nearly six feet, enabled a vast multitude to observe everything enacted thereon. The front and sides of the stage were wrapped around with an American flag, while lesser flags floated from the stanchions.

Before the flag was raised prayer was offered, and in reply to words of welcome addressed to Mr. Lincoln on behalf of the city, through its chosen orator, the President spoke as follows:

Lincoln.

"Fellow Citizens,—I am invited and called before you to participate in raising above Independence Hall the flag of our country, with an additional star upon it. I propose now, in advance of performing this very pleasant and complimentary duty, to say a few words. I propose to say that when that flag was originally raised here, it had but thirteen stars. I wish to call your attention to the fact that, under the blessing of God, each additional star added to that flag has given additional prosperity and happiness to this country, until it has advanced to its present condition; and its welfare in the future, as well as in the past, is in your hands. Cultivating the spirit that animated our fathers, who gave renown and celebrity to this Hall, cherishing that fraternal feeling which has so long characterized us as a nation, excluding passion, ill-temper, and precipitate action on all occasions, I think we may promise ourselves that not only the new star placed upon that flag shall be permitted to remain there to our permanent prosperity for years to come, but additional ones shall from time to time be placed there, until we shall number, as was anticipated by the great historian, five hundred millions of happy and prosperous people. With these remarks, I proceed to the very agreeable duty assigned me."

The excitement was of a fearful character when the President-elect seized the rope to hoist the flag of the country to the crest of the staff over the State House. The souls of all seemed starting from their eyes, and every throat was wide. The shouts of the people were like the roar of waves which do not cease to break. For full three minutes the cheers continued. The expression of the President-elect was that of silent solemnity. His long arms were extended. Each hand alternately pulled at the halyards, and a bundle of bunting, tri-colored, which had never been kissed by the wind before, slowly rose and unfurled itself gracefully aloft. If the shouting had been fearful and tumultuous before, it became absolutely maniacal now. From the smallest urchin to the tall form which rivaled the President's in compass of chest and length of limb, there rose a wild cry,—reminding one of some of the storied shouts which rang among the Scottish hills in the days of clans and clansmen. Suddenly, when the broad bunting had reached the summit of the mast, it unrolled at once in all its amplitude, and blazed magnificently in the sunlight which then spread so brightly upon its gorgeous folds. At the same moment the band struck up the 'Star Spangled Banner,' and a cannon ranged in the square sent up peal after peal. Mr. Lincoln was then escorted to his hotel, and in a short time the crowd had melted away.

### Homage to the Flag by an Eagle.

While they were hoisting the Stars and Stripes over the officers' headquarters at Camp Curtin, near Harrisburgh, Penn, in the spring of 1861, and just as the men had seized the halyards, a large eagle, that came from no one knew where, hovered over the flag, and sailed majestically over the encampment, while the flag was run up. Thousands of eyes were up-

Homage to the Flag by an Eagle.

turned in a moment, and as the noble bird looked down, the cheers of three thousand men rent the air! Never was such ovation paid the "Imperial Bird of Jove." It lingered for a few moments, apparently not a particle frightened at the terrific noise, then, cleaving the air with its pinions, disappeared in the horizon.

### Strange Blotch on Calhoun's Right Hand.

Notwithstanding the long period—some thirty years—which has elapsed since the following political narrative was given to the world, it has still a fresh interest, and all the more striking in view of events which have come upon the American nation in these later years. The 'unobserved spectator' whose pen made record of the scene here described, was a veritable eye-witness of the same:

The other morning, at the breakfast table, when I, an unobserved spectator, happened to be present, Calhoun was observed to gaze frequently at his right hand, and brush it with his left, in a hurried and nervous manner. He did this so often that it excited attention. At length one of the persons composing the breakfast party—his name I think is Toombs, and he is a member of Congress from Georgia—took upon himself to ask the occasion of Mr. Calhoun's disquietude, "Does your hand pain you?" he asked of Mr. Calhoun. To this Mr. Calhoun replied, in rather a hurried manner.

"Pshaw! it is nothing but a dream I had last night, and which makes me see perpetually a large black spot, like an ink blotch, upon the back of my right hand; an optical illusion, I suppose."

Of course these words excited the curiosity of the company, but no one ventured to beg the details of this singular dream, until Toombs asked quietly:

"What was your dream like? I am not very superstitious about dreams; but sometimes they have a great deal of truth in them."

"But this was such a peculiarly absurd dream," said Mr. Calhoun,—again brushing the back of his right hand; "however, if it does not intrude too much on the time of our friends, I will relate it to you."

Of course the company were profuse in their expressions of anxiety to know all about the dream, and Mr. Calhoun related it:

"At a late hour last night, as I was sitting in my room, engaged in writing, I was astonished by the entrance of a visitor who, without a word, took a seat opposite me at my table. This surprised me, as I had given particular orders to the servant that I should on no account be disturbed. The manner in which the intruder entered, so perfectly self-possessed, taking his seat opposite me without a word, as though my room and all within it belonged to him, excited in me as much surprise as indignation. As I raised my head to look into his features, over the top of my shaded lamp, I discovered that he was wrapped in a thin cloak, which effectually concealed his face and features from my view; and as I raised my head, he spoke, 'What are you writing, senator from South Carolina?' I did not think of his impertinence at first, but answered him voluntarily, 'I am writing a plan for the dissolution of the American Union.' (You know, gentlemen, that I am expected to produce a plan of dissolution in the event of certain contingencies.) To this the intruder replied in the coolest manner possible, 'Senator from South Carolina, will you allow me to look at your hand, your right hand?' He rose, the cloak fell, and I beheld his face. Gentlemen, the sight of that face struck me like a thunder clap. It was the face of a dead man, whom extraordinary events had called back to life. The features were those of General GEORGE WASHINGTON. He was dressed in the Revolutionary costume, such as you see in the Patent office."

Here Mr. Calhoun paused, apparently agitated. His agitation, I need not tell you, was shared by the company. Toombs at length broke the embarrassing pause—

"Well what was the issue of this scene?"

Mr. Calhoun resumed:

"The intruder, as I have said, rose and asked to look at my right hand, as though I had not the power to refuse. I extended it. The truth is, I felt a strange thrill pervade me at his touch; he grasped it and held it near the light, thus affording full time to examine every feature. It *was* the face of WASHINGTON! After holding my hand for a moment, he looked at me steadily, and said in a quiet way, 'And with this right hand, senator from South Carolina, you would sign your name to a paper declaring the Union dissolved?' I answered in the affirmative. 'Yes,' I said, 'if a certain contingency arises, I will sign my name to the Declaration of Dissolution.' But at that moment a black blotch appeared on the back of my hand, which I seem to see now. 'What is that?' said I, alarmed, I know not why, at the blotch on my hand. 'That,' said he, dropping my hand, 'is the mark by which Benedict Arnold is known in the next world.' He said no more, gentlemen, but drew from beneath his cloak an object which he laid upon the table—laid upon the very paper on which I was writing. This object, gentlemen, was a skeleton. 'There,' said he, 'there are the bones of Isaac Hayne before you—he was a South Carolinian, and so are you. But there was no blotch on his right hand.' With these words the intruder left the room. I started back from the contact with the dead man's bones and—awoke. Overcome by labor, I had fallen asleep, and had been dreaming. Was it not a singular dream?"

All the company answered in the affirmative, and Toombs muttered, "Singular, very singular," and at the same time looked curiously at the back of his right hand, while Mr. Calhoun placed his head between his hands and seemed buried in thought.

---

## Firm Devotion of a Loyal Southern Woman to the Colors.

A finely independent and successful stand was taken by a woman in New Orleans, on behalf of the Union, in the dawning days of rebellion. She and her husband, a Mississippi steamboat captain, occupied the middle front room of the lowest range of sleeping apartments in the St. Charles Hotel, at the time when the city was to be illuminated in honor of secession. She refused to allow the illuminating candles to be fixed in the windows of her room, and the proprietors remonstrated in vain—she finally ordering them to leave the room, of which she claimed, while its occupant, to have the entire control.

The secessionists, however, determined not to be outdone in a matter of such grave importance, proceeded to find and appeal to the captain,—who was not in the room at the time of the above proceedings. He heard their case; said his wife had reported him correctly on the Union question, nevertheless he would go with them to the room, and see if the matter could be amicably arranged.

But the captain's disposition to yield was not seconded, amicably nor otherwise, by his better half. The proprietors thereupon next proposed to vacate the best chamber in her favor, in some other part of the house, if that would be satisfactory; but the lady's "No!" was still as peremptory as ever. Her point was gained, and the St. Charles was doomed to have a dark front chamber. Pleased with this triumph, Mrs. —— devised the following manœuvre to make the most of her victory. Summoning a servant, she sent him out to procure for her an American flag, which, at dusk, she suspended from her window. When evening came, the streets, animated by a merry throng, were illuminated, but, alas! the St. Charles was disfigured by its sombre chamber—when, suddenly, a succession of lamps, suspended on both sides of the flag, revealing the Stars and Stripes, were lit up, and the ensign of *the Union* waved from the centre of a hotel illuminated in honor of its overthrow! The effect was, to give the impression that the whole house was thus paying homage to the American flag; and, what was a more significant fact still, the old flag was greeted by the passing crowd with vociferous applause. So much for the firmness of a loyal-hearted, true American woman.

---

**Provisional Government of Kentucky on an Excursion.**

The notorious George N. Sanders found himself one day, dilapidated and hungry, under the hospitable roof of Colonel Wm. H. Polk, of Tennessee,—George being well known, even in his own partizan circle, as a sort of political black sheep. After having partaken liberally of the viands set before him by his old friend, George signified by numerous signs, and finally by words, that he wished the servants to leave the room. He then said:

"Polk, I knew you were a man with a heart in your bosom; I told 'em so. I said that no better man than Bill Polk could be found. I told 'em so.

"Told *who* so?" asked Mr. Polk, rather surprised at the sudden and mysterious language, accompanied by the removal of the servants.

"Mr. Polk," said George, "I want your horses and carriage for a time."

"Certainly, Mr. Sanders, if you wish them."

"Mr. Polk," said Sanders, "I do not appear before you in any ordinary character to-day; I am clothed with higher authority; I am an emissary."

The tone and manner indicated something serious—perhaps to arrest his host.

"I am an emissary," repeated Mr. Sanders, speaking in very large capitals, "from THE STATE OF KENTUCKY, and hope to be received as such. The fact is," continued he, coming down to the level of familiar conversation, "I *left the Provisional Government of Kentucky a mile or so back, on foot,* finding its way southwardly, and I demand your horses and carriage in the name of that noble State."

Of course the carriages and horses were harnessed up at once, and Mr. Sanders proceeded to bring the Provisional Government to Mr. Polk's house.

How shall this scene be described? Hon. George W. Johnson, as much a Clay man as the sacred soil of Tennessee could afford, but still preserving his light and active step; McKee, late of the Courier, following; Walter N. Haldeman, with all his industry and perseverance, trying to keep up with his associates; and Willis B. Machen, vigorous, active, slightly sullen, but in earnest, with every boot he drew out of the snowy, muddy soil, giving a groan of fatigue. Imagine this peripatetic "Government" safely ensconced at Mr. Polk's, on their road south!

"Mr. Sanders," said the 'Governor,' with dignified suavity, after the walnuts and wine, "claimed to be an acquaintance of yours, and we were very glad to send him forward."

The Hon. Governor maintained throughout, that easy, self-possessed manner, which characterizes the gentleman.

The emissary shortly after suggested to the Provisional Government that he was "broke," and wished to represent the Seventh Congressional District of Kentucky—that is, the Louisville District; "for," said he, in his persuasive, confidential tones, "that is the only way I know of for a man without money to get to Richmond."

A session was at once held of the "State Council," the result of its deliberations being that Mr. Sanders was authorized to proceed to Richmond and there represent the interests of Louisville in the rebel Congress, *vice* H. W. Bruce.

#### Presidential Prospects.

One of the visitors at the White House took it upon himself to congratulate the President on the almost certain purpose on the part of the people to re-elect "Old Abe" for another term of four years. Mr. Lincoln replied that he had been told this frequently before of late, and that when it was first mentioned to him he was reminded of a farmer in Illinois who determined to try his own hand at blasting. After successfully boring and filling in with powder, he failed in the effort to make the powder go off, and after discussing with a looker-on the cause for this, and failing to detect anything wrong in the powder, the farmer suddenly came to the conclusion *that it would not go off because it had been shot before.*

#### Minister Cameron and his German Africanus.

General Cameron, the American Minister, for a time, at the court of St. Petersburg, traveled extensively in the various countries of Europe, that he might acquaint himself with their manners and customs. One incident which he relates, as occurring during this tour, is, to say the least, not very complimentary to "the great American Republic *as it was*."

Arriving at a small German town on the evening of Whitsuntide—which is a famous and favorite holiday with the Lutherans—the General was struck with the decent and comfortable appearance of the people who crowded the streets; but what just at that time interested him most, was a tall, stout, and impressive negro, far blacker than Othello, even before he was represented as a highly colored gentleman. Supposing him to be an American negro, Mr. Cameron went up to him and said: "How are you, my friend?"—using the Pennsylvania German, in which the General was an adept—when, to his infinite horror, the colored gentleman thus addressed turned upon him and said, in good guttural Dutch, "I am no American, I do not want to talk to you. I won't talk to any man who comes from a country professing to be free, but in which human beings are held as slaves." And this was said by the honest fellow with a magisterial and indignant air that would have been irresistibly severe, if it had not been irresistibly comic.

Minister Cameron made his escape with the best possible grace from his stalwart and sable antagonist, and supposed he had got rid of him; but on passing into an adjoining saloon with his secretary, Bayard Taylor, to take a glass of lager beer, he was again confronted by his German Africanus, who re-opened his vials of wrath, and concluded by turning to the General and asking him in broad German, "*Sagh, bin ich recht, or bin ich unrecht?*" which means:

"Say, am I right, or am I wrong? Answer me!"

Minister Cameron made inquiry as to the negro, and ascertained that one of the nobility in the neighborhood, who had spent some years in Africa in a scientific and hunting tour, brought back with him to Germany a very handsome native, who, in course of time, developed into the individual that sought the opportunity to administer a rebuke to an American who lived in a country professing to be free, but in which human beings are held as slaves.

### Old Abe Hard-up for a Joke for Once.

During a conversation which took place in the summer of 1864, between President Lincoln and a distinguished Western Senator, the various legislative nominations for the Presidency then being made were incidently referred to. "Yes," said Mr. Lincoln, moving his leg with evident gratification—"yes, Senator, the current seems to be setting all one way!" " "It does, really, seem to be setting all one way," was the answer of the Senator, "but, Mr. Lincoln, as you have told me several good stories since I have been here, permit me, if you please, to tell you one:—

"It has always been observed that the Atlantic Ocean at the Straits of Gibraltar, constantly pours into the Mediterrranean, with a tremendous volume. The Bosphorus empties into it, at its other end, and rivers are seen contributing to its waters all along the coast. It was for many years the constant puzzle of geographers, why the Mediterranean, under all these accessions, never got full and overran its banks. After a while, however, a curious fellow took the notion of dropping a plummet in the centre of the Straits, when, lo! he discovered that, though the tremendous body of water on the surface was rushing inward from the ocean, a still more powerful body was passing outward, in a counter current, at some twenty feet below!"

"Oh, ah!" said Old Abe, seriously, and evidently nonplussed for the first time in his life; "that *does not* 'remind' me of any story I ever heard before!"

### Front-Door Confabulations in Arkansas.

A Union man who was visiting Little Rock, Arkansas, under the protecting folds of the Stars and Stripes, which had then taken the place of the Confederate ensign, sat down one evening at the front door of a secession friend, and engaged in a hearty talk about the war, the latter claiming, of course, that the South couldn't be whipped, and the former arguing that that thing was a good deal more than half done already. While thus conversing, a middle aged negro came along, leading a horse

Front Door Confabulations in Arkansas.

that did not seem able to stand without artificial support. Upon nearing them he politely bowed, and said to the secession gentleman,

"Good ebenin' massa."

"Good evening, Joe," was the kind response; and Joe began moving off. Just at this moment "Massa" appeared to think of something else to say, and he remarked,

"Joe, did you hear that Roberts had gone to Texas?"

"Yes, massa. I knew de day he lef'."

"He took all his 'boys,' I believe."

"Yes, massa, he took 'em all: what he go to Texas for?"

"I suppose he went to keep out of the way of the Yankees."

These words had no sooner left "massa's" mouth than a singular change seemed to come over Joe. Before their utterance he was altogether undemonstrative in his manner; but when he caught their full meaning, his countenance evinced pleasure and surprise in about equal proportions. In a moment he began to laugh, but checked himself suddenly, and said:

"Could'nt help laughin', massa. My missus tole me de Yankees could'nt git Memphis; *but dey're dere now.* Den she said dere was'nt enough of 'em lef' to come furder down de riber; *but dey went all de way down.* Den missus say dey can't come up de White, no how; *but dey* DID *come*—and dey went to de Rock (Little Rock), an' dey stayed dar; an' I jes' b'lieve dey mean to stay eberywhar; an' before massa Roberts sees anoder buffalo gnat dey'll be all *ober* Texas, an' he won't hab enough niggas lef' to drive de cow home."

The italicised part of Joe's brief oration was spoken with deep emphasis, and the effect of the words was greatly increased by the appropriate gestures which accompanied them. He did not wait for any mark of approval or censure, but made his adieus rather hurriedly.

"That's a pretty sharp darkie, I should say," remarked Union.

"He is that," was the reply; "he's got any quantity of hard sense; and he's a right good fellow, too—I never heard anything bad of him."

"In case the war were brought to a close on condition that the rebellious States should send Senators and Representatives to Congress, and the Emancipation Proclamation were withdrawn, would it be a possible thing to keep the slaves under the same subjection as before the beginning of the war?"

"Certainly not. The slaves understand that they are, or soon will be, free. But let them be made to believe that the United States government intends to break the solemn promise which it made to them on the first of last January—let them once understand that their anticipations of freedom are not to be realized in the manner which they expected—and they will make a second San Domingo of every Southern State."

"Your ideas agree pretty well with those of the Abolitionists of New England."

"I can't help that," said the secessionist; "I hate an Abolitionist worse than I ever hated a snake, but I believe just what I say, and if the ——— Abolitionists where you came from agree with me, I am not to blame."

### Discussion between Major Downing and Mr. Linkin.

In a letter from the Federal capital, by Major Jack Downing, to the Editors of the Caweashin, the Major thus delivers himself in regard to the great question growing out of the war. The Major says, and even those who venture to differ from his weighty opinions, rarely fail to be interested in his expression of them:

SURS:—I've been kinder sick sence writ you last. The truth is, this clymate in the spring is raely very weakniu to the constitushin. Linkin, too, has been terribully anxus about war noose, and the nigh approach of hot weather. But the great subjeck which the Kernel and I have been considerin, is the "coutrybands." What is to be done with 'em? That's the questshin, and Linkin ses he would like to see the feller that can tell him. One night Linkin got a big map, an he sot down, and "Now," ses he, "Major, let's take a look at all creashin, an see ef ther aint sum place whar we kin send these pesky kinky heds, and get rid of 'em." "Wal," ses I, "Kernel, I'm agreed." So we went at it. First Linkin put his finger on Haty. "Now," ses he, "ther's an iland that jest suits the nigger constitushin. Suppose they go ther?" "But," ses I, "Kernel, they won't go, an ef they did, they wouldn't do nothin." "Wal," ses he, "no matter, ef they won't trouble us here enny longer." "But," ses I, "ther's one more resin. The iland aint large enuff to hold all the niggers—four millions or thereabouts." "Wal," ses he, "ther's Centril Ameriky—what do you think of that spot?" "Wal," ses I, "Kernel, that's a fine country, naterally. The Creator fixed it up on a grand scale, but you can't make a treaty with it, enny more than you can count the spots on a little pig, when he keeps runin about the hull time. The truth is, you can't tell who'll be President of it from one mornin to the next, and the niggers you send ther might all get their throats cut jest as soon as they landed." "Wal," ses Linkin, "that's a *slight* objectshin. But let's turn over to Afriky. Ther's Libery; how would that do, Major?" "Wal," ses I, "Kernel, *that* country is about the biggest humbug of the hull lot. Fust off, sum raely good peopul thought after it was goin to amount to sumthin, but arter forty years of spendin money on it, ther aint enny more chanst of civilizin Afriky in that way than ther is of makin a rifled cannon out of a bass wood log. A few donnays, who can't get enny boddy willin to hear 'em preach, hev got hold of it, an are makin a good thing out of it. As for sendin our niggers ther, why, it would take all the shippin of the world, and more money than Chase could print by steam in a year." "Wal," ses Linkin, "whar on arth *kin* we send 'em?"

"Now," ses I, "Kernel, I've got an idee of my own about that matter. I think they are best off whar they are an jest as they are, but ef you must get rid of 'em, I would send 'em all to Massa-chews-its! Peopul who are so anxus to hev other folks overrun with free niggers, ought to be willin to share sum of the blessins themselves. So let all that are here in Washington be sent rite off to Boston." "Yes, that might do," says Linkin. "But," ses

I, "sum States won't have 'em at all, and they can't go ther. So what's to be done?" "Wal," ses Linkin, "I tell you what it is, Major, this is an almighty tuff subjeck. I know sumthin about splittin rails, and what hard work is ginerally, but this nigger questshin has puzzled me more than enny thing I ever got hold of before." "Wal," ses I. "Kernel, I can explain the reason why." "Wal," ses I. "Kernel, whar do you kerry your pocket book?" Ses he, "What on arth has that to do with the subjeck?" Ses I, "Hold on, you'll see." "Wal," ses he, "I always kerry it right ther, in my left hand trowsers pocket." Ses I, "Didn't you ever hev a hole in that pocket for a day or two, an hev to put your pocket book in sum other?" Ses he, "Major, I hev." Ses I. "What did you do with it then?" "Wal," ses he, "I put it in my right hand pocket, but it kinder chafed my leg ther cause it warn't used to it, an it also felt mity onhandy. So I put it in my side coat pocket, but every time I stooped over it would drop out. Then I put it in my coat tail pocket, but I was kept all the time on the *qui rivers*, afeerd sum pickpocket would steal it. At last, in order to make it safe an sure, I put it in the top of my hat, under sum papers, but the hat was top heavy, an over it went spillin everything. I tell you I was glad when my pocket was fixed, an I got it back in the old spot."

"Now," ses I, "Kernel, that's jest the case with the niggers. The minit you get 'em out of ther place, you don't know what on arth to do with 'em. Now, we've been here all the evenin sarchin over the map to see ef we can't find sum place to put 'em. But it is all no manner of use. You've got to do with 'em jest as you did with your pocket book. Put 'em whar they belong, an then you won't have enny more trubbil."

Linkin didn't see eggzactly how I was gwin to apply the story, an wen he did, he looked kinder struck up. Wen I saw that I had made a hit on him, I follered it up.

Ses I, "Kernel, this government *ain't* out of order, as Seward and Chase kontend. They are only tryin to run it *the rong way* —that's what makes all the trubbil. I once had a thrashin machine, an I sold it to old Jim Dumbutter, an arter he got it he sed it warn't good for nothin—that it wouldn't run, &c. So I went over to see it, an I vow ef he didn't hev the machine all rong eend foremist. I went to work at it, an, arter a little wile, it went off like grease, jest as slick as a whistle. You see, old Dumbutter didn't understand the machine, an, tharfore, he couldn't make it go. Now," ses I, "Kernel, our Constitushin is a Dimmycratic machine, and its got to be run as a Dimmycratic machine, *or it won't run at all!* Now, you see, Seward is tryin to run it on his 'higher law' principle, but it warn't made for that, an the consekence is, the thing is pretty nigh smashed up."

"Wal," ses Linkin, "things do look kinder dark. I don't know whar we will cum out, but I guess I'll issoo a proclamashin for the ministers to pray for us. Perhaps they will do sum good." Ses I, "Kernel, that reminds me of old Elder Doolittle, who cum along the road one day rite whar old Sol Hopkins, a very wicked old sinner, was hoein corn. The season was late, and the corn was mity slim. Ses the Elder: 'Mister Hopkins, your corn is not very forrard this year.' 'No, its monstrous poor,' ses Hopkins, 'an I guess I shan't have half a crop.' 'Wal,' ses the Elder, 'Mister Hopkins, you ought to pray to the Lord for good crops, perhaps he will hear you.' 'Wal, perhaps he will, and perhaps he won't,' ses old Sol, 'but I'll be darned ef I don't believe that this corn needs *manure* a tarnel sight more than it does prayin for.' Now," ses I, "Linkin, I think this country is something like old Hopkinses corn. It needs statesmanship good deal more than prayin for." Linkin didn't seem to like that observation of mine much, for he turned the subjeck, an he ain't axed me what it was best to do with the nigger sence.

### Bad for the Cow.

In the following little story, which is certainly unique in its way, it will not require a great stretch of imagination to consider the Federal Government as representing the locomotive, and the seceding States the cow:

When George Stephenson, the celebrated Scotch engineer, had completed his model of a locomotive, he presented himself before the British parliament, and asked the attention and support of that body. The grave M. P.'s, looking sneeringly at the great mechanic's invention, asked,—

"So you have made a carriage to run only by steam, have you?"

"Yes, my lords."

"And you expect your carriage to run on parallel rails, so that it can't go off, do you?"

"Yes, my lords."

"Well now, Mr. Stephenson, let us show you how absurd your claim is. Suppose when your carriage is running upon these rails at the rate of twenty or thirty miles per hour, if you're extravagant enough to even suppose such a thing is possible, a cow should get in its way. You can't turn out for her—what then?"

"Then 'twill be *bad for the cow*, my lords!"

### Advised to Stick to his Business.

If, through a multitude of counsellors there is safety, President Lincoln may be said never to have run any great risk of not carrying the ship of state securely through all its perils. Their number in his case was always legion. Among these, in the early part of the war, was a Western farmer, who sought the President day after day, until at last he procured the much desired special audience. Like many other visitors at the executive mansion, he, too, had a plan for the successful prosecution of the war, to which Mr. Lincoln listined as patiently as he could. When he was through, he asked the opinion of the President upon his plan.

"Well," said Mr. Lincoln, "I'll answer by telling you a story. You have heard of Mr. Blank, of Chicago? He was an immense loafer in his way—in fact, never did anything in his life. One day he got crazy over a great rise in the price of wheat, upon which many speculators gained large fortunes. Blank started off one morning to one of the most successful of the speculators, and with much enthusiasm laid before him a plan by which he, the said Blank, was certain of becoming independently rich. When he had finished, he asked the opinion of his hearer upon his plan of operations. The reply came as follows: 'My advice is that you stick to your business!' 'But,' asked Blank, 'what is my business?' 'I don't know what it is,' said the merchant, 'but, whatever it is, I advise you to stick to it.' And now," said Mr. Lincoln, "I mean nothing offensive, for I know you mean well, but I think you had better stick to your business, and leave the war to those who have the responsibility of managing it."

### Burlesque on Peace Propositions.

Concerning a certain peace proposition then on the tapis at Washington, Mr. Kerr —his prenomen Orpheus C.,—thus discourseth :—

The Confederacy hastily put on a pair of white cotton gloves, and says he:

"Am I addressing the Democratic Organization?"

"You address the large Kentucky branch," says the Conservative chap, pulling out his ruffles.

"Then," says the Confederacy, "I am prepared to make an indirect proposition for peace. My name is Mr. Lamb, by which title the democratic organization has always known the injured Confederacy, and I propose the following terms: Hostilities shall at once cease, and the two armies be consolidated under the title of the Confederate State forces. The war debts of the North and South shall be so united that the North may be able to pay them without confusion.

"An election for a new President shall at once be held, everybody voting save those who have shown animosity to the sunny South. France shall be driven out of Mexico by the consolidated armies, the expense being so managed that the North may pay it without further trouble. Upon these terms the Confederacy will become a peaceful fellow man."

Fernando Wood

"Hem!" says the Kentucky chap. "What you ask is perfectly reasonable, I will consider the matter after the manner of a dispassionate democrat, and return you my answer in a few days."

Here I hastily stepped up, and says I, "But are you not going to consult the President at all about it, my Jupiter Tonans?"

"The President? the President?" says the Conservative Kentucky chap, with a vague look—"Hem!" says he, "I really forgot all about the President."

"The democratic organization," (adds Kerr, with said prenomen,) "my boy, in its zeal to benefit its distracted country, is occasionally like that eminent fire company in the Sixth Ward, which nobly usurped with its hose the terrible business of putting out a large conflagration, and never remembered until its beautiful machine was all in position, that another company of fellow firemen had exclusive possession of all the water works."

The same sparkling and trenchant pen would find some other peace propositions, emanating from organizations not exactly Democratic or Conservative, first rate material for his side-shaking irony and wit; or, should he lack the necessary material, Mr. Fernando Wood, the "Apostle of Peace," might be able to supply the deficiency.

### Ohio Toll-gate Keeper's Talk with Vallandigham.

As Messrs. Vallandigham and Pendleton, the Pro-Southern or Anti-War members of Congress, from Ohio, were going in a carriage, in the spring of 1863, from Batavia, to fill an appointment at some place in Brown County, they drew up at a toll-gate.

Vallandigham.

Mr. Pendleton, with that amiable familiarity characterizing his intercourse with the poor and lowly voters, asked the venerable gate-keeper how he stood on politics, and was answered: "I am a Democrat; have voted the ticket all my life, and expect to as long as I live."

"That's right, my good man! I am glad to find you all right on politics; now, as an old Democrat, what do you think of the Hon. Mr. Vallandigham for our next Governor?—Vallandigham for our next Governor, eh?"

"Vallandigham is the —— traitor north of Mason and Dixon's line, and I wouldn't help elect him dog pelter!"

"But stop, man, this gentleman with me is Mr. V."

"I don't care who he is; I am a Jackson Democrat, not a Vallandighamcrat."

The worthy pair now drove on, not particularly elated or refreshed in their political feelings by the conversation they themselves had provoked.

### Gov. Andy Johnson's Supplement to one of Lorenzo Dow's Stories.

Governor Andy Johnson—now our President,—at one of the Loyal League meetings in New York, hit the secession sympathizers with the following story. Great complaint, (said the Governor) has been made about the suspension of the writ of *habeas corpus*. Is there any man who has no treason lurking in his bosom that is apprehensive of an arrest? Why are certain persons so nervous in this regard? Because treason is lurking in their bosoms!

Lorenzo Dow, when he was on his way, upon one occasion, to attend an appointment, met a man who complained that his axe had been stolen.

"I will settle that matter for you," said Dow.

Before reaching the meeting house he picked up a large stone, weighing about a pound and a half. After he had concluded his sermon in his peculiar way, looking over the audience, turning the stone over in his hand, he said:

"I have been informed by one of your neighbors that he had his axe stolen last night, and I intend with this stone to knock the man down who did it."

Poising the stone in his hand, as if about to throw it, there was one man who immediately dodged behind his seat, and Dow pointed him out to the audience as the thief. And so I say (continued Gov. Johnson,) if you want to find out traitors, just look around and shake the suspended writ of habeas corpus at them, and you will see them dodge, shrink and complain.

### Napoleon on French Youngsters in the Federal Army.

Archbishop Hughes, on his way to Rome, had an interview with the Emperor Napoleon. After a few commonplaces on the horrors of civil war, pronounced in the slow and monotonous tone of voice peculiar to him, Louis Napoleon abruptly altered his manner. His glassy countenance lit up, his voice rose, and he proceeded with marked accentuation: "But who then advised your President, Mr. Lincoln, what induced him to receive *those two youngsters* (*ces deux jeunes hommes*—king Louis Philippe's sons,) into his army? He might have perceived that it is not to his credit to encourage pretensions like theirs by giving them an opportunity of getting themselves talked of. The cause of the Orleans is not a cause which can be avowed. I found the throne vacant. I took it. *But they! they stole the crown of their relative!*"

### That Card from Willard's Hotel.

An anecdote was told at an out door political meeting, in Washington, one night, by the Hon. Mr. Chittenden, of Vermont, the well known Register of the United States Treasury. It shows what was going on among certain high political characters, to prevent the will of the people from being executed in the inauguration of Mr. Lincoln and to overthrow and usurp the constitutional Government.

Mr. Chittenden remarked that he would state one fact in connection with his experience in Washington, which he believed had never yet been made public: His first visit to the national capital was perhaps an unfortunate one. He was a delegate from the State of Vermont to the peace convention, or conference, which met in that city, in the month of February, 1861, upon the invitation of the Governor of Virginia. In that convention he happened to form the acquaintance of James B. Clay, of Kentucky, William A. Seddon, of Virginia (afterwards the Confederate Secretary of War), Governor Morehead, of Kentucky, (who became a fugitive from the flag that had always protected him,) and others of a similar political stripe. His seat was near those gentlemen. One day, while sitting with them, a servant from Willard's Hotel entered and handed a card to Mr. Seddon, who sat near Mr. Chittenden. He did not know what was on the card, but it was passed around from one to the other in such a manner that he could not help but see what was written upon it. On the card was written these words: '*Lincoln is in Washington!*' He never saw such confusion made by a small piece of card before. They looked at each other with amazement. At last, Waldo P. Johnson, afterwards a Senator from Missouri, who could control himself no longer, exclaimed with vehemence and chagrin, "How the devil did he get through Baltimore?"

It was a part of the secession plot that the bludgeon-mongers of Baltimore should see to it that Mr. Lincoln did not pass through that city alive, on his way to assume the charge of the Government—a graphic account of which will be found on another page of this volume.

### Secret of the Unanimous Vote in the Senate.

The passage of a bill by Congress enlarging the power of the President of the United States in order for him to more effectually meet the necessities, civil and military, of the country, was in the highest degree expedient. But how the bill ever passed the Senate by an unanimous vote, while it received so bitter an opposition in the House, was a point which partook largely of the mysterious, in the view of outsiders. A Democratic Senator, however,—one of those who took their noviriate for senatorial honors in the cells of Fort Lafayette—(Walk, of New Jersey,)—gave a solution of the mystery, one day, and so terse and true as to deserve repetition. "Four of our men"—and he named them, but of course one couldn't be guilty of such disrespect to American Senators as to print them—"four of our men were so drunk they couldn't leave their rooms; and the others, not knowing how drunk these men were, had gone off to Count Mercier's party." That is the whole story, —and a similar tale might be told in connection with many other Congressional bills and measures. It is hardly necessary to add, that more than one section was represented in the drunken quartette in question.

### Price of Chivalry in Hard Cash.

When the Federal troops occupied Winchester, Virginia, a young lady was seen ripping up a Union flag, to turn into a "Secesh streamer." An officer made her give it up. It was repaired and raised over the sidewalk of the surgeon's house, where it was a great trouble to the Winchester ladies, who crossed the street rather than walk under it. One day the Maine Tenth seeing one of them coming down the pavement, placed a bright silver Union "quarter" directly under the flag. Miss Secesh came up and stepped off the curb as usual to go round the "dirty rag," but on seeing the piece of money she retraced her steps, and while she was stooping to pick it up she was greeted by a tremendous shout of laughter. So the price of chivalry was found to be not *more* than twenty-five cents—certain!

### "Spiritual" Revelations on the Conduct of the War.

President Lincoln was induced by some of his friends to hold a "spiritual soiree," one evening, in the crimson room in the White House, to test the alleged wonderful supernatural powers of Mr. Charles E. Shockle. The party consisted of the President, Mrs. Lincoln, Secretaries Welles and Stanton, Mr. D. of New York, Mr. F. of Philadelphia, and Mr. Shockle, accompanied by a friend. They took their seats in the circle about eight o'clock, but the President was called away shortly after the manifestations commenced, and the spirits which had apparently assembled to convince him of their power, gave visible tokens of their displeasure at the President's absence, by pinching Mr. Stanton's ears and twitching Mr. Welles's beard. He soon returned, but it was some time before harmony was restored, for the mishaps to the secretaries caused such bursts of laughter that the influence was very unpropitious. For some half-hour the demonstrations were of a physical character—tables were moved, and the picture of Henry Clay, which hangs on the wall, was swayed more than a foot, and two candelebras, presented by the Dey of Algiers to President Adams, were twice raised nearly to the ceiling.

It was nearly nine o'clock before Shockle was fully under spiritual influence, and so powerful were the subsequent manifestations, that twice during the evening restoratives were applied, for he was much weakened. The following account of what took place is believed to be as correct as possible.

Loud rappings, about nine o'clock, were heard directly beneath the President's feet, and Mr. Shockle stated that an Indian desired to communicate.

"Well, Sir," said the President, "I should be happy to hear what his Indian majesty has to say. We have recently had a visitation from our red brethren, and it was the only delegation, black, white, or blue, which did not volunteer some advice about the conduct of the war."

The medium then called for pencil and paper, and they were laid upon the table in sight of all. A handkerchief was then taken from Mr. Stanton, and the materials were carefully concealed from sight. In a short time, knocks were heard and the paper was uncovered. To the surprise of all present it read as follows:

"Haste makes waste, but delays cause

PATRIOTIC, POLITICAL, CIVIL, JUDICIAL, ETC. 51

vexations. Give vitality by energy. Use every means to subdue. Proclamations are useless; make a bold front and fight the enemy; leave traitors at home to the care of loyal men. Less note of preparation, less parade and policy talk, and more action. HENRY KNOX."

"That is not Indian talk, Mr. Shockle," said the President; who is 'Henry Knox?'

It was suggested to the medium to ask who General Knox was, and before the words were fully uttered, the medium spoke in a strange voice, "The first Secretary of War."

"Oh! yes, General Knox," said the President; who, turning to the Secretary, said: "Stanton, that message is for you; it is from your predecessor."

Mr. Stanton made no reply.

"I should like to ask General Knox," said the President, "if it is within the scope of his ability, to tell us when this rebellion will be put down."

In the same manner as before, this message was received:

"Washington, Lafayette, Franklin, Wilberforce, Napoleon, and myself have held frequent consultation on this point. There is something which our spiritual eyes cannot detect which appears well formed. Evil has come at times by removal of men from high positions, and there are those in retirement whose abilities should be made useful to hasten the end. Napoleon says, concentrate your forces upon one point: Lafayette thinks that the rebellion will die of exhaustion; Franklin sees the end approaching, as the South must give up for want of mechanical ability to compete against Northern mechanics. Wilberforce sees hope only in a negro army.—KNOX."

"Well," exclaimed the President, "opinions differ among the saints as well as among the sinners. They don't seem to understand running the machines among the celestials much better than we do. Their talk and advice sound very much like the talk of my cabinet—don't you think so, Mr. Welles?"

"Well, I don't know—I will think the matter over, and see what conclusion to arrive at."

Heavy raps were heard, and the alphabet was called for, when "That's what's the matter," was spelt out.

There was a shout of laughter, and Mr. Welles stroked his beard.

"That means, Mr. Welles," said the President, "that you are apt to be long-winded, and think the nearest way home is the longest way round. Short cuts in war times. I wish the spirits would tell us how to catch the Alabama."

The lights, which had been partially lowered, almost instantaneously became so dim as to make it difficult to distinguish the features of any one in the room, and on the large mirror over the mantel-piece there appeared the most beautiful though supernatural picture ever beheld. It represented a sea view, the Alabama with all steam up flying from the pursuit of another large steamer. Two merchantmen in the distance were seen, partially destroyed by fire. The picture changed, and the Alabama was seen at anchor under the shadow of an English fort—from which an English flag was waving. The Alabama was floating idly, not a soul on board, and no signs of life visible about her. The picture vanished, and in letters of purple appeared: "The English people demand this of England's aristocracy."

"So England is to seize the Alabama finally?" said Mr. Lincoln: "It may be possible; but, Mr. Welles, don't let one gunboat or monitor less be built."

The spirits called for the alphabet, and again "That's what's the matter," was spelt out.

"I see, I see," said the President: "Mother England thinks that what's sauce for the goose may be sauce for the gander. It may be tit, tat, too, hereafter. But it is not very complimentary to our navy, anyhow."

"We've done our best, Mr. President," said Mr. Welles; "I'm maturing a plan which, when perfected, I think, if it works well, will be a perfect trap for the Alabama."

"Well, Mr. Shockle," remarked the President, "I have seen strange things and heard rather odd remarks; but nothing which convinces me, except the pictures, that there is anything very heavenly about all this. I should like, if possible, to hear what Judge Douglas says about this war."

"I'll try to get his spirit," said Mr. Shockle; "but it sometimes happens, as it did to-night in the case of the Indian, that though first impressed by one spirit, I yield to another more powerful. If perfect silence is maintained, I will see if we cannot induce General Knox to send for Mr. Douglas."

Three raps were given, signifying assent to the proposition. Perfect silence was maintained, and after an interval of perhaps three minutes, Mr. Shockle rose quickly from his chair and stood up behind it, resting his left arm on the back, his right thrust into his bosom. In a voice such as no one could mistake who had ever heard Mr. Douglas, he spoke. The language was eloquent and choice. He urged the President to throw aside all advisers who hesitate about the policy to be pursued, and to listen to the wishes of the people, who would sustain him at all points if his aim was, as he believed it was, to restore the Union. He said that there were Burrs and Blennerhassetts living, but that they would wither before the popular approval which would follow one or two victories, such as he thought must take place ere long. The turning-point in this war will be the proper use of these victories. If wicked men in the first hours of success think it time to devote their attention to party, the war will be prolonged; but if victory is followed up by energetic action, all will be well.

"I believe that," said the President, "whether it comes from spirit or human."

Here closed the interview, at Mrs. Lincoln's request, Mr. Shockle being much prostrated. The account here given is from one who was present; and, though evidently by no one unfriendly to the medium, there has been no denial of the general correctness of the proceedings.

### Putting 'Em Through a Course of Sprouts.

One lively spring day, four young men of the city of Frederick, Maryland, went to the good old town of Liberty, and whilst passing the Stars and Stripes which floated from a pole at the west end of the town, took the idea into their empty heads to *curse* that time-honored emblem with considerable liberality and positiveness, and to even say something about taking it down. Hearing, however, that they would be called to account for such rebellious acts, they loaded their pistols before leaving the hotel, and roisterly declared what they would do if attacked. The "fun" came at last. About five o'clock, a carriage was seen coming up the hill, and when nearly opposite the flag, two citizens walked out into the middle of the street and gave the command, "*Halt*," which was promptly obeyed. The next command was—"Salute that flag!" After an excuse or two about a 'bad cold,' and 'how salute it?' they gave a weak cheer. The answer to this was, "That won't do; a little louder!" The second time their voices raised considerable; but "louder yet!" was commanded, and the third time they gave mighty good proof of pulmonary health. They were then ordered to "Curse secession," and they did so. After having thus passed successfully their exercise on the various points of the political decalogue, they were allowed to move on —wiser and better posted men.

### Carolinian Unionist Showing the Track.

Captain Grant, of the Nineteenth Wisconsin regiment, had the good fortune to escape from the Confederate prison at Columbia, South Carolina, to the Union lines. When he had been twenty days out, and had just crossed the line between

North and South Carolina, he was startled about the middle of the night by hearing voices in the middle of the road and approaching. Stepping aside and listening closely, he was reassured by the discovery that one of the voices was that of a negro, and supposed, of course, the other was a negro also. He called them, and enquired the road to a town not far distant, which was in the direction he wished to go. To this interrogatory, a white man's voice replied:—

Carolina Unionist.

"Men of your stamp don't want to go to that town—you must flank it."

"What do you mean by men of my stamp?" was the reponse.

"Why," said the Carolinian, "I mean that you don't want to go there, that's all; but you must flank it."

"But what do you suspect me of being?" Captain Grant enquired.

"You are a Yankee," replied the Carolinian; "if you go there you will be made a prisoner."

"And if I am a Yankee," said the Captain, "and wanted to flank the town, is there anybody about here who could show me how to do it?—is there such a man?"

"That I be," was the reply, and the Carolinian parted from his negro companion, who turned out to be a woman, and took Captain Grant to his house, and called up his wife and had her get supper for the stranger. Here Captain Grant got his first insight of the faithfulness, earnestness and hopefulness of the real Union party of North Carolina. His host told him where and how to find Union men, and marked out the most favorable roads for him to take, giving many directions, all of which were proven to have been given in good faith.

### Sentiments of a Dying Soldier.

At a public meeting in Boston, Mr. Gough said: "Not long ago I was in a hospital, and saw a young man, twenty-six years of age, pale and emaciated, with his shattered arm resting upon an oil-silk pillow, and there he had been many long and weary weeks, waiting for sufficient strength for an amputation. I knelt by his side and said, "Will you answer me one question?" "Yes sir," was his reply. "Suppose then you were well, at home, in good health, and knew all this would come to you, if you enlisted, would you enlist?" "Yes, Sir," he answered in a whisper; "I would in a minute! What is my arm or my life compared with the safety of the country?"

That was patriotism of the genuine brand.

### Banks's Morning Call at Marshal Kane's Door.

General Banks, on assuming command in Maryland, took his first step in the work of throttling treason by arresting George P. Kane, marshal of the police of Baltimore, who had publicly declared that that city was "red with blood," and boastingly adding, with reference to the Northern troops, "We will fight them, and whip them, or die." Banks accordingly determined to arrest the marshal. Eighteen hundred men marched from Fort McHenry into Baltimore with loaded muskets and fixed bayonets, just before daybreak, for it was well known that the marshal had arms secreted at the head-quarters and the stations of the police, and it seemed that he was only waiting a favorable opportunity to rise with his whole force and begin an insurrection to wrest Baltimore from Federal authority.

The men wore their cartridge boxes, in which were a few rounds, but no knapsacks. They had marched a square, when a policeman, in his cool summer uniform, and swinging his long baton, was observed crossing the street ahead. Instantly the head of the column opened, the body swept on, and the policeman, riveted to the ground in astonishment at this manœuvre, unknown to the tactics of either Matsell or Vidocq, found himself swallowed up and borne along in the resistless advance. Two squares ahead another policeman was discovered—again the column opened and he was engulfed. By the time the column reached the residence of the marshal, not less than fifty-seven of the vigilant guardians of the night had been thus swallowed up; but when they found that their captors had halted at the door of the marshal's house, they began to smell a rat of the largest possible dimensions. An officer now rang the bell. After some delay, a night-capped head popped out of the window, and the well-known voice of Marshal Kane inquired, in a rather gruff tone,—

"What is wanted?"

The officer blandly replied that he himself was the article just then in demand.

"Hum, hum," said the marshal, never at a loss for a joke, "I'll supply that demand."

Did the vision of escape cross the marshal's mind? Possibly. It is certain that he skipped with agility to a back window, raised the curtain and looked out. Alas! the moonbeams played upon five hundred glittering bayonets in the yard below. The game was up, and the marshal knew he must submit to his inevitable fate. He descended the stairs and opened the front door.

"Good God!" he exclaimed to the officer in command. "Why did you not bring five or six more regiments and some artillery? If you had sent me a note and a carriage, I would have come without all this fuss."

It was even then day-break; the column moved briskly forward, and the marshal enjoyed the rare sight of sunrise from the ramparts of Fort McHenry.

### Prospective Value of the War.

An officer from Louisville led one of Rosecrans' regiments into battle, his superior having been called to other duty. In the advance this man's son fell by a rebel bullet. The father saw him fall, but could not stop to care for him. Narrating the circumstances, the bereaved father said, with the tears fast falling from his eyes:

"My boy, you know, is gone. I was in temporary command of the regiment, and as we were pressing on I saw my boy fall. I could not turn back to him, so I said to a soldier, 'Look to Johnny,' and went on, and we did the work we went to do."

"Do you still hold to the idea you expressed when you and I talked over the questions of this war before? Do you feel now as you did then?

"Certainly; I feel we are doing this work for ourselves and children, and for those who are to come after us. Of course, I am very sad, but the cause is just the same as before—*only more sacred than ever.*"

### Comedy of Cabinet Errors.

The following jaunty account is told of an interview with the Cabinet chiefs, just after the Baltimore Republican Nominating Convention:

Immediately upon the adjournment of the Convention, a prominent Republican gentleman paid his respects to Mr. Seward; found him in a pleasant state of mind, with one thumb in vest pocket, and twirling his spectacles with the other hand.

"Ha! ha! Mr. —," said the secretary

PATRIOTIC, POLITICAL, CIVIL, JUDICIAL, ETC.   55

to his visitor, "I see that poor Blair and Chase have been invited to leave the Cabinet by the Baltimore Convention!"

The gentleman was astonished, as he had supposed that this resolution referred to Mr. Seward as much, at least, as to any other member of the Cabinet, and after a few common-place remarks, retired. Immediately after, he paid his respects to Mr. Welles, whom he found awake, and who immediately notified his visitor that he had heard or dreamt that some people, who had recently assembled in Baltimore, had invited Mr. Seward to leave the Cabinet. The next Secretary visited was Mr. Blair, and he was found to be laboring under the delusion that the resolution of the Convention was meant for Mr. Chase, his particular 'friend.' And finally it was discovered, in this amusing Comedy of Cabinet Errors, that every individual member of Old Abe's confidential advisers supposed that he was excepted, while all the others were censured for their part in the conduct of the war.

### Political Courtesies at the White House.

One of the most significant of the many political groupings at one of President Lincoln's 'receptions' during the war, was that in which the President, Mrs. Lincoln, General and Mrs. McClellan, and General and Mrs. Fremont, were parties. The two latter were waiting in the reception room until their carriage should arrive, when the President came up and asked General Fremont if he would be presented to General McClellan. "With pleasure," replied he, "but we are about leaving." "Never mind that," said the President, "I've got him in a corner in the other room, and he's waiting for you." Of course General Fremont did not refuse, so, followed by Senator Sumner and Mrs. Fremont, he walked with Mr. Lincoln the entire length of the East Room, the observed of all the guests, who cheerfully 'gave place.' The introduction was, of course, the ordinary simple ceremony, and after a few moments conversation with General and Mrs. McClellan, the parties retired as they had advanced. Such an occurrence of ceremonial courtesy between two opposed military and political chieftains did not fail to impress the hundreds of lookers on.

### Forgetting his Usual Courtesy.

The instances are rare in which President Lincoln's temper is known to have given way, under the annoyance of persons boring him with their "views" of secession, war, emancipation, &c. One such instance is thus narrated:

A good lady of Ward Beecher's church, doubtless inspired by her pastor's free exhortations about politics, thought she had discovered a sure means of aiding the cause, and became so engrossed with it that, — woman-like — she persuaded her husband to take her to Washington that she might be the first to whisper it in the ear of the President, and so become the honored instrument of the nation's salvation. The patriotic couple called at the White House, and were told that the President was engaged on important business and could not be seen. But the lady thought her mission of too much importance to be postponed for a single day, and sent word back to the President that her business was of the greatest consequence.

Unwilling to send away a lady, and supposing that she had come to ask a personal favor, perhaps in reference to some relative in the army, the President left his conference on State matters, and went down to listen to his lady visitor. He sat patiently while she opened her plan of military and moral strategy for the suppression of the rebellion, and then rising to his full hight, which was some, said, with abruptness and impatience—

"Madam, all this has been thought of a hundred times before!"

Saying which, he hastened out of the room, forgetting his usual courtesy to the other sex.

### Political Rendering of Hamlet.

Hon. John Cochrane is 'some' at sensation making. He got off something in this line, in one of his speeches during the war, which—at one point at least—seemed to 'bring down the house,' friends and opponents alike included. With characteristic vivaciousness of manner and expression, Mr. C. said:

Upon yonder lines, at Windsor Pass, Vallandigham and his friend Horatio—I see the friend of Horatio grasping his cloak about him to screen him from the northern blast; and I also behold Marcellus Wood. It is the peace platform on the Canadian line. They tread the stage and remind me of that scene conceived in the mind of nature's poet, composed undoubtedly with reference to events now transpiring. It was the melancholy Hamlet—Vallandigham—his friend Horatio, and the officer Marcellus Wood, that occupied, upon a dreary night, a brief hour upon the peace platform at Elsinore, [Hisses and applause.]

Hamlet—(Vallandigham)—the air bites shrewdly; it is very cold.

Horatio—it is indeed, an unhappy and an eager air.

Hamlet—What hour now?

Horatio—Methinks it lacks of twelve.

Marcellus Wood—No, it has struck.

Horatio—Indeed! I heard it not.

Heard it not, Horatio? Heard you not Rhode Island, one? two, Vermont? three, Massachusetts? four, New Hampshire? five, Maine? six, California? seven, Wisconsin? eight, Illinois? nine, Pennsylvania? ten, Ohio? eleven, Maryland? and New York, twelve? [Uproarous applause, which lasted for some time, the audience rising to their feet and cheering *en masse.*] And there struck the last syllable of recorded time. If, Horatio, your auricular nerve was dead to that, it must be the dull, cold ear of death with which you are struck. The dead heard it, looked up and wondered at the miracle. The living heard it and rejoiced, and as our army stood shoulder to shoulder in the front, the people were standing shoulder to shoulder in the rear.

### Cheers instead of a Speech.

A very cheerful little speech was given by President Lincoln, one afternoon, while a very large concourse of people was assembled on the grounds of the presidential mansion, listening to the charming music of the Marine Band.

The President, in the midst of the musical entertainment, made his appearance on the balcony of the White House, and after conversing with a few friends, stood up and looked very much like a man who was going to make a speech. The people took the cue from Abraham's countenance, and instantly there was a general rush to the spot where he stood. Mr. Lincoln smiled on the crowd gathered around him, and understanding very well what they wanted, made a low bow and proceeded:

"Ladies and gentlemen, I suppose you want a speech, don't you?"

"Yes, yes!" was the response on all sides.

"Well," said the President, "I propose in lieu of it to give three cheers for General Grant and the army under him."

The cheers were given with a right good will, after which the crowd dispersed, thinking that old Abe had played a joke in pretending that he was going to make a speech. The little episode put everybody into the best of humor. The President knew well how to lead off with "three and a tiger."

### Stirring Scene at the Polls.

At a town meeting held in Newton, Massachusetts, a very black freedman who came from Virginia to the former State about a year and a half previously, and who, for fourteen months, had been in the employ of a gentleman in West Newton, appeared at the polls for the purpose of voting. He had been assessed, his tax was paid, and he was all right on the record, but he held a War ticket, and the presiding member of the board of selectmen at the time, who entertained opposite political views, refused permission for him to vote.

"Upon what grounds?" asked a gentleman present. "Because," said the officer, "he is an escaped slave, and under the fugitive slave law he ought to be sent back." "But," said the gentleman, "we don't live under that dispensation now; the President's Proclamation has settled all that, and the man has a right to vote and should be allowed to do so."

"The President had no right to make such a Proclamation; it is unconstitutional," said the selectman.

The gentleman replied: "It is for the Board to determine the man's right to vote, and I appeal to them;" and with the exception above stated all concurred that the freedman had the right to vote, and he accordingly deposited his first ballot with a grin of delight which was pleasant to witness.

As he was doing this, however, a little Irishman entered his protest, on the ground that he could not read and write. "I beg pardon," said the gentleman who acted the part of friend to the voter, "he can read and write. Since he came here he has been prepared for the duties of a free man, and he can read and write as well as a white man." "Well," said the little Irishman, "I don't care for that; niggers have no right to vote, any way," and so the matter ended.

### General Stewart and Senator Douglas on the "Situation."

A most remarkable prediction was made by Senator Douglas, in January, 1861. Mr. Douglas was asked by General C. B. Stewart, of New York, who was making a New Year's call on the great Illinoisian,—

"What will be the results of the efforts of Jefferson Davis and his associates to divide the Union?"

"The cotton States," Douglas replied, "are making an effort to draw in the border States to their schemes of secession, and I am too fearful they will succeed. If they do succeed, there will be the most terrible civil war the world has ever seen, lasting for years. Virginia will become a charnel house; but the end will be the triumph of the Union cause. One of their first efforts will be to take possession of this capital, to give them prestige abroad, but they will never succeed in taking it;

*Douglas.*

the North will rise *en masse* to defend it; but it will become a city of hospitals; the churches will be used for the sick and wounded, and even the Minnesota block (which afterward did become the Douglas hospital) may be devoted to that purpose before the end of the war."

"What justification is there for all this?" inquired General Stewart.

"There is," said Douglas, "no justification, nor any pretense of any. If they will remain in the Union, I will go as far as the Constitution will permit to maintain their just rights, and I do not doubt but a majority of Congress will do the same. But,"—and this he said rising on his feet and extending his arm, "if the Southern States attempt to secede from this Union without further cause, I am in favor of their having just so many slaves, and just so much slave territory, as they can hold at the point of the bayonet—and no more!"

## Wilkinson's Veteran Minnesota Regiment.

One of the richest scenes afforded by the United States Senate, during the war, was that in which Pitt Fessenden, of Maine, and Wilkinson, of Minnesota, were the principal actors. Wilkinson—a very clever Senator—had been indulging in a little abuse of "the East." The East got everything, he said, and the West nothing. He alluded particularly to a veteran regiment from Minnesota, which from some informality had not yet received its pay, and an appeal was taken to Congress, which was not successful. From one thing to another, the discussion rambled, till at last the Senator (Wilkinson) began to ridicule the army of the Potomac in "Dunn Browne's" best style. He pictured that army swinging to and fro between Washington and Culpepper, and made eastern armies and eastern generals appear in a ridiculous aspect. Pitt Fessenden rose to defend the East.

"How is it," asked Fessenden, "about the veteran Minnesota regiment, which our friend has complimented so highly here? To what army did it belong?"

"To the army of the Potomac," replied Wilkinson.

"Indeed," quoth the Maine senator, "*is it possible?* Has this Minnesota regiment been swinging to and fro between the Potomac and the Rapidan?"

Wilkinson then explained that he did not allude to the soldiers of the army of the Potomac, but to its leaders. Mr. Fessenden took him up on that point.

"Who is the General-in-Chief?" asked Mr. Fessenden; "It is General Halleck, a western man. Who is the Commander-in-Chief, the man responsible for the leadership of all the armies? Is *he* not a western man?"

It was a most amusing colloquial debate, Fessenden coming out in his best style, and Wilkinson doing extremely well, too, but choosing to be in a weak position, he was compelled to throw up the sponge.

## Availing himself of a Joke.

A representative of one of the five Great Powers met Mr. Seward one day, just as he was coming out of his room, on his way to dinner. Of course the diplomat was invited to walk in. He declined, saying:

"Oh, no, I only called to tell you a good joke. One of our Captains has just arrived, and says that, when he reached

Seward.

Charleston and went to my consul's office, and inquired for the consul, he was told that he was drilling his company. What company? inquired the captain of the ship. Why, one of the companies selected to march against Washington. The captain was greatly surprised, and mentioned the fact as evidence of the universal feeling of hostility which pervades Charleston."

*Mr. Seward.* What is the name of your consul at Charleston?

*Diplomat.* ———.

*Mr. Seward,* (opening the door opposite where they were standing.) Mr. Assistant Secretary, draw up an order *recalling* the *exequatur* issued in favor of ———, consul at Charleston. There. That business is disposed of.

*Diplomat.* My ——— Seward! You are not in earnest. I only told you the story as a good joke.

*Mr. Seward.* And I, Mr. ———, avail myself of this "joke," to give you practical evidence of the manner in which we intend to deal with every Foreign Power and their representatives, whenever they interfere, directly or indirectly, between us and the traitors in rebellion against our Government. The exequatur of your consul is recalled; and I sincerely hope that no imprudence on the other side of the Atlantic, will compel me as summarily to terminate the very pleasant relations now existing with all the members of the Diplomatic Corps.

## "And the brother shall deliver up the brother to death."

A man named C—e, lived in Missouri, about fifty miles from the Kansas border. His family, originally from the South, had settled in southwestern Missouri. When the war broke out his two brothers avowed their disloyalty to the Government, joined

"And the brother shall deliver up the brother to death."

the secession army,—and they urged him to do so too. But he was true to his allegiance to the Union and its starry ensign. Hesitating, and with the ties of kindred to distract him, he remained a passive witness of events until at length induced him to take his place in the great struggle. A few days after a younger brother rode up to his house. At the time he was out of his wagon, and had been practising with his rifle at a mark, and had just loaded. The younger brother said: "I'm glad you're thinking about your gun. You'd better join a company." "I have done so," was the calm reply. "Whose?" "Captain ——'s," naming the Captain of a company of Home Guards that had been raised in that county. "Ah! that's what you are at, is it?" cried the younger brother—and, drawing a Colt's navy, he continued, "I've got something for you," and fired. The ball lodged in the breast of the elder brother, who staggered and fell with the violence or suddenness of the shock. Recovering himself, however, for a moment, with superhuman energy, he got upon his knees, and seizing his rifle, pointed it at his murderous brother, who turned and fled, but the rifle-ball in his spine arrested the course of the rebel forever. The family of the Union man gathered a few of their effects hurriedly, and fled with him in a wagon—at last reaching Kansas, where, though severely wounded, he slowly recovered.

## Female Traitors making Ashes of the Glorious Flag.

In the earlier stage of the rebellion, four young gentlemen stopping in Alexandria, engaged apartments there of a highly respectable lady living in Prince street, with her daughters, the latter aged respectively sixteen and eighteen. Although the lady and her daughters were avowed secessionists, the former having two sons in the rebel army, the new-comers were nevertheless not quite prepared to hear them speak so contemptuously and bitterly of the Union. The young gentlemen, it appears, took it into their heads to hoist the Stars and Stripes on the top of their dwelling, one day. The lady and daughters, when they discovered it, raised such a storm of indignation that the gentlemen were afraid to approach them. One of the young ladies clambered to the roof of the house, at the risk of life and limb, and, with the spirit of a tigress, tore down the flag, trampled it beneath her feet, and finally threw the fragments into the stove. Not content with this disrespect to the glorious emblem of the country which had protected herself and family from their birth, this young traitress took the ashes of the burnt flag and pitched them contemptuously into the street.

### Merited Rebuke of a Secessionist by General Dumont.

A good anecdote is told of how a violent secessionist at the Tennessee capital got a merited rebuke from General Dumont. A famous physician's female household deported themselves so rudely to our soldiers, once or twice actually spitting in their faces, that the General ordered the house to be put under guard, with orders to let no one pass in or out. The Doctor, who was in the country at the time, was greatly incensed on finding his access to his own house debarred by a guard of soldiery on his return, and forthwith went to headquarters, boiling over with rage. On hearing the Doctor's representation, the General calmly replied that he was not aware of giving any order to put the complainant's house under guard. The latter insisted, however, that the fact was so, and pointed to his residence, which was in sight and near at hand, as evidence, for the guard could be plainly seen.

"Is that your residence?" inquired the General, blandly.

"To be sure it is."

"Why, I took it for granted, from the conduct of its female occupants, that it was an abode of shameless courtezans, and I ordered a guard to be placed around it to prevent the visitation of our soldiery."

### Confession of a Rebel Officer to General Grant.

One of the majors in the rebel army at Vicksburg had formerly served in the same regiment of the United States army with General Grant, but was then the latter's prisoner of war. Grant treated him kindly, invited him to his private apartment, and extended to him the courtesies of personal friendship. After he left, the General gave a little sketch of the rebel's former life to the members of his staff. He also said, that when the rebel major was in his room and he was talking to him about being in the Confederate service, the major replied:

"Grant, I tell you I ain't much of a rebel, after all, and when I am paroled, I will let the d—— service go to the mischief."

### Dr. Cottman in Butler's Hands.

There is a story of General Butler's administration in New Orleans which does not appear in his excellent biography. By direction of the President, an election for Congressmen was held in the First and Second districts. Dr. Cottman engaged to be a candidate, and was thereupon sent for by General Butler.

The General, after inquiring whether it was really true that the Doctor was a candidate with his own consent, and receiving an affirmative answer, read the oath which he would be required to take before entering upon his Congressional duties—a pretty stringent covenant by the way, declaring that the deponent had never given aid or comfort to the internal or external enemies of the Republic, never held or sought office under the pretended government of the Confederate States, or in any way countenanced the great rebellion. Having thus called the attention of the Doctor to the terrible ordeal which awaited him, the General drew forth a large fac-simile of the Ordinance of Secession, and pointed to the signature, Thos. E. H. Cottman, which appeared thereon in a fair, round, schoolmaster-like hand.

"Now," asked the General, "how can you take that oath after having signed that treasonable document?"

"But I did not assent to it. I opposed separate secession all through."

"But you signed the ordinance—and the signature looks as though you thought it was something to be proud of."

"I signed it merely as a witness to the record!"

"Signed as witness! Bosh! What nonsense! Suppose, Doctor, you really were a Member of Congress, and old Jake Barker, as the representative of Benjamin Franklin, should present a claim for witness fees, on the ground that his ancestor signed the Declaration of Independence only in that capacity—would you vote for it?"

The Doctor appeared to be afflicted with a bronchial disorder, which prevented his making immediate answer.

"Now," says the General. "I tell you I think it an insult to loyal men that a signer of that ordinance should offer to take the oath I have read. You know very well that the signing of that document was made a test of the devotion of members of the Convention to the cause of Secession. You know very well that it was made a test in the case of Mr. Rozier, and you know that he did not meet it as you did by surrendering to treason."

"Very well, Sir, I will announce in the newspapers that I am ordered by the military commander to withdraw my name from the canvass."

"No you wont—nothing of the sort. I have given you no orders; I shall give you none. I have only to say that I think it grossly scandalous that you, after having signed an ordinance of secession, should ask the people of this District to put you in a position to take this oath; and even if you can bring your conscience to allow you to take that oath, certain it is that no House of Representatives would allow you to take it in its presence!"

So the Doctor went his way, and announced in the newspapers that unforeseen circumstances commanded his withdrawal from the canvass.

### Accidents Will Happen.

General Garfield had a bad egg thrown at him by some treason sympathizer while speaking at Chestertown—the same place where, he said, a few weeks since he was face to face with the companions of the miscreant on the field of battle. "They carried more dangerous weapons," said the General, "but as I did not run there, it is not probable that I shall run now; and as I fought then, if necessary, I can fight now!" The mob were intensely gratified by this plucky speech, and proceeded to inflict summary justice upon the egg-thrower, which they did, unfortunately, by administering a tremendous beating to the wrong man! If a true patriot, however, he doubtless forgave the accident, and was willing thus to suffer vicariously in so good a cause.

### Disturbing an Orator.

When the Union lines advanced towards Corinth, in the summer of 1862, a battery was planted on an eminence commanding a considerable portion of the country, but completely shrouded from view, by a dense thicket. Scouts were sent out to discover the exact position of the rebels, and when they were but a short distance in advance, to give a signal as to the direction to fire, if any were discovered.

One of the rebel commanders, unaware of such presence, called around him a brigade, and commenced addressing them in something like the following strain: "Sons of the South! We are here to defend our homes, our wives and daughters, against the horde of Vandals who have come here to possess the first and violate the last. Here, upon this sacred soil, we have assembled to drive back the northern invaders—drive them into the Tennessee.. Will you follow me? If we cannot hold *this* place, we can defend no spot of our cherished Confederacy. Shall we drive the invaders back, and strike to death the men who would desecrate our homes? Is there a man so base among those who hear me as to retreat from the contemptible foe before us? I will never blanch before their fire, nor—"

At this interesting period the signal was given, and six shells fell in the vicinity of the chivalrous officer and his men, who suddenly forgot their red-hot resolves, and fled in confusion to their breastworks.

### One of the Things to be Done.

A very gentlemanly, intelligent Union soldier was one day standing by the side of a 32-pounder, at Annapolis, Maryland, over which, under the military rule of General Butler, there proudly floated the Stars and Stripes. In the course of a conversation with some disunionists who surrounded him, one of them said:

"I would just like to know now, what you all expect to do?"

With the gun for his seat, the flag for his protection, and slaveholders for his audience, he replied:

"We expect to enforce the laws of the United States, in all the States. We intend, that persons living in Charleston, South Carolina, who desire to subscribe for any Northern paper, may, with perfect safety, take such paper from its wrapper, and read it with impunity in the public rooms of your hotels. And when vessels with colored sailors, having regular papers from the United States custom houses, go to Southern ports, we intend that those sailors shall not be molested, in any manner whatever."

"Why, you are an abolitionist!"

"No, Sir, not a bit of it. But I am an American citizen, having certain rights, which have not, heretofore, been protected; but which hereafter, thanks to your folly, will forever be secured. Why, only a year ago, when I was at Wilmington, a colored man, who had bought himself and a small schooner, was engaged in the coasting trade hereabouts, and happened to find himself in trouble, not far from this very point. His vessel ran aground, and he was obliged to stay several days in this place. He was put in jail, had no funds to pay some infernal fine with, and would have been sold by the State into slavery, had not several of us, who happened to hear it, raised $800, and secured his liberty."

"Why, you surprise me; I never heard of that."

"No, and you never would have heard of it under your state of things. But now you will find that papers will print different matter from what they used to. And that, my friend, is *one* of the things that we expect to do."

### Friendly Advice to a Doubtful Unionist.

Colonel Marshall, an old army officer, distinguished by his explorations on the Plains, regarded the valley of the Pamunkey as almost a paradise. The green fields of waving grain were so luxuriant that he was induced to inquire how long the ground was run without change, and was astonished to find that once in six years was the reply. The houses are built of brick, and the barns are of the most substantial character. Upon one occasion he encamped in a clover field, and, as was very natural under the circumstances, the horses, being in clover, lost no time in taking advantage of it. The gentlemanly proprietor of the clover field, having made serious remonstrances without effect, at last demanded payment therefor, when the following brief and conclusive colloquy ensued:

PROPRIETOR. Colonel Marshall, I believe?

COL. M. You believe right, Sir.

PROPRIETOR. Well, Colonel, you have trampled down my clover field and completely destroyed it. Do you intend paying for it?

COL. M. Well, Sir, are you loyal?

PROPRIETOR. Yes, Sir.

COL. M. Are you willing to take the oath of allegiance to the United States?

PATRIOTIC, POLITICAL, CIVIL, JUDICIAL, ETC. 63

PROPRIETOR. No, Sir.
COL. M. Then get Jeff. Davis to pay you, and get out of my tent, you infernal traitor.

### Rousseau's First Step toward making Loyal Men of Rebels.

On General Rousseau's succeeding General Mitchel in his command in Alabama, he was visited by a gentleman requesting permission to go beyond our lines and visit his wife. He had never taken up arms against the Union, but he had aided and abetted those who had, and admitted that he was still a Secessionist.

"You can't go," said the General.

"It seems very hard," replied Secesh, "that I can't go to see my wife."

"No harder for you than it is for me," returned the General; "I want to see my wife. You have compelled me to leave her, by your infernal treason. You surely don't expect me to grant you a favor which your rebellious conduct prevents me from enjoying."

"Well, but General, ——"

"It is useless to talk, Sir. If you will go to work and assist me to return to my wife, I will do all I can to enable you to return to yours."

"What do you wish me to do, General?"

"I wish you to return to your allegiance, and, as far as lies in your power, to discountenance rebellion and treason."

"But, General, my conscience will not allow me to do that."

"Neither, then," replied the Kentucky patriot, "will my conscience allow me to grant you favors which are due only to loyal men."

Of course there was nothing further to be urged; the baffled rebel took up his hat and left. The General turned toward those who were sitting in his tent, and quietly remarked,

"When you have rendered these rebels fully sensible of how much they have lost by their rebellion, you have taken the first step toward making them loyal men."

### Dr. ——'s Loyalty rather Coppery.

Down in old Eastern Massachusetts (town not mentioned), resides a certain Dr. ——, whose loyalty was commonly reputed as rather "coppery," but who is wonderful in his success in transplanting trees and making them thrive—in fact has raised a paradise around his fine old mansion. A clerical guest once making the rounds, said, "Doctor, the United States Marshal ought to have an eye to your proceedings." "How so," asked the Doctor, a trifle startled, and wondering whether he had spoken out a little too plainly any time. "Because you have such a happy way of encouraging trees-on." The Doctor laughed, and "owed him one."

### Raising the Flag.

A great city for Union people, Union speeches, Union flag-raising, etc., is ——. The boys are even more vociferous in cheering for the Union than are their parents, and when the 'Stars and Stripes' are to be unfurled to the breeze, specimens of Young America may always be seen honoring the occasion with their presence. At one of these gatherings, where, with the above described concourse, were assembled the stanch Union men of the city, one among the latter class was chosen to address the assembly. Accordingly, he arose upon the platform, and amidst the deep silence of the expectant audience began, 'slowly but surely,' as follows:

"Countrymen!—friends!—fellow-citizens!—why are we here assembled this evening?"

Scarcely had this question been thus put to the listening crowd when an impatient juvenile patriot, indignant at the very thought that the man selected to address the people should be ignorant of the reason why they had there assembled, answered in a drawling, whining, but perfectly audible voice:

"To raise that flag, ye big fool ye!"

This information was applauded by a general laugh—the orator asking no more such patent questions during that address.

### Judge G——'s Idea of the Rebellion.

Judge G. was a Justice of the Supreme Court in the western part of the State of New York a short time before the rebellion broke out, but while the distant mutterings of its thunders could be heard. The Judge was as renowned for his solid learning and patriotism as he was for a certain quaintness of expression, that ofttimes produced a laugh in court, to the great surprise of the Judge. One day a feigned issue in a divorce suit, involving abandonment and desertion on the part of the guilty party, was on trial at the Circuit, and the counsel for the plaintiff, who sometimes indulged in "spread eagles," was in the very climax of his rhapsody, when, turning a moment from the jury, whom he was addressing, to the Court, he said, "What would your Honor do, I would like to know, if a portion of the States of this glorious Union should 'shoot madly from their spheres,' and attempt the destruction of the nation?" "What would I dew?" asked the Judge; "why, I'd try and *shute* them back again." It may be added that the Judge, who is still upon the bench, adhered unfalteringly to his opinion.

### Devotion to the Stars and Stripes.

Rev. Mr. ——, a man about six feet four in his stockings, and of proportions worthy a grenadier, and whose heart is as stout as his frame, a thorough Union man, and in for the war until all treason was thoroughly crushed out, was conducting a religious conference meeting, when a brother arose to speak, who, after alluding to his hopes and fears in a religious point of view, branched out in reference to the state of the country, saying that so great was his devotion to the Stars and Stripes that he had enlisted; and after a few further patriotic remarks, begged an interest in the prayers of the church, that he might be protected by Divine Providence, on the battle field, and that should he fall a victim to the bullets of the enemy he might be prepared for the change.

Such a speech at any time would thrill with patriotic fervor the brave heart of that worthy minister, and he consequently spoke a few words of encouragement to the hero. After this, the wife of the enlisting brother volunteered her experience, in the course of which, alluding to her husband's enlistment, she expressed a willingness to give him up, even unto death, in the service of his country.

In a few moments after, the meeting came to an end, when the minister, all anxiety for the welfare of the patriot volunteer, proceeded to make some inquiries in reference to his regiment, commencing with the very natural question as to its name and number, when he received the startling reply,

"I've jined the *Home Guard!*"

### Arrest of "Joe Guild" by Colonel Myers.

Colonel Myers, of California, received the appointment of Union Sheriff of Nashville and its vicinity, and in the discharge of his duties was ordered to arrest certain offensive characters—among others a certain Col. Joe Guild. This person was elected Judge of the Chancery District, which embraces Sumner county, after Tennessee was forced into rebellion. He was a lawyer of some ability, and a bilious Breckinridge politician. In the work of treason, no one commenced earlier or ran faster.

When Colonel Myers went in search of "Old Bally," he took a walk around Gallatin in his usual quiet way, and asked some one he met where Colonel Guild lived. "Judge Guild? yonder he goes now," said the citizen, "on that pony." Quickening his pace, the Sheriff soon caught up, and approaching him, inquired if that was Colonel Guild.

"Guild is my name, sir; what will you have?"

"I have visited Gallatin for the purpose of arresting you."

"Arrest me!" said Guild, with well feigned astonishment; I have done nothing worse than thousands have done in this county."

"That may all be very true, Colonel Guild; but we are determined that those who took front seats in this little show shall keep them throughout."

Colonel Guild desired to see his residence before setting out for Nashville, but our Sheriff was in a hurry. "But the Court is in session," said Guild, "surely you will allow me to sign the records?" "Yes, you can sign them. Send for them and sign them at the Provost Marshal's office."

The Judge sent for the records and for his family. When these came, a number of citizens came as a committee of condolence. Judge Guild's female relatives were demonstrative. Mrs. G. wished she just had the power; she would drive the Yankee Hessians out of the country very quick.

"Yes," said the officer, "but we have the power, and intend to drive the enemies of the country in."

"Very well," replied madam, "you need not think you can force our people into the Union."

"We intend to force the soil in, anyhow," said Colonel Myers, "and if the people cannot afford to come in, they would better get off."

#### Pro-Southern Domine Delineated.

Some one was discussing the character of a pro-Southern clergyman—a timeserving Washington domine—in the presence of Mr. Lincoln. Says Mr. Lincoln to his visitor, I think you are rather hard upon Mr. Blank. He reminds me of a man in Illinois who was tried for passing a counterfeit bill. It was in evidence that before passing it he had taken it to the cashier of a bank and asked his opinion of the bill, and he received a very prompt reply that the bill was a counterfeit. His lawyer, who had heard of the evidence to be brought against his client, asked him just before going into court, "Did you take the bill to the cashier of the bank and ask him if it was good?" "I did," was the reply. "Well, what was the answer of the cashier?" The rascal was in a corner, but he got out of it in this fashion: "He said it was a pretty, tolerable, respectable sort of a bill." Mr. Lincoln thought the clergyman was "a pretty, tolerable, respectable sort of a clergyman." The President said: "We have a good many of that class in Washington, I fear, though, if anybody is going to make me prove this I'll back down at once, for in these times it is hard to prove anything."

#### Hard-Shell Brethren Dealing with a Contumacious Member.

Nobody took a higher reputation for daring and efficiency in the guerrilla war in Missouri than Major Clark Wright. He and his rangers became a terror to rebels in that region. When the roar of secession first went up from South Carolina, he heard it in common with others, but, while avowing his Union sentiments,

Hard Shell Brethren.

attended simply to his business, and avoided giving any offence on account of his views. In course of time, however, at a Baptist meeting near his residence, a few of the "brethren," after refreshing their spiritual appetites with the crumbs of his sanctuary, took his case into consideration, and unanimously determined that he should be made to leave the country, appointing a committee to inform him of their decision.

One of the party, although an ardent secessionist, happened to be a personal friend of Wright, and forewarned him. Wright, knowing that he had done nothing to warrant such proceedings, determined to fight it out, and in this he was backed by his wife. He provided himself with two revolvers, and his wife took one, and awaited further developments.

Monday afternoon, three men rode up and inquired for Mr. Wright. He walked out, with the butt of a revolver sticking warily from his coat pocket, and inquired their wishes. The revolver seemed to upset their ideas. They answered that it was nothing in particular, and proceeded to converse upon every thing in general, but never alluded to their errand. Finally, after a half hour had passed, and the men still talked on without coming to their mission, Wright grew impatient, and asked if they had any special business—if not, he had a pressing engagement, and would like to be excused. Well, they had a little business, said one, with considerable hesitation, as he glanced at the revolver butt.

"Stop!" said Wright, "before you tell it I wish to say a word. I *know* your business, and I just promised my wife on my honor as a man, that I would blow — out of the man who told me of it, and by the Eternal God, I'll do it! Now tell me your errand?"

Saying this, he pulled out his revolver and cocked it. The fellow glanced a moment at the deadly looking pistol, and took in the stalwart form of Wright, who was glaring at him with retribution in his eye, and concluded to postpone the announcement. The three rode away, and reported their reception to their principals. The next Sunday, after another refreshing season, the "brethren" again met and took action upon the contumacy of Mr. Wright. The Captain of a company of secessionists was present, and after due deliberation, it was determined that upon the next Thursday he should take his command, proceed to Wright's, and summarily eject him from the sacred soil of Missouri. Wright's friend was again present, and he soon communicated to Wright the state of affairs, and begged him to save bloodshed by leaving.

Wright lived in a portion of the country remote from the church, and the residence of those who were endeavoring to drive him out, and he determined, if possible, to prepare a surprise for the worthy captain and his gallant forces. To this end he bought a barrel of whiskey, another of crackers, a few cheeses, and some other provisions, and then mounting a black boy upon a swift horse, sent him around the country, inviting his friends to come and see him, and bring their arms. By Wednesday night he had gathered a force of about three hundred men, to whom he told the state of things, and asked their aid. They promised to back him to the death. The next day they concealed themselves in a cornfield, back of the house, and waited the development of events. So, a little after noon, the captain and some eighty men rode up to the place and inquired for Mr. Wright. That gentleman immediately made his appearance, when the Captain informed him that, being satisfied of his abolitionism, they had come to eject him from the State.

"Won't you give me two days to settle up my affairs?" asked Wright.

"Two days be —! I'll give you just five minutes to pack up your traps and leave!"

"But I can't get ready in five minutes, I have a fine property here, a happy home, and if you drive me off you make me a beggar. I have done nothing. If I go, my wife and children must starve."

"To hell with your beggars! You must travel!"

"Give me two hours?"

"I'll give you just five minutes, not a second longer. If you ai'nt out by that time (here the gallant soldier swore a most fearful oath,) I'll blow out your cursed abolition heart!"

"Well, if I must, I must!" and Wright turned toward the house, as if in deep despair, gave a preconcerted whistle, and almost instantly after the concealed forces rushed out and surrounded the astounded Captain and his braves.

"Ah, Captain!" said Wright, as he turned imploringly towards him, "won't you grant me two days—two hours, at least, my brave friend, only two hours in which to prepare myself and family for beggary and starvation—now do, won't you?"

The Captain could give no reply, but sat upon his horse as if ague-smitten. He at length found voice to say—

"Don't kill me!"

"Kill you! No, you black-livered coward, I won't dirty my hands with any such filthy work. If I kill you, I'll have one of my niggers do it. Get down from that horse!"

The gallant Captain obeyed, imploring only for life. The result of the matter was that the whole company dismounted, laid down their arms, and then as they filed out were sworn to preserve their allegiance inviolate to the United States. An hour after, Mr. Wright had organized a force of two hundred and forty men for the war, and by acclamation was elected Captain. The next Sunday he started with his command to join the National troops under Lyon, stopping long enough on his way to surround the Hard-shell church, at which his miseries had all been so augmented. After the service was over, he administered the oath of allegiance to every one present, including the Reverend Pecksniff, who officiated, and then left them to plot Treason and worship God in their own peculiar and pious manner.

He soon became Major Wright, doing brave and valuable service for his country.

### Noble Greeting by a Loyal Southerner to a Green Mountain Boy.

A tall, splendid-looking man, dressed in the uniform of the Allen Greys, Vermont, stood one day conversing with a friend on Broadway, New York city. He was entirely unconscious that his superior height was attracting universal attention on that crowded thoroughfare, until a splendid barouche drove up to the sidewalk, and a young man sprang from it and grasped the soldier's hand, saying,

"You are the most splendid specimen of humanity I ever saw. I am a Southerner, but my heart is with the Union; if it were not, such noble-looking fellows as yourself would enlist me in the cause."

The subject of this salutation, although surprised, was perfectly self-possessed, and answered the cordial greeting of the young Southerner with warm enthusiasm. He was of superb stature — several inches above six feet, and his noble, open countenance, beamed with the ancient patriotism of the Green Mountain Boys, of which he was so fine a specimen. He had walked fifteen miles from the village of Chittenden to enlist, and was the only representative of that village; but he was a host in himself.

### Parson Brownlow expressing his Sentiments in Jail.

Parson Brownlow's sufferings while in jail for his fidelity to his country are well known, as well as his unflinching endurance of them. General Carroll, of the Confederate army, who was at one time a great friend of his, visited the parson in jail, and said to him,

"Brownlow, you ought not to be here."

"So I think," responded the Parson; "but here I am."

"The Confederate Court is sitting within a hundred yards of the jail, and if you will take the oath of allegiance you shall be immediately liberated."

"Sir," said the Parson, looking him steadily in the eye, "before I will take the oath of allegiance to your bogus Government I will rot in jail, or die here of old age. I don't acknowledge you have a Court. I don't acknowledge you have a Government. It has never been acknowledged by any power on earth, and never will be. Before I would take the oath I would see the whole Southern Confederacy in the infernal regions, and you on top of it."

"That is — plain talk," said the General, indignantly leaving the jail.

"Yes, Sir-ee," said the Parson; "I am a plain man, and them's my sentiments."

#### Confederate Notes in Maryland.

The rebel officers treated the citizens of Frederick with a great deal of courtesy, but generally forced upon them their worthless Confederate notes and scrip, in exchange for provisions, or any thing else they desired. The merchants and others who had articles to sell, upon the rebel forces entering the town, closed their places of business and refused to sell. Stuart threatened to use force unless the stores were opened, and then the merchants concealed the bulk of their stocks, and opened their doors. At one store Colonel Gordon called, and insisted upon paying for goods he wanted in Confederate notes. The merchant happened to be a man who did not hesitate to utter his Union sentiments freely, and he told the gallant rebel that Confederate notes were not worth the paper they were printed on. The Colonel, in reply to this, asked,

"And pray what may be your political sentiments?"

"I am a Union man, Sir, and always intend to remain one."

"Indeed! are there many people like you here?"

"Yes, Sir. We have voted on secession, and this district gave three thousand majority for the Union."

"Yes, at the point of the bayonet."

"No, Sir. There were neither bayonets nor muskets to intimidate us. Every man was free to vote as he pleased."

"Then we have been most damnably deceived."

#### "Hail Columbia," and the "Star Spangled Banner," at Fort Sumter.

It is familiar to all, that, on leaving Fort Moultrie, Major Anderson brought away with him the flag which he had been in the habit of hoisting over that fort. He entered Sumter on the night of 26–27th December, 1860, and determined to hoist the flag at noon on 27th.

Anderson.

A short time before noon Major Anderson assembled the whole of his little force, with the workmen employed on the fort, around the foot of the flag-staff. The national ensign was attached to the cord, and Major Anderson, holding the ends of the lines in his hands, knelt reverently down. The officers, soldiers, and men clustered around, many of them on their knees, and all deeply impressed with the solemnity of the scene. The chaplain made an earnest prayer—such an appeal for support, encouragement and mercy, as one would make who felt that 'Man's extremity is God's opportunity.' As the earnest, solemn words of the speaker ceased, and the men responded "Amen" with a fervency that perhaps they had never before experienced. Major Anderson drew the 'Star Spangled Banner' up to the top of the staff, the band broke out with the national air of 'Hail Columbia,' and loud and exultant cheers, repeated again and again, were given by the officers, soldiers, and workmen.

### Cities built and in Embryo: Schaffer and Ould at a Joke.

Colonel Schaffer, chief of staff to General Butler, and General Ould, the rebel Commissioner of exchange, were the best of friends, personally, and, in their official interviews, always very pleasant and agreeable to each other. On one of these occasions, when chatting at City Point on matters and things in general, Colonel Schaffer picked up a map of Virginia, and glancing at it casually, it occurred to him that there was a good site for a city in the neighborhood of City Point, and expressed his astonishment that it had been overlooked so long. Said he, with great seriousness, "If I had the capital, I would invest it right here. It's bound to be a great city some day or other." Ould kept his eyes for awhile on the map, and then looking at the Colonel, remarked, hardly able to suppress a smile that was trying to force its way out, "It seems to me, Colonel, that instead of building a new city, *you had better take one already built.*" "Sam," said the Union Colonel to the servant, "get that black bottle out of my basket;" and the rebel joke was washed down with old rye.

### Blondin's Art Serving a good Figure.

Some gentlemen from the West obtained an interview with President Lincoln, at the executive mansion, when things looked dark for the national cause, and gave vent, in an excited and troubled manner, to their feelings as to the commissions and omissions of the administration. The President, as usual, heard patiently all that was said, and then replied: "Suppose, gentlemen, all the property you were worth was in gold, and you had put it in the hands of Blondin to carry across the Niagara river on a rope, would you shake the cable, and keep shouting to him, 'Blondin, stand up a little straighter—Blondin, stoop a little more—go a little faster—lean a little more to the North—lean a little more to the South!' No, you would hold your breath, as well as your tongue, and keep your hands off till he was safe over. The Government is carrying an immense weight. Untold treasures are in their hands. They are doing the best they can. Don't badger them. Keep silence, and we'll carry you safe across." This simple but wonderfully graphic idea answered the complaints of half an hour, and not only silenced but charmed the auditors.

### Cabinet Pictures Before and After the Election.

President Lincoln took it into his head to call one day at the studio of the artist who at that time was engaged in painting the Cabinet group. Mr. Lincoln inquired how he was getting along with the happy family. The artist informed him that he was progressing finely, and would soon have it completed. Mr. Lincoln, after scanning closely the arrangement of the group, expressed his admiration of the work. "Yes," said the artist, "it will be a fine painting, and as soon as I get it completed, I intend to travel through the country and exhibit it." "What!" says the President, "exhibit that all over the country? It will ruin my chances for re-election. Everybody expects me to change my Cabinet."

### Danger of Freedmen Voting.

Some southern gentlemen were discussing the question of the possibility and propriety of giving votes to the freedmen of the South; a measure in the expediency of which the Southern Unionists—

more particularly those from the far South—appear to be tolerably unanimous. One of the gentlemen present—a loyal Texan—announced himself inflexibly opposed to any such a grant of votes to the blacks, "because," said he, "in six months after you give the right to negroes to vote, half the politicians in the country will go about swearing that they have negro blood in their veins."

### Didn't like Vallandigham's Defeat.

The news of Vallandigham's gubernatorial defeat, when announced to the Ohio troops, caused a good deal of lusty cheering,—such as would have been heard after the reading of an official dispatch on dress parade, proclaiming a signal victory for our troops. The noise attracted the attention of the rebel pickets in front, and many of them inquired what it all meant. The following conversation on the subject took place in front of Fort Wood:

*Rebel*—Say, Yank, what's all that noise about?

*Union*—The boys are cheering for Brough's election. Vallandigham is whipped.

*Reb.*—How do you know Vallandigham ain't elected? your telegraph's out, ain't it?

*Union*—I don't know about that. Rosey says Brough's elected.

*Reb.*—Rosey's a d—n liar, I guess. But is Brough elected, honest?

*Union*—Yes, he is, honest.

*Reb.* (vociferously)—Officer of the guard, No. 6!

The officer of the guard made his appearance very shortly, and asked what was wanted. The rebel picket replied—

"Brough's elected and Vallandigham's whipped like h—l. You had better send word to General Bragg."

The pickets were told to find out how the election went, if they could, and send word to head-quarters.

### Vanity of Patriotism and Honor.

A humorous colloquy took place upon the hurricane deck of one of the Cumberland river craft, between a newspaper correspondent and an elderly darkey. The latter possessed a philosophical and retrospective cast of countenance, was squatted upon his bundle, toasting himself against the chimney, and apparently plunged in a profound state of meditation. Finding upon inquiry that he belonged to the Ninth Illinois, one of the most gallantly behaved and heavy-losing regiments at the Fort Donelson battle, and part of which was aboard, the correspondent interrogated him somewhat on the subject. That the Ethiop's philosophy was much in the Falstaffian vein, the following will show:

"Were you in the fight?"

"Had a little taste of it, sa."

"Stood your ground, did you?"

"No, sa, I runs."

"Run at the first fire, did you?"

"Yes, sa; and would have run sooner, had I known it war comin'."

"Why, that was not very creditable to your courage!"

"Dat isn't in my line, sa—cookin's my perfeshun."

"Well, but have you no regard for your reputation?"

"Reputation's nuffin to me by de side ob life."

"Do you consider your life worth more than other people's?"

"It's worth more to me, sa."

"Then you must value it very highly."

"Yes, sa, I does—more dan all dis wuld—more dan a million of dollars, sa; for what would even dat be worth to a man wid de bref out of him? Self-preserbashun am de just law wid me."

"Then patriotism and honor are nothing to you?"

"Nuffin, whatever, sa; I regard dem as among de vanities."

It is safe to say that the dusky corpse

of that African will never darken the field of carnage.

## "Mustered In."

The boys of the One Hundred and Seventeenth New York tell a good joke in regard to the "mustering in" of a darkey attached to that regiment, who became fearful he would be deprived of his pay unless he was joined to the service. A huge mustard plaster was applied to his back, about a foot below where the rear buttons of his coat were placed, and, under the belief that all soldiers were served in the same manner, as a sort of military institution, he wore it until the pain became unendurable, at which time he was formerly declared "mustered in," according to the law in such cases made and provided. If that darkey didn't get his wages, it was not because he failed to suffer for his country as a patriot duly put through by the One Hundred and Seventeenth.

## "Benefit of Clergy."

The "Volunteer" was the title of a 'broadside', published by the boys of the Iowa Tenth, then stationed at the little secesh town of Charleston, about twenty-five miles west of Cairo. The following story tells the way in which, the day after the Tenth took possession of the village, the people thereof went to church: On his arrival, on Sunday, General Payne found the churches vacant, and no evidences of that devotion on the Sabbath so necessary to all well-regulated communities; he accordingly summoned the inhabitants of the place and its surroundings to meet him at the Court-house, at half-past one in the afternoon, where he proposed to expound to them the weightier matters of the law. The house was filled (the General occasionally sending after a prominent absentee), and after giving them some good advice, he called on a reverend divine to conduct the services, quietly informing the audience that his services were required elsewhere, and that it would be necessary for them to remain until six o'clock. On turning to the door they were surprised to find that the house was closely guarded, and that for the balance of the day they were prisoners. By this ruse the General not only succeeded in preventing information of his movements being carried to the rebels, but brought many an old sinner to the altar who had not seen it for years.

## Prompt Administration of the Law.

After General Schenck's arrival in Cumberland, one of his first decisions was very characteristic. A secesh Colonel had sold his negro to the Confederate government, taking pay, of course, in scrip. The negro, employed in fortifications, managed to escape to Cumberland, where he spread himself considerably. A constable, knowing the circumstances, and wishing to turn a penny, had the negro thrown into prison as an escaped slave. General Schenck, hearing the facts, sent for the parties. "By what right," he asked of the constable, "do you hold this man in prison?"

"As a fugitive from service."

"Don't you know that he escaped from the service of the rebels?"

"Yes, but we have a law in Maryland that covers the case, General."

"And I have a law upon which it can be decided. Colonel Porter, set that negro at large and put this constable in his place."

The astonished snapper up of trifles was marched off to the cell lately occupied by his proposed victim. After being detained there precisely the same number of days he had imprisoned the poor darkey, he was set at large, fully impressed with the belief that the grim-visaged General had never learnt to be trifled with.

## Command of the Virginia Forces tendered to General Scott.

Judge Douglas stated, soon after the breaking out of the rebellion, that one day while walking down the streets of Washington, he met a distinguished gentleman, a member of the Virginia Disunion Convention, whom he knew personally, and had a few minutes conversation with him. "He told me," said Judge D., "that he had just had an interview with General Scott; that he was chairman of the committee ap-

General Scott.

pointed by the Virginia Convention, to wait upon General Scott, and *tender him the command of the Virginia forces in this struggle.* General Scott received him kindly, listened to him patiently, and said to him:

"I have served my country, under the flag of the Union, for more than fifty years; and as long as God permits me to live, I will defend that flag with my sword, even if my own native State assails it."

### Minute Men of Massachusetts. 1775 and 1861.

As one of the Massachusetts regiments was passing through New York on its way to Washington, under the President's first call for seventy-five thousand men, a gentleman of the first-named city met one of its members on the street.

"Is there anything I can do for you?" said the New Yorker, whose heart warmed toward the brave representative of the brave Massachusetts militia who had been so prompt to shoulder the musket.

The soldier hesitated a moment, and finally, raising one of his feet, exhibited a boot with a hole in the toe, and, in other respects, decidedly the worse for wear.

"How came you here with such boots as those, my friend?" asked the patriotic citizen.

"When the order came for me to join my company, sir," replied the soldier, "I was plowing in the same field at Concord,

Minute Men of Massachusetts—1775 and 1861.

where my grandfather was plowing when the British fired on the Massachusetts men at Lexington. He did not wait a minute; and I did not, sir."

That noble soldier was furnished at once with every thing that could meet a soldier's wants.

### Patriotism of the Rarest Kind.

Messrs. Nathaniel Davis, Robert Davis, and William Robertson, co-partners in business in Montreal, Canada, abandoned their establishment immediately on receipt of the President's proclamation calling for troops, and issued the following card:

"The business of Nathaniel Davis & Co., 1058 McGill street, will cease on Thursday of this week, as the proprietors leave for the scene of war on Friday. Our landlord, Mr. Flynn, kindly releases us from our agreement to occupy his store for another year. The President of the United States has issued his call for volunteers. As Americans we respond at once. Every drop of blood in our veins belongs to our country. We are thankful to Divine Providence that we are alive and in good health to do duty to our government. The name of Washington will receive new lustre from the glorious deeds about to transpire in the trial of the cause of freedom and a republican government."

### They Had Heard of Him.

When the steamer Maryland reached Locust Point, Baltimore, carrying Captain Sherman's Light Artillery, and a regiment of Pennsylvania volunteers, the troops were met by the noted Mr. Kane, Marshal of the city, when the following colloquy took place:

"Major, can I be of any assistance?"

"Who are you, Sir?"

"I am Marshal of the Police of Baltimore, and would render any assistance."

"Oh, yes! we have heard of you in the region from whence we came. We have no need of you. We can take care of ourselves."

The secession-hearted Marshal retired, and the disembarkation of the troops took place immediately, the Harriet Lane presenting her broadside to the point where the cars waited to convey the passengers to the Relay House.

### Retort Courteous from an American in Paris to M. Thouvenel.

A distinguished American, conversing in the city of Paris, with M. Thouvenel, the French Minister of State, was asked rather impatiently by that distinguished French official,

"But, Sir, how much time do you want to take Richmond? How long must we wait?"

"I think, Monsieur, with great respect," was the courteous reply of our countryman, "that we shall be satisfied if we are granted as much time as the allies took to reduce Sebastopol."

M. Thouvenel changed the subject.

### Compromising the Capitol Flag.

Under the administration of Mr. Buchanan, a man named Duddington was captain of the Capitol police at Washington. Though he held an important and responsible office connected with the safety of the Capitol, he was a secessionist—a decided but not an obtrusive one; he made little display of his Southern patriotism, and his politics were practically of that mild type which was not inconsistent with a willingness to retain office after the accession of Lincoln. In fact, he was not indisposed to mediation and compromise, and was inclined to bring back our misguided and rather impetuous Southern brethren by gentle and conciliatory means. So he visited Senator King, during the special executive session of the Senate called to consider the nominations of the new President, and suggested as a measure of reasonable compromise that the American flag, which always floats over each house of Congress, when it is in session, should not be raised. "Not raise the American flag! Why not?" asked the sturdy Republican Senator. "Because," said the official, "it *irritates* the Southern people." The careful compromiser soon after—about as soon as a note could reach the Secretary of the Interior from Mr. King—fell a victim to "this proscriptive Administration," and the places that had known him in Washington knew him no more. He was next, and very soon afterwards, heard of in command of a rebel battery, one of those which so long blockaded the Potomac, and were unfortunately left so long without being "irritated" by our arms.

### Under the Star-Spangled Banner.

Over the large gate at the Provost Marshal's splendid head-quarters in Nashville—Elliott's female school—waved a Union flag. A very ardent secesh lady, who wished to see Colonel Matthews, was about to pass through the gateway, when, looking up, she beheld the proud flag flapping like an eagle's wing over his eyrie.

Starting back horror-struck, she held up her hands and exclaimed to the guard:

"Dear me! I can't go under that dreadful Lincoln flag. Is there no other way for me to enter?"

"Yes, madam," promptly replied the soldier, and turning to his comrade he said—

"Here, orderly, bring out that rebel flag and lay it on the ground at the little gate, and let this lady walk over it!"

The lady looked bewildered, and after hesitating a moment, concluded to bow her head to the invincible Goddess of Freedom, whose immaculate shrine is the folds of the Star Spangled Banner.

### Description of South Carolina by Mr. Pettigru.

The late Judge Pettigru, of Charleston, South Carolina, stood, solitary and alone, among his peers in that treasonable city, for his undisguised and persistent anti-secessionism, facing with an unblenching

Col. Rhett.

eye the social and political tide of antagonism which rolled against him in his venerable years and whitened locks. A person meeting him in the street one day, accosted him, and said:

"Will you be so kind as to direct me to the lunatic asylum?"

"Certainly," answered Mr. Pettigru: "There it is," pointing to the east; "and there," turning and pointing to the south; "and there," pointing to the west; "and there again," pointing to the north: "You cannot possibly go amiss."

When asked an explanation of this singular direction, he said, not having the fear of Rhett, Pickens, Magrath & Co., before his eyes:

"The whole State is a lunatic asylum, and the people are all lunatics."

When prayers were offered in the Charleston churches for "President Davis," Judge Pettigru took his hat and left the place of worship where such jargon sounds fell upon his ear. It seems almost impossible that such a noble-minded man could have been a fellow townsman and walked the same streets with that "architect of ruin," Colonel Rhett, who so boldly boasted of having "fired the Southern heart."

### National Oath of Allegiance according to Southern Honor.

There is no doubt that much false swearing was "done" under the feint of loyalty, in order to serve ulterior ends, by citizens of the States in rebellion, and many likewise took the oath under avowed compulsion. The following will serve as an illustration of the circumstances under which many in Louisiana attested *their* "loyalty." A young man, well known in New Orleans, was anxious to send down some goods on a boat from Memphis. He applied to the Provost Marshal there for a permit, and the following form was gone through with as preliminary: "Are you a loyal citizen?" "No, sir." "You must take the oath of allegiance." "Very well, Sir." (Takes it without sugar.) "There, you have taken the oath. Do you know what that means?" "Perfectly. It means a padlock on my mouth, and a bayonet in my rear."

### Shaky Abutments.

President Lincoln's repeated reference to the irreconcilable antagonism between the demands of the south and the spirit

PATRIOTIC, POLITICAL, CIVIL, JUDICIAL, ETC.    75

of the Constitution is well known. On a certain occasion he illustrated this antagonism by an anecdote not less apt than amusing. "I once knew," said Mr. Lincoln, "a good sound churchman, whom we will call Brown, who was on a committee to erect a bridge over a very rapid and dangerous river. Architect after architect failed, and, at last, Brown said he had a friend named Jones, who had built several bridges, and could build this. 'Let us have him in,' said the committee. In came Jones. 'Can you build this bridge, Sir?' 'Yes,' replied Jones, ' I could build a bridge to the infernal regions, if necessary.' The sober committee were horrified. But when Jones retired, Brown thought it but fair to defend his friend. 'I know Jones so well,' said he, 'and he is so honest a man, and so good an architect, that if he states, soberly and positively, that he can build a bridge to Hades, why, I believe it. But I have my doubts about the abutment on the infernal side.' And so it is with me. When politicians said they could harmonize the northern and southern wings of the democracy, why, I believed them. But I had no doubt about the abutment on the southern side."

### Dr. Rucker—his Capture and Escape.

The arrival at Fayettville, West Virginia, of Dr. Rucker, the Union refugee, was an exciting event in the history of that remarkable man—renowned as he had become for his persevering loyalty under circumstances that would ordinarily cause the stoutest heart to quail. He came up from Kanawha county, making his appearance in company with Colonel Duval, of the Ninth West Virginia regiment of infantry.

Dr. Rucker resided in Covington, Virginia, and was regarded as a radical Union man. He was several times formally requested by the authorities to take the oath of allegiance to the Southern Confederacy, but this he unyieldingly refused to do. At last a squad of men, headed by a desperate leader, were sent to take him by force. He still refused to heed their demands, when the leader of the party struck him a blow upon the head with a cane, producing an ugly wound, from which the blood flowed freely. The doctor deliberately drew a knife, telling his assailant he intended to kill him, and proceeded to execute his threat by cutting the fellow until he died. Dr. R. soon found himself with twelve Confederate indictments pending against him, for murder, horse stealing, treason, and almost all the crimes known to the law.

His escape from the jail at Pittsylvania, in the southern part of Virginia, was made partly by means of a key obtained from a two year old child and partly through the assistance of an unknown lady who procured a carriage and drove him to Lynchburg, where he remained some days and until the excitement growing out of his escape had subsided. From the time he was arrested until the time of his escape he was confined in twelve different jails, and was threatened with mob violence every time he was removed from one prison to another. In all these jails he communicated with unknown friends—Union men,—who made him proffers of assistance. While in Pittsylvania jail he received from different persons yarn and aquafortis, and other means of sawing or cutting his way out. He was also presented with a pair of shoes, in the soles of which he found watch springs which had been converted into saws. No more heroic instance of making political loyalty a point of life or death can be found than this of Dr. Rucker.

### Where is Your Heart?

The case of Rev. William J. Hoge, D. D., forms a sad page in the incidents and outgrowths of the rebellion. He was born in Athens, Ohio, in 1826, and was for some years a clergyman in that State, removing thence to Richmond, Virginia, where he taught for several years. In 1858-9 he was called to be colleague to the Rev. Dr. Spring, of the Brick Church, New York city, which he accepted and was settled. In the midst of these labors, the rebellion burst upon the country. Dr. Hoge was not at once decided as to his course of action. His sympathies were with the South, but he hesitated as to the line of ministerial duty. On the 17th of July, 1861, he went to the study of Rev. Dr. Prime, at whose invitation Dr. H. originally came to New York, and solicited Dr. P's advice as to his duty—should he go to the South, or should he remain in New York? Dr. Prime had often argued the political question with him before, and vainly endeavored to convince him that secession was a crime, and would be the ruin of the South. Dr. P. therefore said to him,

"Where is your heart?"

"It is with the South."

"Then, go there; and, if my heart was there, I would go with you."

"When shall I go?"

"Go this week; to-day, if possible."

The result of this conversation was his immediate resignation of his pastoral charge. He preached his farewell sermon on the Sabbath following, while the disastrous battle of Bull Run was in progress. He left for the South, and was soon heard of as settled at Charlottsville. He threw himself into the cause of the rebellion with his accustomed zeal, but died in a short time, in the midst of his years and of the gigantic conspiracy against a nation's life.

---

**Questions and Replies: "Nothing agin the Old Flag."**

*Unionist to a Virginian prisoner.*—Are you not ashamed to fight against the Union, and the Government which has done so much for you?

*Virginian.*—I never fought agin the Union, and I never will.

*Unionist.*—What were you doing at Fort Donelson?

*Virginian.*—I hugged the ground closer nor ever I did before in my life.

*Unionist.*—Were you forced into the army?

*Virginian.*—Wall, no, not exactly forced; I knew I would be, so I j'ined. I thought I'd feel better to go myself!

*Unionist.*—What do you expect to gain by the rebellion?

*Virginian.*—We find our lenders have lied to us. Our big men, like Tyler, Wise, Letcher, and others, wanted to get rich and get into high office, and so they have got us into this mess by their lies. We have *nothing agin the old flag.* All we want is

John Tyler.

our constitutional rights, according to the instrument under which our forefathers lived. They told us that the election of Lincoln would deprive us of these, and we believed them. But we now know that they were lies."

Poor Tyler, in the midst of his efforts to destroy the nation over which he once presided, in the chair of state consecrated by the immortal Washington, died an outlaw and fills a traitor's grave.

---

**Slave Insurrections Foiled by Union Generals.**

One day (says "Edmund Kirke," in his racy volume, "Down in Tennessee,") as I was sitting alone with Rosecrans, an aide handed him a letter. He opened it, ceased doing half a dozen other things, and became at once absorbed in its contents. He re-read it, and then, handing it to me, said:

"Read that. Tell me what you think of it." I read it. Its outside indicated it had come from "over Jordan," and had "a hard road to travel," but its inside startled me. It was written in a round, unpracticed hand, and though badly spelled, showed its author familiar with good Southern English. Its date was May 18th, 1863, and it began thus :

"GENERAL :—A plan has been adopted for a simultaneous movement or rising to sever the rebel communications throughout the whole South, which is now disclosed to some General in each military department in the Secesh States, in order that they may act in concert, and thus insure us success.

The plan is for the blacks to make a concerted and simultaneous rising, on the night of the first of August next, over the whole States in rebellion. To arm themselves with any and every kind of weapon that may come to hand, and commence operations by burning all railroad and county bridges, tearing up all railroad tracks, and cutting and destroying telegraph wires,—and when this is done take to the woods, the swamps, or the mountains, whence they may emerge, as occasions may offer, for provisions or for further depredations. No blood is to be shed except in self defence.

The corn will be in roasting ear about the first of August, and upon this, and by foraging on the farms at night, we can subsist. Concerted movement at the time named would be successful, and the rebellion be brought suddenly to an end."

The letter went on with some details which I cannot repeat, and ended thus :

"The plan will be simultaneous over the whole South, and yet few of all engaged will know its whole extent. Please write 'I' and "approved" and send by the bearer, that we may know *you are with us.*

Be assured, General, that a copy of this letter has been sent to every military department in the rebel States, that the time of the movement may thus be general over the entire South."

I was re-reading the letter when the General again said : "What do you think of it ?"

"It would end the rebellion. It taps the great negro organization, of which I speak in 'Among the Pines,' and co-operated with by our forces would certainly succeed, but—the South would run with blood."

"Innocent blood! Women and children !"

"Yes, women and children. If you let the blacks loose, they will rush into carnage like horses into a burning barn. St. Domingo will be multiplied by a million."

"But he says no blood is to be shed except in self-defence."

"He says so, and the leaders may mean so, but they cannot restrain the rabble. Every slave has some real or fancied wrong, and he would take such a time to avenge it."

"Well, I must talk with Garfield. Come, go with me."

We crossed the street to Garfield's lodgings, and found him bolstered up in bed, quite sick with a fever. The General sat down at the foot of his bed, and handed him the letter. Garfield read it over carefully, and then laying it down, said :

"It will never do, General. *We* don't want to whip by such means. If the slaves, of their own accord, rise and assert their original right to themselves, that will be their own affair; but we can have no complicity with them without outraging the moral sense of the civilized world."

"I knew you'd say so ; but he speaks of other department commanders—may they not come into it ?"

"Yes, they may, and that should be looked to. Send this letter to ——, and let him head off 'the movement.'"

It was not thought prudent to intrust the letter to the mails ; nor with the railway, infested with guerillas, was it a safe document to carry about the person. A short shrift and a long rope might have been the consequence of its being found on a traveler. So, ripping open the top of my boot, I stowed it snugly away in the lining, and took it North. On the 4th of June following, Garfield wrote me that he had just heard from the writer of the letter; that five out of our nine department commanders had come into the project, and, subsequently, that another general had also promised it his support.

But I can say no more. All the world knows that the insurrection did not take place. The outbreaks in September, among the blacks of Georgia and Alabama, were only parts of the plan, the work of subordinate leaders, who, maddened at the miscarriage of the grand scheme, determined to carry out their own share of the programme at all hazards. It was a gigantic project, and the trains were all laid, the matches all lighted.

### Ratifying the Ordinance: Startling Scene.

On the ratification of the South Carolina Ordinance of Secession, Rev. Dr. Bachman was selected by the Secession Convention to offer a prayer before them, in religious observance of the act. Dr. Bachman's name had become quite distinguished in scientific circles, he being an eminent naturalist; but he had also become even more conspicuous by his strong political leanings to the side of Disunion. The scene was one that partook alike of the startling and the impressive. Most of the men there assembled to commit the highest and gravest act against their country, were those upon whose heads the snow of sixty winters had been shed—patriarchs in age—the dignitaries of the land—the high priests of the Church—reverend statesmen—and the judges of the law. In the midst of deep silence an old man, with bowed form and hair as white as snow, the Rev. Dr. Bachman, advanced forward, with upraised hands, in prayer to Almighty God for his blessings and favor on the great act about to be consummated. The whole assembly at once arose to its feet, and, with hats off, listened to the prayer. At the close of this performance, the President advanced with the consecrated parchment upon which was inscribed the decision of the State, with the great seal attached. Slowly and solemnly it was read until the last word—'dissolved'; when men could contain themselves no longer, and a shout that shook the very building, reverberating long continued, rose up, and ceased only with the loss of breath. Such was the scene, in the midst of which

P. S. Brooks

no portrait could have been suspended with more appropriateness, than that of Preston S. Brooks, South Carolina's arch-assassin of liberty of speech on the floor of the United States Senate.

### Non-Combatant—but a Tough One.

Mr. Mark R. Cockrill, was an old man of great wealth living near Nashville, Tennessee; he was reputed to be worth two million dollars, and owned twelve miles of land lying on the Cumberland river. It was reported to the Federal Chief of Army Police, that this Mr. Cockrill had induced guerrillas to lie in wait near his place for the purpose of seizing upon and destroying Union forage trains, &c., and that he was a very bitter rebel. Having been ordered to appear at the office of the

## PATRIOTIC, POLITICAL, CIVIL, JUDICIAL, ETC. 79

Chief of Police, he made the subjoined statement:—

"I am upwards of seventy-four years of age, and have six children,—three of them being sons, and one of them is in the Confederate army. I was born near this city. I had about ninety-eight slaves, but most all have left me. My son has been in the Confederate service since the war began; is twenty-two years old; was captain in that service; think he is now in the commissary department. I voted for separation every time; was not a member of any public committee; have had nothing to do with getting up companies or any thing else connected with the army. Have talked a good deal; was opposed to guerrillaism; have ordered them away from my house. I have lost twenty thousand bushels of corn, thirty-six head of horses and mules; sixty head of Durham Cattle, two hundred and twenty sheep,— very fine ones, valued at one hundred dollars each,—two hundred tons of hay. The Federals have taken all this. I have two thousand sheep left, and I have a few milch cows and five or six heifers. I was worth about two million dollars before the war commenced. The Confederates have taken three horses from me only. I have loaned the Confederates twenty-five thousand dollars in gold. They have pressed from me no other property. I have their bonds at eight per cent interest, payable semi-annually in gold, for this twenty-five thousand dollars. I thought when I loaned the money that the South would succeed, and I think so now. I do not think that the two sections can ever be brought together. The Federals also took two thousand pounds of bacon from me; also two thousand bushels of oats. Some twenty-five or thirty of my men negroes ran away,—six of them, however, being pressed. I have about five thousand six hundred acres of land. My son, James R., is with the South; lives on a place belonging to me; but he has never taken any active part. The Federals have taken over three thousand dollars worth of wood from me. I have never received any pay for anything taken from me. I came in yesterday to get a negro blacksmith of mine to go out with me, he consented to go if I could get a pass for him; have not been in town before for four months. I paid one thousand dollars as an assessment by General Negley, about four months since, to the United States government, as a loan. I have been very much aggravated by the taking of my property, and have been very harsh in my expressions towards those who have visited my place for such purposes. I will not give bond for loyal conduct, or that I will not aid or abet by word or deed the Southern cause. The loan to the South was made voluntarily, and supposing it to be a good investment. While I was loaning to individuals the loan was made to the Southern government just as I would have loaned to any other party."

When brought into the police office, Mr. Cockrill was almost beside himself with passion. The language he used with respect to the Federal troops was, "Kill 'em! Plant 'em out! Manure the soil with 'em ——— 'em!" &c. He utterly refused to give the non-combatant's oath and bond; and when assured by General Rosecrans that he must do so or he would be sent out of the State, and perhaps to a Northern prison, he struck his hands against his breast, and exclaimed,—

"Take my heart out,—kill me if you will; I will not give any bond by which enemies here can swear falsely and I be prosecuted for its forfeiture."

The General assured him that he had but a choice of two evils,—to give the bond or be sent away. He preferred the former.

---

**Interesting Historical Episode, Civil and Military.**

It is a fact of some interest, that General Robert E. Lee, of the Confederate army, commanded in person the small body of marines sent to Harper's Ferry from Washington, on the occasion of John Brown's attack upon that place, and that it was to Colonel Lee that the old man surrendered. The Virginia militiamen having driven Brown and his gang into the engine house, awaited anxiously the arrival of government troops, known to be on their way from Washington, the greatest excitement in the mean time prevailing at Harper's Ferry, as several citizens who had shown themselves near the engine house had been shot by the invaders.

By three o'clock the following morning, sixty marines, under the immediate command of Lieut. Green, but directed by Col. Robert E. Lee, reached the Ferry by cars from the capital. Colonel Lee ordered his detail to stand under arms in the public streets until sunrise, when he conducted the men, leading them himself to the front of the building fortified and occupied by Brown. The lookers-on viewed this soldierly movement with astonishment and awe, expecting to see Colonel Lee shot down as other leaders had been. But not a shot was fired. Lieutenant Green was ordered to demand a surrender. He knocked at the door of the engine house. John Brown asked—

"Who goes there?"

"Lieutenant Green, United States Marines, who, by authority of Colonel Lee, demands an immediate surrender."

"I refuse it;" said Brown, "unless I, with my men, are allowed to cross the bridge again into Maryland, unmolested, after which you can take us prisoners if you can."

Lee refused to allow this, and ordered Lieutenant Green to renew his demand for an immediate and unconditional surrender. John Brown refused those terms, and four of the marines, who had got tremendous sledge-hammers from the works, began battering at the door of the engine house. The engine had been moved against the door, and it would not yield.

"Ten of you," said Lee, "take that ladder and break down the door."

Five on each side, the soldiers drove the ladder against the door, and at the third stroke it yielded and fell back. Colonel Lee and the marines jumped in—one man John Brown shot through the heart—and then was overpowered and surrendered. Colonel Washington, with other citizens, in Brown's hands, was released, and John Brown was handed over to the civil authorities, after which, Colonel Lee took the train to Washington again.

Who knows how much this episode, in its civil and military bearings, may have influenced Robert E. Lee to forsake the flag of the United States and become a chieftain in the rebel cause!

### The Boy Father to the Man.

When General Grant was a boy, he attended the same school with his cousin John, a Canadian, who had come to the States to be educated. The two youths mingled as relatives; and, whenever the Canadian restrained his inherited prejudices, their intercourse was pleasant. Ulysses felt all the true impulse of patri-

The Boy Father to the Man.

otism when a student at school. It was his conviction, born and nourished in his boy's heart, that his country was the equal of any other, and that his countrymen were the equals of the best of mankind.

"Speaking of Washington," said his Canadian cousin, one day, "it seems to me,

PATRIOTIC, POLITICAL, CIVIL, JUDICIAL, ETC.   81

Ulysses, you appear to think a great deal of him."

"And why shouldn't I?" quickly replied the tanner boy; "he is the father of my country, and was raised up by the Almighty to lead it to independence."

"All very fine," retorted John; "but he was a traitor to his king!"

"A what?" asked Ulysses, raising his voice.

"Washington was a traitor, a rebel!" continued the Canadian.

"Cousin John," calmly replied Ulysses, "would you like to have your sovereign called hard names?"

"Why, no; I can't say I should."

"Well, then, let me tell you plainly, that I will not allow you or any one to insult the memory of Washington!"

"What are you going to do about it?" queried John with a sneer.

"I shall resent it as I have a right to do. You may take advantage of me; for you are older than I am. My mother has told me not to quarrel with my schoolmates; and I mean to mind her, and shall not attack them on my own account. But when Washington is assailed, and especially by an English boy, I shall defend the father of my country. Cousin or no cousin, I am ready to fight for Washington."

So saying, Ulysses laid off his jacket, and soon convinced the Canadian reviler that he was in earnest. Blow quickly followed blow, until young Grant was the victor. The false assertion of the elder boy was corrected, and he compelled to admit that he had done wrong. As he would have defended his own chief ruler, so he was forced to acknowledge that Ulysses had done right in not submitting to hear Washington insulted.

**Ohio Battle Flag in the Hands of a Bishop.**

The autumnal session of the Pittsburg Annual Conference of the Methodist Church, 1864, was characterized by an incident of patriotic and thrilling interest.

Bishop Simpson followed the introductory exercises with a speech, an hour and a half long, without manuscript, in which he held his vast audience of cultivated Christian gentlemen spell bound, under his discussion of the four questions—" Shall our government be destroyed and swept from the earth? Can we be divided into two or more governments? Shall we have a new form of government? Is not the nation to rise out of its present troubles better, firmer and more powerful?" During the whole of this magnificent address, the assembly, in deep silence, hung upon his lips save when applause was struck out of them as with blows of magnetism. But a scene ensued, in the delivery of his peroration, that was well nigh sublime.

Laying his hands on the torn and ball-riddled colors of the Seventy-third Ohio regiment, the impassioned orator spoke of the battle-fields where they had been baptised in blood, and described their beauty as some small patch of azure, filled with stars, that an angel had snatched from the heavenly canopy to set the stripes in blood. With this description began a scene that Demosthenes might have envied. All over the vast assembly handkerchiefs and hats were waved, and before the speaker sat down the whole throng arose, as by a magic influence, and screamed and shouted, and saluted, and stamped, and clapped, and wept, and laughed in wild excitement. Colonel Moody sprang to the top of a bench and called for the "Star Spangled Banner," which was sung, or rather shouted, until the audience dispersed.

**Northern Instructors of Southern Teachers.**

As touching the subject of loyalty, one of the most unique and characteristic letters of General Butler will be found in the following correspondence between him and a southern woman whose patriotism had failed her:

LOCUSTVILLE, ACCOMAC CO., VA., March 10.—General B. F. Butler, Sir: My school has been closed since Christmas, because as I understood the oath required of us, I could not conscientiously take it. Having heard since then that one of your officers explains the oath as meaning simply that we *consent* to the acts of the United States government, and pledge *passive obedience* to the same, I take the liberty of addressing this to you to ascertain if you so construe the oath. I cannot understand how a woman can "support, protect and defend the Union," except by speaking or writing in favor of the present war, which I could never do, because my sympathies are with the south.

If by those words you understand merely *passive submission*, I am ready to take the oath, and abide by it sacredly.

Very respectfully,
MARY R. GRAVES.

General Butler's reply to the foregoing certainly leaves Miss Graves in no doubt as to what an oath to support the government of her country implies.

FORTRESS MONROE, March 14.—My Dear Madam: I am truly sorry that any Union officer of mine has attempted to fritter away the effect of the oath of allegiance to the government of the United States, and to inform you that it means nothing more than passive obedience to the same. That officer is surely mistaken. The oath of allegiance means fealty, pledge of faith to love, affection and reverence for the government, all comprised in the word patriotism, in its highest and truest sense, which every true American feels for his or her government.

You say, "I cannot understand how a woman can 'support, protect and defend the Union,' except by speaking or writing in favor of the present war, which I could never do, because my sympathies are with the south." That last phrase, madam, shows why you cannot understand "how a woman can support, protect and defend the Union."

Were you loyal at heart, you would at once understand. The southern women who are rebels understand well "how to support, protect and defend" the Confederacy "without speaking or writing." Some of them act as spies, some smuggle quinine in their under-clothes, some smuggle information through the lines in their dresses, some tend sick soldiers for the Confederacy, and some get up subscriptions for rebel gunboats.

Perhaps it may all be comprised in the phrase, "Where there is a will there is a way."

Now, then, you could "support, protect and defend the Union" by teaching the scholars of your school to love and reverence the government, to be proud of their country, to glory in its flag, and to be true to its Constitution. But, as you don't understand that yourself, you can't teach it to them, and, therefore, I am glad to learn from your letter that your school has been closed since Christmas; and with my consent, until you change your sentiments, and are a loyal woman in heart, it never shall be opened. I would advise you, madam, forthwith to go where your "sympathies" are. I am only doubtful whether it is not my duty to send you. I have the honor to be,

Very respectfully,
your obedient servant,
B. F. BUTLER, Maj. Gen. Com'g.
To MISS MARY R GRAVES,
Locustville, Accomac County, Virginia.

### Loyalty of one of Jeff. Davis's Fellow Citisens in Mississippi.

Andrew Jackson Donelson's name was, for more than a generation, prominent and respected in the region where he lived, as well as far beyond that limited sphere of political influence. In 1856 he was a candidate for the Vice Presidency of the United States, by one of the great parties which then swayed the country. During the rebellion, Mr. Donelson's case was a hard one, as appears from a conversation which he had with a Union man, on board a gunboat going from Memphis down the Mississippi. In a frank, hearty, and open manner, Mr. D. spoke of his ineffectual efforts to induce his friends in Mississippi to keep clear of the rebellion; of his many predictions to them that the sacrifice of their "peculiar institution" would certainly follow their attempt to destroy the Government; of the ban under which he was placed in consequence of his loyalty; of the many little annoyances to which he was subjected by those whom he had previously befriended; and finally, of his arrest and transportation to Vicksburg, to answer a charge of high treason to the Confederate Government. On the last topic he was very bitter, and used language too expressive to look well in print. He said that upon his arrival in Vicksburg, he demanded the charges against him, and that after considerable delay they were furnished. There were thirteen specifications, one of which intimated that he would not trust Jeff. Davis further than a blind mule could kick,—or words to that effect. He admitted that he had said so, and offered to substantiate his opinion by evidence bearing upon certain events connected with that functionary's political dishonesty in former years; but his proposition was ruled out. In regard to the other specifications, he said he was ready to prove any statement which they charged him with making in reference to the rebellion, if time were allowed him in which to bring his witnesses. The result of the matter was, that he was not brought to any trial, but was told, after several day's stay in Vicksburg, that he was at liberty to return to his plantation. He was not slow to avail himself of this permission.

### Predictions of Beckerdite, the "Southern Prophet."

In the year 1832, as appears from authentic statements, a man named Beckerdite, who resided at Lawnhill, Mississippi, began to prophesy on national affairs and the future of the southern States. He was a man of reputable character, of grave manners, and of profound religious feeling. Conscious that the "visions" he had to reveal would be very unpopular if made public, he made them known only to influential persons, and these subsequently corroborated his statements. His visions had one burden—southern ruin.

On the 27th of March, 1864, he felt impelled to communicate to Jeff. Davis, through the Hon. J. A. Orr, of Mississippi, the predestined taking of Richmond, and utter defeat of the South. The rebel authorities regarded Beckerdite as a dangerous man, whose prophetic words tended to discourage rebel efforts, and they ordered that he should be hung; he was however warned, and escaped. His daughter subsequently placed copies of the paper sent to Jeff. Davis, in the hands of Captain Jean, of the Sixty-first United States infantry (colored,) and through him they were made to see the light,—the following quotations being samples:

"At this writing Richmond is threatened by the armies that will take it, after which it may be called the city of Blood."

"No memory can be strong enough to retain all the moans of so great a war. Be it sufficient that I have given you the great events to prove to you that the whole was laid out by the Master of the Universe, before the sectional conventions of 1860. There will be an implied armistice by the northern power, believing the rebellion at an end, during which, God gives you time to consider your welfare. If you repent, humbling yourself in prayers and supplications for His mercy and re-instate yourselves in the Union, peace will ensue; but the States of South Carolina, Georgia, Alabama and Mississippi will not, and the vision of 25th of March, 1864, will take place and be fulfilled by three northern armies crossing in the radius of, and east of Mobile, and prostrating the Confederacy to its ultimate destruction.

A curious trait of this southern prophet was his attachment to the South, his dislike of Yankees, an indisposition to condemn slavery, and his belief that great evils would ensue to the Union people of the country unless they provided a home for the blacks and induced them to emigrate to it.

### Scouting the Doctrine that Majorities are to Rule.

Mr. Gilmore, who visited Richmond in the summer of 1864, and sought by interviews with Jefferson Davis, to bring about an arrangement for a cessation of hostilities, was at one point in the conversation with that official completely "stuck"—and no wonder. This dead-lock between the two was occasioned by Davis's plump denial that "majorities" should rule in political or State affairs.

*Gilmore*—If I understand you, the dispute between your government and ours is narrowed down to this: Union or disunion.

*Davis*—Yes; or to put it in other words: Independence or subjugation.

*Gilmore*—Then the two governments are irreconcilably apart. They have no alternative but to fight it out. But it is not so with the people. They are tired of fighting and want peace; and as they bear all the burden and suffering of the war, is it not right they should have peace, and have it on such terms as they like?

*Davis*—I don't understand you. Be a little more explicit.

*Gilmore*—Well, suppose the two governments should agree to something like this: To go to the people with two propositions—say, peace, with disunion and southern independence, as your proposition; and peace, with union, emancipation, no confiscation, and universal amnesty, as ours. Let the citizens of all the United States (as they existed before the war) vote 'Yes' or 'No' on these two propositions, at a special election, within sixty days. If a majority votes disunion, our government to be bound by it, and to let you go in peace. If a majority votes Union, yours to be bound by it, and to stay in peace. The two governments can contract in this way, and the people, though constitutionally unable to decide on peace or war, can elect which of the two propositions shall govern their rulers. Let Lee and Grant, meanwhile, agree to an armistice. This would sheath the sword; and if once sheathed, it would never again be drawn by this generation.

*Davis*—The plan is altogether impracticable. If the South were only one State, it might work; but as it is, if one southern State objected to emancipation, it would nullify the whole thing; for you are aware the people of Virginia cannot vote slavery out of South Carolina, or the people of South Carolina vote it out of Virginia.

*Gilmore*—But three-fourths of the States can amend the Constitution. Let it be done in that way, so that it be done by the people. I am not a statesman or a politician, and I do not know just how such a plan could be carried out; but you get the idea—that the people should decide the question.

*Davis*—That the majority shall decide it, you mean. We seceded to rid ourselves of the rule of the majority, and this would subject us to it again.

*Gilmore*—But the majority must rule finally, either with bullets or ballots.

*Davis*—I am not so sure of that. Neither current events nor history shows that the majority rules, or ever did rule. The contrary, I think, is true. Why, Sir, the man who should go before the Southern people with such a proposition, with any proposition which implied that the North was to have a voice in determining the domestic relations of the South, could not live here a day. He would be hanged to the first tree, without judge or jury.

*Gilmore* (smiling)—Allow me to doubt that. I think it more likely he would be hanged if he let the Southern people know the majority couldn't rule.

*Davis* (also smiling most good humoredly)—I have no fear of that. I give you leave to proclaim it from every house-top in the South.

### Crossing Fox River.

Mr. Lincoln's story in reply to a Springfield (Illinois) clergyman, who asked him what was to be his policy on the slavery question, in connection with the war, must certainly be regarded as sufficiently expressive:

"Well, your question is rather a cool one, but I will answer it by telling you a story. You know Father B., the old Methodist preacher? and you know Fox river and its freshets? Well, once in the presence of Father B., a young Methodist was worrying about Fox river, and expressing fears that he should be prevented from fulfilling some of his appointments by a freshet in the river. Father B. checked him in his gravest manner. Said he 'Young man, I have always made it a rule in my life not to cross Fox river till I get to it.' And," said the President, "I am not going to worry myself over the slavery question till I get to it." A few days afterwards, a Methodist minister called on the President, and on being presented to him, said, simply: "Mr. President, I have come to tell you that I think we have got to Fox River." Mr. Lincoln relished the point thoroughly, thanked the clergyman, and laughed heartily.

### Three Hundred Ladies with their Union Flags.

The good people of Cleveland, East Tennessee, suffered much from the power of the rebellion, and for a time the flood-gates of secession were opened wide upon them, with the accompanying tide of persecution and spoliation. But in course of time the "powers that be" were changed, and they once more breathed the salubrious atmosphere of olden times, for the law of the Union and the Constitution was again established among them. Colonel Waters, of the Eighty-fourth Illinois regiment, was in command, and one of his first acts was to give notice that the loyal citizens of Cleveland and vicinity desired to resurrect the same identical flag that was lowered two and a half years previously, in obedience to the revolutionists, but which had been securely buried in the southern portion of the county, that it might escape insult and destruction.

At the time appointed for this interesting patriotic ceremony, a procession of ladies, numbering some three hundred, and displaying their gay Union flags, marched to the public square, where their long banished idol was to be unfurled to the pure breeze that played so calmly over the beautiful town of Cleveland. It was one of the most imposing spectacles of loyalty and true patriotism ever witnessed. Gray-haired mothers, whose eyes were dimmed by age, were there; and there, too, was the middle-aged matron, whose sober gaze told the observer that a husband and father was at that time imperiling his life upon the field or in the dreary camp, to sustain the honor and dignity of that banner about to flap its cherished folds in the breeze where it was once scoffed and derided; and there were those who had bade farewell to brother or lover, with a God-speed to the glorious cause.

Of these was that jubilant procession composed, while five hundred, at least, refugees from rebellion, and loyal East Tennesseans, who had taken refuge within the Federal lines, were there to assist in unfurling "the gorgeous ensign of the Republic." The procession halted at the Public Square, the band discoursed 'Hail Columbia,' and amid the swelling jubilee of cheers from the vast multitude, that beautiful emblem of a great people's nationality was run up to the staff-head. Each star appeared more brilliant, and each stripe more attractive, for having been so long buried from the hands of those who would have dishonored it.

### Presidential Favor at last for Everybody.

Not long after the issue of his Proclamation of Emancipation, the President had a fit of illness, though happily of short duration. Notwithstanding this disability, however, he was greatly bored by visitors. The Honorable Mr. Blowhard and the Honorable Mr. Toolittle did not fail to call on his Excellency, to congratulate him on his message and his proclamation; gentlemen in the humble walks of civil life were at the capital for the first time, and couldn't leave without seeing the successor of George Washington; persons with axes to grind insisted upon a little

Presidential Favor at last for Everybody.

aid from the great American rail-splitter; and between them all they gave the convalescent Chief Magistrate very little leisure or peace of mind. One individual, whom the President knew to be a tedious sort of customer, called at the White House about this time, and insisted upon an interview. Just as he had taken his seat, Mr. Lincoln sent for his physician, who immediately made his appearance.

"Doctor," said he, holding out his hand, "what are those marks?"

"That's varioloid, or mild small-pox," said the doctor.

"They're all over me! It is contagious, I believe," said Mr. Lincoln.

"Very contagious, indeed," replied the Esculapian attendant.

"Well, I can't stop, Mr. Lincoln; I just called to see how you were," said the visitor.

"Oh, don't be in any hurry, Sir!" placidly remarked the Executive.

"Thank you, Sir, I'll call again," replied the visitor, executing a masterly retreat from a fearful contagion.

"Do, Sir," said the President: "Some people said they could take very well to my Proclamation, but now, I am happy to say, I have something that *everybody* can take." By this time the visitor was making a desperate break for Pennsylvania Avenue, which he reached on the double quick.

### French Sensibility.

Amongst the gentlemen present on the platform when Mr. Beecher addressed the people of Edinburgh on the American question, were M. Garnier Pagès, M. Desmarest (a distinguished member of the French bar), and M. Henri Martin, the French historian. These eminent foreigners had been attending the social science meetings in Edinburgh, and they had arranged to leave for Paris early that evening; but at the request of somebody they consented to attend Mr. Beecher's meeting to testify their detestation of slavery. Near the close of the proceedings, the chairman stated that M. Desmarest had intended to address the meeting, but owing to an allusion to the Peninsular War in the course of Mr. Beecher's remarks, he thought his national sensibilities had been offended, and had left the room before the reverend gentleman had concluded. The following passage is supposed to have wounded the Frenchman:—

In the beginning of the war we were peculiarly English—for I have observed that England goes into wars and makes blunders in the first part—["hear, hear," cheers and hissing.]—for it is generally found, I say, that England has blundered in the beginning. [Renewed cheers and hissing.] That is mere punctuation, I suppose. I will make all the noise that is necessary. I have noticed that in the Peninsular War for months—for a whole year—there was a series of rude endeavors—misunderstandings at home, and want of support to the armies—money squandered like water—contracts, and contractors making themselves rich — ["hear," cheers and hissings]—but if I recollect, at last [cheers and disturbance]—at last Wellington drove every Frenchman out of the Peninsula, and did not stop his course until he had swept every Frenchman out of Spain. And I say that we have not lost so much of the English blood, from which we are derived, and which yet flows in Yankee veins; but that we began by blundering and blundering—[laughter]—but I think we are doing better and better at every step. [Loud cheers.]

### Right kind of Government to be Established Down South.

Colonel Hanson, of the Kentucky Second, was one of the prisoners that fell into Union hands at Fort Donelson. Not so taciturn as some of his comrades he entered into an animated conversation with the Union Lieutenant who had him in charge, on "the situation," telling frankly some bad truth:

*Colonel*—Well, you were too hefty for us.

*Lieutenant*—Yes, but you were protected by these splended defences.

*Col*—Your troops fought like tigers.

*Lieut*—Do you think now one Southern man can whip five Northern men?

*Col*—Not Western men. Your troops are better than Yankee troops—fight harder—endure more. The devil and all hell can't stand before such fellows. But we drove you back.

*Lieut*—Why didn't you keep us back?

*Col*—You had too many reinforcements.

*Lieut*—But we had no more troops engaged in the fight than you had.

*Col*—Well, you whipped us, but you havn't conquered us. You can never conquer the South.

*Lieut*—We don't wish to conquer the South; but we'll restore the Stars and Stripes to Tennessee, if we have to hang ten thousand such dare-devils as you are.

*Col*—Never mind, Sir, you will never get up to Nashville.

*Lieut*—Then Nashville will surrender before we start.

*Col*—Well, well, the old United States flag is played out—we intend to have a right Government down here.

*Lieut*—What am I to understand by a 'right Government?'

*Col*—A Government based on property, and not a damned mechanic in it.

*Lieut*—Do these poor fellows, who have been fighting for you, understand then that they *have no voice in the 'right Government' that you seek to establish?*

*Col*—They don't care. They have no property to protect.

### Tracing his Political Pedigree.

A northern sympathizer with the South was denouncing, in immeasurable terms, the United States Government and the war, when the company was joined by a neighbor, a strong Union man, and after listening for a time, he interrupted him with the remark: "You came honestly by your principles—you are a tory, naturally." "What do you mean?" said Secesh. "You know," said Union, "that during the war with Great Britain, the British entered the harbor and burned the town of New London." "Well, what of that." said S. "Why, somebody piloted them in, and when his dirty work was done, he came home with the British gold, and his neighbors, hearing of his presence, provided themselves with ropes and made him an evening call, when he made his escape by the back door, and fled to the island of Bermuda, and died there." "Well," said S., "what has all that to do with it?" "Well," said Union, "that pilot was your grandfather."

### Pelicans vs. Eagles.

A little incident in connection with the custom-house at New Orleans, would seem to show that secession was a thing thought of by some of the southern leaders many years ago. This was not done merely to assert the doctrine of State Rights, but rather with the deliberate purpose and expectation that Louisiana would one day become an independent nation. The custom-house in question has been in the course of erection some sixteen years or so, and, more than ten years ago, there were put up the heraldic ornamentations and devices which usually give to such an edifice the indications of its nationality. An examination, however, shows that there is not on the building the slightest indication that it was erected and owned by the United States. As many as ten or twelve years ago, Beauregard and Slidell displayed their propensity to treason by ignoring the arms of the United States and substituting in their stead the Pelican of Louisiana. And there to this day is the sectional symbol, occupying the place of right and honor in the great room, where should be the eagle and the shield.

### Mistook his Man.

Rev. Mr. —— was a priest of the Catholic church in Missouri, his parochial precinct embracing several counties. A staunch Union man from the beginning, he hoisted the Stars and Stripes over the door of his church at the commencement of the war, and there he kept them flying. His life was threatened, he was warned to flee, but he maintained his ground. He knew the views and sentiments of every man in his parish, which extended from the Iowa line to Missouri river.

One day he saw a man moving about from house to house and having business with rebel sympathizers. He watched the fellow's course. He noticed also a wagon filled with bedding, with a woman and children, as if the family were on the move. It stopped at the houses of rebel sympathizers. He took notes and kept his own counsel. One night he was waited upon by a ruffianly looking fellow, who advised him to flee, as there was to be an uprising of the rebels, and his life might be in danger. Out of respect for the Catholic religion, he had called to give him timely warning. "The wagon which you may have seen filled with bedding," said the fellow, "contained guns and ammunition. Our friends (rebels) are supplied with arms, and will soon be in possession of the country."

"Sir," said the priest, "you have come voluntarily into my house and told what I had already mistrusted. I give you two hours to leave this town. If you are found here at the expiration of that time you need not appeal to me to save your life. Go, Sir!"

The ruffian had mistaken his man. He disappeared, and the rebel sympathizers did *not* rise. The nearest Federal officers were at once informed of what was going on, and the Union citizens were immediately supplied with arms.

### Sprinkling Blood in the Face of the People.

Jere. Clemens, of Alabama, in a public address given by him, related an interesting circumstance in connection with the early history of the Rebellion, as illustrating the predetermination of the leaders to plunge the country into war. He was in Montgomery soon after the Ordinance of Secession was passed, and was present at an interview between Jeff. Davis, Memminger and others. They were discussing the propriety of firing upon Sumter. Two or three of them withdrew to the corner of the room, and, said Mr. C., "I heard Gilchrist say to the Secretary of War, 'It must be done. Delay two months and Alabama stays in the Union. You must sprinkle blood in the face of the people.' The meeting then adjourned."

The traitor chieftains were as good as their word. Sumter was fired upon. Blood *was* sprinkled "in the face of the people," and from this sprinkling the best blood of the nation, in both sections, was made to flow as a river. "Sprinkle blood in the face of the people!"—a trim and

Howell Cobb.

polished phrase which filled a continent with woes unutterable! It was doctrine such as this, that Howell Cobb taught in Georgia, and, by carrying that glorious old State over to secession, gave force and prestige to the disloyal movement in its first stages, and thus reddened the history of the whole country with four years of blood.

**Andy Johnson and the Clerical Secessionists.**

The State of Tennessee had a watchful pilot at the helm when Andrew Johnson was its Governor. He was early called to deal with secessionists and traitors in this capacity. One day a pair of citizens belonging, professionally, to 'the cloth,' stood before him, and the following dialogue between the respective parties, 'spiritual' and ' secular,' will throw some light on the question ' Who was the truer man?'

*Gov. Johnson*—Well, gentlemen, what is your desire?

*Rev. Mr. Sehon*—I speak but for myself. I do not know what the other gentlemen wish. My request is that I may have a few days to consider on the subject of signing this paper. I wish to gather my family together and talk over the subject for this purpose, I desire about fourteen days.

*Gov. Johnson*—It seems to me there should be but little hesitation about the matter. All that is required of you is to sign the oath of allegiance. If you are loyal citizens, you can have no reason to refuse to do so. If you are disloyal, and working to obstruct the operations of the Government, it is my duty, as the representative of that Government, to see that you are placed in a position so that the least possible harm shall result from your proceedings. You certainly cannot reasonably refuse to renew your allegiance to the Government that is now protecting you and your families and property.

*Rev. Mr. Elliott*—As a non-combatant, Governor, I considered that under the stipulations of the surrender of the city, I should be no further annoyed. As a non-combatant, I do not know that I have committed an act, since the Federals occupied the city, that would require me to take the oath required.

*Gov. Johnson*—I believe, Mr. Elliott, you have two brothers in Ohio.

*Mr. Elliott*—Yes, Governor, I have two noble brothers, there. They did not agree with me in the course I pursued in regard to secession. But I have lived in Tennessee so many years that I have considered the State my home, and am willing to follow her fortunes. Tennessee is a good State.

*Gov. Johnson*—I know Tennessee is a good State; and I believe the best way to improve her fortunes is to remove those from her borders who prove disloyal and traitors to her interest, as they are traitors to the interest of that Government which has fostered and protected them. By your inflammatory remarks and conversation, and by your disloyal behavior, in weaning the young under your charge from their allegiance to the Government, you have won a name that will never be placed on the roll of patriots. A visit to the North may be of benefit to you.

### Loyal Demonstration with a Crutch.

At one of the fashionable hotels in New York, there boarded for a time, during the war, a somewhat wrathful secession sympathizer—one of the New England and consequently one of the worst kind,—and a chivalric, spirited Major-General of the army, minus a leg, and hobbling about on his crutch. Fired by natural folly and a luxurious dinner, the former insulted the latter, as he was passing through the halls, with loud and coarse denunciations of the war, and all who fought on the loyal side in it. The cripple turned and faced the coward, demanding apology and retraction. They were denied. The man of crutch and soul then asked the name of the poltroon traducer of his country and her patriots. With natural instinct, a wrong one was given. Other words followed; another insult was added by the traducer; whereupon the hero of Chancellorsville and Gettysburg "shouldered his crutch and showed how fields were won," by breaking it over the head of said degenerate son of Adam, who then took himself off, with at least one new idea in his head, namely, that the next crippled soldier of the army he insulted had better be somebody else than Dan Sickles.

---

### First Oath and Testimony of a Slave in Virginia.

A few miles from Fortress Monroe, toward Back river, there is a place called Fox Hill, in the neighborhood of which are or were several excellent farms, one of these being the "Hudgins place." The Hudgins family had absconded when General Magruder retired from Hampton, and, under permission from General Wool, Captain Wilder (superintendent of the colored inhabitants) had allowed a colored man named Anthony Bright to occupy and cultivate the Hudgins farm. Under this permission Anthony had carried on the place in 1861, and up to August, 1862, assisted by other industrious and well-behaved negroes.

In July or August, 1862, Mrs. Hudgins and her two children had unexpectedly returned to the farm, taken possession of the mansion, and set up a claim to the harvest of 1862. She came with her claim to the provost judge, John A. Bolles. On the other hand, Anthony Bright, in behalf of himself and his black co-laborers, presented his claims to the fruit of his labors, and called on the judge for protection. A day and hour was appointed for the trial. Mrs. Hudgins was an intelligent lady, and in all her conduct and conversation made a very pleasant impression on those who observed them. Anthony Bright was a tall, finely-formed, and very bright young man of perhaps thirty years of age. He was a slave. His master had been many years in California, and during that period Anthony had been left in charge of Mr. and Mrs. Hudgins, who had allowed him on payment of $75 a year to work for himself and to act as though he were a freeman.

About half an hour before the trial was to begin, Col. Joseph Segar, the member of Congress from that district, called upon the provost judge in behalf of Mrs. Hudgins, and among other things inquired if the judge was intending to allow Anthony or any other slave to testify. The judge answered yes. But the Colonel begged him to reconsider his determination, reminding him of the exclusionary rule of the Virginia law of evidence, and remarking that in his own judgment the admission of colored witnesses would, more than almost anything else that could happen, displease the Union men among his (Segar's) constituency, and prejudice the cause of the federal government. The judge, however, was unmoved by that suggestion, and ventured to express the belief that never again in the Old Dominion would a colored man be banished, as unworthy of belief or as unfit to be heard, from a court of justice. "However, Colonel," said he, "I will first examine Mrs. Hudgins, and possibly she may save me the necessity of shocking the prejudice of your constituents. If she places the case beyond the need of further evidence, or is herself desirous to hear what Anthony will say, your difficulty will be obviated."

Accordingly Mrs. Hudgins appeared in court, and after being sworn, proceeded to relate her story. From her statements and the documents which she produced, it appeared that the farm, which formerly belonged to her father, had been devised by him to her two minor children, and that she was the executrix of the will, and guardian of the little girls. Her husband, then with the rebels, had no interest in the farm. She went on to state what "Anthony said," and what "Anthony told me," and was interrupted by the judge, who inquired, " But who is Anthony, Mrs. Hudgins?" "Anthony," answered she, with much surprise, "why, judge, Anthony is the colored man that claims the harvest." " Yes," said the judge, " but isn't he a slave, and would you think of believing what he said, or of wishing me to hear his story?" "Of course, Sir," replied Mrs. H., " why should not I believe him? He was brought up in the family. I would believe him as quickly as I would one of my children." "And have you no objections to my examining Anthony, and attaching such credit as I please to what he may say?" "No objection in the world, judge; I *want* you to hear him."

Here the judge exchanged glances with Colonel Segar, and said, " Well, Colonel, I don't see but that I must gratify Mrs. Hudgins;" and the Colonel, in a tone that was almost amusing, responded, "I suppose you must."

Anthony was accordingly called into court, and told all that Mrs. Hudgins had said, to which he assented as strictly true. He was then asked if he had ever testified under oath. " No, Sir," said he, very respectfully, " I never has." He was further asked if he knew what an oath was, and what would be the consequences of false swearing. "I s'pose so master," was his answer: " If I ask God to hear me tell lie, God will punish me for lying." "Very well, Anthony; very truly answered," said the judge.

"*And now, Anthony,*" continued Judge Bolles, rising as he spoke, " *I am about to administer to you the oath to tell the truth, the whole truth, and nothing but the truth. Hold up your right hand.*"

It was worthy of a long journey to behold Anthony in that supreme moment of his life. As he lifted his hand and arm aloft, he seemed to gain several inches in height; his broad chest expanded and his dark eye lighted up as with the inspiration of a new manhood. He was a noble specimen, physically and intellectually, of his race, and most favorably impressed all who saw him.

Anthony produced the permission of Captain Wilder and of General Wool, and then told his story clearly and intelligibly and with a modesty as pleasing as his intelligence was remarkable. When he had finished his statement, the judge asked the lady if she wished to cross-examine Anthony; but she said, " No, I believe he has told the truth." And there, so far as the evidence was concerned, the case was ended. The judge gave the parties a short time to settle the matter among themselves, and at the end of that period, as they had not come to a settlement, appointed a commissioner to divide the products of the farm, awarding one half of the harvest to the executrix and guardian, as the representative of the land, and the other half to Anthony and his associates, as the representatives of the labor. This decision was satisfactory to both the parties in interest, and even Colonel Segar was content with the result, though not entirely pleased with the process by which it was attained.

### Two Kings at the South.

Senator Hammond, of South Carolina, will long be remembered for his famous " mudsill " speech in the United States Senate, in the palmy days of Union, when the lion and the lamb there commingled. In that speech, the vivacious Senator declared that by means of her cotton crop the South could "bring the whole world to her feet." With a defiant air he went on to say: "What would happen if no cotton was furnished for three years? I will not stop to depict what every one can imagine, but this is certain—England would topple headlong and carry the whole civilized world with her, save the South. No, you dare not make war upon cotton. No power on earth dares to make war upon it. *Cotton is King!*" Senator Hammond, as well as many others, unquestionably believed this, and acted accordingly. But there were and are a much greater number believing, with Senator Clark, of New Hampshire, who, in his review of the astute South Carolinian's argument, remarked: "Cotton is King! Sir, there is another King besides Cotton—*Humbug* is King!"

### Which Side?

Walking one day on the beach at Birattz, Louis Napoleon happened to meet an intel-

Which Side?

ligent looking boy, about eight or nine years old, who took off his hat as he passed. The Emperor courteously returned the salute, and said, "Are you English?" "No," answered the boy, very quickly, and drawing himself up, "I'm American." "Oh! American, are you? Well, tell me, which are you for, North or South?" "Well, father's for the North, I believe; but I am certainly for the South. For which of them are you, Sir?" The Emperor stroked his moustache, smiled, hesitated a little, and then said, "I'm for both!" "For both, are you? Well, that's not so easy, and it will please nobody!" His Majesty let the conversation drop and walked on.

### Diseases of the Brain and Heart.

In one of the upper townships of Ohio were two farmers, their places being separated by a small creek. They were well-to-do people, but diametrically opposed in politics, and each noted for the zeal with which he defended his sentiments, Mr. M. being a straight uncompromising Union man, and Mr. S. an anti-war Democrat. Meeting a few days before the State election, Mr. S. accosted his neighbor, saying:

"How is it, friend M.,—I hear there is a very prevalent disease on your side of the creek!"

"Ah!" said Mr. M., "what is the disease?"

"N-i-g-g-e-r on the brain," replied Mr. S.

"Well," said Mr. M., "that is a mere trifle compared to the malady existing on the other side."

"Indeed!" exclaimed Mr. S., "and pray what can *that* be?"

"Treason on the heart!" retorted M. The conversation "took a turn."

### Treason in an Unexpected Quarter.

As one of the boats containing Federal prisoners was on its way to the point where an exchange was to be made, the rebel Captain essayed a conversation with one of the passengers on board, the circumstances and situation furnishing the theme.

"I am a Northern man myself; my name is Samuel Todd; I am Mrs. Lincoln's brother," said the Captain. "And what are you doing here?" asked the passenger. "Yes, Sir," he repeated, in a musing manner, "I am Mrs. Lincoln's brother. I was

Mrs. Lincoln.

born and brought up in the North; but I am into this thing on the Southern side, and I mean to see it through." To this the Captain received answer: "Now, you know very well that the cause of the Union, for which the United States are fighting, will be successful in the end, and what in the world are you doing down here, fighting against the lawful government of the Union—fighting against your own historic flag, which you know has been respected and honored by the civilized world?" This allusion to the Stars and Stripes seemed to touch him; but he answered, "I came down here several years ago, made some money, bought some property, and my home and interest are here. We consider that the Northern people are encroaching on our rights, and of course we feel bound to protect them, or die in the attempt." And yet, there was no truer-hearted loyal woman, during the war, than Mrs. Lincoln, whose misguided brother was thus willing to "die in the attempt" to destroy the best and most benign government in the world.

### Hatred of Southern Unionists to Southern Rebels.

In one of the tents of a Union Maryland regiment a man was found who had been wounded in an engagement with a rebel Maryland regiment, in which were two of his cousins, "the same as brothers to him—they had all gone to school together and lived on the next farm to each other all their lives, till the war broke out." The Unionist was asked if it would not have been very disagreeable to him if he had learnt that either of them had been shot by a bullet from him. "No," he answered savagely, "I was on the lookout for them all the time, so that I might aim at them. I was hoping and praying all the time that my shot might by chance reach them. I would ask for nothing better than to shoot them, or to stick them with my bayonet—curse the traitors!" When thrown together on picket or in hospital, the Yankee boys from Massachusetts or Ohio, and the Johnnies from Alabama and Mississippi were the best of friends; but the loyal Virginian scowled darkly on the rebel Virginian, and the rebel Tennessean had only a curse for the loyal Tennessean —and so of the other border States.

### "To the Manor Born."

At one of the receptions at Secretary Seward's, the dusky representative of Haytien government was present as one of the diplomatic corps. This distinguished colored gentleman figured conspicuously among the richly attired ladies and official dignitaries in attendance; but at the refreshment table an awkward incident occurred in connection with him. One of the representatives from Missouri, upon reaching the table with a lady upon his arm, observed a well dressed negro helping the ladies to oysters, and supposing him to be one of the waiters, the Missourian, holding out his plate, directed the supposed servant to "put some oysters on that plate." The colored gentleman hesitated. The Missourian then became more imperative, when the colored individual, whom he addressed as "waiter"—looking daggers at him—finally obeyed the order. The incident was generally observed, and the Missourian was soon after informed that the colored personage whom he had commanded as a servant and addressed as "waiter," was "His Excellency" the Haytien Minister. "I am very sorry for the mistake," replied the gentleman from Missouri; "But as I own an hundred as good looking negroes as he, I can not afford to apologize for so natural a misconception of his position." Such an occurrence seems in keeping with the domination at Washington which preceded the Rebellion, but not subsequently. It may, however, have taken place, and at all events illustrate the manner of those who are "to the manor born."

### Welcome to the Troops at Port Royal.

Our troops at Port Royal were accompanied in their first reconnoissance into the island by Dr. J. J. Craven, who reported the negroes on the plantations further inland as almost wild with delight at the advent of our soldiers and the hasty flight of their masters, which they described with great gusto. Said one of them to the Doctor:

"O, Lord! massa, we're so glad to see you. We'se prayed and prayed the good Lord that he would send yer Yankees, and we know'd you'se was coming."

"How could you know that?" asked Dr. Craven; "You can't read the paper; how did you get the news?"

"No, massa, we'se can't read, but we'se can listen. Massa and missus used to read, and sometimes they'se would read loud, and then we would listen so" (making an expressive gesture indicative of close attention at a key hole); "when I'se get a chance I'se would list'n, and Jim, him would list'n, and we put the bits together, and we knowed the Yankees were coming. Bress the Lord, massa."

### Constructive Parole Rights.

A detective officer belonging to the New York police force, named Hart, who accompanied Mrs. Anderson on her visit to her husband at Fort Sumter, obtained permission to remain there on condition that he should not fight. He faithfully observed his parole, but when the barracks took fire, he exclaimed, "I didn't promise not to fight fire!" and devoted himself with almost superhuman energy, to extinguish the flames. With balls hissing and shells bursting around him, he worked on undaunted, and could with the utmost difficulty be forced away from the burning buildings, even when it was death to remain. When the flag was shot down, the Charlestonians concentrated their fire upon the flag staff, to prevent its being replaced; but unmindful of the shot, which whizzed by him every second, Hart *nailed the flag to the wall*, amid cheers from the United States troops.

### That Flag Presentation in New Orleans.

General Butler had a dandy regiment in New Orleans—one a little nicer in uniform and personal habits than any other; and so ably commanded, that it had not lost a man by disease since leaving New England. One day the Colonel of this fine regiment came to head-quarters, wearing the expression of a man who had something exceedingly pleasant to communicate. It was just before the fourth of July, and this is Mr. Parton's apt narration of what followed:

"General," said he "two young ladies have been to me—beautiful girls—who say they have made a set of colors for the regiment, which they wish to present on the fourth of July."

"But is their father willing?" asked the General, well knowing what it must cost two young ladies of New Orleans, at that early time, to range themselves so conspicuously on the side of the Union.

"Oh, yes," replied the Colonel; "their father gave them the money, and will attend at the ceremony. But have you any objections?"

"Not the least, if their father is willing."

"Will you ride out and review the regiment on the occasion?"

"With pleasure."

So, in the cool twilight of the evening of the fourth, the General, in his best uniform, with chapeau and feathers, worn then for the first time in New Orleans, reviewed the regiment amid a concourse of spectators. One of the young ladies made a pretty presentation speech, to which the gallant Colonel handsomely replied. The General made a brief address. It was a gay and joyful scene; everything passed off with the highest *eclat*, and was chronicled with all the due editorial flourish in the *Delta*.

Subsequently, the young ladies addressed a note to the regiment, of which the following is a copy:

NEW ORLEANS, July 5, 1862.

"GENTLEMEN:—We congratulate and thank you all for the manner in which you have received our flag. We did not expect such a reception. We offered the flag to you as a gift from our hearts, as a reward to your noble conduct. Be assured, gentlemen, that that day will be always present in our minds, and that we will never forget that we gave it to the bravest of the brave; but if ever danger threatens your heads, rally under that banner, call again your courage to defend it, as you have promised, and remember that those from whom you received it will help you by their prayers to win the palms of victory and triumph over your enemies. We tender our thanks to General Butler for lending his presence to the occasion, and for his courtesies to us. May he continue his noble work, and ere long may we behold the Union victorious over his foes and reunited throughout our great and glorious country. Very respectfully."

A few days later, an officer of the regiment came into the office of the commanding General, his countenance not clad in smiles. He looked like a man who had seen a ghost, or one who had suddenly heard of some entirely crushing calamity.

"General," he gasped, "we have been sold. THEY WERE NEGROES!"

"What! Those lovely blondes, with blue eyes and light hair? Impossible!"

"General, it's as true as there's a heaven above. The whole town is laughing at us."

"Well," said the General, "there's no harm done. Say nothing about it. I suppose we must keep it out of the papers, and hush it up as well as we can."

They did not quite succeed in keeping it out of the papers, for one of the "foreign neutrals" of the city sent an account of the affair to the Courier des Etats Unis, in New York, with the inevitable French decorations.

---

**Original Conspiracy to Assassinate Mr. Lincoln.**

That Mr. Lincoln, the President-elect, was to feel the sting of Southern steel—as proclaimed by his political enemies—on his way to Washington, to take the oath of office, is now historical. A detective of great experience, who had been employed by Mr. Lincoln's friends, discovered a combination of men banded together under a most solemn oath, to do the deed of assassination. The leader of the conspirators was an Italian refugee, a barber, well known in Baltimore, who assumed the name of Orsini, as indicative of the part he was to assume.

The assistants employed by the detective of this plot, who, like himself, were strangers in Baltimore, by assuming to be secessionists from Louisiana and other seceding States, gained the confidence of some of the conspirators, and were thus intrusted with their plans. It was arranged, in case Mr. Lincoln should pass safely over the railroad to Baltimore, that the conspirators should mingle with the crowd which might surround his carriage, and by pretending to be his friends, be enabled to approach his person, when, upon a signal from their leader, some of them would shoot at Mr. Lincoln with their pistols, and others would throw into his carriage hand-grenades filled with detonating powder, similar to those used in the attempted assassination of the Emperor Louis Napoleon. It was also intended that in the confusion which should result from this attack, the assailants should escape to a vessel which was waiting in the harbor to receive them, and be carried to Mobile, in the seceding State of Alabama.

Upon Mr. Lincoln's arrival in Philadelphia, upon Thursday, February 21st, the detective visited Philadelphia, and submitted to certain friends of the President-elect the information he had collected as to the conspirators and their plans. An interview was immediately arranged for between Mr. Lincoln and the detective. The interview took place in Mr. Lincoln's room, in the Continental Hotel, where he was staying. Mr. Lincoln, having heard the officer's statement, replied:

"I have promised to raise the American flag on Independence Hall to-morrow morning—the morning of the anniversary of Washington's birthday—and have accepted the invitation of the Pennsylvania Legislature to be publicly received by that body in the afternoon. *Both of these engagements I will keep if it costs me my life.* If, however, after I shall have concluded these engagements, you can take me in safety to Washington, I will place myself at your disposal, and authorize you to make such arrangements as you may deem proper for that purpose."

On the next day he gallantly performed the ceremony of raising the American flag on Independence Hall; he then went to Harrisburg, where he was formally welcomed by the Legislature, and at six o'clock in the evening he, in company with Col. Lamon, quietly entered a carriage without observation, and was driven to the Pennsylvania railroad, where a special train was waiting to take him to Philadelphia. On his departure, the telegraph wires were cut, so that no communication of his movements could be made.

The special train arrived in Philadelphia at a quarter to eleven at night. Here he was met by the detective, who had a carriage in readiness, into which the party entered, and were driven to the depot of the Philadelphia, Wilmington and Baltimore railroad.

They did not reach the depot until a quarter past eleven; but fortunately for them, the regular train, the hour of which for starting was eleven, had been detained. The party then took berths in the sleeping car, and without change of cars passed directly through to Washington, where they arrived at the usual hour, half-past six o'clock, on the morning of Saturday, the 23d. Mr. Lincoln wore no disguise whatever, but journeyed in an ordinary traveling dress.

#### Protection under the Constitution.

Among the incidents attending the operations of the celebrated Mackerelville Brigade, at or near the seat of war, is the following, recounted by the historiographer-extraordinary of the corps, Mr. Kerr. It seems that just at the moment when the Comic Section was proceeding to make a "masterly movement," an aged chap came dashing down from a First Family country seat, near by, and says he to the General of the Mackerel Brigade:

"I demand a guard for my premises immediately. My wife," says he with dignity, "has just been making a custard pie for the sick Confederacies in the hospital, and as she has just set it out to cool near where my little boy shot one of your vandals this morning, she is afraid it might be taken by your thieving mudsills when they come after the body. I, therefore, demand a guard for my premises in the name of the Constitution of our forefathers."

Here Capt. Bob Shorty stepped forward, and says he:

"What does the Constitution say about custard pie, Mr. Davis?"

The aged chap spat at him, and says he:

"I claim protection under that clause which refers to the pursuits of happiness. Custard pies," says he reasoningly, "are included in the pursuits of happiness."

"That's very true," says the General, looking kindly over his fan at the venerable petitioner. "Let a guard be detailed to protect this good old man's premises. We are fighting for the Constitution, not against it."

A guard was detailed, with orders to make no resistance if they were fired upon occasionally from the windows of the house; and then Captain Brown pushed forward with what was left of Company 3, to engage the Confederacy on the edge of Duck Lake, supported by the Orange County Howitzers.

### Unacquainted with Politics.

No small pains were taken by certain partisan leaders, while General Grant was at Vicksburg, to inveigle him into some debate, or the expression of some definite idea or opinion relative to the state of the various political parties of the country, and their professed tenets. The General, however, was not thus to be drawn out. He had never attached himself to any mere partisan organization, and all the various political issues or questions were, to him, entirely subordinate to the great and single object of crushing the rebellion.

While operating in the vicinity of Vicksburg, his professed political friends paid a visit to his head-quarters, and after a short time spent in compliments, they touched upon the never-ending subject of politics. One of the party was in the midst of a very flowery speech, using all his rhetorical powers to induce the General, if possible, to view matters in the same light as himself, when he was suddenly stopped by Grant.

"There is no use of talking politics to me. I know nothing about them, and, furthermore, I do not know of any person among my acquaintances who does. But," continued he, "there is one subject with which I am perfectly acquainted; talk of that, and I am your man."

"What is that, General?" asked the politicians, in great surprise.

"Tanning leather," was the reply.

The subject was immediately changed.

### Secesh Taming.

War, like nearly every other sort of human experience, has its comical side. 'Old Ben Butler's' management of New Orleans was "as good as a play,"—a spice of humor in it, a certain apt felicitousness in turning the tables, calculated to make even the victim smile while he yet winced.

It was the New Orleanaise who gave the General his *soubriquet* of 'Picayune Butler'—that being the well known appellative of the colored barber in the basement of the St. Charles. The fourpence ha'penny epithet of course implied how very cheap they held the commander at Ship Island. The Yankee General *fetched up* at the St. Charles. 'Twas empty and barred. Where was the landlord? Off. The house must be opened. Impossible. It shall be forced. Well, here are the keys. So the first thing was to show he could keep a hotel.

Next he sends word to the Mayor that he must see him at his parlor. Back comes word that His Honor does business at the City Hall. Straight goes a peremptory message by an orderly, and Mayor Monroe and a whole bevy of dignitaries make their appearance, hats in hand. The hotel-keeper is induced to draw it mild, and arranges that the civil government of the city shall remain in their hands on the condition that all the police and sanitary duties shall be faithfully performed.

For a little while matters go on smoothly. But it soon became apparent that the streets were neglected, as if on purpose to invite Yellow Jack to come and make short work of the "Hessians." A sharp word goes from the St. Charles to the City Hall to start the hoes, and, at a jump, the hoes were started. But it went against the grain. The aldermen could not sleep o'nights. Yellow Jack out of the question, they thought they would try *la belle France*. So they passed a resolution tendering the officers of the French frigate Catinet the freedom and hospitalities of the city. Up comes word from the St. Charles that this sort of thing don't answer—that 'the freedom of a captured city by the captives would merit letters patent for its novelty, were there not doubts of its usefulness as an invention, and that the tender of hospitalities by a government to which police duties and sanitary regulations only are intrusted is simply an invitation to the calaboose or the sewer.'

The women next bridle up. They are not content with leaving our quiet soldiers to themselves, but must needs insult and abuse them. The General determines that this unfeminine practice, so provocative of ill blood, shall stop. He proclaims that all women guilty of it shall be treated as disorderly women. Thereupon Mayor Monroe steps again upon the scene, and as 'chief magistrate of this city, chargeable with its peace and dignity,' protests against an order 'so extraordinary and astonishing.' The immediate reply is that 'John T. Monroe, late Mayor of the city of New Orleans, is relieved from all responsibility for the peace of the city, and committed to Fort Jackson until further orders.' Straightway the Mayor hurries down to the St. Charles, and makes a written retraction, to wit: 'This communication having been sent under a mistake of fact, and being improper in language, I desire to apologize for the same, and to withdraw it.' The retraction is accepted, and the Mayor retires; but on the next day, having been taken to task by his clique, he again presents himself, with several backers, to get a modification of the 'woman order,' or to take back his apology. He receives for reply, that a modification is impossible, and with it an argument from the good-natured General showing its propriety and necessity. The Mayor bows, convinced, and leaves. Two days afterwards again he comes down with his friends and *insists* upon having back his apology. The General, being of a yielding nature, politely hands it back, and, at the same moment, gives an order committing the whole set to Fort Jackson, and there they ruminated.

### Romantic Adventure of a Tennessee Loyalist.

Of a similar character for boldness and intrepidity to Parson Brownlow, was Hurst, the indomitable Unionist of Purdy, Tennessee. On returning from West Tennessee, to make his periodical report of himself—being under heavy bonds to the rebel powers to do so—and stopping at his home, he had no sooner entered his

Romantic Adventure.

house than he was told to fly for his life, as a new accusation of being a traitor and a spy had been made against him by a malicious old rebel neighbor.

He had barely time to make an appointment with a bound boy, who loved him more than he did his own father, to bring a favorite horse—that somehow escaped the thieving confiscations of the rebels—to the entrance of a certain alley in the town. Scarcely had he made the arrangement when a file of Confederate soldiers was seen coming towards the house. He slipped out at the back door, passed through a neighboring garden, and in a minute more was walking composedly down the principal street of the town. His bold and unconcerned appearance created quite a stir in the town. Men whispered together, and winked and wagged their heads significantly, and now and then would dart off to give information to the rebel guard, who were searching for him. He knew his time was short, that in a few minutes they would come in upon him from all sides, and his chance for life would not be worth a straw. He quickened his pace a little, and suddenly entered an apothecary's shop; dozens of men were watching him, and said—

"Now he is trapped; he'll be nabbed as he comes out."

Hurst walked quickly through into the back room, and called the proprietor in after him. The apothecary entered smilingly, thinking, doubtless, of how soon he should see his guest dancing upon nothing in the air. The moment he had entered, Hurst grasped him suddenly by the throat, and placing a pistol at his ear, told him that if he attempted to raise the slightest alarm, and did not do exactly as he told him, he would fire.

By this time a crowd had collected in front of the shop, and as they could not see what was passing in the back room, they waited until the guard should come up to arrest him. Hurst now opened the back door, and looking up the alley, he saw the faithful bound boy with the horse standing partly concealed in the entrance of the alley. He beckoned to the boy, who quickly brought the horse to him. He then turned to the trembling fellow, and said—

"Now, sir, in the spot where you stand, the rifles of four of my faithful friends are covering you—they are hid in places that you least suspect, and if you move within the next ten minutes they will fire; but if you remain perfectly quiet they will not harm you."

The apothecary had become so completely 'frickened,' as the Irish would say, by the touch of cold steel at his ears, that he did not recognize at once the improbability of Hurst's story. In an instant more, Hurst had put spurs to his horse, and dashed out of the alley, leaving the terrified 'pothecary gaping after him, and the bound boy absolutely crying at his master's danger, and in another instant the rebel soldiers and the crowd entered the store, rushed through the back room and out at the back door, just in time to see Hurst dashing out of the alley at full speed. Horses without number were at once in requisition, but Hurst distanced them all. He soon joined the Union army, and on its subsequent triumphant entry to Nashville, Hurst was on hand with them, naively remarking that he came so as to "*defend his bondsmen from any damage they might suffer by his non-appearance, and 'report' himself as he had agreed!*"

### Them and Theirs—not Us.

One of the most interesting cases among the rebel prisoners at Camp Denison, Ohio, was a wounded youth, whose heart was evidently busy doing poetic justice to the Yankees he had been taught to hate, though he still was anxious about Southern rights. Parson Clayton talked to him for some time concerning religious matters, and the young man at last broke in by saying, "We've talked about religion long enough, now let's talk politics." There was a peculiar Southernism about his look and tone that excited a smile all around. "Well," replied Mr. Clayton, "I'm not much on politics; I'd rather not talk about them—tell me how you felt when you were wounded." He did so:

"Thought it would be a sharp pain, Sir, but it wasn't. I was wounded in the legs, and it was just like my being knocked off my pins by a strong blow from a log of wood. Fell flat on my belly, and my knees drew themselves up under my chin. Made sure I was dead, but thought it didn't make much difference, for I saw our men retreating, and knew that the Yankees would get me and kill me sure; always was told, Sir, the Yankees had horns. Well, there I lay; and up came a Colonel leading his men—he was in front, Sir; he jumped down from his horse, and ran to me drawing something from his belt, so I gave up; but it wasn't a pistol, Sir," (and here the boy's eyes moistened) "it was a canteen! He put it to my lips, I drank. He jumped on his horse again, and said, 'Charge, boys, they're fleeing!' Then some soldiers on foot came toward me, and I thought they're not all like that officer, and I gave up again. But, Sir, they said, 'Comrade, get up.' They lifted me up and said, 'Put your arms around our necks, and we'll lead you away from these bullets.' And these were the 'damned Yankees!' I tell you, Sir, no man ever hugged his sweetheart harder or more friendly than I hugged those Yankees' necks."

After a few more remarks the youth showed a determination to "talk politics," and asked Mr. Clayton, "What are you fighting us for?" Mr. Clayton calmly, and in good humor, gave him his ideas of the issue, and in ending asked him what they were fighting for. "To hold property, Sir," replied the youth,—"our slave property." "How many slaves did you have?" "None." "And you?" (to the next). "None." He then went around to all the thirty-four rebels, and but one was found who had owned a slave. "Now," said Mr. Clayton, "where are the men who have these slaves which they are so afraid of losing?" Here a man named McLellan, who soon afterwards died, raised himself up on his cot, and stretching out his thin hand said, in a sepulchral voice, "They are at home enjoying themselves, and have sent us to die for them and theirs." And to this the echoes around the room were, "That's so!" "That's God's truth!"

## Vice-President Hamlin a Private in Company A.

There was at Fort McClary, in Portsmouth harbor, New Hampshire, during the dark days of the war, a soldier who performed all the duties of a private in the ranks and a guard, and was not even clothed with the power of a fourth corporal,—but who, in the event of the death of President Lincoln, would at once have become the commander-in-chief of the army and navy of the United States. And yet, with that necessary consciousness, he was willing to place himself in the position of a common soldier, share with them in their messes, bear about his own tin dipper, and reside in their barracks. This was the position of the Hon. Hannibal Hamlin, Vice-President of the United States (and formerly Governor of Maine and United States Senator), and private in Company A, of the State Guard of Bangor. Such may be said to be one of the beauties of republicanism; but it requires a sound-cored man thus to display the most beautiful features of the simplicity of our institutions.

## Col. Polk, and Sanders, the Refugee.

Colonel William H. Polk, of Tennessee, the well known scholar, politician and wit, of Tennessee, had a plantation some forty miles from Nashville, lived comfortably, had a joke for every one, and was, withal, a resolute man in his opinions.

A few days before the arrival of the U. S. army at Nashville, in 1862, and, indeed, before he heard of the fall of Fort Donelson, in going down the road from his farm, he descried a fat, ragged, bushy-headed, tangled-mustached, dilapidated-looking creature, (something like an Italian organ-grinder in distress,) so disguised in mud as to be scarcely recognizable. What was his surprise, on a nearer approach, to see that it was the redoubtable George N. Sanders.

George had met the enemy and he was theirs—not in person, but in feeling. His heart was lost, his breeches were ragged, and his boots showed a set of fat, gouty toes protruding from them. The better part of him was gone, and gone a good distance.

"In the name of God, George, is that you?" said the ex-Congressman.

"Me!" said the immortal George: "I wish it wasn't; I wish I was anything but me. But what is the news here—is there any one running? They are all running back there," pointing over his shoulder with his thumb.

"No," said Mr. Polk, "not that I know of. You needn't mind pulling up the seat of your pantaloons. I'm not noticing. What in —— are you doing here, looking like a muddy Lazarus in the painted cloth?"

"Bill," said George to the Tennesseean, confidentially, and his tones would have moved a heart of stone, "Bill, you always was a friend of mine. I know'd you a long while ago, and honored you—cuss me if I didn't. I said you was a man bound to rise. I told Jimmy Polk so; me and Jimmy was familiar friends. I intended to have got up a biographical notice of you in the Democratic Review, but that —— Corby stopped it. I'm glad to see you; I'll swear I am."

"Of course, old fellow," said the charitable Tennesseean, more in pity of his tones than even of the flattering eloquence; "but what is the matter?"

"Matter!" said George; "the d——d Lincolnites have seized Bowling Green, Fort Donelson, and have by this time taken Nashville. Why," continued he, in a burst of confidence, "when I left, hacks was worth $100 an hour, and, Polk, (in a whisper,) I didn't have a —— cent."

The touching pathos of this last remark was added to by the sincere vehemence with which it was uttered, and the mute eloquence with which he lifted up a ragged flap in the rear of his person that some envious rail or briar had torn from its position of covering a glorious retreat.

"Not a d——d cent," repeated he; "and, Polk, I walked that hard-hearted town up and down, all day, with bomb-shells dropping on the street at every lamp-post—I'll swear I did—trying to borrow some money; and, Polk, do you think, there wasn't a scoundrel there would lend anything, not even Harris, and he got the money out of the banks, too!"

"No," interjected Polk, who dropped in a word occasionally, as a sort of encourager.

"Bill," repeated Sanders, "Bill, I said you was a friend of mine—and a talented one—always said so, Bill. I didn't have a red, and I've walked forty-five miles in the last day, by the mile-stones, and I havn't had anything to buy a bit to eat; and," he added, with impassioned eloquence, "what is a cussed sight worse, not a single drop to drink."

This is complete. It is unnecessary to tell how the gallant and clever Tennesseean took the wayfarer home, gave him numerous, if not innumerable drinks, and filled him with fruits of the gardens and flesh of the flocks.

**Unfortunate Absence at the Siege of Fort Sumter.**

On the news of the fall of Sumter, the fires of patriotic enthusiasm were kindled throughout all the loyal States. In one of the small towns of Western Pennsylvania the excitement became intense—patriotic speeches were made, companies for the war speedily formed, etc., etc. It was at this time, when the public excitement was at its height, that there was a flag-raising at a school-house two miles from A——, the orator of the occasion being a young collegiate, fresh from his Alma Mater. After the speech had been made a sheet of foolscap was produced, and twelve big. noble-looking fellows walked boldly up and enrolled their names among the brave detenders of their country. As each man put his name upon the paper he was greeted by three lusty cheers and the rolling of the drum. Finally, when the twelve recruits had taken their seats, and no one seemed to manifest any inclination of following their example of enlisting, a young man was called upon to speak. He was a strong, dashing, dark-eyed youth, and evidently much excited. He seemed determined, however, to acquit himself with applause, and he spread out accordingly.

After stating numerous, and, as he urged, strong reasons for not going to the war himself—that 'he couldn't leave his business'—'would go if they couldn't get along without him'—'if he found it to be his duty,' etc., he waxed warm. He glowed in his overflowing patriotism, and having depicted in flaming colors the outrage practiced on our flag by the rebels, he closed his impressive speech with, in effect, the following:

Edmund Ruffin.

"Gentlemen! do you know what I'd have done had I been down there when that glorious flag was torn by these traitors from its lofty height? I would have snatched it from their bloody hands—I would have mounted the flag-staff—and, regardless of the hail of bullets that might have stormed around me, I would have *nailed* it there—ay! with my own hands would I have nailed it there! and have— have—gentlemen—*desired it to remain!*" The absence of this patriotic orator at the siege of Sumter must, of course, have been the cause of its unfortunate surrender. Edmund Ruffin, the hoary traitor, who fired the first shot at Sumter, should have had a clinch at that tonguy and softpated orator. The odds would have been of little account, which of the two went down.

### Application of the Term "Contraband" by General Butler.

The rebel Colonel Mallory had the misfortune to lose some of his 'servants,' who used their legs to convey themselves from the custody of their master. Though a traitor to his country, Col. M. had the audacity to go with a flag of truce to Fortress Monroe and demand of his old political friend, Butler, the delivering up of said escaped servants, under the Fugitive Slave Law.

"You hold, Colonel Mallory, do you not," said General Butler, "that negro slaves are property; and that Virginia is no longer a part of the United States."

"I do, Sir."

"You are a lawyer, Sir," Gen. Butler replied, "and I ask you, if you claim that the Fugitive Slave Act of the United States is binding in a foreign nation? And if a foreign nation uses this kind of property to destroy the lives and property of citizens of the United States, if that species of property ought not to be regarded as *contraband?*"

Such was the origin of the term contraband, as applied to fugitive slaves, and its acceptance became at once universal.

### "Newport News."

The operations of the two great armies, from time to time, at "Newport News Point," have given that place quite a celebrity in military annals, and its peculiar name has given rise to much curiosity as to how it could have originated. In reference to this, it appears that the early colony on James river was at one time reduced to a straightened condition, and some of its members started down the James river, with the intention of proceeding to England. They reached the bend in the river which has since become an object of so much interest, and paused for some days. When they were about to set sail, they saw a ship coming up the roads, bearing the British ensign. They delayed till it should arrive. It proved to be Lord Newport's ship, with his lordship on board, who brought the intelligence that the ship which the colony had long before dispatched to England for supplies, and which was many months overdue, was near at hand, bringing much needed relief. Meantime, his lordship distributed provisions among the colonists, who, from these circumstances, named the place "Newport News," on account of the good tidings which his lordship brought to them.

### Tigers and Treason.

Colonel Boernstein, a German commander at the West, became somewhat noted for his logical method of dealing with traitors. While holding possession of Jefferson City, Missouri, his patriotic and magisterial traits were made conspicuous by not a few well-remembered cases of summary discipline. One day he heard of a desperado being in town, from Clark township, who had led a company of disunionists known and dreaded as the "Tigers."

"If anybodies vill make ze affidavit," said Colonel B., "I vill arrest him if he izh a tiger. I don't believe in tigers; zey d——d humbugs!"

Some one inquired of the Colonel how long he should remain in that place. With a French shrug of the shoulder, he replied:

"I don't know—perhaps a year; so long as the Governor chooses to stay away; I am Governor now, you see, 'till he come back."

His notions of freedom of speech and the press, he gave expression to as follows:

"All people zall speak vat dey tink—write vat dey pleaze, and be free to do anytink dey pleazhe—*only dey zall speak and write no treason!*"

### Gould, the Hero of Corinth.

In the heat of the conflict, the Ninth Texas regiment bore down upon the left centre of the Twenty-Seventh Ohio regiment, with their battle flag at the head of the column, when Orrin B. Gould, a private of Company G. shot down the color-bearer and rushed forward for the rebel flag. A rebel officer shouted to his men to "*save the colors!*" and, at the same moment, put a bullet into the breast of Gould. But the young hero was not to be intimidated. With his flag-staff in his hand, and the bullet in his breast, he returned to his regiment, waving the former defiantly in the faces of the enemy. After the battle, on visiting the hospitals, Colonel Fuller of the Twenty-Seventh Ohio, (commanding first brigade, second division) found young Gould stretched upon a cot, apparently in great pain. Upon seeing him, his face became radiant, and, pointing to his wound, he said, "Colonel, I don't care for this, since I got their flag!"

### John Bell's Tennessee Iron Works.

On the evening of Feb. 16th, 1862, Commodore Foote sent the gun-boat St. Louis on a reconnoitreing expedition towards Clarksville, Tenn. Six miles above Dover, they came in sight of the Tennessee Iron Works, an extensive establishment owned by Hon. John Bell, Mr. Lewis, and others. Not a person was in sight, and to ascertain if anybody was at home, a shell was thrown at a high elevation, and burst directly over the establishment, too high to do any damage. It had the desired effect—the workmen streamed out of their hive like a swarm of bees.

It having been reported that the mill

had been engaged extensively in the manufacture of iron plates for rebel gunboats, officer Johnson, of the St. Louis, was sent ashore to find the proprietors and inquire about it. He found Mr. Lewis, who at once presented himself as the proprietor, and in response to the officer's inquiries, stated that the mill had been occupied lately in the manufacture of a good deal of iron of various patterns; but it had been done for contractors and other individuals, and not directly for the rebel 'Government.'

Mr. Lewis was asked if he did not know from the pattern of the iron that it was for war purposes. He said that a good deal of it had been square iron, which he supposed was for wagon axles, and a considerable part had been heavy plates which might be for gunboats. He stated that he had been a strong and decided Union man as long as he could be with safety from mobs, which threatened his person and property, and likewise applied the rather doubtful assertion to Mr. Bell. He was asked why he did not decline orders for making war materials, as Mr. Hinman—proprietor of the Cumberland Iron Works, lower down the river—had done; to which his reply was, that Mr. Hinman was in Kentucky, which did not secede, while he was in Tennessee, and above the fortification of Donelson, which was erected in May, thus shutting up the Cumberland river at the Tennessee line.

In view of the inevitable fact that the works had been engaged in making and furnishing materials of war to the rebels, Commodore Foote considered it his duty to disable them, not knowing then that the Union lines would soon embrace them, and the river beyond, to Clarksville. He informed Mr. Lewis that this would be necessary and also that he must require him to go on board as a prisoner. An attempt was first made to disable the machinery of the establishment, the desire being not to utterly destroy the property if it could be avoided. But the machinery was so heavy that no means could be found of confining powder sufficient to blow it up. It was, therefore, set on fire and consumed. When Mr. Lewis beheld his property in flames, he said—

"I hope that my private residence will be spared."

"Sir," said the noble Commodore, "we came not to destroy any particle of your property which has not been used in the carrying on of this most unnatural war against the Government."

### Other Side of the Case.

A New York journal in one of its issues published the opinions of respectable colored people, favoring the President's Emancipation Proclamation. In the afternoon the reporter met a well-known colored man, named Cooley, who whitewashes for a living, and is generally found about Ann street. The reporter said:

"Well, Cooley, what do you think of the Proclamation?"

Cooley—"The —— worse thing for the black man that ever was done."

Reporter—"Why?"

Cooley—(coming close up, and in a mysterious whisper.)—"There's too many niggers starving here now. By'-n-bye these fellows will come down on us from the South, and drive us out, for then I tell you, *then* there would not be a place where a decent colored man can put down his foot! Mark my words!"

### Another of the Uncle Toms.

During the secession conflict in Kentucky, a Union gentleman on the other side of Green River had his attention attracted, one morning, to a little group coming up the hill. First were two intelligent looking contrabands, next, a little 'go-cart,' drawn by a mule, in which was a female slave and about a dozen little negroes, carefully wrapped in sundry and divers coats. An Uncle Tom sort of a chap, with a Miss Dinah, brought up the rear. "As they came by," says the gentleman, "I addressed Tom.'

"Well, Uncle, where did your party come from?"

"We's from de town, dar, sah."

"And where are you going?"

"Gwine home, sah."

"Then you do not live in the village?"

"No; we lib right ober yonder, 'bout a mile: de secesh draw us from home."

"Ah! well now stop a minute, and tell me all about it."

"Dat I do, sure, massa. Jim (to the other leader of the mule-cart,) you go on wid the wagon, an I kotch you fore you gits home. Now, I tells you, massa, all 'bout um. My massa am Union, an' so is all de niggers. Yesterday, massa war away in de town, an de first ting we know, 'long come two or free hundred ob dem seceshers, on hosses, an' lookin' like cut-froats. Golly, but de gals wor scared. Jus' back ob us war de Union sogers—God bress (reverentially.) for dey keep de secesh from killin' nigger. De gals know dat, an' when dey see de secesh comin' dey pitch de little nigger in de go-cart, an' den we all broke for de Union sogers."

"So you are not afraid of the Union soldiers?"

"God bress you. massa, nebber. Nigger gits ahind dem Union sojers, secesh nebber gits um. Secesh steal nigger—Union man nebber steal um. Dat's a fac, massa."

And with a chuckling smile on his face, the clever old darkey bade good morning, and trotted on after the go-cart.

### On the Road to Dixie.

When Mr. Vallandigham was being conducted to his Southern friends, by order of the United States government, because of his treasonable utterances, a halt was made by the escort, on nearing the out posts, for rest and refreshment. After an hour passed in conversation there was an effort made to obtain a little sleep, and Mr. Vallandigham himself had just fallen into a doze, when Colonel McKibben waked him, informing him that it was daylight, and time to move. Some poetical remark had been made about the morning. Mr. Vallandigham hereupon raised himself upon his elbow, and said, dramatically,

'Night's candles are burnt out, and jocund day Stands tip-toe on the mountain tops.'

He had evidently forgotten the remaining line of the quotation; but it seemed so applicable to his own case, in view of the wrathful feeling of the soldiers toward him, that some one near by could not forbear adding aloud,

'I must be gone and live, or stay and die.'

The extreme appositeness of this quotation startled every one who heard it, including Mr. Vallandigham himself.

### Good Charlie, the Union Guide.

A Union man named Smith had resided about six miles from Fayetteville, Arkansas, the owner of a tract of six hundred acres of land, with comfortable dwelling, stock, etc. Obnoxious to the secessionists, his property was plundered by their foraging and other parties during the winter, his place being only about a mile from McCulloch's head-quarters. The family consisted of Mr. Smith, his wife and child, his mother-in-law, and also his brother-in-law, James Watkins and wife, married only about a year previously. Besides these, Charlie, the slave of Mr. Smith.

Upon news of the approach of Curtis's forces to Springfield, the secessionists began pursuing all the Union men to hang them, and Smith and Watkins fled, hoping to make their way to some of the Union camps. The women thus left behind, being in fear of outrage and torture on their husbands' account—if not death—departed from their home on the night of Feb. 8th, with Charlie as their guide and protector, leaving the aged mother and child, who were unable to move. On foot they wended their way, sleeping what they did sleep in the open air, upon such straw or litter as Charlie could gather for them, and covered by the single blanket which he carried,—subsisting on the food which he had stowed in a pair of saddle-bags. He would have been seized as marketable property belonging to a Union man, and the women regarded their own jeopardy as something more than that of their lives, if met or caught by the secessionists. They traveled about eight miles the first day—the women being feeble, and one of them in a delicate situation,—fording creeks, and avoiding the traveled roads.

On one occasion, crossing a creek upon a log, one of the ladies fell in, and was with difficulty extricated by Charlie, who, as he said, "cooned it on de log," so that his mistress got hold of him, and when she reached the bank he pulled her out. Thus for nearly a week, foot-sore and with short and painful journeys, having no shelter, and not seeing a fire, subsisting on the scant provision which Charlie carried, they slowly made their way until they first met the advance guard of the Union forces at Mudtown. Here the ladies were at once cared for by the Colonel, while Charlie was taken some miles on horseback to "Mister Sigel," who examined him at great length, as a General knows how, comparing his stories with his own maps of the country. He was satisfied of Charlie's truthfulness, and gave him a pass for himself and the two ladies. He was rightly termed "good Charlie."

### Refusing to Volunteer in the Rebel Army.

In the same prison with Parson Brownlow and other Unionists in Tennessee, was a venerable clergyman named Cate, and his three sons. One of them, James Madison Cate, a most exemplary and worthy member of the Baptist church, was there for having committed no other crime than that of refusing to volunteer in the rebel army. He lay stretched at full length upon the floor, with one thickness of a piece of carpet under him, and an old overcoat doubled up for a pillow,—and he in the agonies of death. His wife came to visit him, bringing her youngest child, which was but a babe. They were refused admittance. Parson Brownlow here put his head out of the jail window, and entreated them, for God's sake, to let the poor woman come in, as her husband was dying. The jailer at last consented that she might see him for the limited time of fifteen minutes. As she came in, and

Refusing to Volunteer.

looked upon her husband's wan and emaciated face, and saw how rapidly he was sinking, she gave evident signs of fainting, and would have fallen to the floor with the babe in her arms, had not Parson B. rushed up to her and seized the babe. Then she sank down upon the breast of her dying husband, unable to speak. When the fifteen minutes had expired, the officer came in, and in an insulting and peremptory manner, notified her that the interview was to close.

### Entombment of a Virginia Loyalist.

Mr. John A. Ford, a respectable merchant of Petersburg, Va., having expressed a wish that the Boston troops had killed "fourteen or fifteen hundred" of the mob in Baltimore, instead of "fourteen or fifteen," was soon after waited on by an excited crowd of people, who demanded to know if he had used this language. He replied in the affirmative, whereupon a cry was raised of "shoot him! hang him! kill him!" and demonstrations were made to carry out the demand of the excited mob.

Meantime, however, it had become quite dark, of which some friends of Mr. Ford, fellow members of a Masonic Lodge, took advantage, in dragging Mr. Ford out into an open store, through which he was urged into an alley-way in the rear, while the crowd in the street who had lost sight of him, were clamorously in search. A friend and Masonic brother accompanied him rapidly through the alley, and conducted him to the only place of safety which probably could have concealed him —a tomb in his family burial ground!

Taking the key from the vault hastily from his pocket he opened it, urged Mr. Ford in among the coffins, locked the door upon him, and quickly disappeared. That night and the following day every place and by-place in the town was ransacked in the eager search of the mob for the victim who had so terribly and so narrowly escaped their clutches. They finally concluded that he had been spirited away, and relaxed their vigilance. Meantime Mr. Ford remained undisturbed, with darkness and the dead. There were several bodies deposited there—far less feared, however, by him than the living.

At three o'clock the following Monday morning, the train was to leave for Richmond. At an earlier hour, Mr. Ford's protector and friend came to deliver his friend from the charnel house, where, for two nights and a day, he had fasted with the dead. He was faint and weak from exhaustion, but the emergency lent him strength. While his friend went for his daughter, a little girl seven years of age, Mr. Ford wended his way cautiously and alone to the depot. Here they met again, and when the train rolled out of the station on its way north, Mr. Ford sat on one of the car seats, with his child wrapped closely in his arms. Arriving at Richmond, he attempted to procure a ticket, but was told that no passenger could leave for the North, unless exhibiting a pass from Governor Letcher. With many misgivings, Mr. Ford (it was still early in the morning,) wended his way to the executive mansion. He represented to the Governor that his business called him out of the State, and desired credentials which would enable him to continue the journey. Mr. Letcher asked no questions, but promptly made out the papers and handed them to him, by the aid of which he in due time arrived in Washington.

### Unwilling to Forfeit his Right to Escape.

One of the prisoners at Fort Warren, Boston, managed to escape about the time he was sent there from Fort Lafayette. He then enlisted in the navy under an assumed name, in the hopes of being placed upon a vessel from which he could escape, and join his friends at the South. Finding that his chances of success in this project were small, and not wishing to serve against the Confederate States, he revealed his true name, and the fact that he had escaped from custody, whereupon he was sent to Fort Warren. Col. Dimmick, of that institution, had an interview with him, and told him that he might have the same privileges as the other prisoners, if he would give his parole of honor not to attempt to escape again. The man hesitated a moment, and then frankly replied:

"No, Colonel, I cannot do it; if I make the promise I shall feel bound by it; but really, I cannot consent to give up the right to escape if an opportunity occurs."

The Colonel told the man that if he did not give his parole, he should put him where escape would be impossible, but he remained spunky, and was placed in close confinement.

### Left to Dine Alone.

A person from Baltimore, temporarily a resident in the city of Boston, invited five of his friends to dine at the house of a female relation,—which invitation was duly accepted. On going to the dinner table, the party found the rebel flag topping a piece of ornamental pastry, in the centre of the festive board. The insult was at once noticed by the guests, before they were seated, and, as it appeared, by all of them nearly at the same moment. Not a word was spoken, but every man left as by a mutual impulse, and the Baltimore secessionist had to dine alone. Next morning he was waited upon for an explanation of his misconduct, but his discretion had prompted him to take the first westward train for home.

### Circumstances alter Principles.

An anecdote is told of a Union officer, by Prentice, which is somewhat illustrative of the fact that circumstances not only alter cases but principles also. The gentleman in question was a violent Republican, and both before and after going into the army opposed, with all the zeal and ability of which he was capable, the Crittenden Compromise. At the battle of Chickamauga, when our routed wing was falling back in great disorder, and the mass of the enemy pushing forward with a shower of shell, grape, canister and musketry, this officer, who was in the midst of the deadly torrent, and who stuttered somewhat in his speech, turned to a fellow-soldier and said:

"G-g-g-george, if G-g-g-governor Crittenden were to r-r-r-rise up now f-f-f-from his g-g-g-rave, and offer me the C-c-c-crittenden com-com-compromise, by —— I would take it!"

### Old Cotton Beard and his Girls.

Among those who took the oath of allegiance to the United States Government, may be named Mr. V. B. Marmillon, one of the richest and most extensive sugar planters in the whole valley of the Mississippi. He refused, however, to work his plantation, unless he could have his own negroes returned to him. He had about fifteen hundred acres of cane under cultivation, but his whole family of plantation hands left him and went to New Orleans, reporting themselves to the Union officer. Among them could be found every species of mechanic and artisan. They were called up and informed that the Government had taken possession of their old master's crop, and that they were needed to take it off, and would be paid for their labor. All consented to return; but next morning, when the time came for their departure, not one of them would go. One of them said: "I will go anywhere else to work, but you may shoot me before I will return to the old plantation." It was afterwards ascertained that Marmillon, whom they called "Old Cotton Beard," had boasted in the presence of two colored girls, house servants, how he would serve the hands when he once more had them in his power. These girls had walked more than thirty miles in the night, with all the risks of personal safety staring them in the face, to bring the information to their friends. The hands were set to work elsewhere.

### Conciliatory Mesmerism.

General Garfield aptly illustrated, by the following quotation from an old English nursery rhyme, the policy of those extra-bleached and super-superior patriots who sought to put down the rebellion with conciliatory mesmerism:

"There was an old man who said, how
Shall I flee from this horrible cow?
I will sit on the stile,
And continue to smile,
Which may soften the heart of this cow."

## Circulation of Union Proclamations in South Carolina.

Lieutenant Magner, of General Sherman's staff, accompanied by Dr. Bacon, of the Seventh Connecticut, was detailed by General Sherman to perform the *rather* delicate duty of conveying to the rebels, under a flag of truce, his proclamation, which was addressed to the loyal citizens of South Carolina, inviting them to return to their homes and promising them protection. The bearers were placed ashore in the cutter, under a flag of truce, accompanied by a negro, who was picked up while ascending the river, and who, being acquainted with the country, was to act as guide. Mules were found, and, led by the negro, they proceeded into the country, and after penetrating about ten miles they were met by a Rev. Mr. Walker, a Baptist clergyman, formerly of Beaufort. To their inquiries, whether there were any rebel camps in the vicinity, he informed them that the camps they were looking after were a number of miles on, and advised them not to proceed further, as he did not deem it prudent or safe. They were not quite satisfied, however, with the information he gave, as his conduct was somewhat suspicious, and they inquired of the negro guide as to the distance. He informed them that it was about half a mile further on. They concluded to proceed. They had continued about half a mile further on, when they were met by two rebel officers, one of whom bore a white handkerchief on an oar, which he had brought from a small boat in a creek near by, in which they had evidently come. They proved to be a First Lieutenant and a Second Lieutenant from a Charleston company.

The object of the mission was explained by the bearers of the flag, and they were politely informed that there *were* no "loyal citizens" in South Carolina, and that their mission was fruitless. The business being completed, a luncheon was partaken of, which was furnished by the bearer of the flag; the mules were fed by order of the rebel officers. During the lunch, Lieutenant Barnwell, one of the scions of the aristocratic stock of South Carolina, made his appearance and joined the company. He was excessively haughty and distant in his demeanor, and appeared to regard himself as one of the most important personages the world had yet produced. During the conversation he haughtily and impertinently inquired:

"Have you permission, sirs, to return?"

Naturally enough the question was regarded as insulting, and Dr. Bacon quietly replied:

"I have already communicated with your superior officer."

This sarcastically worded reply effectually squelched the upstart, and he subsided immediately thereafter.

## Letting them Judge by the Tunes.

A good story is told of an old patriot who was employed at the Kentucky Military Institute as a fifer. The old fellow had served in the Northwest, in the second war with Great Britain, taking a part in the battle of the Thames and other fights. During the secession tornado which at first swept over Kentucky, the cadets at the Institute, becoming affected with the fever, talked pretty severely against those devoted to the stars and stripes. Our old veteran listened, but said nothing. One evening he went into a room, and was observed to be in something of a passion. He paced backward and forward, saying nothing, and refusing to answer all questions. At last he pulled out his fife, and, sitting down, sent forth Yankee Doodle with its shrillest strains. Then he played Hail Columbia, and then The Star Spangled Banner, until the whole premises were made alive to the jubilant sounds,— the tears meanwhile rolling down his aged and weather-beaten cheeks. Concluding the last named exhilarating melody he jumped to his feet, and exclaimed: "*Now*,

—— 'em, I guess they know which side I'm on!"

### Old Hickory's Three Swords and Three Injunctions.

Among the multiplied testimonials that honored the glorious career, civil and military, of Andrew Jackson, were the three magnificent swords presented to him—one by the State of Tennessee, another by the citizens of Philadelphia, and a third by the riflemen of New Orleans. By his will the General bequeathed the first of these swords to his nephew and adopted son, Andrew Jackson Donelson; the sec-

Jackson

ond to his grandson, Andrew Jackson; and the third to his grand-nephew, Andrew Jackson Coffee. The clause relative to the first runs thus:—

"*Seventh*—I bequeath to my well-beloved nephew, Andrew J. Donelson, son of Samuel Donelson, deceased, the elegant sword presented to me by the State of Tennessee, *with this injunction*, that he fail not to use it, when necessary, in support and protection of our glorious Union, and for the protection of the constitutional rights of our beloved country, should they be assailed by foreign enemies or *domestic traitors*."

That same Andrew J. Donelson *did* fail thus to use the sword thus received from his great kinsman, and even ranged himself at the side of those very "traitors" who fought to destroy both the glorious Union and the Constitution itself. Again:

"I bequeath to my beloved grandson, Andrew Jackson, son of Andrew Jackson, Jr., and Sarah, his wife, the sword presented to me by the citizens of Philadelphia, *with this injunction*, that he will always use it in defence of the Constitution and our glorious Union, and the perpetuation of our Republican system."

This same Andrew Jackson, thus honored by his patriotic grandfather, put himself in the ranks of the traitors, aiding by his influence and his money the conspirators who sought the overthrow of that same "Republican system." And again:

"To my grand-nephew, Andrew Jackson Coffee, I bequeath the elegant sword presented to me by the Rifle Company of New Orleans, commanded by Captain Beal, as a memento of my regard, and to bring to his recollection the gallant services of his deceased father, Gen. John Coffee, in the late Indian and British wars, under my command, and his gallant conduct in defence of New Orleans in 1814 '15, *with this injunction, that he wield it in protection of the rights secured to the American citizen under our glorious Constitution, against all invaders, whether foreign foes or intestine traitors.*"

Where, then, was Andrew Jackson Coffee, when the Union was in its life and death struggle? He, too, was among the traitors, and the sword placed in his hands for the "protection of the rights secured to American citizens under our glorious Constitution," was pointed at the hearts of loyal men!

### Broadbrim's Method with Secessionists.

A secession minister comes into the store kept by a Quaker, and talks loudly against the country, until Broadbrim tells him he must stop or leave the store. The clerical brawler keeps on, till the Quaker tells him he will put him out of the store if he does not go out. "What," exclaimed the minister, "I thought you Quakers did

PATRIOTIC, POLITICAL, CIVIL, JUDICIAL, ETC.    111

not fight." "The sanctified do not fight, but I have not been sanctified yet; and I will put thee out of the store in a minute!" The minister fled from the wicked Quaker.

### Badge of Treason in a New York Ball Room.

Quite a flutter in the political world was occasioned by a little act which transpired at a convivial gathering in New York, one winter's evening in 1863. The Marquis of Hartington, a young gentleman from England, had been traveling for some months in this country, and had run the lines to Richmond. In returning, his companion, or one of them, was taken, and imprisoned. The Marquis was more fortunate, and escaped.

Before sailing for England from New York a masquerade was given by a gentleman of the city, to which the young man was invited. While chatting with a 'domino' (one of the characters assumed by a lady in the masquerade,) the wearer insisted that he, the Marquis, should wear a rebel badge upon his coat. He refused, good humoredly. She pressed. He declined. At last she said, "Well, then, at least, while you are talking with me." It was the old story: "The woman tempted me, and I did yield." She paraded her triumph through the rooms until meeting suddenly his guide, philosopher, and friend, that gentleman said abruptly to the Marquis, as his eye fell upon the badge, "Good God! my good fellow—you must'nt do that;" and exhorted him in the most stringent way to remove the badge. The young man obeyed; but not of course until it was known throughout the rooms that he had plainly displayed a badge which was inexpressibly offensive to the feelings of every loyal heart in the house. There were several officers of various grades present. General McClellan was one of the guests. It was therefore not surprising that a little later a young officer, whose only knowledge of that badge was that it was the symbol of the murder of his friends and the attempted ruin of his country, brushed violently against the Marquis. That gentleman, thinking probably that it was an inadvertence, took no notice of the collision. But upon its repetition, when the intention was palpable, he turned, and said,

"Well, sir, what am I to understand by that?"

"You know very well what it means," was the prompt and crisp reply.

At the same instant friends interfered, and begged that if any difficulty were pending, its consideration should be deferred until the morning. The gentlemen assented. Before the morning full explanations were made, and when the two gentlemen met at the club-house an understanding satisfactory to both sides concluded the affair. A few days afterwards the Marquis sailed for England.

It was a proceeding which grossly insulted every loyal American in the rooms; and it is not to be doubted that the host—a conspicuous member of the gayer circles of the city—took occasion to inform the light-headed youth of the great abuse of courtesy and hospitality of which he had been guilty. If the host himself had been dining a few years since at the house of the Marquis of Hartington's father—an English duke—and had said or implied (as he certainly never would have done), intentionally or unintentionally, that he hoped Great Britain, which was then contending for India in the persons of the children and brothers and friends of the company at table, would not succeed; or if he had worn at table the colors, had there been any, of Nena Sahib—if there had been a single gentleman present whose son had been massacred in that war, it is not rash to presume, despite British phlegm, that the offender would have left the dining-room more rapidly than he entered.

### Senator Lane and the Stage Driver.

A story is told of Senator Joseph Lane, of Oregon, which will bear repetition.

Accounts of the Senator's pro-southern sentiments and movements preceded his return from the Congressional session of 1861, and, it is said, rendered him very unpopular; particularly after the attack on Fort Sumter. When he reached the shores of the Pacific, he began to feel his unpopularity in various ways; but no remark that was made to him and in his hearing was more cutting than that of a stage driver with whom he had entered into conversation without disclosing his name. In the course of his talk the Senator took occasion to remark that he considered himself the worst-abused man in the State. "Well, I don't know about that," replied the driver; "but if you are any worse than that rascal, Jo. Lane, God help you."

### Loyal Breeze from Port Hudson.

In order to enjoy a sight of the fleet of busy steamers at Port Hudson, soon after the capture of Vicksburg, a Union gentleman took a station on a cliff, commanding a fine view of the newly-conquered territory and of the Union flags, as their graceful forms waved sharp and clear against the blue sky. While thus stationed, a rebel Captain gaily dressed, came up to the gentleman and said, thoughtfully—

"It is a long time, Sir, since we have seen so many vessels lying there."

"Yes, Sir, and I am glad of it, for *your* sake as well as *ours*."

"How so?" asked the Captain, in a somewhat surprised tone.

"Because it looks to me very much like the beginning of the end; and that is what we all wish to see."

"The *end* is very far off yet," he continued, in a proud manner; "In the first place I do not believe, even now, that Vicksburg is lost to us; and you never yet knew a rebellion of such magnitude to fail in achieving its object."

"Nor did you ever know a rebellion so causeless and unnatural to succeed. If you were like the Poles or Circassians, and we Russians, trying to crush out your existing nationality—if this were a war of religion or races, I could imagine it lasting through many, many years. But it is not so. Instead of trying to crush out your nationality, we are merely fighting to prevent you from crushing out our mutual one; and every acre, every liberty we save from destruction, is as much yours as ours. War for such a cause was never waged before, and therefore cannot last. When a few more decisive successes like the present shall have proved beyond all doubt to the Southern people that the cause of separation is utterly hopeless, I think we shall all be glad to meet again as citizens of a common country, greater for the very ordeal through which it has passed. The only difference will be that Slavery—the cause of all this trouble—will have died during the progress of the war."

"We shall see," said the Captain, either unwilling or unable to maintain his position further; "I suppose you will allow we defended our position here well?"

"Too well,' was the answer; 'I think a great many good lives, on both sides, might have been saved by sooner surrendering a place which, it must have been evident, you could not possibly retain."

"We should have done so," he candidly avowed, "only we were all the while hoping for reinforcements."

### Familiar Chat about Generals.

President Lincoln expressed his troubles to a gentleman who was visiting him on a certain occasion, in the following language:

"The military men, it seems to me, will keep me in trouble all the time on their account. One day Senator Lane, of Indiana, calls on me and asks me why I don't give Lew. Wallace a command. I tell him that Halleck says Wallace is of no account, and ought not to have a command He goes at me then, and says Halleck isn't worth a cent, and oughtn't to have a command. Halleck wants to kick Wallace out, and Lane wants me to kick Halleck out."

"Well," said the visitor, "I'll tell you how to fix it to the satisfaction of both parties."

"How is that?" inquired the President.

"Why, kick 'em *both* out," was the reply.

"No," said Mr. Lincoln, "that won't do. I think Halleck is a good man. He may not be—of course; I don't know much about such things. I may be a judge of good lawyers, but I don't know much about Generals. Those who ought to know, say he is good."

"Well," said the visitor, "if you don't know, you ought to know; and if the people don't know that Halleck is a fool, they think they do, and it's all the same."

### Pen with which the Emancipation Proclamation was Signed.

The identity of the pen with which the Emancipation Proclamation was signed by President Lincoln cannot be made good. This appears from the statement of a gentleman who happened to be in Washington a few days after the signing of that paper, and who, by appointment, had an interview with President Lincoln, on matters of official business. Just after he had entered the room and taken a seat, Mr. Lincoln opened and read aloud a letter from a Boston gentleman applying to him for the pen with which he signed the proclamation, and stating, in glowing words, what great value he should place upon it, could he obtain the prize.

The President remarked, after he had read the letter, that he did not think he could comply with the request of the writer, as he was not sure which of his pens was the right one. He knew it was one of a lot (this was the word) of a dozen or so, and he would do the best he could. To finish up the matter, Mr. Lincoln—according to custom—told a story. He asked the gentleman at his side if he had ever read or seen a book or story called Squibob, and went on to give some account of it. But the point of the story was that Squibob was asked by some one for his autograph, which was sent with the remark that " it must be genuine, for it was written by his brother-in-law."

### When will the War End?

This question was answered by a little miss at one of the school examinations in Troy, in a manner that did credit to her intelligence and loyalty—her head and heart. After the exercises of the afternoon had concluded, the Principal stated that he should be pleased if the committee would examine the class in reference to matters of recent history, such as the events of the present war,—to show that they kept their eyes and ears open, and were posted in matters transpiring around them. One of the Committee said to the President of the Board of Education, who was conducting the exercises, "Ask 'em when the war will end. Guess that will puzzle 'em."

Mr Kemp, in his blandest tones, said to the class—

"It is asked, by a visitor, 'when this war will end.' Can any of you answer the question?"

Up went a show of hands, as at least fifteen boys and girls manifested a willingness to solve the problem that statesmen, financiers and politicians were supposed to have puzzled over in vain.

"*You* may answer," said President Kemp to a bright-eyed little girl near him: "When will the war end?"

Rising from her seat, the little patriot, in a clear unfaltering voice, with enthusiasm flashing from her eye, answered:

"*When the rebels lay down their arms and sue for peace!*"

The gentleman who had suggested the inquiry said: " I guess we won't have any more questions." 'We are all loyal in this school,' was the comment of the Principal, echoed by the large audience present.

### Swear him in, and let him go!

A characteristic story is said to have been told by General Butler, one day, in Washington. The General, speaking of the farce of administering the oath to captured rebels, and then turning them loose, related an incident that occurred at Fortress Monroe. A scouting party having captured and brought in a live rattlesnake, a question arose as to the disposal to be made of the dangerous customer, when a partially intoxicated soldier hiccoughed, "— him! *swear him in, and let him go!*"

Swear him, &c.

### "Mudsills" on the Sacred Soil.

Mr. Orpheus Kerr, of the "Mackerelville Brigade," relates his experience with the soldiers of the Potomac army as follows:

I never really knew what the term "mudsill" meant, my boy, until I saw Capt. Bob Shorty on Tuesday. I was out in a field, just this side of Fort Corcoran, trimming down the ears of my gothic steed Pegasus, that he might look less like a Titanic rabbit, when I saw approaching me an object resembling a brown stone monument. As it came nearer, I discovered an eruption of brass buttons at intervals in front, and presently I observed the lineaments of a Federal face.

"Strange being!" says I, taking down a pistol from the natural rack on the side of my steed, and at the same time motioning towards my sword, which I had hung on one of his hip-bones, "Art thou the shade of Metamora, or the disembodied spirit of a sandbank?"

"My ducky darling," responded the eolian voice of Capt. Bob Shorty, "you behold a mudsill, just emerged from a liquified portion of the sacred soil. The mud at present inclosing the Mackerel Brigade is unpleasant to the personal feelings of the corps, but the effect at a distance is unique. As you survey that expanse of mud from Arlington Heights," continued Bob Shorty, "with the veterans of the Mackerel Brigade wading about in it up to their chins, you are forcibly reminded of a limitless plum-pudding, well stocked with animated raisins."

"My friend," says I, "the comparison is apt, and reminds me of Shakespeare's happier efforts. But tell me, my Pylades, has the dredging for those missing regiments near Alexandria proved successful?"

Capt. Bob Shorty took the mire from his ears, and then, says he:

"Two brigades were excavated this morning, and are at present building rafts to go down to Washington to get some soap. Let us not utter complaints against the mud," continued Capt. Bob Shorty, reflectively, "for it has served to develope the genius of New England. We dug out a Yankee regiment from Boston first, and the moment these wooden-nutmeg chaps got their breath, they went to work at the mud that had almost suffocated them, mixed up some spoiled flour with it, and are now making their eternal fortunes by peddling it out for patent cement!"

### Davis's Chairs in Readiness for Ulysses.

During the siege of Vicksburg, some of the Sixth Missouri Cavalry visited the former residence of "President" Davis, and found the blacks all very much alarmed

PATRIOTIC, POLITICAL, CIVIL, JUDICIAL, ETC. 115

at the near approach of General Grant, who they believed would immediately devour them. The frightened creatures asked numberless questions of the boys, as to what they should do to appease him if he should visit them. The boys told them the General was not very frightful, and if they would assemble in the yard and give him three cheers, when he made his appearance, they would be safe. They were very much amused on returning, to find that the darkeys had nicely swept a place under the tree in the yard, and had set there three of the best chairs the mansion afforded—presuming that "cheers" meant *chairs*,—in readiness for the great Ulysses. The best part of this joke is not given, viz., the reply which Grant made when the joke-loving General was informed of said preparations to receive him.

### John Wells's "Idee" as to Splitting the Union.

At one of the stations on the Georgia Central Railroad, Sherman's men came across an old man named Wells—a very original character,—who was formerly a depot-master on that line. He was a shrewd old man, and seemed to understand the merits of the war question perfectly.

They say, (remarked the old man,) that you are retreating, but it is the strangest sort of retreat *I* ever saw. Why, dog bite 'em, the newspapers have been lying in this way all along. They allers are whipping the Federal armies, and they allers fall back after the battle is over. It was that ar' idea that first opened my eyes. Our army was allers whipping the Feds, and we allers fell back. I allers told 'em it was a — humbug, and now by —, I know it, for here you are right on old John Wells's place ; hogs, potatoes, corn and fences all gone. I don't find any fault. I expected it all.

Jeff. Davis and the rest (he continued) talk about splitting the Union. Why, if South Carolina had gone out by herself, she would have been split in four pieces by this time. Splitting the Union! Why, — it, the State of Georgia is being split right through, from end to end. It is these rich fellows who are making this war, and keeping their precious bodies out of harm's way. There's John Franklin, went through here the other day, running away from your army. I could have played dominoes on his coat tails. There's my poor brother, sick with small-pox at Macon, working for eleven dollars a month, and has'nt got a cent of the — stuff for a year. 'Leven dollars a month and eleven thousand bullets a minute. I don't believe in it, Sir.

My wife (added the old Georgian) came from Canada, and I kind o'thought I would some time go there to live, but was allers afraid of the ice and cold; but I can tell you this country is getting too cussed hot, for me. Look at my fence rails a-burning there. I think I can stand the cold better. I heard as how they cut down the trees across your road up country and burn the bridges ; why, dog bite their hides, one of you Yankees can take up a tree and carry it off, tops and all; and there's that bridge you put across the river in less than two hours—they might as well try to stop the Ogeechee, as yon Yankees. The blasted rascals who burnt this yere bridge thought they did a big thing ; a natural born fool cut in two had more sense in either end than any of them.

To bring back the good old time, (he concluded) it'll take the help of Divine Providence, a heap of rain, and a deal of elbow grease, to fix things up again.

### Oath-Taking in St. Louis.

The St. Louis newspapers published long lists of the persons in that city who took the oath of allegiance to the Government in compliance with General Halleck's recommendation. Some of them appended remarks to their signatures. The following is an instance :—

Truman M. Post, pastor of the First Trinitarian Congregational church of St.

Louis. "As a minister of the Gospel, and a trustee of a State charity, I recognize the fitness of the call on me for my oath of allegiance. Cordially and gratefully do I give in this my adhesion to my country in this hour of terrible trial, regarding it as the source of innumerable blessings to myself, and the millions of my countrymen, and fully believing the present attempt to destroy it to be a curse against both God and men, against the present and future, against ourselves and the human race, with hardly a parallel in the history of the world."

That was good text and comment for every lover of his country and his race.

### Knotty Argument for Secession Ladies.

Quite an entertaining dialogue occurred one day in the Governor's office in Nashville, Tennessee, between Governor Johnson and two secession ladies of that city, who came to complain of the occupation of a residence belonging to the Confederate husband of one of the ladies by a United States officer. The conversation was substantially as follows :—

*Lady.*—I think it is too dreadful for a woman in my lonesome condition to have her property exposed to injury and destruction.

*Gov.*—Well, Madam, I will enquire into the matter, and if any injustice has been done, will try to have it corrected. But your husband, you admit, has gone off with the rebels, and you abandoned your dwelling.

*Lady.*—My husband went off South, because it was his interest to do so. You mustn't find fault with anybody for taking care of himself these times. You know, Governor, that all things are justifiable in war.

*Gov.*—Well, Madam, it appears to me that this broad rule of yours will justify taking possession of your house. According to your maxim, I don't see any reason for helping you out of your difficulty.

*Lady.*—Oh! but I didn't mean it that way.

*Gov.*—No, Madam, I suppose not. I will try to be more generous to you than your own rule would make me. I do not believe in your rule that "all things are justifiable in time of war." But that is just what you rebels insist upon. It is perfectly right and proper for you to *violate* the laws, to *destroy* this Government, but it is all wrong for us to *execute* the laws to *maintain* the Government.

The secession ladies looked around in various directions, and seemed to think that they had opened a knotty argument on a dangerous subject, with a very bristling adversary. Heaving a long sigh, they retired.

### "Come from 'Ginny, Sure!"

At Point Lookout, where the Union army encamped, the blacks were nearly all from Virginia. Some, however, ran in there from the State of Maryland, pretending to have come from Virginia, that thus they might not stand any chance of being returned, in any contingency. On a certain occasion, a rich Marylander came down to the Point, to look after one of his boys; finding him, he said, "Jack, you rascal, what are you here for?" Jack very coolly replied, "Who be you, Massa? I never seed you 'fore." "Yes you have too, you lying scamp, I raised you and you must go home with me." "Yah! yah! Massa nebber can don fool dis nigger. I's come from 'ginny, sure," replied the darkey, and utterly refused to know his old master at all. General Marston was asked to send the negro back, but respectfully declined, and "Massa" went off one darkey short.

### Literal "Stump" Speech of a Soldier.

One of the attendants at the great Union meeting held in Troy, Miami county, Ohio, during the gubernatorial canvass between Vallandigham the anti-war candidate, and Brough the Union Republican candidate, was a returned soldier who had lost one leg at Vicksburgh. He was welcomed by his friends, and one of them—a

Vallandigham democrat—entering into conversation with the soldier, remarked, "You were a Democrat when you enlisted, and I suppose you have come back a Democrat." The soldier replied, "Yes, I was a Democrat when I left, and I am a Democrat still." "That's right!" replied his friend, triumphantly; "and of course you will vote for Vallandigham,"— looking around to gain the attention of the crowd to the answer. It came. "My God! how can I?" said the soldier, as he raised his eyes to the crowd, and *put his hand on the unhealed stump of his leg.* Was not that an eloquent "stump" speech?

### Bogus Yankee Legislature in Georgia.

When the Twentieth Corps of Sherman's grand army of invasion through Georgia marched into the capital of that State, to the music of the Union, the officers, to the number of about one hundred, assembled at the Senate chamber, called the roll of the House, appointed a speaker and clerks, and opened the 'Legislature' with prayer, the facetious chaplain praying for the overthrow of the Confederate Government, the return of Georgia to the old Union, fine weather and little fighting on their march to the coast, and concluding with, "All of which is respectfully submitted."

A lobby member very gravely arose in the gallery, and asked if this honorable body would hear from the gallery.

Half an hour's discussion followed, and on a parliamentary division, it was decided that the gallery should be heard.

Rising with all the dignity and polish of a Chesterfield, he quietly put his hand in a side pocket, drew out a flask, placed it to his lips, replaced it in his pocket, and resumed his seat.

*The Speaker.*—I must raise a point of order. I believe it is always customary to treat the Speaker.

*Lobby Member.*—I beg the pardon of the honorable House for my thoughtlessness. I believe it *is* customary to treat the Speaker.

Here he produced the flask, and proceeded: 'Yes, I beg to inform the House that I shall treat the Speaker—respectfully.'

The flask dropped into his pocket and he into his seat, amid cheers from the gallery and smiles from the honorable Speaker's colleagues.

After the organization of the Legislature the question of reconstructing the State was taken up and discussed for some time, with all the gravity conceivable, by the Yankee 'representatives' from the various counties. The result of the deliberations was that the State was led back like a conquered child into the Union, and a committee appointed to kick Governor Brown and President Davis at their most accessible point—which committee retired, and soon after returned and reported that they were animated by a progressive spirit, but that the articles upon which they were to exercise their pedal extremities were *non est.*

The Legislature adjourned after the style of Governor Brown's Legislature of the previous Friday—by taking a square drink and a handful of "hognuts."

### Tableau Political.

In a letter dated from Murfreesboro', N. C., January twenty-second, 1862, is a description of a tableau given there for the benefit of the soldiers. It must have its place among the political *olla podrida* of the war of the rebellion :—

We should not do justice to the tableau unless we were to describe the first scene. A young gentleman representing King Cotton, sat upon a throne resembling a bale of cotton. Down on one side of the throne sat a representative of the ebon race, with a basket of cotton. The king held a cotton cloth as a sceptre, and one of his feet rested on a globe. Around him stood young ladies dressed in white, with scarfs of red and white looped on the shoulder with blue. On their heads they wore appropriate crowns. These represented the Confederate States; Missouri and Kentucky were guarded by armed soldiers.

While we were gazing on this picture a dark-haired maiden, robed in black, with brow encircled by a cypress-wreath, and her delicate wrists bound by clanking chains, came on and knelt before his majesty. He extended his sceptre, and she arose. He waved his wand again, and an armed soldier appeared with a scarf and crown, like those worn by her sister States. He unchained this gentle girl at the bidding of his monarch, changed her crown of mourning for one of joy and liberty, and threw the Confederate flag across her,—raised the flag over her and led her forward; then Kentucky advanced, took her by the hand, and led her into the ranks. Need we tell you who this maiden of sable garments was intended to represent? We leave that to be understood. If your readers cannot divine, it is owing to our description, and not to the scene. The ceremony was performed in pantomime. The representative of Virginia had inscribed on her crown, '*Mater Heroruan;*' and North Carolina wore on her brow a white crown, on which was the word 'Bethel.' Both of these States were represented by their own daughters.

### President Washington's Summary Dealing with Rebellion.

When the Whisky Insurrection broke out in the eastern counties of Pennsylvania in 1794, Washington said: "If the laws are to be so trampled upon with impunity, and a minority, a small one too, is to dictate to the majority, there is an end put at one stroke to republican government."

Washington issued his proclamation on the 7th of August, 1794, declaring that, if tranquillity were not previously restored, on the first of September force would be employed to compel submission to the laws. On the same day he made a requisition for twelve thousand men, afterward increased to fifteen thousand. He appointed Governor Lee, of Virginia, to the chief command, and Lee marched with the fifteen thousand men in two divisions. This great military array, says the historian, extinguished at once the kindling elements of a civil war by making resistance desperate.

Every thing that Washington said and did at that period became of singular interest to those who lived in the times of the great Southern Rebellion, just two generations following. In writing of the soldiers to Governor Lee he speaks of "the enlightened and patriotic zeal for the Constitution and the laws, which had led them cheerfully to quit their families, homes, and the comforts of a private life, to undertake and thus far to perform, a long and fatiguing march, and to encounter and endure the hardships and privations of a military life. No citizen of the United States can ever be engaged in a service more important to their country. It is nothing less than to consolidate and preserve the blessings of that revolution which at much expense of blood and treasure, constituted us a free and independent nation."

When the disturbance was quelled, he said: "It has afforded an occasion for the people of this country to show their abhorrence of the attempt and their attachment to the Constitution and the laws; for I believe that five times the number of militia that was required would have come forward, if it had been necessary, in support of them."

Governor Lee, of Virginia, was the "Light Horse Harry" of the Revolution —peculiarly dear to Washington, who in youth had loved Lee's mother before her marriage. He was also the father of General Robert E. Lee, the great Confederate chieftain in arms against that same Constitution and those laws. Could General Lee doubt where Washington, had he been alive in 1861, would have been found? Would he have been found standing side by side with the Virginian Lee, striking deadly blows at the heart and life of his country?

### Same old Planter's Crotchet.

To General Mitchell and his brave troops belongs the distinguished honor of being the first Federal commander to penetrate to the great Charleston and Memphis railroad, and the first to break through the enemy's line of defence, extending from Chattanooga to Corinth. A strong Union feeling was discovered by the Nationals as they entered the State of Alabama, but it was mingled with the usual Southern political crotchet of State sovereignty, and the duty of submission thereto. One old Gentleman, a planter, with an extensive estate, expressed the views of the majority of the people of Madison county. Said he—

"It seems like tearing out my heart, to give up the old Union, but when Alabama voted to separate, I thought it my duty to sustain her."

"But," said his Union interlocutor, "Alabama, in attempting to break up the nation, did what she had no right to do."

"Ah," responded the old gentleman, "passion and prejudice blinded our eyes to that truth."

"Are you then willing,' he was asked, "to see the authority of the National Government restored?"

"Yes, and to pray from this time forth that all her people may be willing to return to their allegiance."

This final answer of the old planter indicated his resolution to abide by the action of his State, whether the majority of her people became loyal or remained treasonable. It was the old planter's blinding and blundering crotchet, as it was of the South generally, among the planters.

### "Old Zack" and his Son-in-Law.

When the usual committee was appointed by Congress to wait upon General Taylor, the President-elect, and announce to him his election by the people as Chief Magistrate, an incident occurred which the events of 1861 served strongly to recall in the minds of those who were knowing to it.

It was doubtless with a courteous intent that those who moved the springs in this little matter induced Congress to appoint as chairman of that committee Jefferson Davis,—his previous domestic relations with General Taylor suggesting him as an acceptable medium; though, had the public been as well informed as the private mind, such a choice would have been the last adopted. The duty in question is, of course, only a form, to be fulfilled with the gravity and the grace adapted to the occasion, but calling for no display of rhetoric, and no assumption of official dignity; it is simply a constitutional observance, whereby the representatives of the nation testify to the result of the ballot, and state the same to the successful candidate.

General Taylor's want of oratorical accomplishments, his aversion to display, his modest demeanor, and his conscientiousness, were known as well as his bravery and patriotism, and would have been delicately respected by a thorough gentleman in the discharge of this simple duty, which needed for its performance only quiet courtesy and respectful consideration.

Instead thereof, Jefferson Davis, entering the hotel parlor, where General Taylor was seated, with the aspect of a quiet, honest old farmer, threw back his shoulders, turned out his right foot, and with precisely the air of a complacent sophomore, began a loud harangue about the "highest office in the gift of a free people," the "responsibility of an oath," and other rhetorical platitudes;—the needless pitch of his voice and dogmatism of his emphasis, the complacency and elaboration of his manner and assumption of his tone, in connection with the meek attitude and deprecatory air of his auditor, made the tableau resemble a prosecutor and prisoner at the bar. The difference of age and the former relations of the parties, (Davis having by a runaway match married General Taylor's daughter, who died a few months after,) and the utter novelty of the good old man's position, made the scene, to say the least, a flagrant violation of good taste not less than good feeling.

It was one of those unconscious and therefore authentic revelations of character, which reveal a man's disposition and temper better than a biography. Though ostensibly doing him honor, the speaker seemed to half defy the gray-haired soldier, whose eyes were cast down, and whose hands were listlessly folded—to challenge, as it were, with his fluent self-confidence the uneloquent but intrepid man of action, and ungraciously make him feel how alien to his habits and capacity was the arena to which popular enthusiasm had elevated him

### Magic of Washington's Name.

While the disunion Senate of Maryland were in session in the State House at Annapolis, in 1861, a number of soldiers entered the ante-room and inquired if the Senate Chamber was not the place where General Washington once stood? An employee of the house answered that it was, and showed one of them as near as he could the very spot where Washington stood when he resigned his commission. The young man reverently approached the spot, and standing for several minutes apparently fixed to the place, hastily turned and left the chamber, exclaiming that he could stand it no longer, for he "felt his Fourth of July rising too fast." Would that all whose names are familiar with the scenes enacted in that Chamber in 1861, had been susceptible to the spell of that same great name.

### Witnessing and Dying for the Truth in Mississippi.

About fifty miles from Natchez, Mississippi, lived an unflinching Union man. During the war, his residence was approached by an armed gang of guerillas,

Witnessing and Dying for the Truth.

who soon succeeded in securing him as a prisoner, and told him, that if he did not immediately and in their presence, recant his former sentiments, and take an oath that he never by word or deed would again favor the principles that he had formerly all along adhered to, his fate would be instant death. His reply was: "In the sight of God and man, I am clear of the crime of treason to so glorious a nation as this was till your wicked and selfish designs have caused it to be what it is; and while I draw the breath of life, I intend never to give my children cause to brand me as a traitor."

They then replied that they had a long

time had him under their special notice, and that the words he had now uttered fixed their determination to make an example of him, in order that his doom might serve as a warning to others. Whereupon they immediately killed him, in spite of the entreaties, the agony and utter despair of his grief-stricken wife, and in the presence of herself and children.

Turning to the widow, they gave her ten days to get inside of the Yankee lines, and if she failed to do so, she would share the fate of her husband,—after which they rode away, leaving her to her gloomy forebodings and lonely wretchedness. The cries and sobs of her fatherless children fell in doleful accents upon her ear, which added, of course, still more to her wretched state. The sense of duty that she was now under to her children, together with the fortitude that woman is not unfrequently known to exhibit in extreme cases of peril, nerved her to the task of consigning her husband to his blood-wet grave. And then, remembering the words of his murderers, their parting threat also to herself, she procured an ox team, and after a trip of a few weary days, such as may easily be imagined, she arrived in Natchez, where she sold her oxen, and by the assistance of the Government procured transportation to her kindred in Indiana.

### Union Men Safe in South Carolina in Jackson's Day.

What a scene it would have been,— said Edward Everett in one of his speeches before the citizens of Boston in the autumn of 1864,—to witness the flash of President Jackson's eye and to hear the thunder of his voice, when he heard of the attack on Sumter. What that scene *would* have been, the following anecdote of 'Old Hickory,' as related by Mr. Everett, will pretty fairly show: When the nullification phrenzy was at its height in South Carolina, the Union men in Charleston sent a deputation to Washington, to inform the President that they were daily threatened with an outbreak, and did not consider their lives safe. Scarcely waiting to hear the words uttered, the General sprung to his feet, and with a voice and a look of almost superhuman energy, exclaimed,

Edward Everett.

"The lives of Union men not safe, while Andrew Jackson is President! Go back to Charleston, and tell the nullifiers that if a hair on the head of a Union man is harmed, that moment I order General Coffee to march on Carolina with fifty thousand Tennessee volunteers, and if that does not settle the business, tell them (he added with an attestation that need not be repeated) that I will take the field myself with fifty thousand more."

### Purging the Prayer-Book.

The venerable Judge Pettigru, for four score years one of South Carolina's noblest names, continued, to the day of his death, to bear witness to the value of the Union against the traitors who surrounded him. He had no faith in the practicability of their measures, and predicted from them the worst results to the State and the country. One day, while attending church, where, by his presence, he for so many years showed that the character of a statesman was most complete when religion gave it grace and solidity, he found that the services were purged (by nullification) of the usual prayer for the President of the United States. The stern old patriot rose from his seat and left the church, thus giving a silent but most pointed rebuke to treason in its most rampant locality.

### General Paine's Conversation with the Wife of a Secessionist.

General Paine, with fifteen hundred men, occupied the town of Mansfield, Kentucky, to the great delight of its loyal citizens. It is a place situated twenty-eight miles from Paducah, containing one thousand inhabitants and many fine residences and public buildings. Soon after taking possession, General Paine and his staff went to make a call upon Mr. John Eaker, an old resident of the town, and one of the wealthiest rebels in it. They all walked into the parlor and took seats, when the General turning to Colonel McChesney, said:—

"Colonel, you will occupy this room as your head-quarters, allowing Mrs. Eaker and family the privilege of remaining in the house ten days, when she, her family and husband, if he can be found, will report to me at Paducah, and I will furnish them transportation to New Orleans, and thence to Central America, where they will live hereafter."

"Madam, Mr. Eaker has been our enemy; he has done all that he could to destroy the Government of the United States —that Government which has raised him in the lap of luxury, giving him slaves, rich crops, tobacco warehouses—all that his heart could desire, and did he, could he, think that he could raise his two sons and send them out to murder that Government, and yet go unpunished? Is it possible that he could have been so insane? Now, madam, I want you to send your husband word to report himself to me immediately, and I will spare his life and let him go with you?"

"General, won't *you* write to him?"

"No, madam, I have no correspondence with rebels, except at the cannon's mouth. You put your boy on a horse and send him to him to-day, and tell him that he is to pay Major Bartling, Provost-Marshal at Paducah, the sum of ten thousand dollars, which is the fine I have levied upon him. This money, madam, is to go to make up a fund that I am raising from you rebels, from which to pay something toward the support of the widows and orphans your husband has made. Five thousand of it will be paid to the widow Happy. You know, madam, how the old man was led out in the front yard, across the street there, and *shot dead!* not for having wronged any human being—no, not for this,—but because, and only because, he was unconditionally true to his Government. Oh! madam, it makes the blood boil to think of these things."

"General, I have a very sick child in the other room, and don't think I can possibly move with it. Won't you let me visit my friends, five miles above Paducah? I have a daughter living there."

"No, madam, I cannot; think of the four thousand widows in Illinois—think of *their* little orphan children coming to me for help and protection! You must go with your husband. God and nature have ordained that woman links her fate with her husband, for weal or woe. You have shared his prosperity, you have sympathized with him in his rebellion, and now you must abide with him in his exile. I am sorry to say these things, to you, madam, but the outraged law must be avenged. How can you expect to live in a country you have robbed and murdered as you have this? Did you think that the hand of justice would never reach you? Madam, you will pack your trunks, take all your silver plate, and your linen, bed-clothes, all your ready money, (except the ten thousand dollars which I fine you,) but your heavy goods, such as that elegant bedstead, and this sofa, you cannot take; it would cost too much to freight them. All your lands and tobacco will go to the United States, and this will be the end of John Eaker, his estate and family, in the United States; and you will not go alone, madam, one hundred families from Graves county will go with you—these rebels who cannot live under our Government must go out of it. And, madam, for every day your husband refuses to report to me after to-day, I shall increase his fine five hundred dollars."

Then turning to Colonel McChesney, the General said:

"Colonel, I want you to act as commander of this post. You must levy on as many men, white or black (not soldiers) as you may need, first to sink a well that shall supply all your wants; then repair this railroad, so that trains can run regularly to Paducah; after that, you will send your cavalry out with instructions to rebel farmers who have been raising crops to feed the southern army, to bring all their hay, corn and oats, and fat cattle in here, and send to Paducah all the grain and provisions you collect, so that I can operate my whole district free of cost to the Government. For I tell you, Sir, these rebels must pay the cost of this war, pay five hundred dollars for every widow they make or cause to be made, support and educate the orphan children of our soldiers, and finally go to Central America, South America, or the jungles of Africa, to eat the apple of their discontent, and die despised of men."

"Good morning, madam."

"Good morning, sir."

### John Quincy Adams Foretelling the Future to Calhoun.

One day, during the debate upon the Missouri bill in Congress, Mr. Calhoun, the great South Carolina leader, remarked to John Quincy Adams that he did not think the slave question, then pending in the nation's councils, would produce a dissolution of the Union; but if it should, the South would, from necessity, be compelled to form an alliance, offensive and defensive, with Great Britain. Mr. Adams asked if that would not be returning to the old colonial state. Calhoun said, "Yes, pretty much; but it would be forced upon them."

Mr. Adams inquired whether he thought if, by the effect of this alliance, the population of the North should be cut off from its natural outlet upon the ocean, it would fall back upon its rocks, bound hand and foot, to starve; or whether it would retain its power of locomotion to move Southward by land.

Mr. Calhoun replied that in the latter event it would be necessary for the South to make their communities all military.

Mr. Adams pressed the conversation no farther, but remarked, "If the dissolution of the Union should result from the slave question, it is as obvious as anything that can be foreseen of futurity that it must shortly afterward be followed by a universal emancipation of the slaves. A more remote, but perhaps not less certain consequence would be the extirpation of the African race on this continent by the gradually bleaching process of intermixture, where the white is already so predominant, and by the destructive process of emancipation, which, like all great religious and political reformations, is terrible in its means, though happy and glorious in its end."

### Hard-Up for a Blacksmith.

On the 4th of March, 1864, the citizens of Fort Smith, Arkansas, raised a palmetto flag in town, and one of the soldiers, private Bates, company E, First cavalry, went out and climbed up the tree upon which the flag was suspended, took it down, and brought it into the garrison. Captain Sturgiss ordered him to take it and put it back where he got it. He said he never would. The Captain ordered him to the guard house, and in going he tore the flag in pieces. He was then ordered to be put in irons, and was sent to the blacksmith shop for that purpose; but the smith, a citizen, refused to put them on, and he was discharged in consequence. D company, First cavalry, farrier, was then ordered to put them on, and he refused, and was also sent to the guard-house. E company, First cavalry, farrier, then put them on. The soldiery gave three shouts for Bates, and for the blacksmiths who refused to put the irons on.

### Reading the Amnesty Proclamation at "Buzzard's Roost."

When Sherman's men were climbing the sides of "Buzzard's Roost," in their gallant and successful movement at that point, the rebels attempted to resist the advance by rolling down heavy stones from the cliffs and rocky sides of the mountain. The following story is told of the occasion, on the authority of a staff officer:

A corporal of the Sixty-fourth Illinois hallooed to the rebels, and told them if they would stop firing stones he would read to them the President's Proclamation. The offer was at first received with derisive yells, but they soon became quiet, and the corporal then read to them the Amnesty Proclamation. When he came to some part they did not approve, they would set up a fiendish yell, as if in defiance, and then sent down an installment of rocks by way of interlude. But the corporal kept on in spite of such uncivil demonstrations, and finished the document, when there was another outburst of yells, mingled with laughter, and the old business of tumbling down the rocks and firing was again resumed. That corporal deserved an appointment as President Lincoln's Secretary-at-large.

### Official Farewell to General Scott.

An event of profound interest to the country occurred Oct. 31st, 1861, namely, the resignation of Lieutenant-General Scott, the veteran commander-in-chief. This was owing to his advanced years and various bodily infirmities. The request, on such grounds, could not, of course, but be complied with, and General McClellan was at once notified that he had been selected as the successor of the late Commander-in-chief.

The President, accompanied by every member of the cabinet, now visited General Scott at his own residence, and read to him the order of retirney, accompanied with highly eulogistic expressions of the national gratitude for his brilliant services in times past, and regret at the necessity of officially parting with him. The aged General stood up, and with him rose the President and the members of the cabinet. Deeply affected by the occasion, the old veteran said:

"President, this hour overwhelms me. It overpays all services I have attempted to render to my country. If I had any claims before, they are all obliterated by this expression of approval by the President, with the remaining support of his cabinet. I know the President and his cabinet well. I know that the country has placed its interests in this trying crisis in safe keeping. Their counsels are wise; their labors are as untiring as they are loyal, and their course is the right one."

After these few words, overcome by emotion, and tottering from the effects of wounds and infirmities, the old hero sat down.

The President and each member of his cabinet now bade farewell to the General and retired.

### Preaching the Sword—and Using It.

The following telegraphic correspondence passed between a mother in Baltimore, and her son, the pastor of a church in Boston:

BALTIMORE, April 17th.

MY DEAR SON: Your remarks of last Sabbath were telegraphed to Baltimore, and published in an extra. Has God sent you to preach the sword or to preach Christ? Your MOTHER.

BOSTON, April 22d.

MY DEAR MOTHER: "God has sent" me not only "to preach the sword," but to

USE IT. When this Government tumbles, look amongst the ruins for your SON.

### Irish Military Imagination.

The following took place at a flag presentation in the Army of the Cumberland, May 1, 1863. The flag was presented to the Fifteenth Indiana Volunteers (on behalf of the young ladies of Hascall, Indiana,) by the chaplain, and received for the regiment by General Wagner. The regiment was in line, and the rest of the brigade assembled to witness the ceremony. The General, in the course of his speech, said:

"Tell the young ladies of Hascall that when the war is over their then sanctified gift shall be returned to them, unless torn to shreds by the enemy's bullets."

"An' thin we'll take 'em back the pole!" cried an Irishman in the regiment.

The brigade, officers and men, created a breach of discipline by laughing immoderately, and Pat received a pass to go to town next day.

### Brownlow Prefers the "Direct" Route to Hell.

Parson Brownlow, at that time editor of the Knoxville (Tenn.,) Whig, was requested by General Pillow, in the early part of the secession movement, to act as chaplain for that General's brigade in the rebel service. The Parson replied in his usual scathing and trenchant rhetoric, as follows : "Sir—I have just received your message through Mr. Sale, requesting me to serve as chaplain to your brigade in the southern army; and in the spirit of kindness in which this request is made, but in all candor I return for an answer, that when I shall have made up my mind to go to hell, I will cut my throat and go *direct*, and not travel round by way of the Southern Confederacy."

### Legislative Scene for a Painter.

The secret schemes of secession undertaken by certain members of the Kentucky legislature gave great impetus, at one time, to the rebel movements in that State, especially as it was known that John C. Breckinridge, one of the political idols of the Kentuckians, would, under certain circumstances, be found on the conspirators' side. During the session of that body, there appeared one day in the Legislative Hall, a patriarchal old farmer from a neighboring county,—one of that kind for whom Kentucky has an instinctive veneration,—who uncovered his snowy

John C. Breckinridge.

locks and sat down. At the first lull in the debate, he rose slowly and said he had a word to say, but was aware it was out of order for him to speak before the legislature while in session. His dignified and venerable appearance arrested attention, and "Go on!" "Go on!" from several voices, seemed to keep him on his feet. Again expressing his diffidence at speaking out of propriety — "Hear! hear!" resounded generally over the room. The members' curiosity as well as respect for the appearance and manner of the man, was up, and a silence followed the "Hear! hear!" when the old hero delivered the following eloquent but laconic speech:

"Gentlemen; I am delegated by my county to inform you, that if you hold a secret session here, as you threaten to do, not one stone of this capital will rest upon another twenty-four hours after — good

126   THE BOOK OF ANECDOTES OF THE REBELLION.

day," and he left. Alas! that those words were derided, as they were, by that band of misguided men, and that Breckinridge, voluntarily falling from his high estate, should at last find himself an outlawed fugitive on a foreign shore.

### George Peabody Repudiating the Rebel Commissioner.

Mr. Dudley Mann, one of the representatives of the rebel cause in England, waited in behalf of that cause on our countryman Peabody, who happens to hold some $300,000 of repudiated Mississippi Bonds, on which there is due more than $600,000 of interest. Mr. Mann was very magnificent and grandiloquent, but withal, prosy; and Peabody, suffering from gout and Mississippi Repudiation, lost his temper. Shaking his clenched fist at the rebel, he said, emphatically: "If I were to go on 'Change and hunt up the suffering and starved widows and orphans who have been ruined by your infamous repudiation of honest debts, and proclaim that you are here to borrow more of our gold and silver to be again paid by repudiation, (as I believe it is my duty to do,) you would inevitably be mobbed, and find it difficult to escape with your life. Good morning, Sir."

### Stating the Exact Alternative.

The active operations of General Butler's army in Louisiana were confined, at first, to sudden incursions into the enemy's country, either for the purpose of rescuing Union men, who were threatened by their neighbors with destruction, or of breaking up camps and roving gangs of guerillas. The guerillas were numerous, enterprising, and wholly devoid of every kind of scruple. The first dash by the Federals into the inhabited country was made by Colonel Kinsman, who went fifty miles or more up the Opelousas railroad to bring away the families of some Union men who had fled to the city, asking protection. He crossed the river to Algiers, and took possession of the depot and cars. He inquired of the bystanders where the engineers were to be found. "There goes one," a man replied. Colonel Kinsman hailed him, and he approached. A conversation ensued, which showed something of the quality of the more demonstrative secesh.

Stating the Exact Alternative.

"Are you an engineer?" asked Colonel Kinsman.

"Yes."

"Do you run on this road?"

"Yes."

"How long have you been on this road?"

"Six years."

"I want you to run a train of cars for me."

"I won't run a train for any d—— Yankee."

"Yes you will."

"No I won't."

"You will, and without the slightest accident too."

"I'll die first."

"Precisely. You have *stated the exact alternative*. The first thing that goes wrong, you're a dead man. So march along with us."

The man obeyed. Upon getting out of hearing of his townsmen, he appeared more pliant, and the conversation was resumed.

"What is your name?"

"Pierce."

"Pierce? Why that is a Yankee name. Where were you born?"

"In Boston."

"Are you married?"

"Yes."

"Where was your wife born?"

"At East Cambridge."

"How long have you been at the South?"

"About six years."

"And *you* are the man who would'nt run a train for a ' — Yankee.' You are, indeed, a ' — Yankee.' Go home, and see that you are promptly on hand to-morrow morning."

He was promptly on hand in the morning, ready to run the train for his condemned countrymen. But as competent engineers were found among the troops, it was thought best not to risk the success of the expedition by trusting the renegade, and the objects of the party were accomplished without his aid.

### Senator Douglas's Last Message to his Sons.

For a considerable time previous to his death, Senator Douglas was in a semi-

Mrs. S. A. Douglas.

conscious condition; but on the morning of that event his mind and energies rallied somewhat. Lying at apparent ease in his bed, but with the marks of death upon his pale countenance, Mrs. Douglas, who sat, soothing him gently, by his bedside, painfully aware that the dreadful moment of final separation was approaching, asked him what message he wished to send to his sons, Robert and Stephen, who were then students at Georgetown. He answered not at first, and she tenderly repeated the question. He then replied with a full voice, and emphatic tone—

"Tell them to obey the laws, and support the Constitution of the United States."

### Death Preferred to the Southern Oath.

John Beman, a watchman on board one of the Western steamers, was deliberately hung at Mound City for his patriotic fidelity to the flag of his adopted country. He was a native of Norway, came to this country more than fifty years ago, and lived in Boston, where his children still reside. He was first examined by a "committee," was proven to have said that he hoped Lincoln would come down the river and take every thing; that he would die rather than live in the Southern States, and much more of the same sort. The committee proposed to forgive him if he would take an oath to support the Southern States. He indignantly repelled the proposition, and said he would die first. Finding that he was determined, beyond all appeals, they threw a rope over the limb of a tree, and, stringing the venerable patriot up twenty-five feet, they left him to a halter's doom.

### Nature in Council upon the Union.

The Rev. Bishop Ames, of the Methodist Episcopal Church, while preaching in his usual fervid manner at a Western camp-meeting, remarked that there had been one grand Union Convention, the proceedings of which had not been reported by telegraph. Said the eloquent Bishop: "It was held amid the fastnesses of the everlasting hills. The Rocky Moun-

128    THE BOOK OF ANECDOTES OF THE REBELLION.

tains presided, the mighty Mississippi made the motion, the Alleghany Mountains seconded it, and every mountain and hill, and river and valley, in this vast country, sent up a unanimous voice—*Resolved,* That we are one and inseparable, and what God hath joined together, no man shall put asunder."

#### "Nothing agin the Old Flag."

After the battle of Fort Donelson, one of the rebel prisoners was asked if he was not ashamed to fight against the Union, and the Government which had done so much for them. He replied, "I never fought agin the Union, and I never will." "What then were you doing at Fort Donelson?" "I hugged the ground closer nor ever I did before in my life." "Yes," peeped up a little shrill voice by his side, "and you ran three miles to get out of the way. You ran until you got tired and then sat down and rested, and ran again." "Were you forced into the army?" "Wal, no, not exactly forced; I knew I would be, so I j'ined. I thought I'd feel better to go myself!" "What do you expect to gain by the rebellion?" "We find our leaders have lied to us. Our big men wanted to get rich and get into office, and so they have got us into this mess by their lies. We have nothing agin the old flag. All we want is our constitutional rights, according to the instrument under which our forefathers lived. They told us the election of Lincoln would deprive us of these, and we believed them. But we now know that they were lies."

#### Calhoun's Escape from the Gallows.

The relative position of the National Government and South Carolina, and of the President of the United States and John C. Calhoun, in the winter of 1833, placed the latter in great personal peril, which his friends perceived and tried to avert. Among others consulted on the subject was Letcher, of Kentucky, Clay's warm personal friend. He knew that South Carolina must yield, on some terms, to the authority and power of the National Government, and he conceived the idea of a compromise by which, in so yielding, she might preserve her dignity. He proposed it to Mr. Clay, who, sincerely desiring reconciliation, entertained the idea, and submitted it to Webster. The amazing intellectual plummet of the latter had fathomed the turbid waters of Nullification deeper than had even the brilliant Kentuckian, and he instantly said:

"No!—it will be yielding great principles to faction. The time has come to test the strength of the Constitution and the Government."

He was utterly opposed to compromising and temporising measures with a rebellious faction, and told Mr. Clay so; and from that time he was not approached by those who were willing to shield conspirators from the sword of justice.

Mr. Clay drew up a compromise bill and sent it to Mr. Calhoun, by Mr. Letcher. Calhoun objected to parts of the bill most decidedly, and remarked that if Clay knew the nature of his objections he would at least modify those portions of the bill. Letcher then made arrangements for a personal interview between these eminent Senators, who had not been on speaking terms for some time. The imperious Clay demanded that it should be at his own room. The imperilled Calhoun consented to go there. The meeting was civil but icy. The business was immediately entered upon. The principals were unyielding, and the conference ended without results. Letcher now hastened to President Jackson and sounded him on the subject of compromise:

"Compromise!" said the stern old man, "I will make no compromise with traitors. I will have no negotiations. I will execute the laws. Calhoun shall be tried for treason, and hanged if found guilty, if he does not instantly cease his rebellious course."

Letcher now flew to M'Duffie, Calhoun's ardent friend, and alarmed him with a startling picture of the President's wrath. That night, after he had retired to bed, Letcher was aroused by a Senator from Louisiana, who informed him that Jackson would not allow any more delay, and that Calhoun's arrest might take place at any hour. He begged Letcher to warn Calhoun of his danger. He did so. He found the South Carolinian in bed. He told him of the temper and intentions of the President, and the conspirator was much alarmed.

Meanwhile Mr. Clay, and Senator Clayton, of Delaware, had been in frequent consultations on the subject. Clayton had said to Clay, while the bill was lingering in the House, "These South Carolinians act very badly, but they are good fellows, and it is a pity to let Jackson hang them;" and advised him to get his compromise bill referred to a new committee, and so modify it as to make it acceptable to a majority. Clay did so, and Clayton exerted all his influence to avert the calamity which hung over Calhoun and his friends. He assembled the manufacturers who had hurried to the capital when they heard of the compromise bill, to see whether they would not yield something for the sake of conciliation and the Union. At a sacrifice of their interests, these loyal men did yield, and agreed to withdraw all opposition to the bill, and let it pass the Senate, providing all the nullifiers should vote for certain amendments made by the Lower House, as well as for the bill itself. The nullifiers in committee would not yield. The crisis had arrived. The gallows was placed before Calhoun. Clayton earnestly remonstrated with him.

Finally, they concluded to vote as Mr. Clayton demanded, but begged that gentleman to spare Mr. Calhoun the mortification of appearing on the record in favor of a measure against which at that very time, and at his instance, troops were being raised in South Carolina, and because of which the politicians of that State were preparing to declare their secession from the Union. Mr. Clayton would not yield a jot. Calhoun was the chief of sinners in this matter, and he, of all others, must give the world public and recorded evidence of penitence, whatever his mental reservations might be. "Nothing would be secured," Mr. Clayton said, "unless his vote appeared in favor of the measure."

The Senate met; the bill was taken up; and the nullifiers and their friends, one after another, yielded their objections on various pretences. At length, when all had acted but Mr. Calhoun, he arose, pale and haggard, for he had had a most terrible struggle. He declared that he had then to determine which way he should vote, and at the termination of his brief remarks he gave his voice in the affirmative with the rest. It was a bitter pill for that proud man to swallow. The alternative presented to him was absolute humiliation or a course that would bring him to the gallows. He chose the former. With that act fell the great conspiracy to break up the government of the United States in 1832.

## Minister Faulkner and the Emperor Napoleon on Secession.

The following interesting conversation took place on New Year's day, 1861, between the Emperor of the French and Mr. Faulkner, United States Minister to the French Government. The conversation possesses a special interest in view of the fact that Mr. Faulkner, on his return home became himself an avowed and influential secessionist, participating intimately in the counsels of the leading conspirators. After the usual greetings, the Emperor said:

"What is the latest intelligence you have received from the United States? Not so alarming, I trust, as the papers represent it?"

"Like most nations, Sire," replied Mr. Faulkner, "we have our troubles, which have lost none of their coloring, as described in the European press."

"I hope it is not true that any of the States have separated from the General Confederation," added Napoleon.

"The States still form one common government, as heretofore. There is excitement in portions of the Confederacy, and there are indications of extreme

Chas. J. Faulkner

measures being adopted by one or two States. But we are familiar with the excitement, as we are with the vigor, which belong to the institutions of a free people. We have already more than once passed through commotions which would have shattered into fragments any other government on earth; and this fact justifies the inference that the strength of the Union will now be found equal to the strain upon it."

"I sincerely hope it may be so," rejoined the Emperor, "and that you may long continue a united and prosperous people."

#### Such a Sight as Thrills the Nerves.

The vestry of Grace Church, Episcopal, in New York, was desirous that an American flag should wave from the very apex of the spire of that magnificent structure, the height being two hundred and sixty feet from the ground. Several persons offered to undertake the dangerous feat, but on mounting by the interior staircase to the highest window in the steeple, thought they would scarcely have nerve to undertake it. At last, William O'Donnell and Charles McLaughlin, two young painters in the employ of Richard B. Fosdick, of Fifth avenue, decided to make the attempt. Getting out of the little diamond-shaped window about half way up, they climbed up the lightning rod on the east side of the spire, to the top. Here one of the men fastened the pole securely to the cross, although quite a gale was blowing at the time. The flag thus secured, the daring young man mounted the cross, and, taking off his hat, calmly and gracefully bowed to the immense crowd which were watching his movements from Broadway. As the flag floated freely in the air, they burst into loud and repeated cheers. It was a sight to thrill the nerves of any patriot.

#### Clerical Prisoners of State.

An event occurred one day during General Butler's career in New Orleans, which brought that officer into such direct collision with the Episcopal clergy, that New Orleans was not considered by the General large enough to contain both parties in the controversy.

On a Sunday morning, early in October, Major Strong entered the office of the General in plain clothes, and said:

"I have'nt been able to go to church since we came to New Orleans. This morning I am going."

He crossed the street and took a front seat in the Episcopal church of Dr. Goodrich, opposite the mansion of General Twiggs. He joined in the exercises with the earnestness which was natural to his devout mind, until the clergyman reached that part of the service where the prayer for the President of the United States occurs. That prayer was omitted, and the minister invited the congregation to spend a few moments in silent prayer. The young officer had not previously heard of this mode of evading, at once, the requirements of the church and the orders of the commanding General. He rose in his place and said:

"Stop, sir. It is my duty to bring these exercises to a close. I came here for the purpose, and the sole purpose, of worshipping God; but inasmuch as your minister has seen fit to omit invoking a blessing, as our church service requires, upon the President of the United States, I propose to close the services. This house will be shut within ten minutes."

The clergyman, astounded, began to remonstrate.

"This is no time for discussion, sir," said the Major.

The minister was speechless and indignant. The ladies flashed wrath upon the officer, who stood motionless with folded arms. The men scowled at him. The minister soon pronounced the benediction, the congregation dispersed, and Major Strong retired to report the circumstances at head-quarters.

This brought the matter to a crisis. General Butler sent for the Episcopal clergymen, Dr. Leacock, Dr. Goodrich, Dr. Fulton, and others, who were all accustomed to omit the prayer for the President, and pray in silence for the triumph of treason. The General patiently and courteously argued the point with them at great length, quoting Bible, rubricks and history, with his wonted fluency. They replied that, in omitting the prayer, they were only obeying the orders of the Right Reverend Major-General Polk, their ecclesiastical superior. The General denied the authority of that military prelate to change the liturgy, and contended that the omission of the prayer, in the peculiar circumstances of the time and place, was an overt act of treason.

"But, General," said Dr. Leacock, "your insisting upon the taking of the oath of allegiance is causing half of my church members to perjure themselves."

"Well," replied the General, "if that is the result of your nine years' preaching; if your people will commit perjury so freely, the sooner you leave your pulpit the better."

After further conversation, Dr. Leacock asked:

"Well, General, are you going to shut up the churches?"

"No, sir, I am more likely to shut up the ministers."

The clergymen showing no disposition to yield, General Butler ended the interview by stating his ultimatum: "Read the prayer for the President, omit the silent act of devotion, or leave New Orleans prisoners of state for Fort Lafayette."

They chose the latter—Dr. Leacock, Dr. Goodrich and Mr. Fulton—and were duly shipped on board one of the transports.

### Curiosity of Rebel Soldiers to hear President Lincoln's Message.

A few days after the publication of the President's message and Amnesty Proclamation, the fact of its promulgation having been made known to the rebel pickets of the Army of the Potomac, they manifested great curiosity to hear it, and one of the Union soldiers consenting to read it to them, quite a considerable party collected on the opposite bank to listen. While it was being read the utmost silence and attention were observed by the listening rebels; and after it was finished one of them called out, "We'll go back to camp and tell the boys about it." Papers had been frequently exchanged by the pickets, but about this time the rebels told our men that their officers did not like them to get our papers, as "there was nothing encouraging in them."

### Slidell's Consolation.

In one of the great imperial soirees at Biarritz, one of the courtiers of the Empire, seeing the emissary Slidell alone crossing one of the reception parlors, exclaimed: "Ah, Mr. Slidell! you may show yourself as much as you please; you will never be recognized." "I beg your pardon," said the Southern diplomat, "I have been recognized long since for a patriot; a few more Southern victories and I will be called the representative of a great nation. As to you, Sir, I acknowledge, you are too well known to need recognition; and this is what *consoles* me for not being recognized!" Bah!

### Handsome Rebuke from an Alabamian.

A highly instructive as well as amusing incident took place in a business house on one of the principal streets of Nashville, Tennessee, while a colored regiment was marching along to the music of the national airs. Several gentlemen were looking on the parade, among them a wealthy planter of Alabama, the owner of a large number of slaves. One of the group stepped out to the door, looking on for a few minutes, and then indignantly turning on his heel, addressed himself to the grave Alabamian, to the following purport:

"Well, I'll be d—— if that is not a burning disgrace, which no decent white man can tolerate. Isn't that nigger regiment too great an insult?"

The Alabamian jumped to his feet, and replied, while his eyes flashed fire:

"Sir, there is not a negro in that regiment who is not a better man than a rebel to this Government, and for whom I have not a thousand times more respect than I have for a traitor to his country. I think that the best possible use the Government can make of negroes is to take them and make them fight against the rebels. No traitor is too good to be killed by a negro, no weapon too severe to use against the wretches who are endeavoring to overthrow the Government. Now, Sir, swallow that, whether you like it or not."

The rebel stepped off in utter amazement, without uttering a syllable in reply, leaving the sturdy Alabamian, who cherished the jewel of patriotism as something rather more precious than flocks of slaves, "alone in his glory."

### John Minor Botts between Two Fires.

While the Third Indiana cavalry were engaged in one of the bloody skirmishes which fell to their lot in Virginia, Major McClure, seeing a hale-looking, oldish gentleman in a doorway by the roadside, hailed him, and inquired: "Which way did the rebel cavalry, that a moment since passed here, go?" "Sir," was the reply, "I am under parole to the Confederate Government to tell nothing I see. But, Sir, my name is John Minor Botts—as devoted a Union man as the world can find. I put no 'ifs' nor 'buts' in the case."

### Political Dialogue in Camp.

In the rear of General Grant's headquarters at City Point was the camp of Head-quarters Cavalry Escort. While passing through said camp on a certain occasion, a visitor overheard the following dialogue-politico, coming from a group of soldiers lounging under a shelter of pine boughs:

Says A.—"I tell you that a majority *don't* elect the President."

Says B.—"I know better; it *does* elect, and there ain't nothing else can elect."

A.—"Well, it ain't so in *our* State, any how."

B.—"Well, if the majority don't elect, I should like to know who does?"

A.—"Well, I'll tell you who does elect: it's the *Pleurisy*."

B.—"The what-i-sy? What the —— is that?"

A.—"Well, I don't know exactly, but I know it ain't the *majority*."

A. was right. He only got the pleurisy for *plurality*; that's all.

### Money Couldn't Buy his Vote.

Up in Morris County, New Jersey, lives old Uncle Pete, who always votes the ticket that bids the highest. A few evenings before the presidential election of 1864, some Republicans went to his house to outbid some Democrats who had been there. But Uncle Pete informed them he had sold his vote three days before to the Democrats for ten dollars. He was told that if he would carry his ticket and the ten dollars back to the one who gave them, and vote the Republican ticket, they would give him *twenty* dollars, which offer Uncle Pete immediately accepted. Just as the party had left the house they heard a couple of men coming up whom they knew to be Democrats. Being convinced they were on their way to Uncle Pete's, they hid themselves till the second party had passed into the house, and went back to listen. The Democrats had hardly become seated when Uncle Pete said:

"Gentlemen, you called upon me the other day, and offered ten dollars if I would vote the McLellan ticket. I am poor, and took your money and the ticket. Here are both; take them back—I never sell my vote!"

They tried to induce him to stick to his first promise to them, but it was no go; for Uncle Pete said.

"There is no use to talk, gentlemen. I am a Lincoln man, and have been for over ten years!" And getting a little warmed up at the thought of the twenty dollars, he continued, "No, gentlemen, there is no use trying to change my mind, as I always vote unflinchingly on *principle*, and money can't buy *my* vote. I am a Lincoln man, and have been a Lincoln man all my life!"

The Democrats left in disappointment, the Lincoln men of course feeling sure of Uncle Pete's vote;—unless a higher bid came before election!

---

**Northern Present to Jefferson Davis.**

The editor of one of the newspapers published in Norwich, Connecticut, sent Jefferson Davis, the "President" of the then "Six Nations," a pen-holder made from a rafter of the house in which his forerunner, Benedict Arnold, was born. In closing his letter of presentation accompanying the gift, the editor said:—"I have taken occasion to present you this pen-holder, as a relic whose associations are linked most closely to the movement of which you are the head. Let it lie upon your desk for use in your official duties. In the 'eternal fitness of things,' let that be its appropriate place. It links 1780 with 1861. Through it, West Point speaks to Montgomery. And if we may believe that spirits do ever return and haunt this mundane sphere, we may reckon with what delight Benedict Arnold's immortal part will follow this fragment of his paternal roof-tree to the hands in which is being consummated the work which he began."

---

**Scene at Fort Warren: Exit of Mason and Slidell.**

On the receipt, at Fort Warren, Boston, of the news that Messrs. Mason and Slidell were to be surrendered to the British Government, there was general dissatisfaction among both officers and men, and expressions very much against their personal safety were freely indulged in; but upon reading the very cool and logical deduction of the Secretary of State, especially the latter part of his reply, where the insignificance of the worth of the custody of the Commissioners in this country is asserted, and the fact that were it essential to the welfare or the safety of the Government they would be retained at all hazards, a general acquiescence was as freely manifested.

On the morning of their departure, the battalion was called out as usual, at 8:45, for dress parade, and were kept upon the parade-ground, manœuvring slightly, till after the rebels left. The guards were strengthened to prevent any from going upon the parapets, either soldiers or prisoners, and thus they left as quietly as a dog could—perhaps with not so much notice as a noble specimen of the Newfoundland ordinarily attracts. As they passed down to the wharf, they were accompanied by Colonel Dimmick, who kindly waved all ceremony at the guard-house, save to simply turn out the guard—as our men were unwilling and doubtless would have refused to salute the Colonel, for in thus doing, they would have had to salute the rebels; but when the Colonel came back, the thing was done to a nicety.

When taking leave of Colonel Dimmick, Mr. Mason was somewhat affected, and said, "God bless you, Colonel; God bless you!" and cordially shook hands with him. Mr. Slidell shook hands with the Colonel, and said: "Under whatever circumstances and in whatever relations in the future we may meet, I shall always esteem you as a dear friend."

During the morning many rebels thronged the rooms of Messrs. Mason and Slidell to get their autographs, and Mr. Mason's hand was so unsteady as to be noticed through the window out doors. Some of the political prisoners said to Mason: "We hope when you get to England you will represent our case, imprisoned on this island for no offence save differing from others in political opinions." He replied that if ever he arrived in Europe he would faithfully represent their case.

### President Lincoln at the Play of Macbeth.

One evening at the Washington theatre, while Macbeth was being rendered upon the stage by Mr. Wallack and Mr. Davenport, President Lincoln was observed to be present with his little "Tad" (Thaddeus Lincoln) with him. It being Mr. Lincoln's favorite play, one could not repress a certain curiosity to know—though he was familiar with them as with stump-speaking, doubtless—how certain passages would strike him. When the following passage between Malcolm and Macduff was pronounced the audience was suddenly silent as the grave:

*Mal.* Let us seek out some desolate shade and there
Weep our sad bosoms empty.
*Macd.*            Let us rather
Hold fast the mortal sword and like good men
Bestride our down-fall'n birthdom. Each new morn
New widows howl, new orphans cry; new sorrows
Strike heaven on the face, that it resounds
As if it felt with Scotland and yelled out
Like syllable of dolour.

Mr. Lincoln leaned back in his chair in the shade after this passage was pronounced, and for a long time wore a sad, sober face, as if suddenly his thoughts had wandered from the playroom far away to where his great armies were contesting with the rebellion a vast empire.

### Interceding for her Father: Elizabeth Self and Jeff. Davis.

Poor Hessing Self was one of the many loyalists in Tennessee who were imprisoned and barbarously treated by the rebels because of their fidelity to the Stars and Stripes. He was told that a halter was in preparation for him, only a few hours previous to the time appointed. His daughter, who had come down to administer to his comfort and consolation—a most estimable girl, about twenty-one years of age—Elizabeth Self, a tall, spare-made

Interceding for her Father.

girl, modest, handsomely attired, begged leave to enter the jail to see her father. They permitted her, contrary to their usual custom and savage barbarity, to go in. They had him in a small iron cage, a terrible affair; they opened a little door, and the jailor admitted her. As she entered the cage were her father was, she clasped him around the neck, and he embraced her also, throwing his arms across her shoulders. They sobbed and cried; shed their tears and made their moans. When they had parted, wringing each other by the hand, as she came out of the cage, stammering and trying to utter something intelligible, she lisped the name of Mr. Brownlow, who was confined within the same walls. She knew his face, and he could understand as much as that she desired him to write a dispatch to Jefferson Davis, and sign her name, begging him to pardon her father. Mr. B. worded about this: "HON. JEFFERSON DAVIS.—My father, Hessing Self, is sentenced to be hanged at four o'clock to-day. I am living at home, and my mother is dead. My father is my earthly all; upon him my hopes are centered; and, friend, I pray you to pardon him. Respectfully, ELIZABETH SELF." Jefferson Davis, who then had a better heart than some of his coadjutors, immediately responded by commuting his sentence to imprisonment.

### Clerks of the President.

Some clever patriot, anxious that things political should square a little more nicely with his ideas of the necessities of the public welfare, went to Washington, and there sought the occupant of the White House. He said to Mr. Lincoln, "Sir, you must get rid of Mr. Seward—throw him overboard." "Mr. Seward," said the President, "is Secretary of State. He conducts the diplomacy of the country. Have you read his diplomatic correspondence?" "Yes, Sir." "Have you any fault to find with it?" "No, Sir." "Well, Sir, he is my clerk; I got him for that purpose." "Well, but you should throw Blair overboard." "Sir, Mr. Blair is Postmaster General. Do you get your papers and letters regularly?" "Yes, Sir." "Well, Sir, he is my clerk for that purpose; and I am President of the United States." That was pretty much the idea entertained by President Jackson of his cabinet.

### "Mr. Lincoln Forgot It!"

The capture of Mason and Slidell created intense excitement throughout Europe, and in no country perhaps was this excitement more mercurial than in Paris. Public opinion was in painful suspense in regard to the forthcoming Presidential Message, which it was supposed would contain a broad and national enunciation relative to the event which held almost the whole world by the ears. The anxiously awaited document duly arrived, but no word did it contain about the affair of the Trent. The surprise of the volatile Parisians knew no bounds. A speculator at the Bourse, more *spirituelle* than his colleagues, found an explanation of the enigma: "Mr. Lincoln forgot it!" The word was taken up at once, and had an immense success. Here was England about to fall on the American coast with an armada such as the world had never seen, all Europe was in consternation at the disasters that were to follow such a struggle, commerce was already paralyzed, the funds were fluctuating like the needle of a barometer before a storm, and—Mr. Lincoln had forgotten even to speak of the circumstance! The joke was too chilling; and people swore while they laughed. Was there ever such a people on the face of the earth? *Ils ne se doutent de rien!* They fiddle while Rome is burning!

### Examining one of the Baltimore Unconquerables.

Considering the source from which the following narration comes—the columns of the Charleston Mercury—it may perhaps be regarded as 'drawn rather mild,' though the veraciousness of the affair, even as thus given, is more than doubtful. It however gives the rebels a chance to set off the "unconquerable *spirit* of the women of Baltimore," and this is at least instructive to the student of feminine benignity. But to the "unconquerable":—

A Mrs. W., of Baltimore, about to pay a visit of a few days to the country, to some relatives, was driving through the city in her own carriage, with her trunks strapped behind. Suddenly the vehicle was stopped by a policeman, who assured the lady she was under arrest, and would be obliged to repair immediately to the office of the Provost-Marshal. Mrs. W., somewhat indignant at the request, refused to go, alleging as an excuse, that such a public place was unfit for a lady to frequent; she said that she would go to the Commanding General, Dix, at Fort McHenry, but if the policeman attempted to take her to the Provost Marshal she would shoot him.

"As you please, madam; I will get into the carriage and go to the fort with you."

"You are mistaken," replied Mrs. W., "this carriage is mine, and if you attempt to get into it I will immediately fire upon you."

The policeman took a seat with her coachman, in whom Mrs. W. confided as her protector, and they drove to Fort McHenry. On reaching the Fort, she sent for General Dix, and seeing her he said:

"Madam, I do not know how to address you."

"It is time you did, Sir, since I am arrested, I suppose, by your authority."

"Madam, you look wearied; walk into my office."

Ordering some regulars to bring in the trunk and search it, the General remarked to Mrs. W. :

"This is a military necessity, madam, I would these things were not, but the Government must be supported. 'United we stand,' you know. Madam, have you any sons in the Confederate army?"

"I have three, Sir."

"Did you aid and encourage them to enlist in that service?"

"General Dix, are you a married man?"

"I am, madam."

"Then ask your wife what she would have done under similar circumstances."

"Madam, you look faint and weary; let me order you some refreshments."

"What! eat here? I, a Southern woman, break bread with the *Yankees?* Never! while they are the miserable foes they have proved themselves. Every day I see more clearly the necessity of an eternal separation. And where the dividing line is fixed I want a wall built so high that a Yankee can never scale it!"

The trunk breakers having satisfied themselves that nothing objectionable to the Administration could be found, reported the same to General Dix, who, on consultation, determined to have the person of Mrs. W. searched. The gallant General remarked:

"Madam, it is necessary now that your person be searched; you will not object, I hope?"

"Oh, no, Sir, if the person to perform that ignoble office is a female."

"Oh, yes, madam, a lady, your equal."

"Sir, you are mistaken—not a lady, nor my equal. Were she either, she would not do the degrading work you assign her."

Mrs. W. was taken to a private apartment, and the search was begun. Finding the woman delinquent, Mrs. W. threatened to report her, if she did not perform her duty faithfully. "Pull off my shoes," she continued; "look well into them; make a thorough search, and see if you can find a combination of red and white, or anything inimical to the Union-savers; look well, or I will report you."

The woman finding nothing treasonable upon Mrs. W., returned with her to the gallant General, telling him she would not search another lady for five hundred dollars; that such a persevering character she had never encountered.

General Dix, shocked, no doubt, at Mrs. W's agitated appearance, again proposed refreshments, saying,

"Madam, do have a glass of wine."

"Only on the condition, Sir, that you will drink with me to the health and success of General Beauregard!"

The wine, it is believed, was not taken. Mrs. W. then, turning to General Dix, said:

"Sir, I hope you are satisfied that I have nothing traitorous to your righteous (!) cause. You thought to find the Confederate flag in my trunk, or on my person; indeed, you are not good at hide and seek. Your soldiers are too little interested in your righteous cause to serve you faithfully. They searched my house a fortnight since for the flag. Both you and they have been foiled. I sent that flag to Virginia ten days since under a load of wood; it now waves over the glorious Confederates at Manassas. Sir, it seems the Yankees' peculiar pleasure is to try to frighten women and children. They cannot gain battles, so they revenge themselves in this ignoble manner. And now, Sir, I imagine you have done."

"I regret, madam, that we should have met under these unfortunate circumstances. I will detain you no longer."

"Sir, I demand one thing of you, before I depart. I have been arrested on suspicion. I desire now an honorable discharge."

"Oh, madam, that is unnecessary; it is a mere form, and therefore useless."

"I like forms, General Dix, particularly when connected with official documents."

The General, seeing Mrs. W. determined, ordered the Secretary to write the discharge, and, handing it to Mrs. W., said:

"Madam, I believe that is all."

"No, Sir, not all yet. I wish your name added. I believe that it is essential to such a document."

The General, more reluctant to sign his name than to grant the discharge, was finally brought to the point.

"And now, General Dix," said Mrs. W., "do you know what I intend doing with this discharge? I shall send it to my sons at Manassas, and if they have any of the spirit of their mother, they will one day make you rue this encounter."

After Mrs. W. left, they say the General vowed he would not see another woman for three years, three months, and three days, calling, no doubt, to mind, Richard Cœur de Lion's famous truce with Saladin.

#### Poor Pat's Idea of the Thing.

There is a story told of an Irishman who, landing in New York harbor, was met and welcomed by a countryman who had been longer here.

"Welcome, Pat," said the latter, "I'm glad to see ye; you've come just in time, for to-morrow's election day."

Pat and his friend took some refreshment together, and presently the newly-arrived began to make some inquiries about voting.

"Ye'll vote for who ye plaize," said his friend, "sure it's a free country."

"Well, thin, be-gorra," rejoined Pat, "I go agin the government—that's what I always did at home."

#### Juvenile Political Sentiments.

An artist from the North was sitting on a bluff, at New Orleans, making a sketch of a river scene, when a whole bevy of little children came round to watch him, conversing freely upon the merits and demerits of the picture, with all the acuteness and correctness of any full-grown critic. A conversation between the artist and the little ones soon commenced, and as the lighter end the straw the better can be seen the way the wind blows, these little fellows gave the man of the pencil as good an insight into the real state of political feeling there as could have been obtained from the older and more wily population.

"What are you all, youngsters—Union or Secesh?" asked the artist.

"Union, Sir," simultaneously exclaimed the half-dozen tiny voices, with a decision that was surprising.

"Oh, yes, it's very well to tell me that, with all those blue-coats coming up the hill; but were you not all Secesh yesterday?"

"No, Sir! we were always Union," firmly replied the leader—the same who had been reading from the note-book—

"we ain't afraid of your soldiers, either; when they come here we know we are going to have something to eat."

"Don't you have any thing to eat, then, when the rebels are here?"

"Scarcely any thing, Sir; there is'nt a thing they see they don't take;" and then the whole of them began eagerly, at once, to give his individual experience of cases of extortion and oppression among poor families.

"But though you are for the Union, my little friends," continued the artist, "I guess your parents are all Secesh."

"No, Sir; mine ain't," cried one, "they took the oath."

"So did mine," chimed in all the others.

"Don't you think your parents took it because they were afraid of us?" asked the artist, turning to his young friend of the note-book.

"No, Sir; father and mother were always Union. I wish you could have seen how she took care of a sick Michigan soldier for three months; he used to call her mother, and the soldiers always loved father and mother. I wish I could show you my mother, Sir."

The artist said he would be glad to see her, and shortly after set out with the boy to show him through the town, which he did most effectually, pointing out not only every building and thing of note, but every well-known Union or Secesh dwelling. The former appeared to be in a lamentable minority; and others again he said had taken the oath, but he didn't think they were "good for much."

### Where are They?

General Butler, during the interval of his military duties, made a visit to the White Mountains in New Hampshire, and while there he was compelled to make a speech. He enumerated the various points gained by the Union armies, and the work which had been accomplished, in the following strain: "The flag of the Union to-day floats in every State of the Union but Texas. The rebellion came upon us when we were possessed of an army less than any other country keeps for an armed police. Traitorous hands had so disposed of it, and scattered our navy, that neither was available to immediately crush the incipient rebellion. But in two years we have seen three-quarters of a million of men raised." Before this last sentence was completed, one of the audience asked in a sneering tone,

"Where are they now?"

"WHERE ARE THEY NOW?" replied General Butler, with his customary promptness, "Some of them lie sleeping beneath the sod; and others are still fighting the battles of their country; while you remain at home aiding the cause of traitors!"

### Rosecrans and Vallandigham coming to an Understanding.

When Vallandigham arrived at Murfreesboro', General Rosecrans went to see him. "I wanted to see you," said the General; "I wanted to see you, Vallandigham, to see if you had a rascal's face." Then changing the subject rather abruptly, and bringing down the forefinger of his right hand in that rapier-like style which is a conspicuous feature of his gesticulation when he is in terrible earnest, he said: "Vallandigham, don't you come back here. If—you—do—Vallandigham, I'll be——, and may God forgive me for the expression—I'll be —— if I don't hang you!"

People will be pleased to remember that the General claims that he "never blasphemes, but sometimes swears."

### John Letcher's Views on a Very Personal Subject.

When the boys of the Fifteenth West Virginia regiment went into Lexington, Va., they paid a visit to the home of Ex-Gov. Letcher, and among other things found in his dwelling was a composition read by him during his school days. As the composition is on a subject that might have proved of no small *personal* interest to the author, it is here given word for word, and letter for letter. The subject is that of Capital Punishment.

The manuscript bears the following indorsement on its back, and is also signed by its author, viz:

"John Letcher, Composition read Sept. 25th, 1830.

I have often thought if capital punishments were abolished, our Constitution would be rendered more wholesome.

To hang a man looks too much like barbarism among a people who call themselves a civilized nation, when we consider the manner in which publick executions are attended. They are generally if not always attended with riot and drunkenness, which is very prejudicial to morality. whereas if there were no publick executions this not be the case. A great multitude of people from a distance attend these executions whose families are on the eve of starving.

It would have been better J. M. Jones had been confined in the penitentiary than to have been hung he would have had a chance to repent and the State would have been paid for keeping him the time he was confined in Lynchburg. Upon the whole I am inclined to think if capital punishments were abolished our constitution would be rendered more wholesome. J. Letcher.

September 24th, 1830."

#### Mr. Cass's Backbone.

Colonel Eastman of Chicago, having paid a visit to General Cass, narrates his political conversation with that venerable statesman, in substance as follows:

Colonel Eastman—I have always admired and supported you as a Democrat, but perhaps you will not regard me as a Democrat now, as I have pledged my support to the present officers of the Government, and to all the war measures.

General Cass—You are right. The Government is right. You young men must sustain it.

Col. E.—But I approve of the Emancipation Proclamation, and all.

Gen. C.—So do I. Whether or not the President had the constitutional right to declare the slaves free, the President's friends do not strengthen the measure by claiming it to be constitutional. I do not deny that there is that in the Constitution to justify the act; but the circumstances of the country clearly justify it. I do not fear its effect in the South—I only hope it will prove effectual. I cannot understand how any old Democrat can have any sympathy with the South; and I hope that if there are any persons in the North who would ever consent to a separation, they will not be permitted to have any position or influence.

The old general and statesman showed a good stiff backbone.

#### Cavender, the Martyr Preacher.

There was in Van Buren County, Tennessee, an old Methodist preacher, of a great deal of ability, named Cavender. He was from the first, a most determined Union man, and as his influence in the County was great, they determined to make an example of him and get him out of the way. So the most rabid among the rebels took the aged and service-worn preacher out of his house, put a rope around his neck, and, setting him upon a horse, led him out into a forest. They then told him that unless he would publicly renounce his Unionism they were ready to hang him. Poor Cavender replied:

"God gave me breath to bear witness to His truth, and when I must turn it to the work of lies and crime, it is well enough to yield it up to Him who gave it."

They then asked him if he had any parting request. He said " he had no hope that they would attend to any thing he might ask." They said they would. He then requested that they would take his body to his daughter with a request that she would lay it beside the remains of his departed wife. They then said:

"It's time to go to your prayers."

"I'm not one of the sort," he replied, "who has to wait until a rope is around his neck to pray."

"Come, old man; no nonsense; if you don't swear to stand by the Southern Confederacy you'll have to hang," at the same time tying the rope to a branch.

"Hang away," said the old man.

One of them then gave a blow with a whip to the horse upon which poor Cavender sat—the horse sprang forward, and the faithful servant of God and his country passed into eternity. As already recorded, they said they would fulfil his last request. Well, they cut the flesh off his bones and threw it to the hogs; his heart was cut out and lay in a public place till it rotted.

#### Bad Atmosphere for a Patriot's Lungs.

In one of the Chelsea (Mass.) horse cars, there one day exhibited himself an original 'secesh' sympathizer—and afterwards a groaner, of course—who commenced the usual doleful lament common to that class, about the great rise in prices in this article and that, with the gold groan as a clincher to the whole story. There was not a word of hope or cheer for the country; nothing but the evils from which civil wars are inseparable, could he see. Presently a returned soldier spoke something in this wise:—

"All you say may be true, sir, but we have no such sort of talk in the army. No man would be allowed to utter such sentiments by the troops who are fighting the battles of their country to save it. I have served in the field three years. My time has expired. I joined the army from patriotic motives—because I believe we have a country worth fighting for, and the Union is our only hope. I am sick and tired of hearing such talk as I have just heard from you; and I am going to the field again, partly to *get away from on atmosphere that tolerates such people.*"

Secesh sympathizer dumbed.

#### "God's Flag."

As one of the brigades of the reserve corps which came up to the rescue of General Thomas at Chickamauga was marching through the town of Athens, a bright-eyed girl of four summers was looking intently at the sturdy fellows as they tramped by. When she saw the sun glancing through the stripes of dazzling red and on the golden stars of the flag, she

"God's Flag."

exclaimed, clapping her hands: "Oh, pa! pa! God made that flag!—see the stars! —it's God's flag!" A shout, deep and loud, went up from that column, and many a bronzed veteran lifted his hat as he passed the sunny-haired child of bright and happy thoughts, resolving, if his good right arm availed anything, God's flag should conquer. What a sweet and happy christening the glorious ensign received from those artless lips—'God's flag!' and so it is.

#### Taking his Choice.

The proffering of the Union oath of allegiance to the people of Tennessee, in the infected districts, proved a severe *experi-*

*mentum crucis* to the professed patriotism of some of the people there. As a specimen of the amusing scenes witnessed in the provost-marshal's office, the following will illustrate the 'situation:' A surly planter presented himself, desiring to transfer himself or his goods to the North.

"Certainly, sir;" responded the marshal, "you will be obliged to take the oath of allegiance to the United States Government."

After some hesitation, and considerable inward squirming, the applicant gruffly remarked—

"Well, I'll take it."

The oath was propounded. As it was read out, the applicant's face assumed an expression of mingled surprise and indignation, almost sublime in its intensity.

"Why, sir, I can not take *that* oath. It compels me to discountenance and discourage secession forever."

"Yes, sir."

"And then it binds me to maintain the National authority over that of my own State. No, sir, I can not take that oath."

"Very well, sir, there is no compulsion in the matter. But until you do, I shall be obliged to refuse you permission to leave town, or to ship or receive goods by the river."

### Object of the War on the Union Side.

When the train from Corinth arrived at the Memphis and Charleston railroad depot, having on board General Prentiss and a portion of his brigade captured at the battle of Shiloh, a large crowd assembled to see the Yankees; but no disrespect was shown them. On the contrary, bread, cakes, pies, tobacco and cigars were given them without stint. Said a rebel Colonel to General Prentiss:

"What are the Federals fighting *for*?"

"*For the restoration of the Union as it was*," replied the General.

"You don't think reconstruction is possible, do you?" continued the Colonel.

"Yes," said the General, "and the event is not far distant. If you wish to hold us (meaning his brigade) prisoners very long, you had better send us further South, for before the month is out Memphis will be in our possession, and then the Mississippi valley will be lost to you and the backbone of the rebellion broken."

### Object of the War on the Rebel Side.

On the Louisville and Nashville railroad, when the cars were conveying the gallant Union soldiers and the rebel prisoners, a Union officer coming along said to a Confederate chap, "Will you answer me one question? What are you fighting for?" "What are *yous*?" was the immediate reply of 'Alabammy,' and some others. "That is not answering my question. I asked you first," said the officer. At this there were mutterings of 'liberty bills,' 'abolitionists,' 'unconstitutional,' and some such expressions. "*We are fighting for the rich man's niggers*," finally spoke up an intelligent-looking Corporal, in a clear-ringing and decided voice. There were some 'constitutional' mutterings

R. M. T. Hunter.

against this, on the Confederate side of the house, but they were entirely too feeble to neutralize the impression of truthfulness which the first remark made upon all the crowd, both Confederates and Unionists. "That is all you need to say," observed the officer; "that short sentence covers the whole ground." In reply to the remark that "there would be a large number in the South who had never been in the habit of working before the war, who would be found to have learned to do so since," Reb. said: "Oh, yes, one good thing about this war is that it will teach many of the rich, lazy fellows how to work and take care of themselves, which they never knew how to do before." Had R. M. T. Hunter's famous pronunciamento to the people of Virginia been accompanied with those last two lines, it would have been an antidote to his polished falsifications that would have saved the "old mother State" from plunging into a four years' war that soaked every acre of her soil with blood—yea, would have deprived the Confederacy of its first, strongest and most vital foothold.

### Investigation by General Butler into General Phelps's Insanity.

While in command at Fortress Monroe, some officers told General Butler that they had been conversing with General Phelps, and that he (Gen. P.) was manifestly crazy. General Butler, with his characteristic promptness, went over at once and conversed with General Phelps, and found him as usual quite sensible. A few days after that, some Vermont gentlemen arrived, to urge the appointment of General Phelps to some expedition. General Butler said, with great solemnity, "But, gentlemen, have you not heard the sad reports of the *insanity* of General Phelps?" The Vermont friends of Gen. P. were very indignant, and were denouncing the charge as malicious, when General Butler interrupted them by saying, "Stop, gentlemen, I have looked thoroughly into the matter of General Phelps's insanity, and find that it is only that he has become an Abolitionist two months before you and I."

### American Soldiers Then and Now.

After the capture of Brownsville, Texas, General Banks paid an official visit to the American Consul at Matamoras. The Mexicans, having previously learned of his intention to do so, decided to give him a public reception. A deputation was dispatched to invite him to the Public Hall. The military were paraded, a salute was fired, and all the enthusiasm of a gala day was manifested. Speeches were made by Srs. Argues, Cartina, and others, expressing their sympathy with the Federal cause in the United States, and their belief that the result would be favorable to the cause represented by General Banks. General Banks replied, hoping that Mexico would come out of her present troubles triumphant, and, after a great many mutual expressions of friendship and sympathy, the party adjourned to the office of the American Consul. The citizens of Matamoras were highly pleased with the quiet, unassuming manner of the American General. One poor fellow, however, seemed greatly disappointed. He was an old Mexican soldier, had fought at Palo Alto and Resaca de la Palma. He evidently expected to see something more than human.

"Ah, Senor," said he, "the Americans are not what they were at Palo Alto. I remember them well there; their horses were larger than elephants, and the head of a mounted American reached the heavens!"

### Unexpected Rebuff.

Emerson Etheridge, formerly clerk of the House of Representatives, at Washington, was introduced to Brutus J. Clay of Kentucky, and immediately began to denounce the government. Mr. Clay, after hearing his tempest a few moments, replied:

"Well, Mr. Etheridge, this is pretty rough. Before the war, when I was a Democrat, I used to hear of you down in Tennessee as an Abolitionist. You must have lately changed your views."

This was somewhat wilting to the retiring clerk, who supposed that he had got a man after his own heart. He plucked up

PATRIOTIC, POLITICAL, CIVIL, JUDICIAL, ETC.    143

courage, however, and went into another tirade. Mr. Clay, thereupon, with calmness mingled with manifest indignation, rising to his full height, interrupted—

"Well, sir, this is our first meeting. Your language, sir, seems to me atrocious, and all I have to say to you is, that when men talk thus down in Kentucky, we regard them as secessionists, and treat them accordingly."

### Mutability of Public Reputation.

The sudden changes in the popularity of our political and military chieftains have been most remarkable,—so much so as to lead to the inquiry, " What is lasting distinction?" There are, for instance, not many people in Boston who will fail to recollect the part they bore in the spontaneous triumph which overwhelmed General Banks on his return to Massachusetts during the war. On the very day in question, that favorite of the people was congratulated by a friend on the hold which he had on the public favor. " Yes, madam," said he, with his grave and expressive smile, " and the first mistake I make,

Sheridan.

they will forget it all."—a prediction that more than one General's experience most amply verified during the struggle, not excepting the General who thus so philosophically expressed himself. But, what Banks, through unavoidable obstacles, failed to execute, of his well planned campaign in the Shenandoah, the gallant Sheridan abundantly retrieved by his brilliant and successful tactics—his name and fame encrowned with ineffaceable splendor.

### Coming Events Cast their Shadows Before.

When Marcus Morton was Governor of Massachusetts for the first time, he one day addressed his Council in the executive apartment at the State House upon his intended appointments, and among other matters he alluded to a petition from a young man who desired to fill the situation of messenger to the Governor and Council. The applicant had then just commenced his public career, having spoken at political meetings with excellent effect. The Governor remarked with reference to the matter: " I have considered his case and I shall not appoint him, for he is too smart a man and too good a mechanic to fill the position." " What did you say was his name?" asked a councillor, who had not listened very attentively: " His name," replied the Governor, "is Nathaniel P. Banks." That General Banks was one of the truest-hearted, though not always the most successful, of patriots, in the hour of his country's wo, no one will deny

### Length of the War according to Floridan Chronology.

The sublime ignorance in which the poor non-slaveholding whites of the South are steeped is pretty fairly exemplified in the following:

In the month of February, 1864, when the United States troops penetrated to Jacksonville, Florida, some Confederate soldiers were captured. A motley crew they were, whose picturesque variety of raggedness bore here and there some indications of aim at military style, but nothing of what could be called "uniform." Two men claimed exemption from capture as being civilians. One of the two owned to having been impressed into the Confederate army, but alleged that he had got his discharge and was then a civilian.

"How long were you a soldier?" asked Captain Randolph.

"Three years," replied the prisoner.

"The Confederate army has been three years in the field—eh?" asked the Captain.

"No," answered the 'cracker,' "but I was in the State of Florida service part of the time."

Length of the War.

"How long were you a soldier for Florida?"

"Two years," said the ex-conscript.

"And how long has the war been going forward?" asks the Captain again.

"Well, I suppose going on fifteen years," replied the prisoner.

"Are you sure of that?" his captor inquired.

"Now, I hain't kept no strict tally," the Floridan veteran answers, "but this I do know, sarten; we've ben hangin' the darned Ab'lishnists a darned sight longer time nor that; well, 'bout's long's I kin remember!"

### Interesting Scrap of History.

While on the hights of Fredericksburg, the attention of our men was often attracted by the shaft of an imposing monument in full view, and many took occasion to visit and examine it. Though its commemorative object belonged, as is well known, to the past, there is a strange reminiscence connected with its history,—an act of brutality to a high official, which in later days found its counterpart in Brooks's assault on Senator Sumner.

The inauguration of the monument was marred by a brutal and cowardly assault on the President of the United States. In the early part of May, 1833, the steamer Cygnet was bearing Andrew Jackson, on his way from the Capital to lay its corner stone. The Cabinet and many guests were on board, and the beauty of the day, and the music of peace charmed the company. While he sat over his newspaper smoking in the cabin, a dismissed Lieutenant of the Navy suddenly attacked the President, striking the General in the face with his gloved hand, but was instantly seized by the bystanders. In the *melée* the table behind which the President sat was broken down. The old hero only remarked: "No villain has ever escaped me before, and he would not had it not been for the table." It seemed as if the sacred errand of the President was about to be defeated, but the boat sailed on and he accomplished his duty, as was his wont, forgetful of himself.

### Mrs. Polk Defining her Political Position.

Much has been said of the secession proclivities of Mrs. Polk, the widow of the late President. A writer in one of the western journals gives an account of an interview which he had with that distinguished lady, while he was on a visit to Nashville, during high disunion times. He remarked to her:

"Mrs. Polk, I have heard you accused, since I have been in Nashville, of being a bitter secessionist: how is this?"

She quickly and warmly responded in substance as follows:

"Mr. G——, that is a wrongful accusation. I never was a secessionist, and I don't think I ever will be one. I always said there was no excuse for the course taken by my misguided Southern friends. I said that Mr. Lincoln was constitutionally elected, and that that election should be acquiesced in by every true patriot. I go, Sir, for my Government—my whole Government."

"In other words, Mrs. Polk, you go for that *United* States of which your late honored husband was once the President."

"Yes, Sir," she responded, with marked emphasis, "I do. I know my name has been placed before the public—once at least—in a connection that may have engendered in some minds doubts of my loyalty; but was so placed against my wishes and remonstrances. But inasmuch as it was done for a humane and charitable purpose, I said nothing publicly about it. I do not deny," she added, "that my womanly sympathies are with the South, and that I often catch myself *exulting over the success of the Confederate arms*, but this is only when my reason is taken prisoner and my judgment temporarily suspended at the bidding of my sympathies, prejudices and affections. I was born in the South. From infancy to old age—for my days now, you know, 'are in the sere and yellow leaf,'—my surroundings have all been Southern. My relatives, my friends, and more than all, my late loved and honored husband, were all of that 'sunny clime.' Is it, then, reasonable to suppose that, 'in a moment, in the twinkling of an eye,' with the frosts of many winters upon my head, I can throw off, as I would a garment, all the affections, all the endearing associations, all the prejudices (if you please) of a long life? No! No! this cannot be. And yet, dear Sir, notwithstanding all this, I long, and pray, and yearn for a restoration of my distracted country to its former peaceful and happy condition; for a restoration of the 'Union as it was.'"

The words italicized in the above afford a pretty direct clue to the alleged disloyal proclivities of the venerable lady.

### Armstrong, the Rebel Dominie, before General Butler.

One of the most interesting cases that came before General Butler to decide, in respect to loyalty, was that of Rev. Geo. D. Armstrong, of Norfolk, Virginia, the same clergyman upon whom sentence of imprisonment at Fort Hatteras was pronounced, for his rebel sentiments. An aide of General Butler conducted the first examination, but the General himself afterwards made a careful personal investigation, cross-questioning Mr. Armstrong very closely.

General Butler—I perceive that in your former examination you declined answering the question: "Do you call yourself a loyal man in letter and spirit to day?"

Mr. Armstrong—I do not decline to answer now; if I were to put my own interpretation upon it, I should say I am; but I don't know, Sir.

General—Well, Sir, perhaps I can teach you. Now, Sir, what is the name of that gentleman who had taken the oath, and while coming out of the Custom House with you, made the remark that he "would like to spit upon the Northern Yankees?"

Mr. A.—Mr. Charles Reid. I declined to answer on my former examination, because I had not his consent to tell, Sir; but since that, I have seen him, and he has given me his consent to mention his name.

General—Where is Mr. Reid?

Mr. A.—He is in Norfolk.

General—(to an aid)—Telegraph to Colonel Weldon, provost-marshal, Norfolk, to arrest Mr. Charles Reid and send him here. He lives on Main street.

General—He stated that as he came out from taking the oath?

Mr. A.—Yes, Sir.

General—With the oath fresh on his lips and the words hardly dry in his mouth, he said he "wanted to spit in the face of the Northern Yankees!"

Mr. A.—Well, General, he took it with the same view as I did.

General—I agree to that, Sir.

Mr. A.—I meant to say—

General—Stop, Sir, I don't like to be insulted. You said, Sir, that that infernal

146    THE BOOK OF ANECDOTES OF THE REBELLION.

secessionist wanted to spit in the faces of loyal men of this Union, and that you took the oath with the same view as he did, or rather he took it with the same view that you did—it makes no difference which. I agree, Sir, that you did. I have treated you, Sir, during this interview, with propriety and courtesy up to this moment, and yet you, Sir, here tell me, in order to clear this vile wretch, who shall be punished as he deserves, that you took the oath to my Government with the same view that he did.

Mr. A.—Well, Sir, it was a mortifying fact to confess that we were a conquered people, and it was the irritation growing out of that fact.

General—You have not helped it, Sir. You had not better go on in that direction any further, Sir, for your own sake. Now, Sir, while you did preach a very virulent sermon upon "The Victory of Manassas," at the recommendation of the Confederate Congress, have you ever since preached in your pulpit a sermon favorable to the Union cause, or one that would be likely to please the loyal, and displease the disloyal?

Mr. A.—No, Sir, I never have.

After some further sharp questioning, the examination was continued and concluded as follows:

General—You said you looked upon the hanging of John Brown as just and right, because he interfered with the peace of the country.

Mr. A.—Yes, Sir.

General—Very good, Sir. Now, then, would you look upon the hanging of prominent rebels, Jefferson Davis, for instance, as just and right? You know that the rebels have 'interfered with the peace of the country' and have caused rivers of blood to flow where John Brown only caused pints. What do you say to that?

Mr. A.—I would not, Sir.

General—Are your sympathies with the Union or the Confederate cause?

Mr. A.—With the Confederates.

The examination was terminated by the following order from the General:

"Make an order that this man be committed to the guard-house in close confinement, there to remain until further orders; and send a copy of this examination to the officer in command there."

### A "Long" Portrait.

Some curious reminiscences attach to the career of Alexander Long, of Ohio, whose well-known pro-southern speech and course in Congress, during the war, raised him to such bad eminence.

He was a candidate for Congress during the dark days of 1862, when McClellan retreated from the Peninsula, when Pope transferred his head-quarters from the saddle to the fortifications at Washington, and when Kirby Smith was besieging Cincinnati—Alexander's home. He was wonderfully patriotic; was a member of the military committee of Hamilton County, and gave liberally toward the payment of bounty for recruits; he made speeches urging men to enlist in the glorious cause of his country; talked war, and declared he was prepared to act war, if his bleeding country demanded such a sacrifice; and, by way of earnest, induced a young law partner to enter the army; he went around among his religious brethren—for Alexander the Long was a devoted member of the church—and urged them to support him from personal considerations, as he was as good a war man as his competitor—Gurley, the then sitting member.

He held tickets all day at the polls in his own Ward—the Eighth—in Cincinnati; and persistently importuned all his friends and acquaintances to vote for him, pledging his word that he was for the suppression of the Rebellion at all hazards, and declaring that to compromise with traitors would be dishonorable in the highest degree.

Gurley had many enemies among members of his own party, and the consequence was that Alexander the Long overreached his rival, and was accredited a Representative from the IId Congressional District of Cincinnati, by a majority of a little rising one hundred votes out of a poll of sixteen thousand.

A few days after his election, a good brother in Alexander's church, who had always been a Republican, but who had voted for him out of personal considerations, upon solicitation, and a pledge that he was a good war man, called upon him to offer congratulations. Alexander proffered his hand, and vouchsafed one of his best smiles; but he was a little horrified when asked something about his views relative to the details of the war.

"*I had better not talk with you,*" said he; "*you are for war—I for peace; we can't agree, and, as brethren in the church, we should not quarrel.*"

The 'brother' left the Congressman, feeling that he had been completely sold, and conveyed the intelligence to others, who, like himself, had been deceived; and they all resolved that never again should personal considerations induce them to vote for a doubtful candidate. The result was, that at the succeeding election for Governor, Brough, the straight Republican candidate, carried the District by about seven thousand majority.

### Chronicles of a Railway Trip.

The ride over the Great Western road was amusingly diversified one day by the mouthings and antics of a big-whiskered, French-brogue jackanapes, who claimed to be a Southerner, and, of course, a rebel. He met his match, however, and a big dog under the wagon to spare, in the person of a plain, intelligent looking, and gentlemanly-appearing farmer from near Pontiac, Michigan.

The "lordly Southron" opened the ball with the farmer, by leading off in a "forward two" movement upon the subject of the rebellion. The farmer sat directly behind the Southron, and the latter being anxious to know what "you Yankees think of us rebels," the farmer retorted by assuring him that " we think you are a miserable set of rascals, and we mean to clean you out." This of course roused the ire of ye rebel, and he began to make a lusty display of tongue and muscle,—brandishing his arms wildly, pulling off his overcoat, advancing and then falling back grotesquely, and exhausting the rebel vocabulary of tirade and insult. The Michigander remained all the while as calm and composed as Bunker Hill monument, and although some of the occupants of the car were for holding back the French rebel, yet Michigan bade them let him advance just as soon as he pleased, or in any shape he pleased.

Finding that bluff wouldn't win, the Frenchman began to plead that the sympathy of the car was against him, but boastingly said:

" I'l be d—d if you can crush me, any more than Abe Lincoln and the d—d Yankees can crush the Southern Confederacy."

The old game of injured innocence and Northern cruelty here began to manifest itself, but it wouldn't work in the least. The Michigander carried too many Columbiads for the chivalry, and beat him on every tack he took — muscle, cut-and-thrust argument, and every other way. Frenchy insisted that he must whip somebody, even after he had blown off two or three times, and apparently got cooled down to milk heat—a new degree of Fahrenheit, indicating a milk and water state of mental temperature. Michigan put a poser to him by inquiring:

" If you are so full of fight, why don't you go back South, and help your friends out of their troubles!"

Frenchy said he had been in the Southern service for fifteen months, and became so enfeebled that he was discharged. (He presented a '*feeble*' picture, he did!) Michigan assured him that from appearances he had thoroughly recuperated, and as he was so full of fight, he ought to go back again now, and re-enter the service, where he could have all the chance he wanted, to whip somebody. Frenchy couldn't stand this kind of 'lip,' and so he culminated all the mean things that he could think of, by venting forth the following against his Michigan friend:

"My opinion of *you* is that you are a — miserable, ranting, black-hearted Yankee abolitionist."

"My opinion of *you* is," retorted Michigan, "that you are a sneaking, cowardly rebel, and a God-forsaken man-stealer, and a *thief*," (accent particularly heavy on the last noun.)

"Right!" "right!" exclaimed several who were within the car. The sympathy was evidently with Michigan, and Frenchy saw it and had to wilt.

A spruce-looking little fellow approached Frenchy after the worst of the storm was over, and informing him that he was on his way to join the Federal Army, and was anxious to obtain recruits, made a vigorous appeal to Frenchy to go with him and join our army, promising him a handsome bounty, and a splendid chance for a fight. This was the last feather upon the camel's back, and it broke Frenchy "clean down."

### Billy Shelton, the Martyr Patriot Boy.

The sway of the rebels in East Tennessee was characterized by a trail of blood which flowed from the veins of men, women and children alike. The case of poor little Billy Shelton, the patriot martyr boy, will never cease to be remembered and wept over by every true Union heart. He was but a mere child, only twelve years old, but with five others was ordered to kneel and receive the assassin's fire. He implored the men not to shoot him in the face. "You have killed my father and brothers," said he, "you have shot my father in the face; *do* not shoot me in the face!" He covered his face with his hands. The soldiers received the order to fire, and five more fell. Poor little Billy was shot in both arms. He then ran to an officer, clasped him around the legs, and besought him to spare his life: "You have killed my old father and my three brothers; you have shot me in both arms—I forgive you all this—I can get well. Let me go home to my mother and sisters." His appeal was disregarded. The little boy was dragged to the place of execution; again the stern word "Fire!" was given, and he fell dead, eight balls having entered his body.

### Memorable Interview at the White House.

As a bit of political history that will always stand connected with the great money crisis during the rebellion, the change in the Treasury department caused by the resignation of Secretary Chase, may here be noticed, especially in its personal developments, showing that 'all men are but mortal.'

The President was very low-spirited on Thursday—the day on which he sent in the nomination of Dave Tod. The feeling, whether well-founded or not, was universal in Congress, that for such a man to succeed Mr. Chase was ruinous to the finances. On Thursday night Gov. Tod sent his declination by telegraph — the same as it was received by him. Mr. Lincoln went to bed upon it, and, as he said, before morning he was satisfied that Pitt Fessenden was the man. Early Friday he ordered the nomination to be made out, and Major Hay took it down to the Senate. Only five minutes after he had left, Senator Fessenden entered the Presidential apartment and was soon discussing the "situation." Mr. Lincoln did not tell him what he had done, but discussed Mr. Chase's resignation for a short time and then said:

"Mr. Fessenden, I have made a new nomination this morning which I trust you will approve; I have sent your own name in!"

The Senator was greatly surprised and amazed. He replied:

"You must recall it; you can overtake Hay with a messenger now if you will. Please send for him at once for I can not possibly undertake it. My health will not permit me to think of it for a moment."

But the President was firm. "You must take it," he said, and later in the day he sent word as follows: "Tell Fessenden to stick." Meantime telegrams from all parts of the country came pouring in upon him, congratulating him upon his admirable selection. At night Mr. Lincoln was in fine spirits, and he exclaimed to Mr. Seward who was present:

"The Lord has never yet deserted me, and I did not believe he would this time!"

The strain which the Ship of State suffered during this sudden financial complication will not be forgotten.

---

**Master and Servant meeting in a Strange Place.**

There is a quaint old negro to be seen every day in the City Building Park, Cincinnati, who is known and called by the name of James Morgan. He acts as a sort of Cerberus of the gates, or kind of Major Domo of the grounds, sprinkling water upon the grass when needed, and clearing away the litter that accumulates in the paths. Well, James was originally a slave to the father of Morgan, the rebel chief, but some years ago he contrived to make his escape, and found his way to Cincinnati, where he has lived ever since. Hearing that his young master—the notorious guerilla Morgan—was in the city prison, he made application to the Chief of Police to see him, and was admitted. The General treated him warmly, shook hands with him, and congratulated him upon his having his freedom. "Yes, Massa John," broke in Jim, "you mout hab yourn too, if you hadn't gwine in to broke up de Union; but you is in a tight place now, Massa John; you is in a tight place now! Good bye, Massa John!" and Jim swung away at his usual limping gait.

---

**Beauty of Nullification and of the Guillotine.**

Napoleon, on one occasion, when speaking of the French Revolution, called it '*natre belle revolution.*' This will do to go along with a little occurrence in 1835, soon after the excited times of nullification.

Mr. Calhoun, in a conversation with Senator—then Judge—Butler, repeatedly called nullification a 'beautiful remedy.' The assertion of State sovereignty, against an unconstitutional act of Congress, appeared beautiful in the eyes of Mr. Calhoun.

"Mr. Calhoun," replied Judge Butler, "I am as determined a nullifer as any one, and I am as ready to go as far in the assertion of State sovereignty as you can possibly be;" (Judge Butler and many others had, indeed, preceded Mr. Calhoun in the open avowal of nullification,) but, to save my life, I cannot see the beauty of it. Nullification is all right, but as to its being beautiful that is another thing. It is not unreasonable to suppose that a man might have replied to Napoleon—

"Sire, whatever the French revolution may have effected, leaving aside all discussions of this sort—to save my life, your Majesty, as to the beauty of the guillotine, I have never been able to see that!"

---

**Stanton and the "Old General."**

Secretary Stanton will be recognized by all who ever saw him when in his prime, by the following portrait: Stout, thick-set, about five feet eight inches high; hair and beard very black, the latter worn thick and long; head set very erect on his shoulders—if anything a little thrown back; face round and solid in expression, with blunt features; address prompt and practical—voice full, distinct and unmusical. He never studied the art of pleasing and this left him without the gift of paying compliments in conversation. An exhibition of his thoughtlessness in this regard was exhibited when the officers of the army called to pay their respects to him on his induction into the War Department. An officer well sprinkled with gray, but yet with quite a vigorous step and clear eye, was presented to Mr. Stanton. The latter recognized him, and shook him warmly by the hand, saying: "I remember you well. I saw you *many years ago, when you were in the prime of life,* and I was a little boy about so high,"— and the new Secretary measured with his hand, as he said this, an imaginary lad of not over ten years old. The sturdy old General turned and walked off without a word in reply, evidently not disposed to regard himself so 'old' as Mr. Stanton's remarks would have implied.

### Quality of Secessionist Oaths.

The following conversation, which occurred not far from Nashville, Tenn., will give some idea of the estimation in which the oath of allegiance to the United States is held by many of the chivalry. A wealthy secessionist, of high social position, was summoned as a witness before a military board:

*Officer.*—Are you a loyal man?

*Secessionist.*—I have taken the oath.

*Offi.*—Are you a friend to the Federal Government?

*Secess.*—I cannot say that I am.

*Offi.*—Well, then, are you a friend of the Southern Confederacy?

*Secess.*—Yes, I am.

*Offi.*—And you want its armies to whip ours?

*Secess.*—I have always lived in the South; all my property is here, I have sons in the Confederate army, and it is natural that I should have a desire for our side to succeed.

*Offi.*—So you want the Confederacy to succeed?

*Secess.*—Yes, I do.

*Offi.*—Well, Sir, you have a strange misconception of your oath of allegiance. You have solemnly sworn to support the United States, and now you avow that you are for the Rebel Confederacy. This is nothing but perjury. I shall have to commit you for trial.

### Backing the Commander-in-Chief.

The story seems to have become quite a favorite one, that a well known Senator took it into his head to have a special interview with the President, in order to ask a change in a certain particular, relative to military operations. The President agreed that it was a good one, and promised that he would make it. Some time, however, intervened, and nothing was done, when the Senator again visited the executive mansion, and accosted the President with, "Well, I see you have not made the change.' "No, Sir, General Halleck would not consent." "Well, then, why don't you dispose of Halleck, if he is always in the way?" "Well," said the President, "the fact is, the man who has no friends should be taken care of." The Senator retired, appreciating the President's dry compliment to the Commander-in-Chief.

### Big Job in Prospect.

A brisk and spirited dialogue was that which took place between an East Tennessean loyalist and a Mississippi 'Butternut' who had been taken prisoner and brought into Federal custody.

"What do you expect to do with us Southerners?" asked the Mississippian.

"Why, we mean to whip you, Sir; we mean to whip you badly," replied the loyalist.

"But if you are so sure you can whip us, why is it that you have to call in the niggers to help you out of the scrape?"

"Why, our white men are too valuable to risk in battles against rebels. We want to save 'em, Sir! But niggers are plenty good enough to shoot traitors with. We mean to save our white folks, and whip you, like the very devil, with your own niggers. And the niggers will do the job up brown. Before the war is over, they will knock the handsights off you, and we intend to stand by and see the job well done!"

### Garrison at the Grave of Calhoun.

One of the most impressive scenes—because so eminently historical—growing out of the war of the rebellion, was that of William Lloyd Garrison, the life-long Abolition Agitator, upon whose head a price in southern gold had for more than a quarter of a century rested, standing at the grave of the great Apostle of Slavery and Secession, John C. Calhoun. It was on the very morning, too, April fifteenth, 1865, when Abraham Lincoln died. The cemetery where the mighty senator's remains repose is a small one, opposite St. Philip's church, in the heart of the city of Charleston; and the monument of the great advocate of slavery and nullification is built of brick and covered with a large, plain slab of marble, inscribed with the simple name—CALHOUN. He who sleeps beneath was the very soul of the "peculiar institution," when Garrison began his intense warfare against it. The latter had now lived to see the power of his great antagonist pass away, and just as the illustrious Emancipator, who gave to the system its final blow, was breathing his last, Garrison laid his hand upon the monument before him, and said, impressively, "Down into a deeper grave than this, slavery has gone, and for it there is no resurrection." It was a scene, take it for all in all, that a painter might well attempt to reproduce upon canvass.

### War Dispatches in Church.

Having been requested by President Lincoln to proceed to Fort Sumter, and deliver an oration on the fourteenth of April, 1865, at the unfurling of the national flag once more over that renowned spot, Rev. Henry Ward Beecher gave notice of the fact from his pulpit, on the Sabbath previous, in the following words:

"I am called to accompany the members of the Government and the officers of the army, as they go to lift again, over the ruins of Fort Sumter, our national ensign. At other times, when the prospect of any such mission seemed to me almost visionary—remote, certainly—I spoke of it with some jubilation; but as the thing itself draws near, it comes with solemn shadows to me. And the sense of the magnitude of the work that seemingly, then, like a girdle, will have clasped itself upon this nation, and buckled itself in peace, so impresses me, that the greatness of the mission seems such that, though I am unaccustomed to tremor, my soul trembles within me. There will be many that will go to participate in that solemn and wonderful event in the history of this people; and I should be sorry if there was one that went with any other feeling than that of the most profound Christian patriotism. And if any man goes, supposing that he accompanies me upon an errand of triumph and exaltation over a fallen foe, he does not know the first letter of my feelings. For I go as a brother, to say to brethren misled, 'I appeal to you from yourselves, and from the day of your information to the better day of your knowledge.' I go, not to triumph over the South, but to say to them, 'Brethren, after four long years of blood and darkness, we bring back to you the same hearts of love that you smote at in the beginning of this conflict, and are your brethren still, if ye will.' If there be any minded in that spirit, let them go; and those that may not go, let them tarry at home, praying the blessing of God to rest, not upon the North, but upon this whole undivided land."

When he had closed the sermon of the morning—the subject of which was, the Body-man and the Soul-man, or, the Old Man and the New Man,—and sat down, and when the singing was about to commence, Mr. Beecher rose and said—

"Stop! Turn to 'America.' We will sing that; and I will read a telegraphic dispatch that I have just received, while you are finding the place!"

The reading of the dispatch—which was from the Secretary of War to Mr. Beecher, and which announced the triumphant success of the National forces under General Grant—was greeted with prolonged and enthusiastic applause.—When the excitement, which was very intense, had subsided, and quiet was restored, Mr. Beecher said:—

"The Old Man is being conquered, and the New Man of Liberty is going to rule after this." America was then sung with a depth of feeling such as the occasion may be supposed to have inspired, after which the congregation was dismissed, by the pastor, with these words:

"In the name of Almighty God, of Justice, and of Humanity, now, men, go, and be worthy of your country!"

---

**Accommodating Himself to Circumstances.**

Immediately after the battle of Prairie Grove, some rebel officers of rank were sent up to Cane Hill, Arkansas, to negotiate for exchange of prisoners. It was during their visit that the amusing scene narrated below occurred:

In a small building close on the only street of that crooked village, three Confederate officers, in their best gray uniform, were sitting on one side of a table, and three Federal officers, in blue, on the other. An old gray-headed and gray-bearded man came to the door, and incontinently walked in, with the query—

"Es this the Provo's offis?"

He was dressed in brown homespun, and had an old white wool hat on his head, tied on with a handkerchief, and he leaned on a brown stick.

"Es this the Provo's offis? I want a pass."

Some one here attempted to explain to the old gentleman that he was in the wrong shop; but the old fellow, who was a little deaf, it seems, mistook this as a

Accommodating Himself to Circumstances.

hesitation to give him what he wanted.

"I'm a good l'yal citizen. I've got my pertection papers. I've ben to get paid for my forage. It's all right."

There was a slight inclination to laugh by several present; but the old gentleman continued to make the most earnest protestations as to his "l'yalty."

"Look here, my friend," said Colonel W——, with a smile, "you had better take care what you say about loyalty. Look at these gentlemen"—pointing over the table—"don't you see they are Southern officers?"

The old man's hand trembled as he now adjusted a dilapidated pair of spectacles to his eyes, and closely examined the gray uniforms with the velvet collars and brass stars. His hands trembled more violently. For the time being he seemed to forget the place and surroundings in his fear and bewilderment. At last, in great distress, he turned to the gentlemen, and began to stammer out his explanations:

"Well, gentlemen, I didn't think. I— I didn't mean any thing. I've allers ben a Southern man. I've jest got one son, and he's with Marmaduke. The only other man grown that's fit for sarvice is my darter's husband and he's with Rector, and—and—"

"Hold on, old fellow!" cried Colonel W——, "what about your being a loyal citizen?"

"Will you inform me," asked Colonel P——, who sat next to Colonel W——, "who paid you for your forage?"

The old man turned to look at t'other side of the table. Again he adjusted his spectacles, and looked at the blue coats, and in an agony of distress he took off his spectacles and his handkerchief and hat, and while he leaned on both hands on the table, the tears ran down the wrinkles of his old face.

"Well, well, gentlemen," he at last found words to say, "you go on an' fight it out among yourselves. I can live in any government."

### Important Witness on the Stand.

In a council held in the city of Charleston, just preceding the attack on Fort Sumter, two commissioners were appointed to go to Washington; one on the part of the army from Fort Sumter, and one on the part of the Confederates. The Lieutenant who was designated to go for the Loyalists said it seemed to him that it would be of little use for him to go, as his opinion was immovably fixed in favor of maintaining the government in whose service he was employed. Then Governor Pickens took him aside, detaining, for an hour and a half, the railroad train that was to convey them on their errand. He opened to him the whole plan and secret of the Southern conspiracy, and said to him, distinctly and repeatedly—for it was needful, he said, to lay aside disguises,—that the South had never been wronged, and that all their pretences of grievance in the matter of tariffs, or anything else, were invalid.

"But," said Governor Pickens, "we must carry the people with us; and we allege these things, as all statesmen do many things that they do not believe, because they are the only instruments by which the people can be managed."

Governor Pickens then and there declared that the two sections of country were so antagonistic in ideas and policies that they could not live together,—that it was foreordained that northern and southern men must keep apart on account of differences in ideas and policies, and that all the pretences of the South about wrongs suffered were but pretences, as they very well knew.

### Brief but Eventful History.

The history of a Federal soldier, named Robert Lane, who entered the service as a private in Loomis's battery, has some features which characterize it as one of extraordinary qualities. Briefly summed up, Lane's chronicles, military and otherwise, may be given as follows: After being a member of the above-named company nearly a year, he was discharged for physical disability. He then returned to the city of Detroit, where, however, his stay was limited, and the next heard of him he was in Nashville, connected with some sutler. Shortly after this he was acting as chief clown in a circus—swallowed the sword, and performed other gastronomic feats of more or less wonderful nature. After this, according to report, he entered a Kentucky regiment of cavalry, but soon closed his connection with this troop, whether by discharge or desertion is not known. When next heard from he was a sergeant in an Indiana regiment of Infantry, from which he deserted to enlist in another, in which greater bounties were paid. Another regiment, offering a still higher bonus, induced him to risk the chances again. He did so, and the next heard of him he was a prisoner in the Indiana penitentiary, awaiting court martial for his numerous enlistments. The trial resulted in conviction, and he was sentenced to be shot. The extreme penalty, however, was commuted by the President to one year's hard labor with chain and ball.

### Rather Doubtful Allegiance.

The capture of the Confederate General Jeff Thompson revived many anecdotes of his eccentricities of speech and manner. The General is a great talker, and is bound to tell a good thing, no matter whom it hits. On his arrival at Pilot Knob, Missouri, as a prisoner, he had a long conversation with General Fisk, the commander at that post. Jeff swore on his honor that the Confederacy was a sure thing, bound to succeed, and all that. He continued: "But confound these fellows in south-east Missouri! When I was cavorting around Bird's Point two years ago they were all friendly enough; but as I came through the country here as a prisoner, and told a few of them that I supposed they were right yet, hang me if they didn't have to stop and think *which oath of allegiance they took last!*"

### No Heart in the Cause.

A young man, about twenty years of age, of marked intelligence and pleasing address, made his appearance one day in Louisville, as a refugee from the South, and from the rebel army, into whose service he had been drawn. He described himself as of wealthy parentage, and, before the war, was the idolized heir of a large plantation in the vicinity of Charleston, South Carolina. He served nearly two years in the rebel army, but, having no heart in the cause, he concluded to break off, leave his native sunny clime, and find a home beneath the colder skies of the North. With this determination, and having but a scanty wardrobe in his possession, he bade adieu to Charleston, and set out on foot on his weary journey North. He dared not travel on the public thoroughfares, for he knew the relentless conscripting officers would not let him pass. He therefore pursued his lonely journey along unfrequented paths, often making his bed on the ground, with only the starry canopy for a covering. Weary steps lengthened into weary miles, and he finally arrived in Louisville, Kentucky, having traveled the whole of the distance, excepting about forty miles, on foot from Charleston.

### Wash Litchtiter, one of Morgan's Converts.

Wash Litchtiter, of Indiana, was converted from secesh into a warm Union man. Wash had been flogged once or twice for cheering for Jeff Davis, but he stuck to his principles. One day Morgan and his band of thieves came along, and Wash gave them a cordial welcome. He brought out all the liquor he had and treated them well; told them how he loved the South, and hoped that the Yankees would be whipped out. The banditti then asked him for money. He begged off, but Morgan said, "Come, old Butternut, shell out; we want all the spondulics you've got!"

Wash had to put his nose to the grindstone this time, and fork over; he was however so slow about it that they pitched in and gave him a thrashing, and then carried off everything he had. Wash went in for a 'vigorous prosecution of the war' ever after, and was mighty glad when Morgan went to the State prison, where all such fellows belong.

PART II.—HO! FOR THE WAR!

# PART SECOND.

## ANECDOTES OF THE REBELLION—VOLUNTEERING, DRAFTING, COMMUTING, SUBSTITUTING, DESERTING, ETC.

Noble Instances of Rallying to the Ranks, and of Enlistment among the Aged and Young; Hearings, Ludicrous and Perplexing, before the Commissioners; Raw Recruits and Eccentric Characters; Applicants for Exemption; Ruses and Quibbles to Escape Duty—Strange Phenomena of Nativity, Age, and Infirmities; Bewildered Surgeons; Luckless Conscripts; Rare Brokerage and Bounty Dealings; Flush Purses, Hardships and Miseries; Side-shaking Gaieties, Jests, Puns, &c., &c.

---

"Sound, bugle, sound! and rally round
 The Star-flag of the Free!"
"Lock the shop and lock the store,
 Chalk this down upon the door—
 *We're enlisted for the war!*"
  Put it through!"

When the order came for me to join my company, sir, I was plowing in the same field in Concord where my grandfather was plowing when the British fired on the Massachusetts men at Lexington. He did not wait a minute; and I did not, sir.—*Concord (Mass.) Volunteer.*

I can't do anything for *him*, but I'll tell you what I'll do for you: In case he's drafted and gets killed,—I'll marry you myself!—*Gov. Tod, of Ohio, to an aged woman soliciting her husband's exemption.*

He is my all, but I freely give him to my country.—*Consent of a Maine mother for her 'only boy,' a minor, to enlist.*

---

### How does he Grow 'Em?

An old colored female one day approached Howard's column of Sherman's Georgia army, and entering into conversation, expressed great surprise as to where they all came from.

A wag informed her that old Lincoln had a very productive field away up North, where he raised them at the rate of a million per year. Turning up her white eyes in blank astonishment, she exclaimed:—

"For de Lord's sake, you don't say so! How does he grow 'em?"

"Oh," was the reply, "*that* is very simple. He gathers up all the dead rebels from the battle fields, plants them down in Massachusetts—after a while they begin to sprout, and the moment they see a chicken they make for it, when Lincoln's provost guard catches them and grafts them into the army."

"Bless ye, say so! And are you 'uns dead rebels?" replied the bewildered creature, completely transfixed to the spot where she stood.

"No, we used to be, but we're now live Yankees. I'm Bishop Polk, who preached down here in Dixie."

"De debil you aire!" exclaimed the now excited wench—"and what are you doin' here? Come after Misses Bishop and de chilen?"

"No ——— the children!" was the profane reply; "we've come to assist in whaling ——— out of Jeff Davis."

"You'll hab to cotch him fust," was the

quick response; "guess it's done gone job."

"Well, we'll see," said the soldier; "it's a race between us and the devil, and may be Old Nick will win the heat."

"How does he grow 'em?"

"Should'nt wonder. Dis nigger don't care neder," remarked the dusky matron, as she right-wheeled and double-quicked it back to the house.

### Old Men Turning Out when England Pitches In.

The attention of travelers on one of the Western railroads was considerably attracted, one day, by the appearance of a rather oldish man among a company of recruits for the Seventeenth (Irish) Wisconsin regiment, who were on board the cars, on the way to camp; he gave his name, as follows:—

"My name is Rufus Brockway, and I am in the seventieth year of my age. I am a Yankee from the State of New Hampshire; was a volunteer in the last war with England for nearly three years. I have served under Gens. Izard, McNeil, and Macomb, being transferred from one command to another, as the circumstances then required. I was at the battle of Plattsburg, at the battle of French Creek in Canada, and at the battle of Chateaugay, on the fourteenth day of October, 1813, and was present at the surrender of McDonough.

I am now a farmer, in the town of Beaver Dam, Dodge county, and, with my son, the owner of three hundred acres of land; my son was a volunteer in the Federal army at the battle of Bull Run, had his nose badly barked and his hips broken in and disabled for life, by a charge of the rebel cavalry, and now I am going to see if the rebels can bark the *old* man's nose.

I tell you (said the old man,) if England pitches in, you'll see a great many old men like me turning out, but the greatest of my fears is, that I shall not be permitted to take an active part in the *present* war."

It was the opinion entertained by all those who listened to the old man's remarks, that, if he ever should be "permitted" to be in an engagement with the enemy, he would "take an active part," and not be found to have received any wound in the back,—but on the "nose" side, rather.

### Two Desertions—A Double Tragedy.

A striking and most sad illustration of the effects of civil war in the domestic and affectional sphere is that which the following event discloses. A lady had resided with an only daughter for many years in Alexandria. In the course of time, a mutual friend introduced a young gentleman of his acquaintance, belonging to Richmond, to the family. The young people soon became quite intimate in their social relations, and, very naturally, fell in love. The parents on both sides consenting, the parties were betrothed, and the marriage day fixed for the fourth of July. In the meantime, however, the Virginians were called upon to decide on which side they would range themselves in the great political and military conflict then spreading its dark wings over the land. The ladies declared themselves heartily on the side of the Government, but the gentleman joined the forces of his State. Such was the rapid and widening progress of events, that no opportunity was afforded for any interchange of sentiments between the young folks, or anything settled as to their future movements. Matters thus remained till the fourth of July, when, exactly within an hour of the time originally fixed for the marriage, intelligence was received at the residence of the ladies that the young man had been shot by a sentry two days before, while attempting to desert and join his bride. His betrothed did not shed a tear at this sudden and overwhelming information; but, standing erect, smiled, and then remarking to her mother, "I am going to desert, too," fell to the floor, while the blood bubbled from her lips, and she was soon in the embrace of death.

### Jenkins's Mode of Paroling Deserters.

Notwithstanding the sympathy excited in behalf of the people of Hagerstown, at the time of the rebel raid upon them, some of the inhabitants were observed to receive the rebels with joy, spreading before them the best to be obtained for the morning meal.

On Tuesday, about noon, a lieutenant and five men, wearing the uniform of Union soldiers, crept out of some of the houses of the town where they had been concealed, and delivered themselves up. When they made their appearance before General Jenkins, the following conversation occurred:—

*Jenkins.*—Halloa! who are you, and where did you come from?

*Lieutenant.*—We belong to the Union army, or did belong to it, but we don't wish to fight any longer against our Southern brethren; so when our forces left here, we staid behind, and to-day we came out to be paroled.

*Jenkins.*—What did you say about "Southern brethren?" By ——! if I thought I had a twenty-fifth cousin who was as white-livered as you are, I would kill him and set him up in my barnyard to make sheep own their births. I'll show you how I parole such pukes as you are. You are too miserable to be paroled in military style.

So saying, he ordered a detail of six men and a sergeant—"good lusty fellows, with thick boots"—who paroled the recreant federals to the west border of the town, where the paroling process ceased, and the detail and crowd came back highly pleased with Jenkins's mode of paroling cowards of that genus. Jenkins's military stomach was just then in poor condition for rabbit flesh.

### Marian and her Brave Boy in Blue.

An affair which took place in connection with the First regiment of Michigan engineers and mechanics, goes far to illustrate the old and never-questioned proverb that "when a woman will, she will, depend on't," &c.

In the fall of 1861, a young man conceived the idea of joining the above-named regiment. He had previously formed the acquaintance of a young girl living in the same village, whose proper name was Marian Green—and, in fact, became enamored of her. They were engaged to be married, and she protested against his going into the army. He, however, had made up his mind to go, and go he did. She threatened to follow, but was finally prevailed upon to remain at home, which, however, she only consented to do after a solemn promise that her "brave boy in blue" would ever cherish and regard her as his affianced. The following December, Marian Green bade good-bye to her lover at Ypsilanti, having gone there to see him "off for the wars."

Letters passed regularly, for months, between the parties, but Marian grew tired of being absent from her lover, and finally resolved to join him. This time she kept the matter a profound secret. An opportunity was soon offered, and she set her wits to work to accomplish her long-desired wish. By an arrangement known only to herself and a certain surgeon, she managed to enlist in a detachment that was subsequently recruited for the regiment, and in the summer of 1862, she, together with many other new recruits, joined the main organization, then engaged in rebuilding some bridges on the Memphis and Charleston railroad.

Although Marian had informed her parents that she was going to leave home on a visit to some friends in Illinois, she was soon missed, and anxious inquiries were made concerning her prolonged absence from home. No tidings of her could be learned, and the sorrow-stricken parents remained ignorant of her whereabouts until she suddenly made her appearance in person, having apparently enjoyed soldier life amazingly. She, owing to her boyish appearance, while with the regiment managed to avoid the more arduous labors incident to that organization, and thus was enabled to bear up under the fatigue and exertions of a soldier's life.

As letters written by her lover remained unanswered, save by her parents, he became sad and lonely. Could she have deserted him and eloped with another, after having so frequently assured him to the contrary? He could not, for a moment, entertain any such idea. That she would eventually prove true to her declarations, he felt no doubt. Strange forebodings, however, crept over his mind, and so worked upon his feelings that, in the fall, he was taken sick, and was sent to the hospital.

But imagine his surprise, when, after a day or two in his dreary quarters, a familiar countenance there met his anxious gaze. It was none other than the one he cherished so much—that of Marian Green. What transpired at the recognition of each other at that time and place may possibly be imagined, but would be difficult to describe. Suffice it to say, however, that mutual explanations followed never to reveal the discovery then and there made. Months passed on, and still Marian Green remained in the hospital, kindly nursing the patients. She kept her sex a secret for a time, and would doubtless have done so for the whole term of her enlistment, had not the young man himself proved recreant to his trust. He wrote a letter to her parents, informing them of the discovery, and they soon found means to bring home their long-lost daughter. She was loth to depart for home, but obedience to her parents rendered it necessary that she should lose no time in doing their bidding, especially since her sex had been discovered.

In due course of time her lover returned home, and Marian Green, learning that a portion of the regiment had been discharged, proceeded to Detroit, where she met the idol of her heart. A justice of the peace was soon visited, and the happy pair were made one. After the ceremony, they returned home to the inland town from whence they came, with their hearts full of joy and their pockets lined with greenbacks.

All this was accomplished by Marian Green's enlistment as one of Uncle Sam's "brave boys in blue."

### Taken In and Done For.

An entertaining affair occurred at the Provost Marshal's office in Springfield, Massachusetts, illustrating the truth of the well-known adage, "the best laid schemes o' mice and men," &c. A citizen of that place, desiring to put a representative into the grand army, bargained for one at nine hundred and fifty dollars with the brokers who hung around the office, ready to "take in and do for" any timid wight wishing to be patriotic by proxy. Two or three candidates were examined, and rejected, and the buyer was about to withdraw in despair, when the brokers announced that for nine hundred and seventy-five dollars they could "stop a man"—a healthy darkey, who was on his way North, but could be induced to enlist in Springfield, for the sum named.

The money was promised, and soon the

VOLUNTEERING, DRAFTING, DESERTING, ETC.   161

substitute elect was produced, bearing a letter from his employer—a Captain in a returned Massachusetts regiment—to the Provost Marshal, stating that the boy, his servant, brought from Dixie, wished to go as a soldier, and that the money he received was to be placed in a savings-bank for his benefit. This philanthropy on the Captain's part met the approval of the board of enrollment, the young contraband proved to be able-bodied, and, as the sequel shows, of sound and disposing mind also.

While undergoing the usual sharp questioning characteristic of the Marshal's office, it came out that two hundred dollars was the sum total which he was to receive, while the disinterested Captain and the brokers were graciously to pocket the difference. Furthermore, he did not wish to go as "sub" for any man, but it was his delight to march and fight as a Yankee volunteer,—and draw the bounties incident thereto. He was accordingly enlisted as he wished, and when the citizen and brokers came for their expected papers, they were politely informed that the intended "sub" was already a soldier in the service of the United States. The citizen cursed his luck, the brokers gave vent to their wrath in true Flemish style, and claimed the boy to return to the man who "owned him." Property in man not being recognized in the Marshal's office, he was not given up, and the brokers went their way, sadder but wiser men, threatening never to bring another "sub" to that office till "this matter was made right." The lofty indignation of the Captain on ascertaining the failure of his nice little project for filling his purse, would have overwhelmed any smaller men than those same United States officials, and the depth of his patriotism was sounded when he declared that he would not have allowed his servant to enlist had he been informed of the intention.

The new recruit was jubilant over his unexpected good fortune, and, determined to make the most of his opportunities, elected to go as a volunteer for one of the wards of the city, receiving thereby the ward and city bounties, which, with the State and Government bounties, made him up a purse of nearly one thousand dollars. Could he have now found a dark-skinned beauty, willing to have foregone the pleasures of honey-moon, he would have entered into partnership, sharing fame and fortune, for the benefit of the State aid that a married man is entitled to. The last that was seen of the shrewd volunteer, he was marching through Boston with his "knapsack strapped upon his back," having given to his former master and Captain a generous gratuity as a "memento nigri."

### All a Mother Can Do.

At the time of the first call for volunteers to strike down the rebellion, a matronly lady, accompanied by her son, a fine youth of about nineteen years, entered a gun-store on Broadway, New York, and purchased a full outfit for him. Selecting the best weapons and other articles for a soldier's use, that could be found in the store, she paid the bill, remarking, with evident emotion, "This, my son, is all that I can do. I have given you up to serve your country, and may God go with you! It is all a mother can do." The scene attracted considerable attention, and tearful eyes followed that patriotic mother and her son, as they departed from the place.

### Maiden, Wife, Volunteer and Widow—Love and Patriotism.

An undaunted woman was Mary Owens. This remarkable person accompanied her husband to the army, fought by his side until he fell by the hand of his country's enemy, and then returned home in full uniform, to tell the adventurous tale of her devotion and sufferings. She was in the service eighteen months, took part in three battles, and was wounded twice,—first in the face above the right eye, and then in her arm; this required her to be taken to the hospital, where she was obliged to confess her true sex and the circumstances of her being in the ranks. She had enlisted in the town of Danville, Montour county, Pennsylvania, under the name of John Evans, and gave as her reason for such a romantic and hazardous undertaking, the fact that her father was uncompromising in his hostility to her marriage

Love and Patriotism.

with Mr. Owens, threatening violence in case she disobeyed his commands; whereupon, after having been secretly married, she donned the United States uniform, enlisted in the same company with her husband, endured all the hardships of the camp, and the dangers of the field, saw her husband fall dead by her side, and returned home wounded and a widow—young, rather pretty, and, of course, the heroine of the neighborhood. Though of Welsh parentage, she was a genuine Yankee in patriotism and "smartness."

### Got the Point Twisted Around Wrong.

A rural conscript appeared before the Eastern Board of Enrolment, Providence, Rhode Island, and desired to be exempted forthwith, in order that he might return to his country home. "What are your claims?" demanded the Doctor. "*I'm entirely dependent upon my mother for support!*" was the innocent reply. Whereupon, thus the Doctor rejoined, while a smile faintly illumined the face of the Board: "I am happy to assure you, my honest-hearted friend, that the Government is prepared at once to relieve your mother of so unsuitable a burden, and assume your entire charge and expenses during the next three years, without the slightest recourse to the maternal fount for support or succor." The young draftee appeared a little bewildered, and, referring to the papers to ascertain what was the matter, found that the humanitarian clause in the Enrolment Act was not precisely in his favor, though he had thought it to be. He had innocently got the point twisted round just contrary to its word and intent, and found, greatly to his— 'satisfaction,' that he was just the kind of young buck to do his country a favor.

### No Fancy for Salt Pork, Hard Tack, and Minie Bullets.

Katie Maxwell, with as loyal a spirit in her bosom as ever an American maiden owned, sat knitting alone in the parlor one evening; she heard the bell ring, and knew by the sound whose hand had pulled the wire. Her fingers grew unsteady, and she began to drop stitches. So she let the stocking upon which she was at work fall into her lap. She sat very still now, her heart beating strongly. The heavy tread of George Mason was in the hall. Then the door opened, and the young man entered. She did not rise. In fact, so strong was her inward disturbance that she felt the necessity for remaining as externally quiet as possible, in order to keep from betraying her actual state of mind.

"Good evening," said Mason, almost gaily, as he stepped into the room. Then pausing suddenly, and lifting both hands in mock surprise, he exclaimed,

"Blue yarn and soldiers' stockings—blue yarn and soldiers' stockings! Oh, Katie Maxwell!"

Katie did not move nor reply. Her heart was fluttering when he came in, but in an instant it regained an even beat. There was more in his tone even than in his words. The clear, strong eyes were on his face.

"Ha! ha!" he laughed, gaily, now advancing until he had come within a few feet of the maiden. Then she rose and moved back a pace or two, with a strange, cold dignity of manner that surprised her visitor.

"What a good actress you would make!" he said, still speaking lightly, for he did not think her in earnest. "A Goddess of Liberty! Here is my cane; raise your stocking and the representation will be perfect."

"I am not acting, George."

She spoke with an air of severity that sobered him.

"You are not?"

"No; I cautioned you this morning about trifling with things which should be held out of the region of trifling," she answered steadily; "If you are not sufficiently inspired with love of country to lift an arm in her defense, don't, I pray you, hinder, with light words even, the feeble service that a woman's hands may render. I am not a man, and can not, therefore, fight for liberty and good government, but what I am able to do I am doing from a state of mind that is hurt by levity. I am in earnest; if you are not, it is time that you looked down into your heart and made some effort to understand its springs of action. You are of man's estate, you are in good health, you are not trammeled by any legal or social hindrances. Why, then, are you not in the field, George Mason? I have asked myself a hundred times since morning this question, and can reach no satisfactory answer."

Katie Maxwell stood before the young man like one inspired, her eyes flashing, her face in a glow, her lips firmly set but arched, her slender form drawn up to its full height, almost imperiously.

"In the field!" he said in astonishment, and not without confusion of manner.

"Yes, in the field! in arms for your country!"

He shrugged his shoulders with an affected indifference that was mingled with something of contempt, saying blandly— for he did not give himself space to reflect—

"I've no particular fancy for salt pork, hard tack, and Minie bullets."

"Nor I for *cowards!*" exclaimed Katie, borne away by her feelings; and she pointed sternly to the door.

The young man went out. As she shut the door she sank into the chair from which she had arisen, weak and quivering. The blue yarn stocking did not grow under her hand that night; but her fingers moved with unwearied diligence through all the next day, and a soldier's sock, thick, and soft, and warm, was laid beside her father's plate when he came to the evening meal. Very sweet were the approving sentences that fell from his lips, and they had balm in them for the pain which had wrought at her heart for many hours.

### For Life, if the Nation will Take Me.

On the Sunday afternoon after the fall of Fort Sumter, Theodore Winthrop was walking with a friend in the woods upon Staten Island, near his home. No man could have a clearer conception of the significance of that event. An American in the noblest sense, he felt that the time had come in which the nation's liberties could be maintained only as they were won. "To-morrow," said his friend, "we shall have a proclamation from the President." "Then to-morrow," he answered, "I shall enlist. I wish to enroll myself at once in the police of the nation, and *for life, if the nation will take me.* I do not see that I can put myself—experience and character—to any more useful use." In this spirit he acted, and such was his evident ability that in a month he was aid and military secretary to General Butler, and held at his disposal a first lieutenancy in the army. He lost his life in the expedition that left Fort Monroe June 9, 1861, at Bethel, the rebel riflemen stating that they several times took deliberate aim at him, as he was all the time conspicuous at the head of the advancing Federal troops, loudly cheering them on to the assault. He was shot in the side.

### Making a Family Matter of It.

Before the departure of the Fourteenth Brooklyn regiment for the seat of war, a man who carried on a blacksmith shop in connection with two of his own sons, went to head-quarters and concluded to enlist. He said that he could leave the blacksmith business in the hands of the boys—"he could'nt stand it any longer, and go he must." He was accepted. Next day down came the oldest of the boys. The blacksmith business "wasn't very drivin', and he guessed John would take care of it." "Well," said the old man, "go it." And the oldest son went it. But the day following, John made his appearance. He felt lonesome, and had shut up the shop. The father remonstrated, but the boy would enlist, and enlist he did. Now the old gentleman had two more sons, who "worked the farm," near Flushing. The military fever seems to have run in the family, for no sooner had the father and the two older brothers enlisted, than the younger sons came in for a like purpose. The father was a man of few words, but he said that be "wonld'nt stand that anyhow." The blacksmithing business might go to the d——l, but the farm must be looked after. So the boys were sent home. Presently one of them re-appeared. They had concluded, on the whole, that one could manage the farm, and had tossed up to see who should go with the Fourteenth, and he had won the chance. This arrangement was finally and definitely agreed to. But lo! on the day of departure the last boy of the family was on hand to join, and on foot for marching. The old man was somewhat puzzled to know what possible arrangement could have been made which would allow *all* of the family to go, but the explanation of the boy solved the difficulty. "Father, said he, with a confidential chuckle in the old man's ear, "the fact is, I've let the farm on shares!" Father and four sons went with the Fourteenth regiment.

### Something to Cogitate Upon.

The movements of the Mackerel Brigade have engaged to such an extent the pen of that eminent historiographer, Mr. Kerr, that no additional fact need be stated in speaking of their interest and importance with reference to the war, in which the brigade played so distinguished a part. One commemorative scene is thus portrayed:—

Knowing that the Mackerel Brigade was making preparation to entrap the Southern Confederacy at Molasses Junction, I ascended to the upper gallery of my architectural steed, Pegasus, on Tuesday, in order that I might not be unduly hurried on my journey. Taking Accomac on my way to the battle-field,—my boy,—I called upon Colonel Wobert Wobinson, who is superintending preparations for the draft there, and was witness to an incident suitable to be recorded in profane history.

The draft in Accomac, my boy, is positively to take place on the eleventh of September; but it is believed that the enrolment can be finished before the fifteenth, in which case the draft must not take place on the twentieth. In fact, the Judge Advocate of Accomae states positively that the conscription will take place on the first of October; and volunteering is so brisk that no draft may be required. At least, such is the report of those best acquainted with the more decisive plans of the War Department, which thinks of joining the temperance society.

The exempts were filing their papers of exemption with Colonel Wobert Wobinson, my boy, and among them was one chap with a swelled eye, a deranged necktie, and a hat that looked as though it might have been an elephant's foot-pad. The chap came in with a weary walk, and says he:

"Being a married man, war has no terrors for me; but I am obliged to exempt myself from military affairs on account of cataract in my eyes."

Colonel Wobert Wobinson looked at him sympathizingly, and says he:

"You might possibly do for a Major-General, my son; it is principally business that characterizes a majority of our present Major-Generals in the field; but fearing that your absence from home might cause a prostration in the liquor business, I will accept your cataract as valid."

The poor chap sighed until he reached the first hiccup, and then says he:

"I wish I could cure this here cataract, which causes my eye to weep even in the absence of woe."

"Do your orbs liquidate so freely?" says the Colonel, with the air of a family physician.

"Yes," said the poor chap, gloomily, "they are like two continual mill streams."

"Mill streams!" said Colonel Wobinson, meditatively; "mill streams! Why, then, you had better dam your eyes."

I think, my boy, I say I *think*, that this kind advice of Colonel Wobert Wobinson must have been misunderstood in some way, for an instant departure of severally piously inclined recruits took place precipitately, and the poor chap chuckled like a fiend.

It is a grate misfortune of your mother tongue, my boy, that words of widely different meaning have precisely the same sound, and in using one you seem to be abusing another.

### Ira's Wife and his Breeches.

While Mr. Ely was addressing a patriotic meeting in Gosport, N. Y., a little scene occurred which created much merriment. He had been urging the men to come forward and sign the roll, and told the women to hurry them up. At this, a woman arose in the meeting and addressed her husband substantially as follows: "Ira, you know that you said before you came

Ira's Wife and his Breeches.

here to-night, that you would enlist. If you don't do it, go straight home and take off those breeches, and let *me* have them, and I will go myself!" This brought down the house and brought up Ira, who put his name down and became a volunteer.

### Hard Work for a Drafting-Colonel in Savannah.

The scene which ensued on the occasion of the Confederate draft for four hundred men in Savannah, Georgia, to complete a requisition for troops, the requisite number not having volunteered, is thus amusingly described by an eye witness:

Fifteen hundred of the business men and mechanics of the city were drawn up in a hollow square, on the parade ground, all in a high state of excitement. The Colonel now took his place in the centre, and from the back of a magnificent horse, in a few well-timed remarks, called for volunteers. He said it was a shame that a Georgian should submit to be drafted,

166   THE BOOK OF ANECDOTES OF THE REBELLION.

and dishonorable to a citizen of Savannah to be forced into the service of his country. He appealed to their patriotism, their pluck, and their—pelf. He told them of good clothes, good living, and fifty dollars bounty; and on the strength of these—as he thought—conclusive considerations, invited everybody to walk three paces in front. Nobody did it. An ugly pause ensued, worse than a dead silence between the ticking of a conversation.

The Colonel thought he might not have been heard or understood, and he repeated his catalogue of persuasions. At this point one of the sides of the square opened, and in marched a company of about forty stalwart Irishmen, whom their Captain, in a loud and exultant tone, announced as the "Mitchell Guards; we volunteer, Colonel, in a body." The Colonel was delighted. He proposed "three cheers for the Mitchell Guards," and the crowd indulged not inordinately in the pulmonary exercise. The requisite number did not seem to be forthcoming, however, and the Colonel made another little speech, winding up with an invitation to the black drummer and fifer to perambulate the quadrangle and play Dixie, which they did, but they came as they went—solitary and alone; not the ghost of a volunteer being anywhere visible in the Ethiopian wake. The Colonel looked as blank as if he was getting desperate, and a draft seemed inevitable.

As a dernier resort the Colonel directed all who had excuses to advance to the centre, and submit them for examination. Those who have ever seen a crowd run away from a falling building at a fire, or toward a dog-fight, or a street show, can form some idea of the tempestuous nature of the wave that swept toward the little table in the centre of the square around which were gathered the four grave gentlemen who were to examine the documents.

It was a scene which, as an uninterested outsider, one could only hold his sides and laugh at. Hats were crushed into every imaginable misshape, ribs punched, corns smashed, clothes torn, and canes lost. Every hand held its magical bit of paper, from the begrimed digits of the individual just from a stable or a foundry, to the filbert-tapering and dainty-gloved extremity of the dry goods clerk, just from his counter. Young and old, rich and poor, neat and nasty, Americans, Englishmen, Irishmen, Germans, Frenchmen, Italians, Israelites, and Gentiles, all went to make up the motley mass. What a pretty lot of sick and disabled individuals there were, to be sure. Swelled arms, limping legs, spine diseases, corns and bunions, bad eyes, toothaches, constitutional debility in the bread-basket, eruptive diseases, deafness, rheumatism, not well generally—these, and a thousand other complaints, were represented as variously and heterogeneously as by any procession of pilgrims that ever visited the Holy Land.

And so the day progressed, nearly ten hours being consumed in the endeavor to secure a draft. In the afternoon, the absentees were gathered together, and the efforts renewed, when, strange to say, every man who found the liability imminent of his being forced to enlist, protested that he was just on the point of doing so, and "willingly" put his name to the roll. The state of things in Savannah, in respect to volunteering in defence of "outraged Southern rights," was about on a par with the feeling in other cities of the South.

---

### Settling an Irish Volunteer Case.

A buxom Irish woman came one day to the room of the Supervisors' Volunteering Committee, New York, with three Emerald lads in tow, about six, eight and ten years of age respectively. She pushed rather brusquely up to the table where sat Mr. Chairman Blunt, with all the qualities of lawyer, judge and jury blended harmoniously into one, and said :—

"Is Misther Bloont within? Come along up here, ye childers," turning to her trio.

## VOLUNTEERING, DRAFTING, DESERTING, ETC. 167

"Yes, I am the man," says the jury, judge and counsellor.

"Wal, I've fetched the three boys for yees."

"Whose boys?"

"Your own, to be sure. Take them and make the best ye can of them."

Here was a nice pickle of fish. The clerks in the vicinity and the numerous spectators about pricked up their ears, and looked knowingly at each other and then at Mr. Blunt.

The latter gentleman for a moment appeared a little staggered, looked about him generally, and ejaculated "Ahem." It was an interesting moment, and all waited for the next development.

"My boys! what do you mean?"

"Mane?" said she; "I mane that they are yer own, and ye must take the care of them, for I won't. Didn't ye enlist me husband here without me consent? Put him in the nasty army, where I suppose he is shot by this time? Yes; he's left me and left me childers. As ye took him, so may ye take me boys, and support them, too. He's the father of me childers, and he has left them and their mither, and without a cint to feed them with, and ye—ye—*ye did it!*"

"Oh! be calm, my good woman," says Mr. Blunt; "let us look into this matter. Your husband enlisted, did he?"

"Yees, sur."

"Well, I do not enlist any one; I only pay the bounty. Did he get his bounty money?"

"Yees, sur; he did—three hundred dollars; but niver a divil of a cint did he give to me. Ye had no business to give him the money. Now ye've got him, take the childers wid ye."

"Well, if you insist upon it, I'll take your children and put them in excellent quarters."

"And what will ye did with them?"

"Why, put them in the Orphan Asylum."

"The Orfen Asylum! The divil ye will! And do ye think I will have them in the Orfen Asylum, and their father isn't dead yit, and I am a living soul, their own honest mither, standing afore ye? The Orfen Asylum!"

The very idea seemed abhorrent to her, and she still insisted on "Misther Bloont" taking upon himself the care of her "childers."

"Have you not seen your husband since he enlisted?"

"No, sur."

"How do you know I paid him three hundred dollars bounty?"

"Michael McGuire, who went with him, told me so."

"Now, what is your name?" says Mr. B.

"Me name is Margaret Phelin."

"And your husband's name?"

"Patrick Phelin; and these are the three little Phelins—all we have."

The Supervisor directed one of his clerks to refer to the books for that name. It was soon found, with the fact also that Mr. Blunt had, at Patrick's request, deposited the money in the savings bank to the credit of his wife Margaret. Here, then, was a discovery. Says Mr. B. to Margaret:

"Patrick, you say, left you no money?"

"No, sur, and the more shame to him; for he was a good man, Patrick."

"What would you do with the three hundred dollars, if you had it?"

"Bless yer Honor, I'd put it in the praist's hands or the savings bank, and keep it safe for Pat and the boys."

"You wouldn't spend it, nor fool it away?"

"In faith, I would not."

"And you would bring up your boys well and send them to school?"

"Indade I would."

"Well, my good woman, the money is all safe in the bank and belongs to you. I placed it there for you at Patrick's request. It shows he is a good man, and you see to it that you make him a good wife while he is away."

The woman was overwhelmed with astonishment as well as gratitude at this piece of unexpected good luck, and poured out her thanks upon him whom she was a few minutes before anathematizing, and in such a demonstrative manner as the native Irish alone can evince. The tables were fairly turned, and no father was wanted for the "childers."

### Girl-Recruit for the Cavalry.

A dashing young woman in male attire visited the city of Rochester, New York, and sought admission to the army as a volunteer. She was dressed in dark clothes and wore a soft hat with a gilt cord around it, and had the general air of a soldier. She went to the head-quarters of the Third Cavalry, in the Arcade, and there made her application to Sergeant White, of Company H, to be enlisted as a soldier. She stated to the officer that she had served eighteen months in the infantry, and had been wounded in one of her limbs, was put into hospital, and then discharged. Sergeant White thought she was rather light for the service, but said she might perhaps go in as bugler. She replied that it was just what she would like, and to show her capacity she whistled one or two calls.

The Sergeant, not at all suspecting that he was dealing with a female, familiarly put his hands upon her chest and arms, and remarked that she was *rather* queerly made. Finally he started with her for the office of the surgeon, to be examined, she having signed her name as —— Johnson, on the roll. Just before reaching the office of the surgeon, the recruit said to the Sergeant that she could not be examined, and if she went in it must be without that. The Sergeant replied that the law was imperative. She then disclosed her sex as a reason why she craved exemption from the customary examination. This ended the matter so far as Sergeant White was concerned. He introduced the recruit to a number of officers, and none of them suspected her sex. The Sergeant did not betray the confidence reposed in him by the girl, until she had time to get out of the way. One of the lieutenants of the Third, who conversed with this recruit, expressed his doubts as to the young man being old enough or tall enough for such service. A measurement, however, showed that he was over five feet high, and though he claimed to be eighteen years of age, the lieutenant protested that he could not be over sixteen.

### Fate of a Coward.

The following is one among the many curious cases resulting from the draft. In the month of July, 1863, a man in Amesbury, Massachusetts, was drafted, and on the 27th of that month he presented a claim for exemption as the only son of an aged and dependent mother. On this, an investigation took place, which proved that the woman he called his mother was only one who had adopted him, and the claim was not allowed. He then suggest-

Fate of a Coward.

ed that perhaps his teeth might exempt him; but an examination caused that also to be dismissed. The next day or the day after he went to Newburyport and had eight teeth extracted, and in four or five days afterward he called at the office for exemption, and was duly exempted for loss of teeth. A short time after, these facts came to the knowledge of the provost officers, the man was at once arrested, and the allegations substantiated. The case was now reported to the Provost-Marshal-General, who ordered that the man be held to service and assigned to the artillery, without the privilege of commutation or furnishing a substitute. He was soon on his way to Gallop's Island.

### "I likes de Job."

A stalwart descendant of the Nubian race, buttoned to his chin with nine brass eagles, his Burnside hat surmounted with a feeble plagiarism of the "Prince's feather," his feet encased snugly in a pair of "broadhorn" coal boots, built of leather, and his lips of a character not especially commented on in the "Song of Solomon," pleasantly vouchsafed to those around him the following little military apostrophe. Striking the most graceful attitude of Dick Swiveller, puffing a weed fresh from the *remarkably choice* stock of an army sutler, he cocked one eye condescendingly upon his listeners, as he defined his position: "Yer see," said he, "dis life is diff'ent from what I used to live—no pickin' cotton in de field now—no sore shins, no jeens clothes—no oberseer—no lickins. I'se a soger now—thirteen dollars a month, plenty grub, and good clothes. I always 'haves myself, and gits furlough. I likes de job, myself! Ha, ha, ha!"

### Sad Result of Patriotic Courage in a Youth.

Robert —— was a conscientious, likely young man, who was one of those persons honored by the draft, in one of the pleasant villages of New England. His state of bodily health was such that he could have availed himself, if he had chosen, of one of the 'humane clauses' of the original conscription act, but being patriotic and honest, he felt it to be his duty to obey the call of his government. Before leaving his village home, he married the girl of his choice, and then left her and his doting mother to pray for his early return to them. In the course of time it was rumored that the young soldier was sick in a Washington hospital. Now, Robert was never fit to enter the service, and the severe marches between the Potomac and the Rapidan were too heavy a tax upon his slender frame. Sure enough, he fell sick, and was lucky enough to get into a Washington hospital. One Sunday morning, afterwards, a friend went to Harewood hospital, to find Robert. In reply to his inquiries, he was told that the young soldier had recovered, and had been transferred to the invalid corps. The friend was rejoiced at this announcement, but as he was leaving, he met a surgeon, and asked him more particularly respecting the soldier in question. He replied very quickly, "You have been misinformed. Charles —— has been transferred to the invalid corps, but Robert died last night of typhoid fever!" This is one of ten thousand incidents, of a similar kind, in the heart-history of America's great rebellion.

### Jim Morgan and the New Recruit.

The arrival of new recruits always was taken advantage of by the old soldiers, as an excellent opportunity to gratify their love for jokes and sells, of which they did not fail to have an abundant and varied supply, to suit different cases and circumstances.

On one of these occasions of camp hazing, General James Morgan, from Illinois, and commanding a brigade in Davis's Division, was drawn in as one of the *dramatis personæ*. The General being one of those men who would be very apt to be mistaken for a wagon-master, on account of his plain and unassuming manner and dress, advantage was duly taken of this for a 'lark.' A new recruit of his brigade lost some books, and made inquiry of a Veteran where he would be likely to find them. Veteran informed him that the only thief in the brigade was Jim

Morgan, who did the teaming, and who occupied a tent near the blue flag. Away ran recruit to Morgan's tent, shoved his head in, and asked,

"Does Jim Morgan live here?"

"Yes," was the reply, "my name is James Morgan."

"Then I want you to hand over those books you stole from me."

"I have none of your books, my man."

"It's a — lie," indignantly exclaimed the recruit. The boys say you are the only thief in camp; turn out them books, or I'll grind your infernal carcass into apple sass."

The General relished the joke much, but seeing the sinewy recruit peeling off his coat, thought it time to inform him of his relations to the brigade,—at which the astonished recruit walked off, merely remarking, "Wall, — me if I'd taken you for a Brigadier. Excuse me, General, I don't know the ropes yet."

### Wanted to Draw on the Blue Clothes.

Commissioner Blunt, of New York, while superintending the local bureau of drafting in that city, received the following note in "fair and gentle lines:" —

"O. BLUNT—SIR: Pardon me for the liberty I have taken; but I am an ablebodied woman, and if you will enlist me I will put on soldier's clothing and go. There shall never be any one the wiser until my time has expired, if I could secure the doctor, and that is done very easy, I suppose. I think I should make a better soldier than a great many who draw on the blue clothes, and are always talking but won't fight. Yours, etc.,

MISS HATTIE ——, 55 —— street."

Of course the fair Hattie was allowed to dispense her charms in her accustomed sphere instead of donning the "blue clothes" and to show "fight" with her pen instead of with the sword or bayonet.

### Fannie and Nellie of the Twenty-fourth New Jersey.

Miss Fanny Wilson was a native of Williamsburg, Long Island, and about one year prior to the war she went to the West, visiting a relative who resided at Lafayette, Indiana. While there, her leisure moments were frequently employed in communicating by affectionate epistles with one to whom her heart had been given and her hand had been promised before leaving her native city—a young man from New Jersey. After a residence of about one year with her western relative, and just as the war was beginning to prove a reality, Fanny, in company with a certain Miss Nellie Graves, who also had come from the East, and there left a lover, set out upon her return to her home and family. While on their way thither, the two young ladies concocted a scheme, the romantic nature of which was doubtless its most attractive feature.

Fannie and Nellie.

The call for troops having been issued, and the several States coming quickly forward with their first brave boys, it so had happened that those two youths whose hearts had been exchanged for those of the pair who then were on their happy way toward them, enlisted in a certain and the same regiment. Having obtained cognizance of this fact, Fanny and her companion conceived the idea of assuming the uniform, enlisting in the service, and following their lovers to the field. Their plans were soon matured and carried into effect. A sufficient change having been made in their personal appearance,—their hair cut to the requisite shortness, and themselves re-clothed to suit their purpose,—they sought the locality of the chosen regiment, offered their services, and were accepted and mustered in. In just another company from their own, of the same regiment —the Twenty-fourth New Jersey—were their patriotic lovers, 'known though all unknowing.' On parade, in the drill, they were together; they obeyed the same command. In the quick evolutions of the field they came as close as they had in other days, even on the floor of the dancing school; and yet, notwithstanding all this, the facts of the case were not made known.

But the Twenty-fourth, by the fate of war, was ordered before Vicksburg, having already served through the first campaign in Western Virginia; and here, alas, for Fanny, she was to suffer by one blow. Here her brave lover was wounded. She sought his cot, watched over him, and half revealed her true sex or nature in her devotion and gentleness. She nursed him faithfully and long—but he died.

Next after this, by the reverse of fortune, Fanny herself and her companion were both thrown upon their hospital cots, exhausted and sick. With others, both wounded and debilitated, they were sent to Cairo. Their attendants were more constant and scrutinizing. Suspicion began to be excited,—the discovery of Fanny's and Nellie's true sex was made. Of course the next event in their romantic history was a dismissal from the service. But not until her health had improved sufficiently was Fanny dismissed from the sick ward of the hospital. This happened, however, a week or two after her sex had become known. Nellie, who up to this time had shared the fate of her companion, was now no longer allowed to do so; her illness became serious, she was detained in the hospital, and Fanny and she parted—their histories no longer being linked.

Having again entered society as a member of her real sex, Fanny was next heard of on the stage of a theatre at Cairo, serving an engagement as a ballet girl. But this was for only a few days. She turns up in Memphis, even as a soldier again! But she had changed her branch of the military service, having become a private in the Third Illinois *cavalry*. Only two weeks, however, had she been enlisted in this capacity, when, to her utter surprise, she was stopped by a guard and arrested for being a woman in men's clothing. She was taken to the office of the detective police and questioned until no doubt remained as to her identity, not proving herself, as was suspected, a rebel spy, but a Federal soldier. An appropriate wardrobe was procured her, and her word given that she would not again attempt a disguise. A brief description of Fanny would be that of a young lady of about nineteen years, of a fair but somewhat tanned face, rather masculine voice, sprightly and somewhat educated mind—being very easily able to pass herself off for a boy of about seventeen or eighteen years.

### Table Turning at the Recruiting Office.

The idea had become pretty general that no one was sharp enough to outwit or cheat a broker in bounties for army recruits; but, in one instance at least, this illusion was dispelled in the goodly village of Gotham—sometimes known as the city of New York,—where one of the fraternity was more than matched at the rooms of the municipal committee or commission on the draft.

The broker in question attempted to take a man into the State of Connecticut as a substitute, for which act he confessed he was to receive the little sum of seven hundred dollars. He was on the point of being arrested, but earnestly declared that he did not know of any law against it, and, promising fairly for the future, was let off. His next effort was with a party to whom he offered to give five hundred dollars to go as a substitute. The parties appeared at the rooms of the city committee; matters looked all right; the broker deposited the three hundred and thirty-five dollars with the committee, as usual, (which was of course to be paid over to the substitute when he had passed,) and he paid to the substitute, into his own hands, the balance, one hundred and sixty-five dollars,—which made the five hundred.

They now proceeded to the surgeon's apartment, for examination of the man's bodily condition, the substitute in the meantime having quietly and secretly given his one hundred and sixty-five dollars 'hand money' to some sly friend, who was probably hanging about for the purpose. The examination progressed in the usual manner, when the surgeon announced that the substitute would not pass! Substitute probably knew this before he started. Now the broker wanted his one hundred and sixty-five dollars back again; but the substitute had not got it—he had just sent it home to his wife. The wife was sent for; she had seen no money from any quarter, and had received nothing but a black eye, which she said her husband gave her when a little how-come-ye-so. Substitute was again questioned, then stripped and thoroughly examined, but nothing turned up but a certificate pledging him an extra hundred to go to Brooklyn; " But," said substitute, " my honor was at stake, and I would not leave the city."

The broker was of course dumbfounded and amazed—silent with sorrow that he had at last found a man who could "do" him. But he *was* "done" most effectually—done out of his 'one hundred and sixty-five' clean, and also out of the two hundred dollars which he would have secured from his principal. He withdrew his three hundred and thirty-five dollars, from the hands of the committe, bade an affectionate farewell to Supervisor Blunt, declaring that ' There were two things he never expected to see in his day, viz., any one getting ahead of the supervisor, or being himself cheated. The last sad event he had experienced to-day, much to his grief, the other might yet happen, for it now appeared there were sharper ones to look after than the bounty-brokers— farewell!'

With a wave of the hand the honest broker retired—to meditate, probably, over the gross and open-handed corruptions of the day.

### Nervous Customer in the Red Tape Department.

When Washington was being besieged by the rebel raiders, there came into the Adjutant-General's office a man anxious to serve the country. He was old and bent, long and gray of hair, coarse and strong of features, nervous and trembling of hand, slow and shambling of step, husky and uncertain of voice, quick and wandering of eye. " I want to go into the service; aren't we to have a chance? Isn't there to be any call on the people of the city to rise against the invaders?" " Please step up to the Provost-Marshal-General's office, Sir," answered one of the clerks, as he winked at his neighbor. " But I don't want to run around—I want to go into service to help repel the invaders of our homes." " Certainly, Sir, certainly; but you'll have to go up there to be enrolled," replied the clerk. The old man left. Half an hour later he was seen up stairs, talking with Colonel McBeever. " It's a damnable shame that the rebels have got into Maryland," said he; " the invaders must be driven out, and I want to help do it. I am an old man, but I can handle a musket yet." " Certainly, Sir, certainly; just step over to the Quartermaster's Department, and you'll find them organizing a company for immediate service, into which you can go at once. Shall I send a messenger to show you over there, Sir?" "Oh, no—I'll find it; I'll find it." He went out, muttering something about the invaders; but showed his confidence in official movements and directions, by turning deliberately and going the other way from the Quartermaster General's Department.

### Career of Frank Henderson.

The war produced many heroines, and turned up from the humbler walks of life many rough stones that proved to be the genuine diamonds. But probably no army ever opened so many doors for romance as did the army of the United States during the southern rebellion. Accounts presented themselves almost daily to the eye, of the valorous deeds of females fighting in the ranks for months, without their sex being divulged; and in most of these cases there was connected with their history some love experience or matter of romance that had an important bearing upon their action. The following case of triple enlistment shows a military penchant quite rare and remarkable.

Career of Frank Henderson.

While our army was at Chattanooga, Colonel Burke, of the Tenth Ohio, went out to Graysville, Georgia, under flag of truce, with authority from General Thomas to exchange twenty-seven prisoners in our hands for an equal number in the hands of the rebels, the preliminaries of which had been previously arranged. Among the number in the hands of the enemy was a member of the Ninetieth Illinois, who may be called Frank Henderson.

Frank's history was briefly this: On the breaking out of the rebellion she had an only brother, the only relative, living in Chicago, Illinois. The brother enlisted in the Eleventh Illinois infantry, and being left alone in the world she resolved to enlist in the service in order to be near her brother. She enlisted in the Eleventh, participated in its engagements, and on the mustering out of the regiment for the three months' service she was discharged, without her sex having been discovered. She next enlisted in the Third Illinois regiment, and served for several months, during which time she managed to retain her secret, and by her staid habits won the universal esteem of the officers.

Wounded in one of the battles in which she participated, she was discharged. But Frank's love for the service did not permit her long to pursue the inert life incident to home, and the organization of the Ninetieth Illinois regiment offered her an opportunity to gratify her love for a military life. She enlisted as a private in Colonel O'Mara's regiment, and proved herself an excellent soldier. She served in all the battles of that regiment, and was present at the capture of Holly Springs by the rebels—denounced by her as a disgraceful proceeding on the part of our forces, who could have held the place. In the latter part of the summer, while the regiment was marching through Florence, Alabama, she asked and obtained permission of her Colonel to enter a house in search of something to eat; her regiment moved on, and while waiting for the supper to be prepared in the house where she was, two rebels crawled out from under a bed, and presenting themselves before her, ordered her to surrender.

Thus in their power, she was forced to yield herself a prisoner, and was taken to Atlanta, Georgia, and there placed in duress. In a few weeks after her arrival, Frank made a desperate attempt to escape, and when ordered to halt by the guard, paid not the least attention to the demand, and was fired upon. The ball took effect in her leg, and she continued to suffer from the wound. Colonel Burke, while out with the flag of truce, effected her exchange, among others, and she became an inmate of the hospital, where in due time she happily recovered from her wounds. From the time of her first enlistment, which was in June, 1861, until some weeks after her capture, she kept her sex a secret from everybody, nor was there ever any suspicion excited in regard to her not being of the sex whose attire she wore. In personal appearance she was prepossessing, and her whole demeanor was such as would have done no discredit to the best man in the ranks.

### Fearful Ordeal for a Deserter.

One of the privates in the Nineteenth Indiana regiment having deserted his post, was tried by a court martial, and found guilty, the punishment being death for such a crime. His execution was deferred for some time, and he was kept in a painful state of suspense. At last, the time was fixed for his execution, and five regiments were drawn up in line to witness it, while a file of twelve men were in advance to execute the sentence of death by shooting him.

The prisoner was led forward blindfolded, and the usual words of preparation and command were given in a low, measured tone, by the officer in charge of the proceedings. During the interval between the orders, "Take aim," and "Fire," and before the last was given, a horseman rode rapidly up the road, waving in the air a paper, which was understood by all present to be a reprieve. Covered with dust and perspiration, the officer rode hurriedly up to the officer in command, and delivered to him what really proved to be a reprieve.

The shout, "Reprieve!" fell upon the poor soldier's ear, which was already strained to the utmost in anticipation of hearing the last and final word that was to usher his soul into the presence of his Creator; it was too much for him, and he fell back upon his coffin apparently dead. The bandage was removed from his eyes, but reason had taken its flight, and he became a hopeless maniac. He was discharged and sent home to his friends. His death had really never been intended; but it was deemed necessary for the good order and discipline of the army to make an impression not only upon himself, but the whole brigade; for that purpose the forms of the execution were regularly gone through with, in presence of five regiments, and the reprieve arrived in good time, as it was intended. It was sought by this means to solemnly impress upon the whole assemblage of soldiers the necessity of a strict observance of duty and obedience, under the penalty of an ignominious death. It was a fearful ordeal for the deserter, but it was certainly better than to have completed the tragedy by sending his soul into "that world which no mortal doth know."

### From Deck to Camp.

As some of the prisoners captured from Grant's Virginia Army were halting, when on their way to the Libby Prison, a southerner, observing a rather good looking foreigner among the number—and stepping up to him, said, "What! are you down here fighting us—you are no Yankee." "No, Sir," said the soldier, hanging his head. "Why, then, do you come to fight us," continued reb, "if you have no common sympathy with the Yankees?" "Well, Sir," said the prisoner, "I will tell you. I am a foreigner. I landed in New York not more than a month ago. I got drunk, and the first thing I knew I found myself in camp." This shrewd make-up did not save him from entering the portals of the rebel prison-house.

### Noble Words and Acts of a Slavemaster.

Hon. Mr. McClurg, the well known member of the United States House of Representatives from Missouri, showed his patriotism by giving written permits to several of his slaves to go into the army, securing to each of them whatever compensation he himself might be entitled to as a loyal owner, and stipulating that in case of the death of the men, their wives and children should receive the money. He also wrote a letter to his "yellow man," Caswell, in which he said to him: "Make your own choice. If you go into the army, let me hear frequently from you. Make peace with your God and you need not fear death. Be temperate; save your earnings. If you ever fight, fight with desperation, and never surrender. Enroll your name as Caswell McClurg, and try to give honor to it. In the army use your idle hours in learning to read and write."

### Strong Case of Conscience.

A remarkable instance of honesty—remarkable especially on account of its connection with the war and Government—happened in Cincinnati. A woman in almost destitute circumstances came to that city, a stranger, from Canada, and being a Presbyterian herself, she sought out a minister of that denomination, Rev. Dr. Thompson, to whom she confided the fact that her husband had volunteered in the United States army, obtained Government and local bounty to the amount of three hundred dollars, and then deserted. He had left the money with her and then gone off, perhaps to enlist again. Her conscience would not allow her to use the money, and she had come all that distance to return it to the proper authorities, which she besought Dr. Thompson to do for her. The Dr. took it to Colonel Roberts, of the second district, who however declined to receive it, on the ground that it had been paid to the recruit legally, and if he had committed any subsequent act that was not right, the return of his money would not make it so. If arrested as a deserter, he would have to suffer the consequences. So the woman received back the money she had so conscientiously brought with her.

### Poorer Pay but Better Business.

The following remarks were made by a non-commissioned officer of the —— New York artillery, in a hotel in that city. The officer was at home on a twenty days' leave, given him on account of his remarkably good conduct and bravery. Though he describes himself as a "loafer," no one will deny him the character of a true man and patriotic soldier. The conversation was started by the entrance into the room of a black French poodle. He said:

"*There's* a French poodle, *I* know it is. I used to be in the fancy dog business myself, before I went to soldiering. Did I find soldiering pay better? Yes, I did! I always spend all I can get. I can't help it. You see I am a loafer, I am. I get my little seventeen dollars a month for the little place I have in the battery, and I spend it all and I fight for my country. Here, in New York, I used to get more money, but I spent it all and it didn't do me any more good than what I get now. And then I know all the time I am doing my country's work. You see there are soldiers and there are 'sogers?' I'm a *soldier* clear through. We have lost two batteries since this war began, and I have been all through the fighting from the first. We came out of one fight with seven men, and out of another with five. It seems strange to me that while I saw men laid out all around me, who had wives, and mothers and babies, I shouldn't be hit. I am a loafer: I haven't got a mother, or a wife, or a baby, or a sister, or a brother. But they spared me, and killed hundreds of men who had lots of folks to mourn for them. I wish, sometimes, that I could have been laid out in the place of any of those poor fellows. Nobody would cry for me, but there would be some honor in dying for my country. I am going back in a few days, and if I should get an arm or a leg shot off, I should have to come back to New York and beg for my living. I hope if they hit me they will kill me. I am ready to die any time for my country."

Had every man who enlisted in the war for the Union been of the above stamp, the conflict would have been a short one.

#### Sole Condition for Re-enlisting.

While a visitor to General Butler's army before Richmond was threading his way through one of the camps, a good looking, cleanly dressed, full bearded soldier attracted his attention by a gesture which was half salute and half beckon. Reining up, for there seemed to be a desire to speak, the soldier advanced, and, folding his arms and standing at his full length, began:

"Sir, do I look like a beggar? Look at me and say if I appear as if I were in the habit of begging?"

The visitor answered in the negative, and desiring to know whether he had anything to beg for then, got his story. Said he—

"Do you chew or smoke? Now I don't know whether you are an officer, or a chaplain, or a sutler, or a quartermaster's clerk, but if you have any tobacco with you, for God's sake divide with me. You see I've not been paid for five months, so I can't buy any, and I *must* have a smoke —can't stand it any longer, am homesick as a school girl, be hanged if I haven't come confounded near deserting. (Here he stopped short to light a segar the visitor had handed him, along with a more or less of Killikinnick.) When (puff,) I get back (puff, puff,) to Connecticut, I mean to raise (puff, puff,) raise tobacco by the acre, and, hang me, (puff, puff,)—hang me, if I don't give it all away to poor devils that haven't money to—(puff, puff, puff,) —poor devils that haven't money to buy any."

In further conversation, he declared that he would *re-enlist* if he could be *sure* of obtaining tobacco regularly, and he would *not* re-enlist—not he!—unless he *could* be sure of it.

#### After the Firing on Old Sumter.

"Well, father! the traitors have fired on old Sumter!" exclaimed Captain Grant, as he entered the store in Galena, on the morning of the 15th of April, 1861.

"What! fired on the American flag?"

"Yes! a body of seven thousand rebels have attacked Major Anderson in the fort, set the barracks on fire, and driven our brave boys out!"

"Did Anderson give up the colors?"

"No, Sir: he has carried them with him, and brought them off in triumph. God bless him."

"This is startling news, my son. What shall we do to restore the flag?"

"I tell you what I shall do, Sir! I shall volunteer!"

"Good. I like your pluck. I would do the same, if I were not too old. But what will your wife say to it?"

"My family, father, are in the hands of my God and my country. I believe that both God and country are calling me to volunteer; and I am not afraid to have my family in such good hands."

In a few moments more our hero was across the threshold of his house.

"Wife, what do you say? I am going again to war."

There was an answering look that met his at that moment. It was more tender than that of the father in the store. Its

## VOLUNTEERING, DRAFTING, DESERTING, ETC. 177

brief glance told a sweet story of home joys. The witnessing tears that gushed silently to the eyelashes, and trembled a moment there ere they were dashed gently away, spoke louder than the father's words had spoken. But a moment more, and the firm consent followed. It was such a consent as a hero's wife loves to give a hero. In yet another moment the mother steps quietly forward:

General Grant.

"Go, Ulysses, go, my dear son. And may the blessing of Jehovah of hosts go with you!"

"I knew you would all consent," said the Captain, as he glanced his eye quickly and firmly to where some portions of his former armor were suspended; "for, if ever there was a just cause for fighting, it is this in which I now volunteer."

In a few hours more Captain Grant was on his way to the capital and governor of the State.

### Black, the Scotch Deserter at Leesburg.

One of the Confederate soldiers in the Virginia army was a rough Scotchman named Black. His relatives were at the South, and, desiring to get to them, he had joined the Northern army, with the intention of deserting at the first opportunity. When on picket guard at the river, therefore, he pretended to bathe, and being a good swimmer, dexterously struck out for the Virginia shore. When midway, the rogue turned and shouted: "Good bye, boys; I'm bound for Dixie!" "Come back, or we'll shoot!" answered the guard. "Shoot and be ——, you white livered nigger-thieves," shouted Black, and in the midst of a shower of Minie balls he reached his destination. He entered at once the Confederate ranks, and proved an active fighter. During the battle he performed many feats of daring, and at night formed one of a corporal's guard who escorted a full company of captured Federals off the hotly-contested ground. As Black was laughing and joking, the Captain of the Federals remarked to him:

"I ought to know that voice!—is that you, Black?"

"That's me!" jocosely replied the renegade Scotchman. "I couldn't stay with you, you see; it wasn't because I feared to fight, but I like to fight in the right cause always."

Singular enough, Black was escorting his old company, officers and all.

### Hopeful Tackett—his Mark.

Hopeful Tackett sang the inspiring national anthem—

"An' the Star-Spangler' Banger in triumph shall wave
O! the lan dov the free-e-e, an' the ho mov the brave,"

as he sat on his little bench in the little shop of Herr Kordwaner, the village shoemaker. Thus he sang, not artistically, but with much fervor and unction, keeping time with his hammer, as he hammered away at an immense "stoga." And as he sang, the prophetic words rose upon the air, and were wafted, together with an odor of new leather and paste-pot, out of the window, and fell upon the ear of a ragged urchin with an armful of hand-bills.

"Would you lose a leg for it, Hope?" he asked, bringing to bear upon Hopeful a pair of crossed-eyes, a full complement of white teeth, and a face spotted with its kindred dust.

"For the Banger?" replied Hopeful;

"guess I would. Both on 'em—an' a head, too."

"Well, here's a chance for you." And he tossed him a hand-bill.

Hopeful laid aside his hammer and his work, and picked up the hand-bill; and while he is reading it, take a look at him. Hopeful is not a beauty, and he knows it; and though some of the rustic wits call him "Beaut," he is well aware that they intend it for irony. His countenance runs too much to nose—rude, amorphous nose at that—to be classic, and is withal rugged in

Hopeful Tackett.

outline and pimply in spots. His hair is decidedly too dingy a red to be called, even by the uttermost stretch of courtesy, auburn; dry, coarse, and pertinaciously obstinate in its resistance to the civilizing efforts of comb and brush. But there is a great deal of big, honest bone and muscle in him, which are of great value in a good cause.

By the time he had spelled out the hand-bill, and found that Lieut. —— was in town and wished to enlist recruits for Company —, — Regiment, it was nearly sunset; and he took off his apron, washed his hands, looked at himself in the piece of looking-glass that stuck in the window —a defiant look, that said that he was not afraid of all that nose—took his hat down from its peg behind the door, and in spite of the bristling resistance of his hair, crowded it down over his head, and started for his supper. And as he walked he mused aloud, as was his custom, addressing himself in the second person, as follows:

'Hopeful, what do you think of it? They want more soldiers, eh? Guess them fights at Donelson and Pittsburg Lannen 'bout used up some o' them ridgiments. By Jing! (Hopeful had been piously brought up, and his emphatic declarations took a mild form.) Hopeful, 'xpect you'll have to go an' stan' in some poor feller's shoes. T'won't do for them there blasted Secesh-ers to be killin' off our boys, an' no one there to pay them back. It's time this here thing was busted! Hopeful, you an't pretty, an' you an't smart; but you used to be a mighty nasty hand with a shot gun. Guess you'll have to try your hand on old Borey's (Beauregard's) chaps, an' if you ever git a bead on one, he'll enter his land mighty shortly. What do you say to goin'?—you wanted to go last year, but mother was sick, an' you couldn't; an' now mother's gone to glory, why, show your grit an' go. Think about it, any how.'

And Hopeful did think about it—thought till late at night of the insulted flag, of the fierce fights and glorious victories, of the dead and the dying lying out in the pitiless storm, of the dastardly outrages of the enemy—thought of all this, with his great warm heart overflowing with love for the dear old "Banger," and resolved to go. The next morning he notified the "boss" of his intention to quit his service for that of Uncle Sam. The old fellow only opened his eyes very wide, grunted, brought out the stocking (a striped relic of the departed Frau Kordwaner,) and from it counted out and paid Hopeful every cent that was due him.

But there was one thing that sat heavily upon Hopeful's mind. He was in a predicament that all are liable to fall into—he was in love, and with Christina, Herr Kordwaner's daughter. Christina was a plump maiden, with a round, rosy face, an extensive latitude of shoulders, and a general plentitude and solidity of figure. All these she had; but what had captivated Hopeful's eye was her trim ankle, as it appeared to him one morning, encased in a warm white yarn stocking of her own knitting. From this small beginning, his great heart had taken in the whole of her, and now he was desperately in love. Two or three times he had essayed to tell her of his proposed departure; but every time that the words were coming to his lips, something rushed up into his throat ahead of them, and he couldn't speak. At last, after walking home from church with her one Sunday evening, he held out his hand and blurted out—

"Well, good-bye. We're off to-morrow."

"Off! Where?"

"I've enlisted."

Christina didn't faint. She didn't take out her delicate and daintily perfumed mouchoir to hide the tears that were not there. She looked at him for a moment, while two great real tears rolled down her cheeks, and then—precipitated all her charms right into his arms. Hopeful stood it manfully—rather liked it, in fact. But that is a tableau that may be left to the imagination,—the tears and embraces, protestations of undying affection, promises of eternal remembrance, etc.

The next morning found Hopeful with a dozen others, in charge of the Lieutenant, and on their way to join the regiment, and as he went through the various duties and changing experiences of soldier life he would say, "Hopeful, the Banger's took care of you all your life, and now you're here to take care of it. See that you do it the best you know how." But in his case the path to glory was not amid the roar of cannon and muskets, through a storm of shot and shell, over a serried line of glistening bayonets—it was only a skirmish, a bushwacking fight for the possession of a swamp. A few companies were deployed as skirmishers, to drive out the enemy.

"Now, boys," shouted the Captain, "after 'em! Shoot to kill, not to scare 'em!"

"Ping! Ping!" rang the rifles.

"Z-z-z-z-oit!" sang the bullets.

On they went, crouching among the bushes, creeping along under the banks of the brook, cautiously peering from behind trees in search of "butternuts." Hopeful was in the advance; his hat was lost, and his hair more defiantly bristling than ever. Firmly grasping his rifle, he pushed on, carefully watching every tree and bush. A rebel sharpshooter started to run from one tree to another, when, quick as thought, Hopeful's rifle was at his shoulder, a puff of blue smoke rose from its mouth, and the rebel sprang in the air and fell back—dead. Almost at the same instant, as Hopeful leaned forward to see the effect of his shot, he felt a sudden shock, a sharp burning pain, grasped at a bush, reeled, and sank to the ground.

"Are you hurt much, Hope?" asked one of his comrades, kneeling beside him and staunching the blood that flowed from his wounded leg.

"Yes, I expect I am; but that red warms over yonder's redder'n ever now. That feller won't need a pension."

They carried "Hope" back to the hospital, and the old surgeon looked at the wound, shook his head, and briefly made his prognosis:—

"Bone shattered—vessel injured—bad leg—have to come off. Good constitution, though; he'll stand it."

And he did stand it; always cheerful, never complaining, only regretting that he must be discharged—that he was no longer able to serve his country.

Once more Hopeful is sitting on his little bench in Mynheer Kordwaner's little shop, pegging away at the coarse boots, singing the same glorious prophecy that he was first heard singing. He had but two troubles after his return. One, the lingering regret and restlessness that attend a civil life, after an experience of the rough, independent life in camp. The other trouble was when he first saw Christina after his return. The loving warmth with which she greeted him pained him; and when the worthy Herr considerately went out of the room, leaving them alone, Hopeful relapsed into gloomy silence. At length, speaking rapidly, and with choked utterance, he said :

"Christie, you know I love you now, as I always have, better'n all the world. But I'm a cripple now—no account to nobody —just a dead weight—an' I don't want you, 'cause o' your promise before I went away, to tie yourself to a load that'll be a drag on you all your life. That contract —ah—promise—an't—is—is hereby repealed! There!"

And he leaned his head upon his hands and wept bitter tears, wrung by a great agony from his loving heart.

Christie gently laid her hand upon his shoulder, and spoke, calmly and slowly—

"Hopeful, your soul was in that leg, was it?"

It would seem as if Hopeful had always thought that such was the case, and was just receiving new light upon the subject, he started up so suddenly.

"By Jing! Christie!"

And he grasped her hand, and—but that is also one of those scenes to be left to the imagination. And Christie promised the next Christmas to take the name, as she already had the heart, of Tackett. Herr Kordwaner, too, had come to the conclusion that he wanted a partner, and on the day of the wedding a new sign was to be put up over a new and larger shop, on which "Co." would mean Hopeful Tackett. In the mean time, Hopeful hammered away lustily, merrily, whistling and singing the praises of the "Banger." Occasionally, when resting, he would tenderly embrace his stump of a leg, gently patting and stroking it, and talking to it as to a pet. If a stranger was in the shop, he would hold it out admiringly, and ask:

"Do you know what I call that? I call that '*Hopeful Tackett—his mark!*'"

And a mark of distinction—a badge of patriotism and honor—it might well be called.

### Substitute Broker Sold—"Indians" for the Army.

Along the dock near the foot of First Street, Detroit, is a large wooden figure of an Indian, embellished with all the trappings of a Chippewa chief, and leaning against the warehouse of ———. Well, one day a stranger appeared in front of the provost-marshal's office, and beckoning to one of the substitute brokers hanging around there, said to him, "You are in the substitute business, I believe?" Being answered affirmatively, he continued, "Do you take Indians?" "Oh, yes," said the broker. "Well," inquired the stranger, "what will you give me if I tell you where you can get one, sound in every respect, not liable to draft, and will go as a substitute, if accepted?" "Give you?" replied the broker, every feature in his face beaming with delight at the prospect of making a lucky strike, "give you! why, I'll give you a hundred dollars in greenbacks." "It's a bargain," said the stranger, and here they clasped hands fraternally over it. "Here's my name,' he continued, handing the broker a card, on which was pencilled "Enoch Ketchum." "Take this to ———, near the foot of First street, and tell them that I sent you after *that* Indian; they will understand it; and don't forget the hundred dollars when you get him through." "All right," shouted the broker, as he jumped on board of a street car, on his way to the foot of First street. Having reached the warehouse, he presented his card, and informed the attendants of his mission. "Go right through the back door on to the dock, and turn to the left, and you will find the only Indian that I know anything about in this neighborhood," said the attendant. Having followed directions, he soon came face to face with the Chippewa chief heretofore referred to. Fully realizing the joke which had been played upon him, he went back to the warehouse, and finding the party laughing at his expense, he bawled out: "That was — well done, but that wooden Indian is better than some live men that have gone in as substitutes," and left said dock in a hurry, occasionally casting a furtive glance around to see if any one he knew was interested in the sell.

### Union Recruits among the Negroes.

Some queer things now and then turn up, and the following is a pretty fair sample of the best:

A Tennessee slaveholder from the country approached an old acquaintance, also a slaveholder, residing in Nashville, and said in quite a friendly and confiding manner:

"I have several negro men lurking about this city somewhere. I wish you would look out for them, and when you find them, do with them for me as if they were your own."

"Certainly, I will," replied his friend.

A few days afterward the parties met again, and the planter asked—

"Have you found my slaves?"

"I have."

"And where are they?"

"Well, you told me to do with them just as if they were my own, and, as I made my men enlist in the Union army, I did the same with yours."

The astonished planter thoughtfully absquatulated.

### Putting his Hand to the Roll.

In one of the counties of Indiana a meeting was held by the patriotic citizens, for the purpose of getting volunteers, by the usual means of encouragement and promise. After the matter had progressed some time in the usual manner, a pleasant incident occurred which seemed to warm and gladden every loyal heart. A young lady stepped from the crowd, went up to her betrothed, took him by the hand, and led him up to the stand, where the recruiting officers were taking the names of those who desired to enlist in the service of their country. Having done this, and without seeming in the least abashed in the presence of the large assembly, the fair girl kissed him warmly, and then with her own plighted hand gracefully placed his hand on the roll, for him to sign his name. It was the rarest scene and subject for a painter—a fair and beautiful girl inspiring her lover to go forth to noble deeds for their common country! There was enthusiasm in *that* meeting.

### Beauties of Rebel Conscripting.

Early in the morning of Nov. 6th, 1861, the outside picket belonging to our army at Newport News, on the river, was hailed by a man who approached in a skiff of small size · he proved to be a Virginian, by the name of Peter White, who escaped from a rebel prison at Williamsburg, Va.,

He used to own a little schooner, the Maria Louisa, and traded up and down the James and York rivers, especially during the oyster season. He hardly ever slept on shore, making the schooner his real home, having his wife and two children with him. In April, 1861, when the enlistment in the rebel army was progressing favorably, some one made overtures to White about enlisting. Being at heart a Union man, he did not feel inclined to do so, yet he wished, if possible, to save the schooner and its contents, that being all the property he owned in the world. He therefore ran into a little bay in the Chickahominy river, a small branch of the James, where he found a safe hiding-place. At this time his wife died, and he had a good excuse in the care of his children for refusing to accept the offers of enlistment, which were still occasionally made to him.

He remained at this place until the 9th of September, when he ventured out of his retreat, to go up to Jamestown, hoping that, as the patriotic enthusiasm among the Southerners had considerably died away, he would be granted the necessary pass for following up the oyster business at Hogg's Island. However, poor Peter soon found himself mistaken on this score. The authorities at Jamestown, in pursuance of Governor Letcher's mandates, under confederate law, at once demanded that he should unconditionally enlist in the army, and when he refused to do this they confiscated his schooner with all its contents, including $150 in gold, and sent him as a prisoner to Williamsburg. Here he remained for forty two days, without being once permitted to have a fair hear-

Gov Letcher

ing. He was confined in a cell next to three negroes, who had previously attempted to run away, and with their assistance, a hole was dug sufficiently large, under the wall, to admit one man at a time.

On Thursday evening he made good his escape. That night he walked twelve miles, and during Friday hid himself in a cornfield. Towards midnight he reached the house of Becky Simpson, an old acquaintance of his, and a woman with strong Union feelings, who offered him shelter, and further volunteered to go, on the following Monday, to Williamsburg to endeavor to bring his children back. He consequently remained at her house, purposing to await her return; but on Sunday he saw a certain Mr. Slader, a well known slave hunter in those regions, come towards the house, and knowing that a price of $500 had been put upon his head, he thought it best to 'vamose' as quickly as possible; therefore, when he came in at the front door Peter ran out at the back, and, it being dusk at the time, he safely reached the shore, where he soon found a skiff, and pushed off into the river. In thirty-two hours he rowed between forty and fifty miles.

**Effect of Crinoline on 'Union' Sentiments.**

William Growman, a rebel deserter, who was drafted in Michigan, escaped from the provost-marshal by concealing himself under the crinoline of his intended. After the marshal left, it was hard to persuade the man to run the risk of coming forth

Effect of Crinoline.

from his hiding-place, fearing, so he said, that the officer was still on the look-out for him. But when he did finally emerge from the friendly shelter thus afforded him, he wanted—out of gratitude, probably—to marry the girl on the spot, and did so

## VOLUNTEERING, DRAFTING, DESERTING, ETC.

the next day, after paying his three hundred dollars commutation. He thus, at least in a constructive sense, proved himself a prompt 'Union' man.

#### Married Applicants for Exemption.

*Commissioner.*—"What have you to say?"

*Applicant.*—"I'm forty-eight years old."

"Where were you born?"

"Don't know."

"How old were you when you came to this country?"

"Don't know."

"How do you know you are forty-eight years old?"

"I know it. I'm sure of it."

The Commissioner, after various ineffectual trials to make applicant show what reasons he had for his belief, now asks, "Are you married?"

(Applicant very sulky, but no answer.)

"I asked you if you are married. Did you hear?"

"I don't wish to be insulted."

"No one wishes to insult you. Are you married?"

Applicant, in a very loud voice,—"Of course I am!"

#### No Appeal Left.

At Newport, R. I., on mustering in the new companies for military service, several minors were finally rejected, because they did not produce the certificate of consent from their parents. One young man—his mother a widow—had first enlisted and then went to his mother with a certificate for her signature. But she, not being willing for him to go, withheld her consent, yet finally, after much persuasion, said she would agree to do it on one condition, namely, that her son should thrust his finger at random through the leaves of the closed Bible, and the language of the text upon which it rested should decide her action in the matter. He did as she requested, and his finger, when the Bible was opened, was found resting over the two following verses: 2d book of Chronicles, 20th chapter, 16th and 17th verses: "To-morrow go ye down against them: behold they come up by the cliff of Ziz; and ye shall find them at the edge of the brook before the wilderness of Jeruel. Ye shall not need to fight in this battle; set yourselves, stand ye still, and see the salvation of the lord with you. O, Judah and Jerusalem: fear not, nor be dismayed; to-morrow go out against them; for the Lord will be with you." The thing was settled—the mother consented. There was no appeal from the very pointed text which had been resorted to as the arbiter.

#### Enlistment of Stonewall Jackson in the Union Army.

One morning, a young farmer from Ogdensburg, N. Y., applied at the recruiting office in Brooklyn for a place in the Union ranks. The attending surgeon gave a favorable opinion of applicant's physique and he was accepted. When asked to sign his name he wrote, in very legible characters, "Stonewall Jackson." The commissioner very naturally asked him, on seeing the signa-

Stonewall Jackson

ture, if that was really his name. "Everybody asks me that question," said the young volunteer; "it riles my blood. It *is* my name, and I mean to let the rebels know that there is a Stonewall Jackson North." We would like to adorn these pages with a likeness of that noble youth, side by side with that of his epauleted but treacherous namesake who threw away his valuable life in so ignoble a cause.

#### Commissioner Deciding a Question of Age.

*Commissioner*, (a young lawyer, looking very grave and dignified): "Well, Sir, how do you claim to be an exempt?"

*Applicant*, (an Irishman, in the prime of life, with a bewildered look): "I am forty-six years old."

"Where were you born?"

"Don't know."

"How old were you, when you left Ireland?"

"By Gorra, I don't know."

"How do you know you are forty-six years old?"

"I am grandfather of four children."

"I don't see what that has to do with your age."

"By Gorra, I believe you don't know much about it (eyeing the Commissioner contemptuously, as if he were a boy)."

#### Billy Wilson's Zouaves—Extraordinary Scene.

Billy Wilson's Zouaves composed a regiment made up from what are called the "Roughs" or "B'hoys," of New York city, and were formally mustered at Tammany Hall, the evening before their departure for their encampment at Staten Island. On this occasion the following extraordinary scene was enacted:

The men were ranged round the hall three deep, with Colonel Wilson and the other officers in the centre of the room. The men had all clad themselves in the gray shirts and pantaloons which had been provided for their uniform, and which was completed by a common brown felt hat, brogans and leather belt. They carried a short knife, about seven inches in length, between a sort of bowie knife and butcher knife in shape. Many also had revolvers, —one or two being intended for the arms of each man, as well as a slung shot and a Minie rifle.

All the men being ranged against the walls, Colonel Wilson, with a drawn sabre in one hand and an American flag in the other, stood forth uncovered, and addressed his men amidst deafening cheers. After a short adjuration to the flag, for which he declared his devotion, he called upon all to kneel and swear with him. Waving the banner and flourishing his sabre, he knelt on one knee. All present knelt with him and repeated the oath which he put to them to support the flag, and never flinch from its path through blood or death. He said he would lead them to Baltimore, and they would march through it or die; at which they all arose with a tremendous yell, flung up their hats, and brandished their glittering knives, amidst prolonged

Colonel Wilson.

and frantic cheers. He then denounced death to the Baltimore traitor secessionists and Plug Uglies, and said they would leave a monument of their bones in the streets of Baltimore. Amid yells of "Death to the Plug Uglies!" he said, though he might be the first man slain, he had but one thing to ask, which was that each one of his followers should secure his man and avenge his blood. That they would do so, he again called upon them to swear, and marched around the hall holding up the flag and his sword, and accompanied by two officers, the one on the right bearing a banner inscribed—"THE UNION BATTALION OF ZOUAVES: DEATH

TO SECESSIONISTS!"—while the other officer, on his left, held up, in both hands, a bowie knife and revolver. Wilson shouted to them to swear, and they responded with shouts of "Blood!" "Blood!" "Blood!" "We swear!"

### Governor Tod and the Applicant for Exemption.

A good thing is told of Governor Tod, of Ohio, whose labor in the great work of suppressing the rebellion may be characterized as of the heartiest and most telling character. An old lady, between fifty and sixty years of age, entered the Governor's office, and made an effort to induce that personage to exempt her husband from the draft. Mr. Tod looked at her an instant and exclaimed,

"Why, the old gentleman *is* exempt, isn't he?"

"Ah, but he ar'nt an old gentleman," added the applicant, "he's only 35!"

"In that case," said the Governor, "I can't do anything for *him*, but I'll tell you what I'll do for you; in case he's drafted and gets killed,—I'll marry you myself."

This seemed to satisfy the old lady, and she accordingly departed.

### Quite the Youngest Recruit for Uncle Sam.

One of the principal recruiting factories was once on a time enlivened by one of those amusing episodes which help the appetite and spirits.

"So, Sir, you've clapped your dirty sojer trappings on my husband, have you?"

"Who is your husband?" asked the officer.

"Billy McCurtee, an' shure, an' a bould boy he is, so plaze ye. But it's a dirty thing of ye, my pretty man, to take him from his wife an' childers."

"Can't be helped," said the officer; "it's too late now."

"Then take the baby, too," she cried, as she forced the little one into the arms of Lieutenant Adams: "Take them all— I'll send ye four more to-day."

Off she ran at a rapid pace, leaving the

Quite the youngest recruit for Uncle Sam.

unfortunate officer with the squirming and squalling recruit in his arms. Doubtful of its services to Uncle Sam, he sent it home by its father.

### Happy Ending to a Sad Mistake.

One day, during the stringent pressure for men to fill the ranks and the rigid activity to prevent the draft being baulked, Captain Maddox, of Brooklyn, New York, sent a provost guard to arrest a German, a deserter, whose name sounded very much like Ferral, and who was at work somewhere in South Second street, near the residence of Mr. John Ferral. The guard took it for granted that Mr. Ferral was the man they had been sent to take into their custody, and straightway made known to him that his bodily presence was required at the office of the Provost-Marshal. Mr. Ferral, who was just in the act of sitting down to a most toothsome dinner, which it seems had been prepared with especial pains, "didn't see it;" he thought there must be a mistake or a joke somewhere. He was told that it was sober earnest. Then he said he would see Mr. Maddox very cheerfully, but—he must see his dinner first. But the guard's instructions were positive, and nothing would do but that Mr. F. should go forthwith. So he was duly marched off, according to the manner provided for deserters and similar culprits, between two muskets, down to the office of Captain Maddox, of whom he demanded an explanation. said, "You will pass, Sir; a dollar, if you please." "But, doctor," said the man, "let me run down stairs once more, and then try me." The doctor said "Oh, yes;" the man ran down stairs again, but this time with such increased velocity that he forgot to come back.

Drafting Scene.

The Captain was much amused at the mistake, which he explained to Mr. F. The latter couldn't see the joke of the thing, but concluded to make the best of it, and a hearty "smile" all round rectified everything, even to the loss of a good dinner,—or rather it was worth the loss of that savory meal to have the matter turn out a mistake instead of a reality, in those times.

### Unintentional Trick taught by an Examining Physician.

An applicant for exemption in one of our towns, on account of physical disability, informed the examining physician that he was troubled with heart disease. The doctor told him to run up and down the stairs leading to his office once or twice. This the applicant did, when the physician, after listening to the motions of the heart,

### Western Zeal in Volunteering.

Soon after the formation of Camp Morton, in Indiana, an old man of sixty years of age, with gray hair and flowing white beard, presented himself at head-quarters, full of the fire of patriotism, and offered himself as a volunteer soldier in defence of his country's flag. The officer in command was obliged, however, to refuse the old patriot's offer, on account of his advanced age; whereupon, quick as thought, he went to a barber's, had his beard cropped, and his hair and beard dyed, and again applied for admission to the coveted ranks of his country's defenders. Not being detected, he was at once received, and being asked his age, for enrolment, modestly replied, "*Rising* thirty-five." At the same camp might have been seen a young man on horseback, looking wishfully upon the scene before him. Speaking to the crowd he said: "If I could only dispose of my wife and children, I'd go in a minute." A gentleman who knew him well stepped up and said, "I'll look after them!" "Hold my horse," cried the other, and with one bound he was in the camp, and a volunteer.

**Wisconsin Body-Guard for the President.**

"Brick" Pomeroy, an editor—and wag—in La Crosse, Wisconsin, on being invited to assist in forming a body guard for President Lincoln, after due consideration decided to "go in," provided the following basis could be adopted and rigidly adhered to throughout the war.

The company shall be entirely composed of colonels, who shall draw pay and rations in advance.

Every man shall have a commission, two servants, and white kids.

Each man shall be mounted in a covered buggy, drawn by two white stallions.

Under the seat of each buggy shall be a cupboard, containing cold chicken, pounded ice, and champagne, *a la* members of Congress and military officers at Bull Run.

Each man shall have plenty of cards and red chips to play poker with.

The only side-arms to be opera glasses, champagne glasses, and gold-headed canes.

The duty of the company shall be to take observations of battle, and on no account shall it be allowed to approach nearer than ten miles to the seat of war.

Behind each buggy shall be an ambulance, so arranged as to be converted into a first-class boarding house in the daytime, and a sumptuous sleeping and dressing room at night.

The regimental band must be composed of pianos and guitars, played by young ladies, who shall never play a quickstep except in case of retreat.

Reveille shall not be sounded till late breakfast time, and not then if any one of the regiment has a headache.

In case of a forced march into an enemy's country, two miles a week shall be the maximum, and no marches shall be made except the country abound in game, or if any member of the regiment object.

Kid gloves, gold toothpicks, cologne, hair-dressing, silk underclothes, cosmetics, and all other rations, to be furnished by the Government.

Each member of the regiment shall be allowed a reporter for some New York paper, who shall draw a salary of two hundred dollars a week, for puffs, from the incidental fund.

Every member shall be in command, and when one is promoted all are to be. Commissions never to be revoked.

**Rejected because he could not Fight.**

James Leonard, of Upper Gilmanton, N. H., who had been rejected as a volunteer on account of his being over forty-five years of age, thus expressed his views of his own case and the *et ceteras* pertaining thereto:—

"After accepting several men over forty-five years of age, and several *infants*, such as a man like me could whip a dozen of, I was rejected because I had the honesty to acknowledge I was more than forty-five years of age. The mustering-officer was a very good-looking man, about thirty-five years old, but I guess I can run faster and jump higher than he; also take him down, whip him, endure more hardships, and kill three rebels to his one."

Poor Jeems *ought* to have been allowed the chance of trying his hand—at least on the last-mentioned class.

**Mrs. Smith's Husband to be Exchanged.**

At the battle of Ball's Bluff, one of the gallant boys of the Twentieth Massachusetts regiment was taken prisoner, and confined with many others at Salisbury, N. C. His name was—say Tom Smith—and he had a wife and children living not a thousand miles from New Bedford. When it became pretty certain that there

188    THE BOOK OF ANECDOTES OF THE REBELLION.

would be a general exchange of prisoners, some kind friend, desirous of relieving the terrible anxiety of the wife, called and informed Mrs. Smith that her husband would probably be exchanged. "Well," said the lonely woman, "I love Tom, and —the children love Tom, and I don't want him exchanged. *I won't have a rebel husband, so now.*" The poor woman thought the exchange was a swap, and that she was to have some chap from the South in lieu of her real husband. Tom, however, reached home by-and-by, to the great delight of Mrs. S., who was afraid that exchange, in this case, was to prove robbery —and worse than that

### A Mother Puts Out the Eyes of her own Son to keep him from the War.

A deed to make humanity shudder was enacted in the neighborhood of Terre Haute, in connection with the drafting of recruits for the army. Mrs. John Eastwick, the wife of a respectable farmer, was the mother of seven children, all boys. In the early part of the war, two of these enlisted and served with General Buell in Kentucky. One of them, the eldest, Ezra, died of exposure in camp, and his brother Thomas soon after suffered an amputation of the right leg, from injuries received in a cavalry skirmish. These casualties operated upon Mrs. Eastwick's mind to such a degree that she lost all fortitude and presence of mind, and sat during whole days weeping and full of forebodings. Among her premonitions was a curious one, namely, that her third son, Stark, would also die in battle. As the war advanced and conscription began, Mrs. Eastwick's fear on this point grew intense.

Finally, the first draft came; the State had filled its quota in almost every district, and Stark promised his mother that, under no circumstances, would he go to the field. But a second draft being projected, the mother's fears and excitement augmented. She endeavored to persuade her son to leave the country and make a voyage to sea. He endeavored to pacify her, and left home for a time. On his return, finding her in the same melancholy frame of mind, he threatened, in jest, that if she made further reference to the matter, he would enlist voluntarily.

Mrs. Eastwick, doubtless laboring under some hallucination, or uncontrollable operation of her mind, seems now to have resolved upon the sad act of mutilating her son in such a manner as to prevent his being accepted for military service, whether as a volunteer or conscript. She deliberately pressed a burning coal upon his right eye, while he slept upon a lounge, and the optic nerve was thus destroyed with but a momentary pang of pain to poor Stark. He became entirely blind. It may well be supposed that this unfortunate issue from her fears did not contribute to the mother's peace of mind. On the contrary, insanity took hold upon her, her sane moments being marked with melancholy regret at her frenzied act.

### My Gift to My Country.

From more than one heart—yea, from multitudes—came forth the same sweet, sad sentiments of domestic love mingled with patriotic self-sacrifice, which utter themselves so earnestly in the following sentences:—

It was little more than three years ago that I met him for the first time. Alike in thought, feeling and action, we seemed exactly united to each other; at least, *we* thought so; and hope painted the future with roseate hues. Our home might be an humble one, but love and confidence, with a mutual trust in our Heavenly Father, and each other, would well make up for the lack of worldly fortune; and many a bright hour did we spend together, dreaming fairy dreams of the future. But, thank God, we did not set our hearts upon them, for both of us had learned to say, "Thy will be done!" Together we studied God's holy word, and "walked to the house of God in company"; together we courted the society of the Muses, and many a glad hour have we passed writing for each other. He was *everything* to me! Many friends are very, *very* dear, but none can fill *his* place! IT IS VACANT NOW.

It was a beautiful summer evening, nearly midnight; the moon sailed majestically overhead, and seemed to look laughingly down upon us, as, arm in arm, we wended our way home from spending the evening with a friend; but my heart was very heavy, for the call for six hundred thousand more soldiers had just been made, and we had been speaking of a draft. My only brother is not a Christian, and it lay heavy on my heart that perhaps he might be taken from us, and die without hope. I said some such words, and he (I cannot write the familiar name yet), drew me closer to him, and said earnestly, "If the draft comes, I will go instead of Ben."

The draft did *not* come, for bravely, and of their own free wills, the sons of New Jersey responded to the call of their President, and hundreds left their pleasant homes to go forth boldly and fight the battles of their country. Oh, methinks I can still see his proud, elastic step; still feel the pressure of his warm hand as we said our last good-bye; still see the dear form as he rose in the stern of the boat to call it yet once more to the sad little group on the shore; still see the boat dwindling in the mist as it bears him away from me forever —*the gift I gave my country!* O, Fredericksburg! thou that didst drink the blood of my cherished one!

They have laid him to rest near Falmouth; but *he* is not there. Sometimes in the shadowy twilight, I feel him near me, and he seems to whisper sweet thoughts of *another* meeting. I can not see him, but I feel his presence. When I speak his name it dies in a hollow echo; but I *know* he hears it, and will some day answer. *My gift to my country*—I gave thee freely! Heaven has accepted the sacrifice! We'll meet again—ah, yes!

### Gottlieb Klobbergoss on the Draft.

I dink muchs about de war und de draft, und de rebils, und all about dese dings. I dinks about 'em more as about anyding else. Sometimes I sets mits myself all day on de front stoop, und schmokes, und drinks hard cider, und does noting else only drink; den my vife she gifs me de teufel for drinkin so much, und ses I vas petter go und see atter Jacop, our hired man, und not bodder my head mit more as I can understood. But I tells her what shall vomens know about war? better she goes und mindts her own piseness. I drubles myself more about Abraham as about Jacop.

Ven I gits tired mit drinkin on my own stoop, I goes down to Hans Butterfoos's tavern, und I drinks dere, und I tells my obinion, und some oder one tells his obinion, und we makes him out togedder. De oder day begins de draft. Dat lodders me agin. Some goes in for de draft, mostly dem as is too olt, und von't be took demself; some goes agin de draft; und some don't know vich vay to goes, but ony goes roundt und roundt, und gits boddered like dam so as I do.

But, nefer mind, I dinks I must find dis ding out, und down I goes to Hans Butterfoos und hears de fellers blo. I don't make notin mit dat; dey all blos some uder vay, und I don't dink dey hef him rite in dere own mind to. So I begins und asks a questchun; und I ses to Bill Puffenshtock:

"Vot you dinks von de draft, dat it is rite?"

And ses Bill: "No, I dinks et ain't rite."

Vell, I don't believes him, caus he sheated me vonce mit a plind mare he sells on me. So I dries agin und shpeaks mit Fritz Hoerkenshphicer.

"Vot you dinks von de draft, Frith, ef it's rite or not?"

And Fritz, he ses, dat he "Dinks it is shust so as it ought to be."

But I don't believes him neder, 'cause

he run'd aginst me last year for de peace of shustice, und dey makes him de peace —dat is de shustice. Und he is no more good for shquire as my old cat. So I gifs up askin somebody, und makes him out myself. I dinks in dis shtyle; de reason dey go mid de draft, is becos dey want sojers. Ef dey don't git no sojers den dey can't bring on de war. Ef dey don't bring on de war den dey don't licks de rebils. Ef dey don't licks de rebils, den de rebels licks dem. Ef de rebils licks dem den we all go to ter tuyfel. Dat's pooty straight. So much.

Now I must dink of some more; vot is de next ding? I dink dat's all rite; but now I shtops, someding else comes doe. Let me sees. Oh, yes; dry hunderd tollars—dat's de ding—dey all blos about de dry hunderd tollars. I dinks so myself. Dry hunderd tollars don't licks de r'bils no more as dry hunderd cenths. Vot's de goot mit tollars? Petter a good shmart sojer, like my Shorge, he licks de rebils more tan shix hunderd tollars, yes. Now, I know more as Bill Puffershtock und Fritz Hockenshplicer, both togedder. We want de *sojers*, not de tollars. Dat's where de bodder is. We pooty soon makes money enuff; but paper sojers is ony goot mit wooden guns, so when de draft comes und ven men ses, "here is dry hunderd tollars," I shtays behindt und dont fight de rebils, den if I was de draft I takes dat man by his preeches und I ses, "Go to ter tuyfel mit your tollars und come along mit me like some oder man as has got no tollars und don't like to go sojerin so bad as not you do," den pooty soon I gits so much as I vants; dat's my ideas. I tells my olt voman, if dey drafts me I goes myself. To be sure, I don't dink dey will, 'cause I am more as fiwfty years; but nefer mindt. I should go a long while, like my Shorge, ony deres two dings I don't like, und one is de marshin und de oder is de fitin. I sooner marshes down to Hans Butterfoos und fites dere. Ef Sheff Davis comes dere on me, I gifs him dam, you petter had believe; but ef I goes to Richmond, may be Sheff Davis gifs me dam. So onyhow, I shtays home. De oder day, my Shorge he comes back mit a furlow. He is so much a corporal as ever he vas, und I shpeaks mit him about dese dings, und I gifs you now what he ses:

"Shorge," I asks him, "you've bin mit de rebils und mit de army, und mit Olt Abe, und dese fellers; vat you dinks von dis draft dat all de beeples blos about?"

Und he ses to me, "Oh, tunder!"

Well, dats his obinions. May be he shall know somedings to. He's pooty shmart sence he goes for a sojer. He shwears like a man shix foots high, und calls mudder "olt voman," und he calls me "cap," and he kisses de ghals, und he calls Jacop "dam phool." I dinks he gits some high offis before de war is gone.

GOTTLIEB KLOBBERGOSS.

### Quid Pro Quo.

Before the close of the "peace" interview between President Lincoln and the three Richmond Commissioners, in February, 1865, "Vice President" Stephens spoke to President Lincoln on the subject of the exchange of prisoners, and asked him what was proposed to be done in the matter. The President replied that every thing connected with that subject had been confided to the care of General Grant, and that all information must come from him, through the regularly established channels of communication. Mr. Stephens then said he had a favor to ask of Mr. Lincoln, and which, if he could grant, he would esteem a personal obligation. The President, of course, inquired what the favor was. Mr. Stephens said it was in reference to a nephew of his who had been taken prisoner some time ago, and still continued in the North. His desire was to have him released.

"Well," said Mr. Lincoln, after a little reflection, "I don't think I have the power to do that; but I will give you a note to

General Grant, who will, no doubt, do all he can to oblige you. But, by the way," he added, "there is, I believe, a young man, a Union Lieutenant, in one of your prisons in the South, of about the same rank as the young man you wish to get released. If you will try and get him out of prison I will use my influence for the liberation of your nephew, and they can be easily exchanged one for the other."

Mr. Stephens asked the name of the young Lieutenant, and, on being informed, borrowed a pencil, and, tearing a slip of paper, took a note of it, saying that he would do what he could in the matter.

"Very well," said Old Abe; "send him to us, and your nephew shall go down to you."

## "I've Enlisted, Sir."

A wealthy citizen of Philadelphia had been supplied with butter twice a week by a young farmer living on the edge of Philadelphia county. He came on one of his usual days to the house with his butter, received his pay, and then asked for a brief interview with the head of the household. The gentleman complied with the request thus made, and the young agriculturalist was duly ushered into the parlor.

"I just wished to thank you, Sir, for your custom for these three years, and to say that after to-day I can not longer serve you."

"I'm sorry for that. Your butter and eggs have always been very fine. What's the matter?"

"I've enlisted, Sir."

"Enlisted?"

"Yes, Sir. A mortgage of eleven hundred dollars has been hanging over my place. I purchased it from a lady— Mrs. B."

"Yes. I know her very well."

"Well, Sir, she holds the mortgage. She offered, last Saturday, if I would enlist as a representative substitute for her, and transfer my bounty to her, she would cancel the mortgage and present my wife with two hundred and fifty dollars in greenbacks."

"And you accepted the offer?"

"Indeed I did, most gladly. I go for one year. I come back with a farm clear of incumbrance. My wife and boy can take care of it for a year. My pay will keep me, and my family can live without me for at least that time. Besides, I am glad to go. I wanted to go all along, but couldn't leave my folks."

"And you are glad to go!"

"Indeed I am. I feel just as contented and free from care as my red cow when Sally is milking her. If I can be with Grant when he goes into Richmond, it will be the very happiest day of my life."

## Representative Recruit for President Lincoln.

President Lincoln caused himself to be represented in the great army of which, by virtue of his office, he was Commander-in-Chief, by obtaining a recruit—Mr. John S. Staples. Mr. S., arrayed in the uniform of the United States army, and accompanied by General Fry, Provost-Marshal-General, Mr. N. D. Larner, of the Third Ward, Washington, and the recruit's father, was taken to the Executive Mansion, where he was received by President Lincoln. General Fry introduced him by saying: "Mr. President, this is the man who is to represent you in the army for the next year." Mr. Lincoln shook hands heartily with Mr. Staples, remarked that he was a good-looking, stout and healthy-appearing man, and believed he would do his duty. He asked Staples if he had been mustered in, and he replied that he had. Mr. Larner then presented the President with a framed official notice of the fact that he had put in a representative recruit, and the President again shook hands with Staples, expressing to him his kind personal

192    THE BOOK OF ANECDOTES OF THE REBELLION.

regard, and the hope that he would be one of the fortunate ones in the conflict in which he had entered.

### Cheers and a Tiger for Harry Bumm.

There was at one time a hitch in the management of affairs in Philadelphia, producing difficulty and delay in paying out bounties to the fresh volunteers. Besides, there was no very great amount of money to be found in the treasury. On the whole, the duties of Mr. Henry Bumm, the popular treasurer of the Quaker City, were more difficult than those of any previous incumbent of the office. Under these circumstances, Captain Cameron, with a hundred and seventy-five recruits, marched one day to Mr. Bumm's office to draw their bounty. The aggregate was a large sum. The treasury was something like the Susquehanna at low water—its bottom was plainly visible. Mr. Bumm, however, did not keep the gallant boys waiting. They stepped up, one by one, and received their emerald-backed portraits of Secretary Chase. When all had been paid, a color-sergeant stepped forward and called "Three cheers for City Treasurer, Mr. Harry Bumm." All mouths opened, and the cheers were given loudly and lustily. This done, Captain Cameron said, "Boys, three more, if you like." The three more were given, when all hands put in the largest "tiger" seen since Van Amburg's caravan left Philadelphia. The men then formed into line, giving another *feu de joie* of cheers as they moved off.

### Deserting a Bad Cause.

Lieutenant Foster, of the Third Maine Heavy Artillery, arrived at Philadelphia with forty rebels who had taken the oath of allegiance to the Union. One of these had one thousand dollars in genuine Confederate scrip, of one hundred dollars each. He supposed they were worth nothing in Philadelphia, and on being told that possibly some of the sympathizers of the South, in that city, might buy them, he replied that of all classes of people they were the worst, and should receive merited condemnation. He was asked what he did for a living before the war broke out. He replied that he was a clerk at Atlanta, Georgia. He was then told—

"Perhaps you can get a clerkship in Philadelphia." At this, he looked thoughtfully for a moment, and then said,

"No, no; do you think any sensible man would trust me with his business affairs, believing that I am a *deserter?* I have deserted the Confederate army; most of us have done the same thing. If I can get work at laboring, I shall be satisfied. I want to go to some remote place, where I shall never hear the word 'war' mentioned."

"Could you make yourself useful on a farm?" interrupted an elderly man from New Jersey.

"Yes Sir," replied the rebel oath-taker.

"I will give you plenty to do," responded the farmer, "get into my wagon."

The repentant got into the wagon, and was soon on the sandy soil of New Jersey.

### Equal to the Emergency.

Secretary Stanton is stated to have settled a little point with the President of the Baltimore and Ohio Railroad, as follows:

President—The draft has fallen with great severity upon the employees of our company.

Stanton—Indeed!

President—If something is not done to relieve us, it is hard to foresee the consequences.

Stanton—Let them pay the commutation.

President—Impossible! The men can't stand such a tax.

Stanton—They have a rich company at their back, and that's more than other people have.

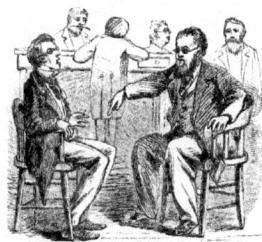

Equal to the Emergency.

President—They ought to be exempted, because they are necessary to the working of the road for the Government.

Stanton—That can't be.

President—Then I will stop the road.

Stanton—If you do, I will take it up and carry it on.

The discussion is said to have been dropped at this point, and the very worthy president still worked the road as successfully as ever.

### Anglo-African Daughter of the Regiment.

While the Twelfth Rhode Island regiment was on duty in the town of Lancaster, Kentucky, a chubby young Anglo-African, answering to the name of Tommy, came into camp, and desired to enter the service of some one of Uncle Sam's officers, and was taken by one of the Captains as a body-servant. In this capacity the fugitive followed the regiment through all the experiences and vicissitudes of the campaign, and then home to Rhode Island, always faithful, attentive, cheerful. But the refinements of civilized life were too much for Tommy, and the Captain's body servant proved to be a veritable daughter of the regiment,—a *bona fide* girl of less than twenty summers,—who had been able, during all the period of her military service, successfully to conceal her sex in the guise of a boy.

### Yankee Forever!

Colonel Lawson, like every other loyal prisoner in the hands of the rebels, was not unwilling to accept the privilege of parole in lieu of a dose of cold lead. The Colonel was taken prisoner by a gang of Missouri guerillas, who at first proposed a little target practice upon him with their rifles, but at last concluded to let him off on his parole. Upon investigation, however, it proved that of the rebels who then had him in charge—about a dozen—not one could write a parole, nor any thing else. Through their whole youth they had never been subjected to the pernicious influence of free schools. At last they requested Colonel Lawson himself to make out the parole and sign it. He immediately wrote an agreement, solemnly pledging himself never to take up arms against *the United States of America*, or in any way give aid and comfort to their enemies,—signed it, and was set at liberty. He made the best of his way to our lines, and was not overtaken.

### Mr. S., the Countryman, and his Substitute.

During the drafting time in New York, a Mr. S., from Putnam County, arrived in New York city full of hope, and eager in pursuit of a good substitute to take his place in the army, and four hundred dollars in his pocket to pay for him. Of course he did not call at the rooms of the Supervisors' Committee. Had he done so he would have been made by Mr. Blunt a wiser, if not a better, man, and also saved his money. But he preferred going into the street, into the highways and byways, and through an 'honest' agent or broker succeeded in a way not altogether agreeable. The active and persevering agent whom S. secured to aid him, soon found a capital fellow—strong, hale and hearty, and an alien—just what he wanted, and moreover named Stander—a good name, under the circumstances.

The agent did all the business for S., made his own bargain with Stander, and received from S. four hundred dollars in cash. How much of this the substitute was to receive was a secret between him and the agent.

S. was delighted. He took possession of his substitute and started in the first train for Putnam County; but before he reached the Provost-Marshal's office there was a sergeant of marines after him, who, notwithstanding the remonstrances of S., took him by force of arms, and conveyed him back to New York and to the naval rendezvous, where he had already enlisted for the navy. S. was of course disconsolate. He had lost his substitute, lost his four hundred dollars, and lost sight of the agent who had fleeced him. Neither knew he of his whereabouts, or even his name. All was gone, and he had nothing to do but to cast about for another substitute or go into the ranks himself.

#### Cause for Rejecting a Recruit.

One of the recruiting agents in the city of New York carried a finely proportioned man to the surgeon for examination, telling the man to return to the ward room as soon as he had been passed. In due time the man arrived at official head-quarters, bringing his own rejection. There was indignation among the recruiting committee, who immediately began to feel of the muscles of this really promising specimen of a man, and point out the beauties of his structure. Loud were the complaints and bitter their denunciations of Dr. H—, and what overt act they might have committed it would be impossible to tell, had not a bystander asked the man what *cause* the Doctor gave for rejecting him. "Well, I believe," calmly replied the man, "that he said I had the itch." The wardroom was clear in a moment—muscle-feelers and all.

#### Rebuff to a Trafficker in Exemption Papers.

At Plattsburgh, New York, while the drafting was going on, a man of no very great loyal pretensions called on a widow and informed her that her only son was drafted, and then hastened to assure her that he could secure his exemption if she would certify that she was a widow, and that he was her only son, upon whom she made her dependence for support. The patriotic lady made the following Spartan reply to the mercenary: "I can certify to no such thing. I am *not* dependent on my son for support, and I never expect to be. Besides, I think he ought to go, if he is able to perform military duty, and so ought every other able-bodied man, till this wicked rebellion is put down. Nothing but the necessity of wearing these skirts has kept me from going." And the patriotic trafficker in white-livered merchandize evaporated.

#### Puzzling a Draft Commissioner.

Commissioner: "Well, young man, have you come to volunteer?"

Applicant—a bright French boy of nineteen: "No, Sir; I'm exempt. I am not a citizen—I am a French subject." (Handing to the Commissioner the certificate of such fact, signed by the French Consul.)

Commissioner: "You speak English well. Where were you born?"

Applicant: "In New York, Sir."

Commissioner: "Then you are an American citizen."

Applicant: "No, Sir; I am not."

Commissioner: "Why not?"

Applicant: "My father was naturalized before I was born."

Commissioner: "Well, what has that to do with making you a French subject?"

Applicant: "Why, when he was naturalized, *I was not in the country.*"

#### Fightin' ober a Bone.

The following dialogue actually took place in war times, between a guest at one of our metropolitan hotels and a sable waiter connected with the establishment:

Guest: "Well, Jim, you are going to join a colored regiment at once, I suppose?"

Jim: "Me, Massa? O no, me nebber tink ob it at all."

Guest: "Never thought of it? I am surprised! I supposed all your people would embrace the first opportunity to take up arms eagerly. But *why* are you not going to fight?"

Jim: "Well, Massa, I tell yer. Did yer ebber see two dogs fightin' ober a bone?"

Guest: "Yes, of course; but what has that to do with it?"

Jim: "Why, don't yer see, Massa? de *bone* nebber fight; de bone take no part in de conflic'. *De Norf an' Souf are de two dogs fightin' ober a bone; we niggers are de bone; we don't take no part in de conflic'!*"

Fightin' ober a Bone.

### Queer Drafting in Maryland.

The enrolling officer for Salisbury District, Maryland, was very active and thorough in the performance of his duties. One day he went to the house of a countryman, and finding none of the male members of the family at home, made inquiry of an old woman about the number and age of the "males" of the family. After naming several, the old lady stopped. "Is there *no one else*?" asked the officer. "No," replied the woman, "none, except Billy Bray." "Billy Bray! where is he?" "He was at the barn a moment ago," said the old lady. Out went the officer, but could not find the *man*. Coming back, the worthy officer questioned the old lady as to the age of Billy, and went away, after enrolling his name among those to be drafted. The time of the drafting came, and among those on whom the lot fell was the veritable Billy Bray. No one knew him. Where did he live? The officer who enrolled him was called on to produce him; and, lo and behold, Billy Bray was a *Jackass* (not a human one, like the enroller, but with four genuine legs and ears of the usual length) —regularly recorded on the list of drafted men as forming one of the quota of Maryland.

### Complimentary Salutations to his General.

The Thirty-eighth Ohio Regiment once on a time went home as veterans. They obtained many recruits, among whom was a young man recruited in Dayton. He was paid the usual Government and local bounties, dressed out in a suit of blue, and after a good time on furlough, returned to the front. On Saturday his Regiment was on picket, and our new recruit was put on an outpost, as he was rather a sharp fellow. Soon, however, he was missed, and it was found he had deserted to the enemy. In a short time, nothing more was thought of it. The matter was somewhat revived, however, when, with the flag of truce that subsequently came in, there were brought, among other things, the compliments of Captain ——, late of Johnson's Island, to General Baird. He was one of the escaped prisoners, who had taken this means of again getting among his friends in Dixie. He was also too well posted not to be able to give the rebels almost as much valuable information as they could obtain from a northern newspaper.

196  THE BOOK OF ANECDOTES OF THE REBELLION.

### Indiana Volunteer Ninety-two Years Old.

Indiana has accorded to her the honor of furnishing the oldest volunteer of any State in the Union. Mr. Bates, of Pendleton, *ninety-two years old*, volunteered with a company from Madison County, and went into Camp Morton on Saturday, full of patriotic fire. Of course he was rejected, on account of age. When asked why he volunteered, he replied that he wanted to show the young men that old men were not afraid to fight, and expressed his determination to remain with the company, if permitted to do so. Men ninety-two years old are seldom to be found in these days, and especially in a military camp. Mr. Bates is said to be the father of twenty-two children. No wonder that he feels some interest in preserving the nation from destruction.

### Deaf and Dumb Soldier.

Connected with the Springfield City Guard, Captain Lombard, Tenth regiment of Massachusetts volunteers, stationed at Camp Brightwood, Virginia, was a deaf mute, named John Donovan, who was a regularly enlisted soldier, and detailed as the regimental tailor. He learned the trade of tailor in Brooklyn, N. Y. He went to Springfield, Massachusetts, from which city he enlisted at the commencement of the rebellion. His infirmity, of course, precluded him from performing the ordinary military duties of a soldier; and, being employed as the regimental tailor, he had many leisure moments, which he improved by the practice of a natural gift for drawing. In that art he was a self-taught man, and in it he attained a truly astonishing degree of proficiency. An accurate draft of Camp Brightwood was made by him, and subsequently lithographed. John was always spoken of in the highest terms of praise by the officers of his regiment, and, notwithstanding his infirmity, was fully equal, bodily and mentally, to the rank and file of the grand army of the Union.

### Donning the Breeches.

In Clinton county, Ohio, there is a certain township, Richland, which, at the opening period or year of the war, had not, it would seem, raised a very large crop of patriotic young men,—judging from the proceedings of a meeting of irate females held there to consider the call made upon the country for troops. It was stated that not more than two volunteers had been furnished by the township up to that time, and the resolutions adopted and the speeches made at the meeting referred to, not only called the patriotism but the courage of the men of Richland in question. So stung were the female population by what they termed the disgraceful and unmasculine spirit manifested by the male population—the young men, especially,—that seven young ladies, determined if possible to retrieve the character of the community and set an example befitting the crisis through which the country was passing, stepped forward and requested to have their names then and there enrolled as volunteers in defence of the nation. They added, that as soon as they could be furnished with uniforms, they would leave their clothing to the young men, who lacked the manliness to defend the flag of their country when it was assailed.

### Recruiting Extraordinary.

At the time when the Federal troops were quartered at Blue Licks, Kentucky, the monotony of camp-life was broken by a rather romantic incident. Several recruits were coming in daily, and were immediately sworn into service, but one spruce little fellow arriving Sunday evening, refused to take the oath on the Lord's day, wishing to postpone it until next morning, which modest request was granted. The young recruit sauntered leisurely around among the men, apparently perfectly at home. When the time came to "turn in," he was shown a bed with three or four soldiers in the same room, which he readily accepted. His fellow-lodgers attempted to converse, but found him quite silent, and, observing him kneel for prayer before retiring, they concluded he was too pious for a soldier, but was perhaps to be chaplain. Next morning the surgeon was sent to have a conversation with the recruit before the oath was administered, and he being rather observing than otherwise, concluded, after a short "confab," that the young soldier was a very pretty female. After considerable blushing, she acknowledged the fact, stating that her intended was in the ranks, and that she was determined to accompany him. It seems that "cruel parients," as usual, were the cause, they having refused to let the young folks marry, and, in the desperation of the moment, the young swain sought the army, and a night or two following, the lovestricken maiden donned a suit of her brother's clothes, and joined her lover at Camp Blue Lick. The Colonel discharged the young Romeo the next morning, and that evening the fortunates were made one.

### Why John Rawley became a Substitute.

During the battle of Olustee, Florida, Jerome Dupoy, of Company D, Seventh C. V., was shot in the back of the head, evidently by some one in his own ranks, and suspicion fell upon a substitute for a drafted man, named John Rawley, of the same company, who had a quarrel with Dupoy and been stabbed by him. Sergeant Broes charged Rawley with the crime, when he confessed, and is reported to have made the following statement: Well, Sergeant, I did kill Dupoy; he stabbed me at St. Helena; I swore if ever I got a chance I'd kill him. I had one at Olustee, and I killed him. Nor is he the only man I have killed or caused to die. I cut out the entrails of a sailor on a gunboat, since this war begun; and I killed, by stabbing, a man in New York, which caused me to leave my family and go as a substitute for a drafted man last Fall. But the ghost of Dupoy is the only one that ever troubled me. Since the battle I have dreaded night, for they are horrible nights. When on picket I always see Dupoy stand a little way front, his face all bloody, and the bullet hole in his head. At night, when in my dreams, he stands at the entrance. I awake, he is there, pale and bloody, but vanishes as soon as I see him. I could not keep the horrible crime a secret any longer.

### Pat's Compliments to "Desarters."

The following dialogue really took place between Lieutenant A. C. C——d, then recently of the United States Texan army, and Pat Fletcher, one of the privates of the Second Cavalry at Carlisle, but then near Fort Bliss:—

*Officer*—Well, Pat, ain't you going to follow the General (Twiggs)?

*Pat*—If Gineral Scott ordhers us to folly him, Sir, begor Toby (Pat's horse) can gallop as well as the best of 'em.

*Officer*—I mean, won't you leave the abolition army, and join the free South?

*Pat*—Begor, I never enlisted in th' abolition army, and never will. I agreed to sarve Uncle Sam for five years, and the divil a pin mark was made in the contract, with my consint, ever since. When my time is up, if the army is'nt the same as it is now, I won't join it agin.

*Officer*—Pat, the "Second" (Cavalry) was eighteen months old when you and I joined. The man who raised our gallant regiment is now the Southern President; the man who so lately commanded it, is now a Southern General. Can you remain in it, when they are gone?

*Pat*—Well, you see, the fact of the matter is, Lieut. C., I ain't much of a scholar; I can't argue the question with you, but what would my mother say if I desarted my colors? Oh! the divil a give-in I'll ever give in, now, and that's the end of it. I tried to run away once, after enlistin', but a man wouldn't be missed thin. It's quite different now, Lieutenant, and I'm not going to disgrace naither iv my countries.

*Officer*—Do you know that you will have to fire on green Irish colors, in the Southern ranks?

*Pat*—And won't you have to fire on them colors, (pointing to the flag at Fort Bliss,) that yerself and five of us licked nineteen rangers under? Sure, it isn't a greater shame for an Irishman to fire on Irish colors, than for an American to fire on American colors. An' th' oath'll be on my side, you know, Lieutenant.

*Officer*—D——n the man that relies on Paddies, I say.

*Pat*—The same compliments to desarters, your honor.

### Worse than being Drafted.

One of the earliest names drawn in the South District of St Louis, Missouri, for the war, in the draft of 1864, was that of George R. B——, a young man who had recently commenced business in the city, and who not long before had married a very respectable young lady. At noon on the day of the publication of the list of drafted men, in which his name appeared, he received notice from a substitute agent, that he—the agent—had eight hundred dollars in hand with which a substitute was to be procured. This seemingly eccentric proceeding was no cause of surprise to the young man, inasmuch as he had from his very cradle been the recipient of bounties from an unknown source, having been left an orphan by the ravages of the cholera in 1848, and placed in one of the benevolent institutions of the city. He was put in the best schools as soon as he arrived at a proper age, and ever since he had been supplied with a sufficiency of means, the institution which had guarded his infancy being the trustee of the funds. Since commencing business he had been able to live independently, and whatever sums he was informed were placed to his credit at his *alma mater* he generously donated to the charity fund. But when he was drafted his hopes of the future became clouded. His wife wept upon his bosom, and his heart sank within him at the prospect. Too poor to pay a substitute, he saw nothing left to him but to be put in the front and fight, perhaps die, just as life was blooming into the brightness of springtime. Under these circumstances, the notification above referred to, brought sunshine back to the young and despondent couple. But the strangest point in all this experience was yet to be developed—one, too, partaking largely of the romantic. Two days after the examination of the young man, at about the hour of nine, a carriage drove up to the door of his residence, and the driver placed the following note in the hero's hands:

"OCTOBER 21, 1864.

"Come with the bearer of this. A dying friend wishes to see you. Be quick, or you may be too late."

L. G."

Bidding his wife adieu, telling her business called him away for a short time, he stepped into the carriage, and after driving for near half an hour, stopped in front of a comfortable-looking cottage in the suburbs. In a few moments he was ushered into a room in which was every evidence of a tasteful but modest luxury. On a low couch in the centre of the room lay an emaciated woman, of perhaps forty years of age, who, roused from an unrestful doze, opened her languid eyes and looked upon the young man as he neared her. A wild, peculiar expression lit up her countenance, and she seemed deeply affected. But the interview was short, for her strength was fast failing. Said she:

"George, I am dying. You are my son. I have been wicked, but suffering has purified me; and because I am worthy to hope for God's forgiveness, I have sent for you to-night to see you, and let you know the mystery and history of your life. Father ———, who is here, will tell you all. I have supported you all your life, and to me you are indebted for your exemption from the draft. All I ask is, that you will not curse the memory of your mother. For years I have lived secluded, and endeavored to retrieve the errors of other days. Be virtuous!"

The dying woman here became exhausted beyond the power of utterance, and not long after breathed her last. The young man learned that she had been a notorious character in St. Louis, and was divorced from her husband soon after her son's birth, the father having died about two years after, previously placing the boy in the orphan asylum spoken of. Knowing the whereabouts of her son, however, she superintended his education and furnished means for his proper maintenance, by her vicious course, but at last, with amended life, dying in the hope of a happy future. But the young man was so deeply affected by this knowledge, that his reason for a time was almost overthrown. The next day, without even informing his wife, he left the city for parts unknown.

### Changed his Mind.

A tall and good looking fellow made his appearance before Supervisor Blunt, in New York, intending to volunteer. To all appearance, he was well to do in the world, and, passing through most of the forms usual in enlisting, he reached the chairman of the committee, of whom he expected to get his bounty. At this point another character stepped upon the scene.

A tidy looking young woman, who claimed to be, and doubtless was, his wife, appeared unexpectedly before the would-be recruit, and in a modest, yet determined manner, protested against his taking the money. She appealed to him with tears in her eyes, to remain at home with her and the children. "You know, John," said she, "that I am not strong," and her delicate frame indicated this to be true, "and what can I do without you? How can I take care of and support myself and our three dear, dear children, without you to assist? The three hundred dollars will soon be gone, and then where shall we be, and you perhaps dead—dead?" Her poor little heart seemed ready to burst with grief, and her sobs were painfully affecting. Flinging herself upon his neck she again exclaimed, "John! do not, do not leave me." Then she repeated her tale of sorrow, present and prospective, to Mr. Blunt. But John, as most self-willed husbands are, they say, was stoical and indifferent to all these feeling appeals, unmoved and unimpassioned. Mr. Blunt looked on all this, while hesitating what to do. Finally, without paying the bounty, he allowed them both to pass out of the surrounding crowd into the more private apartments provided for the new recruits, there to consult together alone on the subject.

With what arguments she assailed her John here, what appeals she made, or what witchery she practised, are not known; but, like most intelligent women who accompany their strong protestations with a copious flow of tears—real tears—she triumphed at last. She obtained his consent to remain with his fond wife and family. Then they appeared again before Mr. Blunt—she with a triumphant air, and her face all aglow with joyful smiles, he looking as an obedient husband should, resigned and satisfied. She announced that her husband had changed his mind and concluded not to go. The little rogue knew very well that it was she who had changed his mind. He was asked if he had determined not to volunteer. He said he had. "Why?" says Mr. Blunt.

"Why, you see this little natty wife of mine has fairly persuaded me out of it, and she would control the devil himself, I believe, if he stood in her way."

As the enlistment was not consummated fully, the Supervisor allowed him to go, and a happier woman never left the presence of a woman's court than was that young wife as she passed out of the presence of those who came so near sending her husband to the "front." Husbands, obey your wives.

### Scene of Domestic Sadness: Woman's Firmness.

In a New York village resided a widow named Smith, who had sent four sons to the war, two of whom were minors, leaving behind them only two sisters. After a while two of them returned home, Nathaniel Smith, a member of the Eighteenth regiment, and the other a member of the Seventh artillery, the latter on a furlough. On Thursday night following this, there was to have been a jubilee at the house of their uncle, given in honor of the boys' return, and they had set off to meet companions, when, unexpectedly, officer Burt stepped up to Nathaniel and arrested him as a deserter. This was so unlooked-for that he almost fainted on the spot. It appears that Nathaniel deserted the regiment just previous to the second Bull Run battle, and since that time had been loitering about Washington and Alexandria, wholly unknown to the authorities in those places. Had he enlisted at the breaking out of the rebellion, and had he remained with his regiment he would have been mustered out of service in May. But he deserted eight months before his time was out, and consequently was compelled to make good that loss. After a parley with the officer who arrested him, the latter consented to go with him back to his mother's house, and here a scene ensued which shows the earnest patriotism of a true woman's heart.

When taken back to his mother's house as a deserter, and she being informed of the fact, she burst into a flood of tears and said:

"I have sacrificed four sons to my country—two minors; I have buried my husband and children; but I never knew what trouble and grief were before. To have one brought back as a deserter is more—more than I can stand. I do not blame the officers for doing their duty, but I do you for deserting. Go, my son, you are bone of my bone and flesh of my flesh. I would rather have seen you brought home as a corpse, than to find you alive, branded as a deserter. But go, my son; do your duty as a man and a soldier, remembering that your mother's prayers are with you, and do not come home again until you can come as a man who has nothing to fear."

While his mother was still engaged in talking to him in strains of sorrow and regret, his aunt came in—feeble in health, but strong in feeling. Mortified that he had deserted his comrades, she appealed to him as a lover of his country and a member of the family to go back to the army and do his whole duty as a soldier, and not return again until he had served his time out. The mother and aunt's tears were too much for the soldier, for they both wept tears of regret. With their blessings, the soldier left his mother and aunt, promising them henceforth to be a man, a true soldier, and not to return home until discharged.

### Bounty-Jumper Captured by a Dog.

The good deeds of a dog have more than once had to be put in contrast with the mean tricks of the human kind, and

Bounty Jumper captured by a dog.

here is an additional illustration of this truth. A man who had in charge a bounty-jumper, stopped at the Union House, Wheeling, with his prisoner. The man left his charge in the hall in order to look into an adjoining room for a person he wished to see, when the nimble jumper jumped out of the door, upon the sidewalk, ran up the street with great rapidity and darted down the alley in the rear of the Union House. A Newfoundland dog—honest patriot !—observing that the jumper was being followed, with loyal instinct joined in the pursuit. The dog soon overtook the fleeing rascal, seized him by the boot leg, and squatted down in the mud. The jumper kicked the dog off, but he had no sooner extricated himself than the faithful animal caught him again, and continued to hang on and delay the culprit until his pursuers came up and captured him.

#### Peculiar Question of Bounty.

A party of raw recruits—very raw—were on their way home from a tavern in the town of ———, where they had spent a portion of the evening in revelry, when they brought up at a church where a revival was in progress. They marched into the crowded aisle of the sanctuary, and for a few minutes closely observed the minister, who was urging his unconverted hearers to at once " enlist in the army of the Lord !" At length the worthy minister, noticing the uniformed men standing in the aisle, approached one of them, who was pretty near oblivious to the scene before him, and remarked—

" I am glad to see by your uniform that you are soldiers of your country ! That is right—glorious ! But you should now join the army of the Lord !"

" Eh ?" queried the soldier, whose tavern entertainment had put him in such a state that he but imperfectly comprehended the invitation—" eh ? join the Lord's army ? What bounty does he give, eh ?"

The minister attempted to explain, but soon gave it up as a bad job, the recruit being really *too* raw for 'impression.'

#### Re-enlisting, but on a Different Side.

Captain Crane, who commanded at Fort Meyers, tells a good story, illustrative of the value of time—in this instance viewed from a military point. When the Captain landed at Fort Meade he found a solitary sentinel marching back and forth, with a chip hat on his head, a dingy blouse on his back, and a double-barreled shot gun across his shoulder. This sentinel marched up and down, while Captain Crane and his men were busily removing the stores and doing other things usual on such occasions.

At length the sentinel looked that way, and called out, " I say, fellows, who in hell are you ?" Captain Crane, with the brevity of a soldier, replied with the one word, " Yanks." " Are you genuine Yanks ?" was the rejoiner. " We are that same," was the answer. The rebel sentinel passed up and down a few times more, and then called out, " I say, fellows, will you allow a fellow to come up to you ?" Captain Crane replied that he might. At this the sentinel laid down his two barreled gun and went to where the Union men stood, when he again addressed Captain Crane —" Will you allow a fellow to take arms with you ?" The answer was in the affirmative ; upon which the rebel expressed himself in this manner : " Well, I reckon my time with old Jeff. is out this day ; and, as I don't like to waste time, I will enlist with you." And enlisted he was on the instant. Captain Crane said he had not a better soldier in his corps than the one who thus so readily ' re-enlisted.'

This puts one in mind of Sir Walter Scott's Captain Dugald Dalgetty, who, when taken prisoner by the Marquis of Montrose (or Argyle), refused to serve the Covenanters, on the ground that he had stipulated to serve the king for the space of six months, but averred that, after his six months had expired he was open to any offer from the most noble marquis.

### Private Notions and Public Laws.

Governor Bramlette, of Kentucky, at one time had actually gone so far as to prepare a proclamation calling on the people of that State to resist by force the negro enrollment. This was before his visit to Washington, and he was only dissuaded from issuing the document through the appeals of Rev. Dr. Breckinridge. General Grant treated the matter in his accustomed cool and soldierly way. When the General was at Louisville, he said, in reply to a distinguished Union man who asked him what he would do if Bramlette and others "made trouble about the enrollment?" "Do?"—looking at his interrogator a moment with stern surprise—"My God, Sir! what have I to do with their notions about slaves? This is a law of Congress. It shall be executed, if I have to bring up the entire army from Chattanooga. Tell them so."

### Hercules-Africanus going to the War.

A stalwart specimen of colored humanity, just enlisted for the war, and incased in a military uniform,—a perfect Hercules in appearance,—was accosted by a gentleman who happened in his way, and the following conversation took place:

"Where did you come from?"

"Lycoming county, sah," replied the candidate for military honors.

"What business did you follow?"

"I am a raftsman."

"Then you are used to pretty hard work?"

"De Lor' knows I is."

"Do you feel anxious to go South?"

"De Lor' knows I does."

"Do you ever expect to come back?"

"No, sah; 'xpect to be killed."

"You know the rebels will have no mercy on you if they take you a prisoner."

"Aint gwang to be tuk prisoner—am gwang to fight till de bressed life falls out o'me."

"Well, you don't intend, if you have the chance, to kill all the white people down south, do you, women and children?"

"Look yere, my chile, you doesn't understand culled folks. We aint gwang to fight anybody, unless they fight us. You doesn't 'spose I is gwang to kill a little baby or a woman; I is'nt much educated, but I knows de Lor' is above all; and I knows right from wrong—aint gwang to do nuffin to displease de Lor.' I'm gwang to fight Jeff. Davis and his rebels, and I feel as if I could kill ebery one on 'm. I could bite Jeff. Davis to def. I tell you I could lib a week without eating nothing, if that could only gib me a chance to smash the rebels. I tell you, I don't intend to hab much mercy on 'em, nohow."

"Suppose a rebel surrendered to you; what would you do then—would you kill him?"

"I tell you what I'd do under them ar kind of a circumstance. I'd say, look here, Mister Rebel, I'se got you in my power, and could smash you, but I aint gwang to do it; but I'm gwang to tuk you prisoner—and off I'll tote him; you better believe it."

### War's doings to One Family.

There arrived, one day, at the sanitary rooms, a woman with the remains of her son, who had served in the army three years, and who, had he lived a few months longer, would have been sixteen years of age. The circumstances of this case show the doings of war in one family.

In August, 1861, being then twelve years old, James Henry ——, enlisted as drummer in the Seventeenth New Hampshire regiment, where he served fourteen months. He then re-enlisted, and served nine months in the Nineteenth New Hampshire regiment; and again, in January, 1864, enlisted for three years in the First Maine Heavy Artillery. He died in March, at Fort Sumner Hospital. The mother stated that this boy, who was evidently her pet—her Benjamin—had been the first of the family to enlist; shortly after, his father enlisted, served a year in the Tenth Maine regiment, and died at Lynchburg. In the same month of the father's death, another son enlisted, in the Seventeenth Maine regiment, was in battle at Gettysburg, and was never heard from again.

During the same year, too, the third and last son enlisted in the Eleventh United States regulars, was wounded in the head at Gettysburg, discharged for permanent disability, becoming imbecile in consequence of his wound. The care of the mother, and of an infirm grandparent, and of an imbecile brother, had fallen upon the little drummer-boy. Being small of stature, besides his extreme youth, he could not earn a man's wages, and therefore proposed re-enlisting. His mother had her forebodings, and remonstrated; but he reminded her of his former good fortune, of the bounty money, of a time when the war should be over, and every thing be all right.

She consented. He served two months, and here were his ashes! The mother behaved with Roman firmness. She would not say that she regretted giving up her all to the war: "The country needed them, and it was only right that they should go," was the patriotic language of this American mother. Drawing nearer the fire, she remarked, "I feel chilly; I sat at the end of the car last night, for the sake of bringing home Jimmy's drum; I did not like to take so much room by the stove." Ah, that little lone home in Maine, with nothing left in it so dear as Jimmy's silent drum! How many such desolate homes in the land!

"Divil a Macarthy drawn at-all-at-all."

The editor of the Oshkosh Northwestern attended the drawing of the names for the draft in that district. While watching the progress of the draft, as one by one the names of the honored conscripts were announced, he was much amused by the evolutions of a tall, stalwart son of Erin. He was a man of somewhere about fifty years of age, was dressed in the long-tailed, high-collared coat of the last century, and, by way of jewelry, carried a 'gem' of blackthorn, about the size of a stick of cord-wood, in his right hand. His occupation seemed to consist in addressing to every corner, the one question: "Do yez think it's fair?" On an answer given in the affirmative he would eye his shillalah most affectionately, and respond, "Yiz, I think it's fair." A conversation with him proved that his anxiety arose from the fact that he had three sons, all liable to the draft, and he was concerned that they should have fair play. When his own town was being drawn, he stood all alert, listening to the names as they were read out, and on the list being completed, with a wave of his shillalah and a pigeon-wing that would have done credit to a younger man—"Hurroo!" exclaimed he, "I *know* its fair; divil a Macarthy drawn at-all-at-all; sure, I *know* its fair!"

Happy to Make General Gordon's Acquaintance.

General Gordon was a strict disciplinarian, who would never have any words with a private; and hence a joke. One day, one of the 107th New York Volunteers got ahead of the brigade, when the General halted him and ordered him back. The soldier stopped, turned around, stared at General Gordon, and replied, "Who are you?" "I am General Gordon." "Ah, General, I am very happy to make your acquaintance!" was the complacent answer. A roar of laughter burst from the General's staff.

Branding Deserters at Castle Thunder.

Branding deserters, as performed at Castle Thunder, in Richmond, must be set down as decidedly one of the most beautiful of rebel military practices, and as humane as beautiful. The culprit was fastened to a large table, with his face downward, and a large "D" scarred upon his posteriors. A plain bar of iron, about an inch in diameter, narrowed down a little at the point, was heated to incandescence, and then used as a sign-painter would use a brush in lettering, only in a very slow and bungling manner. A greasy smoke with a sickly stench arose during the performance of the operation, accompanied with crackling sounds, and the groans of the victim as the hot iron sank deep into the flesh. On pretense of rendering the mark of disgrace plain and indelible, but in reality to torture the unfortunate culprit, the hot iron was drawn many times through the wound, making it larger and deeper, until the victim, unable to endure the exerneiation longer, would faint, and be carried away. The operation was always performed by old Pard, the executioner of Kellogg, the greatest demon in human form outside of Pluto's realms.

### Eager to be a Soldier: Handsome Lizzie.

The hospital matron at Benton Barracks, St. Louis, one day had the routine of her official duties varied by detecting the form of a young lady in the habiliments of a young man, the wearer of which was an applicant for enlistment. She was sent to the office of the Department Provost-Marshal, where she declined to make any statement as to her name, history, etc. At length, however, she concluded to tell her story. Her proper name was Lizzie Cook, and her home lay in Aponoose county, Iowa. Her father was in the First Missouri State Militia, and met his death in a skirmish at Walnut Creek, Linn county, Mo. Her brother held the position of sergeant in the Fifth Kansas. A desire to reach him, and a disgust at the monotony of woman's life, with a wish to serve her country, led her to determine to assume male attire and volunteer as a soldier.

She accordingly left her home and proceeded to Keokuk, where she worked as house servant for a family needing such help, till she had earned money enough to buy a suit of boys' clothes. She bought and donned them, and as soon as she had done so, started for St. Louis. Here she put up at the Everett House, registering her name as Wm. Ross. In the morning she took the cars for Benton Barracks, and was there proposing to enlist, when, failing to carry out her disguise to the requisite degree of nicety, she was detected.

Lizzie was a young lady of about twenty summers, tall, fine-looking, intelligent, animated in conversation, and expressed a strong desire to shoulder a musket and do with it what she could for the glorious cause of the Union. It was concluded, however, to commend her to the attention of the Union Aid Society, and, greatly to her disappointment, Lizzie was denied the satisfaction of engaging in her country's cause in the way she had marked out. A fine specimen of a whole-hearted, finely formed, patriotic, Western girl, was handsome Miss Lizzie.

### Had to Acknowledge the Breed.

An old farmer from the West, who knew President Lincoln in by-gone times, called one day to pay his respects at the Presidential mansion. Slapping the Chief Magistrate upon the back, he exclaimed, "Well, old hoss, how are you?" Old Abe, being thoroughly democratic in his ideas, and withal relishing a joke, responded: "So I'm an old hoss, am I? What kind of a hoss, pray?" "Why, an old draft-hoss, to be sure," was the rejoinder. Old Abe had to acknowledge the breed.

### Unquestionably a Hard Case.

The following inarticulate certificate got a man a discharge from the draft at Louisville. As he could not step squarely, he took the oblique. Puffiness ought to have excused him alone. But to the document—a model of its kind, as will be seen:

"I hereby certify that —— —— had one of his feet caught in the cylinder of a threshing machine on the 4th of last September, and severely injured, particularly the metatarsophalongial articulation of the great toe and a spot on the dorsum of the foot—perhaps the articulation of the cuboid bone with the scaphoid slightly interrupted. I have examined the foot lately, and have no doubt of the truth of his statement when he says he can not step squarely on his foot on account of not being able to bear his weight on the ball of the great toe in walking. There also remains a puffiness in the region of the instep. He has hemorrhoids."

Poor fellow!

### Regimental Clothes-washer for the Sixteenth Illinois.

He who gives a little spice to the ordinary flatness of camp life loses no friends. Acting upon this idea, a clever joke was perpetrated one dull day, at the expense of Lieutenant C., of the Sixteenth Illinois regiment, and a company of recently arrived recruits.

The raw recruits, some twenty in number, in a short time after their arrival, wished their linen washed, and made inquiry of a veteran comrade as to the location of the quarters of the washerwoman.

"We don't keep any washerwoman here," was the reply, "but there is a fellow up in that tent (pointing to Lieutenant C.'s,) who washes for the regiment."

Away to their quarters went the boys, gathered up their linen, and in a body repaired to the tent of the Lieutenant, who unfortunately was not in. The unclean articles were left on his cot, with the names of the owners attached to each bundle. Whether Lieutenant C. washed the clothes or returned them to their owners, is a question by no means so difficult of an answer as 'Who struck Billy Patterson?'

### Sixteen Brothers in One Regiment.

Perhaps no incident in the way of practical family patriotism, bearing upon the war of the rebellion, was more remarkable than the following: One of the companies connected with the Ohio regiments raised at the commencement of the war contained *sixteen brothers* by the name of Finch, residents of Dayton, Ohio. They were born in Durkheim, Germany, the family numbering in all nineteen children—sixteen being boys, all of whom enlisted as soldiers for the defence of their adopted country, in the regiment named above. Their parents had taken up their residence in New York, and their children obtained leave to visit them in Philadelphia. Such an instance as this is certainly without a parallel in the annals of war.

### Fiction left in the Shade—the Corporal of the Tenth Connecticut.

There was in the Second Connecticut regiment, before Richmond, a Corporal, the story of whose life outdid romance itself, and even left fiction in the shade. Seven years previously and more he enlisted into the British army in York. His first night as a recruit he passed with a fellow German, who had also just enlisted, and the two talked together as countrymen thus situated would be likely to. The next day they left for London, and there they were separated. Time passed on. This soldier was ordered to India. He was nearly five years in service. Receiving his discharge, he returned to England, shipped on a vessel for Norway, was, later, on a Norwegian vessel, and in that was shipwrecked on the coast of Sweden; barely escaping with his life, he went to Wales; again, he was on a Prussian vessel; he visited Constantinople, Odessa, and the West Indies.

Coming to New York, he was, after one or two brief voyages, led to Connecticut. Enlisting there, he joined his regiment at Gloucester Point, and was subsequently in all the battles of the army of the James. One day—or night,—in the winter of 1864, while Corporal of the guard, he was calling the relief at midnight; in passing a tent he heard a voice, the peculiar tones of which attracted his special attention and revived remembered associations of that first night as a recruit in old York, more than seven years before. He was sure that the voice was that of his then companion, and inquiry proved him not mistaken in his belief. Strange meeting—that of these two men!

His comrade's experience had been hardly less varied than his own. After several years' service on special duty in Great Britain, he also had taken to the sea. Coming to America, the opening of the war had found him at the South, and there he joined the Confederate army. For a time he was an orderly of a well-known Confederate General, and as such he on one occasion carried messages back and forth in a battle where the Tenth Connecticut fought prominently and victoriously. Later, he escaped from Charleston to the Federal gunboats, and after various experiences at Morris Island, Hilton Head and in New York, entered the Union army as a substitute, and there he found himself in the very regiment before the pressure of whose gallant charge he had two years before fled in precipitous haste after his chivalrous and fleet-footed commander, on a battlefield in another State; and now his voice was recognized and his name was called by a fellow-countryman who had been for a single night his comrade in the long gone years in a distant land. Would it be strange if he rubbed his eyes and asked if it were all a dream?

### Maryland Slaveholder Driving his Slaves to the Recruiting Office.

When the recruiting ball for the Union ranks had been fairly set in motion in Maryland, a slaveholder in Dorchester county, in that State, said to his slaves one day that they had permission to volunteer in the army if they so desired. He requested them, however, when they had made up their minds really to go, to inform him, and as they had driven him many a time to Cambridge, he would himself drive them in his carriage hither on that important mission. Sure enough they heeded his request, and he drove them to town in his carriage on their way to Baltimore, after fitting them out quite liberally. He subsequently came to the city and went to Camp Birney, to get his certificates for the three hundred dollars substitute money for each slave, and to grant his obligation to free them when the State laws would allow him to do so. The slaves met him, on this visit, as affectionately and demonstratively as sons could meet a father.

### Girl-Boy Drummer.

A fair and sprightly girl, of but twelve dimpled summers, and giving the name of Charles Martin, enlisted in one of the Pennsylvania regiments, in the early period of the war, as a drummer boy. She had evidently enjoyed the advantage of education, could write a good hand, and even composed very well. She made herself useful to officers of the regiment in the capacity of a clerk; and though involved in the scenes and chances of no less than five battles, she escaped unwounded and unharmed. The officers never dreamed of any hitch as to her sex. After a while, she was taken down sick with the typhoid fever, a disease then quite prevalent in Philadelphia, and was removed to Pennsylvania Hospital. It was while there that the worthy matron of the institution discovered the drummer boy, who had passed through so many fatigues, perils and rough experiences, to be no more nor less than a girl not yet in her teens.

### Just the kind of Arms a Young Quaker Could Bear.

Among the drafted men who presented themselves for examination before the recruiting Board at Providence, Rhode Island, was a young Quaker, whose conscientious regard for his faith would not allow him to send a substitute, or purchase a discharge, or take any personal part in bearing arms himself. But he proved a clear case of exemption from military duty under the law, as made and provided, and was discharged accordingly. Soon after the case had been decided, and before the young Friend had left the room, a letter came directed to the Board, and was opened by the officer. It proved to be an appeal in behalf of the young man, in a most delicate "hand of writ," and couched in most pure and winsome language. The commissioner playfully submitted the letter to the inspection of the young man, who with unfeigned surprise marked the well-known tracery of a dear young Friend who, on the next "Firstday," in open meeting, would surrender to him "arms" that he could bear conscientiously.

### Tender in Years but Strong in his Devotion to his Country.

Edward Lee, or "Little Eddie," as he was dotingly called, will never be forgotten among the reminiscences of Wilson's Creek, in the winter of 1861. A few days before the First Iowa regiment received orders to join General Lyon, on his march to Wilson's Creek, the drummer of one of the companies was taken sick and conveyed to the hospital. On the evening preceding the day of the march, a negro was arrested within the lines of the camp —Camp Benton—and brought before the Captain, who asked him:

"What business have you within the lines?"

"I know a drummer," he replied, "that you would like to enlist in your company, and I have come to tell you of it."

He was immediately requested to inform the drummer that if he would enlist for their short time of service, he would be allowed extra pay, and to do this, he must be on the ground early in the morning. The negro was then passed beyond the guard.

On the following morning there appeared before the Captain's quarters during the beating of the *reveille*, a good-looking, middle-aged woman, dressed in deep mourning, and leading by the hand a sharp, sprightly-looking boy, apparently about twelve or thirteen years of age. Her story was soon told. She was from East Tennessee, where her husband had been killed by the rebels, and all their property destroyed. She had come to St. Louis in search of her sister, but not finding her, and being destitute of money, she thought if she could procure a situation for her boy as a drummer, for the short time the company had to remain in the service, she could find employment for

Tender in years but strong in devotion to his country.

herself, and perhaps find her sister by the time the men were discharged.

During the rehearsal of her story the little fellow kept his eyes intently fixed upon the countenance of the Captain, who was about to express a determination not to take so small a boy, when he spoke out: "Don't be afraid, Captain, I can drum." This was spoken with so much confidence, that the Captain immediately observed, with a smile, "Well, well, Sergeant, bring the drum, and order our fifer to come forward." In a few moments the drum was produced, and the fifer, a tall, round-shouldered, good natured fellow, from the Dubuque mines, who stood, when erect, something over six feet in height, soon made his appearance. Upon being introduced to his new colleague, or comrade, he stooped down, with his hands resting upon his knees, that were thrown forward into an acute angle, and after peering into the little fellow's face a moment, he observed:

"My little man, can you drum?"

"Yes, Sir," he replied, "I drummed for Captain Hill, in Tennessee."

The fifer immediately commenced straightening himself upward until all the angles in his person had disappeared, when he placed his fife in his mouth, and played the "Flowers of Edenborough," one of the most difficult things to follow with the drum that could have been selected, and nobly did the little fellow follow him, showing himself to be a master of the drum. When the music ceased, the Captain turned to the mother and observed:

"Madam, I will take your boy. What is his name?"

"Edward Lee," she replied; then placing her hand upon the Captain's arm, she continued, "Captain, if he is not killed ——" here her maternal feelings overcame her utterances, and she bent down over her boy and kissed him upon the forehead. As she arose, she observed:

"Captain, you will bring him back with you, won't you?"

"Yes, yes, we will be certain to bring him back with us. We shall be discharged in six weeks."

In an hour after, that company led the Iowa First out of camp, the drum and fife playing, "The Girl I left behind me." Eddie, as he was called, soon became a great favorite with all the men in the company. When any of the boys had returned from a "horticultural excursion," Eddie's share of the peaches and melons was the first apportioned; and during the heavy and fatiguing march from Rolla to Springfield, it was often amusing to see that long-legged fifer wading through the mud with the little drummer mounted upon his back —and always in that position when fording streams. But, though thus far sunny and unscathed in his military career, the dark side of the picture was soon to be turned to Eddie's gaze. Says a comrade:—

During the fight at Wilson's Creek I was stationed with a part of our company on the right of Totten's battery, while the balance of our company, with a part of the Illinois regiment, was ordered down into a deep ravine upon our left, in which it was known a portion of the enemy was concealed, and with whom they were soon engaged. The contest in the ravine continued some time. Totten suddenly wheeled his battery upon the enemy in that quarter, when they soon retreated to the high ground beyond their lines. In less than twenty minutes after Totten had driven the enemy from the ravine, the word passed from man to man throughout the army, "Lyon is killed!" and soon after, hostilities having ceased upon both sides, the order came for our main force to fall back upon Springfield, while a part of the Iowa First and two companies of the Missouri regiment were to camp upon the ground and cover the retreat next morning.

That night I was detailed for guard duty, my turn of guard closing with the morning call. When I went out with the officer as relief, I found that my post was upon a high eminence that overlooked the deep ravine in which our men had engaged the enemy, until Totten's battery came to their assistance. It was a dreary, lonesome beat. The moon had gone down in the early part of the night, while the stars twinkled dimly through a hazy atmosphere, lighting up imperfectly the surrounding objects. Occasionally I would place my ear near the ground and listen for the sound of footsteps, but all was silent save the far off howling wolf, that seemed to scent upon the evening air the banquet that we had been preparing for him. The hours passed slowly away, when at length the morning light began to streak along the eastern sky. Presently I heard a drum beat up the morning call. At first I thought it came from the camp of the enemy across the creek; but as I listened, I found that it came up from the deep ravine; for a few minutes it was silent, and then as it became more light I heard it again. I listened—the sound of the drum was familiar to me—and I knew that it was our

Drummer boy from Tennessee<br>Beating for help the *reveille*.

I was about to desert my post to go to his assistance, when I discovered the officer of the guard approaching with two men. We all listened to the sound, and were satisfied that it was Eddie's drum. I asked permission to go to his assistance. The officer hesitated, saying that the orders were to march in twenty minutes. I promised to be back in that time, and he consented. I immediately started down the hill through the thick undergrowth, and upon reaching the valley I followed the sound of the drum and soon found him seated upon the ground, his back leaning against the trunk of a fallen tree, while his drum hung upon a bush in front of him, reaching nearly to the ground. As soon as he discovered me he dropped his drum-sticks and exclaimed, "O, Corporal, I am so glad to see you. Give me a drink,"—reaching out his hand for my canteen, which was empty. I immediately turned to bring him some water from the brook that I could hear rippling through the bushes near by, when thinking that I was about to leave him, he commenced crying, saying: "Don't leave me, Corporal, I can't walk." I was soon back with the water, when I discovered that both of his feet had been shot away by a cannon ball. After satisfying his thirst, he looked up into my face and said:

"You don't think I will die, Corporal, do you? This man said I would not—he said the surgeon could cure my feet."

I now discovered a man lying in the grass near him. By his dress I recognized him as belonging to the enemy. It appeared that he had been shot through the bowels, and had fallen near where Eddie lay. Knowing that he could not live, and seeing the condition of the boy, he had crawled to him, taken off his buckskin suspenders, and corded the little fellow's legs below the knee, and then lay down and died. While Eddie was telling me these particulars, I heard the tramp of cavalry coming down the ravine, and in a moment a scout of the enemy was upon us, and I was taken prisoner. I requested the officer to take Eddie up in front of him, and he did so, carrying him with great tenderness and care.

*When we reached the camp of the enemy the little fellow was dead.*

### No Title of Soldier given to the Devil.

Among the multitudinous developments of one kind and another made by the war of the rebellion, the light which it has thrown upon certain points and passages of Scripture is not to be reckoned as insignificant. At the funeral of an army Sergeant in the Federal ranks, who was murdered, Rev. Mr. Healitt, who preached the funeral sermon, said he would not call the murderer a soldier, because the word soldier was an honorable title, borne by Joshua and David and others mentioned in the Bible; he wished every one to remember that the devil is nowhere in Scripture called by the honorable title of soldier—a fact of no mean bearing upon the course of those who enlisted in the army of the Union to put down a sectional rebellion.

### "Sweet Sixteen" on the Male Side, and a "Darling" too.

A lad of less than sixteen years, named Darling, from Pittsfield, Mass., enlisted in the early period of the war in Captain Cromwell's company, in the Northern Black Horse Cavalry. On learning that he had a sick mother at home, who was sadly afflicted at his departure, the Captain discharged the youngster and sent him home, as the brave lad supposed on a furlough. The Captain received the following acknowledgment of his kindness from the sister of the "bold soldier boy." It is certainly worth reading:

PITTSFIELD, MASS., Oct. 20, 1861.

CAPTAIN CROMWELL—DEAR SIR: My brother, David H. Darling, a lad of sixteen, left home and joined your command without the consent or even knowledge of our parents. I went from school to see him last Thursday, and stated these facts to your second lieutenant. Our young soldier returned home Friday, on furlough, as he supposed, and seeing the effect of his conduct upon my mother and a sick sister, gave his consent to remain. But he is very much afraid you will think that he did not promise to return in good faith, or, to use his own term, that he has "backed out," so he made me promise, before I returned, that I would explain it to you.

This, then, "is to certify," gentlemen, that the young Darling aforesaid has not abated his desire in the least degree to serve his country under your especial guidance, although he has consented to devote himself in the more humble capacity of staying at home and minding his mother. Having reached the advanced age of sixteen, he possesses the strength of Hercules, and sagacity of Tacinaque, Aguilier's bravery, and the patriotism of Washington, whom you have probably heard mentioned before. Would that he could add to these a few of Methuselah's superfluous years, for youth, though no crime, is very inconvenient in his case. Of course, the advancement of the Black Horse Cavalry is materially retarded, and its glory dimmed for a season; but wherever you are at the end of two years, he is determined to join you. If thou wouldst take me in his place, I would be very happy to go. I believe not only in this war, but fighting in general, and think that if women were permitted to use 'knock down arguments,' it would civilize not only their mutual relations, but also their treatment of your much abused sex.

Meantime, awaiting thy orders, I am respectfully thine,

JENNIE DARLING.

P. S.—If you are married, please hand this over to your Second Lieutenant.

J. D.

So much for Jennie. The Captain's response to this winsome epistle, failed, alas! to greet the public eye.

### Sharp Practice among Volunteers.

That all the rogues were not in the army nor out of the State Prison was very clearly made to appear—and by the following fact among others, the scene of which was New York city. Mr. Blunt, the head of the Committee on Drafting in that city, took in multitudes of volunteers —black and white—paying the three hundred dollars, without being able to determine whether they were, in all cases, honest and acquainted with their catechism. One was taken of this class, who appeared especially loose on both those points. A black fellow, who had been enlisted for the navy and received his three hundred dollars, applied in the course of an hour or so to Mr. B. for the privilege of putting his money into the savings bank. It was of course granted. The Supervisor, on counting over the darkey's money, found that there was only two hundred and thirty-five dollars.

"Where is the rest of it?" says Mr. Blunt.

"Dat's all," says Snowball.

"No, it's not all. You have sixty-five dollars more. Turn your pockets wrong side out."

Darkey complied, but not another greenback was found. This was a staggerer, for Blunt well knew he had paid him three hundred dollars.

"Now, you horse marine," says the chairman, "what have you done with the balance of your money?—here are some notes I never gave you."

"Well, Massa Cap'n, I didn't do noffin

with 'em greenbacks; I jis ask a feller in dare to change me one hundred dollar bill, and de sailor he did it; and dat are is de money."

"Ah, ha!" says B., "Bring out that fellow."

Wide trowsers came out, looking very innocent. His money, too, was examined, and sure enough, there lay ensconced the identical sixty-five dollars the darkey was minus of.

"How is this?" says Mr. B.

"Well, you see, Boss, that piece of ebony wanted me to change one hundred dollars for him, and I did it, but I ain't very good at cyphering, and I rather guess I counted wrong. Here's your dust, old boy; let's tack ship and put back to port."

This impudent piece of rascality was corrected by the Supervisor, the darkey's money banked, and the parties again turned into their quarters.

### "How are you, Conscript?"

Not the least singular among the great variety of incidents in connection with the draft, is the following, which occurred among the good citizens of Vigo county, in the State of Indiana. During the drawing for one of the sub-districts of that region, the proceedings were watched with eager interest by at least one person, a "patriotic" resident of the locality under draft. As the names were drawn he betrayed considerable nervousness—was particularly anxious about the price of substitutes, and thought it the duty of all "veterans" to *re*-enlist. Finally, impatient under such critical suspense, and unable longer to control his anxiety, he made bold to ask permission of Colonel Thompson, the provost-marshal, to place his hand in the box, and draw forth the unfortunate prize. The Colonel, with his accustomed suavity and willingness to accommodate, kindly granted the request. The individual accordingly reached forth his hand, placed it in the box, and drew forth a card on which was written—his own name! That his curiosity was now fully satisfied, was no matter of doubt; and the good-humored salutation of " How are you, conscript?" regaled his patriotic ear from every quarter.

### Nasby's Reasons why he should not be Drafted.

Petroleum V. Nasby, in order to place himself in his proper position before the public, felt called upon to give his reasons —weighty and cogent ones, too,—why he should not be drafted. Says he:—

I see in the papers last nite, that the government haz institooted a draft, that in a few weeks hundreds uv thousands uv peaceable citizens will be dragged to the tented feeld. I know not wat uthers may do, but ez fer me, I can't go. Upon a rigid eggsaminashun uv my fizzikle man, I find it wood be wus ner madnis fer me 2 undertake a campane, to wit :—

1. I'm bald-heded, and hev bin obliged to ware a wig these 22 years.

2. I hev dandruff in wat scanty hair still hangs round my venerable temples.

3. I hev a kronic katarr.

4. I hev lost, since Stanton's order to draft, the use uv one eye entirely, and hev kronic inflammashun in the other.

5. My teeth is all unsound, my palit ain't eggsactly rite, and I hev hed bronkeetis 34 yeres last Joon. At present I hev a koff, the paroxisms uv which is frightful 2 behold.

6. I'm holler chestid, and short-winded, and hev allus hed panes in my back and side.

7. I'm afflicted with kronic diarrear and kostivniss. The money I hev paid fer Jayneses karminnytive balsam and pills wooed astonish almost ennybody.

8. I am rupehured in 9 places, and am entirely enveloped with trusses.

9. I hev varrykose vanes, hev a white swellin on wun leg and a fever sore on the uther—also wnn leg is shorter than tother, though I handle it so expert that nobody never noticed it.

10. I hev korns and bunyuns on both feet, which wooed prevent me from marchin.

I don't suppose that my political opinions, which are ferninst the prosekooshun uv this unconstitooshnel war, wooed hev enny wate with a draftin osifer, but the above reasons why I can't go, will, I maik no doubt, be suffishent.

### Clever Use of the Countersign.

During the fight at Gauley Bridge, Virginia, on the 10th of November, 1861, a glorious instance of personal bravery was afforded in the conduct of Sergeant Carter, of Tippecanoe, Ohio. The Sergeant was upon the post first attacked by the Confederates. The advance guard of the Second Virginia, consisting of twelve men, came suddenly upon him and his three companions. The bright moonlight revealed the flashing bayonets of the advancing regiment. He was surrounded and separated from his reserve. With great presence of mind he stepped out and challenged, "Halt! Who goes there?" The advance guard of the Second Virginia, consisting of twelve men, supposing that they had come upon a scouting party of their own men, answered, "Friends, with the countersign."

At his order, "Advance one, and give the countersign," they hesitated. He repeated the order peremptorily, "Advance and give the countersign, or I'll blow you through." They answered, without advancing, "Mississippi." "Where do you belong?" he demanded. "To the Second Virginia regiment." "Where are you going?" "Along the ridge."

They then in turn questioned him, "Who are you?" "That's my own business," he answered, and taking deliberate aim he shot down his questioner. He called for his boys to follow him, and leaped down a ledge of rock, while a full volley went over his head. He heard his companions summoned to surrender, and the order given to the Major to advance with the regiment. Several started in pursuit of him. He had to descend the hill on the side toward the enemy's camp. While he eluded his pursuers, he found himself in a new danger. He had gotten within the enemy's camp pickets! He had, while running, torn the 'U. S.' from his cartridge box, and covered his belt plate with his cap box, and torn the stripe from his pantaloons. He was challenged by their sentinels while making his way out, and answered, giving the countersign, "Mississippi," Second Virginia regiment. They asked him what he was doing there. He said that the boys had gone off on a scout after the Yankees; that he had been detained in camp, and in trying to find them had got bewildered. As he passed through, to prevent further questioning, he said, "Our boys are up on the ridge,—which is the best way up?" They answered, "Bear to the left, and you'll find it easier to climb." Soon again his pursuers were after him, as he expressed it, "breaking brush behind him."

This time, with a hound on his trail, he made his way to a brook, and running down the shallow stream, threw the dog off the scent, and as the day was dawning he came suddenly upon four pickets, who brought their arms to a ready, and challenged him. He gave the countersign "Mississippi;" claimed to belong to the Second Virginia. His cap box had slipped from his belt plate. They asked him where he got that belt. He told them he had captured it that night from a Yankee. They told him to advance, and as he approached, he recognized their accoutrements and knew he was among his own men, a *picket guard from the First Kentucky.* He was taken before Colonel Engart and dismissed to his regiment. When the brave fellow was asked what was his motive in halting a whole column of the enemy, he said his plan was to give intimation to the reserve, of their advance, that they might open upon them on their left flank, and so, perhaps, arrest their progress. If ever a fellow escaped by the skin of

## VOLUNTEERING, DRAFTING, DESERTING, ETC.

his teeth, from his enemies—and if ever a brave fellow deserved to—that man was the gallant Sergeant Carter. It was a courageous thing to obtain the countersign, and nothing but his courage made it afterwards available.

### Bridegroom and Volunteer the same Night.

Crime and outrage, in all their various phases, are the concomitants of war. An illustration in point is afforded in the adventures of an ex-Confederate soldier from Alabama, the scene of his exploits being in Chicago, Illinois. It seems that one day a young man waited upon the police authorities at the central station in that city, to obtain advice in a search for his sister, a young girl of seventeen years, who had fled from Oshkosh, Wisconsin, to Chicago, after having fallen a victim to the wiles of a seducer. On this representation being made, one of the detectives took charge of the case, and in the course of time found the girl living with an Alabamian, of the name of Jones. The officer arrested both of them, and then called in the brother, the interview resulting in a refusal on the girl's part to leave Jones, and Jones not only refused to leave her, but expressed his willingness to marry her at once. In addition to his offer of marriage, the man proposed to enlist in the Federal army as a substitute, and leave the money with his bride. The brother was satisfied with this proposition, and the ex-rebel Jones, having become a virtuous Jones, instantly fulfilled his promise,—a justice of the peace performing the marriage ceremony. Jones thereupon went to a recruiting office, enlisted, received two hundred and fifty dollars bounty money, paid it over plumply to the brother, and left Chicago the same night for Springfield, to be assigned to a regiment. The bridegroom declared that he did not mind what regiment he entered, so long as he avoided being sent into Virginia, where, he stated, he was so well known that if captured he would assuredly be hung.

### Snaked Away, and Drummed In.

One of the "sufferers" at Camp Dennison, which for a time was used for the care of the sick and wounded, was an Irish soldier. The attendant approached him and said:

"Well, Sir, what's the matter with you?"

"Wounded, Sir; slight wound in the groin—worse one in the heel."

"Where were you wounded?"

"Pittsburg Landing, Sir."

"What part of the battle?"

"Second fire of the last round, Sir."

Snaked away and drummed in.

"What, Monday? Why it was rather hard, wasn't it; to fight two days and then get hurt at the very last?"

"Devil a two days did I fight at all Sir."

"Why, how was that?"

"Why, you see, Sir, I didn't know what I was fighting for, and I didn't want to blow a fellow creature's brains out without knowing what I was blowing 'em out for, d'ye see; no more did I want a fellow creature to blow my brains out without knowing what they was blown out for—so, Sir, I just *snaked away* Sir! But on Monday they found me, Sir, and drummed me in." He was from Texas.

### Melancholy End of Johnson, the Deserter.

The execution of poor Johnson, for the crime of desertion, constituted a melancholy page in the history of the army in Virginia. Of this crime, the unfortunate culprit said: I had not the slightest intention of deserting, up to a few minutes before I started in the direction of the enemy's lines. The way I came to leave our army was this: I was on the outposts, and after dinner, when watering my horse, I thought I would go to the first house on the Braddock road and get a drink of milk. When I rode up to the house I saw a man and a boy. I asked the man for some milk, and he said he had none; and to my enquiry as to where I could get some, he said he did not know except I should go some distance further on. I said I thought it would be dangerous to go far, and he remarked that none of the rebels had been seen in that vicinity for some time. It was then that I conceived the idea of deserting. I thought I could ride right up to the rebel pickets and inside the enemy's line, go and see my mother in New Orleans, stay for a few weeks in the South, and then be able to get back to our regiment again, perhaps with some valuable information. I never had any idea of going over to the rebels, and as it is I would rather be hung on a tree than go and join the rebel army. I don't see what under heaven put it into my head to go away. I acted upon the impulse of the moment. When the man at the house said none of the enemy had been seen lately in that vicinity, I asked where it was that the five rebels I had heard of had been seen some time ago, and he said it was at the round house on the left hand side of the road. I asked him where the road led to. He said to Centreville, and so I went that way. Riding along on the Braddock road, some miles beyond our pickets, I suddenly came across Colonel Taylor, of the Third New Jersey regiment, with his scouting party. I thought they were the rebels, but at first was so scared that I did not know what to say. However, I asked him who they were, and he said they were the enemy. Said I to him,

"I'm all right, then."

"Why so?" said he.

"Because we are all friends," said I; "I am a rebel too—I want to go down to New Orleans to see my mother."

Then he asked me how our pickets were stationed. I told him two of our companies which had been out went in that day toward the camps. He asked if I thought he could capture any of them, and I told him I did not think he could. He asked why, and I replied that there were a number of mounted riflemen around. The head scout asked me what kind of arms the Lincoln men received, and at the same time said,

"Let me see your pistol."

I handed him my revolver. Colonel Taylor took it, and cocking it, said to me,

"Dismount, or I will blow your brains out."

I was so much frightened I thought my brains had been blown out already. I dismounted, delivered up my belt and sabre, while at the same time they searched my pockets, but there was nothing in them except a piece of an old New York *Ledger*, I believe. Then he tied my hands before me, and sent me back to camp in charge of three men, besides another who took my horse.

Johnson was duly tried by court-martial and found guilty. The place chosen for his execution was a spacious field near the Fairfax Seminary. The Provost-Marshal, mounted and wearing a crimson scarf across his breast, led the mournful cortege. He was immediately followed by the buglers of the regiment, four abreast, dismounted. Then came the twelve men—one from each company in the regiment, selected by ballot,—who constituted the firing party. The arms, Sharps' breech-loading rifle, had been previously loaded under the direction of the

Marshal. One was loaded with a blank cartridge, according to the usual custom, so that neither of the men could positively state that the shot from his rifle killed the unfortunate man. The coffin, which was of pine wood stained, and without any inscription, came next, in a one-horse wagon. Immediately behind followed the doomed man, in an open wagon. About five feet six inches in height, with light hair and whiskers, his eyebrows joining each other, Johnson indeed presented a most forlorn appearance. He was dressed in cavalry uniform, with the regulation overcoat and black gloves. He was supported by Father McAtee, who was in constant conversation with him, while Father Willett rode behind on horseback. The rear was brought up by Company C, of the Lincoln Cavalry, forming the escort.

Arriving on the ground at half-past three o'clock, the musicians and the escort took a position a little to the left, while the criminal descended from the wagon. The coffin was placed on the ground, and he took his position beside it. The firing party was marched up to within six paces of the prisoner, who stood between the clergymen. The final order of execution was then read to the condemned.

While the order was being read, Johnson stood with his hat on, his head a little inclined to the left, and his eyes fixed in a steady gaze on the ground. Near the close of the reading, one of his spiritual attendants whispered something in his ear. Johnson had expressed a desire to say a few final words before he should leave this world to appear before his Maker. He was conducted close to the firing party, and in an almost inaudible voice, spoke as follows:

"BOYS,—I ask forgiveness from Almighty God and from my fellow-men for what I have done. I did not know what I was doing. May God forgive me, and may the Almighty keep all of you from all such sin."

He was then placed beside the coffin again. The troops were witnessing the whole of these proceedings with the intensest interest. Then the Marshal and the chaplains began to prepare the culprit for his death. He was too weak to stand. He sat down on the foot of the coffin. Captain Boyd then bandaged his eyes with a white handkerchief. A few minutes of painful suspense intervened while the Catholic clergymen were having their final interview with the unfortunate man. All being ready, the Marshal waved his handkerchief as the signal, and the firing party discharged the volley. Johnson did not move, remaining in a sitting posture for several seconds after the rifles were discharged. Then he quivered a little, and fell over beside his coffin. He was still alive, however, and the four reserves were called to complete the work. It was found that two of the firing party, Germans, had not discharged their pieces, and they were immediately put in irons. Johnson was shot several times in the heart by the first volley. Each of the four shots fired by the reserves took effect in his head, and he died instantly. One penetrated his chin, another his left cheek, while two entered the brain just above the left eyebrow.

The troops then all marched round, and each man looked on the bloody corpse of his misguided comrade.

### Maternal Love and Patriotic Duty.

An old lady residing in Johnstown, Cambria county, Penn., had an only son, a strapping minor, to whom she was most warmly attached. This lad, however, having some of the war fever in him, was induced to join a corps from the mountains, and, hoping to deceive the old lady, he invented a very plausible tale, and came away. The love of the mother was, however, too great to be deceived, and after a week had elapsed, the true story was revealed to her. She started upon the railroad with a bundle and a small sum of money, and walked to Harrisburg alone,

—a distance of more than one hundred and fifty miles. At Harrisburg she took the train, and her money carried her to Downington, where she again resumed her tramp, and turned up, much to the lad's astonishment, at Camp Coleman, near Frankford. There the old lady, utterly wearied out, fell sick, and the men, hearing of the case, made up a collection, and provided her a bed and attendance in the neighborhood. But her strength revived with her anxiety, and she proceeded to the railroad with her boy, and kissed him a good-bye at the cars, with the tears falling free and warm upon her cheeks.

#### Distribution of his Bounty.

The better part of man's nature as well as its worst features, could be seen very palpably in the volunteering room, as the following among many kindred instances will show. A whole family, mother and five children, led by their stalwart head, the husband and father, presented themselves one day to Supervisor Blunt, in New York city, for the six hundred dollars bounty, he, the husband, having just been examined and mustered in as a recruit.

It was a large family and a sorrowful one—all except the little tow-headed fellow in its mother's arms, who was leaping and crowing as though he really thought it was excellent fun, a capital joke. The family appeared like a respectable one, though the hand of poverty evidently rested heavily upon it, and this, most likely, was the last resort, the last hope, the throwing of one overboard to save the rest. As Mr. Blunt counted the money—one, two, three, four, five, six hundred dollars, and presented it, a kind of sickly, faint smile was visible through the unbidden tears which were coursing down the volunteer's cheeks; for his time, he knew, with his family—its joys and hopes—was now about up. His children were clinging to his legs, begging him not to leave them; his wife, too full to speak, looked unutterable griefs, and clung all the closer to her babe. The money was all right; he held it in his hand—more than he had owned at once, perhaps, during all his lifetime. Said he—

"God bless you, wife and children; we must now part, perhaps forever. This money, wife, is yours—but let me give some to each; it will gratify me, and will go to you whenever you are in want of it. Here, wife, is one hundred dollars for you; may heaven bless it and you! Here, Billy, is one hundred dollars for you; be good and true to your mother, and, as you are the oldest, watch faithfully over your brothers and sisters. James, here is one hundred dollars for you; give it to your mother whenever she wants it. Mary, take this one hundred dollars, be a good girl, and in your prayers remember your father. Come here, my pet Alice, here is one hundred dollars for you to keep until good mamma requires it. And now, my little toad without a name—yes, let us call him Hope; do you say so, wife?" It was assented to. "Then here, you little crowing cock,—bless the little fellow! I may never see him again. Kiss me, boy. Here, put this hundred dollars in your little hand, and don't eat it, but pass it over to your mother as soon as possible."

The noble-hearted fellow's heavy frame seemed to quiver all over as he finished his distribution and knew that his time had come. He embraced each and all separately, and declared himself ready to go.

"But," says Mr. Blunt, "there is another hundred dollars coming to you—the hand money. Who brought you here!"

"That wee bit of a babe, your honor; I'd never come in the world had it not been for that dear babe."

"Well, then, the hand money or premium belongs to him!"

"Bless me, is it so? Wife, put that one hundred dollars into the savings bank for Hope, and never touch it if you can help it—if you can help it, mind—until

### Tenderness of the President toward the Lowly.

A woman in a faded shawl and hood, somewhat advanced in life, was admitted one day, in her turn, to see President Lincoln, in his office.

Her husband and three sons, all she had in the world, had enlisted in the war. But her husband having lost his life in the service, she had come to ask the President to release to her the oldest son. Being satisfied of the truthfulness of her story, he said, "Certainly, if her prop was taken away she was justly entitled to one of her boys." He immediately wrote an order for the discharge of the young man. The poor woman thanked him very gratefully, and went away. On reaching the army she found that this son had been in a recent engagement, was wounded and taken to a hospital. She found the hospital, but

Tenderness of the President toward the Lowly.

the boy was dead, or died while she was there. The surgeon in charge made a memorandum of the facts upon the back of the President's order, and, almost broken-hearted, the poor woman found her way again into his presence. He was much affected by her appearance and story, and said,

"I know what you wish me to do now, and I shall do it without your asking; I shall release to you your second son."

Upon this he took up his pen and commenced writing the order. While he was writing the poor woman stood by his side, the tears running down her face, and passed her hand softly over his head, stroking tenderly his rough hair—as a fond mother will do to a son. By the time he had finished writing, his own heart and eyes were full. He handed her the paper, saying, "Now *you* have one and *I* one of the other two left; that is no more than right." She took the paper, and reverently placing her hand again upon his head, the tears still upon her cheeks, said,

"The Lord bless you, Mr. President. May you live a thousand years, and may you always be the head of this great nation."

### It was the Baby that did It.

A touching incident of President Lincoln's kindness of heart is the following, as told by one of the servants attached to the presidential mansion. A poor woman from Philadelphia had been waiting, with a baby in her arms, for three days, to see the President. Her husband had furnished a substitute for the army, but some time afterward was one day made intoxicated by some companions, and in this state induced to enlist. Soon after he reached the army he deserted, thinking that as he had provided a substitute, the Government was not entitled to his services. Returning home, he was, of course, arrested, tried, convicted, and sentenced to be shot. The sentence was to be executed on a Saturday. On Monday, preceding, his wife left her home with her baby to endeavor to see the President. Said old Daniel: "She had been waiting here three days, and there was no chance for her to get in. Late in the afternoon of the third day the President was going through the back passage to his private rooms, to get a cup of tea or take some rest. On his way through this passage-way, (which shuts the person passing entirely out of view of the occupants of the ante-room,) he heard the little baby cry. He instantly went back to the office and rang the bell. 'Daniel,' said he, 'is there a woman with a baby in the ante-room?' I said there was, and, if he would allow me to say it, I thought it a case he ought to see; for it was a matter of life and death. Said he, 'Send her to me at once.' She went in, told her story, and the President pardoned her husband. As the woman came out from his presence, her eyes were lifted and her lips moving in prayer, the tears streaming down her cheeks." Daniel added: "I went up to her and pulling her shawl said, 'Madam, it was the baby that did it!'"

#### Sold by his intended Victim.

The employes and habitues of the Provost-Marshal's office in the city of Troy, New York, were one day considerably amused by a little episode, showing the manner in which a substitute broker could be victimized—done for!—by his intended victim. It seems that broker became acquainted with a countryman who had some notion about enlistment. "Oh, you're my man—I can pocket two or three hundred dollars on you," muttered the joyous broker, at the same time inviting Greeny to "take a walk and see the town." Greeny accepted, and off the two started. They not long after imbibed freely—in fact, very freely. Broker was anxious to have Greeny drink often, while his plan was to keep sober. Broker had plenty of money, and would not permit "his friend from the country" to spend a single dime. Finally, Broker—contrary altogether to his original plan—became weak in the knees, while Greeny was growing sober. Result: Greeny marched Mr. Broker to the Marshal's office, had *him* examined, was accepted and sworn in as a substitute. Greeny pocketed the profits, and started for the country. Mr. Broker became a sojourner on Hart's Island, in company with several of his victims. Verdict—served him right.

PART III  BOMBARDMENT OF FORT SUMTER APRIL 12 1861

# PART THIRD:

## ANECDOTES OF THE REBELLION—GREAT CONFLICTS AND ACHIEVEMENTS OF THE ARMY, AND ILLUSTRIOUS EXAMPLES OF INDIVIDUAL HEROISM IN THE RANK AND FILE; ETC.

BRILLIANT BATTLE SCENES; MILITARY CHARACTERISTICS OF THE LEADING GENERALS.—THEIR APPEARANCE, CONVERSATIONS, ORDERS, TACTICS AND BRAVERY, WHEN CONFRONTING THE ENEMY; MARTYRS ON THE GORY FIELD; UNPARALLELED FORTITUDE AND ENDURANCE; COOLNESS AND INTREPIDITY IN DANGER; BOLD MOVEMENTS OF ARTILLERY, CAVALRY, AND INFANTRY; SPLENDID CHARGES; DESPERATE HAND-TO-HAND ENCOUNTERS; EXTRAORDINARY SHARPSHOOTING; EXAMPLES OF YOUTHFUL COURAGE; DEALINGS WITH BUSHWHACKERS AND GUERILLAS; CELEBRITIES AND ADVENTURES OF CAMP, PICKET, SPY, SCOUT, AND STAFF; PERIL, TERROR, PANIC AND DISASTER; MIRTH-PROVOKING SIGHTS, SCENES, WHIMS, SQUIBS, ODDITIES, &c., &c.

---

"Strike for that broad and goodly land
Blow after blow; till men shall see
That *Might* and *Right* move hand in hand,
And glorious must their triumph be!"

"He sleeps where he fell, 'mid the battle's roar,
With his comrades true and brave ;
And his noble form we shall see no more,—
It rests in a hero's grave."

No enemy can withstand you, and no defences, however formidable, can check your onward march.—GENERAL GRANT *to his army.*

Boys, your field officers are all gone! I will lead you.—GENERAL WILLIAMS, *at Baton Rouge, just before he fell mortally wounded.*

Men, don't run till *I* run!—*The lamented* COL. E. D. BAKER, *at Ball's Bluff.*

Why don't you go after 'em? Don't mind me, I'll catch up,—I'm a little cold, but running will warm me.—*Dying words of* ALBERT, *the Mass. drummer boy.*

---

### Planting the Flag on Mission Ridge Crest.

The story of the battle of Mission Ridge is struck with immortality; the gray quarry there still firmly belted itself; the rebel army was terribly battered at the edges, but yet full in our front it grimly waited, biding out its time.

The base attained, what then? A heavy rebel work, packed with the enemy, rimming it like a battlement!

That work carried, and what then? A hill, struggling up out of the valley, four hundred feet, rained on by bullets, swept by shot and shell!

Another line of works—and then, up like a Gothic roof, rough with rocks, a wreck with fallen trees, four hundred feet more!

Another ring of fire and iron, and then the crest, and then—the enemy!

To dream of such a journey would be madness; to devise it a thing incredible ; to do it a deed impossible. But Grant was guilty of them all, and Granger was equal to the work.

At half-past three a group of generals

stood upon Orchard Knob. The hero of Vicksburg was there, calm, clear, persistent, far-seeing; Thomas, Meigs, Hunter, Granger, Reynolds. *Generals Grant, Thomas, and Granger conferred, an order was given, and in an instant the Knob was cleared like a ship's deck for action.* At twenty minutes of four, Granger stood upon the parapet; six guns at intervals of two seconds, the signal to advance. Strong and steady his voice rang out: "Number one, fire! Number two, fire! of rifle pits, as calmly as a chess player. An aid rode up with an order. "Avery, that flask," said the General. Quietly filling the pewter cup, Sheridan looked up at the battery that frowned above him, by Bragg's headquarters, shook his cap amid that storm of everything that killed, when one could hardly hold their hand without catching a bullet in it, and with a "How are you?" tosses off the cup. The blue battle-flag of the rebels fluttered a response to the cool salute, and the next instant the battery let fly its six guns, showering Sheridan with earth. Alluding to that compliment with anything but a blank

Rallying around the flag.

Maj. Gen. George H. Thomas.

Number three, fire!"—like the toll of the clock of destiny; and when at "Number six, fire!" the roar throbbed out with the flash, the line that had been lying behind the works all day, all night, and all day again, leaped like a blade from its scabbard, and swept with a two-mile stroke towards the ridge. From divisions to brigades, from brigades to regiments, the order ran. The tempest that now broke upon their heads was terrible to the rebels. General Granger's aids radiated over the field, to left, right, and front.

"*Take the Ridge if you can*"—"*Take the Ridge if you can!*"—and so it went along the line.

Sheridan, one of the most gallant of leaders, rode to and fro along the first line cartridge, the General remarked to one near him, in his usual quiet way, "I thought it —— ungenerous!"

Wheeling towards the men, he cheered them to the charge, and made at the hill like a bold-riding hunter. Amid sheets of flame, plunging shot, and mangled comrades, they wrestled for the Ridge, clambering steadily on—up—upward still! The race of the Union flags grew every moment more terrible. Just as the sun, weary of the scene, was sinking out of sight, with magnificent bursts of exultation all along the line—exactly as the crested seas leap up at the breakwater, *the advance surged over the crest,* and in a minute those Union flags fluttered along the fringe where fifty rebel guns were kenneled.

GREAT CONFLICTS, INDIVIDUAL HEROISM, ETC.     223

**Not a single General on the Battlefield.**

The regiments constituting the reserve, at the battle of Bull Run, under acting Major-General Miles, had an experience which, in one respect, was without a parallel in that or any other battle of equal importance. At 5 o'clock in the afternoon, the New York Sixteenth and Thirty-first, being well in advance toward Blackburn's Ford, were called upon to stem the tide of the Virginia cavalry, who were swooping at our retreating forces. An order from Miles, consequently, sent the First California regiment, under Colonel Mathewson, of the New York Thirty-second, forward to their support; but though the cavalry was thus turned to the right about, it was found to be impossible to stem the mad career of the extraordinary mass that came pouring back from Centreville.

The best that could be done, therefore, was for the California regiment to stay just where it was, and in absence of further orders, lend what aid it could to the protection of Green's battery, which was busily plying its fire upon the harrassing approaches of the Virginia horse. While the Thirty-second was in this position, the Sixteenth and Thirty-first having passed within its range, a youthful Orderly rode up to Colonel Mathewson to inform him that the Black Cavalry, sheltered from his observation by a piece of woods, were coming upon the right, and if he would take a cut with his regiment across the fields, they would be turned back upon their errand.

The evolution was performed, gave the protection that was desired, and the Black Horse gave up its purpose in that quarter. While the regiment, however, was adhering to this position, the same youth who had imparted the previous suggestion rode up to that regiment again, and told Mathewson he had better fall back on Centreville, as his duty at that spot had been thoroughly performed. As this was about the first sign of orders (with one single exception) he had received during the entire day, Mathewson felt some curiosity to learn who this young Lieutenant was, and whence these orders came; he therefore turned sharply on the youth, who, he now perceived, could not be more than twenty-two or twenty-three, and said:

"Young man, I would like to know your name."

"I am a son of Quartermaster-General Meigs," replied the youth.

"By whose authority then do you deliver me these orders?" was the Californian's next inquiry.

The young man smiled and remarked—

"*Well, Sir, the truth is, that for the last few hours I have been giving all the orders for this division, and acting as General too, for there is not a single General on the field.*"

This incident is surely worthy of notice among the lessons of that eventful day.

---

**His Knapsack Told the Tale.**

The day before General Grant attacked Fort Donelson, the troops had had a march of twenty miles, part of it during a bitter cold night. Grant called a council of war to consider whether they should attack the fort at once, or should give the troops a day or two of rest. The officers were in favor of resting. Grant said nothing until they had all given their opinion; then he said: "There is a deserter who came in this morning, let us see him and hear what he has to say." When he came in, Grant looked into his knapsack. "Where are you from?" "Fort Donelson." "Six days' rations in your knapsack, have you not, my man?" "Yes, Sir." "When were they served out?" "Yesterday morning." "Were the same rations served out to all the troops?" "Yes, Sir."

"Gentlemen," said Grant, "troops do not have six days' rations served out to them in a fort if they mean to stay there. These men mean to retreat, not to fight; we will attack at once."

### Explaining the Initials "O. V. M."

An incident worth narrating occurred soon after the first occupation by the Union forces of the country around Falls Church and Vienna, the brigade of General Tyler being on picket in that vicinity. The Ohio boys under General Schenck had been fired upon from a masked battery at the last named place, and some of the brave fellows were murdered. The remainder were anxious for a sight of the "gray backs;" and when Lieutenant Upton, a brave officer on General Tyler's staff, called for a party for a scout, they were ready. Lieutenant U. went some distance into the country, and obtained much valuable information. At one place he visited the house of a well-known secessionist, and succeeded in making the inmates believe the party were all "secesh." He found out the whereabouts and strength of the enemy, and feasted on the best the gardens and cellars afforded. All went well till a cap-pouch, that had been very carefully placed over the letters O. V. M. (Ohio Volunteer Militia) on the waist-belt plates of the men, became misplaced, and one of the young ladies, who had been very forward in giving the desired information, became alarmed, and asked the meaning of the letters. The Lieutenant was as ready with a reply as he would have been if it had been an order to surrender.

"They mean," said he, "Old Virginia Militia."

The explanation was perfectly satisfactory, and the Lieutenant took his departure. But the household soon occupied apartments in Washington at the expense of the Government.

### Lyon's Bravery and Sacrifice.

The battle of Wilson's Creek raged with unabated fury for more than an hour, and the scales seemed all the time nearly equally balanced. It was almost inconceivably fierce, and the Union cause lost one of its bravest and most beloved defenders—General Lyon, who was carried from the field a corpse. While he was standing where bullets flew thickest, just after his favorite horse was shot from under him, some of his officers interposed and begged that he would retire from the spot and seek one less exposed. Scarcely raising his eyes from the enemy, he said:

"It is well enough that I stand here. I am satisfied."

Lyon had been wounded in the early part of the engagement. He had been struck by three shots; one in the heel, a second in the fleshy part of his thigh, and a third in the back of his head, which had cut it open to the skull. His surgeon begged him to retire to the rear and have his wounds dressed. "No—these are nothing," was the General's reply, and, though wounded and streaming with blood, he mounted his horse and led the Kansas and Iowa regiments to the fatal charge, saying:

"I fear that the day is lost; if Colonel Sigel had been successful, he would have joined us before this. I think I will lead this charge; *Forward, men! I will lead you!*"

His horse had hardly sprung forward, when a minié ball struck Lyon in the breast, and passing out at the back severed in its course the aorta, the principal blood-vessel of the heart. He fell into the arms of his body-servant, saying, "Lehman, I am killed; take care of my body,"—and instantly expired.

One of the bravest of the brave was Nat. Lyon!

### Duel on Horseback in one of the Peninsular Battles.

Colonel Estoan, a Confederate officer, and author of "Notes from the South," gives the following very graphic account of an episode in one of the fights that took place during McClellan's operations on the peninsular:—Meantime an episode in the fight occured, in the shape of a duel between one of the enemy's dragoons and one of our Texans on a small field close by. The dragoon evidently scorned to join in the fight of his comrades, and displayed such skill in the management of his horse and the use of his sword that it was quite a pleasure to watch him.

In vain did the Texan make lunge after lunge, and try all sorts of expedients to overcome his antagonist. The dragoon sat as firm as a rock in his saddle, wielding his sword like a brand of lightning. By the manner in which he handled his horse and weapon I judged at a glance that he was a German trooper, and I could not help watching the exciting contest with great interest. The Texan still continued to wheel round his opponent on his fleet barb, eagerly seeking to deal a home thrust, whilst the dragoon, with a cool steady eye, followed all the movements of his impetuous antagonist. At last they close in earnest. A blow—a parry—a thrust—follow close on each other!

The Texan had slashed the dragoon's shoulder, so that the blood began to flow, which aroused a cheer from the Texans looking on, but at the same moment the former received a back stroke, which cut through the sleeve and flesh of his left arm. The Texan now backed his horse like lightning, and his fellow troopers rushed forward to look at his wound; but without paying any heed to his hurt, he again dashed at his opponent, and made a lunge at his breast. The dragoon parried it with great dexterity, and at the same time let fly a "quarte," which caused a slashing wound in the Texan's back. The latter spurred on his horse to a little distance, and before I could take means to prevent the cowardly act, he deliberately took out a pistol and shot the brave dragoon, who fell dead from his saddle. The bullet had entered just below the region of the heart.

Much grieved at his fate, I ordered a grave to be dug to receive the remains of the brave German trooper. We buried him in his regimentals, with his trusty sword on his breast and his pistol by his side. This sad act having been performed, I sent for the Texan, and after reprimanding him severely for his cowardly conduct, I ordered him to seek service in some other corps, telling him that I could not think of allowing a fellow of his stamp to remain in my regiment. The Texan scowled at me with his wild cat-like eyes, and muttering a curse, mounted his horse and rode away.

### Stray Leaf in the Vicksburg Campaign.

On the first of April, 1863, Generals Grant, Sherman, Oglesby, Secretary of State Hatch and Auditor Jesse R. Dubois, of Illinois, with some others, were on board the flag-ship of Commodore Porter's squadron, the party having been up the Yazoo River to Haines's Bluff, on a reconnoissance of the fortifications. While the other gentlemen were in the cabin, discussing public questions, General Grant and Mr. Dubois withdrew, and being in company on the deck, the following conversation ensued between the two:

*General Grant.*—Uncle Jesse, to tell you the truth, I have come to my wit's end as regards the capture of Vicksburg. I really do not know what next move to make. I have tried everything I could think of, and here we are yet. I have been advised that we go back to Memphis, and commence an overland march from that point.

*Mr. Dubois.*—General Grant, you cannot do that. If you take this army back to Memphis, with all this array of gunboats and transports and all your material of war, the effect will be disastrous on the country. This infernal constitution in our State was only defeated by superhuman exertions. Another election is almost upon us, and the whole Northwest is on the verge of revolution. If you go back, you strengthen the hands of the traitors and K. G. C.'s at home. They will call your movement a retreat, and more loudly than ever assert that the South cannot be conquered. If you can do no better, you must storm Vicksburg. If it costs the lives of forty thousand men it must be taken. It is a terrible thing to think of, but it must be done.

General Grant replied that he would reflect upon the matter during the night, and let Mr. Dubois know of his determination in the morning. When the morning came, General Grant met Mr. Dubois with a cheerful countenance, and the following conversation took place:—

*General Grant.*—Uncle Jesse, you are going home to-day; tell Governor Yates and the people of Illinois for me, that I will take Vicksburg in sixty days.

*Mr. Dubois.*—General Grant, I am glad to hear you say this; but all I ask you to allow me to tell them is, that you will take Vicksburg.—I don't care whether in sixty days or in six months.

*General Grant.*—I am bound to take it. I have decided on my plans. I will not tell you what they are. Even with the best intentions, you might disclose them to the detriment of the movement.

They then parted, and General Grant detailed his plan to General Sherman, who protested in writing, but placed himself under the General's orders.

Auditor Dubois went home and told Governor Yates that Grant would take Vicksburg; that he had no doubt of it; that General Grant told him to tell him so, and that he must tell it to the people as coming from General Grant. It will be remembered that the promise of General Grant was published in the papers at the time, and that Governor Yates repeated it from the stump.

General Grant's next move was to send for General John A. McClernand, and ordered him to march his corps from Milliken's Bend to the Grand Gulf. General McClernand proposed some changes in the details of the plan; but General Grant cut him short by saying that he had digested and arranged the entire details for the movement, and only required him—General McC.—to execute his orders. McClernand said he would do that to the best of his ability, and departed on his expedition.

There are those who know that, at this very time, strenuous efforts were being made at Washington for the removal of General Grant. Not only West Point was arranged against him, but Republican members of Congress, some of them from Illinois, went to Mr. Lincoln and urged his removal, taking back their former indorsements of him. Leading Republican papers also loudly denounced him, and clamored for his supersedure. At this time, a prominent Republican and retired officeholder from Illinois, who had been down the river buying cotton, wrote a letter to Mr. Lincoln, denouncing General Grant, predicting his failure, and urging the appointment of General Pope to his command. He brought the letter to Hon. C. M. Hatch, then Illinois Secretary of State, and one of Mr. Lincoln's most intimate friends, and asked him to direct it, but did not show him its contents. He represented to Mr. Hatch that Mr. Nicolay, who had been Mr. Hatch's deputy-clerk, seeing the handwriting, would hand it to Mr. Lincoln. Hearing of the occurrence, and suspecting a trick, Mr. Dubois made Mr. Hatch write a letter to the President, which both signed, and which urged him to do nothing against Grant; that they had been down the river, and, so far as they had anything to say in the matter, they were perfectly satisfied with him.

Not the least interesting incidents connected with this "inside view" of matters, are, the written protest by General Sherman against General Grant's circuitous march around Vicksburg, and by which he cut himself off from his base of supplies; General Sherman's direction that the protest be forwarded to Washington, and

General Grant's never so forwarding it; and afterward, when Vicksburg was about to surrender, the tearing-up of said protest, by General Grant, in General Sherman's presence, much to the satisfaction of the latter.

#### Deathly Encounter between Hunt and Loughborough.

Among the prisoners released from Richmond, in January, 1862, was Captain Ralph Hunt, of the First Kentucky regiment,—Captain H. belonging himself in Clark county, Ohio. In September, 1861, his regiment formed a part of the force under General Cox, encamped near Gauley's Bridge, in Western Virginia. The enemy were desirous of dislodging the General, and about the 3d of September attempted a reconnoissance in some force. Our pickets were driven in, and Captain Hunt was ordered out with his company to make observations of the force and movements of the enemy and report thereon. The whole country thereabouts is thickly covered with scrubby pine and cedar, so that a man may escape notice at a few yards distance. Pushing his way through the bushes and scrubby trees until he obtained a position commanding the road by which the rebels must advance, the Captain halted his men where they were concealed from observation, and ordered them to lie quiet and await orders; a few men had been sent in advance as scouts, but it seems that these were bewildered amidst the dwarf pines and bushes, and, in making their way back, unfortunately got into the Captain's rear.

The Captain, after posting his men, had gone forward a few yards, accompanied by two of his men, and, hearing an advance upon the road, stepped forward a few paces, in expectation of seeing his returning scouts, but the party advancing along the road turned out to be the leading files of the advanced guard of the rebel forces. With these was a fine-looking officer named Loughborough, who had been sent out to drill the Confederate troops in that region. This officer was marching some distance in advance of his men, and, catching sight of Captain Hunt, poured forth a torrent of imprecations,—exclaiming—

"Come out, you —— Yankee son of a ——, and be shot!"

Saying this, the rebel fiend raised to his shoulder instantly his Mississippi rifle. Captain Hunt had a musket with him—the ordinary smooth bore, which he immediately leveled at his adversary. The combatants were about fifty yards apart—each fired at the same instant; the Adjutant's ball whistled close by the Captain's ear, but the Adjutant himself, with a curse upon his lips, fell dead with a bullet through his brain. So instantaneous was his death, that not a limb quivered after the body touched the earth.

Not less than seven shots were instantly fired at Captain Hunt, none of them, however, taking effect. The enemy, enraged at the loss of a favorite officer, were at first inclined to be revengeful; but the gallantry he had just displayed, and the coolness with which he bore himself when in their power, finally won their respect. The men of Captain Hunt's company supposed their leader to be killed, and made good their escape to camp. Hunt and the two men with him were so surrounded that escape was impossible. Refusing to give his parole, Captain Hunt was ironed, and, after visiting several of the towns in Virginia, was confined in the tobacco factory at Richmond.

#### "Young America" at Fort Donelson.

In a little open field in the woods which had been the scene of the hottest portion of the Fort Donelson conflict, there was afterward found one living mortal among the multitudinous dead. On approaching this person, he was found to be a mere stripling with the garb of a Federal soldier, and at least, in his own estimation, just then, a pretty formidable one at that. "Do you see that old secesh?" said he, pointing to a stalwart body at least six feet in length, stretched out a short distance from him,—"well, I killed him;" and with evident pride he went on to say how the dead rebel enemy was the color-bearer of a rebel regiment, and as he was lying there beside that stump, had taunted him with

Young America.

being an Abolitionist, and told him to 'come out of there.' He *did* come out, and to the sad detriment of his Goliah-like antagonist. The boy had come a mile or more from his camp to get a glimpse of his fallen foe.

### "Thpit on It."

A good story is told of a lisping officer in the army having been victimized by a brother officer (noted for his cool deliberation and strong nerves), and his getting square with him in the following manner. The cool joker, the Captain, was always quizzing the lisping officer, a Lieutenant, for his nervousness.

"Why," said he, one day, in the presence of his company, "nervousness is all nonsense; I tell you, Lieutenant, no brave man will be nervous."

"Well," inquired his lisping friend, "How would you do, thpose a shell with an inch futhe thould drop itthelf into a walled angle, in which you had taken thelter from a company of tharpthoot- herth, and where it wath thertain, if you put your nothe, you'd get peppered."

"How?" said the Captain, winking at the circle; "why take it cool, and *spit* on the fuse."

The party broke up, and all retired except the patrol. The next morning a number of soldiers were assembled on the parade and talking in clusters, when along came the lisping Lieutenant. Lazily opening his eyes he remarked:

"I want to try an experiment thith morning, and thee how exceedingly cool you can be."

Saying this, he walked deliberately into the Captain's quarters, where a fire was burning on the hearth, and placing in the hottest centre a powder canister, instantly retreated. There was but one mode of egress from the quarters, and that was upon the parade ground, the road being built up for defence. The occupant took one look at the canister, comprehended the situation, and in a moment dashed at the door, but it was fastened on the outside.

"Charley, let me out, for your love for me!" shouted the Captain.

"*Thpit* on the canister!" shouted he in return.

Not a moment was to be lost. He had first caught up a blanket to cover h's egress; but now, dropping it, he raised the window and out he bounded, *sans compliments*, *sans* everything but a very short undergarment; and thus, with hair almost on end, he dashed upon a full parade ground. The shouts which hailed him called out the whole barracks to see what was the matter, and the dignified Captain pulled a Sergeant in front of him to hide himself.

"Why didn't you thpit on it?" inquired the Lieutenant.

"Because there were no sharpshooters in front to stop a retreat," answered the redoubtable Captain.

"All I got to thay, then, ith," said the Lieutenant, "that you might thafely have

## Two College-Mates Colonels in Opposing Armies.

In the class of 185-, at Waterville College, Maine, were two young men who had been chums while fitting for college, at the same school, and were chums through the entire college course, and after graduating pursued their legal studies at the same law school, and were chums during that period also. After admission to the bar, one went South to seek his fortune, the other West. After the breaking out of the rebellion, the one who went South enlisted in the Confederate army, the other in the Union army. They both afterward rose to the rank of Colonel, and both took part in the battle of Mission Ridge, in command of their respective regiments. It so happened, that the Confederate Colonel, at the head of a Tennessee regiment, was in support of a battery which the regiment in command of the Union Colonel was ordered to take at the point of the bayonet.

The battery was taken; but so desperate had been the conflict, that both Colonels fell mortally wounded. After the fight was over, a Union Captain, himself a classmate of the two Colonels, being detailed to bury the dead, found the two college classmates and chums lying side by side on the battle-field, with their right hands clasped and both dead. They had evidently recognized each other after being wounded, and the old ties of friendship had asserted their supremacy, and together their spirits had passed into the eternal world. Side by side, in the same grave, they sleep their last sleep.

## Traitor Generals conferring over the "Last Ditch."

On the morning of February 16th, 1862, about one o'clock, it had been determined by the rebel officers in command at Fort Donelson to cut their way through the rebel lines, destroy the army stores, and retreat to Nashville. But scouts were sent out and reported that it would be impossible to effect the communication planned, on account of Union troops at all points and the impassable condition of the *slough* to be crossed,—that "last ditch," it is presumed!

A conference of the rebel Generals was now held, and notwithstanding the fact of communication being thus cut off, General Pillow urged the attempt to cut their way out or make a fight for one day more, in which time he thought they could get steamboats enough to cross the river, and escape by Clarksville.

General Buckner then said that, from the worn out and distressed condition of his men, and the occupation of the rifle-pits on the extreme right by the enemy, he could not hold his position for half an hour if attacked by the enemy at daylight, which he would certainly do.

"Why can't you?" asked General Pillow; "I think you can, sir," and added that the occupation of their rifle-pits by the Federals left an open gateway to the river battery, and he thought they ought to cut their way through, at all hazards.

"I know my position," retorted Buckner; "I can only bring to bear against the enemy 4,000 men, while he can oppose me with any given number."

"Well, gentlemen, what do you intend to do? I am in favor of fighting out," responded Pillow.

General Floyd then asked General Buckner what he had to say. General Buckner replied quickly, that to attempt to cut their way out through the enemy's lines would cost a sacrifice of three-fourths of his command, and that no General had a right to make such a sacrifice of human life. General Floyd admitted the fact and concurred with General Buckner on this point. General Pillow then remarked that there was but one alternative left, and that was capitulation; and addressing himself to General Floyd, said:

"Sir, I shall neither surrender the command nor myself; I will die first."

"Neither will I surrender myself," replied General Floyd; "you know my relation with the Federal Government, and it would not do."

Buckner replied that he thought no personal feeling ought to control official action. Floyd admitted this, and said, nevertheless, it was his determination.

"Then, gentlemen," said Buckner, "I suppose the surrender will devolve on me."

"General," said Floyd to Buckner, "if you are put in command, will you allow me to take out my brigade?"

"Yes, sir, if you move your command before I send my offer of capitulation to the enemy."

"Then," said General Floyd, "I surrender the command."

"I will not accept it, as my purpose is never to surrender," said Pillow, upon whom the command next devolved.

"I will accept it," immediately replied Buckner, "and will share the fate of my command,"—and at once called for pen, ink and paper, and a bugler to sound a parley, it being too dark to send a flag of truce.

Pillow then asked if it would be proper for him to make his escape. To which Floyd replied, that was a question for every man to decide for himself, but that he would be glad for every man to make his escape that could.

Colonel Forrest now addressed General Buckner, saying, "General, I think there is more fight in our men than you suppose; but if you will let me, I will also take out my command."—to which Buckner and Floyd both assented. Turning to General Pillow, Forrest then said:

"General, I have fought under your command, what shall I do?"

"Cut your way out!" answered Pillow.

"I will, by G—!" replied Forrest.

All the officers then retired, leaving Buckner in command. The sequel is well known.

### Is the Colonel at Home?

Captain Kemper, at the head of a squad of cavalry, went down into Platte county, Missouri, one day, on an amateur scout, and was rewarded by scaring up a full-grown Confederate Colonel, whom he captured under the following rather "domestic" circumstances:

The name of the captured officer was John W. Hinston, 'Colonel of the First

Is the Colonel at home?

Missouri Rifles, C. S. A.' The Captain heard of the Colonel's being in the neighborhood of Platte City, and therefore "put" for his residence, about six miles below that point. On nearing the Colonel's abode, the Captain was somewhat in advance of his men, and on riding up to the back of the house saw a man put his head out of the window, and then with a quick dodge draw it in again. The men, in the meantime, came up in front of the house, and by this means "out flanked" the Colonel, and completely cut off his retreat.

Captain Kemper now alighted, entered the house, and asked a lady, "Is the Colonel at home?" She replied, "No; there are no gentlemen about the house." But she could not "come the giraffe" over the Captain in that kind of style, for his loyal eyes had already seen the "human face divine" of a gentleman ornamenting the window.

He therefore instituted a search, his men even going under the house with lighted candles. Still, sure enough, there could be found "no gentleman about the house." At last, some bedding lying in the corner of a room was examined, and—there lay the Colonel between the upper and nether ticks, dressed in the Confederate uniform, and as bright as a cricket! He immediately and unconditionally surrendered himself a prisoner of war, acknowledging in the person of Captain Kemper, the "one man power," and that his little domestic arrangement was a "goner."

### Dick Bowles Parting with his Revolver.

The noted guerilla chief, Dick Bowles, met with an end as unexpected as it was tragical in the last degree. He was killed about seven miles from Gilbertsville, Limestone county, Alabama, by Ira O. Tuttle, the young and daring chief of scouts of the Army of the Cumberland. Tuttle sought Bowles, and represented himself as willing to engage in any scheme of murder and plunder which might be proposed. Bowles was disarmed of suspicion, and related to Tuttle a short history of his life, in which he boasted of the many acts of plunder in which he had engaged, and the deliberate murders he had committed. Tuttle heard him through, and carelessly asked to examine the revolver with which Bowles was idly toying. Without any thought of suspicion, the revolver changed hands. Tuttle coolly cocked the pistol, and informed Bowles who he was, and, drawing his watch from his pocket, said:

"You have just one minute and a half to live; if you wish to humbly pray to God, kneel down, and be expeditious, for, by my soul, you die!"

Quick as a flash of lightning, Bowles made a forward movement to grasp the pistol, when Tuttle as quickly pulled the trigger, and the ball penetrated the brain of the guerilla chief. He fell and died without a groan. Tuttle immediately retreated from the place, and safely arrived inside of the Federal lines.

### One Obscure Patriot Baffling a Whole Rebel Army.

The fact that General Buckner did not take the city of Louisville instead of stopping at Green River, where he invaded Kentucky on the line of the Louisville and Nashville railroad, was due, not to any foresight or force of the United States authorities or of the Union men of Kentucky, but to the loyalty, courage and tact of one obscure individual.

The secessionists had laid their plans to appear suddenly in Louisville with a powerful force. They had provided for transportation four hundred cars and fifteen locomotives, and had eight thousand men, with artillery and camp equipage, on board. They had secured the services of the telegraph operators, one of whom forwarded to Louisville a dispatch explaining the detention of trains on the road, and things were moving forward at a grand rate. Everything was going well with them, and Louisville, with perhaps the exception of a few secessionists, was unsuspected and unguarded.—General Anderson being innocent of any knowledge of the movement; James Guthrie, President of the road, totally in the dark, and General Rousseau lingering in camp on the Indiana shore. Nothing could have been better planned—nothing more swimmingly and romantically in process of execution. Buckner felt as though walking through a bed of June daisies.

But at a station just beyond Green River, there was a young man in the service of the road, who was a warm friend for the Union, and who, comprehending the meaning of the monster train, when it came up, seized a crowbar used for taking up rails to make repairs, and while the locomotives were being wooded and watered, ran across a curve, and, in a deep narrow cut, wrenched the spikes from four rails,

The train came along at good speed, the rails spread, the locomotive plunged into the ground, the cars crashed on the top of it, and it was twenty-four hours before the train could go ahead. In the meantime Louisville was saved. The hero of the occasion had not had time to get out of the cut before the crash came, and was taken, but in the general confusion and excitement got away, and was safe.

That obscure individual did much more for his country than some who wore straps and stars.

### Scott's Plan of the War.

The account given by Hon. Mr. Richardson, of Illinois, of the interview which took place, after the battle of Bull Run, between himself, his Congressional colleagues, Messrs. Logan and Washburne, and the President, Secretary of War, and General Scott, is of peculiar interest, as

War and Navy Buildings, Washington.

showing how that battle came to be fought. Mr. Richardson's statement, as made by him in Congress, was as follows:—

In the course of our conversation, General Scott remarked, 'I am the biggest coward in the world.' I rose from my seat. 'Stay,' said General Scott; 'I will prove it. I have fought the battle against my judgment, and I think the President ought to remove me to-day for doing it. As God is my judge,' he added, after an interval of silence, 'I did all in my power to make the army efficient, and I deserve removal because I did not stand up when I could, and did not.'

On a subsequent occasion, in the summer of 1861, the glorious old General said, that if the plan and conduct of the war had rested solely with him, he would have commenced by a perfect blockade of every Southern port on the Atlantic and the Gulf. Then he would have collected a large force at the Capital for defensive purposes, and another large one on the Mississippi for offensive operations. The summer months, during which it is madness to take troops south of St. Louis, should have been devoted to tactical instruction; and with the first frosts of autumn he would have taken a column of eighty thousand well-disciplined troops down the Mississippi, and taken every important point on that river, New Orleans included. It could have been done with greater ease, with less loss of life, and with far more important results than would attend the marching of an army to Richmond. At eight points the river would probably have been defended, and eight batteries would have been necessary; but in every one of them success could have been made certain for us. The Mississippi and the Atlantic once ours, the Southern States would have been compelled, by the natural and inevitable pressure of events, to seek, by a return to the Union, escape from the ruin that would speedily overwhelm them if out of it. 'This,' said the General, 'was my plan.'

### Poor Bragg and his Supposed Army.

While General Bragg's troops were on their retreat from Murfreesborough, ragged, hungry, and weary, they straggled along the road for miles, with an eye to their own comfort, but a most unmilitary neglect of rules and regulations. Presently one of them espied, in the woods near by, a miserable broken-down mule, which he at once seized and proceeded to put to his use, by improvising, from stray pieces of rope, a halter and stirrups. This done, he mounted, with grim satisfaction, and pursued his way. He was a wild Texas tatterdemalion, bareheaded, barefooted, and wore in lieu of a coat, a rusty looking hunting-shirt. With hair unkempt, beard unshorn, and face unwashed, his appearance was grotesque enough; but, to add to it, he drew from some receptacle, his corn-cob pipe, and made perfect his happiness by indulging in a comfortable smoke.

While thus sauntering along, a company of bestarred and bespangled horsemen—General Bragg and staff—rode up, and were about to pass on, when the rather unusual appearance of the man attracted their notice. The object of their attention, however, apparently neither knew nor cared to know them, but looked and smoked ahead with careless indifference.

"Who are you?" asked the Major-General.

"Nobody," was the answer.

"Where did you come from?"

"Nowhere."

"Where are you going?"

"I don't know."

"Where do you belong?"

"Don't belong anywhere."

"Don't you belong to Bragg's army?"

"Bragg's army! Bragg's army!" replied the chap, "Why, he's got no army! One half of it he shot in Kentucky, and the other half has just been whipped to death at Murfreesborough."

Bragg asked no more questions, but turned and spurred away.

### Redfield's Stolen March.

The capture of the rebel forge at Henderson's Hill, by the Sixteenth Indiana mounted infantry, under Lieutenant Colonel Redfield, was a notable instance of stealing a march. After a detour of sixteen miles, Colonel Redfield reached the rear of the enemy's position. Here he captured a courier with despatches from General Taylor, who was advancing with a supporting force. A squadron of Colonel Redfield's was at times completely surrounded by Taylor's men, but managed to keep them in check, while Captain Doxey, with two companies, engaged the enemy's pickets. This was cleverly done. His men dismounted, advanced in small squads directly up to the rebel pickets, greeting them heartily with—

"How are you, boys?"

This was accompanied with various slaps on the back, &c., after the manner of friends rather than enemies—a confidence which quite disarmed the rebels, who said—

"Why, who are you?"

"Why, the Third Texas, don't you know us? We have come to help you against these —— Yankees."

"Hurrah! Bully for you!" &c.

In such a cold, rainy night, what could be pleasanter than friends, and especially friends to help against the confounded Yankees?

After getting well warmed, our boys said to them—

"Now, boys, you must surrender, for we are the —— Yankees themselves!"

"No you don't."

"But we *do*; surrender and sit down!"

And so the disagreeable truth came upon those damp Louisiana fellows. Picket after picket was in this way successfully captured and sent to the rear, without the firing of a shot or alarming the main body.

Captain Doxey then entered the rebel camp with his cavalry, while a body of infantry supports were deployed on his right. There he captured, almost without resistance, the surprised and astonished enemy. Four pieces of artillery were captured, two just as they were being brought into line—one of their officers saying, "Don't fire! they are our own boys." Unfortunately for him it did not prove correct, and the four guns were soon in the possession of the Yankees, as was also the too confiding officer.

A squad of Redfield's command surrounded a house in which a party of rebels were engaged in preparing their frugal repast, and the sounds from within indicated that they were quite comfortable in their minds at least, if their bodies were not. One of his men then knocked at the door.

"Who's there?"

"Federals."

"None of your joking—come in."

The door was opened, and the graybacks were not a little astonished at the sight of the "blue bellies," as they were pleased to call the Yankees in their sportive moods.

"By ——, that's so;" said one of them, who drew and discharged his pistol.

His arm was at once disabled by a shot from one of our men, and the order was given them to surrender at once, or they would be sent to another and hotter place.

They quietly obeyed, and our men took the whole party prisoners, and found the wounded man to be the famous scout Bailey Smith.

Redfield, with a few of his men, were guarding a squad of some twenty prisoners about a camp fire, when a rebel officer dashed up and said—

"Good evening, gentlemen—enjoying yourselves, eh?" and seemed to have an impulse to dismount, but suddenly seeing the condition of affairs, his impulse was quite strong to ride away, so he said: "Good evening and good night," and put his horse into a gallop; but it so happened that two of Redfield's men, of a polite turn, galloped by his side and soon brought him back, and allowed him to sit around the cheerful fire with the rest. Colonel Redfield, not unmindful of the duties of hospitality, endeavored to engage him in conversation, but to which he did not respond with that urbanity for which the Southern people have usually prided themselves. He said—

"You think it all very fine, I suppose, but in five minutes it will be all right, and you will be *my* prisoners."

It did not turn out that way.

### Startling Adventure of General Birney.

A personal adventure of General Birney, at Centreville, in the summer of 1862, showed the heroism of that officer. Our forces were following the rebel Jackson from Manassas, which he had evacuated in his own time and in his own way. "Whither had he gone?" was the question. "Was he at Centreville?" was the second question. Cavalry should inquire. "I have no cavalry," or "I can't lay my hand on any cavalry," said General Pope, when General Kearney suggested this to him. It was mentioned that there was one company in General Birney's brigade. "Let it feel the enemy if he be at Centreville," said General Kearney. "Go with it, General Birney, yourself," he added; "I don't like to risk a general officer, but his report is worth very much more than that of a subordinate."

General Birney galloped away in the direction of Centreville, at the head of his company, which, by the time he reached Centreville, mustered some forty men. With this small command at his back, General Birney proceeded to feel the enemy: felt his way into Centreville street, and into the tavern, where he stopped to make inquiries. He was lecturing the landlord on his rebel proclivities, when one of the videttes, whom he had posted on the hill to the right and left of the town, reported a cavalry regiment approaching with the Stars and Stripes flying. He was sure that it was the Stars and Stripes.

"What regiment?"

"Can't tell; but it must be one of the new regiments, its ranks are so full."

General Birney sent another man to

make sure it was one of our regiments. The report again came that the Stars and Stripes waved at its head. General B. stepped out to look for himself. The front line was forty rods distant. The Stars and Stripes were there, sure enough; but a large infantry flag, almost new. Every sabre was drawn, a thing not done by our cavalry when entering a town. The caps were different from ours; the uniform differed. It was the enemy—the flag a capture from one of our regiments. It was time to evacuate the town just retaken. General Birney ordered the bugle to sound, and at the head of his command of forty men moved *rather* rapidly toward Bull Run.

In response to his bugle the enemy sounded a charge, and a race began. A regiment had been posted at the Run three miles distant, and toward that our General hastened, after paying his farewell respects from the muzzles of his carbines. The enemy returned the compliment, with little or no effect. "Forward!" was the word, along a road not over good. Occasionally a horse stumbled; over his body and that of his rider the company galloped. The best horses of the regiment in pursuit were gaining—gaining; but the Run and the regiment on guard were in sight.

"Spurs to your horses, my men!" shouted the General. More stumbled and fell, but the rest kept on. Still the enemy gained—gained! upon them; and now one bold rebel just reaches General Birney's shoulder with his sabre. The General draws his pistol, and the rebel falls dead. Another moment, and the General is in the rear of the regiment at the Run, and orders them to fire at the rebel pursuers, who were unable to draw rein in season to escape.

### Howe, the little Drummer Boy in the Fifty-fifth Illinois.

In the spring of 1864, President Lincoln placed Orion P. Howe, who was for a time the little drummer boy for the 55th Illinois Volunteers, in the Naval School at Newport. This act was in consideration of the little fellow's bravery, as narrated by General Sherman. General S. wrote to the Secretary of War of him, saying that at the assault on Vicksburg he came to him at the front, crying out: "Gen. Sherman, send some cartridges to Col. Malmborg, the men are nearly out." "What is the matter, my boy?" "They shot me in the leg, Sir; but I can go to the hospital. Send the cartridges right away." Even where we stood, the shot

Old Capitol Prison, Washington.

fell thick, and I told him to go to the rear at once, I would attend to the cartridges, and off he limped. Just before he disappeared on the hill, he turned and called as loudly as he could, "Caliber 54." "I have not seen the boy since, and his Colonel (Malmborg,) on inquiry, gives me his address as above, and says he is a bright, intelligent boy, with a fair preliminary education. What" continues the General, "arrested my attention then was—and what renewed my memory of the fact now—that one so young, carrying a musket ball through his leg, should have found his way to me on that fatal spot, and delivered his message, not forgetting the very important part, even, of the caliber of his musket, 54, which you know is an unusual one."

### Portable Iron-Clad Breastworks.

While search was being made of the passengers on the Central Railroad train, one evening in June, 1863, a soldier noticed that a lady's dress appeared more full breasted than it naturally should be; and his quick eye also detected the fact that the artificial contents of the lady's bosom were pressed out against the folds of the dress, so as to make it almost certain that pistols were there. He was a very polite soldier, and in the most gentlemanly manner approached the lady and said—

"Madam, I want those revolvers."

"Sir," she replied indignantly, "I am a respectable woman, and have no revolvers."

"Madam," again said the soldier, very coolly, "I wish you would give me those revolvers,"—pointing to her bosom.

She again denied that she had any; whereupon, without further parleying, the soldier, in discharge of his duty, thrust his hand into the place of concealment and drew out a revolver, and kept on repeating the operation until seven were captured from their sacred citadel. Then gathering up the pistols, he politely remarked to the fair but utterly discomfited deceiver,

"Madam, your breastworks seem to have been iron clad."

### Gathering Violets on the Battlefield.

The battle fought by General Grant on the first Friday, while on his way to Richmond, was fruitful of incident, not excepting the romantic. Far down the plank road where Hancock fought, beyond the thickest rebel dead, lay a boy severely wounded,—perhaps not less a soldier, that he was but a boy. He had fallen the day before, when the Union army was farthest advanced, and had remained unmolested within the rebel lines. They had not removed him, and he was alone, making his company among the dead. When first discovered, the little fellow was crawling about, gathering violets. Faint with the loss of blood, unable to stand, he could not resist the tempting flowers, and had already made a beautiful bouquet. When a stretcher had been sent for and arrived, he was taken up tenderly and borne away, wearing a brave, sweet, touching smile. Could the violet bouquet thus made by that brave young patriot have been on sale at any of the great Soldiers' Fairs it would have been transmuted into a golden double-eagle.

### "California Joe" and his Telescopic Rifle.

"California Joe" will always be remembered as the very apostle of sharpshooters. While before Richmond, a rebel

California Joe.

sharpshooter had been amusing himself and annoying our General and some other officers by firing several times in that direction, and sending the bullets whistling in unwelcome proximity to their heads.

"My man, can't you get your piece on that fellow, who is firing on us, and stop his impertinence?" asked the General.

"I think so," replied Joe; and he brought his telescopic rifle to a horizontal position.

"Do you see him?" inquired the General.

"I do."

"How far is he away?"

"Fifteen hundred yards."

"Can you fetch him?"

"I'll try."

And Joe did try. He brought his piece to a steady aim, pulled the trigger, and sent the bullet whizzing on its experimental tour, the officers meantime looking through their field glasses. Joe hit the fellow in the leg or foot. He went hobbling up the hill on one leg and two hands, in a style of locomotion that was amusing. Our General was so tickled—there is no better word—at the style and celerity of the fellow's retreat, that it was some time before he could get command of his risibles sufficiently to thank Joe for what he had done.

### Zouaves on Picket Duty.

An industrious and shrewd typo from the Queen City of the Lakes, under Colonel Ellsworth, was out on picket duty in the Old Dominion, when a haughty son of the chivalry rode up, driven of course by his servant. Zoo-zoo stepped into the road, holding his bayonet in such a way as to threaten horse, negro and white man, at one charge, and roared out "Tickets!" Mr. " F. F. V." (he was one of 'em) turned up his lip, set down his brows, and by other gestures indicated his contempt for such mudsills as the soldier before him, ending by handing his pass over to the darkey, and motioning him to get out and show it to Zoo-zoo.

"All right," said the latter, glancing at it, "move on,"—accompanying the remark with a jerk at the coat-collar of the colored person, which sent him spinning several paces down the road.

"Now, Sir, what do *you* want?" said Zoo-zoo, addressing the astonished white man,—who now showed that he had recovered his tongue.

"What? I want to go on, of course. That was my pass."

"Can't help it," replied Zoo; "it says 'pass the bearer,' and the bearer of it has already passed. You can't get two men through this picket on one man's pass, *no how.*"

Mr. V. reflected a moment, glanced at the bayonet in front of him, and then called out to his black man to come back. Sambo approached cautiously, but fell back in confusion when the 'shooting stick' was brandished toward his own breast.

"Where's your pass, Sirrah?"

"Here, massa," presenting the same one he had received from the gent in the carriage.

"Won't do," replied the holder of the bayonet; "that passes you to Fairfax. Can't let any one come from Fairfax on that ticket. Move on!" A stamp of the foot sent Sambo down the road at a smart gallop.

"Now, Sir, if *you* stay here any longer, I shall take you under arrest to headquarters," continued Zoo-zoo.

Mr. V. caught up his reins, wheeled around, and went off at the best trot his horse could manage, over the "sacred soil." Whether Sambo ever hunted his master up, is not known.

### Zollicoffer's Death at the hands of Colonel Fry.

Colonel Fry, of the Fourth Kentucky Regiment, who killed the rebel General Zollicoffer, was for many years a personal friend of the latter, and in their youthful days the two were associates in school. Col. F.'s regiment came up and formed along a fence which separated the road from the field on the left, and the Tenth was on the right. The two regiments here formed in the shape of a V. The regiments which attacked Colonel Fry were Battle's Tennessee and the Fifteenth Mississippi, the Wigfall Rifles, and the Mississippi Tigers. These were the crack regiments of the rebels, and were only driven back by the terrible fire of the Kentucky Fourth.

It was at the point of the V, that General Zollicoffer died. He fell nearer the Union camp than any other man of his army. He was with Battle's regiment, his own home friends, born and brought up around him at Nashville. A short distance from him, to his right, a party of his men had broken from their comrades, and were herding together like frightened deer. Colonel Fry's men were just about to fire on them, Colonel Fry himself being at the right of his regiment, at the point of greatest danger. General Zollicoffer was on foot and within a few feet of the Colonel, an extra coat concealing his uniform. Upon discovering Colonel Fry across his path, General Zollicoffer threw up both hands and exclaimed:

"Hold, Fry! You are not going to fight your friends, are you? These men (pointing to the Mississippians) are all your friends."

Colonel Fry supposed, from the General's manner and remark, that he was one of our own officers, and at once replied:

Gen Felix K. Zollicoffer.

"Certainly not, Sir; I have no such intention."

Colonel Fry now turned and rode a few steps, when one of the General's aids fired at him, wounding his horse. Believing that he was tricked, Col. Fry at once wheeled and fired at the General, with deadly effect, the latter raising his hand to his breast and falling dead. His last words were, "I am killed; all's well," and with a groan expired.

The country people who had suffered from his lawless soldiery, or feared their ravages, were wild with delight at the report of his death. One old woman exclaimed, "I've got two children in the fight, but I don't trouble myself about them. I'm so glad that Zollicoffer is dead."

General Zollicoffer was a tall and rather slender man, with thin, brown hair, high forehead, somewhat bald, Roman nose, firm, wide mouth, and clean-shaved face. His face in death, bore no expression of malice, reckless hate, nor even a shadow of physical pain; but never was a countenance so marked with sadness.

### Southern Black-Horse Guards and Yankee Fire Zouaves.

The terrible tragedy of Greek meeting Greek was realized in all its fearful horrors at the battle of Bull Run, in the combat between the Union Fire Zouaves and the Black Horse Cavalry—the latter known as the "bloody pride" of the rebel army. They came upon the Zouave regiment at a gallop, and were received by the brave firemen upon their poised bayonets, followed instantly by a volley, from which they broke and fled, though several of the Zouaves were cut down in the assault. They quickly returned, with their forces doubled—perhaps six or seven hundred—and again they dashed with fearful yells upon the excited Zouaves. This time they bore an American flag, and a part of the Zouaves supposed for an instant that they were friends, whom they had originally

## GREAT CONFLICTS, INDIVIDUAL HEROISM, ETC.

mistaken. The flag was quickly thrown down, however, the horses dashed upon the regiment, the *ruse* was discovered, and the slaughter commenced. No quarter, no halting, no flinching now, marked the rapid and death-dealing blows of our men, as they closed in upon the foe, in their madness and desperation. Our brave fellows fell, the ranks filled up, the sabres, bowie-knives and bayonets glistened in the sunlight, horse after horse went down, platoon after platoon disappeared—the rattle of musketry, the screams of the rebels, the shout of "Remember Ellsworth!" from the lungs of the Zouaves, and the yells of the wounded and crushed belligerents filled the air, and a terrible carnage succeeded. The gallant Zouaves fought to the death, and were sadly cut up; but of those hundreds of Black Horse Guards, not many left that bloody encounter.

### Terrible Encounter—Texas and Iowa.

At the battle of Pea Ridge, one of the Texas soldiers was advancing with his bayonet upon a Lieutenant of the Ninth Iowa, whose sword had been broken; the officer saw his intention, avoided the thrust, fell down at his foeman's feet, caught hold of his legs, threw him heavily to the ground, and before he could rise, drew a long knife from his adversary's belt and buried it in his bosom. The Texan with dying grasp seized the Lieutenant by the hair, and sank down lifeless, bathing the brown leaves with his blood. So deadly stiff and firm was the hold of the grasp of his hand that it was necessary to cut the hair close from the head of the officer before he could be freed from the corpse of his slain foe.

### "Father, I will never Surrender to a Rebel!"

The First and Second Ohio Regiments, did glorious service at the battle of Bull Run. Colonel McCook had command of the First. His younger brother—only seventeen years old—was a member of the Second, and was left as a guard to the hospital. One of the enemy's cavalry dashed upon him and ordered him to surrender. The brave youth, with fixed bayonet, steady nerve and cool bearing, replied:

"I never surrender!"

The father, Judge McCook, who had all the day been arduously engaged in assisting and taking care of the wounded, bringing them in from the field, and that, too, at the imminent peril of his own life, was in the hospital tent and heard the order to his son. Seeing others of the enemy's cavalry near by, he rushed out, and shouted:

"Charley, surrender, for God's sake, or you are lost!"

Charley turned to his father, and with all the lion in his countenance replied:

"Father, I will *never* surrender to a rebel!"

In a moment a ball pierced his spine, but he instantly discharged his musket at the rebel horseman, and laid him low in death, and then fell himself, mortally wounded. The rebels now undertook to drag him off, but his father succeeded in obtaining his release.

### Fremont's whole Body-Guard Charged upon by One Rebel.

One of the Southern soldiers engaged in the conflict at Springfield, Missouri, where Fremont's Body-Guard achieved such a grand success, exhibited the gamest courage of which there is any record during the war. He was a young officer, was superbly mounted, and charged single-handed upon a large body of the Guard. He passed through the line unscathed, killing one man. He wheeled, charged back, and again broke through, killing another man. A third time he rushed upon the Federal line, a score of sabre points confronting him, and a cloud of bullets flying all around him; but he pushed on—on, until he reached Zagonyi, the Major of the Guards. He pressed his pistol so close to the Major's side, that the latter felt it and drew convulsively back, the bullet passing through the front of Zagonyi's coat, but who at the instant ran the daring rebel through the body; he fell, and the men,

Maj Gen. John C. Fremont.

thinking their commander hurt, killed the rebel with a dozen wounds.

"He was a brave man," said Zagonyi afterwards, "and I did wish to make him prisoner."

**Silence of a Drummer-Boy before the Flag.**

One of the volunteer military companies organized in Chicago, had a drummer-boy thirteen years old, a member of a Sabbath School in that city. As the company on drill were marching through one of the streets, a fine flag bearing the stars and stripes, was displayed from one of the many drinking-saloons which, unhappily, are to be found in that as in other cities. The Captain, with patriotic enthusiasm at the sight of the national ensign, ordered his men to halt, and give it a hearty salute. The drummer-boy, supposing the salute to be intended for the place, as well as for the flag, held his drum in perfect silence. The Captain, in a reproving tone, inquired the cause: "Sir," said the boy, "I would not go into such a place as that, and I certainly can not salute it." "My good boy," said the Captain, patting him on the shoulder, "my good boy, you are right, and I am wrong."

**Our Dear Old Flag Never Touched the Ground.**

When the brave Colonel Shaw, commanding the Fifty-fourth colored Massachusetts regiment, fell in the charge upon Fort Wagner, Charleston, S. C., most of his guard also fell with him. Sergeant Carney was also one of the bravest of his race on that eventful day. When Governor Andrew, of Massachusetts, presented the flag to that colored man, he said he gave it with undoubting faith that he would bring it back again without a stain.

On the eighteenth of July, 1863, the memorable assault was made on Fort Wagner. When the Sergeant arrived to within about one hundred yards of the fort — he was with the first battalion, which was in the advance of the storming column — he received the regimental colors, and pressed forward to the front rank, near the Colonel, who was leading the men over the ditch. As they ascended the walls of the fort, the ranks were full, but as soon as they reached the top, they "melted away" before the enemy's fire, almost instantly. Carney received a severe wound in the thigh, but fell only upon his knees. He planted the flag upon the parapet, lay down on the outer slope, that he might get as much shelter as possible, and thus he remained for over half an hour, till the second brigade came up. He kept the colors flying till the second conflict was ended. When the Federal forces retired, he followed, creeping on one knee, and still holding up the flag.

It was in this manner that the brave colored sergeant came from the field, having held the emblem of liberty over the walls of Fort Wagner during the sanguinary conflict of the two brigades, and having received two very severe wounds, one in the thigh and one in the head. Still he refused to give up his sacred trust until he found an officer of his regiment. When he entered the field hospital, where his wounded comrades were being brought in, both white men and black sat up in their beds, and cheered him and the colors until, exhausted, they could cheer no longer. Though nearly exhausted with the loss of blood, the brave standard-bearer said:

"Boys, I could not walk, but I did my duty; our dear old flag never touched the ground!"

### Eleven-Year Old Warrior Picking off the Enemy.

A boy about eleven years old, cut what might be called a tall figure in the Fort Donelson fight. His father, a volunteer, had been taken prisoner by the confederates some time previously. The boy smuggled himself on board one of the transports at Cincinnati, laden with troops for the scene of conflict. On the field, the morning of the great fight, he joined the Seventy-eighth Ohio, and being questioned by one of the officers, he told him of his father having been taken prisoner, and, having no mother, he had no one to care for him, and he wanted to fight his father's captors. The officer tried to get him to turn back, but he was not to be denied. So he succeeded in obtaining a musket, and went into the thickest of the battle. He finally by degrees crept up within a short distance of the Confederate intrenchments, and posted himself behind a tree, from which he kept firing as often as he could see a head to fire at. He was soon discovered by the enemy's sharp-shooters, who endeavored to drive him away from his position, as he kept picking them off very frequently. One of the secessionists, who was outside of the work, got sight of the boy with his rifle, but before he got his piece off, the little warrior fired, and down went Mr. Rebel. As the latter had a fine Minie rifle, the boy ran out and picked it up, taking time to get pouch and balls, together with his knapsack, while the bullets were flying on all sides of him, and then he retreated to his wooden breastwork, where he renewed his fire, and with a little better success. After being in the fight all day he returned to the Seventy-eighth at night with his prizes. This story might appear incredible for one so young to be the hero, but it is vouched for by a number of officers and men who saw the boy on the field and in the position mentioned, and many saw him shoot the man referred to, besides several others.

### "Don't Shoot there any more—that's Father."

An eye and ear witness relates an occurrence at the battle of Shiloh, which shows, by one of innumerable similar instances, the peculiar frightfulness of the "family war" growing out of the Southern rebellion:—Two Kentucky regiments met face to face, and fought each other with terrible resolution. It happened that one of the Federal soldiers wounded and captured a man who proved to be his brother, and, after handing him back, began firing at a man near a tree, when the captured brother called to him and said: "Don't shoot *there* any more—*that's* father." Such the war inaugurated by the fire upon Sumter's embattled walls. At Pittsburgh, two brothers fought on opposite sides, and in regiments directly confronting each other. It so happened that the Confederate brother was found mortally wounded, and was brought into the very hospital where his loyal brother had been detailed to nurse, and died in his brother's arms.

### Going in Quest of Satisfaction.

Just after the firing of musketry at the battle of Cedar Mountain had become interesting, a private soldier was noticed going off the field, and it being suspected that possibly he was running away to avoid danger, he was spoken to, when it was found that he had two fingers of his left hand shot away and a third dreadfully lacerated. It was seen at once that he had at least a hand in the fight. He was assisted to dress his wound as well as circumstances would permit, he in the meantime propping up the pluck of his assistant by various quaint remarks. Said he, "I don't keer a darn for that third finger; for it wa'nt of no 'count no how; but the pinter and t'other one were right good ones, and I hate to lose 'em. I should'nt have come to the rear if I had been able to load my gun, but I was'nt." After

Going in quest of satisfaction.

having his hand dressed, he looked over in the direction of the firing and stood a moment. Turning presently, he said, "Stranger, I wish you would jist load up my shooting iron for me; I want to have a little satisfaction out of them cusses for spiling my fore paw." His gun was loaded for him, and he started back for the top of the hill at a double-quick, in quest of "satisfaction." His name was Lappin, or Lapham, of the Ohio Seventh.

**Root Hog or Die: "Music hath Charms."**

At the battle of Lookout Mountain, a soldier belonging to an Ohio Regiment coolly sat down on a rock during the thickest of the engagement, to wait for his gun to cool off, as he had fired it very often and effectively. The boys who were fighting around him deliberately ceased their firing, and waited until he sung for them an old and familiar song, "Root Hog or Die," and which he is said to have sung with such humor as to make all merry and forgetful of the fearful scenes around them. When the song was finished, they reloaded their guns and again entered the fight, to the special damage of the rebels, who had to pay for the "charms" which "music hath."

**Joe Parsons' "Little Favor" from a Rebel Soldier.**

Here is all that need be said of "Joe Parsons, of Baltimore," as told by a newspaper correspondent:—Joe enlisted in the First Maryland regiment, and was plainly a "rough" originally. As we passed along the hall we first saw him crouched near an open window, lustily singing, "I'm a bold soldier boy," and observing the broad bandage over his eyes, I said,—

"What's your name, my good fellow?"

"Joe, Sir," he answered, "Joe Parsons."

"And what is the matter with you?"

"Blind, Sir—blind as a bat."

"In battle?"

"Yes—at Antietam. Both eyes shot out at one clip."

"I was hit" he said, "and it knocked me down. I lay there all night, and next day the fight was renewed. I could stand the pain yer see, but the balls was flyin' all round, and I wanted to get away. I couldn't see nothin' though. So I waited, and listened; and at last I heard a feller groan' beyond me. 'Hello,' says I. 'Hello yourself,' says he. 'Who be yer,' said I, 'a rebel?' 'You're a Yankee,' said he. 'So I am,' says I, 'what's the matter with you?' 'My leg's smashed,' says he. 'Can't yer walk?' 'No.' 'Can yer *see*?' 'Yes,' 'Well,' says I, 'you're a — rebel, but will you do me a *little favor*?' 'I will,' says he, 'ef I ken.' Then, I says, 'Well, ole butternut, I can't see nothin'; my eyes is knocked out; but I ken walk. Come over yere. Let's git out o' this. You p'int the way, an' I'll tote yer off the field, on my back.' 'Bully for you!' says he. And so we managed to get together. We shook hands on it. I took a wink outen his canteen, and he got onto my shoulders. I did the walkin' for both, an' he did the navigatin'. An' ef he didn't make me carry him straight into a rebel Colonel's tent, a mile away, I'm a liar!"

### Nerving his Hand One Instant More.

On that memorable hill where the army of the Union paused in the last of the Seven Days' Battles and hurled back the shattered hosts of the enemy, a soldier lay gasping, while life ebbed away with his fast flowing blood. The roar of the battle was around him, and the dying man heard the sounds of the strife strangely intermingled—it cannot be doubted—with those home sounds that come to the ears of the departing, in whatever scenes they meet the final summons. For him the war was over. To him peace was coming—the peace that passes human understanding. It was in this solemn moment, the soldier saw his General riding swiftly down into the battle. The sight caused his ebbing life for one instant—only one—to flow backward. Gathering his strength, the soldier seized his bloody cap in his freshly nerved hand, and raising it in the air waved it as the warrior passed him, cheered lustily, as of old in the camp when he was hale and strong, then smiled, laid his head back on the sod, and went away forever from battle-fields and the sound of human strife. It was not the person of his commander alone that the soldier cheered—not the General merely,—that the dying man recognized and loved even in death. It was the representative defender of the American Union and of the American Constitution,—the great cause for which men lay dying,—which inspired him.

### Out of Ammunition for a Time.

The following is a specimen of Sigel's strategy at Pea Ridge: A considerable force of the Confederate army was sent to charge some batteries which Sigel had stationed a little in front of a wood. The force was somewhat too formidable to oppose with the infantry he had at command, but the General was not at all at loss, and did not think of retreat. He ordered his men to lie down in the wood, ready to rise up in a moment and deliver their fire. Then he ordered his cannoniers to fire a few rounds of ball, and afterwards a number of blank cartridge.

The Confederates, cautiously advancing, at once guessed that poor Sigel had got out of ammunition. Their commander, with a shout of triumph, gave the order to charge in a body upon what he thought were empty guns. But when the screaming secessionists got within less than a hundred yards of Sigel's guns, his cannoniers were ordered to use grape and canister, and fire as quickly and accurately as possible.

At the same moment the infantry rose, advanced out of the wood, and poured in their volleys upon the bewildered enemy. The result was not to be doubted. The Confederates, dismayed at the storm which tore their ranks in pieces at such close distance, halted, shook for a moment, then broke and fled with cries of horror, leaving their dead heaped upon the field. A young farmer lad, belonging to a dragoon regiment which was sent to charge upon the flying enemy, remarked, "They lay there like grass cut down by a scythe, in great swaths."

### "God bless the old Fla—."

Major Barnum, of the Twelfth New York regiment, was one of the many brave officers who were mortally wounded in the battles of the Peninsula. While lying down breathing his last, in the agony of his bodily suffering, a friend asked him if he had any message to send home. He replied—

"Tell my wife that in my last thoughts were blended my wife, my boy and my flag."

He asked of the physician how the battle went, and when told that it was favorable to the Union cause, he said, "God bless the old fla—," and expired with the prayer finishing inaudibly with his closing lips. A noble prayer and a noble death.

### "Shackasses" just at the Right Moment.

One of General Fremont's batteries of eight Parrott guns, supported by a squadron of horse, and commanded by Major Richards of the First Pennsylvania cavalry, was in sharp conflict with a battery of the enemy near at hand, and both shell and shot were flying thick and fast, when the commander of the battery, a German, one of Fremont's staff, rode suddenly up to the cavalry, exclaiming in loud and excited tones,

"Pring up de shackasses, pring up de shackasses, for Cot sake, hurry up de shackasses, im-me-di-ately!"

The necessity of this order, though not quite apparent to the reader, will be more obvious when it is mentioned that the 'shackasses' were mules carrying mountain howitzers, which are fired from the backs of those much-abused but valuable animals; and the immediate occasion for the 'shackasses' in this exigency was, that two regiments of Confederate infantry were at that moment discovered descending a hill immediately behind the Federal batteries. The 'shackasses,' with the howitzers loaded with grape and canister, were soon on the ground. The mules squared themselves, as they well knew how, for the shock. A terrific volley was poured into the advancing column, which immediately broke and retreated. Nearly three hundred dead bodies were found in the ravine the next day, the effects of that volley from the backs of the 'shackasses.'

### Morgan! Morgan!

Morgan, the Confederate guerrilla chief, created terror wherever he stepped foot. *Apropos* of this wide-spread sensitiveness, is the following account of a scene which occurred at the City Hotel, Nashville, Tenn. A tall gentleman entered, pushed through the crowd rather unceremoniously, and registered his name 'Morgan—Cavalry;'—desiring dinner, supper, a bed and his bill, at the same time throwing down a twenty dollar note of Confederate scrip. "We are not taking that money now," said the polite clerk. "The hell you ain't; then, Sir, we don't trade," and with a pompous 'Ahem' he moved off. The conversation and demeanor of the officer attracted the attention of the crowd, and several looked at the name, among others, Lieutenant ——, who, on glancing at the register, was observed to change color, and with a nervous motion to hurry from the room. A murmur of surprise and amazement soon swelled into a cry of "Morgan! Morgan!" but the stranger was not to be seen. Scarcely twenty minutes elapsed when a company of infantry, fresh from the office of the Provost Marshal, rushed into the room with bayonets fixed and determined countenances. "Where is he?" inquired the commanding officer. "He passed out the back way," replied a wag, "and is now at the Sewanee House." "Right about face," and away they went at double quick—the last report representing them as still going. The originator of the cock-and-bull ruse was Captain Morgan, of one of the brave Ohio regiments of cavalry, a worthy officer and an inveterate wag.

### Behind the Trees: Maine and Georgia.

At the siege of Yorktown, and during the first day's skirmish on the Federals' right, two soldiers, one from Maine, and the other from Georgia, posted themselves each behind a tree, and indulged in sundry shots, without effect on either, at the same time keeping up a lively chat. Finally, that getting a little tedious, Georgia called out to Maine, "Give me a show," meaning step out and give an opportunity to hit. Maine, in response, poked out his head a few inches, and Georgia cracked away and missed. "Too high," said Maine,—"now give *me* a show." Georgia poked out his head and Maine blazed away. "Too lŏw," cried Georgia. In this way the two alternated several times, without hitting. Finally, Maine sent a ball so as to graze the tree within an inch or two of the ear of Georgia. "Cease firing," shouted Georgia. "Cease it is," responded Maine. "Look here," says one, "we have carried on this business long enough for one day; 'spose we adjourn for rations?" "Agreed," said the other. And so the two marched away in different directions, one whistling 'Yankee Doodle,' the other 'Dixie.'

#### Family Quarrel Settled on the Battlefield.

In the Confederate charge upon McCook's right, at the battle of Stone River, the Confederate Third Kentucky was advancing full upon one of the loyal Kentucky regiments. These two regiments were brought from the same county, and consequently were old neighbors, now about to meet for the first time as enemies. As soon as they came near enough for recognition they mutually ceased firing, and began abusing, and cursing, and swearing at each other; using the utmost license of denunciatory and outlandish names; and all this time the battle was roaring around them, without much attention from either side. It was hard to tell which regiment would come off victor in the wordy battle, for both sides were terrible in the use of profane nouns, adjectives, verbs, etc. But this could not always last; by mutual consent they finally ceased cursing, and grasping their muskets, charged into each other with the most unearthly yell ever heard, even on a field of battle. Muskets were clubbed, bayonet met bayonet, and in many instances, when old personal or local feuds made the belligerents rank-crazy with passion, the musket was thrown away, and at it they went with nature's weapons, pummelling, pulling, gouging, and clinching, in rough and tumble style, and in a manner that any looker-on would consider a free fight indeed. The secessionists were getting rather the better of the fight, when the Twenty-third Kentucky succeeded in giving a flanking fire, when they retreated with quite a number of prisoners in their possession. The Confederates had got fairly under weigh, when the Ninth Ohio came up on the double-quick, and charging on their now disordered ranks, succeeded in capturing all their prisoners, besides taking in return a great many of the Con-

Humphrey Marshall.

federates. As the recent belligerents were conducted to the rear they appeared to have forgotten their late animosity, and were soon on the best terms imaginable, laughing, and chatting, and joking, and, as the Confederates were well supplied with whiskey, the canteens were readily handed about from one to the other, until they all became as jolly as possible under the circumstances.

#### Two noble Women saving a Regiment.

When traveling on the cars from Bethel to Jackson, Tennessee, the Twenty-seventh Iowa regiment was saved from a fearful loss of life by the heroism of a couple of Union women. The train was running in the night at a high rate of speed, and just before reaching a railroad bridge the engineer saw a couple of lanterns being vigorously waved in the distance, directly on the track. He stopped the locomotive, and men were sent ahead to ascertain the cause of the alarm. They found that the lanterns were held by two women, who explained to them that a party of guerrillas in that vicinity had been informed of the coming of the regiment, and that about eight o'clock that evening the villains had set the bridge on fire, and allowed the main timbers to burn so much that they could not bear the weight of the train, and then put out the flames and went away, hoping, of course, that the cars would run on the bridge, that it would break down with the weight, and thus kill and injure many of the soldiers, and prevent the regiment from going through. The noble women had learned of these intentions, and had walked ten miles through the darkness and mud to save the Union soldiers.

#### Thirteen Battles and Three Flags.

At the battle and capture of Port Gibson, Sergeant Charles Bruner, a Pennsylvanian, of Northampton County, with a squad of fifty men of the Twenty-third regiment Wisconsin volunteers, was the first to enter said fort. The flag-sergeant being wounded, Sergeant Bruner seized the colors, and, amid cheers and a rain of bullets, planted the Stars and Stripes upon the ramparts.

Again, at Champion Hill, the Twenty-third was about breaking, when Sergeant Bruner took the colors in his hand, and cried, "Boys, follow! don't flinch from your duty!" and on they went, following their brave color-bearer; and the intrenchment was taken.

Again, at the battle of Big Black, Company B, of the Twenty-third Wisconsin, got orders from General Grant to plant a cannon and try to silence a battery, which was bravely done, when the cannon was dismantled, Captain and First Lieutenant were gone and wounded. Sergeant Bruner again cheered on his men, and, in a hand-to-hand fight, the enemy were routed. The Sergeant was made prisoner twice, but his captors were soon put *hors du combat* by his brave followers, who would die for the brave Sergeant—afterwards Captain. The Confederates were driven back with lost colors.

Singular to say, Sergeant Bruner, who, up to June, 1863, had led on his men in more than thirteen battles, and always in front, had the good fortune to escape being wounded. He captured, with his own hands, three Confederate flags, which he handed over to General Grant.

#### Well Done for a Youth.

The gallant conduct of Henry Shaler, of Indianapolis, Indiana, at the battle of Gettysburgh, was worthy of all praise and remembrance. He seems to have more than equaled the self-told mythical performance of the Irishman who "surrounded" a half-dizen of the enemy and bagged them plump. Henry's parents reside in Indianapolis, and are Germans. Harry is a brick; he did more, that is, he took more prisoners in the battle of Gettysburgh, than any other man in the army.

Gen. Meade's Headquarters.

He took in all twenty-five men,—one Lieutenant and eighteen men at one time; he took them by strategy that was strategy—he surrounded them, and they had to give up. On the morning of the fourth he went out with his poncho over his shoulders, so that the rebs couldn't see his coat, and thus they thought he was one of their own men. He went up and told them to lay down their arms and come and help carry some wounded off the field; they did so. When he got them away from their arms he rode up to the Lieutenant, and told him to give up his sword; the Lieutenant refused at first, but

Well Done for a Youth.

Harry drew his pepper-box, and like Crockett's coon, the Lieutenant came down without a shot. Harry then took them all into camp. He took a Captain and five men at another time, making twenty-five in all. Pretty well for a little Dutchman, like Harry—one of Meade's noblest fighters.

### Rallying Again for the Battle.

At the battle of Chickamauga, the chivalrous courage of General Reynolds enabled him not only to keep his own division in effective order, but to give effective assistance to the forces around him. A tremendous onslaught of the enemy broke General Palmer's lines, and scattered several of his regiments in wild dismay toward the rear. Amongst these was the Sixth Ohio, which, in charge of the fine-spirited Anderson, had, up to that moment, nobly maintained its ground. General Reynolds perceiving the danger, quick as lightning threw himself amongst the brave but broken Guthries.

"Boys!" he shouted, "are you the soldiers of the Sixth Ohio, who fought with me at Cheat Mountain? You never turned your backs upon traitors in Virginia. Will you do it here?"

"No! no!" they screamed almost frantically; "Lead us back! lead us back!!"

From every quarter came rushing back the scattered fragments of the regiment; with magic swiftness they re-formed the ranks; with General Reynolds at their head, they charged the jubilant enemy, and, after a moment's struggle, every Confederate in front of them, not killed or wounded, was in confused retreat.

The example of the Sixth Ohio was communicated to the flying fragments of other regiments, and it is a memorable fact in the history of this battle, that these rallied stragglers, principally from one division, re-formed ranks almost of their own accord, and drove back the forces of the enemy which at that point had been victoriously pressing on.

### Kilpatrick's Battle-Flag at Hagerstown.

On Monday, the thirteenth of July, 1863, General Kilpatrick was anxious to make an advance, but could not obtain orders. Some of the Pennsylvania militia were placed at his disposal, and he thought he would try one regiment under fire. The Philadelphia Blues were selected, and, accompanied by the First Vermont cavalry, a demonstration was made on the right—the Confederates then occupying a fortified position. The militia were now deployed, the General desiring them to move to the crest of a knoll, where the bullets were flying pretty lively. There was some hesitancy at first, whereupon the battle-flag presented to the division by the ladies of Boonsboro was sent to the front. Sergeant Judy, bearer of the flag, cried out—

"*This is General Kilpatrick's battle-flag; follow it!*"

The militia obeyed the summons promptly, and fell some distance in front of the line, and it was supposed for some time that the enemy had captured the flag; but at night, when Judy was brought in on a litter, he proudly waved the battle-flag.

The novelty of being thus under fire for the first time was keenly felt by the militia. About the first man touched had the top of his head grazed just close enough to draw blood. He halted—threw down his musket—truly an astonished

Maj. Gen. Judson Kilpatrick.

man! One or two officers and a dozen or more privates ran up hurriedly to see what the matter was. Running both hands over his pate, and seeing blood, he exclaimed, "A ball! A ball!"—while the others stood on agape with astonishment, until the shrill voice of the General sounded in their ears: "Move on there!"

### "I'll Do It, tell General Grant."

One of the Fort Donelson correspondents, writing from Cairo, gives a most graphic description of the attack by General C. F. Smith's division upon the enemy's works in that splendid fight. Captain Hillyer, General Grant's Aide de Camp, rode down to General Smith, with the order to charge at the point of the bayonet. It had been long and impatiently expected. "I'll do it, tell General Grant, I'll do it," was the reply; and then, facing his men, he shouted: "Soldiers, we are ordered to take those works by assault; are you ready?" "Ay, ay, Sir. Ready! Hurrah!" burst from the ranks. Then, placing himself at their head, he thundered — "*Charge bayonets! forward! double-quick!* MARCH!" The double-quick soon became a run, but, never faltering, the solid column charged through a storm of shells, solid shot and bullets, over the parapet into the fort, like a thunder-bolt, upon the panic-struck foe.

### Nothing Lost by True Courage.

An illustration of the spirit of the brave men who fought the battles of good government against treason will be found in the following,—though this is but one of a thousand similar noble and heroic instances.

A New Hampshire regiment had been engaged in several successive battles, very bloody and very desperate, and in each engagement had been distinguishing themselves more and more; but their successes had been very dearly bought, both in men and officers. Just before the taps, the word came that the fort they had been investing was to be stormed by daybreak the next morning, and they were invited to lead the 'forlorn hope.' For a time the brain of the Colonel fairly reeled with anxiety. The post of honor was the post of danger, but in view of all circumstances, would it be right, by the acceptance of such a proposition, to involve his already decimated regiment in utter annihilation? He called his long and well-tried chaplain into council with him, and, asking what was best to be done, the chaplain advised him to let the men decide it for themselves.

At the Colonel's request, he stated to the regiment all the circumstances. Not one in twenty probably would be left alive after the first charge. Scarcely one of the entire number would escape death, except as they were wounded or taken prisoners. No one would be compelled to go, if he did not go with all his heart. "Think it over, men, calmly and deliberately, and come back at twelve o'clock and let us know your answer." True to the appointed time, they all returned.

"All?" was the interrogatory.

"Yes, Sir, all, without exception, and all of them ready for service or for sacrifice."

"Now," said the chaplain, "go to your tents and write your letters—settle all your worldly business, and whatever sins you have upon your consciences unconfessed and unforgiven, ask God to forgive them. As usual, I will go with you, and the Lord do with us as seemeth Him good."

The hour came, the assault was made, onward those noble spirits rushed into "the imminent deadly breach," right into the jaws of death. But, like Daniel, when he was thrown into the lions' den, it pleased God that the lions' mouths should be shut. Scarcely one hour before, the enemy had secretly evacuated the fort, and the 'forlorn hope' entered into full possession, without the loss of a single man!

### Fighting, Dying, and Buried "with his Niggers."

Few military names among the fallen brave in the war against rebellion will maintain a more endearing freshness and hallowed association, than that of Colonel Robert G. Shaw. Of the most aristocratic family connections, wealthy, accomplished, he must have possessed the truest moral courage to have enabled him to march out of New York city, at the head of the Massachusetts Fifty-fourth regiment, all black or colored men, amidst the jeers and scoffings of the "roughs," and the contemptuous pity of many far removed from that class. Yet this did Colonel Shaw, one dawning spring day, with a brave, trustful heart, leaving mother and the beauteous young being whom he had just wedded, to go forth with those poor, despised men, the first regiment of "niggers" called into the field, and to share their hardships, and teach them the same knowledge that he himself possessed of things present and of events and duties to come.

Two months afterwards he was with them before Fort Wagner, sitting on the ground and talking to his men, very familiarly and kindly. He told them how the eyes of thousands would look on the night's work on which they were about to enter; and he said, "Now, boys, I want you to be men!" He would walk along the line, and speak words of cheer to his men. It could be seen, too, that he was a man who had counted the cost of the undertaking before him, for his words were spoken so ominously.—the Confederates having openly threatened to make an especial aim of any white officer leading colored troops,—his lips were compressed, and now and then there was visible a slight twitching of the corners of the mouth, like one bent on accomplishing or dying. One poor fellow, struck, no doubt, by the Colonel's determined bearing, exclaimed as he was passing him, "Colonel, I will stay with you till I die;" and he kept his word—he was never seen again after the charge.

The Fifty-fourth colored Massachusetts regiment held the right of the storming column that attacked Fort Wagner. It went into action six hundred and fifty strong, and came out with a loss of a third of the men, and a still larger proportion of officers, but eight out of twenty-three coming out uninjured. The regiment was marched up in column by wings, the first being under the command of Colonel Shaw. When about one thousand yards from the fort, the enemy opened upon them with shot, shell, and canister. They pressed through this storm, and cheered and shouted as they advanced. When within a hundred yards of the fort, the musketry from it opened with such terrible effect that the first battalion hesitated—only for an instant. Colonel Shaw sprang forward, and, waving his sword, cried—

"FORWARD! MY BRAVE BOYS!"

With another cheer and shout, they rushed through the ditch, gained the parapet on the right, and were soon hand to hand with the foe. The brave Shaw was one of the first to scale the walls. There he stood erect to urge forward his men, and, while shouting to them to press forward, he was shot dead, and fell into the fort. His body was found with twenty of his men lying dead around him, two lying on his own body. In the morning they were all buried together in the same pit. When the Federals asked for the gallant officer's body the next day after the fight, they said—

"Colonel Shaw! we buried him below his niggers!"

Thus died Robert G. Shaw—the rich, prosperous, accomplished member of one of the choicest circles of refined and elegant society in America, and who might have lived at his ease in the beautiful companionship and surroundings of his home on Staten Island. He who might have fought gallantly in splendid uniform on a noble charger among his fellows in riches and station, died fighting side by side with a race who, for generations, have been unstintedly despised and "cast out"—spending the last months of his life in friendly contact with them—and finally buried beneath "his niggers" with contempt and insult. There is no thread or filament of fiction interwoven with this sketch. It is reality unadorned with fancy.

---

### Good Samaritan in an Unexpected Hour and Place.

Soon after the battle of Bull Run, a gentleman who happened in at the quarters of the Michigan Fourth regiment, one morning, came in contact with a very intelligent Corporal, who became separated from his regiment during the retreat, and was obliged to seek shelter among the bushes. When night came, he wandered along and lost his way in the woods. Being slightly wounded in the leg, his progress was somewhat slow, so that by Wednesday night he had only reached the environs of Fairfax. Exhausted and completely dispirited, he espied a Confederate picket, and deliberately walked up and

Good Samaritan.

told the sentry who he was. To his grateful surprise the southern soldier poured out some whisky, gave him food, told him where he could find a stack of arms, and where he could sleep in perfect security in a negro hut. He added: "I am a Union man, but preferred to volunteer to fight rather than to be impressed. I thus save my property, and will trust to luck. If we meet again in battle, I will not try very hard to shoot you, and mind you don't me." Truly a good Samaritan and a wise man.

---

### Skulking and Fourth-of-July Speeches at Pittsburg Landing.

On the bluffs above the river there was—at the battle of Pittsburg Landing—a sight that made many a brave man's cheek tingle. There were not less than five thousand skulkers lining the banks! If asked why they didn't go to their places in the line, their reply was: "Oh! our regiment is all cut to pieces." If asked, "Why don't you go to where it is forming again?" "I can't find it," was the skulker's answer,—and he looked as if that would be the very last thing he would want to do. Officers were around among them, trying to hunt up their men, storming, coaxing, commanding—cursing. One strange fellow—understood to be a Major, undertook to make a sort of elevated, superfine Fourth of July speech to everybody that would listen to him. He meant well, certainly—as for example: "Men of Kentucky, of Illinois, of Ohio, of Iowa, of Indiana, I implore you, I beg of you, come up now. Help us through two hours more. By all that you hold dear, by the homes you hope to defend, by the flag you love, by the States you honor, by all your love of country, by all your hatred of treason, I conjure you, come up and do your duty now!"—and so on for quality. "That feller's a good speaker," was the only response heard, and the soldier who gave it nestled more snugly behind his tree as he uttered it. Enough is known of the nature of the skulking animal in an army during a battle; their performances show but little variation of programme, but rarely have they been known to "come off" on so large and heart-sickening a scale, as on this occasion. Still, it was a big army, and perhaps the skulking did not much exceed the average percentage. The runaways all sought the Landing.

### Escape of General Tyler and Staff.

The scene at the military head-quarters in Baltimore, July 13th, 1864, on the arrival of Brigadier-General Tyler, commanding the first separate brigade of the Eighth Army Corps, and who was reported to have been either killed or captured in the action at Monocacy Junction on the Saturday previous, was most exhilarating. Accompanying him were Captain Webb and Lieutenant Goldsborough, of his staff.

It appeared that on Saturday, after the Federal troops had retired from the Monocacy Bridge, General Tyler and his staff made a stand on the hill on the east side of the bridge, but were not there long before they discovered themselves to be surrounded by the rebels. The General and his party succeeeded in making their escape on the north side, closely pursued by the enemy, who fired upon them repeatedly, killing one of the General's orderlies, a German. To this fact, the General attributed his escape, as, when the soldier fell from his saddle into the road, the pursuers stopped to see who it was, and to inquire if General Tyler was not of the party. During this time, the General reached a clump of woods, and the three officers secreted themselves from their pursuers. A negro, who was endeavoring to make his escape from the rebel lines, pointed out the way to the house of a well known and patriotic citizen of Frederick county, whose family were unremitting in their attentions to the fugitives, concealing them until Tuesday, when they took their departure for Frederick, which they reached early in the morning.

The appearance of General Tyler in the streets of Frederick created the greatest surprise. The rebels had boasted that he had been killed by them, and it was believed to be a fact until the loyal citizens saw to the contrary themselves.

### Fruit in Old Age.

The name of Ishmael Day will long be remembered in Baltimore county, as that of one who, without fear of man, but in the fear of God, used the limbs and faculties with which God had endowed him, to the noblest advantage, in his old age.

On Sunday evening, July 10th, 1864, Day heard that Dulaney's valley, Maryland, was filled with rebels stealing horses and cattle, but did not give credit to the report, thinking they were Federal troops pressing horses. About sun-down the same day he heard that the rebels were on the Hartford pike, about a mile distant, the people living thereon being much excited. He went to bed, leaving a lamp dimly burning all night, and arose early

252    THE BOOK OF ANECDOTES OF THE REBELLION.

on Monday morning and ran up the glorious old Stars and Stripes rather earlier than usual, then sat down on the front porch. About six o'clock A. M., the sound of horses' feet coming down the road was heard, and in a short time two of them came at full tilt up to the door. Mr. Day moved down to the lower step to see if there were any more near, and, seeing none, resumed his seat.

By this time the foremost one had dismounted, seized hold of the foot of the flag, jerked it down and broke the rope, cursing and calling it a 'damned old rag.' Day coolly asked him, "What do you mean? What are you about?" Without waiting, however, a reply, he ran immediately up stairs, seized one of his two guns, already loaded in a bedroom. With this gun, he shot the foremost one of the rebels, direct-

Brigadier-General Wm. W. Averill.

ing his shot out of the second story window, which was standing open. When shot, the rebel was in the act of folding up the flag for his departure, but raised his hands and fell back, exclaiming, "I am shot!"

Mr. Day now seized the other gun, and ran down stairs, when he was met by Mrs. Day, crying, and imploring that he would not shoot again or they would kill him. He however pressed out into the yard to take a shot at the other marauder, but he was among the missing, having clapped spurs to his horse on the fall of his comrade. This was a matter of keen regret to the old patriot, as it failed him of the opportunity to give him his dose of metallic bitters also. Seeing none of the squad at the time, he walked up to the wounded man, and, in his patriotic anger, said, "You rebel rascal, I will now finish you!" Day cocked his gun for that purpose, but the rebel asked for mercy and surrendered. Knowing that he had received the whole charge, Day was satisfied that he could not live, and therefore did not shoot again,—seeing he would never be able again to haul down and dishonor the flag under which Averill 'led to conquer.'

The whole troop was now heard coming down the road. Day returned forthwith to his bedroom, got a six-barrelled revolver, and with the loaded gun started for a hiding-place, about two hundred and fifty yards northeast of his house,—hardly doing so before they were all at the house, at once firing his buildings, sparing only a small corn and hen-house. Everything was burnt by them, including all the personal property. At the end of the conflagration, which he was an eye witness to, Mr. Day went to one of his nearest neighbors to get some breakfast, and afterward to a second one to get his dinner, and was conveyed to Baltimore the same day. On the next Thursday, he had his name enrolled in the company of the Old Defenders, commanded by Captain Childs, for the defence of Baltimore, and on the same day obtained a guard from headquarters, to bring in the wounded rebel, who afterwards died.

A short time previous to this occurrence, Mr. Day, on being asked if he would keep his flag floating in case of an invasion by the rebels, said, emphatically—

"Yes, and I'll shoot the first of them who attempts to take it down, if it costs me my life the next instant!"

### Heroism of Sherman on the Battle-field of Shiloh.

At the battle of Shiloh, a cavalry officer having occasion to report personally to General Sherman about noon of the first day at that place, found him dismounted, his arm in a sling, his hand bleeding, his horse dead, himself covered with dust, his face besmeared with powder and blood; he was giving directions at the moment to Major Taylor, his chief of artillery, who had just brought a battery into position. Mounted orderlies were coming and going in haste; staff officers were making anxious inquiries; everybody but himself was excited. The battle raged terrifically in every direction. Just then there seemed to be universal commotion on our right, when it was observed that our men were giving back, General Sherman said—

"I was looking for that, but I am ready for them."

His quick, sharp eyes gleamed, and his war-begrimmed face beamed with satisfaction. The enemy's packed columns now made their appearance, and as quickly the guns which Sherman had so carefully placed in position began to speak. The deadly effect on the enemy was apparent. While Sherman was still managing the artillery, Major Sanger, a staff officer, called his attention to the fact that the enemy's cavalry were charging towards the battery. The General's quick reply to this was—

"Order up those two companies of infantry."

The General coolly went on with his guns, and the cavalry made a gallant charge—but their horses carried back empty saddles. The enemy was evidently foiled. Our men, gaining fresh courage, rallied again, and for the first time that day the enemy was held stubbornly in check. A moment more, and he fell back over the piles of his dead and wounded.

### Close of McPherson's Noble Career.

General McPherson's Grand Division held the left of the line in the fighting before Atlanta, on the day when his death occurred. About noon, the General received a report from one of his officers that the enemy were approaching upon the left—the extreme of his line—in heavy force. Arrangements were immediately set in motion to meet the expected attack, but as the blow was delayed, apprehension for a time was lulled. The General had ridden from left to right in superintending the advance of his skirmish line, and was returning again to the right. He was alone, or had with him only one of his orderlies, a faithful sergeant. Not being aware of the presence of the rebels so near him, he came upon a party lying in ambush, who, running from their covert between the Sixteenth and Seventeenth corps, cried out wildly—

"There they come; give 'em hell!"

A volley accompanied this, and the General was shot through the breast, the ball entering his right side and lodging in his body. He fell from his horse. A party of half a dozen rebels ran out from the woods, and coming up to where the sergeant was already bending over the body, they snatched a handful of papers from the General's side-pocket, took his gold watch, and, calling to the sergeant to follow them as a prisoner, were starting off. The sergeant feigned to be wounded, and was left to care for the dying General. Immediately afterward, officers and orderlies meeting Colonel Strong, Inspector-General, and Captain Buell, both of General McPherson's staff, accompanied by a few orderlies, related the whole circumstance. Colonel Strong instantly drew the party into line, and ordered a charge. This handful of brave and impetuous men, regardless of the foemen in front, dashed gallantly ahead, and drove off the thieving enemy. But the thieving was not all done by the enemy. Improving their chance, two Federal soldiers came up and took the General's pocket-book, containing three hundred dollars in money. One of them expressing a wish to see that it was safely kept to be restored, asked the other his name, at the same time giving his own. The only reply he received was to let him see the pocket-book, which the miscreant took, extracted the money, and then throwing the pocket-book down, ran away. General McPherson all this time was still alive, but unconscious. While Captain Buell, with his revolver, kept the enemy at bay, Colonel Strong, assisted by the orderlies, lifted the nude body, stripped of every article of clothing save a glove and a sock, to his own horse, and bore it safely from the field. Beneath the light glove covering the left hand was a diamond ring, which the vandals failed to discover. All this occurred in less time than it takes to describe it, and the daring and determined charge made by Colonel Strong for the body of his noble and loved chief formed one of the most gallant episodes of the war.

The General's body was conveyed in an ambulance to the head-quarters of General Sherman at Howard's house, where the officers who had heard of the sad event hurriedly assembled, to take a farewell view of their honored General. The body was still warm. General Sherman, who, up to this moment, had appeared unmoved by the untoward events of the hour, and by all the alarming reports brought to him, became deeply moved at the sight of the dead body of the General. He reverently uncovered his head as the corpse was brought in, all present doing the same, and gathered around the body. The noble features were as placid as if the dead were reposing in calm sleep. Officers and men, and the servants and orderlies of the departed, mingled their tears over the lifeless form of the great and good man who lay before them. Thus closed the noble career of one of the most brilliant officers in the national cause.

### Missing their Booty.

A narrow escape was that of Major Hale's, who was paying the troops stationed between Nashville and Murfreesboro'. He was, however, not doomed to 'fall by the sword,' nor yet by the rifle. The Major had been to Lavergne, and paid the Union troops there, and was on his way to Stockade No. 2, six miles from Nashville, in an ambulance, accompanied by a Lieutenant and two or three men. Before arriving at the stockade he sent the men forward to reconnoitre, feeling that such a precaution was necessary. Suddenly, half a dozen guerrillas made a dash on his ambulance,—the Major seized the safe key and took out all the large bills, and fled with them to the bushes.

The Lieutenant took a Henry rifle with him, and fled also. The horses attached to the ambulance immediately took fright, and had gone but a few rods when the safe fell out on the ground; at this the marauders dismounted, one of them exclaiming with gusto, "Here is what we are after!" They at once threw down the guns, and were about helping themselves to the money, when the Lieutenant, who, with the paymaster, was secreted in some bushes near by, fired and wounded one of the men. A comrade immediately went to his assistance, when a second shot brought the fellow to the ground, a corpse. The others, warned by this example, then fled without securing any of the coveted booty.

In the dead guerrilla, Major Hale recognized a man who was at Lavergne that very morning, trying to get a pass to Nashville as a loyal citizen!

### Anderson and his brave little Company leaving Fort Sumter.

Having defended Fort Sumter for thirty-four hours, until the quarters were entirely burned, the main gates destroyed by fire, the gorge wall seriously injured, the magazine surrounded by flames, and its door closed from the effects of the heat, four barrels and three cartridges of powder only being available, and no provisions but pork remaining, Major Anderson accepted the terms of evacuation offered by General Beauregard, and marched out of the fort Sunday afternoon, April 14th, 1861, with colors flying and drums beating.

The terms of evacuation were, that the garrison should take all their individual and company's property with them; that they should march out with their side and other arms, with all the honors in their own way and in their own time, and that they should salute their flag and bear it away with them. Beauregard previously had asked Major Anderson if he would not accept of the terms without the salute. Major Anderson replied, "No!" It was late on Saturday night when the terms demanded were finally agreed to; and then Beauregard sent word to Major Anderson that he would furnish the Isabel, or any other vessel at his command, to convey him and his men to any port in the United States he should choose.

On Sunday, therefore, the Isabel came down from Charleston, and anchored near Fort Sumter, and the little steamer Clinch lay alongside the wharf to transport Major Anderson and his men to the larger vessel.

When the baggage had been all put on board the Clinch, the soldiers being inside the fort under arms, a number were detailed to salute the United States flag. At the fiftieth gun the flag was lowered and the men set up a loud cheer. In firing, however, this last discharge, a premature explosion took place which killed one man instantly, seriously wounded another, and injured less seriously two other men. These were the only casualties of moment during the whole conflict.

The troops, having now been formed, were marched out, while the band played merrily "Yankee Doodle" and " Hail to the Chief." Remaining on board the Isabel during the night, in consequence of the state of the tide, Major Anderson and his men were transferred next morning to the Baltic, and during the evening of the day after sailed for New York.

### Safe Across the River.

The escape of a portion of the Massachusetts Twentieth, at the Ball's Bluff struggle, constituted one of the most memorable of the events connected with that awful tragedy.

After all was finished, and the fragments of the regiment were brought together on the water's edge, it was determined to push upward along the shore with the uncertain hope of finding some means of re-crossing to the Maryland side. In the event of meeting the enemy, however, it was decided to surrender at once, since any contest under the circumstances would be a useless sacrifice of life. After progressing a mile or so, the officers (Captains Bartlett and Tremlett, and Lieutenants Whittier and Abbott,) discovered a mill surrounded by cottages, about which numbers of persons were seen moving. Here it seemed that they must yield themselves. The officers ordered a halt, and directed the men to cast all their arms into the river, so that the enemy should gain as little as possible by the surrender.

"Shall we be accountable if we throw them away?" asked one or two.

"Guess not, if an officer orders us," said others.

So everything went over. Lieutenant Whittier went on in advance with a white handkerchief tied on his sword, to be used when occasion should demand. The first person met was an old negro, who, though greatly terrified at encountering so large and unexpected an assemblage, contrived to reveal that an old boat was stored near the mill, which might be bailed out and used to convey the fugitives across the river. A gift of five dollars insured his services, and the boat was in due time launched and ready for use. It was small, and only a few could pass each trip, but they were all transferred in safety.

### Hoax upon Rebel Sharpshooters.

One morning, some boys of the Fifteenth Illinois, who were doing duty in the rifle-pits at Vicksburg, manufactured an imitation soldier and accoutred him in the regulation uniform. When the bogus imitation was completed, they raised it up slightly above the work, when whizz—whizz—whizz—went the rifles of the rebel sharpshooters, and two bullets penetrated the spot where the brains ought to have been. Dropping him down, they soon exposed the figure again, and repeated it several times to the great amusement of the soldiers, who were delighted to see the rebels so completely humbugged into wasting their time as well as powder, in firing at a log of wood. The hoax was at length discovered by a lynx-eyed rebel, who, in clear clarion tones which were distinctly heard in our lines, shouted out, "Oh, you — Yankees, no more of your infernal wooden nutmeg and white oak cheese jokes. They are played out, and be — to you!"

### Generals Grant and Meade in Consultation before Richmond.

When the first terrible climax of the battle between Grant and Lee was over, Generals Grant and Meade established their personal head-quarters on the site of Cold Harbor. The great question was: Will the assault be renewed? To those looking into the face of General Grant for an answer to this query, there was no legible response. His is a face that tells no tales—a face impassive in victory or defeat; face of stone; a sphinx face! Not of him can it be said, as Lady Macbeth to her lord: "Thy face, my thane, is as a book, wherein one may read strange things." Rather is it a palimpsest, whose obscured characters escape the scrutiny of the keenest-eyed searcher.

Nothing, indeed, could be more striking than the contrast presented by these two commanders, as they stood in consultation on that bare hill, with their faces turned Richmond-ward. The small form with the slight stoop in the shoulders, sunken gray eyes, still, reserved demeanor, impassive face and chin as of a bull-dog or close-set steel trap—that is Grant; the tall figure, with the nervous, emphatic articulation and action, and face as of antique parchment—that is Meade,—and the antipodes could not bring together a greater contrast.

Whether it was that General Grant himself was in doubt as to the path which should be pursued, or that he felt the need of seeing for himself the actual situation —for from the thickness of the woods everything was hid as by a veil—is not known, but he suddenly mounted his horse, and rode rapidly down (an occasional shot or shell passing over his head and falling around at head-quarters) to the head-quarters of General Hancock, and afterward to those of General Wright; and when he came back it was plain there would be no renewal of the battle, for they all rode leisurely again to the old camp occupied the night before.

### Friendship's Strongest Test.

In the terrible engagement at Fort Donelson, an orderly sergeant, seeing a rebel point a rifle at the Captain of his company, threw himself before his beloved officer, received the bullet in his breast, and fell dead in the arms of him he had saved. The brave fellow had been reared and generously treated by the Captain's father, and had declared, when enlisting, that he would be happy to die to save the life of his benefactor's son. The affection shown by Damon and Pythias did not exceed that of this nameless soldier on the battlefield of his loved country.

### Four Strapping Confederates Bagged by a Union Captain.

One night in June the rebels about Vicksburg came out in force, and by making a long detour got in the rear of three companies which had been sent out to protect the men at work in digging Union rifle-pits. They killed, wounded and captured upwards of one hundred of our soldiers, and got back to their works just before daylight, with small loss. Captain G—, discovering that they were completely surrounded and that there was no chance of escape, contrived to climb a tree, and there he remained undiscovered until the rebels retreated, when he came down and started towards our lines. He had gone but a short distance when he suddenly came upon four rebels armed with rifles, who at the same moment saw him. It was a critical situation, but the Captain was equal to it. Marching directly up to them he said: "What the devil are you doing here?" The secesh were rather taken aback by his authoritative and bold manner, and never doubting for a moment that his Company were at hand, unhesitatingly laid down their arms upon his ordering them to do so. Soon after, our troops and pickets were greatly puzzled by the sight of four strapping Confederates marching in line in the direction of camp with a Federal officer immediately behind, a revolver in one hand, his sword in the other. It was Captain G—, marching his four prisoners to head-quarters.

### "Forward! March!"—Last Words of a Federal Lieutenant at Newbern.

A touching scene on the battle-field is the following, which occurred at Newbern, North Carolina: The Lieutenant was in advance of his men in the bayonet charge, when a volley from the enemy shattered his right leg and the Captain's left. They were both removed and laid side by side, when William called to the Surgeon and said, "Surgeon, you must amputate my leg, I cannot stand this." The Captain tried to persuade him not to have it removed, but he was determined, and said it must be done. The surgeon then administered chloroform and amputated his leg. As soon as the operation was performed, William called for a cigar, and smoked it very leisurely until the fire was near to his lips. The surgeon then came along, and inquired, "How do you feel now, Lieutenant?" To which he replied, "Very comfortable; but I feel as if that stump of a leg you cut off was on again and the toes were cold." The Captain said it made him shudder to hear William speak so coolly, and he turned his head so as to look in his face. As he gazed at him he thought his eyes looked strangely. At that moment William sat up, and in a voice which never sounded louder or clearer, shouted to his men, "Forward—march!" and fell back dead.

### Prayers for the President by a Dying Soldier.

The attack on Lee's Mills, near Yorktown, by the Fourth and Sixth Vermont regiments will be long remembered, and there was at least one incident connected with that attack which proves how much stranger is truth than fiction. In the summer of 1861, a private was court-martialed for sleeping on his post, out near Chain Bridge on the Upper Potomac. He was convicted, and his sentence was death; the finding was approved of by the General, and the day fixed for his execution. He was a youth of more than ordinary intelligence; he did not beg for pardon, but was willing to meet his fate. The time drew near; the stern necessity of war required that an example should be made of some one; his was an aggravated case. But the facts reached the ears of the President; he resolved to save him; he signed a pardon and sent it out; the day came. "Suppose," thought the President, "my pardon has not reached him." The telegraph was called into requisition; an answer did not come promptly. "Bring up my carriage," he ordered. It came, and soon the important State papers were dropped, and through the hot broiling sun and dusty roads he rode to the camp, about ten miles, and saw that the soldier was saved. He perhaps forgot the incident, but the soldier did not. When the Vermont regiments charged upon the rifle-pits, the enemy poured a volley upon them.

The first man who fell, with six bullets in his body, was William Scott, of Company K. His comrades caught him up, and as his life blood ebbed away, he raised to heaven, amid the din of war, the cries of the dying, and the shouts of the enemy, a prayer for the President, and as he died he remarked to his comrade that he had shown he was no coward and not afraid to die.

### Wigs on Rebel Majors.

Colonel A. K. Johnson, of the Twenty-eighth Illinois, shared in the dangers of many a bold adventure. On the last day of the action at Pittsburg Landing, and while the rebels were flying in confusion from their works, three of the officers in their flight passed very near the place where Colonel Johnson was stationed. The Colonel instantly started in pursuit. Coming within pistol range, he fired at the nearest of his flying foes; this brought the rebel officer down on his horse's neck. Colonel Johnson believing this to be a feint to avoid a second shot, determined to drag him from his saddle by main force. Riding up to his side for this purpose, he seized him by the hair of his head, but to his astonishment and disgust, he only brought off the rebel Major's wig. Instantly recovering his headway, he again started for the delinquent, but his pistol had done its work, and before the Colonel reached him his lifeless body had fallen from the saddle.

### He was Too Big not to be a Soldier.

When the present war commenced [says a contributor to Harper's Drawer,] I was practicing law in the State of Georgia. I was a strong Union man, and concluded to leave the land of secession and return to my native city. I started for Mobile to run the blockade; when I reached Montgomery, Alabama, I found I would have to remain until the next day. That evening, after tea, there was a large crowd in the rotunda of the hotel, and the war was, of course, the general theme of conversation. "War!—war to the death!" was nearly the only expression that could be heard. Every body was volunteering, and the whole city seemed to be in uniform. In the midst of the excitement a little boy, about five years old, came out of one of the

He was too big not to be a soldier

parlors, dressed in the full uniform of a Confederate Captain. He looked so pretty and smart that I patted him on the head, saying, "You're a very little man to be a soldier." He turned, measured me with his eye, and replied, "You're a very *big* man *not* to be a soldier!" The crowd appreciated it, and I paid for the liquor.

### Military Notation according to President Lincoln.

Somebody asked President Lincoln how many men the rebels had in the field. He replied very seriously, "Twelve hundred thousand, according to the best authority." The interrogator blanched in the face, at this reply, and ejaculated despairingly, "My God!" "Yes, Sir, twelve hundred thousand—no doubt of it! You see, all of our Generals, when they get whipped, say the enemy outnumbers them from three or five to one, and I must believe them. We have four hundred thousand men in the field, and three times four make twelve. Don't you see it?" The inquisitive man looked for his hat soon after "seeing it." The President's arithmetical logic was altogether too square and simple to be withstood, without questioning the veracity of *somebody's* statements. Perhaps Mr. L. P. Walker, or Mr. Judah P. Benjamin, the Confederate secretaries of war—and so well known as 'gentlemen of undoubted veracity!' could explain the discrepancy in numbers which so puzzled the good President.

Judah P. Benjamin.

**Captain Strong Delivering his Revolvers.**

While on duty extending the line of pickets, three miles north-west of Chain Bridge, Captain Strong, of the Second Regiment, Wisconsin Volunteers, was taken prisoner. As he neared the river he left three men, while, according to the orders of Major Larrabee, he reconnoitered, preparatory to assigning them positions. Having proceeded about a quarter of a mile without discovering the slightest trace of the enemy, he returned by a slightly different route, to avoid the rough road he had passed over, when he suddenly was surrounded by six rebel pickets —two cavalry and four infantry. The Captain surrendered; and while they marched him about twenty rods, amused themselves by applying the choicest epithets, and promising themselves the pleasure of a hanging bee. The Captain wondered they did not disarm him, but still did not see any way of escape until one of them, noticing his splendid pair of revolvers, said they would relieve him of them. "Certainly, gentlemen," said the Captain, drawing them from his belt behind him, and cocking them silently; "here they are!" As he said these words, he fired each, and two men fell dead at his feet, while he wheeled and secured cover in some thick bushes, eluding the immediate pursuit of all but two bullets, one of which pierced his canteen, the other, a small round pistol ball, passing through his left cheek, and coming out of his mouth, without injuring a single tooth, but slightly cutting his tongue!

**Carter's Polite Mode of Giving Information.**

General Carter's expeditionary tour into East Tennessee, in the winter of 1862–3, was attended with many brilliant successes as well as noteworthy incidents. Among the latter was a little occurrence, brief and decisive, at Blountsville and Zollicoffer, the former being the county-seat of Sullivan County. As the forces, or a portion of them, entered that town, a lady was observed at her door, throwing up her hands, and exclaiming: "The Yankees! the Yankees! Great God, we are lost!" After stopping at Blountsville, a few minutes, to feed their horses, they proceeded toward Zollicoffer, formerly called Union Station, on the Virginia and East Tennessee railroad. At this station were encamped about one hundred and fifty of the Sixty-second North Carolina regiment, Confederate soldiers, under command of Major McDowell. Colonel Carter, being in advance, met three citizens, and, after passing the salutations of the morning, inquired the news of the day, when one of them replied that there was "a rumor of there being a lot of — Yankees within a few miles of Blountsville."

"Ah! indeed," said Colonel Carter; "who is in command at the station below?"

"Major McDowell, Sir, and he is now coming up to find out the truth of the report."

"Well, gentlemen, you are all my prisoners. Guards, take them to the rear," said the Colonel.

In a few minutes Major McDowell rode in sight, and four of the Union troops filed across the road in his rear, when Colonel Carter approached him, saying:

"Major McDowell, I believe?"

"Yes, Sir, that is my name."

"You are my prisoner, Sir."

"Pray, Sir, who may you be?"

"Colonel Carter, Second Tennessee regiment, Federal troops!"

The Major looked utterly blank and down-hearted, but concluded that resistance was useless, when the Colonel informed him that he would impart to him, with the greatest pleasure in the world, the information he was seeking, namely, that there was a large Federal force in his rear—and, in order to prevent the effusion of blood, it would be policy to advise a surrender of the post. The poor Major agreed to this, and accordingly advised Lieutenant Inloes to surrender, which he did. It was a big day's business both for Carter and McDowell, though a little more satisfactory to the former than the latter.

### Disguised as a Bell-Wether.

Among the loyal Tennesseeans who, in 'the times that tried men's souls,' came into the Union Camp in Kentucky, was a little fellow of about five feet four inches, with gray and grizzled beard, dilapidated nose, and an eye as keen as a fish-hawk's. The manner of his escape from the military clutches of the secessionists was remarkable and highly ingenious. He headed a large squad of his neighbors, and eluded the Confederate pickets, by wearing a big sheep's bell on his head, and bleating away over the mountains, followed by a herd of men who did likewise. By this stratagem he deceived the Confederate scouts, and passed within a few feet of them through one of the most important of the mountain passes. Old Macfarland—the name of the hero of the bell—thus won the soubriquet of the bell-wether, by which name he became known all through the camps. He was a rough, and good humored old man, with a full supply of mother-wit, and was accustomed to speak of himself as 'under size and over age for a soldier,' which he literally was.

### Bishops Meade and Polk in Consultation.

The Right Rev. Leonidas Polk, Episcopal Bishop of the Diocese of Louisiana, forsook the gown for the sword at an early stage of the rebellion, having been commissioned a Major-General in the army of the Confederate States. The appointment was urged upon him for a considerable time before he accepted it, and previously to his doing so he paid a visit to the venerable Bishop Meade, at his home near Winchester, to consult with him about it.

Bishop Meade told him truly that he 'already held a commission in a very different army, to which he owed allegiance 'till life's journey ends.'

"I know that very well," replied Bishop Polk, "and I do not intend to resign it. On the contrary, I shall only prove the more faithful to it by doing all that in me lies to bring this unhallowed and unnatural war to a speedy and happy close. We of the Confederate States are the last bulwarks of civil and religious liberty; we fight for our hearthstones and our altars; above all, we fight for a race that has been by Divine Providence entrusted to our most sacred keeping. When I accept a commission in the Confederate army, therefore, I not only perform the duties of a good citizen, but contend for the principles which lie at the foundation of our social, political, and religious polity."

The result of this conversation was, that the Bishop soon afterwards accepted

GREAT CONFLICTS, INDIVIDUAL HEROISM, ETC.     261

the appointment which so soon cost him his life.

Polk was a native of Tennessee, and at an early age entered the Military Academy at West Point, where he graduated with distinguished honors,—a contemporary of Jefferson Davis, General Lee, General Johnston, and General Magruder, all birds of the same feather and hatched in the same nest.

### Yielding only when He Lost His Head.

Of the many instances of personal bravery among the *privates*, in the fight at Fort Donelson, probably but a small proportion will ever be recorded in the printed page. Here is one instance, too memorable to allow to pass unnoticed: A private in the Ninth Illinois regiment was shot through the arm in the early part of that sanguinary engagement, which paralyzed the limb for a moment. Leaving the ranks, he went back a short distance to where the temporary hospital was placed, had his arm dressed, and returned to take his place. Shortly afterward he received a shot in the thigh, which prostrated him. To some of his companions who came up to render him assistance, he remarked, "I guess I can manage to get back," and by the assistance of his gun he once more limped to the hospital. Feeling considerably better after his wound was dressed, he again sought his regiment and took his place in the ranks. While in a stooping position as a skirmisher, a ball entered the back part of his neck, and passed lengthwise through his body. Before he fell headlong to the ground, four or five other balls struck him in the head, literally shattering it to pieces, and scattering his brains in every direction. The name of those whom no extremity of danger and blood could daunt, in the war against rebellion, was Legion.

### Change of Tune and Position.

A gentleman whose slave accompanied a young Confederate officer on the Wild Cat expedition, asked the darkey on his return to Nashville, how long the army was on the march from its encampment to the battle-field.

"About four days," was the reply.

"Well, how long were they in marching back?"

"About two days, massa."

"Why, how is that, Joe? Could the men travel any faster back, when they were broken down with their four days' march and a severe fight, than they traveled forward after a good rest in camp?"

"Oh, I'll tell you what made the difference, massa," said Old Joe; "it was the music. They marched toward Wild Cat to the tune of Dixie. When they marched back, the tune was—'Fire in the mountains—run, boys, run!'"

### Firing Twenty-two Rounds with a Ball in his Thigh.

A very remarkable and praiseworthy case is recorded of a young man attached to the Thirty-first regiment of Illinois volunteers, when in battle. He received a musket shot wound in the right thigh, the ball passing through the intervening flesh, and lodging in the left thigh. The boy repaired to the rear and applied to the doctor to dress his wound. He however was observed to manifest a peculiar reserve in the matter, requesting the doctor to keep his misfortune a secret from his comrades and officers. He then asked the surgeon if he would dress his wound at once, in order that he might be enabled to return to the fight. The doctor told him that he was not in a condition to admit of his return, and that he had better go to the hospital; but the young brave insisted upon going back, offering as an argument in favor of it the fact that he had fired twenty-two rounds after receiving his wound, and he was confident he could fire as many more after his wound should be dressed. The surgeon found he could not prevent his returning to the field, so he attended to his wants, and the young soldier went off to rejoin his

262    THE BOOK OF ANECDOTES OF THE REBELLION.

comrades in their struggle, and remained, dealing out his ammunition to good account until the day was over, as if nothing had happened to him. Several days after, he returned to the doctor to have his wound re-dressed, and continued to pay him daily visits in his leisure hours, attending to duty in the mean time.

### Montgomery's Ride into the Hampton Legion's Nest.

West Point, Va., was the scene of one of the bloodiest of battles, May seventh, 1862. Of the various incidents by which it was distinguished, none was more notable than the escape of Captain Montgomery, General Newton's chief-of-staff, from the Hampton Legion.

It was about one o'clock in the afternoon, when the Captain received an order from General Newton to go forward into the woods to ascertain whether the secessionists were falling back, and whether a certain Federal regiment held its position there. Captain Montgomery went forward at once as fast as his well tried horse could run, and upon entering the woods moved cautiously until near a barricade, when, hearing voices, he plunged into the woods, thinking, of course, it was a Federal regiment—the Thirty-first New York —but was surprised to find that he had gone right into a perfect nest of the Hampton Legion, from South Carolina, who were lying behind trees, standing behind bushes, and kneeling behind stumps like bees.

At once perceiving his mistake, and aware that nothing but the most consummate coolness could save him, Captain M. saluted them, and they, taking him for a Confederate officer, inquired how far General Hampton was then. Without hesitation, and with *rather* more assurance than he ever thought he possessed, Captain M. replied, " I left him about ten rods below here—and now, boys! the General expects you to do your duty to-day !" He then turned his horse slowly to lull suspicion, and was congratulating himself on the probable success of the ruse, when the soldiers seeing the U. S. on his cap, yelled out: " That's a —— Yankee son of a ——, give him —— !" On hearing this, Montgomery dashed the spurs into his horse, threw his head over the animal's neck, and made for the road. A perfect volley of Minie balls passed over and around the Captain—killing the horse, who rolled over, carrying his brave rider with him down to the ground. Knowing that apparently nothing but time would save him, Montgomery lay with his head back in a ditch, as he fell, and appeared *dead* for some ten minutes, not moving a muscle or a feature, although the soldiers were swarming around and threatening to " end him." He remained in this way until they came up, took away his pistol and commenced a general plundering; as they thus fingered away he could not suppress a smile—and then rising, said:

" Well, men, I yield as a prisoner of war."

' You have been shamming," they said, "you d—— Yankee scoundrel, have you?"

" Certainly, everything is fair in war."

They then commenced to abuse him as a d—— Yankee this and a d—— Yankee that, when the Captain turned upon them and said—

" I have yielded as a prisoner of war: I demand to be used as such. We in the North know now to treat dogs better than you do men; now lead me to your commanding officer."

They gave him another volley of abuse, at which he merely smiled, and then a *shell*, fired by the Federal artillery to the place where the Captain was seen to enter, burst like the wind amongst them—*skinning the Captain's nose* and scattering the Confederates like chaff. Seizing their muskets, they pointed two of them at him, and said, " come along. you d—— Yankee !" He still continued conversation, in order to gain time, when another shell bursting amongst them, they moved on further, calling to their prisoner to "come on," the latter responding: "Go ahead, lead the way, quick."

Montgomery now saw a favorable moment, and preferring freedom to a Southern prison, made one bound into the woods and went back as fast as one leg would carry him, to the Federal lines. He was very much exhausted, and was carried to the rear by some men and placed under a tree, when, with suitable stimulants and care, he soon gained strength, and, calling for an extra horse, was lifted upon his back, and returned to the field, where he had the pleasure of once more reporting himself to General Newton for duty, and received the warmest greeting from that officer.

#### Lieutenant Davis's delicate little Task.

Lieutenant Frank C. Davis, Company D, Third Pennsylvania cavalry, performed a gallant exploit when the army of the Potomac was at Fair Oak station, in May, 1862. General McClellan was very anxious to communicate with the gunboats on the James river; and Lieutenant Davis, with one sergeant and ten men, was detailed for this purpose by Colonel Averill.

It was of the utmost importance that the communication should be opened. It was a known fact that the enemy were picketed all through that region, and the danger of capture was imminent. It was only by shrewd dodging from point to point that the Lieutenant consummated his errand successfully. The distance was some fifteen miles, but the party were obliged to make some twenty-five miles before reaching their destination. It was on a Sunday morning that Lieutenant Davis and Sergeant Vandergrift, with the command of ten picked men, started in the direction of the James river, to reach the point opposite City Point. After proceeding about four miles, he learned that six of the enemy's pickets were posted in the woods near by. He avoided these, and about one mile further on came across a negro, who stated that about three hundred yards further on were twelve mounted rebel pickets at a house. The Lieutenant avoided the latter by making a detour to the left, and took a by-road, leading over to the Richmond and Charles City road. The night before, some seventy-five Confederate cavalry passed up this road, but were not in sight at this time. The white

Lieut Davis.

people all along the way were terrified at the sight of Union soldiers, as this small party was the first they had ever seen.

A short time previous to the arrival of the Union party at this point, a secession foraging party had passed down the road; and the Union troops were now between two parties. In no wise daunted, they proceeded up the road toward Richmond, about four miles, through a deep wood, and came out at an opening and caught sight of the river, some three miles in the distance. The Lieutenant halted here and hid his men in the woods, then proceeded alone to a cross-road, to reach an eminence that gave him a view of the country around; while there, one of the

Union gunboats threw a shell into a secession party some distance above.

The Lieutenant then returned to his command, avoiding the Richmond road, as it was full of the enemy, apparently. He got a negro, belonging to Mr. Hill Carter, to pilot him down to the landing. The darkey stated that his master had acted as Colonel in the Confederate army at Williamsburg, but he got enough of it, and had left the service. While passing through this man's plantation the old chap himself rode down and demanded,

"Are you Yankee troops or Confederate?"

The Lieutenant answered that they were Union troops. Mr. Carter then stated that he did not allow Confederate troops to come on his plantation, as the gunboats shelled them, and would soon destroy his house. The Lieutenant assured him that he should be protected as far as they went. The Lieutenant got an old boat and two slaves to row him out to the Galena, Captain Rodgers; and when about half a mile from the boat he was met by a cutter from the ship. The message delivered was verbal, as the undertaking was very hazardous, and no writing was given. It was a gallant exploit all through, and was the first communication opened with the army. The party returned in the night, and reached camp at eleven o'clock on Monday morning, where a warm and deserved greeting awaited them, and the commanding General signified his appreciation of the importance of the undertaking, and the promptness and skill with which it was consummated, by an official letter of thanks. While the Lieutenant was on board the Galena, a squadron of the Confederate cavalry entered the small town on the opposite side of the James river at City Point, at the mouth of the Appomattox river. Two shells were thrown amongst them, as additions to their number, but they hastily ignored the new 'company.'

### Too Brave a Man to Disarm.

One of the earliest acts in the great drama of the rebellion was the capture of the United States arsenal at Apalachicola, at the mouth of the Chattahoochee river, by the troops of the State of Florida. In consequence of the weakness of the command, an entrance was gained. Mr. Powell, who had been in the service of the United States some twenty years, and had command of the place, acted in a gallant manner. After the troops had entered, he faced the line and thus addressed them:

"OFFICERS AND SOLDIERS: Five minutes ago I was the commander of this arsenal; but, in consequence of the weakness of my command, I am obliged to surrender—an act which I have hitherto never had to do during my whole military career. If I had had a force equal to, or even half the strength of your own, I'll be —— if you would have entered that gate until you walked over my dead body. You see that I have but *three* men. These are laborers, and can not contend against you. I now consider myself a prisoner of war. Take my sword, Captain Jones!"

Captain Jones received Commander Powell's sword, and then returned it to him, addressing him as follows:

"My dear sir! take your sword! You are too brave a man to disarm!"

The whole command then gave three cheers for the gallant Powell.

### Promises of Bravery in Advance.

Among the secession flags captured by the Federals in their rout of the Confederates at Philippi, Western Virginia, was a very beautiful silk banner which had been presented to a brave secession Captain, only the evening before the rout, by some fair secession ladies. On receiving the flag, the captain had made a gallant speech, assuring the bewitching donors that it should lead him and his company ever to victory or death; that where the battle was thickest there it should wave; that it should never trail dishonored in the mire—that rather would he spill his life's blood in its defence, and, dying, wrap his body in its gorgeous and defiant folds. But, alas! when that unmannerly cannon ball from the Cleveland artillery on the hill went crashing through the camp, this heroic Captain forgot all about the flag he had received with such exquisite gallantry the night before, and led the column—out of danger as fast as their legs could carry them.

#### "Go on with the Fight—Don't Stop for Me."

In the fight at Great Bethel, Orderly Sergeant Goodfellow, of Colonel Allen's regiment, was mortally wounded in the breast. He handed his musket to a comrade, and several flocked around him. "Oh," said he, "I guess I've got to go," and he placed his hand upon the wound. "Oh, don't mind me, boys," he continued, "go on with the fight; don't stop for me!" and pressing away those who attempted to support him, he sank down upon the ground. Just at that instant his Colonel passed, and looking up to him he gasped, "Good bye, Colonel!" Colonel Allen turned ghastly white as he observed it. He bit his lips, too much moved to speak, and rushed on to avenge his death.

#### "Oh, for Four Regiments!"

It is a fact acknowledged even by the rebel commanders themselves, that at the battle of Bull Run, the fortunes of the day were for a time evidently against them. Between two and three o'clock large numbers of men were leaving the field, some of them wounded, others exhausted by the long struggle; some of the best Confederate officers had been slain, and the flower of their army lay strewn upon the field. The result of that hour hung trembling in the balance. Among other high officers wounded was Colonel Hampton; but there was at hand the General whose reputation as a commander was in the die, on this battle,—General Beauregard,—who promptly led the Hampton Legion into battle. Just at this critical moment, General Johnston was heard to exclaim in agonizing energy to General Cock, "*Oh, for four Regiments!*" His wish was answered, for in the distance the rebel re-enforcements appeared. The tide of battle turned in their favor by the arrival of General Kirby Smith, from Winchester, with four thousand men of General Johnston's division. General Smith heard, while on the Manassas railroad cars, the roar of battle. He stopped the train and hurried his troops across the fields, to the point just where he was most needed. They were at first supposed by the rebels to be Federal troops, their arrival at that point of the field being so entirely unexpected. Cheer after cheer went up from the Confederate lines, and by them the battle was won.

#### Ben. Phillips, the Hoary Old Bloodhound.

An old Virginia trapper of considerable notoriety 'in his way,' Ben. Phillips by name, and for many years a resident of Hampton, was coming up the road near that town one afternoon, armed with a double-barrelled gun. Seeing a buggy some distance ahead of him, he slipped into the woods and waited its approach. He soon discovered two Federal officers seated in a buggy, and saw from their distressed appearance that they were in no condition to do him much damage. They hailed him as they passed, asking who he was, to which he responded in a way to suit his own purpose. As soon as they passed on, the old man let fly both barrels of his gun in rapid succession into the back of the buggy. A death-yell was heard, and one of the officers leaped out and took to the woods. The other fell forward, and the buggy passed on. Ben. had previously killed, at different times, nine of the Federal scouts,—affording a good specimen of Virginia Chivalry; a hoary old bloodhound.

### Western Regiments on a Charge at Fort Donelson.

At the battle of Fort Donelson, General Wallace ordered the Eighth Missouri and Eleventh Indiana to retake the hill from which the first brigade had been driven in the morning. Colonel Smith, commanding the second brigade, rode up, and in a clear, loud, ringing voice, gave the word of command. Colonel McGinnis, as calm and self-possessed as if on dress parade, repeated the order, and in double-quick the two regiments, the Missouri in the lead, moved forward. The hill proposed to be stormed was about a mile to the right of the Union position when the order was given. As they went forward they met bands of straggling soldiers of the various regiments that had been engaged in the morning, and who would shout out—

"Boys, you'll catch hell there on the hill!" "We were cut to pieces there this morning!" "There are seven regiments there all armed!" etc., etc.

But the two regiments moved steadily onward, notwithstanding the foreboding fears so freely and earnestly expressed by those who were just freed from the field of strife—and not a soldier of the little brigade seemed to hesitate or falter in the least.

"No man was there dismayed—
Take the hill!" Wallace said.

The ravine was reached, the two regiments in line, the Missouri in the lead, and up the hill they start. When about half way up they were met by a most fearful volley of musketry, while a sheet of flame seemed to burst from every bush and tree and log, and the leaden messengers of death sped in every direction. Our men saved their lives by their faithful practice of the Zouave drill—throwing themselves flat on their faces when the rebels poured in their hottest volleys—loading while on their backs, and never, indeed, upon their feet except when upon the advance after receiving the enemy's fire, or in returning fire. This was a new thing to the rebels, and in which they were not prepared to imitate. Seeing that our brave Zouaves were comparatively unharmed by their fiercest volleys, they began to give ground, and were evidently panic-stricken.

"On, men, on!" cried Colonel Smith.
"Forward, Zouaves!" repeated McGinnis.

With a cheer which made the old hills ring again, and which struck terror to the hearts of the retreating rebels, the two regiments rushed up the hill, driving the enemy straight into their entrenchments. So soon as they were fairly behind their fortifications the rebels opened upon the Eighth and Eleventh with grape shot and shell. Here several of the Eleventh were killed while lying flat upon their faces. One of the rebel gunners, a Hoosier from Evansville, and who knew the Eleventh Indiana when they approached, cried out, "Here comes those — Zouaves—fire low, boys, if you wish to do any good!" They accordingly depressed their guns, and began to throw shells right into our ranks. Night intervening, our men were drawn back a few hundred feet under the brow of the hill, where they slept with their arms in their hands, ardently wishing for the morning, when, under the protection of our guns, which General Wallace ordered up, they expected to storm the fortifications.

Alas! for the poor wounded soldier on the battle-field! Every possible aid was given them, yet all night long their groans could be heard, and their cries for water and for help. Many of the Eleventh wounded lay out in the open field exposed twenty-four hours to the cold and the tender mercies of the rebels, who stripped many of them nearly naked.

### Whiz-z-z and Whist.

One of the most daring feats performed in connection with the Island No. 10 struggle, was the planting of a battery by the boys of the Forty-third Indiana, at Rud-

## GREAT CONFLICTS, INDIVIDUAL HEROISM, ETC. 267

dle's Point, on the Missouri shore—in the very eyes and teeth of the rebels. Until they opened fire, the rebels did not appear to be aware, even, of their new position. Their gunboats soon fired up, however, to attack them, as the new position would cut them off from an important military depot, unless the Federals were driven away. Their attack by five heavy gunboats was terrific. So thick and fast they sent their shot and shell that the Union artillery were at times for fifteen or twenty minutes unable to show a head above the parapet to load or fire. The Federal guns, however, were well manned, and though only two against twenty, the enemy finally hauled off. Only one man—an artillery man—was killed on our side. The men in the pits took the thing very coolly. In the intervals between the discharges, more or less of them would rise up to look around; but when the smoke on one of the boats told them that shot or shell was coming, the cry was "Down!" and every head disappeared. Notwithstanding the hissing, screaming and whistling of the shot, round and conical, and the bursting of shells around and over them, they indulged in jests, and many of them were found deeply engrossed in games of cards. The remnants of shells fell into several of the pits. One pit was knocked in by a thirty-two pound shot, and buried the men in it a foot deep in sand. They kicked out, and laughingly dug their pit anew.

### Capital Ruse to Save Springfield.

Previous to the attack on Springfield by Major Zagonyi, Major White of the Prairie Scouts was captured by the enemy, but was recaptured on the same night by a detachment of Home Guards, and proceeded to Springfield, then held by only eleven men. Of these he at once assumed command.

While holding the town with this scant force, the rebels sent in a flag of truce, asking permission to bury their dead. Nine of his men were on picket duty—his whole garrison force consisted of him-self and two others. At first he scarcely knew what to do, for had the enemy supposed there were no greater force in town they would have retaken it, and perhaps massacred every man. In this strait he resorted to a ruse, which met with good success. Getting the bearer of the flag

Major Zagonyi.

into the hospital, under the pretense that it would be unsafe were any of his men to see him, he told him that General Sigel was in command of the town, and it would be necessary to send the request to him. He then took one of his men outside, gave him proper instructions, and then re-entered and engaged the confederate in conversation. In an hour or so, the man returned, and expressing General Sigel's regrets that, being mounted, he could not return a written answer to the request, gave the desired permission to bury the dead. The flag soon left, firm in the belief that an immense National force were encamped on the south and east of the town.

### Albert, the Drummer Boy of the Massachusetts Twenty-third.

Albert Munson, of Marblehead, was a little hero, fifteen years of age, who could merrily play Yankee Doodle and the Star Spangled Banner, and, struck by his bold and inspiring manner, Colonel Kurtz appointed him as a drummer in one of the companies of the Massachusetts Twenty-third. His father was attached to the same regiment.

They sailed in the Burnside expedition; and at the battle of Roanoke Island, after a weary march through slime and water, they came in sight of the enemy's battery. "Who will go and take it?" asked the General commanding. "The Massachusetts Twenty-third," was the quick reply. "Forward, then, double-quick!" and in the teeth of a galling fire they rushed to their death as it had been to their bridal. The father fell wounded by his side, but the son heeded him not; his whole soul had lost itself in the work before him. "Look at that child!" said one officer to another; "no wonder we conquer when boys fight so."

"Didn't I say they should run to the old tunes?" and seizing a disabled revolver for a drum-stick, he struck up, in a wondrously defiant way, our impudent old strain of Yankee Doodle. A flying rebel heard it, and looking back, took sure aim at Albert. A man near the boy saw the deadly aim, but tried to pull Albert down, but he stood his ground, and the ball did not fail to do its fatal work. His knightly Colonel's arms held the brave boy, and all bent eagerly to hear his last words;—"Which beat—quick, tell me?" Tears ran down the blackened faces, and one, in a voice husky with sobs, said, "We, Albert, the field is ours." The ears death had already deadened caught no sound, and his slight hand fluttered impatiently as again he gasped, "What? tell quick!" "We beat 'em intirely, me boy," said a big Irish sergeant, who was crying like a child. Albert heard then, and his voice was as strong as ever as he answered, "Why don't you go after 'em? Don't mind me, I'll catch up—I'm a little cold, but running will warm me." He never spoke again.

### Mrs. Brownell, the Heroine of Newbern.

Mrs. Brownell, wife of Orderly-Sergeant R. S. Brownell, of the Fifth Rhode Island Volunteers, accompanied her husband to the war, and he was severely wounded at Newbern. Mrs. Brownell was with the Third Rhode Island regiment at the battle of Bull Run, having been adopted as the 'child of the regiment' by General Burnside, then Colonel. She was on the field at the battle of Roanoke Island, in spite of the many efforts to keep her out of the way of danger. At

Mrs. Brownell.

the battle of Newbern she exhibited that presence of mind and bravery which proved her a woman of the most heroic character. She was on the field during the whole of the engagement, attending to the wounded, and giving encouragement by her fortitude and presence to the soldiers. When the standard-bearer of the Sixth regiment fell, she seized the banner, and, carrying it across the field, received a flesh-wound. She brought with her to the North a Secessia rifle, which she found after the battle—a prize of no little value.

### Appointment of Mrs. Reynolds as Major in the Army.

Governor Yates, of Illinois, paid a rather unusual but well-merited compliment to Mrs. Reynolds, wife of Lieutenant Reynolds, of Company A, Seventeenth Illinois regiment, and a resident of that city.

Mrs. Reynolds accompanied her husband through the greater part of the campaign through which the Seventeenth passed, sharing with him the dangers and privations of a soldier's life. She was present at the battle of Pittsburg Landing, and like a ministering angel attended to the wants of as many of the wounded and dying soldiers as she could, thus winning the gratitude and esteem of the brave fellows by whom she was surrounded. Governor Yates, hearing of her heroic and praiseworthy conduct, presented her with a commission as Major in the army, the document conferring the well-merited honor being made out with all due formality, and having attached the great seal of the State. Probably no lady in America ever before had such a distinguished military honor conferred upon her.

### Safeguard for Body and Soul.

Charlie Merrill, a young Massachusetts soldier, had an ounce ball pass through his head during the battle of Fredericksburg. It entered near his right eye and was extracted behind his left ear. Another ball would have entered a vital part of his body had it not been arrested by a Testament, in which it lodged. When this safeguard was shown the President, he sent to the hospital a handsome pocket Bible, in which, as an evidence of his warm regard, he caused to be inscribed: "Charles W. Merrill, Co. A., 19th Massachusetts, from A. Lincoln."

### One of the Most Brilliant Achievements of the War.

An incident occurred to the rebel forces stationed in the shore batteries at Island No. 10, which illustrates how easily, fortuitously, or perhaps it ought rather in this case to be said providentially, an army may be caught in a position from which it is impossible to escape. About five thousand men were stationed in and about the shore batteries. On Sunday night, as soon as they saw the Pittsburg run the blockade in safety, and knowing that the transports to convey General Pope's forces across the Mississippi had been got through the slough, and that very soon a strong force would be in their rear, they abandoned their camp and all its contents on Monday afternoon, and left for Tiptonville, only five miles distant by land, but by the river fifteen miles below New Madrid, hoping thence to escape by their transports. But on reaching the little town, what was their surprise to find the gunboats Carondelet and Pittsburg moored to the shore. On the left was a swamp through which runs the outlet of Reelfoot Lake, in front were the gunboats, on the right was the Mississippi, and they found, when too late, General Paine, with a strong force, posted in their rear. The rebels were caught in a trap from which there was no possible escape. A bloodless victory, with two thousand prisoners, was the immediate result. Great numbers fled to the swamps, but were soon glad to surrender, raising the whole number of prisoners taken there, at the Island, and other places, to near five thousand men. Thus, what the rebels acknowledged to be the key to the Mississippi, a position strong by nature, and fortified with consummate skill and great expense, and defended by five thousand men and one hundred cannon in battery, most of them very heavy, and numbers of them rifled, was taken, and the whole army captured by General Pope and Commodore Foote, without the loss of a single man. History will record it as, taken all in all, one of the most wonderful and brilliant achievements of the war.

### Sources of Merriment in Camp.

The funniest animal in the world is a little negro when he "lets himself out," and their antics are a continual source of merriment in camp—a monkey is nowhere in comparison. Nor are they lacking in shrewdness, and that readiness in repartee which characterizes the native-born Irishman.

A Chaplain in General Grant's army—when the latter was falling back from Oxford, Mississippi, after Van Dorn's movement on Holly Springs—gives an account of the motions of two little yellow fellows who had caught an old mule, and were following the rear of a regiment in advance. The older was probably ten years of age, and the other — his brother — a year younger.

Passing through a strip of woods, the younger, who rode behind, holding to his brother with both hands, had his cap knocked off by the protruding limb of a tree, and he began to cry. "Riding up," says the Chaplain, "I told him not to cry, and asked a soldier to hand him his cap, which was done cheerfully. The little fellow was "all right" in a moment, and politely thanked us. 'Now,' says I, 'you must take better care, and not lose your cap again. When you are traveling under trees, hold on to your brother with one hand and your cap with the other."

The older one turned around, and with a very dignified and grateful air said, "Thanky, Sar; thanky, Sar. Dat's jist it, Sar. Dat's what I tell 'im, Sar. But ye see, Sar, he never trabble none before, Sar!"

The Chaplain concluded that, under this combined advice, the little fellow long since became an experienced "trabbler."

### Black Squalls.

The Lieutenant-Colonel and Major of the —— Ohio Regiment of Infantry, had each a 'contraband' as servant. 'Jim' belonged to the Lieutenant-Colonel, and 'Harvey' to the Major. One day the Lieutenant-Colonel, hearing a disturbance in the rear of his tent, went out and found Jim and Harvey engaged in the amicable occupation of throwing boulders at each others' heads. After quelling the disorder the Lieutenant-Colonel demanded an explanation of the row. Jim replied in his justification as follows: That boy Harvey is de most ungratefulest nigger I ever saw. He had'nt no good place, and I brought him up to the Major, and introduced him to de Major, and spoke well of him to de Major, and got him a good place wid de Major, and now he's puttin' on more airs dan de Major."

### Failed to Hold his Position: General Palmer to General Pope.

As the Army of the Mississippi, under General Halleck, was approaching Corinth, General Pope, commanding the left wing, threw out a force toward Farmington, and General Palmer was ordered to occupy the ground with his brigade, the rest of the force returning to camp. The next morning the enemy, under Generals Price and Van Dorn, made an advance in force, and General Pope sent an orderly to inquire if Palmer could hold his position.

"Tell General Pope that I can hold my position against the world, the flesh, and the devil!"

Gen. Pope.

Before long, however, the rebels—for they were many thousand strong—compelled the brigade to fall back upon the reinforcements which were ordered up.

The affair being over, General Palmer rode to the head-quarters to report, and his appearance was the signal for a hearty laugh from the officers present.

"How is it, Palmer?" said General Pope, as he entered the tent.

"Well, General," said the gallant Palmer, "I can stand the world, but the devil was too much for me!"

#### Hoosier Straightforwardness.

An Indiana Chaplain at one of the camps near Corinth selected, for singing, the hymn commencing—

'Show pity, Lord, Oh, Lord, forgive;<br>Let a repentant rebel live.'

He had scarcely uttered the last word of this line, when a private soldier in his congregation—an old man and a zealous Christian—earnestly cried out, "No, Lord, unless they lay down their arms." While the clergyman was offering the concluding prayer, a rifle shot was heard as if from our pickets a mile beyond. The report of the gun was immediately followed by an exclamation from the same venerable Hoosier—" Lord, if that's a Union shot, send the bullet straight; an' if it ain't, hit a tree with it, Lord!"

#### Strong Professional Illustration.

The New York One-hundred and Seventh supported Cotheren's battery, at the battle of Antietam. During the hottest part of the fight, the enemy massed themselves opposite our front, for an assault on Cotheren's position. The battery was short of ammunition, and so reserved their fire, while throughout the whole field there came a lull in the tumult. The rebels advanced in a solid mass, with a precision of movement perfectly beautiful. It was a moment which tried the nerves of the bravest. In the mean time one of the lads—a noted sporting character from Elmira—becoming quite interested in the affair, had climbed a rock where he could view the whole scene. He occupied the place unmindful of the bullets which were buzzing like bees all around. The rebels came on until the boys could see their faces and then Cotheren poured the canister into them. The advancing column was literally torn to pieces by the fire. At this, the lad on the rock became frantic in his demonstrations of delight, and as one of the battery sections sent a shrapnel which mowed down a long row of Johnnies, he swung his cap, and, shouting so that the flying rebs could have heard him, sung out, Bull-e-e-e-e! Set 'em up on the other alley!"

#### Encounter of Picket Wits.

At times, the rebel and Union pickets were quite communicative, as the following dialogue which occurred at Yorktown between Joe D., of Leeds, Wiscousin, and one of the graybacks, when within ten rods of each other, will show. The parties were separated by a low, deep swale, covered with water and thick brush, completely concealing the parties. Joe hearing a noise on the other side, yelled out in a loud voice,

Hallo, Mike! Have you got any tobacco?

Secesh—with a strong Hibernian accent —Yes, be jabers, and whiskey too.

Joe—Come over, we'll have a quiet smoke!

Secesh—I'll meet you half way.

Joe agreed to do so, and advanced some distance through brush and water, and then stopped.

Secesh—Where the divil are ye? Are ye comin'?

Joe—I'm half way now. Can't go any further without swimming.

Secesh—Hav'nt ye a boat?

Joe—No, I have not.

Secesh—Where's yer gunboat?

Joe—Down taking care of the Merrimac.

Secesh—Then come over in that big balloon.

[Much laughter along the rebel lines.]

Joe—Have you a boat?

Secesh—I have, sure, and I'm coming over.

Joe then inquires the news of the day, and if his companion had a Norfolk *Day Book*.

Secesh replied—I have. Have you got a *Tribune*?

Joe answered that he had not.

Secesh—Where is General Buell?

Joe—Buell's all right, and surrounds Beauregard.

Secesh—Where's General Prentiss? Where's Saxton?

Joe—Where's Johnston?

[Another rebel laugh.]

Joe—How about Island No. 10?

Secesh—That's evacuated.

Joe—How is it that you left one hundred guns and six thousand prisoners?

General Saxton.

Secesh—Sure, they (the prisoners) were not much account.

Joe—How about Fort Pulaski?

Secesh—That be blowed! It was only a rebel sand bank. But tell me, what made ye leave Bull Run?

Dick B. (Union)—We had marching orders!

This caused great laughter among the rebels, some exclaiming, "Bully Boy!"

Dick B.—Where's Zollicoffer?

Secesh—Gone up the spout.

Joe—Why don't you come over?

Secesh—Can't get through the brush!

At this moment a rebel bullet came whizzing over by our men, and Joe angrily inquired who fired.

Secesh—Some fool over this way.

An order was then issued to cease firing.

Joe—Ain't you coming? What regiment do you belong to?

Secesh—Eighteenth Florida. What regiment do you?

Joe—Berdan's First regiment Sharpshooters.

Some of his comrades here warned him to look out.

Secesh—Would you shoot a fellow?

Joe—No! but I will stack arms and smoke with you, if you will come over.

Here a rebel officer ordered him back, and the secessionist refused to communicate further.

---

### "Glorious to Die for One's Country."

In the sanguinary battle of Antietam an officer of a Massachusetts regiment was mortally wounded. He had passed unhurt through the thickest of the fight. At one time, when his regiment had captured a flag from the enemy, he seized it, and, waving it proudly in the air, galloped fearlessly up and down the lines, his men cheering most lustily, and the bullets falling about him like hail. Later in the day, and when in a comparatively sheltered position, a random shot struck him, from the effects of which he died two days afterward.

As he lay near to death, and conscious of his approaching end, the musicians of the regiment happened to pass by. He called to them with a cheerful voice, and asked them to play the Star Spangled Banner. They played the grand old tune, and as he listened, the countenance of the dying soldier beamed with joy. He heard no more music until he heard that of heaven. He inquired the result of the battle, and, when told it was a victory, triumphantly exclaimed, "Oh! it is glorious to die for one's country at such a time as this!" Then, speaking in the most

## GREAT CONFLICTS, INDIVIDUAL HEROISM, ETC. 273

affecting manner to his Chaplain, who was with him to the last moment, he said, "Tell my mother I love her. Tell her I feel I have a God and Father in heaven. Tell her I trust fully in my Lord Jesus Christ." These were the last words he uttered.

### Courtesies of Picket Life.

When our army was in the Chickahominy swamps, before Richmond, just at the breakfast hour, when the aroma of good coffee is doubly delicious, our pickets were accosted by a voice from the rebel side, only a few rods distant, with—"Hallo, there!" "Hallo yourself!" "What you doing over there?" "Making some coffee. Have some?" "Will you let me come over?" "Yes." "Will you let me come back?" "Yes." "Honor bright?" "Yes." And over he came. His coffee drank, he smacked his lips, and said: "Well, that's very nice. We don't get any of that on our side;" then casting his eyes around, scrutinizing the neat appearance of our men, he continued: "Well, you look very comfortable. All of you live so?" "Yes." A few moments more of silence, and he broke out: "Well, I like the looks of things here. I believe I won't go back." And he didn't.

### Raw Recruits on Camp-Guard.

It happens to the new recruit that, sooner or later, he has to be posted on camp guard for the first time, and this was the lot of our "intelligent" friend who figures below. Rebel cavalry was known to be in the vicinity of the Federals, and as there were expectations of an attack, the new recruit placed on guard was instructed, if there was any firing on the picket line, to report it instantly. In the course of the evening he observed a fire in the direction of the pickets, which the "reserve" had built for their personal comfort. Supposing this to be the very thing he was cautioned about, 'Raw' dropped his gun and started through camp yelling at the top of his voice, "Fire on the pickets! fire on the pickets!" Thus summoned, every man was in line in a twinkling, breathlessly awaiting the expected foe. But when the cause of alarm was explained, the yells and shouts that greeted our new soldier can only be understood by

Courtesies of Picket Life.

those who have heard a battalion of soldiers cheer.

#### Jeff. Davis's Trap for Grant.

On the 6th of November, 1863, one of the rebel journals in Richmond said that "whether General Grant intends to advance or is preparing to retreat from Chattanooga, he must be defeated either on the south side of the Tennessee or on his retreat to Nashville."

General Grant had, however, no intention of retreating.

About this time the rebel President paid a visit to Bragg's army, to ascertain the true condition of affairs, and it is reported that the following scene occurred on the summit of Lookout Mountain:

Looking down one bright day from the lofty eminence commanding a clear view into four States, and a very distant view into a fifth, Davis saw Grant's army almost beneath his feet; across the valley, working like beavers on their fortifications:

"I have them now," said he, "in just the trap I set for them."

To which Lieutenant-General Pemberton, who was sitting on horseback beside him, replied:

"Mr. Davis, you are Commander-in-Chief, and you are here. You think the enemy are in a trap, and can be captured by vigorous assault. I have been blamed for not having ordered a general attack on the enemy when they were drawing around me their lines of circumvallation at Vicksburg. Do you now order an attack on those troops down there below us, and I will set you my life that not one —— —— man of the attacking column will ever come back across that valley, except as a prisoner."

#### Sherman's Courage before the Enemy.

The advance of General Grant's army before Chattanooga commenced Nov. 23d, 1863. It involved one of the hardest fought and most protracted struggles of the war, and one which crowned the Union arms with undying renown. General Howard's corps was selected by Grant to open communications by the east side of the Tennessee river with General Sherman. Learning that General Sherman's position was not over two miles and a half distant, General Howard sent one of his staff on the dangerous mission of finding General Sherman alone. The skirmishers were thrown forward until the line became dangerously extended, and none of General Sherman's troops were found. The staff officer departed on his mission of danger; but by keeping close to the river succeeded in crossing and re-crossing the gap without being captured. General Howard, on receiving his report, ordered the division to push further to the left, and started out to seek General Sherman. They soon met. Sherman, on the north end of the bridge, dressed loosely, with a worn overcoat thrown around him, was directing the completion of the bridge; and, as soon as the boat was put in, sprang over and shook the hand of the princely Howard. It was exactly at noon.

In about an hour after the meeting of Howard and Sherman, the latter gave his orders to prepare for an attack. The drizzly rain began to fall, and the object of the assault was soon hid from view. General Sherman stood on a prominent hill to the left of the pontoon bridge, and having succeeded, with the aid of two orderlies, and in despite of the rain, in lighting a cigar, stood puffing away at one end, chewing at the other, and observing all that could be seen in the country before him. Around him were gathered at this time Generals Frank Blair, Morgan L. Smith, Ewing, John W. Corse, and Howard. The troops of the several divisions were encamped just in front of him, while on the left and rear Davis's artillery was thundering over the bridge.

In a very quiet tone Sherman gave his orders to form for the assault, remarking that the enemy was reported heavy on his front. The formation as ordered, was *echelon* on the left, General Morgan L. Smith's division being the left, John E. Smith the centre, and Ewing the right. The left was to keep well toward the Chicamauga Creek, Sherman remarking:

"I want you to keep up the formation, four hundred yards distance, until you get to the foot of the hill."

"And shall we keep it after that?" asked Ewing.

"You may go up the hill," answered Sherman, "*if* you like, and can."

General Davis having got into position, and the troops having been arranged as ordered, General Sherman gave the orders to move to the assault. They were couched in calm, laconic, unpretentious terms, as follows:

"I see Davis is up. *I guess you may as well go on, and take the hill.*"

In a few moments after, the three columns were moving.

But it was not destined that Tuesday should witness the great conflict for those hills. The doings of that day were more of a preliminary than a decisive cast, the latter being reserved for the succeeding day's history. The sequel of the fight—the next morning's handsome epilogue to the night's drama—is well known; its laurels are yet fresh and green. Sherman carried the end of Missionary Ridge, and the troops from Lookout Valley carried the point of the mountain.

---

**Battle with Snow Balls at Chattanooga.**

On the 22d of March, while our army was at Chattanooga, the earth was covered with a beautiful sheet of snow, measuring one foot deep on a level. Such a thing was never known before, at such a time of year, and the residents there, including that inevitable "oldest inhabitant," all agreed that such a thing was never known before at the season—indeed, no such depth of snow, at any part of the year, in that region of the "sunny South," had been known for twenty-three years past. The soldiers found an inconceivable amount of fun in it.

Early in the morning the town was alive with the merry shouts of Uncle Samuel's blue coats, engaged in the exhilarating pastime of snow-balling. Gradually the fun assumed immense proportions. The fight waxed hot and furious; and whole regiments were ranged in battle array, opposed in friendly combat. Officers and men partook of the sport; breastworks were formed of the snow, and the boys, led on by their officers, threw out their skirmishers, formed the flanking parties, and opened the fight. The battle, though a sham one, was most exciting.

One regiment had formed behind breastworks, had thrown out its pickets, and was all ready, awaiting the attack of its opponents. Each of the gallant lads was armed with a ball in each hand, and several lying ready at his feet. Soon another body was seen to come over the top of a hill in front of the fort, with skirmishers thrown out, and in a few minutes the skirmishers of the advancing party were engaged with the pickets of the army in the front. They fought for some minutes, when the skirmishers being heavily reinforced, the pickets retired to the interior of the fort, and prepared with the main body for the siege. It was not long delayed, for the besiegers advanced actually to the fort, and with a yell rushed up to the very mouth of the embrasures. Then the fight commenced in earnest. For a time the boys in the fort had the best of it, for they had a good supply of ammunition on hand; but soon this was exhausted, and the army inside had to manufacture their hand grenades of snow, the same as those on the outside. The besiegers climbed up the fort walls, making shot of the walls as they went, and such fun—such a scene for a few minutes! It ended in the attacking party being driven off.

The battle was gone through with a second time, and on the third trial the besiegers were more successful, for, detaching a party from the main body, and winding them around the rear of the fort, they awaited patiently for the signal of the flanking party. The signal was not long in coming, and the two parties attacking the fort simultaneously from front and rear, compelled the garrison to surrender. The surrender was done in good military style, the victors allowing them to evacuate with all the honors of war, and fists and necks and ears full of snow to boot.

### Splendid Service in a Bad Cause.

Lamar Fontain proved himself one of the most daring of the many brave rebels in the Southwest, and his name will long be remembered with satisfaction by those whom he served so well in a bad cause.

One of the most hazardous feats undertaken by Fontain was that by order of General Johnston—to bear a verbal dispatch to General Pemberton, in Vicksburg, and to carry a supply of percussion caps to the rebel troops in that besieged

Gen. A. Sidney Johnston.

city. It was an enterprise of great peril, for Vicksburg was closely invested on all sides. The Federal lines of circumvallation extended from Snyder's Bluff, on the Yazoo, to Warrenton, on the Missis-ippi, and the rivers and their opposite shores were filled and lined with their forces. He was well mounted, and was burdened with forty pounds of percussion caps, besides his blanket and crutches. He had no use of his broken leg, and could not walk a step without a crutch; and in mounting his horse, he had to lift it over the saddle with his right hand. All this, however, he accomplished with much dexterity and without assistance.

He crossed Big Black River that night, and the next day got between the Federal lines and the division of their army, which was at Mechanicsburg. He hid his horse in a ravine, and ensconced himself in a fallen tree, overlooking the road, during the day. From his hiding place, he witnessed the retreat of the Yankees, who passed him in considerable haste and confusion.

After their columns had gone by, and the night had made it safe for him to move, he continued his route in the direction of Snyder's Bluff. As he entered the telegraphic road from Yazoo City to Vicksburg, he was hailed by a picket, but dashed by him. A volley was fired at him by the Yankees, but he escaped unhurt, though a minie ball wounded his horse mortally—not, however, until the spirited animal had carried him safely to the bank of the Yazoo river, where he died, and left his rider afoot. He lost one of his crutches in making his escape, it being jerked from him by the limb of a tree, and he had no time to pick it up.

With the assistance of one crutch, he carried his baggage, and groped along the Yazoo, until he providentially discovered a small log canoe, tied by a rope, within his reach. He pressed this into his service, and paddled down the river until he met three Yankee gunboats coming up to Yazoo City. These he avoided by running under some willows overhanging the water, and lying concealed until they passed. Soon after he floated past Snyder's Bluff, which was illuminated, and alive with amusement on the part of the Yankees. He lay flat in his canoe, and could hardly be distinguished from a piece of drift wood—and thus he glided safely through the gunboats and barges of his foes. Before day, he reached the backwater of the Mississippi, and in the darkness missed the outlet of the Yazoo, and got into what is called "Old River."

After searching in vain for a pass into the Mississippi, day dawned, and he discovered his mistake. He was forced to conceal his boat and himself, and lie by for another day. He had been two days and nights without food, and began to suffer the pangs of hunger. At night he paddled back into the Yazoo, and descended it to the Mississippi, passing forty or fifty of the Federal transports. Only one man hailed him from the stern of a steamboat, and asked him where he was going. He replied that he was going to his fishing lines. In the bend, above Vicksburg, he floated by the mortar-fleet, lying flat in his canoe. The mortars were in full blast, bombarding the city. The next morning he tied a white handkerchief to his paddle, raised himself up, in the midst of the rebel picket-boats at Vicksburg, and gave a loud huzza for Jeff. Davis and the Southern Confederacy, amid the *vivas* of the rebel sailors, who gave him a joyful reception, and assisted him to General Pemberton's head-quarters.

Having rested a day and a night in the city, he started forth with a dispatch from General Pemberton to General Johnston. He embarked in his same canoe, and soon reached the Union fleet below the city. He avoided their picket-boats on both shores, and floated near their gunboats. He passed so near one of these, that through an open port-hole he could see men playing cards and hear them converse.

At Diamond Place he landed, and bade adieu to his faithful "dugout." After hobbling through the bottom to the hills, he reached the residence of a man who had been robbed of all his mules and horses, except an old, worthless gelding, and a half-broken colt. He gave him the choice of them, and he mounted the colt, but soon found that he traveled badly. Unexpectedly he came upon a very fine horse in the bottom, tied by a blind-bridle, without a saddle. As a basket and old bag were lying near him, he inferred that a negro had left him there, and that a Yankee camp was not far distant. He exchanged bridles, and saddled the horse, and mounted him, after turning loose the colt.

After riding so as to avoid the supposed position of the Yankees, he encountered one of them, who was returning from a successful plundering expedition, being loaded with chickens, and a bucket of honey. He commenced catechizing Fontain, who shot him dead by a pistol-bullet through his forehead.

Fontain approached with caution the next settlement, where he hired a guide for fifty dollars, to pilot him to Haukerson's Ferry, on Big Black River, which he wished to reach near that point, without following any road. The fellow he hired proved to be a traitor. When he got near the ferry, Fontain sent him ahead, to ascertain whether any Yankees were in the vicinity. The conversation and manners of the man had excited his suspicions, and as soon as he left him he concealed himself, but remained where he could watch his return. The man was gone much longer than Fontain expected; but returned, and reported that the way was open and that no Yankees were near the ferry.

After paying him, Fontain took the precaution to avoid the ferry, and to approach the river above it, instead of following the guide's directions. By this he flanked a force of the Yankees posted to intercept him; but as he entered the road near the river bank, one of them, who seemed to be on the right flank of a long line of sentinels, suddenly rose up within ten feet of him, and ordered him to halt.

He replied with a pistol shot, which killed the sentinel dead, and, wheeling his horse, galloped through the bottom up the river; but the Federals sent a shower of ball after him, two of which wounded his right hand, injuring four of his fingers. One grazed his right leg, cutting two holes through his pantaloons, and another cut through one side of the sword scabbard. Seven bullets struck the horse, which reeled under him, but had strength and speed enough to bear him a mile from his pursuers, before he fell and died. Fontain then divided his clothes and arms into two packages, and swam Big Black River safely. He did not walk far before a lady supplied him with the only horse she had. On this he reached Raymond at two o'clock in the morning, changed his horse for a fresh one, carried his dispatch to Jackson that morning, and landed safely down home again.

### No Respect for the Tender Passion.

When the Third Massachusetts cavalry was at Louisiana, Private C. P. Philbrick, of that regiment, rode out alone one day, within the enemy's lines, and captured a rebel Colonel, with an audacity that put chivalry to an immense disadvantage. Colonel Bradford was visiting his lovely affianced, at a plantation house four miles from Jackson, where he supposed himself entirely safe in her agreeable company, for the rebel pickets were right within call. Philbrick, however, late at night, stole into the negro quarters, and learned from the slaves, who were always friendly, all that he wished to know. Quietly fastening his horse, he crept to the front door, burst it open, and pistol in hand, astonished the assembled party with the sight of a Union soldier on the rampage. The scout thundered out his orders to an imaginary company, through the back window, kicked over the whist table, smashing the goblets and a bottle of "Widow Cliquot" that had probably paid recent duty at Baton Rouge, disarmed the Colonel and took both him and his servant prisoners, mounted them on their own horses, and brought them off amid the tears and lamentations of the 'affianced' and her friends. Through by-roads the unlucky Colonel was brought safely to camp, and was soon on his way, with a letter of introduction, to head-quarters. The prisoner nearly ground up a fine set of natural teeth when he learnt that his amours had been broken in upon, and his capture effected, by a single soldier, armed no better than himself. Alas! that war should have no respect even for the tender passion!

### Fierce Artillery Duel.

Probably one of the most spirited and hotly contested artillery duels of the war was the fight, one Friday afternoon in June, 1864, between Battery D, First Ohio, Captain Cockerell, and the enemy in Georgia, who had just got into position on the Marietta road,—as the enemy fell back behind his works.

For over two hours these antagonistic batteries, within six hundred yards of each other, kept up an incessant fire of shell and shot, during which Captain Cockerell threw at the enemy a full supply of ammunition, emptying his limbers and caissons. His guns were protected by the crest of the hill, his horses, also, being under cover. The rebel finally gave up to superior metal, moral and physical, and yielded the contest.

Meantime, the Thirteenth New York Independent Battery of light twelves, connected with General Geary's division of Hooker's corps, was brought forward down the hill upon the run, and advanced to the top of a ridge confronting the enemy's works at a distance of four hundred yards, in fact on the very skirmish line. Here, sinking their guns so as partially to find protection under the hill, Captain Wheeler and Lieutenant Bundy kept up a steady cannonade on the enemy's battery of eight guns on the opposite crest, doing terrible execution, cutting down whole forest trees, knocking away the logs and earthworks, killing the rebel gunners, and so disabling them that they were compelled to detail men from the ranks to supply gunners.

At one or two of the enemy's eight gun battery all the men but two were killed, and they crawled into a hole from the dreadful, annihilating fire.

### Midnight Charge of the Mule Brigade.

During the advance of General Hooker's command upon the enemy, near Lookout Mountain, an incident occurred which caused much merriment at the expense of the rebels. Hooker moved on Lookout Mountain very cautiously from the west side; and it was while engaged in the movement up the valley, that a great stampede among the mules took place. It was in the dead of night, when both armies were resting from the fatigues of the previous day, and the sentinel's tread was the only sound that disturbed the universal quiet.

Rushing from the wagons, to the number of about thirty, the mules made for the enemy's lines like frightened sheep. The drivers were awakened by the noise, just in time to witness the disappearance of the animals through our advanced pickets. The enemy's pickets were not caught napping. Hearing the mule brigade tearing across the valley, they mistook them for Yankee cavalry charging, discharged their muskets at the supposed 'Yanks,' and fell back upon a battalion stationed a little in the rear of them, with the cry that the enemy was upon them.

The battalion, partaking of the alarm, sprang to arms only in time to hear the sound of the frightened mules, whose race was not checked by the volley from the pickets. They retreated also a short distance to a point where a whole rebel brigade had stacked their arms, and were calmly dreaming of home and battle scenes. In rushed the battalion, more dead than alive from fright, with the exclamation—"*Hooker has surprised us; his cavalry is upon us!*" The valiant sons of Mars did not wait to gather up their blankets or guns, but made the fastest pedestrian time on record back to the main force, leaving upon the field, for the mule brigade, over one thousand stand of arms, among which were three hundred new Enfield rifles, blankets, small arms, knapsacks, etc. Meantime, our teamsters had given the alarm, and a force was sent out for the recovery of the mules, and in a few hours the expedition, inaugurated by the mules, returned to our lines with the valuable spoils.

This midnight charge of the mule brigade is well worthy of a place in history. Through its aid a large amount of valuable stores and arms was secured, and Hooker was enabled to push his advance much nearer the point of ground contended for.

### Won his Wager.

A Seneca Indian, belonging to the fourteenth New York artillery, made a bet that he would capture a rebel sharpshooter who was in a tree in front of our line in Virginia. He enveloped himself in pine boughs till he looked like a tree, and by

Won his Wager.

slow movements advanced near the sharpshooter's roost. Here, Indian like, he patiently waited until his prey had emptied his piece at one of our men, when he suddenly brought his musket to bear upon the reb, giving him no time to reload. The sharpshooter was taken at a disadvantage.

To the command to come down he readily assented, when the Indian triumphantly marched him a prisoner into camp, and won his wager.

#### No Dead Cavalry-Men.

An anecdote is told of General Hooker, which shows that his opinion of one branch of the military service was just right. Soon after he assumed command of the Army of the Potomac, he summoned to head-quarters all the principal cavalry officers in his command, twenty-five or thirty in number. Arranged in a semi-circle facing him, he addressed them after this manner, very coolly and with low voice at first, but warming as he proceeded:—" Gentlemen : I have called you together to consult with you in regard to the cavalry arm of the service. I think it should be, and may be, made more efficient. It seems to me to be at present a very costly show—very expensive and very useless. Why, gentlemen," moving up and taking a step forward—" I'll be —— if I have ever seen or have ever heard of a dead cavalry-man !"

#### Sheridan and the Moonlight Picture.

The night after the battle of Mission Ridge, General Sheridan went in pursuit of the flying enemy, and met with a sharp resistance near Chickamauga Station, some two miles beyond the Ridge. At about seven o'clock of that November evening he sent a regiment to take possession of a little promontory jutting out into the valley, which would give him a vast advantage. The musketry were briskly playing all the while, time was precious, the position important, the regiment a long time executing the movement, and Sheridan, anxious and impatient, was watching the sky line to see the troops emerge from the shadows and move along the clear-cut crest of the promontory. The moon, then near the full, had just risen above the edge of the hill, when the battalions moved out of the darkness, and exactly across the moon's disc. There, for an instant, was the regiment, colors and gleaming arms in bold relief and motionless—a regiment transferred to heaven ! And there was the moon, a great medallion struck in the twinkling of an eye, as if in honor of that deathless day. The General's eye brightened at the sight. Even there and then it was something to be thought of; to be seen but a moment—to be remembered forever.

#### Very obliging Picket at Morris Island.

A somewhat singular circumstance occurred on picket one night at Morris Island. During the night a man named Henry Grand, of Company E, One Hundredth New York regiment, was killed while in discharge of his duty, and his body lay between the lines. Captain Ayres of the Third Rhode Island, shortly after the event had been made known, leaped upon the top of the last parallel and shouted to a rebel picket, " Here, you; we have a man killed out there and want to bring his body in." " Well," replied the rebel, " three of you may come over for it." Whereupon Captain Ayres started with three men, making, including himself, four altogether. The rebel observing four men approaching him cried out before they had proceeded far, " Halt." The command having been complied with, the rebel continued thus :—" I said but three might come over—one must go back." Captain Ayres then returned, and was followed soon after by the three men bearing the dead body of their comrade. The rebel was certainly very obliging, and what motive prompted him to extend such a privilege could not be easily accounted for.

#### Incident of the One Hundred and Nineteenth New York Regiment.

There was a small detachment of the One Hundred and Nineteenth New York which had advanced close up to the enemy—so close that they had been compelled to halt for the time and throw up light breastworks of logs as a defence. By some untoward mistake a party of twelve or fifteen men were ordered to advance beyond these works on picket duty.

Though knowing that it was almost certain death to show their heads above the walls of their little fort, still they obeyed without question or hesitation. They had advanced scarcely more than a rod beyond their comrades, when a heavy volley of musketry prostrated to the ground every man save two. Two were killed instantly, and the rest wounded more or less severely. All of the wounded, however, were able to drag themselves back and escape, except one poor fellow, Sergeant Guider, who was so badly wounded that he could not stir from his place. There he lay almost within arm's length of his comrades, and yet they were powerless to rescue him or give him aid, so galling was the rebel fire. One bolder than the rest made the hazardous attempt; but scarcely had he got over the breastworks when he fell severely wounded. They endeavored to allay his raging thirst by throwing to him canteens of water, and even one of those was pierced by a rebel bullet.

Finally, as they could not go over the breastworks, they dug a way under them with no other implements than their bayonets, and through this, two men crawled and succeeded in reaching him unhurt. Just as they reached him, their comrades in the rear gave an exulting cheer, which elicited from the rebels another volley. A fatal ball pierced the poor fellow's breast for a second time, and he had only breath to murmur feebly to his rescuers, "Now I die content—I am in your hands," and expired.

### "Boys, I'm for the Union Still."

Daniel Sullivan, of the Ohio volunteers, had his arm shattered by a ball, when the Federal troops were surprised at Vienna. This was the brave boy, who, when ordered to fall in, replied, "I wish I could," at the same time showing his arm. Sullivan was taken up and carried back with the retreating force. He died before leaving Alexandria, but his heroism was shown to the last. A handkerchief was bound upon his arm, near the shoulder, to check, in a measure, the flow of blood. This rude bandage Sullivan himself adjusted several times, tightening it to check the blood, and again loosening it when the pain became too great. While he was lying in this condition, some of his comrades approached, and one asked, "Dan, how do you feel?" "Boys," said the young hero, lifting with the other hand his shattered arm, and then laying it gently down, "Boys, I'm for the Union still!" Poor Dan died very soon after, but his last words were a mighty spell and watchword to his comrades.

### Emphatically a Bootless Undertaking.

In the earlier days of the rebellion there lived in southeastern Missouri one Ogilvie B. Young. He was a wild, graceless, Southern cavalier, who plunged madly into the first waves of rebellion, and, while Sterling Price was yet a Union General, and Claiborne F. Jackson a loyal Governor, dared to avow and advocate opinions of the most ultra Southern character. Fine-drawn theoretical arguments on the right and duty of secession were spread before the people of the State, in column after column of letters published in newspapers, and to which was attached the full signature, "Ogilvie Byron Young." He was sent to the Missouri State Convention; and though the State did not secede, he did.

In the fall of 1861 he was arrested in Cincinnati as a spy, but escaped conviction; and the same thing, with a similar result, occurred at Covington. In November, 1862, he was in Nashville, as a paroled prisoner, but acting all the while as a smuggler and spy. But about the last of that month, Young was introduced to a gentleman who represented himself as a hostage for the return of certain loyal

Mississippians captured at Iuka, and treated by Price as traitors, contrary to the terms of the cartel between the Federal and Confederate authorities. At first he was shy and suspicious, but was finally convinced that his new acquaintance was really what he purported to be, and heartily entered into all his plans for the advancement of the Confederate cause. As his confidence grew stronger, he remarked that he had been of more benefit to the South, as a spy, than any brigade of rebel soldiers. He had encouraged desertions in the Federal camps, and made out paroles in the names of Morgan and Kirby Smith; The business was getting a little dangerous now, however, and he should get beyond the lines as soon as possible. He would have gone long ago, only that he had expected to be saved the trouble and expense of the trip by the fall of Nashville.

The Iuka hostage then informed him that Mrs. Major Ranney, wife of Major Ranney, of the Sixth Texas regiment, was in the city, under his charge, and just returned from Europe, whither she had been on diplomatic business for the Confederate Government. She had in her possession very important despatches, and was anxious to get safely through the lines with them. Young said, in reply, that he would bring his influence to bear upon the army officials in her favor, but in case she should be searched it would be well to provide for such a contingency. There was, he said, in the city, a man by the name of Thompson, ostensibly a citizen, but really a rebel Lieutenant in Bragg's army, and then acting as a spy. He had made the trip through the lines ten or twelve times, and could do it again. He was then engaged in drawing a map of the fortifications around Nashville and procuring information as to the number of the troops, &c., which should be forthcoming in due season. These secret despatches of Mrs. Ranney's, together with the map and other papers, could be hidden in the heel of a boot, which would be made for them by a bootmaker of the city in the employ of the Confederate Government. His name was C. J. Zeutzschell, and his shop was on Union street.

This plan was agreed to, and Young was to assist in the execution of it,—in return for which, he was to be placed in a high position at Richmond. The reputation of Young, however, was not of the best, and the bootmaker would do nothing for him, when called upon, without first making inquiry among his friends and consulting with the hostage, for whom the boots were wanted.

Accordingly, Zeutzschell went to his room one evening and said that Young had been to his house and wished him to make a pair of boots and to secrete some important documents in them so as to defy detection. He had no confidence in Young's honor, and did not wish to do it for *him*. He knew him as identified with the Confederates, indeed, but he was a bad man, low in his habits and associates, never had any money, &c. He, Zeutzschell, had been inquiring of the *friends* of the South—undoubted secessionists, concerning him (the Iuka hostage), and was convinced that he was a gentleman and true southerner. He would do anything to promote the cause,—money was no object,—he would lay down his life for it. If Young could be thrown off the track, he would make the boots and secrete in them a map of the fortifications about Nashville. His brother-in-law, Harris, would go out and see if any new ones had been erected. If not, he had a perfect plan of them in his head, to prove which he immediately sat down and drafted one. He remarked that he had recently sent several such to General Morgan. He had made the boots for all the spies in the same way, and not one had ever been detected. He had sent valuable information in a common pipe.

"Can you get a pass for your man?" asked the hostage.

"Certainly," was the reply; "as many as you like. There is a German at head-quarters who steals blank passes for me, and I fill them up myself. I give him whiskey for them."

He would like to go South, too, he said, in conclusion. He could describe the fortifications so much better than in a map.

Both parties being satisfied, an arrangement for the boots was made. Zeutzschell was to get the exact distances of the defences, the number and disposition of the troops, &c., and secrete them, together with Mrs. Ranney's despatches, in one of the heels of the boots. This he did, according to promise; the boots were made and delivered on the evening appointed. Instead of reaching Generals Bragg and Morgan, however, as intended, the maps, papers, boots, owner, maker, and spy, suddenly found themselves in the hands of the army police, much to the astonishment and utter chagrin of all parties concerned. Zeutzschell and Young were sent to the military prison.

### Northern Muscle and Southern Chivalry.

After the Federal forces had flanked Johnston's army from Dallas, it was contrary to the usual custom, the fortune of the First Brigade—Sheridan's old Division—to be left behind the army a few days, as a guard for an ambulance train. One day two of the men—one of them Jack Tyrrell, Commissary of the Brigade—went out to take a bath beyond and in sight of the Federal picket line, in a small bayou, which temerity was observed by some of Ferguson's cavalry hovering in the vicinity, who detached two men, armed with sabres and carbines, to bring them in. Being without arms they were surprised, and started off, *en dishabille*, in the very face of the pickets, who dared not fire for fear of injuring the prisoners. Each rebel started in a different direction with his charge. After going a short distance, Tyrrell dodged to one side, exposing his captor to the Federal pickets, who gave him a volley but missed, on which the Johnny, out of spite, returned the shot; when Tyrrell, taking advantage of his empty carbine, sprang and caught him by his abundant whiskers and dragged him from his horse. Here a short struggle ensued, in which the 'chivalry' had to give way to Northern muscle, although they were both good types of their respective regions, and Johnny, minus his gun and sabre, was marched to the picket lines by his escort, who guided him by walking behind him with one hand in each side of his whiskers. It is useless to say that he was received by the pickets with considerable merriment. The other reb, on seeing his comrade's fate, and hearing the whirr of a few random shots, fled, and left his charge to come back at his will.

### Shaking Hands in the Middle of the River.

A detachment of Federal troops was stationed on the northern bank of the Potomac river; and on the opposite, or southern bank, was stationed a detachment of the Confederate troops,—all within hailing distance, the river being not more than one quarter of a mile wide at that point (Conrad's Ferry). A challenge was proclaimed by some two or three of the Federal troops to meet the same number of the Confederate troops in the middle of the river, where it was fordable, to shake hands and drink each other's health. The challenge was accepted, and divesting themselves of their arms and a portion of their clothing, they met, exchanged salutations, and drank together in mutual friendship. These troops had been skirmishing across the river some six or eight days previous, with cannon, rifles, and musketry.

### Longstreet's Instant Detection of a Spy.

The feverishness of the Confederates in regard to spies, during the eventful days of the Manassas conflict, was greatly intensified by the following occurrence, as related by one of their officers:

While Longstreet's corps was hurrying forward to Jackson's relief, several brigades in advance on different roads were observed to halt, thereby stopping all further progress of the corps. Very angry at this, Longstreet trotted to the front, and was informed that a courier had brought orders from General Lee to that effect!

"From General Lee?" said Longstreet, his eyes glowing with rage: "Where *is* that courier?"

Gen Longstreet.

"There he goes now, General, galloping down the road."

"Keep your eyes on him, overtake him, and bring him here,"—which was soon accomplished.

"By whose orders did you halt my brigade?" asked a Brigadier.

"As I have already told you—by General Lee's! I have orders for Longstreet, and must be off to the rear!"

"Here is Longstreet,"—said that General, now moving forward,—"Where are your orders?"

The spy was caught! He turned red and pale, his lip quivered—he was self condemned.

"Give this man ten minutes, and hang him! Let the columns push forward immediately."

In fifteen minutes the spy was lifeless, hanging from a tree by the roadside; but before death, confessed that although a Virginian and a Confederate soldier, he had been in communication with the enemy over ten months, and was then acting for General Pope.

### More than a Match against Six.

The brilliant exploit of Captain Strong, of the Belle City Rifles, Second Wisconsin regiment, in escaping, as he did, from the Confederates, into whose clutches he unfortunately fell, was the theme of congratulation on the part of every one who knew the gallant Captain's worth. When he enlisted as a Union soldier, he was a student in Racine College, about twenty-one years of age, well built, and very agile and active. He was regarded in college as the best jumper, runner, &c., and withal an excellent shot, as well as a popular comrade of the students. Of his remarkable escape he says:—

As I was passing through a thicket, I was surrounded by six rebel soldiers—four infantry and two cavalry. The footmen were poorly dressed, and badly armed, having old rusty altered muskets. The cavalry were well mounted and well armed.

Seeing I was caught, I thought it best to surrender at once. So I said, "Gentlemen, you have me." I was asked various questions as to who I was, where I was going, what regiment I belonged to, &c., all of which I refused to answer. One of the footmen said 'Let's hang the — Yankee scoundrel,' and pointed to a convenient limb. Another said, 'No, let's take him to camp, and hang him there.' One of the cavalry, who seemed to be the leader, said, 'We will take him to camp.' They then marched me through an open place—two footmen in front, two in the rear, and a cavalry man on each side of me. I was armed with two revolvers and my sword. After going some twenty rods, the sergeant, who was on my right, noticing my pistols, commanded me to halt and give them up, together with my sword. I said, 'Certainly, gentlemen,' and immediately halted. As I stopped, they all filed past me, and of course were in front.

We were at this time in an open part of the woods, but about sixty yards to the rear was a thicket of undergrowth. Thus everything was in my favor. I was quick of foot and a passable shot. Yet the design of escape was not formed until I brought my pistol pouches to the front part of my body, and my hands touched the stocks. The grasping of the pistols suggested my cocking them as I drew them out. This I did, and the moment I got command of them I shot down the two footmen nearest me—about six feet off—one with each hand. I immediately turned and ran toward the thicket in the rear. The confusion of my captors was apparently so great that I had nearly reached cover before shots were fired at me. One ball passed through my left cheek, passing out of my mouth. Another one—a musket ball—went through my canteen.

Immediately upon this volley, the two cavalry separated, one to my right and the other to my left, to cut off my retreat—the remaining two footmen charging directly toward me. I turned when the horsemen got up, and fired three or four shots; but the balls flew wild. I still ran on; got over a small knoll, and had nearly regained one of our pickets, when I was headed off by both of the mounted men.

The Sergeant called to me to halt and surrender. I gave no reply, but fired at him and ran in the opposite direction. He pursued and overtook me, and just as his horse's head was abreast of me, I turned, took good aim and pulled the trigger, but the cap snapped. At this time his carbine was unslung, and he was holding it with both hands on the left side of his horse. He fired at my breast without raising the piece to his shoulder, and the shot passed from the right side of my coat, through it and my shirt to the left, just grazing the skin. The piece was so near as to burn the cloth about the size of one's hand. I was, however, uninjured this time, save the shot through my cheek. I then fired at him again and brought him to the ground—hanging by his foot in the left stirrup, and his horse galloping toward his camp. I saw no more of the horseman on my left, nor of the two footmen—but running on soon came to our own pickets, uninjured save the shot through my cheek, but otherwise much exhausted from my exertions.

### Rockafellow's Right Arm left Still.

Judge Kelley entered the office of Mr. Stanton, Secretary of War, one day, having with him a youthful-looking officer, whose empty coat-sleeve hung from his left shoulder. He was introduced to the Secretary as Brevet Lieut. Harry Rockafellow, of Philadelphia.

"My friend," said the Judge, "left a situation worth eight hundred dollars a year, three days after the President's proclamation for troops, to carry a musket at eleven dollars a month, with his regiment, the New York Seventy-first. After the term of his enlistment had expired, he marched with his regiment to Bull Run. Early in the day he received that ugly rifle-ball in his mouth (pointing to a Minie ball that was hung to his watch-key), and for two hours and a half he carried it in his fractured jawbone, fighting like a true hero, until a cannon-ball took off his arm and rendered him powerless. He was captured, and for three months lay in a mangled condition in a tobacco warehouse in Richmond, without proper surgical treatment. He was breveted a lieutenant by his Colonel, for his bravery, and is now filling a small clerkship. I beg of you to appoint him in the regular service."

"But where could I put him, if I were to?" said Mr. Stanton.

The Judge was about to reply, when the young man raised his arm and said with an anxious look:

"See, I have a right arm still, and General Kearney has only his left; send me into the line where there is fighting to be done! I have letters from ——," he tried to draw a bundle of letters from his pocket. Mr. Stanton stopped him—

"Put up your letters, Sir; you have spoken for yourself. Your wish shall be granted. The country cannot afford to neglect such men as you!"

Ere the soldier could thank him for his kindness, his case was noted. He turned to leave, and remarked to the Judge as they left, "I shall be proud of my commission, for I feel that I have earned it! This day is the proudest one of my whole life." His heart seemed so light that he appeared not to realize the loss he had met with, nor the weary nights, and long, long days he had suffered in the vile prisons of the enemy. Congressman Ely came in just as he passed along the aisle and remarked, "There goes the noblest and most heroic of all our prisoners. He was the pride of the boys—all loved him as though he were a brother."

### By-Scene at the Battle of Leesburg.

One of the terrible personal encounters at the battle of Leesburg, is thus related: As Captain Jones, of Company B, Seventeenth Mississippi regiment, was passing through the woods at the head of his men, he met another party headed by an officer. The two halting instantly upon discovering their close proximity, Jones exclaimed, "For God Almighty's sake, tell me quick—friends or enemies—who are you?" The other replied, "We are friends," and at the same time advanced. A little boy, named Joseph Ware, who was behind the Mississippian, instantly cried out, "Captain, they are not friends; don't you see they have not guns like ours? They are Yankees, let me shout." Again Jones exclaimed, "Who are you? Speak quick, for I can't keep my men from firing." "I'll let you know who we are, you d—— rebel," said the Federal officer, for such he was, and suiting the action to the word, he sprang upon and seized Captain Jones by the collar. For a second or two a scuffle ensued between the officers, when the latter broke loose. At the same instant one of the Mississippians dashed out the Federal officer's brains with the point of his musket.

### Uncomfortably Warm Place for a Soldier.

A good story is told about a soldier, who, in dodging away from a patrol, hid himself in a restaurant, by jumping into a large box used for steaming oysters. The lid closed with a spring lock, and the disappointed patrol went on his way baffled. In a little while the colored man attending the apparatus turned on a full head of

Uncomfortably Warm Place.

steam in order to prepare a mess for some customers. The soldier began to grow uncomfortably warm, and soon kicked and yelled lustily for liberation, until the frightened negro ran away shouting that "de debbil was in de steamer." Other employees gathered around, hearing the noise, and released the perspiring soldier, who bounded with the speed of a machine whose motive power is steam.

### Stating it Just Right.

When it was as well known as that the world exists, that Grant had forced Lee to retreat for scores of miles right steady to the very walls of Richmond, the rebel papers declared with the coolest effrontery that Lee was getting Grant just where he wanted him, that Grant was really retreating, and Lee in close pursuit. This was about equal to the facetious Iowa editor who got a downright whaling in his printing office, and described it next day —giving all the facts, but making himself the hero:—There was a blow. *Somebody fell. We got up.* Turning upon our antagonist, we then succeeded in winding his arms around our waist, and by a quick manœuvre threw him on top of us, bringing our back, at the same time, in contact with the solid bed of the printing press. Then inserting our nose between his teeth and his hands in our hair, we had him!

### Glorious Effect of National Music upon the Troops.

When General Kearney's troops were being brought into action at the battle of Williamsburg, they met the lengthened files of General Hooker's wounded being carried to the rear. The shrieks of the lacerated soldiers, bleeding and ghastly, who had been fighting so long and so well, pierced the air, and this, joined to the mud and rain, and the exhaustion of those who had come several miles with so much speed, was not calculated to produce a favorable impression on them as they were going into action. General Heintzelman, however, ordered several of the bands to strike up national and martial airs, and when the strains of the familiar tunes reached the ears of the wounded as they were being carried from the field, their cheers mingled with those of the soldiers who were just rushing into the battle. The effect, too, was great on the other side; for some of the prisoners stated that when they heard the bands strike up the *Star Spangled Banner,* and heard our soldiers cheer, they knew that the victory would be ours.

### Bleeding, but Had His Colors With Him.

A sight at once horrible and sublime, was witnessed after the Gettysburg battle, among the wounded heroes whose deeds had crowned with imperishable honor the history of that all-memorable day. A strong, stalwart fellow, with the chevrons of a sergeant on his arm, ragged and torn, was limping along slowly, with agony terribly depicted upon his visage. The shoe on his right foot was covered with blood,

Head-quarters of Lee at Gettysburg

and a large rent in his pantaloons, just above the knee, from which the blood was also trickling, solved the question of the location of his wound. He was hatless, his hair was disordered, his face and hands were begrimed with smoke and powder, and he looked altogether maniac-like and exhausted. But he *had his colors with him!* His regiment, or the greater part of it, had been either killed or captured; he had lost his colors once, and was afterward captured himself. He watched his opportunity, killed the rebel who held his flag, and escaped with it safely into the Union lines. Ought not the name of one so brave as he to be chiseled in monumental marble? It was against such heroes as this, that Lee and his myrmidons frantically but vainly fought.

### "I Told You I Could Do It."

The commander of Williston's battery observing that when the rebels fired there was one particular piece that was very annoying, on account of its shelling the head-quarters, turned to General Devens, and said, "For God's sake, General, let us knock that gun over, for I can do it." The General replied that he was afraid that he might hit some of Custer's men, who were but recently ordered out on the left. "They are not there," replied Williston, "I should see them if they were. I know where I am going to shoot. I will not hit any one. I only want to knock that gun over." General Devens still hesitating, Williston said, "Let me fire on my own responsibility, for God's sake. Will you do it?" At last the General consented, when—bang! went one of the pieces, and over went the doomed gun, the carriage shattered and dispersed instantly. "There," said the keen-eyed Williston, with a smile of triumph, "I told you I could do it!"

### Song of Patriotism in the Forest.

During one of those eventful nights in Virginia, when the Federal troops lay in line of imminent battle behind their temporary fortifications of dirt, mud, logs and rails, and the continuous crack of the sharp-shooter's rifle rolled startlingly along their front, a solitary voice struck in shrill but blithesome and melodious tone, the patriotic song, "Rally round the flag, boys!" —and, almost instantly, those hundreds of men, who seemed to have been waiting, as it were, for something to dissipate the gloom which thoughts of the day's carnage had engendered, were shouting in a chorus which shook the depth of the forest's gloom,—

"The Union, forever, hurrah, boys, hurrah!
Down, down with the traitors, and up with the stars!"

As down the line the strain of jubilee sped its electric course, the sound swelled into one vast diapason of deep-toned, exultant song. The only reply of the enemy was the spiteful whistle of extra bullets from the skirmishing line—but whizzing harmlessly by. This unexpected but refreshing little episode tended greatly to inspire the hearts of the troops in that dismal locality.

### Humphreys' Deadly Charge at Fredericksburg.

At the terrible battle of Fredericksburg, in 1862, Humphreys' division of Butterfield's corps was at one juncture resting on its arms in the streets of that city. General Butterfield sent an order to move it to the front. At the head of Allabach's second brigade, Humphreys crossed the mill-race, formed his men behind the crest ready for the charge, and Tyler's first brigade was following closely after, ready to support. The line was formed, the column moved gallantly forward, reached the line of battle, passed fifty yards beyond, when a deadly fire from behind the stone wall caused it to recoil, and finally to fall back, re-forming under the crest from which it started. Humphreys and staff were dismounted in this charge, their horses being killed, while the brigade lost five hundred men in fifteen minutes.

There was but one more chance. Tyler's brigade had come up, and notwithstanding the turmoil, General Humphreys had succeeded in forming it in gallant style. The only hope now was with the bayonet. The men were ordered not to fire—to rely solely upon their trusty steel. Then, with great exertion, the batteries and the line of troops on the crest were persuaded to cease firing while the charge was being made; then General Hooker exhorted his men not to quail, not to look back; to disregard the men in front who were lying down covered by every projection; to ride over them.

The officers were ordered to the front; then the brigade, led in person by Generals Tyler and Humphreys, moved forward with a glorious cheer. They reached the little rise in the ground, within eighty yards of the stone wall, where line after line of the Federals lay flat upon the ground: they began to move over the living mass, when suddenly the prostrate men cried out, "Don't go there, 'tis certain death!" and, rising, began to impede the progress of the column, and by protests of every nature implored the men not to go forward. Then the crisis came. The division was fighting its maiden battle; older troops than they quailed before the murderous volleys now making great gaps through their ranks; the head of the charging column was enveloped in a sheet of living flame; the hideous shells were bursting all around and in their midst. Was it any wonder that they faltered? The men began to load and fire; the momentum of the charge was gone; the column began to retire slowly, falling back to its place of formation.

"Oh, men!" said Humphreys, "if you had only gone forward as well as you come back!"

And then, again dismounted, his second horse having been killed, he reported the result to General Butterfield, who ordered him to withdraw his troops to a place of shelter.

### Price and Van Dorn Pitted Against Rosecrans.

The battle of Corinth commenced on the third day of October, 1862, the Confederates under Price and Van Dorn being the attacking party. That day they seemed to have rather had the advantage. On the fourth, the contest was renewed at daybreak, and for some hours continued to be waged with indifferent success. At length the great struggle followed, of which the annexed is an account;—a struggle exhibiting the masterworkings of modern generalship in the highest degree:

For a time there were no demonstrations on the part of the Confederates, and they remained altogether quiet in the angle of the woods near the railroad. Presently two lines were formed, one at right angles to the other—the one destined with its reserves to sweep over the railroad, through the abattis into the village—the other with its reserves to attack battery 'Robinett,' which was the key to the whole position. If once taken and held, Corinth was undeniably in rebel possession. The line destined for the occupation of the village came rapidly forward at a charge across the railroad, over the fallen timber, driving the Union line before them like chaff. All that grape and canister could do to impede their progress was attempted, but still their irresistible progress was not stayed. Batteries of light artillery played upon their front and left incessantly; their colors were thrice shot away; but they came still onward, nor halted until they reached the public square, and formed in line of battle directly in front of General Halleck's old headquarters. The Federal line of battle was formed directly opposite, in the street leading past General Rosecrans's head-quarters.

The two armies advanced. A terrible hand-to-hand encounter was engaged in, and for a time the destruction of the Union line seemed inevitable. It gradually yielded, and fell back until the enemy had nearly reached the Corinth House. Here General Rosecrans rode along the line, and in a few cheering words revived the drooping courage of the wearied soldiers. The Confederate reserve was at this time directly in range of the guns on the redoubts to the left; and huge shells began to drop in their midst, whose explosion in the solid masses began to create considerable confusion and loss of life. At the same time the order was given to "*Charge bayonets.*" At this command the brave Union soldiers sprang to their work with a will. They attacked vigorously, and soon the enemy were flying across the public square in wild confusion. The explosion of the fiery missiles from the two batteries added haste to their movements, and by the time they had reached the cover of the timber, their retreat had become a rout.

By the time this line was driven back, the other line with their reserves were well advanced in the direction of battery Robinett.

During the period of seeming inaction when the Confederates had withdrawn to the cover of the timber, while preparing to make the two charges in question, General Price and his principal officers held a consultation to devise ways and means to take the battery. The importance of its capture was admitted, and the risk and danger of the attempt thoroughly canvassed. General Price would not undertake the responsibility of ordering the attack, but called for volunteers. Colonel Rogers, of Arkansas, immediately tendered his brigade as the forlorn hope, and Colonel Ross his brigade as a support.

They massed their troops eight deep, and advanced under a heavy fire of double charges of grape and canister. A terrible enfilading and flanking fire was poured upon them from every battery bearing in that direction, aided by incessant volleys of musketry from the supports of the batteries and the Union regiments drawn up in line parallel with them.

The first shell from Battery William exploded in the centre of the advancing column, sending thirty or forty to their long home. Every discharge caused huge gaps in their ranks. The effect of the Federal fire was like the falling of grain before the scythe. But this tremendous mortality did not affect their irresistible onward march. As fast as one man fell his comrade stepped forward in his place. Twice did they approach almost to the outer works of the battery, and twice they were compelled to fall back. The third time they reached the battery and planted their flag upon the edge. It was shot down—raised again—again shot down. They swarmed about the battery; they climbed over the parapets; they fired through the escarpments, and for a time it seemed as if they had secured the victory their valor had so richly earned.

When they obtained the battery, the Federals who were working it fell back behind the projecting earth-works, out of reach from the Federal shells, and immediately all the batteries bearing upon the position were turned upon Battery Robinett, and soon a shower of missiles was falling like hail upon the brave intruders. No mortal man could stand the fire, and they retreated. Slowly the brave remnant turned their unwilling steps toward the forest from which they started, when the order was given to the two regiments supporting the battery to charge. This order was splendidly executed. The miserable remnant of troops which the batteries had nearly destroyed was now almost annihilated. A few scattering troops were all that remained of the column which so valiantly attacked the battery scarcely an hour before. The dead bodies of rebels were piled up in and about the intrenchments, in some places eight and ten deep. In one place directly in front of the point of assault, two hundred and sixteen dead bodies were found within a space of a hundred feet by four, among them the commanders of both brigades making the assault—Colonel Rogers and Colonel Ross.

This was the termination of the engagement.

### Holding the Hill—Valor of Burnside.

At four o'clock on the 17th of September, during the great battle of Antietam, McClellan sent simultaneous orders to Burnside and Franklin; to the former to advance and carry the batteries in his front at all hazards and at any cost; to the latter to carry the woods next in front of him to the right, which the rebels still held. The order to Franklin, however, was practically countermanded, in consequence of a message from General Sumner that if Franklin went on and was repulsed, his own corps was not yet sufficiently reorganized to be depended on as a reserve.

Burnside obeyed the order most gallantly. Getting his troops well in hand, and sending a portion of his artillery to the front, he advanced them with rapidity and the most determined vigor, straight up the hill in front, on top of which the rebels had maintained their most dangerous battery. The movement was in plain view of McClellan's position, and as Franklin on the other side sent his batteries into the field about the same time, the battle seemed to open in all directions with greater activity than ever.

The fight in the ravine was in full progress, the batteries which Porter supported were firing with new vigor, Franklin was blazing away on the right, and every hill-top, ridge, and wood along the whole line was crested and veiled with white clouds of smoke. All day had been clear and bright since the early cloudy morning, and now this whole magnificent, unequaled scene shone with the splendor of an afternoon September sun. Four miles of battle, its glory all visible, its horrors all veiled, the fate of the Republic hanging on the hour!

There are two hills on the left of the road, the furthest the lowest. The rebels have batteries on both. Burnside is ordered to carry the nearest to him, which is the furthest from the road. His guns opening first from this new position in front, soon entirely controlled and silenced the enemy's artillery. The infantry came on at once, moving rapidly and steadily up, long dark lines, and broad dark masses, being plainly visible without a glass, as they moved over the green hill-side. The next moment the road in which the rebel battery was planted was canopied with clouds of dust swiftly descending into the valley. Underneath was a tumult of wagons, guns, horses, and men flying at speed down the road. Blue flashes of smoke burst now and then among them, a horse, or a man, or half a dozen went down, and then the whirlwind swept on.

*The hill was carried!* But could it be held? The rebel columns, before seen moving to the left, increased their pace.

The guns, on the hill above, sent an angry tempest of shell down among Burnside's guns and men. He had formed his columns apparently in the near angles of two fields bordering the road—high ground about them everywhere except in rear. In another moment a rebel battle-line appears on the brow of the ridge above them, moves swiftly down in the most perfect order, and though met by incessant discharges of musketry, of which the flashes are plainly seen, does not fire a gun. White spaces show where men are falling, but they close up instantly, and still the line advances. The brigades of Burnside are in heavy column; they will not give way before a bayonet charge in line. The rebels think twice before they dash into these two hostile masses.

Now there is a halt; the rebel left gives way and scatters over the field; the rest stand fast and fire. More infantry comes up; Burnside is out-numbered, flanked, compelled to yield the hill he took so bravely. His position is no longer one of attack; he defends himself with unfaltering firmness, but he sends to McClellan for help. McClellan's glass for the last half-hour has seldom been turned from the left. He sees clearly enough that Burnside is pressed—needs no messenger to tell him that. His face grows darker with anxious thought. Looking down to the valley where fifteen thousand troops are lying, he turns a half-questioning look on Fitz John Porter, who stands by his side, gravely scanning the field. They are Porter's troops below, are fresh, and only impatient to share in this fight. But Porter slowly shakes his head, and one may believe that the same thought is passing through the minds of both Generals: 'They are the only reserves of the army; they can not be spared.' McClellan remounts his horse, and with Porter and a dozen officers of his staff rides away to the left in Burnside's direction. Sykes meets them on the road —a good soldier, whose opinion is worth taking. The three Generals talk briefly together. It is easy to see that the moment has come when everything may turn on an order given or withheld, when the history of the battle is only to be written in thoughts and words and purposes of the General. Burnside's messenger rides up. His message is—

"I want troops and guns. If you do not send them I can not hold my position for half an hour."

McClellan's only answer for the moment is a glance at the western sky. Then he turns and speaks very slowly:

"Tell General Burnside that this is the battle of the war. He must hold his ground till dark at any cost. I will send him Miller's battery. I can do nothing more. I have no infantry." Then, as the messenger was riding away, he called him back—

"Tell him if he *can not* hold his ground, then the bridge to the last man!—always the bridge! If the bridge is lost, all is lost."

The sun is already down; not half an hour of daylight is left. Till Burnside's message came it had seemed plain to every one that the battle could not be finished that day. None suspected how near was the peril of defeat, of sudden attack on exhausted forces—how vital to the safety of the army and the nation were those fifteen thousand waiting troops in the hollow. But—the rebels halted instead of pushing on; their vindictive cannonade died away as the light faded. Before it was quite dark the battle was over. Only a solitary gun of Burnside's thundered against the enemy, and presently this also ceased, and the field was still.

### Preferred to Die in the Field.

On Sunday, June 14th, 1863, orders were issued to pursue Lee's army, then moving toward Pennsylvania. At a distance of fifteen miles from Gettysburg, where the armies were massing, were first caught the murmurs of the opening battle, and from that time the scene was all enthusiasm among the weary, footsore braves, who counted as nothing all the pains of a march of one hundred and ninety-eight miles, now that they were within striking distance of the foe. Most of the way the ambulance train had been crowded with both officers and men, weary, worn and haggard; but the cannon's rattle, as it became more and more distinct, changed them in a twinkling into new creatures. The New Jersey Brigade, in General

Preferred to die in the field.

Sedgwick's corp, was of this body. At about three o'clock on the afternoon of the third of July, the head of the column arrived upon the battle-ground. As it came to a halt, a poor fellow, who looked the very image of death, hobbled out of the ambulance in which he had been lying, and, shouldering his musket, was just starting forward, when the surgeon in charge stopped him with—

"Where are you going, Sir?"

"To the front, Doctor," and the brave fellow tried hard to stand firm and speak boldly as he saluted the surgeon.

"To the front! What! a man in your condition? Why, Sir, you can't march half a mile; you haven't the strength to carry yourself, let alone your knapsack, musket, and equipments. You must be crazy, surely."

"But, Doctor, my division are in the fight," (here he grasped the wheel of an ambulance to support himself,) "and I have a younger brother in my company. I *must* go."

"But I am your surgeon, and I forbid you. You have every symptom of typhoid fever; a little over-exertion will kill you."

"Well, Doctor, if I *must* die, I would rather die in the field than in an ambulance."

The Doctor saw it was useless to debate the point, and the soldier went as he desired. But on the evening of the next day he was buried where he fell—for fall he did,—his right arm blown off at the elbow, and his forehead pierced by a Minie ball. His name could not then be learned; but the heroic soldier belonged to the Third Division of the Sixth Corps, and that mark was placed at the head of his last resting-place. Peace to the brave.

### Phil. Sheridan at Stone River.

On the dreadful morning which made Stone River memorable in the annals of blood and death, General Sheridan, when he emerged from his mangled division in solid phalanx from the frightful cedars, loomed up like a very giant. He was grave, firm and strong, and as Rosecrans dashed up to him in the tumult of battle, his deportment seemed to express: "You see, General, it was not the fault of my Division that we did not stay." He had lost his hat and fought bareheaded until a trooper handed him a covering—a dead soldier's cap, no doubt. Sunday morning, after the enemy had gone, Sheridan sitting on an old stump told the story quietly but graphically;

"General, I lost seventeen hundred and ninety-six men, seventeen of them being officers, with my three brigade commanders. These were the noble Sill, Roberts and Shaeffer—than whom more gallant fellows never fought under the flag!"

Stone River made Sheridan a Major General, and they always said in the army of the Cumberland, " Phil Sheridan is the rising man in the army;" and when Grant put him in command of the cavalry in the Army of the Potomac, those who knew him said he was the right man in the right place. In the Shenandoah Valley, Sheridan's record is equal to that of Napoleon for successive brilliant victories.

### "No Quarter"—the Black Flag.

A genuine 'black flag' was captured by the Federals, between Harpers' Ferry and Martinsburg, Virginia, the act being performed by one of the scouts of General Tyler, and by the latter was presented as a memorial of the Rebellion to the city of Philadelphia. It was the production of the ladies of Winchester, during the early part of 1862,—instigated, it is to be presumed, by the more sanguinary among the other sex,—and placed in the hands of one of the gangs of guerrillas afterwards under the command of the redoubtable Mosby. At the time the flag was thus put in possession of the chivalric sons of the sunny south, they were sworn to give no quarter to any Yankee who might fall into their hands, and they kept their oath up to the time of their memorable defeat at Winchester. The scout who captured the flag had enlisted with Mosby, and made himself very useful in stealing all the 'secesh' horses that he could lay his hands on. After remaining with the Confederate band for some three weeks, he left, and brought into the Federal lines the celebrated flag, which he tore from its staff. It is of black alpaca, measuring about one yard and a quarter, with a star in the centre measuring some twenty-nine inches, and with the word 'Winchester' printed in large letters. The words 'No quarter' are written with lead pencil in one corner. The flag was officially presented to Mayor Henry, of Philadelphia, on behalf of General Tyler, by Lieutenant Rankel, of the Third Pennsylvania Artillery,—to be finally placed in Independence Hall.

### Following their Leader.

The crossing of Rolling Fork, by General Rousseau, was an act every way in keeping with the character of that fine soldier. "We cross this ford," he exclaimed, "never to retreat again to this side. We are to march forward. There is to be no backward movement. It is victory or death."

The command was about to be given and repeated through the lines, when General Rousseau, in the van, rising in the saddle, exclaimed, "Men, follow me! I expect none of you to do what I am not willing to do myself," and, springing from his horse, he stepped briskly into the stream, and crossed the breast-high ford on foot. His men, cheering wildly, followed their General, crying they would "follow wherever he dared to lead." He did not falter until he had gained his end — nor did they.

### Eighth Ohio "Blazing Away."

While the National forces were standing under the enemy's fire, on the day of the battle at Romney, Virginia, and the shot and shell went murderously in every direction, there was one 'personage' who deliberately 'stumped' it.

Captain Butterfield, of the Eighth Ohio regiment—being one of the ranking Captains—acted as Major upon that occasion, and was obliged to ride an old sorrel horse, which had been used as a team horse, and required both spurs and whip, which the Captain had provided himself with, the latter cut from a tree, and about five feet long. It was found that the six pound guns of the Federals could not reach the Confederate battery, and Colonel Mason ordered Captain Butterfield to bring forward a brass twelve-pounder which was in the rear.

Off sped the old sorrel and his brave rider, and in a few moments up came the gun. Its position was assigned and made ready for the match, but the Captain came dashing back in front of the gun, and the smell of powder or something else had made the old sorrel unmanageable almost, for in trying to wheel him to the front of the gun, the more the Captain applied the whip and spur, the more old sorrel refused to go. This kept the gunners in terrible suspense, for much depended on that shot. Finally, the Captain finding his efforts to move his steed fruitless, he sang out at the top of his voice, "Never mind the old horse, blaze away!" And sure enough, they did blaze away, and it proved a good shot, for it caused the Confederates to limber up their battery and take to their heels. At that moment orders came to charge, and off dashed the old sorrel frightened at the discharge of the gun, which had scorched his tail, and mingled in the charge. He was lost to view until his arrival in town, where he was soon brought to a stand, the Captain standing in his stirrups, with his cap flying, cheering for the glorious victory that had been achieved.

### Delivery of their Ammunition before Surrendering.

The surrender of Lexington to the Confederate forces was rendered a necessity by the want of ammunition, as well as by the want of water. A few of the companies had one or two rounds left, but the majority had fired their last bullet. After the surrender, an officer was detailed by Price to collect the ammunition, and place it in safe charge. The officer, addressing Adjutant Cosgrove, asked him to have the ammunition delivered. Cosgrove called up a dozen men, one after the other, and exhibiting the empty cartridge-boxes, said to the astonished Confederate officer, "I believe, Sir, we gave you all the ammunition we had before we had stopped fighting. Had there been any more, upon my word, you should have had it, Sir. But I will inquire, and if, by accident, there is a cartridge left, I will let you know." The expectant officer turned

GREAT CONFLICTS, INDIVIDUAL HEROISM, ETC.    295

away, doubtless reflecting upon the "glorious" victory of having captured men who had fired their last shot.

### Sherman Watching the Capture of Fort McAllister.

On the evening of the 12th December, 1864, General Howard, commanding one of the wings of Sherman's grand army in Georgia, relieved Hazen's Second Division of the Fifteenth Corps by a part of the Seventeenth, and threw it across the Little Ogeechee, toward the Great Ogeechee, with the view of crossing it to Ossabaw Island, and reducing Fort McAllister, which held the river. The Confederates had destroyed King's bridge, across the Great Ogeechee, and this had to be repaired. Captain Reese, topographical engineer of Howard's Staff, with the Missouri Engineers, prepared the timber and bridged the one thousand feet of river during the night, and, on the morning of the 13th, Hazen crossed and moved toward the point where Fort McAllister obstructed the river. Kilpatrick, in the meantime, had moved down to St. Catharine's Sound, opened communication with the fleet, and asked permission to storm Fort McAllister; but Sherman did not give his consent, considering it questionable whether the cavalry, with its poor facilities and small supply of artillery, could succeed.

Hazen made his arrangements to storm the fort on the afternoon of the 13th, Generals Sherman and Howard being at Cheroe's rice mill, on the Ogeechee, opposite Fort McAllister. Sherman was on the roof of the mill, surrounded by his staff and signal officers, Beckley and Cole, waiting to communicate with Hazen, on the Island. While patiently waiting for Hazen's signals, Sherman's keen eye detected smoke in the horizon, seaward. Up to this time he had received no intelligence from the fleet. In a moment the countenance of the bronzed chieftain lightened up, and he exclaimed:

"Look! Howard; there is the gunboat!"

Time passed on, and the vessel now became visible, yet no signal from the fleet or Hazen. Half an hour passed, and the guns of the fort opened simultaneously with puffs of smoke that rose a few hundred yards from the fort, showing that Hazen's skirmishers had opened. A moment after, Hazen signaled—

"I have invested the fort, and will assault immediately." At this moment Beckley announces, "A signal from the gunboat." All eyes are turned from the fort to the gunboat that is coming to their assistance with news from home. A few messages pass, which apprise that Foster and Dahlgren are within speaking distance. The gunboat now halts and asks—

"Can we run up? Is Fort McAllister ours?"

"No," is the reply; "Hazen is just ready to storm it. Can you assist?"

"Yes," is the reply; "What will you have us do?"

But before Sherman can reply to Dahlgren the thunders of the fort are heard, and the low sound of small arms is borne across the three miles of marsh and river. Field glasses are opened, and, sitting flat upon the roof, the hero of Atlanta gazes away off to the fort. "There they go grandly—not a waver," he remarks.

Twenty seconds pass, and again he exclaims,

"See that flag in the advance, Howard; how steadily it moves; not a man falters, * * There they go still; see the roll of musketry. Grand, grand."

Still he strained his eyes, and a moment after spoke without raising his eyes—

"That flag still goes forward; there is no flinching there."

A pause for a minute.

"Look!" he exclaims, "it has halted. They waver—no! it's the parapet! There they go again; now they scale it; some are over. Look! there's a flag on the works! Another, another. It's ours! The fort's ours!"

The glass dropped by his side; and in an instant the joy of the great leader at the possession of the river and the opening of the road to his new base burst forth in words:—

"As the old darkey remarked, dis chile don't sleep dis night!"—and turning to one of his aids, Captain Auderied, he remarked, "Have a boat for me at once; I must go there!"—pointing to the fort from which half a dozen battle-flags floated grandly in the sunset.

And well might William Tecumseh Sherman rejoice, for here, as the setting sun went down on Fort McAllister reduced, and kissed a fond good night to the starry banner, Sherman witnessed the culmination of all his plans and marches, that had involved such desperate resistance and risk—the opening up of a new and shorter route to his base. Here, at sunset, on the memorable 13th of December, the dark waters of the Great Ogeechee bore witness to the fulfillment of the covenant Sherman made with his iron heroes at Atlanta twenty-nine days before, to lead them victorious to a new base.

### Characteristic Pluck of a Western Soldier.

One December day, a Federal squad of some half-dozen soldiers left Col. Shackleford's regiment, at Calhoun, Green river, Ky., to bring back three soldiers who had gone to Todd county. While on their route, after night, they came upon some Confederate cavalry, and the Nationals seeing that resistance would be useless, took the woods. One of them, named Wilkins, was separated from his companions, and in winding through the woods, came several times in close proximity to Confederate squads, but succeeded in eluding them. He at last overtook three of them, and seeing that his chances were desperate, he determined to join them and pass himself off as one of their number. By keeping a little in the rear he watched a favorable opportunity, when he drew his revolver, and firing rapidly, killed one, badly wounded another, and caused the third to take to flight. Wilkins succeeded in making his escape, and returned to camp at Calhoun, where

Characteristic Pluck.

a gentleman arrived the next day from Elkton, and stated that the Confederate cavalry reported that the country was overrun with Federal troops, and that they had been forced to retreat before a superior force.

### Loved the Old Flag Still.

After the battle of Mill Spring, when the Minnesota regiment returned to its quarters at Camp Hamilton, they marched past the Colonel's marquee with banners flying, and their splendid band playing "Hail Columbia." Standing in front of the tent were Dr. Cliff, Zollicoffer's Brigade Surgeon, Lieutenant Colonel Carter, of the Twentieth Tennessee (Confederate) regiment, and several of the Federal officers. It was observed that "Hail Columbia" affected both the Confederate officers to tears—they wept like children—and Carter remarked that: "Although compelled to fight against the old flag, he loved it still."

### Fiendish Deeds of a Western Amazon.

The operations of Sue Munday, the female guerrilla, will long be remembered in Kentucky. About the middle of October, 1864, Sue, in company with Captain Berry, made a descent at the head of their marauding gang, upon Jeffersontown, and took possession of the place. Sue Munday dismounted at the Davis House and had her canteen filled with whisky. A negro boy was mounted on horse, armed in the most complete manner, and rode with the gang. He stood guard over the horses, while the scoundrels were scattered about the town engaged in robbing the people.

The discharge of fire arms was heard by several parties residing in the vicinity, but they were ignorant of the cause. A short time, however, after these reports were heard, Mr. James Simpson, on his way to Jeffersontown, was met in the road by the outlaws and robbed of twenty-seven dollars in money. He observed that Sue Munday's pistol was empty, and the fresh stains showed that it had very recently been discharged. While Mr. S. was being robbed, she was engaged in reloading her revolver. She pointed the muzzle at the breast of Mr. S., and smiled with fiendish satisfaction at his embarrassment as she capped the tube of each barrel of the cylinder. After being released, Mr. Simpson rode directly to Jeffersontown and related his adventure. He was informed that, with the prisoner in Federal uniform, the party numbered eight when in town. He met but seven on the road, and no prisoners.

The citizens at once surmised that the soldier had been murdered, and, following the trail of the guerrillas, they approached the dark ravine, and found their worst apprehensions too true. His body was marked with five pistol-shot wounds, and two deep stabs, as if made by the keen blade of a dagger. All the circumstances went to prove that the murder was committed by one hand, and that hand Sue Munday's, the outlaw woman, and the wild, daring leader of the gang. By a record in a small memorandum book, found upon the dead body, it was learned that the name of the murdered man was Hugh Wilson. Upon his person was also found a letter dated Mount Vernon, Illinois, and presumed to be from his wife, as it commenced with 'My dear husband.' She wrote in an affectionate manner, and spoke with loving fondness of their pleasant home and the little darling ones who 'sent love to pa.' This letter was found in his bosom, pierced by balls and stained with blood gushed in warm life-streams from his heart.

### Saved a Comrade's Life, but Lost His Own.

In one of the battles of the autumn campaign of 1864, there was a young man killed, a member of the Massachusetts Fifty-Eighth regiment, who used to live in the town of Concord. His name was Broad, and, on account of his having been connected with the ambulance train, he had never been in battle before. He met his death, at last, in the following manner, —than which no instance of braver self-devotion is anywhere on record: There was a man struck by a solid shot, it cutting one of his legs nearly off. The poor fellow was bleeding to death, but if brought off, would in all probability get well. Broad proved to be the only man who would volunteer to go out and fetch him in. It was almost certain death for any man; but, said Broad, in the generosity and self-sacrifice of his noble nature,

"I have neither wife nor child to suffer if I am killed."

So out he went, and picked the bleeding soldier up, put him on his strong and willing shoulder, and brought him safely in, though the bullets flew like hail around him. He came in so promptly that they all thought he had escaped the bullets. But, alas! poor Broad himself was a mortally wounded man. He laid his burden tenderly on the ground, saying, as he did so,

"I may have saved your life, but I have lost my own."

He had been shot through the bowels,

and died very soon after. He was as brave a man as ever lived.

### "O'Meara is Dead."

"O'Meara is dead, then?" said the General, at Chattanooga. "Yes, sir," replied the officer of the day, to whom the inquiry was addressed, "his body is about being sent forward." "Gallant O'Meara!" continued Grant, as if communing with his own spirit, and the spirits of the brave around him, "Gone! A braver man never filled a saddle." "He is at the landing now, waiting to be put on the boat." "I knew him well," the General spoke on, as if he heeded not what was said by his companion—" he was with us in the Army of the Tennessee. I shall never forget his noble defence of the trestle-work at Holly Springs. He saved us all from starvation. Noble O'Meara! Brave Irish Legion!" "Would you like to see him, General?" "I should, let us go." The two officers passed together to the little steamer by the levee of the river. It was a touching sight. A group of officers and men had gathered on the deck and levee, while others stood looking on along the adjacent heights. The coffin, covered with the American flag, lay on the army bier. The procession had halted, and the boat was about to start. "Stop the steamer a moment," said the General, solemnly: "I want to see him." An orderly removed the colors and the coffin-lid. The hero bent over his departed comrade, and dropped a silent tear on the cold face. His lip quivered, as it always did when he was experiencing deep emotion. He clasped his hands over the breast of the brave young Irish volunteer, who had come so willingly with him from the same State, who had stood so gallantly by his side in the deadly hurtlings of battle, who had fought so bravely to save his whole army from death by starvation, and who had now offered up a youthful life as a sweet, rich sacrifice on the altar of his country. An exile and a pilgrim from his own native land, he had come to America to die for the flag that is the emblem of liberty throughout the world.

### All Through a Mistake.

The first battle of Bull Run broke the calm of a peaceful Sabbath in such a manner as was never known before in Virginia, and terrible must have been the scene at the farm houses of Mr. Lewis and Mrs. Henry, upon the knolls beyond the breastworks, where the awful carnage opened up. For hours the fighting goes on, with ghastly horror and varying success to both armies. There is marching to and fro of regiments. There is not much order. Regiments are scattered. The lines are not even. This is the first battle, and officers and men are inexperienced. There are a great many stragglers on both sides; more, probably, from the rebel ranks than from McDowell's army, for thus far the battle has gone against them. You can see them scattered over the fields, beyond Mr. Lewis's. The fight goes on. The artillery crashes louder than before. There is a continuous rattle of musketry. It is like the roaring of a hail storm. Sherman and Keyes move down to the foot of the hill, near Mr. Lewis's. Burnside and Porter march across the turnpike. Franklin and Howard and Wilcox, who have been pushing south, turn toward the southeast. There are desperate hand-to-hand encounters. Cannon are taken and re-taken. Gunners on both sides are shot while loading their pieces. Hundreds fall, and other hundreds leave the ranks. The woods towards Sudley Springs are filled with wounded men and fugitives, weak, thirsty, hungry, exhausted, worn down by the long morning march, want of sleep, lack of food, and the excitement of the hour. Across the plains, towards Manassas, are *other* crowds,—disappointed, faint-hearted, defeated soldiers, fleeing for safety.

"We are defeated!"

"Our regiments are cut to pieces!"

GREAT CONFLICTS, INDIVIDUAL HEROISM, ETC.   299

"General Bartow is wounded and General Bee is killed!"

Thus they cry as they hasten towards Manassas. Officers and men in the rebel ranks feel that the battle is all but lost. Union officers and men feel that it is almost won.

The rebel right wing, far out upon the turnpike, has been folded back upon the centre; the centre has been driven in upon the left wing, and the left wing has been pushed back beyond Mr. Lewis's house. Griffin's and Rickett's batteries, which had been firing from the ridge west of the toll gate, were ordered forward to the knoll from which the rebel batteries had been driven.

"It is too far in advance," said General Griffin.

"The Fire Zouaves will support you," said General Barry.

"It is better to have them go in advance till we come into position; then they can fall back," Griffin replied.

"No; you are to move first, those are the orders. The Zouaves are all ready to follow on the double quick."

"I will go; but, mark my words, they will not support me."

The battery galloped over the fields, descended the hill, crossed the ravine, advancing to the brow of the hill near Mrs. Henry's, followed by Rickett's battery, the Fire Zouaves, and the Fourteenth New York. In front of them, about forty or fifty rods distant, were the rebel batteries, supported by infantry. Griffin and Ricketts came into position, and opened a fire so terrible and destructive that the rebel batteries and infantry were driven beyond the crest of the hill.

The field was almost won by the National troops; the Confederate troops acknowledged that at this time "all seemed about to be lost."

The battle surges around the house of Mrs. Henry. She is lying there amidst its thunders. Rebel sharpshooters take possession of it, and pick off Rickett's gunners. He turns his guns upon the house. Crash! crash! crash! It is riddled with grape and canister. Sides, roof, doors, and windows are pierced, broken, and splintered. The bed-clothes are cut into rags, and the aged woman instantly killed. The rebel regiments melt away. The stream of fugitives toward Manassas grows more dense. Johnston has had more men and more guns engaged than McDowell; but he has been steadily driven. But rebel reinforcements arrive from an unexpected quarter,—General Smith's brigade from the Shenandoah. It comes into action in front of Wilcox. There are from two to three thousand men. General Smith is wounded almost at the first fire, and Colonel Elzey takes command. General Bonham sends two regiments, the Second and Eighth South Carolina. They keep south of Mrs. Henry's, and march on till they are in position to fire almost upon the backs of Griffin's and Rickett's gunners. They march through a piece of woods, reach the top of the hill, and come into line. Captain Imboden, of the rebel battery, who is replying to Griffin, sees them. Who are they? He thinks they are Yankees flanking him. He wheels his guns, and is ready to cut them down with grape and canister. Captain Griffin also sees them, and wheels his guns. Another instant and he will sweep them away. He believes them to be rebels. His gunners load with grape and canister.

"Do not fire upon them; they are your supports!" shouts Major Barry, alas! riding up.

"No, sir, they are rebels," replied the hawk-eyed Griffin.

"They are your supports, just ordered up."

"As sure as the world, they are rebels," insists Griffin.

"You are mistaken, Captain, they are your supports."

The cannoneers stand ready to pull the lanyards, which will send a tornado through those ranks.

"Don't fire!" shouts the Captain.

The guns are wheeled again towards Mrs. Henry's, and the supposed 'supports' are saved from destruction at the hand of Captain Griffin.

Captain Imboden, before ordering his men to fire upon the supposed Yankees, gallops nearer to them, to *see* who they are. He sees them raise their guns. There is a flash, a rattle and roll—Griffin's and Rickett's men and their horses go down in an instant! They rush on with a yell. There is sharp, but decisive work. Close musket-shots and sabre-strokes. Men are trampled beneath the straggling horses. There are shouts and hurrahs. The few soldiers remaining to support Griffin and Rickett fire at the advancing rebel brigade, but the contest is unequal; they are not able to hold in check the three thousand fresh troops. They fall back. The guns are in the hands of the rebels. The day is lost. At the very moment of victory the line is broken. In an instant all is changed. A moment ago we were pressing on, but now we are falling back. Quick almost as the lightning's flash is the turning of the tide. *All through a mistake!*

### Reporting at the Front.

At Stone River, during the second day's fight, a young cavalry officer rode up to General Thomas for orders. "Report to Morton at the front," said the General, and shouting to his men, the young man dashed on to where the battle was raging hotly. Morton was not there. On again he went, through the thick smoke and the hurtling fire, to where Hazen was reaping a harvest of death on that terrible "half-acre"; but—Morton was not there. "Where is Morton?" he cried. "At the front!" came back from out of the smoke, and again he rode on—rode on past the Burnt House—past where Rosecrans sat like a statue amid a hail-storm of fire—past where a reeking funeral pile marked the outer line of intrenchments—on to the cannon-ploughed, death-strewed cotton-field. "Is he mad? Call him back! Call him back!" shouted the General, but the bugle was drowned in the awful uproar, and still he rode onward. Amazed, the rebel gunners stood at their pieces, but straight at them he rode with his handful of men. "I say, rebs," he shouted, "where is Morton?" "Gone where you are going," they answered, and the cannon echoed "Gone," and he went back again; not a man wounded. That young officer was Lieutenant Kelly, Fourth United States cavalry.

### One Day Before the Battle: Last Talk of Johnston with his Generals.

The rebel army had warmed up to the highest point, in expectation of being the conquerors at Pittsburg Landing. The troops had received five days' rations on Friday, meat and bread in their haversacks. They were not permitted to kindle a fire, except in holes in the ground. No loud talking was allowed; no drums beat the tattoo, no bugle-note rang through the forest. They rolled themselves in their blankets, knowing at daybreak they were to strike the terrible blow. They were confident of success. They were assured by their officers it would be an easy victory, and that on Sunday night they should sleep in the Yankee camp, eat Yankee bread, drink real coffee, and have new suits of clothes.

In the evening, General Johnston called his corps commanders around his bivouac fire for a last talk before the battle. Although Johnston was commander-in-chief, Beauregard planned the battle. Johnston was Beauregard's senior, but the battle-ground was in Beauregard's department. He gave directions to the officers.

Mr. William G. Stevenson, of Kentucky, who was in Arkansas when the war broke out, was impressed into the rebel service. He acted as special aide-de-camp to General Breckinridge in that battle. He escaped from the rebel service a few months later, and published an interesting narrative of what he saw. He stood outside the circle of Generals, waiting by his horse in the darkness to carry any despatch for his commander. He says:

In an open space, with a dim fire in the midst, and a drum on which to write, you could see grouped around their 'Little Napoleon,' as Beauregard was sometimes fondly called, ten or twelve Generals, the flickering light playing over their eager faces, while they listened to his plans, and made suggestions as to the conduct of the fight.

Beauregard soon warmed with his subject, and, throwing off his cloak, to give free play to his arms, he walked about the group, gesticulating rapidly, and jerking out his sentences with a strong French accent. All listened attentively, and the dim light, just revealing their countenances, showed their different emotions of confidence or distrust of his plans.

General Sidney Johnston stood apart from the rest, with his tall, straight form standing out like a spectre against the dim sky, and the illusion was fully sustained by the light-gray military cloak which he folded around him. His face was pale, but wore a determined expression, and at times he drew nearer the centre of the ring, and said a few words, which were listened to with great attention. It may be be had some foreboding of the fate he was to meet on the morrow, for he did not seem to take much part in the discussion.

General Breckinridge lay stretched out on a blanket near the fire, and occasionally sat upright and added a few words of counsel. General Bragg spoke frequently, and with earnestness. General Polk sat on a camp-stool at the outside of the circle, and held his head between his hands, buried in thought. Others reclined or sat in various positions.

For two hours the council lasted, and as it broke up, and the Generals were ready to return to their respective commands, General Beauregard said, raising his hand and pointing in the direction of the Federal camp, whose drums could be plainly heard:

"Gentlemen, we sleep in the enemy's camp to-morrow night!"

The brilliant result to the Union forces of this great conflict is well known.

### Work of a Second.

There was in the trenches in front of Fort Donelson a rebel soldier with a rifle-shot through his head, whose case was indeed an interesting one. He was an excellent marksman, and had killed or wounded several Union officers. One of Colonel Birges's sharpshooters, an old hunter, who had killed many bears and wolves, crept up towards the breastworks to try his hand upon the rebel. They fired at each other again and again, but both were shrewd and careful. The rebel raised his hat above the breastwork,— whi-z! The sharpshooter out in the bushes had put a bullet through it. "Ha! ha! ha!" laughed the rebel, sending his own bullet into the little puff of smoke down in the ravine. The Rocky Mountain hunter was as still as a mouse. He knew that the rebel had outwitted him, and expected the return shot. It was aimed a little too high, and he was safe.

"You cheated me that time, but I will be even with you yet," said the sharpshooter, whirling upon his back, and loading his rifle and whirling back again. He rested his rifle upon the ground, aimed it, and lay with his eye along the barrel, his finger upon the trigger. Five minutes passed. "I reckon that that last shot fixed him," said the rebel; "he hasn't moved this five minutes."

He raised his head, peeped over the embankment,—fell back lifeless! The unerring rifle-bullet of the old hunter had passed instantly through his head. It was but the deadly work of one swift-fleeting second.

### Ragged Texans: Boots and Booty.

In one of the frightful contests near Yorktown, Virginia, some notable instances of bravery and reckless daring occurred, nor was this confined to one of the great armies only. Conspicuous among these cases was the conduct of a tall, hard-fisted, and very ragged Texan soldier, who was hunting up, very cautiously, "a pair of boots and pants." He was warned by his Confederate comrades not to show his head above the parapet, for the Yankee sharp- and delighted at these discoveries; but when he examined the haversack and found it well stored with capital rations, including a canteen full of fine rye whisky, he was electrified with sudden joy, dropped boots, haversack, and money, upon the ground, and half emptied the canteen at a draught. Setting down the can, he smacked his lips, and thus soliloquized upon his rare adventure:

"Well, poor devil, he's gone, like a mighty big sight of 'em; but *he* was a

Ragged Texans.

shooters, armed with rifles of a long range, with telescopic "sights," were "thick as blackberries" in the woods to the front, and were excellent shots. "Darn the blue-skins, any how; who's scared of the blue-bellies? (That is, Eastern men.) Let all the Yankees go to ——, for all *I* care. Let 'em shoot, and be ——! I'm bound to have a pair of boots, any how!" And so saying, the rash fellow passed over the parapet, down its face, and returned with the body of a Federal, which he had fished out of the water. He first pulled off the boots, which proved to be an excellent pair; then, proceeding to rifle the pockets, he found the handsome booty of sixty dollars in gold. He was much astonished gentleman, and deserved better luck. If he'd been a Massachusetts Yankee, I wouldn't cared a darn! but these fellows are the right kind. They come along, as they should, with good boots and pants, lots to eat, money in their pockets, and are no mean judges of whisky. These are the kind of fellows I like to fight!"

### Bleeding to Death, but Sound as a Trout.

After the fight at Manassas had terminated, Adjutant Flint, of the Confederate ranks, was detailed as one of a burying party, and was out all night and most of the following day. As his regiment had been engaged near Centreville, he was hunting along the slopes for any poor fellow who required assistance, when his attention was called to moans in the bushes near by. Calling some comrades, search was made for the sufferer. They found him leaning against a tree, near which a shell had exploded—his countenance was ghastly pale, and he rolled his eyes apparently in great torture. "What's the matter, Lieutenant?" he was asked; but he groaned and fell on his face. "What can we do for you?" inquired another. "Oh! leave me to my fate, boys," was the sorrowful and faint reply. "I am dying every minute, and can't last long—I'm bleeding internally, and my blood is flowing fast! Farewell to my own sunny South; good bye, boys, and if any body shall ever visit Holly Springs, tell 'em that Shanks died like a patriot for his country, and shot four Yankees before he fell! Give my love to the Colonel and all the rest of the boys, and when you write, don't fail to give my last dying regards to Miss Sally Smith, if any on ye know her, and say I was faithful to the last—faithful to the last."

Affected beyond all words by the poor Lieutenant's simplicity and sufferings, they determined to carry him to the nearest ambulance, and ask a doctor to look at his wound. They placed him in a blanket, and in solemn procession had proceeded about half a mile, when he positively refused to go farther. "Let me down gently, boys, I can't stand shaking—there isn't much blood in me now, anyhow, and I feel I'm passing away from this vale of tears and wicked world every minute, and can't last long." A doctor was passing at the time, with sleeves rolled up, looking more like a gentleman butcher than anything else, and in whispers he was told of the condition of poor Shanks, who was now groaning more piteously than ever. "I think he's bleeding internally, doc.," said Adjutant Flint, "for I don't see any blood, although his momentary contortions are awful to look at—if he wasn't suffering so much I should be tempted to laugh."

"Where are you hit, Lieutenant?" inquired the surgeon tenderly. "Oh! don't touch me, doc., pray don't—I'm mortally wounded under the left shoulder blade, the ball has ranged downwards, and I'm bleeding internally!"

In a trice, Shanks's coat was cut in all directions, but yet there was no wound visible, until, to stop his lamentable groans, the surgeon asked again: "Where *are* you hit,—don't groan everlastingly, Shanks, but place your hand upon the wound, and let's see what can be done for you." The place indicated was as sound as any part of his body, and after searching in vain for half an hour, and cutting the clothes off his back in search of blood, the doctor gave Shanks a slap, laughing as he said—

"Get up, Shanks, and don't make a fool of yourself any longer; you are *as sound as a trout*, man—your wound is all imaginary."

They all began to laugh heartily, and were about to take signal vengeance on him for making them carry him half a mile through the mud and bushes, when Shanks jumped up as lively as ever and threatened to whip any man who should dare laugh at him—a threat that would have been fulfilled to the letter. It seems that a shell had burst within a few feet of him, and feeling certain that he was wounded by a fragment, he suffered all the symptoms of a wounded and dying man. In proof of his sincerity, poor Shanks had lain out in the rain all night, and when found he looked the most lamentable object for a first Lieutenant that could be imagined. The story got wind pretty universally, and Shanks always had an engagement on hand to 'whip somebody,' until at Gaines' Mill he at last fell mortally wounded.

**Waving the Stars and Stripes from the Summit of Lost Mountain.**

The battle of Lost Mountain, in Georgia, was one of the most severe battles of the war of the rebellion. At daylight on the seventeenth of June, 1864, the Union right was in motion from the third line of rifle-pits on Lost Mountain; and as Hooker advanced steadily, he was only supported by Schofield, immediately on his left. From the beginning the battle raged furiously; each succeeding line of rebel works was found stronger, and the ascent, as the National forces neared the top of the mountain, grew more difficult and dangerous. The rebels, too, fought more obstinately the further they retired, and their fire continued to increase in deadly fury and power.

At eight o'clock, the fourth line of rifle-pits was carried, resulting in the capture of a few rebel prisoners, and of nearly all their wounded. The troops who occupied the works only left them when absolutely pushed out; for in many places the assailants and assailed were mingled together in a hand-to-hand encounter for several minutes, before the Union troops could obtain positive possession. Schofield moved forward toward Pine Hill, carefully keeping up the unity between his right and Hooker's left, and, after a pretty stubborn resistance on the part of the rebels, he carried two lines of their earthworks.

After so furious an onslaught as was made in the morning, it became necessary to rest and recuperate the men for an hour or more, which was done by the lines lying down in the ditches from which they had just dispossessed the enemy. About eight o'clock the onset was renewed, and more furious fighting occurred; but the Union march was onward, with steady tread, and the resistance of the rebels only availed to sacrifice thousands of lives on both sides—nothing more. From that time there was no halt, no real check; and by one o'clock, at high noon, the Stars and Stripes waved from the summit of Lost Mountain, and Hooker stood proudly on the top, greeted by the voices of ten thousand of as gallant soldiers as ever fired a shot or charged a bayonet.

### Bloody Sabre-Charge by Colonel Minty.

General Kilpatrick made a brilliant raid upon the rebel region around Atlanta, Georgia, in August, just preceding the fall of that place. Four days of constant fighting was had under Kilpatrick, and the damage and destruction was great.

Suddenly, however, the Union forces were surrounded. With wild yells a whole division of Confederate cavalry (Jackson's,) five thousand strong, were seen coming down on the keen run, accompanied by ten pieces of artillery. Ere Kilpatrick had time to learn what was coming, a spirited attack was made upon the rear, and shells came tearing over the fields and bursting over the columns. Kilpatrick's keen eye soon comprehended the situation.

Minty's brigade was instantly withdrawn and hastily formed along the road, in line of regimental column. While other regiments which were to charge simultaneously with Minty's, were being manœuvred into position to meet the onslaught of the rebels, who were sweeping down upon them, the men had time to see the danger that surrounded them—rebels to the right of them, rebels to the left of them, rebels in the rear of them, rebels in front of them—surrounded, there was no salvation but to cut their way out. Spectres of Libby prison and starvation flitted across their vision, and they saw that the deadly conflict could not be avoided. Placing himself at the head of his brigade, the gallant and fearless Minty drew his sabre, and his voice rung out clear and loud,

"*Attention, column; forward, trot, regulate by the centre regiment, march, gallop march!*"

Away the brigade went with a yell that echoed loud across the valleys. The ground from which the start was made, and over which they charged, was a plantation of about two square miles, thickly strewn with patches of woods, deep water cuts, fences, ditches, and morasses. At the word, away went the bold dragoons, at the height of their speed. Fences were jumped, ditches were no impediment. The rattle of the sabres, mingled with that of the mess kettles and frying-pans, that jingled at the sides of the pack mule brigade, which were madly pushed forward by the frightened darkies who straddled them.

Charging for their very lives, and yelling like unchained devils, Minty and his troopers encountered the rebels behind a hastily erected barricade of rails. Pressing their rowels deep into their horses' flanks, and raising their sabres aloft, on, on—on, nearer and nearer to the rebels they plunged. The terror-stricken enemy could not withstand the thunderous wave of men and horses that threatened to engulf them. They broke and ran, just as Minty and his troopers were urging their horses for the decisive blow. In an instant all was confusion. The yells of the horsemen were drowned in the clashing of steel and the groans of the dying. On pressed Minty in pursuit, his men's sabres striking right and left and cutting down everything in their path. The rebel horsemen were seen to reel and pitch headlong to the earth, while their frightened steeds rushed pell-mell over their bodies. Many of the rebels defended themselves with almost superhuman strength, yet it was all in vain. The charge of Federal steel was irresistible. The heads and limbs of some of the poor rebels were actually severed from the bodies—the head of the rider falling on one side of the horse, the lifeless trunk upon the other. Hardly a Union man flinched, in the work of death, and when the brigade came out, more than half the sabres were stained or clotted with blood. Three stands of colors were captured—the Fourth United States taking two, and the Fourth Michigan one. Colonel Minty, whose soldierly form was conspicuous in the charge, urging his men to follow his lead, had his horse shot under him.

## Remember Fort Pillow!

The terrible butchery of colored Union soldiers at Fort Pillow—killed in cold blood, instead of being treated as prisoners of war—by General Forrest, the Confederate commander at that post, sent a feeling of horror throughout the entire country. It did not, however, excite astonishment on the part of those acquainted with the antecedents of the rebel chieftain. About the middle of the summer of 1862, Forrest surprised the post of Murfreesboro, commanded by Brigadier-General

"Remember Fort Pillow."

Crittenden, of Indiana. The garrison was composed mostly of the Ninth Michigan and Second Minnesota infantry and the Seventh Pennsylvania cavalry. After some little fighting, the troops were surrendered. A mulatto man, who was a servant of one of the officers of the Union forces, was brought to Forrest on horseback. The latter enquired of him, with many oaths, 'What he was doing there?' The latter answered that he was a free man, and came out as a servant to an officer—naming the officer. Forrest, who was on horseback, deliberately put his hand to his holster, drew his pistol, and blew the man's brains out. This statement was made by a Confederate officer, with the additional fact that the mulatto man came from Pennsylvania, that the murdered man was not a soldier, and, indeed, the occurrence took place before the United States Government determined to arm negroes for military service.

But the example set by General Forrest at Fort Pillow furnished the colored troops with an avenging watch-word, when, some time afterwards, a force of Union black troops was sent out, opposite Natchez, Mississippi, to disperse a similar force of rebels. The latter were badly whipped and routed. The blacks went into battle with the rallying cry of "*Remember Fort Pillow.*" Eleven men were captured, but were immediately put to the sword on the spot where they surrendered. One rebel dropped upon his knees before a black soldier, and begged for his life. The soldier turned to his Captain and said,

"Captain, what shall I do with this man?"

"Do with him as he would do with you if he was in your place and you was in his," was the quick reply.

Swift as thought, a loyal bullet was sent from a Colt revolver through the rebel's head, and he fell dead at the hands of one who, to that extent, had avenged the wrongs of his race. It was the example set at Fort Pillow and the policy there initiated, legitimately carried out.

### How the Flag was Planted at Vicksburg.

For two long hours a terrible cannonade was carried on during one of the eventful days before Vicksburg, when on the left, in Smith's, Carr's, and Osterhaus' division, a charge was made. Winding through the valleys, clambering over the hills, everywhere subjected to a murderous enfilading and cross fire, they pressed up close to the rebel works to find that a deep ditch, protected by sharp stakes along the outer edge, lay between them and the intrenchments. They planted their flag directly before the fort, and crouched down behind the embankment, out of range of the rebel fire, as calmly as possible, to await developments. The soldiers within the fort could not raise above the parapet to fire at them, for if they did a hundred bullets came whizzing through the air, and the adventurers were 'nowhere.'

Use for a Shell.

They adopted another plan. *Taking a shell, they cut the fuse close off, lighted it, and rolled it over the outer slope of the embankment.* Subsequently, with picks and shovels, a way was dug into one fort, and through the breach the boys walked bravely in.

### One of Bill Myers's Capers in Missouri.

Bill Myers was one of the earliest and most notorious bushwhackers and horse thieves in Missouri; his stealing of horses, guns, and everything else that came in the way, being all done in the name of the "Southern Confederacy," and he was a kind of mean fac-simile of Jeff. Thompson, and other 'Generals' of the same stripe in that region, in those dark days of war and persecution.

Soon after Bill commenced his patriotic career, he stole from a Union man one of the finest horses in the neighborhood, and continued to use him as his war-horse through many hard chases, both in pursuit of plunder and in retreat from the pursuit of the avenging Union soldiers, until he was completely broken down and used up. In this condition, Bill rode him into the neighborhood whence he stole him, and where he (Myers) had previously lived.

Bill had a particular friend named M'Fadden, who owned a fine farm, plenty of fine horses, cattle, etc., and a few lively darkies; and there Bill went by night, confident of a warm reception and good lodgings for himself and his broken-down horse.

M'Fadden was like thousands in Missouri, who "took no sides—no part nor lot in the war" publicly, but would privately

Jeff. Thompson.

aid and encourage the bushwhackers in every way possible, when it could be done without detection. A watch being set to guard against any sudden surprise, Bill entertained his host with many an adventure and hairbreadth escape from capture and death, in which his listener was greatly interested and deeply sympathized. M'Fadden noticed the wretched condition of Bill's horse, the property of a former intimate friend, but now abused as "a black Republican," who had contributed but a very small amount of what he ought to do in support of Southern rights; and urged Bill by all means to get a better horse—that one doing the service and running the risks he did, in support of "our cause," ought to be well mounted all the time, and that not at his own expense—it being understood, of course, at the expense of "black Republicans."

The justice of these ideas was admitted by Bill, who, however, spoke of the risks of thus taking horses wherever he could find them, the exasperation of the community at that kind of war, and of the injury it had done to their cause, however proper in itself. M'Fadden thought all such qualms of conscience out of place, and urged, "Every thing for the cause; nothing for men." But it was growing late, and as Bill had to be up and off before daylight, as the "Feds" might be about, with many kind wishes and hopes of success each retired to bed with the understanding that Bill, knowing where to find his poor broken-down horse, would wait on himself when he should leave before the light of dawn.

M'Fadden had got too much exhilarated by the exciting scenes narrated by his friend Bill to sleep soundly. He was wakeful, and distinctly heard the soft footsteps of Bill as he retired quietly, in order not to awake his friend or his family, or to arouse the suspicion of any thing "wrong in Denmark." But M'Fadden was rejoiced to know that Bill was again safely "at sea" in the bush, and that nothing had occurred to betray him, M'F., as the harborer of a bushwhacker.

*But alas for the sequel!* Quite early in the morning the contraband whose business it was to feed the horses and prepare for the work of the day came thundering at his master's door, with—

"Master, master! your fine bay hoss, Ned Buntline, is dun bin stole and gone, and dat old broke-down gray hoss what Massa Bill rode is thar in the stable whar your hoss was!"

Springing from the bed as if an earthquake was just beginning to rumble, M'Fadden cried out, "Oh, surely, Jack, you are mistaken!" But quickly as possible he hauled on his trowsers and ran to the stable; and, sure enough, there *was* old gray—once the elegant charger of his old friend and neighbor, but now a hated "black Republican," the designation of all Union men in that region—and his own fine bay was out and gone, "and if forever," "then still forever," etc. If the quotations be not right, readers can hunt up the documents for themselves; but the *facts* of the case are too palpable to be misunderstood. Bill had taken his friend's advice, and merely exchanged old gray for a better charger,— fully agreeing with M'F., " Every thing for the cause—nothing for men," and that qualms of conscience were, after all, decidedly out of place.

But the misfortune did not stop here. Had it been in a distant neighborhood from the old home of Bill, M'Fadden might have retained " old gray," as a stray waiting for the call of his proper owner; but, being right at home, old gray, though badly broken-down, was too easily recognized to be retained on the farm, and was forthwith sent home to his proper owner, with the singular explanation that he was found in the stable in place of his own fine bay, which was supposed to be stolen by some unknown bushwhacker.

### Long Table-Cloths for Southern Cavalrymen.

Private Reed, of the Seventh Ohio regiment, while making a reconnoissance with other soldiers, in Virginia, was sent to search a house about eight hundred yards from the road. He went up to the house and walked in, but on opening the door could not see anybody in the house. The table was set, ready for breakfast, the table-cloth hanging down, touching the floor. He first looked under the bed, but in vain. As he was about to go away he thought he would look under the table; so he lifted the cloth, and, lo! a pair of spurs and also a cavalryman attached to them! He lay there so quiet, that death would not have been more so. As soon as he discovered him, Reed, cocking his piece, presented it to the hiding man's breast, at the same time ordering him to come out. After looking at Reed for a second, he complied with the order. On their leaving the house together, the prisoner stated that he was a member of Ashby's cavalry, and had stopped there to get something to eat. He then said: " Since you have got me, you may as well have my horse." So they walked round to the barn and got his horse, also a sabre and a carbine. They then proceeded to where the boys had quartered themselves, and the gallant private delivered to General Geary the prisoner whom he had taken from his very domestic retreat.

### Not Yankees, but—Wolford's Cavalry.

Wolford's cavalry distinguished itself by some dashing and remarkable exploits in its campaign of 1862, in Tennessee and that region. That which took place in the neighborhood of New Haven was one of the most brilliant and successful. Coming upon the enemy suddenly, Captain Adams shouted: " Halt! and present arms!" All, with the precision and coolness of veterans, in a moment leveled their guns upon the now panic-stricken, confused enemy; and the Captain at the top of his voice called out: " I demand your immediate, unconditional surrender." " To whom must I surrender?" called out Colonel Crawford in command of the Third Georgia cavalry, as he now stepped forward. " To Captain Adams, commanding the First Kentucky cavalry," replied the Captain. " Give me a few moments to consult my officers, will you?" said the Colonel. " I have no time to fool away," said the Captain. " Two minutes and a half, Sir, and I will order my men to work upon you." " If I have only that time, Captain," said the Colonel, " I will surrender at once, expecting good treatment from so gallant an officer and such brave men as you have the honor to command." The camp was accordingly surrendered, and the whole force, consisting of nearly all the Third Georgia cavalry, a few of the First Kentucky secession cavalry, and some of the Texas Rangers,—and all without the firing of a gun. Before the other gallant fellows could come up, the whole affair was over, and they only had the pleasure of feeling that they had also gallantly done their part, in coming up to the support of the more fortunate advance, to whom the main credit of the exploit belonged. As the advance dashed around the camp, a group stood near them looking on in wonder. As they halted, one exclaimed: "You are not Yankees, are you?" "No," answered Sergeant Humphrey. He turned to his fellows and, clapping his hands, exclaimed: "Didn't I tell you they were not Yankees? Didn't I tell you so? Who are you?" he called out again. "Wolford's cavalry," replied the Sergeant. Then raising his hands in utter despair, the poor Georgian exclaimed: "Good heavens! then we are gone." They were marched over to Elizabethtown.

### Bearing the Standard through Baltimore.

Previously to the departure of the Sixth Massachusetts regiment for the defence of Washington, they were gathered in front of the State House, Boston, to hear the parting words of Governor Andrew. At the end of his remarks, the Governor presented the regiment with a standard, telling them to see to it that no foe should ever take it from them. They received it with cheers, and swore to die in its defence.

Well, when they got out of the cars at Baltimore, to march across the city, the colors were given to the breeze, and borne aloft in defiance of every foe. The standard-bearer, as noble a fellow as ever wore the uniform of the Old Bay State, was Timothy Crowley. His two aids were Sergeants Derril and Marland. Unused, as, indeed, all the soldiers then were, to the rough usage of actual warfare, it would not have been strange if Crowley had shown some signs of fear. Indeed, he might have rolled up the colors, which would inevitably call down upon him the hatred of the vast and murderous mob. But Crowley was not made of such stuff. He had sworn to stand by his standard, and with him it was either succeed, or die in the attempt. Pistols were freely fired, but the company saw at their head that standard proudly leading them on. No one who has never been in actual service can imagine how the colors of a regiment keep up its courage. So long as they are defiant, the company have light hearts; if they should be taken away, a strange distrust runs through the whole force.

As it was, the troops had lost their band, —they did not even have a fife and drum, —and so they kept their eyes upon this standard. Tramp, tramp, tramp—left, left, left,—the music of their own steady, measured tread,—this was all they had. Crowley was the target for many a missile, for the mob knew that to disgrace the regiment, it was only necessary to down with the standard. Paving-stones flew thick and fast, some just grazing Crowley's head, and some hitting the standard itself. Amid all this, the everlasting pluck of Crowley showed itself without a taint. One large stone struck him, just between the shoulders, a terrible blow, and then rested on his knapsack. And yet Crowley did not budge. With a firm step he went on, carrying the rock on his knapsack for several yards, until one of the sergeants stepped up and knocked it off. His coolness showed him to possess the very highest qualities of a soldier.

### Fate of Two German Brothers.

A member of the Second Connecticut regiment captured a German, belonging to the Eighth South Carolina regiment—at the battle of Bull Run—and took him to Major Colburn for instructions as to how to dispose of the prisoner. The latter requested one privilege as his last, which the Major very readily granted. He said his brother lay a short distance off, in a dying condition, and he wished to see him. His captor bade him lead the way, and the two proceeded, the prisoner going to an old log hut but a few rods from where the regiment was halted. On the north side, in the shade, the wounded man was found.

Fate of two Germans.

The prisoner spoke to him—he opened his eyes—the film of death had already overspread them, and the tide of life was fast ebbing. He was covered with blood, and the swarms of flies and mosquitoes, which were fattening upon his life's blood, indicated that he had lain there, helpless, in agony, and uncared for, for some time. The two unfortunate victims of the war clasped hands warmly together, muttered a few words in the German language, supplicating the favor of heaven upon their families at home, kissed each other, and mutually exchanged the final adieux,—the prisoner remarking, as he was taken by the arm to be led away, for the column was moving, "Brother, you are dying, and I am a prisoner." The man was shot with a musket-ball, in the back, just over the hip.

### Zou! Zou! Zou!

The battle of Roanoke Island was marked by more than one exhibition of great and decided bravery. General Foster was in active command on the ground. His brave and collected manner, the skillfulness with which he, as well as General Reno and General Parks, manœuvred their forces, their example in front of the line, and their conduct in any aspect, inspired the troops to stand where even older soldiers would have wavered. In this they were seconded nobly by officers of every grade. General Parks, who had come up with the Fourth Rhode Island, Eighth Connecticut, and Ninth New York, gave timely and gallant support to the Twenty-third and Twenty-seventh Massachusetts. The ammunition of the artillery getting short, and the men having suffered severely, a charge was the only method of dislodging the enemy. At this juncture, Major Kimball, of Hawkins's Zouaves—New York Ninth—offered to lead the charge, and storm the battery with the bayonet. General Foster's reply was—

"You are the man, the Ninth the regiment, and this the moment! Zouaves! storm the battery! Forward."

They started on the run, yelling like devils, cheered by the federal forces on every side. Colonel Hawkins, who was leading two companies in the flank movement, joined his regiment on the way. On they went, with fixed bayonets, shouting "Zou! Zou! Zou!" into the battery, cheered more loudly than ever. The rebels taking fright as the Zouaves started, went out when they went in, leaving pretty much everything behind them, and not even stopping to spike their guns, and take away their dead and wounded that had not been removed.

### Blenker Scorning to Retreat.

The retreat from Bull Run on the twenty-first of July, 1861, will ever be memorable for its illustrations of the fortunes of war. Stretching far across the road, long before the hoped-for refuge of Centreville was reached, was a firm unswerving line of men, to whom the sight of the thousands who dashed by them was only a wonder or a scorn. This was the German rifle regiment; and to see the manly bearing of their General, and feel the inspiration which his presence gave at that moment, was like relief to those ready to perish in a desert. Steady and watchful, Blenker held his line throughout the evening, advancing his skirmishers at every token of attack, and spreading a sure protection over the multitudes who fled disordered through his columns. With three regiments he stood to fight against an outnumbering enemy already flushed with victory, and eager to complete its triumph. As the darkness increased, his post became more perilous and more honorable. At eleven o'clock the attack came upon the advance company of Colonel Stahel's rifles, not in force, but from a body of cavalry whose successful passage would have been followed by a full force, and the consequent destruction of the broken Federal host. The rebel cavalry was driven back, and never returned; and at two in the morning, the great body of Federal troops having passed and found their road to safety, the command was given to retreat in order, and the brigade fell slowly and regularly back, with the same precision as if on parade, and as thoroughly at the will of their leader as if no danger had ever come near them. Over and over again Blenker begged permission to maintain his post, or even to advance. "Retreat!" said he, scornfully, to the messenger; "bring me the word to GO ON, sir!" But the command was peremptory, and he was left no alternative.

### Hooker's Battle Above the Clouds.

Quartermaster-General Meigs, in his lively account of the three days' conflict before Chattanooga, mentions the notable fact that in General Hooker's fight up the slopes of Lookout Mountain, "much of the battle was fought *above the clouds,* which concealed him from our view, but from which his musketry was heard." There is on record at least one case parallel to this, in the campaign of Napoleon in the Carnic Alps, in 1797. The battle of the Col de Tarvis, March 22, 1797, was fought above the clouds—the artillery thundering in the very laboratory of storms and arsenals of the electric batteries—while the cavalry charged and performed their evolutions on the ice, and the infantry floundered to the attack through snow three feet deep.

### Sleeper's Saucy Battery.

Towards the end of Friday's battle in the Wilderness, about nightfall, a desperate charge was made by the rebels upon the extreme left of the Federals, where a number of batteries of the Second Corps were in position, being a part of Hancock's line. In front of these guns, and below their level, was an open field. Rather more than half way across this space ran the Union line of breastworks—at this point not more than one hundred yards from those held by the enemy. Everything was perfectly quiet,—mutual respect for each other's fire preventing unnecessary exposure. Suddenly, however, a perfectly devilish volley of musketry was delivered from their works, accompanied by the dismal howling which, in Dixie, had quite superseded honest cheering, and out they came, piling over the breastworks, and for a short time having things just as they wanted them. Their success was very short lived, for in a moment Sleeper's Tenth Massachusetts battery, Adams's Rhode Island battery, the Sixth Maine battery, and others, were pouring canister into them in so effective a manner that they were forced to protect themselves in front of the Federal breastworks, from which, later in the evening, they were expelled, losing terribly in their 'forlorn hope' of a charge. The Tenth Massachusetts battery, commanded by Captain J. Henry Sleeper, proved itself one of the best in the service. It was engaged seventeen times since the army crossed the Rapidan, and was one of the very few batteries which managed to get into the memorable Wilderness fight of Thursday and Friday. It had come to be called the "saucy battery" in Hancock's corps, of which it was part.

### Texas Flag Captured by the Sixteenth Indiana.

When flags are captured in the height of battle, it shows close and severe fighting. A New Orleans paper states that in the bloody engagement which took place near Mansfield, the battle-worn and weather-beaten banner of a Texas regiment of rebels was captured by Captain Doxie, of the Sixteenth Indiana mounted regiment, attached to the first brigade of Lee's cavalry, after one of the most desperate hand-to-hand encounters of the war. When the stalwart Indianians met the rough riders of Texas, there could of course be no child's play, and consequently the ground was piled with slain in the struggle for the possession of that flag, which bore the inscription—"Texans never can be slaves." Captain Doxie, the hero of the fight, came forth from the battle covered with wounds, inflicted by sabre-stroke and pistol-shot. The flag was brought down to New Orleans by Colonel Brisbane, of General Lee's staff, and was presented to Miss Mary Binny Banks, the "daughter of the brigade," in presence of her mother, at the residence of the General. The young lady showed a great deal of emotion as she took the battle-stained trophy—which had so long waved triumphantly in the centre of a hecatomb of heroes slain—in her hands. Mrs. Banks made a few feeling and commendatory remarks, complimenting the gallantry of Captain Doxie and his brave men, and promising to interest herself in securing the promotion of those who had so nobly contended for the prize and torn it from the possession of a desperate foe. It was a white and red banner, with blue union, but so old, faded, and battle-worn, that the colors could scarcely be distinguished. Perhaps it had waved on every field from Wilson's Creek to Pleasant Hill.

### Court-Martialing a whole Division.

It was near sundown when General T. J. Wood, whose conduct all through the three days' battle of Lookout Mountain, marked him as one of the ablest leaders of the National armies, rode along the lines of his superb division. Loud shouts of enthusiasm everywhere greeted his appearance, until at last his feelings, no longer controllable, broke out in a speech:—

"Brave men," said he "you were ordered to go forward and take the rebel rifle pits at the foot of these hills; you did so; and then, by the Eternal! *without orders*, you pushed forward and took all the enemy's works on top! Here is a fine chance for having you all court-martialed! and I myself will appear as the principal witness against you, unless you promise me one thing."

"What is it? what is it?" laughingly inquired the men.

"It is," resumed the General, "that as you are now in possession of these works, you will continue, against all opposition of Bragg, Johnston, Jeff. Davis and the devil, steadfastly to hold them!"

At the conclusion of this speech, the enthusiasm of the soldiers knew no bounds. They left the ranks and crowded around their General. "We promise! we promise!" they cried, and amid such exclamations as, "Of course we'll hold them!" "Let any one try to take them from us!" "Bully for you!" "Three cheers for old Wood!" the gallant officer rode off the field.

### Brilliant Strategy of General Smith at Red River.

The brilliant and successful strategy of General Smith at the close of the second day's fighting at Red River, is well known. The whole two days had been full of disaster, when suddenly, in the midst of retreat, a favorable point and a happy thought struck the mind of General Smith, an educated soldier, and he at once availed himself of it. He placed a division in front in line of battle, and arranging his artillery and the residue of his forces along the ridges in the valley between which the road ran, he awaited the approach of the confederates.

On they came, yelling and foaming with the flush of success, and with rebounding speed they rushed upon the troops they saw before them. Then, apparently alarmed at their overwhelming force, retreated, first in order, and then at a trot, and the enemy followed. When the gorge was completely filled, grape, canister, and musket shot opened upon them, and the destruction was appalling; those who could, fell back to their main body, the few who passed through were taken prisoners, and the Federal troops re-formed, the forces under Smith continuing to cover their retreat until all safely reached Grand Ecore. As soon as the army had thus been extricated from its crushing danger, General Banks rode up to General Smith and said—

"God bless you, General! You have saved the army from destruction."

"I hope he will bless all of us," was the brave soldier's terse and significant reply.

### Falstaff in the Cavalry Service.

In one of the Union cavalry regiments there was a Major whose character more resembled that of Fal-taff in some respects than that of any other officer. The Major blustered when there was no danger, and when in a tight place he either *showed* the white feather or attempted to conceal it by some act that seemed like blind desperation. Being an arrant coward, he feared the reputation of a coward as much as he did death itself, and therefore would make a terrific charge—but without judgment,—if he supposed that people whose opinion he feared were looking on. One of his exploits may here be cited.

Some fortune, kind to him but cruel to his regiment, which was composed of tough, brave veterans, frequently placed him in command—seniority of rank doing the business. On the occasion referred to he was leading his regiment, under orders, on an expedition in Western Virginia, when he came near the town of ———. He had felt his way cautiously toward the town, with skirmishers thrown forward, and employing all the precautions necessary when a strong force of an enemy is in the neighborhood. Thus the valiant Major proceeded until he met some of the residents of the town, who assured him that no rebels were there—that the citizens of the place were prepared to receive the Union troops with a welcome.

Upon receiving this information, the Major was almost instantly transformed from an anxious, cautious skirmisher, into a terrible son of Mars. His eyes protruded, his pursy form swelled, he flourished his saber high in the air, and in a stentorian voice ordered his command to close up, to trot, and to gallop. Away went the Major, followed by his regiment, charging directly through the town pell-mell, with great rattling of hoofs and clanging of sabers; nor did he draw rein and order a halt until he was a clear mile beyond the limits of the village. Once safe beyond the possibility of an ambush, beyond a town where he had supposed secesh were lurking, the indomitable Major kept on his way rejoicing.

But, oh! the wonderment and terror of the women and children of the town, and the rage of the Major's veteran troopers! The ladies had prepared a collation for the yankee soldiers—either from a friendly feeling or a desire to propitiate them, tables were spread in front of their houses, and women and children were in the streets to welcome the hungry warriors and their 'gallant chieftain' to their repast,—and what was their dismay, when the whole body galloped furiously through the streets, actually endangering the lives of the inno-

### Hurrah for the Gunspiker.

Colonel Roberts, of the Forty-second Illinois, rendered himself conspicuous for his bravery at Island No. 10, (where he so gloriously spiked the battery,) and at Farmington; services so distinguished, that, in the subsequent battle in which he engaged, he acted as Brigadier-General. His regiment was also noted for its coolness and bravery. When ordered to fall back, they did so under a terrible crossfire of grape and shell, with all the regularity of a parade. Halting occasionally and facing about, they would check the onward rush of the enemy, and then quietly resume their retreat. Their coolness was so conspicuous, that General Palmer, struck with admiration, galloped along their lines, hat in hand, shouting: "Brave Forty-second, I wish I could be the father of every one of you!" Colonel Roberts exposed himself constantly with perfect *sang froid* to the hottest fire of the enemy, and when the last regiment, the Forty-second, passed through the gap, he in person commanded the rear guard. Several times during the fight, as the Colonel rode along the lines, the boys ceased from their labors to "hurrah for the gunspiker!"

### Owning Up.

Major McKee, at the head of a Union force, hunted up a great many secessionists of the rampant sort, in Southern Missouri,—so actively, indeed, as to nearly fill the various county jails. When he caught one of this type, he said:

"Well, how much of a rebel have you been? You know more about what you have done than I do. I know some, and you know it all."

One old man said, as he trembled, "Major, I have not done any thing."

"Stop," said the Major, "you know you have got some powder hid."

"Oh, yes, there is some."

Owning up.

"Tell it all now," said the Major.

"Well, I will. I have got twenty-one kegs of powder and one gun. I furnished four horses to Price, and went down to Smith's Chapel to fight the Feds, and I have fed any amount of rebels. I won't lie any more! You have got it all. I have done all I could to aid the South."

The Major had come down so hard on them that they feared to lie to him. Another man came in at the same time as the above, to take the oath.

"Well, Sir, what have you done?"

"Nothing."

"Well, Sir, I will put you in jail for not doing something."

After he had been in jail about two hours, he sent for the Major, and told him where there were eleven kegs of powder, and a Government wagon, and owned to helping cut up a ferry boat on the Missouri river, in the summer.

### Seven Rebels Captured by One Fed.

One of the neatest of military exploits during the war, was that performed by Captain Drake DeKay of General Mansfield's staff, while awaiting the General's arrival at a house called Moore's Ranche, a kind of summer hotel kept by a man named Moore, at Ocean View. All the white men, and most of the women of the vicinity had fled—it was said by those they had left behind—to the woods, to prevent being forced into the rebel service.

Captain DeKay, while supper was being prepared, mounted his horse and determined to explore the country, followed only by his negro servant. As he was passing a swamp toward evening, he came suddenly upon *seven* of the secession troops, who were lurking by the roadside, and were armed with double-barreled guns. The Captain turned instantaneously and shouted to his (imaginary) company to prepare to charge—and then riding forward rapidly, revolver in hand, told the men they were his prisoners, as his cavalry would soon be upon them, ordered them to discharge their pieces and deliver them to him, which they did without delay. He then informed them that his only 'company' was his negro servant, and directed them to follow him into camp.

An hour later, just after General Wool had returned from Norfolk, the Captain rode to the beach and informed Colonel Cram, as Chief of the General's Staff, that the seven prisoners, whom he had marched to the beach, were at his disposal. Their arms were taken away, and on promising to take the oath of allegiance, the men were at once dismissed. One of them proved to be Moore himself, who came over to his house, where he found half a dozen Feds in full possession, and just preparing to discuss a most comfortable supper which his obliging colored cook had got ready for them. Like nearly all the rebel soldiers in that section, he said that he had been *forced* into the service, and was only waiting a chance to run away; but his statements on this point did not obtain, to say the least, any *more* credit than they deserved.

### Sheridan Riding to the Front.

The victory gained by General Sheridan at Cedar Creek, Va., October 19th, 1864, surpassed in interest the victory gained precisely one month earlier at Winchester. It was a victory following upon the heels of apparent reverse, and therefore reflecting peculiar credit on the brave commander to whose timely arrival upon the field the final success of the day must be attributed.

The General was at Winchester in the early morning when the enemy attacked—fifteen miles distant from the field of operations. General Wright was in command. The enemy had approached under cover of a heavy fog, and flanking the extreme right of the Federal line, held by Crook's Corps, and attacking in the centre, had thrown the entire line into confusion, and driven it several miles. The stragglers to the rear were fearfully numerous, and the enemy was pushing on, turning against the Federals a score of guns already captured from them.

This was the situation a little before noon when Sheridan came on the field, riding, said one of his staff, so that the devil himself could not have kept up. A staff officer meeting him, pronounced the situation of the army to be "awful."

"Pshaw," said Sheridan, "it's nothing of the sort. It's all right, or we'll fix it right!"

Sheridan hastened to his cavalry on the extreme left. Galloping past the batteries to the extreme left of the line held by the cavalry, he rode to the front, took off his hat and waved it, while a cheer went up from the ranks not less hearty and enthusiastic than that which greeted him after the battle of Winchester. Generals rode out to meet him, officers waved their swords, men threw up their hats in an extremity of glee. General Custer, discovering Sheridan at the moment he arrived, rode up to him, threw his arms around his neck, and kissed him on the cheek. Waiting for no other parley than simply to exchange greeting, and to say "This retreat must be stopped!" Sheridan broke loose and began galloping down the lines, along the whole front of the army. Everywhere the enthusiasm caused by his appearance was the same.

The line was speedily re-formed; provost-marshals brought in stragglers by the scores; the retreating army turned its face to the foe. An attack just about to be made by the latter was repulsed, and the tide of battle turned. Then Sheridan's time was come. A cavalry charge was ordered against right and left flank of the enemy, and then a grand advance of the three infantry corps from left to right on the enemy's centre. On through Middletown, and beyond, the Confederates hurried, and the Army of the Shenandoah pursued. The roar of musketry now had a gleeful, dancing sound. The guns fired shotted salutes of victory. Custer and Merritt, charging in on right and left, doubled up the flanks of the foe, taking prisoners, slashing, killing, driving as they went. The march of the infantry was more majestic and terrible. The lines of the foe swayed and broke before it everywhere. Beyond Middletown, on the battle-field fought over in the morning, their columns were completely overthrown and disorganized. They fled along the pike and over the fields like sheep.

Thus on through Strasburg with two brigades of cavalry at their heels. Two thousand prisoners were gathered together, though there was not a sufficient guard to send them all to the rear. The guns lost in the morning were recaptured, and as many more taken, making fifty in all, and according to Sheridan's report, the enemy reached Mount Jackson without an organized regiment. The scene at Sheridan's head-quarters at night, after the battle, was wildly exciting. General Custer arrived about nine o'clock. The first thing he did was to hug General Sheridan with all his might, lifting him in the air, and whirling him around and around, with the shout: "By —, we've cleaned them out and got the guns!" Catching sight of General Torbert, Custer went through the same proceeding with him, until Torbert was forced to cry out, "There, there, old fellow; don't capture me!"

Sheridan's ride to the front, October 19th, 1864, will go down in history as one of the most important and exciting events which have ever given interest to a battle scene; and to this event is to be attributed the victory of the day.

### Boy Soldiers at the Old Ones' Trade.

Knoxville, Tennessee, is a town well known. Across a little creek is a place called Shieldstown. The spirit of war exhibited itself warmly among the boys six, eight, and ten years old, and the fight raged fiercely between the Shieldstowners and Knoxvillers. They used slings and minie balls, which they handled with great dexterity. They had camp-fires built along in a line. Every morning each party appeared on its own side of the stream, drawn up in array, ammunition was distributed out of a bag, fifteen rounds to the man, and they commenced. Old soldiers of the Ninth Corps, who had been through many a storm of shot and shell, kept at a respectable distance as they hurled their minies with vigor. One day the Shieldstowners made a charge at the single plank that crossed the stream, the Knoxvillers ran, all except one little fellow about eight years old—he stood at the end of the plank, swearing oaths like Parrott shells, calling them cowards, and, by a vigorous discharge of minies, repulsed the assault. The casualties amounted to bruises and cuts in all parts of the body, rather serious to look at, or to think what they might have been; but every little fellow was proud of his wound. So it went on for several days, when one bright morning, as they were drawn up in full-fighting array, and only awaited the military signal to commence, suddenly appeared some women in rear of each—a half dozen were caught up, severely spanked, and led off. The rest were disconcerted and dispersed.

### Foolhardiness and its Terrible Penalty.

When our forces were at Tybee, a party of Germans went one day up to Goat's Point. One of the privates stood on the summit of a sandhill, perhaps a hundred yards less than a mile from Pulaski, (which was as near as the Federals could get,) and waved his hat. The others went back out of sight, but could see the rebels bringing a gun to bear. They warned their comrade, but he would not heed. As he stood with his back to the fort, a barbette gun sent out a little cloud. Then came the thunder, the rushing ball, *and the rash man lay disemboweled and cut in two on the sand.* It was a splendid shot, such as could not be equaled in a month's practice.

### Cost of a Canteen of Water.

Mr. Hepworth, Chaplain to one of the Massachusetts regiments, relates the story of a curious capture, as follows:

One of our men was captured by a very neat piece of strategy. About a hundred and fifty yards from the front of one of our regiments was a spring of clear cold water. After having drunk the vile fluid which oozes through a clay bank, oftentimes impregnated with a very disagreeable odor, and always having the appearance of mud paste, (being chiefly composed of that very necessary but not always palatable substance,) the boys were willing to run some little risk for the sake of a draught of genuine water. One day a sick man asked a chum to fill his canteen. Without hesitation he promised to do so; and so, crawling up with all due caution, he at length reached the spring.

It so happened, however, that a rebel sharpshooter had seen him. He waited quietly till the canteen was filled, and then drawing a bead on the soldier, cried out—

"I say, Yank!"

The startled Unionist at once saw his predicament, and began to think that his last minute had come. He at last got voice enough to cry out—

"Well, what do you want?"

"Want you. Walk over this way, please."

It was certainly a very courteous invitation, and there seemed no way to avoid accepting it; for the rebel kept him covered with his rifle. He was in an unpleasant predicament; and, when the rebel had enjoyed his embarrassment long enough, he cried out—

"I say, Yank, aren't you coming? or shall I send some lead after you?"

This was a very pointed remark. Nothing was left the poor Unionist but to obey; and so, with unwilling steps, he walked over to the jocose rebel and gave himself up.

### Steedman taking the Flag.

It was about four o'clock of that afternoon on which occurred the battle of Chickamauga, when a part of General Steedman's division of the Reserve Corps bowed their heads to the fierce storm of lead as if it had been rain, and betrayed signs of breaking. The line wavered like a great flag in a breath of wind. They were as splendid material as ever shouldered a musket, but then—what could they do in such a blinding tempest? General Steedman rode up. A great, hearty man, broad-breasted, broad-shouldered, a face written all over with sturdy sense and stout courage; no lady's man to make bouquets for showy fingers, and sing 'Meet me by moonlight alone,' like some fancy Generals, but realizing fully the description given of the stout old Morgan of the Revolution. Well, up rode old Steedman, took the flag from the color-bearer, glanced along the wavering front, and with that voice of his, that could talk against a small rattle of musketry cried out, "Go back, boys, go back; I the flag can't go with you!" grasped staff, wheeled his horse, and rode on. it necessary to say that the column close.. up and grew firm, and moved resistlessly on like a great strong river, and swept down upon the foe, and made a record that shall live when their graves are as empty as the cave of Macpelah?

### Glad for Burnside.

When the telegram from Cumberland Gap reached President Lincoln that "firing was heard in the direction of Knoxville," he remarked that he was "glad of it." Some person present, who had the perils of Burnside's position uppermost in his mind, could not see *why* Mr. Lincoln should be "*glad* of it," and so expressed himself. "Why, you see," responded the President, "it reminds me of Mrs. Sallie Ward, a neighbor of mine, who had a large family. Occasionally one of her numerous progeny would be heard crying in some out-of-the-way place, upon which Mistress Sallie would exclaim, 'There's *one* of my children that *isn't dead yet*.'"

### Bowie-Knife Conflict at the Battle of Pea-Ridge.

While the fight was raging about Miser's farmhouse, at the battle of Pea-Ridge, on Friday morning, a Union soldier belonging to the Twenty-fifth Missouri regiment and a member of a rebel Mississippi company, became separated from their commands, and found each other climbing the same fence. The rebel had one of those long knives made of a file, which the South has so extensively paraded, but so rarely used, and the Missourian had one also, having picked it up on the field.

The rebel challenged his enemy to a fair open combat with the knife, intending to bully him, no doubt, but the challenge was promptly accepted. The two removed their coats, rolled up their sleeves, and began. The Mississippian had more skill, but his opponent more strength, and consequently the latter could not strike his enemy, while he received several cuts on the head and breast. The blood began trickling rapidly down the Unionist's face and running into his eyes, almost blinding him. The Union man became desperate, for he saw the secessionist was unhurt. He made a feint; the rebel leaned forward to arrest the blow, but employing too much energy, he could not recover himself at once. The Missourian perceived his advantage, and knew he could not lose it. In five seconds more it would be too late. His enemy glared at him like a wild beast, and was on the eve of striking again. Another feint; another dodge on the rebel's part, and then the heavy blade of the Missourian hurtled through the air, and fell with tremendous force upon the Mississippian's neck. The blood spurted from the throat, and the head fell over, almost entirely severed from the body. Ghastly sight—too ghastly even for the doer of the deed! He fainted at the spectacle, weakened by the loss of his own blood, and was soon after butchered by a Seminole who saw him sink to the earth.

### Kearney, the "One-Armed Devil."

Of the many noble Generals who took part in the battles of the Peninsula, one of the most active and efficient was General Kearney.

Maj Gen. Phil. Kearney

He was always foremost in the fray, and many times it is said he was observed with his bridle in his teeth, while with his right arm, the only one he had, grasping his sword, he charged at a furious rate among the enemy. The Confederates styled him the "one-armed devil," and at the battle of Williamsburg he was watched by them and their officers, some of the most accurate sharpshooters being ordered to "draw a bead on that one-armed devil;" yet they did not bring him down. Finally, a rebel Colonel ordered his entire regiment—according to the statement of a prisoner taken at the battle—to withdraw their fire from everything else and centre it "on that officer with one arm." His order was obeyed, and the entire regiment—the Fifth Carolina—discharged a volley at General Kearney, but he was unhurt.

### Negro Rifleman Brought Down at Yorktown.

One of the best morning's work done at Yorktown was that of reducing to a state of perfect inutility in this mundane sphere, a rebel negro rifleman, who, through his skill as a marksman, had done more injury

Negro Rifleman.

to our men than any dozen of his white compeers, in the attempted labor of trimming off the complement of Union sharpshooters. The latter had known him a long time, had kept an eye on him, and lain in wait to pick him off. His habit was to perch himself in a big tree, and, keeping himself hid behind the body, annoy the Union men by firing upon them. He climbed the tree as usual one morning, but in advance of the others coming out, and, snuggling himself into his position, was anticipating his usual day of quietude. The Union men might have killed him as he came out, but purposely avoided shooting, so as not to alarm the others. His tree was about twenty rods from one of the Union pits. When our men fired on the advancing rebel pickets, he of course saw the fix he was in—that he was indeed and decidedly up a tree.

"I say, big nigger," called out one of the Union soldiers, "you better come down from there."

"What for?" returned the big nigger.

"I want you as prisoner."

"Not as this chile knows of," replied the concealed Ethiop.

"Just as you say," replied our sharpshooter.

In about an hour the darkey poked his head out. Our man was on the lookout for him; he had his rifle on the bead-line ready—pulled the trigger—whiz-z went the bullet, down came the negro. He was shot through the head.

### Tragical Death of General Baker.

At the battle of Ball's Bluff, while Colonel Wistar was doing glorious service in council and action at the crisis hour in that hard-fought struggle, a ball shattered his sword arm—he dropped his weapon, picked it up with his left hand, and General Baker himself restored it to its scabbard. Alas! that the chivalric leader should never again do such a kindly service for a brother in arms! The yelling enemy began to pour in overwhelmingly, a large body of them pressing down from the left. The General ordered the troops around him to stand firm, and cried—

"Who are those men?"

"Confederate troops, you —Yankees!"

No sooner did they give this reply than they rushed almost within bayonet distance. One huge, red-haired ruffian now stepped from behind the trees, and drawing a revolver, came within five feet of General Baker, and fired four balls at the General's head, every one of which took effect, and a glorious soul fled through their ghastly openings, for he fell on his back against a tree and died instantly. Captain Beiral seized the slayer by the throat and blew out his brains—the hero and the traitor falling within the same minute, and face to face. In a second the enemy swarmed over the spot. "For God's sake, boys,"

General E. D. Baker.

cried Adjutant Harvey, in his hot English way, "are you going to let them have the General's body?" An angry howl was the answer, when a dozen of our fellows charged, with set teeth and bayonets fixed, upon the rebels, who surrendered their priceless trophy.

Colonel Baker was in plain dress, wearing a regulation hat with a black plume. He had no distinguishing mark as Colonel, and was not unnecessarily conspicuous. His right hand had been maimed a week or two before the fight, and he kept it in his breast. He constantly passed up and down the ranks encouraging his soldiers, saying,— "Men, don't run till I run," "Keep your courage up," and other words of cheer. He was exceedingly anxious for a bayonet charge, having more faith in that than in any other weapon. Indeed, he was constantly drilling his men in the bayonet exercise, and, when on parade or drill, he insisted upon their going through every movement. He was a whole-souled hero, but his bravery cost him his life. His was that "good gray head which all men knew and loved." He fell gloriously with the "light of battle" on his features.

### Too Fond of Chestnuts.

The capture of Lieutenant Segal, of the Confederate army in Virginia, was a neat and amusing affair. On Friday, the 4th October, 1861, a scouting party of eighteen men, under Lieutenant-Colonel B. Winslow and Captain L. B. Shattuck, of the Thirty-seventh New York Regiment, were out in the vicinity of the enemy's lines, about five miles from Fall's Church in the direction of Fairfax. As they were proceeding in silence and caution, through dense woods, they heard the tramp of horses and the jingle of sabre scabbards. The Lieutenant-Colonel and Captain, ordering their men to halt, went to reconnoitre. In a short time, one of them came upon an open space where they saw four rebels seated under a large chestnut tree, by the side of a road, and engaged in eating chestnuts. The Confederates saw him, and sprang upon their horses. The officer crying in a loud voice "Charge!" by the time the scouting party had got up, the four "gallant" horsemen were beyond pursuit. Our men were about gathering up the spoils of victory, which consisted of four sabres, two revolvers, four coats and

Fairfax Court House.

blankets, when they saw a horse tied to a tree by the wayside. A further search revealed its master, perched upon the lower limb of a large chestnut—whither he had climbed with his sabre to lop off the tempting fruit. A dozen rifles pointed at his breast soon brought him to reason, and he surrendered himself a prisoner. When he got down, and felt safe, he began to "blow," with true southern chivalry; and, when brought before General McDowell, coolly boasted that in the battle of Bull Run he had aimed repeatedly at the General, but had always missed. General McDowell smiled, and said that "he would send him somewhere where he would not have another such chance for some time."

### No Calculation of that Sort.

After the battle of Pittsburg Landing and General Grant's complete victory at that point, General Buell, a thorough soldier, began criticising in a friendly way the impolicy of his having fought a battle with the Tennessee river behind him.

"Where, if beaten, could you have retreated, General?" asked Buell.

"I didn't mean to be beaten," was Grant's sententious reply.

"But suppose you had been defeated, despite all your exertions?"

"Well, there were the transports to carry the remains of the command across the river."

"But, General," urged Buell, "your whole transports could not contain over ten thousand men; and it would be impossible for them to make more than one trip in the face of the enemy."

"Well, if I had been beaten," said General Grant, pausing to light another cigar as he spoke, "transportation for ten thousand men would have been abundant for all that would be left of us."

This anecdote is eminently characteristic, the data for the proper appreciation of it being that General Grant had about fifty thousand men over the river.

### Tragedy of Ellsworth's Assassination.

It was 2 o'clock in the morning of the 24th of May, when the expedition planned by General Scott started secretly from Washington to take military possession of Alexandria. One half of the troops crossed the Long Bridge, and marched down the right bank of the Potomac, to enter Alexandria by the rear, and to cut off any rebel troops who might be lurking about the city. The other half, including the Fire Zouaves under Colonel Ellsworth, descended the river in steamers, from the Washington Navy Yard. It was in the first gray of the morning, when the steamers touched at the wharves. Of this division Colonel Ellsworth was in command. He was one of the first to land. While

Col. Ellsworth.

the regiment was forming in line, one company was sent, post haste, to seize the telegraph station, that no communication could be sent to Richmond of their landing. This was of such vital importance, that Col. Ellsworth himself accompanied the party, passing through the streets on the full run.

On their way they went by the Marshall House, a hotel kept by one Jackson, over the roof of which a secession flag was flaunted. "We must have that flag," said Col. Ellsworth, and, rushing in, he found a white man, in the front room, half dressed, and a negro. "Who raised that flag?" inquired the Colonel. "I do not know," was the reply, "I am a boarder here." Followed by two or three he sprang up stairs to the roof of the house, seized the rebel banner, and was descending with it in his hands, hardly a moment having been occupied in the movement, when the same half-dressed man, who had said that he was a boarder, but who proved to be Jackson himself, a brutal desperado, jumped from a dark passage, and leveling a double-barreled gun at Col. Ellsworth's breast, at a distance of not more than two yards, fired a couple of slugs directly into his heart, and which of course, proved fatal.

Ellsworth was on the second or third step from the landing, and he dropped forward with that heavy, horrible, headlong weight, which always comes of sudden death inflicted in such a manner. His assailant had turned like a flash to give the contents of the other barrel to Francis E. Brownell, a private, but either he could not command his aim, or the Zouave was too quick with him, for the slugs went over his head, and passed through the panels and wainscot of the door, which sheltered some sleeping lodgers. Simultaneously with his second shot, and sounding like the echo of the first, Brownell's rifle was heard, and the assassin staggered backward. His wound—exactly in the middle of the face, was frightful beyond description. Of course Brownell did not know how fatal his shot had been, and so, before the man dropped, he thrust his sabre bayonet through and through the body, the force of the blow sending the dead man violently down the upper section of the second flight of stairs.

The body of the murdered Colonel was laid upon a bed; and the rebel flag, stained with his blood, and purified by this contact from the baseness of its former meaning, was fitly laid about his feet.

### Harp and Shamrock, Stars and Stripes.

At the fearful battle which opened the way to the crossing of the Pamunkey by Grant's army, Maurice Collins, of the Twelfth Massachusetts, was brought off with an ugly wound in the shoulder. He was a Catholic, and the priest was showing him the crucifix. "Will it be mortal?" he asked. "Perhaps not, if you lie still and keep quiet. But you have to lose your arm." "Well, I'm *willing* to give an arm to my country," was the reply of one who, though born in the ever-green isle, and still loving the Harp and Shamrock of Fatherland, was willing to uphold to the last the Stars and Stripes of his adopted country.

### Massachusetts and South Carolina Pitted against each other in Battle.

A very curious coincidence happened on the left, in the Eighteenth Corps, Butler's army, when engaged in the spring campaign of 1864. In General Hickman's brigade were the Twenty-third, Twenty-fifth and Twenty-seventh Massachusetts regiments. Opposed to them, and in a brigade opposite to them in the line of battle, were the Twenty-third, Twenty-fifth and Twenty-seventh South Carolina regiments; and the Twenty-fifth South Carolina charged upon the Twenty-fifth Massachusetts. They got used up by the Yankees they are accustomed to despise. The two Twenty-fifths charged each other three times, South Carolina getting most thoroughly worsted. These facts were ascertained from a Captain of the Twenty-fifth South Carolina, who was wounded and brought in a prisoner.

### "Leatherbreeches" in the Federal Service.

Captain Dilger, or " Leatherbreeches," as he was familiarly called, earned an honorable name, as one of the most skillful and plucky officers in the Union service. When the war broke out, Captain Dilger was an artillery officer in the Prussian service. A short time after the battle of Bull Run, an uncle of Dilger (a merchant in New York) wrote that the present was an opportune time to visit America, etc.

Dilger was desirous of studying war as carried on in the Western world, and to this end procured leave of absence for a year. As soon as he arrived he joined the army of the Potomac, as an artillerist, and commanded a battery. As his year drew to a close he managed to get his leave indefinitely extended. The term of his battery, the First Ohio artillery, having expired, he was ordered to Cincinnati, to be mustered out of the service.

His next appearance with his battery was under General Hooker, and by the name of "Leatherbreeches" he became known to every officer and soldier in the army of the Cumberland. In all the battles which occurred, from Lookout Mountain to Peachtree Creek, Dilger was on hand. He was the first to open fire upon the eve of a battle, taking his guns nearly up to the skirmish line. So often had he done this, that some officer, appreciating the frightful destruction which his practice wrought, presented the Captain *with bayonets for his pieces.*

At one time, upon the eventful day of the Hooker and Johnston contest, Captain Dilger took his "smooth bores" up to General Johnston's line of battle, and for half an hour poured a raking fire of grape and canister into the enemy in front of Hooker. So conspicuous and deadly was his movement, that he became at one time the target for three rebel batteries, and lost seven men during the day. He fired by volley when he got a 'good thing,' and the acclamations of the infantry drowned the reverberation of the cannon's roar on all such occasions. Captain Dilger impressed every one by his fine appearance; he always wore close buckskin breeches, with top boots, and stood by his gun in his shirtsleeves during battle, eliciting the admiration of the whole army by his coolness and intrepidity when in action.

**Horrors of the Old Bull Run Battle-Field.**

At the old Bull Run battle-field, adjacent to the Warrenton pike, as described by a visitor fourteen months after, bullets are still picked up and exhibited by the handful. In the long, luxuriant grass, the visitor strikes his foot against skulls and bones, mingled with the deadly missiles that brought them to the earth. Hollow skulls lie contiguous to hemispheres of ex-

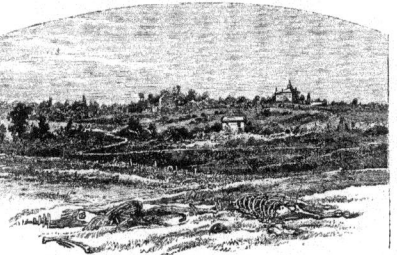

Bull Run Battlefield, Va.

ploded shells. The shallow graves rise here and there above the grass, sometimes in rows, sometimes alone, or scattered at irregular intervals. Through the thin layer of soil one sees the protruding ribs whence the rain has washed their covering, a foot or an arm reaching out beyond its earthy bed; and in one case one of these long sleepers was seen covered snugly up to the chin, but with the entire face exposed and turned up to the passer by,—one could imagine him a soldier lying on the field wrapped up in his blanket, but the blanket was of clay and the face was fleshless and eyeless.

In one case a foot protruded, with the flesh still partially preserved; in another, an entire skeleton, lay exposed upon the surface, without any covering whatever. The tatters of what had been his uniform showed that he had been a cavalryman. The flesh was decomposed; but the tanned and shrivelled skin still incased the bony framework of the body, and even the finger-nails were in their places. The ligaments that fasten the joints must have been preserved, for he was lifted by the belt which was still around the waist, and not a bone fell out of its place. When found, he lay in the attitude of calm repose, like one who had fallen asleep from weariness. This was in the camp of the Ninth Massachusetts regiment. He was buried, as were more that night, who had waited a long fourteen months for their funeral rites. In fact, the different pioneer corps were engaged some time in paying this last tribute to the gallant dead.

The Pennsylvania reserves bivouacked, fourteen months afterwards, for a night, on the same ground where they themselves were engaged in the deadly strife of battle, and the skulls and bones of some of their former companions in arms lay around within the light of their camp fires. It may even have happened that men pitched their tents over the grave of a lost comrade, and again unwittingly rested under the same shelter with one who had often before shared their couch on the tented field. A soldier of the First regiment struck his foot against a cartridge box, near his tent, and, picking it up, read on it the name of an old associate who had been among the missing, and whose death was only known from his prolonged absence. His resting place had at length been found.

### Shotted Salute at Midnight from Grant to Lee.

Sherman's victories and the fall of Atlanta were celebrated in true military style in the army of General Grant before Petersburg. By special order of the General, thirty-six shotted guns from each battery was fired at midnight, directly into the city or into the enemy's works, while the bands at the rear played "Hail Columbia,' 'Star Spangled Banner,' and 'Red, White and Blue.' Pleasant and soldierly way of celebrating victory, certainly. Of course, the shrieks of the dying or the maimed and mangled sufferers beyond the federal lines, formed no part of the chorus as heard by the celebrants; but what was heard was novel and warlike, in the highest degree.

Away, above all, in its majestic sweep, the "Petersburg Express" sped on its way from the far rear to the devoted city in the far front. Curve crossed curve of fire. Blazing ball passed blazing ball. Hiss, and howl, and crash, and crackle, mingled in the burdened air. Ragged fragments of iron fell all around. Bits of singing lead flew by or dropped briskly about.

When the salute was finished, there was some cross-firing of words between the aroused pickets along the vidette line. "How are you, Atlanta?" cried out one of the Yankee boys. "You'd better try and take Petersburg, now," was the rebel response. "Sherman is after you fellows, sharp," said Yank. "Won't you send some more of your colored brudders into another mine?" asked Johnny. "Don't you want some coffee and sugar?" inquired the Yankees, tauntingly. "Wouldn't you like to exchange your wormy hard tack for our johnny cake?" was the response. This last hit was a hard one, and unexpected,—the poor soldiers having for some little time had shockingly bad bread; and though the worms in it were very large and lively, it was not known that they had been seen from the enemy's works! There was much more of this verbal sharp-shooting.

### Do They Miss Me at Home?

After one of the battles in Louisiana, a boy of sixteen was lying on his cot, motionless, from a ball that passed through the brain. The worthy surgeon in charge was probing the wound, during which, to the astonishment of all, for his young life was ebbing fast away, he sang sweetly, clearly and strong, the tender strain, "Do they miss me at home?" Poor little fellow, *he* missed the warm hands and hearts of his far-off home, which he thus recalled in that gentle fireside song.

### Neutral Cornfield before Petersburg.

There was a cornfield between the Union and Confederate lines at a certain point before Petersburg, during Grant's autumn campaign,—a little to the left of Cemetery Hill. The opposing pickets of the two great confronting armies would, in spite of all, occasionally creep into that field for a friendly chat, or for a barter, or for a game of cards! Two of them were playing a game one day, with Abe Lincoln and Jeff Davis as imaginary stakes. The Lincolnite lost. "There" says the winner, "Old Abe belongs to me." "Well, I'll send him over by the 'Petersburg

Neutral Cornfield.

express,' responded the defeated Yank. At another time there had been lively shelling and some musketry firing during the forenoon—of course but little talking. After dinner there was a slack of hostilities. A Johnny rose up on the parapet of his line, and shook a paper as a sign of truce, then sprang over into the cornfield. At once a hundred men from either line were over their works and side by side, swapping papers for papers, tobacco for coffee or jack-knives, hard tack or sugar for corn cake. New acquaintances were made. In some instances old acquaintances were revived. A Connecticut sergeant found a townsman and schoolmate in a sergeant from over the way. A Connecticut officer found a kinsman in a rebel officer. A loyal Maryland regiment was *vis-a-vis* with a Maryland secession regiment. Many links of union were there. One found a brother on the other side, and yet another his own father! After a little time the swapping of the day was done, and officers and men returned to their respective lines. All was quiet again until the artillery re-opened fire. Then a half score of loiterers sprang up from their concealment in the corn and scrambled back to their places behind the works. Thus the fighting and the chatting alternated.

### Mower's Successful Trick upon the Rebel Dispatch Bearer.

A capital manœuvre was practiced by General Mower upon the rebels, at Henderson's Hill, and by means of which he gained that little victory over the bewildered chivalry. Overtaking one of the couriers, General Mower, in very indignant terms accused him of being a d—— Yankee spy, at which the rebel dispatch bearer became alarmed, and protested his innocence, asserting that he was a good Confederate, on his way with highly important dispatches. As a proof of his identity he handed over his papers for the General to examine, asking him to read them quickly, as he did not wish to be detained. General Mower pronounced the documents forgeries, and said—

"You are a Yankee, sir, and I intend to take you before the Colonel. I am General Walker, and you can not deceive me in this way."

"Very well, General," replied the astonished soldier, "I will lead you to the Colonel's head-quarters, and he will explain that I am not a Yankee."

Suiting the action to the word, the deluded rebel piloted General Mower and his staff some two miles. As fast as the

General neared the cavalry pickets, who were seated in picturesque groups around their camp fires, scarcely noticing our troops as they passed, they were ordered to the rear. Approaching the encampment on Henderson's Hill, General Mower sent for two companies of infantry to march forward. Before giving this order, he questioned the courier as to the disposition of the cavalry and artillery, telling him the Yankees were not far off. Eager to be of service, the messenger explained the precise location of each gun to 'his General.'

As soon as the courier overheard the order for infantry to advance, made under such circumstances, he discovered the terrible situation and its consequences into which he had been brought, but it was too late. The terrified soldier expected to be shot, and he became highly excited, telling the General to "hurry and take that gun on that road,"—pointing out the various positions of each cannon.

### Joe Johnston's Whipping at Resaca.

The battle of Resaca, Georgia, was one of the handsomest operations performed under the splendid leading of General Sherman.

Let any one imagine the army of McPherson, with the able corps commanders, Dodge and Logan, on the right, the army of Schofield on the left, and the grand army of the Cumberland, with Thomas, Hooker, Howard and Palmer in the centre, with immense bodies of cavalry upon the flanks,—and there is Sherman's complete army in line of battle.

Opposite, on splendid ground, were seventy thousand Confederates, commanded by Joe Johnston, with Hardee on the right, the Right Rev. Bishop Polk on the left, and the one-legged, one-armed fighting devil, Hood, in the centre. The Federal army being a few thousand stronger, but Johnston having the ground.

This was on Saturday. Early in the morning, skirmishing commenced all along the line. A short time before noon, Bishop Polk made an artillery bark at McPherson, who reciprocated in magnificent style. At this time, Howard's corps was on the extreme left, Schofield to the right of him, then old Palmer, and Joe Hooker between him and McPherson. The thunders commenced rolling to the left, and Hooker was in for it, throwing the bulk of his corps to the right, as McPherson was being most

General J. E. Johnston.

vigorously assaulted; the thundering war increased in fury, and the whole line eventually were using artillery. It was the diapason of five hundred cannon!

All of a sudden the brigades were shifted from the right to the left, and considerable changing took place on the left and in the centre. Presently the Federal line wavered, the greater part of it fell back, and some portions of it in confusion. General Judah made a good fight, got severely handled, and was obliged to get out, which he did with confused ranks. Hardee was at work, and was very vicious. General Cox got into a snarl, too, and couldn't be found for some time.

But ah! now the Federals get at them again handsomely, and the rebels go back the way they came, and more rapidly. The gallant Generals Manson and Harker receive wounds. Everything is going on well at the left now; both parties recover and maintain their own ground, and bang away at each other at a respectful distance. Considerable hand-to-hand fighting took place during the day, and brigades were pitted against brigades upon several occasions. The happiest thing of the day was the thrashing which General King's Brigade of Regulars administered to a Mississippi Brigade under General Anderson, and an Alabama Brigade under General Deas.

The heaviest fighting of the day occurred in the centre, Palmer's corps bearing the brunt. Baird's division achieved a multiplicity of successes, and Turchin and Carlin fought like butchers. Wood's splendid division also added to its world-wide renown by its spirited behaviour, and little Willich pitched in, in his usual style, during the afternoon. At a critical moment, Joe Hooker came around with his whole corps, and some magnificent fighting took place, the engagement lasting above an hour.

It was near midnight when the conflict ceased—one of the most remarkable day's fight, and one of the most interesting battles of the war. From eight until ten o'clock P. M., the roar of artillery and small arms, and the additional din, was tumultuous, especially upon the extreme right, where Dodge and Osterhaus had several pitched engagements with the enemy in the moonlight. About an equal number were engaged on both sides, and it was at last settled by the respective parties remaining in the positions which they occupied at the commencement. There was no slaughter whatever compared with the excessive fighting—the entire line being nearly all day at work.

Notwithstanding that with midnight came the cessation of the hostilities of the day before, the battle of Sunday opened at sunrise, and before nine o'clock the fighting was general. Hooker was the man of the day. Early in the conflict his corps was ordered to the extreme left, and there it was that the most brilliant events of the Sabbath transpired. Hooker stormed a fort, and carried the works handsomely, capturing a number of guns and several hundred prisoners. During this time, however, a terrible conflict was going on—the National troops gaining ground. Slowly but surely were the disciplined forces of Joe Johnston relinquishing their claims to the field. On, on marched the enthusiastic columns of the Federals, seemingly attempting to drown the terrific roar of their guns with shouts and yells, while back— back moved the mad columns of the foe, the valor and desperation of the participants degenerating into despair, at times almost precipitating them upon certain destruction.

The day ended with the Federal troops occupants of the rebel ground.

### Vice President Breckinridge's Son.

John Tyler, of Virginia, formerly President of the United States, and John C. Breckinridge, formerly Vice President, were the only persons at any time holding those distinguished offices, who raised their voice or their sword against the National Government, and openly sided with its armed enemies. Breckinridge's son, Lieutenant James C., at one time bid fair to duplicate his father's consummate prowess as a leader, but was captured in one of the battles of the Southwest—or rather, was captured in the National lines, having made a mistake while carrying a dispatch. He bore a remarkable resemblance to his father, and was quite youthful in appearance; possessed the fascinating deportment of his sire, and, in conversation, was quite winning. He was on his father's staff, and had been in service during the past two years. Like the rest of the Confederate officers, he was attired in a coarse, but neat-fitting suit of gray clothes, with a blue military cap. He did not appear to be more than eighteen or twenty years of age, though evidently a young man of more than ordinary ability.

### Bravo for Pea Ridge.

Pea Ridge battle crowned with honor the military skill of General Curtis and his brave comrades in arms for the good old Union flag. In the midst of the conflict, or during a cessation of the terrible

Climbing the Mountains.

cannonade, the question came regarding the name of the battlefield. Somebody proposed Sugar Creek, to which General Curtis objected, because what he considered an important battle had been fought three weeks previous on that stream, and the two battles would be confounded. Mr. Knox, correspondent of the New York Herald, suggested the name of "Ozark Mountain," because of the place being in the midst of that extensive range. The name had a rich sound, but was objected to, on account of its not being sufficiently specific. The name of a battlefield should indicate with all possible precision, its locality. The name of Leetown, a small hamlet, with half a dozen poor tenements, was proposed, but owing to the insignificance of the place, the appellation was not received with favor. At length, General Curtis inquired of one of the natives standing by, and who was dressed in Confederate clothes, but who had sided with the Union army,—

"What name do you call your country here?"

"This," said the man, "is Pea Ridge."

"That," responded Curtis, "is the name I want. I like the name. It is something new."

Some opposition was made to this christening, but the General stood firm, and adhered to the name of Pea Ridge. The next day, therefore, he sent a Major of the Third Iowa cavalry, through to Kietsville, with a dispatch to Halleck, announcing the victory of "Pea Ridge,"

GREAT CONFLICTS, INDIVIDUAL HEROISM, ETC.    329

and it was not long before brave fellows were making the welkin ring with "*Bravo for Pea Ridge!*"

#### New Federal Troops against Rebel Veterans.

On the 19th of May, 1864, the First Massachusetts and First Maine heavy artillery, which were armed as infantry, were lying in the woods west of Spottsylvania and Fredericksburg road, two miles in rear of the Federal front line, when they rode to Stannard's brigade, composed of the First Massachusetts and First Maine.

"The sons of Maine and Massachusetts are not cowards!" shouted the General.

"No! No!" was the response.

"Follow me, then!"

Away they went with a cheer. They came within musket range, and the contest began. Ewell's old veterans on the one hand, and the troops who until the previous week had not handled a musket, on the

Union Bushwhackers attacking Rebel Cavalry.

were startled by the appearance of a body of rebels which were coming upon them from the west. It was Rhodes's division of Ewell's corps, who had moved out from Spottsylvania up the Beach road to the north-west, starting at one P. M. Their advance was most unexpected to the Union forces.

General Tyler, who commanded the division of heavy artillery, called upon his men to move against the enemy. The troops never had been under fire. They had arrived, some of them only the day before. They hesitated. General Tyler other. The heavy artillery knew little about infantry tactics, of handling muskets, of loading and firing, but they poured in their volleys—or, rather, each man loaded a piece, irrespective of all orders. It was a continous roll. Meanwhile the rest of Tyler's division—four regiments—joined, and the contest became furious. The Second Corps, which was near at hand, was swung round to form a second line, but before it could be brought into action, the heavy artillery had repulsed the rebels. It was a short, sharp, decisive engagement. The result had a great effect on

21

the army, raising its spirits to the highest pitch.

**Devotion of a Private to General McPherson.**

There were thousands of instances of bravery displayed by the real heroes of this war—the gallant privates—that never found their way into print. Here is one of this class which is happily, however, rescued from oblivion, namely, the gallantry displayed by Private George D. Reynolds, Company D, of the Fifteenth Iowa

Maj Gen McPherson.

regiment, on the battlefield before Atlanta, in the summer of 1864. This tried and trusty veteran had been engaged in the savage contest for several hours, and at last was severely wounded in the arm, the bullet fracturing the bone so that amputation of the fore-arm seemed to be necessary to save his valuable life. This George Reynolds saw the noble McPherson when he fell mortally wounded, and remained with his General till the brave heart ceased to beat longer for the land he loved, and the pulse, which ever throbbed with heroic blood, grew silent. The storm of shot and shell did not intimidate the soldier, but growing faint from the loss of blood and the pain of his wound, he was compelled to start for the hospital to get his wound properly dressed. After marching nearly a mile in the hot sun and dust, he met Lieutenant-Colonel Strong, Inspector-General on McPherson's staff, and Captain Buell, Chief Ordnance Officer of the Department and Army of Tennessee, who were anxiously inquiring for the General's body. Reynolds volunteered to pilot them to the spot where he had left the body, notwithstanding the Confederates were rapidly advancing, and the bullets whistled through the branches of the trees. The entire party had a very narrow escape from death or capture, for they had barely placed the body of their inanimate chieftain in an ambulance when a squad of rebels fired several shots after them.

**Compliments of the Season.**

During a temporary lull in the conflict attending the rebel attack on Franklin, Tennessee, General Forrest, who had seen one of Lieutenant Hopkins' white signal flags working, sent a flag of truce to Colonel Baird. The flag was borne by what passed for an extremely courteous young rebel officer, whose first benign salutation was, "Ah! you've surrendered, have you, —— —— you?" Colonel Baird's officer, under the influence of passion thus provoked, with more regard for strength than beauty or blandness in his reply, remarked to the rebel, "Not much, you —— —— fool!" This ended the peaceful conference, and warlike operations were at once resumed. *Query*: How many and what kind of religious tracts were sent to *that* army?

**Fight for the Flag at Petersburg.**

Among the many incidents of bravery and personal daring exhibited in storming the enemy's intrenchments at Petersburg, under General Grant, the capture of a rebel battle-flag by a private in the Third New York Regiment, in General Smith's corps, was one of the most notable. While the contest was at its height, and the tide of battle swaying to and fro, he espied the flag, borne by a rebel captain, who picked it up as its former bearer fell at his side. The gallant New Yorker singled him out for personal encounter, and, after a hard hand-to-hand fight, succeeded in capturing the flag and its bearer, and emerged from the dust and smoke of the conflict victoriously bearing the banner and driving the Captain before him.

General Butler heard of this incident, sent for the daring man, ascertained that he was formerly a mechanic, but then a humble soldier in the ranks; obtained a specimen of his handwriting; found by conversation that he was sensible and intelligent, and commissioned him a lieutenant of volunteers on the spot. The battle-flag was of blue bunting, about four feet square, with white banding, two inches wide, around the edges; had a white diagonal cross, six inches wide, with thirteen blue stars on both arms, extending from corner to corner, and well mounted on a staff about ten feet in length—the whole presenting an elegant and well finished appearance, though somewhat soiled and worn.

The banner was neatly folded around the staff and given in charge of Lieutenant-Colonel Babcock, of General Grant's staff, to convey to head-quarters. On the way from Petersburg, the soldiers he passed in the road were unusually demonstrative and exultant, which occasionally broke out in vociferous cheering as he passed along the line. The Colonel was unable to account for his sudden popularity, until he discovered that his orderly had unfurled the rebel colors, and was explaining its capture to all the troops he passed, by grimaces and pantomine.

#### Our Generals among the Bullets.

General Grant afforded a remarkable illustration of the fortune through which some men, in the thickest showers of bullets, always escape. He had participated in two skirmishes and fourteen pitched battles, up to the time of the Pittsburg Landing conflict, and was universally pronounced, by those who had seen him on the field, daring even to rashness; but he never received even a scratch. One Sunday evening, or afternoon, he was sitting upon his horse, just in the rear of our line of batteries, when Captain Carson, the scout who had reported to him a moment before, had fallen back, and was holding his horse by the bridle, about seven feet behind him—instantly a six-pound shot, which flew very near General Grant, *carried away all of poor Carson's head, except a portion of the chin,*—then passed just behind Lieutenant Graves, volunteer aid to General Wilson, tearing away the cantle of his saddle, cutting his clothing, but not injuring him, and then took clean off the legs of a soldier in one of General Nelson's regiments, which were just ascending the bluff.

About the same hour, further up to the right, General Sherman, who had been standing for a moment while Major Hammond, his chief of staff, was holding his bridle, remounted. By the prancing of his horse, as he mounted, General Sherman's reins were thrown over his neck, and he was leaning forward in the saddle, with his head lowered, while Major Hammond was bringing them back over his head, when a rifle ball struck the line in Major Hammond's hand, severing it within two inches of his fingers, and passing through the top and back of General Sherman's hat. Had he been sitting, as usual, upright, it would have taken his head clean off. At another time, a ball struck General Sherman on the shoulder, but his metallic shoulder-strap warded it off. With a third he was less fortunate, for it passed through his hand. General Sherman had three horses shot under him, two with three balls each, and the last with two. General Hurlbut had a six-pound shot pass between his horse's head and his arm; a bullet passed through his horse's mane, and one of his horses was killed under him.

#### Told the Truth at the Right Time.

When General Sturgis went on his great expedition at the southwest, the main body of his command halted at Salem, and a detachment of three hundred men was sent out to reconnoitre the road to Ripley, a little town southwest of Corinth. When within a few miles of that place, the advance guard of the detachment came upon and captured a squad of half a dozen rebel cavalry without firing a gun. As is customary, the prisoners were closely examined, with a view to eliciting such in-

General Barksdale

formation of the enemy's whereabouts and intentions as they might be able to give. A gaunt, stringy haired man, who seemed to be the leader of the rebel party, was conducted to the officer in command of our advance, who asked him,

"What regiment do you belong to?"

"I won't tell," was the pointed reply of the rebel.

"How far is it to Ripley?" was the next question.

"Don't know," answered the man, sullenly, with the true Barksdale grit.

"Who is your commander?"

"Won't tell."

"How far off is the command to which you belong?" still inquired the persevering Federal, pretending not to notice the crusty demeanor of his prisoner. Here the rebel informed him in terms that would not be altogether comely in print, that he would see him in a much hotter region than Mississippi before he would tell him any thing at all.

"Very well," said the officer, drawing and cocking a revolver, "I will send you there to wait for me."

"You may shoot me if you want to," said the Confederate, "but you will be sorry for it."

"Why?"

"Because there are a hundred men over yonder in the woods, and if they hear you shoot they will come up and murder every man of you."

"Well," said the officer, "since you have told me just what I wanted to find out I guess I won't shoot you."

In thirty minutes the whole hundred men were prisoners.

### Kind o' wanted to be in the Front.

Sergeant Hunter, of the Kentucky soldiery, exhibited the bravest soldierly qualities in the conflict at Springfield, Mo. His superb figure never failed to attract the eye in the ranks of the Guard. He had served in the regular cavalry, and the Body Guard (Fremont's noted men) had profited greatly from his skill as a drill-master. He lost three horses killed under him in the fight. As soon as one was killed, he caught another from the rebels; the third horse taken by him in this way he rode into St. Louis. The Sergeant slew five men. Said he—

"I won't speak of those I shot—another may have hit them; but those I touched with my sabre I am sure of, because I felt them."

At the beginning of the charge he came to the extreme right and took position next to Major Zagonyi, whom he followed closely through the battle. The Major, seeing him, said:

"Why are you here, Sergeant? Your place is with your company on the left."

"I kind o' wanted to be in front," was the answer.

"What could I say to such a man!" exclaimed Zagonyi, speaking of the matter afterwards.

### An Hibernian's Tustle with a "Mississippi Tiger."

The dogged, obstinate, and bitter character of the rebel Gulf troops was one of the familiar facts of the war, as the following incident which happened near Martinsburg, Va., will show. A son of Erin captured one of the famous 'Mississippi Tigers,' but while bringing him to the Union camp, the 'Tiger,' an immense fellow, managed to free himself and run. The plucky Hibernian disdained to use his musket, but chased him with the wildest speed. At last, seizing him, at it they went, in the most logical style of rough-and-tumble. The 'Tiger,' maddened by the stinging whacks which the lusty Hibernian dealt, basely bit him, nearly severing his thumb. The Celt dropped the soldier then, and retaliated in the same way; finally he conquered him after a tremendous whaling, which dislocated his shoulder. The next day he visited the son of the "Repudiation State," in the hospital, went up to him, and shaking his well arm with a hearty grip, observed, with his 'rich Irish brogue,' "I haven't a bit of a grudge agin ye; be jabers! ye are almost as good as meself."

### "Old Rosy," and not "Old Pap."

General Rosecrans was one of those wide-awake commanders who could not be caught napping. He was accustomed to visit all the camps and outposts, to see that the soldiers under him were thoroughly on the alert. One night, the General, accompanied by Major Bond, mounted his horse and galloped out to Camp Sheridan, the stamping ground of General Pike's enrolled militia. It was midnight when the two officers arrived at the camp, and not being hailed, they dashed into the centre of the camp, and dismounted. A soldier came forward from some place of concealment and hailed the officers—

"Who goes there?"

"Friends," answered the General.

"Friends, heh? Well, what next?"

"Nothing next; but you are all prisoners."

The militiaman got his eyes open by this time, and seeing the stars of a Major General before him, supposed the veritable old Pap Price had him in hand. He dropped his gun by his side, folded his arms, and appeared resigned to his fate. A German soldier now came up and asked what was going on. He was told that the camp had been captured, and he had to surrender.

"We will see about that!" said the German, tightening his belt and preparing for a fight. The two soldiers then escorted the General and his aid to head-quarters, and when they discovered that it was "Old Rosy," and not "Old Pap," who had captured the camp, they felt greatly relieved and made up their minds not to be caught napping again.

### Mighty Big Risk.

The Union pickets near the James river, while one night quietly sitting around their fires, were startled by the report of a single rifle from the enemy's line, followed by an irregular volley. Of course every man sprang to his arms in an instant, ready to repel any assault of the enemy. "Don't fire, boys," was the order given in a low tone by the Lieutenant in command, who had received instructions not to fire unless the Johnnies saw fit to thoroughly initiate the barbarous practice. For a few seconds the enemy's bullets continued to whistle spitefully by, and the Lieutenant was about giving the order returning the fire, when three Johnnies came 'piling' over the works into the Federal lines, and with a fervent 'Thank God!' sank down behind the embankment. This occurrence accounted for the sudden outbreak of the Confederate pickets, who upon discovering the flight of their treacherous videttes, had opened fire upon them. Out of eight who attempted to run the perilous gauntlet, only the three succeeded, the remaining five being either killed or disabled by the shots of their companions. By a preconcerted arrangement, three cartridges were elevated and successively flashed above the Federal works by the lucky Johnnies, to indicate to their less fortunate friends the number reaching the Union lines in safety. On being invited to warm themselves at the picket fire, they refused, fearing lest the light might reveal them to their former companions, but a few yards from the line. "We un's run a *mighty big risk* in getting to you un's, and now we's safe, we don't care to run any more," was their reply, and so they remained shivering under cover of the federal works, until sent to head-quarters.

### Delirious Bravery of a Southern Hotspur.

On the last day of the fight at Pea Ridge, while the force under General Sigel was gallantly charging the rebels, and driving them from the heights they had occupied, one rebel officer, Captain of a Louisiana company, seemed resolved to throw away his life. As his fellow soldiers retreated, he advanced further towards our troops until he was almost alone. He waved his sword and cried in a loud ringing voice for his men to follow him, denouncing them as cowards if they retreated. They heeded not his appeals, and seeing himself deserted he ran towards our advance, shouting like a madman and saying something that sounded like, "I am brave as Cæsar. If we are whipped, I do not want to live. Come on, you —— Yankees!" The Union infantry were anxious to take this southern hotspur prisoner, and would have done so had not one of their batteries opened from the left, and in its storm of iron swept down the single life which, so full of fierceness, ebbed itself away in the sodden and unpitying ground. He was the son of a sugar planter living up the Bayou La Fourche, and was given to drunkenness—which perhaps accounts for his delirious conduct.

### Delivering up their Swords at Fort Pulaski.

After a truly heroic defence, Fort Pulaski yielded to the superior prowess of its assailants, and became again part of the possessions, as well as of the property of the glorious Union it was designed to protect and preserve.

First, an interview of one hour took place between Colonel Olmsted, the rebel commandant, and General Gillmore on the Union side. The terms of capitulation having been settled, General Gillmore was shown over the fort by the Colonel, and

Gen. David Hunter.

took his leave, accompanied by Colonel Rust. Messengers from General Hunter had meantime arrived. These, together with General Gillmore's aid, made the rounds of the fort under the escort of Colonel Olmsted, who introduced them to his officers, and comprised the only persons present when the swords were delivered.

Major Halpine, as the representative of General Hunter, received the weapons. The ceremony was performed in the Colonel's head-quarters, all standing. It was just at dark, and the candles gave only a sombre half-light. The weapons were laid on the table, each officer advancing in turn, according to his rank, and mentioning his name and title; nearly every one added some remark, the Colonel's being defined: "I yield my sword, but I trust I have not disgraced it." Major Alpine, in reply, spoke gracefully of the painfulness of the duty he had been called upon to perform —to receive the swords of men who had shown by their bravery that they deserved to wear them. As soon as the surrender was complete, the Stars and Stripes once more flapped their glorious folds in the secession breezes of that famed region of the 'Sunny South.' The officers invited the Unionists to their quarters, where several took supper, and some even slept with the rebels whom they had been fighting with such bloody desperation only a few hours before.

### Picket Repartee at Vicksburg.

The richness of rebel repartee and fecundity of Federal fun during the long and familiar *vis a vis* at Vicksburg is pretty well illustrated in the following verbatim colloquy:

*Rebel Picket.*—What are you men doing over there?

*Union Picket.*—Guarding about twenty to thirty thousand rebels in and about Vicksburg. Guarding your army as prisoners, and *moking you board yourselves*.

*Reb.*—Why, you —— fools, Pemberton has a strong line of guards for the same purpose.

*Reb.*—How's Hooker? He had to recross the river, did he not?

*Fed.*—Yes, but he was not as big a fool as your General was. He did not burn the bridges before his men all got across!

*Reb.*—What do you think of the gunboat Cincinnati?

*Fed.*—Gunboat? Why, don't you know the difference between a gunboat and a hay-rack?

*Reb.*—(just in the act of throwing a hand-grenade)—Antn'y, over!

*Fed.*—(in the act of hurling it back) —Look out for the skillets and camp-kettles!

*Fed.*—(addressing a rebel lieutenant of artillery)—Where's your gun?

*Reb.*—Turned it over to Grant at the Big Black, and I guess its now in active service, by the way it plays into these works.

*Reb.*—Why don't you come and take Vicksburg?

Union and Rebel Pickets.

*Fed*—Oh, we're in no particular hurry. General Grant is not yet ready to transfer you North.

*Reb.*—(boastingly)—We've got a lot of your —— old flags over here.

*Fed.*—Have you, though? You'd better make shirts of 'em, for they'd look better'n that butternut.

*Reb.*—(in a husky voice)—I want to trade some corn-meal for some coffee.

*Fed.*—What did you say?

*Reb.*—(louder)—Won't you trade some coffee for some corn-meal?

*Fed.*—You'd better get some coffee, or something else, for you've eat corn-meal till you can't talk plain.

*Reb.*—When are you going to make a change?

*Fed.*—Oh, in about two years. We are in no hurry—are living fine over here— have a pleasant place, and ammunition to last us the rest of the time.

### Six Generals Waiting to Receive Battle.

Six Union Generals waiting upon Pleasant Hill, for the second day's attack of the enemy, formed a war picture of rare interest. The plateau had the appearance of a parade-ground on a holiday. Regiments marching to the right, and regiments marching to the left, batteries being moved and shifted, cavalry squads moving in single file through the brush, now and then an aid galloping madly, or an orderly at full speed, driving his spurs, and holding an order or a dispatch between his teeth, bugles sounding the different cavalry calls, and drums repeating the orders of the Captains,—all passed and re-passed, and controlled the vision, making very much the impression that a spectator in the theatre receives as he looks upon a melodrama.

In an enclosure near the roadside was a small cluster of gentlemen, to whom all this phantasmagoria had the meaning of life and death, power and force.

General Banks, with his light-blue overcoat buttoned closely around his chin, was strolling up and down, occasionally conversing with one of his staff, or returning with his accustomed suavity the salute of a passing subaltern. No one could possibly forget Banks after once seeing him.

Near Banks was General W. B. Franklin—his face as rough and rugged as when he rode through the thick and furious storms of the Peninsula,—the ideal of a bold, daring, resolute, indomitable fighting soldier.

There were few braver men in that group, or elsewhere, than Major General Charles O'Malley. He had two horses shot under him the day before. His face was very calm that morning, and occasionally he pulled his whiskers nervously, as though he scented the battle afar off, and was impatient to be in the midst of the fray.

General Charles P. Stone, the chief of staff, a quiet, retiring man, and regarded by the few that knew him as one of the finest soldiers in the service, was sitting on a rail smoking cigarettes, and apparently more interested in the puffs of smoke that curled around him than in the noise and bustle that filled the air.

There, too, was General Smith, with his bushy, grayish beard, and his eager eye, as it appeared through spectacles, giving him a strong resemblance to a schoolmaster, as indeed he was, in the military sense, to the enemies of his country.

General Arnold, the chief of artillery, with his high boots, and slouched hat thrown over his head, seemed the busiest man of all.

#### Burnside Directing a Retreat.

A wounded soldier who served in Burnside's expedition in North Carolina, mentions that at Newbern, on one occasion, the Federal troops, on account of the numerous batteries they had to encounter,

Gen A E Burnside

became discouraged, and were falling back; thereupon an officer rode up in haste to Burnside, and asked if he would order a retreat. "Retreat!" said Burnside, "yes, right into the face of the enemy. That is how I want you to retreat." A forward movement was immediately ordered, and by a *forward retreat*, the Union troops carried all before them, driving the enemy from their entrenchments, and capturing all their strongholds.

### Three Soldiers Captured by a Boy with a Coffee Pot.

An amusing instance of the value of a ready wit and presence of mind occurred during the advance of the Second Corps of Federal troops, near Hatcher's Run. A young lad in the Fourteenth Connecticut regiment, going with a coffee-pot to get water from the stream, suddenly found himself surrounded by three of the enemy.

Soldiers Captured by a Boy

With all the fierceness of voice the little fellow could muster, he commanded them to throw down their arms and surrender. Supposing that the brave youth had companions near to enforce his command, they complied, when he seized one of their muskets and marched them into camp in great triumph. This story was related in his camp as the capture of three Johnnies with a coffee-pot.

### Career of the "Handsomest Man in the Southwest."

Albert Pike is a name which will long be remembered in the Southwest, as that of one of the most remarkable men who have lived in that region. It was not to be expected that he would be otherwise than conspicuous in the great rebellion which enveloped that section with the rest. In the battle of Pea Ridge, he led the Cherokee Indians, whom he had seduced from their allegiance to the Government of the United States. A noble looking, white-haired man, of very imposing appearance, he nevertheless proved an utter failure as a military leader, running like a coward before the veterans of Curtis and Sigel on that bloody day.

Albert Pike

It was in another sphere, and a totally different one, that Pike was destined to shine; and shine he did. He was a man of extraordinary genius, and had pocketed a hundred thousand dollars as the fees of a single lawsuit. He had been known, during a term of court, to meet his brother lawyers for an evening carousal, drink with them till the stoutest was 'laid out' under the table, and then seat himself, and, in the midst of their convivial singing and roaring, draw up a most intricate bill in chancery, without an erasure or interlineation. He would do this same thing in court, apparently undisturbed by the noise of a trial in progress. But, with all his genius and wonderful versatility of talent, he was utterly and persistently wayward in his habits, and half a dozen fortunes passed from his hands—spent in reckless and prodigal excesses. Once young, highly educated, graced with personal accomplishments and a physique which won for him the distinction of being called the "handsomest man in the Southwest," his magic touch had swept the lyre of the gods, compelling a busy, din-resounding nation to stop and listen in enraptured silence.

But from all this eminence, he became an exile from his home, a traitor to his country, the pusillanimous leader of red-handed savages against the valiant defenders of the Union and the noblest flag that ever floated, and, to cap the climax, deserted the savage victims of his own silver-tongued eloquence, and ran like a coward in the day of battle!

### General Howard on the Wrong Side of the Battle-field.

A short time subsequent to the magnificent charge made on the rebel breastworks, in the midnight conflict at Lookout Valley, by General Geary, General Howard, taking with him a small escort of cavalry, started for that part of the field where General Geary was supposed to be. He had not gone far, when he came up with a body of infantry. "What cavalry is that?" was the hail. "All right," responded General Howard, at the same time calling out, "What men are these?" "Longstreet's," was the reply. "All right —come here," said General Howard. The men approached. "Have we whipped those fellows?" asked the General, in a manner to keep up the deception. "No, — them, they were too much for us, and drove us from our rifle-pits, like devils. We're whipped ourselves." By this time the rebels had gathered nearer. "Lay down your arms!" demanded General H., in a stern voice. The men surrendered.

Taking his prisoners in charge, General Howard proceeded on his way. He had not gone far, before another party of rebel infantry called out, "What cavalry is that?" "All right," was the response again, of General Howard, as he proceeded. On approaching the position occupied by Geary, that officer had observed the advancing horsemen, and infantry, as he supposed the prisoners to be, and taking them to be rebels, he had ordered his guns to be loaded with canister, and in a moment more would have given the intrepid Howard and his little force the benefit of it. But the general who had successfully deceived the enemy, found a way to make himself known to his friends, and so escaped a reception of that kind.

### Intrepid Conduct of Two Drummer Boys.

Two drummer boys of the Tenth Connecticut Volunteers, while off duty, and while Gillmore was pounding Fort Wagner, determined to discover the effect made upon the fort, and for this purpose borrowed an opera glass and went out a distance from camp, to obtain a favorable site to witness the operations. They had proceeded about three-quarters of a mile, when they came suddenly upon a burly rebel, who upon sight of the boys, snap-

Intrepid Conduct.

ped his gun at them, which however did not explode, the piece not being capped. One of the boys at that moment, thrusting the glass into the case which hung at his side, the rebel thought he was drawing a revolver, and immediately threw down his gun, crying out, "I surrender!" The boys immediately sprang forward, seized his gun, and at a "charge bayonet" drove the big fellow into camp. When he discovered that the only appearance of a weapon in the boys' possession was an opera glass, he was much incensed, declar-

## GREAT CONFLICTS, INDIVIDUAL HEROISM, ETC.

ing he could not be held as a prisoner of war. The fact was witnessed by the Colonel of the regiment, who highly commended the intrepid conduct of the boys.

### Bob, the Spunky Drummer Boy.

The battle of Fredericksburg was attended by many memorable instances of individual heroism. It is known that, for several days a curtain of thick fog rose up from the waters of the Rappahannock, completely hiding from view the artillery that crowned the opposite hills, and the infantry that crowded the sheltering ravines. But the preparation for the great fight, so hopefully commenced, was continued amid the thunder of cannon and the eruptions of exploding batteries.

Bob, the Drummer Boy.

The hazardous work of laying the pontoon bridges was frequently interrupted by the murderous fire of Confederate sharpshooters, concealed in the stores and dwelling-houses on the bank of the river. To dislodge these men, and drive them out of their hiding-places, seemed an impossible task. At a given signal, the Union batteries opened with a terrific fire upon the city, crashing through the walls of houses and public buildings. But in this storm of shot and shell, which ploughed the streets and set the buildings on fire, the sharpshooters survived, like salamanders in the flames, and continued to pour a deadly fire upon the Federal engineers and bridge-builders.

In this dilemma it became evident that the bridges could not be laid except by a bold dash. Volunteers were called for to cross in small boats; forthwith, hundreds stepped forward and offered their services. One hundred men were chosen, and at once started for the boats. Robert Henry Hendershot was then a member of the Eighth Michigan—acting as drummer boy. Seeing a part of the Michigan Seventh preparing to cross the river, he ran ahead, and leaped into the boat. One of the officers ordered him out, saying he would be shot. The boy replied that he didn't care, that he was willing to die for his country. When the boy found that the Captain would not permit him to remain in the boat, he begged the privilege of pushing the boat off, and the request was granted. Whereupon, instead of remaining on shore, he clung to the stern of the boat, and, submerged to the waist in water, he crossed the Rappahannock. Soon as he landed, a fragment of a shell struck his old drum, and knocked it to pieces. Picking up a musket, he went in search of relics, and obtained a secesh flag, a clock, a knife, and a bone ring. On opening a back door in one of the enemy's houses, he found a Confederate wounded in the hand, and ordered him to surrender. He did so, and was taken by the boy-soldier to the Seventh Michigan. When the drummer boy recrossed the river from Fredericksburg, General Burnside said to him, in the presence of the army:

"Boy, I glory in your spunk; if you keep on this way a few more years, you will be in my place."

Robert is a native of New York, but moved with his parents to Michigan when he was an infant. His father died, leaving the mother in destitute circumstances, and with a family of four children to support and educate. Bob went from Jackson (Michigan) to Detroit, with Captain Deland, in the capacity of waiter in the Ninth Michi-

840 THE BOOK OF ANECDOTES OF THE REBELLION.

gan. With that regiment he went to Louisville, West Point, Ky., and Elizabethtown, Ky.,—at the last named place being appointed drummer boy. Subsequently he was in six battles, namely, Lebanon, Murfreesboro, Chattanooga, Shelbyville, McMinnsville, and Fredericksburg. At the battle of Murfreesboro, where the Union forces were taken by surprise before daylight, in the morning, after beating the long-roll, and pulling the fifer out of bed to assist him, he threw aside his drum, and seizing a gun, fired sixteen rounds at the enemy from the window of the court-house in which his regiment was quartered; but the Union men were compelled to surrender, and they were all taken prisoners, though immediately paroled, and afterward sent to Camp Chase, Ohio. Soon as the news came from the Rappahannock that Bob had lost his drum in that terrible tempest of fire and iron, the New York Tribune Association promised to make good his loss and give him a new drum. If ever a little fellow deserved both drum and drumsticks, it was Robert Hendershot, the gallant little Western drummer boy, whose "spunk" elicited the admiration of Burnside.

### Heavy Firing—No Casualties: and Why.

It was almost always observed that when the Confederate and Union troops were lying near one another for any length of time, they became quite communicative and friendly. They forgot that they were enemies, and a kind of chivalric honor and courtesy was strictly observed during their self-appointed truce. If they were compelled to fire during the existence of this self-constituted armistice, they fired the first volley in the air, so as to give the others time to get back. The following incident, which happened in front of the Fourteenth Corps, at Atlanta, Georgia, shows how much ticklishness there was about 'honor' on such occasions:

The Federal works were pretty close to those of the Confederates, and the pickets nearly met in the centre. There was no firing along the lines, and it occurred to the poor fellows on both sides that it would be pleasant to get up out of their rifle-pits, stretch their cramped limbs, and have a little friendly intercourse with their neighbors. So a sort of ventriloquism conversation ensued from the pits, and, all preliminaries being satisfactorily arranged, a regular truce was agreed upon. They jumped up, shook off the dirt, and met in so friendly a way that one would have thought they were the best and most loving neighbors in the world. Trade was carried on on a small scale, escapes and adventures recounted, and home friends and scenes warmly discussed. In the midst of all this, the rebels in the rear called out to their comrades,

"Boys, come back, the Major is coming."

Now it happened that "the Major" was an old, rusty, crusty customer, and had no hand in the truce at all, so when he came up he was in a fume, and called out,

" — you, come back here; and why the — don't you fire?"

The men went back, but refused to fire on the Federals until they had got to their pits, which set the major in such a boiling rage that he snatched a gun and popped at one of the Yankees, slightly wounding him. A regular cry of indignation at such a violation of faith was raised by his men, and five of them actually walked out of his lines into the Union, owning that they could not, in justice to their honor, serve any longer in an army where honorable treaties were so grossly violated. Their comrades refused to interfere, and evidently deeply sympathized with their offended dignity. The Union boys received them warmly; even the wounded man joined in the welcome. The following day the rebel picket called out in a quiet way to the Yankees,

"Boys, we ain't allowed to hold any intercourse with you; but if you attack us to-night, we ain't going to fight hard."

It was settled to the satisfaction of all parties that the Federals were to attack them, and both parties to fire in the air, and while the firing was hottest the Federal boys was to capture them. Accordingly at night the Federals made a vigorous attack, and, after some very heavy firing, captured over one hundred men and seven officers. What sounded strange to the uninitiated was—"*heavy firing, no casualties.*"

General H. W. Slocum.

**Paying to have a Hand in the Fight.**

In the conflict that took place at West Point in the spring of 1862, as General Franklin came on the ground, (late in the afternoon,) he discovered a soldier scrambling up the sand bank, and hailed him. "What are you doing there, Sir; where is your regiment?" thundered the General. "From that transport, yer honor, and I paid the fellow three dollars to bring me over, so that I could take a hand in the fight." "You're a brave fellow," remarks the General, "and I will see you cared for." He was directed to his regiment. The General subsequently ascertained that the man was so anxious to take part in the fight, that he had paid the boatman three dollars to land him, so that he might take a hand in it. General Franklin sent him a five dollar gold piece, and promised to reward him for his bravery.

**Ignoble End of a Washington.**

The death of John A. Washington created quite a sensation throughout the whole country, on account of his identification with the great name and family of the Father of his Country. He fell, on the afternoon of September 15th, 1861, about seven miles south of Elk Water camp. It seems that, in company with three other Rebel officers he was approaching the Federal fortifications with a view of making a reconnoissance. Secreted in the bushes, by the road-side, were a number of the Seventeenth Indiana regiment, and, as Washington and his companions came up the road, the Indiana boys rose from their concealment and fired. Washington fell from his horse, on the first round, having received three bullets, two of which passed entirely through his body, entering at the right breast. One of the other officers was also hit, but the two remaining unhurt managed to get him away by supporting him on his horse.

The body of Washington was conveyed to the quarters of Colonel Waggoner. He lived for the space of half an hour, and never spoke save to utter once, "O, my God!" The next day his body was sent to the rebel camp, under a flag of truce. In the pockets of Washington were found one hundred dollars in United States gold currency, and a splendid gold watch. His dress was new, and of the most elegant make, broadcloth coat and pants, and a white satin vest. His shoulder-straps denoted him to be a Colonel. He early paid the penalty of treason to that Government, in defence of which he, above all other American citizens, ought willingly and proudly to have raised his arm and poured forth his blood, instead of fatuitously following the lead of such men as Letcher, Wise, and other Virginia high-priests of treason and blood. To Wise's example and threats, in especial, is due the sacrifice of the noblest blood of the Old Dominion, for to none more than to him did the chivalry of Virginia look for their political cue.

Shade of GEORGE WASHINGTON—*pater patriæ*—alas!

Gen. Henry A. Wise.

### Determined Capture of a Texan Battle-Flag.

On the 9th of October, 1862, Colonel Fuller, commander of the First Brigade, Second Division, of the Mississippi Army, forwarded to Governor Tod, of Ohio, the battle-flag of the Sixth Texas Regiment, which was captured by a private of the Twenty-seventh Ohio Infantry, at the battle of Corinth, October 4th. The history of the capture of this flag is most interesting.

The rebels, in four close columns, were pressing with gallantry, amounting to recklessness, upon the Ohio Brigade, with the evident intention of breaking our lines, when the terrible and incessant fire of our men drove them back in the utmost confusion.

The Sixth Texas bore down upon the left centre of the Twenty-seventh Ohio, with this flag at the head of their column, and advanced to within six or eight yards of our lines, when Orrin B. Gould, a private of Company G, shot down the color-bearer, and rushed forward for the rebel flag.

A rebel officer shouted to his men to "save the color," and at the same moment put a bullet into the breast of Gould, but the young hero was not to be intimidated. With the flag-staff in his hand, and the bullet in his breast, he returned to his regiment, waving the former defiantly in the faces of the enemy. After the battle, Colonel Fuller visited the hospital, and found young Gould stretched upon a cot, evidently in great pain. Upon seeing the Colonel, his pale face was instantly radiant with smiles, and pointing to his wound, he said, "Colonel, I don't care for this, since I got their flag."

### Captain Tilden's Lucky Escape.

Captain Tilden, of the Sixteenth Maine regiment, was taken prisoner in the fight for the Weldon Railroad, in August, 1864, and carried on the way to Richmond about four miles from Petersburg, when he slipped from a car and escaped. Having on a light colored and broad brimmed Kossuth hat, and a rubber overcoat, was unquestionably his bodily salvation. The fact that it rained nearly all the time he was a prisoner gave no look of strangeness or ground for suspicion in his wearing his rubber coat, while his broad brimmed beaver gave him the air and tone of a true southerner "to the manor born." At all events, he walked freely through

Captain Tilden's Lucky Escape.

the streets and public places of Petersburg, picking up much valuable informa-

# GREAT CONFLICTS, INDIVIDUAL HEROISM, ETC.

tion, which he afterwards imparted to the Union commanding generals. When he first struck the rebel lines with a view to get through them, he was fortunate enough in his plan of concealment and observation to hear a Confederate soldier remark to another: "The yanks will have hard work getting through our three battle lines here, but down below, where there is only a thin skirmish line, it ain't so safe, I reckon." The Captain thought he would take a look after that "thin skirmish line," and he found it. The heavy storm and dense darkness of the night enabled him to get through the line. He did not get through any too quick, for two shots were fired at him while between the Confederate skirmish line and his own. He finally came upon the pickets of his own brigade—a piece of good fortune pleasingly agreeable, and quite as remarkable as agreeable.

### A Milesian's Plucky Defence of the Flag.

The transport of the Confederate prisoners from New Orleans, to Baton Rouge, on board the steamer Empire Parish, elicited many a merry incident. In the saloon of the steamer there was noticed a lubberly rebel with a little flag, to which he seemed desirous to attract attention, as he occasionally flourished it, with remarks disparaging to the Union cause. An under-sized Union soldier was on guard, apparently indifferent to what was going on; but the sequel proved that, though his mouth was shut, his ears were open, for suddenly he dropped his musket, and, quick as lightning, "let go his left mawley," and the frontispiece of the rebel color-bearer being in the way, there was a collision, in which the frontispiece got the worst of it, its owner trying the while to secure his flag by hiding it in his bosom. He was foiled, as the plucky little Milesian (for he proved by his brogue that he was a "broth of a boy,") went down after it, secured it, and flapping the well-earned trophy in the face of his foe, remarked, "You bloody ribil, you can't flap that bastard flag in these lines. Who's got another?" That was the last of the flag insults.

### As Good as a Captured Gun.

There was an odd character among Berdan's Sharpshooters, near Yorktown, known as "Old Seth." He was quite an 'individooal,' and a crack shot—one of the best in the regiment. "His "instrument," as he termed it, was one of the heaviest telescopic rifles. One night, at the time of roll call, Old Seth was *non est*. This was somewhat unusual, as the old chap was always up to time. A sergeant went out to hunt him up, he being somewhat fearful that the old man had been hit. After

As good as a Captured Gun.

perambulating around in the advance of the picket line, he heard a low "Halloo!" "Who's there?" inquired the sergeant. "It's me," responded Seth, "and I've captured a secesh gun." "Bring it in," said the sergeant. "Can't do it," exclaimed Seth. It soon became apparent to the sergeant, that "Old Seth" had the exact range of one of the enemy's heaviest guns, and they could not load it for fear of being picked off by him. Again the old man shouted, "Fetch me a couple of haversacks full of grub, as this is my gun, and the cussed varmints sha'nt fire it agin, while the scrimmage lasts." This was done, and the old patriot kept a good watch over that gun. In fact it was a captured gun —or as good as that.

### Pemberton's Question about Grant Answered.

In one of the assaults upon Vicksburg Lieutenant-Colonel Graham, of the Twenty-second Iowa infantry, was taken prisoner. This officer, with three companies, had gained a position in the ditch in front of the rebel works. Sending for spades, he commenced to throw up traverses to protect him from an enfilading fire, and then sent for reinforcements. The Lieutenant-Colonel, however, had barely time to congratulate himself on the security of his position, and the fact that the colors of the Twenty-second had been planted on the parapet of the fort before them, ere an awkward turn was given to his reflections, by the ingenious enemy. Unable to reach our men with musket, bayonet or artillery, they resorted to the effective mode of lighting the fuses of shells and dropping them over the parapet into the ditch below. Unable to either run or stay, our men took a middle course, and surrendered.

The party was conducted to the county jail, with the exception of Colonel Graham, who was taken before General Pemberton. The rebel commander propounded the following questions:

"What regiment do you belong to?"

"Is the Twenty-second Iowa an Abolition regiment?"

"How many nigger regiments have you fellows got out there?"

"What is that fellow Grant trying to do?"

"How many men have you got in your army?"

The answers of the indignant officer at these interrogatories can be readily imagined; assuring Pemberton that "that fellow Grant" meant to and *would* take Vicksburg, and receiving the reply, "No, by ——, he won't!" Colonel Graham was sent to join his friends in the prison.

Gen. John C. Pemberton.

### Emptying a Hawk's Nest.

At one point in the battle of Chattanooga there was a lull—at least it had gone chattering and thundering down the line, and the boys were as much "at ease" as boys can be upon whom, at any moment, the storm may roll back again. To be sure occasional shots, and now and then a cometary shell, kept them alive; but one of the boys ran down to a little spring, and towards the woods where the enemy lay, for water. He had just stopped and swung down his canteen, when, 'tick!' —a rifle ball struck it at an angle and bounded away. He looked around an instant, discovered nobody, thought it was a chance shot—a piece of lead, that goes at a killing rate without malice prepense; and so, nowise infirm of purpose, he again bent to get the water. 'Ping!' a second bullet cuts the cord of his canteen, and the boy "got the idea"—a sharpshooter was after him—and he went to the right-about on the double quick to the ranks. A soldier from another part of the line made a pilgrimage to the spring, was struck, and fell by its brink. But where was the marksman? Two or three boys ran out to draw his fire, while others watched: 'Crack!' went the unseen piece again, and some keen-eyed fellow spied a smoke rolling out from a little cedar. This was the spot, then, where the rebel had made him a hawk's nest—in choice Indian, a Chattanooga in the tree—and drawing the covert around him, was taking a quiet hand at 'steeple-shooting' at long range.

A big, blue-eyed German, tall enough to look into the third generation, and a sharp-shooter withal, volunteered to dislodge him. Dropping into a little runway that neared the tree diagonally, he turned upon his back, and worked himself cautiously along; reaching a point perilously close, he whipped over, took him as he lay, and God and his true right hand "gave him good deliverance." Away flew the bullet, an instant elapsed, the volume of the cedar parted, and, "like a big frog," as the boys described it, out leaped a gray-back, the hawk's nest was empty, and a dead rebel lay under the tree. It was neatly done by the German man grown. May he live to tell the story a thousand times to his moon-faced grandchildren.

### Polk, the Reverend General, in the very Tightest Place.

An English officer, Colonel Freemantle, who served for some time in the rebel army, and lived long enough in the South to make the acquaintance of a number of the prominent men there, afterward published a book relating his experience. In this book he tells the following story, as it was told him by Lieutenant-General Polk:—Well, sir, it was at the battle of Perryville, late in the evening—in fact, it was almost dark, when Lindell's battery came into action. Shortly after the arrival, I observed a body of men, whom I thought to be Confederates, standing at an angle to this brigade, and firing obliquely at the newly arrived troops. I said, "Dear me, this is very sad and must be stopped;" so I turned round, but could find none of my young men, so I determined to ride myself and settle the matter. Having cantered to the Colonel of the regiment that was firing, I asked him, in angry tones, what he meant by shooting his own friends. He answered with surprise,

"I don't think there can be any mistake about it; I am sure they are the enemy."

"Enemy! Why, I have only just left them myself. Cease firing, sir. What is your name?"

"My name is Colonel ——, of the —— Indiana; I pray, sir, who are you?"

Then I saw, to my astonishment, that I was in the rear of a regiment of Yankees. Well, I saw there was no hope but to

Gen. Leonidas Polk.

brazen it out; my dark blouse and the increasing obscurity befriended me; so I approached quite close to him, and shook my fist in his face, saying.

"I'll show you who I am, sir! Cease firing, sir, at once!"

I then turned my horse and cantered slowly down the line, shouting authoritatively to the Yankees to cease firing; at the same time I experienced a disagreeable sensation, like screwing up my back, and calculating how many bullets would be between my shoulders every minute. I was afraid to increase my pace till I got to a small copse. When I put the spurs in and galloped back to my own. I went up to the nearest Colonel, and said: "Colonel, I have reconnoitered those fellows pretty closely, and there is no mistake who they are; you may get up and go at them." And I assure you, sir, that the slaughter of that Indiana regiment was the greatest I have seen in this war.

### Hovey's Brilliant Charge—the Preachers' Regiment.

One of the most brilliant and daring operations in the fight at Vicksburg, was performed by General Hovey, at the head of several of his regiments. He had met with varied success all the morning—sometimes gaining a little, and again being driven. The heights were steep, the enemy numerous, their positions almost inaccessible and protected by timber, while from every crest on the heights their batteries rained hurricanes of death upon his thirsty, weary column. Finally, about noon, the General arranged a storming party, and heading them in person, moved directly up a gorge in the hills, every inch of which was swept by the musketry and artillery of the enemy. Two four and one six gun battery commanded the gorge, and on both sides of it were massed heavy supports of infantry. On went the storming party, and in twenty minutes the gallant remnant of those who started were hurrahing over the possession of all the guns, the crest of the hills, and the total rout of the infantry. In this charge the Twenty-fourth Iowa—a regiment made up largely of clergymen, and hence known as the " preachers' regiment "—was foremost, and was nearly annihilated. No more gallant thing has been done in the history of gallant efforts.

### Ahead of his Troops.

During the fog and darkness of the night on which Decatur was taken, General Dodge, Colonel Spencer, of his staff, and a few others, thinking that the troops, who were to cross at another point, had quietly occupied the place, started in a little boat to row directly across to the town. The fog was so close that it was impossible to see anything. As the boat neared the Decatur shore, a sentinel on shore heard it splashing and hailed, "Who goes there?" Thinking it to be a Union soldier, the General sang out, " General Dodge." *Bang!* went the gun of the sentinel—he was a rebel picket. The boat was instantly put to the right-about, and got safely away, although fired at by all the guard. The General wisely

Ahead of his Troops.

determined not to take Decatur without the aid of troops, and waited until he knew they had made a landing.

### Lee's Great Army Surrendered and the Rebellion in its Final Gasp.

The first week in April—immediately following the evacuation and surrender of Richmond to General Grant—General Lee found himself in a position from which he could not possibly extricate himself. His army lay massed a short distance west of Appomattox Court House; his last avenue of escape toward Danville on the southwest was gone; Mead was in his rear on the east and on his right flank north of Appomattox Court House; Sheridan had headed him off completely, by getting between him and Lynchburg; General Ord was on the south of the court-house, near the railroad; the troops were in the most enthusiastic

Surrender of Gen. Lee and his Army to Gen. Grant.

spirits, and the rebel army was doomed. Lee's last effort was that of attempting to cut his way through Sheridan's lines, but it totally failed.

On the seventh, a correspondence, looking to the surrender of Lee's army, commenced between himself and General Grant, the purport of General Lee's first note being to ascertain the best terms on which he could surrender his army. General Grant's reply not being to Lee's mind, the latter communicated to General Grant a request for a personal interview at a certain place, at ten o'clock on the morning of the ninth, to arrange "terms of peace." As this was changing the question at issue, and under discussion, and one which General Grant had neither the inclination nor the authority to decide, he replied in a note which admitted of no misconstruction, and which virtually ended the negotiations.

On receipt of this, General Lee at once dispatched another, requesting a personal interview for the object named in General Grant's previous communication, viz., the surrender of the entire rebel army. A flag of truce proceeded to Appomattox Court House shortly after noon, and at about two o'clock the two generals met at the house of Mr. W. McLean. General Lee was attended by General Marshall, his adjutant-general; General Grant, by Colonel Parker, one of his chief aids-de-camp. General Grant arrived about fifteen minutes later than General Lee, and entered the parlor where the latter was awaiting him.

The two generals greeted each other with dignified courtesy, and after a few moments conversation, proceeded to the business before them. Lee immediately alluded to the conditions named by General Grant for the surrender, characterized them as exceedingly lenient, and said he would gladly leave all the details to General Grant's own discretion. The latter stated the terms of parole—that the arms should be stacked, the artillery parked, and the supplies and munitions turned over to him, the officers retaining their side arms, horses, and personal effects. General Lee promptly assented to the conditions, and the agreement of surrender was engrossed and signed by General Lee at half-past three o'clock.

Thus substantially ended the interview. Both generals wore the very impersonation of dignity and courtesy in their bearing. Lee looked very much jaded and worn, but, nevertheless, presented the same magnificent *physique* for which he was always noted. He was neatly dressed

348     THE BOOK OF ANECDOTES OF THE REBELLION.

in gray cloth, without embroidery or any insignia of rank, except three stars worn on the turned portion of his coat collar. He also wore a very fine sword. Grant had no side arms.

The large marble-topped centre table on which the two generals signed the minutes, was of a somewhat antiquated style, and was afterwards purchased by

Gen Geo. A. Custer

General Ord for fifty dollars. General Custer purchased the other table, of small size, on which the documents were prepared, for twenty-five dollars. The only trophies left Mr. McLean were the chairs occupied by the two generals and the room itself in which the meeting took place. Numerous offers were made for the chairs, but Mr. McLean steadily refused to part with them. Finally, two cavalry officers, one of them a Colonel, finding that they could not obtain the chairs by any other means, seized them by force and made off with them. They had endeavored to make the owner take money for them, but he had thrown the proffered greenbacks on the floor. After they had been gone some time a cavalry officer rode up to the house, called Mr. McLean out, thrust a ten dollar note in his hand, and shouting, "that is for the Colonel's chair," rode off in hot haste.

After the interview, General Lee returned to his own camp, about half a mile distant, where his leading officers were assembled awaiting his return. He announced the result and the terms, whereupon they expressed great satisfaction at the leniency of the conditions. They then approached him in order of rank, shook hands, expressing satisfaction at his course, and their regret at parting. The fact of surrender and the liberal terms were then announced to the troops, and when General Lee appeared among them he was loudly cheered.

On Monday, between nine and ten o'clock in the forenoon, General Grant and staff rode out in the direction of the rebel lines, and on a hill just beyond the court-house, where a full view of the rebel army could be obtained, General Lee was met, attended by but one staff officer and orderlies. The Generals halted, and, seated on their horses, conversed for nearly an hour upon the prospects for the future, each seeming to realize the mighty influence which the events of the present were to have upon it. General Lee signified very emphatically his desire for a total cessation of hostilities, and indicated his intention to do all in his power to effect that end. This was the last interview between the two great commanders.

PART IV.—NAVAL SCENES AND EXPLOITS.

## PART FOURTH

ANECDOTES OF THE REBELLION—NAVAL AND COMMERCIAL. SQUADRON, FLEET, FLOTILLA, STEAMER, GUNBOAT, TRANSPORT, AND PRIVATEER,—THEIR CRUISES, OFFICERS, CREWS. PERFORMANCES, ETC.

TERRIBLE ENGAGEMENTS; SUFFERING AND DEATH FOR THE FLAG; HORRORS AND HAVOC OF MODERN BOMBARDMENT; BLOCKADE EXPLOITS; DARING FEATS OF SEAMANSHIP; FURIOUS PERSONAL COMBATS; LONG AND EXCITING CHASES; ESCAPES, RESCUES, PRIZES; THRILLING CATASTROPHES AND TRAGEDIES; CAPTURES, SINKINGS, AND SURRENDERS; AWKWARD LANDSMEN, RAW MARINES, JOLLY VETERANS, AND TREACHEROUS PILOTS; JACK AFLOAT AND ASHORE; FREAKS, DROLLERIES, HAPS AND MISHAPS, AMONG THE TARPAULINS AND BLUE JACKETS; &C., &C.

> "Shall we give her a broadside once more, my brave men?
> 'Ay! ay!' ran the full, earnest cry;
> A broadside! a broadside! we'll give them again,
> Then for God and the Right nobly die!'"
> Never, never will we surrender the ship."—LIEUT. MORRIS, *of the "Cumberland."*
> Before I will permit any other flag than the Stars and Stripes to fly at her peak, I will fire a pistol into her magazine and blow her up.—CAPT PORTER'S *reply to the demand to surrender the U. S. ship "St. Mary."*
> I hope we'll win it! I hope we'll win it!'—*Dying words of* COXSWAIN JACKSON, *of the "Wabash," at Port Royal.*

**Tarpaulin Raking a Traitor Fore and Aft.**

IN the early days of the rebellion, there were at the United States Marshal's office in San Francisco, several models of ships which had been ornamented with little secession flags about half the size of one's hand. They were made of paper, and colored with red and blue ink. One, at the mast head of the largest ship, bore the name of Jeff. Davis, and the others were the ordinary three-striped rag, adopted as the Confederate ensign. On account of the display of these flags, the only public place in the city, the Marshal's office became a sort of privileged quarters for secessionists, and nothing was more common than to hear secession talk there. This was particularly the case after the news of the breaking out of hostilities.

The story goes, that while several gentlemen were sitting in the Marshal's office, attending to business, a big strapping fellow, all the way from South Carolina, with a revolver peeping out from under his coat-tail, strode into the place, with the air of a Tarquin, and exclaimed:

"Well, at last, thank God! we've got these —— nutmeg-selling, mackerel-catching, cod-livered Yankee sons —— —— to come to it. That's just what I've been wanting this many a day!—the nigger-thieving, psalm-singing abolitionists! We'll skin 'em out of their boots."

The braggart had scarcely finished his low-lived tirade, when one of the gentlemen, Captain ——, of the ship ——, who was observed to be getting nervous, suddenly jumped up, and taking his place in front of the fellow, and shaking his fists, replied:

"Now, sir, I don't know you, and don't want to know you; but I suppose you designate me as one of those nutmeg-selling, mackerel-catching, cod-livered Yankee —— ——. I am captain of the ship ——, and I want you to understand that I will not allow any man to use such language respecting me and my people, in my presence. And if you don't recant, I'll whip you here and now. I see your pistol, but I don't care for it. You have insulted me, sir, and you shall answer for it."

Licking a Traitor.

The boaster, seeing the Captain's determined bearing, and finding that he was in downright earnest, replied by saying that his remarks were general in their nature, and not by any means intended to apply to any particular person. Nothing was further from his purpose than to insult any person present, and particularly a stranger.

To this the irate captain retorted: "The language, sir, is an insult to the American name, and I for one will not stand it from any living man. No one but a traitor and a coward can talk in that way. Retract it! retract it!"—and with this he commenced advancing upon the secessionist Hercules, who began weakening in the knees, and finally wilted, while tarpaulin raked the traitor's fore and aft without mercy.

#### Not a Star Obscured.

There were many touching illustrations evoked during the rebellion, of the love cherished by some for the power under which they had been nurtured from their very cradle, notwithstanding the contrary pressure of circumstances and surroundings. One of these illustrations took the following form: When Captain Armstrong was about to surrender the navy yard at Pensacola, his daughter, after vain endeavors to persuade him not so to act, demanded of him a dozen men, and *she* would protect the place until aid came; but no—he was untrue and disloyal, and determined to act as he had decided; the old flag was hauled down from where it had so long waved, and the renegade Renshaw ran his sword through it, venting his spleen upon the flag by which he had so long lived in competence and luxury. Human nature could not stand it, and the brave, glorious-hearted woman, seizing the flag, took her scissors and cut from it the 'Union,' telling them that the time was not far distant when she would replace it unsullied; but for the *stripes*, she left them as their legacy, being their just deserts. Not a star on that flag would she allow to be obscured or destroyed by the hand of treason. Brave-hearted, noble woman!

#### Last Gun of the Cumberland.

One of the greatest instances of patriotic devotion ever recorded in our own or any other nation's naval history, is that of the last broadside of the Cumberland, in her struggle with the Merrimac. Amid the dying thunders of those memorable guns, the noble vessel sank with her devoted crew, with the Stars and Stripes still proudly waving above their heads.

Neither the shots of the Congress, nor of the Cumberland, had any more effect upon the Merrimac than if they had been so many peas or peanuts. But if they could have kept the Merrimac off, she never could have sunk the Cumberland.

Naval Peacemaker.

They had then, nothing to do but stand and fight and die like men. Buchanan asked their commander, Lieutenant Morris,

"Will you surrender the ship?"

"Never," said Morris, "never will we surrender the ship."

Buchanan backed his infernal machine off again, and the Cumberland fired as rapidly as she could, but the Merrimac once more ran her steel prow in; and now it was that Buchanan asked Lieutenant Morris, calling him by name,

"Mr. Morris, will you surrender that ship?"

"Never," said Morris; "sink her!"

The remaining act in this startling drama is well known. The guns of the Cumberland were coolly manned, loaded and discharged, while the vessel was in a sinking condition, and the good ship went down with the flag flying defiantly at the gaff, and many a heroic patriot perished with her.

### Going to See the Rebel Ram.

A captured Confederate vessel, iron clad, and of the style commonly denominated "a ram," lay for several weeks in the Delaware, off the Philadelphia navy yard. She was something of a curiosity, and was visited by many hundreds of citizens and strangers. Prompted by this feeling, the keeper of a restaurant proposed one day to follow the track of the multitude and treat his wife with a sight of the rebel "ram." She consented, and off they sailed. They duly reached the iron deck of the vessel, went into her iron hold, examined her armament, inspected the damages wrought upon her by the guns of Uncle Sam, gazed upon her iron nose, which was constructed to be thrust impertinently into the affairs of our aforesaid Uncle's webfooted property, and, in short, investigated her, inside and out. Having satisfied his curiosity, the husband proposed to return to shore, when the following conversation occurred:

"Now, my dear, we have seen the vessel, let us go," said the husband.

"Well, yes,—but as we have taken the trouble to come so far, we might as well see what we came to look at," said the wife.

"You have seen enough of it, I should think," said he.

"Why, no! I have not seen it at all," she replied.

"Seen what?" he at last inquired with surprise.

"Why, the animal that we came to see —the sheep, or ram, or what you call it."

Then there was an explosion.

The story was too good to be kept. It was told to a visitor who called in the morning for one of the capital 'stews' got up at the friendly establishment in question. The visitor enjoyed it very much— he did; and, after finishing his repast, directed the waiter to inquire of his mistress whether she had in her larder any nice chops cut from the rebel "ram." The simpleton actually delivered the message, and the consequence was, that the last seen of the impertinent inquirer was the tail of his coat, as he was leaving the premises precipitately, with sundry broomsticks, boot-jacks, three-legged stools, long-handled sauce pans, and other missiles flying after him. At last accounts he was only too glad to be still running.

### Final Answer of Farragut to the Emissaries of Treason.

Just previous to the fall of Norfolk, Va., Admiral Farragut, himself of Southern birth, as was also his true and noble wife, was invited by the emissaries of the insurgent chiefs to join his fortune to their cause. He promptly declined. The effort to change his purpose was repeated. He was urged by every consideration that it was supposed could influence his pride or ambition, by the ties of consanguinity and place of birth, to side with his native South; he still refused. Those chiefs well knew the man. They knew him better than his own government then did, and they knew the lion-like qualities that slumbered beneath his modest and habitually retiring demeanor, and the achievements of which he was capable when the latent powers of the man should be roused to active energy. As a last effort to win him over to their cause, they offered him any position which he should be pleased to name. Admiral Farragut is a man of sincere but unobtrusive piety, a piety as modest as his own habitual deportment; but this assault upon his loyal virtue was more than his nature could endure, and, with a sudden and sailor-like burst of indignation, he replied, as he pointed to the emblem of the republic, which floated near him,—

"Gentlemen, your efforts are useless. I tell you I would see every man of you ——, before I would raise my arm against that flag." This answer was an extinguisher.

Norfolk soon fell, and Farragut was warned that the South was no place for him. A few hours only were allowed him for escape with his family, leaving, as he was compelled to do, all his property behind, which was immediately absorbed by the relentless confiscation of the foe. He reached the house of a friend, northward of the Potomac, exclaiming, as he did to him,—

"Here I am, without a farthing, or a place where I can lay my head!"

In this way came Farragut to the North —to the government to which he gave his allegiance—to the flag he so nobly upheld in many a fierce conflict with armed treason.

### Unknown Lady Visitor at the New Orleans Fleet.

Just before the city of New Orleans had been definitely surrendered by the authorities, and while the national fleet was anchored off in sight, a small boat, pulled by one pair of oars, was observed leaving the levee. A closely veiled lady was noticed in the stern. When she reached one of the vessels, she drew back her veil and beckoned to the officer of the watch. The Captain, who had remarked that she was young and apparently very winsome, dreaded the influence of the fair syren upon his subordinate, as with a gesture he forbade his responding to the mute appeal, and repaired himself to the gangway. Probably he imagined that forty odd years were more secure than twenty from treasonable temptation.

"Pray, Sir," she asked, in the most musical voice imaginable, "might I inquire if a person named McLellan is on board?"

At the same time she made him a brief but imperative sign, which he construed to signify that he was expected to reply in the affirmative.

"Certainly there is, Madam!"

(The white lie is accounted for by the

brilliancy of the flashing eyes which partially bewildered the Captain.)

"Might I trouble you to give him this letter?"

As the Captain descended to take it from one of the smallest and most delicately gloved hands he had ever seen, he partially recovered that presence of mind which had not deserted him once during the fierce struggle of the preceding days. He was unwilling that the first pair of bright eyes he had seen for weeks should vanish so quickly. Fluttered and perspiring with excitement, he managed to say—

"Would you not wish to step on board, Madam, and speak with him?"

A wicked smile flitted over the charming face before him, and but for his age, and the wife he had left in the North, he would infallibly have lost his heart. As it was, he felt it almost going, and laid his heavy hand upon it to check its disposition for levanting from its legitimate owner.

"No; I thank you"; she said, "such an unexpected pleasure might prove somewhat embarrassing."

Saying this, she again sat down, drew her veil over her face, and making a sign to the colored boatman, was pulled once more towards the levee.

The Captain gazed after her, sighed, and then looked at the letter.

"I suppose I must do duty for 'McLellan' on this occasion," he said; "But who the deuce can she be!" He then opened it.

The letter contained a great deal of valuable information respecting the temper of the population of the city. It also stated that Forts Pike and Livingston had been evacuated, and their garrisons dispatched to join Beauregard at Corinth, and distinctly affirmed that no Union sentiment could find expression in New Orleans until those who felt it could be guaranteed the protection of United States troops against the temper of the populace. Subsequent events proved that the fair correspondent was right; and the young subaltern, who was only able to catch an occasional glimpse of those magnetic eyes, as she was speaking to his commanding officer, said that, "Never before was the flashing glance of beauty one half so agreeable."

There was more than one on board that craft that night, whose pair of eyes willingly forgot their accustomed slumber in the deeper reverie caused by the charming lady visitor.

### Majer Downing on the Merrymac.

The prowess of the monster Merrimac, and the fate which she met at the hands of the brave and gallant Worden, has been the theme for many pens, both grave and satirical. A good specimen of the latter will be found below.

It was a good joke, (according to Majer Jack Downing) that the Kernel got off

Lieut. Worden.

one day on Seward. You know (quoth the Majer) what a solemn looking chap he is naterally. Wal, since he has got to be Chief Clerk to the President, he seems to look solemer than ever. He cum into Linkin's room, and the Kernel ses, "Have you heard the news, Boss?" "No," ses Seward, "what is it?" "Wal," ses Linkin, "the Giascutis is loose." "What's that?" ses Seward. "Why," ses Linkin, "ain't you never heard the story of the Giascutis?" Seward sed he never had. "Wal," ses the Kernel, "I must tell you. Several yeas ago a couple of Yankees were travelin out West, an' they got out of money. So they konkluded to 'raise the wind' as follers: They were to go into a village an' announce a show, pretendin that they had a remarkabal animil, which they had jest captured on the Rocky Mountings. A bran new beast, such as was never seen before. The name was the 'Giascutis.' It was to be shown in a room, and one of the fellers was to play Giascutis. He was put behind a screen, an' had some chains to shake, an' he also contrived to growl or howl as no critter ever did before. Wal, the people of the village all cum to see the Giascutis, an' after the room was filled, his companion began to explain to the audience what a terribal beast he had, how he killed ten men, two boys an' five hosses in ketchin him, an' now how he had got him, at 'enormous expense,' to show him. Jest as everybody was gapin an' starin, thar was, all at once, a most terrific growlin and howlin, an' rattlin of chains, an' in the excitement the showman almost breathless, yelled out at the top of his voice, "the Giascutis is loose! Run! run! run!" An' away went the people down stairs, heels over head, losin all they had paid, an' seein nothin." "Now," ses Linkin, "the Merrymac is out, an' wen I read about the wessels, an' tug boats an' steamers all scamperin off as soon as she was seen, I thought she was the Giascutis sure, only I'm afraid she is real Giascutis an' no mistake." Since then, Linkin calls the Merrymac the Giascutis all the time.

### Yankee Doodle in the Storm of Shot.

Master's Mate Arbane, of the Owasco, had a very narrow escape from death at the battle of Galveston, three shot having struck him in different places. One of the bullets passed completely through the crown of his cap, another penetrated his pantaloons just below the right knee, taking the piece of cloth with it. The third shot struck the gallant fellow's sword just as he raised it in the air, and was ordering his men to give a rousing cheer for "Yankee Doodle." The cheer was given in the storm of shot.

### "Charge! Chester, Charge!"

Captain Chester was a man of grit; without any of the oleaginious mixture. He belonged to Pittsburg, and used to carry coal to Memphis. When the war broke out, the Confederates seized his steamboats and his coal-barges, and refused to pay him for the coal they had already purchased. The act roused all his ire. He was a tall, athletic man, and had followed the river thirty years. Although surrounded by enemies, he gave them plain

"Charge! Chester, Charge!"

words.

"You are a set of thieves and rascals! You are cowards, every one of you!" he shouted.

He took off his coat, rolled up his shirt-sleeves, bared his great brawny arms, dashed his hat upon the ground.

"Now come on! I'll fight every one of you, you infernal rascals. I'll whip you all. I challenge you to fight me. You call yourselves chivalrous people. You say you believe in fair play. If I whip you shall give up my boats, but if I am beaten, you are welcome to them."

They laughed in his face, and said, "Blow away, old fellow. We have got your boats. Help yourself if you can." A hot-headed secessionist cried out, "Hang the Yankee." The crowd hustled him about, but he had a few old friends, who took his part, and succeeded in making his escape.

### Thirty Tremendous Minutes.

The bombardment of Fort Sumter by the iron-clads under Admiral Dupont was equally magnificent and terrible. Unfortunately, the *Ironsides* got disabled by the current at a most critical hour. In this plight, however, it only remained for Admiral Dupont to signal to the fleet to disregard the movements of the flagship. This he did, and the ships then assumed such positions as were available and they could gain, the whole number being at the

Admiral S. F. Dupont

mouth of the harbor, between Cumming's Point and Sullivan's Island, and opposite the northeast and eastern face of Fort Sumter, at distances of from six hundred to a thousand yards. While the manœuvres of the Admiral were thus going on, the enemy was not inactive. The powerful work on Cumming's Point, named Battery B, opened; the long range rifle ordnance of Fort Beauregard joined in; Moultrie hurled its heavy metal, the fifty guns lining the Redan swelled the fire; and the tremendous armament of Sumter vomited forth its fiery hail.

There now ensued a period of not more than thirty minutes, which formed the climax and white heat of the fight; for though, from the time when the fire was opened on the head of the approaching line, to the time when the retiring fleet passed out of the enemy's range, there was an interval of two hours and a half, yet the essence of the fight was shut up in those *thirty tremendous minutes*.

The best resources of the descriptive art, are feeble to paint so terrific and awful a reality. Such a fire, or anything even approaching it, was simply never seen before. The mailed ships were in the focus of a concentric fire of those five powerful works, from which they were removed only some five to eight hundred yards, and which in all could not have mounted less than three hundred guns, viz., the finest and largest guns from the spoils of the Norfolk navy-yard, the splendid and heavy ten and eleven inch guns cast at the Tredegar Works, and the most approved English rifled guns, Whitworth and others, of the largest calibre made. There was something almost pathetic in the spectacle of those little floating circular towers, exposed to the crushing weight of those tons of metal, hurled against them with the terrific force of modern projectiles, and with such charges of powder as were never before dreamed of in artillery firing. During the climax of the fire a hundred and sixty shots were counted in a single minute, and the shot struck the iron-clads as fast as the ticking of a watch.

It was less of the character of an ordinary artillery duel, and more of the proportions of a war of the Titans in the elder mythologies.

### Final Scene Aboard the Steamer Mississippi.

There is a startling combination of the romantic and tragical in the destruction of the United States steam frigate

Mississippi. The most exciting scenes portrayed in the best English and American naval novels hardly exceed in vividness of description the matter-of-fact narrative of this staggering event.

The Mississippi was the last in the line of the fleet which attempted the passage of the Port Hudson batteries, on the night of March 14th. In going up, she was struck by three or four shot only, and the damage done was comparatively insignificant. But when she was at a point nearly in the centre of the range of batteries, the smoke and steam from the boats in advance, and from the batteries on shore, so enveloped the ship that her pilot lost his bearings, and the frigate grounded on the right bank of the river.

For forty minutes she was exposed to a terrific fire from all the batteries. During this time she fired two hundred and fifty rounds; but her guns, one after another, were nearly all dismounted; her portholes on the starboard side were knocked into one; twenty-five or thirty men were killed, and four wounded; she was riddled through and through with shot; there was no prospect of her ever floating again—and, at last, in the utter hopelessness of the case, Captain Smith gave the order for her abandonment.

It is said that during all the time she was under fire there was no particular excitement on board. The orders were quietly given and executed. The crew were told to load and fire at the batteries as rapidly as possible, and they did so as long as there was a mounted gun to fire. After the order to abandon the ship had been given, and the crew had all left, Captain Smith and Lieutenant Dewey went around to see if there were any living men among those lying on the deck, and sprinkled turpentine in the ward-room, setting it on fire. The Captain of the forehold was ordered to fire the ship forward, and they then abandoned her, leaving the dead on deck. The Captain and Lieutenant pulled in a boat for the Essex. The abandoned ship was soon wrapt in flames, and presently the fire reached the magazine, blowing up the ship with a tremendous explosion;—and that was the *finale* of the United States steam frigate Mississippi.

### Roberts's Half-Hour's Visit at Island No. 10.

One Wednesday night, five launches, one from each gunboat, and carrying in all fifty seamen and soldiers, armed to the teeth, "might have been seen," a little after dark, pushing out from the various gunboats at Island No. 10, and gathering under the shadows of the willows that fringe the Kentucky shore. Each boat had an officer in command, and the whole were in charge of Lieutenant-Colonel Roberts, of the Forty-second Illinois infantry.

The strictest silence was observed—not a whisper nor even the splash of an oar broke the stillness. At length everything was ready, and giving themselves to the

Half-hour's visit at Island No. 10.

current, the boats started down the stream, the oarsmen quietly giving each boat sufficient motion only to enable the steersman to it to keep close within the shadows. In this mysterious manner they departed, and speedily disappeared in the darkness.

An hour later, and the solitary rebel sentry, who, musket in hand, paced forward and backward along the parapet of the upper battery, had his thoughts disturbed by a remarkable appearance. He had just entered the depths of a cogitation, the main features of which probably were that Yankees are vulgar, base, low-born mud-sills; that Southerners are chivalrous, noble, knightly, superior; and that one of the latter is just an equal match for from five to twenty-five of the former,—when suddenly happening to glance toward the river, his eyes caught sight of numberless black objects drifting slowly toward him, and above these dark masses were luminous points and flashes, which seemed to envelope them like a net-work of ghostly phosphorescent flame. He rubbed his eyes, looked again at these mysterious phenomena, and was about to conclude that something was abroad, when suddenly a voice was heard, "*Give way!*"—fifty oars dropped in the water, and the dark-looking objects, with the swiftness of thought, shot straight for his position. He had only time to see that the supernatural light was the gleam of bayonets, and then to his disordered vision there appeared to be coming at him a hundred boats, each carrying a thousand Yankees. With a yell of horror he pulled off his piece in the air, and fled with the darkness, no more to be seen.

He had no more than left when the five boats struck the bank, their contents poured ashore and took possession of the battery, guards were posted around, and their rat-tail files and sledge-hammers were brought into requisition with a success that, in the course of half an hour, effectually spiked every gun—there were seven—in the battery. The party remained in the works about an hour, and then, without hearing a word from the enemy, returned to the fleet. A very profitable evening call at 'No. 10.'

### Western Steamboat Saved by a Woman.

The steamer City of Alton, belonging to St. Louis, and plying between that city and Cairo, was nearly surprised and taken by the rebels under Jeff. Thompson, who had stolen down the river at the town of Commerce, and were prepared to board the boat on its arrival at that place,—and which would all have been carried out but for the interposition of a brave woman.

On approaching Commerce, the mate, who was on the watch, saw a woman (Mrs. Eversoll) on the bank, gesticulating violently, surrounded by a few men, and ever and anon her two little girls would tug at her dress, as if to induce her to keep quiet. The mate was uncharitable enough to think that the woman had been indulging in liquor, and knew not what she did; but there was 'method in her madness.' The mail was to be put out, and wood to be taken, and despite the continued waving of the woman's hand northward, the boat stood into shore. At last the boat was about to touch the shore, and the plank was half way over the bow, when—the knot of persons of which the 'guardian angel' formed the most attractive object, being about fifty steps from the water—the mate heard her exclaim:

"Go back! go back!" Jeff. Thompson is here with soldiers!"

The mate instantly appreciated the state of affairs on shore, and rapidly gave the order to "back her strong." Captain Barnes at this moment rushed out of his room, coat and boots off, to find the boat backing out and the balls plunging into his room and all around. When the mate issued the order mentioned above, he retreated behind the chimney, in time to escape a ball which struck the bell with a thud and broke into fragments. He then saw the full force of the assailants springing up from behind the wood pile, and rushing like madmen down a lane to the bank of the river. One of the balls went through the pilot house directly over the head of the pilot. There were Minie balls, musket balls, and buck-shot. One ball struck the office bulkhead between the clerk and barkeeper, who were in quiet conversation; they prudently ceased talking and went to the other side of the bulkhead.

The boat swiftly sped to an island below, where lived a loyal Frenchman, and procured forty muskets and one pistol. The boat returned, her crew eager for the fray, and determined to give Jeff. and his rascals battle,—but all were gone, leaving not a wreck behind. The lady who thus saved the boat, as well as saved lives, resided in Commerce, and her husband was made a prisoner by the bandits that same day. When they were cutting down a pole, from which had floated a loyal flag, she boldly said to them, with flashing eyes, and in a tone which all could hear, that if she was a man she would kill at least one of them, and if she had no better weapon, she would break their heads with a brick. She herself was a glorious "brick."

### Glorious Success of General Butler in saving "Old Ironsides."

One of General Butler's first acts, on taking possession of the city of Annapolis, was to save the glorious old ship Constitution—used by the cadets of the Naval School as an exercise ship, and universally known as "Old Ironsides," one of the most revered of our national relics—from the clutch of some insurgents who were about to pounce upon her, after the usual fashion of Southern honesty and chivalric honor. The General, learning of the helpless condition, from want of a crew, of the old ship of historic fame, mustered his men and declared to them that "if there are any men in the ranks who understand how to manage a ship, let them step forward." Fifty-three presented themselves, and they were immediately put on board. The steam ferry-boat Maryland, which General Butler had seized on the Susquehanna, then took her in tow, and she was safely borne out of harm's way.

The honored frigate had for a long time lain at Annapolis, substantially at the mercy of an armed rebel mob. For four days and nights, previous to the arrival of General Butler, her crew had been at quarters with the guns shotted. The insurgents of Maryland were plotting her destruction or capture. She had four anchors and seven chains out when the Maryland was ordered by General Butler alongside. One anchor alone was hove up, the rest were slipped, and finally by lighting and careening, and by dint of hard labor, she was dragged over the bar. The crew of the Maryland were only kept to their work and duty by placing a guard over them with armed revolvers. After dragging her over the bar, the vessel grounded on the Outer Spit. About ten P. M., information having been brought off that the channel outside the ship would be obstructed, kedges were laid out, and it was endeavored to warp the ship over the Spit, part of the men being at the guns. The Maryland having been run aground by her officers during the warping, a squall came up and drove the ship ashore again. At daylight, a steam-tug from Havre de Grace came in sight, and was taken at once to tow the ship out. She was then taken in tow by the R. R. Cuyler, and brought to New York. Subsequently she was sent to Newport, Rhode Island, whither the Naval School formerly at Annapolis was removed. Surely, it was worth a greenback of the largest numeral, to see the plucky General, as he presented himself at the Navy Department, and narrated to white-bearded Gideon, this glorious achievement.

### Generosity of Poor Jack.

There were present almost every day of the Sailors' Fair in Boston, some of the gallant but unfortunate fellows whose names and deeds on the sea had given them renown—such as Walter Greenwood, U. S. gunboat Massasoit, of Nashua, N. H.; R. D. Dunphy, coal passer, U. S. ship Hartford, of New York City; and A. Mack, of the U. S. ship of war Brooklyn. Greenwood was struck blind by the intense heat of the fires in the fireroom while in search of the privateer Tallahassee; Dunphy had both arms carried away

## NAVAL EXPLOITS, CHASES, ESCAPES, PRIZES, ETC.

above the elbows by a shell from the ram Tennessee, in the engagement in Mobile Bay; and Mack lost his left arm during the engagement with the same vessel. The visitors to the Fair were very generous to these brave and shattered heroes, handing

Light House at Fort Morgan, Mobile Harbor.

them in all some hundreds of dollars. But, said the blind man of his friend, "He needs the money more than I do, and unless our friends distinctly state that what they give is to be equally divided, I take care that he has the whole." What words —other than that it is just like Jack—can do justice to such a generous spirit!

### Admiral Porter's Big Scare.

The sham Monitor contrived by Admiral Porter, for a double purpose, proved, as is well known, a big scare. An old coal barge, picked up in the river, was the foundation to build on. It was constructed in twelve hours, of old boards, with old pork barrels piled on top of each other for a smoke-stack, and two old canoes for quarter boats. Her furnaces were built of mud, and only intended to make black smoke, and not steam.

On the eventful night of the 24th, at nine o'clock, heavy guns were heard about fifteen miles below. It was known that the rebels had nothing but light guns there, which could not be heard at any distance. So they thought it was the Indianola engaging the batteries at Carthage, fifteen miles below Vicksburg. Not knowing that Brown was in peril, the Monitor was now let loose. It was towed to within a couple of miles of the first battery and let go, when it was discovered by the dim light of the moon that Vicksburg was in a stew. Never did her batteries open with such a vim. The earth fairly trembled, and the shot flew thickly around the devoted Monitor, which returned no shot with her long wooden guns. The Monitor ran safely past all the batteries, though under a heavy fire for an hour, and drifted safely down to the lower mouth of the canal, where she was tucked into an eddy.

The rebels were completely deceived by her. As soon as they saw her by daylight they opened on her again with all the guns they could bring to bear, but without a shot hitting her to do any harm,—for the shot went at their convenience through one side and came out the other, without causing the vessel to sink, as she was full of water already. Our soldiers shouted and

Admiral Porter.

laughed like mad men; but the laugh was somewhat against them, when, at daylight, the ram Queen of the West was discovered lying at Warrenton; and the question at once arose, what had happened to the In-

362        THE BOOK OF ANECDOTES OF THE REBELLION.

dianola. That the two rams sunk her or captured her in the engagement they had heard the night before. One or two of the soldiers got the Monitor out in the stream, and let her go down on the ram Queen. All the forts hereupon began firing and signalizing, and as the Monitor approached her the ram turned tail and ran down the river as fast as she could go, the Monitor after her, making all the speed that was given her by a five-knot current.

tion just north of the town, opened upon her.

At first the aim was too high, and the balls passed over without doing any damage; but as the boat neared the batteries, it became more accurate, as the sound of the passing balls, growing sharper at every shot, plainly indicated.

In order to attack the upper batteries it was necessary to drop below them, and round-to, with the head up stream. This

Before Vicksburg.

**Sunk, with the Stars and Stripes still Waving.**

On the 26th of May, 1863, it was determined to make an attack upon the rebel batteries to the north of Vicksburg, and opposite General Steele's column. The gunboat Cincinnati, Lieutenant Bache, was to co-operate and attempt to silence the water-batteries, previous to the assault from the land side. Accordingly, a little after eight in the morning, she commenced dropping down below Young's Point. When about two miles from Vicksburg, the famous gun, 'Whistling Dick,' in posi-

position was a most unfortunate one, as it exposed the vessel to a raking fire, from one battery in front, and another from behind. The first shot which struck her, hit the iron plating, and did no material damage. But the Captain had given orders to push up to within three hundred yards, and by the time she had reached that proximity, the shot hit her with fearful accuracy, generally passing directly through her port-holes.

One battery, which fired from an elevation and at some distance, threw plunging shot, which went through her upper deck, and did great damage. Lieutenant Sokalski, of General Steele's staff, who had been sent to point out the position to be taken in the assault, stated that when Lieutenant Bache and two others beside himself, were standing in the pilot-house, one of these plunging balls entered the port-hole of the pilot-house, passed through the thigh of the pilot, and then sheered down through the floor on the gun-deck, at the same time breaking the wheel, and wounding another man through the hand and arm, with the splinters. Lifting the hatchway and rushing down the gun-deck, Lieutenant Sokalski found it filled with the mangled and dead. It was a slaughter-pen. Blood and fragments of bodies, shot away, were scattered over the floor.

It was discovered that one ball had passed through the boat below the water-line, and that the boat was sinking. It was evident that to continue the fight longer would be to throw away the lives of the crew, and orders were given to start up the river as fast as possible. Lieutenant Starr, who was second in command, went to the pilot-house and directed movements as best he could with a broken wheel and sinking craft. In the meantime she was riddled by shot after shot, and was fast sinking. For three-quarters of an hour she was toiling, crippled, up stream; while the enemy, seeing her condition, redoubled the fury of the cannonading. More than fifty shots struck her before she reached the shore. But Lieutenant Bache refused to allow the colors to be lowered, and she sunk, like the Cumberland, with the Stars and Stripes still waving.

### Man of Experience—Sure.

Lewis A. Horton, of Plainfield, Connecticut, may be set down as a man of 'experience' during the war. At the breaking out of the rebellion, he enlisted in the navy, and was wrecked on the Bahamas. He afterwards undertook to take a prize into port, but was himself taken and confined in the Libby. When he was exchanged, he went on board the ship that was to tow the Monitor to Charleston, and when that vessel went down, he, while attempting to rescue the crew, was drifted off into the gulf, and was not picked up till the next day. Afterward, while firing a salute at St. Domingo, both his arms were blown off by the explosion of a gun; and "last of all"—and, it is to be hoped, the safest of his many risks—he *got married*. But further, the tale readeth not.

### Pleasant Hoax all Round.

After the battle between the Kearsage and Alabama, there was great excitement in Liverpool at the expected arrival there of Captain Semmes, and for several hours the neighborhood of the Exchange was crowded with persons anxious to get at least a glimpse of the famous sea raider.

About one o'clock, a double hoax was played in a highly successful manner. A

Pleasant Hoax all Round.

middle aged man, who had passed several years in tropical climates, and delighted in sporting a white blouse and a Panama hat during summer time, was often to be found lounging about one of the landing stages, having some connexion with shipping. Possessing a bronzed complexion, clean shaved cheeks and chin, and a pair of fierce mustaches, some mad wag conceived the idea of palming him off upon the public as "Captain Raphael Semmes, Confederate States Navy." Accordingly he was got hold of, treated very hospitably, and then asked to go on 'Change, in order to see the redoubtable hero of the Sunday's sea-fight arrive. One or two outdoor officials connected with the Underwriter's room were also got in tow, and under some rather nonplussed at first; but readily catering the drift of the joke, he raised his straw hat, 'bobbed around,' and by his extemporized gracious demeanor, after the manner of 'lions,' raised the enthusiasm to fever heat, —a special cheer rewarding a reverential obeisance that he made on passing Nelson's monument. He disappeared, not at the main entrance to the newsroom, but at the foot of the stairs leading to the Underwriter's room, and in a little time it leaked

Wreck of the Iron Clad Monitor.

pretence or other the fictitious Captain Semmes was taken through Brown's buildings, where the Southern Club's headquarters were, and was then brought out at the entrance which abuts on the Exchange flags.

This ruse was quite enough. Coming from such a neighborhood, followed by the Underwriter's officials, and making across the flags in the direction of the newsroom, the expectant crowd at once made up their minds that this was the man they were on the lookout for, and they clapped their hands, waved their hats and caps, and cheered vociferously.

The object of all this demonstration was out that the public had been hoaxed, that the object of their ovation was not Captain Semmes at all, but a 'highly respectable' sailor's boarding-house keeper, living in Leeds street, of the name of ———. But never mind, if he is allowed to be nameless.

#### Scared before being Hurt.

The commanders of the great Burnside expedition, on reaching the Southern coast, had to apply themselves very busily to obtain guides and pilots from among the loyal natives inhabiting that region. They had about a dozen of these chaps, from time to time, in the lower cabin of the Commodore's ship, calling them up one after another and disposing of them according to circumstances. They were decidedly as hard looking a set of men as could be gathered together. Their conversation was very amusing. They were all strong Union men, but none of them were willing to enter the service. A fellow was called up who had been recommended for his knowledge of Croatian Sound, when the following conversation transpired:

*Commodore.*—Well, Sir, they say you know something about this Sound.

*North Carolinian.*—Well, yes, mebbe four or five years ago I had a smart knowledge of that strip of water, Sir.

*Com.*—How much water (pointing to the chart) is there on this shoal?

*N. C.*—Wal, I reck'n there's a right smart chance of water there, Sir.

*Com.*—Did you pilot boats up and down the Sound?

*N. C.*—Wal, yes; I reck'n I've driv a few flat-boats up thar, Sir.

*Com.*—Can you give us assistance in pointing out the safest way to get up there?

*N. C.*—Wal, I reck'n I could help you a right small chance, Sir.

*Com.*—Well, then, we want you.

*N. C.*—But, yer honor, I rather wouldn't, Sir.

*Com.*—What! don't you want to serve your country?

*N. C.*—Wal, yes, but the old woman and young 'uns have got powerful little to live on, Sir.

*Com.*—But we will pay you good wages.

*N. C.*—And I haven't anything but these ragged, yeller old sou'-westers, Sir,— (pointing to his clothes.)

*Com.*—And will give you good clothes.

*N. C.*—B-b-b-but ——

*Com.*—But what, Sir?

*N. C.*—Wal, you see, yer honor, you see, that mebbe ef you shouldn't get up thar, them ar secesshers would use me powerful bad, Sir!

The 'devoted Union man' was dismissed, with orders to hold himself ready to lend a 'right smart chance' of aid to the expedition—probably preferring, however, a chance of picking up the expedition in pieces on the coast, that being the chief business of himself and co-loyalists.

### Clinging to the Guns.

The scenes on board the Cumberland, when she went down, were almost past description. There was scarcely an instance in the war of more desperate and devoted spirit. Two of the gunners at the bow guns, when the ship was sinking, clasped their guns in their arms, and would not be removed, but went down embracing them. One gunner had both his legs shot away, and his bowels open and protruding, but he made three steps on his raw and bloody thighs, seized the lanyard and fired his gun, falling back dead. Another lost both arms and legs, yet lived, and when they would assist him, cried out, "Back to your gun, boys! Give 'em —! Hurrah for the flag!" He lived till she sunk.

### Combat between the Kearsarge and the Alabama.

No volume of reminiscences of the war of the rebellion would be complete without an account of the memorable naval com-

Captain John A. Winslow.

bat between the United States steamship Kearsarge, Captain John A. Winslow, and the Confederate privateer Alabama, Captain Raphael Semmes, on the morning of June 19th, 1864, off Cherbourg, France.

The Kearsarge was lying at Flushing, Holland, when a telegram came from Mr. Dayton, the American Minister in Paris, stating that the Alabama had arrived at Cherbourg. The Kearsarge immediately put to sea, and arrived at Cherbourg in quick time, taking the Alabama quite by surprise by so sudden an appearance on her track. Through the Consular Agent there, a sort of challenge was received by Captain Winslow from Captain Semmes, the latter stating that if the Kearsarge remained off the port he would come out and fight her,—and that he would not detain the vessel long.

After cruising off the port for five days, until the 19th of June, Captain Winslow at twenty minutes after ten o'clock descried the starry ensign of the Alabama floating in the breeze, as she came boldly out of the western entrance, under the escort of the French iron-clad Couronne. The latter retired into port after seeing the combatants outside of French waters. Captain Winslow had previously had an interview with the Admiral of Cherbourg, assuring him that, in the event of an action occurring with the Alabama, the position of the ships should be so far off shore that no question would be advanced about the line of jurisdiction.

The Alabama came down at full speed until within a distance of about three-quarters of a mile, when she opened her guns upon the Kearsarge. The Kearsarge made no reply for some minutes, but ranged up nearer, and then opened her starboard battery, fighting six guns, and leaving only one thirty-two pounder idle. The Alabama fought seven guns, working them with the greatest rapidity, sending shot and shell in a constant stream over her adversary. Both vessels used their starboard batteries, the ships being manœuvered in a circle about each other at a distance of from five hundred to one thousand yards. Seven complete circles were made during the action, which lasted a little over one hour. At the last of the action, when the Alabama would have made off, she was near five miles from the shore; and, had the action continued from the first in parallel lines, with her head in shore, the line of jurisdiction would, no doubt, have been reached. From the first, the firing of the Alabama was rapid and wild; toward the close of the action her firing became better. The Kearsarge gunners, who had been cautioned against firing rapidly, without direct aim, were much more deliberate; and the instructions given to point the heavy guns below rather than above the water line, and clear the deck with lighter ones, was fully observed.

Captain Winslow had endeavored, with a port helm, to close in with the Alabama; but it was not until just before the close of the action that he was in position to use grape. This was avoided, however, by the Alabama's surrender. The effect of the training of the Kearsarge's men was evident; nearly every shot from their guns told fearfully on the Alabama, and on the seventh rotation in the circular track she winded, setting fore-trysail and two jibs, with head in shore. Her speed was now retarded, and by winding her port broadside was presented to the Kearsarge, with only two guns bearing, not having been able to shift over but one. Captain Winslow now saw that she was at his mercy, and a few more guns, well directed, brought down her flag, though it was difficult to ascertain whether it had been hauled down or shot away; but a white flag having been displayed over the stern, the fire of the Kearsarge was reserved.

Two minutes had not more than elapsed before the Alabama again opened fire on the Kearsarge, with the two guns on the port side. This drew Captain Winslow's fire again, and the Kearsarge was immediately steamed ahead and laid across her bows for raking. The white flag was still flying, and the Kearsarge's fire was again

## NAVAL EXPLOITS, CHASES, ESCAPES, PRIZES, ETC. 367

reserved. Shortly after this, her boats were to be seen lowering, and an officer in one of them came alongside and stated that the ship had surrendered, and was fast sinking. In twenty minutes from this time the Alabama went down, her mainmast, which had been shot, breaking near the head as she sunk, and her bow rising high out of the water, as her stern rapidly settled.

### Admiral Foote's Terms to General Tilghman.

When the surrender of Fort Henry was found to be no longer avoidable, General Tilghman had an interview with Admiral Foote, having been conveyed to the latter's ship for this purpose. Hoping to

Admiral A. H. Foote.

render his doom a little softer and more bearable, the rebel chieftain desired to be informed what terms of capitulation would be allowed. "Unconditional surrender," laconically responded the fearless Admiral.

"Well, Sir," said General Tilghman, "if I must surrender, it gives me pleasure to surrender to so brave an officer as you."

"You do perfectly right to surrender," answered the Admiral; "but I should not have surrendered to you on any condition."

"Why so? I do not understand you."

"Because I was fully determined to capture the fort, or go to the bottom."

### Exploits of the "French Lady."

The seizure of the steamer St. Nicholas, in Chesapeake Bay, was a successful rebel exploit, accomplished by means of a clever ruse, in the enactment of which the female sex was made a convenient scapegoat.

The St. Nicholas, Captain Jacob Kirwan, left Baltimore one Friday morning in June, 1861, having on board about forty-five passengers. Among those who went aboard the boat previous to her departure, was a very respectable "French Lady," who was heavily veiled, and, pleading indisposition, she was immediately shown to her state room. There was also a party of about twenty-five men dressed in the garb of mechanics, carrying with them carpenters', tinners', blacksmiths', and other tools.

At the usual hour the boat left for Point Lookout, and other points on the Potomac River, and every thing passed off as usual until the boat arrived at Point Lookout, on Saturday morning.

When near the latter place, the 'French Lady' appeared on deck, not in crinoline, but in the person of a stalwart man, who was immediately surrounded by the party of mechanics above named. Captain Kirwan demanded an explanation, when the 'lady-man' coolly informed him that he designed confiscating the steamer and going on a privateering expedition. Finding himself overpowered, Captain Kirwan was compelled to submit quietly, and the boat was formally handed over to the man and his crew, who took possession, and proceeded to run the steamer to a point known as 'The Cone,' on the Virginia shore.

Upon landing at 'The Cone,' the steamer was boarded by about one thousand Virginia troops, when the passengers were all landed and allowed to go on their way unmolested. About one hundred and fifty of the troops were then placed on board the steamer, Captain Kirwan and fourteen of the crew being detained as prisoners. Her subsequent success in taking prizes, under her 'new Captain,' is well-known.

It is satisfactory to record that this "artful dodger," variously known as Colonel Richard Thomas, Zouave, and the 'French Lady,' was caught in a second attempt. Having returned to Maryland, he took passage on board the steamer May Washington, bound to Baltimore, but was detected before he was able to carry out his purpose of capturing her. He strove to outface his captors by a protest against the invasion of his rights as a passenger. This failing, he escaped from those who had seized him, and tried to hide himself from further pursuit by taking to a chest of drawers. He was, however, dragged out, and securely held until the arrival of the vessel at Baltimore, when he was thrust into Fort McHenry.

#### Just like Jack.

In the explosion on the gunboat Essex at Fort Henry, one of the noble-hearted seamen was most shockingly scalded. His clothing was at once removed, linseed oil and flour applied to his parboiled flesh, and he was carefully wrapped in blankets and placed in bed. A few moments after, the news came that the rebel flag was struck and the fort surrendered. In his enthusiasm, and notwithstanding his awful condition, Jack sprang out of his berth, ran up on deck, and waved his blanket in the air, huzzaring for the Stars and Stripes. The poor fellow, after the first excitement was over, was assisted below, and in the night he died, full of rejoicing to the last, at the triumph of the old flag.

#### Blue-jacket on the Quarter-deck of his Mule.

On the capture of Morris Island by Gillmore's gallant army, the whole mass of men was thoroughly pervaded by that feeling of hilarity that follows a quickly successful engagement — soldiers shouting, singing, happy. The sturdy Jack Tars, in quest of adventure or abandoned "toot," doing and saying as only they can when thoroughly buoyant in spirit, came upon the subject of the following yarn:

A bronzed blue-jacket had captured a mule, and, not without difficulty, mounted

Blue-jacket on the quarter-deck of his mule.

it, perching himself as near the animal's tail as there was a shadow of a chance — the mule objecting in every known way of a mule, and in some ways until then unexhibited.

"Jack, sit more amidships," said Hardy, the first engineer of the Weehawken, "and you'll ride easier."

"Captain," quoth old Salty, "this is the first craft I was ever in command of, and it is a pity if I can't stay on the *quarterdeck*."

#### Umbrellas in Military Service.

"Are you going to keep that poor soldier out there in the rain all night?" said Captain C's wife to her husband, on seeing a sentinel on duty in the rain.

When it was understood who she meant it was explained to her that it was necessary to do so; but that he didn't have to remain there all the time, being relieved by two others in turn. But she didn't seem quite satisfied, and presently asked again —

"Couldn't you let him come in on the boat and stand under shelter?"

This proposition was necessarily negatived, and her innocent solicitude on account of the presumed hardship to that "poor soldier" became so apparent as to cause a smile among the listeners. A short silence followed, during which it was evident she was devising in her tender little heart some scheme for his relief, when suddenly a bright idea seemed to have struck her, and looking up into her husband's face with a countenance full of anxious hope, she said—

"Dear, couldn't you lend him your umbrella?"

### Pleasant little Trade.

A little trading used to go on between the blockading fleets and the coast, notwithstanding the vigilance of the rebel authorities,—as the following note sent from a feminine 'rebel' to one of the ships off Charleston will show:

"Madame L. G—— sends her compliments to the officers of the United States man-of-war, now anchored off the harbor. If they are agreeable, she will exchange all sorts of garden vegetables for ice."

Although the Union stock of frozen water was very short, two pailsful of the best "Rockland Lake" went to the lady,

"And blest forever is she who relied
On northern honor and northern pride."

### River Steamers and Yankee Pilots.

The Captain of one of the Mississippi river steamers one morning, while his boat was lying at her moorings at New Orleans, waiting for the tardy pilot, who, it appears, was a rather uncertain sort of fellow, saw a tall, gaunt Yankee make his appearance before the Captain's office, and sung out—

"Hello, Cap'n! you don't want a pilot, nor nothin' about this 'ere craft, do ye?"

"How do you know I don't?" responded the Captain.

"Oh, you don't understand; I axed you s'posin' you did?"

"Then, supposing I do, what of it?"

"Well," said the Yankee. "I reckon I know suthin' about that ere sort of business, provided you wanted a feller of jest about my size."

The Captain gave him a scrutinizing glance, and with an expression of countenance which seemed to say, "I should pity the steamer that you piloted," asked—

"Are you acquainted with the river, and do you know where the snags are?"

"Well, ye-as," responded the Yankee, rather hesitatingly, "I'm pretty well acquainted with the river, but the snags, I don't know exactly so much about them."

"Don't know about the snags?" exclaimed the Captain contemptuously, "don't know about the snags! you'd make a pretty pilot!"

At this the Yankee's countenance assumed anything but an angelic expression, and with a darkened brow and a fiercely flashing eye, he drew himself up to his full heighth, and indignantly roared back in a voice of thunder:

"What do I want to know where the snags are for, old sea-hoss? I know where they ain't, and there's where I do my sailing!"

It is sufficient to know that the Yankee was promptly engaged, proving himself, according to the Captain's report, one of the best.

### Farragut when a Midshipman.

Whatever relates to the career of Admiral Farragut possesses a value to every loyal reader. The following anecdote is therefore given, as illustrating the connection between the twig and the tree. When only nine years old, little David determined to be a sailor, and was taken by Commodore Porter on board the Essex as a midshipman. He shared the fortunes of that historic craft in her memorable cruises in the Pacific, and took part in the battle of Valparaiso.

While that famous contest was at its height, he was ordered by the Commodore to go below and bring up some friction-tubes, that were needed for the guns. While descending the ward-room ladder, the captain of the gun directly opposite was struck full upon the face by an 18-pounder shot. He fell back against Farragut, and they both tumbled down the hatchway. The man was a stout, heavy fellow, and it was fortunate for the young midshipman that his full weight did not fall upon him as they reached the deck. As it was, the lad was severely stunned; and recovering, as if awakening from a dream, he ran up on deck. Commodore Porter, seeing him covered with blood, inquired,—

"Are you wounded?"

"I believe not," was the reply.

"Then where are the tubes?"

The words brought him to his senses, and he immediately went below and got them.

When the brave little brig was surrendered, Farragut sobbed like a child, to see the American colors hauled down. From this heavy grief he was soon aroused, however, by hearing an English middy exultingly shout to his men, "Prize-oh, boys! here's a fine grunter, by Jove!" He knew the young reefer alluded to a young porker that had been petted by himself and all the sailors, and had helped to beguile away many a weary hour; therefore he energetically laid claim to the animal.

"But," said the Englishmen, "you're a prisoner, and your pig, too."

"We always respect private property,' said Farragut, and he seized the squealing bone of contention, asserting that he should retain possession until compelled to yield to superior force. Here was sport for the older officers, who called out,—

"Go it, little Yankee; and if you can thrash 'Shorty' (a *sobriquet* for English middies) you shall have your pig."

"Agreed!" said Farragut; and the lads went at it in pugilistic style. 'Shorty' soon failed to come to time, and the victor walked off with piggy under his arm. He afterward remarked that he felt, in mastering the young Englishman, that he had wiped out the disgrace of being captured.

### Death Smiling in Victory's Embrace.

Orderly Sergeant C. H. Plummer, of the 51st N. Y., was on the gunboat Pioneer, mortally sick with typhoid fever, at the time of the Burnside Expedition battle, North Carolina. Late in the evening a boat came off from the shore, and the news of our success was told. Plummer, whose life was just hanging in the balance, turned to the chaplain and asked, "Is our side winning?" On being told that it was, he smiled, gasped out the words "Thank God!" and died. This brave man's real name was Charles Plummer Tidd, and he was one of those famous nineteen men who undertook to capture Virginia, under John Brown.

### "Dem Rotten Shell."

An officer in the Mississippi fleet is authority for the following: After the battle and capture of Forts Henry and Donelson, the fleet were lying at Cairo. The prisoners were passing the fleet, and among them there was a contraband, an old servant of one of the officers. In passing the 'Essex' he shook his head, and remarked, "I doesn't like dat one-pipe boat, for when she cum along and throwed dem rotten shell ob hers we couldn't stan' it no longer; den massa run, and after dat I left, too!" Just previous to the battle I had filled my shells with an incendiary matter of my own invention, which had not the most agreeable *smell*, and hence the old darkey's remark. I used the same shell on my attack and destruction of the Arkansas.

### Sailing into the Jaws of the Mohican.

One day Lieutenant Howe, while in command of the Tuscaloosa, learnt that the Federal gunboat Mohican was "somewhere about," lying in wait for him, and he received a particular description of her

## NAVAL EXPLOITS, CHASES, ESCAPES, PRIZES, ETC.

rig and general appearance Next day his masthead look-out reported a steamer in sight to leeward. The Tuscaloosa held on her course until her commander was near enough to make out sufficient of the hull and rigging of the distant craft to find that he was pleasantly sailing into the jaws of the Mohican. Of course he immediately ran up in the wind and made as long a leg as possible, had the precious good fortune not to be observed, and having a handy, smart sailing craft under him, was soon out of sight and of danger,—the reward of unsleeping wariness.

### Billiards on board the Ironsides.

The gunners on the Ironsides at Morris Island had a neat way of exploding their projectiles within the fort. It was impossible to drive them through the sand and cotton of which the work was made, nor could the guns be so elevated as to toss them in as from a mortar. So the pieces were depressed, and the shot, striking the water about fifty yards from the beach, jumped in. In nearly every instance this manner of making the missiles effective was successful. "Those are what I call billiards," said the Captain, watching the firing, "they carom on the bay and beach and pocket the ball in the fort every time!"

### Sinking the Albemarle Ram in the Bottom of the Roanoke.

To Lieutenant William B. Cushing, a young officer of great bravery, coolness and resources, was due the sinking of the ram Albemarle to the bottom of Roanoke River. He submitted a project to Admiral Lee, in June, 1864, in conjunction with Admiral Gregory, Captain Boggs and Chief Engineer William W. Wood, and having arranged one of the new steam picket boats (of about the size of a frigate's launch) with a torpedo, took her down the Sound for duty, at first making due reconnoissances.

At about midnight, the little picket boat entered the narrow river, and steamed cautiously and silently up without giving the least alarm. The Southfield, and three schooners alongside of her engaged in raising her up, were passed, almost within biscuit toss, without a challenge or hail. It was not until Lieutenant Cushing reached within pistol shot of the Albemarle, which lay alongside the dock at Plymouth, that he was hailed, and then in an uncertain sort of a way, as though the lookouts doubted the accuracy of their vision. He made no reply, but continued to press towards the great monster, and was for the second time hailed. He paid no attention to the challenge, but kept straight on his way, first detaching the Shamrock's cutter to go below and secure the Confederate pickets on the Southfield.

In another instant, as he closed in on the ram, her Captain, Walley, in a very dignified, pompous and studied manner, shouted, "What boat is that?" The reply was an invitation for him to go to —! Thereupon arose a terrible clamor. The rattle was vigorously sprung, the bells on the ship were sharply rung, and all hands

Lieut. Cushing's Great Exploit.

were called to quarters, evidently in the greatest consternation.

A musketry fire was immediately opened upon the torpedo boat, and a charge of canister fired, injuring some of the crew.

Along the dock to which the Albemarle was tied were a large number of soldiers, evidently stationed there to guard against the landing of any Federal force after a surprise. And in front of their lines blazed cheerily up a number of camp-fires, which threw a strong light upon the Albemarle and the bosom of the river. By the aid of this glare, Lieutenant Cushing discovered the pier of floating timbers which surrounded the ram on the accessible sides, to guard against the approach of rams and torpedoes. By the aid of the same light he plainly saw a large body of soldiers thronging to the wharf and blazing away at his boat. To quiet these fellows he brought the bow of his boat around a little, and discharged a heavy stand of canister into them from his twelve-pounder howitzer mounted at the bow, and sent them flying. Making a complete circle, under a scorching musketry fire at less than thirty yards, he came around, bow on, at full steam, and struck the floating guard of timbers, pressing them in towards the ram. His boat soon lost headway, and came to a stand-still, refusing to back off or move ahead.

*The moment for decisive action had now arrived.*

The enemy fired muskets and pistols almost in Cushing's face from the ports of the ram, and from the hundred small arms on shore. Several of his men were injured, and Paymaster Swan had fallen severely wounded. The officers and crew of the Albemarle cried out, "Now we've got him; surrender, surrender, or we will blow you to pieces." The case looked desperate indeed; but Lieutenant Cushing was as cool and determined at the moment as one could be under the most agreeable circumstances. He knew that the moment of all moments had come, and he did not allow it to glide from his hands. Seizing the lanyard to the torpedo and the line of the spar, and crowding the spar until he had brought the torpedo under the overhang of the Albemarle, he detached it by one effort, and the next second he pulled the lanyard of the torpedo and exploded it fairly under the vessel on her port side, just below the porthole of the two hundred pounder Brooke's rifle, which at that moment was discharged at the boat. An immense volume of water was thrown out by the explosion of the torpedo, almost drowning all in the boat, and, to add to the peril of the moment, the heavy shell from the enemy's gun had gone crashing through the bottom of the boat, knocking the splinters about in a terrible style.

She at once began to sink in the most rapid manner, and Lieutenant Cushing ordered all hands to save themselves as best they might.

Cushing divested himself of his coat and shoes, and plunged into the river, followed by those of his men who were able to do so. All struck for the middle of the river, under a hot fire of musketry, the balls penetrating their clothing and striking all about them. The rebels took to boats and pushed after the survivors, demanding their surrender. Many gave up. Lieutenant Cushing swam down the river half a mile, until, exhausted and chilled by the cold water, he was compelled to struggle to the shore, which he reached about daylight. After lying in the weeds along the river bank for some time, he recovered his strength sufficiently to crawl into the swamp farther, till daylight found him lying in the swamp grass, between two paths and in speaking distance of the enemy's fort. While thus only partially screened by the low sedge, he saw some rebel officers and men walk by, and heard their conversation, which was entirely devoted to the affairs of the morning. From their remarks he learned that the torpedo had done its work effectively and thoroughly, and that his great object was accomplished. A short time after, he luckily discovered a skiff, and in this succeeded in reaching the squadron which lay twelve miles distant.

### Lucky Moment on Board the Sumter.

One of the officers of the privateer Sumter gives the following account, in his private journal, of an hour of trepidation on board that craft,—with a little 'brag' to boot. Under date of August 18, 1861, he writes:—After leaving Cayenne the vessel's course was shaped for Paramaribo, Dutch Guiana, off which port she signaled for a pilot until sundown; none having arrived at that hour she came to anchor. About twilight a sail was seen in the distance approaching the Sumter. It was soon apparent that she was a steam war-vessel. Steam was raised, the anchor hove up, all hands beat to quarters, the guns manned, the old charges drawn and fresh ones put in their places. By the time all these preliminaries had been arranged it was ascertained by the aid of the night telescope, that the strange vessel had anchored. The Sumter followed suit, but a vigilant look-out was kept upon the movements of the supposed enemy.

Early on the morning of the 19th, the look-outs had reported that the steamer outside was under way. Slowly she steamed toward the Sumter, seeming to have made every preparation for attack. She had not yet hoisted her flag, neither had the Sumter—each commander being apparently desirous of learning the nationality of the other first, and of letting him know, by a death-dealing broadside, that an enemy was at hand. The stranger looked like an American-built vessel, having long mast-heads and a sharp overhanging bow. Yes, there was no mistaking her—she must be one of the gunboats sent in search of the Sumter. When she was near enough for the number of her guns to be determined, we were glad to find that she carried but one gun more than the Sumter, and that the disparity was no greater. Slowly and cautiously the vessels neared each other. When not more than a cable's length off, our first Lieutenant hailed her in a loud voice—

"Ship ahoy!"
"Hallo!" was promptly answered.
"This is the Confederate States steamer *Sumter*—what vessel is that?"

After waiting about half a minute, which seemed an age, the 'enemy' replied—

"The French steamer *Abbeville!*"

Here was a disappointment—after all this preparation for mortal combat, to find at last that the supposed enemy was a friend! There was not a single man who would not freely have relinquished all the prize-money then due to him could he have transformed the Frenchman into a Yankee. She was nearer the equal of the Sumter than they ever expected to meet again, and the Sumter had captured so many merchantmen that it might be said she did not care to meet any other class of vessels."

The advantage to the Sumter of meeting one so 'nearly her equal' may be judged of by the good luck which befel the Alabama in her encounter with the Kearsarge, where the 'equality' was nearer still!

### Presentation to a Brave Woman.

On the evening of the fifth February, 1862, at Cape Girardeau, Captain Ben Sousley, in behalf of the Alton Packet Company, presented to the loyal and heroic Mrs. Eversol, the sum of two hundred dollars, in acknowledgment of her courage, humanity and patriotism, in having saved the passengers of the steamboat City of Alton from being captured by Jeff. Thompson's marauding band of Confederates. As that boat was approaching the shore where the secessionists waited to seize her, Mrs. Eversol ran to the levee, and by her shoutings and gesticulations warned those on board of the danger, and enabled them to escape. The handsome testimonial to her merit was richly deserved, but a richer one is assured to her in the memories of her countrymen and countrywomen, for such an unusual, brave, hazardous, and fortunate act.

Captain Sousley subsequently received from Mrs. Eversol the following appropriate note:—

COMMERCE. MO., February 5th.

J. J. Mitchell, President Alton Packet Company: DEAR SIR; Permit me, through you, to tender to the members of your Company my thanks for the unmerited token of respect which they were pleased to convey to me through the hands of Captain Sousley, and received by me to-day. In reply to their earnest solicitations to visit St. Louis and Alton, allow me to say that I would be most happy to do so when the weather and traveling are pleasant; although I would again assure them, that, in any part I may have taken on the twenty-ninth day of December, in the preservation of the lives of my fellow-beings and their property, I only obeyed the impulse of a loyal heart.

With my kindest wishes for the prosperity and happiness of the members of your Company and yourself, I remain yours, respectfully,

SARAH L. EVERSOL.

**Laconic Hint to a Pilot by General Butler.**

General Butler one day sent a man of the name of Curtis, who had been a pilot on the James river, and who professed to know the position of the torpedoes, to Admiral Lee, with the characteristic suggestion: "If he faithfully and truly performs his duty, and answers all queries, return him to me at Bermuda Landing; if not, hang him at the yard-arm." This was dictated in the presence of Curtis, to whom the General then remarked: "Now, my good man, go; you have your life in your own hands." The individual certainly seemed to realize the fact as thus laconically stated.

**Another Cassabianca.**

In an account, by a Confederate prisoner who participated in the affair, of the capture of the U. S. ship Harriet Lane, the following interesting incident is g'ven, as we find it in the papers:—Almost the first men struck down were the gallant Captain Wainwright and Lieutenant Lee, who both fought with a desperation and valor no mortal could surpass. Though bleeding and prostrate upon the deck, they were seen to still continue to deal death among their enemies. One young son of

Another Cassabianca.

Captain Wainwright—only ten years old!—stood at the cabin door, a revolver in each hand, and never ceased firing until he had expended every shot. One of his poor little hands became disabled by a ball, shattering his four fingers, and then his infantile soul gave way: he burst into tears, and cried—"Do you want to kill me?" Blessed young hero—may his country never forget him! And where is the Hemans to wed his name to immortal verse, like another Cassabianca, or the artist to portray the scene on historic canvas?

**Devotion of Farragut's Men to their Admiral.**

After the flagship Hartford, with the brave Farragut, had hauled off from her first fierce assault upon the rebel flagship Tennessee, in Mobile Bay, and as she was again pointed fair for her, and thunderingly coming down upon her to dash into her a second time—suddenly, to the surprise of all, she was herself tremendously struck by one of our own heavy vessels, also heavily coming down upon the rebel Admiral, and it was thought for a brief moment, so fearful was the blow, she must go down. Immediately, and high above the din of battle, hoarse, anxious voices were heard crying,

"*The Admiral! the Admiral! save the Admiral! Get the Admiral out of the ship!*"

The brave men utterly forgot themselves—thought not a moment of their own safety, but only of their glorious old Admiral, who was all in all to them! Nothing could better illustrate the love and devotion of the whole squadron for their Admiral than this. When they themselves were in imminent peril of death, they only cared for him! Finding the vessel would float, notwithstanding the possible ultimate serious results, the brave old Admiral turned to his gallant fleet Captain with the order—

"*Go on with speed! Ram her again!*"

Onward the Hartford sped, determined to 'do and die,' if need be; but just before she reached her the white flag of surrender was hoisted above the discomfited Tennessee, and soon all the victory was with Farragut and his noble men.

### Pictorial Humors of the War.

The benefit of having one's picture in *Harper* is thus illustrated in an amusing account given by a naval officer: A few days ago I was standing on the steps of one of the hotels of this city, (New York,) when several boys applied to black my boots, with the well-known cry of "Black yer boots, Sir? Shine them up!" etc. One little fellow had a very dirty face, and I told him if he would wash it he should black my boots. "What will you give me to do it?" was the prompt reply. "Five cents," I said. He hesitated for a moment, and then asked, "Who will stand your security?" I applied to each boy, and all refused with the exception of one little ragged fellow, who, after steadily looking at me for some time, suddenly exclaimed, "I'll stand! I've seen that chap's picter in *Harper!*" The boy's face was washed and my boots cleaned.

Pictorial humors of the war.

The beauty, accuracy and profusion of pictorial illustrations of the scenes and heroes of the war, afforded in the pages of the above named and kindred serials, have constituted one of the most marked facts in its history.

### Seeking a Naval Appointment.

Mr. —— was an applicant for an official berth in the navy, and, as usual, permission was granted by the Secretary of the Navy to him to be examined for the position to which he aspired. He presented himself in due form before the Examining Board, and was duly "put through" by the venerable members. At last the final question was put:

"Now, Sir, your vessel being anchored in New York harbor, how would you proceed if ordered to take her to Key West?"

The aspirant proceeded, by aid of chart, rule, and compass, to show to the attentive Board the courses he would steer, etc., and, at the end of a long (imaginary) voyage, brought his charge safely into Key

West harbor. The member who had asked the question astonished the would-be Ensign by requesting him to recommence his voyage, as he would never get to Key West in the manner he had just tried. The long description was again gone through with, the same as before, and at

Secretary Welles.

its close Mr. —— looked triumphantly at the querist, who shook his head, smiled, and said:

"Well, Sir, that is precisely your previous voyage; and again I must say that you could by no possibility arrive at Key West, in the way you describe, *until you had heaved up your anchor in the harbor of New York.*"

Suffice to say, the little omission was overlooked, and Mr. —— was soon in the full enjoyment of his honors as an Ensign, often relating the above as a good joke.

#### Bailey's Dam for Saving the Mississippi Squadron.

Immediately after the Union army received its check at Sabine cross-roads, and the retreat commenced, Colonel Bailey, engineer of the Nineteenth Corps, learned that the Red River was rapidly falling, and became assured that by the time Admiral Porter's fleet could reach Alexandria, there would not be sufficient water to float the gunboats over the Alexandria Falls. It was evident, therefore, that they were in imminent danger. Colonel Bailey, believing that their capture or destruction would involve the destruction of the Union army, the blockade of the Mississippi, and even greater disaster, proposed to Major-General Franklin, on the 9th of April, 1864, previous to the battle of Pleasant Hill, to increase the depth of the water by means of a dam, and submitted to him a plan of the same, which was approved.

General Banks placed at the disposal of Colonel Bailey all the force he required, consisting of some three thousand men and two or three hundred wagons. All the neighboring steam-mills were torn down for material—two or three regiments of Maine men were set at work felling trees, teams were moving in all directions bringing in brick and stone, quarries were opened, flat-boats were built to bring stone down from above, and every man seemed to be working with unequaled vigor, probably not one in fifty believed in the success of the undertaking,—the falls being

Col. Bailey.

about a mile in length, filled with ragged rocks, and over which at the existing stage of water it seemed impossible to make a channel.

The work was commenced by running out from the left bank of the river a tree dam, made of the bodies of very large trees, brush, brick, and stone, cross-tied with heavy timber, and strengthened in every way which ingenuity could devise. This was run out about three hundred feet into the river; four large coal barges were then fitted with brick and sunk at the end of it. From the right bank of the river, cribs filled with stone were built out to meet the barges, all of which was successfully accomplished, notwithstanding there was a current running of nine miles an hour, threatening to sweep everything before it.

After eight days of hard labor it was found that one day more would raise the water sufficiently to enable all the vessels to pass the upper falls. Unfortunately, the pressure of the water became so great that it swept away two of the stone barges which swung in below the dam on one side. Seeing this, Admiral Porter jumped on a horse and rode up to where the upper vessels were anchored, and ordered the Lexington to pass the upper falls if possible, and immediately attempt to go through the dam,—thinking to save the four vessels below, and not knowing whether the persons employed on the work would ever have the heart to renew the enterprise.

The Lexington succeeded in getting over the upper falls just in time, the water rapidly falling as she was passing over. She then steered directly for the opening in the dam, through which the water was rushing so furiously that it seemed as if nothing but destruction awaited her. Thousands of beating hearts looked on, anxious for the result. The silence was so great as the Lexington approached the dam that a pin might almost have been heard to fall. She entered the gap with a full head of steam on, pitched down the roaring torrent, made two or three spasmodic rolls, hung for a moment on the rocks below, was then swept into deep water by the current, and rounded to safely into the bank.

Thirty thousand voices rose in one deafening cheer, and universal joy seemed to pervade the sea of faces there present.

The Neosho followed next — all her hatches battened down, and every precaution taken against accident. She did not fare so well as the Lexington, her pilot having become frightened as he approached the abyss, and stopped her engine, when a full head of steam had been particularly ordered. The result was that for a moment her hull disappeared from sight, under the water. Every one thought she was lost. She rose, however, swept along over the rocks with the current, and fortunately escaped with only one hole in her bottom, which was stopped in the course of an hour. The Hindman and Osage both came through beautifully without touching a thing, and the Admiral thought that if he was only fortunate to get the large vessels as well over the falls, his fleet would once more do good service on the Mississippi.

Colonel Bailey and his men set cheerfully to work to repair the damage, although they had been working for eight days and nights, up to their necks in water, in the broiling sun, cutting trees and wheeling bricks. The Admiral also made the best of the mishap, saying that it was on the whole very fortunate, as the two barges that were swept away from the centre swung around against some rocks on the left and made a fine cushion for the vessels, preventing them, as it afterward appeared, from running on certain destruction.

The force of the water and the current being too great to construct a continuous dam of six hundred feet across the river in so short a time, Colonel Bailey determined to leave a gap of fifty-five feet in the dam, and build a series of wing dams on the Upper Falls. This was accomplished in three days' time, and the Mound City, the Carondelet and Pittsburgh, came over the Upper Falls, a good deal of labor being necessary, however, to haul them through, the channel being very crooked, and scarcely wide enough for them. Other vessels followed these in safety. The passage of these vessels was a most beautiful sight, only to be realized by seeing. They passed over without an accident, except the unshipping of one or two rudders. The scene was witnessed by all the troops, and the vessels were heartily cheered as they went over. Next morning, at ten o'clock, the Louisville, Chillicothe, Ozark, and two tugs passed over without any accident except the loss of a man, who was swept off the deck of one of the tugs. By three o'clock that afternoon the vessels were all coaled, ammunition replaced, and all steamed down the river with the convoy of transports in company. A good deal of difficulty was anticipated in getting over the bars in Lower Red River, the depth of water reported being only five feet, while the gunboats were drawing six. But there was fortunately a rise from the back-water of the Mississippi—that river being very high just then,—the back-water extending to Alexandria, one hundred and fifty miles distant, enabling them to pass all the bars and obstructions with safety. Eight valuable gunboats were thus saved from destruction.

### His Favorite Flag for a Winding Sheet.

The brave Captain Rodgers, as if under a presentiment of what was awaiting him in the conflict soon to take place, the night before he was killed wrote a letter to his wife, which he left with his servant, to be handed to the Admiral in case any thing should happen to him. After his vessel, the Catskill, had moved up toward her fighting position, Captain Rodgers withdrew her from range, and taking a small boat, returned to the flag-ship to get a flag which he denominated as "his own flag." It was the one which he fought under, on the Catskill, in the April attack on Sumter; and, wishing praise for the same flag on the Catskill during the coming, he went to the flag-ship, secured it, and returning to the Catskill, again moved up into action, and in ten minutes was a corpse. Strange to say, his body wrapped up in that same flag, was conveyed on board the flag-ship, which but a few minutes before he had left with countenance smiling as was his wont.

### Farewell Scene among the Tars.

On the departure of Commodore Foote, of the Mississippi Flotilla, in 1862, on account of his impaired health, produced by too laborious service, a scene was presented which abundantly showed the strong hold which that gallant officer had upon the hearts of his brave and noble men. About three o'clock, the officers and crew of the flag-ship were assembled in one of the gunrooms, when the Commodore presented Captain Davis to them, assuring him that a more gallant crew never trod the deck of a ship. As the friend of his boyhood, manhood and age, he hoped the Captain would never forget that these sun-browned, weather-beaten tars, were also his friends, and that their best interests would always be near his heart. The old hero then took leave of his men in a few touching remarks, which brought tears to many an eye unaccustomed to weeping.

An hour later he hobbled on board the Cairo packet, De Soto, and seated himself on the guards of the boat, in full view of his men, who all crowded the decks of the flag-ship to see him off. The scene was affecting in the extreme. The Commodore was agitated and very nervous. He looked emaciated and worn, bit his fingernails, and frequently raised a palm-leaf fan to his face to conceal the briny drops which would force themselves, in spite of all he could do, from his sunken eyes and roll down his hollow cheeks. As the packet moved off, he rose to say a few farewell words, but the hissing of the steam prevented his being distinctly heard. There could only be caught such fragmentary sentences as "God bless you!" "You are engaged in a holy cause!" "I know you will succeed!" &c. Then the Lieutenant-Commanding said, "Now, three hearty cheers, my lads," and they

NAVAL EXPLOITS, CHASES, ESCAPES, PRIZES, ETC. 379

were given with a will, although the poor tars felt more like weeping than cheering. The order was in questionable taste, but the applause was infectious, and the crews of other gunboats took it up and made the welkin ring, till the steamer turned the point and was lost to view. A few months elapsed, and a nation mourned the death of one of its most heroic officers.

### Gallantry of Commodore Farragut to Miss Victor.

The truly brave are always good,—and the following is one among many instances which confirm the adage. Miss Victor, Principal of St. Mary's Female Academy, at Baton Rouge, Louisiana, was one of those who really adorned the society of the South. She was a northern-born lady, of excellent standing as a teacher, and before secession swept over the land, she was a much courted member of the refined circle in which she moved. The lady was true to the instincts and principles of her northern birth, and, of course, received the favors of old friends, and the hatred of those who sympathized with the plotters of the nation's ruin. Enough to say, the lady suffered so much at the hands of this latter class, that she welcomed the advent of Commodore Farragut's fleet.

The guerrilla band which fired upon the boat of the Hartford, and for which act the city was shelled by that ship, designed to take a last revenge on Miss Victor, by destroying her fine estate. But their fear of Federal vengeance induced them to flee before Miss Victor's place was reached. Unfortunately, the shells from the fleet found in the Academy a prominent target, and a number of shells were put through it. The inmates fled in dismay, and the fine building was ruined. Miss Victor and a younger sister fled to the river bank, and signaled for help. A boat put off from the Hartford and bore them on board. Commodore Farragut, hearing the circumstances, acted a noble part. The ladies were assigned the Captain's cabin, and treated with such consideration as their condition merited. Every officer vied in acts of kindness, and offered the protection of the flag to those who, shorn of their property, were thankful to escape from the outrages of guerrillas and the shells of the Union fleet.

### Semmes Outwitting the Vanderbilt.

The intelligence that the Confederate privateer Alabama was cruising about the Cape of Good Hope, created much excitement. In the Straits of Sunda she captured some United States merchant vessels, and was put upon her speed by the Vanderbilt. When night came on, the Alabama was about twenty miles ahead of her pursuer, and, under cover of darkness, she unshipped her funnel, put out her fires, and set sail. The ship was then put about, and stood in the direction of where

Captain Raphael Semmes.

they had last seen the Vanderbilt. At daybreak she was within only a mile of her enemy, who actually bore down and inquired if they had seen a large steamer standing to the norward. Captain Semmes graciously replied, "Yes; she was going ahead, full speed, and must be one hundred miles away by this." At this information, so opportunely obtained, the Vanderbilt immediately put on all steam, and went on a wild goose chase, while

Semmes quietly shipped his funnel and bore away in an opposite direction.

### Taking a Hint.

In one of our squadrons—which may as well be nameless—one of the officers, wanting to get leave of absence, went up to the Commandant's office, where he found no one in but the clerk. The Commandant very soon came in, and anticipating at a glance the errand, and pretending not to see the officer, at once cried out to the clerk, "If any officer comes to-day for leave of absence, order him at once on board the *Starling*,"—which was about to go on active service. Then turning to the startled officer, he added, "Ah! what can I do for *you* to day?" "Nothing—nothing at all, thank you," he replied, and made a masterly retreat.

### Literal Understanding of Terms.

A surgeon who officiated on one of the ships composing the blockading squadron off Wilmington, North Carolina, states that one day a number of contrabands came on board. One of them wore a masonic pin, and the Captain, who was a "G man," became some troubled by the fact, for a slave can not be a *free* mason. So he called up the intelligent 'contraband,' and said, "You are not a mason." "Oh, yes, massa, I is, I'se a bricklayer!" If there was any difference there, Cuffie 'didn't see it.'

### Buchanan's Sword Yielded with a Bad Grace.

When it was reported to Admiral Farragut that the rebel monster ram Tennessee had surrendered, and that Admiral Buchanan was wounded, he sent a staff-officer off to receive the rebel Admiral's sword. Some one asked Farragut if he would not go off himself and see Buchanan. The former merely replied: "No, Sir, he is my enemy." Subsequently, when the staff-officer returned with Buchanan's sword, it was represented to the Admiral that Buchanan had expressed a wish to see him. "Well, Sir, he shan't see me," replied the old Salamander. Then looking with most concentrated expression

Buchanan's Sword yielded with a bad grace.

of countenance upon the bloody decks of his ship, he added: "I suppose he would be friends; but with these brave men, my comrades, mangled, dying and dead about me, and, looking upon the destruction he has caused in the fleet, I can only consider him an enemy." On the staff-officer getting on board, Admiral Buchanan was found to be severely wounded in the leg. He yielded with a very bad grace—in fact, it was said that, after receiving his wound, he gave orders to his next in command to continue the fight as long as there was a man left; and then, when he found he could do no more, to run the vessel ashore and blow her up. But there was no alternative. The ram must be surrendered; and this was done. The Stars and Stripes were hoisted upon the staff of the magnificent ram, greeted, as they went up, by the hearty cheers of the whole fleet.

### Sharp Practice of Confederate Cruisers in English Waters.

One Saturday morning a channel steamer put into Plymouth, England, and landed eighteen persons from the Confederate cruiser, Virginia, formerly the Japan. Two of these persons were men who had been scalded through the bursting of a feed-pipe in the engine-room of the Virginia, whilst they had been acting as firemen. In consequence of this arrival, something was learnt respecting the manner, the escape, and the arming of that notorious Confederate cruiser, and the tale is a curious one.

It appears that the well-known firm of the Dennys, of Dennys, of Dumbartown, built the Japan for, *it was supposed*, the Emperor of China. She was a very fine steamer, of seven hundred tons burthen, and fitted with engines of 250-horse power. When she left the Clyde, she had been named the Virginia, and some forty carpenters went out in her to construct a magazine. These returned to Greenock in the tug steamer that towed the Virginia out. The day after she had sailed, an order arrived at Greenock, directing that she be seized. After the Virginia left the Clyde she made her way round into the English Channel. In the meantime, one of the steamers that ply between Newhaven and France, chiefly for the conveyance of French produce, intended for the London markets, had been taken up by 'a gentleman' to carry some packages and hardware across the Channel. This 'gentleman' stipulated for the power of taking the steamer to another port than the one to which he ordinarily traded, or to discharge the cargo into another vessel, if he thought fit to do so. The steamer, however, did take some passengers for France, and left Newhaven as if on her regular voyage across the Channel. The Captain, however, had instructions from the owners to follow the direction given by the 'gentleman.'

Well, when they got fairly into the Channel, the latter said, that before going across he wished to make for a certain point, meaning the latitude and longitude somewhere between Plymouth and Falmouth. "All right," said the skipper, and away they went and soon arrived at the point indicated, and there found a steam vessel, with which the 'gentleman' said he would like to communicate. He went on board the new steamer, but soon returned and told the Captain that he had sold the cargo, and it must be put on board that vessel. The Newhaven man brought his craft alongside, having the misfortune to carry away his boom in so doing. The cargo was then transferred to the large steamer, which was no other than the Confederate cruiser Virginia, and said cargo of the Newhaven steamer was guns, arms and ammunition. The cargo thus safely transferred, some seventeen men were transhipped from the Virginia to the Newhaven steamer, and these included the two men injured by scalding. With these men, on the 'gentleman's' directions, the Newhaven steamer made for Plymouth; and the Virginia went westward on her Confederate cruise.

### Impressive Sight aboard Ship on Sunday.

Ten o'clock was the hour for Divine service on board the Union fleet at Island No. 10. The church flag was flung out on the flag-staff of the Benton, and all the commanders called their crews together for worship. On board the Pittsburg, Captain Thompson, the crew consisted of men from Maine, New Hampshire, Massachusetts, Rhode Island—from the Eastern as well as the Western States. Some of them were scholars and teachers in Sabbath Schools at home. They were dressed in dark blue, and each sailor appeared in his Sunday suit. A small table was brought up from the cabin, and the Stars and Stripes spread upon it. A Bible was brought. They stood around the Captain with uncovered heads, while he read the twenty-seventh Psalm. Beautiful and appropriate was that service:—

"The Lord is my light and my salvation; The Lord is the strength of my life; of whom shall I be afraid?"

After the Psalm, the prayer, "Our Father which art in heaven."

How impressive! The uncovered group standing around the open Bible, and the low voices of a hundred men in prayer. On the right hand, looking down the river, were the mortars in play, jarring the earth with their heavy thunders. The shells were sweeping in graceful curves through the air. Upon the left hand, the Benton and Carondelet were covering themselves with white clouds, which slowly floated away over the woodlands, fragrant with the early buds and blossoms of spring. The rebel batteries below were flaming and smoking. Solid shot screamed past—shells exploded above. Away beyond the island, beyond the dark green of the forest, rose the cloud of another bombardment, where Commodore Hollins was vainly endeavoring to drive Colonel Plummer from his position. So the prayer was mingled with the deep, wild thunders of the cannonade.

### Sumter and the little Paul Jones.

The wooden gunboat Paul Jones, commanded by Captain Rhind, was one of the vessels engaged in the attack on Charleston. Captain Rhind steamed right up to Sumter, utterly regardless of fear. He was implored to be careful, but as in the Keokuk, he was determined to get nearest "the crater." Having delivered two or three effective broadsides, a rebel ball flew over the quarter deck, almost grazing the shoulders of the gallant Captain, who once more let fly vigorously at the fort, and then triumphantly steamed back with flying colors.

The brave old salt was never nearer being a martyr in his life.

### Had no White Flag on Board.

The Federal steamer Star was on her way up the James River, from Fort Wool, with military and political prisoners, the former to be left at Aikin's Landing. The Captain, pilot, and all hands of the crew did not number fifteen, the prisoners one hundred. Though none of the former were armed, there was no feeling of fear or thought of danger. Nothing whatever was apprehended of warlike peril.

The matter of hoisting said 'snowy banner' proved, however, of some interest. *There was no such white flag on board.* It had not occurred to Quartermaster or Captain to procure one. Indeed, until they were half a dozen miles up river, nothing had been said or done on the subject. Approaching the Union fleet off Newport News, the Captain was inquired of why he did not run up the *drapeau blanc*, to avoid being hailed and stopped, and called on to announce his character and errand. "Besides," it was added, "Admiral Wilkes may wish to forward letters by us to ships farther up, and if he sees the white flag approaching he will send a barge to deliver them without delay,"—and he did, as the event proved; wished not only to forward such letters, but to deliver certain packages of gold and bills of exchange for several Union officers imprisoned in Richmond,—" and moreover, Captain, we may in less than an hour, be within range of secesh rifles; and you had better get up your white pocket-handkerchief before giving those rascals a chance to mistake our character."

"Gracious!" was his first exclamation, "I have not got any flag. What shall I do?"

"Have you any sheets?"

"Plenty; but they are very small—single berth sheets."

"Stitch four of them together; make the flag too large not to be seen a mile off; it is sometimes well to have more than 'three sheets in the wind.'"

It was done very promptly, and probably no larger flag of truce, ("to use," as Mr. Everett said, in his magnificent Gettysburg funeral oration, "the language of the Confederate Secretary of War,") ever "flaunted the breeze," than that flaunted on this memorable occasion, and which was kept displayed aloft, both day and night, until the steamer's return from Aikin's Landing to the cover of the Federal gunboats in the lower and wider portion of James River.

### River Devils for Carrying on War.

The principal diver employed at Port Royal for cleaning the bottoms of the monitors, was named—and quite appropriately—Waters. A man of herculean strength and proportions, he became, when clad in his submarine armor, positively monstrous in size and appearance. A more singular sight than to see him roll or tumble into the water and disappear from sight, or popping up, blowing, as the air escaped from his helmet, like a young whale, could scarcely be imagined. Remaining for five

River Devils for carrying on War.

or six hours at a time under water, he had become almost amphibious.

Waters had his own ideas of a joke, and when he had a curious audience would wave his scraper about as he bobbed around on the water, with the air of a veritable river god. One summer day, while he was employed scraping the hull of a monitor, a negro from one of the up-river plantations came along-side with a boat-load of water melons. While busy selling his melons, the diver came up, and rested himself on the side of the boat. The negro stared at the extraordinary appearance thus suddenly coming out of the water, with alarmed wonder, but when the diver, with gigantic motion, seized one of the plumpest melons in the boat and disappeared under the water, the gurgling of the air from the helmet mixing with his muffled laughter, the fright of the negro reached a climax. Hastily seizing his oars, without a thought of being paid for his melons, he put off at his best speed, nor was he ever seen in the vicinity of Station Creek again. Believing that the Yankees had brought river devils to aid them in carrying on the war, no persuasion could tempt him again beyond the bounds of the plantation.

### Coffee for Jack.

Everybody admired Admiral Farragut's heroism in climbing the top-mast and fastening himself thereto, in order to direct the great battle before Mobile. But there was another little incident in that contest which no less forcibly illustrated his high, heroic character, as a man and officer, and exhibited the secret of his courage and self-command, no matter what the stress or pressure of circumstances around him.

"Admiral," said one of his officers, the night before the battle, "won't you consent to give Jack a glass of grog in the morning—not enough to make him drunk, but just enough to make him fight cheerfully?"

"Well," replied the Admiral, "I have been to sea considerable, and have seen a battle or two, but I have never found that I wanted rum to enable me to do my duty. I will order two cups of good coffee to each man, at two o'clock, and at eight

384    THE BOOK OF ANECDOTES OF THE REBELLION.

o'clock I will pipe all hands to breakfast in Mobile Bay."

And he did give Jack the coffee, and then went up to the mast-head and did the rest.

#### Expensive Joke on Commander Bankhead by a Southern Dame.

While the gunboat Pembina was at Beaufort, as one of the naval force stationed there, a negro came one day, as the bearer of a package from his owner, a Mrs. Chisholm, to commander Bankhead. Commander B. had been very active with his vessel, performing many important services in the conduct of the war, where the naval arm of his country had been brought into requisition. Some of these services, indeed, had been more than usually painful, as it had been necessary for him to take up arms against personal friends, and even relatives, living in that vicinity. But for all that, he did not flinch from the paramount duty he owed to his country, as one of its sworn officers, intrusted with its honor and defence. Among his acquaintances in that region was a Mrs. Chisholm, wife of a planter, who now wished to express her appreciation of his patriotism by sending him—what? —a set of expensive *coffin-handles!* with the intimation that the box they were intended to adorn was ready for his reception, as soon as he should come that way. In order to play this unique joke, the fair rebel actually sacrificed one of her trusty slaves as the messenger, and who, finding himself thus conveniently among the candidates for funeral honors, was contented to remain with them.

#### Place for the Watch in Battle.

In the fight in Mobile Bay, under Farragut, a piece of a rebel shell struck the after 11-inch gun carriage of one of the Union vessels, embedding itself in it, and a solid shot struck a marine, taking off his head as clean as though with a large sabre, at the same time striking the gun itself, deeply indenting and cracking it.

The Captain of this gun was badly wounded by the splinters and by *pieces of the man's head* striking him in various parts of the body, bespattering him with blood and brains. But he experienced a most remarkable escape, similar instances of which have been occasionally recorded in the annals of war. His name was James Sheridan—a quarter-master, and a man of far more intelligence than is usually found among foremast men, being pretty well versed in navigation, understanding the use of all the ordinary nautical instruments, and was frequently to be seen on the forecastle of the vessel with watch and sextant in hand, either practicing himself, or imparting instruction to any one who was willing to receive it.

The watch Sheridan always wore in the left breast pocket of his blue shirt, consequently directly over the region of the heart, and when the shot struck the marine's head off, it carried with it one of the brass buttons of his cap. This button, striking Sheridan's watch, produced a deep indentation on the outer edge or rim of it; imparting a brassy hue to the furrow it made in its passage; and there were also two other marks of blows on the back of the watch, which reached to the inner case.

Had it not been for the watch, there is no doubt but that button would have caused another deep and painful wound, if not his death. But although severely wounded and bleeding, he would not leave his gun, and even though the gun had been struck, and rendered unsafe, if not unfit for use, he fired two more rounds of solid shot from it, and then went up on the poop to assist at the signals. The escape of Sheridan, by his watch being worn in the left breast pocket, shows that to be the right place for that instrument, instead of lower down on the right side—at least in battle.

### Fight with the Iron Monster Tennessee.

When it was reported to Admiral Farragut that the monster iron ram Tennessee was bearing down upon him, he hastened on deck with the remark,

"*He is after me; let him come on if it must be so; admiral for admiral—flagship for flagship—I'll fight him!*"

The enemy was close at hand, and coming with all speed directly at the Hartford, evidently with the intention of running her down. The Admiral mounted to the maintop and surveyed his ground, arranging hastily his plan of battle. This settled quietly in his own mind, he awaited the approach of the monster. Buchanan must have fancied that he had caught his adversary napping, from the apparent quiet that prevailed on Farragut's flagship. Not a gun was fired; no crew was to be seen; her broadside lay plumply exposed to the tremendous blow he was hastening to give. But suddenly there was a change.

When the rebel had approached near enough to make these observations and fully appreciate them, the helm of the Hartford was put hard a port, her machinery started, she described a segment of a circle, and, just as Buchanan had thought to strike her squarely amidship and cut her in two, as he was capable of doing, the towering brow of the noble old ship struck him a tremendous blow on his port quarter forward, that knocked every man aboard his craft off his feet. The force of the collision checked the headway of both vessels. The blow given by the Hartford was a glancing one, and the two vessels came up broadside to broadside. At this moment a full broadside from the Hartford was let go at her antagonist, but it was like throwing rubber balls against a brick wall,—nine-inch solid shot, though they were, and fired from the muzzles of her guns scarcely ten feet distant. Simultaneously, Buchanan also discharged his broadside of four Brookes' rifles, which passed completely through the Hartford, and expended their force in the water beyond.

The Tennessee immediately put on steam again, and started to try her strength with some other of the wooden vessels. The Brooklyn lay nearest, and for that ship she headed. Here she was met with almost precisely the same reception as with the Hartford. Instead of butting, she received a butt—both vessels came together, broadside to broadside; both broadsides were discharged, and the ram went on her way to try another, and another, and all of them, but with no better success.

She now started to run back through the fleet, but here a new combination awaited her. *The Monitors had come up*, the appearance of which seemed for a moment to disconcert the rebel. From the first he had shown a wholesome dread of them, and by skillful manoeuvring and his greater speed had managed to avoid them. Now they hammered him to the utmost of their ability. The three had managed each to get a position in a different direction from each other, and whichever way the ram turned he met these ugly and yet invincible foes. At first he was shy, and seemed irresolute as to what course to pursue, but finally seemed determined to get out of the bad scrape by running through the fleet back to the friendly protection of Fort Morgan.

Now, then, Admiral Farragut's admirable tactics developed themselves, and which he signaled to the whole fleet. The little Monitor Manhattan appeared directly in front of the ram to head him off. The rest of the fleet formed a circle about the rebel craft, and all commenced paying him their heaviest compliments. It was a terrible fire—every rebel ball that struck the Union vessels did execution, making great holes in their sides and reddening their decks with blood; but every shot that struck the monster ram, glanced away like a rubber ball. To meet the exigency at this critical state of affairs, Farragut's vessels were put in motion, describing a circle about the rebel, the sloops and monitors being directed to ram her every time they came around, which was done with deadly effect. Each vessel chased its leader about, throwing a broadside into the enemy at every opportunity, and at every chance getting a ball at her. In this way the plucky fellow was terribly used. Every time one of the sloops came on to him the concussion was such as to throw the crew of the monster off their feet. The frequency with which she was thus rammed, and the continuous artillery fire that was rained upon her, so demoralized her men, that they are said to have begged to surrender, fearing, at every new shock, that they would be sent to the bottom. The course pursued by the vessels was such that the ram was unable to get range upon any of them so as to run them down, thus compelling the ram to remain passive. Or, if she attempted to escape the tormentors, an unlooked for enemy would come and strike her on the quarter, and throw her out of her course. During this melee, the Manhattan got one good shot in directly at the ram's broadside. The huge ball of iron struck fairly at the lower angle of the heavy casemates and penetrated into the inside, spending its force in the effort. This was the only shot that ever passed through her iron.

Against such odds in number, such cannonading and punching and entanglement, the ram could not continue, and the formidable craft finally succumbed, after a fight of something more than an hour. Buchanan directed his flag to be struck, the Chickasaw having the honor of receiving the surrender of the ship.

### Good Natured Jerry.

One of the gunboats which was employed in blockading the port of Wilmington, North Carolina, had for second boatswain's-mate a comical little carroty-haired Irishman called Jerry, who would eat more souse, chew more tobacco, and do more growling than any two men in the ship. Jerry had had no previous experience in his duties, having been rated to the position a day or two after he came aboard; and great was the merriment, fore and aft, at the dismal squeaks he elicited from his boatswain's-whistle, when ordered to call away a boat or pipe "all hands up anchor;" or, in the richest brogue, bawl out, "D'ye hear, there, forre an' aft, the meal-bag will lave to-morrow mornin', an' thar'll be an opportunity to sind away letthers!" Jerry, however, was good-natured, and generally bore all the fun at his expense without remonstrance; but on one occasion the laugh was so uproarious against him, that, if possible, he would never permit any allusion to it. Some men of his watch were at work down in the fore-hold breaking out provisions, when duty on deck required a few more hands. Jerry went to the fore-hatch and sung out:

"Forre-hould, there!"

"Hallo!" came up from the depths.

"How many of yez is there down there!"

"Three of us."

"Come up the half o' yez!"

### Rigging up a "Long Tom" out of Billy Luly.

A vessel which went from New York bound for St. Thomas, one morning found herself being pursued by a Confederate privateer off King's Channels. The villain was close in under land, in a small sloop, with about twenty-five men, and when he discovered his prey, the latter was nearly becalmed. He gave chase, and bore down very fast upon his supposed prize. There appeared to be no chance for the vessel to effect her escape, under these circumstances, except by stratagem; and there happening to be on board a man who could be metamorphosed into almost anything, some one proposed to the Captain of the seemingly fated craft that he had better make a gun of Billy Luly, and give chase in turn. They accordingly went to work, put a black cap on Billy's head, stretched him fore and aft on the keel of the boat, with a rope made fast to his heels, so that they could slide him on the centre of gravity freely, and pointed his head to the enemy. Having thus rigged up a 'Long Tom,' the next thing was to fire it; and this was done by discharging a pistol into a barrel, and raising a smoke by throwing ashes into the air. The trick succeeded—the sloop tacked and made off; the vessel hauled on the wind and pursued her close in under land, then tacked ship and stood into St. Thomas. Thus were twenty-five men driven off by four.

#### Heroism of a Naval Engineer.

During the engagement between the rebel ram Albemarle, and the Sassacus, a wooden gunboat, the latter received a shot through her boiler, which caused a large quantity of steam to escape directly into the ship. The situation was appalling. The shrieks of the scalded and dying, as they frantically rushed up from below, with their shrivelled flesh hanging in shreds upon their tortured limbs, the engine beyond control, surging and revolving without guide or check, abandoned by all save *one*, who, scalded, blackened, sightless, still stood like a hero to his post. Alone, amidst that mass of unloosed steam and uncontrollable machinery, the chief engineer of the Sassacus, James M. Hobby, remained, calling to his men to return with him into the fire-room, to drag the fires from beneath the uninjured boiler, which was now in imminent danger of explosion. Let his name be long remembered by the two hundred beings whose lives were saved in that fearful moment by his more than heroic fortitude and exertion. There were no means of instantly cutting off communication between the two boilers, and all the steam contained in both rushed out like a flash, exposing the ship to a most fearful catastrophe, had the brave engineers been too late in drawing the heavy fires which threatened such destruction. Even after Mr. Hobby had been severely scalded by steam escaping from a shot-hole in the boiler, he stood by and worked the ship out of the reach of the enemy.

#### Two Things that Sounded Alike.

There was a laughable story frequently repeated at Fortress Monroe, concerning a certain high Commander, who was pious enough in creed, but on certain occasions, when his dander was up, could do full jus-

The Merrimac.

tice to his feeling by giving them mouth. When, therefore, the Merrimac came down, the high official in question, was all motion; he was highly excited, and now and then he eased his feelings by certain forcible ejaculations in the shape of solid balls of nouns substantive. A contraband, who heard him, gave a very good description of how the white-haired old man moved about in the storm of shells. "By golly, Boss," said he, "but de way dat old mass' off'cer moved about day war a caution. He went dis way and dat way; he went hea' an' he went dar; but to hab hearn de old mass' swar!—Bo-s, its de solemn truf, dat de way de old un swar war plumb nigh like preaching."

#### Sailors and Sweethearts on the Ohio.

A sailor belonging to one of the United States gunboats doing Government service on the Ohio river, became enamored of a fair young damsel who superintended a sewing machine in a certain dress-making establishment in Cincinnati. A description of the youthful pair, will be first in place. The sailor was tall, and exposure to the Southern Confederacy and plug tobacco had given an Olivia tinge to his cuticle. He donned his suit of Federal blue with becoming grace, and wore his cowhide boots thick upon him. The third day comes a frost—but this need not be anticipated.

As the young lady was not wrapped up in the sailor to any alarming extent, in short, had not the tender passion within her excited toward him, a description of her is scarcely necessary to the point of the story. It may just be said, however, that she was exceedingly intellectual with that sewing machine, and had an engaging way in doing general housework and fulfilling the multifarious little duties peculiar to her sex.

The sailor, however, loved her, and what's more he didn't know it. She never told her love—nor anybody else—what her feelings were toward the sailor, till one autumnal afternoon, during the fore part of October, when—but this is anticipating.

One day, while her maiden meditations were fancy-freeing to the hum of her machine, (she was wont to hum there) a billet-doux, enclosed in a Government envelope, was placed before her. It came from her would-be love—the gallant sailor-boy—and notified her to be in readiness, for on the coming afternoon she might expect him to "call for her." Anticipating a visit to the matinee at Pike's, or a street railroad excursion at least, she paid a little more attention to her personal appearance than usual, on the afternoon named, and when the tall, tanned, timid, trembling tar appeared, fresh and trim in Uncle Sam's naval insignia, she was resplendent in new harness, with all her perfections on her head. The loyal tar, so true to the 'Union' sentiment, had a shipmate with him—had she caught a tar-tar?—and was accompanied by a third person, who proved to be a justice of the peace.

Explanations set in. Her sailor boy, clad in loyal garb, had come to marry her; that's what he meant by calling for her. He wanted her to be the sharer of his shares, and the jawer of his joys. She shrieked, tore the basting out of a dress-waist that had been cut bias, laughed hysterically, and said she "couldn't see it." Alas for the cause of the Union! The sailor implored. Her attention was persuasively solicited to several packages of postal currency, two dollars and a half in each package, the savings of six months gunboating in behalf of the Stars and Stripes. She gazed upon said packages with undazzled eye. He assumed a despairing look, and darkly hinted at the aqueous facilities always in the reach of gunboaters, for washing off this mortal evil! She was inexorable still. The sailor, finding his matrimonial scheme a dead failure, fled from the destroyer of his peace, and was last seen burying his woes (also his nose) in a tumbler. The maiden, happy and free, still continued to paddle her own —sewing machine.

### Chase of the Sovereign.

Commodore Davis's fleet of Federal vessels left Fort Pillow for Memphis, on the 5th of June. I was sitting at dinner, (says 'Carleton,' a spirited and agreeable writer, and author of one of the best books on the war,) with the Commodore and Captain Phelps, on board the Benton, when an orderly thrust his head into the cabin, and said:

"Sir, there is a fine steamer ahead of us."

We are on deck in an instant. The boatswain is piping all hands to quarters. "Out with that gun! Quick!" shouts Lieutenant Bishop. The brave tars seize the ropes, the trucks creak, and the great eleven-inch gun, already loaded, is out in a twinkling. Men are bringing up shot and shell. The deck is cleared of all superfluous furniture.

NAVAL EXPLOITS, CHASES, ESCAPES, PRIZES, ETC.     389

There she is, a mile distant, a beautiful steamer, head up-stream. She sees us, and turns her bow. Her broadside comes round, and we read "Sovereign" upon her wheelhouse. We are on the upper deck, and the muzzle of the eleven-inch gun is immediately beneath us. A great flash comes in our faces. We are in a cloud, stifled, stunned, gasping for breath, our ears ringing; but the cloud is blown go, the tug puffing and wheezing as if it had the asthma.

"Through the *chute!*" shouts Captain Phelps. *Chute* is a French word, meaning a narrow passage, not the main channel of the river. The Sovereign is in the main channel, but the Spitfire has the shortest distance. The tug cuts the water like a knife. She comes out just astern of the steamer.

Gunboat Fight at Fort Pillow.

away, and we see the shot throw up the water a mile beyond the Sovereign. Glorious! We will have her. Another, not so good. Another, still worse.

The Louisville, Carondelet, and Cairo opened fire. But the Sovereign is a fast sailer, and is increasing the distance.

"The Spitfire will catch her!" says the Pilot. A wave of the hand, and the Spitfire is alongside, running up like a dog to its master. Lieutenant Bishop, Pilot Bixby, and a gun crew jump on board the tug, which carries a boat howitzer. Away they

"Bang!" goes the howitzer. The shot falls short. "Bang!" again in a twinkling. Better. "Bang!" It goes over the Sovereign.

"Hurrah! Bishop will get her!" The crews of the gunboats dance with delight, and swing their caps. "Bang!" Right through her cabin. The Sovereign turns towards the shore, and runs plump against the bank. The crew, all but the cook, take to the woods, and the steamer is ours.

The crew on board the Sovereign had

been stopping at the farm-houses along the river, setting fire to the cotton on the plantations. They did it in the name of the Confederate government, that it might not fall into the hands of the Yankees.

### Eagle at the Mast-Head.

As the fleet of Federal transports was passing down the Chesapeake Bay to Hampton Roads, on that beautiful day in October when the vessels first got under weigh at Annapolis, a large bald eagle came sweeping out from the shore of Maryland, and, soaring grandly high in the air above the fleet, finally alighted on the mast-head of the Atlantic, the head-quarters of the army. In an instant, all eyes were upon the great and graceful visitor, and conjectures were busy as to whether he were a loyal bird, come to give his blessing at parting, or some cunning secession rooster, intent on spying out the Federal strength. The brave men gave the bird the benefit of the doubt; an officer peremptorily staying the hand of a soldier who would have shot him, and the omen of his appearance at such a time and in such a manner was accepted as auguring the full success of the enterprise.

### Rather too Spunky for Them.

Something may be learned of the spirit which is in woman, when she will or when she won't, by the courageous conduct of the wife of Captain McGilvery, master of the ship Mary Goodell, which was captured by a rebel privateer and subsequently released, and arrived at Portland. Mrs. McGilvery was on the voyage with her husband, and when the ship was boarded by the privateers, she was asked by them for a supply of small stores for their use, as they were rather short. She immediately replied that she had nothing but arsenic, and would gladly give them a supply, but that they could have nothing else from her. Seeing the national flag near at hand, they started to secure it, when she sprung forward, and grasping the flag, threw it into a chest, and placing herself over it, declared they should not have it unless they took her with it. Finding the lady rather too spunky for them, the desperadoes were content to retire without further molesting her.

Fleet of Gunboats in the James River.

### Tete-a-Tete with the Old Admiral.

At the gathering in the Brooklyn Academy of Music, in honor of Admiral Farragut, in December, 1864, on his return after his brilliant naval achievements in the South, a most enthusiastic ovation was given him. While the main portion of the company were enjoying themselves up stairs, a pleasant scene was enacting for a short period, in one of the private apartments below—the Admiral and a few ladies and gentlemen partaking of a collation prepared for the distinguished guest. In a *tete-a-tete* with a lady, an explanation was elicited from the Admiral of his being lashed at the mast-head of the Hartford.

"Admiral," said the lady, "do tell me

if it was true, as they said, that you were lashed to the mast down at Mobile Bay?"

"Well," said the Admiral, with the artlessness of a child, "I'll tell you all about it. You know in a fight the smoke of the guns lies on the water, and, naturally, I would want to see over it to know what was going on. Well, I would jump upon a box—so high." (indicating with his hand); "then I would get up a little

Farragut Lashed to the Mast.

higher; and by and by I got up to where they said. I suppose I was two hours getting as high as that. I had a little rope that I had lashed around me, just to keep me from falling, in case I should get hurt. Every one, you know, is liable to get hurt in a fight."

"When have you heard from your friend Admiral Buchanan?" asked a gentleman.

"Oh, I saw a letter from him yesterday. He complains bitterly of his hard treatment, as he calls it, in Fort Lafayette, and wants me to use my influence to get him in the Naval Hospital. They (the rebels) all seem to think a good deal of me," continued the Admiral, with charming *naïveté*, "although I have done so much to hurt them."

"Buchanan didn't lose his leg," he re- marked, in correction of an observation of one of the company; "the surgeon saved that for him, although we tried our best to knock it off. Tell you what," he went on, "I was glad enough to see that flag come down on the ram."

"Which do you like best, Admiral—being afloat or ashore?" inquired another lady.

"Well," he replied, "I enjoy life everywhere. I take the world as I find it."

"Well, Admiral, what do you think of the war?" was another question—there not being often a chance to "pump" at such an illustrious handle.

"It's all right. We've got 'em. They'll begin to show it soon." He expressed great hopes of the success of the expedition that had recently sailed. "Porter," said he, "is a noble fellow. I know him well, and he will not disappoint the country."

He was congratulated on his probable elevation to the rank of Vice Admiral, in pursuance of the resolution before Congress. He replied: "Yes, I'm much obliged to them. I'm thankful to everybody."

About twelve o'clock the old hero rose to go, and upon being offered an escort to New York he said playfully,

"When I am poking around down South, then I often want a pilot; but around here I am at home, and can paddle my own canoe."

He at length consented to accept a "convoy," as he called it, but insisted that it should be a "single" man. Said he, jocosely, "I know what good wives say sometimes when their husbands are out too late."

### Astonishing Ignorance on board a Gun-boat.

The humors of the Federal Navy were neither few nor inferior during the period of its splendid service in behalf of the old flag. But not all of these humors were strictly in the belligerent line, as the following will show. The excellent gunboat

'We-no-shepokes-slow' had been out of port quite a considerable length of time. One of the messes was the owner of some butter, which, following rules and regulations naval, outranked by seniority all other butter that came upon the ship. While admitting its abstract right to do so, they nevertheless voted that it had clearly no right to outrank *them* to the extent it did; and consequently various curious chemical processes were detailed, each of which was equal to the task of deceiving them into the belief that the new product would "taste like butter just from the churn." The caterer, being a man of extensive family experience, had the ear of the mess, and boldly asserted that first washing in diluted chlorid of lime, followed by a cleansing bath of pure water, was an infallible cure. But where should they get the chlorid aforesaid? The doctor was appealed to, who had no chlorid of lime, but had what was just as good— chlorid potassium. Caterer was not posted on chlorid potassium, but, considering the authority good, gave the steward instructions how to manipulate the strong. At dinner time he brought upon the table two plates *in appearance* of yellow butter, in *reality* of beautiful soap. The imperturbable Ensign H— got the first mouthful, but with a slight grimace swallowed his disgust and the soap together. With an anathema on that hollow tooth, he passed the dish to the fastidious paymaster with eloquent laudations. Paymaster took the bait unsuspiciously, but without making a sign was taken sea-sick, and rushed frantically to the side. When all that could be were sold and marked, the joke was saddled upon the doctor and caterer, each of whom accuse the other of immense chemical ignorance to this day.

### Signaling for Sherman—Meeting of the Warriors.

The United States revenue cutter, Nemaha, Lieutenant Commanding Samuel S. Warner, General Foster's flag-boat, left Hilton Head on the morning of December 12th, 1864, to go down the coast with General Foster and staff, to endeavor to open communication with General Sherman, (who was expected to have arrived at the head of his great army just marched through Georgia,) going through to Fort Pulaski and thence through the marsh to Warsaw Sound, looking toward the main canal to discover some traces of Sherman's advance. None were observed, so the General proceeded outside and entered Ossabaw Sound, where the gunboat Flag, on blockading duty, was communicated with. Lieutenant George A Fisher, of the Signal Corps, United States Army, was here left on board the Flag to proceed with his party up the Ogeechee, and endeavor to communicate with Sherman, if he should approach the coast at that point.

The Nemaha returned to Warsaw and moved up the Wilmington river, anchoring just out of range of a Confederate battery. During the night, rockets were thrown up by Captain Jesse Merrill, Chief of the Signal Corps, to announce his presence to General Sherman's signal officers, but elicited no response.

Lieutenant Fisher was more successful. The Flag fired six guns in rapid succession, from a heavy gun, as a signal, and then Lieutenant Fisher threw up several rockets and closely examined the horizon over the mainland for the response. At about three o'clock on the morning of the 13th, after a rocket had been discharged from the Flag, a little stream of light was observed to shoot up in the direction of the Ogeechee, and quickly die away. Another rocket was immediately sent up from the flag-ship, and a second stream of light was seen in the same position as the first. It then became a question whether or not they were rebel signals to delude the Federal officers.

At about seven o'clock, the navy tug Dandelion, Acting Master Williams, took Lieutenant Fisher and his party, and Captain Williamson, of the flag-ship, and proceeded up the Ogeechee to a point within sight of Fort McAllister and the batteries on the Little Ogeechee. Here Lieutenant Fisher took a small boat and proceeded up as far as possible without drawing the enemy's fire. A careful reconnoisance was made of the fort and the surrounding woods, from which proceeded the reports of musketry, and the attention of the garrison seemed to be directed inland entirely. A flag, which seemed like that of the Union, was seen flying from a house four miles off, and on more careful examination the stars were plainly visible, and all doubt of the character of the flag was at once removed. It was the flag that had floated over General Howard's headquarters at Atlanta, and now flamed out on the sea coast, within eight miles of the city of Savannah. Lieutenant Fisher at once returned to the tug, and moved up to an opening out of range of Fort McAllister, when, from the top of the pilot-house of the Dandelion, the American flag could be distinctly seen. A white signal flag was as once raised by Lieutenant Fisher, and at once a signal flag of like nature was waved, and communication opened.

Lieutenant Fisher signalled—

"Who are you?"

"McClintock, chief signal officer of General Howard," was signalled back.

A message was at once sent to General Sherman, tendering all aid from General Foster and Admiral Dahlgren.

General Sherman then signalled that he was investing Fort McAllister, and wanted to know if the boat could help with her heavy guns. Before any reply could be given, General Sherman had signalled to General Hazen, of the Fifteenth Corps, to take the fort immediately.

In five minutes the rally had been sounded by the bugles. One volley of musketry was heard, and the next moment the three brigade flags of Hazen's Division were placed almost simultaneously on the parapets of Fort McAllister. The fort was captured in twenty minutes after General Sherman's order to take it was given. General Sherman then sent word that he would be down that night and to look out for his boat. The tug immediately steamed down to Ossabaw Sound, to find General Foster or Admiral Dahlgren; but they not being there, despatches were sent to them at Warsaw, announcing General Sherman's intended visit, and the tug returned to its old position. While approaching the fort again a small boat was seen coming down. It was hailed with—

"What boat is that?" and the welcome response came back—

"Sherman."

It soon came alongside, and out of the little dugout, paddled by two men, stepped General Sherman and General Howard, and stood on the deck of the Dandelion. The great leader was received with cheer after cheer.

The correspondents for the press who accompanied General Sherman, have published, in vol. form, their admirable reports.

### Bibles on Shipboard,—Touching Scene.

What may well be called a pleasing scene occurred on board the steamer Canada during her passage from Dubuque toward St. Louis, in the fall of 1861. One Saturday evening, while many of the passengers were engaged in conversation, others whiling away their time at 'euchre,' while some, more rude, perhaps, with the ribald jest and ungentlemanly oath, were using up the evening, a young man seated himself at one of the tables, and engaged in reading his Bible. Another, and still another, took his place around this temporary altar, untill nearly all of that little band of soldiers, numbering about twenty, were reading the Scriptures. An aged man took his station in their midst. He had a benign and venerable air, his hoary locks proclaiming that many a winter had passed over his head. There, those boys, with that old man, formed a group, the sight of which was indeed adapted to enchain the eye and to win the heart. The creaking machinery of the boat, the dirge-like music of the wind, were loud; but, above the clatter and confusion, the prayers of those boys assuredly were heard by the Highest.

### The Day and the Event.

"Day 19.— Morning prayer: Psalm XCV.— *Venite, exultemus*— 'O come, let us sing unto the Lord; let us heartily rejoice in the strength of our salvation. Let us come before his presence with thanksgiving, and show ourselves glad in him with psalms.'" This was the opening psalm for the day, said or sung in many Christian churches, by minister and people responsively, at the hour when the Kearsarge, just out of French waters, was rounding-to to meet the Alabama. When the morning service was closing, the Alabama lay a harmless mass of wood and iron at the bottom of the ocean, and her commander, saved from drowning by the clemency of his conqueror, was, with his treacherous ally, approaching the British shore, where he might, had he been piously inclined, have listened to the evening service for that day, closing with the last response of the *Misericordium et judicium* —" I shall soon destroy all the ungodly that are in the land; that I may root out all the wicked doers from the city of the Lord." It is well known that the fact of the fight between the Kearsarge and the Alabama, on the Sabbath day, was not sought or arranged for by Captain Winslow to take place then. Having received notice that Captain Semmes, of the Alabama, encouraged by Mason, Slidell, and other Confederate minions abroad, intended to come out, at some time, and fight, Captain Winslow held himself in readiness to meet his antagonist at any day or hour. Perhaps the holy day could in no other way have been so peculiarly hallowed as by the summary and complete destruction of such a craft as the Alabama. Query: Did that very devout man, John Slidell, who was so busy with his secession schemes in that part of Europe, join in the '*Venite exultemus*,' as his morning devotional exercise for the day in question? It would be interesting, too, to know the hoary intriguer's religious meditations when night closed in upon him!

### Up the Cumberland—Grit of the Old Major.

The opening of the Cumberland river, free from secession enemies, was a joyous event to the Tennessee Unionists, and the demonstrations were enthusiastic beyond

Gunboat Kansas.

all description. Here and there, however, a contrary spirit was manifested. As one of the Federal gunboats passed up the river, there was at one of the large houses a group of ladies observed, who stood looking at the boat. "Hurrah for the Union!" yelled old Major —, from the roof of the pilot-house. No response from the ladies. "Hurrah for the Stars and Stripes!" yelled the Major again. Still no response. "Why don't you wave your handkerchiefs?" angrily roared the Major, while the decks and guards now exploded with uncontrollable roars of laughter. "Haven't you got any feelings? Secesh! Secesh! (pointing the finger, after the manner of little boys, crying shame,) Secesh! Secesh! O you villains! Hurrah for the Union! Death to rebels! Hail Columbia!" &c., &c.

### Reinforcement of Fort Pickens—How it was Done.

Why and how Fort Pickens was so skillfully reinforced is thus made to appear: The gallant Slemmer, with a handful of men to garrison an extensive fortification, having for some time suspected that the secessionists were tampering with his men, intercepted a couple of letters which had been smuggled into Pickens and addressed to a sergeant. The writer offered this man the sum of two thousand dollars, and a commission, which would make him the companion of the gentleman of the South in arms; and, as an inducement to the faithful fellows who so long had held those stone walls against thousands, five hundred dollars were promised to every private who at that price would become a traitor to the United States. The men, true soldiers as they were, remained steadfast to their colors. The sergeant was forthwith sent a prisoner to the commander of the naval force lying off the harbor. That very day, a messenger arrived from Washington, bringing a verbal order to reinforce; this messenger had been captured, but had destroyed his dispatches, the contents of which luckily he knew. The order was now passed to throw into Pickens all the artillery, soldiers, and marines in the squadron. How the work was done, the surgeon's story which here follows will tell :—

We had shoved off, and were struggling hard against the tide to reach the steam frigate that was to tow us in. At length we reached her, and I seized the man-ropes to climb her steep sides. "Sure, and that's a cruel limb, Docther, an' you wid yere sthiff ould legs." "Watch till she rises," said the coxswain, "now's your time, Sir." I hauled my rheumatic limbs painfully up, trusting to my hand, and reached the deck. Here artillery-men and marines were assembled ; and on deck I left them to go below, where cigars, coffee, and chat awaited me, and in which I indulged until the steamer came to anchor, and I was summoned to repair to another and smaller steam vessel which was to tow us in further. It was two o'clock in the morning when we got aboard the small steamer, and ran in toward the shore of Santa Rosa. The first detachment of boats must have landed its party under cover of the obscurity; for the young moon had long since gone down, leaving the sentinel stars to give us a faint light. On we steamed, and by-and-by came to and dropped anchor at least two miles from Fort Pickens. "Come, men, bear a hand —no time to lose!" said the Captain ; and down the steamer's sides tumbled the men into the boats. A senior surgeon and I jumped into the Captain's gig, into which he followed, and away we went—two long miles to pull against a tideway. "Lively stroke, lads, give way!" The oars bent, and every blade shone as it flashed through the phosphorescent water. On, on, on! How long those miles seemed ! We conversed gravely, occasionally looking aft to see whether the boats were keeping way with us. We conversed gravely, for I suppose we were all speculating on what might be the manner of our return. I take no shame to myself in confessing that I did not hold a very cheerful view of the expedition. The first detachment of boats was returning as we started. Night had favored them, while we —! "Rather bright to the eastward," said I. "Yes," said the Captain, "we'll have morning on us directly; strike out, men!" Morning, thought I, and we were not more than half way. The men pulled like good fellows, we keeping near the shore to avoid the strength of the current. Near, yet just without easy rifle range; for the chaparral afforded excellent cover for riflemen. It was so light now that I could see my hands, and morning was coming on more rapidly than I ever knew it to break before.

"Give way, lads!—whose oar is that out of water?"

"Smith's, Sir; he's a haulin' off his pea-jacket, Sir."

"Give way!"

The Captain had been searching with his glass for the fort. At length he said: "AH, THERE IT IS!" An opaline light by this time pervaded the eastern sky, revealing our boats to any watchful eye. I was gazing into the distance to catch a glimpse of the fort. I soon made out its dark outline, and almost at the same moment I, Bob Harding, saw another sight, which to me was of particular interest. It was the white mass of the hostile Fort McRae, on the side of the harbor opposite to Pickens, and, like Pickens, commanding the entrance. The white mass of masonry, dotted regularly with dark embrasures, occupied my attention exceedingly as our boats pulled right for it; for our Captain had, it seems, determined to land in front of Pickens, on a beach that McRae might have swept with a storm of shot and shell. It was quite light enough by this time for the enemy to distinguish every boat, nay, every man. "Give way!" As we rounded a sandy point right under the hostile guns, I kept my eyes fixed on four embrasures in McRae. By Jove! how big and black they seemed! I watched them; for I felt assured that before we should have pulled much farther one or more sheets of red flame would burst forth, and then those who lived would be swimming for it. No one spoke. Bright, brighter, grew the east. The oars buckled and the waters hissed as we dashed toward the beach.

Soon the boats found bottom. Out jumped the men and marines; and we officers, mounted on the shoulders of some of the boat's crew, landed, the surf overtaking and wetting us all. The men drew up on the beach. Surely, thought I, now McRae will open upon us. Now's their chance. We started to lead the men across the sand to the sally-port of the fortress. Bang!

"Who fired that musket?" said the Captain, at whose side I stood.

"It's the ould Docther, Sir," said Private Brennan; "he's filled my muskit wid tebacky euds, an' I'm afther emptyin' it, Sir. Och! but he's a powerful man wid the tebacky, ony way."

"Keep silence there," said the Captain —"come on, men! Here you are! Tumble in! Sailor men, back to the boats?"

Into the fort went the marines, led by my friend, the surgeon, while the Captain and I made for the boats, and started to return to our ships, with the Lieutenant, who had staid on the beach to guard our flotilla. As we passed McRae I said to myself, "Now it's coming, Bob!" I watched the embrasures. They looked twice as ugly as a ship's port-holes, and every gun seemed pointed to my devoted head. I knew that I would be the only one hit, for at me they aimed. The men pulled cheerily, and after a while I made up my mind that we were to get back to our floating homes with unbroken limbs. The east was glowing with a warm, rosy light; the morning was lovely.

"Are you one of those who admire sunrise?" said the Captain.

"No, Sir, I am not; and I must say that this morning it was especially unwelcome. A few minutes since I would have been glad of an hour more of darkness."

The Captain laughed.

"Did not you expect McRae to open on us?" asked I.

"Most certainly," replied he.

*That* is the way that Fort Pickens was reinforced from the Federal squadron on the morning of the thirteenth of April,

1861, by daylight, in face of a fully armed fort and other batteries—reinforced while a large body of men held the opposite shore.

#### Willing to part with his other Leg.

The river at Port Hudson makes a majestic curve. At the memorable siege, resulting in the capture of that stronghold, rebel cannon were planted along the concave brow of the crescent-shaped bluffs of the eastern shore, while beneath the bluff, near the water's edge, there was another series of what were called water-batteries

Willing to part with his other leg.

lining the bank. As the Federal ships entered this curve, following the channel which swept close to the eastern shore, they were, one after the other, exposed to the most terrible enfilading fire from all the batteries following the line of the curve. This was the most desperate point of the conflict; for here it was almost literally fighting muzzle to muzzle. The rebels discharged an incessant cross-fire of grape and canister, to which the heroic squadron replied with double-shotted guns. Never did ships pass a more fiery ordeal.

Lieutenant-Commander Cummings, the executive officer of the ship Richmond, was standing with his speaking-trumpet in his hand cheering the men, with Alden by his side, when there was a simultaneous flash and roar, and a storm of shot came crashing through the bulwarks from a rebel battery, which they could almost touch with their ramrods. Both of the officers fell as if struck by lightning. The Captain was simply struck down by the wind-age, and escaped unharmed. The speaking-trumpet in Commander Cummings' hand was battered flat, and his left leg was torn off just below the knee. As he fell heavily upon the deck, in his gushing blood, he exclaimed—

"Put a tourniquet on my leg, boys. Send my letters to my wife. Tell her that I fell in doing my duty!"

As they took him below, and into the surgeon's room, already filled with the wounded, he looked around upon the unfortunate group, and said—

"If there are any here hurt worse than I am, let them be attended to first!"

His shattered limb was immediately amputated. Soon after, as he lay upon his couch, exhausted by the operation and faint from the loss of blood, he heard the noise of the escape of steam as a rebel shot penetrated the boiler. Inquiring the cause, and learning that the ship had become disabled, he exclaimed, with fervor—

"I would willingly give my other leg, if we could but pass those batteries!"

The hero died of his wound a few days after.

#### Daring Attack upon a Paymaster's Boat.

The following record is only one among very many which illustrate the skill and valor exhibited by our officers, whether duty called them to the performance of gallant deeds on the land or on the sea.

Captain Spencer, aid to General Wool, received information one day, from two ladies who went from Norfolk to Fortress Monroe with a flag of truce, that near midnight a six-oared boat was to leave

PART V.—VARIETIES OF THE WAR.

# PART FIFTH.

ANECDOTES OF THE REBELLION—MILITARY ORGANIZATION AND EQUIPMENT, DISCIPLINE, DRILL AND PARADE, REVEILLE, REVIEWS, ORDNANCE, PASSES, PAROLES, FURLOUGHS, COUNTERSIGNS, ETC.

Mustering in; Splendid Specimens of Soldierly Movement; Dexterous Handling of Arms; Evolutions, Comical and Piquant; Queer Dilemmas; Uncouth Subjects and Verdant Victims; Grotesque Performances; Novel Terms and Phraseology; Bivouac Sights; Tasks and Pleasantries, Mistakes, Jocularities, Facetiæ, &c., &c.

"Twenty millions held at Bay!
Why, Northmen, why?
Less than half maintain the flag!
Why, Northmen, why?"

Haman's gallows ought to be the fate of all such ambitious men who would involve their country in civil war, and all the evils in its train, that they might reign and ride on its whirlwinds and direct the storm.—ANDREW JACKSON.

That's right, boys! make your coffee, break the orders, and—catch the shells.—GENERAL ROSECRANS.

I feel that I was born for something better than mending old clothes.—BURNSIDE, *when a tailor's apprentice*.

You can't go in and *keep your cigar*.—*Soldier on guard duty*, to LIEUTENANT-GENERAL GRANT.

I don't care a ——; if McClellan himself was here without the countersign, he should mark time till the corporal comes. Quick time; march!—*Soldier on guard at Camp Joe Holt*, to GEN. NELSON.

## Challenging the Sentinel.

IT was the custom of the Colonel of the Eighty-fifth Pennsylvania Volunteers, to make the rounds every night in person, and satisfy himself that every sentinel was at his post and doing his duty. On one occasion, while in the discharge of that self-imposed duty, he approached a post, and received the challenge as usual, "Who comes there?"

"Friend with the countersign," was the Colonel's reply.

Here the poor sentinel was at a loss. The rest of his instructions had been forgotten. The Colonel was a very particular man, and insisted that every thing should be done exactly right. So, after spending considerable time in the endeavor to impress the 'role' upon the mind of the sentinel, suggested that *he* would act as sentinel while the other should personate the Colonel. 'Blinky'—for such was this soldier's surname in the regiment—moved back a few paces and then turned to approach the Colonel. "Who comes there?" challenged the Colonel.

"*Why, Blinky; don't you know me, Colonel?*"

This was too much for even so patient and forbearing a man as Colonel Howell. "As green as verdigris," thought he. The gun was handed over, and the Colonel passed on to the next post, meditating upon the vanity of all earthly things in general, and of things military in particular.

### "Mark Time!"—General Nelson in a Fix.

The following story is told of the late General Nelson, of Kentucky. Occasionally some of the shrewd privates would get and use an opportunity to cut the feathers of pompous officers, which always afforded merriment to the whole camp. In

"Mark Time."

fact, officers who clothe themselves with unapproachable dignity, and say, either by word or action, I am General ——, or I am Colonel ——, or, when slightly 'riled,' by (oath,) I'll let you know I am Captain of Company A, or B, or C, naturally become targets for rear rank victims. This was well illustrated at Camp Joe Holt. The camp guards after night were instructed to allow no one to pass in or out without giving a countersign, and to retain as prisoners those who came from outside to the lines without it. General Nelson came to one such guard, on a certain evening, just after the countersign had been given out, and held something like the following conversation:

"Halt! who comes there?" says the guard.

"I am General Nelson, commanding this army."

"I don't care a ——; mark time, march." Corporal of the Guard No. 1," cocking his piece.

"You —— — fool, I'll have you punished like ——," replied the General, commencing to mark time slowly. (He was a *bad* swearer.)

"I don't care a ——; if McClellan was here without the countersign, he should mark time till the Corporal comes. Quick time, march."

"Let me rest," said Nelson, swearing and sweating.

"No Siree; mark time," was the inexorable reply.

By this time the news had spread like wildfire through the camp, that one of the guards had Nelson out at Post No. 1, marking time, and half of the regiment was collected on that side, enjoying the joke hugely. The Corporal was very slow in coming, and every time Nelson would slacken speed, the guard would cock his gun and command, "Mark time." There was a dreadful crash of oaths just around there,—the atmosphere was black and blue with them. The above are but faint samples.

By the arrival of the Corporal, the General's rage had so far subsided, that he, too, began to enjoy the humorous side of the joke.

---

### Sentry Encounter with a Regular.

When Sherman's famous Battery passed

General Sherman.

through Perryville, one of the soldiers, while the horses were feeding, went into a tavern outside the camp limits, and filled his canteen with the villainous mixture of camphene and strychnine, which is called "whiskey." In coming back within the limits, the sentry challenged him, and put a firmly held musket across his path, to bar his progress. With a quick motion the artilleryman grasped the musket barrel, closed with the astonished sentry, and before he could recover from his stupefaction, grasped him tightly by the throat. His useless musket dropped from his nerveless hand. The artilleryman, still holding him by the throat with his left hand, drew from his girdle a long and sharp knife, which glittered in the light of the distant watchfire before the eyes of the terrified sentry. The latter sank upon his knees in a paroxysm of terror. He would have begged for mercy but he could not speak. Suddenly the artilleryman hurled him from him, caught up his gun, and brought it to a charge.

"Now, you rascal," said he to the trembling sentry, "listen to me. I am a regular—mind, a regular. Now, don't you go for to stop a regular agin. Regulars never stop. In the bright lexicon of a regular's vocabulary, there's no such word as *stop*. Regulars is on the go all the time. They go with the password, and they goes without the password; passwords is nothin' to them, and they is nothin' to passwords. My friend, (in a softer tone,) take yer gun. The night is dark, the air is chill. Take some," (pouring from his canteen into a tin cup.)

"What is it?" faltered the sentry.

"Water, you lobster, you; or more properly, whiskey and water."

The sentry took a long and deep draught, and the regular passed on. Soon after, when the relief guard came around, they found the sentry in a condition not easily described. He was taken to the guardhouse, and thence to the hospital. The poisonous liquor made him nearly mad. On getting well, he swore, first that he would never again try to stop a "regular;" and, second, that he would never touch Perryville whiskey again; third, that he would give Sherman's artillerymen a specially wide berth.

Sentry's Encounter with a Regular.

#### Putting him through the Discipline.

One summer's day, about one o'clock, a long, gaunt, bony man, with a queer admixture of the comical and doleful in his countenance, that fairly reminded one of a professional undertaker cracking a dry joke, undertook to reach General Grant's tent, by scrambling promiscuously through a hedgerow and coming in the back way alone. He was stopped in his venturesome career, however, by one of the hostlers, who cried out to some purpose, "Keep out o' here!" The individual in black replied that he thought General Grant would allow him inside, and strode ahead. 'You'll — soon find out," was yelled in reply. On reaching the guard, who very naturally took him to be one of the Sanitary or Christian Commission folks, he was stopped instanter with—

"No sanitary folks allowed inside."

After some parleying, of the usual character, the intruder was compelled, hit or miss, to give his name, and at last did so, announcing himself as—

"Abraham Lincoln, President of the United States, desiring an interview with General Grant."

The guard saluted the Commander-in-Chief, and allowed him to pass.

General Grant recognized him as he stepped under the large "fly" in front of his tent, rose and shook hands with him cordially, and then introduced him to such members of his staff as were present and unacquainted. The President had just arrived on the City of Baltimore, and was accompanied by his son 'Tad,' Assistant Secretary of the Navy—Fox, Mr. Chadwick, proprietor of Willard's Hotel, and a marine guard. No one relished the little affair with the guard more keenly than the amiable President.

### Sold!

Soldiers are, it is well known, averse to the drill, and yet dislike to work still more. During the siege of Corinth it became necessary to go some ten miles over the worst of roads to Pittsburg Landing, to draw forage and provisions, and many were the expedients resorted to by the boys to escape the hard task. One morning at roll-call the Lieutenant said, "Any of the boys who would like a drill, step to the front." Not many came forward. "Now, you rear rank men, each take a horse, go to the Landing, and bring back a sack of oats." The boys acknowledged that they were flatly 'sold,' but ever afterwards volunteers for drill were more numerous than scarce.

### Paying his Penalty, Cash Down.

"Slick" was known as a *case* in Company I, and was familiarly called by the *sobriquet* in question, when the army was at Murfreesboro'.

Slick was passing General Johnson's head-quarters one day, and without any ceremony fired his gun almost in the face of the General himself.

"What?" says the General; "Do you not know the penalty of firing your gun without orders to do so?"

"Why, no, sir!" says Slick, very innocently.

"Well," replied the General, "I will tell you. It is the loss of a month's pay."

"You don't say so!" says Slick, and very coolly puts his hand in his pocket and draws therefrom an old greasy wallet, opens it, and offers the General *thirteen dollars* in greenbacks, saying, "Well, General, I guess I am able to stand the pressure!"

It is needless to say that the General discontinued the conversation immediately. Slick was not fined.

### Halting Effect of "the Ardent."

During the winter campaign in Tennessee, as C. S. Beath, quartermaster-sergeant of the One Hundred and Seventeenth Illinois, was passing along one of the principal streets in Memphis, he saw a soldier coming toward him struggling with the

Halting effect of the Ardent.

spirit within him. Just in advance of Sergeant B. was a "freeman of African descent." The soldier saw him coming, and with some difficulty managed to ejaculate

"Halt!" Darkey didn't heed his authority, and marched ahead. The soldier squared himself, and as the darkey was passing made a dive at him; but the darkey, aided by the soldier's inward foe, easily dodged the blow, and the soldier plunged over the curbing into the gutter, his head striking first. As soon as he could recover his speech he said, "There, now; lie there. I g-g-guess y-y-you'll h-h-halt the next time I tell you to!"

### Stuttering when on Guard-Duty.

When Colonel Daniel M'Cook's regiment was lying at Camp Dennison, a brawny recruit from one of the Eastern counties, who stuttered badly, was put on guard-duty for the first time. A citizen attempted to pass the line. Recruit yelled out, "H-h-h-alt!" The citizen, who either did not understand him or paid no attention, when the sentinel carefully laid his bright "Springfield" upon the ground, and knocked the intruder down, saying, in his stuttering way, "There, now, mind the next time. If I ain't much with the frog-sticker, yet I'm heavy with the fist."

### Mr. Beecher's Case of Muskets for the South.

Among the passengers by the steamship Asia from England, was the Rev. Henry Ward Beecher, just returned from his sojourn in the land of "Neutrality." The steamer stopped at Halifax, Nova Scotia, and there landed a portion of her cargo. Mr. Beecher, who had just come on shore, and was stretching his legs by a walk on the pier, seeing that the first case of goods came hard, with characteristic impulse volunteered a helping hand. The force of his additional muscle—which is 'some' —quickly brought the case bang upon the wharf. He stood aghast, however, to find, as he and his friends gathered around to examine it, that he had lent a hand to land a case of muskets intended for the Southern Confederacy. A Boston paper is responsible for this story—which, at all events, is too good *not* to be true, though no one will ever suspect Henry (as he speaks of himself in his pulpit) of thwarting Secretary Chase in his laudable efforts

Secretary Chase.

to prevent arms from passing through *any* custom-house, *en route* to Davisdom.

### Governor Yates giving Grant a Desk in his Office.

Soon after Grant's first application to Governor Yates for a commission in the army, which was declined on account of there being no vacancy at that time, the Governor was very much distressed in regard to the raising of the quota of the State. He had plenty of offers for officers' positions, but he personally did not know the minutiæ of regimental organization,—how many men composed a company, or how many subordinate officers there should be in a regiment. In his distress, he asked the Representative of the plain little man to whom he had been introduced, if he knew any of these matters. The Representative replied by bringing Grant into the presence of the Governor.

"Do you understand the organization of troops?" inquired the Governor of Grant.

"I do, Sir."

"Will you accept a desk in my office for that purpose?"

"Anything to serve my country," was Grant's reply.

And to work he at once went; and but for this, Grant might still have been unknown to the world as a military chieftain. By his energy, Illinois became noted for the alacrity with which she filled her quota. Some of the best things of this kind concerning Grant, together with the other great heroes of the war, are contained in the series of volumes, written with such fine taste, by Rev. W. M. Thayer, and issued in such attractive style for young readers, as to take the highest place in the popular estimation.

### Ruse to Obtain a Furlough.

Joe Robinson enlisted in the 199th Regiment of New York Volunteers. The men were in camp on the island, and their friends were often visiting them. Joe's brother, John, came to see him, and found Joe very homesick. He begged so hard for John to get him a furlough that his brother went to the Colonel and told him his sister was dead, and he wished leave for his brother to go home for a few days. Consent was given; and as they were leaving the ground, one of the men who heard of Joe's affliction, and wished to say something, asked him how long his sister had been dead?" Joe said, "About ten years!" and went on his way rejoicing.

### Couldn't Pass with his Cigar.

A little incident, as related by Lieutenant James Hutchinson, of the veteran reserved corps, and formerly of the Thirteenth New York Volunteers, exhibits General Grant in one of his characteristic qualities as a man and soldier. Lieutenant H. was stationed for a time at Washington, and on the occasion in question was on duty as officer of the day at the War Department. An order was in force which forbade smoking in the building, and the sentries were instructed to enforce it. It so happened that among those who called to see General Halleck was Lieutenant-General Grant, who approached the door confidently, cigar in mouth, expecting, doubtless, to pass without question; but the veteran soldier on guard knew his duty better. Bringing his piece down to a charge, he barred the General out, and said to him, respectfully, "You can't go in and keep your cigar!" The Lieutenant-General of the United States Armies was too good a disciplinarian to dispute such a point, so he yielded with true soldierly grace, threw the obnoxious weed away, and went in. After his departure, an order came from General Halleck—but which those who know General Grant will be slow to believe came through his instigation—rescinding the rule about smoking, so far as it affected army officers.

### Snake-Hunters' Style of Drill.

Among the rebel guerrilla organizations, the most noted band was that known by the name of "Moccasin Rangers." They had a good time, too, until Captain Baggs got up his 'counter-irritant' in the shape of a company of "Snake-Hunters," a delicate allusion to said venomous reptile—the moccasin. As to their arms, these were of every variety; and as to toggery, no two were dressed alike. As to parades, their extraordinary system of tactics included no such dandyism.

But most peculiar of all was their drill. Every movement was accomplished on the double-quick, or in a run. They acknowledged no "common time," and if reduced to a dead march they would surely have mutinied. This, for instance, was Captain Baggs' very original style of dismissing his company:

"Put down them thar blasted old guns, and be — to you!"

(Which being interpreted, is "Stack arms!")

"Now to your holes, you ugly rats, and don't let me see you again till I want you!"

(Which, being reduced to the Hardee vernacular, means, "Break ranks—march!")

*Exeunt* Snake-Hunters on the run, with

grand divertissement of whoops, yells and squeals, interspersed with life-like imitations of birds and beasts.

Once, when the Snake-Hunters were detailed to guard some stores between Fairmount and Beverly, two elaborate gentlemen from Philadelphia, who were making a tour of that country, had the good fortune to witness their very original style of drill, and at the close of the performance invited Captain Baggs to take a drink in a neighboring rummery. As the tin cups were laid out, one of the aforesaid gents expressed his astonishment, not to say admiration, of this peculiar style of dismissing, "which looked to him very much like a stampede," and was curious to know where in the world they were all gone to, and how the Captain expected to get them back if he wanted them in a hurry. Baggs replied that the process was rather difficult to explain verbally, but "if they'd jest let that 'ere rum wait a minute, he'd show 'em;" whereupon going to the door, he fired three barrels of his revolver. The echo of the third report was still lingering among the cliffs when every blessed Snake-Hunter burst into the bar-room with a whole menagerie of roars and screeches and hee-haws, and without question or apology called for tin cups. This demonstration of Captain Baggs' style of "falling in," cost the elaborate gentlemen from the Quaker City $5, the very thought of which almost turns their brains to this day.

### Giving 'em Fits.

Fresh recruits are a little behindhand in their drill, as may naturally be supposed. At one of these morning exercises, Captain M'D. was marching his squad past the Colonel's tent. The Colonel says, "Captain, I wish you to put those boys through. Give 'em fits." In a short time the Colonel went out to supervise the drilling on the beach (Folly Island) of the different squads. He at once observed one squad huddled together in a formation that his practiced eye told him was not to be found in tactics. He hurried up but to see a man writhing in convulsions.

"What's the matter? What have you been doing?" queried the Colonel.

"I obeyed your orders," said the Captain.

"What orders?"

"I've given 'em fits."

### Colonel Owen's Squad Drill.

Great difficulty was experienced in furnishing the Pennsylvania troops with shoes at the commencement of the three months service. Those that were furnished were generally much too large for the wearers —a fault which occasioned much merriment and some inconvenience. A raw re-

Colonel Owen's Squad Drill.

cruit in Colonel Owen's regiment was being put through the squad drill, when the following colloquy took place.

SERGEANT. "Why don't ye mind the orthers there, Patrick Kelly? There ye've bin standin' like a spalpeen iver since ye come out, and niver a once faced to the right or left! Shure an' I'll arrist ye! D'ye mind that?"

PRIVATE. "Ye're mistaken altogether, sargeant. Shure an' ye've been lookin' at me shoes. *Divil a bit can I turn thim around!*"

### Raw Captains.

A raw captain of one of the rural companies of Ohio volunteers marched his men into the long narrow mess-booth for the first time, under somewhat peculiar circumstances. After dinner, feeling anxious to bring them out in military order, and thinking it wrong to have the left in front under any circumstances, he ordered the separated ranks to countermarch where there was not room to execute the movement. The result, of course, was great confusion. The captain raved, swore, and commanded impossible things. Result, still greater confusion. At last the men poured out of the doors pell-mell like sheep. The disgusted captain, placing his back against a tree, shouted the only command they could obey, thus: "*Any way you please, hang you*—MARCH!" About as laughable an incident occurred in the case of another captain (formerly a railroad conductor,) who was drilling a squad, and while marching them by flank turned to speak to a friend for a moment. On looking again toward his squad he saw they were in the act of 'butting up' against a fence. In his hurry to halt them he cried out—true to his former calling—'Down brakes! down brakes!'

### New-comer into Camp.

One day, the Federal pickets near Charlestown, Va., descried a solitary horseman, with a bucket on his arm, jogging soberly towards them. He proved to be a dark mulatto, of about thirty-five; as he approached they ordered a halt.

"Where are you from?"

"Southern army, Cap'n," giving the military salute.

"Where are you going?"

"Coming to yours all."

"What do you want?"

"Protection, boss. You won't send me back, will you?"

"No; come in. Whose servant are you?"

"Cap'n Rhett's of South Cariliny—you's heerd of Mr. Barnwell Rhett, editor of the Charleston Mercury. His brother commands a battery."

"How did you get away?"

"Cap'n gave me fifteen dollars this morning, and said, 'John, go out and forage for butter and eggs.' So you see, boss (with a broad grin,) I'se out foraging! I pulled my hat over my eyes and jogged along on the Cap'ns horse (see the brand S. C. on him) with this basket on my arm, right by our guard and pickets. They never challenged me once. If they had, though, I brought the Capn's pass,"—and the new-comer produced the following document from his pocket-book, written in pencil, and carefully folded:—

"Pass my servant, John, on horseback, anywhere between Winchester and Martinsburg, in search of butter, &c., &c.
A. BURNETT RHETT,
*Capt. Light Artillery, Lee's Battalion.*"

"Are there many negroes in the rebel corps?"

"Heaps, boss."

"Would the most of them come to us if they could?"

"All of them, Cap'n. There is'nt a little pickaniny so high"—waving his hand two feet from the ground, "that would'n."

"Why did you expect protection?"

"Heerd so in Maryland, before the Proclamation."

"Where did you hear about the Proclamation."

"Read it, Sir, in a Richmond paper."

"What is it?"

"That every slave is to be emancipated on and after the 13th day of January. I can't state it, boss!"

"Something like it. When did you learn to read?"

"In '49, Sir. I was head waiter at Mrs. Nevitt's boarding-house in Savannah; and Miss Walcott, a New York lady who was stopping there, taught me."

"Does your master know it?"

"Cap'n Rhett dosn't know it, Sir; but

DISCIPLINE, DRILL, PAROLES, FURLOUGHS, ETC.   409

he isn't my master. He thinks I'm free, and hired me at twenty-five dollars a month, but he never payed me a cent of it. I belong to Mrs. John Spring, of ———, Connecticut. She used to hire me out summers, and had me wait on her winters, when she came South. After the war, she could'nt come, and they were going to sell me for Government because I belonged to a northerner. I slipped away to the army. Have tried to come to you twice before in Maryland, but could'nt pass our pickets."

"Were you at Antietam?"

"Yes, boss. Mighty hard battle."

"Who whipped?"

"Yours all, Massa. They say you didn't; but I saw it, and know. If you had fought us that next day—Thursday—you would have captured our whole army. They say so themselves."

"Who?"

"Our officers, Sir."

"What do the slaves think about the war?"

"Well, boss, they all wish the Yankee army would come. The white folks tell them all sorts of bad stories about you all; but they dont believe them. They know that Mr. Fremont, and Mr. McClellan, and Mr. Burnside won't hurt them."

**Brave and Good, but Must be Shot.**

A lady of high social standing in New Orleans had two sons in the Confederate army in Mississippi. A lady, when she is determined, can accomplish almost anything, and will surmount difficulties before which many a brave man would stand appalled and turn back from his purpose.

This lady determined to visit her two sons, as they could not visit their parent, and by some means or other, having obtained a passport, she crossed the lines, and made her way to the camp of the Confederate General under whose banner her sons were serving. She was entertained at head-quarters, and found that the General and his staff officers fared sumptuously, living on the very fat of the land. But the common soldiers had only bread and molasses for their fare.

It so happened that while this lady was with the Confederates, the time for which a certain Tennessee regiment had enlisted expired, and the soldiers, anxious to see wives and little ones once more, began to make preparations to start home. Who so well as the soldier, can tell the emotions which must throb at a soldier's heart, who has been in front of the thickest battles, who has heard the roar and rattle of the cannon and musketry, and seen his comrades fall all around him, but who has himself been miraculously preserved on the field of carnage! Who, but a soldier, can tell the emotions which must swell his heart at the near prospect of being welcomed to his home once more, and clasping to his arms the dear ones who have occupied his thoughts day and night. But it was not so to be.

The brave men of this Tennessee regiment, who had been a whole year in the service, during which time one half the number which had started with them, flushed with health and the hope of victory, had either fallen on the bloody field, or sadder still, been pierced by the arrows of slow and lingering disease, caused by exposure and hardship, were not to be allowed the pleasure of visiting their loved homes.

The General, in making his daily rounds, and seeing the men of this regiment busily engaged in making preparations for their intended departure, inquired what it meant: and on being acquainted with their determination, he immediately gave orders that not a single man of them should leave his encampment. The whole brigade or division of the army was at once ordered under arms; cannon and musket were brought menacingly against this devoted regiment, and they were told by the General, that unless they took up their arms, which they had thrown down, within three minutes, they should be fired on. With death thus staring them in the face, they obeyed the order to take up their arms—all but eight. It was decreed that these eight should be court-martialed and shot!

Before the time came that the military court was to be held, seven of the eight followed the example of their comrades, and agreed to resume their arms. One soldier alone remained firm in his purpose; one soldier alone was willing to brave death rather than yield to the despotic demands of a tyrant. He pleaded his own cause with all the fervor of which a soldier is capable. With struggling but manly utterance he said to his General:

"I have served out the time for which I enlisted, faithfully; I have been in every battle; I have been at all times at the post of duty assigned me, in rain and sunshine, in summer and winter. I have served and am willing to serve my country. But, General, I have a wife and four small children at home, who depend on me alone for support and protection, and who have no one besides me to look to their interests. Allow me thirty days, the law allows a furlough of sixty days, but allow me half that time to visit my family, whom I have not seen for a year, and make some necessary arrangements for their welfare, and I promise to return within that time and to take my former position in my regiment. I make but a just and reasonable request. It is essential to the welfare of my family that you grant it. I cannot enter the service again till I have visited my family."

He was sentenced to be shot. The decree was pronounced on Saturday, and was to have been executed the next day. The soldier and hero—for he was a hero —the bravest man in his regiment,—asked for a little longer time to make the preparation necessary for a change of worlds; and the time was graciously extended one brief day, the sentence to be executed on Monday, instead of Sunday.

When the fatal hour arrived, following his coffin which was in full view, he was marched to the place of execution, and arrived there, the General pointed him to the new-made grave, and commanded him to kneel down upon its margin. The soldier and martyr simply replied that he had never kneeled to any but his Maker, and that he could not consent to kneel now to a man. As he said this the order was given to fire, and, in the act of making the sign of the cross—the Christian's emblem—on his breast, the martyr and soldier was in eternity. Ah, how many there were there, who, though unaccustomed to weep, shed bitter tears at the enactment of this tragedy!

### McClellan Dismounting to the Guard.

As General McClellan was riding along the lines of his army one day, examining the condition of the men, a little incident in the way of "military rule" occurred,— the same, it may be remarked, which has been related of Napoleon, Wellington, and Washington,—and of course very

General McClellan.

likely to take place. In this case, a young Pennsylvanian was on guard when McClellan rode up. The guard demanded the countersign. "I am the commander-in-chief, George B. McClellan," was the answer. "Well, then, commander-in-chief George B. McClellan, get down from your horse and give the countersign, or I will see what kind of a hole the musket which J. K. Morehead prepared for us will make in the body of the commander-in-chief George B. McClellan." The General, like a good soldier, calmly dismounted, and proved his identity, gave the word, and praised the young man for his conduct, telling him whenever he wanted a favor, just to let him know.

### Worse to lose Five than One.

In the first action in which Grant commanded, his troops at first gained a slight advantage over the Confederates. They began to plunder the Confederate camp, in spite of all that Grant could do to stop them. At last Grant, who knew that Confederate reinforcements were coming up, got some of his friends to set fire to the camp so as to stop the plundering. Then he got his troops together as well as he could, and retreated; but, in the mean time, the Confederate reinforcements came up, attacked Grant, and defeated him. There were five Colonels under Grant who had not by any means supported him efficiently in his attempts to stop the plundering and collect his troops. Mr. Osborn saw Grant a day or two afterwards, when he expected to be deprived of his command on account of the defeat. He said:

"Why do you not report these Colonels? They are the men to blame for not carrying out your orders."

"Why," said Grant, "these officers had never before been under fire; they did not know how serious an affair it was; they have had a lesson which they will not forget. I will answer for it they will never make the same mistake again. I can see by the way they behaved in the subsequent action that they are of the right stuff, and it is better that I should lose my command, if that must be, than the country should lose the services of five such officers when good men are scarce."

Grant did not lose his command, and three out of the five officers subsequently greatly distinguished themselves.

### General Rosecrans and Pat's Furlo'.

General Rosecrans was reviewing the lamented Brigadier-General Nelson's old division. He took unusual interest in that band of veterans, who so long and so nobly had defended their country. He rode

Gen. Rosecrans.

along alone between the ranks, talking to the men, and inquiring into their individual wants. Some wanted shoes, some blankets, some an increase of rations, etc. Finally the General stopped in front of an Irishman, apparently well pleased with his soldierly appearance.

"Well, Pat," says the General, "and what do you want?"

"*A furlo' plase your honor!*" answered Pat.

"You'll do, Pat!" said the General, as he rode away, laughing.

A fund of exceedingly readable incidents concerning 'Old Rosy' and his soldier boys, may be found in the very racy volume by 'W. D. B.,' entitled *Rosecrans' Campaigns*.

### Mother-Corporal on a Ten Days' Furlough.

The lady friends of a certain Corporal sent him a box; and among the many good things packed by fair but roguish hands was a life-size doll, dressed in full Zouave uniform, which the fun-loving damsels won at a soldiers' fair. The Corporal, after getting the box, was taken sick. The boys now started the rumor that the Corporal was a woman and had given birth to a boy. The rumor spread like wildfire; hundreds flocked to said quarters to see the wonderful phenomenon—a new born babe—but the insiders guarded the tent with zealous care, only allowing pryers to catch a passing glimpse of the supposed mother and babe. A number of men were to be found who would swear they had seen both. But the cream of the joke was yet to come off; the Corporal received a ten days' furlough—all thought now, for certain, it was the mother going home with her babe; some had it that she was a rich heiress escaping from a tyrant father; but hundreds believed in the mother-corporal and young recruit of Company I, of the Zouaves d'Afrique.

### Obeying Orders in his Own Way.

Just before the charge made by Fremont's Body Guard at Springfield, Mo., Major Zagonyi directed one of his buglers, a Frenchman, to sound a signal. The bugler did not seem to pay any attention whatsoever to the order, but darted off with Lieutenant Maythenyi. A few moments afterwards he was observed in another part of the field vigorously pursuing the flying infantry. His active form was always seen in the thickest of the fight. When the line was formed in the *Plaza*, Zagonyi noticed the bugler, and approaching him, said: "In the midst of battle you disobeyed my order. You are unworthy to be a member of the Guard. I dismiss you." The bugler showed his bugle to his indignant commander—the mouthpiece of the instrument was shot away. He said: "The mouth was shoot off. I could not bugle viz mon bugle, and so I bugle viz mon pistol and sabre." It is unnecessary to add, the brave Frenchman was not dismissed.

### Shaken Down among the Pickets.

A Confederate officer who had been detached from the ranks on some special service, at the battle of Manassas, having discharged his duty, received orders to return to the army. He started towards Manassas at a rattling pace, but had not proceeded many miles along his circuitous route, ere he fell in with the Confederate cavalry patrols and pickets, who were extremely vigilant; and although custom had made the officer sharp-sighted at night, they frequently halted him before he had the slightest notion of being within many miles of their vicinity. To add to his misery and delay, he had not the countersign, and therefore was marched off to the nearest guard-post to account for himself.

"Can't help it, comrade," said the cavalry-man, "I believe your words, and think I have frequently seen you before; but orders are orders, you know, and we must obey."

He was handed over to the next picket, and so on, until, reaching the central picket station, the Captain commanding examined him rigorously, and upon the officer presenting papers of identity, the Captain politely gave him the countersign, saying:

"It was well, perhaps, you fell in with our men, for the road you were taking must have led you nearer the present lines of the enemy than you care about finding yourself, I know; the countersign I have given you is good among the outer pickets; when you reach the infantry, be careful how you act, for they have another one, and are particularly wakeful to-night, and thick as flies!"

Acting upon this advice, he plunged forward boldly, and was in high spirits, singing right heartily, for the numerous Confederate encampments were visible for many miles around. But—"Halt! halt!" was the challenge suddenly given by half-a-dozen; and from their guns leveled at him, he saw there was no fun about them.

"Who goes there!" "Officer without the countersign!" "Advance officer!"—which he did, very meekly, for could they have seen him even wink improperly, he would have been instantly riddled with half-a-dozen shots. Here he went through the operation of being handed over from one to another, until fairly out of patience. The corporal of the guard would do no more than hand him to the sergeant, the latter to the lieutenant of the guard; the last to the officer of the night, and he to the officer of the day—so that, from being handed from one to another, it got rumored about among some of the soldiers that he was a spy and soon there was a large crowd at his heels, bestowing all manner of uncomplimentary epithets. The rumor spread among the regiments through which he was then passing; and while in the tent of the officer of the day making explanations, one loquacious gentleman, who stood peeping through a rent in the tent, was heard to exclaim—

"The Captain's got him, he's a spy, and they've got the papers on him! I hope they'll detail me as one of the firing party; *won't* I let him have it good!"

After a few moments of explanation, he remounted again; and his sudden transformation into a good and true Southerner seemed to cause infinite disgust to many, but particularly to the ragged gentleman who was so anxious to make one of the "firing party."

### Tragical Encounter between Generals Nelson and Davis.

When the alarm was raised in Louisville, Ky., in the autumn of 1862, that the Confederates were marching on that city, General Davis, who could not reach his command under General Buell, then at Bowling Green, went to General Nelson and tendered his services. General Nelson gave him the command of the city militia so soon as they were organized. General Davis opened an office and went to work in assisting the organization. On Wednesday, General Davis called upon General Nelson in his room at the Galt House, when the following conversation took place, as reported in the newspapers:

GEN. DAVIS. I have the brigade, General, you assigned me, ready for service, and have called to inquire if I can obtain arms for them.

GEN. NELSON. How many men have you?

DAVIS. About twenty-five hundred, General.

NELSON (roughly and angrily). About twenty-five hundred! *About* twenty-five hundred! By G—! you are a regular

Gen. J. C. Davis.

officer, and come here to me and report *about* the number of men in your command! — —— you, don't you know, sir, you should furnish me the exact number?

DAVIS. General, I didn't expect to get the guns now, and only wanted to learn if I could get them, and where; and, having learned the exact number needed, would then draw them.

NELSON (pacing the room in a rage). About twenty-five hundred? By ——, I suspend you from your command, and order you to report to General Wright; and. I've a —— good mind to put you under arrest. Leave my room, sir!

DAVIS. I will not leave, General, until you give me an order.

NELSON. The — you won't! By — I'll put you under arrest, and send you out of the city under a provost guard! Leave my room, sir!

General Davis left the room, and, in order to avoid an arrest, crossed over the river to Jeffersonville, where he remained until the next day, when he was joined by General Burbridge, who had also been relieved by Nelson from his command. General Davis went to Cincinnati with General Burbridge, and reported to General Wright, who ordered General Davis to return to Louisville and report to General Buell, and General Burbridge to remain at Cincinnati. So General Davis returned and reported to General Buell. Nothing further occurred until the morning

Encounter between Gens. Nelson and Davis.

when General Davis, seeing General Nelson in the main hall of the Galt House, fronting the office, went up to Governor Morton and requested him to step up with him to General Nelson and witness the conversation that might pass between Nelson and him. The Governor consented, and the two walked up to General Nelson, when the following took place:—

GEN. DAVIS. Sir, you seemed to take advantage of your authority the other day.

GEN. NELSON (sneeringly, and placing his hand to his ear). Speak louder, I don't hear very well.

DAVIS (in a louder tone). You seemed to take advantage of your authority the other day.

NELSON (indignantly). I don't know that I did, sir.

DAVIS. You threatened to arrest and send me out of the State under a provost guard.

NELSON (striking Davis with the back of his hand twice in the face). There, d—— you, take that.

DAVIS (retreating). This is not the last of it; you will hear from me again.

Nelson then turned to Governor Morton, and said: By G—d, did you come here also to insult me?

GOV. MORTON. No, sir; but I was requested to be present and listen to the conversation between you and General Davis.

GEN. NELSON (violently to the by-standers). Did you hear the d—— rascal insult me? He then walked into the ladies' parlor.

In three minutes General Davis returned, with a pistol he had borrowed of Captain Gibson, of Louisville, and walking toward the door that Nelson had passed through, he saw Nelson walking out of the parlor into the hall separating the main hall from the parlor. The two were face to face, and about ten yards apart, when General Davis drew his pistol and fired, the ball entering Nelson's heart, or in the immediate vicinity.

Gen. Nelson.

General Nelson then threw up both hands and caught a gentleman near by around the neck, and exclaimed, "I am shot!" He then walked up the flight of stairs toward General Buell's room, but sank at the top of the stairs, and was unable to proceed further. He was then conveyed to his room, and when laid on his bed requested that the Rev. Mr. Talbott, an Episcopal clergyman stopping in the house, might be sent to him at once. The reverend gentleman arrived in about five minutes, and found the General extremely anxious as to his future welfare. He knew that he must die immediately, and requested that the ordinance of baptism might be administered, which was done. The General then whispered, "It's all over," and his spirit at once returned unto its Maker.

### When General Buckner Hung his Head.

Some of the Confederate officers at Fort Donelson took their surrender very much to heart. They were proud, insolent, and defiant. Their surrender was unconditional, but they thought it very hard to give up their swords and pistols. One of them fired a pistol at Major Mudd, of the Second Illinois regiment, wounding him in the back. The Major belonged in St. Louis, and had been, from the beginning, an ardent friend of the Union. He had hunted the guerrillas in Missouri, and had fought bravely at Wilson's Creek. He was probably shot by an old enemy. General Grant at once issued orders that all the rebel officers should be disarmed. General Buckner, in insolent tones, said to General Grant, that it was barbarous, inhuman, brutal, unchivalrous, and at variance with the rules of civilized warfare. General Grant replied—

"You have dared to come here to complain of my acts, without the right to make an objection. You *do not appear to remember that your surrender was unconditional.* Yet, if we compare the acts of the different armies in this war, how will yours bear inspection? You have cowardly shot my officers in cold blood. As I rode over the field, I saw the dead of my army brutally insulted by your men, their clothing stripped off of them, and their bodies exposed without the slightest regard for common decency. Humanity has seldom marked your course whenever our men have been unfortunate enough to fall into your hands. At Belmont, your authorities disregarded all the usages of civilized warfare. My officers were crowded into cotton pens with my brave soldiers, and then thrust into prison, while your officers were permitted to enjoy their parole, and live at the hotel in Cairo. Your men are given the same fare as my own, and your wounded receive our best attention. These are incontrovertible facts. I have simply taken the precaution to disarm your officers and men, because necessity compelled me to protect my own from assassination."

General Buckner had no reply to make. He hung his head in shame at the rebuke.

### Weitzel Satisfied with the Twelfth Connecticut.

The Twelfth Connecticut had lain for ten days within hearing of the bombardment of Fort Jackson, within sight of the bursting shells and of the smoke of that great torment, but still they had not as a regiment been under fire. Though they were the first troops to reach the conquered city of New Orleans, they had never yet heard the whistling of balls, excepting in a trifling skirmish on Pearl River, where five of the companies received a harmless volley from forty or fifty invisible guerrillas. Almost all that they knew of war was the routine of drill and guard duty, and the false night alarms with which the brigadier used to try and season them; though they wilted under a southern sun, and were daubed with Louisiana mud, and were sick by hundreds and died by scores.

But they were at last to quit garrison duty behind the great earthworks of Camp Parapet, and go into active offensive operations. Lieutenant Godfrey Weitzel of the Engineers, the chief military adviser of General Butler, had lately been created Brigadier-General, and the extenuated forces of the department were exhausted to furnish him with a brigade suitable to the execution of the plans which he proposed.

Weitzel did not want the Twelfth Connecticut. It was generally believed that the regiments which garrisoned Camp Parapet were not only sickly but broken in spirit and undisciplined, which, in a qualified but not disparaging sense, had some foundation. At any rate, the word had gone abroad that the regiment was undisciplined, and so General Weitzel did not want the Twelfth Connecticut.

But shortly after the regiment had joined his brigade, he came upon it in one of its battalion drills, and, taking command, hurried them on the double-quick through movement after movement, with the intention as it seemed, of puzzling them, and so finding occasion to report their unfitness for immediate field service. It was, "Double column at half distance; battalion, inward face; double-quick; march!" And then, — "Form square; right and left into line, wheel; double-quick, march!" And then, — "Reduce square; double-quick, march!" And then, — "Column forward, guide right; double-quick, march!" And then,—"Deploy column; right companies, right into line, wheel; left companies, on the right into line; battalion, guide right, double-quick, ma-r-c-h!" And so on for half an hour, as fast as the men could trot, and the officers drill, the ranks. But there was not an instant's tangle in reeling and unreeling the difficult skein. If there was any thing that the Lieutenant-Colonel commanding loved, if there was any thing the old General excelled in, it was tactical evolution. The regiment had been drilled in battalion and drilled in brigade, till it went like a watch. Weitzel rode off satisfied with the Twelfth Connecticut; and the regiment was equally pleased with its smart young general. We believe that to that excellent chaplain and popular writer, Mr. Trumbull, is due this first-rate narrative; or, at any rate, every Connecticut reader will find himself deficient in some of the best written and always truthful memorabilia of the war, who has not Trumbull's racy sketches, as penned by him in the camp and on the field of battle.

### Tom. Taylor's Flag of Truce.

On the 8th of July, 1861, a singular affair, in the way of a rebel flag of truce, took place at Washington. It appears that while Colonel Andrew Porter, of the United States army, was scouting at the head of a party of eighteen in the immediate vicinity of the disunion lines on the other side of the river, a party of twenty-two mounted disunion troops was observed approaching them. Colonel Porter immediately placed his men in position for a brush, and awaited their nearer approach. Perceiving, when they got in hailing distance of him, that one of them had in his hand trailing, a white flag, he demanded that they should halt where they were, and explain their errand. They came to a halt, and declared that they bore an important communication from Davis to the President of the United States.

Colonel Porter requested them to dismount, and approach with it on foot, a measure of precaution rendered necessary by the fact that the officer bearing the flag, was accompanied by a larger escort than that (twelve men,) incident to the presence of a flag of truce. His request was complied with, and he found their representation correct. The disunion officer proved to be Captain Tom. Taylor, of Frankfort, Kentucky, a kinsman of Old Zack's, who bore a sealed letter from Jeff. Davis to President Lincoln, according to a representation upon its back, written and signed by Beauregard at Manassas, explaining the fact, and asking that Captain Taylor might be facilitated in his mission.

Accordingly, Colonel Porter sent Captain Taylor and his missive forward with an officer and an orderly, and directed the disunion escort to return forthwith into their own lines—himself and the picket guard with him, following them for some distance, to see that that direction was properly carried out.

Captain Taylor was carried immediately to General McDowell's head-quarters, where, by telegraph, directions were received to send him to General Scott's head-quarters at Washington. He arrived under a guard at seven P. M., and after a brief interview with General Scott, wherein Captain Tom. Taylor told his story as he had doubtless been instructed to tell it, he was sent to the President, bearing the sealed missive from Jeff. Davis to that functionary.

His business was disposed of at the White House in a very few minutes; for in that time he was sent back to General Scott with one letter less than he bore on his person on entering the Union lines, the President not deeming the communication he brought such as required him to enter into any correspondence with Davis.

Captain Tom. Taylor, of Uncle Sambo's cavalry, was next immediately faced in the direction from which he came, and marched back to General McDowell's head-quarters, where, though courteously and kindly treated, he was kept under a strict guard until an early hour the next morning, when he was escorted back to Uncle Sambo's lines, and turned loose to find his way back to Beauregard, without having accomplished what was evidently a main point to be attained by his mission —viz.: to communicate with traitors in Washington, who had doubtless prepared to send to Beauregard, through him, important information concerning contemplated military movements.

### McCook's Pass for Old Buz.

A man named Buz Rowe, well known in the neighborhood of Bacon Creek, was early afflicted with the secession fever, and when the Confederates occupied that portion of Kentucky, the sickness assumed a malignant form. It was his practice to lie around a tavern at Bacon Creek Station, drink whisky, swagger, blow about Southern rights, and insult Union men. When, however, the Union troops advanced to Nevin, and the Confederates fell back to Green River, Buz changed his tune. He was not disposed to take up arms in behalf of the cause he represented. In fact, to secure peace and safety at home, he expressed his willingness to "take the oath."

On being lectured by Union men, he stated that he was only 'going through the form, to prevent being troubled at home, that when he could do good for the rebel

Gen. Alex McCook.

cause he would not regard the obligation in the least.' It was some time before Buz could get a Union man to go to the camp with him, but finally, in company with such, he called on General McCook, and asked for the privilege of taking the oath and obtaining a pass. The General knew his man, and addressing the Union man who accompanied him, said :

"Administer the oath to *him*—a ready traitor to his country! What regard do you suppose he would have for the solemn obligations of the oath? A man, sir, who would betray his country, has no respect for his oath."

Buz turned pale. The truth cut him deep, and he began to see that his time had come.

The General absolutely refused to have the oath administered, or to grant a pass. He could not get out of camp without some sort of a document, and he besought the interference of those whom he had so greatly cursed, pursued and abused, when they were without protection. At last General McCook agreed to pass him out of camp, and gave him a document which read something in this way:

"To the guards and pickets. The bearer is a traitor to his country. Pass him; but, in doing so, mark him well, and if you see him hereafter prowling about our lines, shoot him at once."

This pass the brawling disunionist had to show to the whole line of guards and pickets, who all marked him well before they let him pass. Though he had previously been at Bacon Creek every day, he was not known to show his 'bacon' there again. One interview with General McCook caused him to subside. 'Doctor' McCook's medicine was the only kind that proved a cure in such cases.

#### Colonel Gazley Doing a little Guard Duty.

Lieutenant ———, of one of the Ohio regiments, was making a detail of men to guard a lot of army stores captured from the enemy. He approached a crowd of men all wearing overcoats, such as Uncle Sam gives his 'soger boys,' and selected four or five for special duty. It happened that Lieutenant-Colonel Gazley, of the thirty-seventh Indiana, was in the crowd, and was selected by the Lieutenant. This was fun for the Colonel, and without a word he shouldered his gun and went to his post of duty. Not long afterward, the Lieutenant, going his rounds, discovered by the firelight the bugle upon Gazley's cap. He rather authoritatively inquired where he got that bugle? The Colonel drily replied that he "must have picked up an officer's cap somewhere," and with this very reasonable explanation the Lieutenant passed on.

The Colonel stood his turn of 'special detail' all night long and was found in the morning walking his post with true soldierly gait and pace. Having laid off

Colonel Gazley doing a little Guard Duty.

his overcoat, his shoulder-straps appeared very conspicuously in connection with the musket on his shoulder. As soon as the Lieutenant discovered a Colonel on guard, he approached him and courteously inquired how he came to be there upon guard. "Well, sir, you placed me here." With no little agitation the Lieutenant inquired who he was? "My name is Carter Gazley, and I am Lieutenant-Colonel of the Thirty-seventh Indiana regiment." The Colonel was speedily "released," but the Lieutenant was not so speedily relieved from his embarrassment. It is to be supposed that the Lieutenant "stood treat" in this case.

#### "Hail Columbia" in a New Version.

Colonel Granville Moody, a well known Methodist preacher, entered the Union army with a will. He did not ask or seek a chaplaincy—not he; he commanded the Seventy-fourth Ohio regiment, and proved himself a tremendous fighter as well as a good preacher. Fifty years, or more, of age, he was of magnificent port, and six feet two or three inches of stature; fine, genial face, fiery dark eyes, and a vocal range that would have excited the envy of Roaring Ralph Stackpole. He carried into battle a spirit of enthusiasm which inflamed his "boys" to the highest pitch of daring, and won for him the admiration of thousands. Thus, Lieutenant-Colonel Van Schrader, Inspector-General on the staff of General Thomas, had not been on friendly terms with Moody for some months, but admiring his splendid gallantry, he approached him in the heat of desperate conflict, extended his hand, expressed his earnest approbation of the Colonel's heroism, and begged that ever after peace might exist between them. A little later, Moody's "boys," as he paternally addressed them, were obliged to withstand a terrific fire without enjoying opportunity to return it. Moody galloped to General Negley and protested. "This fire, General, is positively murderous; it will kill all my boys." But there was no help for it. His martial flock, imposing upon his benevolent nature, sometimes indulged a little sly humor at his expense. In the midst of battle, an Irishman in the regiment shouted, "His riverence, the Colonel, has been fightin' Satan all his life ; I reckon he thinks hell's broke loose now." Not long after the battle, General Negley merrily accused him of having indulged heterodox expletives in the ardor of engagement.

"Is it a fact, Colonel," inquired the General, "that you told the boys to give them hell?"

"Now," replied the Colonel, reproachfully, "there's some more of the boys' mischief. I told the boys to give the rebels *Hail* Columbia, and they have wickedly perverted my language."

The fighting parson explained the matter, however, with such a sly twinkle in the corner of his eye, that all he said only tended to cast a doubt upon the subject. But there was no doubt that one of his injunctions to his regiment sounded marvellously like a fervent ejaculation swelling up from the depths of the "Amen" corner in an old fashioned Methodist church. This fact must be imagined, that the anecdote may be appreciated. The Colonel's mind was saturated with piety and pugnacity. He praised God and pitched into the rebels alternately. He had been struck by bullets four times already. He had given the enemy "H—ail Columbia" once, and they had reeled back to cover. Now they were swarming back to renew the contest. Moody's regiment were lying on their bellies waiting for them to come up. He had a moment to spare, and thought he would exhort them. The rebels were advancing swiftly, and probably cut him short. But as they approached he said quietly—" Now, boys, fight for your country and your God "—'and,' said one of his boys, 'we all surely thought he was going to say Amen, but at that instant the rebels let fly, and the old hero roared with the voice of a Stentor, "AIM LOW!"' Weeks afterward, when the Colonel passed through his camp, the mischievous rascals would shout behind him, "Fight for your country and your God—AIM LOW!"

### Ingenuity of a Yankee Wife in Getting a Pass.

An order was issued by the General of the Army of the Cumberland, that officers' and soldiers' wives should stay at home,— or, at least, advising them that they better not visit the army at Murfreesborough, there being no hotels, no nice eatables, none of the comforts of life, there ; on the contrary, many disagreeable things would have to be encountered. Hence, the dear ladies could get no passes to that army,— sad fact, but very necessary denial.

But an officer's wife is shrewd. If she can circumvent the epaulet and shoulder-straps, 'tis done ; and she takes not a little delight in the operation. One of them, accordingly, telegraphed from Louisville to General Garfield, Chief of Staff, that her husband, an artillery officer, was very sick,—perhaps dying,—and that she *must* see him, and requested the General to authorize the issuing to her of a pass to Murfreesborough. The General's heart was touched; but, knowing nothing of the matter, he referred it to Colonel Barnett, Chief of Artillery. The Colonel, too, sympathized with the distressed wife, and kindly sent an orderly out to the husband's battery to inquire into his condition, that the devoted wife might be advised thereof. Speedily the husband himself came in, with astonishment depicted upon his face. Something's the matter, somehow or somewhere, he does'nt exactly know what.

"How do you do?" asked the Artillery Chief.

"First-rate, sir."

"Where have you been of late?"

"At my battery,—on duty."

"Have you not been sick lately?"

"No, indeed! Never had better health in my life."

"Quite sure of it, are you?"

"Of course I am."

"You have been on duty all the time? Have'nt you been absent from your command at all?"

"Not a day."

"Perfectly well now,—no consumption, liver complaint, fever, spleen, or Tennessee quickstep? eh?"

"Certainly not. Why do you ask?"

In reply to this query, the telegram of his anxious wife was handed to him. He read it, looked down and pondered for a moment in silent wonder at the ingenuity of the woman, then called for a bottle of wine, and a general "smile" circulated among the by-standers. The loving wife was informed by telegraph that her husband was in no danger,—in fact, was doing remarkably well. Thus she was circumvented for a time. Yet, to "vindicate the truth of history," it needs to be added that she gained her point in some other way,—what Yankee wife will not?—and made her visit successfully.

### Matronly Opinion of "Corduroy."

Mrs. W., an old lady residing in the town of O——, was, just after one of the battles in the Southwest, listening to an account of General Grant's operations, in which, among other things, it was stated that he had caused several miles of new road to be constructed, and had covered it here and there with *corduroy*. "Why, bless me!" she exclaimed, "what a waste! Did a body ever *hear* the like! There's our boys, poor creatures! some of 'em most naked, and the pesky officers using up on them secessioners' roads all that stuff that was sent to make breeches! I kin tell you," she concluded, with an indignant flourish worthy of the best days of Mrs. Partington, "*we havn't got the right kind of Ginerals!*" The honest matron was not aware that the "corduroy" referred to was not exactly the stuff for the boys' "breeches," but that stout timber construction employed to cover otherwise impassable highways.

### Halleck and the Teamster.

That General Halleck, like General Sherman, is, in military as well as personal affairs, a man of some odd ways, is saying nothing to his damage as a soldier. When in camp, he was accustomed to put on citizen's dress and privately take a look at men and things. During one of these tours—not unknowing but unknown—he helped a teamster out of the mud, then gave him a severe lecture for not driving carefully. He laughed heartily to hear the witticisms of a teamster upon himself. The high water in the river made a slough all but impassable. The teamster had floundered through it, and, having reached the top of the bluff, and being in sight of head-quarters, relieved himself of volley after volley of oaths upon the creek, his horses, the roads, and lastly upon General Halleck for not having the creek bridged. The criticism was just; but the General had already ordered the construction of a bridge, and, being incog., could enjoy the verbal castigation.

#### Down upon the Table-Waiters.

The illustration afforded of General Butler's pluck, in what follows, could hardly be exceeded by the most graphic sketches of that always graphic and brilliant writer, Mr. Parton, to whom we are indebted for one of the very best military biographies in the whole range of war literature, possessing, as it does, almost the fascination of romance. It appears that a respectable colored woman, named Clara Duncan, left New York city, in company with a Mr. Walker and a Miss Bassett (white), for Norfolk, being sent by the American Missionary Association as teachers to the freed people. It was the desire of the Secretary, Rev. Mr. Whipple, that the two female passengers, white and black, on arriving at Baltimore, should occupy the same state room on board of the boat.

All passed pleasantly; they were seated in the upper saloon when the gong sounded for tea. The clerk invited all down, Miss Duncan with the others. After tea, the clerk called Mr. Walker aside and inquired whether he knew the regulations of the boat. Mr. Walker replied that he did not. The clerk then said, "We don't allow niggers to eat at the first table. And you go and tell her to come out of that saloon to a place prepared for her, or I shall take her down publicly." During the conversation, the mail agent, by the name of Rollins, stepped up and said that Mr. Walker "was no gentleman for traveling with a nigger wench," neither was Miss Bassett a lady for occupying the same state room. Arrangements were made for Miss Duncan to remain in her state room until the boat arrived at Fortress Monroe. All parties were indignant. On arriving at Norfolk the case was submitted to General Wild, who told Mr. Walker to write out a statement and submit it to Prof. Woodbury, Superintendent of Schools. Prof. Woodbury submitted it to General Butler, and the parties were duly summoned before that official.

The officiating clerk of the boat, Mr. Wilson, was asked by General Butler what he had to say for himself.

Wilson—I remember seeing those persons on the boat, and remember some complaint being made about a mulatto eating at the first table.

General—Who made those complaints?

Wilson—I do not know, General, all that were on board. I can not remember all the names and faces.

General—You must remember some of them.

Wilson—Gov. Pierpont was on board and he—

Gen.—Then you say Gov. Pierpont complained? If Governor Pierpont had anything to do with it he shall not remain in my lines. Did Gov. Pierpont complain?

Wilson—No, sir.

Gen.—Who did complain, then?

Wilson—I do not know that any one complained.

Gen.—They either complained or did not complain—which was it?

Wilson—They did not complain; but, General, it has always been the rule—

Gen.—Has been, is not now; there's where the trouble lies—has been.

The General then, turning to the mail agent, remarked, "Mr. Rollins, you run on the steamer Louisiana?"

Rollins—I do.

Gen.—Your employment is to tend to the mail and express, I believe. You, sir, are charged with calling that young lady (pointing to Miss Duncan,) improper names. Miss Duncan has not the power to change her color; that she can not control, but her character; and to call her a nigger-wench implies that she is of disreputable character.

Rollins—I never said so.

Gen.—You say your business is to tend to the mail and express.

Rollins—Yes, and to wait on table.

Gen.—It does not seem probable that you should say anything of the kind. The waiters are generally colored persons. You are a waiter, you say; therefore it is not natural that you should say anything against your associates. May I ask, Mr. Rollins, what business you had to say anything? The clerk had spoken; that was sufficient.

Mr. Rollins said nothing.

The General, then turning to Mr. Wilson : "When John or Susan traveled with master or mistress, they could stay in the saloons or sleep in the same state-room, could they not?"

Wilson—Yes.

Gen.—Well, now I would like to ask one more question: Which do you consider in the highest state of civilization, the slave in his chains or the free person of color?

Wilson—I do not know—I guess—I think—well, I suppose, the free person.

Gen.—You admit, then, the free man. Well, all I want is that the free man shall have the same rights the slave once enjoyed; they shall sit in saloons, sleep in state-rooms, and go to the first table, if they desire.

Wilson—I suppose I may tell them they may be insulted?

Gen.—Oh, yes! and I shall excuse you, Mr. Wilson, if I never hear the same thing again. You were trying to promote your employers' interest. Remember what I have said. Now, Mr. Rollins, am I to believe your assertions? How much do you receive per month?

Rollins—Twenty-five dollars.

Gen.—How much do you receive from Government?

Rollins—Not anything, Sir.

Gen.—Where were you born?

Rollins—In Baltimore.

General—And brought up in Baltimore, too, I suppose.

Rollins—Yes.

Gen.—Well, now, Mr. Rollins, your employment on the Baltimore boats is at an end. Clerk, write an order to that effect, write one also to the Captain. Good afternoon, ladies and gentlemen.

## "Abe" and "Andy."

The drift of the communication given below will be found explained in the universal domestic dictionary.

The applicant, Normain Doane, an Indiana volunteer, asked for a furlough of twenty or thirty days in order to visit his wife and twins, boys, recently born, which he designed having christened "Abe" and "Andy." The document had passed through the War Department, from which place it was referred to the Adjutant General's office, then to the Medical Director's Department, where it was reported that he had been transferred to Philadelphia. The document was then sent back to the Military Commander at Washington, from thence to the Adjutant General's office, and then to General Couch's Department. The Medical Director of the latter finally referred the matter to the surgeon in charge of the hospital in which the patient was confined, who immediately granted the applicant the furlough:

Judiciary Square Hospital, Ward 15.
Washington City, D C, June 28, 1864.

DEAR SIR: The Union is saved. Hurrah!

Make room in Abraham's bosom!

My wife has twins. Both boys!

Do please grant me a furlough for twenty or thirty days to go to Fort Wayne, Ind., to christen 'em Abe and Andy; and besides, I would like to know if they look like me.

I am not so sick now. A few days at home will do me more good than six months in the hospital. Should any ref-

crence be required on patriotism and public service, Schuyler Colfax; on domestic relations, Mrs. Doane.
Very respectfully,
NORMAIN DOANE,
Private, signed Corporal U. S. A.
P. S.—The little presents necessary upon such occasions need not be sent till after the 4th of March next, when Andy will be present also. N. D.

### Impromptu Enforcement of Discipline.

General Grant was one day busy with his military plans in the inner part of his tent. His maps, rules, and compasses, were all in use. His mind ranged over the vast extent of country under his control. Mountains were scaled, rivers forded, swamps bridged, deserts traversed, forests threaded, storms and sunshine were overcome, and he was master of the situation. He was just laying out his plan of a projected battle, intensely occupied with the marshalling of his troops in their best positions for victory, when his ear caught the inquiry, put to his orderly, in a strong foreign accent,—

"Is de Generawl in?"

Then came the reply, in a firm, decided tone, which General Grant understood instantly—

"Yes, Sir, the Commanding General is in; but he is very busy, Sir."

"Could I zee him a vew momenz?"

"He ordered me to say, Sir, that he would be very much occupied for some time"—

"On de advance, eh?" interrupted the intruder; "Den he is going down furder to de coddon regione?"

"I can't say where he is going, Sir: I don't know. You must leave."

Stranger became more excited, and his accent more peculiar.

"Mine young vrend, I have one important proposals to make de Generawl,—a proposals, mine young vrend"—

"I can't hear your 'proposal.' Step out, Sir!"

"Sdop, mine young vrend,—sdop one letle momend. You zay to de Generawl dat I will make it one gran' objecs for 'im,— one rich speculadion! You understan', eh?"

The orderly was about to force the base interloper out, with an added word of military admonition, when General Grant came quickly forward. He had heard the whole conversation, and comprehended the entire case in a moment. It was a covert assault on his nice sense of honor, and he was determined to punish it on the spot. Stepping to the open front of his tent, the General seized the rascally operator by the collar, and, lifting him several inches from the ground, applied the toe of his boot to him in such a manner that he was pitched out headlong, falling on the muddy ground at a distance of nearly ten feet. Before the orderly could recover from his surprise, the General had quietly retired to his inner apartment, and the next moment was as busily engaged with his maps, and plan of campaign, as if nothing had happened.

### Password as Understood by the German Guard.

In the Union army of the West, one of the officers,—a wag, too, in his way,—whose duty it was to furnish the guards with a password for the night, gave the word "Potomac." A German on guard, not understanding distinctly the difference between the B's and P's, understood it to be 'Bottomic,' and this, on being transferred to another, was corrupted to 'Buttermilk.' Soon afterward the officer who had given the word wished to return through the lines, and approaching the sentinel, was ordered to halt, and the word demanded. He gave "Potomac."

"Nicht right: you don't pass mit me dis way."

"But this is the word, and I will pass."

"No, you stan' "; at the same time placing a bayonet at his breast in a manner that told Mr. Officer that "Potomac" didn't pass in Missouri.

"What is the word then?"
"Buttermilk."
"Well, then, 'Buttermilk.'"
"Dat is right; now you pass mit yourself all about your pizness."

#### Congressman Ely at the Confederate Passport Office.

When Congressman Ely, of New York, but for a time a prisoner in Richmond, was finally released, in exchange for Hon. Mr. Faulkner, of Virginia, on calling at the office for his passport, a hearty laugh occurred over the brown paper on which it was printed, and which had been contracted for by the superintendent of public printing. He asked if it was Southern manufacture. The passport officer replied in the affirmative, and suggested that he should exhibit it, the specimen, in the North, and say that although crude in its origin, they—the South—would refine upon it, and never cease striving for independence until they could make as good

Congressman Ely.

paper as the Yankees. Congressman Ely naively replied that he had no doubt they would arrive at the dignity of *white paper*.

#### Caught in his own Trap.

The sergeant of one of the Union picket guards suddenly had his attention drawn to the tinkling of a cow-bell in the bushes. With visions of new milk running through his head, he examined carefully, and to his astonishment found himself euchered of his milk; but he made the discovery that as he advanced the cow-bell retreated. The sergeant smelt a moderate sized mice, and made a double-quick retrograde movement. He immediately reported the affair to Colonel Hays. The Colonel secreted a squad of men in the woods, and

Caught in his own Trap.

the sergeant again made himself conspicuous. He brushed about among the bushes, and the cow-bell approached. The squad soon had the satisfaction of seeing—not the cow-bell, but a secesher, with a cow-bell hung to his neck and a six-shooter in his belt. When he got within easy range, and in sight of the squad, the sergeant hailed him: "I say, old fellow, would you rather go to —, or to Washington?" The squad at the same time stepped forward. "To Washington, I reckon," drawled the rebel—"I ain't clothed for a warm climate." And he accordingly delivered himself up with the best possible grace.

#### Marshall's "Demijohn Drill."

Colonel Marshall, when stationed at Baltimore, proved himself a prompt and efficient officer, according to the testimony of his men, over whom he exercised not only a military but moral oversight. On a certain occasion, at dress parade, he gave them what he called the "demijohn drill." Some one had been permitted to set up a tent inside our lines, and sell eatables to the soldiers. This individual dared to sell rum, which made a few drunk and noisy. This drunkard-maker was arrested by the Colonel's orders, and taken into the guard-house. His liquor was also seized. He was then drummed out to the tune of the "Rogue's March," presenting a most laughable appearance, with a bottle slung over each shoulder, a toddy-stick in his rear, soldiers ahead of him and soldiers behind him with bayonets charged close to his person. After this the sound of shattered glass testified that the demijohn was drilled, and its contents spilled.

#### No Passes to Official Speculators.

A little affair transpired in General Banks's head-quarters one day, as related by an eye witness, which furnishes a rather sorry idea as to how much actual interest was felt in the war by some of the "patriotic" men who got up regiments and companies for the service.

Enter an Ex-Colonel of a Massachusetts regiment, and after waiting an interview, a colloquy something like the following occurred:

Ex-Col.—Good morning, General.

Gen. B.—Good morning, Sir, I am very happy to see you.

Ex-Col.—General, I called to ask you for a pass to go to New Iberia.

Gen. B.—Your name is ——.

Ex-Col.—Yes, Sir.

Gen. B.—You were Colonel of the Massachusetts — regiment?

Ex-Col.—Yes, Sir, I did command that regiment.

Gen. B.—And you resigned your commission to engage in speculation?

Ex-Col.—Why, General, you would not suppose I should continue in the service when I saw a chance to make twenty or thirty thousand dollars in a few months?

Gen. B.—Sir, I did not come here to make money by speculation, and it is because men like yourself are willing to see my command broken up, if they can accomplish their own purposes, that this department is in no better condition to-day. I give no passes to New Iberia, Sir, and especially I shall not grant one to you. Good morning, Sir.

Exit Ex-Colonel—violently considering how he shall get to New Iberia *without* General Banks's pass.

#### Honorable Commendation instead of Ignominious Death.

It appears that information reached the President that a young man belonging to the Army of the Potomac had been sentenced by court-martial to be shot for desertion. The boy was doomed to die in a few hours when the dispatch was received. A telegram was sent to General Meade, suspending the execution of the sentence. An examination of the case was ordered by the President, when it was ascertained that the young man ought, in justice, to have been promoted long ago for gallant and meritorious service, instead of being shot! It was proved that upon the march of the Army of the Potomac towards Maryland, on the occasion of General Lee's first raid northward, the young man in question became exhausted and fell out of the ranks, and, as soon as he recovered, he proceeded on after his regiment, but not finding it, and there being no time to lose, he fell into the ranks of another regiment and fought gallantly at South Mountain and Antietam, and was wounded in the last named battle. He was sent to the hospital, which fact, owing to the absence of a proper system in such cases, did not reach the officers of his regiment. At last he was arrested as a deserter, tried, condemned, and was about to be shot, when by the interference of the Executive, his life was saved, and a young man, hastily doomed to an ignominious death, was suddenly restored to honor.

### Peggie McCue who Whipped General Cheatham.

A queer specimen of the *genus homo* was Peggie McCue—so they called him—who used to be employed on the river boats, and afterward was a soldier in the rebel army, seeking his fights. During the occupancy of Missionary Ridge, by the Confederates, an incident occurred in which Peggie played a conspicuous and certainly a very characteristic part. Peggie was engaged one day as a teamster, and General Frank Cheatham, riding along, caught him in the act of vigorously pummelling the mules with a billet of wood. Riding up in a terrible rage, Cheatham denounced him with great severity, and ordered him to cease his brutal treatment. Peggie's Irish riz suddenly. Turning about and confronting Frank, he remarked—

"General, you are a — coward. You know your shoulder-straps protect you, or you would never apply that talk to me."

"A coward, am I, you miserable devil!" exclaimed the General, throwing off his coat; look here, McCue; there is General Cheatham and the shoulder-straps; here is Frank Cheatham. Come and take satisfaction."

Peggie was not slow to accept the invitation, made for Frank, and in two minutes had whipped him soundly.

The General, smarting under his defeat, started for his horse, which a sudden application of Peggie's foot assisted him to mount. Picking up the coat, McCue threw it to the General, remarking as he did so, (pointing first to the rider, and then to the coat.)—

"There is the whipped Frank Cheatham, of the Cumberland Army—here is Major-General Cheatham, commander of a division. General, you can repeat that operation as often as you desire; you will always find Peggie ready for you."

### Sticking to the Original Order.

Peter Apple, of Oakland, Marion county, was a recruit for the Eleventh Indiana regiment, and took part in the attempt to storm one of the Vicksburg batteries. The enemy's fire was so destructive, however, that the Union army recoiled. Apple, the raw recruit, having received orders to go "Onward," "didn't see" the backward movement, and, obedient to the original command issued, kept going ahead until he came right up to one of the enemy's guns, caught a gunner by the collar, and brought him within the Federal lines, saying, "By golly, boys, why didn't you come on? Every feller might have got one."

### Toombs's Idea of Passports.

Robert Toombs, formerly a United States Senator, subsequently Secretary of State under Davis, and then a Confederate General, but finally a Colonel in the Georgia militia, at last seceded to his private domain, becoming a citizen without civic or military distinction. Rather disgusted than otherwise with the " powers that be," he returned to the advocacy of Georgia State Rights, in all the radicalness of that ultra Southern school. This, with other acts and speeches, made him obnoxious to dislike, nor was his offence mitigated by the personal assumptions in which he sometimes indulged.

One day, acting up to his original standard of the dignity of a noble patrician, a citizen of the State of Georgia, and in defiance of the law military which he himself helped to ordain, he undertook to travel on a Georgia railroad *without a passport*. In reply to the demand of a rebel soldier to show his passport, he said he had no such document—that he was a citizen of the State of Georgia, which State did not require her railroad passengers to show passports.

The inference from this was that Robert denied his allegiance to the central agent, whose foundations were laid upon the mutual good-will and esteem of the component parts, and cemented with the doctrine of secession. Such language was to the ears of Beauregard little short of treasonable; and he had the Ex-Senator, Ex-

Secretary and the Ex-Brigadier arrested and sent to prison. An old Southern lady, who witnessed the arrest, summed up Robert in this style:

"Well, well, well! they have got Bob Toombs! I heard him say he would swallow the blood of all the Yankees that came South. Well, well, well! he'll swallow all he sheds!"

At which remarks the unfeeling crowd, whose veneration for the illustrious Toombs must have undergone considerable modification since they allowed him to persuade them to secede, burst into loud laughter.

### Hardee's Tactics, with a Point Left Out.

While on a forced march in some of the army movements in Mississippi, General Hardee, of the rebel army, came up with a straggler who had fallen some distance in the rear of his command. The General ordered him forward, when the soldier replied that he was weak and broken down,

General Hardee

not having had even half rations for several days.

"That's hard," replied the General, "but you must push forward, my good fellow, and join your command, or the Provost Guard will take you in hand."

The soldier halted, and, looking up at the General asked—

"Are you General Hardee?"

"Yes," replied the General.

"Didn't you write Hardee's Tactics?"

"Yes."

"Well, General, I have studied them tacticks, and know'em by heart. You've got a order to double column at half distance, ain't you?"

"Well," asked the General, "what has that to do with your case?"

"I'm a good soldier, General, and obey all that is possible to be obeyed; but if your orders can show me a order in your tacticks to double distance on half rations, then I'll give in."

The General, with a hearty laugh, admitted that there were no tactics to meet the case, and putting spurs to his horse, rode forward.

### Sickness after Furlough.

It was a common trick in the army to try and get a medical certificate of illness or incapacity; but very many of those who went to the Medical Director, found they had got to the wrong man. Any one sitting in Dr. Cuyler's office, any five minutes during the day, would been likely to hear an amusing dialogue somewhat after this fashion:

Enter two sturdy soldiers, very stout, rosy and healthy in appearance, but trying to look very lackadaisical.

Dr. Cuyler, (in a brusque but honest tone, to first,)—Well, Sir, what can I do for you to-day?

Soldier, (groaning slightly,)—I'm very sick, doctor; I've chronic rheumatism.

Dr. C.—Chronic rheumatism, eh? My dear Sir, that disease is quite played out here. Try a little exercise with your brave brothers on the James River. Where do you come from?

Soldier—New York, Sir, on return from furlough.

Dr. C.—From furlough, eh? How long?

Soldier—A month, Sir.

Dr. C.—So you go home and enjoy yourself a whole month, at your country's expense, return here to resume your duties, and just at the time your over-worked brothers are needing your assistance most, you come here to desert them. I put it to your conscience, Sir, as a man, is this right?

Dr. C., (sternly.)—No sick man needs explanation to *me*, Sir. I know them too well, and insist upon their being tended like children; but that is not *your* case. (Turning to the other)—What is the matter with *you*, Sir?

Second Soldier, (looking heartier than the first.)—I am very sick, Sir.

Dr. C.—Have you been on furlough, too?

Second Soldier—Yes, Sir, we came together, from New York.

Dr. C.—Strange, you weren't sick in New York, but get sick directly you come back! Pray, how long have you been sick?

Second Soldier—Two days, Sir.

Dr. C.—Only two days, and you consider that enough to throw up your duties? Why, my dear Sir, I don't feel very well to-day, but you see I must keep to my post. Pooh! Pooh! I'm tired of this nonsense. (To his clerk)—Here, Mr. Silva, write an order for these two men. Tell —— that they have just returned from a month's furlough, and wish to rejoin their regiments.

The papers are speedily made out, and *exit* the two "patients," no doubt feeling that Dr. Cuyler is a rather "hard case."

### Tricks to Avoid Duty.

One of the first things a soldier learns to do is to avoid duty. He tires of the daily drill, picket duty, etc., and seeks, through plea of sickness, to escape them. Thus it was in our Union armies; thus it has been in all armies. It would have puzzled Dr. Lieber himself to make out some of the complaints which were "put in" at the morning call of the regimental surgeon, by the soldiers. Thus, knowing that the doctor relies mainly for his judgment of a case upon the condition of the pulse, the soldier would not unfrequently render it unsteady and violent by rapping the elbow severely just before entering his tent. The appearance of the tongue is, of course, another standard criterion of condition. A surgeon of a New York regiment in General Davidson's brigade was much puzzled during the winter of 1861, to account for so many of the men having coated tongues. It was almost a distemper in the regiment. After much diligent inquiry he discovered that among the privates was a druggist who furnished, for a trifle, his comrades with a white mixture, which they applied to their tongues whenever desirous of getting off from duty. The discovery was not made, however, until after nearly the whole regiment had deceived him at one time and another.

### Easy Way of Cutting Red Tape.

The convenient manner in which General Grant sometimes was accustomed to cut red tape was quite refreshing. On one occasion the Ninetieth New York regiment, then in a distant field of military operations, re-enlisted as veteran recruits, but were not able then to take their furlough, on account of a press of business. While, however, General Grant was on his visit to Maryland, the regiment departed for home on furlough. But there were twenty-two of the men, who, as punishment for some trivial offence, were not allowed to go. They were put into other regiments, to serve until their regiment returned, and were still held as veteran recruits. These twenty-two men, being at Monocacy, where General Grant was visiting, concluded to try the heart of their chief, and one of them waited on him in behalf of the party.

A private soldier, grim and travel-stained, bearing in every feature the trace of long service in the field, the Lieutenant-General listened attentively while he told his tale and plead for himself and his companions. A few questions put and answered, and Grant was satisfied that injustice had been done the war-worn men, and on the spot he wrote a telegram to the proper officer, then at Harper's Ferry, instructing him to furlough the men immediately. They left for home at once, with a consciousness that the Commander-in-Chief was one who could mete out equal and exact justice to all.

### Ready Mode of Meeting Difficulties by General Butler.

Two noted characters, C. C. Pearson and James Leary, formerly billiard and liquor-saloon keepers and gamblers in Norfolk, having inveigled themselves into Bermuda Landing without passes, were brought

Head-quarters of Gen. Butler, Baltimore.

before the Commanding General, Butler, who thereupon issued the following order:

"C. C. Pearson having smuggled himself within my lines, contrary to law and without a pass, on board the gunboat Pink, Ensign Kendrick, master, and being, by his own statement, able-bodied and without any business, is ordered to be set to work in the trenches, until further orders, to supply the place of a soldier who has other occupation. There being constant employment for him in Gen. Hinks's line, he will be forwarded there."

The same order was issued in the case of Leary. One of them pleaded that he had served under the General at the beginning of the war.

"Very well," said the General, "serve with me now at the end of it."

Pearson begged off, telling the General to remember his family in Norfolk.

"Well, I am not doing anything to disgrace your family."

"But they won't know what has become of me."

"True. Davenport, print this order in the Norfolk papers, and then his family can see where he is."

### Arrest of one of General Grant's Aids by a Colored Guard.

While General Grant was on a visit to the front of his Potomac Army one day, one of his aids, who happened not to wear any distinguishing mark of office, was arrested by one of the colored soldiers as soon as his presence was discovered. In vain did he put in the plea of his official relations to the Lieutenant-General—they would not believe his story, but took him forthwith to General Grant to corroborate his explanation.

"Well, General," said the prisoner, "I have been arrested by this soldier, who won't believe my story."

The Commander-in-Chief identified and released his aid, telling the soldier he had done his duty. He then remarked to his aid:

"Served you right, Sir; I am glad of it, as it shows the negroes are vigilant. The next time you had better wear something to indicate your rank and profession, or else keep out of their way."

The author of that admirable work, 'Grant and his Campaigns,' could scarcely tell a better thing than the above of his great chieftain.

### Wanted a Furlough.

Colonel Parkhurst, the very efficient Provost Marshal General of the Army of the Cumberland, 'in the course of human events' married an elegant lady of Murfreesboro', Tennessee, and having been home twice within a short time to see her, was informed of a little joke on General Thomas—one, by the way, which the General was only too happy to tell himself.

Once on a time, a High Private, of extraordinary dimensions, lumbered into the presence of General Thomas and asked point blank for a furlough, adding:

"General, I wish to go home and see my wife."

"How long is it since you have seen your wife?" inquired the General.

"Why," he answered, "I have not seen my wife for over three months."

"Three months," exclaimed General Thomas, "three months! why, I haven't seen *my* wife for three years!"

"Well, that may be," rejoined the other, "but you see, General, me and my wife ain't o' that sort."

Whether H. P. got that little furlough or not may easily be guessed.

#### Irish Logic concerning "Shmall Arms."

During the siege of Vicksburg General Grant was in the habit of saying often that the rebels defending the city were his prisoners-of-war, who were *temporarily subsisting themselves.*

One day the Lieutenant-Colonel commanding the —th Wisconsin replied to some observation addressed to him by one Dennis ——, a perfect specimen of an Irishman, with the good-natured remark, "Oh! never mind, Dennis; General Grant says that they [pointing to the rebel lines] are only our prisoners." "Shure, then," said Dennis, "if they're our prisoners, why don't he be after taking away their *shmall arms?*"

#### "Whar's dat Nigger?"

In July, 1863, when the Army of the Cumberland was at Winchester, Tennessee, one of the foraging expeditions had for its guide, old Jim, one of the blackest of the black,—so black that he could be plainly seen in the darkest night,—and the first place he led to was the house of his former master. Riding up the lawn and dismounting, the first sound that was heard was: "Well, there's Jim! Oh, Jim, how could you leave us, when we have always treated you so kindly? Didn't you always say that you loved us dearly?" Jim straightens himself up, and goes up to the porch of the house, and replies, "Yes, Missus, I always lub you, and lub you now a heap: but really, Missus, I lub myself a heap better." Even the good old lady could not help smiling; and Jim conducted the party over the grounds where he had so many years been a slave with as much pride as if he was its real owner.

But Jim showed his peculiar nature more, perhaps, in the following incident, than in any other. During the advance toward Bridgeport a heavy artillery skirmish was had, and Jim was not seen for a whole day. At night, when he came up, he was asked where he had been. He rolled his large eyes in his head, and said, "Oh! massa, I heard something coming through the air, saying, 'Whar's

"Whar's dat Nigger!"

dat nigger? whar's dat nigger? whar's dat nigger?' and putty soon dat ting busted, and little debils went skirmishing all round right arter dis nigger, and I run away!"

Those persons who have heard shells come whizzing through the air will readily see that old Jim's description of them is perfect.

#### Judge Baldwin Soliciting a Pass.

Judge Baldwin, of California, an old and highly respectable and sedate gentleman, called one day on General Halleck, and presuming upon a familiar acquaintance in California a few years ago, solicited a pass outside our lines to see a brother in Virginia, not thinking that he would meet with a refusal, as both his brother and himself were good Union men. "We have been deceived too often," said General Halleck, "and I regret I can't grant it." Judge B. then went to Stanton, and was very briefly disposed of with the same result. Finally he obtained an interview with Mr. Lincoln, and stated the case. "Have you applied to General Halleck?" inquired the President. "Yes, and met with a refusal," said Judge B. "Then you must see Stanton," continued the President. "I have, and with the same result," was the reply. "Well, then," said Old Abe, with a smile of good humor, "I can do nothing; for you must know *that I have very little influence with this Administration!*"

#### Serious Indisposition of Two Uncles.

General Rosecrans was chary of giving passes. A lady one day approached him, and began with a pitiful story in regard to her "poor, dear, sick uncle." "I condole with you, madam," said the General, in his well known quiet way; "it is unfortunate that uncles will sometimes get seriously indisposed. I, too, have a dear afflicted uncle." "Then you can sympathize with me," she said. "Yes, madam, I do, and when my Uncle Sam gets over his present serious indisposition, I will give you a pass." It would of course be an anti-climax, which would ruin the story, to tell what the lady did.

#### Troubles of a Feminine "Secesh."

Galena, Illinois, is justly celebrated for its lead mines and pretty ladies,—quoth an officer of the Sixteenth United States infantry, who also furnishes the very readable 'local item' which follows: In this town resides a very interesting family, the father a native of New England, the mother of Tennessee. The daughters, grown to womanhood, are accomplished and lovely. The eldest daughter, Bell, married last fall a chaplain in a rebel Tennessee regiment, who, when the rebels evacuated Murfreesboro', went with his regiment, leaving his wife to return home. The father was a loyal man, but the rest of the family were badly "secesh." The married daughter, during the spring and summer, was continually teasing her father to get her a "military pass," to go South to her husband, which, however, he was not inclined to do. She got the pass, nevertheless, and commenced packing her things, preparatory to leaving. About this time the news of the fall of Vicksburg came, and a horse, a very great favorite in the family, was taken violently sick, and his life despaired of. One afternoon, while a social chat was going on in the parlor, with the daughters, the mother came in looking extremely dejected.

"Ma," asked the youngest daughter, "what is the matter?"

"Oh dear, my daughter," she replied, at the same time straightening herself up in her chair in a peculiar manner, which would have done honor to Mrs. Partington, "Vicksburg has fallen, Bell is going down South, the horse is going to die, and the dear Lord only knows what will come upon us next!"

#### Hard on Negley.

Quite a joke was played off upon General Negley by an audacious secession wag —a whiskey-drinking, facetious joker residing in the town of Goolettsville, a strong secesh hole, in which there never was but one Union man, and he died. Well, this wag wagered a gallon of whiskey that he could go into Nashville, and go all over the city, notwithstanding the strictness of General Negley's orders; further, that he would see Negley personally, and have a talk with him. The bet was taken, and this fellow, whose name was Paul, and well known in John Bell's State as a violent secessionist, the next day took a flag of truce, rode into the city, saw crowds of his friends, rode up to the head-quarters of General Negley and demanded the surrender of the city, stating that he was Assistant Adjutant Paul, and that there was an immense quantity of troops ready to enforce the demand. General Negley refused to entertain the thought of a surrender, and Paul returned to Goolettsville, having won his audacious bet. Negley was not 'cute, but a brave man and true patriot, who did great service for his country in Tennessee, the State so wofully plunged into secession anarchy by her Bells, Polks, and kindred spirits.

### Impositions upon Furloughed Men.

The impositions practiced upon soldiers by the cormorants that generally hang upon the trail of an army are well known. When, therefore, General Grant issued his order, No. 45, granting furloughs to the soldiers, he also issued a special order forbidding steamboat men to charge more than five dollars to enlisted men, and seven dollars to officers, as fare between Vicksburg and Cairo.

Immediately after Vicksburg had fallen, a large number of steamboats cleared from Northern ports for that place, and were in the habit of charging soldiers going home on furlough from fifteen to thirty dollars' fare to Cairo. One of these steamers was compelled by general Grant to disgorge its ill-gotten gains under the following circumstances:

The boat had about one thousand enlisted soldiers and nearly two hundred and fifty officers on board, *en route* for home on short leave of absence, after the fatigues of their protracted but glorious campaign.

The captain had charged these men and officers from ten to twenty-five dollars each as fare to Cairo. Just, however, as the boat was about to push off from the wharf at Vicksburg, an order came from General Grant, requiring the captain to pay back to his passengers all money received by him as fare in excess of five dollars to enlisted men, and seven dollars to officers, or submit to imprisonment for disobedience, and have his boat confiscated. The order certainly caused an amount of disagreeable astonishment to the captain; but the presence of a guard rendered it useless to refuse, and so, amid the shouts of the soldiers over their General's care of their interests, he complied with as good grace as possible, and paid back the money. A gentleman who was a passenger on this occasion had been present when General Grant issued the order above referred to. The General, upon being informed of the impositions practiced upon furloughed men and officers by steamboat men, was very indignant:

"I will teach them, if they need the lesson," said the gallant General, "that the men who have periled their lives to open the Mississippi River for their benefit cannot be imposed upon with impunity."

### Complimentary Responses of a Soldier to his General.

General Warren had the reputation not only of commanding a gallant corps but of making first-rate soldiers of his men, and meeting all sorts of cases in a manner that showed that he was not only a commander of soldiers but a man among men. When falling back during the night after the fight at Bristow, he saw a conscript straggling along, apparently without any weapon.

"To what command do you belong?" asked General Warren.

"Second corps," replied the man, with strong nasal twang denoting his recent departure from the Eastern States.

"What are you doing here without a gun?" was the next question put by the General, but to which the man gave an evasive reply, indicating that that was his business.

"What have you got under your coat there?" demanded General Warren.

"A gun, you ——— fool," returned the conscript, partly revealing a gun beneath the folds of his ample coat.

"There's no discount on that man," remarked General Warren to an Aid, and passed on.

rades, was instantly adopted. Every man loaded his piece, and pointed it over the parapet or through one of the many small portholes made by placing ammunition boxes in the wall. Then the author of the plan began to shout orders as though commanding at least a brigade:

"'Colonel, connect your line with the Forty-seventh!' 'Give way to the right.' 'Close ranks!' 'Right dress!' 'Fix bayonet!' 'Double-quick!' 'Ch-a-a-rge!'"

Instantly five hundred men rise into plain sight behind the rebel works, expect-

Belligerent Work.

Should this meet the brave fellow's eye, he will learn that he addressed his complimentary response to General Warren, and will wonder perhaps why he was not punished.

### Tricks and Tactics in the Ranks.

While the two armies—Grant's and Lee's—lay opposite each other, with their lines in close proximity, one Sunday, one of our men conceived a brilliant scheme, or ruse, which, when unfolded to his com-

ing to see an advancing line. Not so, but five hundred men from safe cover fire upon them on the instant. The volley, which must have inflicted considerable loss, is followed up with cheers and jeers, laughter, and much chaffing, as—'What do y' think o' Yankee tricks?' 'That's the way John Brown's soul is marching on!' 'No use o' baitin' hooks when you're fishin' for gudgeons!'

The trick was repeated several times during the day, with ingenious variations, always to crowded houses, and always eliciting much applause from the performers. Such pleasantries were a grateful offset to the belligerent work which the brave fellows of the national army were called to engage in, before and after, and of which they proved themselves masters worthy of the noble cause in which they fought.

### Widow Shultz's Appeal to the President.

Benjamin Shultz, of Newark, and who was a member of the Eighth New Jersey regiment, had the misfortune to fall into the hands of the rebels on two different occasions, as a prisoner. On his return from his first imprisonment, on parole, young Shultz was sent to Camp Parole, at Alexandria. Having had no furlough since the war commenced, efforts were made, but without success, to obtain for him liberty to pay a brief visit to his friends. But, not disheartened, and having faith in the warm-heartedness of the President, the young soldier's widowed mother wrote to Mr. Lincoln, stating that he had been in nearly every battle fought by the Army of the Potomac; had never asked a furlough; was now a paroled prisoner, and in consequence was unable to perform active duties; that two of his brothers had also served in the army; and asking that he be allowed to visit home, that she might see him once more. Her trust in the President was not unfounded. He immediately caused a furlough to be granted to her son.

### A Pass that Would'nt Pass.

"Traveling on a pass," among the negro soldiers on the Mississippi, must have been rather a difficult business, if any judgment can be formed from the narrative of personal experience given by a sojourner in that region— which serves also to illustrate in an amusing manner the esteem cherished by them for letters and their unwillingness to reveal their own ignorance:—I floated down to Port Hudson (wrote the traveler), where I arrived at a late hour in the night. At the end of the plank where I disembarked I met an unbleached American soldier, with a bayonet, who expressed a desire to read my pass, and ordered the steamboat to " hol on " till he did so. But the boat rounded out, and was well on her way toward New Orleans, before the member of the *Corps d' Afrique* came to the conclusion that he " didn't know whedder dat pass all right or no—may be good enough for soldiers, but may-be not for a citizen," he said. I asked him what he proposed to do about it; whereupon he called for " de Sahgent ob de ga'ad "; and the Sergeant appearing, I was graciously permitted to go aboard the steamer North America, lying at the landing, and stay till morning.

Next morning, with my trunk in one hand and my pass in the other, I essayed to land, and found in my way the same bayonet. The Sergeant was again called, and he took a long look at the pass, holding it wrong end up. Another Sergeant came, who mistaking it for Hebrew, read it from right to left. Both concurred in the opinion that it was "no account." I asked for the officer of the guard, and was told he was in camp, about a mile off. I then asked the Sergeants if they had read the pass. This somewhat stunned the Hebrew scholar; but the wrong-end-up gentleman, with a dignity intended to be overwhelming, remarked —" I glanced over it, sah!" Now, respect for sentinels is my strong point; so, without saying a crooked word, I laid down my plunder, and commenced to reason the case with my sable fellow citizens. I first asked them what were their instructions? and was told—

"Our instructions is to let nobody land without he's got the right kind of a pass." I then read them my pass, which concluded, " By order of Major-General U. S. Grant." "Does General Banks sign his

## DISCIPLINE, DRILL, PAROLES, FURLOUGHS, ETC.   435

name to dat?" No, said I; this was a pass from General Grant. "Don't know who dat is, sah; don't know him." I then gave them a biographical sketch of General Grant, and in order to impress them with some faint idea of his importance, I stated that he was a greater General than their commander, General 'Andrews.' But there's just when I overdid the thing and ruined my character for veracity. Their look of incredulity and astonishment was unmistakable; and when the sentinel here chimed in, " I tole you not for to get off de boat not till I seed your pass," I think I did some "discoorsin" that reminded them of old times.

#### Military Etiquette.

Lieutenant W., of the Third Rhode Island heavy artillery, at one of the out-posts in the Department of the South, while on duty in a carriage, had the kindness to fa-

Military Etiquette.

vor a staff officer with a ride. On meeting a private of a colored regiment who paid the required salute, which was properly returned by the Lieutenant, the following dialogue, in substance, ensued:

Staff Officer—Do you salute niggers?

Lieutenant—He is a soldier; and he saluted me.

Staff Officer—I swear I won't salute a nigger.

Lieutenant—The Regulations require us to return a salute.

Staff Officer—Curse such Regulations; I'll never salute a nigger; and I don't think much of a man that will.

Lieutenant (coolly reining in his horse) —You can get out and walk, Sir.

The official was consigned to shoe leather and the sand, with the reflection that one who assumes to command and govern by law ought not to set the example himself of disobedience.

#### Appeal for a Furlough—with an Appendage.

Appended to an application for a furlough, forwarded to General Joe Johnston's head-quarters, was a letter, of which the following is a copy. The application for absence was made for the purpose of getting leave to go to Georgia, to carry out a matrimonial engagement, and was approved by the Confederate general for fifteen days. The writer's authography is retained.

"MY MOAST ESTEEMED FRIEND: I am awair that you will be surprised to that father and mother have consented for myself and you to get married, which affords me great pleasure ; for I don't feel as though I could every give my consent to marry any other gentleman, for you know yourself that I always esteemed you higher than any one else.

Mr. ———, bear in mind—you know you once said that you never could live and see me in the arms of Another man. Know is the time to prove it. You will haf to come home immediately. I am shure that the commanding officer will not object to your having a furlow to come home on such important business as that. Ma and pa has given their consent, thinking that you would hardly get a furlow, and then they could say it was not their fault; but I want you to take them on a surprise. I know if you love me as you say you do, you will not fail to come. Give my kindest regards to General Johnston, and tell him to be a friend to matrimony this time for my sake.

Nothing more until I hear from you; an be asshured that I shall await your arrival with the greatest anxiety.

Yours as ever, Ton Ami,
H. T. W."

**Sweetmeats and Patriotism at the South.**

The committee appointed to collect metal for cannon for the rebel army—the scarcity of ordnance in the Confederacy having at that time become a serious matter—applied to a planter in Adams county, Mississippi, for his bell. Not having such an article, he mentioned it to his wife, when she very patriotically offered her brass kettle. The little ones rather demurred to the sacrifice, and one of them, with a sweet tooth, said, "'Lor, pa, what will we do for preserves?" "My daughter, said the wag of a father, our whole duty now is to *preserve* our country."

**Leave of Absence for a Novel Reason.**

The Confederate Generals, Bragg, Walker, Magruder, Hill, and some others, were not only fond of uncorking bottles, but appeared to be very well posted on the military and political bearings of physiological science; that they made due use of this knowledge is evident from the case given below:

An application was made for temporary leave of absence by a soldier serving in General Walker's division of General Hill's corps. On being presented to General Walker, that officer simply endorsed the application with the words (they would have done honor to Bragg himself,) which follow:

"*Disapproved*, but respectfully forwarded to head-quarters of General D. H. Hill." On receiving the document, General H. endorsed it in words which it is safe to assume are without a parallel in military language or reasoning:

"*Approved*, upon the ground that brave men of the army should be permitted to go home whenever practicable; otherwise the children to be born during the war and the usual period afterward will be the offspring of the cowards at home who have substitutes and otherwise exempt."

**Secretary Stanton and General Butler on an Official Point.**

General Butler dropped in at the War Department a few days after his return from New Orleans, and while there the following conversation took place between him and the Secretary.

*General Butler*—I have called, Mr. Stanton, to learn why I was removed from the Department of the Gulf.

*Secretary Stanton*—I assure you, General, that it was from no lack of confidence in your patriotism, capacity or integrity.

*Gen. Butler*—I did not ask you, Mr. Secretary, why I was not removed, but why I was.

*Sec. Stanton*—You are a lawyer, General, and so am I, and you are aware that it is not always polite to tell all we know.

*Gen. Butler*—Well, what are you going to do with me now?

*Sec. Stanton*—How would you like to take the Army of the Potomac?

*Gen. Butler*—Did you ever know a merchant to invest largely in an old stock of goods?

This was the responsive and suggestive poser to the Secretary. Whereupon General Butler made his exit from the Department, confident, doubtless, of his being 'quits' with the Pennsylvania pleader.

**Absence of Colonel M. from the Court-Martial —and Why.**

Colonel M. and Colonel J. were one night placed in adjoining rooms in one of the principal hotels in ————. On retiring for the night, their boots were placed on the outside of the door, in order that they might be blacked by the waiter. Now, Colonel J. had *two* pairs of boots, while Colonel M. had but a *single* pair,— a fact which showed its importance in due course of time.

DISCIPLINE, DRILL, PAROLES, FURLOUGHS, ETC.     487

On rising in the morning, Colonel J., putting one pair of boots on, placed the other pair in his own room and went down town to his work. Colonel M., not quite so early a riser, on taking in *his* boots an hour or so later, found—oh, horror!—that they belonged to his neighbor. Here was a predicament, another man's boots—and his own missing—the only pair he had, too, and a Court-Martial, of which he was President, momentarily awaiting his attendance. Waiters were summoned. Colonel J. had his boots, and must be found. Messengers were dispatched to all the various haunts; word sent to the Court-Martial explaining that he was unavoidably detained; and the Colonel seated himself, in no very happy frame of mind, to await patiently the appearance of—his boots. Three long hours spent in that solitary hotel chamber, sans boots—fretting, foaming and hungry (for a man can't go to breakfast, *cum dignitas*, without covering for his feet, when), at last, the Colonel heard the joyful sound of his neighbor's approaching footsteps. Eagerly he hailed him; the dilemma was explained, and Colonel J., looking into his room, found there Colonel M.'s boots, which had by some unaccountable mistake been substituted for a pair of his in the morning. Morale—have an extra pair of boots.

### Doctor ———'s Dismissal for Drunkenness and Kissing.

An army surgeon was dismissed from the service by Court-Martial, on a charge of drunkenness and insulting a lady. It came out, in the evidence, that the doctor, in common with a great many others in the army, and out of it, imbibed a little too freely on New Year's day. Under this state of things, while riding in one of the street railroad cars, he attempted to kiss a lady passenger, and was only prevented therefrom by the timely interference of the conductor. The Court-Martial found him guilty on both counts in the indictment—intoxication and attempt to kiss—and sentenced him to dismissal. The men and officers of the doctor's regiment, on hearing his fate, unanimously petitioned the President to re-instate him. The evidence was handed to Mr. Lincoln for his perusal, by the defendant's attorney. The President read on till he came to "drunkenness." "That's bad," said he —"very bad." A little further down he came to "insulting a lady." "That's bad, too. An officer shouldn't insult a lady, by any means. I'm afraid I can't re-instate this man," said Mr. Lincoln. "Read the specifications, if you please, Mr. President," said the attorney. Mr. Lincoln proceeded with the papers. Pretty soon he came to a specification about the kissing. He paused, scratched his head a little, and remarked, looking at the attorney,

"Really, I don't know about this. There are exceptions to every rule, but as a general thing it is very hard to insult a lady by kissing her. But, it seems the doctor only attempted to kiss her—perhaps the insult consisted in his not fully succeeding. I don't know as I ought to interfere in behalf of a man who attempts to kiss a lady and doesn't do it," said the President, drily.

"You see, Mr. President," said the attorney, "that the complaint is made by a third party. There's no evidence that the lady felt insulted."

"That's a fact," said Mr. Lincoln, "we can easily dispose of the kissing part. But I must look into the drunkenness a little—I can't overlook that. I'll have to get good evidence that it was strictly a New Year's offence, and is not a common occurrence with the doctor."

The case was taken under advisement.

### Mending a Faulty Pass.

One of the delegates of the Christian Commission, Rev. Dr. ———, on arriving at City Point, in the spring of 1865, found that it was considered best that no more of the delegates should, at that time, be sent "on to Richmond." His pass was, therefore, likely to be of but little service. This talk he was bound to have remedied, and it was. After spending a night at City Point, he was bright and early out of bed the next morning, to find a friend, who was a member of Mr. Lincoln's excursion party, to get his influence in mending up the faulty pass. The steamer River Queen, in which the President and his company were making their home, lay in the stream. But the staff boat was right at the wharf. Said the Rev. Dr. ———,

"Say, my friend, is there any way of getting out to the President's boat? Is Mr. H—— there?"

"*That*," answered the colored friend, "is the President's boat. Don't know about Mr. H——. But don't you see that little black tug, lying by the side of the Queen? Her steam's on. She is coming now to this wharf, and you can learn all that you want to know."

The brave little tug came proudly dancing over the water, seeming almost conscious of the dignity of her freight. She touched the wharf, and out stepped the man himself—not Mr. H., but Mr. L., the commander-in-chief of the army and navy of the United States.

"Good morning, Mr. President. My passes are in a bad way. I wanted to see Mr. H., to get him to help me out of the scrape."

"What is the matter with the passes?" asked the commander-in-chief, smiling.

"Why—so and so; perhaps you could help me."

Suiting the action to the word, the Dr. handed him a scrap of paper torn from the flap of a large envelope. He fumbled for his pencil, but the delegate presented him with his. Putting the paper up against a rough plank, far out of ordinary reach, he wrote the following:

"Let the Rev. Dr. ——— pass as he desires.

A. LINCOLN."

Doing this, the man of the nation strode off; and, with a smirk and a snap of his finger at the provost-marshal, so did the reverend doctor.

#### Outflanked for Once.

When General Sherman was in command at Benton Barracks, St. Louis, he was in the habit of visiting every part of that institution, and making himself familiar with everything that was going on. He wore an old brown coat and a "stove-pipe hat," and was not generally recognized by the minor officials or the soldiers. One day, while walking through the grounds, he met with a soldier who was unmercifully beating a mule.

"Stop pounding that mule!" said the General.

"Git eout!" said the soldier, in blissful ignorance of the person to whom he was speaking.

"I tell you to stop," reiterated the General.

"You mind your business and I will mind mine," replied the soldier, continuing his flank movement upon the mule.

"I tell you again to stop!" said General S. Do you know who I am? I am General Sherman."

"That's played out!" said the soldier. "Every man who comes along here with an old brown coat and a stove-pipe hat on claims to be General Sherman."

It is presumed that for once General Sherman considered himself outflanked.

#### Orders on the Battlefield.

The idea generally prevails that commanding generals are very oracular and didactic on the battle-field, and give their orders in precise language and stentorian voice. A little familiarity with actual war, in company with General Sherman on the field of conflict, must have served to dispel such an impression. Thus, at Chattanooga, he gave his orders for his advance to his brother-in-law, General Hugh Ewing, in the words, uttered between two

## DISCIPLINE, DRILL, PAROLES, FURLOUGHS, ETC. 439

puffs at a bad cigar, "I guess, Ewing, if you are ready, you might as well go ahead." Ewing asked a few questions in regard to retaining the *echelon* formation of his command as then marshaled for the advance. Sherman replied : "I want you to keep the left well toward the creek

Orders on the Battle-field.

(the Chickamauga), and keep up the formation, four hundred yards distance until you get to the foot of the hill." "And shall we keep it after that," asked Ewing. "Oh! you may go up the hill as you like —if you can;" and then he added, hastily, as he pushed Ewing away, "I say, Ewing, don't call for help until you actually need it." Such was the unstrained language of one of the greatest of modern commanders, in the very crisis of unparalleled conflict.

### McClellan and Darkey John.

John, a bright-spoken and honest-faced incomer from the Confederate ranks, made his appearance before General McClellan, and made some military reports on "the situation." At the close of the interview, he asked, anxiously :

"General, you won't send me back; will you?"

"Yes," replied the General, with a smile; "I believe I will."

"I hope you won't, General. If you say so, I know I will have to go; but I come to you all for protection, and I hope you won't."

"Well, then, I suppose we will not. No, John, you are at liberty to go where you please. Stay with the army if you like. No one can ever take you against your will."

"May the Lord bless you, General! I thought you wouldn't drive me out. You are the best friend I ever had; I shall never forget you till I die."

And John made the salute, remounted his horse and rode back to the rear, his darkey face almost white with radiance. An hour later, he was on duty as the servant of Captain Bachelor, Quartermaster of Couch's Second division; and it was feared that a long time would elapse before "Captain Rhett" saw the butter and eggs for which his palate evidently yearned—to say nothing of the horse or of John himself— for John had been sent to forage for those articles by said Rhett, and had improved his opportunity to come into the Federal lines.

### Advantage of Military Firmness.

A little circumstance, of a ludicrous nature, is related by Mr. Parton, in his capital biography of the conqueror of New Orleans, as serving to show something of the disposition of the people of that place. Among a batch of captured letters was found one from a certain Edward Wright, a resident of New Orleans, to a lady in Secessia, full of the most ridiculous lies. He told his correspondent that the Yankee officers were the most craven creatures on earth. One of them, he said, had insulted a lady on the streets, which Wright perceiving, he had slapped the officer's face and kicked him, and then offered to meet him in the field; but the officer gave some "rigmarole excuse" and declined. For this, he continued, he was taken before Picayune Butler, and came near being sent to Fort Jackson.

General Butler caused the writer of this

440    THE BOOK OF ANECDOTES OF THE REBELLION.

epistle to be brought before him, when the following conversation occurred between them:

"What is your name?"

"Edward Wright."

"Have I ever had the pleasure of seeing you before?"

"Not that I know of."

"Have you ever been before an officer of the United States charged with any offence?"

"No, sir."

"Have you ever had any difficulty or misunderstanding with an officer of the United States, in the streets or elsewhere?"

"Never, sir."

"Have you any complaint to make of the conduct of any of my officers or men?"

"None, sir."

"Have you ever observed any misconduct on their part, since we arrived in the city?"

"Never, sir."

The General now produced the letter, and handed it to the prisoner.

"Did you write that letter?"

"It looks like my hand-writing."

"*Did you write the letter?*"

"Yes; I wrote it."

"Is not the story of your slapping and kicking the officer, an unmitigated and malicious lie, designed to bring the army of the United States into contempt?"

"Well, sir, it isn't true, I admit."

The General then dictated a sentence like this, which was written at the bottom of the letter: "I, Edward Wright, acknowledge that this letter is basely and abominably false, and that I wrote it for the purpose of bringing the army of the United States into contempt."

"Sign that, sir."

"I won't. I am a British subject, and claim the protection of the British consul."

"*Sign it, sir.*"

"General Butler, you may put every ball of that pistol through my brain, but I will never sign that paper."

"Captain Davis, make out an order to the Provost Marshal, to hang this man at daybreak to-morrow. In the meantime, let him have any priest he chooses to send for. Gentlemen, I am going to dinner."

Before the General had reached his quarters, an orderly came running up.

"General, he has signed."

"Well, keep him in the guard-house all night, and let him go in the morning."

Mr. Parton might perhaps have added to his capital narration, that the Southern "patriots" of the Wright stamp were indeed only too glad to have Butler dis-

Gen. N. P. Banks.

placed by General Banks,—a gentleman of the most bland courtliness, and whose civil and military administration was of just the right stamp, after the wild elements had been so effectively subdued by his firm-minded predecessor.

PART VI.—OUR COLORED SOLDIERS.

# PART SIXTH.

ANECDOTES OF THE REBELLION—COMMISSARY AND RATIONS, FINANCE AND CURRENCY, THE PRESS, THE TELEGRAPH, POST-OFFICE, ETC.

UNCLE SAM'S SUPPLIES; SUBSISTENCE UNDER DIFFICULTIES; "HARD TACK" AND MULE-BEEF LEGENDS; FORAGING RAIDS; DISLOYAL FOWLS AND CONTRABAND DAINTIES; IMPROMPTU CONFISCATIONS IN A SMALL WAY; DIALOGUES WITH THE QUARTERMASTER; SHAMEFUL IMPOSITIONS; SCRIP AND CURRENCY VARIETIES; UNIQUE BANKING OPERATIONS, COLLECTION EXCURSIONS AT THE SOUTH; CHIVALRIC REPUDIATION, TRICKS, ARTIFICES AND ACHIEVEMENTS OF EDITORS, REPORTERS AND CORRESPONDENTS; TELEGRAPHIC ODDS AND ENDS; MISCELLANIES OF POST-OFFICE EXPERIENCE; &c., &c.

> "Weave no more silks, ye Lyons looms,
> To deck our girls for gay delights!
> The crimson flower of battle blooms,
> And solemn marches fill the nights."

I must decline furnishing both armies any more. Let me know *which* army is to be supplied, and the Department will be able to meet the requisition.—*Ironical reply of* GENERAL RIPLEY.

It was a perfect reproduction of the scene and all its incidents; and it is a marvel to me how you writers can perform such tasks.—GENERAL HOOKER *on the reports of the Battle of Antietam.*

I would sooner face all the cannon of the enemy than taste that glass of wine.—*One of the heroes of Ball's Bluff.*

Be gorra! I thought yez was gintlemin, and paid for what yez wanted. Divil a bit of money have I seen for a year, and "Confederate" scrip has brought me wife and childers to starvation almost.—*Irish peddler at the South, to Union soldiers who jocosely offered him "Confederate" currency.*

I will teach them, if they need the lesson, that the men who have periled their lives to open the Mississippi River, for their benefit, cannot be imposed upon with impunity.—GEN GRANT *on river captains' exactions.*

---

### One of the Best.

——, was a sort of political prisoner, on his way to some point where, with others of his plumage, he might be out of harm's-doing. As he was being thus taken, his imagination wandered away among the horrors of 'Swamp Angels,' his limbs became tremulous, his voice husky, his eyes were fountains of involuntary tears, and his hat-rim overhung them like a weeping-willow, whose broad shadow kept them in a cool, refreshing twilight. They called him "Doctor," and the Major with the flag of truce was directed to leave him at some "landing" above Jamestown Island.

The "Doctor" had contrived to procure somehow, and had somehow brought on board the steamer, a quantity of sugar and coffee, contrary to regulation and without authority. The dinner-hour arrived and passed. Every hungry rebel had done ample justice to the occasion, and had eaten as an Esquimaux eats when he sees before his bodily eyes one huge meal of walrus or whale blubber, and before his mind's eye a week or month of probable starvation or "short commons." The boat was nearing the "Doctor's" landing, and the Major was looking in vain for any appearance of village, or house even, which could give rise to the name of "Macox's Landing"—his point of destination—or induce any boat to stop in such a wilderness, when the steward approached with a scared look, saying,—

"I beg pardon, Major, but we're in a — of a scrape about that coffee and sugar."

"Indeed," said the Major, "what is the matter? Were they bad? Wasn't there enough of them for all hands?"

"Oh, yes, Sir, there was enough; but we've eaten them pretty nearly all up; and, Major, they didn't belong to us at all,

Swamp Angel.

they wa'n't Government property, Sir; they all belonged to the "Doctor," and he's found it out, and is swearing like the —, like a pirate about it."

"Is that all, Steward?" said the Major, after a hearty laugh at such a panic.

"*All!* Major; yes, Major, that's all. But what shall I do about it?" He's awfully mad, and threatens all sorts of —"

"Ask the 'Doctor' to come up on the hurricane deck, and speak to me, Steward. I think I can pacify him."

He went, and presently returned with the angry "Doctor," who did not, however, exhibit any signs of passion in this stage of the adventure.

"Ah, Doctor," said the Major, "I am sorry to learn that you have forgotten what is due to a flag of truce, and have exposed yourself to the risk of further imprisonment, and us to the danger of being treated as culprits, and possibly shot by the Confederates, for carrying on trade under pretext of being a flag-of-truce boat. It was very wrong, very; and if I had known it before leaving the Rip-Raps, I should have seized your coffee and sugar, and left you in prison until further orders. But, in consideration of *our* mistake, and as most of the contraband articles have been consumed, and as we are within a quarter of a mile of your landing-place, I will not be too severe upon you. You can keep what remains, enough now to last your family some weeks, and I will let you take them ashore."

He was extremely grateful, and the steward danced with delight. The "Doctor" shook the Major's hand very heartily as he left the boat, and the Steward came up with the broadest of grins, rubbing his hands, and saying, "By Jim! Major, you got out of *that* snarl completely—slick!"

How are you, "Doctor?"

### The Last Message to his Father.

A soldier went into the rooms of the Sanitary Commission, to procure an envelope, saying that he had a letter to send home for one of his comrades. He drew from his blouse a small package, carefully

Sanitary Commission.

wrapped; and opening it, held up a scrap of a leaf from a memorandum book. It had bloody finger-prints on it, and a few words hastily written with a pencil. The writer was the soldier's partner, he said. In the charge on Kenesaw, he found him staggering back from the line, the blood streaming from his mouth, and covering his hands and clothes. A Minie ball had cut off his tongue at the root. He tried to speak, but could not. Finally, by motions, he made his partner understand his want—paper and pencil. A scrap was torn from the diary, and on it the boy, held up by his comrade, with fingers dripping with blood, and trembling in death, wrote—

"Father, meet me in heaven."

He tried to write his name, but it was too late. Life had fled.

### Dutch Landlord's Use of Greyback Twenties.

During General Lee's summer invasion of Pennsylvania, a detachment of the rebel army had possession for a few days of the thriving town of Hanover, in the county of York, lying some twenty or more miles west of Gettysburg. Apprised of their coming, the merchants and business men of the town mostly placed their movable goods safely out of the reach of the pilferers. They secured but little booty. What they did lay their hands on, however, they did not fail to *bag*.

Among the heaviest losers was one of the landlords of the town, the proprietor of a well-stocked and well-conducted country tavern. At his house the hungry rebels made themselves well "at home." Without leave or license, they devoured his stock of bacon, beef and poultry; consumed all his flour, which they forced the landlady to bake into bread and pies; used his forage, occupied his beds, and, of course, used up every drop of his stock of liquors. Of this latter, before they came, he had ten or a dozen barrels—when they left, not so many pints; for, what they could not guzzle on the spot, they contrived to take along.

As they were about taking their departure for Gettysburg, a Georgia Colonel, exhibiting a degree of conscientiousness not shared by any of his associates, remarked to the landlord that it was "a pity" to consume so much of his property without any compensation, and that if no one else would extend justice to him, *he* would —at the same time throwing on the bar-counter a bill of the denomination of twenty dollars.

"There," said the magnanimous rebel chieftain, "my good fellow, take that as *my* share of our indebtedness."

"Vot kind of monish is dat?" inquired the landlord,—one of the class of Pennsylvanian Germans so proverbial alike for sagacity and integrity.

"That, Sir, is a *grey*back; in other words, a note of the Confederate States of America."

"O, stranger," said the hotel keeper, "if you hash not got no petter monish dan dat, you'll better keeps it. I don't vont none of it; it is good for nix; no petter dan plank paper!"

"Sir!" rejoined the somewhat indignant epauletted Georgian, "I advise you to take it and be glad for the opportunity. You will soon find that it is the best money in the world. Keep it, Sir, keep it, by all means."

"Nein, nein," retorted mynheer of the swinging sign; "dat monish will never be wort anything here nor anywhere. I would not give von silver thaler for a bread basket full. I von't be seen mit it in my hand; and if you don't take it along, I rolls it up, holds it at the candle, un *lites my pipe mit it*."

He was about suiting the action to the word, when the Georgian took the note up from the counter and returned it to his wallet.

### Uncle Sam's Mule Cleaners.

One of General Nelson's teamsters—a green hand—gloried in the charge of six large, shaggy mules. John was also the proprietor of two bottles of 'Old Bourbon' —a contraband article in camp—which a wag discovered, and resolved to possess.

Being well aware that the driver's presence was a very natural impediment to such a theft, he hit upon the following plan to get rid of him: Approaching the driver, who was just then busy currying his mules, he accosted him with—

"I say, old fellow, what are you doing there?"

"Can't you see?" replied John, gruffly.

"Certainly," responded wag, "but that is not your business. It is after tattoo, and there is a fellow hired here, by the General who curries all the mules and horses brought in after tattoo."

The mule-driver bit at once, and desired to know where the hair-dresser kept himself. Whereupon he was directed to General Nelson's tent, with the assurance that there was where the fellow "hung out."

"You can't mistake the man," said wag, "he is a large fellow, and puts on a thundering sight of airs for a man in his business. He will probably refuse to do it, and tell you to go to the —; but don't mind that, he has been drinking to-day. Make him come out, sure."

John posted off, and entering the tent where our Napoleon of the Fourth Division sat in deep reverie, probably considering the most expeditions method of expelling the rebel Buckner from his native State, slapped him on the back with a force sufficient to annihilate a man of ordinary size. Springing to his feet, the General, powerful and spirited, accosted his uninvited guest with—

"Well, Sir, who are you, and what the — do you want?"

"Old hoss, I've got a job for you now—six mules to be curried, and right off, too," said the Captain of the mules, nothing daunted at the flashing eye of the General which was turned at him and pierced him through.

"Do you know whom you are addressing, Sir?" asked the indignant commander.

"Yes," said John, elevating his voice to a pitch which rendered the words audible a square off; "you are the fellow hired by Uncle Sam to clean mules, and I won't have any foolishness. Clean them mules, and I'll give you a drink of busthead."

"You infernal villain!" exclaimed the General, now perfectly furious, "I am General Nelson, commander of this Division!"

John here placed the thumb of his right hand against his nose, and extending his four digits, waved and twirled them slowly, in a manner supposed by some to be equivalent to the expression, "How are you old fellow?" The General's sword leaped from its scabbard, and John sprang from the tent just in time to save his head.

It would be needless to add that the boys drank the "big mule driver's health" in Old Bourbon, and quite as needless to state the source whence said Bourbon was derived.

---

**Wicked Joke upon a Regimental Postmaster.**

There was a joke—though possibly a wicked one—perpetrated on a certain Chaplain in the army, which ought not to be lost to the clerical portion of the world. It was the Chaplain's business to look after

Joke on a Chaplain.

the regimental mail. This Chaplain, however, had been annoyed exceedingly by the

RATIONS, CURRENCY, ORDNANCE, MAILS, ETC.   447

great number of warriors who were constantly running to him and inquiring about the arrival and departure of mails. To save time and patience, the testy official at last posted a notice outside his tent, which read: "The Chaplain does not know when the mail will go," and with this he imagined his troubles at an end. The reverend postmaster was absent from the camp that day, and on returning and glancing at his notice, was horrified to see there conspicuously written upon his own door, read by multitudes during the day, in a hand exactly counterfeiting his, following the words "THE CHAPLAIN DOES NOT KNOW WHEN THE MAIL WILL GO," this addition by some honest wretch: "NEITHER DOES HE CARE A DAMN." It was a case of depravity the obliging and godly man was unprepared for,—but perhaps he and his warriors were now "quits."

### Revenge upon a Goose for Hissing at the National Air.

The secesh farmers, in a well-known locality in Maryland, raised a great outcry, while the Fifth Excelsior Regiment was camping near by, about a few chickens which had been missed from their poultry yards. Stringent orders were accordingly issued against foraging. Still, now and then an unlucky fowl would find its way into the mess kitchen, but nobody could account for its presence there. At last an unlucky wight was caught in the very act of bearing a goose into camp. He was brought to the Captain of his company, who in tones of severity demanded how in the face of such stringent orders, he dare steal geese.

"I didn't steal it," indignantly retorted the culprit.

"Did you buy it?"

"No. I'll tell you how it was: I was

Relay House.

coming up from the village whistling Yankee Doodle, when out came one of old Farrell's geese, and hearing the tune I was whistling, commenced hissing. I couldn't stand *that*, and so I up and knocked it over. Well, as I found I had 'accidentally, killed it, I thought that like as not a detail would be ordered out in the morning to bury offal, and I thought I might as well, being right on the spot, bring the goose up to camp and have it handy."

The Captain could *hardly* "see it:" nevertheless, Farrell never got paid for *that* goose.

### Swearing-in a Cook for the First Iowa Cavalry.

The master of a fugitive slave appeared at Camp Benton, St. Louis, to recover him, when he was ordered off by a corporal of the First Iowa Cavalry. So, soon as he was gone, the negro appeared from under a bundle of sacks in one corner of the

28

corporal's quarters. Innumerable questions were being propounded to him, when the corporal advanced, and the following colloquy ensued, as given by a writer

Army Kitchen.

whose name certainly deserves to be known.

"See here, Dixie! before you can enter the service of the United States, you must be sworn."

"Yes, massa, I do dat," he replied; when the corporal continued—

"Well, then, take hold of the Bible," holding out a letter envelope upon which was delineated the Goddess of Liberty standing upon a Suffolk pig, wearing the emblem of our country. The negro grasped the envelope cautiously with his thumb and forefinger, when the corporal proceeded to administer the oath by saying:

"You do solemnly swear that you will support the Constitution of the United States, and see that there are no grounds floating upon the coffee, at all times."

"Yes, massa, I do dat," he replied, "I allers settles him in de coffee-pot."

Here he let go the envelope to gesticulate by a downward thrust of his forefinger the direction that would be given to the coffee-grounds for the future.

"Never mind how you do it," shouted the corporal, "but *hold on to the Bible!*"

"Lordy, massa, I forgot," said the negro, as he darted forward and grasped the envelope with a firmer clutch; when corporal continued—

"And you do solemnly swear that you will support the Constitution of *all* the loyal States, and not spit upon the plates when cleaning them, nor wipe them with your shirt sleeve."

Here a frown lowered upon the brow of the negro, his eyes expanded to their largest dimensions, while his lips protruded with a rounded form, as he exclaimed:

"Lordy, massa, I *neber*, neber do dat— I allers washes him nice. Ole missus mighty 'tickler 'bout dat."

"Never mind ole missus," shouted the corporal, as he resumed,—"and you do solemnly swear that you will put milk in the coffee every morning, and see that the ham and eggs are not cooked too much or too little."

"Yes, I do dat; I'se a good cook."

"And lastly," continued the corporal, "you do solemnly swear that when this

Swearing-in a Cook.

war is over, you'll make tracks for Africa almighty fast."

"Yes, massa, I do dat. I allers wanted to go to Chee-cargo."

Here the regimental drums beat up for

RATIONS, CURRENCY, ORDNANCE, MAILS, ETC.   449

dress parade, when Tom Benton—that being his name—was declared duly sworn in and commissioned as "Chief Cook in Company K, of the First Iowa Cavalry."

The above will do to go along with the laughter-provoking effusions of Artemas Ward, Orpheus C. Kerr, Petroleum V. Nasby, Major Jack Downing, Philander Doesticks, and Shillaber, who are certainly not excelled in this line, even by the wits of London Punch, or Vanity Fair, and whose names are familiar household words throughout Britannia's isle.

---

### Old Magruder Sharing his Liquor.

Magruder, the secession General, and who for some time was in command at Yorktown, did not belong to the temperance society, and the boys, who were now and then very thirsty, did not fail to discover the fact—and perhaps to speak pretty freely of it sometimes. Among these same was private Winship Stedman, of Fayetteville, N. C. On the day after Stedman had performed an act of great gallantry, in the scouting party from Bethel Church, he was commanded to appear before the General, and the order was enforced by a section of soldiers. He was unable to decide whether he was to be shot or reprimanded, until he reached the General's tent, and was sternly addressed thus: "Private Stedman, I understand that you have said that Old Magruder drinks all the liquor in Yorktown, and wont let you have a drop. You shall say so no longer, sir. Walk in and take a drink. I commend you for your bravery!"

---

### What Mr. Lincoln said to a New Orleans Editor.

The facetious editor of the New Orleans Delta was favored with a familiar *tete-a-tete* with President Lincoln, of which the following is an account by said Delta wag:

When we entered the White House the weather was fine. We sent our card up to Mr. Lincoln, who was sitting in his office, at the head of the stairs. We say our card; we did, in words and figures as follows—"The Daily Delta, New Orleans."

The President sent his compliments through his favorite butler—he calls all of his servants 'Butlers' now—which, as Mrs. T. D. Delta, who accompanied us to the National Mansion, in her bright woman's way, remarked, was "significant"—and requested our wife and us to come up. We went up. There was the President at the head of the stairs waiting to receive us. He was dressed like a gentleman, and his head was uncovered. "I thank you for your visit," said Mr. Lincoln to us, and thereupon we introduced our wife. The President conducted Mrs. Delta into Mrs. Lincoln's apartments, where the two ladies talked together for an hour or two; but the President himself returned instantly, and, with a countenance full of meaning, asked thoughtfully, "How do you do again?" We replied, that we were "very well, we thank you. How are you, in these perilous times, yourself, Mr. President?" said we to Mr. Lincoln. He answered, with a slight addition of language, "I am 'very well' too." Then, in almost the very words of Napoleon to the Irishman, Mr. Lincoln spoke: "Tell me, Mr. Delta, tell me, how is Louisiana, and how does she stand?" We, to show our own knowledge of the royal language of the great Frenchman, answered in almost the words of Pat; we answered—"She is as poor a distressed country as ever you have seen, for the rebels are hanging men and women wherever they are seen."

The President laughed, but became grave in a moment. "I thank you," said he to us; "I thank you for sending two able men to Congress. I thank you for defeating Mr. Jacob Barker. Who is Lee Percy? Is he not a Virginian?" We answered all these questions with our usual felicity, and then gave the President some very useful hints in regard to the culture of the turnip—a vegetable. He seemed greatly interested and instructed. From turnips, we naturally fell upon the culture of cotton and sugar cane. We enlightened him upon these subjects, too; for he was as polite as to say to us, "I assure you, Mr. Delta, I am getting wiser every moment."

The cotton question led us on to the war, and upon this we talked an hour, the President being silent nearly all the time. We gave 'the Executive of the United States' to understand the status of Louisiana. We told him what we thought of men and things in New Orleans, and we condemned the arrest and incarceration of Soule. The President, now, in his dry way, said:

"Mr. Delta, there is danger, if you keep on in this mood, of your getting into Fort Lafayette."

We laughed immoderately; but the President was grave and seemed weary; and finding him in right good humor, we asked him if he had heard our great conundrum, which was known in New Orleans as the Delta conundrum. He said he had not. Thereupon we told him. "Why," said we to the President. "Why are greenbacks like the Jews?" Mr. Lincoln smiled, crossed his legs, and smiled again. "I give it up," said he. We then roared, but having recovered our gravity, gave the answer. "Because," said we, laughing again, for the joke was our best, "Because they are the issues of Father Abraham, waiting for a redeemer." The President shook his sides, and remarked, "I owe you one, and here it is. You remind me of a cow in Illinois:" and here Mr. Stanton entered. The President excused himself, and said he must withdraw. We called Mrs. Delta, and we took our departure. Subsequently, the butler told us what transpired between the President and the Secretary of War:

"Who is that lean cur at Butler's heels, he has been boreing me these three days back about the management of the army of the Gulf?" inquired Mr. Stanton.

"He is not a cur," replied Mr. Lincoln; "you are too severe, Stanton; he is only a bur. Some one flung him at Butler, in sport, and the fellow has the faculty of sticking."

Our wife, who was present during the relation of this, observed, in her woman's way, "The gentlemen were, darling Delta, sarcastic." We said "no, that they were simply indulging in a little humor, to relieve themselves, for a moment, from the austere thoughts of war." "If that was all," said she to us, "I'm glad they've honored you by making you the but of their joke."

### What One Noble Woman Did.

Mrs. Eliza Gray Fisher, a lady of Boston, Mass., going on in years to the allotted period of life, deserves to have a record made of her patriotic enthusiasm and industry. Knowing from experience the necessities of the volunteer soldier,—having lost a grandfather in the Revolutionary war, and a father in the war of 1812,—determined, immediately upon President Lincoln's call for volunteers, to provide a *complete outfit of under-clothing for an entire company*. This, notwithstanding the severe pressure of domestic duties, with the aid of several ladies in Rev. Dr. Dewey's society, she accomplished seasonably and in the most satisfactory manner. The articles—all of the best materials and most thorough workmanship—were as follows: 130 shirts, 130 pairs of drawers, 130 towels, 130 pocket handkerchiefs, 130 pairs of socks, 12 hospital gowns, 55 bags containing needles, pins, thread, &c., 65 Havelock caps, 500 yards bandages. Such women are of the true Revolutionary stock,—all honor to them.

### Milk, with Accompaniments.

Hopeville Gap will long be remembered, particularly by those two clever corporals, Lutten and Hodges, who figured so neatly in the little affair which appears in the following narration. The said corporals were on duty near a house in the vicinity

## RATIONS, CURRENCY, ORDNANCE, MAILS, ETC. 451

of the said classic Gap. They were nearly out of provisions. Fortune, however, threw in their way early one morning, a cow, and the lacteal fluid had too many temptations for them to resist the desire to milk the animal. While Lutten held the cow by the horns, Hodges manipulated the udders in the usual rural style. He had filled one tin cup and was rapidly filling another, when a chamber window

Milking the Cow.

in the house was smartly raised, and a woman with a voice pitched at least *one* octave higher than they had been accustomed to hear from that sex, indulged in the following language.

Q.—What on airth are ye doin *thar!*

No answer from the men at the cow.

Q.—Milking my cow, eh? What ails you? what in the world is the matter on ye—are ye *starving?* Ain't ye ashamed of yourselves?

Receiving still no response from the men at the cow, who continued their labors with the *sang froid* that only troopers can assume, madame became considerably 'exasperated,' and continued her harrangue as follows:

"There is four of you Yankees laying up there on the hill, *with their souls in hell.* *Think of that!*"

This eliciting no response, she continued:

"And you may be there too in less than an hour? Think of *that!*"

No response—Hodges blandly continuing his operations at the udder—

"And I hope you will, and when you are drinking that milk. *Think of that!*"

No response at all, and the woman 'let on:'

"What are you Yankees all doing here, any way?"

The corporals having filled their pint cups, Hodges deigned to answer the last question by saying:

"To protect *you* and maintain the honor of the glorious old flag!".

The reply brought upon them a tirade of billingsgate that made the atmosphere almost blue, amid which the troopers retreated to their camp. To "Dunn Browne," one of the most pleasing and accomplished, as well as widely read war correspondents, we find the above amusing *morceau* attributed, and would be glad to find more of the same side-shaking pencillings, which gave him so wide and enviable a repute previous to his lamentable decease.

### Brandy for a Sick Lieutenant.

No pen could draw a more vivid and life-like picture of the scenes of the war, than that of the Rev. A. H. Quint, one of the most efficient chaplains and military co-laborers in the army of the Union, honoring, in every sense of the word, as he did, the Old Bay State that sought his services and sent him forth. His deeply interesting work, recounting his army experiences, has passed through many editions. He knew the coolness, bravery, and withal the ingenuity which characterized the soldiers of the Union, and of which so many anecdotes are told,—like the following:

One night Lieutenant Clark, Lieutenant Soule, and Captain Wilson, of the First —————— regiment, were very dry. A most stringent order against the introduction of any ardent into camp being then most rigorously executed, they had been discussing the ways and means of procuring something, "hot," when Soule cried out, "I've got it! You, Clark, are very sick—you must go to bed—you have got cramps—you must be covered up—you must have some brandy immediately!" In a moment Clark was very sick abed, covered with all the blankets at command, and Soule was off in breathless haste to the hospital steward for brandy. There he met the conscientious objections of the steward, by the most earnest representations of the urgency of the case. He could wait for no surgeon's order—Lieut. Clark might die! In a moment he was again with the "boys," flourishing a bottle of brandy in the air in triumph, and a right jolly time they had drinking it. But—shade of Bacchus!—what was one bottle to them after a fortnight's total abstinence? They were still dry—of course they were! Before the bottle was quite empty, Soule snatched it out of the hands of Clark, held it up to the light, eyeing it critically, took one more swig, and then said, "Now, boys, for another bottle!" Raising the window curtain, it was but the work of a moment to catch a hundred flies and put them in the bottle, to be drowned by the small amount of brandy remaining. Rushing back to the hospital steward in as breathless haste as before—this time holding up the bottle containing a spoonful of brandy and an equal amount of flies—he cried out, "See there! Is that the kind of brandy you dispense to a sick man here?" With as many apologies as Soule would wait to listen to, the poor steward handed him another bottle of brandy, with which he returned to his comrades. The noise which soon issued from Lieutenant Clark's "sick" quarters attracted attention, and a good many other officers took a taste of the second bottle, with a hearty guffaw.

### Tough Time with a Mule.

In repartee and fun American soldiers are never behind any class of men, and their appreciation of the ludicrous and sarcastic is as keen as a briar. Mr. Chapman, one of the most gifted of the numerous army correspondents of the press, in 1864, stated that he was riding from Brandy Station to Stevensburg, in company with Colonel A., of the Michigan —— regiment, and had reached a point opposite General P.'s head-quarters, when they were overtaken by a couple of soldiers mounted on two decidedly un-Rareyfied mules. The boys had evidently been up to the sutler's, for they were a trifle top-heavy, and only kept their places by dint of the most persevering industry. At that point the road crosses a considerable creek, which the mules seemed to hold in strong aversion. Nevertheless, through the persuasive eloquence of two ragged sticks, they were urged on to the middle of the stream, and then they doggedly refused to advance. The boys plied all the expedients at hand, but it was "no go," and when at length one of them caught the tail of the other's mule in his hand and attempted to twist a forward movement out of him, the refractory animal reared, whirled to one side, kicked and snorted, and, depositing his rider in the dirty creek, he started on a keen run back. Zouave gathered himself up, and seeing that he could not overtake his frightened steed, he only followed with sundry expletives and execrations, not found in the Westminster Catechism. Colonel A., by the way, being a very pious man, took it upon himself to chide the exasperated and unfortunate "vet" for using such unchristianlike language; but the soldier would have his joke—so, shaking what water he could out of his red pants, he waded to a dry spot on shore and muttered, gratingly, that it was "— hard if a feller couldn't cuss a mule." But soon appreciating the utter ludicrousness of his condition, he turned to the Colonel and offered to lay a bet that that was the first time he ever saw a mule tear, (muleteer) shed. It was some time before either the Colonel or Chapman was able to see the *pungency* of the challenge, but it came to them after awhile, and it helped amazingly to dry up the mud between there and Strasburg.

### Sergeant Davis's Tender Beef.

In March, 1862, General Banks advanced upon Winchester in two columns—one by way of Martinsburg, and the other by way of Harper's Ferry and Berryville. In the latter column, Brigadier-General Abercrombie commanded the first brigade, and Cothran's Battery was with him. Abercrombie was very strict, not allowing his men to forage, or to burn rails to cook with, but compelling them to burn green timber. The next morning, after camping near Berryville, he rode

Tender Beef.

around the different camps to ascertain who had burned the rails. When he rode through Cothran's Battery, the Captain was in his tent. Approaching it he discovered the quarters of a fine young beef that the men had "foraged" the night previous, lying against a tree. The old General's brow contracted as he demanded of Sergeant Leander E. Davis,

"Where the —, did you get that beef? I gave the commissary no order to issue fresh beef here."

Davis, who was a very polite soldier, removed his cap and saluted the General, and said, in a tone, evincing perfect coolness and sincerity:

"General, I was sergeant of the guard last night, and about ten o'clock I heard a terrible commotion in the camp of the Twelfth Massachusetts, (Colonel Webster's regiment,) across the road. I rushed out to see what was going on, and just as I passed the Captain's tent I saw a fine steer coming through the camp of the Twelfth Massachusetts, with about a hundred men after it. The animal appeared very much frightened, General, and true as you live, it jumped clear across the road, [about two rods,] over both stone fences, and as it alighted in this lot it struck its head against this tree, and, being so terribly scared, its head, hide and legs, kept right on running, while the quarters dropped down here, where they have remained ever since. It is very fine, tender beef, General, and I had just come here for the purpose of cutting off and sending you a fine sirloin roast for dinner. Will you be so obliging as to accept it?"

"How long have you been a soldier?" demanded the old General.

"About six months, General."

"Well, Sir, I perceive that you thoroughly appreciate the Art of War, and have become a *veteran* in half a year. Were you a green soldier I should order you under arrest and have you court-martialed; but on account of your *veteran* proclivities I shall recommend you for promotion!" And putting spurs to his horse he rode away, shaking his sides with laughter.

### Cotton Burners in Louisiana.

The cotton burners came, they saw, they departed.—at least in *one* instance.

"I have come to burn your cotton, Sir."

"By what authority?"

"By the authority of General Beauregard."

"You will *not* burn my cotton."

"We *will* burn your cotton."

"Go about it, then. But it is my opinion, gentlemen, that you will not burn it."

"What do you propose to do? You don't mean to say that you will show any opposition to our authority?"

"I simply mean to say that you will not burn my cotton. Bob, bring a coal of fire."

The fire is brought.

"Gentlemen, there is the fire, and yonder are one hundred bales of cotton. Proceed."

"Your conduct is very extraordinary, Sir. I should like to know what you mean?"

"Well, Sir, I mean that if you attempt to burn that cotton I will scatter your brains so far and wide that no power in heaven or earth can bring them together again. (Here, boys! that cotton is yours; defend it or starve.")

"—— strange conduct," mutters Mr. Officer, sullenly; "We'll attend to your case, Sir. We are going down the river we will give you a visit on our return."

"Do. Whenever you make up your mind to burn my cotton, by all means come and burn."

The cowed officer and his posse "fell back in good order." The valiant Louisianian saved his cotton. He had no second visit from Beauregard's cotton burners.

---

**Running an Engine in the Confederate Service.**

The popular author of "Thirteen Months in the Rebel Army," one of the most readable of books, must be allowed to tell his own story about 'that engine,' and here it is:

The engineer, Charles Little, refused to run the train on during the night, as he was not well acquainted with the road, and thought it dangerous. In addition, the head-light of the locomotive being out of order, and the oil frozen, he could not make it burn, and he could not possibly run without it. Colonel Williams grew angry, probably suspecting him of Union sentiments and of wishing to delay the train, cursed him rather roundly, and at length told him he should run it under guard, adding to the guard already on the engine: "If any accident occurs, shoot the cursed Yankee." Little was a Northern man. Upon the threat thus enforced, the engineer seemed to yield, and prepared to start the train. As if having forgotten an important matter, he said hastily, "Oh, I must have some oil," and stepping down off the locomotive, walked toward the engine-house. When he was about twenty yards from the cars, the guard thought of their duty, and one of them followed Little, and called upon him to halt; but in a moment he was behind the machine shop, and off in the dense woods, in the deep darkness. The commotion soon brought the Colonel and a crowd, and, while they were cursing each other all around, the fireman and most of the brakemen slipped off, and here we were with no means of getting ahead. All this time I had stood on the engine, rather enjoying the melee, but taking no part in it, when Colonel Williams, turning to me, said:

"Can not you run the engine?"

"No, Sir," I replied.

"You have been on it, as you came down."

"Yes, Sir, as a matter of curiosity."

"Don't you know how to start and stop her?"

"Yes, that is easy enough; but if any thing should be wrong I could not adjust it."

"No difference, no difference, Sir; I must be at Bowling Green to-morrow, and you must put us through."

"Colonel Williams" said I, calmly looking him in the eye, "I can not voluntarily take the responsibility of managing a train with a thousand men aboard, nor will I be forced to do it under a guard who know nothing about an engine, and who would be as likely to shoot me for doing my duty as failing to do it; but if you will find among the men a fireman, and send away this guard, and come yourself on the locomotive, I will do the best I can."

And now commenced my apprenticeship to running a secession railroad train, with rebel regiment on board. The engine behaved admirably, and I began to feel quite safe, for she obeyed every command I gave her, as if she acknowledged me her rightful lord.

I could not but be startled at the position in which I was placed, holding in my hand the lives of more than a thousand men, running a train of twenty-five cars over a road I had never seen, running without a headlight, and the road so dark that I could only see a rod or two ahead, and, to crown all, knowing almost nothing of the business. Of course I ran slowly, about ten miles an hour, and never took my hand off the throttle, or my eye from the road. The Colonel at length grew confident, and almost confidential, and did most of the talking, as I had no time for conversation.

When we had run about thirty miles, and every thing was going well, Colonel Williams concluded to walk back, on the top of the box cars, to a passenger car which was attached to the rear of the train, and occupied by the officers. This somewhat hazardous move he commenced just as we struck a stretch of trestle-work which carried the road over a gorge of some fifty feet deep. As the locomotive reached the end of the trestle-work the grade rose a little, and I could see through or in a deep cut, which the road run into, an obstruction. What it was, or how far ahead, I had almost no conception; but, quick as thought,—and thought is as quick as lightning in such circumstances—I whistled for the brakes, shut off the steam, and awaited the collision. I would have reversed the engine, but a fear that a reversal of its action would crowd up the cars on the trestle work, and throw them into the gorge below, forbade, nor was there wisdom in jumping off, as the steep embankment on either side would prevent escape from the wreck of the cars when the collision came. All this was decided in an instant of time, and I calmly awaited the shock which I saw was unavoidable. Though the speed, which was very moderate before, was considerably diminished. in the fifty yards between the obstacle and the head of the train, I saw that we would certainly run into the rear of another train, which was the obstruction I had seen.

The first car struck was loaded with hay and grain. My engine literally split it in two, throwing the hay right and left, and scattering the grain like chaff. The next car, loaded with horses, was in like manner torn to pieces, and the horses piled upon the sides of the road. The third car, loaded with tents and camp equipage, seemed to present greater resistance, as the locomotive only reached it, and came to a stand still.

My emotions during these moments were most peculiar. I watched the remorseless pressure of the engine with almost admiration. It appeared to be deliberate, and resolute, and insatiable. The shock was not great, the advance seemed very slow; but it plowed on through car after car with a steady and resistless course which suggested at that critical moment a vast and determined living agent. When motion ceased, I knew my time of trial was near; for if Colonel Williams had not been thrown from the top of the cars into the gorge below, he would soon be forward to execute his threat,—to shoot me if any accident occurred. I stepped out of the cab on the railing running along to the smokestack, so as to be out of view to any one coming forward toward the engine, and yet to have him in the full light of the lantern which hung in the cab. Exactly as I had surmised—for I had seen a specimen of his temper and recklessness,—he came stamping and cursing; and jumping from the car to the tender, he drew a pistol, and cried out,

"Where is that cursed engineer, that did this pretty job? I'll shoot him the minute I lay my eyes upon him."

I threw up my six shooter so that the light of the lantern shone upon it, where he could see but indistinctly, if at all, and said with deliberation,

"Colonel Williams, if you raise your pistol, you are a dead man; don't stir, but listen to me. I have done just what any man must have done under the circumstances. I stopped the train as soon as possible, and I'll convince you of it, if you are a responsible man; but not another word of shooting, or you go down."

"Don't shoot, don't shoot!" he cried.

"Put up your pistol, and so will I," I replied.

He did so, and came forward, and I explained the impossibility of seeing the train sooner, as I had no head light; and they had carelessly neglected to leave a light on the rear of the other train. I advised the choleric Colonel to go forward and expend his wrath and curses on the conductor of the forward train, that had stopped in such a place, and sent out no signal man in the rear, nor even left a red light. He acknowledged that I was right. I then informed him that I was an officer in the ordnance department, and was in charge of a shipment of ammunition for Bowling Green, and would have him court-martialed when he reached there, unless he apologized for the threats he had made. This information had a calming effect on the Colonel, who at heart was really a clever fellow.

### Paid his Assessment on the Spot.

The summary method pursued by Colonel Metcalfe, in Kentucky, is well illustrated by the following incident which occurred in Paris, Kentucky. A customer was brought in and told that he was assessed a thousand dollars. "Well, said the rich Secesh, "How long will you give me to raise it?" "*Three years or during the war*," answered the Colonel. "Oh, well, well," said Secesh, "you are not so hard with us after all. I will have it for you in time," and started leisurely for the door. "But," said the Colonel, "you must accept of our hospitality during that time, at your own expense. Guard," continued the Colonel, "take Mr. —— to that mansion that was made with hands, down on the classic bluffs of Stoner." "Stop, stop!" said Secesh; "now I think of it, I happen to have that amount in my pocket, and have not the least objection to helping our country in her hour of need." He escaped a hard bed and bare walls that night.

### Terry's Colored Cook and his Shell.

While at Morris Island, South Carolina, General Terry's colored cook, whose bump of curiosity must certainly have been developed to an alarming degree, undertook to investigate the contents of a 10-inch shell by placing the portion containing the

General Alfred H. Terry.

fuse-cap before the fire of his stove, for the purpose of melting the lead and releasing the cap from the shell. As may be naturally supposed, the heat of the fire soon occasioned an explosion, which seriously wounded the over-curious cook in different portions of his body, to say nothing of the

RATIONS, CURRENCY, ORDNANCE, MAILS, ETC.   457

very promiscuous damage done to the stove and to the kettles and pans resting thereon, the fragments of which it would have been quite impossible to count in any short space of time. A colored soldier, named David, a native of South Carolina, having been made acquainted with the circumstances of this occurrence, drew himself up and pompously remarked, with characteristic vernacular, that "white folks need not offer any more comparisons between the Boston and the South Carolina darkies which were unfavorable to the latter, for it was now clearly demonstrated that the Boston chaps were both simple, and ignorant, while a South Carolinian, if put to the same test, would never have made such a fool of himself as to stick a loaded shell into the fire of a stove and stick his face into it!" It would have been interesting, doubtless, to listen to the Yankee cook's comments upon his adventure—if indeed any comments were needed in view of his knocked-up appearance.

#### Commissaries and Chemists.

The editor of the Baltimore American took it into his head one day to visit the commissary department of one of the large military hospitals conveniently accessible, and in the course of his observations noticed several barrels of dried coffee grounds, the purpose whereof naturally excited his curiosity. The polite Commissary informed him that he received twelve dollars per barrel for the grounds. "But what is it purchased for?" inquired the editor, with that curiosity for information natural to his profession. "Well," said the Commissary, hesitatingly, "it is *re-aromatized* by the transforming hand of modern chemistry, and put up in pound papers, which are decorated with attractive labels and high-sounding names." Yes, re-aromatized! Comment is unnecessary.

#### Halleck's Use of a Bad Report.

Connected with General Grant's great victory on the rivers Tennessee and Cumberland, an interesting incident is told, as follows:

Several rumors had appeared in the newspaper press, and had otherwise been publicly proclaimed, that General Grant was in the habit of getting intoxicated. This idea may have arisen from his slovenly mode of attiring himself, or from some other equally unreliable cause. The friends of the Illinois troops under General Grant's command, being anxious for their safety, selected a delegation to visit

Major-General Halleck.

General Halleck, and have Grant removed.

"You see, General," said the spokesman, "we have a number of Illinois volunteers under General Grant, and it is not safe that their lives should be entrusted to the care of a man who so constantly indulges in intoxicating liquors. Who knows what blunders he may commit."

"Well, gentlemen," said General Halleck, "I am satisfied with General Grant, and I have no doubt you also soon will be."

While the deputation were staying at the hotel, the news arrived of the capture of Fort Donelson and thirteen thousand prisoners. General Halleck posted the intelligence himself on the hotel bulletin, and as he did so he remarked, loud enough for all to hear:

"If General Grant is such a drunkard

as he is reported to be, and can win such victories as these, I think it is my duty to issue an order that any man found sober in St. Louis to-night shall be punished with fine and imprisonment!"

### Shoe-Raid by General Wadsworth.

One of the cleverest Union raids during the war was that undertaken—and successfully carried through—by General Wadsworth, one of the heroes killed while serving in Grant's Richmond campaign. The General in giving an account of this 'shoe raid' to a companion, said:—I remember during the march through Maryland, before the battle of South Mountain,

General Wadsworth.

we passed over a tract of country extremely rugged and stony, and I saw not only men but officers walking along with bleeding feet. The men's shoes gave out entirely. It hurt my feelings more than I can tell you, to see the good fellows trudge along so. We came to a town on the line of march, and I, who was riding at the head of the column, spurred ahead to see if there were not some shoe stores where I could purchase what was needed for the men. All the shops were closed; the first men I saw were two sitting outside of a closed shop. "Are there any shoe stores in this town?" I asked. They replied in a gruff way, that they could not tell—there might be and there might not.

I told them that I wanted to buy some shoes for my troops, who were barefooted. They replied they guessed I would'nt get many. At that I got angry. Said I, "There are two pair of shoes at any rate, which I see on your feet. Take them off instantly!" They were obliged to do it. I went through the town, and took the shoes off every man's feet I could see, and thus I raised about two hundred pairs in all. One fine old fellow, a miller, whom I met, I did not deprive of his own pair; I rode up to him, and asked if he had any shoes he could spare me, describing the pitiful condition of my men. The old man said, "I don't know if there's any shoes in the house or not, but"—looking down at his feet—"here's a pair you're welcome to at any rate." I would not let him take them off, but he gave me some from his house. All the rest I stripped.

### Bad Habit amongst Mules.

When our troops at Paducah first received their teams, they were troubled to procure forage, so that the mules were turned loose or tethered in the outskirts of the town. Occasionally a few would be missing, until Uncle Sam found himself minus some twenty-five or thirty. Those which strayed away were caught up by the rebel speculators and taken to Blandville, back of Columbus, where they had accumulated some fifty stolen and purchased animals, which were under five or six keepers.

Two privates, members of the Fourteenth Illinois Volunteers, hearing of the whereabouts of said stock, asked General Smith's permission to attempt their recapture, which, with some misgivings, was granted. The boys, dressed in the garb of Kentucky farmers, went and surveyed the field and fold, and set to work. They had whiskey with them—whiskey such as Kentucky rebels liked to get drunk on—good old Bourbon, and the first object was to get them as comfortably tight as possible, which was not long in being accomplished. Then the boys went to the mule yard, let down the bars, mounted two of the best, without saddle or bridle, and started for Paducah, the whole lot following at break-neck pace, and braying in the most diabolical chorus. The keepers were not long in discovering the trick, and gave chase as far as they deemed it prudent toward our lines, but to no purpose; and in good season Saturday afternoon the boys made their appearance at General Smith's headquarters to report, their faces beaming with a glow of satisfaction hard to describe. Their report was a clarified condensation of Laconism, in dialogue shape:

General Smith—Well, boys, what luck?

Soldier—We got 'em, and more too!

General S.—How many did you get?

Soldier—Forty, I reckon; haint counted 'em.

General S.—But that is more than we have lost. You did'nt steal any, I hope?

Soldier—Steal! C-ristopher, steal! No, siree, but you see we did'nt have time to put the bars up after we had got Uncle Sam's out, and the —— things would foller; a very bad habit with some mules.

The General drew on an elongated countenance, and as sternly as though he had been judge, and was sentencing a culprit to a life-time of imprisonment, lectured the soldier roundly for using profane language in the quarters and presence of a general officer. The soldier took the lecture uneasily, twirling his hat nervously the while, and when the General had 'subsided,' apologized as follows:

"You see, General, we have had to cuss the —— things all day to get 'em into camp, and its' mighty hard to quit off all of a suddenly."

Then the General's rigidity relaxed; a smile, or rather a laugh, came up from his heart, and tried to escape from the corners of his mouth—but discipline is discipline with an old army officer, and it would not do to allow such a breach of decorum to pass unnoticed. Still, in consideration of the recaptured twenty-five mules, "and more too," he did not inflict any severe castigation or put them in arrest, but, thanking them for the services rendered, dismissed them with a caution to leave their profanity behind when they came again to head-quarters, and the boys left, declaring, as they closed the door, that "such a pious old cuss had'nt any business to be around amongst sojers."

### Half-hour's Experience of a Pedler with General Nelson.

General Nelson occasionally went dashing through the camp, bestowing a gratuitous cursing upon some offender, and was then off again like a shot. The General followed the seas many years and had become a great, rough, profane old fellow. He had a plain, good, old fashioned fire-place kindness about him that was always shown to those who did their duty. But offenders met with no mercy at his hands. The General conceived an awful hatred against pedlers. There were many that

Pedler and Gen. Nelson.

came about the camp, selling hoe-cakes, pies, milk, etc., at exorbitant prices. Cracker-fed soldiers would naturally be free with their money—willing to pay ten times the value of an article if in want of it. One day the General came across a pedler selling something that he called pies—not the delicious kind of pies that an absent soldier is made home-sick at the thought of, but an indigestible combination of flattened dough and woolly peaches, minus sugar, minus spice, minus everything that is good, and any of which the General swore up and down "would kill a hyena deader than the d——."

"What do you charge for those pies?" belched out the General.

"Fifty cents a-piece," responded the pie-man.

"Fifty cents a-piece for pies!" roared the infuriated General: "Now, you infernal swindling pirate," roared he, letting fly, in black and blue, one of his great rifled oaths, that fairly made the fellow tremble, "I want you to go to work and cram every one of those pies down you as quick as the Lord will let you. Double-quick, you villain!"

Expostulations, appeals, or promises, were of no avail, and the pedler was forced, to the great entertainment of the soldiers whom he had been so ready to gouge, to down half a dozen of his own pies—all he had left.

"Now," said the General to the fellow, after he had finished his repast, and stood looking as death-like as the certain doctor who was forced to swallow his own medicine—"leave! and if ever, *ever* I catch you back here again, swindling my men, I'll hang you." The rat departed.

### Zealous for the Cause but not for the Scrip.

Mr. ——, a rebel farmer, living near Bear Creek, in Baltimore county, Maryland, was so elated at the rebel incursion in Maryland, that he determined to visit "our deliverers," and for that purpose hooked up his horse and wagon and started merrily agog. He alighted at a hotel near Frederick, and was drinking a bumper to Jeff, when a Confederate officer came in and inquired for the owner of the team. Bear Creek farmer was delighted, and with smiles, said—

"I am, sir; and that team is Southern all over, sir—horse, wagon, and driver, sir."

"And what is the price?" interrupted the son of Mars, pulling out a roll of Confederate scrip.

"Oh," said farmer, "I would not like to sell now, 'cause I can't use your kind of money in Baltimore."

"Nonsense," says the officer; "haven't you declared over and over in your letters that the bankers and rich men of Baltimore are in the cause; they'll buy, sir."

And handing over the price in Confederate scrip, he left the zealous farmer patriot to toddle home afoot, with a pocket full of confederate treasure. He arrived in town in due time, and stopped several persons with, "Show me the man that buys Confederate scrip!" Up to the latest accounts it was not known that the individual so eagerly sought for had been found.

### Secession Damsels and Federal Foragers.

Quartermaster S. and Commissary B., of one of the regiments in McClellan's army, were both of them very good fellows, and also very brave soldiers, when either of their departments of transportation and supply were brought into conflict with the enemy. One morning they mounted their mettled steeds and started out in company, to forage for the officers' mess. Well provided with money to meet the exorbitant demands of the egg and strawberry hucksters of the section of country to which they were going, they gaily vaulted into their saddles, and bidding good bye to their friends, briskly trotted along on the road towards Richardson's house. Having reached there, they turned off on the White House road, and after a short ride, stopped at a small house by the roadside, to inquire what articles they had for sale. B. was the spokesman, and at his summons out came a blooming damsel, of eighteen summers, to answer the inquiry.

"Have you any eggs, or butter, or milk, or anything of the sort to sell, ma'am?"

"Whereabouts do you come from?"

"About four miles from here. We come from the Yankee army."

"You do, hey? Well, I don't allow a Yankee to come within twenty yards of me, much less to speak to me."

The officers opened their eyes at this desperate declaration, and riding into the yard the Commissary continued:

"Say, look-a-here, don't you know that such folks as you are the only kind of meat we have down in our camp?"

"Yes, indeed," broke in fair Secessia, "I've heard that much about you."

"Well, I suppose you have, and it's all true. Why, at the battle of Fair Oaks the Yankees eat hundreds just such looking rebels as you, and it took ever so many soldiers to guard the three thousand dead ones and keep us off."

At this barbarous speech, which might have provoked most terrible results, if the young lady's eyes were any index of her state of mind, her parents appeared, and gently checking her, accosted the Union officers, and said they had nothing to sell. The father seemed somewhat amused at his daughter's spirit, and exclaimed:

"That ere gal's got a beau in the Confederate army, don't you see, and you know that's a good reason for her being so much opposed to the Yankees. Just you make an offer to capture her, and see if she don't haul down her colors."

But Federal officers don't do such unmanly things, and so, finding they could procure no eatables at that domicil, they withdrew to the road, leaving their plucky little feminine enemy in her glory, and continued their journey.

**Mrs. Partington on the New Military Crop.**

A shadow passed our window, the door opened, and looking up we saw the form of Mrs. Partington before us. "I've just dropped in," she said. 'Dropped' in!—she weighs one hundred and fifty if she does an ounce. She held out her snuffbox as she said "Good morning," filled with Rhode's delectable. Ike was by her side, and before we had time to prevent it, he had both arms stuck to the fly paper on the desks before us. "I've just dropped in to ask," she said, as she looked up inquiringly, "what sort of a crop the cessationists will be likely to get from *planting cannon*, that I see something about in the papers? *I* don't believe it will come up."

"Perhaps it may," we said, favoring the idea, "as we see so many sprouts about us in uniform that are evidently sons of guns, and if, as Mr. Field has said, a soldier's sire and grandsire may be a sword, why not a gun have *its* descendants?"

"May be so," said she, brightening up, "may be so, it isn't the most unlikely thing that never came to pass, and that may be why guns wear breeches. I declare that I never thought of *that* before." Mrs. Partington, the merry and garrulous ward of B. P. Shillaber, was by no means idle during the war, in the good city of Boston, of which she is one of the noted spokes*men*.

**Visit of General Jenkins at a Pennsylvania Editor's.**

The raid of General Jenkins into Pennsylvania was the occasion of a call at the domicil of the editor of the Chambersburg Repository, by that renowned chief, and there had good cheer, though the "landlord" had "stepped out." The editor's remarks on this visit were as follows:

However earnest an enemy Jenkins may be, he don't seem to keep spite, but is capable of being very jolly and sociable when he is treated hospitably. For prudential reasons the editor was not at home to do the honors at his own table; but Jenkins was not particular, nor was his appetite impaired thereby. He called upon the ladies of the house, shared their hospitality, behaved in all respects like a gentleman, and expressed very earnest regrets that he had not been able to make the personal acquaintance of the editor. We beg to say that we reciprocate the wish of the General, and shall be glad to make his acquaintance personally—"when this cruel war is over." Colonel French and Surgeon Bee spent much of their time with Mrs. McClure, and the former showed his appreciation of her hospitality by taking her revolver from her when he left. An order having been made for the citizens to surrender all the guns and pistols they had, Colonel French took the pistol of his hostess. How many rifles he didn't get that were in her keeping, we "dinna choose to tell." General Jenkins had the fullest information of the movements of the editor of this paper. He told at our own house, when we had left, the direction we had gone, and described the horse we rode, and added that there were people in Chambersburg sufficiently cowardly and treacherous to give such information of their neighbors. When it was suggested that such people should be sent within the rebel lines, he insisted that the South should not be made a Botany Bay for Northern scoundrels. We had not the felicity of a personal interview with the distinguished guerrilla chief, but our special reporters took his dimensions and autobiography with general accuracy. He was born of his mother at a very early age, and is supposed to be the son of his father. He was flogged through school in his boyhood years much as other children; and may have startling traditions touching his early character, such as the hatchet and cherry-tree which proved that Washington could not lie; but it is for the present regarded as doubtful. He subsequently graduated at Jefferson College, in this State, and gave promise of future usefulness and greatness. His downward career commenced some five years ago, when in an evil hour he became a member of Congress from Western Virginia, and from thence may be dated his decline and fall. From Congress he naturally enough turned fire-eater, secessionist and guerrilla.

## Lending to the Government.

The use of United States compound interest notes in paying off employees gave rise, in a certain case, to the following little dialogue, as related by one of the parties concerned.

*Boss*—How would you like to lend part of your wages to Government, Patrick?

*Patrick*—Ah, you see, I just make out to live on what ye pay me,—things is so high! I can't save a dollar.

*Boss*—But, Patrick, you know I raised your wages, and you ought to lay by something for a rainy day. Better put by $10 and get $11.94 for it three years hence; or $20, and get $23.88 for it, instead of getting nothing or lending it to a savings bank at only five per cent.

*Patrick*—(Looking at the table of interest on $10 compounded, and asking some questions as to what currency the savings bank would pay in)—Well, I'd like to take $50 in compound interest notes.

*Boss*—But, Patrick, if you can spare $50, you had better put your money into 7-30 notes, which pay more interest, and entitle you to gold-bearing bonds if you want them, or greenbacks if you please.

*Patrick*—Would you please to just let me have one hundred dollars in the Seven-Thirties?

## Agreeable Inducements to Travellers.

Below is a bill of fare "found" in the Confederate camp at Vicksburg, which is of interest to all epicures, as well as to those who are not of that class:

HOTEL DE VICKSBURG.—*Bill of Fare for July,* 1863: *Soup*—mule tail. *Boiled*—mule bacon with poke greens; mule ham canvassed. *Roast*—mule sirloin. *Vegetables*—peas and rice. *Entrees*—mule head stuffed a la mode; mule beef jerked a la Mexicana; mule ears fricasseed a la gotch; mule side stewed, new style, hair on; mule spare-ribs plain; mule liver hashed. *Side Dishes*—mule salad; mule hoof soused; mule brains a la omelette; mule kidneys stuffed with peas; mule tripe fried in pea

## RATIONS, CURRENCY, ORDNANCE, MAILS, ETC.

meal batter; mule tongue cold a la Bray. *Jellies*—mule foot. *Pastry*—pea-meal pudding, blackberry sauce; cotton-wood berry pies; China berry tart. *Dessert*—white oak acorns; beech nuts; blackberry leaf tea; genuine Confederate coffee. *Liquors*—Mississippi Water, vintage of 1492, superior, $3; Lime Stone Water, late importation, very fine, $2.75; Spring Water, Vicksburg brand, $1.50. Meals at all hours. Gentlemen to wait upon themselves. Any inattention on the part of the servants to be promptly reported at the office.

JEFF. DAVIS & Co., Proprietors.

CARD.—The proprietors of the justly celebrated Hotel de Vicksburg, having enlarged and refitted the same, are now prepared to accommodate all who favor them with a call. Parties arriving by the river or Grant's inland route, will find Grape, Canister & Co.'s carriages at the landing, or any depot on the line of intrenchments. Buck, Ball & Co., take charge of all baggage. No effort will be spared to make the visit of all as interesting as possible.

### Pumpkin-Pie Story of Lieutenant Wickfield and General Grant.

The hero and veteran—Grant—who was citizen, Captain, Colonel, Brigadier and Major-General within a space of nine months, though a rigid disciplinarian, and a perfect Ironsides in the discharge of his official duties, could enjoy a joke, and was always ready to perpetrate one when an opportunity offered. Indeed, among his acquaintances, he is as much renowned for his eccentric humor, as for his skill and bravery as a commander.

When Grant was a Brigadier in Southwest Missouri, he commanded an expedition against the Confederates, under Jeff. Thompson, in northeast Arkansas. The distance from the starting point of the expedition to the supposed rendezvous of the Confederates was about one hundred and ten miles, and the greater portion of the route lay through a howling wilderness. The imaginary suffering that the Union soldiers endured during the first two days of their march, was enormous. It was impossible to steal or confiscate uncultivated real estate, and not a hog or a chicken, or an ear of corn, was anywhere to be seen. On the third day, however, things looked a little more helpful, for a few small specks of ground, in a state of partial cultivation, were here and there visible.

On that day, Lieutenant Wickfield, of an Indiana cavalry regiment, commanded the advance guard, consisting of eighty mounted men. At about noon he came up to a small farm-house, from the outward appearance of which he judged that there might be something fit to eat inside. He halted his company, dismounted, and with two second Lieutenants entered the dwelling. He knew that Grant's incipient fame had already gone forth throughout all that region of country, and it occurred to him that by representing himself to be

Pumpkin Pie.

the General he might obtain the best the house afforded. So, assuming a very martial demeanor, he accosted the inmates of the house, and told them he must have something for himself and staff to eat. They desired to know who he was, and he told them that he was General Grant. At the sound of that name, they flew around with alarming alacrity, and served up about all they had in the house, taking great pains all the while to make loud professions of loyalty. The Lieutenants ate

464    THE BOOK OF ANECDOTES OF THE REBELLION.

as much as they could of the not over sumptuous meal, but which was, nevertheless, good for that country, whether in times of war or peace, and demanded what was to pay for their "entertainment."

"Nothing," was the reply, and they went on their way rejoicing.

In the meantime, General Grant, who had halted his army a few miles further back, for a brief resting-spell, came in sight of and was rather favorably impressed —as had been his Lieutenant—with the appearance of this same house. Riding up to the fence in front of the door he desired to know if they would cook him a meal.

"No," said the female, in a gruff voice, "General Grant and his staff have just been here and eaten everything in the house except one pumpkin pie."

"Humph," murmured Grant, "what is your name?"

"Selvidge," replied the woman.

Casting a half dollar in at the door, he asked if she would keep that pie till he sent an officer for it, to which she replied that she would.

That evening, after the camping ground had been selected, the various regiments were notified that there would be a grand parade at half past six, for orders. Officers would see that their men all turned out, &c. In five minutes the camp was in a perfect uproar, and filled with all sorts of rumors; some thought that the enemy was upon them, it being so unusual to have parade when on a march.

At half past six the parade was formed, ten columns deep, and nearly a quarter of a mile in length. After the usual routine of ceremonies, the Assistant Adjutant General read the following order:—

"HEAD-QUARTERS ARMY IN THE FIELD, SPECIAL ORDER, No. —. Lieutenant Wickfield, of the — Indiana cavalry, having on this day eaten everything in Mrs. Selvidge's house, at the crossing of the Ironton and Pocahontas, and Black River and Cape Girardeau roads, except one pumpkin pie, Lieutenant Wickfield is hereby ordered to return with an escort of one hundred cavalry, and eat that pie also.

U. S. GRANT.
Brig. Gen'l Commanding."

Grant's orders were law, and no soldier willingly attempted to evade them. At seven o'clock the gastronomic Lieutenant filed out of camp with his hundred men, amid the cheers of the entire army. The escort concurred in stating that he devoured the whole of the pie, and seemed to relish it.

### General Stuart Too Late to Dinner.

Rather a palatable circumstance of the war was that which General Stuart, were he still living, would probably remember more vividly than anybody else. At the time this circumstance transpired, some there were who contended that Stuart no longer had command of the rebel cavalry, but that Fitzhugh Lee was the chief of that branch of the rebel army. Whether so or not will not change the fact that Stuart fought Buford on that eventful Saturday, for Buford ate his dinner in a cosy little house, nestled among pines, cedars, and jessamine, about one and a half miles from Culpepper, where General Stuart and staff were going to dine. Every luxury and delicacy that could be procured in that poor, ransacked country, was smiling on the white, spotless linen which covered the table. The fair occupant of the stool had no doubt hurried on a sun-bonnet, and slipped off to Culpepper. The 'Bonnie Blue Flag' would not sound so well in the old parlor, and she feared General Buford and Staff could not appreciate her selection of songs. However, the dinner was appreciated; and if smacking of lips, and looks of regret at the fragments they could not eat, were of any significance, the dishes prepared by those kind people met with the appreciation of all the partakers.

### Joke of the President on Secretary Chase.

It was not reported what joke old Abe got off when he heard the news of the surrender of Plymouth, which gave such joy to northern hearts. In regard to the Fort Pillow affair he made a Bunsby speech, but no joke. The latter would appear to have been reserved for the benefit of Secretary Chase, as he was starting on a financial trip to New York. Old Abe, like Cromwell,—though without the latter's military genius—seemed very fond of playing practical jokes upon his associates. It is said that after Cromwell signed the warrant for the execution of King Charles, he turned round to one of his colleagues and smeared his face with ink. This he thought capital fun. Old Abe's jokes have been pronounced as smacking somewhat of the same quality. When Chase called upon him to say good-bye, he, as Secretary of the Treasury, asked for some information about the probable end of the war, saying it would help him in getting more money in Wall street. "Do you want more money?" asked Old Abe, and then quickly added, "What! has the printing machine gin out?" This joke must be set down as fully equal to Cromwell's, and was not unworthy that famous American 'Cruikshank,' Mr. Orpheus C. Kerr, whose *penchant* in this line is a boon to human nature, and—a fortune to his pocket.

### Hooker's Magnificent War-Horse, "Lookout."

Major-General Joseph Hooker claimed the name of "Lookout" for his seven year old battle horse, which bore him through the perils of the fight above the clouds, so memorable in the annals of the war, and an account of which will be found in its appropriate department in these pages. Lookout, according to the description given of him, was a rich chestnut color, standing nearly seventeen hands high, and possessing all the dainty and elastic action of the most delicately-fashioned colt. He was three-quarters bred, being by Mambrino out of a half bred mare; and notwithstanding his ponderous size, he had been known to trot, under saddle, in 2.45. He was bred in Kentucky, and selected when a five-year old, for Mr. Ten Broeck, as the finest horse that could be sent to England to exhibit style in a *coupee*. For some reason he was not forwarded further eastward than New York city; but when there, was seen by the horse agent of the Emperor of the French, who repeatedly offered a thousand dollars to obtain possession of him. It was at this time that General Hooker came in competition with His Majesty, Louis Napoleon, and finally succeeded in purchasing the horse.

Lookout was undoubtedly the finest charger in the army of the Union; and, in grandeur of form and action, dwarfed all other horses which approached him. Backed by his rider, the General—universally acknowledged as a matchless rider—the people, could they have but beheld him moving up Broadway, would have pronounced it the finest equestrian statue they had ever seen.

### War News from Richmond Wanted.

A gentleman of the press once dropped in at the War Department, and in the course of the conversation with the Secretary mentioned casually to him that he had just telegraphed certain information concerning army movements to the New York journals, with which he was connected. The Secretary looked at him in dismay, and replied: "Sir, I will give you one hundred thousand dollars from the army secret service fund, if you will give me the same information concerning the enemy's disposition and movements which you have just conveyed indirectly, but surely, to Richmond."

### "Reliable Information."

A visitor to the army of the Potomac called upon General Grant one morning, and found the great commander sitting in his tent, smoking and talking to one of his staff officers. The stranger approached the chieftain and enquired of him as follows: "General, if you flank Lee and get between him and Richmond, will you not uncover Washington and leave it a prey to the enemy?

General Grant, discharging a cloud of smoke with "a silver lining," from his mouth, indifferently replied, " Yes, I reckon so."

Stranger, encouraged by the reply he thus received, propounded question number two :—

" General, do you not think Lee can detach sufficient force from his army to reinforce Beauregard and overwhelm Butler ? "

" Not a doubt of it," replied the General.

Stranger, becoming fortified by his success, propounded question number three, as follows :—

" General, is there not danger that Johnston may come up and reinforce Lee, so that the latter will swing around and cut your communications and seize your supplies ? "

" Very likely," was the cool reply of the General, as he knocked the ashes from the end of his cigar with his little finger.

Stranger, horrified at the awful fate about to befall General Grant and his army, made his exit and hastened to Washington to communicate the "news." Of such stuff comes much of the "reliable intelligence" and "authentic information" to which the public is treated.

### Material of which "Mudsill" Regiments are Made Up.

Great admiration was excited by the readiness of the men of the Eighth Massachusetts Regiment, under General Butler, for whatever services they were called on to perform during their passage from New York to Washington. Whether men were required to act as engineers, machinists, carpenters, or sailors, they were to be had on demand. Volunteers from every department of industry, there could scarcely be found a trade or profession, from butchers to lawyers, which was not represented in the regiment, by men ready for special service whenever required. On reaching the railway station at Annapolis, General Butler found that the secessionists had taken apart and broken the only locomotive there, so as to render it unserviceable. " Who knows how to repair this engine ? " demanded the General. Six practical machinists stepped forward; but one claimed the job—" Because you see, General," he said, " I made that engine," and he pointed to his private mark on the machinery. These 'mudsill' regiments, as Gov. Hammond would call them, are somehow strangely intelligent.

### Fresh Pork for the Eighth Illinois.

When the Union army was stationed at Bird's Point, Missouri, secessionists were rather supposed to have "rights that a soldier must respect," and there were stringent orders against jayhawking. Colonel (afterward General) Oglesby was then in command of the Eighth Illinois.

"Fresh Pork."

Well, one day his fife and drum majors went out into the woods to practice a new tune. Attracted no doubt by the melody, a fine fat shote, of musical proclivities, came near—alas! for the safety of his bacon, *too* near—for the bass-drummer, by a change of base, made a base attack on his front; while the fifer, by a bold and rapid flank movement, charged him in the rear. 'Twas soon over; a few well directed volleys of clubs and other persuasives were applied, and piggy went dead again—a martyr to his love for music! But how to get the deceased pork into camp?— "That's what's the matter " *now*. After considerable discussion an idea 'strikes' the drummer (not so as to hurt him): "We will put him in the drum." "Just the thing, by hokey!" said the fifer. One head was taken out, and the hog stowed, and our heroes started for their quarters, carrying the drum between them. In the mean time the regiment went out for a dress parade; and the Colonel, somewhat vexed at the absence of the principal musicians, no sooner saw the gents than, in a voice of reprimand, he ordered them to take their places with the music. The drum-bearers halted, looked at each other, then at the Colonel,—but said never a word. The Colonel repeated his order in a style so emphatic that it could not be misunderstood. The dealers in pork felt a crisis had arrived, and that an explanation had become a "military necessity." So the drummer, going up close to the Colonel, in a low voice made him acquainted with the *status* of affairs, winding up with, "We 'low, Colonel, to bring the best quarter over to your mess." " Sick, eh ?" thundered the Colonel. "Why didn'. you say so at first? Go to your 'qnarters?' —of course! Bat-tal-ion, r i-g-h-t f-a-c-e!" The Colonel had fresh pork for supper.

---

**Newspaporial Forestalling of Dying Sentiments, etc.**

The representative of a now defunct newspaper is jocosely stated to have run up to a wounded officer who believed himself mortally hurt, at the battle of Fort Donelson, and begged him not to die yet for the sake of the ———, (naming his journal,) which he had the honor to represent; remarking to the sufferer, that, if he had any last words to utter, they should appear in the best form in the earliest possible issue of his widely-circulated and highly influential paper. The officer turned away his head in abhorrence and disgust, and some of his friends compelled the persevering reporter to retire. But the professor of the quill insisted, true to his craft, that he could make a better speech for the wounded soldier than he could for himself; and hoped he would remember not to give any other member of the press the least hint of his dying sentiments.

Another correspondent is said to have locked General Buckner up in a room at Dover, and insisted on having a sketch of his life. The General demurred, when he was threatened with being printed as one of the most horrible antecedents unless he complied. He blustered a little, but when the newspaper scribbler began putting down and reading off "General Buckner, a native of Massachusetts, formerly one of the editors of Lloyd Garrison's anti-slavery journal; but compelled to fly to Tennessee on account of having been detected in a forgery of his father's name," etc., the General became a suppliant, and gave the irrepressible fellow the main events of his life. But, jokes aside, nothing in the newspaper system of all Europe was ever equal to the splendid manner of marshaling their great array of facts, sketches, etc., during the four years war, by the correspondents of those princely journals, the New York Herald, Times, Tribune, and World; the Philadelphia Ledger, Bulletin, North American, Press, and Inquirer; the Boston Journal, Traveller, etc.; the Springfield Republican; the Cincinnati Gazette, Enquirer, Times, and Commercial; the Chicago Tribune, Journal, and Times; the St. Louis Democrat, Republican, &c. It is not saying too much, that, from the materials furnished by the able and intrepid correspondents of any one of the great journals here named, a history of the war might be written which, for vigor of style, skilfulness of construction, and amplitude of scope, would leave nothing to be desired.

### Hard to tell Pork from Tomatoes.

While the Brooklyn Fourteenth were in Virginia, it was noticed that where they were the enemy's pigs got scared, and that in the promiscuous state of things thereabouts, an accident would sometimes occur by which pig was turned into pork, and then—

"Hallo, my man! where did you get that pork?" called out the Major to a soldier staggering along with something wrapped up in his shelter tent, and crimsoning the ground as he passed.

"It is'nt pork, Sir, it's tomatoes; you don't know, Sir, how hard it is to tell pork from tomatoes in this country."

The Major, a pleasant hand at a joke himself, was conquered at once, and did not press his inquiries.

### Refusal to Receive Pay for Fighting for his Country.

Paymaster Rochester, feeling his lips to be unsealed by the death of General Wadsworth, of New York, stated that he always paid the General from his first entry into the service; and that when the General called on him for money on the eve of starting to the Mississippi Valley on a special mission connected with the arming and organization of the slaves of that region, he casually remarked to him that when he got to New Orleans he would find there Paymaster Vedder, to whom he would recommend him as a gentlemanly officer to apply to for any moneys he might need.

"No, Sir!" said General Wadsworth, "I shall not apply to Major Vedder. While I am in the service I shall be paid only by you. And my reason for that is, that I wish my account with the Government to be kept with one Paymaster only; for it is my purpose at the close of the war to call on you for an accurate statement of all the money I have received from the United States. The amount, whatever it is, I shall give to some permanent institution founded for the life relief of disabled soldiers. This is the least invidious way in which I can refuse pay for fighting for my country in her hour of danger." It has been stated that Gen. 'Stonewall' Jackson, of the Confederate army, acted upon the same principle of pecuniary disinterestedness; but as no mention is made of the circumstances by Mr. Orville J. Victor, in his standard and admirable work, the "History of the Southern Rebellion," in which Gen. Jackson's character is so graphically portrayed, the statement needs to be verified.

### Anxious for a Trade.

An incident which may be characterized as very Yankee-like occurred one morning in front of the Potomac Army—General Turner's lines. A sergeant deliberately stepped out from our rifle-pits and moved towards the rebels, waving a late paper, and regardless of the probability that he would at any moment be shot dead. A rebel officer shouted to him to go back, but the sergeant was unmindful of the warning, and asked—

"Wont you exchange newspapers?"

"No!" said the rebel, "I have no paper and I want you to go back." With singular persistence, however, the sergeant continued to advance, saying—

"Well, if you hain't a paper, I reckon some of your men have, and I want to exchange, I tell you."

"My men have not got anything of the kind, and you must go back."

This the officer said in a louder tone and with great emphasis. Nothing daunted, the Yankee sergeant still advanced, until he stood plumply before the indignant officer, and said—

"I tell ye now you need'nt get your dander up.—I don't mean no harm no way. P'raps if ye aint got no newspapers ye might give me suthin else. May-be you men would like some coffee for some tobacco. I'm dredful anxious for a trade." The astonished officer could only repeat his command—

"Go back, you rascal, or I'll take you a prisoner. I tell you we have nothing to exchange, and we don't want anything to do with you Yankees."

"Well, then," said the sergeant ruefully, "if ye hain't got nothin', why, here's the paper anyway, and if you get one from Richmond this afternoon, you can send it over. You'll find my name there on that."

The man's impudence or the officer's eagerness for news made the latter accept. He took the paper and asked the sergeant what was the news from Petersburg.

"Oh! our folks say we can go in there just when we want to, but we are waiting to gobble all you fellows first," was the reply.

"Well, I don't know but what you can do it!" said the Lieutenant, turning on his heel and re-entering his rifle-pit; "but meanwhile, my man, you had better go back."

This time the sergeant obeyed the oft-repeated order, and, on telling his adventure, was the hero of the morning among his comrades.

### Helping a Poor Soldier.

When Parson Brownlow was in the town of ——, a good many people grumbled about the high price of admission to his lecture. A very rich, but stingy man, who had been all the time very profuse with expressions of his patriotism, exclaimed, in a crowd.

"Give Parson Brownlow half a dollar? No, Sir-ree! I'd a good deal sooner give it to a poor soldier!"

"Oh!" said a bystander, "then give your half dollar to Captain H—— (an officer dismissed from the army for cowardice); they say he's a *mighty poor soldier!*"

### Banking Operations of General Schoepf in Kentucky.

An excellent operation in banking is that related of General Schoepf, in Kentucky. When the General arrived in the neighborhood of London after the Wildcat fight, he found that Zollicoffer had been levying on Union men for provisions, forage, transportation, etc., and had paid them in Confederate bonds. Imitating an example which the secessionists thought so unexceptionable, General Schoepf commenced levying on the secessionists for similar supplies. In the meantime, he assembled the Union men, and, opening an exchange office for their benefit, set at defiance all banking rules, by taking Confederate bonds at par, and supplying the Union men with good Ohio and Indiana money instead. Then when the secessionists presented their bills, he paid them off with the utmost politeness in their own currency. They didn't know enough to be thankful for the arrangement, but that wasn't his fault.

### Good Luck for an Iowan Soldier.

When the Federal troops made one of their raids into the State of Mississippi, in pursuit of Chalmers' forces, one of the privates of the Seventh Iowa Infantry, while excavating the ruins of an old house, for the purpose of fixing a bed for the night, suddenly struck upon a bottle, which on being brought to light and examined, was found to exhibit the refreshing spectacle of seventy dollars in silver coin. Amazed at his un-dreamed-of good luck, he determined to follow the "lead," which soon changed from silver into gold—for, upon further digging, he turned up the glorious sum of seven hundred and eighty dollars in massive gold. A large and precious haul indeed for a 'hard-up' soldier in an enemy's land. It had probably been deposited there for safe keeping by some of the 'natives,' who ludicrously expected it could thus escape a 'Yankee's' scent.

### How to Spike a Gun.

A characteristic incident is related of Captain George T. Hebard, formerly a private in Company A., of the Chicago Light Infantry, and subsequently commander of the First Vermont Battery, which participated in the hard contested battle near Grand Encore. During the progress of the bloody engagement, Major General Banks rode up and said, energetically: "Captain Hebard, your battery will probably be taken; spike your guns!" As the General rode off, the Captain addressed the men, saying: "Not by a — sight! This battery isn't to be taken nor spiked. Give them double canister, boys!" The battery was charged upon terribly three times after that; the last time, they thought they would wait until the enemy had approached quite near, when they let fly a storm of deadly grape and canister, literally killing *every* man within range of the guns. The battery brought off every gun and caisson, showing that to be the best way of "spiking" —unless the General himself knew of a better one.

---

### Specimen of Ninth Corps Discipline.

While Brigadier-General Robert Potter, commanding the Ninth Corps, in East Tennessee, was once riding along with his orderly, he saw a man running with something in his hand, followed by a woman crying out after him. Stopping him, he found he had stolen some article, and asked him his corps. "Ninth Corps." "Very well," said the General; and he instructed his orderly to tie him up to a tree, and give him a smart strapping with a stirrup-strap. Amid his howls it came out that he belonged to the Fourth Corps. "Very well," said the General; "I am commander of the Ninth Corps; if you belong to it, all right—if not, you'll know how we treat fellows that steal in the Ninth Corps."

### That Dinner at General Holt's.

A Senator from the Western States was invited one day in the midst of war times, by the Judge Advocate-General, Mr. Holt, to dine at the latter's house in Washington, and accepted the invitation in due form. Having been up late at a whist party, he was reminded next morning by a friend that he was to dine that day with Mr. Holt, in company with other civilians and military characters. He arranged his toilet accordingly, was shaved by one of the barbers at the Capitol, and proceeded at the proper hour, after the Senate adjourned, to General Holt's residence, there to partake of the General's viands, and to discuss, with kindred dignitaries, "the situation." He rang the bell, was shown into a parlor with no fire, and was soon joined by General Holt. After conversing some time, General Holt suggested that they would be more comfortable in an adjoining apartment, where a fire was burning in the grate. Here they sat, one upon each side of the fireplace, and talked, and talked, and talked!

The Senator kept up the fire of conversation briskly for an hour or so, and his host responded as briskly. But at last the talk began to flag. General Holt was evidently tired of the task of entertaining the Senator, and the latter began to be very hungry. The conversation became rather fragmentary, then monosyllabic, and finally died out altogether, the Senator meanwhile wondering what in the deuce was the matter with General Holt's cook. The General looked at his watch once or twice, and asking to be excused a moment while he delivered an order, left the room. "High time you hurried up your kitchen forces!" thought the Senator, who having eaten a light breakfast, and no lunch, had long before

"Begun to feel, as well he might,
The keen demands of appetite."

General Holt re-entered, and made an attempt to renew the conversation, with but partial success. At last a carriage arrived at the door and the General took out his watch and remarked, apologetically, that he had a business call to make, and begging therefore to be excused, adding—"I shall have the honor of seeing you *at dinner to-morrow*, of course?"

A light flashed instantaneously upon the mind of the Senator; he was a day before "the fair!" He declined the courteously proffered seat in General Holt's carriage, and, as soon as out of the house, he rushed for the nearest restaurant in a famished state. It was ten o'clock! Next day he attended the dinner, and some of the party having got an inkling of his unhappy blunder, he was induced to tell the story at table, which he did with such effect that the "table was set in a roar" with "inextinguishable laughter," which was repeated more than once afterward,—wherever the Senator related, in his inimitable way, the funny circumstances of his dining out. The war 'situation,' unfortunately, was not discussed with that gravity and profit to the nation which would otherwise have been the case, on account of this senatorial *faux pas*.

#### Unsuccessful Search for Information at Head-quarters.

A good story is told of a curious fellow enjoying considerable popularity in a certain town in New York, and upon the basis of such popularity, he conceived it eminently proper that he should be informed of the plans for the spring campaign in the conduct of the various military operations. So he called on the Secretary of War, and, in his largest style of assurance, asked, in the blandest manner, what Grant was going to do. For final answer he got:

"I don't know; and if I did, it wouldn't be my business to tell you."

Surely, thought the politician, these officials are very short and snappish. A day or two afterward he met General Halleck, with whom he had a slight acquaintance, at Willard's, and asked him if Grant meant to move direct upon Richmond, or would he take the Peninsula route, as some of the papers asserted.

"Yes, I think so," confidently answered Halleck. Mr. Politician pricked up his ears for an instant, but soon said—

"Ah' did you say he was going straight down, or by the Peninsula!"

"Oh!" said General Halleck, "I don't know."

His next effort was at the President, on the occasion of a levee at the White House. Standing familiarly at his right in the blue room, he pleasantly remarked:

"I suppose, Mr. Lincoln, you expect stirring times over here on the Rapidan, in a week or two?"

"Possibly," answered the President.

"Possibly!" echoed the New Yorker.

"I don't know much about it," replied the President, "but I heard to-day that General Grant meant to take Richmond from the Charleston side."

The fellow withdrew. There was, however, yet one source more. Representative Washburne ought to know all about it — dead sure. He, therefore, caught Washburne in the House, early in the morning, before it was called to order, and said to him—

"Can you tell me if I will be likely to find General Grant over on the Rapidan, say early week after next, if I go over there with my Congressman?"

"Can't tell you, Sir," answered Washburne, "General Grant didn't tell me *what* he was going to do, or where he was going to be, at any given time."

The New Yorker concluded that things were in a very, *very* bad way, because no one knew what Grant was about nor what he was going to do.

#### Misfortunes of a Cotton Speculator.

No sympathy was felt for the cotton speculators in New Orleans, who swarmed there during the rebellion, and when one of them was fleeced it seemed to be a matter of rejoicing among both parties—Federals as well as rebs. Something of this sort happened to a citizen of that city—one of those neutral individuals who were always on the fence, ready to jump on either side which policy might dictate to be for their interest for the time being. He—Brown—left New Orleans, on one occasion, bound for the Confederate lines, with the intention of investing what money he had in cotton. Just before starting, he met a friend in the street, with whom, after exchanging the usual common place remarks, he entered into the following conversation:

"What are you up to now, Brown?"

"Oh, I've just made a good thing; been into the Confederacy and bought out thirty bales of Cotton. Bound up again to-morrow, and if nothing happens I'll bring back four times that quantity."

"Be careful, Brown, or you'll get gobbled up. They'll have you in the rebel army."

"Oh, no fear of that. They all know me to be a good Confederate. Besides, I've got British papers."

A month later the two friends met, Brown looking decidedly downcast and seedy. Wallace accosted him with—

"Well, Brown, how about that cotton?"

"Don't talk to me about cotton. Lost everything."

"How's that?"

"Well, you see, I got up to Bayou Sara the same night the rebels made their raid into the place. I had plenty of time to escape, same as a good many others did, but I thought I was all right, and so with a friend sat down to a game of poker, just to show that we didn't feel at all alarmed. Presently in came some rebs, and began to search us. On my partner they found a lot of Confederate money, and they wanted to know what right he had in the Federal lines with Confederate money? So they just took it. Of course I was convinced now that *I* was all right —my money was all greenbacks. 'What are you doing in the Confederacy with Federal money?' they asked. And they took mine too!"

"That was rough. Is that all they done to you?"

"All! No, *sir;* they stripped me of everything, and one strapping big fellow gave me such a spirited kick, while my back was turned, as to take me off my feet, accompanied with the remark all round that if they ever caught me in the Confederacy again with so little money, they'd hang me,—'——if they wouldn't!"

### Woman's Trials and Triumphs.

The wife of an officer in the army, living in Williamson county, Illinois, received from her husband a package containing seven hundred dollars, a portion of which belonged to the families of soldiers living in that vicinity. A few days after the reception of the money there came a sick soldier to the house of the officer's wife, and asked permission to remain over night. The woman refused, but the soldier insisting, she finally consented. During the night the family was aroused by the violent knocking of parties outside, who demanded the door to be opened, and if not opened they would break it down,—that the officer's wife had a lot of money and they were bound to have it. The woman was terrified, and giving the money to the soldier inside, secreted herself and her children, when the soldier exclaimed in a voice loud enough to be heard by the villains outside, "I am unarmed, but if I had a pistol I would fix the villains." The door was then bursted open, and the men, disguised as negroes, entered the house. Five shots were instantly fired at them, killing three of the party and wounding another; the remainder fled. The blacking having been removed from the faces of the dead, they were discovered to be the woman's nearest neighbors—one of them her brother-in-law.

### An Honor to her Sex.

A lady appeared before a Federal Provost-Marshal in Tennessee, as an applicant for pecuniary assistance. She was evidently a lady 'to the manor born,' with a chirography that would have done credit to any one, and her language was entirely free from that peculiarity of dialect so characteristic of the region from which she hailed. The case stood as follows:

Provost Marshal—You are an applicant for relief?

Lady—Yes, sir.

Provost—Where is your husband?

Lady—He is dead, sir.

Provost—When did he die?

Lady—In 1859.

Provost—Have you a plantation?

Lady—Yes, sir, four hundred acres.

Provost—Where are your slaves?

Lady—We had but four; one of them is a decrepit, old woman, and is now with me. The remainder were carried off by Bragg's army, to keep them from falling into the hands of the Union troops.

Provost—Were they carried away by your consent?

Lady—They were not.

Provost—Have you any objection to taking the oath of allegiance.

Lady—I have not; I have always consistently opposed secession. I did so in the presence of Bragg's army, even more loudly than I oppose it now.

This case shows that the chaff in that section was not unmixed with wheat.

### Affecting Appeal to a Union Commissary.

The distress produced in some portions of Kentucky and Tennessee by the secession heresy almost exceeded description. At Bridgeport might frequently have been seen a crowd of females around the United States Commissary, applicants for relief. They were in many instances wretched creatures. Of forty-seven females present on one occasion, only three possessed any money to make purchases; the remainder were all pensioners upon the bounty of the much despised Federal Government. Of course the whole throng had first to apply to the Provost-Marshal, and when the proper hour had arrived they were ushered into his tent, one by one, to relate

Affecting Appeal to a Union Commissary.

their sufferings and the causes which had brought them to distress. They were all new applicants, the old ones getting supplies at regular intervals, without the intervention of the Provost-Marshal. The first whose fortune it was to be called, on this occasion, was a Mrs. Ricard. The Marshal asked her—

"Are you a widow?"

"No, sir."

"Where is your husband?"

"With Bragg, in the Third Tennessee cavalry."

"Your husband is in the rebel army; when did he join it?"

"Two years since."

"Did he volunteer?"

"Yes, to keep from being conscripted."

"But the rebel conscription law was not then in force."

"But they told him that it would soon be, and he had better volunteer."

"Was he not a strong secessionist from the start?"

"Yes; he thought you wanted to deprive us of our rights, and take all our slaves."

"How many slaves did he own?"

"None."

"Had he a plantation?"

"No, sir."

"What property had he?"

"Nothing; he lived by days' work."

"Why, then, was he so fearful about the slaves?"

"Because he was afraid the North would put the niggers on an equality with us."

"Your husband is in the *rebel* army, and you ask *us* to supply you with bread. Why do you do this?"

Mrs. Ricard threw aside the fly of the tent and just outside stood five small children, who had but a single article of clothing—a light, home-spun cotton wrapper—on each, though the wind was blowing chilly cold from the north. "They have not had a mouthful since yesterday morning," said Mrs. R., "and not half enough for six months." The appeal was irresistible—the Provost-Marshal told her he would administer the oath and get her relief.

### From a Palace to the Attic.

As an example of the financial inflation caused by the war and a redundant currency, the following is not at all an exaggeration: An ex-mayor of New York, who lived in an elegant residence and in sumptuous style, was visited one day by two ladies, who asked permission to look at his house, stating that the house next door was for sale, but the occupants would not allow them to view it. His Honor courteously informed them that the houses in that block were exactly alike, and they might examine his house as fully as they pleased. On leaving, one of the ladies said to him, "I suppose you would not sell your house?" "Oh, yes," said His Honor, "I'll sell anything but my wife and children." That afternoon he received a note from a leading real estate house, asking him if he would sell his house, and at what price. He offered it at thirty thousand dollars. The offer was taken at once. The papers were passed and the money paid that night. The next day the house was sold for forty thousand dollars. Two or three things in this transaction made His Honor a little unquiet. He offered his house ten thousand dollars less than his next door neighbor asked. He had to abandon his comfortable and luxurious home instanter. He was literally turned into the street. Somebody made ten thousand dollars out of him. Getting a fashionable residence at any reasonable price was out of the question. Nothing remained for him but the overcrowded Fifth Avenue Hotel, where, with his family, in an attic story, he was at last accounts waiting for something to turn up.

### Cord for Cord—Secession Currency.

Quite a 'good un' is told of a steamboat Captain who stopped with his boat at a wood yard, coming down the river, and who thought to try the pretended loyalty of the owner of the yard by an offer of Confederate money, of which the boat had a good supply.

"Will you take Confederate money for your wood?" shouted the Captain, to the man on shore.

"Yes," was the laconic reply.

The boat hauled to, was made fast, and a stage thrown out, when it occurred to the Captain to inquire about the rate he was to pay.

"What do you ask for wood now?" he asked.

"What kind of money did you say you would pay in?" inquired the wood vender.

"Confederate."

"Well, then, I want *cord for cord!*"

### Present of a Turkey to General Sedgwick.

A woman came into the head-quarters of the Virginia army, from the country, and going to General Sedgwick, who was sitting *en dishabille* on the steps of a house, inquired for the General, saying she had brought him a turkey, because he had sent a guard to her house to protect her property. "Won't you sell me the turkey?" said the General, "I will pay you well for it." "No," replied the woman, "I have brought it for the General, and no one else can have it." The discussion was kept up some time, till finally the General pointed out an officer in full uniform, saying, "There, go give it to him." She immediately went and delivered the turkey to the officer, who took it in amazement, while she gave utterance to some voluble thanks. Some of the bystanders, who had heard the whole matter, subsequently illumined the woman's conceptions, and she came up to the General, blushing and apologizing—expressing her regrets that she had given the turkey to the wrong person. The matter was rectified, very much to her satisfaction.

#### Grant's Objection to having any Trade-Partnership.

Quite a characteristic anecdote is told of General Grant, relative to his refusal to engage in or authorize any movements for the reopening of trade with the rebellious States. On one occasion, especially, after his protests and orders suppressing such traffic, he was eagerly entreated by the agents of the Treasury Department to authorize some system of trade. For a long time he refused, for the reason that he could not successfully conduct his military operations while such persons were moving around him; but at last he conceded that a certain amount of trade in the recaptured districts of the South would be safe, proper, and even highly useful to the Union—provided it could be conducted through honest, unimpeachable Union hands. He was asked to name the persons to whom he would be willing to intrust such traffic:

"I will do no such thing," was Grant's reply; "for if I did, it would appear in less than a week that I was a partner of every one of the persons trading under my authority."

Instances of the General's unbending integrity might be given in sufficient number to fill a volume. They will be found amply and admirably displayed in that excellently prepared work, "Grant and his Campaigns," which exceeds in thrilling interest any similar works in which Napoleon or Wellington are the central heroes.

#### Balance of Power maintained between Turkeys and Chickens.

A company of the —th cavalry of volunteers (no matter what State,) were out on a forage, with the usual orders to respect the enemy's property. But coming upon a plantation where chickens and turkeys were dallying in the sunshine, tired of pork and plaster pies, alias hard tack, gave the boys leave to club over as many of the "two-legged things in feathers," as they could conveniently come at. The result was that a good number were dispatched, and, tied together by the legs, were slung over the pommel of the saddle of "Benny," an old *sabreur*, who had frontiered it for years, been in more Indian fights than you could shake a stick at, and could tell, if he wanted to, of some high-old-hard times with those same Mdewakantonwar, Wahpekute, Ihanktonwannas, and Minnikanyewazhipu, red-skinned friends. Returning to camp, as ill luck would have it, they met the Colonel of their regiment riding out to a neighboring camp. Just before they met him, in fact when they were nearly up to him, for a curve of the road had hid him from sight until then, the officer in command rode by Benny with the command: "—— it now. why don't you sling those chickens the other side your saddle? The Colonel will see them hanging that way." "Can't be done! got fourteen turkeys there on a balance!" By remarkably good fortune the Colonel did not see the chickens, so they and the turkeys were safely smuggled into camp, Benny getting the full credit for 'maintaining the balance of power,' when the odds were dead against him.

### Rare Trick upon a War Correspondent.

When the Union army occupied Frederick, in September, 1862, one or two of the most enterprising correspondents of the press were early on hand, and railroad communication with Baltimore being suspended they were obliged to send their despatches through to Baltimore on horseback. At that time a strong picket was thrown out from Baltimore to Ellicott's Mills, and Burnside's corps lay on the pike near Lisbon. Late one evening, a reporter entered what he *supposed* to be the Provost Marshal's office in Lisbon, and addressing a gentleman in semi-military costume sitting at a table, introduced himself, stated his business, and asked for a pass which would enable him to get through the pickets at Ellicott's Mills after the countersign was out. The reply was that he could not obtain a pass which would take him through the pickets, but he could have a note to the Provost Marshal at Ellicott's Mills which would probably procure him the pass required. He was "very much obliged," and received the following note:

H'DQ'RS, LISBON, Maryland, Sept. 13.

*Provost Marshal, Ellicott's Mills:*

The bearer represents himself as a reporter and messenger for the New York ———. From certain suspicious circumstances, I am strongly of the opinion that

Conference of Newspaper Correspondents.

he is nothing but a Baltimore secessionist spy. He wants a pass, and I have referred him to you; but I think it would be well enough to detain him until he can satisfactorily identify himself.

Yours, etc.,

TIMOTHY JONES,

Captain and Provost Marshal.

The correspondent went on his way rejoicing. Upon being challenged by the pickets at Ellicott's Mills, he presented his letter, whereupon to his astonishment he was forthwith taken into custody, and detained some twenty hours before he could

RATIONS, CURRENCY, ORDNANCE, MAILS, ETC.     477

satisfy the officers that a cruel "sell" had been practiced upon him. Of course, "Timothy Jones" *was nobody less than a lazy correspondent who had got behind in his duties;* and he at once improved his chance, went up to Frederick, and got in his account as soon as his poor competitor whom he had practiced this sorry joke upon.

**Hooker and the Newspaper Correspondents.**

General Hooker always treated every newspaper correspondent who visited him with great politeness, but he cared very

Maj. Gen. Joseph Hooker.

little for their opinion, and was as lenient towards the journals whose language was inimical to him as to those professing to be his friends. The representative of a radical journal once asked him why he allowed a certain "Copperhead" journal to circulate in his army. "Well, I'll see about it," said Hooker. Sometime afterward, when asked by the same party why he did not suppress it, he replied that he "had read it carefully every day for two weeks, and was still looking for the *overt act* which would justify him in doing it." Nothing more was said about the suppression of newspapers by that party.

**Inability to furnish Supplies to both Armies.**

It was regarded as a necessity by our men that they should throw off their blankets and great coats, in order for them to pass through the swampy grounds on the way to Richmond. One of the most noted chief commanders of the Union army was singularly liberal in this respect, and even the good General Steele left supplies for the rebels on a still larger scale. To facts of this kind is probably due the reply attributed to General Ripley, on a requisition for supplies being made upon him, before he was displaced: "Gentlemen," he said, "I must decline furnishing *both* armies any more. Let me know *which* army is to be supplied, and the department will meet, if able, or refuse, if not, the requisition."

**Tapping the Telegraphic Wires.**

The telegraph line between Memphis and Corinth was exceedingly important. General Halleck's messages all passed over it. But little of the line was guarded, for the rebels refrained from cutting the wires; they found a better use for them.

The Memphis operators detected something wrong in the working of the instruments, and surmised that some outsider was sharing their telegraphic secrets. They communicated this suspicion to the superintendent at Corinth, who promised to keep a sharp lookout. They soon after-

Telegraph Station.

wards discovered that their uninvited confidant could talk as well as listen. The transmission of a message was suddenly interrupted by the ejaculation "O pshaw!" A moment after it was again broken with

—"Hurrah for Jeff. Davis!" Individuality shows itself as well in telegraphing as in the footstep, or in handwriting. Mr. Hall, one of the Memphis operators, instantly recognized the performer, not by his tune, but by his time, as a young man formerly in Buffalo and other Northern offices, but then employed by the Confederates. Mr. Hall surprised him by replying promptly—

"Ed. Saville, if you don't want to be hung, you had better leave! Our cavalry is closing in on both sides of you!"

There was a little pause, and then the reply—

"How in the world did you know me? However, I've been here four days, and learned all we want to know. As this is becoming rather a tight place, I think I will leave. You'll see me again, when you least expect it. Good-bye, boys!"

The rebel operator made good his escape. He had cut the wire, inserted a piece of his own, and by a pocket instrument, been reading the official despatches. Some of the utmost importance, giving the very information most desired by the rebels, were passing, and as they were not in cipher, they could easily be read. One from General Hovey, in reply to a question from General Halleck, stated the precise number of our available men in Memphis, (only about 3,000,) and their exact location!

### Lieutenant ——'s Perfumed Breath.

Little Freddy H., a four-year-old, son of Chaplain H., of a New York regiment of volunteers, perpetrated a good thing while said regiment was at camp at Suffolk. A smart looking Lieutenant, with dashing air and *perfumed breath*, came into a tent where Freddy was. The little soldier scanned him very closely, and when a convenient opportunity offered itself he said to the Lieutenant, "You are a *doctor*; I *know* you are a doctor." "No, my little man," replied the officer, "you are mistaken *this* time; I am not a doctor." "Yes, you are a *doctor* too," replied Freddy; "I know you are a doctor; *for I can smell the medicine!*" This was too good a thing to be kept, and half an hour did not elapse before it had spread throughout the regiment.

Lieutenant ——'s Perfumed Breath.

### Sharing General Magruder's Table.

General Magruder always enjoyed the reputation, among his men, of being a brave officer and kind man, but filled with vanity, self-conceit, and pomposity. Shortly after the war commenced he was sitting one day in a restaurant in Richmond, enjoying, *solus*, a twelve o'clock *déjeuner* with rigid dignity, every button of his splendid uniform exactly *in situ*, and his immaculate shirt-collar adjusted at precisely the proper angle. He had hardly tested the merits of his repast when in sauntered a tall, long-haired, red-shirted private of the Louisiana First, which regiment had just arrived in the city. With the utmost coolness red-shirt sat himself down in the vacant chair opposite the General, and let into the good things before him with a zest that plainly told of long marches and previous scanty rations. This was too much for the aristocratic old officer. Drawing himself up *a la* General Scott, and with one of his severest frowns and the harshest voice he could command, he exclaimed, in tones of evident disgust—

"Sir, what do you mean? Do you know at whose table you are sitting?"

The soldier, scarcely looking up replied, in the interval between a bite and a drink, "I know I am dreadful hungry; *and I ain't a bit particular who I eat with since I've gone soldiering!*"

#### All for the Whiskey.

In one of the battles in Mississippi, an Indiana regiment was fiercely attacked by a whole rebel brigade. The Indianians, unable to withstand such odds, were compelled to fall back about thirty or forty yards, losing—to the utter mortification of officers and men—their flag, which remained in the hands of the enemy. Suddenly a tall Irishman, a private of the color company, rushed from the ranks across the vacant ground, attacked the squad of rebels who had possession of the conquered flag, with his musket, felled several to the ground, snatched the flag from them, and returned safely back to his regiment. The bold fellow was, of course, immediately surrounded by his jubilant comrades and greatly praised for his gallantry, his captain appointing him to a sergeancy on the spot; but the hero of the occasion cut every thing short by the reply, "Oh, niver mind, Captin, say no more about it; I dropped me whiskey-flask among the rebels and fetched that back, and I thought I might just as well bring the flag along."

#### Going Over his Battles Again.

Captain McD. arrived in New Orleans about four hours after the battle at Baton Rouge, and as he was a good talker, and had a pretty clear idea of the battle, he was instantly surrounded at his hotel and overwhelmed with questions. The result was that the Captain fought the battle over and refreshed himself with "some of the same," until he got rather confused—so much so, indeed, that he was often caught getting the line of battle in disorder, and doing other very unmilitary movements. In the height of his excitement, Colonel ——, a friend of the Captain's, came in, and the latter, determined that the former should have a clear idea of the action, commenced over again as follows:

"Look here, Colonel—you see the Michiganders were stationed along here;" and the Captain stuck his finger into his neighbor's sherry cobbler, and with the mixture, as it dropped off his finger, drew a short line on the top of the bar counter. "This, gentlemen," said the Captain, warming up, "that's the Michigan-ic-gan-ic Regiment, and here the Vermonters in the rear of the Indi-Indi-an-ians in the centre." Hereupon, the Captain stuck his finger in somebody else's glass, and drew a second line with his finger. "Now, you see," continued the Captain, with a very self-satisfied air, "that the Twentieth Maine was stationed out here;" and pop went the Captain's finger into another glass, the action resulting in the making of a formidable water-line considerably in advance of the other two. "Now," said the Captain, by way of parenthesis, "I believe if General Butler has a fair chance, he can whip the Confederacy or any other man." Just at this moment, one of the barkeepers, a stolid old negro, whose business it was to keep things neat and clean, espied the three marks the Captain had made on the top of the counter, and swinging round his formidable towel the front line disappeared in an instant. The Captain glanced on the darkey for a moment, but most penetratingly, and then wrathfully exclaimed, "You infernal nigger you! don't you observe you have wiped out the Twentieth Maine Regiment?"

The Captain having so suddenly been deprived of one of his most reliable regiments, and the Michiganders at the same time beginning to "dry up," he concluded he would adjourn the description until a more favorable season. The Captain was seen the next day, and seemed to complain of a severe headache—owing to the fact, perhaps, that there was a hole in his mosquito-bar, and he was so bit up the night previous, by the insects, that he could'nt sleep. (Ahem.)

### "Swamp Angel" Incident.

Colonel Serrell, of the New York Engineers, had the charge of the construction of the "Swamp Angel," at Morris Island, S. C., and being of an energetic constitution himself, and not afraid to enter swamps, his surprise can be imagined when one of his lieutenants, whom he had ordered to take twenty men and enter that swamp, said that he "could not do it—the mud was too deep." Colonel Serrell ordered him to try. He did so, and the Lieutenant returned with his men covered with mud, and said :

"Colonel, the mud is over my men's heads ; I can't do it."

The Colonel insisted, and told the Lieutenant to make a requisition for anything that was necessary for the safe passage of the swamp. The Lieutenant *did* make his requisition in writing, and on the spot. It was as follows :

"I want twenty men eighteen feet long to cross a swamp fifteen feet deep."

The joke was a good one. It secured, however, not a cubit to the stature of the Lieutenant, but rather his arrest for disrespect to his superior. The battery, nevertheless, was built with the aid of wheelbarrows and sand. Like Jonah's gourd, it sprang up in a night.

### Reporters on a "Bender."

Immediately after Grant's great victory in the Southwest, three newspaper correspondents, who had been at the scene of conflict, started for their respective destinations, each seeking, of course, to come out in advance of the others with the public report,—one of the gentlemen being connected with the press of Chicago, Illinois, and the others with New York papers. The three arrived together at Nashville, Tennessee, when two of them leagued to play a joke upon their associate. All of them being wearied, they thought it not in bad taste to regale their appetites with some strengthening beverages. The ubiquitous John D—, of the N. Y. ——, boasted that he could drink more and not get drunk than any other knight of the quill in the Army of the Cumberland. The Chicago man and the other New Yorker closed the bet, and soon the three were engaged in their bibulous labors. The boaster tossed them down—the 'slings' and 'skins,'—without regard to what his competitors did, and soon got himself into a condition in which mere terrestrial affairs and worldly vanities gave him very little trouble. Business was the great point with his rivals, and by a *leetle* closer attention to that than to the bowls, succeeded in keeping sober, and when the time to depart had arrived, off they started, leaving the boozy and oblivious gentleman in charge of the chambermaid. Up to the latest date, no 'original' report had appeared in the columns of that enterprising reporter's paper.

### Honesty on the Battlefield.

Lieutenant Tinkham was one among the many brave men who were killed at the second battle of Corinth. It appears that Lieutenant Tinkham was not seriously wounded when the rebels took possession of that part of the field where he fell, but was only shot through the leg ; and as the Union boys were contesting the advance of the enemy with desperate bravery, Lieutenant Tinkham raised himself upon his elbow to see the fighting, when another leaden messenger pierced his body, and he fell to the ground again. Seeing that he

RATIONS, CURRENCY, ORDNANCE, MAILS, ETC.    481

soon must be numbered among the slain, and that his life blood was fast flowing out, he made some sign to a passing rebel—which was said to be a Masonic sign of recognition—who immediately came to Tinkham's side, and rendered him all the assistance in his power. Just before the Lieutenant expired, he handed the rebel his watch and some money, with the instruction to forward it to his family the first opportunity he had,—and in a few moments after saying this he expired. The rebel now pinned a small piece of paper on Tinkham's coat, stating his name and company, and left him. In this condition he was found by his company and by them buried. Time rolled on, and on the fourth of July, 1863, thirty-five thousand rebels surrendered to the victorious Federal army at Vicksburg, and among that vast multitude was to be found Lieutenant Tinkham's rebel friend—all honor to him!—eagerly searching for the Fourteenth Wisconsin regiment. This he at last discovered, and, safely delivering the watch and money to one of its members, disappeared among the throng. The articles were duly received by the Lieutenant's friends. What it is to have an honest foe

### Estimate of Confederate Promises-to-Pay, Down South.

Lieutenant McFadden, of the Seventy-ninth Indiana, was taken prisoner at Chickamauga, and, at Richmond, confined in Libby prison. He survived starvation rations, and after his release gave an account of his amusing experiences, financially, relative to the rebellion. When captured he had two hundred and sixty dollars in greenbacks, concealed, which he hoped to be able to keep. But the rebels either heard of it or suspected it, and made him give it up. They assured him that if he gave it up readily it should be restored to him on his release, but if he refused, and compelled a search, he would lose it entirely, and find that things would not go well with him besides. He gave it up. On his release, he found in the prison office the sum of one thousand eight hundred and twenty dollars, in Confederate money, ready for him, as the return of his own which had been promised him. He "couldn't see it." He said to the Quartermaster that he would rather have his own money. He was replied to that Federal money was not currency in that region, and he could not be allowed to take it. "Why," retorted Lieutenant McFadden, "I read in the Whig of this city only this morning, that the Yankee currency was worthless,—that the treasury was bankrupt; and, if it is, why may I not as well have my own money, especially as I had rather have it?" The officer replied that he wanted "no words about it." "But," persisted McFadden, "if my money is no currency here, it can't do you any good, and if yours is worth anything it will do you some good, and I am willing to take my little pile instead of your big one; why not make the exchange?"

This plain Saxon "poser" was met with the assurance that if he gave any further "lip" he should at once go to a cell and stay there. So he took the "money." The Quartermaster instructed the clerk to count it. Lieutenant McF. interrupted this rather unnecessary operation with the remark, "I am in a great hurry, Sir, and you need not wait to count it—a few hundred dollars more or less will make no difference." This came near sending him back to prison whether or no, but he managed to avoid the peril and get out to find that a hackman refused to carry him to the boat, about a quarter of a mile from the prison, for one hundred dollars of his rebel money. This fact, as well as the more significant one that the Government officials themselves gave *seven* dollars of their money for *one* of the Federal greenbacks, as the legal—or at least the officially recognized—difference, shows that if the Confederacy had not itself "gone under," its currency was certainly about at that point.

### The Newsboy and his Officer Customer.

At a time when the war news was rather scarce, and the Washington newsboys were slightly 'stuck' on their merchandise, one of them planted himself by the Metropolitan Hotel entrance and shouted, "Extra STAR—Great battle in Alabama!" so lustily that he speedily found a shoulder-strapped customer, who ran his eye eagerly over the columns for that 'battle in Alabama.' He didn't find it, and called out, "You little rascal, I can't see any battle!" "No," answered the boy, as he widened the gap between himself and the officer, "I reckon you don't, and you never will see one if you loaf round this 'ere hotel *all* the time!"

### Prompt Settlement of a Claim.

—Old Lady—"Is this where Captain Bragg lives?"

Colonel Brent—"Yes, madam. Can I do anything for you?"

Settling a Claim.

Old Lady—"Well, you see, Mister, I lives over where the fitin' was, and when Captain Bragg's company skered the Yankees, they ran rite peerst my house—rite peerst—when up comes Captain Forrest with his crittur company [cavalry] and makes a line of fight rite through my yard, and oversets my ash hopper, and treads——"

General Bragg (sitting near)—"Colonel Brent, see that the lady's claim is settled *immediately!*"

### His Discharge Confirmed by Heaven.

A solid shot is the most deceptive of projectiles. It may seem to move lazily —to be almost dead,—but, so long as it moves at all, it should be allowed a wide berth. Just before one of the battles in the Southwest, an artilleryman received his discharge for disability, but delaying, for some reason, his Northward journey, he was yet with his battery on the eve of an engagement,—and, true to his instincts, took his old place beside the horse, and was just preparing to mount, when a solid shot came ricocheting across the field, bounded up, and struck him in the lower part of the body. Crying out, "I've got the first ticket, boys!" the poor fellow sank down, and only added, with that strange dread of a little hurt a terribly wounded man always seems to feel, "lay me down by a tree where they won't run over me." They complied with his request, hastened into position, and saw him no more. The wounded man's discharge was confirmed by Heaven. Now, that fatal ball, when, having finished its work there, it leaped lazily on, pushed out the skirt of the artillerist's coat as a hand would move a curtain, without rending it!

### Style of Clearing off a Table by General Butler.

Every lady reader knows—or should know—how to "clear off a table;" in either case, General Butler's style of doing the thing will be found more interesting than instructive. A newspaper reporter had need one day to call upon General Butler, and gave him occasion for about a minute to use writing materials and a table. General Butler ushered the reporter into his sitting-room meanwhile. In the centre of the sitting-room was a table piled with newspapers, pamphlets and books. The General for an instant ran his eye over its area in search of sufficient room to lay a sheet of note paper. There was none. What did Butler do but tilt over the table, spill its contents upon the floor, and then placidly sit down and do his writing. While he did this, an African nimbly removed the conglomerated heap of literature. This spontaneous clearing of the table by the General was suggestive of the manner in which Columbus made the egg stand upon its end, and the incident afforded a clue to the General's whole character. While others are thinking about doing a thing, he does it. The man who buys him for a fool gets a shocking bad bargain.

### Smuggling "the critter" into Camp.

The smuggling of liquors into the Union camps of the Potomac army was carried on very ingeniously and to a very great extent. It was ascertained—and this was but one of the many cute devices resorted to—that parties engaged in bringing liquid offal from the camps in the vicinity of Alexandria, conveyed enormous quantities of liquor across the Potomac, by constructing their tubs with false bottoms—one for the liquor and one for the offal. This little trick was at last exposed by a man engaged in the legitimate part of the business, the offal,—who feared that if the officials should discover the guilty, that all would be adjudged so, and that, in that way, he would be deprived of the lucrative profits which he was then realizing. Another mode of getting liquor to the soldiers on the opposite side of the Potomac was more difficult of prevention. Large numbers of jugs, filled with villainous whisky, were carried across the river in true submarine style. Parties had a small wire, coiled on a tackle, by which means they drew bottles and jugs of the "critter" across, realizing enormous profits in their sale.

### Female Government Contractor.

A married lady residing in the neighborhood of Boston—her husband holding a position in the custom-house of that city—was one of the largest contractors in Massachusetts for furnishing supplies to the army. Her contracts for clothing are said to have amounted during a single year to half a million dollars, and the total amount of all her contracts since the commencement of the war to its third year was estimated as high as two millions of dollars. On one of her contracts she lost some money, but on the others realized handsome profits.

The business of this lady having led her to visit Beaufort, she there saw neglected opportunities for speculation, which she improved to even more advantage than her government contracts. She established two wholesale and retail stores at or near Beaufort and Morehead City, then came back to Boston, and contracted for the materials and machinery of a steam saw mill, the erection of which was carried on under her direction or superintendence, and the mill was soon ready to saw the logs which two hundred contrabands had been cutting for her in the pine forests of North Carolina.

This lady possessed the advantage of being well educated, moving in the best circles of society, and joining with her admirable self-reliance, a sound judgment. She will probably finally retire with an ample fortune.

### Beef Steak and Hot Rolls Every Morning.

Colonel Leve, of the Eleventh Kentucky Cavalry, relates the following conversation which took place between one of the Union and a rebel picket, in Tennessee, showing on which side the 'grub' preponderated.

"Hallo there, Yank, have you got a chew o' tobacco?"

"Yeas—lay down your shootin' iron and I will mine, and will meet you half way."

The next moment they were together, in earnest conversation, sitting on the ground as socially as any two friends.

484        THE BOOK OF ANECDOTES OF THE REBELLION.

Reb.—Got anything to eat over there in Knoxville?

Yank.—Anything to eat! Yes; more'n we know what to do with. Plenty—full rations for thirty days.

Reb.—Do they have sugar and coffee over there?

Yank.—Yes; we've plenty; but General Burnside, not knowing what may happen, is issuing only half rations now. Why, see here (putting his hand into his pocket and hauling out a handful of parched coffee,) you see we carry it with us.

The rebel's eyes stuck out with astonishment.

Reb.—Have you got any cavalry over there?

Yank.—Now, friend, that is hardly a fair question, but I'll answer it the best I know how. I was at Corinth, Murfreesboro', and Perrysville, but I did not see as many cavalry as we have in Knoxville.

Reb.—Why, you astonish me. We thought you were all on quarter rations, and would be starved into surrender in a day or two.

Yank.—Not a bit of it; we can stay there as long as you did at Vicksburg, and have *good beef-steak and hot rolls every morning for breakfast!*

The rebel "gave it up."

---

### "Divide is the Word, or You are a Dead Johnny."

Amidst all the horrors of the war, many instances occurred, amusing in themselves, and which sometimes, under the most trying circumstances, were provocation of mirth, forming subjects for camp-stories months after. Our soldiers would sometimes chase hares and pick blackberries when a shower of the leaden messengers of death were falling thick and fast around them. But the following, which took place at Mine Run, surpasses anything of its kind:

On one of those biting cold mornings, while the armies of Meade and Lee were staring firebolts at each other across the little rivulet known as Mine Run, when moments appeared to be hours and hours days, so near at hand seemed the deadly strife, a solitary sheep leisurely walked along the run on the rebel side. A rebel vidette fired and killed the sheep, and, dropping his gun, advanced to remove the prize. In an instant he was covered by a gun in the hands of a Union vidette, who said—

"Divide is the word, or you are a dead Johnny."

This proposition was assented to, and there, between the two skirmish lines, Mr. Rebel skinned the sheep, took one half and moved back with it to his post, when his challenger, in turn, dropping his gun, crossed the run, got the other half of the sheep, and again resumed the duties of his post amidst the cheers of his comrades, who expected to help him eat it. Of the multitudes of hostile men arrayed against each other on either bank of that run, not one dared to violate the truce thus intuitively agreed upon by these two soldiers.

---

### A Cluster of Little Courtesies.

At the time of making the raid on Newbern, on the first of February, General Pickett captured Lieutenant Kirby, of Angell's battery, with two pieces of artillery. Kirby being a great favorite, his friends made up a purse and clothing, and forwarded to Lieutenant K. by way of an exchanged prisoner, who did not deliver the money and goods, but deserted and made his way back into our lines, minus the articles. General Pickett, hearing of this transaction, felt very much mortified, and indemnified Kirby out of his own purse. General Butler, hearing of this courteous act, would not allow himself to be outdone, and forwarded to General Pickett the amount he had furnished Lieutenant Kirby. Such acts show that the rebellion did not entirely crush out courteous feelings or humane promptings.

### Field-Carriages and Millinery Dispensed With.

While on his way to the front of the Army of the Potomac, preparing for an advance, General Grant met an officer who had been his fellow cadet at West Point. Grant was on horseback, unattended except by his faithful orderly, carefully pursuing his inspections of his position through a heavy storm of rain. The officer was riding in a handsome four-wheeled covered carriage, on easy elliptic springs and softly cushioned seats, with an elegant stud of horses and a guard of out-

Field-carriages dispensed with.

riders. The meeting under such circumstances was a mutual surprise. The recognition and salutes passed, the Lieutenant-General with that quiet humor which sometimes cropped out in his character, politely asked, "May I have the pleasure of your company, Sir?" Now the officer was clad in his best on this occasion. His uniform was a pink of perfection in its fit. His straps were of the broadest and most elegant pattern. His plumes were of the largest and glossiest. His gloves were as clean as yellow buckskin could possibly be. His patent-leather army boots were unsoiled by a single drop of rain or mote of mud. "Certainly, General," he replied, with great blandness and cordiality, "I will turn about and drive along with you. Or, will you not get in with me, General?" "No, I'm obliged to you," replied Grant, "I am in great haste to get to the front, and have not a moment to lose. Besides, I wish to speak with you in private. Do me the favor to walk along this way." The officer left his comfortable seat, plunged out in the mud and rain, and trudged on by the side of the General, he all the while asking him important questions respecting his department until he was wet to the skin. As he turned to go back to his carriage, the General quietly reminded him of the influence of his example on the troops, and politely intimated that there would be no more field-carriages supplied to officers from that day. As the news of this reached the ears of the brave boys in the ranks they cheered it lustily.

### Johnnie and Yank at a Trade.

A member of the Second New York Artillery, writing to a friend in New York, enclosed a ten dollar Confederate bill,—a bill printed on inferior paper, but very good in its mechanical execution. The letter gave the following account of the manner in which the bill came into the writer's possession:—

I send you a ten-dollar Confederate bill; I will not ask you to give me credit for it, any more than the credit of fighting for it. I was out on picket the other night, and my pit was quite close to the rebel line; so much so that I had a talk with a 'Johnnie,' directly opposite. Towards morning we agreed not to fire at each other, and we got on more friendly terms.

He asked me what I would give him for a plug of tobacco? I offered him an old jack-knife, which he agreed to take. He told me to bring it over. I could not "see it," so I told him to come and get it. At length we agreed to meet each other half way. We did so, and made the exchange; but mark his treachery! I had scarcely turned my back to return when he collared me and tried to drag me into the rebel lines. We had quite a scuffle; at last I got the villain by the throat with my left hand; I then threw my right leg behind him, and backed him over it. Down came the Confederacy! As he struck the ground his pocket-book fell from his pocket; also the knife I had given him. These I picked up in quick time, and ran to my pit.

When 'Johnnie Reb' got up he looked daggers. He would liked to have made a rush upon me, but I don't think he liked the looks of my rifle pointing towards him. I found nothing in the pocket-book but twelve dollars, two of which I sent to my mother, and ten I reserved for you.

#### One Man's Service to his Country.

At the time of the Dupont attack upon Charleston, South Carolina, a telegraph operator was placed in charge of an electric battery that was arranged by the rebels so as to explode a torpedo containing several thousand pounds of powder, with instructions to blow up the Federal *Ironsides* should she near the spot. During the engagement the noble ship, in her manœuvring, seemed directly over the infernal machine, and the officers in charge ordered the instant explosion of the torpedo. The operator—who was a loyalist at heart—could not by any means get the machine to work. Soon an order for the fire of every battery to concentrate upon the *Keokuk* was issued to be telegraphed; again the operator could not, 'for the life of him,' make the instruments work! These incidents occasioned so much distrust in the minds of the rebel leaders that the operator was soon after taken into custody and imprisoned. Being released a short time subsequently and sent to Richmond to resume his occupation, he was after a while sent to Winchester, Virginia, to procure some instruments. The visit to Winchester afforded him the long-looked-for opportunity to escape to the Union lines, where he was well contented to remain. He may be said to have done as much for the Federal cause as any single person in the country.

#### Real and Artificial "Cock-tails."

The Alexandria detectives managed to bring to light a curious method of smuggling liquor into that city for the soldiers' use. For a considerable time a certain chicken coop had been observed to have made frequent journeys between Alexandria and Washington, on the ferry boats, going up empty and returning well filled with fine fat shanghais. The poultry traffic had always been considered an honorable one, and no explanation could easily be given as to what first drew suspicion toward the integrity of the dealer in question; but certain it is, that one of those *curious* chaps employed in the detective department took the liberty of inspecting said "coop," for the purpose of ascertaining the features of the latest improvements in that species of rural structure, and his labors were rewarded with the discovery that its bottom was composed of tin, in the shape of a flat shallow box; and a closer inspection revealed the important item of thirty gallons of old rye, contained in the aforesaid box. The 'game' was up; the chickens—alias whisky dealer—was completely over-sloughed. The dodge was certainly an ingenious one, and would probably not have been discovered in this case but for the fact of its having been suggested that in a place where *cock-tails* were so numerous there must be something else at the bottom of it. Hence the discovery of the "critter."

#### Three German Flank-Movements.

One of Sigel's soldiers gives the following account of a foraging adventure he had in Virginia:

"Vell, you zee, I goes down to dat old fellow's blace dat has a beech-orchard, vere ve vas stadhioned, to stheal some beeches, and ven I gets to de vront gate, vat you dinks I zee? I zees dere a pig pull-dog, and he looks mighty savage. So I dinks

I frighdens him, and I zays, 'Look here, Mr. Pull-dog, stand back, I fights on dis line all zummer.' But de pull-dog, he don't care for dat, so I vlanks him!"

"How did you do that?"

"Vy, I goes vay arount again, so de pull-dog couldn't zee me, and ven I gets to de back gate, vat you dinks I zee? Vy, dere I zee dat same old pull-dog! So I vlanks him again."

"How did you do that?"

"Vy, I goes vay arount again, so as he couldn't zee me, to anoder little beech-orchard, and ven I gets dere, vat you dinks I zee? Vy, dere I see dat same old pull-dog! So I vlanks him again."

"How did you do that?"

"Vy, I zays to dat old pull-dog, 'Look here, Meester Pull-dog, I vlanks you dree dimes, and every dimes I find you de same old pull-dog. Tam your old beeches!—who cares for your old beeches. My dime is out next months and de country may go to de debil for beeches,'—so I goes to my dent."

### Bold Female Smuggler and Highwayman.

As four or five citizens of Tennessee were on their way into the interior from Fort Pillow, they were overtaken by a gay and festive woman upon a small sorry looking mule. She rode boldly up to the men, presented a persuader in the shape of a "Colt," and made known her intention of riding her mule no longer, but of confiscating one of their best chargers to supply its place. The demurrer was Claude Duvalish and Dick Turpinish in the extreme, but she failed to make her victims fear and tremble. Her violence was not force enough for men who had faced all the dangers of siege and battle, and they rode off, leaving my lady-robber alone to her destruction. One of the party, striking into another path, returned to Fort Pillow, and there reported the singular adventure with the woman.

Captain Posten, of the Thirteenth Tennessee cavalry, with a squad of men, was despatched in pursuit of the bold rider of the little mule. After riding some five miles she was overtaken near the house of a Mr. Green, and blandly invited to visit the fort—invited in such an insinuating style that she could not find it in her soul to refuse—that is, the pointed arguments used by Captain Posten were more than human logic could fancy or gainsay. The bold feminine said that no two men could have conquered her, but the numbers overpowered her and she must succumb. She then gave up her arms, and was delicately treated by the officer in charge.

Upon being conducted to the fort and properly examined, upon her person were found orders from the rebel Colonel Hicks for a list of contraband supplies, consisting of gunpowder, short cavalry boots, and other articles. On being questioned, she acknowledged she was employed by the rebels in obtaining goods for their comfort and use, and smuggling them through the lines. Her salary was one hundred dollars per month, the rebels supplying the money to pay for her purchases. She usually transacted this business in St. Louis. On the last occasion she had landed from a steamboat at Randolph, and when taken was on her way to the house of a rebel sympathizer.

This female smuggler gave her name as Mary Simpson. At Randolph she called herself Mary Timms, and proved to be a woman well known in the neighboring country, where she had passed under several *aliases* a year before. She was strongly suspected of being a spy for the rebels and carrying intelligence from Jackson, Tennessee, to the Hatchie. Within a few months, it was found she had proposed to the rebel Colonel Stewart to purchase ammunition for his command.

Mary's age was set down as not far from thirty years,—black hair, a brunette complexion, and a deep, dark, penetrating eye. Her intellect quick, and she was not easily disconcerted; and, as her proposed but unsuccessful horse-trade with so many of the more masculine sex showed, fearless and dauntless as an ancient highwayman. She belonged to the married persuasion, her husband being a loyal soldier doing duty for his country at the fort. When she desired to see him after her arrest, he refused, saying she had brought disgrace upon him and their family by aiding the enemies of their country. He only desired that their true names might not be given to the public. The woman refused to tell where the goods were concealed, orders for which she had.

### Question in Infantry Practice.

A few miles beyond Portsmouth there dwelt a sound Union woman, well known for her general kindness to the often passing Federal troops. Her love for them and the Union, indeed, seemed only equalled by her hate of negroes and rebels. As it happened, some colored troops passed her way, on their route to service. Seeing them, she came out, and with a tongue which moved very easily on

Question in Infantry Practice.

its hinges, she spoke as follows: "The soldiers have been over and over this farm, cavalry and infantry, these two years, and I never lost a chicken yet, but as soon as you darkies come I lose them all. I always said you would never make soldiers because you can't shoot. There you are with your foot on the tail of that rooster, after shooting at him three times and never hit him yet. Get out of here and let that rooster be!" Exit soldier laughing. That special darkey was never afterward seen cleaning or handling a gun without being asked by his fellows how many shots it took to kill a rooster "when your foot be on him tail?"

### Perils of Correspondents.

Bullets and shells are no respecters of persons, and have been known to attack the "gentlemen of the fourth estate." A correspondent who was with Sherman's army, was writing in a tent, when a Minie bullet came whistling through the canvas, passing by several of General Wood's staff, who were sitting inside. It completely disturbed their reflective powers for the time being. Another struck him in the breast, passing through both coat and vest, but he fortunately had his portfolio full of paper inside, through which it also passed, but did him no serious injury. Mr. Bearrie, of the Cincinnati Times, had his portfolio shot through in his hand; and Mr. Fury, (though a mild and unoffending man,) of the Cincinnati Gazette, was at supper, when an unceremonious shell came and took away his candle, leaving him a dark subject indeed. To these enterprising correspondents, and their professional colleagues from other cities, like A. D. Richardson, Junius H. Browne, Bickham, Knox, Taylor, Crounse, Colburn, Davis, Carleton, Dunn Browne, and others, the reading public is indebted for the most faithful portraiture of life-scenes in the camp, the march, and on the battlefield, and their works have been eagerly sought for as among the richest and most exhilarating contributions to our war history.

### John Morgan and Mr. Clay's Horses.

An incident is related concerning John Morgan, in Kentucky, and which, whether it be true or untrue, may be taken as quite

## RATIONS, CURRENCY, ORDNANCE, MAILS, ETC. 489

characteristic of that remarkable guerrilla chieftain. After Morgan had stolen the celebrated race horse "Skedaddle," Mr. Clay started in pursuit with two fine animals, worth over five hundred dollars each, and overtook the freebooter, offering him both of these fine horses, together with six hundred dollars in cash, if he

Gen. John Morgan.

would give up the racer to Mr. Clay, who prized it for its particular uses very highly. "These will answer your purpose just as well," said Mr. Clay, pointing to the handsome pair he had brought with him.

John looked at the horses carefully, and said:

"Well, Mr. Clay, they will answer my purpose as well as Skedaddle; and as I am disposed to accommodate you ——"

Here Mr. Clay's countenance brightened.

"As I am disposed to accommodate you, I will partly comply with your request;—"

Mr. Clay was puzzled.

"I will partly comply with your request; I'll take these two horses, but I can't give you the other."

Mr. Clay was completely taken aback; —but he was not allowed to get away even that easy. The soldiers took the six hundred dollars away from him, and he was compelled to leave for home on foot with his pockets empty.

### Interview of a Canadian Editor with the President.

The editor of the Free Press, published in London, Canada, visited Washington while the war was at its height, and thus describes an interview which he had with the man who was sustaining so vast a weight upon his shoulders at that period —President Lincoln:

The President's private room is just over the reception room, and is entered from a sort of square hall, about which there are many waiting rooms for persons seeking audiences with the President. Upon entering this room, I saw persons walking to and fro in waiting. I at once placed in the hands of a messenger my card and letters (previously procured from friends in New York and Cincinnati), to deliver to the President, and, with scarcely a moment's delay, I was ushered into his presence, when he arose and stepped forward in a stooping position, extended his hand and shook mine kindly, but rather loosely, as if he was afraid of hurting it, remarking, at the same time,

"I am glad to see you, Sir; be seated."

"I am a stranger in the capital," I replied, "and have sought an interview with you, Mr. President, and have been much pleased with the easy means of access."

"Yes," said the President, "this ready means of access is, I may say, under our form of government, the only link or cord which connects the people with the governing power; and, however unprofitable much of it is, it must be kept up; as, for instance, a mother in a distant part, who has a son in the army who is regularly enlisted, has not served out his time, but has been away as long as she thinks he ought to stay, will collect together all the little means she can to bring her here to entreat me to grant him his discharge. Of course I cannot interfere, and can only see her and speak kindly to her. How far is your place from Detroit, Sir?"

"About one hundred miles east from Detroit; we have no water communications, but have a very nice inland city. I intend remaining in Washington for a few days; all seems stir and commotion here."

"Yes, there never was anything in history to equal this."

"Your position must indeed be responsible and trying, President."

"Yes, to think of it, it is very strange that I, a boy brought up in the woods, and seeing, as it were, but little of the world, should be drifted to the very apex of this great event."

"I read your proclamation of this morning, calling for more men; it will, no doubt, be filled up."

"Yes, Sir, it will be filled up."

"I thank you, Mr. President, for your kindness and courtesy,"—I said, as I rose. The President shook hands again, and said—

"I am most happy to have made your acquaintance."

### Rich by Shoddy Contracts.

Crossing the ferry between the cities of New York and Brooklyn, might have been seen, one day, a splendid equipage—prancing steeds, liveried coachman and footman, and an elegant coupé. Within was a lady dressed with uncomfortable richness. She was 'fat,' not very 'fair,' and something more than 'forty.' With her was an unlicked cub of eight or ten years, whose fine clothes seemed to be as uncomfortable for him as were the gloves, tight to bursting, upon his mother's hands. Through an open window of the carriage he espied an apple woman with her basket of fruit. "Mam," cried the youthful aristocrat, "I warnt n'arple!" "Hush up! You ain't goin' to have none!" replied the furbelowed mamma. "But wont I though, by gorry!" said the boy; at the same time throwing himself half-way out of the window, and seizing the apple, which he forthwith commenced upon. The gentle lady fell back with an air of resignation, exclaiming, "Well, you darned critter, now you've got it, mind you only chaw it, and spit out the skin!" The coachman and footman looked mortified, and winked slyly at the bystanders, as much as to say, "Rich by shoddy contracts!"

### "Aint no Business wid a Gun."

A good story is told of a colored man employed by Captain Janney, General Sherman's staff-engineer in the Army of the Mississippi: Among the company which was working under Captain J., at Memphis, there was one very active, sharp, industrious, and faithful fellow, who had left his plantation, about twenty miles off. Soon after his good qualities had attracted Janney's attention, his owner, a rank rebel, came, as they often did with complete as-

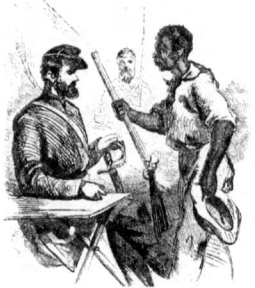

Aint no business wid a gun.

surance, to ask that he should be given up to him. Janney assured him that the country needed his services, and it could not be thought of at such a time. Some weeks after this, the same negro came one morning to Janney's tent, and said:

"There's a right good fowling-piece, Captain, and I want to gib it to you."

"Where did you get it?"

"Got 'im ob my ole massa, Sah."

"How is that? What did he give you his fowling-piece for?"

"Didn't gib 'im me, Sah; I took 'im."

"When?"

"Lass night."

"Has your master been here again?"

"No, Sah. I been down dah, to de ole place, myself, lass night, and I see'd de gun dah, and I tort he was a rebel, and he ort'nt to be let hab a gun, and I ort to take 'im away: tort dat was right, Captain, wasn't it? He ain't no business wid a gun, has he? Only to shoot our teamsters wid it."

"What sent you out there?"

"Well, I went dah, Sah, for to get my wife an' chile dat war dah. I tried to get 'em nodder way, but I was cheated, and had to go myself."

"What other way did you try?"

"I'll tell you Sah. I want my wife and chile; dey was down dah on de ole plantation. Lass Sunday when we'd got our pay, I seen a white man dat libs ober dah, and he tell me if I gib him my money he get my wife for me. I had thirty dollars, Sah, and I gib it to him, but—my wife didn't come. So I went myself. My wife house-servant, Sah, and I creep up to de house, and look into de windah; de windah was open, and I here de ole man and de ole woman dah snorin in de corner, and I put my head in and dah I see de gun standin' by the fi'-place, I jumped right in and coch'd up de gun and turn roun' and hold 'im so. Says I, 'Massa, I want my wife.' 'You can take her,' says he, and he didn't say anodder word nor move a bit, nor Missus either. My wife she heerd me, and she come down wid de chile, and we just walked out ob de door; but I tort I'd take de gun. He ain't no Union man, and he ortn't to had a gun, Captain. You'll take it, Sah, won't you?"

"Yes, I'll turn it in for you."

### Brandy at Fort Sumter.

During the cannonading of Fort Sumter under Beauregard, an incident occurred of a peculiarly Southern character. Roger A. Pryor, of Virginia, ex-member of Congress, was one of the second deputation of secessionists that waited upon Major Anderson, commander of the fort. He was the very embodiment of Southern 'chivalry.' Literally dressed to kill, bristling with bowie-knives and revolvers, like a walking arsenal, he appeared to

General P. G. T. Beauregard.

think himself individually capable of capturing the fort, without any extraneous assistance. Inside the fort he seemed to think himself master of everthing—'monarch of all he surveyed'—and, in keeping with this pretension, seeing upon the table what appeared to be a glass of brandy, drank it without ceremony. Surgeon Crawford, who had witnessed the feat, approached him and said: "Sir, what you have drank is poison—it was the iodide of potassium—*you are a dead man*." The representative of chivalry instantly collapsed, bowie-knives, revolvers and all, and passed into the hands of Surgeon Crawford, who, by purgings, pumpings, and pukings, defeated his own prophecy in regard to Pryor's fate, and thus saved to Beauregard one of his most petted and redoubtable confreres. Both Beauregard and Pryor went up like rockets of fire, in the war of rebellion, and came down like black sticks.

492    THE BOOK OF ANECDOTES OF THE REBELLION.

### "Doughnation" from the Maine Ladies.

The ladies of Augusta, Maine, set in operation and carried out a novel idea, namely, the distribution of over fifty bushels of doughnuts to the Third volunteer regiment of that State. A procession of ladies, headed by music, passed between double lines of troops, who presented arms, and were afterwards drawn up in hollow square to receive from tender and gracious hands the welcome *doughnation*.

Never before was seen such an aggregate of doughnuts since the world began. The circumambient air was redolent of doughnuts. Every breeze sighed—doughnuts; everybody talked of—doughnuts. The display of doughnuts beggared description. There was the molasses doughnut and the sugar doughnut—the long doughnut and the short doughnut—the round doughnut and the square doughnut—the rectangular doughnut and the triangular doughnut—the single-twisted doughnut and the double-twisted doughnut—the 'light riz' and the hard-kneaded doughnut—the straight solid doughnut, and the circular doughnut, with a hole in the centre. There were, in a word, doughnuts of all imaginary kinds, qualities and dimensions. It was emphatically a feast of doughnuts, if not a flow of soul.

### Contraband News—an Editor before the Cabinet.

The editor of the Chautauque, N. Y., Democrat spent some time in Washington, and wrote home letters for publication. One of these was asserted to contain "contraband news," and the editor—if ! his statement may be believed—was summoned before the Cabinet to answer for the heinous offense. Here is his account of the affair:

So many weeks had slipped away since my friends in Jamestown commenced sending the Democrat regularly to the members of the Cabinet and Gen. McClellan, that the visions of a file of soldiers had departed from my imagination, when one morning the subscriber received a gilt-edged jocky-club scented note, requesting his distinguished presence at the White House at a certain hour. I had no doubt that the note was from Mrs. Lincoln, who I supposed wished to apologize for the blunder that she made in my not receiving her invitation to the White House ball.

So giving my boots an extra blacking, and my moustache an extra twist, I wended my way to the President's domicile. After disposing of hat, cane, etc., I was conducted into the room used for Cabinet meetings, and soon found myself in the presence of the President, Messrs. Seward, Stanton, and Welles. Mr. Seward, whom I had met at a dinner-party at Gen. Risley's, in Fredonia, during the campaign of 1860, recognized me, and at once alluded to the excellence of Gen. Risley's brandy, and proposed to Abe that he should send over to his cellar at the State Department, and get a nice article he had there. I noticed three copies of the Chautauque Democrat spread out on the table, bearing certain initials, which for the sake of avoiding personalities I will not mention. I also noticed ominous black lines drawn around certain passages which I recognized as being part of my letter of several weeks ago. They looked like Mr. Benton's expunged resolutions on the Senate Journal.

Mr. Welles was so deeply engaged in reading a fourth copy, that he did not look up as I went in. It seems that the "mailing clerks," at Jamestown, had neglected to furnish the Navy Department with a copy, and the Secretary was deeply absorbed in its perusal. Mr. Stanton was busy writing his recent order, thanking God and Gen. Halleck for the victory and slaughter at Pittsburg Landing, and paid no attention to my entrance.

Mr. Lincoln said : ' A Cabinet meeting has been called at the request of General McClellan, to consider your offence in writing the letter conspicuously marked in the Democrat before us, and which had been kindly furnished several of their number by certain patriotic and high-toned gentlemen in Jamestown, N. Y. But they would have to delay a few minutes, to await the arrival of the Commodore from Yorktown, with despatches from General McClellan, who had telegraphed that the business must not go on till his despatches arrived.'

During the interval, *me*, and Abe, and Seward, sauntered through the rooms, looking at the various objects of interest. On entering the library, we found that the messenger had returned from Seward's cellar, with some of the Secretary's best Auburn brand. The cork was drawn, and we sampled the fluid. We next visited the ladies' parlor, and were presented to "Mary," who came forward and shook me cordially by the hand, and desired to know "how I flourished?" Said "she never should forgive me for not attending her ball." She was greatly shocked to hear that there had been a failure to connect, about getting the card of invitation.

We were soon summoned to the council; the Commodore had arrived, bringing seventeen of Gen. McClellan's staff, who had been delegated by him to transmit to the President his copy of the Democrat, which he had received at Fortress Monroe. On opening it, the same ominous ink-marks were drawn around the passages intended to be brought to the especial notice of the General. The staff officers then withdrew, and the President proposed to proceed to business. At this juncture Mr. Welles looked up from the paper he had been so busily perusing, and inquired of the President—' If he had ever heard anything about the fight the Democrat spoke of, between the Monitor and the Merrimac, and the danger there was of the latter getting out and coming up the Potomac and bombarding Washington?' Mr. Lincoln said, 'It was a fact.' The Secretary seemed greatly surprised, and said, 'he must write to his brother-in-law in New York, to send around a vessel to Hampton Roads, to watch the Merrimac, and also to send him the Weekly Post, so that he could get the news.' He chose the Post, because he had been in the habit, aforetime, of contributing essays for its columns. He also remarked that there was 'much valuable and deeply interesting news in the Democrat,' which was then some four weeks old.

Mr. Stanton here proposed that the contraband article should be read, as he had been so busy of late, he had not read the copy sent him by his patriotic correspondents at Jamestown. So Mr. Seward read the article through carefully. When it was completed, Mr. Stanton brought his fist down on the table with the energy and vigor for which he is celebrated, and, says he, 'Them's my sentiments, by ——.' The Secretary, contrary to the opinion of many who know him only by his short, pungent, pious, pithy, patriotic and peculiar proclamations, profanes pretty profusely when excited. During the reading, he had been fumbling his vest pocket. Says he, 'What's the price of that paper per annum?' I informed him that it was furnished to advance paying subscribers at $1. He handed me a gold dollar, and says he, 'Send it along.' Mr. Welles, who was just then absorbed in reading the account of the 'embarkation' of the army from Alexandria, looked up and said 'He had thought of subscribing himself, but as Mr. Stanton had done so, he would have George send him the Post, and they could exchange.'

The President now called for an opinion from the other members of the Cabinet. Mr. Stanton having *voted*, as I have before remarked. Mr. Seward, who was in a happy frame of mind, said that, ' Perhaps it was impolitic to have written just such an article, as he was always opposed to the expression of any decided opinions, but he thought the editor of the Democrat knew good liquor when he smelt it, and in view of the fact that he hailed from Old Chautauque, whose inhabitants he remembered with pride, having once been a resident there, he voted that the article was not contraband, but that the writer must not do so again.'

Mr. Welles said, 'He did not know enough about the subject under consideration to give an opinion. He had been much interested in the perusal of the article, and had found some useful hints in it in regard to the danger to be apprehended from the Merrimac, which he thought he should act upon by next year—on the whole, he thought the good balanced the evil, and he was for calling it square.'

It was the President's turn, now, to decide the matter. He always gets the opinion of his 'constitutional advisers' all round, and then does as he has a mind to. Abe turned to me with a merry twinkle in his eye, and his lovely and expressive countenance seemed more seraphic than ever, and says he to me, says he, 'Your letter on ——— reminds me of a story that I heard in the days of John Tyler's Administration. There was an editor in Rhode Island, noted for his love of fun—it came to him irresistibly—and he couldn't help saying just what came into his mind. He was appointed postmaster by Tyler. Sometime after Tyler vetoed the Bank Bill and came into disrepute with the Whigs, a conundrum went the rounds of the papers. It was as follows: 'Why is John Tyler like an ass?' This editor copied the conundrum, and could not resist the temptation to answer it, which he did as follows: 'Because he *is* an ass.' This piece of fun cost him his head, *but it was a fact.*'

'On the whole,' said Abe, 'here's a dollar; send me your valuable paper for a year, and be careful in future how you disclose Government secrets that have been published in the Norfolk Day Book only two weeks.'

### Prayer-Books and Scalping-Knives.

The following letter, picked up by an officer of General Cox's staff, on the ground from which Governor Wise's troops fled, shows the affecting tone of true piety that sometimes accompanies transactions of a very nefarious character:

"WAY UP ON THE HILL,

Below Charleston four miles.

"MAT:—I want you to put every thing in the sergeant's room—every thing that belongs to us. And if there is any engagement, break my little trunk open, and take out my Bible and prayer-book, and those Boone County bonds, and save them for me. I have not read my Bible for sixteen years, but I want them saved. Cook all the provender up there, and put all our cooking utensils together in the sergeant's room. The news is that the enemy is coming up on both sides of the river in a ——— strong force. I am the second company to have a shot. The orders are to scalp all we get near to.

J. W. M. SHERRY,

Captain of Boone Rangers."

### Overtaken at Last.

A remarkable instance of retribution was disclosed to the members of the Seventy-ninth Highlanders, on their arrival at Port Royal, in the case of an earnest and most unprincipled traitor. In the early part of the summer of 1861, a man employed in the Washington navy yard was discovered in the practice of filling shells with sand instead of the proper material. This man had received a medical education, and on his escape within the Confederate lines resumed his regular profession as a physician. Singular to relate, when the Seventy-ninth landed at Port Royal, the first object which greeted them on entering the hospital was this man seated at a table, with a splendid case of surgical instruments before him, his left arm resting naturally upon the table and the position of his body indicating perfect ease,—but upon a closer examination it was discovered that the entire upper portion of his head had been cut away, from the crown to the back of his neck, by a cannon ball. His career had been one of ingenious wickedness against his country and its defenders, but, in such an hour as he knew not, he was overtaken at last.

#### No Letter from his Sweetheart for nearly a Year.

The following memorandum note was found in one of the camps at Island No. Ten, and is a decidedly good one of its kind:

"*To any Federal Officer of Comre Foote's Fleet on the Mississippi:*

The finder of this will please hand it to one of the officers and ask him if he PLEASE forward it to its destination in Md. I would enclose a dime or such a matter to pay the postage, but upon my honor I have not got a cent in the world and you will not mind 3 cts to get a letter to one's mother and sweet heart Who has not heard from either for nearly a year.

Yours in every respect except politics,
L. T. H."

This was addressed to "Miss H——b, Hyattsville, Md.," and enclosed in an en-

Writing Home.

velope, addressed as above. Of course, as every one knows what it is to want "to get a letter to one's mother and sweet heart," the tender missive was doubtless put on its due course of destination by the good-hearted Union boys.

#### Dead Lock of Two Bullets in the Air.

The story of two bullets, as related by the Vicksburg correspondent of a St. Louis journal, is most peculiar. He says: I lately saw at the head-quarters of Colonel Slack's brigade, two Minie bullets, which had once told a history. One was a rebel bullet of English manufacture, smuggled over by our dear brethren in Britain to shoot their dear brethren in America. The other was a national ball, of the Springfield rifle type. The former was fired from a rifle pit at Jackson, at our skirmishers. The latter was fired from our line of skirmishers at the rifle pit. They met midway in the air, were welded by the compact, and fell harmlessly to the ground. They are now firm friends, sticking each to the other closer than a brother or a lover.

#### "Shameful Tyranny" of Butler in New Orleans.

The little Count Mejan, formerly French consul at New Orleans, once frantically appealed to the Emperor Napoleon to send an armed force to protect the grog-shop keepers of that city from an "unconstitutional" tax General Butler had levied upon them. The Emperor was so puzzled to know what his consul had to do with the American constitution, and on what principles he made himself the champion of whiskey venders in an American city, that he called the Count home to explain.

It will be seen, however, from what follows, that General Butler's suppositious tyranny did not stop at the mere taxing of grog shops. Thus, after the expulsion of the confederates and their allies, the Thugs, from New Orleans, the dead walls of that city were suddenly covered with conspicuous bills containing the following mandatory sentence :

"*Get your shirts at Moody's, 207 Canal Street.*"

A planter, a secessionist, went to town some months after Butler had taken the reins in his hands, and marvelled much at the cleanliness and good order he found prevailing; also, he was surprised at this notice which stared him everywhere in the face.

"Get your shirts at Moody's"—said he to an acquaintance he met in the street; "what does this mean? I see it everywhere posted up. What does it mean?"

"Oh," was the reply, "that is another of the outrageous acts of that fellow Butler. This is one of the 'orders,' of which you hear so much. Don't you see he has ordered us to get our shirts at Moody's, and we have to do so? It is, of course, suspected that he is the silent partner in that concern, and pockets the profits."

The poor planter listened to this explanation with eyes and mouth open, and, casting one more thoughtful glance at a bill of the kind which stared from the wall near which he then stood, replied impatiently:

"I don't need any shirts just now, and it's a great piece of tyranny; but this Butler enforces his orders so savagely, that it is better for me to give in at once."

He accordingly went to "Moody's," and purchased half a dozen shirts—on compulsion!

### Georgia Girls and Federal Lieutenants.

While Sherman's army was marching through Georgia, the soldiers learned how to rob beehives without the penalty of being stung. The plan was to rapidly approach a hive, take it up suddenly, and hoisting it upon the shoulder, with the open end behind, run like lightning. The bees hustled out, and flew back to the place where the hive stood. The honey belonged to the soldier who thus won it.

One day a cavalry Lieutenant, with his squad, rode up to a plantation house, and were pretty crabbedly received by the girls of the house, who desired to know "Why in thunder you'uns can't let we'uns be?" and hoped the devil would get the Yanks. The Lieutenant was not very well pleased with the reception, and seeing some tempting looking hives of honey in the yard, he ordered one of his men to hoist one up to him. The hive was handed up in a jiffy, and the Lieutenant, bidding the gals good-bye, started off with the hive on his shoulder. But this time, alas! the bees came out the wrong way, and swarmed upon the Lieutenant and his horse, compelling the former to drop the hive, *sans ceremony*, while the taunting Georgian girls on the porch clapped their dainty, tiny hands, stamped their little feet, and screamed "goody! goody!! goody!!!" until they cried for joy.

### Unconsciously a Hero.

The statement made in the newspapers, that General Hooker desired to appoint George W. Smalley, of the New York Tribune, on his staff, as an acknowledgment of the great merit of his report of the battle of Antietam, led to the publication of the following interesting interview between General Hooker and the editor of Wilkes' Spirit of the Times. Mr. Wilkes says:—

The General was laid up with his wound, but, on the occasion referred to, he was well enough to be bolstered up in a chair, and was engaged in writing a letter. Our conversation soon turned to the battle of Antietam, when he referred, with considerable enthusiasm, to what he characterized as the wonderful account of the battle given by the reporter of the Tribune. "It was," said he, "a perfect reproduction of the scene and all its incidents; and it is a marvel to me how you writers can perform such tasks." I asked the General if he knew who the reporter of the Tribune was. He replied:

"I saw him first upon the battle field. I first noticed him when we were in the hottest portion of the fight, early in the morning. My attention was then attracted to a civilian, who sat upon his horse, in advance of my whole staff; and though he was in the hottest of the fire, and the shot and shell were striking and spattering around us like so much hail, he sat gazing on the strife as steady and as undisturbed as if he were in a quiet theatre, looking at a scene upon the stage. In all the experience which I have had of war, I never saw the most experienced and veteran soldier exhibit more tranquil fortitude and unshaken valor than were exhibited by that young man, I was concerned at the needless risk which he invited, and told one of my aids to order him in our rear. Presently, all my aids had left me, on one service and another; whereupon turning to give an order, I found no one but this young stranger by my side. I then asked him if he would oblige me by bearing a dispatch to General McClellan, and by acting as my aid, until some of my staff should come up. He rode off with alacrity, through a most exposed position, returned with the answer, and served me as an aid through the remainder of the fight, till I was carried from the ground."

"And his name, General?"

"He was a young man, recently from college, named George W. Smalley, and I am writing to him now."

Those who know the noble nature of General Hooker, will therefore wonder but little that one of his first acts, when placed in chief command of the army of the Potomac, was to ask to have George W. Smalley placed upon his staff.

**Mary Birkitt and her Two Million Percussion Caps.**

Searching for contraband articles among the passengers' baggage at the Relay House, Maryland, was at one time quite a brisk and busy occupation for the Federal officers. As the train bound for Harper's Ferry came rounding the curve, the guard was drawn up on each side of the track. Soon as the train stopped, a soldier stepped on each platform of every car, to see that no one got off or on. The one whose business it was to "develop" any contraband articles or persons, commenced his labors by entering the forward passenger car. He then asked each person to open their 'traps,' and passed his hand as carefully as practicable through the bundles of varieties with which human beings fill their traveling apparatus.

On one of these rounds, the searcher came across a common-looking, red, wooden trunk. It was marked: Mary Birkitt, Wheeling, Virginia. There was nothing suspicious about it. It looked in keeping with some village aunt, who had foresworn the company of the coarser sex, and had just returned from a visit to some relatives who had lately thrown themselves away by swearing, in presence of a parson, to keep house, neatly and economically, for some one of those worthless creatures called men.

Well, the searcher called out for Mary to come and display her dry goods, but no Mary was to be found. He called again, but with the same result. The conductor was questioned, but he knew nothing about the matter. The thing looked all right enough, but it wouldn't do to let even Mary Birkitt's trunk go out without knowing what was in it. So, having sounded another call for the presumed spinster to make her appearance, the searcher called for a hammer and chisel, and opened the thing. Nothing alarming presented itself. On the top was a very white, and nicely done-up pair of sleeves. Then came a chemisette, and then a dress, and then— *two millions of percussion caps!* Ah, Mary, that was a sorry dodge. No wonder she didn't answer when her name was called by that officious Paul Pry. The trunk was confiscated.

**Silk Petticoats.—Southern Fashion.**

There was a petticoat exhibited at Washington, taken from a feminine secess'onist, the weight of the garment being some fifty pounds avoirdupois. The garment was apparently a quilted one, but instead of the usual filling, it was thickly wadded with the finest quality of sewing silk of assorted colors, the skeins being carefully arranged in layers. It was also provided with straps by which the weight might be supported by the shoulders. Sewing silk was one of the articles most needed, next to quinine, in the South; and this was not the only attempt at smuggling the article by women—ingenious and apparently secure, though it appeared—which the shrewd Government detectives brought to light.

### Pay Day in the Future.

At the breaking out of the rebellion, John Overton was one of the wealthiest men in Tennessee. His plantation, seven miles south of Nashville, embraced several thousand acres of land, with buildings and improvements exhibiting the finest taste. Although the whole family were known to be violent secessionists, the first blast of war swept by without injury to them. Their crops were untouched, their groves and lawns were unscathed, and, while others felt the iron hand of war, theirs was still the abode of luxury and plenty. The plantation was left nominally in the hands of Mrs. Overton, her husband and sons being in the rebel army. This, however, did not prevent her asking and obtaining unlimited protection from the Federal authorities.

Soon after General Negley assumed command of Nashville, information was received that a large amount of rebel stores, consisting of horse shoe iron and nails, was concealed at this place; and a detachment of the Eleventh Michigan infantry, under command of Captain Hood, was sent to seize the goods. Arriving at the house, situated in a beautiful grove at some distance from the road, the Captain halted his men outside of the door-yard, caused them to order arms and remain in place, and announced himself at the door. The summons was answered by a lady, when the following colloquy ensued:—

"Is Mr. Overton at home, madam?"

"No, sir; he is with the Confederate army," was the answer of the lady.

"I presume he is a rebel, then."

"Yes sir; he is a rebel all over."

"Well, madam, I wish to see some person who is in charge of the place. I am ordered to search for articles contraband of war."

"I am Mrs. Overton. You can search the place if you wish; but you will not find anything contraband of war. I wish, however, you would keep the soldiers away from the house."

The Captain assured her that no depredations would be committed by the soldiers, who were still standing at their arms, and added,—

"I will commence by searching under the floor of the meat-house."

The lady opened her eyes with astonishment. Recovering herself she replied, "There is no use of having any words about it. You will find some horse-shoes there."

And they were found. About two tons of valuable iron was unearthed and turned over to the government.

In the fall of 1862, Rosecrans' victorious army relieved Nashville, and remained a few days in the city. Early in December a general advance was made, and the left wing of the army encamped on the Overton place, and it was then known as Camp Hamilton. The camp fires of the Union army were lighted on every part of the farm, and the rights of private property, in disloyal hands, gave way to the stern necessities of war. Grove and woodland resounded with the sturdy strokes of the axeman, and disappeared. Fences were destroyed, and the crops and stock were taken for the necessary use of the army, and receipts given, to be paid when the owner should "establish his loyalty,"—a long time ahead, certainly.

### Horse Incidents at Bull Run.

At the battle of Bull Run, one of the guns of the celebrated Sherman Battery was rescued from capture by the Confederates, and brought off the field by two horses that had been *shot through* by Minie balls. When the order "forward" was given, they resolutely straightened out, and actually brought off the gun. At the commencement of the battle, Lieutenant Hasbrouck, of the West Point Battery, was riding a little sorrel horse. In a short time he was shot three times, and from loss of blood became too weak for further service. He was stripped of bridle and saddle, and turned loose, as his owner supposed, to die. In the heat of the contest nothing more was thought of the little sorrel, nor was he seen again until the remnant of the battery was far toward Washington on the retreat. It paused at Centreville, and while resting there, Lieutenant Hasbrouck was delighted to be joined by his faithful horse, which, by a strong instinct, had obeyed the bugle call to retreat, and had found his true position with the battery, which was more than the most of the human mass engaged on that field could boast of doing. He went safely into Washington, recovered from his wounds, and was soon ready for another fight.

### In Bed with a Shell: Lively Times.

It is stated that a soldier of a Mississippi regiment, at Pensacola, serving in the Confederate army, went to his tent and blankets one day to fight through an ague if possible. A bottle of hot water to his feet—a good domestic application, in such circumstances,—not being convenient, some of his comrades went out and picked up one of the numerous shells which had been sent over to them during the bombardment, heated it at the fire, and put it to bed with the sick man's feet. Unhappily, the shell had lost its cap, but had not exploded. The heat of the camp-fire accomplished what Federal pyrotechny had failed in, to wit,—an explosion. The tent was blown to pieces, and some of the men a little hurt and greatly astonished, though, strange to say, no one was maimed by the mishap.

### Parting and Singular Meeting of Two War Correspondents.

As an evidence of the rapidity of movement and great military strategy of Generals Sherman and Thomas in their splendid winter campaign of 1864—as well as illustrating the enterprise of the newspaper press of New York—the following facts are of peculiar interest.

On the 11th of November two of the *Herald* correspondents shook hands together in the city of Atlanta, Ga., wondering where and under what circumstances they would again meet. One accompanied Sherman on his grand march from Atlanta to Savannah, the other was with Thomas in his great career of triumphs in Tennessee: one South, the other North.

The one who went with Sherman participated in all the prominent events which marked that magnificent undertaking. He was present at the taking of towns, the sacking of treacherous villages, in fights with rebel guerrillas and cavalry, at the capture of thousands of prisoners, negroes, horses, mules, forage, and witnessed the devastation which was spread through forty counties of the richest State within the Southern borders, on a line averaging sixty miles in width and three hundred in length, all the while living on the fat of the land. He was present at the assault and capture of Fort McAllister, on the 14th of December, only a little over four weeks from the time of Sherman's departure from Atlanta, and the date of his junction with General Foster on the seaboard. This representative of the Herald left Hilton Head on the 18th of December, and arrived in New York city on the 21st, with a full budget of stirring intelligence, obtained by all the various devices and ingenuity which the skilled reporters of the Herald, Tribune, Times, World, etc., know so well how to put into requisition.

The correspondent who accompanied General Thomas participated in the first fight with Hood at Franklin, on the 30th of November, retired with the Union troops to Nashville, underwent the brief siege which Hood was crazy enough to lay before that city, advanced when Thomas again advanced, and when that peerless chieftain fell with such terrific force upon the Confederate lines the Herald war correspondent was in the melee. In the bat-

Signaling.

tle of Harpeth, on the 18th of December, the precise date when the Sherman correspondent left Hilton Head, the correspondent with Thomas was taking notes of the unexampled rout of Hood's forces, horse, foot and artillery; and subsequently taking the Louisville cars, made his connections through, and reached the Herald office Dec. 21st, almost at the same moment in the morning that his *confrere* at Atlanta also entered the building. Of course they shook hands again, and congratulated each other upon their fortunate escape from the many perils they had encountered in different parts of the country while upon similar errands. The names of Conyngham and Knox will long be memorable as war correspondents and historians.

### "Nellie," the Brave Battle Horse.

Among 'cavalry people,' in war times, the horse is second in interest only to the man himself. In fact, 'horse and rider' are usually spoken of as one and the same person. Every good cavalry man takes care of his horse, provided he has a good one. And when he secures said kind of animal, the attachment the brave trooper will form for his horse is almost romantic. As gallant a charger of this sort as ever snuffed powder, was owned by a Federal cavalry officer, and mounted upon which he was some scores of times under fire.

'Nellie,' (the name of the fine animal) was born and raised until she was six years old, in Athens county, Ohio, and was then sold to the Union officer, on account of her fondness for her neighbors' pastures and grain-fields, and her total disregard for fences, whether rail, picket or hedge. She was taken into the cavalry service in 1862, but could not be rode in line on account of her high spirit. By reason of her being a 'hard rider'—that is trotting, prancing, and going sideways all the time, making it decidedly uncomfortable for the rider, she was not used—till John Morgan's first raid through Kentucky, Indiana and Ohio, in 1863. Her owner rode her six days on that raid, and was completely worn out by her restlessness and fretting. He then put a black boy on her, who rode her during the remainder of that great raid,—riding her twenty-seven days and most of the nights, from Somerset, Ky., to Buffington Island, Ohio, following the trail of Morgan with General Hobson, and thence back to Stanford, Ky., in all a distance of almost a thousand miles.

After resting only the brief period of two days at Stanford, her owner rode her with General Burnside's advance across the mountains into East Tennessee, and rode her every day during that campaign, lasting from August, 1863, to April, 1864, and in every engagement which his command was in. During one of these engagements, her owner, while riding her, ran into an ambush of the enemy's, and a part of the bridle-bit was shot from her mouth, leaving the rider only one rein; pulling too hard on that, her head was so suddenly turned, that she fell with him, and the rider was made prisoner. Springing up she escaped and swam the Tennessee river, and rejoined the cavalry with the Federal troops. By good fortune her owner also escaped, and came in a few days after. Three times did she cross the Cumberland Mountains, where forage had to be packed on mules for a distance of one hundred miles, and three times did she make the march from Tennessee Valley to the Blue Grass region of Kentucky.

In the memorable engagement at Cynthiana, Ky., June 12th, 1864, with the Confederates under John Morgan, her owner rode her in a cavalry charge upon the rebel retreating column. She leaped a stone wall with him and carried him so close to the rebels that the blood from the wound of a rebel, shot by her rider, splashed over her face and ears. On the subsequent march from the Blue Grass region of Kentucky, to join the army near Atlanta, a distance of over four hundred miles, she had no rider, and was neither bridled nor haltered during the whole march, lasting twenty-four days, keeping her place in the march during the day, and staying close in camp at night. She never made a false step of her own fault, even on the worst of mountain roads and in the darkest nights. She also knew the whistle of a bullet or the shriek of a shell, and the direction of their flight, almost as well as her owner did.

Nellie, the brave Battle Horse.

### Logic of Sugar and Coffee.

John Morgan, after escaping from the Ohio penitentiary, and while on his way, stealthily, to his former field of exploits, came in almost personal contact with a Union picket. His first impulse was to kill the picket, but finding him asleep, he determined to let him sleep on. He made his way to the house of a Union man he knew lived there, and went up and passed himself off as Captain Quartermaster of Hunt's regiment, who was on his way to Athens, Tennessee, to procure supplies of sugar and coffee for the Union men of the country. The lady, who appeared to be asleep while this interview was taking place with her husband, at the mention of sugar and coffee, jumped out of bed in her night clothes, and said:

"Thank God for that, for we ain't seen any rale coffee up here for God knows how long!"

She was so delighted at the prospect that she made up a fire and cooked them a good supper. Supper being over, the General remarked that he understood some rebels had "tried to cross the river this afternoon."

"Yes," said the woman, "but our men killed some on um, and driv the rest back't."

"Now," says the General, "I know that, but didn't some of them get over?"

"Yes," was her reply, "but they are on the mountain, and can't get down without being killed, as every road is stopped up."

"It is very important for me," said Morgan, "to get to Athens by to-morrow night, or I may lose that sugar and coffee, and am afraid to go down any of those roads for fear my own men will kill me."

The fear of losing that sugar and coffee brought her again to an accommodating mood, and she replied—

"Why, Paul, kan't you show the Captain through our farm, that road down by the field?"

"Of course, Paul, you can do it," said the General, "and as the night is very cold, I will give you ten dollars, in gold, to help you along."

The gold, now added to the prospect of sugar and coffee, was too much for any poor man's nerves, and he yielded; so, getting on a horse, he took Morgan seven miles to the big road. The good woman, however, waited in vain for her sugar and "rale coffee."

### Conundrums at the Wrong Time.

Army teamsters have always been proverbial for the scientific volubility of their swearing. Modern times have not altered this fact. A teamster with the Cumberland army got stuck in the mud, and he let fly a stream of black and blue oaths that would have astonished "our army in Flanders," even. A Chaplain, passing at the time, was greatly shocked to hear such solid balls of nouns substantive whizzing around.

"My friend," said he to the teamster, in plaintive accent, "do you know who died for sinners?"

"D— your conundrums! Don't you see I'm stuck in the mud?"

The worthy Chaplain here became so confused, that he tried thirteen times in his mind to make joiner's work of the question and answer, but was obliged, like Dogberry, to "give it up."

### "Strictly Confidential."

Colonel B., of the Eighteenth Wisconsin regiment of volunteers, was, withal, a lawyer and politician, and, like many lawyers, wrote a very poor hand, so that it was almost impossible for a person not acquainted with it to read it. Once upon a time this made bad work all round. The Colonel, it seems, wrote to a political chum at Appleton, in which some important plans for an approaching campaign were divulged; but said Appleton friend was unable to read the letter. Finally, after showing it around to all the leading personages of the place, and getting all the aid he could, he was enabled to make out all the contents of the letter but one line at the bottom. A few days after receiving the Colonel's letter, he was visited by the Colonel himself, at Appleton, and after exchanging the usual salutations, and while surrounded by a bevy of jolly acquaintances, the Appleton friend remarked to the Colonel that he had received the letter, and with the aid of the good folks of Appleton, all of whom had read it and some of them several times, he could read it all but the last line; and producing the letter, remarked to the Colonel that not one of the many to whom he had shown the letter could make out *that*. "Why!" said the Colonel, "that is 'Strictly confidential.'" The Appleton chum stood treat.

### "Old Sortie," the Rebel General.

There was a jolly old Captain in the Eighteenth Missouri regiment of mounted infantry. He was everything good and efficient as an officer, a friend, and a gentleman; but he never deemed a close study of the dictionary as essential to getting a living or subduing a Southern rebellion. One hot day, the Captain, floating around, sat down under the arbor in front of a fellow officer's tent, and, picking up a late paper, commenced to read aloud the heading of the telegraphic column as follows:

"Repulse—of—a—sortie—at—Charleston." Says he, after musing a moment:

"Sortie? Sortie? *A. Sortie?* Cap, have the rebels any General by the name of A. Sortie?"

"Certainly, I've heard of old Sortie frequently."

"Well, I guess I have," said the Cap-

## RATIONS, CURRENCY, ORDNANCE, MAILS, ETC. 503

tain, "come to think now; I've heard of his being repulsed very often."

### Chickamauga and Chattanooga.

The name 'Chickamauga,' in the Cherokee tongue, means "stagnant water," or still water, so named because of the apparent stillness or stagnancy of the water in that river. 'Chattanooga' is the Cherokee for hawk's nest or eagle's nest. The town was originally the head-quarters of John Ross, the Cherokee chief. It received

Indian Mound, Chattanooga.

its name from its location, being surrounded on all sides by mountains, the poetic vision of the red man seeing in it an exact resemblance to a hawk's nest—albeit, General Bragg's definition of it would probably be "hornet's nest."

### Letter to Eight Young Ladies from a Soldier.

The following curious epistle explains itself. Its publication first appeared in one of the daily papers of Chicago, Illinois,—the Tribune.

MEMPHIS, TENN., July 28, 1864.

"To Eight Young Ladies, residing in Illinois, Indiana and Michigan:

Ladies, permit me to address a few lines to you through the Tribune, in regard to 'correspondence' with soldiers and officers serving in the army of our country. We, the officers and soldiers of the army, need and deserve the sympathy and counsel of our mothers, wives, sisters and lady acquaintances, from the dear homes we have left behind. From these, letters are always acceptable, are read with a deep interest, and there is always a deep feeling of respect for the writers and the dear old homes whence they come. There is no levity or expression of vulgar thought, or lewd allusions to the writers of them—holy home thoughts of the dear ones we love so well; and often have I seen the bronzed face of the veteran, as well as the fair cheeks of the young recruit, flushed with manly pride, or over them flowing tears that spoke louder than words of true hearts and brave men. Not so when your cold, insipid and stale letters are received. There is generally a shout of derision from many voices as your carefully written nonsense is retailed out to a corporal, sergeant, private, or may-be a negro servant; and could you hear the vulgar wit and coarse expressions over your letters, and at your expense, I think, ladies, you would answer no more "Wanted, correspondence for mutual cultivation." I trust, ladies, that this article may be of service to you, inasmuch as it will urge you to write only to those whom you know; and you may put it down for a fact that any soldier or officer advertising for lady correspondence, does so for no honorable or noble purpose. Ninety-nine out of every hundred letters received by officers or soldiers are treated with contempt and derision. Thus you see that your tender effusions, gushing out flowery and sentimental platitudes, are used to your disadvantage and injury. In many cases the officer or soldier takes pains to ascertain your true name, and then your letters not only reflect to your disadvantage, but bring disgrace to your friends. I know of one young lady who is the laughing-stock of a whole regiment, and many of them are or were friends and neighbors of hers not two years ago. Her fair name and character are blighted, and one who has counted on her being something more than a friend to him in the future has cast her aside, and her letters of truth to him are unanswered, or returned unopened. Ladies, good-bye. Learn from this to do better. Write to your known and tried soldier friends and relatives, and none other.

I am, ladies, your friend and well-wisher, E. V. WILSON,
1st Lieut., Co. H, 39th Reg't Wis. Vols.

### Canine Patriotism, Sufferings and Honors.

Nearly every company, certainly every regiment, in the Army of the Potomac, had a pet of some kind or other. It mattered not whether the object of their affection was a dog, cat, possum, cow, or horse,—of whatever name or species, the brute was loved by all, and woe be to the outsider who dared to insult or injure one of these pets. More personal encounters were brought on between soldiers about some pet animal than in any other way. Occasionally these pets became great heroes in their way, and then they became general favorites in the whole army. One of this kind was a dog named 'Jack,' photographs of which were as universal as those of the Commanding General. Jack served a regular term with the Niagara Fire Insurance Engine Company in Pittsburg, Penn., before the war broke out; and when volunteers were called to put down the rebellion, several members of the Niagara Company entered the service in the One Hundred and Second Pennsylvania volunteers, and Jack, no doubt prompted by patriotic impulses, also went into the field with some of his old friends, and made a good military record of himself. He was at the siege of Yorktown, battle of Williamsburg, Fair Oaks, battle of the Pickets, Malvern Hill, (where he was wounded,) first and second Fredericksburg; at Salem Church he was captured, after which he was exchanged and returned to the regiment. In the battle of Cedar Creek, Oct. 19, he was again taken prisoner by the Confederates, early in the morning, while on duty at division headquarters, but was recaptured when General Sheridan made his famous advance at four in the afternoon. 'Jack' had to run on three legs, as the penalty of his patriotic services, but in other respects continued as agile as ever,—wearing his honors with the meekness becoming a good dog.

### Dealing with a Rebel Trader.

The case of a German clothier and merchant tailor of Baltimore, who was arrested for engaging in contraband trade with the South, in 1864, excited much public interest at the time, and great efforts were made by his friends to obtain the Executive interference in his behalf. A deputation of nearly a dozen persons presented themselves before President Lincoln, one morning, to interpose in favor of the derelict party, all these persons, except one, being men employed as cutters in some of the establishments carried on by the arrested man. They made a very formidable display, asserting through their speaker, who introduced himself as "an humble tobacconist," but who evidently had had some experience as a speaker, that they were all good Union men—that they had even voted for Mr. Lincoln, and intended to do so again,—consequently they were entitled to a hearing, and that they were sure of the innocence of their employer. A good deal of eloquence was expended, but the President would not be moved. It was even ascertained that this same merchant had given money—some hundreds of dollars—toward carrying on the war. At last the President spoke:

"Gentlemen, this Government is a big machine, even in times of peace; it is no small thing to keep it in good running order—but now, when added to the usual duties of my position, I have on my hands this great rebellion (*which is to be put down,*) I have no time to waste. I have been visited already more than once by parties from Baltimore, urging my interference in this case. You protest that this man is innocent; then let him await his trial, when he can easily prove it."

"But," said the speaker, in behalf of his friend, "but we vote for you."

"Can't help it; it is not so essential that I have votes, as that the rebellion be crushed. To what purpose is it that you vote for me; that you pay a small sum of money to soldiers, as a cover up, while you supply the rebels with goods or arms? I tell you, gentlemen, it will not do. Already has the War Department declared to me that it could not and would not stand by me in this work of subduing the rebels, if every time they catch a rascal, I let him loose. Gentlemen, I ain't going to do it."

"Well, but, your excellency, I am a fighting man. I once paid three hundred dollars for knocking a man down."

The President drew himself back, and with much good nature said—

"Let me beg you not to try that on me."

Then the speaker, in behalf of the accused, took another turn.

"Mr. President, even your enemies say you have much goodness of heart. Will you not parole this man, accepting bonds, which we will procure to any amount?"

The President could not be moved. When appeals were made to his sympathy, he said, with great decision,—

"I will not listen."

"But, Mr. President, you *can* do this thing."

"Certainly I *can*, and I can end this war and let the rebels have their own way; but I am not going to do it."

"Six months in the White House," by Mr. F. B. Carpenter, is a volume of intense interest, as exhibiting, by an eye-witness and familiar household associate, the winsome, *inner-life* traits, of the late beloved President. But for Mr. Carpenter's fortuitous and fortunate residence at the Presidential mansion, in his professional occupation, at a period when Mr. Lincoln's personal and official traits were so strikingly called forth, the world would have lost one of the most authentic and affecting portraitures of the martyred President. Mr. Carpenter's book will happily be accessible to multitudes who may never have the opportunity to look upon his splendid "Emancipation" picture.

### Flight from the Shenandoah.

The order for the desolating of the Shenandoah Valley, issued by General Grant, that it might not afford sustenance to the Confederate raiders, was the source of wide-spread ruin to the inhabitants of that region. Property of all descriptions was swept away as with a besom in an iron hand, and families without number were scattered houseless to poverty, exposure and hunger. An illustration of the scenes attending such a hegira is afforded in the case of a woman—a very Niobe in her distress—who was discovered sitting by the wayside, on an old chest, and with whom the following conversation transpired:

"You look very sad, Ma'am."

"Yes, and I feel so, too, Sir," replied she; "but I've got through crying long ago, Sir; I've no more tears to shed."

"Do you come from the Valley?"

"Yes, we are all from the Valley."

"How far?"

"Nigh fifty miles I reckon we came. Why, we were rich," continued she; "we had a nice farm, a good house and barns, and, let me tell you what we had. We had nine head of young cattle, we had four cows, and four old horses, and six colts. Then there were thirty sheep, and six fatted hogs, and six pigs. Then I had in the house two barrels of apple butter, three hundred pounds of honey, three crocks of butter, and I had silk in the house for two new dresses—to say nothing of my drawers being full of sheets and pillow cases, and all kinds of house linen, and a feather bed on every bedstead. Well, Sir, I was a Union woman, I was; I gave my honey and my apple butter, and all my things to your men, when they came up there scouting, and I never begrudged it. When the order came for your men to clear the Valley, said she; "we sold a colt to one of your men, and he was a kind man, too, for thirty dollars. We had considerable of Confederate money, but that was no good."

"Well, where do you intend to go?"

"Me and the children hope to go to Ohio, but we don't know as we shall. We don't know what to do."

In this same condition, each with its kindred tale of wo, were hundreds of families, on their way from the depopulated Valley of the Shenandoah. In the dark-

Flight from the Shenandoah Valley.

some of them came while I was over to a neighbor's. I saw the light in my direction, and, oh dear! I knew what was going on—I knew my barn was going. I run all the way, and I come on one man with a pot of butter, and another with a pot of honey, and all my things; I knew whose they were, and when I got there they had gutted my house. I just had time to get a few things together—there's all that's left, Sir," pointing with an air of unutterable despondency to a little pile of effects at her feet.

"Have you nothing left but those?"

"Only thirty dollars in money besides," ness of the night, the scene was one that mingled the wretched and the picturesque in a manner that never yet engaged the artist's pencil. An angry sky over their heads, and bleak, cold winds whistling around them; women with children of tender years, often with babes at the breast; young girls and boys and feeble old men—for there were no young or able men among them; such were the scenes and groups which met the eye and wrung the heart.

### Happy Burial Occasion for the Twenty-seventh Illinois.

Early one morning in 1862, while at Farmington, near Corinth, Mississippi, as

General Palmer was riding along his lines to inspect some breastworks that had been thrown up during the previous night, he came suddenly upon some of the boys of Company I, Twenty-seventh Illinois Volunteers, who had just shot a two hundred pound hog, and were engaged in the interesting process of skinning it. The soldiers were startled; their chief looked astonished and sorrowful.

"Ah! a body,—a corpse. Some poor fellow gone to his last home. Well, he must be buried with military honors. Sergeant, call the officer of the guard."

The officer was speedily at hand, and received orders to have a grave dug and the body buried forthwith. The grave was soon prepared, and then the company were mustered. Pall bearers placed the body of the dead upon a stretcher. The order was given to march, and with reversed arms and funeral tread, the solemn procession of sixty men followed the body to the grave. Not a word passed, nor a muscle of the face stirred, while the last rites of sepulture were being performed. The ceremony over, the General and his staff waved their *adieux*, and were soon lost in the distance.

The philosophy of a soldier is usually equal to the emergency. He has read and pondered. He can painfully realize that flesh is as grass, and that life is but a shadow. But he thinks of the resurrection,' and his gloom passes away. So with the philosophic boys of Company I, Twenty-seventh Illinois. Ere the General was fairly seated at his own breakfast table, there was a raising of the dead, and savory pork steaks were frying in many a camp pan.

### "Aunt Charlotte," the Old Cook at Newbern.

"Aunt Charlotte" was one of the institutions within the Union Lines at Newbern, N. C. She was an old family cook. When her master and mistress ran away and deserted her, to join their fortunes and their fates with the disunionists, and their premises were assigned by General Burnside as the headquarters of the Sanitary Commission for his division, "Aunt Charlotte" came into the employ of the Sanitary Inspector for the Department of

Aunt Charlotte, the Old Cook.

North Carolina, and many a sick and wounded soldier from the States of New York, New Jersey, Pennsylvania, and Massachusetts, had reason to bless the culinary accomplishments of this venerable contraband cook, and to praise the alacrity with which, in times of their greatest need, she exerted her skill to save them from suffering.

On one occasion, soon after the battle, when a steamboat load of sick and wounded soldiers from the battle-field were unexpectedly landed in Newbern, and found themselves in a bare hall, with no accommodations for the night, without any provisions or any appliances for cooking, and too late in the evening for any relief from the ordinary "regulation" sources, "our old cook" was appealed to, and the alacrity with which she came to the relief of those sick and wounded men, will never be forgotten.

By the time comfortable beds had been prepared for their occupation, "Aunt Charlotte" had sent over a warm and bountiful supper for some forty or more famished and exhausted patients—a supper of those choice materials with which the noble charity of northern ladies had so generously supplied the service through the Sanitary Commission, and which the skill of "our old cook," on that night of wretchedness, served up to the wan and hungry soldiers with a nicety and a delicacy of flavor which can only come from an accomplished *cuisine*, but which all palates, however unsophisticated, can appreciate. The poor soldiers were no less surprised than gratified at such unexpected relief from the sufferings of that wretched day of exposure and hunger. And their expressions of satisfaction, as they quietly dropped off to sleep after their hunger was appeased and their wants attended to, would almost have paid the old slave woman for her long life of bondage. The next morning, and the next night, and a second morning, did this old "colored lady" add to her ordinary day's labor the preparation of suitable food for this whole hospital of sick and wounded soldiers.

"Aunt Charlotte" was born in Charleston, South Carolina, but came many years ago to Newbern, and was the slave of one of its wealthiest citizens. She is about sixty-five years old; has a great deal of character, and follows a thorough, systematic routine of life—always at her post—always reliable. She possesses no mean administrative abilities, reminding one of an old merchant, habituated to a regular, systematic life, with ability enough to keep all surroundings subordinate to that system. It seemed as if, were she to be superseded in that kitchen, she would lose her hold on life, and the whole "darkey" appendage to the domestic establishment would be deprived of its balance wheel.

When, therefore, on the first occupation of the premises, she was told that so long as she *did right*, she would keep her place in the kitchen, and receive six dollars a month, the "old lady" appreciated her position at once, and from that day forth, without further trouble to her employer, was secured the proper regulation and deportment of all the servants "on the lot"—men, women and children—and of all who visited them. Nothing ever happened among them to annoy or displease, the household being as well ordered as if the white mistress were still there to direct.

"Aunt Charlotte's" domestic relations were as well ordered as the household. She had children, grandchildren, and great grandchildren. Her old husband—"Uncle Sam"—*in propria persona*—but almost superannuated, at the age of seventy-five, was General Burnside's gardener. It was touching to witness the habitual care which "Old Aunty" took of this venerable partner of her life and her bondage. As regular as the clock, the old man, with his staff, came in at mid afternoon from his daily employment. He invariably found a chair set for him on the kitchen piazza, by the side of a well-scoured deal table. On this, "Old Aunty" placed before him a plate well filled from all the dishes which she had that day served from her employer's table.

### Working the Monster Parrott Gun.

There being, of course, no manual laid down for the operating of that novel Philistine in military practice, the "three-hundred-pounder Parrott," the mode of working it will be best understood by an explanation free from technical language—thus: The piece is on its carriage and "from battery." Implements, no two in the same place and no one in its proper place. The instructor gives the command, "Load her up!" At this command the gunner says, "Some of you fellers bring a shell," and "John, bring a cartridge." Some of the 'fellers' take a small hand-barrow and bring a shell. Gunner says, "Stick in that powder." "Now, boys, hold on till I get out a fuse." "Stick it in." All hands by hard heaving get the shell to the embrasure. Gunner says,

"Swab her out." She is swabbed out. "Now, heave and haul, and in it goes." It goes in accordingly. "Now, ram it down." It is rammed down. "Now, run her in." She is run in. "Screw down the recoil-bands." They are screwed down. Gunner aims. "Slew her round a little." "All right!" "Where's that primer?" "Now, git out of the way, everybody." All go to windward, and No. 3 steps round a corner, so as not to be hit if the gun bursts. Gunner says, "*Blaze away!*" She blazes away. Remark of the gunner on returning to the gun: "HOW ARE YOU SUMTER?" Repeat.

### Buford's Method of Spurring up Teamsters.

While Meade's army was on its retrograde movement, an incident occurred which showed that General Buford was as fertile in expedients as he was brave in an

Bridge Across Piatto Creek.

emergency. While bringing up the rear, with the rebels not far behind him, he came up with a train of wagons several miles long, numbering, in all, some eight hundred. The train was stopped, and Buford could find no one in command to start it. No time was to be lost. The enemy were coming—coming! and Buford's command would be cut up and the train captured. The teamsters in that long line could not be made to comprehend and act. But General Buford, in a few seconds, both comprehended and acted. He ordered one of his rifled pieces to be planted in the rear of the train, and began firing shells up the road, over the wagons, at the longest range, and with a good elevation. A few of those "rotten cannon balls" bursting over the train roused the laggards and fixed the business. Believing that the rebels were thus close—*very* close upon them, the wagon-masters and teamsters applied whip and spur, and the whole caravan was moved off safely.

### History of a Sword.

Major William Stubbs captured a sword at the battle of Shiloh, which has a history which pertains to few weapons of its kind, or indeed to any other. It had been presented to him by his fellow-conductors on the Chicago and Rock Island Railroad, and bore an appropriate inscription of respect from the donors to the Major. When captured it fell into the hands of a Confederate Lieutenant-Colonel, who was taken prisoner at the battle of Corinth by a private of the Tenth Missouri regiment. The private, however, having no use for the article, gave it to his Lieutenant. After the fall of Vicksburg the original owner of the sword was exchanged, and the Missouri private, reading a list in a Chicago paper, saw the name of the officer, which was the same as that inscribed upon the sword. He thereupon wrote to the Major, who answered in person, and the sword was returned. It had passed through three campaigns, sometimes wielded for and sometimes against the Union.

### Soldier Mechanics.

Captain Arnold, of company E, Rhode Island Fourth regiment, was one day ordered to take possession of the cross-roads at Havelock station. Near this place he came upon a large and valuable property, in the shape of a corn and flour mill, combined with a saw-mill, belonging to Dr. Master, of Newbern. He found the place deserted, and the machinery purposely thrown out of gear to prevent its use by the Yankees. The turbine wheel had wedges and clogs placed in it, so that it would be both difficult and dangerous to attempt to start the mill. Being a practical mechanic, and withal possessing some experience in the management of mills,

Inflating the Pontoon.

Captain Arnold immediately discovered "what was the matter with the mill." He accordingly first drew down the pond, came to the seat of the difficulty, repaired damages, and in a few hours the mill was jogging along as good as new, doing capital service in the cause of the Union by grinding corn-meal for the use of the troops. After it had been restored, a person, claiming to be an agent of the Doctor, made his appearance, when, everything being made satisfactory, the premises were gracefully turned over to him without any charges for repairs. It was the easiest thing in the world for Union soldiers from the North and West to improvise machinery of all sorts, repair locomotives, build bridges, dig canals, throw up dams, and, as to pontoons, Prof. Airy himself might have taken lessons in the philosophy of that kind of mechanism, from the soldier-boys of the victorious army.

#### Could not Wait for Death.

At the general hospital in Washington, says Prof. Hackett, a soldier from Pennsylvania, who had been severely wounded —so much so as to be beyond recovery— was lying on the floor. When the examining surgeon of the hospital came along and looked at the condition of the sufferer, expressing his hopeless belief as to the recovery of the man, to his assistant, he raised his head and said:

"Doctor, will I recover? is there any hope for me?—for, if not, I want you to kill me."

The surgeon tried to calm him, and he appeared to drop into a doze. In a few moments he took a revolver from his pocket, placed it resting against his temple, and fired; being so feeble he could not hold it firmly, and the ball just glanced over the skin without starting blood, but the discharge blackened his face. The pistol was immediately taken from him, when he said—though then only half an hour before he was a corpse,—

"I do not want to linger in pain without a hope."

#### Four-legged Messenger proving Disloyal.

A Federal officer who came up from City Point, Virginia, one October's day, to Washington, was observed to have with him an ugly-looking specimen of the genus canine, which he guarded very carefully. The dog, it appears, was a great pet with both the Union and Confederate pickets in front of Hancock's corps. The animal had been trained to carry messages from time to time between the pickets. A southern paper would be placed in his mouth, and he would scamper off to the Union lines,

Four-legged Messenger proving Disloyal.

deliver up the paper, and then return with a northern paper. He would at other times be intrusted with packages of coffee and tobacco, which he always delivered promptly and safely. The secessionists, however, after a while undertook to make use of him for transmitting information from one portion of their lines to another, and the four-legged messenger having been caught with one of these contraband messages, he had to suffer the penalty of such disloyalty by being confiscated and brought North.

### Ammunition Sent by the Enemy Just in Time.

Late one night, after the redoubts had been captured, an ammunition wagon, drawn by six mules, was driven up from the direction of Petersburg, to a particular point in the chain of fortifications. General Birney, surprised to see it coming from that direction, asked the driver at once what he had in the wagon? The answer was, "Ammunition for Battery No. 9." "Where did it come from?" inquired the General, supposing that additional ammunition might have been sent for some of the field-pieces he had placed in the breastworks. "From the arsenal," said the driver. "Oh, very well," said Birney, "I'll take charge of it." This was ammunition sent from the city to the rebels; but Birney and some of his troops, unknown to the driver of the ammunition wagon, occupied Battery No. 9. The General duly appreciated such a timely addition to his supplies. It was the right battery but the wrong General.

### Customer for Grant's Biography.

Rather an amusing incident concerning General Grant is related as having occurred while he was on a journey in a railroad train, and where he displayed, as usual, none of the insignia of his military rank. A youthful book peddler traversed the cars, crying, "Life of General Grant." A mischief-loving aid pointed the youngster to the General's seat, suggesting to him that "*that* man might like a copy." General Grant turned over the pages of the book, and casually asked, "Who is it this is all about?" The boy, giving him a most incredulous grimace of indignation and disgust, replied, "You must be a *darned* greeny not to know General Grant!" After this volley the Lieutenant-General of course surrendered, and bought his biography.

### Consul and General matched against each other in Savannah.

The scene which took place between General Sherman and the British Consul at Savannah was one of the richest and most piquant during that general's eventful peregrinations. On his arrival in that city, the General saw a large number of British flags displayed from buildings, and his curiosity was naturally excited to know how many "British Consuls" there were in that important city! He soon ascertained that these flags were on buildings where cotton had been stored away, and he at once ordered it to be seized. Soon after that, while the General was busy at his head-quarters, a pompous gentleman walked in, apparently in great haste, and inquired if he was General Sherman? Having received an affirmative reply, the pompous gentleman remarked:

"Well, sir, when I left my residence, United States troops were engaged in removing my cotton from it, notwithstanding its protection by the British flag."

"Stop, sir!" said General Sherman; "not your cotton, but my cotton; my cotton, in the name of the United States government, sir. I have noticed a great many British flags here, all protecting cotton; I have seized it all in the name of my government."

"But, sir," said the Consul, indignantly, "there is scarcely any cotton in Savannah that does not belong to me."

"There is not a pound of cotton here, sir, that does not belong to me, for the United States," responded Sherman.

"Well, sir," said the Consul, swelling himself up with the dignity of his office and reddening in his face, "my government shall hear of this. I shall report your conduct to my government, sir."

"Ah! pray, who are you, sir?" said the general.

"Consul to her British Majesty, sir."

"Oh! indeed!" responded the General. "I hope you will report me to your government. You will please say to your government, for me, that I have been fighting the English government all the way from the Ohio river to Vicksburg, and thence to this point. At every step I have encountered British arms, British munitions of war, and British goods of all descriptions—yes, at every step, sir. I have met them in all shapes, sir; and now, sir, I find you claiming all the cotton sir. I intend to call upon my government to order me to Nassau at once."

"What do you propose to do there," asked the Consul, somewhat taken aback.

"I would," replied the General, "take with me a quantity of picks and shovels, and throw that cursed sand-hill into the sea, sir. You may tell your government that, sir. I would shovel it to the sea, sir; and then I would pay for it, sir,—if necessary. Good day, sir."

It is needless to say that General Sherman was not again troubled with the official representative of her Majesty's government,—whose mind became confused in the crash of such nouns-substantive as cotton, arms, picks, shovels, sand-hills and the like.

### Shultz's Timely Discovery

An honest Schuylkill county German merchant, who had been prospered somewhat beyond the average, and had accumulated more money than he could employ as capital in his business, went to a patriotic banker in Philadelphia, and said:

"I have got some moneys, and I want you to buy me some gold."

"Why, Shultz! what do you want gold for? That isn't a thing you sell in your store."

"I knows that; but I want to make some money on de rise of gold. Peoples say it is going up, and I tink I may make a tousand dollars."

"Shultz, you dear old fellow, don't you know that if you buy gold you will be a rebel?"

"N-o!" said Shultz, with a tone of resentment in his wonder.

"Suppose you buy ten thousand dollars of gold; suppose that same morning you read in the papers, in big letters—'Terrible disaster to the Union cause! Grant's army routed and destroyed!! The rebels marching on Washington!!!'"

"I should say dat was tam pad news," excitedly interrupted the German.

"Yes, but wouldn't you say right off, 'dis, however, will put gold up—pad for the Union cause, tam pad, but *it is goot for my ten thousand!*' Don't you see Shultz, that in buying gold you instantly make the interests of the rebels your interests—that you bribe yourself to wish them to succeed, and to wish your country and your countrymen to fail? And if these unholy desires, Shultz, don't define you a rebel, there is no language to define one. Don't you see that buying gold *inevitably* turns honest, patriotic, devoted men like you, away from the cause which they ought to support, and which they think they do support, because they have made it for their interest not to support it? Don't you see it, my dear fellow?"

"Be shure I do," said the honest man, with gravity of manner and a humility in keeping with the discovery he had made; "and I ax pardon of the war. Put de whole of dat in Seven-Thirties. My money goes mit my principles." Honest soul!

### Saddling to Suit the Route.

While the Sixth New Hampshire regiment was stationed at Russellville, in southwestern Kentucky, the inhabitants of the surrounding country were frequently annoyed by the incursions of guerrilla bands from Tennessee. News coming in one morning that a band of these outlaws had plundered one of the neighboring villages, Lieutenant-Colonel P., the active

Saddling to suit the Route

and efficient commander, immediately dispatched a small detachment of the regiment, commanded by Major Q., in pursuit of them. On arriving at the village of Middleton it was discovered by the Major that he was too late to intercept the marauders, and he consequently ordered the horses unsaddled and fed. Now, the Major's hostler was a son of the Emerald Isle, entirely ignorant of everything pertaining to the equestrian art, and, coming in from half an hour's scout through the village, in a state closely bordering on intoxication, he put the Major's saddle on facing to the rear. When the horses were brought up for a fresh start, the Major, instantly discovering the mistake, demanded with a wondering scowl why the saddle was put on in that manner.

"An' shure," said Pat, a little terrified, "an' shure, Major, an' I didn't know which way you was going!"

An explosion followed—the Major was abundantly satisfied—and Pat escaped without further rebuke.

### Moderate Ideas of a Competency.

While Mr. Lincoln was visiting New York city, some time previous to the assembling of the presidential Republican nominating convention at Chicago, he met in one of the business establishments in New York, an Illinois acquaintance of former years, to whom he said in his dry and good-natured way:

"Well, B., how have you fared since you left Illinois?"

"I have made," replied B., "one hundred thousand dollars and lost all; how is it with you, Mr. Lincoln?"

"Oh, very well; I have the cottage at Springfield, and about eight thousand dollars in money. If they make me Vice-President with Seward, as some say they will, I hope I shall be able to increase it to twenty thousand, and that is as much as any man ought to want."

### Brandy for all Hands.

When Stuart made his famous cavalry raid around McClellan's lines before Richmond, the appointed rendezvous of the Confederate troops was not far from New Kent Court-House, at a small village where several main roads joined. The first party that arrived found that the place contained several finely furnished suttlers' stores, and depots of goods deposited thus far in the rear of the army, to be conveyed up to the front as circumstances demanded. They were, in fact, central or wholesale Union establishments, to furnish regimental sutlers, stocked with everything that could be required, having tasteful bar-rooms attached, in which were sold champagne, and all sorts of expensive wines and liquors. The fatigued and dusty men hitched their horses and entered, without ceremony, but were so unprepossessing and unpresentable, that all present rose, including several field officers who had trotted to the rear "to spend the day" convivially. "Brandy, gentlemen!" inquired the fat proprietor, urbanely—"certainly!" and presenting decanters, the new comers began to imbibe freely. "Might I inquire to what cavalry you belong, gentlemen?" asked the proprietor, acutely surveying their dusty figures, from head to foot. "We?" answered one, laying his violent hands on a box of Havanas, and emptying the decanter, "oh! *we* are Maryland cavalry, just arrived ; a new regiment raised in Baltimore, just returned on a scouting party after the rebel Stuart!" "Stuart, eh? You don't mean to say that *he* is in our lines ; do you? Well, let him come, that's all, and, although I'm not in the army, I'll show him a thing or two; just see if I don't!" And as his eye glanced over a fine case of revolvers exposed for sale, he seemed as valiant as Ajax. The rest of the company were dressed too finely to shake hands with the dusty strangers, so smoked and talked apart, in dignified reserve. Hearing the approach of a squadron, the cavalry troopers went to the door, and the landlord prepared bottles and glasses for his expected visitors. "Are these coming some of your party, gentlemen?" "Yes," was the reply, "and as 'tis no use fooling any more, *we* are Stuart's cavalry." All present were struck dumb with astonishment, but were soon disarmed and made prisoners.

### Official Likeness of President Lincoln.

Just before Mr. Lincoln was put forward as a candidate for the presidency, a friend fell into conversation with him upon the photographs of his face then before the public, and a regret was expressed to him that none had been found that did him justice. He laughingly suggested that it might not be desirable to have "justice" done to such forbidding features as his, but added that a likeness taken in Springfield a few days before was, in his judgment, and that of his friends, the best ever had. Of that his friend procured four copies, and subsequently asked Mr. Lincoln to append to each his autograph and the date, which he did with apparent pleasure, calling for a pen and ink, and writing upon his knee. Of these pictures, which were the first taken after he had allowed his beard to grow, and the first to give those that had not seen him a belief that he was not "horrid ugly," three were distributed to friends, and from one of them the head of Mr. Lincoln upon the ten dollar Treasury Note was engraved—which may be called the official likeness of the Western President.

PART VII—CHRISTIAN AND SANITARY COMMISSIONS.

# PART SEVENTH.

ANECDOTES OF THE REBELLION—DOMESTIC, MORAL, WOMANLY, SANITARY, AFFECTIONAL, MATRIMONIAL, ROMANTIC, ETC.

EXHIBITION OF PERSONAL TRAITS,—BENEVOLENCE, GENEROSITY, COURTESY, MAGNANIMITY, &c. ILLUSTRATIONS OF THE HOME AFFECTIONS AND HOUSEHOLD ATTACHMENTS; FEMALE SOLDIERS; REGIMENTAL PETS; MARRIAGES IN CAMP; WORDS AND DEEDS OF LOYAL WOMEN; RANCOR AND CRIMINALITIES OF FEMALE SECESSIONISTS; HOSPITAL PATIENTS; MINISTRATIONS TO THE SICK AND WOUNDED; BOGUS INVALIDS; PARTINGS, REUNIONS, BEREAVEMENTS, BURIALS; TOUCHING DEATH-BED SCENES,—LAST WORDS, MEMENTOES, KEEPSAKES AND SOUVENIRS; PRISON CONTACTS, COMPANIONS, AND HORRORS; SAYINGS AND DOINGS OF CHAPLAINS; GENIALITIES, CARICATURES, PATHOS, FANCIES AND REALITIES, &c., &c.

"Sisters, faithful to your vow,
Smooth his finite and cool his brow:
Peace! his soul is passing now—
        Gently! gently!"

"He talked of his mother far away,
And he talked of his gentle wife,
When the fever frenzied his burning head,
And loosened his hold of life."

This flag graced my wedding table, and I love it, and every soldier that fights for it.—*Union Lady in Pensacola.*

The highest duty of a soldier is to be a Christian.—GENERAL MITCHELL *to his troops.*

It isn't much I want; only that you will get something soft to put under my head; this rail is so hard, it has almost worn off my poor scalp.—*Wounded Soldier on the Gettysburg battle-field.*

### Colonel Farrar Winding up a Dance.

Colonel Farrar, commanding at Vidalia, Mississippi, learned one afternoon through a lady, that a military ball was to be given that night at a Mr. Johnston's plantation, on Black river, thirty-three miles distant. Unfortunately, the Colonel's mounted force was on the Natchez side, having been scouting, and it was then too late to undertake to cross them to the Louisiana side. Determined, however, not to let such an opportunity slip, he hastily mounted ten men of the Thirtieth Missouri infantry, and twenty-five of the Second Mississippi heavy artillery, then on duty at that post, and with them, though not an invited guest, the gallant Colonel started for the scene of festivity.

The route pursued led directly through a swamp, which being partially covered with water, rendered a rapid movement almost impossible. Nothing daunted, the little band pushed on, and by four o'clock in the morning, ('tis the early bird catches the worm,) had approached within half a mile of the house. Here, dismounting, they moved cautiously along the unguarded road to within a few rods of the scene of mirth and merriment. The brilliant lights which gleamed so cheerily from the windows, the lightsome forms flitting to and fro, and the sweet cadence of the music, told that all went merrily within.

To rush through the gateway and surround the mansion was the work of but a moment. Colonel Farrar and Captain Orgue dashing into the house, pistol in hand, demanded the surrender of every Confederate officer and soldier there. They did this—it almost passes belief!—followed by a squad of the rebels' own countrymen and brothers from the Second Mississippi heavy Artillery of African descent! Of course the Confederacy surrendered.

Miss Brownlow.

Now, the Colonel, universally known to be a man not less gallant than brave, not wishing to spoil the fun of such a pleasant party too abruptly, kindly requested the guests to continue the dance. The music once more struck up; and not yet being too old for a little of such exhilarating enjoyment, the Colonel himself graciously led upon the floor a fair and blushing daughter of the South, and with her was soon lost in the dizzy mazes of the dance. Daybreak warned the little party of the danger of delay. The prisoners were hastily mounted on their own good steeds, adieus were given to their disconsolate friends, and each, with a sable guard by his side, commenced their northern journey, convinced, doubtless, with the poet, that "each pleasure has its poison too, and every sweet a snare." One can not help being reminded, by this 'military ball' of Mississippi secession belles, of that other military 'ball' with which the noble-hearted Tennessee belle, Miss Brownlow, stood in readiness to entertain a certain 'party' at her father's house, if they dared to desecrate the flag of her country! A portrait of this glorious woman adorns these pages.

**Beautiful but Dead, on the Field of Honor.**

After the battle of Stone Bridge, a staff-officer rode out next day to view the ground, and passed piles of dead in various directions. Under a large tree, a body was seen lying, very handsomely dressed, with a fancy sword, and a handkerchief over the face. Attracting the officer's cu-

Beautiful but Dead.

riosity, he stopped, and removing the handkerchief, there was revealed to him one of the handsomest faces he ever met with, —that of a boy not more than twelve or fourteen years old. His appearance and dress indicated high position, like that of temporary aid to some general officer To ascertain who he was, his pockets were

## DOMESTIC, WOMANLY, HOSPITAL, PRISON, ETC.       519

examined, in which was a Testament, having the inscription—

"James Simmons, New York. *From his loving mother.* My son, remember thy Creator in the days of thy youth."

The officer wished very much to take the body away, but being six miles from quarters and on horseback, it was impossible. Radiant and serene, almost beyond description, was the countenance of that youthful soldier, bespeaking the fact that once, within that fair and winsome casket, was a spirit as bright and pure as the stars. But there lay his face and form of youthful loveliness, soon to change to decay and offensiveness. "Thou makest his beauty to consume away like the moth." Such was some of the "blood" which conspirators declared they would "sprinkle in the face of the nation!"

### "That is my Brother."

Colonel Kinney, of the Fifty-sixth Ohio regiment, was an observer of one of those strange and melancholy scenes which the

"That is my Brother."

'fortunes' of war not unfrequently bring to pass. As he was riding along the breastworks of Fort Donelson, a day or two after the surrender, and while many of the dead were still lying unburied, he noticed before him a private in his regiment, named Bowman, strolling along. As he came up, he observed the latter suddenly start back, with agony depicted in his countenance, as if transfixed at the sight of a body before him. Approaching nearer, the Colonel asked him what it was surprised him, and added that he supposed he would have become accustomed to seeing dead bodies by this time. Turning to his inquirer, with an expression on his face such as only a discovery like this could produce, and pointing to the body, he replied, "Colonel! *that is my brother!*" His brother had been a resident of Tennessee, and had joined the Confederate army, but he had no knowledge of his whereabouts, or any thought of his being one of the victims of the bloody conflict, until he thus accidentally stumbled across his dead body. Procuring a blanket, and the assistance of some comrades, he wrapped him in it, and buried him tenderly in the spot where he had fallen.

### Miss N——'s Copy of Byron, and the Rebel Sergeant.

On the Confederate troops possessing themselves of the town of Martinsburg, in August, 1864, they divided themselves into small squads or "messes," as they called them, and entering the houses of the Union people, ordered dinner, and, while the repast was being prepared, they ransacked bureaus and wardrobes, relieving them of such jewelry, ornaments, and necessaries, as they could conveniently carry off.

One of these messes paid a visit to a house where, after helping themselves to many other things, a sergeant seized an elegantly bound volume of Byron belonging to Miss N——, which had been presented to her by a friend in London. On the clasp, which was of gold, was engraved the name of the donor and donee. Miss N—— begged the sergeant not to carry it away, telling him how greatly she prized it, not on account of its intrinsic worth—though that of course was considerable,—but as a token from a friend. Perceiving that the sergeant did not heed her entreaties, she drew from her finger a diamond ring, which she assured him was of greater value than the book, while he could carry it away with less trouble, and offered it to him if he would leave her keepsake. But the sergeant was inexorable. At length he proposed that if she would read to his "mess" four certain Cantos from Don Juan, he would give her back the book. The young lady did not resent the insult with a disdainful curl of the lip or angry flash of the eye, but gently, almost kindly, said,

"Sergeant, you surely have no sister, and I fear you forget that you ever had a mother, or you would not so insult an unprotected woman. But, sir, you shall not steal my book—I give it to you; take it and go."

And the callous sergeant, laughing at the rebuke he had received, made off with his booty, first making an offer, in his most enticing words and manner, but unsuccessfully, to leave the book if the young lady would kiss him—the rone !

### Military Monomania of a Brooklyn Girl.

Quite a remarkable case of monomania —military, occurred in the army of the west, in the career of a young lady from Brooklyn, N. Y., about nineteen years of age. She became inspired with the idea that she was a second and modern Joan of Arc, called by Providence to lead the armies of the Union to certain victory in saving the life of the nation against its foes. The hallucination acquired great hold upon her mind, and a change of scene being suggested by her physician, she was carried to Ann Arbor, Michigan. Her mania, however, instead of diminishing, as was expected, increased until it was found necessary to confine her to her apartment. She, however, succeeded in making her escape, went to Detroit, where she joined the drum corps of a Michigan regiment, her sex known only to herself, and succeeded in getting with her regiment to the Army of the Cumberland. How the poor girl survived the hardships of the Kentucky campaign, where strong men fell in numbers, must forever remain a mystery.

The regiment to which she was attached had a place in the division of the gallant Van Cleve, and during the bloody battle of Lookout Mountain, the fair girl fell, pierced in the left side by a Minie ball, and when borne to the surgeon's tent her sex was discovered. She was told by the surgeon that her wound was mortal, and he advised her to give her name, in order that her family might be informed of her fate. This she finally, though reluctantly, consented to do, and the Colonel of the regiment, although suffering himself from a painful wound, became interested in her behalf, and prevailed upon her to let him send a dispatch to her father. This she dictated in the following manner :

"Mr. ———, No. — Willoughby street, Brooklyn.

Forgive your dying daughter. I have but a few moments to live. My native soil drinks my blood. I expected to deliver my country, but the fates would not have it so. I am content to die. Pray, pa, forgive me. Tell ma to kiss my daguerreotype, EMILY.

P. S.—Give my gold watch to little Eph." (The youngest brother of the dying girl.)

The poor girl was buried on the field on which she fell in the service of her country, which, in the mania of her patriotic feeling she fondly hoped to save.

### Foreshadowings of their Fate: A Brave Trio.

It would seem as if Ellsworth, Lyon, and Baker, saw the black plumes of the Death Angel in the path before them. Though as live a man as ever breathed, the dauntless Ellsworth penned a solemn farewell to his parents, in the dead of the last midnight that he ever watched. The brave Lyon, too, exhibited a strange and reckless bewilderment, on that disastrous day when his gallant heart was breaking under the double conviction that death had marked him, and the government had forgotten him. Colonel Baker for several days was oppressed by this overhanging consciousness. He became as restless as an eagle in his camp. He came down to Washington and settled all his affairs. He went to say farewell to the family of the President. A lady—who in her high position was still gracefully mindful of early friendships—gave him a bouquet of late flowers. As he took them he said, quietly, and with a pensive eye resting upon the sweet and fragile blossoms,—

"Very beautiful! *These flowers and my memory will wither together!*"

At night he hastily reviewed his papers. He indicated upon each its proper disposition "in case I should not return." He pressed with quiet earnestness upon his friend, Colonel Webb, who, however, deprecated such ghostly instructions, the measures which might become necessary in regard to the resting-place of his mortal remains. All this without any ostentation. He performed these various offices with the quiet coolness of a soldier and a man of affairs, then mounted his horse and rode gaily away to his death. Every man in that ill-starred struggle to which he hastened fought as bravely as if victory were really among possibilities. Their duty was to stand there until they were ordered away. Death was merely an incident of the performance of that duty; and the coolest man there was the Colonel commanding. He talked hopefully and cheerily to his men, even while his heart was sinking with the sun, and the grim presence of disaster and ruin was before him. He was ten paces in their front, where all might see him and take pattern by him. He carried his left hand nonchalantly in his breast, and criticised the firing as quietly as if on parade, saying,

"Lower, boys! Steady, there! Keep cool now and fire low, and the day is ours!"

All at once, as if moved by one impulse, a sudden sheet of fire burst from the curved covert of the enemy, and Edward Dickinson Baker was promoted, by one grand brevet of the God of Battles, above the acclaim of the field, above the applause of the world, to the heaven of the martyr and the hero. But the flowers were still beauteous and fragrant, as will ever be the memory of this most gallant soldier and of his brave compeers, Ellsworth, Lyon, and the long procession of martyr patriots.

### Tracts vs. Pound Cake.

A secession lady visited the hospital at Nashville one morning with a negro servant, who carried a large basket on his arm, covered with a white linen cloth. She approached a German and accosted him thus:

"Are you a good Union man?"

"I ish dat," was the laconic reply of the German, at the same time casting a hopeful glance at the basket aforesaid.

"That is all I wanted to know," replied the lady, and beckoning to the negro to follow, she passed to the opposite side of the room, where a Confederate soldier lay, and asked him the same question, to which he very promptly replied: "Not by a —— sight. The lady thereupon uncovered the basket and laid out a bottle of wine, mince pies, pound cake, and other delicacies, which were greedily devoured in the presence of the soldiers, who felt somewhat indignant at such un-Samaritan-like conduct.

On the following morning however, another lady made her appearance with a large covered basket, and she also accosted our German friend, and desired to know if he was a Union man.

"I ish, by Got; I no care what you got; I bese Union."

522    THE BOOK OF ANECDOTES OF THE REBELLION.

The lady set the basket on the table, and our German friend thought the truth had availed in this case, if it did not in the other. But imagine the length of the poor fellow's countenance when the lady uncovered the basket, and presented him

Tracts vs. Pound Cake.

with about a bushel of tracts. He shook his head dolefully and said;

"I no read English, and, beside, dat rebel on 'se oder side of 'se house need ten so more as me."

The lady distributed them and left.

Not long afterwards along came another richly dressed lady, who propounded the same question to the German. He stood gazing at the basket, apparently at a loss for a reply. At length he answered her in Yankee style, as follows:

"By Got, you no got me dis time; vat you got mit the basket?"

The lady required an unequivocal reply to her question, and was about to move on when Tenton shouted out—

"If you got tracts I bese Union; but if you got mince pie mit pound cake unt vine. I be secesh like de ribel."

**Tender Burial of a Union Drummer Boy by Two Girls.**

After the Battle of Bean Station, the Confederate soldiers gave loose play to all manner of indignities toward the slain. They stripped their bodies, and shot persons who came near the battlefield to show any attention to the dead. The body of a little drummer boy was left naked and exposed. Near by in an humble house, there were two young girls, the eldest but sixteen, who resolved to give the body a decent burial. They took the night for their task. With hammer and nails in hand, and boards on their shoulders, they sought the place where the body of the dead drummer boy lay. From their own scanty wardrobe they clothed the body for the grave. With their own hands they made a rude coffin, in which they tenderly put the dead body. They dug the grave and lowered the body into it, and covered it over. The noise of the hammering brought some of the rebels to the spot. The sight was too much for them. Not a word was spoken, no one interfered, and when the sacred rites of the burial were performed, all separated, and the little drummer boy lay in undisturbed rest in the grave dug by gentle maidens' hands on the battle field. Such tenderness and devotion deserve to run along the line of coming generations with the story of the woman who broke the alabaster box on the loved head of the Saviour, and with her who of her penury cast her two mites into the treasury.

**Talk with a Pretty Secession Miss.**

While stopping at a certain town in Georgia, a Union man on public business found himself, on the invitation of a friend, sitting at meat not only with Republicans and sinners, but also with rebels. A young lady did the honors of the table most gracefully, taking great pains in pouring out the essence of Java into cups of china to display to good advantage the daintiest taper fingers in the world. Withal she was *very* pretty.

The usual table talk began, when the friend referred to, who well understood her secession proclivities, turned to her, and pleasantly remarked:

"Mr. ———, my friend and our guest, has relatives in the South—two brothers in the rebel army."

"Is that true? *They* are fighting in a good cause," she said spiritedly.

"No doubt they *think* so," he simply replied, hoping to avoid the discussion of an unpleasant subject; but in this he was doomed to be disappointed.

"How can you, Mr. ———, fight against them?" she continued half angrily.

"I am not fighting or willing to fight against relatives," he rejoined, "but, for a principle—a flag—a government. Nor am I in the loyal army because I hate the South, for in my opinion that man who can not rise above sectional animosities is not equal to the emergency! One can give no greater proof that he loves his whole country than that he is willing to die for its salvation."

A warm discussion after the usual sort ensued, at which the young lady became angry at everybody in general, and her guest in particular—who, however, neither spoke nor wished any harm to her, any

Alexander H. Stephens.

way. And when, a few days afterwards, her brother was caught in the act of burning a railroad bridge, and she could be seen in her despair, imploringly asking, "Will the authorities hang him, my poor, dear brother?" that same denounced guest was on hand to offer her his heartfelt sympathy.

Sequel: That bright young secession miss, so warm an advocate of Southern rights, subsequently married a full-blooded Yankee officer! Bravo! Like Vice-President Stephens, foremost among Georgia's political law givers, but who so eloquently defended the Union at the first breaking out of secession, then turned a complete summerset the other way, and when last heard from was re-advocating the Union cause,—it is no wonder that similar gyrations should be performed by the other sex. To make up for the loss of her pretty phiz, in a pictorial sense, that of Stephens will at least afford as much food for study, physiologically considered.

### General O.'s Stern Particularity as to his Night Wardrobe.

After the advent of General Logan's splendid corps at Huntsville, the rooms in the principal hotels were quite in demand. A beautiful and accomplished actress had been staying for a while at the Huntsville Hotel, and in about a minute, minute-and-a-half, or two minutes, after she had vacated her room, the gallant General O. was assigned to it by the landlord. The General, on examining his bed previous to retiring, found a snowy *robe de nuit* neatly folded under his pillow, marked in delicate characters with the name of the fair owner. The chambermaid was called and asked by the General, as he held up the pretty garment in his hand, "Do you know Miss ——— ?"

"Yes," answered the bewildered chambermaid. "Then carry this to her with my compliments, and say General O——— is not in the habit of sleeping with empty night-gowns." By a strange oversight, the funds of the Sanitary Fair held at ———, fell short considerably, in default of that snowy *robe de nuit* not having been on raffle, labelled with the General's stern refusal to have it in his night wardrobe.

524   THE BOOK OF ANECDOTES OF THE REBELLION.

### Capt. Dickson's Ride with the Pretty Secesh.

Captain Dickson, of the Ninth New York Cavalry, while at the sunny South, came across an out-and-out 'shecesh' land mermaid—though in the Captain the delectable creature met her match. He was directed to escort said dangerous damsel of eighteen or twenty summers, outside of the Union lines. Having several miles to ride in company, the conversation naturally was upon matters connected with the war. She was good-looking, young, sarcastic, and a member in her mouth evidently hung in the middle, which enabled her to talk with an astounding volubility. Having got fairly started on their way—

"Well," says the little Miss, pertly, "when are you going to Richmond? You did not succeed by the way of Fredericksburg?"

*Captain*—"No, that was only a *feint*; we are going to Richmond by the way of Tennessee."

The smirk that this answer caused mademoiselle to put on cannot be placed on paper.

*Lady*—"Your Colonel (Cesnola) wanted to take me prisoner; I would not like to be a prisoner and live on hard tack and pork as your soldiers do."

*Captain* (complacently)—"Don't know about that; we could feed you well; we are daily supplied with cotton and other delicacies of the season;" naively alluding to the provisions brought in by foraging parties, from whose daily visits the lady herself had suffered as much as any one. Another smirk of her pretty face and a toss of the head was the only reply.

*Captain*—"Under Pope we managed to live well."

*Lady*—"Yes! (Dry emphatic) that old mean Pope; I only wish he was in command *now*, how we would run you back to Washington again?"

*Captain*—"Yes, but it was a great pity that your army had to leave Maryland so abruptly before Little Mac." After a little pause,

*Lady* (resuming)—"You did'nt make much out of Vicksburg?"

*Captain*—"Oh, we only attracted your attention there, while our troops took a little post of eight thousand men in Arkansas!"

*Lady* (changing the attack)—"You are going to cross now at Richard's Ferry?"

*Captain*—"Yes."

*Lady*—"I heard you were going to cross below Fredericksburg."

*Captain*—"Yes, Burnside says it is the most practicable."

The lady at this point, provoked and puzzled beyond measure, exclaimed in the most sarcastic manner imaginable, and with correspondent expression of her pretty phiz,

"I understand that if it remains *muddy* you are all *going back to Washington!*"

*Captain* (with provoking coolness)—"Yes; I believe that is the *latest* order."

The Captain, being a most redoubtable wag, was one too much for Miss Secesh, and before they parted she frankly "owned up" to that much.

### Material for the Novelist's Pen.

There was in one of the Indiana regiments a young girl who did soldier's service for the space of two years, and all under the most peculiar circumstances,—never until the last disclosing her sex. Having, at the end of the period named, got tired of the rough and arduous life she was leading, she procured a supply of feminine apparel, and arraying herself therein, set off for home, after calling on her Colonel, telling who she was and bidding him good-bye—leaving him and all the rest of the officers, as well as the men, who became aware of her identity, utterly dumb with amazement. She had fought bravely, and had done her duty well, all through the two years she had been in the service, and had received two severe wounds, but during all this period her sex was undiscovered. Her reason for entering the service was that she might be near a young man whom she loved; but he proving a coward, she became disgusted with him, and then continued to serve in the hope that some friendly bullet would end her unhappy life. But finally becoming cured of her love, romance and misanthropy, she concluded to return to her proper sphere in life and live like a rational creature.

### Speedy Realization of an Angry Wish.

A correspondent writing from the Yorktown peninsula tells the following:—While coming from a scout this afternoon we called at a house and found a couple of ladies, quite young, and one as handsome as a Hebe. They were secesh to the backbone, and had each a "lovyer" in the rebel army; one of them was at Yorktown, and only left the day before to pick his way back along the York river, and carry such information as he had gotten from us. The young lady showed us his photograph, a good looking Lieutenant, and hoped we should meet him face to face, that he might leave us for dead. "Oh," said she, "if all the Yankees were one man and I had a sword here, I should like to cut his throat!"

And she said it with a *vim*, too. We told her we would take good care of young Lieutenant White, and see that Miss Florill had an opportunity to change her name after the battle was over, hoping for an invitation to the wedding, and as she had called me the 'Divine,' or chaplain of the regiment, I proposed to marry them.

"Never," said she; "*I hope he will come home dead* before you shall take Yorktown. I would wade in blood up to my knees to bury his body."

She spoke of poison in a glass of water we drank, but I replied that "one look of her angel face, one smile from her lovely features would be an antidote to the rankest poison." "Yes," she replied, "and to your hatred of the South, too."

The flirtation nearly made her in favor of 'Union' and us the more so. But we had not gone far when we observed a company of soldiers approaching, who brought with them the 'lovyer'—*a corpse upon a litter*, returning to his sweetheart. He had been shot while trying to avoid the quick eye of our sharpshooters, near a house upon the York river shore, where his father had resided, and where a negro informed the soldier that his mother and sister were at the house where we had been in conversation with the ladies, one of whom was his sister, and our soldiers had, after receiving orders, carried him to be buried. We did not mar the sorrow of the relatives by stopping to witness the reception of the body. Her hasty wish that he might 'come home dead' was speedily and sadly realized

### Kentucky's Joan d' Arc.

A marauding band of secessionists in Kentucky, on their way to Mount Sterling, stopped at the house of a Mr. Oldom, and, he being absent at the time, plundered him of all his horses, and among them a valuable one belonging to his daughter Cornelia. She resisted the outrage as long as she could, but finding all her efforts in vain, she sprang upon another horse and started post haste toward the town to give the alarm. Her first animal gave out, when she seized another, and meeting the messenger from Middletown, she sent him as fast as his horse could carry him to convey the necessary warning to Mount Sterling where he arrived most opportunely. Miss Oldom then retraced her way toward home, taking with her a double-barreled shot-gun. She found a pair of saddle-bags on the road, belonging to a Confederate officer, which contained a pair of revolvers, and soon she came up with the advancing marauders, and ordered them to halt. Perceiving that one of the thieves rode her horse, she ordered him to surrender the animal; this he refused, and finding that persuasion would not gain her ends, she levelled the shot-gun at the rider, commanding him, as Damon did the traveler, "down from his horse," and threatened to fire if he did not comply. Her indomitable spirit at last prevailed, and the robbers, seeing something in her eye that spoke a terrible menace, surrendered her favorite steed. When she had regained his back, and patted him on the neck, he gave a neigh of mingled recognition and triumph, and she turned his head homeward and cantered off as leisurely as if she were taking her morning exercise.

#### Elizabeth Comstock and the Dying Soldier.

Elizabeth Comstock, a lady of English birth, and a resident of Michigan, is an eloquent preacher of the Society of Friends. For some years she had devot-

Eliz Comstock and the Dying Soldier.

ed herself particularly to visiting prisons and hospitals, and with the self-denying spirit of a Howard or a Fry, has ministered to the suffering inmates. She was in attendance at the Yearly Meeting of Friends, at Newport, Rhode Island, in 1864, and at the close it was urged to visit Salem and spend Fast Day with friends there. This invitation she declined, saying that there were no hospitals or prisons there, and to these was her mission. Soon after, however, yielding to a strong impression upon her own mind, that it was her duty, she announced that she would go. She attended Friends' Meeting and preached, her subject being "the value of early religious training." Illustrative of this, she related the following touching incident:—

Soon after the terrible battle of Fredericksburg, she visited one of the hospitals in the vicinity of Washington, going from ward to ward, and from cot to cot, comforting and consoling the wounded sufferers. Upon one bed lay a young man, with eyes closed, and apparently insensible. The attendant remarked that it would be useless to speak to him, as he had been constantly delirious since his arrival, and had now relapsed into a death-like stupor. But the good lady, full of motherly, christian sympathy, stopped by the bedside, and repeated Dr. Watts's hymn, in her sweet tones:

'Jesus can make a dying bed
Feel soft as downy pillows are,' &c.

As she closed, the young man looked up, with an intelligent smile, and seeing the female form, said—"I knew you would come, mother, and speak to me of Jesus." By his side the good woman remained, till the youth's spirit left him, and catching his last accents on earth, "Mother, I am going to Jesus."

But the most remarkable part of this affecting story is to come.

As the meeting broke up, and the Friends were leaving, the preacher's attention was arrested by a female face in the throng, and she remarked to a friend, "That must be the mother of the young soldier, of whom I spoke." They met, the preacher and the mother, and upon comparing notes, the fact was established, that it *was* the son of that mother, to

DOMESTIC, WOMANLY, HOSPITAL, PRISON, ETC.      527

whom good Elizabeth Comstock had ministered in his dying hour, and had thus brought to her the first knowledge of that son's death. Perhaps none but a parent can imagine the consolation thus given by the assurance that, in his dying hour, the young soldier thought of his mother, and coupled her name with that of the Saviour, whom she had taught him to revere. Who shall say, that the Good Spirit did not lead Elizabeth Comstock, out of her chosen path of labor, to carry comfort to the heart of that Salem mother?

### Music in the Hospital.

A young lady was heard to say, " I wish I could do something for my country; I would willingly become a nurse in a hospital, but I have not the physical strength. What can I do?"

" You can sing," a friend replied.

" Yes, I can sing, but what of that?"

" Go to one of the hospitals, and sing for the soldiers."

The idea pleased her. She accompanied a friend who was long used to such visits, and who introduced her by saying to the patients:

"Here is a young lady who has come to sing for you."

At the mere announcement, every face was aglow with animation, every eye was riveted upon her with expectant pleasure. She sang a few songs, commencing with the glorious "Star Spangled Banner." As the thrilling notes of that song rang through the apartment, one poor man, who had been given up by the physician as an almost hopeless case, raised himself in his cot, leaned his head upon his hand, and drank in every note like so much nectar. The effect was electrical. From that moment he began to amend, and finally recovered.

### Five Hundred Dollars for a Plate of Cream.

A treasury note for five hundred dollars was sent to the United States Treasury at Washington, for redemption, in 1863, having upon it the following endorsement: "This bill was paid for one plate of ice cream in Jersey City, at a fair for the benefit of sick and wounded soldiers, by J. A., Esq., April 11, 1863. H. M. H." This raised the little query, "How much change did J. A. get? or, if he did not receive any, then *who* is J. A?" Well, there was, it seems, a fair at Jersey City, for the benefit of sick and wounded soldiers; and among other things provided by the benevolent ladies in charge was a bountiful supply of ice cream. In the course of the evening a well known and excellent gentleman called for a plate of the cream, ate it, and laid down a five hundred dollar treasury note in payment. The lady from whom he had procured the delicacy was thunderstruck—declaring her utter inability to make the change. "Never mind the change!" said the gentleman, and walked away. The gentleman who chose this pleasant mode of contributing to a noble cause was Mr. John Armstrong, of Jersey City.

### Two made One: the Sergeant and the Daughter of the Regiment.

The marriage of a favorite Massachusetts sergeant with the "daughter of the regiment" constituted one of those pleasant episodes in military life which everybody loves to witness or see chronicled. Says 'Carleton,' that admirable delineator,

Six bold riflemen, clad in blue, with scarlet doublets over the left shoulder, and bearing blazing torches, six glittering Zouaves, with brilliant trappings sparkling in the light; and then the hollow square, where march the bridegroom and bride; then seven rows of six groomsmen in a row, all armed *cap-a-pie*, with burnished weapons, flashing back the lustre of the Zouave uniform; and all around the grand regiment darkening the white tent-folds, as their ruddy faces were but half disclosed between the red and yellow glare of the fires, and the soft, silver light of the May moon.

Marching thus, preceded by the two files of sixes, and followed by the glittering rows of groom-men, the little cortege moved out of the great tent on the edge of the circle, and went slowly, amid the bold strains of the "Midsummer Night's Dream," toward the regimental chaplain.

The bride was fair-haired, blue-eyed, rosy-cheeked, darkened in their hue by exposure to the sun, and in just the dress worn by *les filles du regiment.* She was formed in that athletic mould which distinguishes the Amazon from her opposite extreme of frailty. She was, in a word, a young girl apparently about eighteen years of age, with clear, courageous eye, quivering lip, and soldierly tread.

The bridegroom was of the same sanguine, Germanic temperament, as the bride, and full six feet in height; dress—a cocked hat, with blue plume, dark blue frock, with bright scarlet blanket, tartan fashion over the shoulder, and small sword, —looking every inch a hero. And there they stood before the regimental chaplain, with his robe and surplice and great book, amid the stare of a thousand anxious hearts, and to the music of glorious old Mendelsohn. The music ceased; and then a silence, succeeded by the clear voice of the preacher—a few short words, a few heart-felt prayers, the formal legal ceremonial, and the happy "amen." It was done. The pair were man and wife. The grooms-people formed a hollow square around the newly-wedded couple. In one corner a gateway was left for the entrance of the men. Then came one by one the members of that troop, with a kind word each, as each touched the bride lightly on the cheek, and grasped the bridegroom heartily by the hand—of one the sworn fathers, of the other the friends and brothers, comrades in arms.

The drums rolled forth again!

### Anna Manley, the Baltimore Heroine.

The band of the Sixth Massachusetts regiment that left Boston, numbered twenty-four men, who, with their musical instruments, occupied a car by themselves from Philadelphia to Baltimore. By some accident, this car got switched off at Canton Depot, so that instead of being the first, it was left in the rear of all the others, and after the attack had been made by the mob upon the soldiers, they came furiously upon this car of unarmed men, assailing them violently with stones and other missiles, wounding some severely, and demolishing their instruments. Some of the miscreants jumped upon the roof of the car, and, with a bar of iron, beat a hole through it, while others called for powder to blow the whole concern up. The poor fellows had now to jump out and meet their fiendish assailants hand to hand. They were at once stoned furiously, and ran swiftly through the crowd, fighting their way along, and going they knew not where. As they were thus fleeing at random through the streets, a rough looking man suddenly jumped in front of their leader, and exclaimed, "This way, boys! this way!"

It was the first friendly voice they had heard since entering Baltimore; their new guide took them up a narrow court, where they found an open door, into which they rushed, being met inside by a powerful looking woman, who grasped each one by the hand and directed them up stairs. The last of their number was knocked senseless just as he was entering the door, by a stone, which struck him on the head, but the woman who had welcomed them, immediately caught up their fallen comrade, and carried him in her arms up the stairs.

"*You are perfectly safe here, boys,*" said the Amazon, who directly proceeded to wash and bind up their wounds. After having done this she procured them food, and then told them to strip off their uniforms, and put on the clothes she had brought them, —a motley assortment of baize jackets, ragged coats, and old trowsers. Thus equipped, they were enabled to go out in search of their companions, without danger of attack from the Plug Uglies and Blood Tubs.

They then learned the particulars of the attack on the soldiers and of their escape, and saw lying at the station the two men who had been killed, and the others that were wounded. On going back to the house where they were so humanely treated, they found that their clothes had been carefully tied up, and with their battered instruments had been sent to the depot of the Philadelphia railroad, where they were advised to go themselves. They did not long hesitate, but started in the next train, and arrived in Philadelphia just in time to meet the Eighth regiment of Massachusetts Volunteers, under command of General Butler, who told them to hasten back to the Old Bay State to show their battered faces and broken limbs, and that they should yet come back and play "Hail Columbia" in the streets of Baltimore, where they had been so inhumanly assaulted.

The noble-hearted woman who rescued these men, dressed their wounds, fed them at her own cost, and sent them back in safety to their homes, was a well-known public character in Baltimore—an outcast, according to the verdict of Christian society; but she was a true heroine, nevertheless, and entitled to the grateful consideration of the country. "Anna Manley" is the name by which she has been known in the city of Blood Tubs.

---

## Love and Treason.

A young man, belonging to one of the Tennessee regiments—he held the rank of First Lieutenant in his company—received a mortal wound in the Fort Donelson conflict. This young officer was a native of Harrisburg, Penn., and had resided there until the autumn of 1859, when he went to Columbia, Tenn., and there engaged in the practice of law with considerable success.

While in Tennessee he became acquainted with and enamored of a young lady of culture and fortune, a distant relative of General Pillow, and was soon engaged to marry her. The love-stream of the young couple flowed smoothly enough until the fall of Sumter and the secession of Tennessee, when the affianced husband, a strong advocate for the Union, returned home, designing to wed after the troubles were over. The betrothed pair corresponded regularly; but, some weeks after the lover had gone to Harrisburg, the girl, who had suddenly grown a violent secessionist, informed him that she would not become his wife unless he would enlist in the rebel service and fight for the independence of the South.

The young man was exceedingly loth to take such a course, and remonstrated with his beloved to no purpose,—and at last, in the blindness of his attachment, and the goading selfishness of passion, he informed his parents of his intention to win his mistress on the tented field; the field of his country's enemies. In vain they endeavored to dissuade him from such a resolution. He went to Tennessee, raised a company, received the congratulations of his traitorous friends, and the copious caresses of his charming tempter.

The Lieutenant proceeded to Donelson, in December, and, a few days before the fight, heard that his betrothed was the wife of another! His heart had never been in the cause, though it was in another's keeping; and, stung by remorse, and crushed by the perfidy of his mistress, he had no desire to live. Unwilling to desert on the field of battle the cause he had embraced, lest he might be charged with cowardice, he resolved to lose that existence that had become unbearable to him; and in the thickest of the fight, while seeking death without endeavoring to inflict it, he received a mortal wound.

Those who have not read "Edmund Kirke's" marvelous delineations of life and character in the midst of "the institution," have yet to feast themselves from

530   THE BOOK OF ANECDOTES OF THE REBELLION.

one of the rarest of literary dishes yet served up. 'Uncle Tom's Cabin' can not compare with it in point of originality, freshness, pathos, and sparkling narrative; and the same remark is applicable to his later sketches of the scenes and localities of the war.

### Flowers from Lowly Hands for the Fallen Brave.

The killing of the brave and accomplished Captain Howard Dwight, by the hands of guerrillas, was an event which brought sorrow to many a heart, and deprived the nation of one of the most gallant and trusty officers. After he fell, his body was taken to New Orleans, and borne to his former residence there, to await the departure of a steamer which should transport it to his home in Massachusetts. A guard of men detailed for the purpose, from the Forty-seventh Massachusetts regiment of volunteers, was placed around the house both day and night.

The brother and immediate friends of the deceased wrapped the coffin in the American flag, and covered it with flowers. These arrangements being concluded, they left the apartment and retired for the night. When, on the next morning, the afflicted brother entered the room again, a scene presented itself which showed that there were others besides the immediate friends who sought to pay their tribute of respect to the memory of the fallen hero.

Members of "the Union Association of Colored Women" had visited the room early in the morning. They had brought white linen with which they had covered the furniture of the room, and upon which they had sewed green leaves. They had filled the room and covered the coffin with the freshest and sweetest flowers, made into wreaths and bouquets. They had made the scene one upon which the eye rested with delight. Each morning this labor of love was repeated. At each returning dawn the faded flowers of the previous day were removed, and those of fresh beauty and fragrance took their place.

Before Lieutenant Dwight left New Orleans, on his sad mission, he attempted to express his thanks to those who had shown such tender care for him whom he mourned. He therefore said to one of their number, in tender gratitude for their loving offices to the departed;

" I want to thank you, but I know not how to express my thanks."

" You owe us no thanks," was the reply; " Who are your friends, if we are not. All we ask of you is, that when you go home, you will tell the northern people how we feel, and say to them that we want our husbands and our sons to be allowed to fight in this war."

### Medicinal Properties of Blankets Gloriously Illustrated.

In the month of December, 1863, a Vermont regiment was encamped beyond Arlington Heights, in Virginia. The men of the regiment were brawny and robust, but protracted exposure had occasioned an unusual degree of sickness among them; and application was made to the Sanitary Commission for supplies, medical and otherwise. The regiment, for some cause, had never been supplied with blankets, and many of the sick were consequently destitute of the most necessary protection from the cold. The wants of the men once discovered to the Sanitary Commission, arrangements were immediately made to supply them, and in a day or two one hundred and fifty blankets were forwarded; blankets made and given, most of them, by the wives and sisters of volunteers.

In this regiment was a private—Andrews, he may be called,—a large, stalwart fellow, who had been broken down by severe service, and was considered by all as beyond hope of recovery. He had behaved with marked bravery in every engagement in which his regiment had participated, and was a universal favorite among his comrades. Though naturally courageous and stout hearted, his physical prostration had seriously affected his mind, and he was full of despondency, expecting momentarily to die. When the supplies of the Sanitary Commission were conveyed to the camp, the condition of this man was brought particularly to the attention of the agent having them in charge. He, full of sympathy for the suffering fellow, provided him with all possible comforts, such as fruits, medicines, and agreeable food, adding to his supplies a sick blanket, which he carefully folded over the patient, as he lay on his hard, board bed. The following day, visiting the regimental camp a second time, the agent was met by the Colonel with the information that Andrews was much better, and promised, after all, to recover.

"Would you believe it," said the Colonel, "the sight of that blanket seemed to bring the fellow right back to life; his whole manner brightened; his very fingers grew nettlesome, clutching the blanket with a very ecstacy of delight."

The agent hurried to the sick man's tent, and found him, indeed, vastly improved. His face brightened as the agent approached, but he did not take his gaze from the blankets. Presently, pointing with his long, thin finger to a corner of the blanket, he whispered—

"That, Sir, has been better medicine than all your hospital stuff. It has put new life into my veins; if I'm ever a well man it'll be because God sent me this blanket."

The story of that blanket was a simple and yet a surprising one. It had been *made by the soldier's own wife*, living, far away among the Vermont hills, and had been sent with other contributions from the same neighborhood to the Sanitary Commission. The woman was poor, her home was humble, but she had a true heart, and having nothing else to give she had actually cut up the silk dress in which she was married, and applied it to the purpose in question. On one corner she had marked her name, and with that mark only had sent it on its mission, little dreaming what coincidence would attend that mission. The blanket, laid with tender hands over the soldier, immediately caught his eye; the material seemed familiar; he had certainly seen it before, and that thought roused his whole nature. Presently, pulling up the corners to his face—he was too weak to raise himself—and passing the whole slowly before his eyes, he saw the name dearer to him than all the world besides! In an instant the whole story of her sacrifice for the soldiers' sake was daguerreotyped upon his thought. What wonder that, under the flood of memories which that moment came over him, sweeping away all thoughts of self, all despondency and gloom, he grew hopeful again, realizing that he still had something to live for, and work to do—and all because of this precious gift; a tonic which strengthened and saved him when nothing else, it may be, could have brought him safely through.

Yes! Andrews recovered; and to his dying day undoubtedly he will be a believer in the medicinal qualities of blankets.

We know not the source of the above most touching narration, but it sounds so much like the beautiful and winsome delineations penned by Mr. Coffin, ("Carleton,") author of that widely circulated work "Days and Nights on the Battlefield," —contributed to the Boston Journal—that we may safely cite that graphically written volume as the repository of "more of the same sort."

---

**Dalliance and Treachery.—Lieutenant H. and Mrs. C.**

While the Federal army lay before Fredericksburg, in the early part of December, the cavalry of the Left Grand Division picketed the country from Dumfries toward the Rappahannock. The line had been marked out by a staff officer, whose judgment in such matters was very questionable, and only the most incessant watchfulness could secure the advance posts from surprise and capture. A multitude of woodland roads diverged in every direction, so that cavalry forces could easily get into the rear of the

Dalliance and Treachery.

posts. The only thing was to be ready to take advantage of the same intricacy to escape, and give the alarm. Every man must be alert to mount and fight and retreat at a moment's notice. Weapons must be at hand, and girths kept tight enough for service.

Under these circumstances, Lieutenant Jacob H——, with sixteen men, was posted on the road leading from Stafford to Dumfries; his Captain, with even a smaller party, taking a position to support him. Now, there happened to live on that road close to picket head-quarters, a certain Mrs. C——, the wife of a Captain in the rebel artillery. This lady was young, and attractive enough to poor fellows in the army, cut off from all the charms of feminine society during most of the time. Then she was by necessity "a grass widow," and by inclination seemed ready to assume all the privileges of actual widowhood.

So, like a spider waiting for prey, she dwelt there in her house, watching the movements of the Union soldiers.

Presently Jacob, who had been loitering round, thought that he had better see who lived in that house, and went gallantly up the hill. Mrs. C. was all smirks and courtesy. She did not deny that she was Southern in heart. Her husband was in the Southern army, and she thought he was right in being there. But it was hard for a poor lonely woman; and the soldiers were so rude. She would feel so much obliged if Lieutenant H. would protect her. She would be very happy if he could take his meals at her house, for then the men would feel that they must not disturb her, and she was sure that a gentleman of Lieutenant H.'s appearance and manners would see that no harm was done. The poor foolish fly thought the spider a very charming creature, and could not see the web into which he was blundering. He accepted the invitation most cordially, thinking that he must certainly have produced an impression. With an air of hospitality, Mrs. C. then ordered her horse to be saddled, telling H. that she would go at once and provide a pair of chickens for dinner, her own having been all stolen. H. had already arrived at that point when he could see no objection to any thing which she proposed; and, in the meantime, he kept up an animated conversation, saying many tender things, and casting many enamored glances at his hostess. Of course he tangled himself more and more in the web, letting her find out just what she wished to know,— she need not be afraid,—she would not meet any Federal troops; his were the only ones in that neighborhood, and his pickets were placed in such and such directions. So she rode off, and he returned to his post. While he was thus away, his men, as will always be the case when an officer is not attentive, had removed their weapons, and some had even taken off their saddles. H.'s mind was too much engaged in thinking about the lady to take notice of things relating to his duty, and when his Captain rode up to visit the post he found every thing in this careless state. H. forthwith received a stern reprimand, and a peremptory order to see that his men kept armed, and their horses were saddled. For this time he obeyed the order; but by the time two reliefs had gone round all was again in the same condition.

What the fascinating Mrs. C. had been doing may easily be conjectured. She had only to take a short ride to her neighbors, get the chickens, let fall information of the Federal disposition, and return home as innocently as could be. The chickens had not been picked, however, before a clever negro was making his way with a note to the advance post of General Hampton. The chickens were very tender, the lady tenderer, the Lieutenant tenderest of all. He sat for some time after dinner, describing his military career, his hopes and disappointments, meeting with a delicate sympathy which he had never before received. When they parted it was only to be till tea time, when the lady promised him some music. Alas! Jacob, even if he had had brains enough to think of his responsibilities, would have run the risk of capture in order to enjoy the society of a lady who evidently appreciated his excellent qualities far better than the vulgar souls with whom he associated in the regiment. *He* had met with a congenial spirit, and he looked forward with delight to his three days of picket duty, from which he was generally inclined to hang back. He went over in thought all that he had said, and all that she had replied, and constructed an imaginary conversation for the evening which would be still more delightful. He wondered what songs she would sing, and thought of the comments he could subjoin to the most sentimental. In short, without knowing it, Jacob was already in love. The fly had got fatally entangled in love.

As he walked up to *that supper* an old colored woman met him at the door.

"Oh, massa!" she whispered, "don't go in da. Our sodgers come and catch you, shu'!"

"What's that silly creature saying?" said her mistress, who had slipped out and overheard her speech: "She is always fancying the Southern troops are coming to fight you, ever since she was scared at Dumfries some time ago. I have been waiting for you, and it is very ungallant in you to prefer her conversation to mine!"

H. hurried in, and was soon sipping coffee, and thinking of nectar—though it had come from his own haversack originally. The piano was then enlisted in the service, and Mrs. C. was singing some of her sweetest songs with much expression. Suddenly she began to play a march with the full power of the instrument; and it was not until some minutes had passed by that H. distinguished through the music the sound of the galloping of horse. Unfortunate Jacob! His sword was in the supper room, where he had left it as he sat down. He rushed for it, and bearing it in his hand made for the door.

"I will trouble you for that!" said a manly voice.

Poor Jacob had to render his weapon up to an officer in Confederate uniform who stood upon the threshold. Then, oh bitter mortification! he witnessed the charming Mrs. C. rush from the parlor into this officer's arms; and he gnashed his teeth as several unmistakable kisses were given by those lips which had uttered such gentle sounds for him but a little while before! Could he believe his eyes and ears? She was actually laughing at him, joined by her husband!

"Take good care of him, Charlie!" she said: "You don't know how dangerous I found him."

And the aforesaid Charlie, bowing very low, thanked him in a tone of mock courtesy for the attention he had paid his wife; assuring him that he would repay it by carrying him on a little visit to his own camp. Poor Jacob was overwhelmed by these unexpected 'courtesies,' and could not find a word to reply. He was led off like a lamb; and, escorted by three hundred Southern cavalry, made his first reconnoissance of his own picket line. What was worse, on being exchanged he found that he had been summarily dismissed from service, with loss of all pay and allowances; and he had nothing afterward to do but to murmur at the injustice of the Government and the treachery of Southern women.

### Samaritanism of the Genuine Type.

The "good Samaritan" is often heard of. He made his appearance one day in a Jersey ferry omnibus, New York City, under the following circumstances. On one side of the vehicle, near the door, there was a sick soldier. Very ill, wan, and emaciated he looked, with dark circles round his eyes, and the cape of his overcoat put up over his cap to keep off any breath of air, while his thin hands were bare to the winter cold. Some one got out who sat next him; immediately the place was taken by a man from the opposite side, who at once pulled off his own warm gloves and handed them to the soldier. The latter feebly attempted to decline them, but the other insisted, and he gratefully put them on, and looked at his well covered hands with a sigh of satisfaction. The man, (the Samaritan,) was a plain, quiet looking person, and did the little act of kindness without the slightest ostentation, as if it were purely a matter of course with him to clothe the naked. Nor was this all; he asked where the soldier was going. The reply was, 'Albany.' At the corner of Warren street the good man got down and deliberately lifted the poor fellow out in his arms with the greatest care, re-adjusted the cape of his coat over his head, and supported him to the sidewalk. The last seen of the stranger he was conducting the poor soldier down that street. God bless him. He was a noble specimen of the noble legions in the glorious Empire State, who, under the lead of that true hearted man, Governor Morgan, gave their treasure and blood to save the nation's life, and made their names memorable in the annals of victorious warfare. All honor to such a State —to her good Samaritans and soldier— to her noble rulers!

Gov. E. D. Morgan, New York.

### "Ah, Mother—Mother! I knew you would Come!"

The condition of the sick and wounded in Nashville, Tenn., before the occupation of that city by the National troops, was wretched in the extreme. The hospitals were filled, the surgeons worn out, and death everywhere stalked rampant, with neither food nor medicine to bar his approach.

On one of the beds there lay a young officer, burning with fever. He had evidently been delicately nurtured, and his bright eyes were fixed with a diseased, unnatural lustre, upon the miniature of a regal-looking woman, which he held in his hectic, wasted hands, his hot purple lips all the while murmuring, "Mother, mother!" He was covered with a single blanket—enough as long as disease was burning in his veins of fire—and his head rolled from side to side uneasily with the intense pain, vainly trying to find relief or rest, on the hard, unyielding knapsack, which was his only pillow; an attendant knelt by him and bathed his face with some water, while one of the gray-robed ladies placed a pillow under his head. At this the poor fellow said—

"Ah, mother, mother! I knew you would come,—this is the first moment of comfort I have known for a week!"

### Nuptials in Camp: Maine and Maryland.

When the Seventh Maine regiment were encamped in Baltimore, in the summer of 1861, one of the soldiers, named Clapp, fell in love with a young girl who used to peddle apples to the 'boys,' and promised to marry her. Her mother consented, but about the time set for the marriage the regiment left the place. After they had been in their new location, on the Potomac, about three weeks, who should come into camp one day but Clapp's girl! After a week or so the captain of Clapp's company gave his consent, and they were married and had a tent to themselves. But she was a foolish thing, and after a while the Colonel and Captain wanted to get rid of her. It happened that Clapp was one of the men detached from his regiment to go on board the Western gunboats. So his wife packed up and was going back to Baltimore. But, as luck would have it, when Clapp presented himself at head-quarters, they wouldn't accept him, and sent him back to camp. When the time came for the regiment to leave camp, and it started on the advance, they all supposed that was the last they should see of the soldier's girl. But one fine day who should march into camp at its new quarters but Mrs. Clapp, dressed in full military suit, with knapsack on her back, and canteen and haversack by her side! She was indeed a romantic feminine on a 'bender.' Her disguise was seen through at once, and she was sent to the guard house, to be from there sent back to Washington.

### Sixth Massachusetts Regiment's Daughter.

Little Miss Lizzie, the Daughter of the Massachusetts Sixth Regiment, looked charmingly in her regimental costume, as "the child," and was an object of most peculiar interest to all who had an opportunity of observing her pretty form and features amid such novel surroundings. She was but ten years old, yet from the time of her first appearance in camp, she proved a great comfort to the soldiers in the hospital, visiting them daily, and dispensing among the unfortunate many a little delicacy, as well as going frequently through the streets of the camp with strawberries, cherries, etc. Sometimes she distributed as many as sixteen boxes to a company—the market-man, of course, driving his cart to each tent.

The presentation speech accompanying the gift of the uniform, was made by Sergeant Crowley, of Lowell. The "Daughter" took the box containing the dress, and, with canteen upon her person, she tripped lightly into the 'hospital' that was close at hand, and in a few moments appeared in her new and beautiful attire. Standing upon the green, with the beautiful silk banners on each side, she addressed the regiment as follows:—

"Comrades—when you took me, a stranger, and adopted me as your daughter, I had but little idea of what you were doing, and what my duties were; but having been in camp with you two months, and learned to know you all, I have learned to love you all, and I feel that you all love me, because there are none of you when we meet but have a kind word and a pleasant smile for me. And now that you have put me in uniform, I feel still more that I belong to you, and I will try never to forget it. But you do not expect me to talk, but, like this splendid treasure, which I shall prize as a remembrance to the last day of my life—which is full to relieve the parched lips of my sick and wounded comrades—so shall my *heart* be a canteen full of love and sympathy for each and all of you. Comrades, thank you—thank you—thank you."

The little daughter delivered the speech in a very clear and distinct manner, and at its conclusion the regiment gave her three cheers and a "tiger," and escorted her to head-quarters.

### Amours and Fancies of the Camp.

Shortly after the arrival of a certain Union regiment in the suburbs of Martinsburg, Va., the squad messing in one of the tents near a dwelling, were listeners to most beautiful music. The unknown vocalist sang in tones so soft, so pathetic, and so melodious, that the volunteers strained their ears to drink in every note of the air. In daytime they went by squads past the dwelling, but saw no soul. Once they pursued a sylph-like figure to the very gate, but, alas! she was not the lady sought for. And so they lived on, each night hearing the music repeated,

Amours and Fancies of the Camp.

and, when it ceased, ambition and worldly interest went out with them so that their dreams were filled with fancies of the unseen face.

One night, gathered together, the voice struck up again.

"By jove," said one, "this is agonizing. I can't stand it. She must be discovered!"

A dozen eager voices took up the remark, and a certain amorous youth was delegated to reconnoiter the place. He crept on tiptoe toward the dwelling, leaped the garden pales, and finally, undiscovered, but very pallid and remorseful, gained the casement.

Softly raising his head, he peeped within. The room was full of the music. He seemed to grow blind for the moment.

Lo! prone upon the kitchen hearth, sat the mysterious songstress—an ebony-hued negress, scouring the tin kettles!

The soldier's limbs sank beneath him, and the discovered, looking up, said, "Go 'way dar, won't ye, or I'll shy de fryin' pan out o' de winder!" The soldier left —but not to dream, perchance!

### Contempt for Confederate Lines, Paroles, etc.

The heroic conduct of Mrs. Ricketts, the wife of Captain James B. Ricketts, who was severely wounded at the battle of Bull Run, became the theme of much and deserved praise. Mrs. Ricketts pushed through the Confederate lines alone when she heard that her husband was captured by the enemy, and took her place with him in the hospital, remaining there with woman's patience and constancy. When she arrived in Richmond, General Stuart asked her to sign a parole of honor. She contemptuously refused. He persisted in writing it and handed her the document. She tore it up instantly, and carried the fragments to her husband. When Captain Ricketts was carried to Richmond, crowds flocked to see the brave commander of "Sherman's Battery," as they were accustomed to call it.

### Mrs. Douglas's Noble Resistance to Southern Persuasion.

It could very safely be asserted that few persons of the female sex were placed in a more trying political and personal position, or sacrificed more in the way of devotion to the Union, than did Mrs. Douglas, the widow of the great deceased Illinois Senator. She persistently refused to entertain the proposition forwarded to her by a special messenger under a flag of truce from the Governor of North Carolina, asking that the two sons of the late Senator—by his first marriage—be sent South to save their extensive estates in Mississippi from confiscation. If she refused, a large property would be taken from the children, and, in view of her own reduced circumstances, they might thus eventually be placed in a straitened pecuniary situation. Here, then, was an appeal made directly to her tender regard for them, which, in case of her refusal, would work disastrously against them in after years. But her answer was worthy of herself and of her late distinguished husband, viz., 'If the rebels wish to make war upon defenceless children, and take away the all of little orphan boys, it must be so; but she could not for an instant think of surrendering them to the enemies of their country and of their father.' His last words were, 'Tell them to obey the Constitution and the laws of the country,' and Mrs. Douglas would not make herself the instrument of disobeying his dying injunctions. The children, she said, belonged to Illinois, and must remain in the North.

### Verbal Sharpshooting.

"Are you a Massachusetts soldier!" said a woman elegantly dressed, in Baltimore, to one wearing the Federal uniform.

"I am, madam," was the courteous answer of the officer thus addressed.

"Well, thank God, my husband is in the Southern army, ready to kill such hirelings as you!"

"Do you not miss him, madam!" said the officer.

"Oh, yes, I miss him a good deal."

"Very well, madam, we are going South in a few days, and will try to find him and *bring him back* here with his companions."

"You are from that miserable Boston," was the angry reply, "I suppose, where there is nothing but mob law, and they burned down the Ursuline Convent—the Puritan bigots!"

"Some such thing did happen in Charlestown, many years ago, when I was a boy,—at least I have heard so, and am very sorry for it. But can you tell me what street that is?"

"Pratt street," was the unsuspecting reply.

"*What happened there, madam, on the 19th of April this very year?*"

He got no answer from the angry secessionist, but the loud shouts which went up from the Union bystanders, who generally, though not exclusively, were of the humble order, atoned for her silence. The same officer, riding in a chaise with a gentleman who, to his surprise, showed secession proclivities, but was courteous in their demonstration, was told by the gentleman that the horse which was drawing them was called 'Jeff Davis,' in honor of that distinguished rebel, and asked if he 'did not object to driving such a horse?' 'Oh, no, sir,' was the instant reply, 'to drive Jeff. Davis is the very purpose of our coming South.' The secession gentleman imitated his political sister in preserving a discreet silence.

### The Unuttered Thought of a Dying Soldier.

"Bring me my knapsack," said a young soldier, who lay sick in one of the hospitals at Washington,—"Bring me my knapsack."

"What do you want of your knapsack?" inquired the head lady of the band of nurses.

"I want my knapsack," again said the dying young man.

His knapsack was brought to him, and, as he took it, his eye gleamed with pleasure, and his face was covered all over with a smile, as he brought out from it his hidden treasures.

"There," said he, "that is a Bible from

my mother. And this — Washington's Farewell Address — is the gift of my father. And this,"—his voice failed.

The nurse looked down to see what it was, and there was the face of a beautiful maiden.

"Now," said the dying soldier, "I want you to put all these under my pillow." She did as she was requested, and the poor young man laid him down on them to die, requesting that they should be sent to his parents when he was gone. Calm and joyful was he in dying. It was only going from night to endless day—from death to eternal glory. So the young soldier died.

### Spirit of a Kentucky Girl.

Captain Claypool, living about ten miles from Bowling Green, was commander of a company of Home Guards. He had the guns of his company at his house, but on hearing of the arrival of the Confederate General Buckner at Bowling Green, he sent them to Colonel Grider's camp in a neighboring county. The next day a squad, detached by Buckner, called at his house, and, finding only his daughter, demanded the guns of her. She answered that they were not there, and that, if they were, she wouldn't give them up. They handed her General Buckner's order for the weapons; this she tore up instantly before their faces. They went to the bucket and took each a drink of water, whereupon she threw the rest of the water out of the bucket and commenced scouring the dipper. They concluded they could do no better than to go back and tell their General about their adventure and get fresh instructions.

### Laughable Arrest of Colonel H. by Two Young Ladies.

While secessionism was so rampant in Kentucky, about the first year of the rebellion, the daughter and niece of Colonel H——, an influential man in that region, concluded that they would have a little fun in the politico-military line. To carry out their plan, they dressed themselves in men's apparel, procured an old shot gun, and proceeded to the field where the Colonel was occupied. One of the girls, shot gun in hand, took her position a few paces off, while the other stepped up and laid her hand on him and said :

"By the authority and in the name of the United States Army, I arrest you as guilty of treason."

"Gentlemen, in the name of God, what have I done?" said the astonished Colonel.

He however submitted without resistance, and in reply to his question was told that he would learn all about the case, and have all things satisfactorily explained at Camp Chase,—which caused the Colonel to turn very white. They all walked silently to the house, where the children, being well posted in the matter, got into a titter. This soon caused a loud burst of laughter from all hands except the Colonel, who was very belligerent when he found that he had actually been arrested by two young ladies, his daughter and niece.

### Hiding their Infant Moses.

Riding up to a house one day in Scriven county, Georgia, during Sherman's march through that State, a Union soldier met an old woman and three grown-up daughters at the door, uttering frantic appeals for help. On inquiring of the old woman what was wrong, she pointed to a burning cotton-gin, and exclaimed,

"Put it out! You uns are burnin' me child!"

On asking where the child was, the soldier succeeded in learning that it was in the burning gin-house.

Away he went, with some men, to rescue the innocent, and at the door met a ten-year-old boy, who, badly singed, issued forth from the fiery furnace. Returning to the house, inquiry was made as to how and why the boy came there.

Putting the old pipe between her lips, to compose her nerves, the old lady at last ventured an explanation :—

"Well," said she, "we uns heered that you uns killed all the little boys, to keep them out from growing up to fight ye, and we hid 'em."

Strange as this may seem, among the poor, ignorant dupes of the Southern leaders in rebellion, it was nevertheless a common belief that the Yankees made it a practice to slay all the male children they could lay their hands upon in the South. In consequence of this, there were found many infant Moseses and Jeffs hid away in cellars and corncribs—though none in bulrushes.

### Right Word in the Right Place.

As a large-hearted Union lady, resident in Covington, Kentucky, wife of a gentleman of the same character, was distributing a lot of fine apples, of which she had a half-bushel basket full, to the soldiers encamped back of that city, she gave an apple to one soldier of a group who exhibited peculiar emotion as she handed it to him, observing at the same time that it was a pleasant thing to receive gifts from a lady. At this she asked him whether he had a wife, and immediately his eyes filled with tears, which rolled down his cheeks as he replied,

"Yes, Madam, I have a wife and six children."

Observing his emotion, her own eyes rapidly filling at the sight, she quickly remarked to him;

"Well, keep up a good heart."

"Good heart! yes, Madam, that is my name; *Goodheart* is my name!"

Upon the instant their tears were changed to smiles, and Goodheart, the lady, and the soldier's companions, broke into a hearty laugh.

### "My Son—Has he Come?"

There is something most touching in the following narration of the intensity of maternal sorrow and love.—a grandeur, indeed, in the conduct of this poor lone mother, whose affection had made her mad, and who thus yearned for one her poor faded eyes could never see again. During the progress of the war, her son, a member of one of the Connecticut regiments, was taken prisoner and confined with other Union soldiers at Andersonville, Georgia. A short time afterwards several were exchanged. His mother, in Connecticut, hearing of it, and believing that he was among the number, left her desolate home, and went to Camp P'——, which was situated two miles from Annapolis, to seek her treasure among the boat loads landed on the Severn. She waited, wearily waited, day after day, for the coming of her boy; but though many came, he was not among them. "Hope deferred maketh the heart sick," and so it was with her. Broken-hearted by constantly recurring disappointments, her mind, already shaken by grief, at last gave way, and thus months rolled away, and with them the events borne on the wings and waves of time.

During all this period she continued to visit the office of Dr. Vanderkieft, the surgeon in charge, to ascertain whether any boat loads of released prisoners had arrived. When, finally, the last detachment came in, she seemed overjoyed, and went, with throbbing heart, from skeleton to skeleton, scanning them eagerly, anxiously. But, her son was not there; and each day she went, heavy and weary in spirit, back to her home. The good-hearted surgeon—such he truly was—although he knew and had told her many times that her son had been officially reported as dead, still answered her every day with the same monotonous, but very kindly spoken, "No!"

Thus came this broken-hearted, shattered, but loving mother, every day, always provided with a shirt, a pair of drawers, pantaloons, boots and cap, and when informed, regularly, that her son had not yet arrived she would go down the graveled path across the lawn to the very end of the long wharf. There she stood looking over the broad waters of the Chesapeake for fully an hour. Clad ever in the same neat dress and closely fitting bonnet, she would gaze wistfully, longingly, over the blue waste, as if her very eagerness would hasten on the bark she imagined would bear back to her her child. But her tear-swollen eyes at last grew dim, her strength failed, and with the empty void aching in her breast, she slowly and finally turned her steps from that long-accustomed pathway, never again to retrace them, nor again to ask so piteously, " My son—has he come ?"

### "I am proud to Die for my Country."

The eyes of a youth of tender years, by the name of Bullard, belonging to company A, Eighth Illinois regiment, were closed in death one spring morning, at the Marine Hospital in Cincinnati, by the kindly hands of that noble-hearted and faithful woman, Mrs. Caldwell—unwearied and ever watchful in her personal attentions to the sick and wounded since the establishment of the "Marine" as a military hospital. Young Bullard was shot at Fort Donelson. The ball, a Minie, tore his breast open, and lacerated an artery. He bled internally as well as externally. At every gasp, as his end drew near, the blood spirted from his breast. He expired at nine o'clock. Early in the day, when he became fully aware that he could not live long, he showed that he clung to life, and was loth to leave it; but he cried: " If I could only see my mother—if I could only see my mother before I die, I would be better satisfied." He was conscious to the last moment, almost, and after reminding Mrs. Caldwell that there were several letters for his mother in his portfolio, she breathed words of consolation to him: "You die in a glorious cause—you die for your country." " Yes," replied he, " I am proud to die for my country."

### Death Scene of a South Carolina Lieutenant.

Late one afternoon—too late for the cars that were taking the Gettysburg wounded to the hospitals—a train of ambulances arrived at one of the Lodges of the Sanitary Commission with one hundred rebels, to be cared for through the night. Only one among them seemed too weak and faint to take anything. He was badly hurt, and failing. A nurse went to him after his wound was dressed, and found him lying on his blanket stretched over the straw—a fair-haired, blue-eyed young Lieutenant ; a face innocent enough for one of New England's boys. He did not seem like a rebel against earth's best Government; he was too near heaven for such seeming. He wanted nothing—had not been willing to eat for days, his comrades said; but the good nurse coaxed him to try a little milk gruel, made nicely with lemon and brandy, and one of the satisfactions of three weeks arduous service to that kind nurse, was the remembrance of the empty cup she took away and his perfect enjoyment of that supper. He talked about "that good supper" for hours, and with boundless thanks ; " it was so good; the best thing he had had since he was wounded."

Poor fellow ! he had had no care, and it was a surprise and pleasure to find himself thought of ; so, in a pleased, childlike way, he talked about it till midnight—as long as he spoke of anything, for at midnight the change came, and from that time he only thought of the old days before he was a soldier, when he sung hymns in his father's church. He sung them now again in a clear, sweet voice : " Lord have mercy upon me;" and those songs without words—a sort of a low intoning. His father was a Lutheran clergyman in South Carolina, so a comrade said, on the morning when the brave but unfortunate youth was sliding gently from all earthly care.

All day long the attendants watched him,—sometimes fighting his battles over, after singing his Lutheran chants, till in the tent door, close to which he lay, looked a rebel soldier, just arrived with other prisoners. He started when he saw the Lieutenant, and quickly kneeling down by him, called "Henry! Henry!" But Henry was looking fixedly at some one a great way off, and could not hear him, "Do you know this soldier?" he was asked by the nurse. "Oh, yes, ma'am; and his brother is wounded and a prisoner, too, in the cars, now." Two or three men started after him, found him, and carried him from the cars to the tent. Henry did not know him though; and he threw himself down by his side on the straw, and for the rest of the day lay in a sort of apathy, without speaking, except to assure himself that he could stay with his brother, without the risk of being separated from his fellow prisoners.

Those who would read the most spirited narratives portraying Southern bravery, will find Mr. Orville J. Victor's 'History of the Southern Rebellion,' a work of incomparable value, presenting as it does every noteworthy occurrence with the skill of an accomplished historian, and in the best literary dress,—being accepted also as an authoritative work, both North and South, in respect to the Southern side of the great struggle—its military and political bearings,—by the pen of a Southern sympathizer.

### ' Sweet Seventeen " overhauling the Secessionists.

A noble and well nigh tragical act was perpetrated in the spring of 1862, by a young lady of Graves County, Kentucky, —Miss Anna Bassford, a gentle creature of seventeen rosy summers. Her father and family were devotedly for the Union. The old man having information that the notorious H. C. King, expelled from the Kentucky legislature for treason, and his robber band intended to visit the house for the purpose of taking horses, guns, etc., hid the gun and carried the horses to Paducah. Whilst there, three of King's robbing band visited the house, demanded the gun, and alarmed Mrs. Bassford, who ordered a son some fifteen years old, to find the gun and deliver it over. The boy, after considerable search, found the gun; the robbers then demanded a pistol, which they were informed belonged in the family, whereupon the above-named daughter told them she knew where the pistol was, but *they* could not get it. The

Sweet Seventeen Overhauling the Secessionists.

robbers insisted, with loud, vulgar oaths, but the girl was determined. Seeing they were foiled in this, they ordered the feeble, sickly boy, to mount up behind one of their clan, as 'they intended to take him to Camp Beauregard in place of his—Lincolnite father.' The boy and mother in tears protested, but to no effect, and the boy was in the act of mounting, when the heroic sister stepped between her brother and the robbers, and drawing, cocking and presenting the pistol, ordered her brother back to the house, and, with eagle-piercing eye fastened on the robbers, and death-dealing determination in her countenance, *dared* the scoundrels to hinder or touch her brother, and she would lay the robber dead at her feet! There was no parleying after this utterance and attitude—the three brigands scampered off and left the family without further molestation.

### Fighting for his Country and Deserted by his Wife.

In the pleasant little village of Wyoming, Jones County, Iowa, lived a plain-spoken, honest farmer, J——— B——— by name, who removed thither from a small town in Illinois, not far from the city of Galesburg. He had purchased a farm in the latter place, but the title proving defective he had removed to Wyoming, where the person of whom he had bought the land resided, and there in the courts of Jones County prosecuted his claim to judgment.

Twelve years before, in the city of New York, he had married a blooming Celtic damsel, and by her had been made the happy father of two beautiful children—one, a bright, intelligent boy, attained to his eleventh year, and another, a girl, in her sixth year. When he removed to Wyoming he took along with him a young man named G——— M———, because his evidence was necessary to enable him to maintain his suit in the Iowa courts. And from this source came his unexpected and calamitous troubles.

During the summer, B——— and M——— both enlisted in Company H, Fourteenth Iowa infantry, Colonel William Shaw commanding, and together went to the front. Soon after, M——— deserted, and B——— lost all track of him. After a considerable lapse of time, a young man named J——— C——— received a letter which covered one addressed to M———. This was shown to B———, and he and C——— concluded to break it open. Judge of poor B———'s surprise when he found that it was from his own wife, breathing the most intense love and devotion for his quondam comrade. His resolution was soon taken. He obtained a furlough and returned to his home and took his wife to her friends, who were then in Port Sarnia, Canada West. After the expiration of his leave of absence, he returned to his regiment, from which he heard from her but seldom.

Just before his discharge and return he received a letter from his wife, dated Marquette, Michigan, in which she announced her intention of coming to Chicago to meet him. On his reaching that city, he found her at the Eagle Hotel, opposite the Northwestern depot. The two children he had left in 1861, had become three. Upon her bosom slumbered an infant scarcely nine months old, the fruit of her *liaison* with M———. Mr. B——— was naturally indignant, and threatened to take the children and leave the woman to follow her evil inclinations without hindrance. By some means she pacified him, and induced him to take a glass or two of liquor, and he slept. While thus slumbering, the woman, he said, entered his chamber and robbed him of about three hundred dollars, the savings of his three years' service. With this and his two children and the one whose paternity he ascribed to M———, she took the cars for Detroit, accompanied by a miner from Marquette, named McC———, in whose company she arrived in Chicago, and who, unknown to B———, had stopped at the same hotel with her, in the assumed relation of her brother-in-law.

The woman had not been long away before the eldest child, the lad before mentioned, returned to the hotel, having escaped from the custody of his mother, just as the cars were starting. From him the father learned all that was necessary to be known of his wife's temptation and fall. He said that some time after M——— deserted he came to Wyoming, and while there maintained the relations of a husband with his mother. The citizens of that village becoming cognizant of the scandal, it was thought best to remove. They went to Marquette, Michigan, and opened a boarding house. Here the child, the fruit of their morganatic union, was born. He filled the place of husband to the woman, passing well until, tempted by the high price of substitutes, he sold himself to a drafted man, and abandoned the woman he had taught to deviate from the paths of rectitude and virtue. She remained not long inconsolable, but speedily formed another connection with the man McC——, with whom she went to Chicago, and under whose auspices she robbed her husband of his money and his child. The guilty pair then went to Detroit, and finally to Canada.

### Rare Page in Woman's History.

A gentleman in Ithaca, New York, had an idea that women could do more with their needles if they did less with their tongues, and he therefore promised fifty dollars to the Soldiers' aid Society of the village, if twelve women could be found who would sew all day without speaking. Fifteen candidates presented themselves, and, *mirabile dictu*, fourteen of them succeeded in keeping quiet. They were sorely tempted by various lookers-on, but only one yielded to "woman's infirmity." Heroic fourteen! It is doubtful whether such an instance of female silence, in promiscuous company, was ever known before, and the fact speaks well for the earnestness and sincerity of their regard for the soldiers. To no stronger test could their patriotism have been subjected.

### "Jeb" Stuart Playing Orderly to General Bayard.

During the week of battles in front of Washington, General Bayard went forward, under a flag of truce, to meet and confer with his old comrade in arms, the famous J. E. B. Stuart, of the rebel cavalry. Less than two years previously, Jeb was first Lieutenant and Bayard second Lieutenant in the same company; but Jeb was now a Major-General, and Bayard a Brigadier. During the interview a wounded Union soldier lying near was groaning and asked for water.

"Here, Jeb," said Bayard—old time recollections making him familiar, as he tossed his bridle to the rebel officer—"hold my horse a minute, will you, till I fetch that poor fellow some water."

Jeb held the bridle. Bayard went to a stream and brought the wounded man some water. As Bayard mounted his horse, Jeb remarked that he had not for some time "played orderly to a Union

Castle Thunder.

General." The business upon which they met was soon arranged, and the old friends parted—a fight, which had ceased when they were engaged talking, recommencing with great fury on both sides the moment each got back to his own ranks. Jeb's fighting against his country's flag was, after all, a small sin compared with his complicity in the horrors of Libby Prison and Castle Thunder—those modern bastiles, under the *regime* of Davis, Lee, Stuart, and their myrmidons.

Such incidents as the above, however, attest the old adage that 'none are so bad, some good redeemeth not,' and that even Stuart was no exception. "Miles O'Reilly," (the brave Colonel Halpine,) has told many of these good things, and has promised the public a volume full of his fresh and inimitably piquant military jottings, than which nothing could be more acceptable to the " Universal Yankee Nation."

### Racy Conversation between Mrs. Polk and General Mitchell on "the Situation."

When passing through Nashville, General Mitchell, in company with a number of other distinguished officers, called upon Mrs. Polk, the widow of President James K. Polk. The lady made no attempt to conceal her strong sympathies with the rebellion, and singling out General Mitchell, said to him,

"General, I trust this war will speedily terminate by the acknowledgment of Southern independence."

The remark caused a lull in the conversation, and all eyes were turned to General Mitchell, awaiting his response. For a moment he stood in silence, his lips firmly compressed, and then, in tones of deepest earnestness and solemnity, he replied:

"Madam, the man whose name you bear was once President of the United States. He was an honest man and a true patriot. He administered the laws of this Government with equal justice to all. *We know of no independence of one section of our country which does not belong to all others;* and, judging by the past, if the mute lips of the honored dead who lies so near us could speak, they would express the hope that this war might never cease, if that cessation were to be purchased by the dissolution of the Union of States over which he once presided."

The effect of this remark, uttered in a calm, yet firm and dignified tone, was electrical. But Mrs. Polk, nevertheless, on more than one occasion, avowed herself true to the whole country of which her husband was once the elected ruler.

### Merriment in the Wrong Place.

After one of the bloody Virginia engagements, the wounded among the Confederates received all possible attention on the part of the Union soldiers, though the want of suitable accommodations was sadly felt. In one of the spots to which the sufferers had been removed, a Federal soldier came along with a pail of soup to fill the canteens and plates, and stopping before a fine athletic fellow, who, it turned out had been married only three days previously, said:

"Come, pardner! drink yer sup. Now, ould boy, this 'ill warm ye; sock it down, and ye'll see yer sweetheart soon. You dead. Allybammy? Go 'way now! You'll live a hundred years—you wil; that's what you'll do. Won't he, lad? What! Not any? Get out! You'll be slap on your legs next week, and have another shot at me this week a'ter that. You with the butternut trousers! Sa-ay! pardner, wake up!"

Embalming Building before Richmond.

He stirred him gently with his foot: he bent down to touch his face—a grimness came over his mood of merriment; the man was stiff and dumb,—ready to be buried forever from human sight, or be embalmed for conveyance to his once happy home and kindred.

### Miss Captain Taylor, of the First Tennessee.

One of the features of the First Tennessee Regiment, was a brave and accomplished young lady of but eighteen summers, and of prepossessing appearance, named Sarah Taylor, of East Tennessee, the step-daughter of Captain Dowden, of the First Tennessee Regiment. Miss Taylor was an exile from home, having joined the fortunes of her step-father and her wandering companions, accompanying them in their perilous and dreary flight from their hearths and homesteads. She formed the determination to share with her late companions the dangers and fatigues of a military campaign; and to this end, she donned a neat blue chapeau, beneath which her long hair was fantastically arranged, bearing at her side a highly finished regulation sword, and silver-mounted pistols in her belt, all of which gave her a very neat appearance. She became quite the idol of the Tennessee boys, who looked upon her as a second Joan of Arc, believing that victory and glory would perch upon the standards borne in the ranks favored by her presence. Miss Captain Taylor was, indeed, all courage and skill. Having become an adept in the sword exercise, and a sure shot with a pistol, she determined to lead in the van of the march—to return her exiled countrymen to their homes, if it cost the sacrifice of her own life's blood.

When the order was issued to the Tennesseans to march to reinforce Colonel Garrard, the wildest excitement pervaded the whole camp, Miss Taylor mounting her horse, and, cap in hand, galloping along the line like a spirit of flame, cheering on the men. She wore a blue blouse, and was armed with pistols, sword and rifle, and the persecuted Tennesseans looked upon the daring girl who followed their fortunes through sunshine and shadow, with the tenderest feeling of veneration, and each would willingly have offered his life in her defence. There was but little sleep in the camp on Saturday night, so great was the joy of the men at the prospect of meeting the foe, and at a very early hour in the morning they filed away jubilantly, with their Joan of Arc in the van. Just before taking up their line of march, they all knelt, and lifting up their right hands, solemnly swore never to return without seeing their homes and loved ones.

#### Female Loveliness at Fort Henry.

Not a single atom of Union sentiment appeared to present itself when our army reached the neighborhood of Fort Henry. Even the women were as bitter and unrelenting in their hatred of the Yankees, as could be the most unregenerated son of the 'chivalry.'

"*I* shan't run ef my ole man did"—screamed one muscular termagant, in a highly pitched key, as the scouts made up—" shoot if you want to; I just as lieve die now as any time. You think you're goin to take the Fort, but you'll get fooled—thar's a right smart heap o' men thar!"

Just then some of the scouts came in lugging a butternut native, whom they fished out of the bushes, and who proved to be her "ole man."

"I tole you you oughtener done gone and took to the bush! But don't you let down an inch—if they shoot you, don't let down an inch!"—and screaming like an hyena, she banged the door furiously in their face, and was seen no more. She was about an average specimen of the sex as found in the vicinity of Fort Henry.

#### Red, White and Blue,—God's Flag.

When the Federal troops first made their appearance near Bardstown, Kentucky, a little boy, who just then discovered a beautiful rainbow arching the heavens, ran to his mother and exclaimed. "Mother, God is a Union man." His mother questioned him for his reason for thinking so, and the little fellow replied that he had seen his flag, and it was " Red, White, and Blue." Surely, "Out of the mouth of babes and sucklings hast thou ordained strength because of thine enemies."

### Little Overweighted with Cold Lead.

Those who visited the sick soldiers and did good in the hospitals, occasionally got a gleam of fun among all the sad scenes, for any wag who has been to the war seldom loses his humor, though he may have lost all else save that and honor. Witness an illustration from life:

C——, good soul, after taking all the little comforts he could afford to the wounded soldiers, went into the hospitals for the fortieth time, again, with his mite, consisting of several papers of cut chewing tobacco—'solace for the wounded,' as he called it. He came to one bed, where a poor fellow lay cheerfully humming a tune, and studying out faces on the papered wall. "Got a fever?" asked C. "No," answered the soldier. "Got a cold?" "Yes; cold—lead." "Where?" "Well, to tell the truth, it's pretty well scattered. First, there's a bullet in my right arm—they hain't dug that out yet. One in my right leg—hit the bone—that fellow hurts. One through my left hand—that fell out. And, I tell you what, friend, with all this lead in me, I feel, generally speaking, a little heavy all over."

### Faith and its Reward.

Not far from the Capitol in Washington lived an old negro woman, whose only boy enlisted, in the spring of 1864, in the negro regiment organized in that city. He took part in the action of July 30th, in front of Petersburg, and was one of those who fell wounded near the famous crater. "Badly wounded and in the hands of the rebels," was the word that came to his mother. That was in August. The autumn months came and went in succession, but brought no further word of this only son of his mother and she a widow. Her friends and his friends generally believed him dead. It did not seem probable that he had survived his wounds, yet no one had the heart to say as much to his poor old mother.

Court House, Church, and Hospital, of 2d Corps, Fredericksburg, Va.

She continually said, "I trust in de good Lord." She did not appear to even think it possible her boy would die. Much effort was made in the latter half of November and the first half of December to get word from him, but all to no avail. "Some one ought to tell his mother," was often remarked among those who were interested in the case, yet no one spoke discouragingly to her. Who could do it? She wondered why she did not hear from him, she never wearied in devising crude and simple plans for communicating with him. About the middle of December, or a little later, she was heard to say, "De Lord he will pervide, an' I shall hear from him bime-by." That was on a Tuesday. The next Thursday afternoon he opened the door of his old mother's little house, and walked in and threw his arms around her neck! Wasn't that a royal Christmas gift for the trustful old soul? Half an hour later she burst into the house of friends who had aided her, with only "My boy's come! my boy's come!" He had not been wounded, but was taken prisoner and sent to the Libby prison, where he acted as servant for about three months. One afternoon, when he was sent out for wood— "Oh, golly," says he, "I jus den forgot de way back!" He was near three weeks in making his way overland from Richmond to Washington, and brought through three negro women, five children, and two men!

#### Fulfillment of the Sergeant's Prophecy.

Presentments on the battle-field often prove prophetic. Here is an instance: While Colonel Osterhaus was gallantly attacking the centre of the enemy, on the second day of the battle at Pea Ridge, a sergeant of the Twelfth Missouri requested the Captain of his company to send his

Fulfillment of the Sergeant's Prophecy.

wife's portrait, which he had taken from his bosom, to her address in St. Louis, with his dying declaration that he thought of her in his last moments.

"What is that for?" asked his Captain; "you are not wounded, are you?"

"No," answered the sergeant, "but I know I shall be killed to-day. I have been in battles before, but I never felt as I do now. A moment ago I became convinced my time had come, but, how, I cannot tell. Will you gratify my request? Remember I speak to you as a dying man."

"Certainly, my brave fellow; but you will live to a good old age with your wife. Do not grow melancholy over a fancy or a dream!"

"You will see," was the response.

And so the treasured picture changed hands, and the sergeant stepped forward to the front of the column, and was soon beyond recognition.

At the camp-fire that evening the officers after a while made enquiry for the sergeant. He was not present. He had been killed three hours before by a grape-shot from one of the enemy's batteries.

#### Incident in the Battle of Fredericksburg.

Sergeant Charles H. Stevenson, of Henrietta, N. Y., was one of the killed at the battle of Fredericksburg. A strange incident connected with his death is stated to have transpired, and is not unworthy of record as one of the incidents of the war. On the day of that battle his wife was out in the yard, when suddenly she was made aware of a presence behind her, and turning, felt a warm breath on her cheek, and saw her husband, who, how-

Incident in the Battle of Fredericksburg.

ever, almost immediately vanished. As she turned she cried out, 'Oh! Charlie, is that you?" and returned to the house, where she at once told some friends that she had seen her husband, and that she knew she would never see him alive again. As near as could be ascertained, the event occurred just at the time of day when her husband was killed.

#### Chance for a "Lady of Character."

Among the documents left by the editors of the Memphis (Tenn.) "Appeal," when they left that city, was the following gentle epistle from a secessionist woman, who had sent it to that paper for publication:

#### A CHALLENGE.

Where as the wicked policy of the president—Making war upon the South for refusing to submit to wrong too palpable for Southerners to do. And where as it has become necessary for the young Men of our country, My Brother in the number To enlist to do the dirty work of Driving the Mercenarys from our sunny south, whose soil is too holy for such wretches to tramp And whose atmosphere is too pure for them to breathe

For such an indignity offord to Civilization I Merely Challenge any abolition or Black Republican lady of character if there can be such a one found among the negro equality tribe. To Meet me at Masons and dixon line : With a pair of Colt's repeaters or any other weapon they May Choose. That I may receive satisfaction for the insult.

VICTORIA E. GOODWIN,
Springdale Miss April 27, 1861.

#### "Pro-Patria" Pictures at the Soldiers' Fair.

The more celebrated pictures in the superb collection that adorned the great Soldiers' Fair in New York were left for exhibition, through the kindness of their owners; but many most admirable works were given to it to be sold for its benefit. These latter were accordingly distinguished from the others by being marked on the frame with the very appropriate words, "Pro-Patria."

"What does that mean, Ma?" said a young girl at the Fair, to materfamilias, one morning.

"What, my dear?"

"Why, those words," said the little lady, eyeing the picture frames closely, and pointing to "Pro-Patria."

"Oh! that," said materfamilias, inspecting the letters with her eye-glasses, "why, I suppose that must be the name of the artist who paints the pictures—Prof. Patria."

#### Executive Favor well Bestowed.

A postmaster from Illinois having been killed in the Union army at Vicksburg, Mississippi, there was of course some competition for his office, but President Lincoln endorsed the application in behalf of the deceased soldier's widow, and afterwards wrote a note to the Postmaster General, in which he thus most nobly put in a plea for the right person in the right place. Says the President: "Yesterday, little endorsements of mine went to you in two cases of Postmasterships sought for widows whose husbands have fallen in the battles of this war. These cases occurring on the same day, brought me to reflect more attentively then I had before done, as to what is fairly due from us here, in the dispensing of patronage toward the men who, by fighting our battles, bear the chief burden of saving our country. My conclusion is that, other claims and qualifications being equal, they have the better right, and this is especially applicable to the disabled soldier and the deceased soldier's family." Most worthy and discriminating consideration on the part of the President, in behalf of the brave men who fell in defence of their country,—and for the dependent ones whom they left behind them!

#### Childhood's Prayer in the Last Hour.

It was the evening after a great battle. All day long the din of strife had echoed far, and thickly strewn lay the shattered forms of those so lately erect and exultant in the flush and strength of manhood. Among the many who bowed to the conqueror Death that night, was a youth in the first freshness of mature life. The strong limbs lay listless, and the dark hair was matted with gore, on the pale, broad forehead. His eyes were closed. As one who ministered to the sufferer bent over him, he at first thought him dead; but the white lips moved, and slowly in weak tones he repeated—"Now I lay me down to sleep," &c., going through those five sweet and precious lines.

As he finished, he opened his eyes, and, meeting the pitying gaze of a brother soldier, he exclaimed, "My mother taught me that when I was a little boy, and I have said it every night since I can remember. Before the morning dawns, I believe that God will take my soul for 'Jesus' sake,' but before I die, I want to send a message to my mother."

He was carried to a temporary hospital, and a letter was written to his mother, which he dictated, full of Christian faith and filial love. He was calm and peaceful. Just as the sun arose, his spirit went home. His last articulate words were,— "I pray the Lord my soul to take; And this I ask for Jesus' sake." The prayer of childhood was thus the prayer of his manhood. He learned it at his mother's knee in his far distant Northern home, and he whispered it in dying, when his young life ebbed away on a Southern battle-field.

### Miss Major Cushman among her Captors.

Some of the experiences of that remarkable woman, Miss Major Pauline Cushman, the Federal scout and spy, are equal to anything found in the pages of romance. They are of the most thrilling character. Indeed, among the women of America who made themselves famous during the opening of the rebellion, few have suffered more, or rendered more service to the Union cause, than she.

At the commencement of hostilities, Miss Cushman resided in Cleveland, Ohio, and was quite well known as a clever actress. From Cleveland she went to Louisville, where she had an engagement in Wood's Theatre. Here, by her intimacy with certain rebel officers, she incurred the suspicion of being a secessionist, and was arrested by the Federal authorities. She indignantly denied that she was disloyal, although born at the South, and having a brother in a secession Mississippi regiment.

In order to test her love for the old

Miss Pauline Cushman.

flag, she was asked if she would enter the secret service of the government. She readily consented, and was at once employed to carry letters between Louisville and Nashville. She was subsequently employed by General Rosecrans, and was for many months with the army of the Cumberland. She visited the enemy's lines time after time, and was thoroughly acquainted with all the country and roads in Tennessee, Northern Georgia, Alabama and Mississippi, in which sections she rendered the Federal armies invaluable service.

Twice was she suspected of being a spy, and taken prisoner, but managed to escape. At last, however, she was not so fortunate. After the Union forces had captured Nashville, Major Cushman made a scout towards Shelbyville, to obtain information of the strength and position of the enemy, and while returning to Nashville, was captured eleven miles from that city. She was placed on a horse, and, in charge of two scouts, was being taken to Spring Hill, the head-quarters of Forrest. While thus on her way to that place, she feigned sickness and said she could not travel any further without falling from her horse. Her captors stopped at a house on the roadside, when it was ascertained that a Federal scouting party had passed the place an hour before. Knowing that her guards had important papers for General Bragg, the quick-witted spy seized the fact and schemed to use it to her advantage.

Seeing an old negro, who appeared to commiserate her unfortunate plight, she watched her opportunity and placed ten dollars of Tennessee money in his hand, saying,—

"Run up the road, 'Uncle,' and come back in a few minutes, telling us that four hundred Federals are coming down the street."

The faithful negro obeyed the order literally, and soon came back in the greatest excitement, telling the story. The two 'rebs' told him he lied. The old colored man got down imploringly upon his knees, saying,—

"O Massa, dey's comin, sure nuff; de Lord help us, dey is comin."

The scouts at this believed his story, mounted their horses, and 'skedaddled' for the woods. Miss Cushman, seizing a pistol belonging to a wounded soldier in the house, also mounted her horse and fled towards Franklin. She traveled through the rain, and, after nightfall, lost her way. Soon came the challenge of a picket, "Who comes there?" Thinking she had reached the enemy's line she said, "A friend of Jeff. Davis." "All right," was the reply, "advance and give the countersign."

She presented the countersign in the shape of a canteen of whiskey. She passed five pickets in this way, but the sixth and last was obdurate. She pleaded that she was going to see a sick uncle at Franklin, but the sentry 'couldn't see it.' Sick and disheartened she turned back. Seeing a light at a farm house she sought shelter. An old man received her kindly, showed her a room, and said he would awake her at an early hour in the morning, and show her the road to Franklin.

A loud knock awoke her in the morning from her lethean slumbers, and upon arousing, she found her horse saddled and the two guards from whom she had escaped the previous afternoon! She was taken to the head-quarters of Forrest, and, after a critical examination, he sent her to General Bragg. Nothing could be found against her, until a secession woman stole her gaiters, under the inner sole of which were found important documents which clearly proved her to be a spy. She was tried and condemned to be executed as such, but being sick, her execution was postponed. She finally, after lying in prison some three months, sent for General Bragg, and asked him if he had no mercy. She received from him the comforting assurance that he should make an example of her, and that he should hang her as soon as she got well enough to be hung decently.

While in this state of suspense, the grand army of Rosecrans commenced its forward movement, and one fine day the secession town where she was imprisoned, was surprised and captured, and the heroine of this tale was to her great joy released.

### Family Swords not to be Exempted.

An order was issued by General Butler, when in New Orleans, for the surrender of certain private arms held by secessionists. In one house it was said they had been secreted and not surrendered. It was the house of a lady. She was wealthy and in high social position. But she was summoned to give account. Her story was simple and lady-like, and had a touch of sentiment about it which would

DOMESTIC, WOMANLY, HOSPITAL, PRISON, ETC.   551

show her praiseworthy rather, and not to be blamed for not presenting arms according to order. She was a gentlewoman, a lady in fact of the "uppermost seats," and was unused to the ways of men. The arms had been hid—but the truth of the matter was, there was among them a sword—a valuable sword—a family sword. It had a great value from its associations—and it was really to keep that safe, which was a household jewel, that the error had been committed, and not to keep or secrete the other arms. They were of no account and should of course be given up. This was a very pretty story, but something excited that wide-awake General's suspicions, and he said to her, emphatically, that the sword must be produced, and he should retain her until it was done. Whereupon her friends, as the only alternative now remaining, interfered, and it soon appeared that there was no sword anywhere. It was a pure fabrication—an artful lie. But it would have been held a good joke if the Yankee lawyer, keen-scented and acute, had been outwitted by a woman!

#### Interview at "the Libby" between Morgan the Guerrilla Chieftain and Neal Dow.

According to the statements in the Confederate journals, General Morgan, the guerrilla chieftain, after his escape from the Columbus penitentiary, went to Richmond, Virginia, and visited the Libby prison. On arriving up stairs, where the Federal prisoners 'most did congregate,' he was immediately conducted into the presence of the author of the 'Maine Liquor Law,' Brigadier General Neal Dow, a Federal captive. An introduction took place, when Morgan observed, with one of those inimitable smiles for which he was so noted,

"General Dow, I am very happy to see you here; or rather, I should say, since you are here, I am happy to see you looking so well."

Dow's natural astuteness and Yankee

Libby Prison, Richmond.

ingenuity came to his aid, and he quietly replied, without apparent embarrassment,

"General Morgan, I congratulate you on your escape; I cannot say that I am glad you did escape; but since you did, I am glad to see you here."

The conversation then became general between the two.

#### Instance of Loyalty in Virginia.

Private Job H. Wells, of Company C, was lost in the confusion of the troops at the battle of Bull Run. He got into the woods, and soon after the moon was shut in by a cloud. He wandered till he came to a rye-field, where he encamped for the night. Tired and exhausted, he soon fell asleep, but awoke in the morning cold and hungry. He determined to make for a house he saw at a distance, and risk the consequences. He dragged his weary, stiffened limbs along, in a terrible uncertainty as to the reception he should meet with.

Arriving at the house and entering, he was heartily welcomed by the lady occupant, who gave him a sofa to rest upon, and in the mean time directed her servants to prepare breakfast. The table was liberally supplied, and the stranger told to be seated. The lady was a firm Unionist and declared that the National troops were welcome to whatever she had. She said that on the march out, some of the troops stopped at her place and took several ducks; these she cared nothing about, and if they had taken much more they

Instance of Loyalty in Virginia.

would have been welcome. If they had not broken up her sitting hens, she would not have said a word. The good lady did not like to lose her next year's flock.

Soon after breakfast, a troop of secessionists came in sight. The lady put Mr. Wells in a rear room, while she conversed with some of them. She feigned great ignorance of what had been going on, and learned from them the route they were going. After they had gone, Mr. Wells inquired how he was to get away. "That is easy enough," replied the matron; "trust to me." She ordered one of her servants to saddle a horse and bring it to the door. She then brought out a long overcoat, and told him to put it on. The pockets were liberally supplied with delicacies to serve him on the way. The horse was brought to the door, when the lady told Mr. Wells that the horse was at his service, and would safely carry him through. Said she—

"Take the horse, and go to Washington. You may leave him with my son," (giving his name and residence) "and if a secessionist meets you, shoot him; if there is more than one, shoot the first, and trust to the horse for the other, for he will soon carry you out of danger."

Mr. Wells mounted the horse, and safely reached Washington. He left the horse as directed, and was welcomed by the son as he had been by the mother. While Mr. Wells was waiting, a Unionist of the vicinity came into the house, and said he was about to leave for Washington; that he had sent his family over, and had staid behind to see if it was possible to save anything. The lady asked him if he had any money. He said he had not. She then went up stairs, and returning with a purse of silver, gave it to the gentleman, remarking—

"Take this; you may as well have it as the secessionists. They have already divided my property, and apportioned it among themselves; but the first man that makes the attempt to carry that out, I shall shoot."

### Amours of a New Orleans Ex-Judge.

General Butler, in pursuance of his system of redressing the wrongs of Union men, seized the large estates of Judge C——, of Louisiana, and held them for the future liquidation of a claim held against C—— by Major Robert Anderson, but which C—— had personally written to Major A. his intention to repudiate for political reasons. Now, justly thinking that New Orleans, under the rule of General Butler, was no fit place for him to reside in, vanished soon after into the congenial shades of Secessia.

A few days after his departure, a young woman sought an interview with Mrs. Butler, to whom many women came at that time, to relate the story of personal wrongs. So many women, indeed, resorted to her for that purpose, that at length it was found necessary to close that door to the commanding general's attention. The young woman who came to her on this occasion was a *perfect* blonde, her hair of a light shade of brown, her eyes 'clear honest gray,' her complexion remarkably pure and delicate, her bearing modest and refined, her language that of an educated woman. It has been often remarked that the women of the South, who have been made the victims of a master's brutal lust, escape moral contamination. Their souls remain chaste. This woman, so fair to look upon, so engaging in her demeanor, so refined in her address, was a slave, the slave of Judge C——. She told her incredible story—incredible until her superabundant testimony compelled the most incredulous to believe.

She said that Judge C—— was her father as well as her master. At an early age she had been sent to school in New York, the school of the Mechanics' Institute, in Broadway. When she was fifteen years of age, her father came to New York, took her from school to his hotel, and compelled her to live with him as his mistress. She became the mother of a child, of whom her master was father and grandfather.

"I am now twenty-one," said she, "and I am the mother of a boy five years old, who is my father's son."

The Judge took her home with him to New Orleans, where he continued to live with her for awhile; then ordered her to marry a favorite *protégé*. She refused. He had her horsewhipped in the streets, and continued a systematic torture till she consented. When she had been married some time, the *protégé*—a man so nearly white, that he was employed as chief clerk in a wholesale house—discovered the shameless cheat that had been put upon him, and abandoned his wife. Then the master took her again to his incestuous bed, and gave her a deed of manumission, which he afterward took from her and destroyed.

"And now," she added, "he has gone off, and left me and my children without any means of support."

Mrs. Butler, amazed and confounded at this tale of horror, procured her an interview with the General, to whom the story was repeated. He spoke kindly to her, but told her frankly that he could not believe the story.

"It is too much," said he, "to believe on the testimony of one witness. Does any one else know of these things?"

"Yes," she replied, "everybody in New Orleans knows them."

"I will have the case investigated," said the General; "come again in three days."

General Shipley undertook the investigation. He found that the woman's story was as true as it was notorious. The facts were completely substantiated. General Butler gave her her freedom, and assigned her an allowance from her father's estate; and, some time after, Captain Puffer, during his short tenure of power as deputy provost marshal, gave her one of the best of her father's houses to live in, by letting apartments in which she added to her income.

Mr. Parton, in giving the above narrative says: It is now a year since the outline of this story was first published to the world, but no attempt has been made, from any quarter, to controvert any part of it. And, it may be added, that Mr. Parton is not the man to make or repeat questionable statements with his pen.

### Mr. and Mrs. Grant.

It is one of the misfortunes of great personages that they must be talked about, and,—in this free country,—not always with the reverence paid to the Grand Lama. While General Grant was receiving the highest honors which a country grateful for his accumulated victories could shower upon him, Mrs. Grant showed herself to be a plain, sensible, quiet woman, who took the world as a matter of course. Some friends were talking, in her company, of the great responsibility of General Grant's position, and made some remarks tending to awaken any expression of ambition dormant in her woman's heart. No returns! She said,

"Mr. Grant," (so she always called him,) "had succeeded below, and when he was called to this position, he thought it was his duty to try what he could do."

The hope was then expressed that he would succeed, and that he would take Richmond.

Mrs. Gen. Grant.

"Well, I don't know. I think he may —Mr. Grant always was a very obstinate man." (Nobody learns *that* trait of character sooner than a wife.)

Some conversation also took place with regard to the ensuing presidential term:

"If General Grant succeeds, he may want to be President."

"But he is Lieutenant-General."

"Yes, but when a man can be elected President, it must be a strong temptation."

"I don't know. There have never been but two Lieutenant-Generals of the United States, General Washington and General Scott. There have been a number of Presidents, for instance, such men as —— and ——."

Mrs. Grant was pretty unanimously chalked down as a sensible woman, and Mr. Grant was allowed to be an "obstinate man."

### Improving on Acquaintance.

Some of the soldiers belonging to a Rhode Island Regiment in Maryland, wandered off one day to a farm-house, and commenced conversation with a woman, who was greatly frightened. They tried in vain to quiet her apprehensions. They asked for food, and she cried, "Oh, take all I have, take every thing, but spare my sick husband." "Oh," said one of the men, "we ain't going to hurt you; we want something to eat." But the woman persisted in being frightened, in spite of all efforts to reassure her, and hurried whatever food she had on the table. When, however, she saw this company stand about the table with bared heads, and a tall, gaunt man raise his hand and invoke God's blessing on the bounties spread before them, the good woman broke down with a fit of sobbing and crying. She had no longer any fears, but bade them wait, and in a few moments had made hot coffee in abundance. She then emptied their canteens of the muddy water they contained, and filled them with coffee. Her astonishment increased when they insisted upon paying her.

### Rosecrans' Orderly Sergeant Delivered of a Baby in Camp.

The following order, as unique in its way as any that the war gave rise to, can be best explained—if any further expla-

DOMESTIC, WOMANLY, HOSPITAL, PRISON, ETC. 555

nation be needed—by Major-General Rosecrans:

"HEAD-QUARTERS DEPARTMENT OF THE CUMBERLAND, April 17th, 1863.

"GENERAL:—The general commanding directs me to call your attention to a flagrant outrage committed in your command,—a person having been admitted inside your lines, without a pass and in violation of orders. The case is one which calls for your personal attention, and the general commanding directs that you deal with the offending party or parties according to law.

The medical director reports that an orderly-sergeant in Brigadier-General ———'s division *was to-day delivered of a baby,*—which is in violation of all military law and of the army regulations. No such case has been known since the days of Jupiter.

You will apply the proper punishment in this case, and a remedy to prevent a repetition of the act."

For the most complete, brilliant, and authentic narrative of the war and its scenes, in the above-named department, the "Annals of the Army of the Cumberland" must be allowed to be unsurpassed. No volume which the war has called forth, does greater honor to the talents of its author, and no soldier who served in its gallant ranks can well deprive himself of such a storehouse of the annals so memorable in national and personal history. A brave army, a popular general, and a magnificent corps of officers, well deserve commemoration, such as the "Annals, by John Fitch," gives them.

### Home Scene in the Cradle of Rebellion.

A member of one of the Charleston, (S. C.) companies, on leave of absence in the city, received a summons to appear at his post on Sullivan's Island, on one of the nights when the air was rife with the most startling rumors of the coming of an overwhelming Federal fleet. With cheerful promptitude the brave soldier prepared to obey the imperative call. He was a husband, and the father of a blue-eyed little girl, who had just begun to put words together. After the preparation for the camp had been made, the soldier nerved himself for the good-bye. Those present thought that the wife felt the parting less than the husband. Lively words flowed fast, and her fair face was as bright and calm as a morning in May. Her heart *seemed* to be full of gladness.

She cheered him with pleasant earnestness to show himself a man, and running on in a gleeful strain, admonished him *not* to come back if he were shot in the back. With incredible fortitude she bade her child tell papa good-bye, and to say to him that she would not own him her father if he proved to be a coward. The echo of the soldier's footfall through the corridor had hardly passed away, when a ghastly palor was seen spreading over the lady's face. In a voice weak and husky she begged a friend to take her child, and before she could be supported she fell from her chair prostrate on the floor.

By a tremendous effort the noble woman—still loyal at heart, perhaps, to the glorious flag her husband had been summoned to outrage—had controlled her feelings; but nature and conscience could bear the strain no longer, and she fainted. The swoon was deep, and it was sometime before consciousness returned. At length she opened her eyes languidly, and looked around upon the sympathizing group, and in a tremulous voice inquired if she had fainted before her husband left the room. Comment is unnecessary.

### Bread Cast Upon the Waters.

A Southern fugitive, colored, who had, by good fortune, arrived in Boston, from Baltimore, was one day passing through the Doric Hall, at the State House, when he recognized one of the Massachusetts soldiers who was wounded on the 19th of April, in Baltimore, and at once accosted him, inquiring after his

556        THE BOOK OF ANECDOTES OF THE REBELLION.

health, and asking him if he did not know him. The soldier did not at first remember his face, when the fugitive asked him if he did not remember a colored man bringing him water to drink, and rags to bind up his wounds, while he lay wounded in the street. He replied that he did, and at once recognized his Good Samaritan in the person of the fugitive. The peculiar circumstances of the case made the interview deeply touching. It so happened that the fugitive had a wife and two children, and when the Massachusetts soldiers fell wounded in the streets of Baltimore, the fugitive's wife tore up her clothes to make rags to stanch the flow of blood. These rags she threw out of the window in her master's house, when her husband gathered them up and carried them to the wounded soldier.

**Looking out for Hospital Accommodations.**

Before the Federal capture of Atlanta, Georgia, some of the inhabitants had the idea that no Union army would ever be able to take the city. One of these, a lady, Mrs. Zimmerman, afterward stated that she felt perfectly secure from the hands of the Yankees until the night of the evacuation, when, perfectly astonished at the change of things, she asked the Confederate General, Oglesby, how she should act in order to be safe from insult.

He answered, " Keep your mouth shut, and they will not harm you." She acted upon this advice, until one of the Union surgeons politely informed her that her large, commodious mansion was needed as a hospital, and he would find her a smaller one, which would just as well answer her purpose. Her pent-up indignation now found vent in her answer that she would prefer remaining in her own house. But she afterward respected the kindness received from the hands of the Union Soldiery, and while she took the benefit of Sherman's 'depopulating' order, and went South, that she might be near her husband, (a quartermaster in the Confederate army,) the surgeon complaisantly told her, if she made her residence in Montgomery, Alabama, to select a house suitable for hospital purposes, as he would do himself the favor to call upon her there.

**Soldiers' Offering at the Grave of Washington Irving.**

Some Massachusetts soldiers stationed at Yonkers, New York, went up the river to Tarrytown, and looked at the monument to Andre. Thence they visited the cemetery where repose the remains of the peaceful Washington Irving. A hedge is around the burial-plat. Eleven full length graves are in a row — father, mother, brothers, and sisters. One of the stones is lettered, "WASHINGTON, son of William and Sarah S. IRVING, died Nov. 29, 1859, aged 76 years, 8 months, and 25 days." The soldiers laid each a bunch of roses upon this grave, and a wreath of oak leaves, with a written inscription, "Offering of Massachusetts volunteers to the memory of Washington Irving," signed by them all, and bearing the date, was placed upon the headstone. One boy repeated the "Memory of the Dead," and all plucked a spray of clover from the grave. The graceful pen of John S. C. Abbott, the justly eminent writer,—to which we find this touching anecdote attributed,—might well weave into extended detail of fascinating narration, a war incident at once so tender, exquisite, and peculiarly American, in its characteristics. Pausing in the preparations for conflict and blood, to lay upon the tomb of the best beloved of American thinkers and writers, the sweet, womanly tribute of a leaf-bound wreath, and then, shouldering again the weapons of loyalty to the Union which Irving so much loved, returning to the camp!

**General Tilghman and his Loyal Mother.**

While General Tilghman was confined a prisoner of war at Fort Warren,

Boston, in the spring of 1862, Mrs. Tilghman, accompanied by her daughter, Mrs. Lowry, visited Boston and put up at the Revere House, for the purpose of obtaining an interview with the General, at the Fort. There was some difficulty in obtaining the required permission, but on Saturday the mother and sister were allowed to visit his quarters and enjoy the interview which they desired. The first

Gen. Tilghman.

exclamation on meeting him was, "O, my rebel son!" and during their conversation the grieved and suffering woman said: "When I heard you were taken, I thanked God that you were rescued from secession influences; and were I to bear there was any chance of your being exchanged, I would go on my knees to the President to prevent you from again joining the rebels, for I would rather have you remain here during your life than to know you were among the traitors of the country." Truly, "a foolish son is the heaviness of his mother."

### Nashville Ladies Working the Card.

The despair which must have overtaken the hearts of the secession ladies of Nashville, when that city was redeemed by Federal arms, and the "flag of glory" unfurled once more in its streets, may be judged by the pertness and contempt with which they treated the "political guild of blue-coats." Thus, when General McCook, of the Federal army, arrived in the city, he sent up his card, with the request that he might renew his former acquaintance with Miss McNairy. The following is the pert rebuff, written on the back of the card, which the lady sent the gallant soldier:

"Sir, I do not desire to renew my acquaintance with the invaders of my State."

Two other officers whose hearts were untainted with treason to their country, visited the house of Dr. Martin, and sent up their cards to his daughter, Miss Bettie Martin, requesting the renewal of an old acquaintanceship with one whom they recalled as an elegant and accomplished lady. Repairing to the parlor, with a look of ineffable scorn and contempt, she dashed the card into their faces, and said—

"Your absence, sirs, will be much better company to me than your presence."

### General Lander and the Bible.

The beautiful illustrations presented with such painstaking labor and admirable taste by Prof. H. B. Hackett, of the value of religion to the soldier, are in keeping with his own high character as a Christian philanthropist. Everybody will read, with pleasure, the incident here narrated by the excellent author named:

One day a staff officer caught General Lander with a Bible in his hand, and had the curiosity to inquire of him—

"General, do you ever search the Scriptures?" To this plain interrogatory, General Lander promptly replied:

My mother gave me a Bible, which I have always carried with me. Once in the Rocky Mountains I had only fifteen pounds of flour. We used to collect grasshoppers at four o'clock in the day, to catch some fish for our supper at night. It was during the Mormon war, and my men desired to turn back. I was then searching for a route for the wagon road. "I will turn back if the Bible says so." said I, "and we will take it for an inspiration." I opened the book at the following passage:

"Go on, and search the mountain, and the gates of the city shall not be shut against you."

All concurred in the definite statement of the passage, and the heroic explorer once more led his men into the wild country of the Indians.

Gen. Lander and his Bible.

And yet Lander was not one to boast of his devotional practices. That he was "caught" by the staff-officer was doubtless literally true,—" with a Bible in his hand," for he was not one that read his Bible "to be seen of men."

Such 'Memorials of the War' as the above, constitute, at this era, the most interesting and profitable reading for the youth of our families and Sabbath schools.

**Commission of "Major" conferred on a Lady.**

Mrs. Major Belle Reynolds, the wife of Lieutenant Reynolds, of Company A, Seventeenth Illinois regiment, distinguished herself as a brave soldier, in the war against the great rebellion. Her native place was Shelburne Falls, Massachusetts. The Seventeenth Illinois, to which her husband belonged, was one of the most popular regiments in the Western army, being one of the earliest in the field, and continuing almost uninterruptedly in active service. They met the enemy in a terrible encounter, and vanquished him, at Fredericktown, Missouri. They early took possession of Cape Girardeau; they also bore a prominent part, and were terribly cut up, at the battle of Fort Donelson, and were in the thickest of the fight at the battle of Shiloh or Pittsburg Landing. In these last two battles Lieutenant Reynolds was Acting Adjutant.

During the greater part of the campaign Mrs. Reynolds shared with her husband a soldier's fare in camp; many a night, while on long marches, sleeping upon the ground in the open air, with no covering other than her blanket, and frequently drenched with rain—and ofttimes to the order "Fall in," she would hurriedly mount her horse in the darkness of the night, and make long marches without rest or food, except what she happened to have with her. She at all times exhibited a degree of heroism that endeared her greatly to the brave soldiers of the Seventeenth and other regiments that were associated with them, and to the officers of the army whose acquaintance she formed.

Governor Yates, of Illinois, and his staff, were at Pittsburg Landing to look after the Illinois troops, who suffered so severely in that fearful struggle, and learning of Mrs. Reynolds's heroic conduct on the field, and untiring efforts in behalf of the wounded soldiers, by and with the advice of his staff, commissioned her Daughter of the Regiment, to take rank as a Major, "for meritorious conduct on the bloody battle-field of Pittsburg Landing." Mrs. R. left Pittsburg Landing a few days after the battle to attend some wounded soldiers on their way to their homes by the river, leaving the last one at Peoria—Captain Swain, of Illinois, who died as the boat touched the wharf at Peoria. On hearing of her having been commissioned by the Governor, the citizens of Peoria addressed a letter to the latter, thanking him "for the honor conferred upon Peoria by your voluntary act in commissioning Mrs. Belle Reynolds, of this city, to take rank of Major of Illinois State Militia, showing your appreciation of valuable services so nobly rendered by a lady on the bloody battle-field of Pittsburg Landing. And we take pleasure in bearing testimony to the high moral and Christian character of the 'Major,' believing that in whatever circumstances she may be placed she will ever honor her commission and the worthy Executive who gave it."

### "Whisper Good-Night, Love."

The heart of many a loyal wife and mother has been touched by the strains of that exquisite little song—"Whisper Good-Night, Love"—which was composed by a soldier the night before the battle of Stone River. Lieutenant H. Millard, of the Nineteenth United States Army, and aid-de-camp to Major-General Rousseau, was the author. On the night of the 29th December, when the division bivouacked on Stewart's Creek, Lieutenant Millard's wife bade him good-bye. They expected to go into battle next morning. Lieutenant Millard reclined on a shock of corn, looking into the blue skies, thinking of his wife,—for soldiers think of wives and little ones at such periods. His comrades were speculating on the chances of battle, now and then expressing amiable envy that Millard could sleep so soundly. Suddenly he sprang from his couch, and, calling Lieutenant Pirtle, he repeated the result of his fancies to him, in verse, which he entitled, "Whisper Good-Night, Love." Tuesday night, 30th of December, while the division was bivouacked in front of Murfreesborough, he composed and arranged the music for the piano. The next day five hundred and eight of Millard's comrades were bleeding on the field of battle. Such was the origin of a song which touched many a soldier's heart, as it also did the heart of many a loved one at home.

### Yankee Cavalry against Virginia Chivalry.

The coolness and courage with which some of the Virginia women are endowed is a fact which has been too often and too brilliantly illustrated to admit of any doubt. During the rebellion, a Union cavalry straggler, after vainly ransacking the out-buildings of a plantation in search of corn, approached the door in which a young lady was standing, and demanded that "some of the grain, which he knew was concealed in the house, should be given him." "We have none," was the reply. "Stand aside until I go in and see for myself," he rudely retorted, at the same time whipping out of its sheath a heavy Colt's revolver. No sooner done than the fair Virginian planted herself firmly in the doorway, drew a small repeater from her full and throbbing bosom, and deliberately aiming it at the intruder's head, exclaimed,

"Approach one step further towards this house and you are a dead man!"

Baffled in his endeavors by such an exhibition of bravery, the trooper turned on his heel and left, without taking that 'one step further.' He was not aware, at the time, that the maiden who thus placed such a check upon his movements was the betrothed of George B. Davis, a nephew of Jeff.'s, who discharged her pocket pistol with an accuracy which had made her famous in that locality.

### "Dick," the Four-Footed Orderly.

As we were flying about in every direction, now here, now there, (says a pleasing writer and eye-witness of what is here narrated,) with a pad for one, a basin and sponge to wet the wounds of another, cologne for a third, and milk punch for a fourth, I felt Dick (our hospital dog, my faithful friend and ally, a four-footed Vidocq, in his mode of scenting out grievances,) seize my dress in his teeth, pull it hard, and look eagerly up in my face. "What is it, Dick? I am too busy to attend to you just now." Another hard pull and a beseeching look in his eyes.

"Presently, my fine fellow! presently. Gettysburg men must come first."

He wags his tail furiously, and still pulls my dress. Does he mean that he wants me for one of them? Perhaps so. "Come, Dick, I'll go with you." He started off delighted, leads me to the ward where those worst wounded have been placed, travels the whole length of it to the upper corner, where lies a man apparently badly wounded, and crying like a child. I had seen him brought in on a stretcher, but in the confusion had not noticed where he had been taken. Dick halted as we arrived at the bed, looked at me, as much as to say, "There! isn't that a case requiring attention?" and then, as though quite satisfied to resign him into my hands, trotted quietly off.

He did not notice my approach: I therefore stood watching him a little while. His arm and hand, from which the bandage had partially slipped, were terribly swollen; the wound was in the wrist, (or rather, as I afterwards found, the ball had entered the palm of his hand and had come out at his wrist,) and appeared to be, as it subsequently proved, a very severe one.

My boast that I could make a pretty good conjecture what State a man came from by looking at him, did not avail me here. I was utterly at fault. His fair hair, Saxon face, so far as I could judge of it, as he lay sobbing on his pillow, had something feminine—almost child-like—in the innocence and gentleness of its expression, and my first thought was one which has constantly recurred on closer acquaintance, "How utterly unfit for a soldier!" He wanted the quick, nervous energy of the New Englander, who, even when badly wounded, rarely fails to betray his origin; he had none of the rough, offhand dash of our Western brothers, and could never have had it even in health; nor yet the stolidity of our Pennsylvania Germans. No! It was clear that I must wait until he chose to enlighten me as to his home. After a few minutes study, I was convinced that his tears were not from the pain of his wound; there was no contraction of the brow, no tension of the muscles, no quivering of the frame; he seemed simply very weary, very languid, like a tired child, and I resolved to act accordingly.

"I have been so busy with our defenders, this afternoon," said I, "that I have had no time to come and thank you."

He started, raised his tear-stained face, and said, with a wondering air, "To thank me? For what?"

"For what?" said I; "haven't you been keeping the rebels away from us? Don't you know that if it hadn't been for you and many like you, we might at this moment have been flying from our homes, and General Lee and his men occupying our city? You don't seem to know how grateful we are to you—we feel as though we could never do enough for our brave Gettysburg men to return what they have done for us."

This seemed quite a novel idea, and the tears were stopped to muse upon it.

"We tried to do our duty, ma'am, I know that."

"I know it too, and I think I could make a pretty good guess what corps you belong to. Suppose I try. Wasn't it the Second corps? You look to me like one of General Hancock's men; you know they were praised in the papers for their bravery. Am I right?"

The poor tired face brightened instantly. The random shot had hit the mark.

"Yes, Second Corps, do you know by my cap?"

"Your cap? You don't wear your cap in bed, do you? I haven't seen your cap; I guessed by that wound—it must have been made where there was pretty hard fighting, and I knew the Second Corps had done their share of that."

But this was dangerous ground, as I felt the moment the allusion to his wound was made; the sympathy was too direct, and his eyes filled at once. Seeing my mistake, I plunged off rapidly on another tack.

"Did you notice my assistant orderly who came in with me just now? He had been over to see you before, for he came and told me you wanted me."

"I wanted you! No, ma'am, that's a mistake; no one's been near me since they bathed me, and gave me clean clothes—I know there hasn't for I watched them running all about; but none came to me, and I want so much to have my arm dressed." And the ready tea.s once more began to flow.

"There is no mistake. I told you that my assistant orderly came to me in the ladies' room, and told me that you needed me. Think again—who has been here since you were brought in?"

"Not a single soul, ma'am—indeed, not a thing, but a dog, standing looking in my face, and wagging his tail, as if he was pitying me."

"But a dog! Exactly; he's my assistant orderly; he came over to me, pulled my dress, and wouldn't rest till I came to see you. I am surprised you speak so slightingly of poor Dick."

Here was at once a safe and fertile theme. I entered at large upon Dick's merits; his fondness for the men—his greater fondness, occasionally, for their dinners—his having made way with three lunches just prepared for the men who were starting—(the result probably of having heard the old story that the surgeons eat what is intended for the men,) our finding him one day on our table with his head in the pitcher of lemonade, and how I tried to explain to him that such was not the way of proving his regards for his friends, the soldiers, but I feared without much effect—in short, I made a long story out of nothing, till the ward-master arrived with his supper, saying that the doctor's orders were that the new cases should all take something to eat before he examined their wounds. My friend had quite forgotten his own troubles in listening to Dick's varied talents, and allowed me to give him his supper very quietly, as I found he was really too much exhausted even to raise his uninjured arm to his mouth. I had the pleasure of seeing him smile for good-bye.

### Mistook the Genus.

A young officer upon the staff of a Western General, who was temporarily sojourning at head-quarters in the Zollicoffer House, on High Street, Nashville, one day stopped before the door of a neighboring house to admire and caress a beautiful little girl. She was fair, bright, and active, her hair was in ringlets, and

Mistook the Genus.

she was neatly dressed. Imagine the emotions of the kind-hearted officer when a young lady remarked to him, with a perceptible sneer, "You seem to be very fond of kissing niggers." "Good gracious!" was the startled reply, "you don't call that child a nigger, do you?" "Yes, I do; she is nothing else." The young officer took another glance at the child, who seemed even more fair than the young lady. His reflections upon the "peculiarities of custom" may be easily imagined.

### "Lee's Miserables."

While the Federal forces were passing their winter near Brandy Station, some of the officers endeavored to relieve the *ennui* of camp life by frequent visits to the fair secesh maidens of the surrounding country. One of the staff became quite enamored with a young lady in Culpepper, more noted for her secession ideas than for her beauty. On one of his visits she requested the loan of some books, and the next day he sent over a parcel containing, among other volumes, Victor Hugo's "Les Miserables." To his surprise the orderly returned with the books, and a message from the fair one that she "didn't want any of his nasty Yankee trash." Not ex-

General R. E. Lee.

actly understanding it, he rode over in the evening to enquire what was wrong. The young lady's eyes flashed as she demanded to know how he dared to insult her by sending her a book about "Lee's Miserables." She knew that General Lee's men weren't as well dressed as the Yankees, but they weren't miserable one bit, and it was all a Yankee falsehood to say that they were.

### Last Thoughts of the Dying Boy-Soldier.

In one of the large hospitals for the sick of the Union army, surrounded by the wounded and dying, lay a mere boy. One glance at the fever-flush on his fair cheek, the unnatural brilliancy of the beautiful blue eye, together with the painfully restless movement that tossed the bright curls from his heated forehead, told with mournful certainty the tale that his hours were numbered.

Yet only a fellow-soldier sat beside him. No fond mother's or sister's hand bathed that fevered brow; and tender tones whispering words of love and comfort were wanting by the bedside of the dying lad. The physician approached him, and, used as he was to such scenes, said, sadly,

"What a pity! yesterday such a fair prospect of recovery, and to-day no chance. Poor boy!" he continued, in an under tone, "I wonder where his mother is! but she could never get here in time. Ah, well! it's fretting so much has done it."

Here the poor lad interrupted, saying, with feverish eagerness, and that pretty mingling of Scotch and English always so interesting,

"Its na' the fretting; its the vow. Sin I canna see her in the body I maun in the spirit, and before night—oh, me!"

"Delirious," said the doctor, "I feared it;" and, with an injunction to the watching soldier to let him talk on as much as he pleased, passed on—he had really no time to spend by the dying boy. Thus encouraged to talk—for the young soldier had his senses perfectly—he turned to his comrade, saying:

"Will you hear me tell it, James? It wad mak the time seem shorter to speak out what is in my head. Weel, then, I'll begin at the time when father, mither, Jessie, an I all lived in that sweet wee home awa among the Scotch mountains. We had na much, to be sure, but enough to keep oursels, and some'at to spare for our poorer neighbors. Jessie was a very bonnie lass, older than mysel by some years, and it was na long till she was promised to the minister of the place. A nice young man was he, and all the country round was glad when it was known. It cam Jessie's birthday just three months before the wedding-day. She was very sad, an kep saying how happy she had been at home, an how na ither spot cou'd ever be to her what it had been; an then, in the middle of the dancing an fun, she up an threw her arms round my mither's neck, an vowed that always, on that evening, so lang as my mither was alive, she would come—whether 'in the body or in the spirit,' she would never fail. 'Twas a wild word for her to speak, an' many o' the neighbors shook their heads as they heard, an the talk went round the town that Jessie Graeme had bound hersel by sich a strange vow."

Here the boy paused from extreme exhaustion, and, as he rested for a few moments, seemed to be looking at something very far off; then, rousing himself, said—

"I maun be short; it is near the time. Jessie was married, an our hearts were just as glad as children; till one day word cam that Jessie an her husband were drowned. In crossing a little loch to visit some sick folk the boat must 'a overturned, for it was found floating; but we never saw them again. Oh! 'twas a bitter time. My mither fretted much; for, though she kenned it true, she could na think of our bonnie lassie lying dead an' cold in her husband's arms, on the stanes at the bottom o' the loch. My father fretted too. He wad na think that she was dead, but kep saying she wad soon be back to gladden our hearts once mair; but she never cam; an we three, wi' sickening hearts, waited for her birthday; we kenned right weel that, dead or alive, her promise wad be kep. The night cam, an we sat wi' open door an curtain drawn from the window (for when they come i' the spirit it's only through the window they can look). We three by the bright fire sat waiting for the first sound o' her footstep. I heard it first, as, wi' the water dripping from her clothes, she cam swiftly up the walk, an, putting aside the rose-bush, looked in—only for one moment; then she was gone; but by that we kenned she was dead. It seemed to comfort my mither; so that, when I left soon after to come here, I made the same vow, 'that so long as my mither lived, whether in the body or in the spirit, I wad, on the same night, stand by Jessie's side'; and I maun," he added, his eyes brightening, and a cold damp gathering on his brow. "Does no one see? Don't you hear the water dripping frae her dress? My mither, wi' her long gray hair! See, she is putting the roses awa. How cold an clammy her hand is! It is dark!"

With these words, he fell back lifeless

Bodies laid out

on the bed. In awe-struck silence his eyes were closed, and the cheeks of the bravest paled at the thought that the spirit they had so loved and revered for unfailing tenderness and true courage might be, at that moment, standing by the sister it had so dearly loved, looking through the casement on the home and parents of their childhood, while the beautiful frame it had inhabited lay motionless before them.

---

**Great Day's Work for a Scout,—the Misses Scott.**

The ladies of Virginia and Maryland showed themselves to be, as a rule, fiercer in their secessionism than the men, and by their aid many a disaster was brought upon the Union cause, and the gallant officers and men engaged in its defence. In the summer of 1861, two young ladies of the name of Scott, residents of Fairfax County, Virginia, were the means of capturing the Captain of a volunteer regiment from Connecticut. They were at last taken themselves, in the following manner, by a scouting party who were earnestly in pursuit of the two in question.

After getting out of the woods, the party came to a cornfield, and crawling through it on their hands and knees, came at last to a house, which they visited in order to get what information they could. They found an old man, and asked him if any Federal troops were there. He, in return, wanted to know if they were on the Southern side. Lieutenant Upton told him " Yes ;" when he told them they were about a mile from the Union tents, and to look out sharp or they would be captured. The party of course appeared frightened, and posted a man outside to keep a keen watch. Lieutenant Upton told him he was an officer of a South Carolina regiment. The old man then told him all about the United States camp, the names of all the secession neighbors, and finally said he had in his house the two Miss Scotts who took the Yankee Captain,—the old man conducting them into the room and introducing them to the Miss Scotts.

That moment was a blessed one indeed to the scouting party, for right in their hands were those whom the whole brigade had been hunting for. But the gallant Federals continued to play their part, complimenting the ladies highly for their feat, and pumping the old man for more information. After learning the most direct route to the Union camp, Lieutenant Upton told them he and his party must go, but still he would like to see the whole family together to bid them good-bye. Accordingly they all came out in the front porch—the old man, his wife, three sons, and daughter, and the two Miss Scotts.

The party simply formed a circle around the gathered household, when Lieutenant Upton, drawing his sword, demanded their surrender to the United States. No pen could describe the blank and utter astonishment, wonder and heart-sinkings, exhibited at this moment. The two Miss Scotts and the young men were all that were taken along. The excitement was very great when the party went into camp; and in the evening the party was sent for by the General in command, who complimented them highly for their conduct.

### Conditional Offer of his Autograph by General Grant.

The ladies sojourning at Willard's caravansory in Washington beset General Grant, in the true style of their sex, on one of his rare visits to Washington, that they might obtain an autograph from the hand which then held the nation's sword. Partaking of the enthusiasm of the hour, a whole bevy of them congregated in the principal suite of parlors in the hotel, and signified by a messenger to General Grant, who was a guest of the house, that they desired an interview with him. The General came down from his quarters, and a very pleasant levee was held by him. Many of the ladies succeeded by their dexterous and insinuating *modus operandi* in getting the General's autograph,—the object which was so eagerly sought for. In the course of the interview, an elderly lady applied to the General for an autograph, in behalf of a handsome mother of six children who was present; but when his sharp military eye fell upon the applicant, he immediately stipulated that she should make the request in person. She did so, and immediately received the coveted bit of handwriting.

### Unrequited Gallantry in a New Orleans Street Car.

It was a long time before the dainty hauteur of the New Orleans ladies could yield with any decent degree of flexibility to the rising star of General Butler and his Union associates, and many a look and act of lofty defiance were the latter made the recipients of. One evening, a Federal officer—a very handsome man, by the way, and, therefore, a little vain—happened to be in a street railway car, wherein were also two ladies, evidently belonging to the first classes of the Crescent city. One of them dropped her lace pocket handkerchief—he, the officer, stooped most gallantly, and handed it to her. She looked at him with unmeasured contempt, and said, "Do you suppose I will touch anything contaminated by *your* touch?" That insult restored his manhood and his patriotism, which had fairly melted under the bright eyes of the Creole beauty; he took up the handkerchief with the smallest possible touch, as if he felt its possession by her had been a contamination, opened the car window, deliberately dropped it in the street, and sat down. The lady's brusqueness had been more than matched.

### Appointment of Burnside as a Cadet.

About twenty years ago, one of the members of President Lincoln's cabinet—Secretary Smith,—was a member of Congress from a distant Western State. He had the usual right of designating a single candidate for admission to the West Point Military Academy. The applications made to him for a vacancy which then existed were not many, but among them was a letter from a boy of sixteen or seventeen years of age, who, without any accompanying recommendations or references, asked the appointment for himself. The member dismissed the appeal from his mind, with perhaps a passing thought of the forwardness and impudence of the stripling who could aspire to such a place on no other grounds than his desire to get a good education at the public expense.

But happening a short time afterward to be in the little village whence the letter was mailed, the incident was recalled to his memory, and he thought he would beguile the few hours of leisure that he had by looking up the ambitious youth. He made his way, by dint of much inquiry, to a small tailor's shop on the outskirts of the town, and when he was admitted at the door he found a lad sitting cross-legged

Head-quarters of General Burnside, at Roanoke Island.

upon the tailor's bench, mending a rent in an old pair of pantaloons. But this lad had another occupation besides his manual toil. Near by, on a small block of wood, rested a book of abstruse science, to which he turned his eyes whenever they could be transferred from the work in his hands. The member accosted him by the name given in the letter, and the lad replied " I am the person." " You wish, then, to be appointed a cadet at West Point?" "I do," he rejoined. "Why?" asked the Congressman. "Because," answered the tailor youth, " I feel that I was born for something better than mending old clothes." The member talked further with him, and was so well pleased with his frankness, his spirit, and the rare intelligence he evinced, that he procured him the appointment.

Name of the member, Caleb Smith. Name of the appointee, Ambrose E. Burnside. This reminiscence was one which Burnside's comrades at head-quarters (when the cadet had risen to be General,) not unfrequently recounted with a hearty zest, and it doubtless did not fail to cross the memory of the gallant General himself.

### Lizzie's Mark on the Handkerchief.

In one of the hospitals of the Union army in Virginia, there was a young fellow, severely though not painfully wounded. Seeing some clean linen rag-stuff which one of the doctors had left on the floor a little distance off, he asked an attendant to tear him off a piece that would serve for the purpose of a pocket handkerchief. Thinking the surgeon might have set apart the linen for some special use, and preferring in any case to give him a *bona fide* handkerchief, if there was one left, the attendant felt in his pocket, and there at its bottom was the last of his small store. It was rather a nice affair; the cambric not of the finest, but with quite a stylish border round its edge, and he pronounced it "bully," as it was handed to him. The outside fold had, as usual, the Commission's stamp, but it soon appeared that there was still another mark upon it; for he had scarcely unfolded it and held it out for an admiring inspection, before he uttered quite a shriek of delight, and asked the attendant if he knew his folks at home, and if they had given him the handkerchief to be thus handed. It appeared that besides the mark of the Commission, there was marked in thread the name of the relief society in his native place, and the poor fellow gave sundry reasons for his positive assertion that the marking must have been done by none other than the hands of his little sister Lizzie. Of course such a discovery delighted him.

### Birth of Boys and Girls in War Times.

One of the "strong minded" women of New York city—one noted for the acuteness as well as accuracy of her observations of life and society—bore her testimony to a remarkable physiological fact, owing to moral causes, and which is at least worthy of being recorded. She affirmed, after close investigation, that of the births which took place in New York, during the war, those which occurred in families whose attachment to the Union was decided and zealous, were mostly boys, while in families in which there was a decided sympathy for the secession cause, they were mostly girls. Of course, every one's observation or knowledge would furnish them to instances confirming such a statement, or showing it to be a mistake. It has often been said that in countries wasted by long wars, carrying off the male population, there was a large predominance of male births.

### Agreeable Reciprocity of Union Sentiment.

As the ladies in one of the Union Sanitary establishments were one evening at their tea, a Confederate prisoner came in and stated that a sick comrade wanted "something good—some fruit." One of the ladies was just about eating a saucer of raspberries, and turning to the messenger she handed them to him, saying:

"Take these to him, and tell him they come from a *good Union lady*, who deprives herself of them to give them to a Confederate soldier."

In a short while the messenger returned with the saucer, bearing the following message from the recipient of the lady's kindness:

"He wished *they* were *united*."

### Wedding-Table Flag at Pensacola.

On the night of the arrival of Union troops at Pensacola, two or three of the private soldiers were taking a stroll, and during this walk were met by a very fine-looking lady, who immediately grasped one of the party by the hand, and seemed so overjoyed that for a moment she could say nothing. At last she told them how happy she was at their arrival, and that she had long prayed for the coming of that day; then, taking a small silk American flag from her bosom, she presented it to one of them, saying, "For nine months I have carried this flag hidden on my person, praying that an opportunity like this would present itself, that I might offer it to a Union soldier. This flag graced my wedding table, and I love it and every soldier that fights for it." The husband of this lady was obliged to fly for his life on account of his Union principles.

### Girl-Boy Soldier in the Ninetieth Illinois.

Frances Hook's parents died when she was only three years old, and left her, with a brother, in Chicago, Illinois. Soon after the war commenced, she and her brother enlisted in the Sixty-fifth "Home Guards." Frances assumed the name of "Frank Miller." She served three months and was mustered out, without the slightest suspicion of her sex having arisen. She then enlisted in the Ninetieth Illinois, and was taken prisoner in a battle near Chattanooga. She attempted to escape and was shot through the calf of one of her limbs while said limbs were doing their duty in the attempt. The rebels searched her person for papers and discovered her sex. The rascals respected her person as a woman, and gave her a separate room while in prison at Atlanta, Ga. During her captivity she received a letter from Jeff. Davis, offering her a Lieutenant's commission if she would enlist in their army. She had no home and no relatives, but she said she preferred to fight as a private soldier for the stars and stripes rather than be honored with a commission from the "rebs." At last she was exchanged. The insurgents tried to extort from her a promise that she would go home, and not enter the service again. "Go home;" she said, "my only brother was killed at Pittsburg Landing, and I have no home—no friends!" Frank is described as of about medium height, with dark hazel eyes, dark brown hair, rounded features, and feminine voice and appearance.

### Independent Southern Girls.

One of the rebel papers, in publishing the marriage of a young lady, took occasion to give her the recommendation of being what might be called, sure enough, an independent girl. Her bridal outfit was made all with her own hands, from her 'beautiful and elegant straw hat, down to the handsome gaiters upon her feet. Her own delicate hands spun and wove the material of which her wedding dress and traveling cloak were made, so that she had nothing upon her person when she was married which was not made by herself. Nor was she compelled by poverty or necessity to make this exhibition of her independence. She did it for the purpose of showing to the world how independent Southern girls are.'

### Special Aid to General Hunter.

Quite a sensation was created in Jefferson City, Missouri, one evening, by the arrival of Mrs. Colonel Ellis, from Tipton, bearer of dispatches from General Hunter and Colonel Ellis. She was dressed in semi-military riding-habit and hat, with a crimson sash thrown around the left shoulder, as an officer of the day, mounted on a splendid charger, and attended by two orderlies. She had ridden forty-five miles since ten o'clock, and, without taking a moment's rest, delivered her orders at camp, and then waited upon General Price with her dispatches, urging forward two squadrons of Colonel Ellis's command, to join the regiment at Tipton. This *mulier valiente* was attached to the First Missouri Cavalry, as special aid to her husband, Colonel Ellis.

### Love Greetings to the Soldiers.

Some of the marks which were fastened on the blankets, shirts, etc, which were sent to the Sanitary Commission for the soldiers, show the thought and feeling at home. Thus, on a home-spun blanket, warm, and washed as white as snow, was pinned.

a bit of paper, which said, "This blanket was carried by Milly Aldrich (who is 93 years old) down hill and up hill, one and a half miles, to be given to some soldier."

On a bed-quilt was pinned a card, saying—"My son is in the army. Whoever is made warm by this quilt, which I have worked on for six days and most all of six nights, let him remember his own mother's love."

On another blanket was this—"This blanket was used by a soldier in the war of 1812—may it keep some soldier warm in this war against traitors!"

On a pillow was written—"This pillow belonged to my little boy, who died resting on it; it is a precious treasure to me, but I give it for the soldiers."

On a pair of woolen socks was written—"These stockings were knit by a little girl five years old, and she is going to knit some more, for mother says it will help some poor soldier."

On a box of beautiful lint was this mark, "Made in a sick room, where the sunlight has not entered for nine years, but where God has entered, and where two sons have bid their mother good-bye, as they have gone out to the war."

On a bundle containing bandages was written—"This is a poor gift, but it is all I had; I have given my husband and my boy, and only wish I had more to give."

On some eye-shades were marked—"Made by one who is blind. Oh, how I long to see the *dear old flag* that you are fighting for!"

### Mrs. Wade, the Loyal Bread-Baker at Gettysburg.

One of the most touching episodes of the invasion of Pennsylvania, when Lee was met and discomfited at Gettysburg, was the following: Before the battle of Friday, while our forces awaited assault, a woman named Wade was engaged in baking bread for our troops in a house situated directly in range of the guns of both armies. The rebels had repeatedly ordered her to quit the premises, but she had invariably refused to do so. At length the battle opened, and while still engaged in her patriotic work a ball pierced her loyal breast, and she fell. Curiously enough, almost at the same moment a rebel officer of high rank fell near the place where Mrs. Wade had perished. The rebels, obtaining the body of the officer, immediately constructed a rude coffin in which to inter him; but it is recorded, that hardly was it finished, when, in the surging of the conflict, a federal column occupied the ground. The woman's body, discovered by our troops, was at once placed in the coffin awaiting an occupant; and so, as witnesses love still to testify, finally was buried, amidst the tears of hundreds who knew the story of her valor and kindheartedness. No class in the world are more appreciating of woman's good offices to them than soldiers, whether in the camp or in the hospital, in health or in sickness. Mrs. Wade was one of the noblest of her sex. Peace to her goodly memory.

### Pointed Rebuke from a Soldier's Death-bed.

Among the wounded at the battle of Stone River, in Tennessee,—a scene wor-

Monument at Stone River.

thily commemorated by an enduring monument,—was a young man. Over the mortally wounded son hung the anxious mother, in the deepest sorrow that he gave no evidence of fitness for eternal scenes. But the words the dying youth uttered, severely as they condemned himself, showed clearly his dying convictions. To an appeal from a religious friend, he replied,—" If I live to get well, I will be a Christian; but I will not throw the fag-end of my life in the face of the Almighty." He immediately expired. The poor fellow certainly mistook the gospel mode of salvation, for faith in Christ can avail in other cases as it did with the dying thief in his last moments. The 'fag-end' of his life was distinguished by an act which opened to him the gates of Paradise. The time may indeed be short, but much may be done often in a short time. The striking language of the dying soldier, however, contains a stinging rebuke, worthy of pretty general remembrance, and especially by those who practically claim the best of life for themselves, while they venture to put off their Maker with the little that remains when they are about to sink into the grave.

### Solution of a Problem peculiarly Southern.

A pleasant and not uninstructive incident occurred one morning in Vicksburg, at the expense of a gallant young soldier. He was prospecting around town, when his attention was attracted to a stable of very fine horses. While admiring their nice points, he was surprised by the appearance of a very fascinating young lady, as she emerged from another apartment of the horse-house, and bowed politely, and smiled killingly upon him. He stammered out something like an apology for his seeming intrusion, mixing up the words "proclamation" and "confiscation," etc., and ended by asking who was the owner of the place?

"Dr. Neely," replied the lady.

"And you—you are his wife?" asked the soldier doubtfully.

"No," said the lady.

"Then his daughter?"—this was said very smilingly.

"No."

"His niece, perhaps?"—endearingly.

"No; no relation, that I know of."

"Then a lady friend, on a visit?"—puzzlingly.

"No, not that, either."

"Well, then, may I be permitted to ask who you are?"

"Certainly," replied the lady, who had enjoyed the soldier's discomfiture with a piquant relish; "I am his slave!"

### Proof against Federal Gallantry.

One or two rebel victories at Bull Run are matters pretty generally known. Of any female victories, however, in that region, somewhat less has been told. A

Proof against Federal Gallantry.

certain Union Colonel, a staff officer of one of our Generals, noted for his talent at repartee, and for the favorable opinion which he entertained of his own good looks, stopped at the house of a farmer, and discovered there a fine milch cow, and, still better, a pretty girl, attired in a neat calico dress, cut low in the neck and short in the sleeves. After several unsuccessful attempts to engage the young lady in conversation, he proposed to her to have the cow milked for his own special benefit. This she indignantly refused. The Colonel, not wishing to compromise his reputation for gallantry, remarked that if all the young ladies in Virginia were as beautiful as the one he had the pleasure of addressing, he had no desire to conquer the Confederacy. With a toss of her pretty head and a slight but most expressive elevation of her nose, she answered thus: "Well, sir, if all the gentlemen in your army are as ugly as you are, we ladies have no desire to conquer *them!*"

How are you, Colonel?

### Doubtful Loyalty, Political and Matrimonial.

Kansas City is a gay place, and they have queer specimens of humanity down there. If there should exist any doubt on this subject, the following case in point, about a woman of doubtful loyalty who was brought before the Provost Marshal, will help to confirm the assertion. This woman gave as an evidence of her loyalty that her husband had been killed in the One Hundred and Sixth Illinois regiment. "When did your husband go to Illinois?" "About three years ago." "That was before the war, was it not?" "Yes." "Why did you not go to Illinois with him?" "Well, I didn't like to go off so far with a man I wasn't much acquainted with." "You don't mean to say that your own husband was so much of a stranger that you did not like to go with him?" "Yes, I do. I had only been married to him about a year, and I wasn't going to leave my folks and go off to Illinois with a man I didn't know more about." What *could* the Marshal do to get such a case off his hands but to discharge her,—though, estimating her loyalty to her country by that to her husband, she was a somewhat doubtful patriot.

### The Bloody Flag of Fort Pillow.

The widow of Major Booth, formerly commander at Fort Pillow, and who was killed there, having arrived at Fort Pickering, below Memphis, Colonel Jackson of the Sixth United States Heavy Artillery had his regiment formed into line for her reception. In front of its centre stood fourteen men, as fine, brave fellows as ever trod the earth. They were the remnant of the First battalion of the regiment now drawn up—all who had escaped the fiendish scenes at Pillow.

Mrs. Booth came forward. In her hand she bore a flag, red and clotted with human blood. She took a position in front of the fourteen heroes, so lately under her deceased husband's command. The ranks before her observed a silence that was full of solemnity. Many a hard face showed by twitching lips and humid eyes how the sight of the bereaved lady touched bosoms that could meet steel almost unmoved, and drew on the fountain of tears that had remained dry even amid the pitiless sights of a terrific battle. Turning to the men before her, she said: "Boys, I have just come from a visit to the hospital at Mound City. There I saw your comrades wounded at the bloody struggle in Fort Pillow. There I found this flag—you recognize it! One of your comrades saved it from the insulting touch of traitors. I have given to my country all I had to give—my husband—such a gift! Yet I have freely given him for freedom and my country. Next to my husband's cold remains, the dearest object left to me in the world is this flag—the flag that waved in proud defiance over the works of Fort Pillow! Soldiers! this flag I give to you, knowing that you will ever remember the last words of my noble husband, '*Never surrender the flag to traitors.*'"

Colonel Jackson then received from her hand—on behalf of his command—the blood stained flag. He called upon the regiment to receive it as such a gift ought to be received. At that call he and every man of the regiment fell upon their knees, and solemnly appealing to the God of battles, each one swore to avenge their brave and fallen comrades, and never—'*Never surrender the flag to traitors.*'

### Maiden Loveliness at Culpepper.

Some—but happily not all—of the women of Virginia, were positively hideous in their fierce secession sentiments. For instance, when the Union army was retreating through that hot-bed of rebellion, Culpepper, a young girl stood at her father's door and gave utterance to her feelings in this wise: "You're falling back again, you Yankee cut-throats and robbers, are you? I now shall see my 'Bonnie Blue Flag' again"—(here she sang a verse of that song in a shrill, hyena key,)—"you ought to paint a black wench on your dirty Star Draggled Banner, and a Yankee horse-thief embracing her."

### Southern Female Chivalry.

As Colonel Lander was riding ahead of his troops, down the road and reconnoitering, on the way to Phillippi, he came to a house by the road-side, where the woman was up, when, Yankee-like, he began to question her about the number of secessionists in the neighborhood. She wanted to know what side he belonged to. He replied by asking if she supposed he would be in that neighborhood if he did not want to join the secessionists. He learned from her that the rebels had no artillery. Before he returned from his reconnoissance of the town of Phillippi the woman had discovered her mistake, and had a pistol in hand for him, which she discharged at his person, without any damage, however. He took off his hat and bowed to her very gallantly, and begged her not to shoot at his men, as they would kill her. Just then the advance of his reconnoitering party came up, when he ordered a couple of them to seize the woman's son, a lad of about seventeen, to prevent him informing the enemy of their approach. The boy was immediately seized, when the mother came at them with an axe and the fury of a savage, and they had to let the boy go to defend themselves, when he took to the woods and was soon lost to sight. As the main body of troops marched by, she fired her pistol at them also, but without effect, her door receiving in return some half-dozen rifle ball perforations, to remind her that shooting was a dangerous business.

### Fine Trap but no Game.

Mrs. Mills was a genuine Virginia specimen of her sex, and her husband was absent in the Confederate army, of which he was an officer. One day she was visited by two Federal officers, (Quartermaster S. and Commissary B.) who were on a foraging excursion. Mrs. Mills received them in a most bewitchingly friendly manner, spread out a glorious dinner, and offered to sell them oceans of milk and bushels of cherries. With a pleasant smile she invited them into the house, setting chairs for their accommodation. Nothing loth, the two officials entered, and after some pressing consented to unsaddle their horses and turn them out to graze. Nothing could exceed the politeness of Mrs. Mills. She was so glad they had come, and so fearful that their long ride, under a scorching sun, might have fatigued them. And were they not hungry? Wouldn't they allow her to set out something for them to eat? She was so sorry their camp was so distant, for nothing would delight her more than to send them strawberries and milk, and cherries, and everything which her garden could furnish. She thought the Union soldiers were such gentlemen—so gallant and brave—and so considerate towards the poor Virginians who had lost their all in this sorrowful war. And couldn't they stay to dinner, and allow her to treat them with true Virginia hospitality?

Such a loving reception extended by the wife of a secession soldier to two perfect strangers, was so very unlike other earthly things, and so very like the concluding chapters of the "yeller kivered," that it astonished our soldier friends. The commissary looked at the quartermaster, and the quartermaster, thinking he detected a wink in B.'s eye, returned it, and both together they entered the house. With many thanks and protestations that nothing was further from their intention than to give trouble, they took seats, and whilst the lady bustled about to prepare dinner, had time to look about them.

They were in a cleanly, well kept Virginia log-house, with old-fashioned furniture; and were evidently partaking of the hospitalities of a lady of cultivated manners and excellent understanding. Their ride had been a long and troublesome one, and their hearts were almost melted in gratitude towards their fair benefactress. A few moments sufficed for the preparation of the meal, and the lady, placing chairs at the table, invited them to be seated.

Of course, nothing on that humble board could, in her estimation, suit the epicurean palates of two such gallant officers of the Union army. Her bread she was afraid was too heavy, and her butter too soft. Her milk had soured, and, she was almost ashamed to tell it, but the very last piece of fresh meat had been eaten that very morning, and she had nothing but ham to offer the gentlemen,—but then the ham had been of her father's own raising, and she knew they would like it. Perhaps they would taste some of her early cherries and strawberries, and asparagus, too; but no, the cherries were under, and the strawberries over ripe, and that good-for-nothing wench that did the cooking had left the asparagus too long on the fire, and it was boiled all to pieces. She knew the gentlemen wouldn't like it. And her potatoes, too, she had taken such pains with them, and just to think how sodden they were—oh, it was awful!

"My dear madam," broke in the polite quartermaster, "pray don't apologise any more. The meal is excellent. I haven't ever sat down to a better. Have you, B?"

"No, indeed," said the commissary; "why, at home, I never had anything like it. Salt pork and small potatoes are all we get up in our country."

The lady was terribly afraid that the gentlemen were not being suited, and that they really thought her dinner a poor one, "but then you know," she added with a smile, "I am doing my best, and if I could do better I would."

"Of course," said the quartermaster.

"Of course," echoed the commissary.

"And if my butter is soft it is not my fault, is it?"

"Oh, certainly not," exclaimed both in concert.

The lady was so bewitching, that for two hours the guests sat at her table, eating and talking. The quartermaster made the apologies, and the commissary adroitly put the questions. The fair rebel no doubt thought she had effectually caught the two simple hearted gentlemen who sat meekly before her, and glorying in the triumph which afternoon would bring, were slightly unguarded.

"I believe, madam, that your husband is in the Confederate army," said B; "you must be very lonely without him."

"Oh, no—not with such good company as you are, and then, besides, I hear from him every two or three days, and he tells me all what is going on. Only a day or two ago I had word from him."

The quartermaster treasured this up, and the commissary, looking ten times more simple-hearted than previously, ejaculated, "How very nice!"

"Yes, and he says that Beauregard's army, or a good part of it, at least, is at Richmond, and that soon the enemy will be driven from about here, and then he can come and see me whenever he wants to."

The quartermaster took a mouthful of water, and the commissary said, "Indeed!" After a pause, he ventured to ask—

"But, madam, suppose your husband should be shot; how would you take it?"

DOMESTIC, WOMANLY, HOSPITAL, PRISON, ETC. 573

"Oh, never you mind her," broke in B., "she knows very well that if he's killed, I will come down here and marry her."

"Your northern gentlemen are so kind," said the lady, "why, I never did see a finer set of fellows, and every one unmarried, too. How strange!"

"Not strange at all," said the quartermaster, "because only single men come to war, the married ones staying at home to take care of their wives."

The lady thought a moment, and replied—

"I wish that was the case with us. I was so sorry to lose my husband, and he was so sorry to go. Only the other day he was here, and some rough men came along and forced him to leave."

"Don't cry about it," said kind-hearted B., as the lady's tears began to come, "you know very well I'll make it all right for you, if he's taken prisoner."

"Will you?"

"Oh, yes; you see my friend here is a quartermaster, and his sister knows a young man that was present at Gen. McClellan's wedding, and I, too, frequently write letters to him, and he will do anything for me. Why, only the other day, I sent him a letter asking him for a barrel of whiskey, putting 'commissary' after my name, so that he would know it was me, and he sent it to me right away."

"Did he?"

"Yes, and there's no end to the boxes of crackers and barrels of pork, and barrels of sugar and coffee, and boxes of candles and cheese, he sends me, for myself and friends, and when his wagons—you know he keeps three or four—are doing something else, why, my friend, the quartermaster, jumps aboard his, and drives over, and handing the servant a piece of paper from me, comes back with lots of them. Why, the General will do anything for me."

The lady appeared as if she thought she had found a friend, indeed, and gave him her husband's name and regiment. B. took it down, and said if the old gentleman was taken, he would send him over to her "as soon as he could." Just as soon as she saw a man coming along the road with her husband, she might believe it was he coming back.

They sat talking for a long time, each one becoming more interested in the other, until the quartermaster espied a Federal horseman galloping along the road in front of the house. His manner was excited, and the lady suddenly turning towards the door, muttered, "Have they found out so soon what our friends are about?" Neither of the officers changed countenance, as they were fully prepared for what was coming, and had not rode three miles outside the Federal lines to be gulled by any female manœuvres. The commissary continued talking, and after a moment the quartermaster went out, and leading the horses to a point where the lady could not see the movements, briskly saddled them. The work was finished, and he re-entered the house, joining in the conversation as if nothing was suspected.

"But, Mrs. Mills," said he, after a moment's small talk, "haven't you any milk or butter you could sell us? I almost forgot it, but we came here to buy something for the starving fellows at the camp."

Had he seen the starving fellows at camp about this time, perhaps he would not have talked so placidly about them. The telegraph line had signalled danger to them, and with it came the order to prepare for a fight. 'Where is the quartermaster and commissary?' was heard on all sides. They had been gone since early morning, and here, at four o'clock, they had not returned. 'The enemy advancing in force,' had been signalled from the very direction in which they had gone, and their long absence was a sure indication that they had been captured. Heavy bets were staked against it. 'I'll bet two and a half to one they're taken,' cried a Colonel. 'Take it!' said a major, 'they've got fast horses, and can go a streak.' Every one was anxious.

But, with minds far from anxiety, our two officers still staid with Mrs. Mills, procuring all sorts of dainties, and filling their bags and baskets with them. They rose finally, however, saying they must be going, and the commissary took out his pocket-book to pay for the articles they had bought. He flourished its contents very considerably, and the lady higgled about the change, and couldn't calculate, and had no dimes or quarters, and must go up stairs for some small money. B. didn't object, but winked to the quartermaster, who brought up the horses, and they both mounted.

"Mrs. Mills," shouted he, "I have the right money—here it is."

Down stairs came the lady, and sought to engage them in conversation again. She reluctantly took the money, and, finding that they would go, was at loss for further means of detention. But hospitality came to her aid, and she asked them to dinner next day. Of course they consented, and, thanking her, arranged what dainties were to be provided. Two minutes more settled that point, and as they bade her Good-bye, a shadow passed over her countenance. They walked their horses leisurely to the road, and, looking behind them, each one clapped the spur deep into his horse's side, and with lightning speed they galloped off.

Five minutes afterwards a secession troop came riding by, some stopping at the house to hunt for Unionists! Mrs. Mills had set a fine trap, but lost her game.

The above spirited sketch, though floating as a waif upon the tide of newspaper reading, sounds so much like the effusions of 'Sentinel,' of the New York World, and Mr. Shanks, of the New York Herald, that, even if not due to one or the other of the writers named, they may truthfully be spoken of as having laid the country under no slight obligation for the vast amount of information which, from the various seats of war, they daily communicated to their respective journals. Finer specimens of reportorial aptness, vivacity, and felicitous narrative, are seldom met with, whether in newspapers or books, in times of war or of peace. "Camp-Fire and Cotton-Field," by Mr. Thos. W. Knox, one of the reportorial staff of the Herald, deserves special commendation, as being altogether unsurpassed for its panoramic views of the Great War and all those various side scenes and occurrences which constitute the most piquant feature in war narratives.

### Old Hannah and the Restored Soldier.

The hospitals in Jefferson City, Missouri, were at one time in the most fearful condition imaginable. One poor fellow, as he stated to a visitor, had lain there sick on the hard boards, and seen five men carried away dead, one after the other, from his side. He was worn to a skeleton; worn through so that great sores were all over his back, and filthy beyond telling.

Old Hannah.

One day, old Hannah, a black woman who had some washing to do for a doctor, went down the ward to hunt him up. She saw, on her way, this dying man, and had compassion on him, saying, "O, doctor! let me bring to the man my bed, to keep him off the floor." The doctor said, "The man is dying; he will be dead to-morrow." To-morrow came, and old Hannah could not rest. She went to see the man, and he was still alive. Then she got some help, took her bed, put the man on it, and carried him bodily to her shanty; then she washed him all over, as a woman would a baby, and fed him with a spoon, and fought death hand to hand day and night, and beat him back and saved the soldier's life, so that he was soon going on a furlough to his home in Indiana. He besought Hannah to go with him, but she could not spare time—there was all that washing to do. She went with him to the steamboat, got him fixed to her mind, and then she kissed him, and the man lifted up his voice as she left him and wept like a child.

### Hard Tack for the Fifth Excelsior.

Hard bread, or as it has generally been called in camp, 'hard tack,' is the soldier's food on a campaign. It comes in square wooden boxes, on which different makers put their various distinguishing brands. One day a lot of *peculiarly* hard arrived in the camp of the Fifth Excelsior. Several of the boys were wondering the meaning of the brand upon the boxes, which was as follows: B. C., 603; the figures being immediately beneath the initials. Va-

Familiar Soldier Scenes.

rious interpretations were surmised, but all rejected, until one individual who was then in the act of attempting to masticate a piece, declared it was plain enough—"couldn't be misunderstood." "Why, how so?" was the query. "Oh!" he replied, "that is the date when the crackers were made—six hundred and three years before Christ." (603 B. C.)

### Army Matrimonial Advertisements—Hint to Romantic Young Ladies.

As to who the matrimonial advertisers in the army were—some of them, at least, —the following, which was sent to a Philadelphia paper, will serve as a sample. If

576    THE BOOK OF ANECDOTES OF THE REBELLION.

the gallant writer was as hard on the secessionists as he is upon Noah Webster and Lindley Murray, he was a soldier who deserved to be rewarded with as good a wife as his "advertisement" could scare up:—

*Messer Editer :*—If you pleas stick an advertisement in your paper for me, as I have been in the army for a good while, and like to have something to cheer up with in time of truble, and I am the son of a very welthy farmer, and have no bad hapit, such as useing profane language and drinking and useing tobacco; and I would like to open a correspondince with some intelligent young lady, photograph exchanged if desired, and I have went through a number of hard battles, and I want you to put it up the way you think best, and my address is

E. J. G.
93d O. V. I., 2d Brig., 3d Div., 4th A. C.,
via Nashville, Tennessee.

Now I want you to stick in a gay advertisement.

### Record of a Loyal Family: Five Martyr Sons.

In November, 1864, the Boston papers published a communication from Adjutant General Schouler, of Massachusetts, in which he mentioned the case of a Boston lady, a widow, who had had five sons killed in the war, and who was in rather poor circumstances. The lady was about sixty years of age, residing in Ward Eleven. In response to the General's letter a considerable amount of money was received for soldiers' families, and some was sent especially for the lady to whom allusion was made. General Schouler visited her and left the money, and made sure that the afflicted woman had everything comfortable for Thanksgiving.

The names of the five martyr sons are as follows: Sergeant Charles N. Bixby, Company D, Massachusetts Twentieth regiment, killed at Fredericksburg, May 3d, 1863; Corporal Henry Bixby, Company K, Thirty-second regiment, killed at Gettysburg, July 3d, 1863; private Edward Bixby, Twenty-second regiment, died of wounds in the hospital at Folly Island, South Carolina; private Oliver Cromwell Bixby, Company E, Fifty-eighth regiment, killed before Petersburg, July 30th, 1864; private George Way Bixby, Company B, Fifty-sixth regiment, killed before Petersburg, July 30th, 1864. A sixth son, who was wounded in one of the then recent battles, and who belonged to a Massachusetts regiment, was lying ill in one of the hospitals.

General Schouler's letter, it seems, attracted the attention of President Lincoln, who, by some means unknown to the General, ascertained the name of the mother, and an early mail brought the following letter to the Adjutant General for Mrs. Bixby:

EXECUTIVE MANSION,
WASHINGTON, 21st Nov., 1864.

"*Dear Madam:* I have been shown in the files of the War Department a statement of the Adjutant General of Massachusetts that you are the mother of five sons who have died gloriously on the field of battle.

I feel how weak and fruitless must be any words of mine which should attempt to beguile you from the grief of a loss so overwhelming. But I cannot refrain from tendering to you the consolation that may be found in the thanks of the republic they died to save.

I pray that our Heavenly Father may assuage the anguish of your bereavement, and leave you only the cherished memory of the loved and the lost, and the solemn pride that must be yours to have laid so costly a sacrifice upon the altar of freedom

Yours, very sincerely and respectfully,

A. LINCOLN."

"Mrs. Bixby."

### Home and the Battlefield.

In a ramble over the field of battle at Gettysburg, after the awful scenes of carnage enacted there had ceased, the party came across a soldier who, although not apparently a severe sufferer, was anxious

John Burns, the only man in Gettysburg, Pa., who fought at the Battle.

to rehearse his ills. The surgeon, after some cursory examination of his wound, remarked:

"You must have that limb examined, my good fellow; I will send for you to-morrow, and have you brought up."

A look of unutterable longing passed over the soldier's face. He knew the thought of the surgeon's mind; that examination meant amputation, and he exclaimed, half-savagely, but with a childish entreaty mellowing the defiance of his voice:

"I can't lose that leg—I can't, can't!"

"But why?"

He paused a moment, and a startled look passed over his face, as if in a flash he had thought of his dear ones at home and their dependence upon him, and his possible inability to care for them in the future. Then he answered haltingly:

"Because, because, Sir, I have use for it."

Yes, poor fellow, doubtless he *had* use for it. No wonder that brave John Burns —the only man at Gettysburg who fought at the battle in defence of his home—was inspired to do such noble deeds, under such noble examples!

### All for her Lover.

Among the passengers on board the steamer Georgiana, plying between Fortress Monroe and Baltimore, on the night of December 28, 1861, was a lady who registered her name as Mrs. Baxley, and who had been brought 'up to the Fortress from Norfolk, under a flag of truce.

Mrs. Baxley appeared gay on the passage, and at the breakfast table the next morning she made some remarks which attracted the attention of Mr. Brigham, who asked her jocosely whether she was a secessionist—to which she answered, "Yes." After the gang plank was run out, the boat having landed at Baltimore, Mrs. Baxley was heard to say that she "thanked God she had arrived home safe;" and when about stepping ashore, Mr. Brigham tapped her on the shoulder and requested her attendance in the ladies' cabin.

As soon as the room was reached, she took off her bonnet, between the lining of which were found upwards of fifty letters sewed in,—she exclaiming that having been found out she thought it best to deliver the 'contrabands,' and be allowed to proceed on her way. But Mr. Brigham insisted upon it that she had others, when in her shoes and stockings numerous other letters were also found. The lady was closely guarded until the Provost Marshal of Baltimore was informed of the case, when he sent a lady to examine Mrs. Baxley with more scrutiny. Almost every possible place about her clothing was filled with letters from Secessia for rebel sympathizers at Baltimore.

But in her corsets was found a document which, when taken by the lady examining the smuggler, Mrs. Baxley rushed at her, and, getting hold of the paper, tore it in two. The lady examiner rushed at Mrs. B., at the same time calling assistance. Mr. Brigham, who stood outside while the operation was going on, rushed into the saloon and found Mrs. Baxley vanquished, and the document, though torn, in the possession of the Provost Marshal's aid. This document proved to be a commission from Jeff. Davis to a Dr. Septimus Brown, of Baltimore, also passes and direction for him to run the Federal blockade, in order to gain the rebel domains. The Dr. was immediately arrested and sent to Fort McHenry.

Madam Baxley was taken to a hotel and several police officers placed on guard over her. While locked in her room, she dropped a note out of her window addressed to her lover (the rebel doctor) imploring him, for God's sake, to fly, as all was discovered. She was also quite disheartened and said that she had braved all dangers for the sake of her lover, and, when on the point of having accomplished all her cherished desires, the cup of happiness (alas! such is life and such is love!) was dashed from her lips as she was about drinking from it. It seemed to be her only and darling desire to get her lover into the rebel army, and, having succeeded, she was only detected in her nefarious transactions when about completing her mission.

### Supper for All: Woman's Goodness.

One summer night, a lady belonging to Fall River, Massachusetts, a passenger on the Metropolis, while going from New York with some sick and wounded prisoners, seeing they were not cared for as her generous nature would dictate, and learning from them that the wants of the inner man were just then the strongest, called the steward of the boat to her; she says—"Can these men have supper?" "No, ma'am; there has been no provision made of that kind by the Government, and we cannot provide these unless we provide all." "Can you get them all supper if I will pay for it?" "Yes." "Very well, do so." The supper was accordingly got, with all the delicacies on hand. No stint, but the best, for which the sum of $150 was paid. No one was informed of the act, no herald or newspaper reporter was there to proclaim it. One of the recipients of her noble bounty is the narrator of this.

### Mose Bryan paying his Respects to General Burnside.

Among the contrabands who presented themselves to General Burnside were Moses and Africa Bryan. The former asked, on coming into military quarters, for General Burnside. Having his tent pointed out, he entered it, and proceeded

Mose Bryan.

to introduce himself. Bowing to the General, he says:

"I took the liberty to call on you—I am Moses Bryan."

"Well," says the General, "I am General Burnside. Are you a good Union man, Moses?"

"I am that," says Mose.

"Well, then, give me your hand," says the great-hearted hero; and he at once clasped the hand of his sable ally: "Have you been looking for me?" he continued.

"Yes, massa, I and my people have watched, and have prayed for you so long and so often," was the late bondman's answer.

"What, wasn't you afraid we would sell you to Cuba?" the General next asked.

"No, Sir," said the other, "we know you never do that."

And here, after mutual interchanges of good wishes, the visitor, with a native politeness which would have set well on the shoulders of any one, had the good sense to see that the interview had continued long enough, and withdrew.

### Loyalty and Abolitionism supposed Synonimous.

At one of the leading hotels in New Orleans, a party were one day sitting at the breakfast table, before Louisiana had seceded. The question was asked, "Is there any news this morning?" A southerner, one of the most wealthy men in the city, a burly man, accustomed to despotic sway among his negroes, replied coolly, "Nothing, except that some of our boys went down the river last night, and took possession of one of the United States forts." A northern lady who was present, a lady by birth, by education, and by position, hesitatingly inquired, not provokingly, but as a question for information, "Is it not treason to seize a national fort?" This southern rebel burst out upon her with the most intemperate, profane, and vulgar abuse, denouncing her as a d— Yankee and abolitionist, and declaring that if she were a man, he would wring her nose for her, and that, as soon as her husband came in, he would hold him accountable, and wring *his* nose. No one dared to interfere, for such men carried bowie-knives and revolvers; and there was no power of law to punish one for shooting a person accused of abolitionism. The lady was in a state of indescribable terror. She expected, every moment, to see her husband come in, to be first grossly insulted, and then to be shot or stabbed before her eyes. With a face pallid as death, and a voice trembling almost beyond control, she looked up to him, and said:

"Will you accept the apology of a lady, when I assure you that I intended no offense? I merely wished to ask a question for information."

"Yes," was the reply, "I will accept the apology of a lady; but you are no lady— you are a cursed abolitionist, and I will wring your husband's nose for him when I meet him," and so on, until the lady left the table. The gentleman and lady found it expedient to leave New Orleans.

### Heart-rending Scene.

As the severely wounded in the Virginia battles, in the summer of 1864, were being transferred to the ambulances, a lady from Michigan was seen looking anxiously around to ascertain if either of her

Soldiers' Graves, Bull Run.

sons was among the number. Presently she recognized her son among the throng. He was seated on a coffin, and his arm seemed to be shot off, or partly so. "Where is Charles?" said the anxious parent, while her countenance expressed the agony of intense suspense and her voice could only find a choked utterance. "In this, mother," said the wounded man, pointing to the coffin on which he sat. The scene was heart-rending. The stricken mother had also another son in the army.

### "She Loved a Soldier Lad."

The lover of a young Ohio girl had enlisted, and she determined to join him. She was inspected, accepted, and sworn in with the rest of the company; marched to Camp Jackson, Ohio, drilled there several days, when she was sent with the Third Ohio Regiment to Camp Dennison, near Cincinnati. Here she assisted in all the duties of forming a new camp, handling lumber, standing sentry, etc., until Saturday, when, ascertaining for the first time that there were *two* Camp Dennisons, and that while she was in one her lover was in the other, in Lancaster, Penn., she went to Colonel Morrow, and requested to be changed from the company she was in, giving as her reason that she preferred associating with Americans, and her company was composed of Irishmen. Her real design was, when her request should be granted, to choose a place in one of the companies of the Second Regiment, not knowing that it would be impossible to change her from one regiment to another. Col. Morrow discovered the secret of her sex. Marshal Thompson then supplied her with clothing, having enrobed herself in which, she expressed a desire to leave, as she had friends in the city with whom she could sojourn. She was released.

### Very Pleasant Surprise for Two.

A sprightly young wife appeared one day at the office of the Sanitary Commission in Louisville, asking to have a dispatch written for a permit to visit her husband in Nashville. The clerks turned to consult the record for his name, which she at once pronounced a useless delay—" she *knew* he was in Nashville, and all she wanted was a dispatch written, and would be obliged for as much haste as possible." "But," said the clerk, "are you quite sure he is in Nashville?" "Certainly; nothing is more certain." "You would have no objections to meeting him here?" the clerk inquired again, his eye resting on an open page, with his finger at a particular name. The woman flushed as if annoyed. "You are playing with me, Sir. Will you give me the dispatch?" "No; you will not need it. This 'abstract' will please you better. These are directions where to find your husband—a few blocks off," the clerk rejoined, a smile breaking over his face. With one look—such as a woman can give—to be sure that she was not the victim of a deception, the young wife darted away, and a few moments afterward found that, after all, the one she sought was *not* in Nashville, but right within reach of her loving arms. Such is an illustration of the noble Sanitary Commission, to which such men as Bellows and others consecrated their time and talents during the war,—the noblest scheme of military beneficence, and on the most gigantic scale, ever undertaken in the ages of the world.

### Delivered at the Eleventh Hour.

Major Fullerton, of General Granger's staff, developed quite a little romance in Shelbyville, Tennessee. Just as the Confederate forces were being driven out of the town, the General was on horseback galloping through one of the streets, and when passing an old dingy brick house almost hid from view by the cedar trees in the yard, he observed at a window in it a young lady in her *robe de nuit*, beckoning him toward her. Although advised not to stop, he wheeled his horse around and entered the yard. A he rebel endeavored to keep him from entering, while the lady called out to him that he must come. So, pushing Mr. Rebel to one side, the General at once passed into the house and entered the room where the lady was. She proved to be the beautiful Miss Cushman, then quite ill and prostrated by a nervous fever, brought on by the hardships, indignities and insults she had undergone. As he entered the room she caught him by the hand and said—

"Thank God, you all have come at last; I am now safe!"

Her story was short. Her wrongs and sufferings had been long. Two or three months previously, she had occasion to pass through the lines from Nashville to Shelbyville. When she arrived there, it was discovered by the secession authorities that she was a Unionist. These two circumstances taken together were enough to convict her as a spy, under the arbitrary rulings of the Confederate Government. She was arrested, tried, and condemned to be executed. She tried to make her escape to the Federal lines, but could not succeed. Before the day fixed for her execution she was taken dangerously ill, and was then removed to the house in which she was discovered. They left Shelbyville in such haste that they either forgot her or else they had not the transportation to carry her,—the only carriage that could be had, carried General Bragg and family out of town with great speed a few hours before the Federals entered. An ambulance was fitted up for Miss Cushman, and in it she was sent forward by her deliverers.

**Relieved through the Mercy of Death.**

One morning the ambulance brought a load of fourteen Federal prisoners to be immured in a Southern prison. Among them was a young man—young, judging from the skeleton-like but still powerful frame—but old, from the pinched and ghastly face —a dying one, at all events. Somebody near by uttered the word, softly, "Starving!" But low as it was uttered, the poor boy of whom it was spoken caught the word.

"Yes," he said, feebly, "it is quite use-

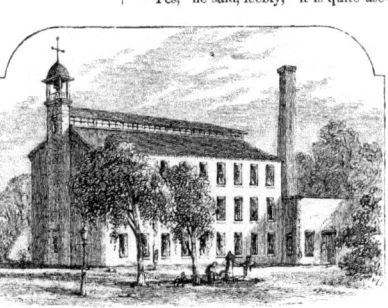

Military Prison at Salisbury, N. C.

less, gentlemen—no," turning from the bread that was offered him, "I loathe it now. For days and days I have been mad for it. I have had murder in my heart. I thought if one died the rest might live. Once we caught a dog and roasted him, and quarreled over the bits. We had no cover; we lay on the scorching sand, and, when the terrible heats were over, came the raw fogs and bitter wind."

He stopped, seemingly from exhaustion, and lay a few moments silent; then the pitiful voice commenced again:

"We were very brave for a while; we thought help was coming. We never dreamed they could go on at home eating, lying soft, and making merry, while we were dying by inches. I think if my brother knew—If ever you get back I charge you, before God, find out Robert

Bence, surgeon of the — Maine. Tell him that his brother Jem starved to death, and that thousands more are—Ah! just Heaven! the pain again! O Christ! help me! have —"

The words died away in inarticulate ravings. He tossed his arms wildly over his head; his whole frame racked with the most awful throes. "And this," says the narrator, "was my poor boy; so wasted, so horribly transformed, that I had not known him. His glazing eyes had not recognized me. His few remaining hours were one long, raving agony. He never knew that his brother was by his side. I died over and over again, standing there in my utter helplessness. I had never so thanked God as when his moaning fell away into the merciful silence of death."

#### Miss Lee and the Yankee Corporal.

After the battle of Manassas, the Union prisoners were conveyed to the Richmond prisons, and, as the train was compelled to halt at every station from one to three hours, the journey occupied two days. Corporal W. H. Merrill, who was one of the prisoners, had the honor of a confabu-

Miss Lee and the Yankee Corporal.

lation with one of the many bright-witted ladies who contributed, by their spirited words and acts, to give such *eclat* to the cause of the South. According to the Corporal:—

Arriving at Culpepper, the daughter of Major Lee, a young and beautiful damsel, came up to the window from which I leaned, and asked if she could do anything for me; and added, "What did you come down here for?" [This had become a stereotyped query.] I replied, "To protect the Stars and Stripes and preserve the Union."

My questioner then proceeded, after the uniform custom, to berate General Scott: "That miserable old Scott—a Virginian by birth—a traitor to his own State—*we all hate him!*"

Miss Lee wore upon her bonnet a miniature silken secession flag, which she handed me, remarking that she thought I could fight as well for the "Stars and Bars" as for the Stars and Stripes. I playfully reminded her that she had just denounced General Scott as a traitor to his own State —and if I should fight for the "Stars and Bars," I should be a traitor to the State of New York! This trivial argument was evidently a poser. "Oh," responded she, "I had not thought of that!" But she insisted upon my acceptance of the emblem of disloyalty, and I still retain it out of kindly regard for the donor. She cut the button from my coat sleeve, and I consented to the "formal exchange," though not fully recognizing her as a "belligerent power."

#### Scarcely Seventeen Years, but a Heroine.

Miss Amelia E. Harmon, a beautiful girl of some seventeen summers, played a prominent part in the thrilling drama of the Gettysburg battles. She occupied with her relatives the best dwelling house in the country round about, and visible from the Seminary Ridge about a mile west of Gettysburg. The destruction of this building was alluded to by Mr. Everett in his celebrated Cemetery Oration.

Early on the eventful Wednesday morning, the signs of the approaching tempest were so numerous and unmistakable that Miss Harmon was prevented from attending the school at Oak Ridge. During the charge of Buford's cavalry, which commenced the battle, the house in question was forcibly occupied by the Federal sharpshooters from which to fire upon the rebels. On the repulse of the Union cavalry the Confederates announced their intention of firing the building, in accordance with the laws of war; it having been used, they said, as a fort. The family and the young lady protested, explaining that the occupation was forcible, and not with their consent,—the young lady adding that 'her mother, who was not now living, was a Southern woman, and that she would blush for her parentage if Southern men could thus fire the house of defenceless females, and turn them out in the midst of battle!'

One of the Confederates then approached her and proposed, in a confidential manner, that if she would prove that she was not a renegade Southerner by hurrahing for the Southern Confederacy, he would see what could be done. The young heroine indignantly refused the mean proposal, and, abandoning her burning home with her aunt, ran the gauntlet of the fire of the two armies.

#### Four-legged Pets in the Army.

The correspondents of the St. Louis Republican, Journal, and Democrat, of the Chicago Tribune, Times, and Journal, the Louisville Journal, and of the Cincinnati Gazette, Enquirer, Times, and Commercial, would do the country a most valuable service by embodying in volume form the diversified and sparkling contributions, through their respective columns, with which they favored the public during the war. No chronicles were so widely read or so greatly praised, especially by those peculiarly interested in the Western troops. 'Bun' and 'Dot' are thus delineated by the same hand that could portray the storm and carnage of battle :

They had the strangest pets in the army —such as nobody would think of taking to at home, and yet they were little touches of the gentler nature as gave one some such cordial feeling, when seeing them, as it is said residents of Bourbon county, Ky., habitually experience at so much a gallon. One of the army boys carried a *red squirrel* through "thick and thin" over a thousand miles, "Bun" eating hard tack like a veteran and having the freedom of the tent. Another's affections overflowed upon a slow-winking, unspeculative little *owl*, captured in Arkansas, and bearing a name with a decidedly classical smack to it— Minerva. A third gave his heart to a young Cumberland mountain *bear*.

But chief among camp-pets were dogs. Riding on the saddle-bow, tucked into a baggage wagon, mounted on a knapsack, growling under a gun, were dogs brought to a premature end as to ears and tails, and yellow at that; pug-nosed, square-headed brutes, sleek terriers, delicate morsels of spaniels—Tray, Blanche, Sweetheart, little dogs and all.

A dog, like a horse, comes to love the rattle and crash of musket and cannon. There was one in an Illinois regiment— and perhaps regarded as belonging to it, though his name might not have appeared on the muster-roll—that chased half-spent shot as a kitten frolics with a ball of worsted. He was under fire, and twice wounded, and left the tip of his tail at the battle of Stone River. Woe to the man that had wantonly killed him! But there was a little white spaniel that messed with one of the batteries, and delighted in the name of "Dot," who was a special favorite. No matter what was up, that fellow's silken coat must be washed every day and there was need enough of it, for when the battery was on the march, they just plunged him into the sponge-bucket—not the tidiest chamber imaginable— that swings, like its more peaceful neighbor, the tar-bucket, under the rear axle of the gun-carriage— plumped him into that, clapped on the cover, and Dot was good for an inside passage. One day the battery crossed a stream, and the water came well up to the guns. Nobody thought of Dot, and, when all across, a gunner looked into the bucket —alas! it was full of water, and Dot was as dead as a little dirty door-mat.

### Mr. Richardson Initiating his Escape.

One of the neatest 'sells' was that practiced by Mr. Richardson, (the brilliant writer for the New York Tribune,) upon the prison guard at Salisbury, N. C., when he—Mr. R.,—made his escape from that southern domicil, together with some similarly situated comrades. In Mr. Richardson's account of his unique experience in this matter, he says:—

Both "Junius" and our esteemed collaborator, Mr. William E. Davis, of the Cincinnati Gazette, had been furnished with passes to visit, during the day, a rebel hospital, outside the fence and inner line of guards, to order in medical supplies for the prisoners. The inflexible rule was, to exact paroles whenever passes were granted, but in the confusion attendant upon the great influx of prisoners, the authorities had neglected to require them. None of us would have given paroles in any event; but my friends had the good fortune not to be asked for them.

On that Sunday evening, half an hour before dark—the latest hour they could pass the guard—they both went outside as usual to the rebel hospital. A few minutes after, taking in my hand a great box full of the bottles in which medicines were brought in, I, too, walked rapidly up to the gate, while a dozen friends, in the secret, were looking on to see the result. I attempted to pass the sentinel, but he halted me and asked:

"Have you a pass, Sir?"

"Certainly I have a pass," I answered. "Have you not seen it often enough to remember by this time?"

"Very likely," he answered, a little nonplussed, "but I was not quite sure, and our orders are very strict."

Thereupon I exhibited to him the genuine pass belonging to my colleague, whose face was so well known to the sentinel—though not his name, as the event proved —that he had been able to go out without showing it. The soldier examined it, reading slowly and with difficulty, "Guards will permit Junius H. Browne, citizen-prisoner, to pass the inner gate, to bring in medical supplies;" and then returned it, saying: "All right, Sir; that pass is correct, for I know Captain Fuqua's handwriting."

Once outside, I hid the medical box behind a fence, and found refuge in a little outbuilding until dark. My two friends there joined me; and we walked through the outer gate into the streets in full view of the guard, who, seeing us come from the rebel hospital, supposed us to be surgeons or their assistants.

By skillful movements, the escape so ingeniously commenced, was carried out to complete success, all of which Mr. Richardson admirably narrates in his book,— "The Field, Dungeon, and Escape."

### Great Act for a Little Girl.

Mr. Herbert, a kind-hearted farmer in Illinois, had a little daughter, who, hearing her father ask others to give in aid of the sick and wounded soldiers, thought of what *she* could do. Of all her playthings she had nothing which could be sold for any amount and so bring money. But she had a very sweet pet lamb, almost as dear to her as a brother or a sister. That surely would bring something. It was of the very finest stock. She had taught it many cunning tricks and winsome ways. The two, child and lamb, had eaten from the same dish, and many hours they had played together upon the sunny hillside, and the lamb, like "little Mary's," knew its name as well as that of its mistress. She proposed, with tears in her eyes, and almost heart-broken to think of it, to give her dear pet to the sick and wounded soldiers. She gave it, and she and the lamb together went in the procession, on one of the wagons. The president of the Soldiers'

Home gave twenty-five dollars for the lamb, and in his speech at the dinner, said he should prize it very much, and through the incident, teach his own daughter a lesson. After they had placed the lamb in a large box to be sent to its purchaser's country residence, its former little mistress took leave of it, fondling and kissing her dear pet. With her eyes full of tears she said she was very sorry to part with it, because it loved her and she loved it so much—but, the soldiers needed the money more than she did the lamb, because they sometimes lost their limbs, and sometimes were killed. Taking all the circumstances into consideration, it was a great act for a little girl.

### Escape from Libby Prison through a Young Lady's Intervention.

A Union prisoner who was confined in the Libby Prison, Richmond, had the good fortune to effect his escape, the means for which were furnished by a young lady, who had taken his case in hand through personal sympathy, and whose plan was as ingenious as it was gracious. This young lady sent the prisoner a bag of tobacco, inclosed in which he found a small Union flag, and a note telling him, if he would be free, to appoint a time and place of meeting. To carry out so cherished a purpose, he affected death, and, having in this feigned condition been carried past the guard, lay in the dead house from noon until dusk. He then scaled a fence ten feet in height, and reached another yard, where he met the young lady with a suit of clothing made from rebel blankets; he then followed the young lady a long distance, safely passing the guards, until he reached the house of the young lady's father. Here he was concealed and cared for in the best manner possible, for nine days, while her father obtained passes for him, paying three thousand dollars in Confederate money for them; and then hiring a carriage for five hundred dollars in the same kind of money, and getting to the Rappahannock by going such a roundabout way as would prevent detection, he finally reached the Union lines—thanks to his kind-hearted deliverer.

### Charleston Women Under Fire.

During the shelling of the city of Charleston, there was a moral sublimity exhibited in many cases by the female portion of that imperilled community, which could but challenge the heart-feeling even of the Federals, whose object it was to destroy or capture that cradle-city of secession. An instance of the calm heroism to which women can rise is thus given: A lady, dressed in deep mourning, was seated in the front verandah of her dwelling, engaged in sewing, when a Parrott shell came screaming up the harbor and burst with an unearthly sound, just above and in front of the position where she was sitting, throwing its fragments in every direction. But this "Mother of Gracchi," as she may be called, remained tranquil in her seat, slowly and sadly raising her eyes toward the point where the shell had burst. She was observed to thoughtfully gaze for an instant upon the deadly scattering missile, and then as calmly to resume her womanly employment, in serene silence. From her mourning apparel it was judged she had felt before the horrors and desolation of war. Perhaps her only son had fallen, in strange fatuity of warfare against his country, at Wagner, at Sumter, or on James Island. Or perhaps the "loved one of her bosom" had fallen, and the Angel of Death had no more terror for her.

### General Lyon leading his Charge at Springfield.

While General Lyon was standing, in the battle at Springfield, Missouri, where bullets flew thickest, just after his favorite horse was shot from under him, some of his officers interposed and begged that he would retire from the spot and seek one less exposed. Scarcely raising his eyes from the enemy, he said:

"It is well enough that I stand here. I am satisfied."

While the line was forming for the charge against the rebels, in which he lost his life, General Lyon turned to Major Sturgis who stood near him, and remarked:

"I fear that the day is lost; if Colonel Sigel had been successful he would have joined us before this. I think I will lead this charge."

He had been wounded in the leg in an early part of the engagement—a flesh wound merely—from which the blood flowed profusely. Major Sturgis during the conversation noticed blood on General

Brig. Gen. Nathaniel Lyon.

Lyon's hat, and at first supposed he had been touching it with his hand, which was wet with blood from his leg. A moment after, perceiving that it was fresh, he removed the General's hat and asked the cause of its appearance. "It is nothing, Major; nothing but a wound in the head," said General Lyon, turning away and mounting his horse. Without taking the hat held out to him by Major Sturgis, he addressed the Iowans he was to command with—

"*Forward men! I will lead you!*"

Two minutes afterward he lay dead on the field, killed by a rifle-ball through the breast, just above the heart.

### Fatal Fulfillment of a Jest.

Just before the war broke out, and before Lincoln's proclamation was issued, a young Virginian, named Summerfield, was visiting the city of New York, where he made the acquaintance of two Misses Holmes, from Waterbury, Vermont. He became somewhat intimate with the young ladies, and the intercourse seemed to be mutually agreeable. The proclamation was issued, and the whole North thrown into a blaze of excitement. Upon visiting the ladies one evening, and at the hour of parting, they remarked to Summerfield that their present meeting would probably be the last; they must hurry home to aid in making up the overcoats and clothing for the volunteers from their town.

Summerfield expressed his regret that they must leave, but at the same time especially requested them to see that the overcoats were *well* made, as it was his intention, if he ever met the Vermont soldiers in battle, to kill one of them and take his coat.

Now for the sequel:

Virginia seceded. The Second Vermont regiment, a portion of which was from the town of Waterbury, were sent to Virginia. The battle of Manassas was fought, in which they were engaged, and so was Summerfield. During the battle, the latter marked his man, not knowing to what State he belonged; the fatal ball was sped on its errand of death; the victim fell at the flash of the gun, and upon rushing up to secure the dead man's arms, Summerfield observed that he had a fine, new overcoat strapped to his back, which he determined to appropriate to his own use. The fight was over, and Summerfield had time to examine his prize, when, remarkable as it may appear, the coat was marked in the lining with the name of Thomas Holmes, and in the pockets were found letters, signed with the name of the sister whom Summerfield had known in New York, and to whom he had made the above quoted remark, in which the now dead man was spoken of as brother. The evidence was conclusive—he had killed the brother of his friend, and the remark which he made in jest had, in the melancholy fortunes of war, a fatal fulfillment.

### Watch kept by a Dog over Lieutenant Pfieff's Grave.

A remarkable incident is related of the manner in which Mrs. Pfieff, the wife of Lieutenant Louis Pfieff, at Chicago, who was killed at Shiloh, was enabled to find her husband's body. No person, when she arrived on the field, could inform her where her husband's body was buried; and after searching among the thousands of graves for half a day, she was about to abandon the pursuit. Suddenly she saw a large dog coming toward her, which she recognized as one that had left Chicago with her husband. The dog seemed delighted to find her, and led her to a distant part of the field, where he stopped

Watch kept by a Dog.

before a single grave. She caused it to be opened, and found the body of her husband. It appeared, by the statements of the soldiers, that the dog was by the side of the Lieutenant when he fell, and remained with him till he was buried. He then took his station by the grave, and there he had remained for twelve days, until relieved by the arrival of his mistress, only leaving his post long enough each day to procure food in order to sustain himself in his faithful service.

### "And a little child shall lead them."

The Boston Sanitary Fair called forth some pleasing illustrations of the sunny side of human nature. Said a pretty girl to a gray-haired gentleman: "Oh, Uncle James, I want you to take a share in this grand piano." "Bless your heart, I've just bought a new one, and you have a piano, and Emma, and every one else, child!" "But you can give it back to the Sanitary." "Bright thought! put me down for two shares; just look in my memorandum-book, though, a minute, Lizzie—share in a plough, a buggy, six dolls, cannon, *piano*, oil painting, sewing machine, four afghans, etchings of Cupid and Psyche, flock of sheep, and—there write it down—*grand* piano!" One of the "solid men of Boston," that, doubtless. He drew a doll, very likely.

### Mrs. Belmont's Concert for the Sanitary Commission.

While the New York Sanitary Fair was engaging the time and generous devices of the good people of that metropolis, several ladies connected with it called upon Mrs. August Belmont, wife of the great banker, and requested her to hold a concert, for the benefit of the Fair, among her friends. She took it under advisement, and consented to do so, and made arrangements accordingly. She found her house would accommodate about three hundred guests. She issued her tickets for that number, at five dollars a ticket. She was shortly visited by the same committee, who informed her that the price of tickets must not exceed two dollars each. They were informed that Mrs. Belmont's friends would as soon give five or ten dollars as two—that the house was small, the expense would be the same, and the receipts to the Fair very much diminished. But the lady managers were persistent—two dollars and no more must be the extent, or they would have nothing to do with the concert. Mrs. Belmont, having much of the spirit of her heroic father, informed the ladies that she was competent to manage her own affairs in her own house, and that they might consider themselves as discharged from all further duty in regard to her concert. Her husband, on learning this state of affairs, handed his wife fifteen hundred dollars in greenbacks, took all her tickets and carried them down town, sold some and gave the rest away to his friends, and made ample provision to have the concert a success. It came off; the rooms were brilliant and crowded; the beauty and fashion and wealth of New York were there in all their glory; Gottschalk and kindred performers charmed the brilliant audience, and Mrs. Belmont had fifteen hundred dollars in her hands to contribute to the Sanitary Commission.

### "That Flag is Doubly Dear to me this Morning."

A poor woman from Wisconsin, whose husband and son were in the ranks, learning that the latter was wounded at Lookout, made her way to Louisville, whence she was sent by the agents of the Sanitary Commission to Nashville. Owing to the interruption of railroad communication it was impossible to send her further front, and the Nashville office accordingly telegraphed to the Commission agent at Chattanooga for information.

The next day, which was Thursday, it was answered that her son was severely wounded, and had been placed in a hospital which was subsequently captured by the enemy, in whose hands he then was. It was sad news, but better than none. It was communicated to her as kindly and gently as possible; but it drove her almost frantic. Two days passed, with no more tidings. The suspense became terrible. Was he alive? were his wounds cared for by the rebels? was he dead? Such were the questions which the poor mother dinned constantly in the ears of the agents. "Oh, that I could hear!" she cried. "Even the worst would be better than this suspense." At last, late on Sunday night, the word so prayed and waited for came. It was this only: "Dead." It was a terrible blow. A very agony of grief settled upon the mother's heart, and for hours her sufferings seemed beyond all human endurance. After a time, carrying her great sorrow with her, she went away; but the next morning she returned to the office, still terribly stricken in heart, but calmer than before, and said, pointing to the flag over the door, with tears in her eyes,

"*That flag is doubly dear to me this morning. IT HAS COST ME SOMETHING.*"

### Quite a Safe Place for the Harper's Ferry Flag.

The War Department was made dramatic one day by an Irish woman, of Amazonian size, and heart as loyal as brave, who came under the auspices of General Schenck, to present to Secretary Stanton the American flag pulled down by Colonel Miles at Harper's Ferry, when that post was surrendered to the rebels. "How did you secure this, my excellent woman?" "Sure, sir, I just lifted my clothes, and wrapped it round me here, just as they flocked into the parade." The Secretary, after gallantly thanking her as her devotion deserved, ordered fifty dollars to be paid to the brave woman. It would not have been safe to have attempted to unwrap *that* flag.

### Baptism for the Dead.

Among the relics of the war upon exhibition at one of the Soldiers' Fairs was a mutilated dollar bill, connected with which was a touching story. A pastor in an inland town had called upon his congregation to contribute to the Sanitary Commission, and had met a liberal response. The next day a woman, dependent upon her daily work for her own support and that of her children, brought him a dollar bill to be added as her mite to the collection. The pastor declined to take it, telling her she ought not to give so much, considering her situation; but the woman insisted, adding, "We've had it in the house many weeks; we can not spend it."

Seeing that the bill was much torn, and supposing that she had found difficulty in passing it, her pastor said, "Oh, I'll give you a good bill for it."

"No, that's not it. It was in brother Sam's pocket when he was wounded. He's dead now, and we have his torn pocket-book, and mother said [the mother was a widow, and he her only son] we will give that dollar to the Sanitary Commission; we can not spend it."

The pastor redeemed the bill for two dollars, and sent it to be disposed of at the Fair. Fifty dollars were at once offered for the bill, but the gift from two widows, of a ball-marked relic of their son and brother, did not stop at that figure, but brought an abundant harvest into the Sanitary treasury. No necessity would have compelled them to spend it; but the cause consecrated it as a holy baptism for the dead,—an affecting and precious offering.

### Woman's Tongue Betraying the Rebel Torpedoes at Fort Henry.

To defeat our attack on Fort Henry, the rebels planted torpedoes of the most formidable description in the principal channels. Their existence and location was revealed by that most irrepressible of all the forces of nature—a woman's tongue. One morning the "Jessie Scouts" —a volatile, daring corps of young men, who inevitably turned up wherever a fight was expected—went into a farm-house, where nearly thirty women had gathered for safety. The inmates, greatly alarmed, begged them not to injure a party of un-

protected females. The scouts allayed their fears, when the women informed them they had frequently heard that Southern wives and daughters had no mercy to hope for at the hands of the Lincoln soldiery. In the conversation which ensued, one stated that her husband was a captain in the rebel army at Fort Henry.

"By about to-morrow night, madam," remarked one of the scouts, "there will be no Fort Henry—our gunboats will dispose of it."

"Not a bit of it," was the reply; "they will be all blown up before they get past the island."

This was said so significantly, that the scout questioned her further, but she refused to explain. He finally told her that unless she revealed all she knew he would be compelled to take her into the camp of "Lincolnites," as a prisoner. This excited her terror, and she explained that torpedoes had been planted, and described their location as well as she was able, though bewailing her slip of the tongue. The information proved accurate enough to enable Lieutenant Phelps to find them; but even had he remained in ignorance, they were of such a character as would have disappointed their makers and done us no harm.

### Sherman's Absence of Mind—the Sergeant's Segar.

One of the most noted characteristics of General Sherman, the hero of Atlanta, was absence of mind in respect to things not immediately affecting his military operations—upon which latter all his thoughts seemed concentrated. This peculiarity of the General found an interesting illustration in a circumstance which occurred at Lebanon Junction, Kentucky, after the following fashion:

General Sherman, with two regiments under Colonel Lovell H. Rousseau—afterwards Major-General, and a detachment under Lieutenant-Colonel R. W. Johnston —afterwards Brigadier,—occupied Lebanon Junction, Ky., on the 17th of September, 1861. While walking up and down the platform of that place, awaiting the repair of the telegraph line, Sherman's segar gave out. He immediately took another from his pocket and asked the orderly sergeant of the marine Zouaves for a light. The home guard sergeant had only a moment before lighted his segar, and, with a bow, handed it to the General —probably the first Brigadier he had seen during the war. Sherman lighted his segar carefully, took a puff or two to assure himself, and abstractedly threw the

Sherman's Absence of Mind.

sergeant's segar away. A short time after, General Rousseau, who saw this scene, mentioned the matter to General Sherman. He could not recollect it, but said—
" I was thinking of something else. It won't do to let to-morrow take care of itself. Your good merchant don't think of the ships that are in, but the ships that are to come in. The evil of to-day is irreparable. Look ahead to avoid breakers. You can't when your ship is on them. All you can then do is to save yourself and retrieve disaster. I was thinking of something else when I threw the sergeant's segar away "—and then he added, laughing, " Did I do that, really ? " Those who would see Sherman's remarkable characteristics, military and personal, most admirably portrayed, will find a fund of such matter in Captain Conyngham's sparkling reminiscences of that great commander, drawn from personal observation, and penned with the hand of a genius not unworthy the chieftain at whose side he rode,— one of the books with which the reader, especially if a soldier, can never tire.

### Ben. McCulloch and Joe Baxter.

General Ben. McCulloch was in many particulars a remarkable man. Though a very common looking person, he was very vain of his personal appearance and proud of his fame. When the General was returning from Richmond, not long before the fatal battle of Pea Ridge, a little incident occurred—such as, perhaps, he was more than once the subject of. The party consisted of the General, Captain Armstrong, his A. A. G., and Colonel Snyder, of the Missouri army, with two or three black servants, traveling in a

Gen. Ben McCulloch.

four mule ambulance. They stopped for lunch by the wayside, about two days travel from Fort Smith, in Arkansas, and were discussing the prospects of the Confederacy and the contents of a basket and a demijohn, when a stranger rode up and inquired the way to Colonel Stone's winter quarters. The stranger was a perfect specimen of the genus ‘butternut.’ He was dressed in bilious looking jeans, with a home-made hat and coarse boots, and wore his hair and beard very long. He was mounted on a good horse, and carried on his shoulder a long, old-fashioned rifle. Before there was any time to answer his inquiries he cast his eyes on General McCulloch, and seemed to recognize him. Dismounting at once, he advanced eagerly to the General, with extended hand and a hearty "Bless my soul, Joe! how do you do?—what on earth are you doing here?" The General saw that the man was mistaken, but answered him pleasantly, and invited him to partake of the lunch, to which said lunch and demijohn the stranger did full and ample justice. He told the General (for to him he addressed all his conversation, as to an old friend) that he was a volunteer, and had joined Colonel Stone's regiment of Texan Rangers, and that he intended to fight with Old Ben McCulloch until we gained our independence." Old Ben enjoyed the man's mistake until they were about ready to start on, when he said to his Texan copatriot,

"My friend, I think you are mistaken as to whom you have been talking to; I don't think you know me, and perhaps have never seen me before."

"You be darned!" said butternut; "I would know you, Joe, if I was to meet you in Africa!"

"Well, now," said the general, getting tired of his new friend's familiarity, "who do you take me for, any way?"

"*Take* you for?" retorted Texas, earnestly; "I don't *take* you for anybody; I *know* you to be Joe Baxter, what staid in the Perkins settlement, in Collins county, all last summer, *a sellin' chain-pumps and puttin' up lightnin'-rods!*"

### Jerry the Genius, looking through General Palmer's Spy-glass.

When General Palmer was on the Tennessee river, there was in Company C, of the Forty-second Illinois, a singular genius, familiarly known as Jerry, an easy, careless, jovial fellow, thinking a man a man anywhere, and paying no attention to the shoulder-strapped gentry any more than if they were not about. One day, General Palmer was among a company of officers, looking with his glass at the battle-ground of Pittsburg Landing. Jerry was near

Jerry and Gen. Palmer's Spy-glass.

by, and stepping up to the General, slapped him familiarly on the shoulder, and said, "Say, old feller, let me see that thing, will yer?" The officers expected to see Jerry sent in on bread and water; but, always ready for fun, Palmer handed Jerry his spy-glass. Jerry took it, and very deliberately looked it over; and, placing it about two feet from his eye, looked through it. One such look was sufficient, and turning to the General, with a look of extreme contempt, he said, "Here, take the tarnal thing; I can see through it!" and retired amidst the shouts of the General and his officers.

### Old Abe fixing the Responsibility.

Mr. Lincoln was naturally very anxious to know who was really responsible for the calamitous surrender of Harper's Ferry. So he summoned Halleck. The General did not know. "Very well," said the President, "then I will ask General Schenck." That General merely knew that *he* was not to blame. The President sent for Milroy. Milroy averred that *he* was not guilty. Hooker was summoned. Fighting Joe hoped it was clear to His Excellency that he had nothing to do with it. "Perfectly clear," said our Uncle Abraham, smiling. So he assembled all the four generals in his room. "Gentlemen," said he, "Harper's Ferry was surrendered, and none of you, it seems, are responsible. I am very anxious to discover the man who is." He walked up and down the room, while they still sat there. Suddenly he stopped. "I have it," he said; "I know who is responsible." The generals crowded about the President, each a little suspicious. "Who is it, who is it, Mr. President?" "Gentlemen," replied our uncle, with a twinkle in his eye, "General Lee is the man." Everybody knows that the good President was exceedingly fond of those witty writers, whose books he was glad to have in his library,—Artemus Ward, Petroleum V. Nasby, Major Jack Downing, Shillaber, Doesticks, and Orpheus C. Kerr, —who helped to keep the nation in good humor, even when the clouds hung black as night. Query: Would it not be interesting to know the opinion of those masters of wit, concerning the jokes of their admirer, "Mr. Linkin?"

### Marriage Scene in the Army of the Potomac.

An event calculated to destroy the monotony of camp life—a marriage—took place in the Seventh New Jersey volunteers, one of Hooker's old regiments in the Army of the Potomac. The camp was very prettily decorated, and being quite trimly arranged among the pines, was just the camp a visitor would like to see. A little before noon the guests began to arrive in considerable numbers. Among them were Generals Hooker, Sickles, Carr, Mott, Hobart, Ward, Revere, Bartlett, Birney, Berry, Colonel Dickinson, and other aids to General Hooker; Colonels Burling, Farnham, Egan, etc. Colonel Francine and Lieutenant-Colonel Price, of the Seventh, with the rest of the officers of that regiment, proceeded to make all welcome, and then the ceremony commenced. In a hollow square formed by the troops a canopy was erected, with an altar of drums, officers grouped on each side of this. On General Hooker's arrival the band played 'Hail to the Chief,' and on the approach of the bridal party the 'Wedding March.' It was rather cold, windy, and threatened snow, altogether tending to produce a slight pink tinge on the noses present, but the ladies bore it with courage, and looked, to the unaccustomed eyes of the soldiers, like real angels in their light clothing. To add to the dramatic force of the scene, the rest of the brigade and other troops were drawn up in line of battle not more than a mile away to repel an expected attack from Fredericksburg. Few persons are wedded under more romantic circumstances than Nellie Lammond and Captain DeHart. He could not get leave of absence, so she came down like a brave girl, and married him in camp. After the wedding was a dinner, a ball, fire-works, etc.; and on the whole it eclipsed entirely an opera at the Academy of Music in dramatic effect and reality.

### "Physical Disability" Exempting from the Draft and from Something Else.

A young man succeeded in getting a certificate of exemption from the draft, from the Board of Enrolment, on the ground of "physical disability," and hastened to his betrothed to announce his escape. Strangely to him, the good news affected her in an unexpected manner, and she withdrew from his presence with but the shadow of an excuse. The young man was confounded, and, visions of rivals rising up before him, he sought an explanation from the lady's father, who always treated him graciously, and was favorable to the proposed alliance. The father in turn was mistified, and immediately seeking his daughter, found her in great grief.

"Oh, father," said the girl, "I have been shamefully deceived. Oh, how mortifying to be known to be engaged to a man who comes shamelessly to me, just before our marriage, and rejoices in 'physical disabilities.' Why did not you tell me that the man was imperfect or sickly before matters went so far? I have no ambition to turn my future home into a domestic hospital, or myself into a perpetual nurse!"

The father tried to persuade her by saying that probably a trifling ailment, magnified by the complaint, might have obtained his exemption from service, and reminded her that her lover was a fine rider, a graceful skater, and very expert in most manly exercises.

"And under all this," added the fair girl, "he hides some dreadful infirmity. Surely, you do not think I would be engaged to him if I knew him to be consumptive, scrofulous, or worse? I thank God that the draft has lifted the mask. And the man actually delights in being advertised as physically disqualified to serve his country. Oh, shame! He shall know," said she, rising with proud indignation, "that he is physically disqualified to husband me!"

And the father, physiologically considering how the seeds of disease are entailed from one generation to another, approved his daughter's decision, and informed the young man that he might henceforth consider himself "exempt" from the proposed marriage, on the ground of acknowledged "physical disability."

### Characteristic Lady's Joke.

A patriotic lady of St. Louis, Missouri, took it into her head to prepare for one of the Military Fairs a wreath, to be composed of locks of hair from the heads of the prominent Union members of Congress. She wrote to the honorable gentlemen, delicately stating her purpose, and requesting the favor of capillary specimens. Among the many, Thad. Stevens was the recipient of a missive on the subject. It was rather a joke on the venerable Thad., unintentional on the part of the lady, no doubt, as the Honorable Chairman of Ways and Means hadn't had a lock of hair that he could call his own for twenty years, but had, during that long period, been a patron of the wig-maker.

### Spirited Fight between Two Girls at Church.

On a Sabbath day in July, while public worship was being held about six miles north of Albany, Gentry county, Missouri, a party of the Union militia force entered that place to secure horses with which to enter the service under the call of General Fisk. A Union girl promptly came forward and placed her horse at the service of the gallant and patriotic boys, and also took the liberty to point out to them another fine steed, which she archly remarked was the property of a secessionist lady friend of hers. A Union trooper was soon snugly astride of the 'contraband,' and was about to leave with him, when the lady owner made her appearance, and plumply protested against giving the animal up to any such rider, for any such or any other purpose whatever.

The Union girl urged the soldiers to go along,—she had voluntarily contributed her horse, and insisted that the secesh horse should also do duty. At this the rebel girl applied all sorts of opprobrious epithets to the Union girl, who in turn became angry and—knocked her opponent, by a spirited thwack, flat on the ground, then jumped upon her, and dealt her sockdologers at a terrible rate. A spectator finally parted the Amazons, but they didn't stay parted, and were soon fighting each other again, accompanying their blows with piercing screams of defiance. Their gay Sunday dresses were soon in shreds; long, beautiful tresses of hair were mixed with blood from dainty noses, etc. Despairing of putting an end to the shameful setto, the bystanders were compelled to form a circle, and seat themselves to await the final result of the she-tiger encounter. The combatants fought long and skilfully, until Miss Union seized Miss Secesh by the throat, when the latter fell to the ground and gave up the struggle. The parties were then duly cared for by their respective friends.

### Robbery by Mistake.

Two ladies, while General McClellan was at dinner at the Massasoit House, Springfield, Mass., on his passage through that city, ventured to rob a military cap, which they supposed to be the General's, of both its buttons, tearing them out in a very unfeminine manner, to be preserved as mementoes of that military chieftain. The mortification of their feelings and the redness of their faces can only be faintly imagined when one of the aids carelessly as usual put on the mutilated cap, and the General put on his own, which was intact. Those buttons were *not* preserved, but the story has been—being told much oftener than was agreeable to the eager but disappointed curiosity-hunters.

### "Meade" and Ale.

At the time the rebel army was on the march from Chambersburg, Pennsylvania, to Gettysburg, several privates stopped at the hotel of Mr. John Brown, in Fayetteville, and inquired for ale. 'Mine host' informed them that he was just out of that article. One of the rebs remarked that they were going to Baltimore, and there they would get plenty. A few days after, when the rebs were retreating from Get-

Maj. Gen. George G. Meade.

tysburg, Brown happened to meet this same man on the South Mountain. He asked him if he had got any Baltimore ale. "No," replied Johnny Reb; "we only got as far as Gettysburg, where the *Meade* was too strong for us, so we had to give up the Baltimore Ale."

### Courage of Woman during Battle.

The millions who never heard the roar and crash of a great battle, but especially *women*, are naturally interested in the feelings inspired—the sensations evoked, by the actual and imminent presence of desperately contending armies. The battle of Gettysburg brought "the noise of the captains, and the shouting," nearer to the people of the Northern States than any other great combat of the present century; and of the many personal reminiscences of that great struggle, the following, from the pen of Miss Carrie Sheades, of the

Oak Ridge Seminary, will be found of peculiar interest. After speaking of the courage of the young ladies during the battle—their assistance in relieving the wounded, when no surgeon could be obtained—she says:

When our forces retreated from Seminary Ridge, many of the prisoners were taken here. At the time, (though a coward before,) it seemed that I was ready to meet the whole rebel army—every vestige of fear had vanished. A Colonel rushed into the breakfast-room, and a rebel after him, demanding him to surrender. The Colonel, being a very large man, could scarcely breathe, (he was asthmatical,) and begged for time to regain his breath; he told them to 'shoot him'—that 'he would not surrender, and if,' said he, 'I had my men here you *could* not take me.' I saw that he would be shot if he resisted any longer, and while the rebels were contending with some prisoners in another part of the breakfast-room, I begged the Colonel to go with him and I would save his sword. He consented, and I concealed his sword in the folds of my dress, and begged them to grant him five minutes, which was granted, and he assured me that he 'would be back for his sword.' It was a sad sight to see them take that gray-headed veteran, but it was a joyful sight to see him return to reclaim his sword, having gone with them as far as Monterey Springs and escaped—'rolled away from them,' he said, for he could not walk.

### Carving His Own Head-Board.

A singular incident is related of Sergeant Major Polley, of the Tenth Massachusetts regiment. A day or two before that regiment left for home, while lying in the trenches before Petersburg, he carved with his knife upon a wooden head-board, similar to those placed at soldiers' graves, the words, " Serg. Maj. George F. Polley, 10th Mass. Vols., killed June —, 1864," remarking to the Colonel, " I guess I'll leave the day blank." The next day he was instantly killed by a shell which struck him in the breast, tearing his body to pieces,—Colonel Parsons, who was standing near by, narrowly escaping. He was buried on the field, and the same head-

Carving his own head-board.

board that he had lettered was placed over his grave. He was not expecting to return with the regiment, for he had re-enlisted. For some of these most touching, as well as brilliant chronicles of the great four years' war, few works will compare, in point of choice discrimination, with " The Bugle Blast," by E. S. S. Rouse, an eye-witness and participant.

### Converting Lady Rebels.

Uncle Sam's nephews in Arkansas found an agreeable and effectual way of crushing the rebellion. It had come to be an axiom, that the women of the South were the most rebellious, and that but for them, the spirit of rebellion would have died out. The Federal boys, therefore, went on the very rational principle of striking at the root of the evil and of conquering the women. The tactics adopted to this end—consisting of wooing and marrying the fair ones—proved highly successful. Whether it was because their secesh lovers were out of sight, and, therefore, out of mind, or that they had lost all hopes of seeing them again, or because the blue coats had such winning ways, was not stated; but, nevertheless, marriages of the soldiers and citizenesses were of daily occurrence. One clergyman married as many as five of these couples in one day; and in the county of Conway, all single women under the fascinating age of sixty were gobbled up as fast as the soldiers found them. This was certainly one of the most effectual means of putting down the rebellion. The fair rebels were, of course, turned over, and became firm believers in the Union, if not unconditional unionists,—a phase of the development of Union feeling in Arkansas that must have been very agreeable, at least to the parties consummating the Union.

### On the Lord's Side.

President Lincoln had various interviews with delegations of clergymen from different sections of the country, during the war of the rebellion. Of one of these delegations it is not related that they had much to say when they were admitted into his presence, but, in taking leave, one of them remarked that he "hoped the Lord was on our side." "I don't agree with you," said the President. Of course they looked amazed. "I hope, indeed, that we are on the *Lord's* side!" he continued.

### Rubbing it in—Scene in the Park Barracks, New York.

(*Dramatis Personæ.*) A sick and wounded, but good-looking soldier, and an anxious lady nurse in search of a subject:

Lady Nurse—My poor fellow, can I do anything for you?

Soldier (emphatically)—No, ma'am! Nothin'!

Lady Nurse—I should like to do something for you. Shall I not sponge your face and brow for you?

Soldier (despairingly)—You may sponge my brow if you want to very bad; but you'll be the fourteenth lady as has done it this blessed mornin'.

It was for the want of such judicious supervision as characterized that gentle and beloved minister of good, Miss Dix, that such annoying scenes as the above sometimes occurred. Wherever she went, her presence was a sweet benediction, but her movements were as harmonious and systematic as though benevolence was a science.

### Sue Munday, the Female Guerrilla.

A band of guerrillas, led by a notorious character, named Berry, formerly of John Morgan's command, attacked the stage near Shawneetown, Kentucky, one Friday evening, robbing the passengers and rifling the mail bag. After this exploit, the band moved in the direction of Harrodsburg, relieved the toll-gate keeper near that place of cash and various articles, and then dashed into town.

The Savings Bank was honored with the first call. The managers of the institution observed the movement, and hastily closed and barred the doors before the scoundrels could gain an entrance. The robbers fired several shots as the doors were being closed, but no injury was done by the same. Finding they could not force the doors, the guerrillas proposed to fire the building, but before they could put the design into execution, the citizens, who had armed themselves and collected to defend their homes, commenced firing on the robber band. The outlaws were taken by surprise, and, greatly alarmed, fled from the town.

One of the peculiar characters or personages composing this band of cut-throats, was the officer second in command, recognized by the men as Lieutenant Flowers. The officer in question was a young woman, her real name being Sue Munday. She dressed herself in male attire, generally sporting a full Confederate uniform. Upon her head she wore a jaunty plumed hat, beneath which there escaped a wealth of dark brown hair, falling around and down her shoulders in luxuriant curls. She was possessed of a comely form, had a dark, piercing eye, was a bold rider and daring leader. Prior to connecting herself with Berry's gang of outlaws, she was associated with the band commanded by Captain Alexander, who met his doom some time previously in Southern Kentucky.

Lieutenant Flowers, or Sue Munday, was a practiced robber, and many ladies, who had been so unfortunate as to meet her on the highway, could testify with what *sang froid* she presented a pistol and commanded "Stand and deliver." Her name had become widely known, and, to the ladies, it was associated with horror. On the evening when the outlaws were at Harrodsburg, Sue dexterously robbed a young lady of her watch and chain; and if the citizens had not so unceremoniously expelled the thieving band from the town, she would doubtless have paid her respects to the jewelry and valuables of all the ladies of the place.

### My Bold Soldier Boy.

"What do the women say about us boys at home?" asked a poor battle-wrecked soldier in the hospital, himself but a lad, of one who sat at his side. That brow of his ached for the touch of a loving hand. He had walked through rough, stony places—temptation, sin, folly had beset him on the right hand and on the left; but he felt still a mother's influence on his soul, leading him into the June paths of old. At the very moment he asked the question "What do the women say of us at home?" he was turning over a little silken needle-book that some laughing girl had one day sent to the Sanitary Commission, working on its cover the words, playfully perhaps, "My bold soldier-boy." The friend, sitting by, simply pointed to the happy inscription. The reply struck home to his heart, and he burst into tears. They were not bitter tears, but tears of joy. His question was answered; the evidence of woman's interest was before his eyes, and he was content. His eyelids closed down, his breathing grew calm, and soon sleep touched him, and he was dreaming.

### "No Wickedness like the Wickedness of a Woman."

The bitter and ferocious spirit of thousands of rebel women in Virginia, Kentucky, Tennessee and other States, as exhibited during the war, towards Unionists, is scarcely, if at all, surpassed by the female monsters that shrieked and howled for victims in the French Revolution.

A wounded soldier, of the Union army, fell out from the ranks retreating through Winchester, Virginia, and sank down upon

No Wickedness like the Wickedness of a Woman

the steps of one of the houses. He had not been sitting there long when a woman came out and asked him if he were not able to walk. He replied that he was not. Seeing a revolver in his belt, she asked him to let her look at it. Suspecting nothing, he handed it to her. She deliberately presented it to his head, and ordered him immediately to leave the steps. He did so; and hobbled along a distance of but a few feet, when she fired the pistol, piercing his side with the bullet. He fell on the street and instantly expired.

The woman threw down the revolver and coolly walked back into the house.

Will it be believed that such events occurred in the heart of Christian civilization, in the middle of the nineteenth century? But this was only one of multiplied cases of the sort.

### Off-Hand Eloquence of a Rough Cavalryman.

When General Custer made his raid into Virginia, in the spring of 1864, all the horses that were valuable which came in his way were taken in the name of the United States. In one place, a very handsome lady, quite young, expostulated loudly with a cavalryman for taking the farm-horses. "My dear Miss," said the soldier, "we do not want to take your horses—ours are much better; and besides it goes against our feelings, but military necessity requires this step, and we are merely the agents of unrelenting destiny." In spite of her concern the pretty creature laughed at such off-hand eloquence from a rough cavalryman.

### Wine and Sentiment for the Hospital Soldiers.

In the Louisville journals of March, 1862, one of the hospital features of the war is thus set forth:—

Mrs. C. M. Love returns her grateful thanks to Miss Breckinridge and other kind ladies of Princeton, New Jersey, for another liberal donation of hospital stores, including a large supply of superior currant-wine, made by a lady of Princeton, with a beautiful, patriotic, Christian sentiment written upon nearly all the bottles, of which the subjoined are specimens:—

Currant wine from the old battle-fields of Princeton, New Jersey. 'Let no traitor's feet pollute the glorious emblem of our freedom.'

'Soldiers! may the stars which float over your heads point you to heaven, and may you be gathered there in brighter and more enduring clusters.'

'Brave soldiers in Kentucky, fighting for us here, we have been, and are now watching you with intense interest. We grasp the papers to read of your deeds of noble daring, and while rejoicing over them, our tears flow at the tales of the hardships, the sufferings, by which they are won. We think of you, we pray for you, and may our heavenly Father bless and save you all.'

'Currant wine from Princeton, New Jersey, may it refresh you brave men from Illinois.'

'Kentucky is almost erect in her struggles; New Jersey's arms entwine her more closely than ever.'

'Forget not the invisible hand that leads you to victory.'

'New Jersey extends her hand to you, brave Tennesseeans: she has watched you with deep interest and warm sympathies; our heavenly Father bless and keep you under the dear old *Stars* and *Stripes*.'

'Let no dark clouds prevent you from seeing the bright sunlight beyond.'

'Forget not, forfeit not, your time-honored name, brave Kentuckians.'

'New Jersey honors the Union soldiers in Kentucky, no matter where from.'

'The ladies of Princeton, New Jersey, think and talk of nothing else scarcely, but the brave soldiers fighting and suffering for our glorious Union.'

'Remember Washington, the great Father of his country, and emulate his virtues.'

'You suffer in a holy cause; may you receive an everlasting reward.'

'Be patient, be hopeful, the day is dawning.'

'This wine was made on the battle-field of Princeton, Mercer county, New Jersey, not far from where Washington led his army on to victory, and where the gallant Mercer fell for this our glorious Union. May it bear to you invigorating, refreshing, and healing virtues, is the prayer of the one who made it.'

'Currant wine for our brave defenders. The Lord thy God, he it is that doth go with thee. He will not fail thee nor forsake thee.'

'The ladies of Princeton, send New Jersey's best wishes for your present and future welfare.'

### Sweetness of Secession Female Temper.

The reporter for a New York paper accidentally stumbled upon a female secesh railer at "the Yankees," in Culpepper. This woman was the unfortunate possessor of considerable property, and failing to secure a guard for it in the quarter where such little favors were sometimes obtained, she vented her indignation by telling all who came in her way and would listen, how "derned mean" Yankees were. Falling into her clutches one day, and hearing her tale of woe, reporter most meekly suggested that she might display the Stars and Stripes over her property, and beneath the folds of that banner it would not be molested. This was the signal for an outburst of furious indignation. She would never raise the Stars and Stripes over *her* property—not she; rather die first. Having thus raised the ire of a "200 pounder," and weighing some forty pounds less than herself, prudence dictated that discretion was the better part of valor, and accordingly he gazed at the creature before him in silence. Now, this very discretion seemed to annoy her exceedingly, and placing her arms akimbo, she swelled up like the frog in the fable, and finally, doubtless feeling that the English language was not copious enough to do the subject justice, she exclaimed :

" *There*, Sir— there's my *barn*, yonder; hay all stolen; pigs all killed; chickens gone; boards off—and I can't get a safeguard from you mean Yankees ! "

Reporter was transfixed—puzzled—and said nothing.

Her indignation continuing to rise, she finally screamed out :

" I'll come up with ye—I'll come up with ye mean Yankees. I'll go intothe barn loft, and burn the barn with myself in it."

Reporter still remained silent, and she ended—after taking breath—with the explodent:

" *Then where will ye— Yankees get boards from ?* "

Having nothing to say, and fearing this original secesh might burn by spontaneous combustion while on his hands, Reporter left. There were many female secesh of that sort.

Bell Boyd.

### Hearts and Swords.

No one, whether loyalist or secession in their political views, will read the following lines penned by one whose cradle was rocked in the dawning days of the Revolution led on by Washington, without the warmest emotions :

Clyde, Ohio, Aug. 3, 1864.
*To General Grant.*

DEAR SIR : I hope you will pardon me for troubling you with the perusal of these few lines from the trembling hand of the aged grandma' of our beloved General Jas. B. McPherson, who fell in battle. When it was announced at his funeral, from the public print, that when General Grant heard of his death, he went into his tent and wept like a child, my heart went out in thanks to you for the interest you manifested in him while he was with you. I have watched his progress from infancy up. In childhood he was obedi-

600 THE BOOK OF ANECDOTES OF THE REBELLION.

ent and kind; in manhood interesting, noble and persevering, looking to the wants of others. Since he entered the war, others can appreciate his worth better than I can.

When it was announced to us by telegraph that our loved one had fallen, our hearts were almost rent asunder; but when we heard the commander-in-chief could weep with us, too, we felt, Sir, that you have been as a father to him, and this whole nation is mourning his early death. I wish to inform you that his remains were conducted by a kind guard to the very parlor where he spent a cheerful evening in 1861, with his widowed mother, two brothers, only sister and his aged grandma', who is now trying to write. In the morning he took his leave at six o'clock, little dreaming he should fall by a ball from the enemy.

His funeral services were attended in his mother's orchard, where his youthful feet had often pressed the soil to gather fruit, and his remains are resting in the silent grave scarce half a mile from the place of his birth. His grave is on an eminence but a few rods from where the funeral services were attended, and near the grave of his father. The grave, no doubt, will be marked, so that passers-by will often pause to drop a tear over the dear departed. And now, dear friend, a few lines from you would be gratefully received by the afflicted friends. I pray that the God of battles may be with you, and go forth with your armies till the rebellion shall cease, the Union be restored, and the old flag wave over our entire land.

With much respect,
I remain your friend,
LYDIA SLOCUM,
Aged 87 years and 4 months.

GEN. GRANT'S REPLY.

Head-quarters, Armies of the U. S.,
City Point, Va., August 10.

MRS. LYDIA SLOCUM: MY DEAR MADAM—Your very welcome letter of the 3d instant has reached me. I am glad to know the relatives of the lamented Major-General McPherson are aware of the more than friendship existing between him and myself. A nation grieves at the loss of one so dear to our nation's cause. It is a selfish grief, because the nation had more to expect from him than from almost any one living. I join in this selfish grief, and add the grief of personal love for the departed. He formed for some time one of my military family. I knew him well. To know him was but to love him. It may be some consolation to you, his aged grandmother, to know that every officer and every soldier who served under your grandson, felt the highest reverence for his patriotism, his zeal, his great, almost unequalled ability, his amiability and all the manly virtues that can adorn a commander. Your bereavement is great, but cannot exceed mine.

Yours truly,
U. S. GRANT, Lieut.-Gen.

**Wooed and Wedded—With Embellishments.**

John Kick, of Buffalo, New York, was a private in the Second New York Mounted rifles, which regiment, notwithstanding its name, was not mounted, but served as infantry "mounted"—on human legs and feet. Pushing along, sunned on and dusted on, during the march from Cold Harbor to James River, John was stricken with deadly sickness. John could go no further—was not simply tired out, exhausted, knocked up, played out and done for, but he was sick. He fell out of the ranks. His comrades thought him now sun-struck. A learned surgeon hazarded the expression of an opinion that the man was suffering from aggravated coup de soliel, induced by exhaustion and the climate.

His comrades bore John to the nearest house,—the residence, formerly, of the late ex-President John Tyler. There John—John Kick—was left, and his fellows went marching on. There was a young lady in the house, Anna Maria Tyler, niece of the once President. A month, nearly two months, passed, and John was not heard from. Was John still sick? Was John lingering in pain and helplessness? Had John gone over to the 'Johnnies' after recovering? Or had he *kicked* the inevitable bucket that awaits all mortals? Would John ever be heard of again? Would Kick ever again pedestriunate with his fellow mounted rifles? Nobody could answer. Kick was supposed to have kicked out of the service. His enemies hinted that he had gone over to the enemy—in fact, been Tylerized. They were mistaken.

Kick had not been Tylerized, but Tyler had been Kicked. Anna Maria took tender care of John. She did pity him like another Desdemona. True, he was a Yankee, but Othello was a Moor. Perhaps Anna loved John for the dangers he had seen. At any rate, she loved John in spite of the fact that he had done the State some service. And John loved Anna Maria. As the flush of returning health came to John's cheek, Maria grew pale; pale, but interesting, John saw, and then John began to feel. And here five chapters might be written, and Tennyson quoted, by way of describing the fusing of their two hearts. But John wasn't agoin' to let concealment feed on his cheek. John spoke. Anna Maria spoke back. She was a rebel, but she did not rebel. Both Barkises were 'willin.' A local preacher lived in a "hard town small by," and the knot was tied.

Kick (prenomen John) and Kick (nee' Tyler) were happy. "Whoso findeth a wife findeth a good thing and obtaineth favor of the Lord," is Scripture. Doubtless the converse should be understood. They were happy, but—a cloud shadowed the honey moon. John must go to his regiment and Kick away his other half. But still he lingered. Duty called, but Anna pleaded. It was kicking against the pricks to think of parting. Four weeks passed at last; John wrenched himself away. Afoot and alone, 'cross lots, and sobbing, Kick left his brided ex-President's niece, and wended his sorrowful but proud way "on this line" till he reached the Union pickets, and so presented himself at General Butler's head-quarters. He told his tale. He was no deserter. On the contrary he was the wedded husband of—his wife, and he told who his wife was and how he came to have her for wife. He produced a letter to the Commanding General, signed "Anna Tyler Kick," begging that her spouse might be granted furlough for thirty days, and pass North for self and wife, "to arrange domestic affairs." The letter was evidently that of a cultivated lady (as she was,)—in an exquisite hand, on exquisite paper, couched in well-considered, well-phrased and touching terms. The regiment, however, happening to be in General Burnside's corps, it was not in General Butler's power to grant the request; but he gave them a letter to Gen. Burnside, recommending that the request of the other half of Kick, late Tyler, be granted, and commending John Kick for successful 'Union' strategy. Furlough and pass were obtained.

Allowance will of course be made for 'embellishments,' in war and newspaper times.

### Florence Nightingale's Contribution.

A gift from Florence Nightingale to the Sanitary Commission in aid of the Union soldiers, seemed peculiarly appropriate, in view of her well known high character, and her self-sacrificing sympathies and efforts in behalf of the soldier's hospital welfare. Mrs. Bancroft Davis, of New York, received through Mrs. Adams, wife of the United States Minister at London, two copies of "Notes on Nursing," from Miss Nightingale, as a contribution to the Sanitary Fair, with her autograph in each, written "from her sick bed," and a copy of "Notes on Nursing for the Laboring Classes," which bears the inscription in her own hand, "Offered to the sick and suffering by their faithful servant, Florence Nightingale." These gifts were also accompanied by views of Miss Nightingale's "two homes," photographed from drawings by her sister, Lady Verney. Of course these gifts, from such a source, possessed a value far beyond their mere material worth.

#### Power of the Tender Passion on a Union Lieutenant.

At the breaking out of the rebellion, Mr. J. S. Searight enlisted in a company of volunteers from the town of Lincoln, Illinois, and which was attached to the Thirty-second regiment of that State. At a later date, Mr. Searight received a Lieutenant's commission. He was generally esteemed as an excellent officer, and did his whole duty in several of the sanguinary engagements in the Southwest. In an unlucky hour he met a young lady of secession proclivities, but, alas! extremely beautiful in her personal appearance, at her home near Nashville, Tennessee. Suffice it to say that they met and loved. All the time the Lieutenant could spare from his duties was spent in the society of this new-found and charming little syren, and she as eagerly returned his burning passion. Lieutenant Searight time and again offered his resignation—he wished to leave the tented field and dwell in the rosy bowers of love—but, unlike his love, it was not accepted. Love at length conquered all his scruples—he deserted! and succeeded in escaping beyond the federal lines with the young lady. The Southern belle who thus captivated the young Lieutenant was enormously wealthy—being the possessor of an ample fortune in sterling gold. They also succeeded in running the blockade at Charleston and arrived at Havana on Christmas day, when they were married. Love has seduced from the path of duty many wiser men than Lieutenant Searight. It is a resistless and overwhelming sentiment, and the best of mortals commit follies and extravagances, and even crimes, when involved in its meshes.

#### First "Union" Demonstration in Old Virginia.

One of the Federal prisoners, Corporal Merrill, who was conveyed to the city of Richmond, found an unexpectedly obliging friend in the person of an Irish woman—true to the generous traits of her nativity. The train of cars arrived at the Confederate capital about nine o'clock in the evening. After the cars had halted, the Corporal heard a low voice at his window, which was partly raised. It was quite dark, and he could not distinguish the speaker, who was an Irish woman.

"Whisht, whisht!" said she; "are ye hungry?"

Corporal M. replied that he was not, but that some of the boys probably were.

"Wait till I go to the house," she continued, and in a moment afterward she was again heard at the window. She handed him a loaf of bread, some meat, and about a dozen bakers' cakes, saying, "That was all I had in the house, but I had a shillin', and I bought the cakes wid it; and if I had more, ye should have it, and welcome! Take it, and God bless ye!"

He thanked her, and said, "You are very kind to enemies."

"Whisht," said she, "and *ain't I from New York meself?*"

This was the first Union demonstration that the Corporal had witnessed in Old Virginia. He thanked God for the consolation which the reflection afforded him, as for the third night he lay sleeplessly in the cars, with clothing still saturated and body thoroughly chilled from the effects of the deluge of rain which fell at Manassas, whither he had come. But the Corporal said he could have desired no sweeter morsel than the good woman's homely loaf, and, proud of the loyal giver, said the Corporal, "I rejoiced that 'I was from New York meself!'"

### Looking After a Soldier's Wife.

The frailty of human nature and the bad policy of trusting too much to human friendships were exemplified in their saddest hue, in a case which happened in the city of Detroit, Michigan, and in which patriotism was made to suffer somewhat severely. A gentleman of that city having become deeply imbued with loyal sentiments, and feeling that he might as well make sacrifices for his country as any one, enlisted in the army. The sacrifice was probably much greater than at first impulse he anticipated. It amounted, indeed, to no less than the ruin of his home and the loss of all hope of future earthly happiness.

He left behind him a lovely and accomplished wife and a family of two interesting children. He made ample provision for their support, and set aside a certain portion of his wages, to be transmitted to them regularly, whenever his regiment was paid. To still further ensure their comfort, he left them in charge of a friend living near, in whom, after a long acquaintance and daily intercourse and friendship, he had gained the utmost confidence, with the injunction to see that they wanted for nothing. Feeling sure, therefore, that his wife and family were in good hands and not likely to suffer under any circumstances, he went cheerfully forth to the hardships and perils of the field.

But, alas for the falsity of human faith. His friend—who, by the way, had always been considered a man of good standing in society and an estimable citizen—obeying the injunction to see that the soldier's family wanted for nothing, paid them almost daily visits. During these visits an intimacy sprang up, which ripened into impropriety, and thus continued through a series of weeks, if not months. In a short time, the soldier-husband, who had gained honor in several campaigns, wrote back to his wife the—to him—joyful intelligence that he had obtained a furlough, and was about to visit his home and family. To the guilty wife this news brought with stunning weight the consciousness of her guilt. Ashamed to meet her husband, she yielded to the suggestions of her seducer, and a few days before the expected return of the soldier, they fled for parts unknown.

The heartless villain left a wife and family behind, who became overwhelmed with grief at the shame and disgrace thus brought upon their good name. The feelings of the soldier on learning the faithlessness of his wife and friend can, of course, be better imagined than described. Finding a suitable home for his children, he returned to the field wiser in many respects, and older and sadder in experience.

---

### Southern "War Widows."

Quite a noticeable institution at Vicksburg and the region thereabout, on its falling into the hands of the Federal powers, was the Southern widow—an article of which there appeared to be an abundance, of all sorts and ages. A partnership, friendship, fellowship, with one of them, proved sometimes profitable, if not pleasant, to the northern newcomers. Gunboat officers, newsmen, merchants and Jews would quit their legitimate spheres to ply these 'lorn women' with their seductive arts, for the sake of the cotton which they were found to have and hold. In one case a penniless adventurer was enriched by his share in a few hundred bales—of course of great value. Another married a scrawny dame, and turned Southern planter, body and soul, quietly softening down from a northern radical to a conservative, meet for "the manor born." A third became encumbered with no less than three women, whom he was anxious to marry off, but found his compensation in the farming of two thousand acres of land. In fact, the rage for turning planter became very great, for the sake of the golden gains of the cotton, exclusive of the innate attractions which the rich southern women possessed for the needy bachelors of Yankee land.

### Leave-taking at the Station.

A squad of 'soldier boys' was about to set off for the seat of war. At the station a large crowd of friends had gathered, and there was the usual amount of kissing, weeping, embracing, and leave-taking. A loud-voiced man was entertaining a group of ladies with his conversation, and he remarked, as one of the soldiers' sweet little wives was passing. "If I was going to the war, and any of my friends should come down to the station to see me off, I would shoot them." The little woman looked up, and very quietly said, "Oh, don't fret; you wouldn't have a chance to fire once!" If one ever saw a man fished out of the raging canal alive—this fellow looked the like.

### "My Mary Ann."

For some time the post commander at Cairo was a certain West Point Colonel of a Northwestern regiment, noted for his soldierly qualities and rigid discipline. One day he passed by the barracks and heard a group of soldiers singing the well known street piece, "My Mary Ann." An angry shade crossed his brow, and he forthwith ordered the men placed in the guard-house, where they remained all night. The next morning he visited them, when one ventured to ask the cause of their confinement.

"Cause enough," said the rigid Colonel; "you were singing a song in derision of Mrs. Col. B——."

The men replied by roars of laughter, and it was some time before the choler of the Colonel could be sufficiently subdued to understand that the song was an old one, and sung by half the school boys in the land, or the risibles of the men be calmed down to learn that the Colonel's wife rejoiced in the name of "Mary Ann."

That Colonel became a Brigadier-General.

### Bright Girls in Missouri.

About fifteen miles northwest from Springfield, Missouri, lived a Union farmer named R. In the spring of 1862, as he was plowing in his field near his little log cabin, a party of a dozen secession marauders, or jayhawkers, as they were there called, rode up. Ten of them hid themselves in the brush; the other two went forward and said,

"We have been here before, at night, and could not get what we wanted, because your stable was locked. We have come now in the daytime and we think we can get them."

"Well," said Mr. R., "you are armed and I am not. It is hard, but I suppose I shall have to give them up."

"And that's not all," replied one of the two, "we mean to take your horses, and we mean to take *you*, too."

"That's what you can't do," replied the sturdy old farmer; "you've got arms, and you can kill me, but you can't take me alive."

Here one of the men stepped back a few paces, cocked his gun and took deliberate aim at the farmer's head. At the same instant Mr. R. heard footsteps in the direction of his house, and saw his daughter coming—a girl nearly grown, with a quiet face, but a look of bright intelligence beaming from her eyes. She had one hand under her apron, in which she carried his revolver—and, what was more to the purpose, she, like many a Missouri girl, knew how to use it. Ah! there were what a Cockney would call "stunning girls" in that neighborhood; one of them had not long since, on coming out of church, horsewhipped a young man in the presence of the congregation, and taken away his horse from him, without the least diffidence or difficulty. This brave daughter never did the like of that; but when near enough to her father, she cast upon him a look of inquiry, which said—

"Shall I shoot that man?"

Her father shook his head. Then she

spoke in a fearless, ordinary tone of voice, and said:

"Father, did you see those Federals come to our house just now?"

"No," said he.

"There were ten of them," she added.

The jayhawker who was threatening her father's life, put up his gun and said:

"Oh, they were just our men who were in the brush. I saw them going that way myself."

"I don't *think* that they were your men," she turned to him and said; "anyway they have got *short jackets* on," (cavalry).

Hereupon the horsethieves turned, remounted their steeds, and incontinently 'vamoused the ranche.'

Meanwhile, the old farmer and his ingeniously bright and bold girl returned to the house; when, without waiting to put on the saddle, he jumped upon his fastest horse, and rode to town to tell his story and seek protection. That there are some bright girls in Missouri no one will doubt who has read Mr. C. C. Coffin's ("Carleton,") admirable sketches of the war in that and other regions.

### Young Feminine Spoiling for Fight.

Lizzie Compton, a smart young Miss of sixteen, presented herself one day at Louisville, for the purpose of being mustered out of the service, she having been for some months a member of the Eleventh Kentucky cavalry. She had served in seven different regiments, and participated in several battles. At Fredericksburg she was seriously wounded, but recovered and followed the fortunes of war, which cast her from the Army of the Potomac to the Army of the Cumberland. She fought in the battles of Green River bridge, on the 4th of July, receiving a wound which disabled her for a short time. Seven or eight times she was discovered and mustered out of service, but immediately re-enlisted in another regiment. She stated that her home was in London, Canada West, that being the place of her parents' residence.

### Falling Back at the Wrong Moment.

Two old ladies were one time conversing on the battle of Chickamauga. Said one (quoth the Columbia 'South Carolinian'):

Two old Ladies conversing about Gen. Bragg

"I wish, as General Bragg is a Christian man, that he were dead and in heaven; I think it would be a God-send to the Confederacy."

"Why, my dear," said the other, "if the General were near the gates of heaven, and invited in, at that moment he would fall back."

### Captain ——'s Trade for a Kiss.

One evening, at the Bazaar held for the soldiers, at Columbus, Ohio, a pretty Indian girl was observed exerting her persuasive powers to their utmost tension, to induce a certain military gent, who ranked as a captain, to buy of her a bead basket, or some other ornament which she had in her possession, for disposal on that occasion. As the gallant Captain had been gouged an unlimited number of times during the evening, he didn't quite yield to the soft and bland appeal; but thinking to startle the maiden a bit, said jokingly—

"Don't want to buy your trinkets, but I'll give you five dollars for a kiss!"

The maid reflected but a moment—she was laboring in a noble cause, for the soldiers, good—"surely in such a case there's no harm;" so, in a twinkling of the eye,

606    THE BOOK OF ANECDOTES OF THE REBELLION.

she said, "*Done, sir,*" and, as she expressed it, gave him a whapper right on his cheek.

Military drew back, abashed. The crowd saw it and laughed. There was but one way of escape—he pulled out his somewhat depleted wallet and forked over a V. He then rushed frantically up stairs and drowned his sorrow in a flowing bowl of oyster soup. The maiden, in the meantime, maintained her accustomed tranquility.

### Became a Soldier After All.

Mrs. Crissey, of Decatur, Illinois, whose husband was chaplain in an Illinois regiment, related to a visitor that many years ago her little baby, while playing in the street, fell down, and began to cry. A very tall young man, who was just then passing by with a yoke of oxen, picked the child up, and handing him inside the gate, said, cheerily, "You will never make a soldier if you cry for that." The little fellow at once banished his grief. The tall young man was Abraham Lincoln, and Mrs. Crissey introduced to the visitor a young Captain, home on furlough, as her son, who had become a soldier after all. Such are the odds and ends which turn up with the whirligig of old Father Time.

### In and Out of the Vicksburg Caves.

The wife of one of the Confederate officers, who was confined within the "wall of fire" which surrounded Vicksburg during the memorable days of April and June, wrote an entertaining volume on the scenes and incidents which there transpired. Like most of her companions, she was compelled to seek shelter from the deluge of iron hail in the caves—these being the fashion—the rage—over besieged Vicksburg. Negroes, who understood their business, hired themselves out to dig them, at from thirty to forty dollars, according to the size. Many persons, considering different localities unsafe, would sell them to others, who had been less fortunate, or less provident; and so great was the demand for cave workmen, that a new branch of industry sprang up and became popular—particularly as the personal safety of the workmen was secure, and money to be made withal.

Finally, the surrender of Vicksburg came, and the husband of the lady entered her cave retreat and informed her of the fact.

"It's all over! the white flag floats from our forts! Vicksburg has surrendered!"

He put on his uniform coat, silently buckled on his sword, and prepared to take out the men, to deliver up their arms in front of the fortification. The lady said of this change of circumstances: "I felt a strange unrest, the quiet of the day was so unnatural. I walked up and down the cave until M—— returned. The day was extremely warm; and he came with a violent headache. He told me that the Federal troops had acted splendidly; they were stationed opposite the place where the Confederate troops marched up and stacked their arms; and they seemed to feel sorry for the poor fellows who had defended the place for so long a time. Far different from what he had expected, not a jeer or taunt came from any one of the Federal soldiers. Occasionally a cheer would be heard, but the majority seemed to regard the poor unsuccessful soldiers with a generous sympathy. After the surrender, the old gray-headed soldier, in passing on the hill near the cave, stopped, and touching his hat, said: "It's a sad day, this, madam; I little thought we'd come to it, when we first stepped into the entrenchments. I hope you'll yet be happy, madam, after the trouble you've seen;" to which I mentally responded, 'Amen.' The poor hunchback soldier, who had been sick, and who, at home in Southern Missouri, is worth a million of dollars, I have been told, yet within Vicksburg has been nearly starved, walked out to-day in the pleasant air, for the first time in many days."

### General Butler as a Young Lawyer.

The shrewd dodge resorted to by Butler, when a young lawyer, in the acquittal of a counterfeiter, and the strange figure cut by Ben on the street, in wresting him from the hands of a constable, are among the memorabilia of the General's former days. It so happened that one of the editors of the Lowell Courier was present and witnessed both scenes of the farce.

Gen. Butler as a Young Lawyer.

The same evening, therefore, a column was devoted to Butler, describing in humorous and sarcastic language his exploits of the forenoon at the court-house. The next morning, Butler appeared in the sanctum of the Courier, armed with a formidable raw-hide, and demanded of Colonel Schouler, the senior editor of the paper—afterwards Adjutant-General of Massachusetts—the name of the author of the offensive article.

"I'm not accustomed to reveal the authorship of any portion of the original matter which appears in my paper," replied the Colonel: "I hold myself, however, personally responsible for the whole of it."

"If you wish to know so very much the author of that article, I wrote it, Mr. Butler," meekly interposed the youthful assistant editor, turning around from his desk at the opposite side of the room.

"I suppose you did, you —— scoundrel," screamed Butler, brandishing his raw-hide, "and I've come up here to thrash you within an inch of your life, unless you promise to publish in this evening's paper a humble apology for it."

"I shall do no such thing," replied the assistant editor: "I have nothing to retract —nothing to apologize for."

"Then take that!" shouted the irate attorney, bringing down his raw-hide *a la* Brooks.

The assistant editor, dodging the badly aimed blow, seized the just filled ink-stand from the desk and let fly. He proved a better marksman than his antagonist. It struck Ben flat as a flounder on the breast, bespattering his bosom and face to a degree his opponent could hardly have hoped for. Just then the door of the printing office opened, and Ben was smartly seized by half a dozen stout printers, hustled down stairs in a most informal kind of gait, and with tattered hat, face smeared with ink, and torn coat, ejected into the street. Whoever saw him, just then, was in no doubt that *somebody* had got into a scrape! The contrast in "plucky Ben's" appearance then and when he afterwards donned his epaulettes and stars, was, to say the least, quite suggestive.

### Conversation with an Atlanta Young Lady.

The order of General Sherman, after the capture of Atlanta, expatriating all the inhabitants of that city, in view of making it a great military depot, or *point d'appui*, was the occasion of many a startling domestic scene. The spirit which it bred is well illustrated in the conversation given below, between a young Southern lady, of refinement, and a Union gentleman, just as the former was starting on her tour of exile.

*Young Lady*—It is very hard to be obliged to leave our home. We have not felt the war before, except in the cost of the luxuries of life. We did not believe that your army would ever penetrate so far south, but I suppose our removal is one of the necessities of the situation, and we would much rather give up our homes than live near the Yankees. We will get far enough away this time.

*Unionist*—May I ask where you intend to go?

*Young Lady*—To Augusta, where your army can't come.

*Unionist*—I would not be sure of that. It is a long way from Nashville to Atlanta,—yet we are here.

*Young Lady* (with ineffable scorn)—Oh, yes, you will '*flank*' us, I suppose.

*Unionist*—Possibly, madam.

*Young Lady*—Look here, sir; there are not two nations on the face of the earth, whose language, customs and habits are different, and who are geographically separated as wide as the poles, but what are nearer to each other than the North and the South. There are no two peoples in the world who hate each other more.

*Unionist*—I hardly think there is the difference you describe, miss. It seems to me just as if you and I were Americans, with no vital points of difference between us which may not be settled some day. And then, I protest against the idea that we 'hate you.' I understand public feeling at the North pretty well, and such a sentiment does not exist there generally.

*Young Lady*—Well, sir, *we hate you*; we will never live with you again. If you whip us, and any of these mean politicians in the South (and there are thousands of them who will be only too glad to do it) offer terms of reconstruction, we will throw ourselves into the arms of France, which only wait the chance to embrace us.

*Unionist*—Reconstruction will undoubtedly come about in time, miss. But we shall not permit France or any other foreign power to interfere. France would embrace you, without doubt, if she gets a chance, but it will be the hug of an anaconda, who will swallow you whole, without mastication.

*Young Lady*—Anything rather than become subject to the North. We will not submit to *that* degradation.

*Unionist*—If you are defeated you will; and then you will have thoroughly learned what your people have never, before the war, in the slightest degree understood—how to *respect us*. I assure you, friendship follows very close upon the heels of mutual respect.

*Young Lady*—There is much truth in that, sir, and we are willing to confess that we never even believed the North would fight; and while there is a certain feeling of respect which has been forced upon us, we hate you all the more now, because we despised you before.

Railroad Depot at Atlanta, Ga.

### Alas! the Poor Soldier.

Shortly after one of the terrible battles on the soil of Virginia, which sent thousands of brave soldiers to their last home, and mangled and mutilated thousands more for life, a wounded soldier was observed wearily making his way along Main street, Worcester, Mass., among the hurrying crowds which thronged the walk. One empty coat sleeve showed that the aim of one rebel musket at least had not been faulty. As he was jostled rudely along, the blood trickled slowly down to the pavement, proving that the wound was far from healed. Presently two young women

—hardly worthy the name of 'ladies,' although attired as such,—approached. They, too, saw the maimed and bleeding soldier, and daintily drawing closer their flowing robes, with their delicate noses elevated in disgust, they shrunk away with sundry little feminine exclamations of disgust and aversion. As the unfortunate soldier stepped within the shadow of a doorway, and leaned his head upon his

Alas, poor Soldier!

remaining arm, to hide the tears which their deeds and words toward one of a sensitive nature had caused to moisten his eyes, a spectacle of lonely desolation, caused by such heartless ingratitude, was presented, which brought pity from more than one passer by.

**Senor B—— and the Confederate Brigadier's Daughter.**

In the summer of 1860, Senor B——, the son of a wealthy Cuban planter, was staying at Saratoga. While there he became acquainted with Miss Eugenie F., daughter of a well known Mobile banker. The parties became enamored of each other, and all things being satisfactory, they became betrothed with the consent of the old folks, and the marriage was appointed to take place on the 16th of August, 1861. The lady returned to her home, while the gentleman went back to Cuba to arrange and settle his private affairs, with a view of permanently residing in the United States. About one month before the time appointed for the nuptials to take place, the Mobile banker received and accepted a commission as Brigadier-General in the Confederate service, and in his first battle, a few weeks after, received a mortal wound. His sudden death involved the family in unexpected embarrassment, and from a state of wealth they were plunged into comparative obscurity and poverty. Upon this state of affairs being made known to the father of Senor B., he broke off the match between the latter and Miss Eugenie, and interdicted even the slight correspondence afforded through the medium of blockade runners. Thus matters remained for a considerable time, until finally the old man died, leaving the son free, of course, to wed the maiden of his choice. He immediately took passage for, and after several days reached, Mobile. He there found that his intended mother-in-law, overcome with grief at her husband's falling in battle, had succumbed to the fell destroyer, and followed her partner to the grave, while Eugenie was conducting a seminary for young ladies. The meeting between the young couple need not be described—it will suffice to say, that the school was given up, the parties married, and in a few days embarking from Wilmington, North Carolina, they arrived in safety at Nassau. From thence they went to New York, and "all went merry as a marriage bell."

### Private W. in Love and Luck.

At the first battle of Bull Run there was a soldier by the name of W——, who, like many others on that memorable occasion, straggled away from his command. After walking, or rather running, for several hours, he became very much fatigued, and after taking good precaution that there were no rebels either within sound or sight, he lay down to sleep by the side of a fence, and slept sweetly and soundly during the night. Late in the morning, when the sun was indeed near midnoon, he woke to find himself in a strange land, and perhaps among the bitterest enemies of the country.

But the demand of hunger soon silenced the voice of prudence and caution. Seeing a mansion on a hill in the distance, surrounded by parks and meadows, orchards and evergreens, artificial fountains and natural streams of clear running water, in fact everything tending to show that it was one of the first-class old Virginia plantations, the home of courtly elegance and refinement, our soldier, tired with a weary step, and a fainting, famishing heart, knocked at the door of the mansion. He was cordially received, for the old Virginia planter was faithful among the faithful few. He remained long enough to recruit his wasted energies and get information as to the most direct route to Washington. But the name of the young soldier was not forgotten by the planter, nor his manly bearing and genial temperament.

W—— re-enlisted in another regiment, and at the second battle of Bull Run was severely though not dangerously wounded. He was taken to the hospital at Washington. His old Virginia friend, who had so highly appreciated his character, learned of his illness. He sent to the hospital and obtained an order for permission to take him to his own home. He was removed, when through the kindness of the planter and the attentions of his daughter, the young man gradually recovered from the effects of his wound, and was himself again.

A tender regard had in the meantime sprung up between the young lady and the young soldier, and, to cut very short the turn the story in such cases made and provided usually takes, they were betrothed. The soldier returned to his northern home on furlough. But while there he learned of the sudden and severe indisposition of her who was soon to become his bride. Shocked at the unexpected intelligence, he hastened on his journey back to her side, but, as the sad result showed, only to bury her loved form in the cold embrace of the grave. The old man, however, still true to the attachment he had formed for the young soldier, told him that he intended to make him his heir,—that he had no children left, and no relatives, except those in rebellion, and that he should now share with him his estate. He at once gave him a deed to a considerable property in Chicago. The young man, a few weeks after, visited that modern miracle and Babylon combined, and found that his little Chicago fortune would realize the handsome sum of two hundred thousand dollars, being offered sixty thousand dollars for a single block to which he had fallen heir. But this is not all of the strange and eventful story. The old man soon after died, leaving all his fortune—more than eight hundred thousand dollars—to the young Union soldier.

---

### Pictures of Mrs. Major G—— and her "Boy."

Mrs. G——, wife of a slain officer, was promoted by the President of the United States to the position of Major in the army, in recognition of her bravery in the field and services in the hospital to the Union soldiers. The female Major afterwards sojourned in Cleveland for some days, and finally was married there to a private in the Forty-ninth New York regiment—a mere boy. The happy couple subsequently visited an artist's studio for the purpose of having their likenesses taken. The lady Major, after inquiring the price of several cases—and failing to be suited thereat—exclaimed: "If you knew who I am, perhaps you would give me a picture!" She then exhibited to the operator several badges, etc., and made known her name and position. "I can see no reason why you should not pay for a picture, and a good round price at that, for you are getting a pretty plump salary," said Mr. Operator. "That may be," archly replied the bright woman, "but do you see that 'ere boy?" pointing to her husband: "In all probability, besides having him to take care of, I shall have his dad and mammy on my hands soon!" Matters were finally "adjusted," and Mrs. Major G—— did not leave without a picture of herself and "boy."

### Northern Schoolma'ams in Georgia.

A body of Federal prisoners had reached Rome, Georgia, en route for Richmond. Weary, famished, thirsting, they were herded like cattle in the street, under the burning sun,—a public show. It was a gala day in that modern Rome. The women, magnificently arrayed, came out and pelted them with balls of cotton, and with such characteristic feminine sneers and taunts as, "So you have come to Rome, have you, you Yankees? How do you like your welcome?"—and then more cotton and more words. The crowds and the hours came and went, but the mockery did not intermit, and the poor fellows were half out of heart. Major P., of an Ohio regiment, faint and ill, had stepped back a pace or two and leaned against a post, when he was lightly touched upon the arm. As he looked around, mentally nerving himself for some more ingenious insult, a fine looking, well dressed boy of twelve stood at his elbow, his frank face turned up to the Major's. With a furtive glance at a rebel guard who stood with his back to them, the lad, pulling the Major's shirt, and catching his breath, boy-fashion, said,

"Are you from New England?"

"I was born in Massachusetts," was the reply.

"So was my mother," returned the boy, brightening up; "She was a New England girl, and she was what you call a 'school-ma'am,' up north; she married my father, and I'm their boy, but how she *does* love New England and the Yankees, and the old United States, and so do I."

The Major was touched, as well he might be, and his heart warmed to the boy as to a young brother; and he took out his knife, severed a button from his coat and handed to him for a remembrance.

"Oh, I've got half a dozen just like it. See here!" and he took from his pocket a little string of them, gifts of other boys in blue. "My mother would like to see you," he added, "and I'll go and tell her."

"*What are you doing there!*" growled the guard, suddenly wheeling around upon him, and the boy slipped away into the crowd and was gone. Not more than half an hour elapsed before a lovely lady, accompanied by the little patriot, passed slowly down the sidewalk next to the curb-stone. She did not pause, she did not

Gov. Andrew, of Mass.

speak; if she smiled at all it was faintly; but she handed to one and another of the prisoners bank notes as she went. As they neared the Major, the boy gave him a significant look, as much as to say, "That's my New England mother." The eyes of the elegant lady and the poor, weary officer met, for an instant, and she passed away like a vision out of sight. Who would not join in fervently breathing two beautitudes: God bless the young Georgian, and blessed forever be the northern school-ma'am!

Yes, she was one of those Massachusetts ministers of wisdom and goodness, so many of whom, under the inspiration of that great-hearted man, Governor Andrew, have left the Old Bay State, and all its attractions of piety, literature, thrift and refinement, to instruct and elevate the children of the South, and reclaim its vast moral wastes.

## "Hopeless Cases."

When the wounded were being brought into the churches at Leesburg, after the battle, friend and foe were accommodated alike with whatever the Confederates had, and the ladies were busy in their various offices of mercy and kindness. Outside one of the churches a tent was raised for the reception of the dead. Lieutenant Small, of the Confederate service, was searching for a poor friend of his among the many bodies, and found two Yankees, thrown in among the others. They were sighing, and he immediately pulled them out, placed a body under their heads for a pillow, and examined their hurts. One had received a shot in the left eye; being a common round musket ball, it had passed round the skull and came out at the left ear. In the second case, the ball had passed in a direction exactly opposite to this. They were not dead, but they had been thrown aside to die, while many of their comrades were comfortably provided for in churches and schools. The doctors in attendance were busy, and treated Lieutenant S. like a Union sympathizer, and to all his appeals in behalf of suffering humanity, swore roundly that they had something more important to attend to, particularly as the two Yankees were pronounced by all the physicians as 'hopeless cases.' But the Lieutenant's appeal to the ladies was answered by instant kindness. They proceeded to the 'dead tent,' and stated that the two sufferers had been there all day, and were considered dead. Lieutenant S. procured some excellent whiskey for them, their faces were washed, more spirit was administered at proper intervals, food was given, and to the astonishment of all the doctors, those two fellows were walking about the streets of Leesburg in less than three days, comfortably smoking their pipes, or fighting their battles over again, around the fire of the mess-rooms.

## Yankee Pris'ner 'Scaped from Richmon'.

"John Bray," of the First New Jersey cavalry, was captured by a band of Mosby's rough-riders, at Warrenton, Va., and duly escorted as a prisoner to Richmond. From this imprisonment he, by great dexterity, managed to escape, one Sabbath— a holy day which blessed his deed. At eleven o'clock that night he was within nine miles of New Kent Court House, having traveled a distance of twenty-one miles since noon. He passed that night in a swamp, asleep, exhausted, chilled, and sore, and had lost his way. The next morning, while pursuing again his devious path, a negro suddenly confronted him. Says "John:"—Whence he came I knew not; I only knew that he stood before me with a look of inquiry in his eyes, as much as to say, Who are you, sir? I was, of course, startled; but I remembered that I wore a rebel uniform, and met him accordingly. But he was not to be deceived.

"Yer can't come dat game on dis chil'," he said with a sparkle in his eye; "I knows you, sar; you'se a Yankee pris'ner 'scaped from Richmon'." Then, as if to reassure me, he hurriedly added, "But Lor' bless yer, massa, I won't tell on yer; I'se real glad yer's got away."

I saw in a moment the fellow could be

trusted—I have never seen a negro yet, in this war, who could not be trusted by the Union soldier; and so I unbosomed myself to him at once, telling him the whole story of my escape, that I had lost my way, that I had not eaten a morsel of food in twenty-four hours, and that if he could help me in any way I would be more indebted than I could describe.

"Dis chil' glad to help yer," he replied, in a tone of real pleasure, and with a bright look in his eyes, and at once started off at a rapid pace, leading me across the fields, a distance of four miles, to the house of another negro, to whom he explained my situation and wishes. Here I was given something to eat, both the man and woman treating me with the greatest kindness; and after a short rest again set out, this time with my host as guide, for the main road, from which I had wandered. This was soon reached, and parting with my black friend, I pushed on, keeping the road as nearly as I could.

At eleven o'clock, Tuesday night, "John Bray" reached the suburbs of Williams-

Enjoying the Negro's Hospitality.

burg, the goal of all his wanderings, but not without passing through many and perilous adventures.

---

### Frankie Bragg, the Boy Patriot at Donelson.

In one of the Union hospitals at Paducah was one of Birges's sharpshooters, who did such excellent service at Fort Donelson. He was a brave and noble boy. There were several kind ladies taking care of the sick. Their presence was like sunshine. Wherever they walked the eyes of the sufferers followed them. One of these ladies thus spoke of little Frankie Bragg:—Many will remember him; the boy of fifteen, who fought valiantly at Donelson,—one of the bravest of Birges's sharpshooters, and whose answer to my questioning in regard to joining the army was—

"I joined because I was so young and strong, and because life would be worth nothing to me unless I offered it for my country!"

I saw him die. I can never forget the pleading gaze of his violet eyes, the brow from which ringlets of light-brown hair were swept by strange fingers bathed in the death-dew, the desire for some one to care for him, some one to love him, in his last hours. I came to his side, and he clasped my hand in his own, fast growing cold and stiff. He said:

"O, I am going to die, and there is no one to love me. I did not think I was going to die till now; but it can't last long. If

Frankie Bragg.

my sisters were only here; but I have no friends near me now, and it is so hard!"

"Frankie, I know it is hard to be away from your relatives, but you are not friendless; I am your friend. Mrs. S—— and the kind doctor are your friends, and we will all take care of you. More than this, God is your friend, and he is nearer to you now than either of us can get. Trust him, my boy. He will help you."

A faint smile passed over the pale sufferer's features, as he asked—

"Oh, do you think he will?"

Then, as he held my hands closer, he turned his face more fully toward me, and said:

"My mother taught me to pray when I was a very little boy, and I never forgot it. I have always said my prayers every day, and tried not to be bad. Do you think God heard me always?"

"Yes, most assuredly. Did he not promise, in his good Book, from which your mother taught you, that he would always hear the prayers of his children? Ask, and ye shall receive. Don't you remember this? One of the worst things we can do is to doubt God's truth. He has promised, and he will fulfil it. Don't you feel so, Frankie?"

He hesitated a moment, and then answered, slowly: "Yes, I do believe it. I am not afraid to die, but I want somebody to love me."

The old cry for love, the strong yearning for sympathy of kindred hearts—it would not be put down.

"Frankie, I love you. Poor boy! you shall not be left alone. Is not this some comfort to you?"

"Do you love me? Will you stay with me, and not leave me?"

"I will not leave you. Be comforted, I will stay as long as you wish."

I kissed the pale forehead as if it had been that of my own child. A glad light flashed over his face.

"Oh, kiss me again; that was given like my sister. Mrs. S——, won't you kiss me, too? I don't think it will be so hard to die, if you will both love me."

It did not last long. With his face nestled against mine, and his large blue eyes fixed in perfect composure upon me to the last moment, he breathed out his life. So he died for his country, and rests on the banks of the beautiful Ohio.

---

### All for Nothing.

The kind of work which was accomplished by the noble women of the North and West, through the agency of the Sanitary Commission, during the war, is well known. Here is an incident in point:—

A Scotch woman, after nursing her

wounded son until he was almost well, found her money so nearly gone that she could not remain with him; yet she could not bear to leave him dependent only on the ordinary hospital supplies, lest, as she said, "he shouldn't be so well." A kind friend took her to a storehouse, to procure a few luxuries for her boy. He ordered a supply of sugar, tea, soft crackers, and canned fruit, then chicken and oysters, then jelly and wine, brandy, milk, and under-clothing, until the basket was full. As the earlier articles nestled under its lids, her face was glowing with satisfaction; but, as the latter lots were being added, she would draw him aside to whisper, that it was too much—really, she hadn't enough money; and when the more expensive items came from the shelves, the shadow of earnestness which gloomed her countenance, grew into one of perplexity, her soul vibrated between motherly yearning for the lad on his bed, and the scant purse in her pocket, until, slowly and with great reluctance, she began to return the costliest of the tempting assortment.

"Hadn't you better ask the price?" asked the guide.

"How much is it?"

"Nothing," replied the storekeeper.

"Sir!" queried she, in the utmost amazement; "*nothing* for all this?"

"My good woman," asked the guide, "have you a Soldiers' Aid Society in your neighborhood?"

Yes, they had; she belonged to it herself.

"Well, what do you suppose becomes of the garments you make, and the fruits you put up?"

She hadn't thought; she supposed they went to the army; but she was evidently bothered to know what connection there should be between their Aid Society and the basket.

"These garments that you see, come from your society, or other societies just like yours; so did these boxes and barrels; those fruits from Boston; that wine was purchased with gold from California; and it is all for sick soldiers—your son, as much as for any one else. This is the kind of work done by the United States Sanitary Commission." This work, indeed, was a peculiar bond of union between the loyal and true-hearted women of our country, enlisting, as it did, the active efforts of such ladies as Mrs. Lincoln, Mrs. Grant, Mrs. Halleck, &c., and reaching to every family, however humble, North and West.

### How to Take the Oath.

A former belle and well known young lady of Louisville, Ky.,—though not too young to marry, was too rebellious to vow the allegiance and fidelity of her heart to the flag of the Union. Hymen held out his hand filled with tempting greenbacks; but military law is very severe and exacting, making no discrimination in favor of the softer sex. The God of domestic bliss had to evacuate his position until the God of war was appeased, and this could only be done by the belle aforesaid taking an oath to support the Union. While the lady was modest enough to look for a union of hearts, she cared nothing for that political Union which a non-clerical law exacted. Rather than forego the joys and delights of married life, however, and waste her sweetness in single solitude, the little rebel beauty took the oath of allegiance to the United States Government, and married—"a Yankee invader!" The joke was considered a good one, especially on the part of the bride; and could the bridegroom be otherwise than a happy man in the companionship of such a loyal woman for a wife?

### General Rice to his Mother.

The following is an extract from the last letter written by General James C. Rice, just before the battles in the Virginia Wilderness, in one of which the noble General lost his life. It was to his aged mother, living in Worthington:—

We are about to commence the campaign, the greatest in magnitude, strength and importance since the beginning of the war. God grant that victory may crown our arms; that this wicked rebellion may be crushed, our Union preserved, and peace and prosperity again be restored to our beloved country. My faith and hope and confidence are in God alone, and I know that you feel the same. I trust that God may again graciously spare my life, as He has in the past, and yet one cannot fall too early if, loving Christ, he dies for his country. My entire hope is in the cross of my Saviour. In this hope I am always happy. We pray here in the army, mother, just the same as at home. The same God who watches over you, also guards me. I always remember you, mother, in my prayers, and I know you never forget me in yours. All that I am, under God, I owe to you, my dear mother. Do you recollect this passage in the Bible: "Thou shalt keep therefore the statutes, that it may go well with thee, and thy children after thee." How true this is in respect to your children, mother. I hope you will read the Bible and trust the promises to the last. There is no book like the Bible for comfort. It is a guide to the steps of the young—a staff to the aged.

Well, my dear mother, good bye. We are going again to do our duty, to bravely offer up our life for that of the country, and "through God we shall do valiantly."

With much love, and many prayers, that, whatever may betide us, we may meet in Heaven at last, I am your very affectionate son,     JAMES.

### Superfluities in War Times among the Fair Sex.

The Provost Marshal of Memphis, Tennessee, one day took several ladies in custody, some of whom were of apparent respectability, suspected of having been engaged in smuggling goods into the Confederacy. As is usual in all such cases of dealing with the fair sex, some strange and curious developements were made, after a little manipulation by a female examiner—"for such cases provided and prepared." One had on a whole bolt of the finest of linen—sufficient for a village haberdasher's stock—adjusted to answer the purpose of a bustle (an article *rather* out of date in a modern woman's wardrobe). Her corset was filled with tempting pieces of gold coin, quilted in, and amounting to twelve hundred dollars. Another had her form winsomely rounded out with padding, made up of the best dress silks, worth five dollars and upward per yard—decidedly extravagant even for so choice a place and purpose. Her hose were found to conceal, besides nature's pedal supports, a quantity of gentlemen's cravats—these being swathed carefully and ingeniously about her rebellious little legs. The third lady's ample hoops were found to cover a number of yards of broadcloth—by no conceivable hypothesis necessary in such a climate; and her bust was filled out to the largest possible maternal fullness with a museum of articles, consisting mainly of jewelry, silk thread, needles and medicines. The fair captives were worth a good deal "as they stood," and were well taken care of.

### Woman as a Dernier Resort.

Women have always been employed to persuade information out of unsuspecting, but not unsuspected persons, and they bring a degree of tact and shrewdness into play that hirsute humanity can never hope to equal. Many a wasp has been caught with their honey of hypocrisy.

Here is an illustration: A subordinate Federal officer in a certain city had long been suspected of disloyalty, but no proof to warrant his arrest could be obtained, and so as a dernier resort a *woman* was set at him. She smiled her way into his confidence, and became his "next best friend," but, finding that ears were of no use,—for he could not be induced to say

## DOMESTIC, WOMANLY, HOSPITAL, PRISON, ETC.

one word of matters pertaining to his office,—she changed her plan of attack, and turned a couple of curious, and, it is said, beautiful eyes upon him. Not unfrequently he would ride out of town into the country, and be absent three or four hours and return.

For all the hours of the twenty-four but just these she could account. Within them, then, lay the mischief, if mischief there was, and she began to watch if he made any preparation for these excursions. None. He loaded his old-fashioned pistol, drew on his gloves, lighted a cigar, bade her a loving good-bye—" only that, and nothing more." Was he deep and she dull? Time would show. At last, she observed that he put an unusual charge into the pistol, one day, and all at once she grew curious in pistols. Would he show her some day how to charge a pistol, how to fire a pistol, how to be a dead shot? And just at that minute she was athirst, and would he bring her a lemonade? She was toying with the weapon, and he went.

The instant the door closed behind him she drew the charge, for she knew quite as much of pistols as he, and substituted another. She was not a minute too soon, for back he came, took the pistol, and rode away. No sooner had he gone than she set about an examination of the charge, and it proved to be plans and details of Federal forces and movements, snugly rolled together. The mischief was in the pistol, then, though none but a woman would have thought of it, and so it was that he carried information to his rebel friends with rural proclivities. The woman's purpose was gained, and when the officer returned, his " next best friend" had vanished like an Arab, or a vision, and he had hardly time to turn about before he was under arrest.

### A Young Woman Shoots a Guerrilla to Avenge the Murder of Her Lover.

The following simple and unvarnished story has hardly a parallel in the page of fiction. Its strict truth is beyond question:

MURFREESBORO', June 28, 1864.
*To the Editor of The Times:*

The original of the following letter is in my possession. The events so graphically narrated, transpired in Overton county, Tenn. I knew Dr. Sadler from a small boy. The men who murdered him were noted guerrillas, and killed him for no personal grudge, but on account of his sentiments. I have no personal acquaintance with the young lady, but have the highest

A Young Woman Shoots a Guerrilla.

authority for stating that she is a pure, high-minded girl, the daughter of a plain farmer in moderate circumstances. It only remains to state that Peteet was killed January 30, and Gordenhire February 4, 1864, so that the vengeance they invoked has overtaken all three of the murderers of M. G. Sadler.

JOHN W. BOWEN.

MARTIN'S CREEK, April 30, 1864.

MAJOR CLIFF: According to promise, I now attempt to give you a statement of the reasons why I killed Turner, and a brief history of the affair. Dr. Sadler had, for two years previous to his death, seemed equally as near and dear to me as a brother, and for several months nearer than any person—my parents not excepted. If he had not, I never would have done what I did—promise to be his.

The men who killed him had threatened

his life often, because he was a Union man; they said he should not live, and after he had taken the oath they arrested him, but Lieut. Oakly released him at Pa's gate. He staid at Pa's till bed-time, and I warned him of the danger he was in; told him I had heard his life threatened that day, and that I felt confident he would be killed if he did not leave the neighborhood, and stay off until these men became reconciled. He promised to go; said he had some business at Carthage, and would leave. He promised us he would leave the neighborhood that night or by daylight next morning, and we felt assured he had gone. But for some unaccountable reason he did not leave.

About 3 o'clock, p. m., next day, news came to me at Mr. Johnson's, where I had gone with my brother, that Dr. Sadler was killed. I had met Peteet, Gordenhire, and Turner on the road, and told my brother that they were searching for Dr. Sadler to kill him. Sure enough they went to the house where he was, and, strange to me after his warning, he permitted them to come in. They met him perfectly friendly, and said they had come to get some brandy from Mr. Yelton, which they obtained, and immediately after drinking they all three drew their pistols and commenced firing at Sadler. He drew his, but it was snatched away from him; he then drew his knife, which was also taken away from him. He then ran round the house and up a stairway, escaping out of their sight. They followed, however, and searched till they found him, and brought him down and laid him on a bed, mortally wounded. He requested some of his people to send for Dr. Dillin to dress his wounds. It is strange to me why, but Sadler's friends had all left the room, when Turner went up and put his pistol against the temple, and shot him through the head. They all rejoiced like demons, and stood by till he made his last struggle. They then pulled his eyes open and asked in a loud voice if he were dead. They then took his horse and saddle and pistols, and robbed him of all his money, and otherwise insulted and abused his remains.

Now, for this, I resolved to have revenge. Peteet and Gordenhire being dead, I determined to kill Turner, and to seek an early opportunity of doing it. But I kept that resolution to myself, knowing that I would be prevented. I went prepared, but never could get to see him.

On the Thursday before I killed him, I learned he was preparing to leave for Louisiana, and I determined he should not escape if I could prevent it. I arose that morning and fixed my pistols, so that they would be sure fire, and determined to hunt him all that day. Then sitting down I wrote a few lines, so that if I fell my friends might know where to look for my remains. I took my knitting, as if I were going to spend the day with a neighbor living on the road toward Turner's. It rained very severely, making the roads muddy, so that I became fatigued, and concluded to go back and ride next day, or Saturday. But Ma rode my horse on Saturday, and left me to keep house.

We had company Sunday a. m., so that I could not leave, but the company left about noon, and I started again in search of Turner. I went to his house about two and a half miles from Pa's. I found no one at home and therefore sat down to await his return. After waiting perhaps one and a half hours, a man came to see Turner, and not finding him he said he supposed that he and his wife had gone to Mrs. Christian's, his sister-in-law, who lived about one-half mile distant.

I concluded to go there and see, fearing the man would tell him I was waiting for him and he would escape me. I found him there, and a number of other persons, including his wife and her father and mother. Most of them left when I entered the house. I asked Mrs. Christian if Turner was gone. She pointed to him

DOMESTIC, WOMANLY, HOSPITAL, PRISON, ETC. 619

at the gate just leaving. I looked at the clock, and it was half-past four o'clock, p. m.

I then walked out into the yard, and as Turner was starting, called to him to stop. He turned and saw I was preparing to shoot him; he started to run. I fired at the distance of about twelve paces, and missed. I fired again as quick as possible, and hit him in the back of the head, and he fell on his face and knees. I fired again and hit him in the back, and he fell on his right side. I fired twice more, only one of these shots taking effect. By this time I was within five steps of him, and stood and watched him till he was dead. I then turned round and walked toward the house, and met Mrs. Christian and her sister, his wife, coming out. They asked me what I did that for? My response was:

"You know what that man did on the 13th of December last—murdered a dear friend of mine. I have been determined to do this deed ever since, and I never shall regret it."

They said no more to me, but commenced hallooing and blowing a horn. I got my horse out and started home, where I shall stay or leave when I please, and say what I please.

L. J. W.

### Bushwhackers Kept at Bay by a Brave Girl.

While Brigadier-General Brown was in command of the Federal forces at Jefferson City, Missouri, an attempt was made by three bushwhackers to enter the house of Mr. Schwartz, twelve miles distant, but who, being resolutely resisted by a young lady of only fifteen years, undertook to break down the door. It appears that on being thwarted in their purpose to enter the house, they declared they *would* come in, at the same time trying to break down the door. While this was going on, the other inmates of the house, viz., Mr. Schwartz, John Wise, Captain Golden, government horse dealer, and a young man in his employ, all left, taking with them—as they supposed—all the arms and ammunition. In their hasty retreat they left behind a revolver, which Miss Schwartz appropriated to her own use. She went to the door, and on opening it, presented the pistol at the leader of the gang, telling them to "come on if they wanted to, and that some of them should fall, or she would." They threatened to kill her if she did not leave the door. She replied:

"The first man who takes one step toward this door dies, for this is the home of my parents, and my brothers and sisters, and I am able to, and shall defend it."

Seeing that she was determined in her purpose, and after holding a consultation together, they left.

Here is one of the many instances of true and brave-hearted courage;—a young girl of but fifteen fresh and tender summers, after all the inmates of the house, even her father, had fled, leaving her alone to her fate,—with the courage worthy a Joan of Arc, boldly defending her native home against three blood-thirsty and cowardly ruffians, and by her coolness and heroic daring, succeeding in turning them at their peril, from their hellish designs. All honor to the heroism of that truly American girl!

### Skull-Bone Memento Kept by a Lady.

Information was one day communicated to the Provost-Marshal of St. Louis, Missouri, that the wife of a well known Confederate officer, Warrack Hugh,—Captain and Assistant-Inspector-General on General Leonidas Polk's staff, was in that city and preparing to go to Jefferson City. Orders were immediately issued for her arrest, and carried out. In her possession were found a number of secession articles, a package of letters, and *a piece of the skull of a Union soldier*, about two inches square, and so thick that it must have been a portion of the occipital bone, on which was the inscription, "Wilson's Creek, Dec. 21st, 1861," and then some obscure chirography, half rubbed out, that looked like 'Found on the spot.' In answer to a question where she obtained it, she replied by telling when she got it. In answer to another, as to whether she knew what it was, she answered in the affirmative,— that she knew it to be a portion of the skull of a Union soldier. When inquired of why she kept it, she replied, "*For a memento*,"—an unaccountable and perverted taste for a lady. She was committed to the female department of the prison, after an examination, and the pleasant souvenirs were retained by the officials.

### Clever Dogs, but both sucked Eggs.

During General Birney's raid through Florida, a bright little girl was found alone in one of the houses, her parents having 'skedaddled.' She was rather non-committal, for she did not know whether the troops were Union or rebel. Two fine dogs made their appearance, while a conversation was being held with the child, and she informed one of her questioners that their names were Gillmore and Beauregard. "Which is the best dog?" asked a bystander. "I don't know," said she, "they're both mighty smart dogs; but they'll either of 'em suck eggs if you don't watch 'em." The troops left without ascertaining whether the family, of which the girl was a hopeful scion, was Union or rebel.

### Rather be a Soldier's Widow than a Coward's Wife.

One day a poor wounded soldier on crutches entered one of the New York city railway cars, which on this occasion happened to be occupied mainly by women. One of them considerately arose and gave the wounded man her place. Her neighbor, seeming to be scandalized by this abdication of feminine privilege, asked her if it were possible that she had voluntarily resigned her seat to 'that man.' She replied she had; that she had a husband who was a soldier in the Union army, and that she had done only what she would wish others should do for him in a similar situation. The other replied that she had no husband in the army, and was glad of it. "Well," retorted the true American wife, "I would rather be a *soldier's widow than a coward's wife*."

### Interesting Contribution to a Sanitary Fair.

One of the contributions to the Cincinnati Sanitary Fair consisted of a letter from Thomas Clay to his father. When the great statesman, Henry Clay, was living, he purchased a farm for his son Thomas, and stocked and prepared it thoroughly for his use. After a few years' residence on the farm, Thomas wrote to his father for more money,—that his farm needed important improvements, and he had not the wherewith to procure what he needed. Mr. Clay replied to the effect that as he (Thomas) had squandered the means he had given him in preparing the farm for his use, he might now go to —. Thomas replied in a brief letter to his father, as follows:

"MY DEAR FATHER: Your kind letter of — instant is before me. I have perused and digested its contents, and am obliged to return you my warmest gratitude for the kindly admonition it contains. The destination you direct me to go will be strange to me, and I have deemed it the part of a dutiful son to request of you a letter of introduction.

Hoping to hear from you, I remain your most obedient and dutiful son,

THOMAS CLAY

### Confederate Brooches not to General Viele's Taste.

General Viele's method of dealing with secession and its abettors was that of the *suaviter in modo, fortitur in re*. For instance, a lady went into his office to consult him or demand some favor. He received her with his usual politeness, but suddenly noticing that she wore the Confederate colors prominently, in the shape of a brooch, he mildly suggested that it would, perhaps, have been better taste to come to his office without such a decoration.

"I have a right, Sir, to consult my own wishes as to what I shall wear."

"Then, Madam," replied the General, "permit me to claim an equal right in choosing with whom I shall converse."

The dignified lady thought it best to make a speedy exit from his presence.

Whoever would read more of these sparkling *morceaux*, will find a rich feast in Dawley's admirable series—the "Camp and Fireside Library."

---

**Annie Lillybridge and Lieutenant W——.**

Annie Lillybridge, of Detroit, was for 'Union,' and in favor of the hardships and dangers of war, if need be, to secure that end. She courted, rather than shrank from, those hardships, and bared her breast to rebel bullets.

According to Annie's account, her parents resided in Hamilton, Canada West. In the spring of 1862, she was employed in a dry goods store in Detroit, where she became acquainted with Lieutenant W——, of one of the Michigan regiments, and an intimacy immediately sprang up between them. They corresponded for some time, and became much attached to each other. But during the ensuing summer season, Lieutenant W. was appointed to a position in the Twenty-first Michigan Infantry, then rendezvousing in Ionia county.

The thought of parting from the gay Lieutenant nearly drove Annie mad, and she resolved to share his dangers and be near him. No sooner had she resolved upon this course than she proceeded to act. Purchasing male attire she visited Ionia, and enlisted in Captain Kavanagh's Company, Twenty-first regiment. While in camp she managed to keep her secret from all; not even the object of her attachment, who met her every day, was aware of her presence so near him.

Annie left with her regiment for Kentucky, passed through all the dangers and temptations of a camp-life, endured long marches, and slept on the cold ground—all without a murmur. At last, before the battle of Pea Ridge, in which her regiment took part, her sex was curiously discovered by a member of her company, upon whom she laid the injunction of secresy, after relating to him her previous history.

On the following day she was under fire, and from a letter in her possession, it appears she behaved with marked gallantry, and by her own hand shot a rebel Captain who was in the act of firing upon Lieutenant W. But the fear of revealing her sex continually haunted her.

After the battle, she was sent out with others, to collect the wounded, and one of the first corpses found by her was the soldier who had discovered her sex. Days and weeks passed on, and she became a universal favorite with the regiment; so much so, that her Colonel, Stephens, frequently detailed her as regimental clerk—a position that brought her in close contact with her lover, who, at this time, was Major, or Adjutant, of the regiment.

A few weeks subsequently she was out on picket duty, when she received a shot in the arm that disabled her, and notwithstanding the efforts of the surgeon, her wound grew worse from day to day. She was sent to the hospital at Louisville, where she remained several months, when she was discharged by the post surgeon, as her arm was stiffened and useless.

Annie implored to be permitted to return to her regiment, but the surgeon was unyielding, and discharged her. Annie immediately hurried toward home. At Cincinnati she told her secret to a benevolent lady, and was supplied with female attire. She declared she would enlist in her old regiment again, if there was a recruiting officer for the Twenty-first in Michigan. She still clung to the Lieutenant—said she must be near him if he fell, or was taken down sick—that where he went she would go—and when he died, she would end her life by her own hands.

### Frank, the Pretty Female Bugler of the Eighth Michigan.

In the spring of 1863, a Union Captain, accompanied by a young soldier apparently about seventeen years of age, arrived in Louisville, Ky., in charge of some rebel prisoners.

During their stay in Louisville, the young soldier alluded to had occasion to visit head-quarters, and at once attracted the attention of Colonel Mundy as being exceedingly sprightly, and possessed of more than ordinary intelligence. Being in need of such a young man at Barracks No. 1, the Colonel detailed him for service in that institution.

A few days subsequently, however, the startling secret was disclosed, that the supposed young man was a young lady, and the fact was established beyond doubt by a soldier who was raised in the same town with her, and knew her parents. She 'acknowledged the corn,' and begged to be retained in the position to which she had been assigned; having been in the service ten months, she desired to serve during the war. Her wish was accordingly granted, and she remained at her post.

Frank was born near Bristol, Penn., and she was raised in Alleghany City, the place of her parents' residence,—highly respectable people, and in good circumstances. She was sent to a convent in Wheeling, Virginia, at twelve years of age, where she remained until the breaking out of the war, having acquired a military education, and all the accomplishments of modern usage.

She visited home after leaving the convent, and, after taking leave of her parents, proceeded to Louisville in July, 1862, with the design of enlisting in the Second East Tennessee Cavalry, which she accomplished, and accompanied the Army of the Cumberland to Nashville. She was in the thickest of the fight at Murfreesboro,' and was severely wounded in the shoulder, but fought gallantly, and waded Stone river into Murfreesboro', on the memorable Sunday on which our forces were driven back. She had her wound dressed, and here her sex was disclosed, General Rosecrans being made acquainted with the fact.

Frank was accordingly mustered out of service, notwithstanding her earnest entreaty to be allowed to serve the cause she loved so well. The General was very favorably impressed with her daring bravery, and superintended the arrangements for her transmission to her parents. She left the Army of the Cumberland, resolved to enlist again in the very first regiment she met. When she arrived at Bowling Green, therefore, she found the Eighth Michigan there, and enlisted, and continued to share its fortunes, being honored with the position of regimental bugler. She was an excellent horseman; saw and bravely endured all the privations and hardships incident to the life of a soldier; and gained an enviable reputation as a scout, having made several remarkable expeditions, which were attended with signal success.

Of only eighteen years of age, quite small, and a beautiful figure, Frank was a decided attraction. She had auburn hair, which she wore quite short, and large blue eyes, beaming with intelligence. Her complexion, naturally very fair, became somewhat bronzed from exposure. In fine, she was exceedingly pretty and amiable. Her conversation denoted more than ordinary accomplishment, and, what was stranger than all, she appeared very refined in her manners, giving no evidence whatever of the rudeness which might naturally be expected from her camp and field contacts.

The pretty bugler stated that she had discovered a great many females in the army, and was intimately acquainted with one such—a young lady holding a commission as Lieutenant in the army. She had assisted in burying three female soldiers at different times, whose sex was unknown to any but herself.

### Eating up the Stars and Bars.

Notwithstanding General Butler's vigilance in terrifying secessionism in the Crescent City, there was revived, in March, 1863, the novelty of an openly avowed secesh lady in the streets. Miss ——, defying the celebrated order " No. 28," made her appearance on the pavement with a handkerchief round her neck, on the corner of which was contemptuously displayed, in conspicuously wrought colors, a rebel flag. It is not probable that any particular notice would have been taken of the circumstance if the fair owner had not defiantly flouted said offensive symbol in the face of a naval officer, who then very promptly escorted the lady before General Bowen. While the examination of the case was going on, the young lady, in her indignation and rancor, absolutely tore the material of the symbolized flag out of the handkerchief with her teeth, and *ate it up*, so she literally put the blessed " Stars and Bars " very near her heart. The handkerchief was confiscated and the young lady was ordered to report once a day, for one month, to Captain Kilborn, Deputy Provost Marshal,—during which time, it is innocently intimated, the Captain had several applications for positions of head clerks.

### Hostage Wanted for his Wife and Family.

When the so-called Provisional Government of Kentucky was on its hegira southward, they stopped and made a political and social call at the house of Colonel Wm. H. Polk, the party being under the convoy of George N. Sanders. Just before leaving, and after receiving the most hospitable treatment at the hands of the Colonel, the latter addressed Sanders, and said that he had a particular favor to ask.

" Bill," said George to his host, speaking out of a full heart and a full chest, " Bill, you are a boy after my own heart; whatever request you make I grant."

" It is only a trifle," said Mr. Polk, " which you can easily grant, and which will please you."

" It is granted," interrupted the grateful Sanders.

" I may be arrested," continued Mr. Polk, " within a few minutes, for disagreeing with some measures which Gov. Harris has urged upon the people."

" Never mind that," said the impetuous Sanders, " I'll stand by you."

" All I want," continued Mr. Polk, " is for you to return to Nashville as a *hostage for my wife and family.*"

" Bill Polk," said George, gravely but firmly, " you are a man I love ; I love you, and I love your wife and family ; *but if ever I go back to Nashville may I be ——!* "

Of course there was no reply to this, and the redoubtable and wife-and-family-loving George, with the Provisional Government, were soon on their way to the dixiest part of Dixie.

### Major B——, en route with the Spanish Widow.

Some of the domestic and extra-personal experiences of the war will, at no distant day, furnish the staple of many a finely-wrought novellette—such, for instance, as the following, narrated by an officer of the Twenty-seventh Corps of the Union Army. Hear him:—

We had (says the narrator,) a very pleasant trip down to the Crescent City, with some political prisoners from the Department of the Missouri, and persons who were allowed to pass into the Confederate lines to see their relations, look after their property, &c.

Among the exiles was Ashton P. Johnston of St. Louis, Marmaduke, late of the Convention, Rev. Father Donnelly, of St. Joseph, and others of less import.

Among the 'voluntaries' were young maids and old maids, wives and widows. Among the young maids was one who *confidentially* told me she was going to Mobile to be married. It looked to me very much like *sending supplies to the enemy;* but I couldn't *help* it, so let it go. They nearly all came to this place in charge of Captain Dwight, Assistant-Inspector General of the Department of the Missouri.

In the party was a young widow. 'Pretty!' In my judgment she was interesting—when was a young and pretty widow not? Being young, pretty, and a widow, is it strange that a young officer, to whose care she was entrusted, should extend to her all the courtesies and atten-

Major B———, en route with the Spanish Widow.

tion proper and consistent with his official position? It was not strange; nor was it strange that in return for his kindness, and at his solicitation, she should confide to him the tale of her woes.

She was from Mexico; her husband had been conscripted in Texas, into the rebel army; had died, leaving her the sole proprietress of numerous droves of mustangs, and the mother of two small children, (mostly boys and girls.)

Her spirits and her person, draped in the habiliments of mourning, for the length of time deemed proper, she resolved to quit the place where each familiar object reminded her of the time spent in conjugal felicity with the dear departed one; that one 'gone to a ranch from which there was no return;' so all the personal property, with the exception of some unruly mustangs, who refused to be 'cotched,' and some colored individual, who, having heard of the Proclamation, refused to be considered personal property, and wouldn't be 'cotched neither,' was converted into Confederate tr—cash, and the ranch vacated.

At Matamoras the Confederate money was exchanged for gold, and passage secured on a Spanish vessel to Havana, which was soon bounding across the Gulf. Tears were shed, as on leaving one's native land they will always be; but it was all for the best—a residence upon the beautiful island of Cuba, a place in the affections and family of the dear relations who anticipated her coming—quiet walks beneath fragrant orange groves,—the air of that delightful and salubrious climate—would go far toward dispelling the gloom which shrouded her young and ardent soul.

But, alas! for the orange groves and ambrosial atmosphere, a storm arose, the ship was driven into an inlet off the coast of Florida, was taken by our blockading squadron off Key West, for a blockade runner, and sent to New York, where, after an examination, she was released, and sent away.

The fair widow, having escaped the dangers of the sea, resolved not to venture again, till her nerves had regained their wonted firmness. Having friends at St. Louis, she resolved to visit that city. Arriving there—there she remained until the fall of Vicksburg and Port Hudson, and the consequent opening of the Mississippi river, when she resolved to attempt Havana, this time *via* New Orleans. Major B. was on the boat. The Major, you must know, is a very gallant man. The ladies, dear creatures, would fall in love with him. In fact, the citadel of their affections invariably capitulated when he laid siege.

The Major was introduced to the fair widow by the Captain in charge, and he had a soul to sympathize with her in her affliction, so to his special care was she assigned. It was soon a mutual discovery that their tastes and sympathies were similar. Did he admire any particular scenery along the shores?—ditto, she. Together they would pass hours in some retired place upon the guards of the boat, in sweet interchange of thought and sentiment.

He had never met one before for whom he had formed an attachment *so* sincere, and she, from the moment when first introduced, felt that she saw in him the realization of her hopes. In him she saw the only one who should ever catch the untamed mustangs, and again bring joy to the ranch.

Thus did this enamored pair pass the long hours of the journey. Arrived in New Orleans. Would the Major be so kind as to secure her rooms at the hotel, and to make some inquiry after her uncle, who resided somewhere in the city? Of course he would. Mine host of the St. Charles provided the proper apartments, and, the widow duly domiciled therein, the Major sallied forth to make inquiries after "our uncle," in which he was entirely unsuccessful, not being able to find any gentleman of that name. The widow felt sad—was disappointed.

Her uncle was formerly a man of wealth and influence, and she had not calculated upon having any difficulty in finding him; but this cruel war had changed everything; and then the beautiful eyes of the fair and fascinating widow filled with tears.

It grew rather embarrassing to the Major. He was expecting to meet his wife, who was waiting in the city for him, having come around *via* the Gulf. But the fair creature whose head was reclining upon his shoulder, and whose heaving bosom was beating against his own, knew nothing of that—she only knew, as she said, that in that great city, among strangers, without the Major her heart would break.

How benevolent the Major's intentions may have been can only be conjectured, for unlooked-for events will sometimes play the deuce with one's arrangements. At least it was so in this case. The fact was, the wife of the Major learning of his arrival made inquiries, and ascertaining that he had taken No. —, resolved upon a pleasant surprise for him, so with two of the little majors in tow she proceeded to No. —. Passing an adjoining room she overheard the voice of the one sought for, and thinking there must be some mistake in the number of the room, and that where that familiar voice was heard must be the right one, she pushed open the door and entered.

Whether the scene which met her eye was calculated to increase her faith in the constancy of her spouse, or otherwise, those who are able to judge must decide. It is known, however, that the Major's baggage was removed to another part of the house before many hours had expired, and that he was the recipient of a note, through the clerk of the house, to the following effect:

'DEAR MAJOR:—Having unexpectedly found my uncle, I will relieve you and yours from any further care upon my part, if you will be so kind as to settle the bill which the clerk will present to you.

    Adios.    L.

P. S. Not having sold my gold yet, it is inconvenient for me to refund you the —— dollars which you so kindly loaned to me.    L.'

The Major is a wiser man: he looks meek, but will fire up upon any allusion being made to mustangs or Spanish widows.

### Grim War and the Innocents.

Rev. Dr. Maginnis stated at the session of the Christian Commission in Saratoga, that he was at Easton, attending a Synod, when Harrisburg was in danger, and the people came rushing down to meet the common enemy. There he saw a company marching resolutely along the street, and among the multitudes who gazed upon them as they passed was a little girl whose tender eye rested upon the forms of those noble men with a strange earnestness. He watched her. As the company came by she clasped her little hands, and then began to shake and quiver, as she scanned closely every soldier's face. Suddenly she wrung her hands, and her childish voice broke out in faint agony—"That's him! that's him! That's papa! Papa! He's going! he's going!" and she bowed her head upon her bosom and wept.

---

### Three Noble Union Girls.

During the advance of Colonel Streight's ill-fated raid in the spring, a portion of his command had a heavy skirmish on the last day of April, near a place called Day's Gap. A Union soldier was killed in this skirmish, and as a matter of necessity, his body was left in possession of the foe. The latter, after stripping the corpse, buried it beside the road on the spot where he fell. They then drove a stake into the ground, evidently intending to have it pierce the body, and attached to it a placard, the blasphemy of which was most barbarous, and totally unfit to be recited. The Union people suppressed their indignation, for it would have been death to interfere. They did not, however, forget where the patriot was buried, and three young ladies, with their own hands, some time after, built a fence around the grave, removed the stake, and planted evergreens and flowers in attractive taste, to bloom and shed their fragrance over the resting place of the defender of his country.

Honor to those noble girls!

### Letter of Sympathy from a Union Soldier to a Confederate Officer's Betrothed.

It was in one of the skirmishes between the Fourteenth Army Corps under General Sherman, and the Confederate forces, that Lieutenant Ross, of Georgia, was wounded and captured. His wound soon proved fatal, but he was carefully nursed to the last by Major Fitzgibbons, of the Fourteenth Michigan regiment. At the request of the dying man, Major Fitzgibbons undertook to forward the personal effects of Ross to a young lady in Oxford, Georgia, to whom he was engaged to be married; and accompanied them by the following letter:—

CAMP 14TH MICH. VET. VOL. INF.,
NEAR ATLANTA, GA., Aug. 8, 1864.
*Miss Emma Jane Kennon, Oxford, Ga.:*

Bereaved Girl: With melancholy pleasure I herewith send to you the valuables and personal effects of the late Lieutenant Ross, Sixty-sixth Georgia. From his dying lips he told me he loved you above all else in the world, and committing these effects to my charge, his last sigh was turned into a prayer that I would, if possible, send you your likeness, which he carried next to and in his heart.

The asperities that demagogues engender in the minds of those separated from the field of battle and the scenes of death—the unnatural bitterness of feeling that has seemingly soured the better natures of our countrymen and women in both extreme sections of our common country—finds neither home nor resting-place in the hearts of this army of ours, and I assure you that I took as tender and respectful hold and care of your betrothed as if he were my own comrade or brother. The innocence depicted in his fair and beautiful face—his heroic efforts at staying the retreat of his fleeing comrades, won my heart and assured him its sympathies and respect.

With this also find his purse and papers, which, 'Vandal' though I am, I feel will be of greater value to you to get than satisfaction to me to withhold. He was conscious to the last, as I learned from the officer who cared for him, and seemed only to deplore his death in parting from that heaven he left in you. Two other Confederate officers lay dead near him, but the necessities of the moment prevented the possibility of my delaying to find out anything in relation to them.

Praying that God will put it into the hearts of your people to return to the allegiance of your father's flag, under which all sections prospered, and which only will prevent the further effusion of blood, and sincerely and from my heart condoling with you and his family in your bereavement,

I am, sad girl, very respectfully,
Your obedient servant,
THOMAS C. FITZGIBBONS,
Major 14th Mich. Vet. Vol. Inf., U. S. A.

### My Mother's Hand!

In one of those fierce engagements which took place near Mechanicsville between the Confederate and Federal forces in the eventful month of May, a young Lieutenant of a Rhode Island battery had his right foot so shattered by a fragment of a shell that, on reaching Washington after one of those horrible ambulance rides, and a journey of a week's duration, he was obliged to undergo amputation of the leg. He telegraphed home, hundreds of miles away, that all was going well, and with a soldier's fortitude, composed himself to bear his sufferings alone. Unknown to him, however, his mother, one of those dear reserves of the army, hastened up to join the main force. She reached the city at midnight, and the nurses would have kept her from him until morning. One sat by his side fanning him as he slept, her hand on the feeble, fluctuating pulsations which foreboded sad results. But what woman's heart could resist the pleading of a mother then? In the darkness, she was finally allowed to glide in and take the place at his side. She touched his pulse as the nurse had done. Not a word had been spoken; but the sleeping boy opened his eyes and said:

"*That feels like my mother's hand! Who is this beside me? It is my mother; turn up the gas and let me see my mother!*"

The two dear faces met in one long joyful sobbing embrace, and the fondness pent up in each heart sobbed and panted and wept forth its expression. The tender-loving but gallant fellow, just twenty-one, his leg amputated on the last day of his three years' service, underwent operation after operation, and at last, when death drew nigh, and he was told by tearful friends that it only remained to make him comfortable, said, "he had looked death in the face too many times to be afraid now," and died as heroically as did the noble men of the famed Cumberland.

### Affecting Mementoes of Gettysburg.

Among the many sad relics of the battlefield in Gettysburg, Pennsylvania, was one which a soldier engaged in that dreadful fight picked up, namely,—a small paper, which contained two separate locks of hair attached thereto, directed to "Mr. Wellerford," from Louisiana, by his wife, in a beautiful handwriting. Below one lock was "Fanny Wellerford," below the other was "Richard Wellerford,"—and below both was "Our Darlings!" These tender mementoes of his name and children had been sent on to him by his attached wife, to cheer his heart in the far distant land to which the fortunes of war had brought him; and probably he wore the tender testimonials near his heart, when the fatal missile separated him from those he loved in his far-off Southern home. The tender relic of domestic love went into the possession of strangers, while the husband and father rested beneath the silent clods of a Northern valley,—his grave probably unmarked and undistinguished from the hundreds around him, who met their death on the bloody field of Gettysburg. His wife and children looked in vain for the return of that loved husband and father! But for the bravery of Meade on that wide field of blood, and the untiring energy of Governor

Governor Curtin

Curtin, who, in the chair of state, gathered together the mighty resources of his people, to beat back that vast tide of southern soldiery, how many *more* battlefields might have been numbered on the soil of the North!

### Buried with his Sister's Picture.

The following incident was related by a Confederate prisoner to an attendant, who by many acts of kindness had won his confidence :—

I was searching for spoils among the dead and dying upon a deserted battlefield, when I discovered a small gold locket upon the person of a dying boy, apparently about fifteen years of age. As I endeavored to loose it from his grasp, he opened his languid eyes and implored me, by all that was good and pure, by the memory of my own mother, not to rob him of his sister's picture:

"Oh," said he, "it was her last gift. I promised her, when she kissed my cheek at parting, that I would always wear it near my heart, in life or death!" (then, as if throwing his whole soul into a plea, he exclaimed :) "Oh, touch not my sister's picture!"

As the last words faltered upon his tongue, his voice hushed in death. By the dim light of the stars I hastily scooped a shallow grave and buried him with his sister's picture lying upon his breast.

### Pretty Widows and Imprisoned Lovers.

A good looking young widow who "bossed" a sewing machine in Wheeling, Virginia, was in love with a notorious rebel bushwhacker who had committed several murders of Unionists, and was confined in the Wheeling jail. His name was George D——, a son of the notorious Dan D——, and the widow's name Mary B——. Mary was allowed to carry delicacies to George, until she was detected in attempting to pass something of a contraband nature through the bars of his cell, after which she was debarred by the jailor from the premises.

One night, about ten o'clock, the jailor heard a noise on the outside of the southern wall of the prison, and going round there with a lantern, he discovered a parcel on the ground. While in the act of picking up the mysterious package, the widow B. alighted sock upon his back from the wall, which was twelve or fifteen feet high, and disputed his possession of the property. In the fall her right leg was broken just above the ankle, but she struggled manfully, and in the contest a bottle of nitric acid was broken, and the contents spilled upon the jailor and Mrs. B., both of whom were stained and burned. The valiant feminine finally sank exhausted, and was carried into the jail and placed under surgical treatment.

Upon examining the parcel, the jailor found that it contained a bottle of chloroform, a bottle of nitric acid, a chisel, a box of steel pens, and two love letters from Mrs. Briggs, and copies of various newspapers. As descriptive of one of the letters, love is stated to be a word of hardly sufficient strength. The infatuated woman had climbed to the wall with a ladder, and was about to attach the package to a long pole and extend it to the window of her 'Dusky's' cell, when she dropped it, and was thus discovered.

#### Pathetic Offering of Genius to the Dead.

Here is a theme for one of the poets. The scene is at Newport News, Virginia; the subject—A Soldier's Grave. The author would have the melody of the moaning sea for inspiration, and his imagination would find material in the tragedy of the Cumberland and Congress. The name of the sleeper it would be difficult to ascertain; nor has the curiosity of the visitor been able to ascertain the name of the unconscious genius, who possessed such power of condensation, poetic feeling and pathos, as are exhibited in the simple epitaph on this lonely grave of an unknown hero. Here it is in words and figure:

It is safe to affirm that one might travel over all the graveyards and the field of the dead in all Virginia—that modern Aceldama—and find nothing more touching in the lapidaric offering.

#### Beware of a Soldier's Wife!

An incident of quite a romantic character—and something more—occurred in Alleghany county, New York, which exhibits human nature in some of its peculiar lights and shades, though perhaps not so very strange, considering that "there is nothing new under the sun." A couple were married. The bride was as beautiful as the morning; her eyes like heaven's orbs. The husband was patriotic; he enlisted and went to war. A libertine from Chautaque county saw the beautiful wife, and exclaimed, "Ye gods, how beautiful!" He sought her society, and ostensibly won her confidence; she consented. He gave her ten fifty-dollar greenbacks to make necessary arrangements. She accepted. The hour was fixed upon. The villain went to his hotel to smoke the impatient hours away, when the following letter was put into his hands:

"MR. ——, have to inform you that circumstances beyond my control will prevent me from fulfilling my engagement to elope with you to-night. I expect my husband home on furlough soon, to spend Christmas and New Year's, when we shall enjoy a hearty laugh at your discomfiture. Meanwhile, I will keep your money as a Christmas present for him, and, when this cruel war is over, it will come handy to assist him to start in business.

Yours 'tenderly,'
C. T. N."

" P. S.—When next you attempt to play the libertine, you would do well to select your victim outside of Alleghany county; and, above all, beware of a soldier's wife."

#### Howard, the Havelock of the War.

Major-General Howard, commanding the Union Department and Army of the Tennessee, was often styled "the Havelock of the war," because of his so closely resembling the great English commander of that name in his habits and manners. He was strictly temperate, never imbibing of alcoholic drinks, or any of a nature intoxicating. His language was always chaste, firm, and right to the point; no word or sound of profanity was allowed about him; tobacco he utterly discarded; and himself and staff held religious meetings for the good of themselves and the country. One who visited the General while engaged in his Georgia campaign, describes the prayer meeting as attended by the officers of his command, in the midst of a pine grove, where his quarters were at that time. The General was in the centre of a semi-circle of staff officers of his command, his good right arm gone, and over his features there played a quiet

Maj Gen O. O. Howard.

yet serene smile as he looked around him upon the assembled guards and escorts upon his left hand, with clerks and orderlies on the right. The exercises consisted of vocal and instrumental music, a short, fervent prayer, a few plain remarks, which all could understand, the singing of the Doxology, and a benediction, to which a solemn Amen was echoed by some distant battery. Before separating, each man was taken by the hand and received a kind word from General Howard.

### Miss Clemmie's Album.

During the last visit of the Federal forces, under Major-General A. J. Smith, to Holly Springs, Mississippi, in August, 1864, the following lines were penned by Colonel A—— on the last page of a young lady's album, all others having been appropriated by real or pretended admirers in 1861. The black crape at the top of five loving epistles, and the broad, dark borders of five cards in the album, proved that ten of Miss Clemmie's admirers had fallen victims to Federal bullets, and that Yankee lead and steel were even more potent than Cupid's arrows. The females of the family being at the time residents of the elegant mansion, the book was returned to the centre-table with these lines—

TO MISS CLEMMIE.

'Tis certain, Miss Clemmie, whether Fed or Confed,
In the plain course of nature you're destined to wed;
Some "Lord of Creation" will lovingly kneel,
And pour forth his tender and fervent appeal,
If the Feds and Confeds will cease this vain strife,
And leave a man living to make you his wife.

FED.

PART VIII.—EARLY HOME AND TRAGIC END OF PRESIDENT LINCOLN

# PART EIGHTH.

## ANECDOTES OF THE REBELLION—FINAL SCENES AND EVENTS IN THE GREAT DRAMA: ASSASSINATION OF PRESIDENT LINCOLN; IGNOMINIOUS DOOM OF JEFFERSON DAVIS; ETC.

THE MOST STRIKING OCCURRENCES RELATING TO THE GREAT ASSASSINATION CONSPIRACY,—THE TRAGEDY, THE ACTORS, AND THEIR DOOM; REMARKABLE PASSAGES AND CONVERSATIONS IN MR. LINCOLN'S PRESIDENTIAL LIFE,—MEMORIAL INCIDENTS OF HIS DEATH, AND OF A NATION'S MOURNING; CAPTURE AND CUSTODY OF JEFFERSON DAVIS,—HIS SAYINGS AND DOINGS, PERSONAL BEARING AMONG HIS CAPTORS, IGNOMINIOUS FATE; INTERESTING REMINISCENCES IN THE CAREER OF ANDREW JOHNSON, &C., &C.

---

IF THIS COUNTRY CAN NOT BE SAVED WITHOUT GIVING UP *that* PRINCIPLE, I WAS ABOUT TO SAY I WOULD RATHER BE ASSASSINATED ON THIS SPOT THAN SURRENDER IT.—*Speech of* MR. LINCOLN, *at Independence Hall, Philadelphia, defending the principle of Liberty contained in the Declaration of Independence: Feb.*, 1861.

"After life's fitful fever, he sleeps well;
Treason has done his worst; nor steel, nor poison,
Malice domestic, foreign levy, nothing
Can touch him further."—"MACBETH," *read twice by* MR. LINCOLN *to some friends, on the Sabbath preceding his death.*

I never willingly planted a thorn in any human bosom.—*Speech of* MR. LINCOLN, *in Washington, on the announcement of his re-election; Nov.,* 1864.

"Judge not, that ye be not judged."—PRESIDENT LINCOLN's *reply, twice repeated, on being urged to hang* JEFFERSON DAVIS, *in case of his capture.*

If it were to be done at all, it were better that it were well done!—JEFFERSON DAVIS *to* GENERAL BRECKINRIDGE *on hearing of* PRESIDENT LINCOLN'S *Assassination.*

He was the best man I ever knew.—SECRETARY SEWARD *to* REV. DR. BELLOWS, *on* ABRAHAM LINCOLN.

---

### Last Day's Incidents in the President's Life.

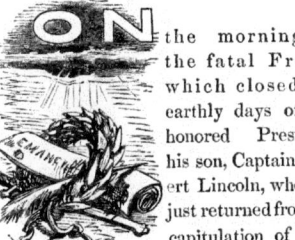

ON the morning of the fatal Friday which closed the earthly days of the honored President, his son, Captain Robert Lincoln, who had just returned from the capitulation of Gen. Lee, breakfasted with his father, and the President passed a happy hour listening to all the details. While thus at breakfast, he heard that Speaker Colfax was in the house, and sent word that he wished to see him immediately in the reception room. He conversed with him nearly an hour, on his future policy as to the rebellion, which he was about to submit to the cabinet. Afterwards he had an interview with Mr. Hale, minister to Spain, and several senators and representatives.

At eleven o'clock, the Cabinet and General Grant met with him, and in one of the most satisfactory and important cabinet sessions held since his first inauguration, the future policy of the administration was harmoniously and unanimously agreed on, Secretary Stanton remarking that he felt that the Government was stronger then than at any previous period since the rebellion commenced. Turning to General

Grant, Mr. Lincoln asked him if he had heard from General Sherman? General Grant replied that he had not, but was in hourly expectation of receiving dispatches from him, announcing the surrender of Johnston. In response to this remark the President replied—

"Well, you will hear very soon now, and the news will be important."

"Why do you think so?" inquired General Grant, somewhat in a curious mood.

"Because," said Mr. Lincoln, "I had a dream last night, and ever since the war began I have invariably had the same dream before any very important military event has occurred." He then instanced Bull Run, Antietam, Gettysburg, &c., and said that before each of those events he had had the same dream, and, turning to Secretary Welles, continued, "It is in your line, too, Mr. Welles. The dream is that I saw a ship sailing very rapidly, and I am sure that it portends some important national event."

In the afternoon, the President had a long and pleasant interview with General Oglesby, Senator Yates, and other leading citizens of Illinois.

At about half-past seven o'clock, in the evening, Hon. George Ashmun, of Massachusetts, who presided over the Chicago Convention in 1860, called at the White House, and was ushered into the parlor, where Hon. Schuyler Colfax was seated, waiting for a short interview with the President on business which had a bearing upon his proposed overland trip. A few moments elapsed, when President Lincoln entered the room, and engaged in conversation upon various matters, appearing to be in a very happy and jovial frame of mind. He spoke of his visit to Richmond, and when they stated that there was much uneasiness at the North while he was at the rebel capital, for fear that some traitor might shoot him, he replied jocularly, that he would have been alarmed himself if any other person had been President and gone there, but that personally he did not feel any danger whatever. Conversing on a matter of business with Mr. Ashmun, he made a remark that he saw Mr. Ashmun was surprised at, and though not very important, he immediately said, with his well known kindness of heart,

"You did not understand me, Ashmun. I did not mean what you inferred, and I take it all back and apologise for it."

Mr. Ashmun desiring to see him again, and there being no time to attend to it then, the President took out a card, and placing it on his knee, wrote as follows:

"Allow Mr. Ashmun and friend to come to me at nine A. M. to-morrow.

April 14, '65.  A. LINCOLN."

These were the last words that he penned. It was the last time that he signed his name to any order, document or message. The last words written by him were thus making an engagement for the morrow—an engagement which he was not allowed to meet. Before the hour had arrived he was no more.

After signing the card, he said, humorously, to Mr. Colfax,—

"Mr. Sumner has the gavel of the Confederate Congress, which he got at Richmond, to hand to the Secretary of War; but I insisted then that he must give it to you, and you tell him for me to hand it over."

Mr. Ashmun here pleasantly alluded to the gavel which he still had—the same one he had used when presiding over the Chicago Nominating Convention of 1860.

Mr. Lincoln finally stated that he must go to the theatre, and, saying "You are going with Mrs. Lincoln and me to the theatre, I hope," warmly pressed Speaker Colfax and Mr. Ashmun to accompany them, but they excused themselves on the score of previous engagements. It was now half an hour after the time they had intended to start, and they spoke about waiting half an hour longer,—the President going with reluctance, as General Grant had that evening gone North, and

FINAL SCENES AND EVENTS IN THE GREAT DRAMA; ETC. 635

he did not wish the people to be disappointed, it having been announced in the afternoon papers that the President, Mrs. Lincoln, and General Grant, would attend the theatre that evening, to witness the representation of the American Cousin. At the door he stopped and said—

"Colfax, do not forget to tell the people in the mining regions, as you pass through them, what I told you this morning about the development when peace comes, and I will telegraph you at San Francisco."

Starting for the carriage, Mrs. Lincoln took the arm of Mr. Ashmun, and the President and Mr. Colfax walked together. As soon as the President and Mrs. Lincoln were seated in the carriage, Mrs. L. gave orders to the coachman to drive around to Senator Harris's residence for Miss Harris. As the carriage rolled away, they both said 'Good-by,—Good-by,' to Messrs. Ashmun and Colfax, and the carriage had in a moment more disappeared from the ground in front of the White House. A few moments later the presidential party of four persons, namely, the President and Mrs. Lincoln, Miss Harris and Major Rathbun, of Albany, step-son of Senator Harris, arrived at the theatre and entered the front and left hand upper private box. There was an immense audience present, as was to be expected, in view of the announcement of the attendance of the President and Lieutenant-General Grant.

Only a short time elapsed, while President Lincoln occupied that box, before the leaden messenger was sped on its fatal errand, and "GOOD FRIDAY," of the 14th April, 1865, was *the last of the beloved President's earthly days.*

Perhaps nothing can be more appropriately presented, in closing this mournful historic page—the last day's incidents of the President's life—than the following lines, written by the President on that same fatal day. It appears that his friend, General Van Alen, had recently written to him not to expose his life unnecessarily, as he had done at Richmond, and assuring him of the earnest desire of all his countrymen to close the war he had so successfully conducted. After acknowledging the receipt of the letter, the President replied, April 14th, the day of his assassination, and said:

I intend to adopt the advice of my friends and use due precaution. * * * I thank you for the assurance you give me that I shall be supported by conservative men like yourself in the efforts I may make to restore the Union, so as to make it, to use your language, a Union of hearts and hands as well as of States.

Yours truly, A. LINCOLN."

**Deathbed Scene of the Murdered President.**

As soon as the discovery was made that the President was shot, the surgeon-general and other physicians were immediately summoned and their skill exhausted in efforts to restore him to consciousness. An examination of his wounds, however, showed that no hopes could be given that his life would be spared.

Preparations were at once made to remove him, and he was conveyed to a house immediately opposite, occupied by Mr. Peterson, a respectable citizen of that locality. He was placed upon the bed, the only evidence of life being an occasional nervous twitching of the hand and heavy breathing. He was entirely unconscious, as he had been ever since the assassination. At about half past eleven the motion of the muscles of his face indicated as if he were trying to speak, but doubtless it was merely muscular. His eyes protruded from their sockets and were suffused with blood. In other respects his countenance was unchanged.

At his bedside were the Secretary of War, Secretary of the Navy, Secretary of the Interior, Postmaster General and Attorney General; Senator Sumner, General Todd, cousin to Mrs. Lincoln; Major Hay, M. B. Field, General Halleck, Major-General Meigs, Rev. Dr. Gurley, Drs.

Abbott, Stone, Hatch, Neal, Hall, and Lieberman, and a few others. All were bathed in tears; and Secretary Stanton, when informed by Surgeon Gen. Barnes, that the President could not live until morning, exclaimed, "Oh, no, General; no—no;" and with an impulse, natural as it was unaffected, immediately sat down on a chair near his bedside, and wept like a child. Senator Sumner was seated on the right of the President, near the head, holding the right hand of the President in his own. He was sobbing like a woman, with his head bowed down almost on the pillow of the bed on which his illustrious friend was dying. In an adjoining room were Mrs. Lincoln, and her son, Capt. Rob't Lincoln; Miss Harris, who was with Mrs. Lincoln at the time of the assassination, and several others.

Mrs. Lincoln was under great excitement and agony, wringing her hands and exclaiming, "Why did he not shoot me instead of my husband? I have tried to be so careful of him, fearing something would happen, and his life seemed to be more precious now than ever. I must go with him," and other expressions of like character. She was constantly going back and forth to the bedside of the President, exclaiming in great agony, "How can it be so!" The scene was heart-rending. Captain Robert Lincoln bore himself with great firmness, and constantly endeavored to assuage the grief of his mother by telling her to put her trust in God and all would be well. Occasionally, however, being entirely overcome, he would retire by himself and give vent to most piteous lamentations. Then, recovering himself, he would return to his mother, and, with remarkable self-possession, try to cheer her broken spirits and lighten her load of sorrow.

At four o'clock the symptoms of restlessness returned, and at six the premonitions of dissolution set in. His face which had been quite pale, began to assume a waxen transparency, the jaw slowly fell, and the teeth became exposed. About a quarter of an hour before the President died, his breathing became very difficult, and in many instances seemed to have entirely ceased. He would again rally and breathe with so great difficulty as to be heard in almost every part of the house. Mrs. Lincoln took her last leave of him about twenty minutes before he expired, and was sitting in the adjoining room when it was announced to her that he was dead. When the announcement was made, she exclaimed, "Oh! why did you not tell me that he was dying!"

The surgeons and the members of the cabinet, Senator Sumner, Captain Robert Lincoln, General Todd, Mr. Field, and Mr. Rufus Andrews, were standing at his bedside when he breathed his last. Senator Sumner, General Todd, Robert Lincoln, and Mr. Andrews, stood leaning over the headboard of the bed, watching every motion of the beating breast of the dying President. Robert Lincoln was resting himself tenderly upon the arm of Senator Sumner, the mutual embrace of the two

Charles Sumner.

having all the affectionateness of father and son. The surgeons were sitting upon the side and foot of the bed, holding the President's hands, and with their watches observing the slow declension of the pulse, and watching the ebbing out of the vital spirit. Such was the solemn stillnes for

FINAL SCENES AND EVENTS IN THE GREAT DRAMA; ETC. 637

the space of five minutes that the ticking of the watches could be heard in the room.

At twenty-two minutes past seven o'clock, in the morning, April fifteenth, gradually and calmly, and without a sigh or a groan, all that bound the soul of Abraham Lincoln was loosened, and the eventful career of one of the most remarkable of men was closed on earth.

As he drew his last breath, the Rev. Dr. Gurley, the President's pastor, offered a fervent prayer of supplication and sympathy. The countenance of the President was beaming with that characteristic smile which only those familiar with him in his happiest moments could appreciate; and except the blackness of his eyes, his face appeared perfectly natural. The morning was calm, and the rain was dropping gently upon the roof of the humble apartment where they laid him down to die. The body servant of the President entered the room just before he died, and as the breath left the body of Mr. Lincoln, this loving and bereaved servant manifested the most indescribable sorrow. Mrs. Lincoln remained but a short time, when she was assisted into her carriage, and with her son Robert and other friends she was driven to the house which but the evening before she left for the last time with her honored husband, who never was again to enter that home alive.

The room, into which the most exalted of mortal rulers was taken to die, was in the rear part of the dwelling, and at the end of the main hall, from which rises a stairway. The dimensions of the room are about ten by fifteen feet, the walls being covered with a brownish paper, figured with a white design. Some engravings and a photograph hung upon the walls. The engravings were copies of the " Village Blacksmith," and " Stable and Barnyard Scenes;" the photograph was one taken from an engraved copy of Rosa Bonheur's " Horse Fair." The furniture of the apartment consisted of a bureau covered with crochet, a table, several chairs of simple construction, adapted for sleeping rooms, and the bed upon which Mr. Lincoln lay when his spirit took its flight. The bedstead was a low walnut, the headboard from two to three feet high. The floor was covered with Brussels carpeting, which had been considerably used. Everything on the bed was stained with the blood of the Chief Magistrate of the nation. A few locks of hair were removed from the President's head for the family, previous to the remains being placed in the coffin temporarily used for removing the remains to the executive mansion.

### Flight, Capture and Death of Booth.

After eleven days had transpired since the death of the President, his murderer, John Wilkes Booth, was discovered in a barn on Garrett's farm, near Port Royal, on the Rappahannock. Immediately after the murder, Colonel Baker, of the detective service, set out to find Booth's hiding-place. He soon succeeded in capturing Atzerodt, the would-be assassin of Vice-President Johnson, and 'Dr.' Mudd. It was Dr. M. who attended to Booth's leg, crippled by his getting entangled with the flag that decorated the President's box, and a boot with Booth's name in it was found in his possession. A negro was then arrested, who said he had seen Booth and another man cross the Potomac in a fishing-boat. Col. Baker sent to Gen. Hancock for twenty-five mounted men to aid him in the pursuit. These were sent under Lieutenant Dougherty, and Baker placed them under the control of Lieutenant-Colonel Conger, and of his cousin, Lieutenant L. B. Baker, and dispatched them to Belle Plain, with orders to scour the country about Port Royal.

The detectives and cavalrymen left Washington at two P. M. on the 23d of April, and at ten o'clock disembarked at Belle Plain, near Fredericksburg. Here they commenced their inquest, but without any result. The next morning they came to Port Royal ferry, and crossed. At Port Royal they found one Rollins, a fisherman, who referred them to a negro named Lucas as having driven two men a short distance toward Bowling Green in a wagon. These men perfectly answered the description of Booth and his accomplice Harold. Some disbanded men, it was learned, belonging to Mosby's command, took Booth under their protection on the way to Bowling Green. On the 25th Baker and his party proceeded to Bowling Green, a small court-house town in Caroline County. Here they found the captain of the rebel cavalry, and extorted from him a statement of Booth's hiding-place. It was found that this was at the house of a Mr. Garrett, which they had passed on their way to Bowling Green.

Returning with the captain for a guide, the worn-out command halted at Garrett's gate, at two o'clock on the morning of the 26th. Without noise the house was surrounded, and Baker went up to the kitchen door on the side and rapped. An old man in half undress undrew the bolts, and had scarcely opened the door before Baker had him by the throat with a pistol at his ear, and asked, "Where are the men who stay with you?" Under the menace of instant death the old man seemed paralyzed, but at Baker's order lit a candle. The question was then repeated. "They are gone," replied the old man. Soon a young boy appeared, and told Baker the men he sought were in the barn. The barn was then surrounded. Baker and Conger went to the door. The former called out signifying his intention to have a surrender on the part of the men inside, or else to fire the barn, and shoot them on the spot. The young boy was sent in to receive their arms. To the boy's appeal Booth answered with a curse, accusing the boy of having betrayed him. The boy then came out, and Baker repeated his demand, giving Booth five minutes to make up his mind. Booth replied—

"Who are you, and what do you want with us?"

"We want you to deliver up your arms and become our prisoners," said Baker.

"But who are you?"

"That makes no difference. We know who you are, and we want you. We have here fifty men with carbines and pistols. You cannot escape."

After a pause, Booth said: "Captain, this is a hard case, I swear. Perhaps I am being taken by my own friends." He then asked time to consider, which was granted. After a little interval, Baker threatened to fire the barn, if they did not come out. Booth replied that he was a cripple, and begged a chance for his life, declaring that he would fight them all at so many yards apace, and that he would never be taken alive. Baker replied that he did not come there to fight but to capture him, and again threatened to fire the barn.

"Well, then, my brave boys," said Booth, "prepare a stretcher for me."

Harold now wanted to surrender, and, in the midst of a shower of imprecations from Booth, did so. Conger then set fire to the barn.

The blaze lit up the black recesses of the great barn till every wasp's nest and cobweb in the roof was luminous, flinging streaks of red and violet across the tumbled farm-gear in the corner, and bathed the murderer's retreat in a vivid illumination, and while in bold outline his figure stood revealed, they rose like an impenetrable wall to guard from sight the dreaded enemy who lit them. Behind the blaze, with his eye to a crack, Conger saw Wilkes Booth standing upright upon a crutch. He likens him at this instant to his eminent brother Edwin, whom he says he so much resembled that he half believed, for the moment, the whole pursuit to have been a mistake. At the gleam of fire Wilkes dropped his crutch and carbine, and on both hands crept up to the spot to

# FINAL SCENES AND EVENTS IN THE GREAT DRAMA; ETC. 639

espy the incendiary and shoot him dead. His eyes were lustrous like fever, and swelled and rolled in terrible anxiety, while his teeth were fixed, and he wore the expression of one in the calmness before frenzy. In vain he peered with vengeance in his look; the blaze that made him visible concealed his enemy. A second he turned glaring at the fire, as if to leap upon and extinguish it, but the flames had made such headway that this was a futile impulse, and he dismissed it. As calmly as upon the battle-field a veteran stands amidst the hail of ball and shell and plunging iron, Booth turned at a man's stride, and pushed for the door, carbine in poise, and the last resolve of death—despair—set on his high, bloodless forehead.

At this instant, Sergeant Boston Corbett fired through a crevice and shot Booth in the neck. They then took him up and carried him out on the grass, a little way from the door, beneath a locust tree. Conger went back to the barn, to see if the fire could be put out, but found it could not, and returned to where Booth was lying. Before this (says Lieutenant-Colonel Conger) I supposed him to be dead; he had all the appearance of a dead man; but when I came back his eyes and mouth were moving. I called immediately for water and put some on his face. He seemed to revive, and attempted to speak. I put my ear down to his mouth, and heard him say, "Tell my mother I died for my country." I repeated the words to him and said, "Is that what you would say?" He said "Yes." They carried him to the porch of Garrett's house, and laid him on a straw bed or tick. At that time he revived considerably, and could talk in a whisper so as to be intelligibly understood. He could not speak above a whisper. He wanted water; I gave it to him. He wanted to turn on his face; I said he could'nt lie on his face. He wanted to be turned on his side; we turned him on his side three times, but he could not lie with any comfort, and asked immediately to be turned back. He asked me to put my hand on his throat, and

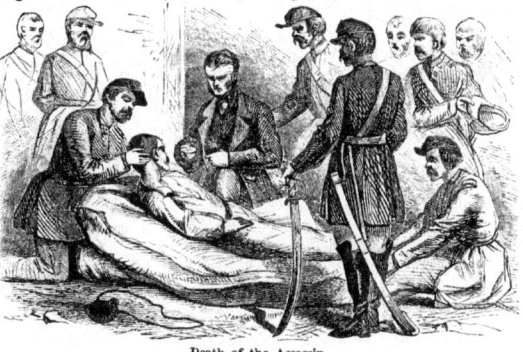

Death of the Assassin.

press down, which I did. He said "Harder"; I pressed as hard as I thought necessary. He made a very strong exertion to cough, but was unable to do so. I suppose he thought there was blood in his throat. I asked him to put out his tongue, which he did. I said, "There is no blood in your throat." He repeated several times—two or three times at least—"Kill me! kill me!" I replied, "I do not want to kill you. I want you to get well."

When the doctor, whom Conger had sent for, arrived, Booth asked to have his hands raised and shown him. When this was done, he muttered "Useless, useless!" These were his last words. He died about four hours after he was shot.

Booth and Harold were dressed in rebel gray uniform. Booth's mustache had been cut off, apparently with scissors, and his beard allowed to grow, thus changing his appearance considerably. His hair had been cut somewhat shorter than he usually wore it. Being taken to Washington, a post-mortem examination of the remains took place on board the monitor Montauk, the body being laid out on a carpenter's bench between the stern and turret. The shot which terminated his life entered on the left side, at the back of the neck, a point not far different from that in which his victim, the lamented President, was shot.

On the night of the 27th of April a small row-boat received the remains of the assassin, and no one save two men—sworn to irrevocable secrecy—it is said, know the place or manner of his sepulture.

The capture and solemn trial of the other accomplices and conspirators in the great crime of simultaneously murdering the President, Vice President, Secretary of State, Secretary of War, and Lieutenant-General Grant—viz., the Surratts, mother and son, Payne, Atzerodt, Harold, O'Loughlin, Arnold, etc.,—constitute the remainder of this darkest chapter in the annals of human crime. Four of these expiated their crime on the gallows, and the blood of the Martyred President was avenged.

### Conversation on his Threatened Assassination.

It is a most noteworthy incident that one of the latest, if not the very last of the letters written by Mr. Lincoln, was in reply to Gen. Van Alen, who wrote to the President a short time previously, asking him not to expose his life unnecessarily, as he had done at Richmond, and assuring him of the earnest desire of all his countrymen for him to close the war he had so successfully conducted. After acknowledging the receipt of the letter—which he did on the 14th of April, the very day of his assassination—Mr. Lincoln said, "I intend to adopt the advice of my friends, and use due precaution." Alas!

Senator Fessenden states that one day he was standing with Mr. Lincoln on the steps of the Secretary of State's office, and, observing that the President looked weary, Mr. Fessenden remarked—

"Mr. President, the people of the United States are praying that God

Secretary Fessenden.

would spare your life to see the end of this rebellion."

"Mr. Fessenden," replied the President,. "it may be that I shall not live to see it, and sometimes I think I shall not; but if I were taken away, there are those who would perform my duties better."

### Patience of Mr. Lincoln Tried too Far.

One day President Lincoln was found in a close and loud conversation with a gentleman from a certain portion of reclaimed southern territory. The visitor professed to be a southern loyalist, and wanted certain papers signed by the President, making good a considerable amount of damage inflicted upon him by the war. The claimant urged his claims in soft, timid tones, and the President answered in a way quite the reverse. He was not pleased, and said—

"Why! this paper does not say you are *entitled* to the money."

"No, Sir, but it recommends my claim for your consideration."

"But, Sir, you do not prove your claim."

"We are loyal, Sir."

"Yes, Sir, and so are the men who stand up in front of Richmond, to be shot at, but they don't come here to plague me."

"We don't wish to worry you, Mr. President."

"No, I know what you want—you are turning, or trying to turn me into a justice of the peace, to put your claims through. There are a hundred thousand men in the country, every one of them as

Patience tried too far.

good as you are, who have just such bills as you present; and you care nothing of what becomes of them, so you get your money."

"We think our claim just, Mr. President."

"Yes, but you know you can't prove what is in this paper by all the people in the United States, and you want me to prove it for you by writing my name on the back of it: yes, in plain words you wish me to lie for you that you may get your money. I shall not do it."

The visitor stood a moment, as if dizzy and undecided; but gathering up slowly, retired to digest his repulse as best he could. Abraham the Just was right. Anybody could go and tell his story, but he had to look to it that he made out a good case, especially if he was after government money.

### Contrast Between the Two.

Mr. William C. Bryant's paper, the Evening Post, says,—An officer of the United States Army, whose authority in such a case we can not question, gives leave to publish the following account of what he heard Jefferson Davis say just before the breaking out of the war:

I heard Mr. Davis utter the following words in a southern town where he delivered an address in November, 1860. I did not hear the whole speech, only the words quoted, as I passed by the crowd of listeners:

"What! coerce a sovereign State! attempt to deprive us of our most inestimable rights! Let Mr. Lincoln try it, or Mr. Douglas either, and we will hang them higher than Haman, and the only difference I should make would be that [humorously] as Mr. Lincoln is considerably taller than Mr. Douglas, we should have to build his gibbet [standing on his toes and reaching up his hand] a leetle higher than that for Douglas."

During the trial of the assassins of President Lincoln, one of the witnesses was Mr. Lewis F. Bates, for several years residing in Charlotte, N. C., and agent of the Adams Express Company, in that place. He testified that Jeff. Davis stopped at his house on the 19th of April, and made a speech from the steps. Davis received and read a dispatch from General Breckinridge, dated Greensborough, April 19th, as follows:—

"President Lincoln was assassinated in the theatre on the night of the 14th. Secretary Seward's house was entered the same night, and he was repeatedly stabbed, and is probably mortally wounded."

Witness said that after reading the dispatch to the crowd, Davis stated, "If it were to be done, it were better it were well done." The day after, Breckinridge and Davis conversed in the house of witness on the subject of the assassination. Breckinridge remarked to Davis that he

Jefferson Davis.

regretted it very much—it was unfortunate for the people of the South, at that time. Davis replied, "Well, General, I don't know that if it were to be done at all it were better it were well done, and if the same were done to Andy Johnson, the beast, and Secretary Stanton, the job would then be complete."

Mr. J. Courtney, telegraph operator, testified that the dispatch in question passed over the wires; and Mr. Bates's testimony was unimpeached.

In contrast with the above, it is refreshing to cite the *animus* of clemency and good will which ever characterized the acts and declarations of the murdered President.

It is well known that, at the very moment of his assassination, he was occupied by thoughts and plans of both lenity and pardon. He was never harsh, even in speaking of Jefferson Davis; and, only a few days before his end, when one who was privileged to speak to him in that way, said, "Do not allow him to escape the law—he must be hanged," the President replied calmly, in the words which he had adopted in his last Inaugural Address, "*Judge not that ye be not judged.*" And when pressed again, by the remark that the sight of Libby Prison made it impossible to pardon him, the President *repeated twice over those same words*, revealing unmistakably the generous sentiments of his heart. Indeed, so disposed was the amiable President to extenuate, or forget, the crimes of even the most active conspirators, civil and military, against the life of the nation, that, on this point, a breach seemed imminent between him and many of his best friends, if not the majority, who elevated him to office. But now that he is dead, the spirit of mercy that actuated him, gives fragrance to his memory. In the words of another —his great Exemplar—Mr. Lincoln might well say of his enemies, "They hated me without a cause."

### Disappointed Expectations.

In the year 1854, a conversation took place at the Smithsonian Institution in Washington, between Jefferson Davis and Professor Jewett, in the course of which Davis predicted that the Union would soon be divided into two republics.

"Where will the division or boundary line be?" interrogated Prof. Jewett.

"The line separating the slave and free states," answered Mr. Davis.

"Then," said the professor, "you expect to claim the national capital."

"Of course," was the reply, "and this very Smithsonian Institute will be within the southern republic."

"But," asked Prof. J., "how will you bring about such a division of the country? Do you think the free states will agree to it without a resort to arms?"

"Sir," said Jefferson Davis, in his sententious manner, "the North will never fight us on that occasion. There will be no bloodshed. When the South says she will secede, and become a distinct nationality, the North will be glad to let us go, and that peaceably. It will be a bloodless revolution." Alas!

#### Comment on Mr. Sloanaker's "Beautiful Portrait."

The genial spirit of the lamented President, which relieved him amidst the toils and anxieties of his dangerous and difficult station, will linger long, in many characteristic anecdotes, to soften in a measure the horror of his death, and mingle light with the dark mourning for his loss to the country he preserved. A significant incident, in illustration of this, is related by a friend of the late President, who happened to be present at the White House the day after the renomination of Mr. Lincoln to the Presidency. Various political organizations called to pay their respects to him. Among the rest was the Philadelphia delegation. The chairman of that body, in presenting one of the members, said—

"Mr. President, this is Mr. A. B. Sloanaker, of the second district of our State; a most active and earnest friend of yours and of the cause. He has, among other things, been good enough to paint and present to our league rooms a most *beautiful* portrait of yourself."

Mr. Lincoln took Mr. Sloanaker's hand in his, and with an earnest cordiality, shook it kindly, saying with a merry voice—

"I presume, Sir, in painting your *beautiful portrait*, you took your idea of me from my *principles*, and *not* from my *person*."

#### Attending to Business in Regular Order.

Andrew Johnson was once announced to speak in Nashville, on one of the exciting questions of the day; and loud threats were uttered that, if he dared to appear, he should not leave the hall alive. At the appointed hour he ascended the platform, and, advancing to the desk, laid his pistol upon it, with the most quiet unconcern of manner. He then addressed the audience in terms as follows:

"Fellow citizens: It is proper when freemen assemble for the discussion of important public interests, that everything should be done decently and in order. I have been informed that part of the business to be transacted on the present occasion is the assassination of the individual who now has the honor of addressing you.

President Johnson.

I beg respectfully to propose that this be the first business in order. Therefore, if any man has come here to-night for the purpose indicated, I do not say to him let him speak, but let him shoot."

Here he paused, with his right hand on his pistol and the other holding open his coat, while with his eyes he blandly surveyed the assembly. After a pause of half a minute, he resumed:—

"Gentlemen, it appears that I have been misinformed. I will now proceed to address you on the subject that has called us together."

#### Reward of a Speech after Fifteen Years from its Delivery.

In an interesting conversation between President Lincoln and Rev. Dr. M'Clintock—as given in a public address by the latter,—Dr. M'C. asked the President if there was any truth in the rumor, at that time quite prevalent, of the removal of Mr. Dayton, American Minister at the French Court, and, if there was, he, Dr. M'C., would like the privilege of discussing the matter a little. President Lincoln said: "As to discussing the matter I have no objection, but as to his removal I have no such idea." He then went on to speak of his reason for appointing Mr. Dayton, and said:

"When I was a member of Congress, in 1846-7, after the close of the Mexican war, a treaty was made, and opposed by Daniel Webster. After Daniel Webster sat down, William L. Dayton arose and made a speech that covered every point that Webster had made. I had been in the habit of regarding Webster as the greatest and most eloquent of men, until Mr. Dayton made that speech (and then with a peculiar humor that belongs to all great natures, Mr. Lincoln added): It may be because Mr. Dayton was on my side that I thought it was a great speech; and one of my first thoughts after my election was that William L. Dayton should occupy one of the best appointments I could give him."

This anecdote shows how tenaciously Mr. Lincoln clung to men he believed to be reliable, remembering that speech and its maker fifteen years.

### "Public Opinion Baths."

Colonel Halpine, one of General Halleck's staff, relates that once, on what was called "a public day"—when Mr. Lincoln received all applicants in their turn—the first thing he saw on being ushered into the President's chamber by Major Hay, was Mr. Lincoln bowing an elderly lady out of the door, the President's remarks to her being, as she still lingered and appeared reluctant to go,—

"I am really very sorry, madam; very sorry. But your own good sense must tell you that I am not here to collect small debts. You must appeal to the courts in regular order."

When she was gone, Mr. Lincoln sat down, crossed his legs, locked his hands over his knees, and commenced to laugh—this being his favorite attitude when much amused.

"What odd kinds of people come in to see me," he said; "and what odd ideas they must have about my office! Would you believe, Major, that the old lady who has just left, came in here to get from me an order for stopping the pay of a Treasury clerk, who owes her a board bill of about seventy dollars!" (And the President rocked himself backward and forward, and appeared intensely amused.) "She may have come in here a loyal woman," continued Mr. Lincoln, "but I'll be bound she has gone away believing that the worst pictures of me in the Richmond press only lack truth in not being half black and bad enough."

This led to a somewhat general conversation, in which surprise was expressed that the President did not adopt the plan in vogue at all military head-quarters, under which every applicant to see the General commanding had to be filtered through a sieve of officers—assistant Adjutant Generals, and so forth,—who allowed none in to take up the General's time, save such as they were satisfied had business of sufficient importance, and which could be transacted in no other manner than by a personal interview. Colonel Halpine remarked—

"Of every hundred people who come to see the General-in-chief daily, not ten have any sufficient business with him, nor are they admitted. On being asked to explain for what purpose they desire to see him, and stating it, it is found in nine cases out of ten, that the business properly belongs to some one or other of the subordinate bureaux. They are then referred, as the case may be, to the quartermaster, commissary, medical, adjutant general, or other departments, with an assurance that—even if they saw the General-in-chief—he could do nothing more for them than give them the same direction. With these points courteously explained, they go away quite content, although refused admittance."

"Ah, yes," replied Mr. Lincoln, gravely —and his words on this matter are important as illustrating a rule of his action, and to some extent, perhaps, the essentially representative character of his mind and of his administration—"ah, yes! such things do very well for you military people, with your arbitrary rule, and in your camps. But the office of President is essentially a civil one, and the affair is very different. For myself, I feel—though the tax on my time is heavy—that no hours of my day are better employed than those which thus bring me again within the direct contact and atmosphere of the average of our whole people. Men moving only in an official circle are apt to become merely official—not to say arbitrary —in their ideas, and are apter and apter, with each passing day, to forget that they only hold power in a representative capacity. Now this is all wrong. I go into these promiscuous receptions of all who claim to have business with me, twice each week, and every applicant for audience has to take his turn, as if waiting to be shaved in a barber's shop. Many of the matters brought to my notice are utterly frivolous, but others are of more or less importance, and all serve to renew in me a clearer and more vivid image of that great popular assemblage out of which I sprang, and to which at the end of two years I must return. I tell you, Major," he said,—appearing at this point to recollect that Halpine was in the room, for the former part of these remarks had been made with half-shut eyes, as if in soliloquy—"I tell you that I call these receptions my *public opinion baths*—for I have little time to read the papers and gather public opinion that way; and though they may not be pleasant in all their particulars, the effect, as a whole, is renovating and invigorating to my perceptions of responsibility and duty. It would never do for a President to have guards with drawn sabres at his door, as if he fancied he were, or were trying to be, or were assuming to be, an emperor."

That original phrase of the President's, "public opinion baths," is not likely ever to be forgotten.

**Pamphlet of Jokes in the Corner of Mr. Lincoln's Desk.**

In a corner of his desk, Mr. Lincoln was accustomed to keep a copy of some humorous work, and it was frequently his habit, when greatly fatigued, annoyed, or depressed, to take this up and read a chapter, with great relief. The Saturday before he left Washington to go to the front, just previous to the capture of Richmond, had been a very hard day with him. The pressure of office-seekers was greater at that juncture than ever before, and he was almost worn out. Among the callers that evening, was a party composed of a senator, a representative, an ex-lieutenant governor of a western State, and several private citizens. They had business of great importance, involving the necessity of the President's examination of voluminous documents. Pushing everything aside, he said to one of the party—

"Have you seen the Nasby papers?"

"No, I have not—who is Nasby?"

"There is a chap out in Ohio," returned the President, "who has been writing a series of letters in the newspapers under the signature of Petroleum V. Nasby. Some one sent me a pamphlet collection of them the other day. I am going to write to 'Petroleum' to come down here, and I intend to tell him if he will communicate his talent to me, I will *swap* places with him!" Thereupon he arose, went to a drawer in his desk, and, taking out the "letters," he sat down and read one to the company, finding in their enjoyment of it the temporary excitement and relief which another man, perhaps, would have found in a glass of grog! The instant he had

### Justice surviving Clemency.

One of the officers employed in investigating the plot of the murder of the President had occasion to question a woman who was in some way connected with the affair. She kept flippantly asserting that "s'help me heaven I don't know anything about it, and s'help me heaven, I don't tell an untruth, for I never told a lie in my life," keeping on in her voluble assertions till at length the officer quietly interrupted her with the assurance that it did not much matter to him what she revealed, but it might be better for her,—at which she became a little indignant, and asked what they could do with her if she knew about the matter and wouldn't tell it. "Why," responded the officer, "in case you prove to be implicated as much as I am afraid you are, you might be hanged." At this reply she was a trifle moved, and said, "Justice should be tempered with clemency." "Ah, yes, my dear madam," replied the officer, "but you forget that the clemency man is dead." For the first time the woman saw it in that light and wept. Justice survived, while mercy lay stricken to the ground by those most in need of its benefit.

### Polly's Baby.

In a rather plain frame building in Raleigh, North Carolina, Andrew Johnson, President of the United States, was born. The house is shown to visitors by the owner, a venerable old lady named Stewart. She will also tell how, in an ecstacy of delight, on returning from her wedding tour, the first news she got was, "Polly has a baby." Full of the feelings and enthusiasm of a young bride, she rushed in and kissed and hugged the baby. "Little I thought," she exclaimed to a visitor, "that I was caressing the future President of the United States." "You, then, knew his father and mother?" "Yes, Sir, I knew them well; they were in our employ for several years." "How did they serve you?" "They were plain, hard-working, honest folks, that attended to their business and nothing more." When leaving, the old lady said to her company, "How I would like to see him, dear me; only it is so far; but then he would not know me. Well, any way, I should like to see; I think he would grant me one little request. I have a grandson in prison in the North, perhaps he'd let him come home to gladden my old heart—would you mention it to him, Sir?"

Andrew Johnson's Tailor Shop.

### Pocket-Full of Coin Ready for Delivery.

The words "Honest Old Abe" have passed into the language of our time and

FINAL SCENES AND EVENTS IN THE GREAT DRAMA; ETC.   647

country as the synonym for all that is just and honest in man. Yet thousands of instances, unknown to the world, might be added to those so often told of Mr. Lincoln's great and crowning virtue. He disliked inuendoes, concealments, and subterfuges; and no sort of approach at official "jobbing" ever had any encouragement from him. He steadily discountenanced all practices of government officers using any part of the public funds for temporary or personal purposes; and he loved to tell of an instance in his own official experience, when he was saved from embarrassment by his rigid adherence to a good rule.

He had been postmaster at Salem, Illinois, during Jackson's administration, William T. Barry being then Postmaster-General, and resigning his office, removed to Springfield, having sent a statement of accounts to the Department at Washington. No notice was taken of his account, which showed a balance due the Government of over one hundred and fifty dollars, until three or four years after, when, Amos Kendall being Postmaster-General, he was presented with a draft for the amount due. Some of Mr. Lincoln's friends, who knew that he was in straightened circumstances then, as he had always been, heard of the draft and offered to help him out with a loan; but he told them not to worry, and producing from his trunk an old pocket, tied up and marked, counted out in sixpences, shillings, and quarters, the exact sum required of him, in the identical coin which he received while in office years before, and which he had sacredly reserved for the Government, whenever the proper official should be pleased to respond to his "account rendered."

---

**Answering the Secretary and the General.**

One of the last stories told by President Lincoln, was to one of the members of his cabinet who went to see him, to ask if it would be a proper proceeding to permit Jake Thompson to slip through Maine in disguise and embark from Portland to a foreign port. The President, as usual, was disposed to be merciful and to permit the arch traitor to pass unmolested. The Secretary, however, urged that he should be arrested as a traitor, saying:

"By permitting him to escape the penalties of treason, you sanction it."

"Well," replied Mr. Lincoln, "let me tell you a story. There was an Irish soldier here last summer who wanted something to drink stronger than water, and stopped at a drug shop, where he espied a soda fountain. 'Mr. Doctor,' said he, 'give me, plase, a glass of soda wather, an' if yees can put in a few dhrops of whiskey unbeknown to meself, I'll be obleeged.' Now," continued Mr. Lincoln, "if Jake Thompson is permitted to go through Maine unbeknown to meself, what's the harm? So don't have him arrested."

Similar was the logic employed by Mr. Lincoln, it appears, in the case of Jefferson Davis. General Sherman, in vindicating himself against what he regarded as the hostile course of the War Department, said that the Government never distinctly explained to him the policy which should guide his actions, and that at City Point he had asked Mr. Lincoln whether he wanted Jefferson Davis captured, and for reply had been told a story. This story is the one, substantially, which Mr. Lincoln had employed in the case narrated above, but its use in connection with Davis, and its repetition by General Sherman, under the circumstances referred to, give it in some measure a historical value.

"I'll tell you, General," Mr. Lincoln is said to have begun, "I'll tell you what I think about taking Jefferson Davis. Out in Sangamon County there was an old temperance lecturer who was very strict in the doctrine and practice of total abstinence. One day, after a long ride in the hot sun, he stopped at the house of a friend, who proposed making him a lemonade. As the mild beverage was being mixed, the friend insinuatingly asked if he wouldn't like just the least drop of something stronger to brace up his nerves after the exhausting heat and exercise. 'No,' replied the lecturer, 'I couldn't think of it; I'm opposed to it on principle. But,' he added, with a longing glance at the black bottle that stood conveniently at hand, 'if you could manage to put in a drop unbeknownst to me, I guess it would not hurt me much.' Now, General," Mr. Lincoln is said to have concluded, "I'm bound to oppose the escape of Jeff. Davis; but if you could manage to let him slip out unbeknownst-like, I guess it wouldn't hurt me much."

"And that," exclaimed General Sherman, "is all I could get out of the Government as to what its policy was concerning the rebel leaders."

The good intentions of the amiable President are appreciated by the whole nation that mourns his loss; but his willingness to allow the escape of the great master-spirit of the rebellion, can scarcely be said to have been shared by many beside himself, even to "save trouble."

### Second Reflection in the Looking Glass.

When Mr. Lincoln received the news of his first election, he went home to tell Mrs. Lincoln about it. She was up stairs in the bed-room, and there he went, throwing himself down on a lounge, in a careless manner. "Opposite where I lay," said Mr. Lincoln, "was a bureau, with a swinging glass upon it,"—and here in relating the matter to a friend he got up and placed the furniture so as to illustrate the position—" and, looking in that glass, I saw myself reflected, nearly at full length, but my face, I noticed, had *two* separate and distinct images, the tip of the nose of one being about three inches from the tip of the other. I was a little bothered, perhaps startled, and got up and looked in the glass, but the illusion vanished. On lying down again, I saw it a second time— plainer, if possible, than before; and then I noticed that one of the faces was a little paler, say five shades, than the other. I got up and the thing melted away, and I went off, and, in the excitement of the hour, forgot all about it—nearly, but not quite, for the thing would once in a while come up, and give me a little pang, as though something uncomfortable had happened. A few days after, I tried the experiment again, when [with a laugh,] sure enough, the thing came back again; but I never succeeded in bringing the ghost back after that, though I once tried very industriously to show it to my wife, who was worried about it somewhat. She thought it was a 'sign' that I was to be elected to a second term of office, and that the paleness of one of the faces was an omen that I should not see life through the last term."

The President, with his usual good sense, saw nothing in all this but an optical illusion; though the flavor of superstition which hangs about every man's composition made him wish that he had never seen it. But there are people who will now believe that this odd coincidence was "a warning," notwithstanding its entire consistency with the laws of nature.

### Tenth of May at Irwinsville.

On arriving at General Johnston's head-quarters, and learning of the terms of the convention between Sherman and Johnston, Jefferson Davis, then on his flight South from Richmond, stopped at Charlotte, N. C. It was frequently remarked that it was dangerous to do so; but he invariably replied that he had two many friends, and knew the country two well, to be caught by any of the forces in the Yankee army. He remained at Charlotte until twelve o'clock on the day that the armistice expired. At eleven o'clock on that day, his horse, a handsome blooded bay, was brought to the door of the private house in which he was stopping. At twelve, having learned that the terms of the aforesaid convention were rejected, he

# FINAL SCENES AND EVENTS IN THE GREAT DRAMA; ETC.

mounted his horse, and, accompanied by numerous friends and officials, rode off. At the same time a force of cavalry, under General Dibrel, moved off with him.

In passing through Lexington, Davis was introduced by Judge Freeman, of Mississippi, who was traveling with him, to Dr. Dusenbury, a native of the place. The doctor invited Davis in to take a drink of apple brandy, and he did so. A brief conversation ensued, the doctor remarking—

"Mr. Davis, our cause is lost."

"Our cause may be lost," replied Davis, "but the principle for which we are contending will present itself at another time, in another shape."

He meant that there would yet be a conflict between the great agricultural interests of the South and the manufacturing and commercial interests of the North and Northwest. The conversation continuing, Dr. Dusenbury again observed—

"The masses of the people of the South are not prepared for self-government."

"Unfortunately it is so," replied Davis.

Davis continued his flight, but General Wilson, who had been put on the fugitive's track, was following hard after him, having left Macon on the evening of May 7th, with orders to push on by forced marches. On the 7th, Lieutenant Colonel Harden, commanding the First Wisconsin, struck the trail of Davis at Dublin, Laurens County, and followed him closely, night and day, through the pine wilderness of Alligator Creek and Green Swamps, *via* Cumberlandsville to Irwinsville. At Cumberlandsville, Colonel Harden met Colonel Pritchard, with his picked men and horses of the Fourth Michigan. Harden followed the trail directly south, while Pritchard, having fresher horses, pushed down the Ocmulgee toward Hopewell, and thence by House Creek to Irwinsville, arriving there at midnight of the ninth. Davis had not arrived; but from a citizen Pritchard learned that his party were encamped two miles out of the town. He made dispositions of his men, and surrounded the camp before day.

The attack was made upon the camp by Colonel Pritchard just as the first streak of dawn began to light the eastern sky. The fugitive party were suddenly startled by the yells of the soldiers, but woke too late to make preparations for even a feeble resistance. After the officers and men were safely under guard, which occupied some time, a corporal went to the door of the tent occupied by defunct royalty, and ordered them to come forth and deliver themselves up. Mrs. Davis appeared at the door, somewhat *en dishabille*, and said:

"Please, gentlemen, do not intrude upon the privacy of ladies. There are no gentlemen here, and you will oblige us greatly by giving us time to dress."

"All right, madam," was the reply; "we will give you time to make your toilet, and then you can take a ride to Macon for your health."

After something of an interval, the monotony outside only being broken by the

Mrs. Jeff. Davis.

demands of the guard to "hurry up," there came to the door Mrs. Davis and Miss Howell, leading an apparently decrepit old lady, dressed in a lady's waterproof cloak, with a tight hood on her head, and her face covered with a small veil. The 'old lady' could walk only with great difficulty, but tottered through the door of the tent with a tin pail on her arm. It appears that Mrs. Davis's keen eyes were the first to recognize the horsemen as they approached in the distance to be Yankee cavalry, and she immediately called to her negro female servant, Ellen Bond, to get the articles of apparel in question, which being done, Mrs. Davis arrayed her liege lord in them, and then said to Mrs. Bond, "Go with Mr. Davis and try to get him off; for God's sake don't refuse me, Ellen; save him if you can."

Mrs. Bond left the tent with Mr. Davis, Mrs. Davis saying, "Soldier, I suppose you have no objection to letting my old mother go to the spring for some water for us to wash with?"

"Well, I reckon I have some little objection to letting that 'old lady' go," was the reply; "she wears boots, don't she?" and with the point of his sabre he raised the frock, discovering a large, coarse pair of calf-skin boots. While doing this, another soldier stripped the veil and hood from off his face, and lo! Davis—it was he! Finding that he was fairly caught, and would be delivered into the hands of his enemies, he waxed exceeding wroth,—declared how he would have defended himself if he had his revolver,—and frequently made use of such sneering remarks as "Valorous soldiers, indeed, to make war upon women and children!" "I thought the Yankee government was a little more valorous than to send its soldiers to steal defenceless women and children out of their beds at night!" He also remarked, among other things, that Lee was one of the boldest Generals of which he had any knowledge—never needing to be urged. This was in comparison with Johnston, of whom his silence was marked.

After a hurried breakfast the party was put in marching order. The prisoners were in ambulances, preceded by the band of the Fourth Michigan cavalry, which played first "Yankee Doodle," and then "John Brown's body's marching on," to inspirit the drooping mood of the captives!

Jeff's last Shift—Capture by the Yanks.

On reaching the steamer that was to convey him to Fortress Monroe, there to be kept under lock and key, the scene of parting with his family took place. They were grouped on the deck, and consisted of Mrs. Davis, a girl just about in her teens, a boy somewhat younger, and an infant. Mrs. Davis was clad in black,—a woman of prepossessing appearance, of the brunette style, though her black hair was sprinkled with gray; her black eyes sparkled clearly, and her features bore a resolute stamp. Mr. Davis, a tall spare man, having a wan, gaunt and depressed look, his whiskers and moustache rather close cut and almost white, was the chief character. He was clad in a suit of fine dark gray cloth, and wore an overcoat of the same material; his head was covered by a soft gray felt hat. He parted

# FINAL SCENES AND EVENTS IN THE GREAT DRAMA; ETC. 651

from his family in rather a formal manner. After embracing them coldly and without any outward show of feeling, he walked on board the other little steamer, the Pierce, which was to convey him to his prison quarters.

### Sir Frederick's Question Answered.

The set speeches of State dignitaries rarely possess an attractive interest to the masses, while their familiar personal intercourse gives an index to the actual state of feeling, which all are pleased to trace. The reception given by President Johnson to the newly appointed British minister, Sir Frederick Bruce, in April, 1865, is an illustration in point. His after interview with President Johnson was as informal and undiplomatic as President Lincoln himself would have made it. The new minister made his appearance with all his stars and decorations on, presented his credentials, and formally read his speech. Mr. Johnson was in the unadorned garb usual to his eminent office, and to Sir Frederick's set speech simply replied, that he was glad to see him, and to welcome to the capital a representative of Great Britain. He afterwards good-humoredly said:

"I am not much used to the diplomatic formalities customary on such occasions. My idea is simply that two great nations ought to conduct their relations very much as two neighbors who sincerely desire peace and goodfellowship between themselves would do, and that the less mere formality about it the better."

"I assure you, Mr. President," interrupted the cordially spoken Sir Frederick, pointing to his uniform and decorations, "that I should feel very much more at ease without these things than with them."

The remark was so thoroughly English, and at the same time so consonant to American prejudice against fuss and feathers, that the President and Minister became friends at once, and sat down for a regular White House chat. Sir Frederick asked about Sherman. President Johnson explained the position.

"What chance is there for Mr. Davis, then?" asked Sir Frederick.

"Oh, a small particle still—doubtless his escape across the country," said the President.

"*Well*," replied the Minister, in an inquiring tone, "*I should think that Mr. Davis and a few members of his cabinet would probably find it well to start pretty soon.*"

"*If they know what is for their own interest,*" responded the President rather grimly, "*they had better lose no time about it. The time has come when traitors must be taught that they are criminals. The country has clearly made up its mind on that point, and it can find no more earnest agent of its will than myself.*"

There was then a renewal of the mutual promise to talk over any difficulties that might arise between Great Britain and the United States like two neighbors sincerely desirous of good terms with each other, and so the interview ended.

### Admiration of Burns.

Mr. Lincoln was an enthusiastic admirer of Robert Burns, always having a copy of the bard's poems by him, and reading them with delight. There was something in the humble origin of Burns and in his checkered life, no less than in his tender, homely songs, that appealed to the heart of the plain man who, transferred from the prairies of Illinois to the executive mansion at Washington at a time of immense responsibility, gave a fresh and memorable illustration of the truth that

> "The rank is but the guinea's stamp,
> The man's the gowd for a' that."

### Familiar Talk with Mr. Lincoln on the Emancipation Proclamation.

The eminent historian, Mr. Bancroft, remarked in his eulogy delivered in New York, on the Life and Character of President Lincoln, that his place in history would centre chiefly in the memorable Proclamation of Emancipation. For one of the most authentic as well as interesting accounts of the origin and forth-putting of that great document, the public are indebted to the exceedingly graphic pen of Mr. F. B. Carpenter, who, through the columns of the Independent, communicated a sketch of the history of the Proclamation, as given to him by Mr. Lincoln himself, while Mr. C. was painting the magnificent picture illustrative of its consideration by the Cabinet.

"It had got to be," said Mr. Lincoln, "mid-summer, 1862. Things had gone on from bad to worse, until I felt that we had reached the end of our rope on the plan of operations we had been pursuing; that we had about played our last card, and must change our tactics, or lose the game!

Familiar Talk with Mr. Lincoln.

I now determined upon the adoption of the emancipation policy; and without consultation with, or the knowledge of the Cabinet, I prepared the original draft of the proclamation, and, after much anxious thought, called a Cabinet meeting upon the subject. This was the last of July, or the first part of the month of August, 1862. (The exact date he did not remember.) This Cabinet meeting took place, I think, upon a Saturday. All were present, excepting Mr. Blair, the Postmaster-General, who was absent at the opening of the discussion, but came in subsequently. I said to the Cabinet that I had resolved upon this step, and had not called them together to ask their advice, but to lay the subject matter of a proclamation before them; suggestions as to which would be in order after they had heard it read. Mr. Lovejoy," said he, "was in error when he informed you that it excited no comment, excepting on the part of Secretary Seward. Various suggestions were offered. Secretary Chase wished the language stronger in reference to the arming of the blacks. Mr. Blair, after he came in, deprecated the policy, on the ground that it would cost the administration the fall elections. Nothing, however, was offered, that I had not fully anticipated and settled in my own mind, until Secretary Seward spoke. Said he: 'Mr. President, *I approve of the proclamation, but I question the expediency of its issue at this juncture.* The depression of the public mind, consequent upon our repeated reverses, is so great, that I fear the effect of so important a step. It may be viewed as the last measure of an exhausted government—a cry for help; the government stretching forth its hands to Ethiopia, instead of Ethiopia stretching forth her hands to the government.' His idea (said the President) was that it would be considered our last *shriek*, on the retreat. ' Now,' continued Mr. Seward, ' while I approve the measure, I suggest, sir, that you postpone its issue, until you can give it to the country supported by military success, instead of issuing it, as would be the case now, upon the greatest disasters of the war!'"

"The wisdom of the view of the Secretary of State," said Mr. Lincoln, "struck me with very great force. It was an aspect of the case that, in all my thought upon the subject, I had entirely overlooked. The result was that I put the draft of the proclamation aside, as you do your sketch for a picture, waiting for a victory. From time to time I added or changed a line, touching it up here and there, waiting the progress of events. Well, the next news we had was of Pope's disaster at Bull Run. Things looked darker than ever. Finally, came the week of the battle of Antietam. I determined to wait no longer. The news came, I think on Wednesday, that the advantage was on our side. I was then staying at the 'Soldiers' Home,' (three miles out of Washington.) Here I finished writing the second draft of the preliminary proclamation; came up on Saturday; called the Cabinet together to hear it, and it was published the following Monday. It was a somewhat remarkable fact, that there were just one hundred days between the dates of the two proclamations, issued upon the 22d of September and the 1st of January. I had not made the calculation at the time."

At the final meeting on Saturday, another interesting incident occurred in connection with Secretary Seward. The President had written the important part of the proclamation—

"That on the first day of January, in the year of our Lord one thousand eight hundred and sixty-three, all persons held as slaves within any State or designated part of a State, the people whereof shall then be in rebellion against the United States, shall be then, thenceforward and forever FREE; and the Executive government of the United States, including the military and naval authority thereof, will *recognize* the freedom of such persons, and will do no act or acts to repress such persons, or any of them, in any efforts they may make for their actual freedom."

"When I finished reading this paragraph," resumed Mr. Lincoln, "Mr. Seward stopped me, and said: 'I think, Mr. President, that you should insert after the word '*recognize*,' in that sentence, the words '*and maintain.*' I replied, that I had already fully considered the import of that expression in this connection, but I had not introduced it, because it was not my way to promise what I was not entirely *sure* that I could perform, and I was not prepared to say that I thought we were exactly able to 'maintain' this. But Mr. Seward insisted that we ought to take this ground, and the words finally went in."

A few days after the passage of the Constitutional Amendment (says Mr. Carpenter,) I was in Washington, and was received by Mr. Lincoln with the kindness and familiarity which had characterized our previous intercourse. I said to him one day that I was very proud to have been the artist to have first conceived of the design of painting a picture commemorative of the act of emancipation—that subsequent occurrences had only confirmed my own first judgment of that act as the most sublime moral event in our history. "Yes," said he, and never do I remember to have noticed in him more earnestness of expression or manner, "as affairs have turned, it is the central act of my administration, and the great event of the nineteenth century."

I remember to have asked him, on one occasion, if there was not some opposition manifested on the part of several members of the Cabinet to the emancipation policy. He said, in reply, "Nothing more than I have stated to you. Mr. Blair thought we should lose the fall elections, and opposed it on that ground only." Said I, "I have understood that Secretary Smith was not in favor of your action. Mr. Blair told me that, when the meeting closed, and he and the Secretary of the Interior went away together, that the latter told him, if the President carried out that policy, he might count on losing Indiana sure!" "He never said anything of the kind to me," returned the President. "And how," said I, "does Mr. Blair feel about it now?" "Oh," was the prompt reply, "he proved right in regard to the fall elections, but he is satisfied that we have since gained more than we lost." "I have been told," said I, "that Judge Bates doubted the constitutionality of the proclamation." "He never expressed such an opinion in my hearing," replied Mr. Lincoln; "no member of the Cabinet ever dissented from the policy, in any conversation with me."

Mr. Chase told me that, at the Cabinet meeting immediately after the battle of Antietam, and just prior to the September proclamation, the President entered upon the business before them by saying that "the time for the enunciation of the emancipation policy could no longer be delayed. Public sentiment," he thought, "would sustain it—many of his warmest friends and supporters demanded it; *and he had promised his God that he would do it!*" The last part of this was uttered in a low tone, and appeared to be heard by no one but Secretary Chase, who was sitting near him. He asked the President if he was correctly understood by him. Mr. Lincoln replied: "*I made a solemn vow before God that, if General Lee was driven back from Pennsylvania, I would crown the result by the declaration of freedom to the slaves!*"

---

**Simple but Effective Point taken by Mr. Lincoln in a Capital Case.**

An instance which occurred during Mr. Lincoln's early professional career as a lawyer, is worthy of record, as showing the simplicity of his character in managing a case that involved nothing less than the life of his client. At a camp meeting held in Menard County, a fight took place which ended in the murder of one of the participants in the quarrel. A young man named Armstrong, a son of the aged couple for whom, many years previously, Abraham Lincoln had worked, was charged with the deed, and being arrested and examined, a true bill was found against him, and he was lodged in jail to await his trial. As soon as Mr. Lincoln received intelligence of the affair, he addressed a kind letter to Mrs. Armstrong, stating his anxiety that her son should have a fair trial, and offering in return for her kindness to him while in adverse circumstances some years before, his professional services gratuitously in defence of her son. Investigation of the matter in its various bearings, convinced the volunteer attorney that the young man was the victim of a conspiracy, and he determined to postpone the trial until the excitement had subsided. The day of trial, however, finally arrived, and the accuser testified positively that he saw the accused plunge the knife into the heart of the murdered man. He declared that he remembered all the circumstances perfectly—that the murder was committed about half-past nine o'clock in the evening, the moon shining brightly, so as to render it easy for him to see the act committed. Mr. Lincoln reviewed all the testimony carefully, and then proved conclusively that the moon, which the accuser had sworn was shining brightly, did not rise until an hour or more after the murder was committed. Other discrepancies were exposed, and in thirty minutes after the jury retired, they returned with a verdict of "Not Guilty."

---

**Life of Lincoln written by Himself.**

The singular modesty of Mr. Lincoln is, perhaps, in no instance more palpably illustrated than in the account given by Mr. Charles Lanman, the well-known editor and author. In 1858, Mr. Lanman commenced his labors on the work known as the "Dictionary of Congress," in the preparation of which he forwarded to every ex-member of Congress whose residence he could ascertain, a circular asking each person for information as to the date and place of his birth, the character of his education, his profession or occupation, and a list of any public positions he may have filled. In looking over the thousands of replies that were sent to him, Mr. Lanman remarks upon the fact that men of the greatest ability invariably told a direct and brief story,—thereby showing their innate modesty, and writing nothing to compromise their dignity. The reply which he

FINAL SCENES AND EVENTS IN THE GREAT DRAMA; ETC. 655

received from Mr. Lincoln was of this character—singularly brief, and yet comprehensive,—as follows:

Born, February 12, 1809, in Hardin county, Kentucky.
Education defective.
Profession, a lawyer.
Have been a captain of volunteers in the Black Hawk war.
Postmaster at a very small office.
Four times a member of the Illinois Legislature.
And was a member of the lower House of Congress.

Yours, &c.,        A. LINCOLN.

Such is the story of his life down to 1858. What a wonderful contrast does it present to his subsequent career!

### Solitary and Alone in Favor of Grant.

Soon after the capture of Vicksburg by General Grant, Hon. Jesse K. Dubois, of Illinois, went to Washington, to obtain a sick furlough for his son, who had been at the siege and was then in a Memphis hospital. Mr. Lincoln himself went to the War Office with Mr. Dubois, to obtain the furlough. Returning from the office, and while Mr. Lincoln, Mr. Dubois, and United States Marshal Phillips were standing at the railing which separates the War Office grounds from those of the White House, the following conversation, in substance, took place:

"Mr. President," said Mr. Dubois, "I do not like General Grant's paroling those prisoners at Vicksburg. We had better feed than fight them."

Mr. Lincoln, straightening himself up to his full height, and his countenance beaming with that peculiar smile which indicated that he was highly pleased, said:

"Dubois, General Grant has done so well, and we are all so pleased at the taking of Vicksburg, let us not quarrel with him about that matter." He then added, placing his foot upon the base of the railing, and taking a less erect posture, "Dubois, do you know that at one time I stood *solitary and alone here in favor of General Grant?* Even —— (naming a member of Congress from Illinois) came and told me that he (Grant) was not worth a ——, and that I would have to remove him. But I remembered that you, and Hatch, and others, had been down there about the first of April, and had not said a word to me on the subject."

In Major Penniman's "Tanner Boy," may be found the happy secret, admirably told, of the good President's confidence in his great General.

### Good Humor towards a Journalist.

A gentleman visited President Lincoln in high dudgeon one night. He was a newspaper proprietor, and one of his editors had been arrested. "Mr. Lincoln," he said, "I have been off electioneering for your re-election, and in my absence you have had my editor arrested. I won't stand it, Sir. I have fought better administrations than yours." "Why, John," said the President, "I don't know much about it. I suppose your boys have been too enterprising. The fact is, I don't interfere with the press much, but I suppose I am responsible." "I want you to order the man's release to-night," said the applicant; "I shan't leave here till I get it. In fact, I am the man who should be arrested. Why don't you send me to Capitol Hill?" This idea pleased the President exceedingly. He laughed the other into good humor. "In fact," he said, "I am under restraint here, and glad of any pretext to release a journalist." So he wrote the order, and the editor got his liberty.

### Under Lock and Key.

On the capture of Jefferson Davis at Irwinsville, he was at once taken to Macon, and thence to Hilton Head, by the steamer Clyde, and then to Fortress Monroe by the little steamer Silas C. Pierce. General Miles was charged by the Secretary of War with the disposal of the captive, and, boarding the Clyde, he despatched an officer of the guard to order the prisoner to report to him. Davis immediately made his appearance, and General Miles at once informed him that he was to be removed from that vessel to Fortress Monroe, and that a few minutes would be allowed him to take leave of his family. He did not evince any surprise at this announcement, but, bidding his family farewell, he walked on board the Pierce, closely attended by General Miles. After reaching the deck of the Pierce he beckoned his son Jeff., and bade him summon Bob, his colored body servant. When Bob made his appearance, Davis shook him warmly by the hand and bade him "Good bye."

Mrs. Davis bore the parting remarkably well, and it did not seem to cost her much effort to do so. As the Pierce was about getting underway she leaned over the rail of the Clyde, and called out to her husband, "Jeff! if they will allow you, write to me and let me know what kind of quarters you have." She also requested him that if it were possible he should remain with Clay—a fellow captive and criminal. Lieutentant-Colonel Pritchard, as the steamer was leaving, stepped up to Mrs. Davis and bade her adieu, when she said to the Colonel, "This is very hard," a remark which very naturally brings to mind the many, many affecting partings which took place between loyal and loving ones—now buried and mourned—during the past four years, all occasioned by the crime of that leading conspirator.

General Miles lavished no needless courtesies upon the offender, indeed, no courtesies whatever were exchanged, nor did any social recognition transpire, with the prisoner. To preclude any attempt at jumping overboard, by Davis or his companions in felony, a strong guard was placed on each side of the gangway; this guard consisted of twenty-five cavalrymen armed with Sharps' rifles.

The Pierce landed at the Engineer's dock, where an additional guard was in waiting, consisting of picked men from the Third Pennsylvania Artillery regiment. As soon as the boat was secured, General Miles took Davis by the arm and led him ashore, at once conducting him within the walls of the fort by the rear sallyport, and placing him in a cell separate by himself.

The conduct of Davis necessitated the placing of irons on his feet, which were subsequently removed, when they had answered the purpose. Not only was he imperious and haughty, but he became absolutely obstreperous, insulting the guard, abusing the officers and their government, throwing his food at his attendants, and tearing a secession passion to tatters generally—sometimes threatening others, and sometimes melo-dramatically courting a bayonet puncture in his bared breast. As a necessity—and possibly as a punishment and warning—orders were given to place manacles on his feet. The Captain in charge, attended by a blacksmith and grim manacles, approached, saying:

"Mr. Davis, I have a very unpleasant duty to perform."

"My God!" exclaimed the conspirator, "you don't intend to put those things on me."

Such were the orders; the Captain could only obey. Davis remonstrated. They

Jeff. and the Blacksmith.

should never be put on. The Captain must go to General Halleck and have the order countermanded. The Captain replied:

"But, Mr. Davis, the order came from General Halleck." Davis still insisted that the order must be countermanded. At this, the Captain finally and resolutely said—

"You are a military man, Mr. Davis, and know that my only course is—to obey orders."

Davis now went off in a more towering passion than before, and declared he would never be ironed alive. After becoming a little cool, and mechanically placing one foot on a stool, the Captain told the blacksmith to proceed. Leaning forward to take to his arms the heels of the anti-coercionist, Davis seized him, and with a vigorous push tumbled him backward on the floor, while the honest son of Vulcan, justly indignant, hurled his hammer at the "president," but missed him. Davis then attempted to seize a gun, and asked to be bayoneted. The guards presented bayonets, and the Captain feared he might rush upon them, and so ordered the guard to fall back. The Captain then called in four stout men and ordered them to lay Davis on his back, which they did, the prisoner resisting with almost preternatural strength, essaying to deal a thwack now to the right and anon to the left, and writhing in their grasp while the blacksmith hammered on the rivet with a will. When placed in his chair again, Davis looked in utter despair upon his manacled limbs, and was unable, even with his well known strong will, to conceal his emotions. The blacksmith's medicine had the desired effect, so that the great fugitive became comparatively docile, far less defiant, but more depressed, and the irons were subsequently removed.

It was feared he would starve himself to death, and, complaining of being sick, he expressed a wish, one day, to see a physician. The officer of the day, after consulting the proper authorities, told his prisoner that a doctor would be allowed him. "What physicians have you here?" asked Davis of Captain Tetlow, the officer on duty. Captain T. mentioned the names of Doctors Bancroft, Janeway, and Craven. "Where is Dr. Bancroft from?" queried Davis. "From Connecticut," answered the Captain. "Don't want him, then. Where's Janeway from? Do you know where Craven is from?" continued Davis. "Yes, he is from New Jersey." "Let me have him then." The doctor—a strong Union man, by the way—found nothing seriously wrong with the prisoner's physical condition. The real reason of Davis's desire for a physician became apparent when his noontide meal was served to him. He who deliberately starved to death thousands of Union prisoners was fed on the regular army rations, precisely of the same quantity and quality as that served to the soldiers at Fortress Monroe. He threw the soup, bread and meat from him, exclaiming, in a loud and angry voice, that he "was not accustomed to such living

Geo. N. Sanders.

and would not put up with it." The physician prescribing a little different diet, it was served accordingly.

---

**Transfer of "President Davis's" Table Service.**

A short time after the evacuation of Richmond, an auction sale took place in that city of a coffee, or tea set, and a quantity of silver plate, formerly used by Jefferson Davis. The set was purchased at the sale by a loyal man, and by him presented, as a souvenir, to President Johnson. The coffee or tea set in question is a perfect minature or fac simile of a railroad locomotive, with tender detached; the locomotive boiler receives the coffee or tea, makes and discharges it through a spiggot, a steam whistle indicating when the tea or coffee is ready. The boiler of the locomotive is of porcelain, and the figure of the fireman, of the same material, appears on the locomotive vigorously ringing the bell, —the breakfast, dinner, or supper bell, as the case may be. The tender, which is an admixture of brass and other metal, carries the sugar in an elegant silver caisson, with goblet for cognias and stunning small cut glasses. The sides of the tender are embellished with racks for cigars. But the most curious contrivance of all is a secret music box, located somewhere in the tender, which, being set, plays eight popular airs, sufficient in duration to entertain a supper, dinner, or breakfast table. The whole establishment, engine and tender, rests upon two beautiful enamelled waiters. Upon the side of the locomotive, in miniature, is emblazoned "President Jefferson Davis," showing that the testimonial—locomotive and tender—combining so peculiarly the useful and agreeable, was especially designed for the use and pleasure of "His Excellency." Upon the front, just above where the "cow catcher" ought to be, appears the confederate national banner and battle flag, entwined with the national ensign of France.

### President Lincoln's First Dollar.

One evening, in the executive chamber, there were present a number of gentlemen, among them Mr. Seward. A point in the conversation suggesting the thought, Mr. Lincoln said, "Seward, you never heard, did you, how I earned my first dollar?" "No," said Mr. Seward. "Well," replied Mr. L... "I was about eighteen years of age. I belonged, you know, to what they call down South the 'scrubs'—people who do not own land and slaves are nobody there. But we had succeeded in raising, chiefly by my labor, sufficient produce, as I thought, to justify me in taking it down the river to sell. After much persuasion I got the consent of my mother to go, and constructed a little flat boat, large enough to take the barrel or two of things that we had gathered, with myself and a little bundle, down to New Orleans. A steamer was coming down the river. We have, you know, no wharves on the western streams, and the custom was, if passengers were at any of the landings, for them to go out in a boat, the steamer stopping and taking them on board. I was contemplating my new flatboat and wondering whether I could make it stronger, or improve it in any particular, when two men came down to the shore in carriages, with trunks, and looking at the different boats, singled out mine, and asked, 'Who owns this?' I answered, somewhat modestly, 'I do.' 'Will you,' said one of them, 'take us and our trunks out to the steamer?' 'Certainly,' said I. I was very glad to have the opportunity of earning something. I supposed that each would give me two or three bits. The trunks were put on my flatboat, the passengers seated themselves on the trunks, and I sculled them out to the steamboat. They got on board, and I lifted up their heavy trunks, and put them on deck. The steamer was about to put on steam again, when I called out that they had forgotten to pay me. Each of them took from his pocket a silver half dollar, and threw it on the floor of my boat. I could scarcely believe my eyes as I picked up the money. Gentlemen, you may think it a very little thing, and in these days it seems to me like a trifle; but it was a most important incident in my life. I could scarcely credit that I, a poor boy, had earned a dollar in less than a day—that by honest work I had earned a dollar. The world seemed wider and fairer before me. I was a more hopeful and confident being from that time."

### Treating his Guests to a Good Drink.

At the interview between Mr. Lincoln and the committee of the Chicago Convention that came to his Springfield home to inform him of his nomination for the presidency, a little incident occurred, of a social nature, which deserves to be repeated.

After the ceremony had passed, Mr. Lincoln remarked to the company that, as an appropriate conclusion to an interview so important and interesting as that which had just transpired, he supposed that good manners would require that he should treat the committee with something to drink; and, opening a door that led into a room in the rear, he called out, 'Mary! Mary!' A girl responded to the call, whom Mr. Lincoln spoke a few words to in an undertone; and, closing the door, returned again to converse with his guests. In a few minutes the maiden entered bearing a large waiter, containing several glass tumblers, and a large pitcher in the midst, and placed it upon the center-table. Mr. Lincoln arose, and gravely addressing the company, said: 'Gentlemen, we must pledge our mutual healths in the most healthy beverage which our God has given to man; it is the only beverage I have ever used or allowed in my family, and I cannot conscientiously depart from it on the present occasion; it is pure Adam's ale from the spring;' and taking a tumbler, he touched it to his lips and pledged them his highest respects in a cup of cold water. Of course, all his guests were constrained to admire his consistency, and to join in his example.

### Dissensions in the "Happy Family."

On Monday, the 6th of February, 1865, after the Peace Commissioners from Richmond had returned from Fortress Monroe, Senator Johnson, of Georgia, waited on Jeff. Davis, and, in substance, the following conversation took place:—

"Well, President Davis, so your peace mission has failed."

"Yes, I knew it would; I hope now the reconstructionists will fight Lincoln instead of fighting me."

Mr. Lincoln, it seems, was not opposed to making peace with the States; but he was not in favor of recognizing the confederate government as an independent power.

"I see, President, that you have withdrawn all the troops from Georgia into Carolina and Virginia. What will the people of Georgia do for protection in the next campaign?"

"The people of Georgia have followed the counsels of Governor Brown and Mr. Stephens; they must now protect themselves."

"Well, President, if you can do without the people of Georgia, *the people of Georgia can do without you!*"

### The Last Battery in Lee's Army: its Doom Sealed by Loyal Virginia Troops.

It is indeed a strange fact, that the last battery which the distinguished commander of the Confederate army, General Robert E. Lee, ever put in position near Appomattox Court-house, was silenced by a skirmish line thrown forward by Brigadier-General T. M. Harris (and commanding at Fredericksburg), under command of Captain Jarbo, of the Tenth West Virginia, and consisted entirely of *West Virginia Union troops*, armed with the Spencer seven-shooter. General Lee, supposing that there was nothing but cavalry in his front, ordered his column to disperse it and move forward. The Twenty-fourth Army Corps having, by a forced march of twenty-four hours' duration, with but a short interval of rest, at the middle of the night been thrown in line across his front in rear of the cavalry, checked his advancing columns.

General Lee had placed a battery in position, and was shelling the line commanded by General Harris (consisting, as before remarked, of West Virginia troops) at a furious rate, when Harris ordered the

660 THE BOOK OF ANECDOTES OF THE REBELLION.

skirmish line forward, under Captain Jarbo, with orders to silence the troublesome battery, which, with the aid of the Spencer rifle, they were enabled to do in half an hour, the line of support following up rapidly. A portion of the battery had been withdrawn, and one or two guns, the horses of which had been killed, fell into the hands of the Federal General.

*These cannon were the last ever ordered into position by General Lee.* Soon after their capture terms were proffered by Grant, and accepted by the Confederate General; the war in Virginia was at an end; and now, at last, upon the long and bloody drama of SOUTHERN REBELLION, —the greatest and most ghastly organized crime that stands out in human history,— fell the white curtain of FEDERAL VICTORY AND NATIONAL PEACE!

"TO WHOM IT MAY CONCERN!"

# LIST OF BATTLES, ENGAGEMENTS, COLLISIONS, CAPTURES, SURRENDERS, SURPRISES, ETC.,

### AND OF NOTABLE LOCALITIES, ON LAND AND SEA, DURING THE REBELLION,

#### CONSULTED IN THE PREPARATION OF THESE ANECDOTES.*

(See also GENERAL INDEX, at the close of the volume.)

## A.

ABACO, 1862, July 7, 16.
ABBEVILLE, La, 1863, Nov. 20.
ABBEVILLE, Miss., 1862, Nov. 30, Dec. 2; 1864, Aug. 10.
ABERDEEN, 1864, Feb. 19.
ABINGDON, 1864, Dec. 14.
ACCATINK, 1863, Aug. 11, Oct. 17.
ACKWORTH, 1864, June 6, Oct. 5.
ACQUIA, see Aquia.
ADAIRSVILLE, 1863, Oct. 24; 1864, May 17.
ADAMSVILLE, 1862, April 6.
AIKEN, 1865, Feb. 10, 11.
AIKEN'S LANDING, 1864, June 21; —.
ALABAMA RIVER; —.
ALBEMARLE SOUND; —.
ALDIE, 1862, Oct. 9; 1863, Feb. 6, Mar. 12, June 4, 17, Aug. 1.
ALEXANDRIA, La. and Miss., 1863, May 6, Nov. 18; 1864, Mar. 15, 21, 26, May 5, 14; 1865, June 2; —.
ALEXANDRIA, Mo., 1862, Aug. 3.
ALEXANDRIA, Va., 1861, May 24, June 1; 1862, Aug. 27.
ALEXANDRIA FALLS, 1864, May 16.
ALIMOSA, 1861, Oct. 4.
ALL SAINT'S PARISH, 1865, Feb. 4.
ALLATOONA, 1864, May 24, June 2, Oct. 6.
ALLEGHANY, and A. Junction, 1861, Dec. 13; 1864, Jan. 2; —.
ALLIGATOR HARBOR, 1863, June 13.
ALTAMAHA RIVER; —.
ALTON, 1864, Jan. 26.
AMELIA COURT HOUSE, 1865, April 3.
AMERICUS, PRISON.
AMITY RIVER, 1863, May 12; —.
ANANDALE, 1861, Dec. 4; 1863, Feb. 14, June 27.

ANDERSON'S CROSS ROADS, 1863, Oct. 2; 1864, Oct. 1, 2.
ANDERSONVILLE, Prison.
ANNAPOLIS, 1861, April 22, 23; —
ANNISVILLE.
ANTIETAM, 1862, Sept. 16, 17; 1863, July 8–11; —.
APACHE CANON, and A. PASS, 1862, Mar. 27, 28.
APALACHIAN RANGE; —.
APPALACHICOLA, 1862, April 3, Oct. 15.
APPOMATTOX, 1862, May 27; 1864, May 10; 1865, April 2–9; —.
AQUIA CREEK, 1861, May 31, June 1, July 29, Oct. 11; 1862, Mar. 7, 15, 18, Aug. 2, Sept. 7; —.
ARANSAS, 1863, Nov. 17.
ARKADELPHIA, 1863, Feb. 15, Oct. 28.
ARKANSAS POST, 1863, Jan. 11, 23.
ARKANSAS RIVER and VALLEY; —.
ARLINGTON, 1861, May 23, June 1;
ARMSTRONG'S MILLS, 1864, Oct. 27.
ASHBY'S GAP, 1862, Sept. 22, Nov. 4; 1863, June 19; 1864, July 18–20.
ASHBYVILLE, 1864, Dec. 17.
ASHEPOO RIVER, 1863, May 3, June 3; 1864, May 25.
ASHLAND, 1862, May 29; 1863, June 7; 1864, May 11.
ATCHAFALAYA, 1863, Oct. 4.
ATHENS, Ala., 1864, Sept. 20, 23, Oct. 1, 2.
ATHENS, Ga. and Tenn., 1862, May 9; 1864, Jan. 26.
ATHENS, Ky., 1863, Feb. 23.
ATHENS, Mo., 1861, Aug. 5.
ATLANTA, 1864, June 5–17, July 20–22, Aug. 5, 6, 10–27, 30, Sept. 2, Nov. 5, 9, 16; —.
AUBRY, 1862, Mar. 7.
AUBURN, 1863, Feb. 3.
AUGUSTA, Ga., 1861, Jan. ; —.
AUGUSTA, Ky., 1862, Sept. 12, 27.

---

*The dates and localities of Battles here recorded, indicate either an actual engagement, or a military movement, at or about the time and place named. Some of the localities, which were the scene of constantly recurring military operations, or of prolonged occupation, investment, or siege, are given with a blank (—) at the right, instead of specifying, in all cases, the numerous data pertaining to such.

AUSTIN, 1863, May 22, 23.
AVERYSBOROUGH, 1865, Mar. 15.
AVOYALLES PRAIRIE, 1864, May 16.
AYLETT'S, 1863, June 4.

**B**

BACHELOR CREEK, 1862, Oct. 1; 1864, Feb. 1.
BACON CREEK, 1862, Sept. 14, Dec. 25.
BAHIA, 1864, Oct. 7.
BAINBRIDGE, 1864, Jan. 14, 17, Dec. 28.
BAKER'S CREEK, 1863, May 16.
BALD HEADED HILL.
BALDWIN, 1864, Feb. 18, 28.
BALL'S BLUFF, CROSS ROADS, FERRY and GAP, 1861, Aug. 27, Oct. 21; 1864, Mar. 31, Nov. 24; —.
BALLINGER MILLS, 1862, July 29, Oct. 22.
BALTIMORE, and B. CROSS ROADS, 1861, Apr. 19; 1863, July 1; —.
BARBEE'S CROSS ROADS, 1862, Nov. 5; 1863, Sept. 1.
BARBOUR, 1862, Nov. 5.
BARBOURSVILLE, 1861, July 12, Sept. 16, 18, Nov. 4.
BARDSTOWN, 1861, Sept. 19; 1862, Oct. 2, 4, 6; 1864, June 18; 1865, Jan. 13.
BARHAMSVILLE.
BARNESVILLE, 1862, Oct. 12.
BATESVILLE, 1862, May 15; 1863, Feb. 4.
BATH, 1862, Jan. 4; 1863, Sept. 8.
BATON ROUGE, 1862, Aug. 5, 6, Dec. 17; 1863, Jan. 1; —.
BATTLE CREEK, 1862, June 21, Aug. 27.
BAXTER'S SPRINGS, 1863, Oct. 6.
BAYLOR'S FARM, 1864, June 15.
BAYOU BARNARD, 1862, July 27; B. BONTOUCA, 1862, Nov. 21; B. BOURBEAUX, 1863, Nov. 3; B. DE CACHE, 1862, July 7; B. DE METEA; B. CATEAU, 1863, Nov. 4; 1863, Aug. 27; B. PIERRE, 1863, May 1; B. SARA, 1862, Aug. 11, 31; B. TECHE, 1862, Nov. 3; 1863, Jan. 13, 14, Apr. 14; B. VERMILLION, 1863, Apr. 17, Oct. 21.
BAYPORT, 1863, Nov. 27.
BEALTON, 1863, Oct. 24, 26, Dec. 25, 27.
BEAN STATION, 1863, Dec. 9, 14.
BEAR BLUFF, 1862, Feb. 24.
BEAR CREEK and INLET, 1863, Feb. 5, April 17, Nov. 15, Dec. 25.
BEAR RIVER, 1863, Jan. 29.
BEAR WALLOW, 1862, Dec. 15, 25.
BEAUFORT, 1861, Nov. 8, 10, Dec. 8; 1862, Mar. 20; —.
BEAVER DAM and B. MILLS, 1862, July 20, 27; 1864, May 9; 1865, Mar. 11.
BECKWITH'S FARM, 1861, Oct. 13.
BEECH GROVE, 1863, June 24, 26.
BEELINGTON, 1861, July 8.

BEHER'S MILL, 1861, Sept. 2.
BELL RIVER, 1862, Nov. 3, Dec. 1.
BELLE ISLE, —.
BELLEFIELD and BELLTOWN, 1863, Oct. 13; 1864 Dec. 9.
BELMONT, 1861, Nov. 7.
BENNETT'S MILLS, 1861, Sept. 1.
BENTON, 1862, Jan. 26, Mar. 6.
BENTONSVILLE, 1865, Mar. 19, 20.
BERLIN, 1861, Sept. 30, Dec. 15.
BERMUDA HUNDRED, 1864, May 4, 5, 11, 20, June 2, 12–19; —.
BERRY'S FERRY, 1863, May 16.
BERRYVILLE, 1862, Mar. 6, 12, May 25, Nov. 26–29, Dec. 1; 1863, Apr. 21, June 6, 13; 1864, Aug. 10, 13, Sept. 4.
BERTIE, 1864, Feb. 26.
BERTRAND, 1861, Dec. 11.
BERWICK BAY and CITY, 1863, Mar. 13–18; —.
BETHANY, 1865, Apr. 4.
BETHEL CHURCH, 1861, June 10.
BETHESDA CHURCH, 1864, May 30.
BEVERLY, 1861, July 12; 1863, Apr. 24, June 8, July 2, Oct. 22–24; 1864, Oct. 29; 1865, Jan. 11; —.
BIG BEAVER CREEK, 1862, Nov. 7.
BIG BETHEL, 1861, June 10; 1862, Jan. 3, Mar. 27.
BIG BLACK BRIDGE and RIVER, 1863, Mar. 16, 17, May 17, July 5, Oct. 13; 1864, Nov. 24; —.
BIG BLUE, 1864, Oct. 25; —.
BIG CAPON.
BIG CREEK, 1862, Mar. 10; 1863, Apr. 20; 1864, July 25.
BIG ELK RIVER BRIDGE, 1863, May 27.
BIG HILL, 1862, Aug. 23, Oct. 23.
BIG HURRICANE CREEK, 1861, Oct. 19.
BIG MIAMI, 1863, July 13; —.
BIG MOUND, 1863, July 24.
BIG SHANTY, 1864, June 8, 25, Oct. 5, 6.
BILOXI, 1861, Dec. 31.
BIRD'S POINT, 1861, Dec. 2; 1863, Aug. 1.
BLACK BAYOU, 1863, April 5.
BLACK JACK FOREST, 1862, Mar.
BLACK RIVER, 1861, Sept. 12; 1863, May 17; 1864, Mar. 1, Sept. 14; —.
BLACK WALNUT CREEK, 1861, Nov. 29.
BLACKBURN'S, or BLACKFORD'S FORD, 1861, July 18, 21; 1862, Sept. 20.
BLACKVILLE, 1865, Feb. 7.
BLACKWATER, 1862 Sept. 28, Oct. 3, 24, Nov. 19; 1863, Mar. 9, 17, Apr. 11; —.
BLAIR'S CROSS ROADS, 1863, Dec. 16.
BLAKELY RIVER.
BLOOMFIELD, 1862, Jan. 26, May 11, Aug. 25, Sept. 11, Nov. 1; 1863, Jan. 27, Mar. 1; 1864, Sept. 23.
BLOOMING GAP, 1862, Feb. 14.

## BATTLES, ENGAGEMENTS, COLLISIONS, ETC.

BLOOMINGDALE, 1864, Dec. 10.
BLOUNT'S MILLS and BLOUNTSVILLE, 1862, Dec.; 1863, Apr. 9, 28, Sept. 22.
BLUE'S GAP, 1862, Jan. 7, 8.
BLUE MILLS LANDING, 1861, Sept. 17.
BLUE RIDGE, —.
BLUE SPRING, Mo., 1863, Mar. 22, Oct. 4.
BLUE SPRINGS, Tenn., 1863, Sept. 28, Oct. 10, 11.
BLUFFTON, 1862, Sept. 30; 1863, May 28, June 3.
BOCO CHICO,* 1865, May 12.
BOLIVAR, Miss., 1862, Sept. 20.
BOLIVAR, Mo., 1862, Oct. 26.
BOLIVAR, Tenn., 1862, July 27, Aug. 30; 1863, Feb. 13, Mar. 9, Dec. 25; 1864, May 2.
BOLIVAR, Va., 1861, Oct. 16, 18; 1862, June 24, Sept. 14, 15, Nov. 4; 1864, July 4.
BOLLINGER, see Ballinger.
BOLTON, 1863, July 5; 1864, Feb. 3.
BONNET CARRE, 1862, Aug. 29.
BONSECOUR BAY, 1864, Sept. 10.
BOONE, and B. COURT HOUSE, 1861, Sept. 1; 1865, Mar. 26.
BOONEVILLE, 1861, June 17, Sept. 13; 1862, May 30, July 1, 19.
BOONSBORO, 1862, Sept. 14; 1863, June 19, July 7-10.
BOSTON, Ky., and B. MOUNTAINS, 1862, Nov. 18, 28; 1863, June 13, 23.
BOTTOM NARROWS, 1863, May 9.
BOTTOM'S BRIDGE, 1862, May 23, June 30; 1863, July 2, Aug. 26; 1864, Feb. 6.
BOWLING GREEN, 1862, Feb. 1, 15, Aug. 21; —.
BOWNERS, 1861, June 29.
BOYD'S STATION, 1862, Sept. 8.
BOYDTOWN, 1864, Oct. 27; 1865, Mar. 29, Apr. 2; —.
BRADYVILLE, 1863, Mar. 1, May 16.
BRANCHVILLE, 1865, Feb. 8.
BRANDENBURGH, 1863, July 7; 1865, Mar. 15.
BRANDON FARMS, 1864, Jan. 23, 25, Mar. 7.
BRANDY STATION, 1862, Aug. 20; 1863, June 9, Aug. 5, Sept. 6, Oct. 12, Nov. 26, 30.
BRASHEAR CITY, 1863, June 20, 23, 26, July 22, 24.
BRAZOS, and B. ISLAND, 1863, Oct. 11, 31; —.
BRENTVILLE, 1862, Dec. 9.
BRENTWOOD, 1863, Mar. 25; 1864, Dec. 15, 16.
BRICK HOUSE POINT, 1862, May 7.
BRIDGEPORT, 1862, Apr. 29, 30; 1863, July 7, Aug. 16, Nov. 17.
BRIER CREEK and FORKS, 1861, July 5; 1864, Dec. 3.
BRISTOE'S STATION, 1862, Aug.; 1863, Oct. 14; 1864, Mar. 9; —.
BRISTOL, 1863, Sept. 21; 1864, Dec. 14.
BRITTON'S LANE, 1862, Aug. 30, Sept. 1.

BROAD RIVER, and B. RUN, 1863, Apr. 1, 8; —.
BROOKVILLE, 1864, Nov. 20.
BROWN'S FERRY, 1863, Oct. 27.
BROWN'S GAP, 1864, Sept. 26.
BROWNSVILLE, Ark., 1863, Aug. 25, Sept. 2.
BROWNSVILLE, Ky., 1861, Dec. 5.
BROWNSVILLE, Mo., 1863, Oct. 16.
BROWNSVILLE, Tenn., 1862, July 29.
BROWNSVILLE, Texas, 1863, Nov. 5, 6; 1865, June 1.
BRUIN'S LAKE, 1863, Apr. 23.
BRUINSBURG, 1863, May 1.
BRUNSWICK, 1862, Mar. 2, 10; 1863, June 8.
BUCKINGHAM, 1861, Nov. 25.
BUCKHANNON, 1861, July 6; 1862, Aug. 30.
BUCKHEAD CREEK, 1864, Dec. 2.
BUCKLAND'S MILLS, 1863, Oct. 19.
BUDD'S FERRY, 1861, Dec. 9.
BUFFALO, and B. SWAMP, 1862, Sept. 27; 1864, Nov. 25.
BUFFALO HILL, Ky., 1861, Oct. 4.
BUFFINGTON ISLAND, 1863, July 19.
BULL PASTURE MOUNTAIN, 1862, May 8.
BULL RUN, (Manassas,) 1861, July 21; 1862, Aug. 26, 30.
BULL'S BAY, 1862, July 7; 1863, Mar. 27; —.
BULL'S GAP, 1864, Jan. 11, Oct. 18, Nov. 13.
BUNKER HILL, 1861, July 15; 1862, Mar. 5, June 2.
BURK'S STATION, 1862, Mar. 9.
BURKITTSVILLE, 1862, Sept. 14.
BURKSVILLE, 1864, Apr. 19, June 23; 1865, April 6.
BURNT ORDINARY, 1863, Jan. 19.
BURTON'S FORD, 1864, Feb. 29.
BUSHY CREEK, 1861, Dec. 9.
BUTE A LA ROSE, 1863, April 20.
BUTLER, 1861, Dec. 13; 1862, Oct. 29.
BUZZARD'S ROOST, 1864, Feb. 24, 25.

### C.

CABIN CREEK, 1863, June 30, July 1.
CACAPON BRIDGE, 1862, Sept. 6, Oct. 11.
CACHE, 1862, May 28, July 7.
CAINESVILLE, 1863, Feb. 12, 15.
CAIRO, 1861, Apr. 24, Aug. 2; —.
CALHOUN, 1862, Nov. 13; 1863, Dec. 28.
CALIFORNIA, Mo., 1864, Oct. 9.
CAMDEN, 1862, Apr. 19; 1864, Apr. 2, 19, 26; 1865, Feb. 24.
CAMERON, 1861, Oct. 11.
CAMP ALLEGHANY, 1861, Dec. 13.
CAMP BECKWITH, 1863, Oct. 5.
CAMP COLE, 1861, June 18.
CAMP DEFIANCE.
CAMP FINEGAN, 1864, Feb. 7.

---

*Last Engagement in the War of the Rebellion.

## BATTLES, ENGAGEMENTS, COLLISIONS, ETC.

CAMP JACKSON, 1861, May 10.
CAMP MOORE, 1863, May 15.
CAMP PRATT, 1863, Nov. 20.
CAMPBELL'S STATION, 1863, Nov. 6, 16.
CAMPBELLVILLE, 1861, Oct. 24.
CAMPTI, 1864, April 4.
CANE HILL, and C. RIVER, 1862, Nov. 28; 1863, Oct. 26; 1864, Mar. 28, Apr. 24.
CANTON, 1862, Aug. 1; 1863, July 18, Oct. 15; 1864, Feb. 4, 14, 21, Mar. 26, July 7, Aug. 22.
CAPE FEAR RIVER, —.
CAPE GIRARDEAU, 1861, July 28; 1862, Aug. 24; 1863, Apr. 26; —.
CAPE HATTERAS, —.
CAPE HENRY, —.
CAPE LOOKOUT, —.
CAPE ROMAINE INLET, 1863, Apr. 18.
CAPITOL HILL.
CARLISLE, 1863, June 25, —, July 1.
CARMEL CHURCH, 1862, July 23.
CARNIFEX FERRY, 1861, Sept. 10, 11.
CARRICK'S FORD, 1861, July 13, 14.
CARRION CROW BAYOU, 1863, Nov. 3.
CARROLL STATION, 1864, Sept. 30.
CARROLLTON, 1864, Mar. 8.
CARRSVILLE, 1862, Oct. 15; 1863, May 15.
CARTER'S CREEK, 1861, June 24.
CARTHAGE, 1861, July 5; 1863, May 30, Oct. 8.
CASEYVILLE, 1862, Oct. 14, 15.
CASHTOWN, June 30, July 3.
CASSVILLE, 1862, Sept. 20; 1864, May 19.
CASTLE ROCK, 1864, Oct. 6.
CATLETT'S STATION, 1862, Aug. 22, Oct. 24, Nov. 16; 1863, Jan. 10; —.
CATOCTIN STATION, 1863, June 17.
CAVE CITY, and C. HILL, 1862, May 11.
CEDAR BLUFF, CREEK, and MOUNTAIN, 1862, Aug. 9; 1863, Apr. 7; 1864, Oct. 19, Nov. 12; —.
CENTRALIA, 1864, Sept. 27.
CENTREVILLE, Mo., 1863, Dec. 24.
CENTREVILLE, Va., 1861, July 21; 1862, Mar. 10, Aug. 28, 30; 1863, Nov. 2; —.
CHAFFIN'S FARM, 1864, Sept. 29, 30.
CHAIN BRIDGE.
CHALK BLUFF, 1863, May 2.
CHAMBERLAIN'S CREEK, 1865, Mar. 30, 31, Apr. 1.
CHAMBERSBURG, 1862, Oct. 10; 1863, June 15, 18, 23, July 5; 1864, July 28-30.
CHAMPION HILLS, 1863, May 16; 1864, Feb. 4.
CHANCELLORSVILLE, 1863, May 2-4; 1864, May 3-8.
CHANTILLY, 1862, Sept. 1; 1863, Oct. 17.
CHAPEL HILL, and C. HOUSE, 1863, Mar. 4; 1864, CHAPLIN'S HILLS, 1862, Oct. 4, 7, 8. [Oct.
CHAPMANVILLE, 1861, Sept. 25; 1862, Sept. 6.
CHARLES CITY COURT HOUSE, 1863, Dec. 9, 13; —.
CHARLES CITY CROSS ROADS, 1862, June 30, July 1; —.

CHARLESTON, Mo., 1861, Aug. 19, Oct. 2.
CHARLESTON, S. C., 1861, Jan. 12, Apr. 13, 14; 1862, Jan. 30, 31; 1863, Jan. 31, Apr. 7, July 24, Aug. 20, 22, Oct. 27, Dec. 25; 1865, Feb. 17, 18; —.
CHARLESTON, Tenn., 1863, Dec. 28.
CHARLESTON, Va., 1861, July 25; '862, Sept. 12.
CHARLESTOWN, 1862, Feb. 28, Oct. 6, 16, Nov. 9, Dec. 1; 1863, Feb. 13, May 16, July 15, Oct. 7, 18, Dec. 28; 1864, Dec. 3; —.
CHARLOTTE, Fla., 1863, Mar. 3.
CHARLOTTE, Tenn., 1863, Feb. 8.
CHARLOTTESVILLE, 1864, Feb. 29; 1865, Mar. 3.
CHATTAHOOCHIE, 1863, June 17; 1864, June 5; —.
CHATTANOOGA, 1862, June 7; 1863, July 14, Aug. 21, Sept. 8, 9, 10, Oct. 5, Nov. 23-27, Dec. 1; 1864, Sept. 29; —.
CHEAT MOUNTAIN, 1861, Sept. 12.
CHECK'S CROSS ROADS, 1864, Mar. 14.
CHELSEA, 1861, Oct. 12.
CHERAW, 1865, Mar. 3.
CHERBOURG, 1864, June 19.
CHEROKEE STATION, 1863, Oct. 21.
CHERRY STONE, 1864, Mar. 7.
CHESAPEAKE BAY, —.
CHESNABURG, 1861, —.
CHESTER'S GAP, 1863, July 22.
CHESTERFIELD, 1865, Mar. 3.
CHEW INLET, 1864, Sept. 29.
CHEWA STATION, 1864, July 17.
CHICKAHOMINY, 1862, May 7, 31, June 1, 25; 1864, May 27, 30; —.
CHICKAMAUGA, 1863, Sept. 19-21, Nov. 26; —.
CHICKASAW, and C. BLUFFS, 1862, Dec. 27-29; 1864, Dec. 27; 1865, Mar. 22; —.
CHICOMACOMICO, 1861, Oct. 5.
CHICOT PASS, and C. LAKE, 1862, Dec. 6; 1864, June 5.
CHILLICOTHE, 1863, July 14.
CHINCOTEAGUE INLET, 1861, Oct. 5, 25.
CHOWAN RIVER, 1862, May 9; 1864, Mar. 4; —.
CHRISTIANSBURG, 1865, Mar. 12.
CHUCKATUCK, 1863, Apr. 23; 1864, Jan. 21, 31, Feb. 1, Mar. 29.
CHUNKY CREEK, 1864, Mar. 17.
CINCINNATI, O., 1862, Sept. 11, 12.
CITICO CREEK, 1863, Nov. 23-25.
CITY POINT, 1862, July 3, Aug. 28; 1864, May 4, 5; 1865, Jan. 21; —.
CITRONVILLE, 1865, May 4.
CLARENDON, 1862, Aug. 11, 13.
CLARK'S HOLLOW, 1862, May 1.
CLARKSBURG, 1861, May 20, June 20.
CLARKSON, 1862, Oct. 26.
CLARKSVILLE, 1862, Feb. 19, Aug. 18, Sept. 7; 1863, Jan. 4, Apr. 8.
CLEAR SPRING, 1861, May 22.
CLEVELAND, 1863, Nov. 27.

BATTLES, ENGAGEMENTS, COLLISIONS, ETC. 665

CLIFTON, 1863, Feb. 18.
CLINCH MOUNTAIN and RIVER, 1863, Dec. 4, 6.
CLINTON, La., 1863, Jan. 19, June 1; 1864, Oct. 6.
CLINTON, Miss., 1864, Aug. 24.
CLINTON, Mo., 1864, Feb. 4.
CLINTON, N. C., 1862, May 19, Dec. 28.
CLINTON FORGE, 1863, Dec. 18.
CLOYD MOUNTAIN, 1864, May 9.
CLYDESDALE, 1864, Dec. 19.
COAL HARBOR, (see Cold Harbor.)
COBB'S POINT, 1862, Feb. 10.
COCKEYSVILLE, 1864, July 10.
COCKPIT POINT, 1862, Mar. 9.
COFFEEVILLE, 1862, Dec. 5, 14.
COGGIN'S POINT, 1862, Aug. 1.
COLD HARBOR, 1862, May 24; 1864, May 30, June 1, 3; —.
COLD KNOB MOUNTAIN, 1862, Nov. 26.
COLDWATER, and C. RIVER, 1862, June 22, July 24, Sept. 10; 1863, Feb. 19, Apr. 19, June 24, Oct. 12; —.
COLE CAMP, and C. ISLAND, 1861, June 19; 1863, Mar. 28.
COLESGATE ISLAND, 1862, May 21.
COLLIERSVILLE, 1863, Oct. 11, 13, 25, Nov. 2, 3.
COLUMBIA, Ark., 1864, June 5, 6.
COLUMBIA, Pa., 1863, June 28.
COLUMBIA, Ky., 1861, Dec. 26; 1863, Oct. 22.
COLUMBIA, S. C., 1865, Feb. 16, 17, 18.
COLUMBIA, Tenn., 1862, July 17; 1863, June 30; 1864, Nov. 24.
COLUMBIA BRIDGE, 1862, May 7.
COLUMBUS, 1861, June 12, Sept. 7, Oct. 7; 1862, Jan. 11, 12, Feb. 27, Mar. 3; 1863, Dec. 24; 1864, Apr. 6, 13; 1865, Jan. 18, Apr. 16.
COMPTON'S FERRY, 1862, Aug. 11.
COMBAHEE RIVER, 1863, June; 1865, Jan. 26; —.
COMMERCE, Miss., 1862, Dec. 18; 1863, Jan. 14.
COMMERCE, Mo., 1861, Aug. 19.
COMMERCE, Tenn., 1862, Oct. 19.
COMO, 1863, Oct. 7.
CONCORDIA, 1862, Dec. 9.
CONRAD'S FERRY, 1861, June 18, Sept. 6.
COOLEYVILLE, 1863, July 19.
COOSAHATCHIE, 1862, Oct. 22.
COOSAW RIVER, 1863, June; 1864, July 13; —.
CORBIN'S BRIDGE, and C. NECK, 1863, Aug. 24.
CORPUS CHRISTI, 1863, Nov. 15.
CORINTH, 1862, Apr. 2, 24, June 4, May 8, 24–30, Oct. 3, 4, 5, Dec. 12, 18; 1863, July 7, 17; 1864, Jan. 25; —.
CORROTOWAN CREEK, 1861, Nov. 6.
CORYDON, 1863, June 17, July 9.
COSBY CREEK, 1864, Jan. 15.
COTTAGE GROVE, 1863, Mar. 21.
COTTON CREEK, PLANT, and HILLS, 1861, Oct. 30–Nov. 7; 1862, Sept. 12, Oct. 28; 1864, Apr. 22, Nov. 16.

COTTONVILLE, 1865, May 5.
COURTABLEAU, 1863, Apr. 22.
COURTLAND, Ala., 1862, July 25; 1863, Apr. 28.
COURTLAND, Tenn., 1862, Aug. 23.
COVE CREEK and COVE MOUNTAIN GAP, 1862, Nov. 18; 1864, May 10.
COVINGTON, Ky., 1862, Sept. 6.
COVINGTON, Tenn., 1863, Mar. 10; 1864, Nov. 17.
COVINGTON, Va., 1863, Nov. 17, Dec. 18.
COX'S BRIDGE, 1865, Mar. 21.
COWAN, 1863, July 3.
CRAB ORCHARD, 1862, Aug. 20–22.
CRAMPTON'S PASS and GAP, 1862, Sept. 14.
CRANEY ISLAND, 1862, May 8–12; —.
CRANSTON'S BLUFF, 1862, Oct. 1.
CRICKET HILL.
CRIPPLE CREEK, 1863, May 16.
CROOKED RUN, 1862, Aug. 16.
CROSS HOLLOWS, 1862, Oct. 28.
CROSS KEYES, 1862, June 8.
CROSS LANES, 1861, Aug. 1.
CROW HOUSE, 1865, Mar. 30–Apr. 2.
CRUMP'S HILL, 1864, Mar. 31.
CRYSTAL SPRINGS, 1863, May 11.
CULP'S FARM, 1864, June 22.
CULPEPPER, 1862, July 12, Aug. 9; 1863, June 8, Sept. 13, Oct. 11, Nov. 8, Dec. 25; —.
CUMBERLAND, Ky., 1863, July 7.
CUMBERLAND, Md. and Va., 1862, May 10, June 17, 22; 1864, Aug. 1; 1865, Feb. 21.
CUMBERLAND FORT, and GAP, 1861, June 28, Nov. 13; 1862, Sept. 4, 17; 1863, Sept. 7, 9; 1864, Jan. 29, Feb. 22; —.
CUMBERLAND ISLAND and SOUND.
CUMBERLAND MOUNTAIN and VALLEY, —.
CUMMING'S POINT, —.
CYNTHIANA, 1861, Sept. 26; 1862, July 14, 17; 1864, June 11, 12.
CYPRESS BEND, 1863, June 21.

D.

DABNEY'S MILLS, 1865, Feb. 6, Mar. 29, 30.
DALLAS, 1862, Aug. 24, Dec. 24; 1864, May 25–28.
DALTON, 1863, Nov. 30; 1864, Jan. 31, Feb. 8, 24, 26, Mar. 1, May 12, 14, Aug. 14, 15, Oct. 12.
DAM NUMBER FOUR.
DANDRIDGE, 1864, Jan. 15, 17.
DANVILLE, 1862, Aug. 25, 26; 1864, Jan. 29; 1865, Apr. 28.
DARBY TOWN, 1864, Oct. 7.
DARDANELLE, 1863, Sept. 9, Oct. 5; 1864, May 30.
DARIEN, 1863, June 11.
DARKESVILLE, 1864, Sept. 3.
DARKEYTOWN 1864, Oct. 7.
DARNESTOWN, 1861, Sept. 15; 1864, July 10.
DAVENPORT, 1865, Jan. 6.
DAY'S GAP, 1863.

666    BATTLES, ENGAGEMENTS, COLLISIONS, ETC.

DAVIS'S FARM, 1864, June 21.
DAVIS'S MILLS, 1862, Dec. 20, 21.
DE SOTO,
DEATONSVILLE, 1865, Apr. 6.
DECATUR, 1863, Dec. 12; 1864, Feb. 14, 21, July 20, Sept. 29, Oct. 26–30, Nov. 26–29.
DECHARD, 1863, June 29, July 1.
DEEP BOTTOM, D. CREEK, and D. RUN, 1863, June 5; 1864, Aug. 15, 16; 1865, Apr. 3; —.
DEER CREEK, 1863, Mar. 21.
DELHI, 1862, Dec. 24.
DENMARK, 1862, Sept. 1.
DES ARC, 1863, Jan. 17.
DESERTED HOUSE, 1863, Jan. 30.
DEVIL'S BACK BONE, 1863, Sept. 1.
DINWIDDIE COURT HOUSE, 1865, Mar. 30, 31.
DISMAL SWAMP.
DOBOY SOUND and RIVER, 1863, Nov. 30, Dec. 16; —.
DONALDSONVILLE, 1862, Aug. 10, Oct. 26; 1863, June 27, 28, July 13, 14, Sept. 25.
DONELSON BLUFFS.
DONIPHAN, Mo., 1863, May 28, Dec. 25.
DONIPHAN, Tenn.
DOVER LANDING, 1863, Sept. 15.
DRANESVILLE, 1861, Nov. 26, Dec. 20; 1864, Feb. 22, 28.
DRESDEN, 1862, May 5.
DRIPPING SPRING, 1862, Dec. 28.
DRIVER'S HILL,
DROOP MOUNTAIN, 1863, Nov. 6.
DRURY'S BLUFF, 1864, May 12–16; —.
DRY FORK, 1861, July 5; 1862, Jan. 8.
DRY SPRINGS and WOOD, 1861, Aug. 2.
DUCK RIVER, 1863, Apr. 25, June 25; 1864, Dec. 19; —.
DUG SPRINGS, 1861, Aug. 2.
DUMFRIES, 1861, Oct. 11; 1862, Mar. 15, 27, Dec. 2, 11, 23, 27; 1863, Jan. 2.
DUNKSBURG, 1861, Dec. 4.
DURHAM'S STATION, 1865, Apr. 17, 18.
DURHAMVILLE, 1862, Sept. 17.
DUTCH GAP, 1864, July 11; 1865, Jan. 1; —.
DUVALL'S BLUFF, 1863, Jan. 16; 1864, Aug. 23; 1865, May 24; —.
DYERSBURG, 1863, Jan. 30.

E.

EAGLESPORT, 1863, July 23.
EAGLEVILLE, 1863, Mar. 2.
EAST BAY, 1864, Feb. 18.
EAST POINT, 1864, Oct. 10.
EASTPORT, 1862, Mar. 24, Apr. 1, 13.
EBENEZER CHURCH, 1865, Apr. 1.
EDENTON, 1862, Feb. 12.
EDGEFIELD JUNCTION, 1862, Aug. 20.
EDINBURG.
EDISTO, 1861, Dec. 18; '62, Apr. 19, 29; '64, July 2.

EDWARDS' FERRY, and STATION, 1861, June 18, Oct. 21, 25; 1862, Sept. 9.
EGYPT, 1864, Feb. 19, Dec. 28.
ELIOTT'S MILLS, 1861, Sept. 22.
ELIZABETH CITY, and RIVER, 1862, Feb. 10, Apr. 8, 19; 1863, Dec. 10; —.
ELIZABETHTOWN, 1862, Dec. 25, 27.
ELK CREEK, 1863, July 16, 17.
ELK FORK, 1862, Dec. 28.
ELK HORN, 1862, Mar. 8.
ELK RIDGE, 1861, Apr. 23.
ELK RIVER, 1862, Sept. 12; 1863, June 25, July 2, 14.
ELK WATER, 1861, Sept. 13.
ELKTON, 1862, May 9.
ELLICOTT'S MILLS, 1861, June 6.
ELLISON'S MILLS, 1862, May 22, 24, June 27.
ELY'S FORD, 1864, Mar. 5.
EMMETSBURG, 1862, Oct. 11.
ENTERPRISE, 1864, Feb. 14–21.
ETOWAH RIVER, 1864, May 18.
ESTELL SPRINGS, 1863, July 1.
EUNICE, 1863, June 13.
EVANSPORT.
EVANSVILLE, 1862, July 15.

F.

FAIR GARDENS, 1864, Jan. 28.
FAIR OAKS, 1862, May 31, June 1, 16, 21, 25, 29.
FAIRBURN, 1864, Aug. 19.
FAIRFAX, 1861, June 1, July 17, Nov. 17, 27; 1863, Mar. 8, June 14, 25, 27, July 30, 31, Aug. 6, 24, Dec. 15; —.
FAIRFIELD, 1863, July 3.
FAIRHAVEN, 1865, Apr. 4.
FAIRMOUNT, Mo., 1862, July 12.
FAIRMOUNT, Va., 1863, Apr. 29.
FAIRVIEW MOUNTAIN.
FALLING CREEK and F. WATERS, 1861, July 2; 1863, July 14, Aug. 30.
FALL'S CHURCH, 1861, June 29, Oct. 8; —.
FALMOUTH, Ky., 1862, Sept. 17.
FALMOUTH, Va., 1862, Apr. 18, Nov. 18, 28; 1863, Feb. 25.
FARMINGTON, Miss., 1862, Apr. 2, May 3, 9; 1863, Oct. 7.
FARMINGTON, Mo., 1861, July 1.
FARMINGTON, Tenn., 1863, Oct. 8.
FARMVILLE, 1865, Apr. 7.
FARRAR'S ISLAND, (see Dutch Gap.)
FAYETTE, 1862, Sept. 10, 14.
FAYETTEVILLE, Ark., 1862, July 15, Oct. 27–29, Dec. 7; 1863, Apr. 18.
FAYETTEVILLE, Ga., 1864, July 29.
FAYETTEVILLE, N. C., 1861, Apr. 22; 1862, Feb. 23; 1864, Mar. 12; 1865, Mar. 9, 11.
FAYETTEVILLE, Va., 1862, Sept., Nov. 15; 1863, May 18–20.

## BATTLES, ENGAGEMENTS, COLLISIONS, ETC. 667

FEDERAL HILL, and F. POINT, 1865, Jan 15.
FERNANDINA, 1862, Mar. 3, 7.
FERNANDO, 1863, June 18.
FIRE ISLAND, 1864, Aug. 11.
FISH SPRINGS, 1863, Jan. 23.
FISHER'S HILL, 1864, Sept. 20-23.
FISHING CREEK, 1863, May 25.
FITZHUGH'S WOODS, 1864, Apr. 1.
FIVE FORKS, 1865, Mar. 30-Apr. 1.
FLAT LICK FORD, 1862, Feb. 14.
FLEMING, 1863, June 16.
FLINT HILL.
FLORENCE, Ala., 1862, July 22; 1863, Feb. 22, Apr. 28, May 27; 1864, Jan. 26, Dec. 5-9.
FLORENCE, Ky., 1862, Sept. 15 17.
FLORENCE, (Prison).
FLORIDA, 1862, July 23.
FLOYD'S FORK, 1862, Oct. 1.
FLUSSELL'S MILL POND.
FOLLY ISLAND and INLET, —.
FORD'S STATION, 1864, June 22.
FORSYTH, 1861, July 22.
FORT ALEXIS, 1865, Apr. 8.
FORT ANDERSON, 1864, Mar. 25; 1865, Jan. 19, Feb. 19.
FORT ANDREW JOHNSON.
FORT BARRANCAS, 1861, Jan. 12, Nov. 22, 23; 1862, Jan. 1.
FORT BARTOW, 1862, Feb. 8; 1864, Dec. 21.
FORT BEAUREGARD '861, Nov. 7; 1862, Mar. 5.
FORT BERTHOLD.
FORT BLAKELY, 1865, Apr. 9.
FORT BLANCHARD.
FORT BLISS.
FORT BRADY, 1865, Jan. 24.
FORT BROWN, 1861, Mar. 6; 1863, Nov. 4, 6; 1864, Dec. 21.
FORT CAMPBELL, 1865, Jan. 16.
FORT CASWELL, 1861, Jan. 8; 1863, Jan. 5; 1865, Jan. 16, 17.
FORT CLARK, 1861, Aug. 29.
FORT CLINCH, 1862, Mar. 7.
FORT CRAIG, 1861, Oct. 4, Dec. 27; 1862, Feb. 21, May 23.
FORT DARLING, 1862, May 15, June 30, July 14; 1864, May 12-14.
FORT DELAWARE.
FORT DE RUSSY, 1863, May 5; 1864, Mar. 14-17.
FORT DONELSON, 1862, Feb. 12-16, Aug. 25, 26; 1863, Feb. 3; —.
FORT ELLSWORTH.
FORT ESPERANZA, 1863, Nov. 27-Dec. 1.
FORT EUGENE, 1865, Apr. 8.
FORT EVANS, 1862, Mar. 8.
FORT FILLMORE, 1861, July 24, Aug. 2; 1862, Aug. 7.
FORT FISHER, 1863, Sept. 23; 1864, Dec. 24-27; 1865, Jan. 13-15, Mar. 25; —

FORT FOSTER, 1865, Apr. 2.
FORT GAINES, 1864, Aug. 5, 8.
FORT GIBSON, 1863, May 20, Dec. 17-19.
FORT GILMORE, 1864, Sept. 29.
FORT GRAY, 1864, Apr. 17.
FORT GREENWOOD, 1863, Mar. 13.
FORT GREGG, 1863, Sept. 6, 7.
FORT GRIFFIN, 1865, May 24.
FORT HALLECK, 1863, July 7; 1864, Apr. 6.
FORT HARRISON, 1864, Sept. 29.
FORT HASKELL, 1865, Mar. 25.
FORT HATTERAS, 1861, Aug. 29.
FORT HENRY, 1862, Feb. 6, 14.
FORT HICKS, 1864, Mar. 25, 26.
FORT HILL.
FORT HINDMAN, 1863, Jan. 11.
FORT HODSON, 1864, Sept. 28.
FORT HOLT, 1861, Sept. 20, Dec. 2.
FORT HUGER, 1865, Apr. 10.
FORT JACKSON, 1862, Apr. 14-28; 1864, Dec. 21.
FORT JEFFERSON, 1862, Jan. 11.
FORT JOHNSON, 1861, Jan. 8; 1863, Sept. 30, Oct. 10; 1864, July 2.
FORT KEARNEY, 1861, Feb. 19.
FORT KELLY, 1864, Nov. 28.
FORT LAFAYETTE.
FORT LEE, 1864, Dec. 21.
FORT LIVINGSTON, 1862, Apr. 27.
FORT LOWRY, 1863, Feb. 21.
FORT MACON, 1862, Mar. 23, Apr. 12, 25, 26.
FORT MAGRUDER, 1863, Apr. 12.
FORT MANNAHASSET, 1865, May 24.
FORT MCALLISTER, 1863, Jan. 27, Feb. 1, Mar. 3; 1864, Dec. 10-13.
FORT MCCRAE, 1861, Nov. 23.
FORT MCGILVERY.
FORT MCHENRY, —.
FORT MEADE.
FORT MONROE, —.
FORT MORGAN, 1861, Jan. 4; 1864, Aug. 5, 9, 23, 26; —.
FORT MOULTRIE, 1860, Dec. 26; 1861, Jan. 9, Apr. 12; 1863, Sept. 9, Oct. 6; 1865, Feb. 18; —.
FORT MYERS, 1865, Feb. 20.
FORT NEGLEY.
FORT NELSON, 1864, Oct. 11.
FORT OREGON, 1861, Sept. 16.
FORT PHILIP, 1862, Apr. 18-28.
FORT PICKENS, 1861, Sept. 14, Nov. 22, 23; 1862, Jan. 1; —.
FORT PILLOW, 1862, Apr. 14, May 10, 24, 27, June 4; 1864, Mar. 16, 25, Apr. 12; —.
FORT POINT, 1862, Oct. 4, 5.
FORT POWELL, 1864, Feb. 16, 26, Mar. 28, Aug. 5; 1865, July.
FORT POWHATAN, 1863, July 14; 1864, May 24.
FORT PULASKI, 1861, Jan. 3; 1862, Apr. 11.

668  BATTLES, ENGAGEMENTS, COLLISIONS, ETC.

FORT RIDGELEY, 1862, Aug. 20, 22, Sept. 4.
FORT SAINT PHILIP, 1862, Apr. 14–28.
FORT SAUNDERS, 1863, Nov. 29–Dec. 1.
FORT SCOTT, 1861, Sept. 2; 1863, Oct. 6, 10; 1864, Oct. 25.
FORT SEDGEWICK, 1864, Nov. 5.
FORT SIMPKINS, 1863, Sept. 30.
FORT SMITH, 1861, Apr. 25, May 4; 1863, Sept. 1, 10, 19; 1864, June 26, Aug. 5.
FORT STANTON, 1861, Aug. 29, Dec. 27.
FORT STEADMAN, 1865, Mar. 25.
FORT STEVENS, 1864, July 11, 12.
FORT SUMNER, 1864, Jan. 4.
FORT SUMTER, 1861, Apr. 12–14*; 1863, Apr. 7, Aug. 17, 20, 22, Sept. 28, 30, Oct. 9, 27, 31, Dec. 11; 1864, May 13, 14; 1865, Feb. 18, Apr. 14, —.
FORT TOTTEN.
FORT TRACY, 1865, Apr. 10.
FORT WAGNER, 1863, July 10–18, 30, Aug. 17, Sept. 1–7; —.
FORT WALKER, 1861, Nov. 7.
FORT WARREN.
FORT WELCH, 1865, Apr. 2.
FORT WESSELL, 1864, Apr. 18.
FORT WHITE, 1865, Feb. 23.
FORT WRIGHT, 1862, Apr. 13, 14, May 10, June 5.
FOUR-MILE CREEK, 1864, June 21, July 28.
FOURTEEN-MILE CREEK, 1863, May 3.
FOX GAP.
FRANKFORD, and FRANKFORT, 1861, June 26; 1862, Sept. 12, Oct. 5–8, Nov. 25; 1864, June 10.
FRANKLIN, La., 1863, Apr. 15, Oct. 2; 1864, Dec. 15.
FRANKLIN, Tenn., 1862, Dec. 12; 1863, Feb. 1, Mar. 5, 25, Apr. 10, 27, May 12, June 4; 1864, Nov. 30, Dec. 17; —.
FRANKLIN, Va., 1862, Oct. 3, 31, Nov. 1, Dec. 2; 1863, Mar. 17.
FRAZIER'S FARM.
FREDERICK, 1862, Sept. 4–14; 1863, June 20, 21, 26; 1864, July 8, 9.
FREDERICKSBURG, 1862, Apr. 18, Aug. 31, Nov. 9, Dec. 11–16; 1863, May 1–5, Aug. 24; 1864, May 7; 1865, Mar. 6; —.
FREDERICKTOWN, 1861, Aug. 16, Oct. 16, 21; 1864, Sept. 24.
FREEMAN'S FORD, 1862, Aug. 22.
FREESTONE, 1861, Sept. 25, Dec. 9, 29.
FRICK'S GAP, 1863, Sept. 8.
FROG'S GAP.
FRONT ROYAL, 1862, May 23–30; 1863, June 12, July 23; 1864, Aug. 13, Nov. 12.
FULTON, Mo., 1862, July 27.
FUNKTOWN, 1863, July 11, 12.

* First Engagement in the War of the Rebellion.

G.

GADSDEN, 1863, May 3.
GAINES' CROSS ROADS, and G. LANDING, 1862, Nov. 8; 1864, May 24, 25, 27.
GAINES' FARM, and G. MILLS, 1862, June 27.
GAINESVILLE, 1862, Aug. 29; 1863, Oct. 19; 1864, Feb. 14.
GALLATIN, 1862, Feb. 23, Aug. 12, 21, Oct. 1, 19; 1863, Nov. 16.
GALLOP'S ISLAND.
GALVESTON, 1861, Aug. 2, 5; 1862, Oct. 4, 9; 1863, Jan. 1, 10; 1865, June 2–5; —.
GARNETT'S HILL.
GARRETTSBURG, 1862, Nov. 11.
GATESVILLE, N. C., 1862, May 29.
GATESVILLE, Va., 1863, Feb. 22.
GAULEY, 1861, Sept. 10, Nov. 10; 1862, Sept. 11.
GEIGER'S CREEK, 1863, July 20.
GENESIS POINT, 1863, Mar. 4.
GEORGETOWN, 1863, Dec. 11; 1864, June 3; 1865, Feb. 23.
GERMANIA FORD, 1863, Nov. 18; 1865, May 4.
GERMANTOWN, 1862, Feb. 7, June 25, Sept. 1, Nov. 1; 1863, Apr. 10.
GETTYSBURG, 1863, June 26–July 3.
GHENT, 1864, Sept. 8.
GILES' COURT HOUSE, 1862, May 7.
GLADE'S SPRING, 1864, Dec. 15.
GLASGOW, 1861, Sept. 19; 1862, Oct. 5; 1863, Oct. 5; 1864, Oct. 14.
GLENDALE, 1862, June 30, July 1.
GLOUCESTER, 1862, May —, Nov. 17; 1863, Apr. 12, May 7, 8, Sept. 3.
GOLDING'S FARM.
GOLDSBORO', 1862, Dec. 17; 1865, Mar. 21, 22.
GOLGOTHA, 1864, June 15.
GONZALES, 1864, July 20.
GOODRICH'S LANDING, 1863, June 29.
GOOSE CREEK, 1861, Oct. 22; 1862, Sept. 17; 1864, Feb. 26.
GORDON, GORDON'S LANDING, and GORDONSVILLE, 1862, July 17; 1863, Jan. 14, Feb. 14; 1864, June 12, Nov. 21, Dec. 23.
GOSPORT.
GRAFTON, 1861, May 27, 30, Aug. 13.
GRAHAMSVILLE, 1864, Nov. 30.
GRAND COTEAU, 1863, Nov. 3.
GRAND ECORE, 1864, Apr. 5–14; —.
GRAND GULF, 1862, May 26, June 1, 8; 1863, Feb. 24, Apr. 1, 29, May 3; 1864, July 17; —.
GRAND HAZE, 1862, July 4.
GRAND JUNCTION, 1862, June 9, July 28.
GRAND PRAIRIE, 1862, July 6, Oct. 24.
GRANT'S PASS, CREEK, and MILLS, 1863, Sept. 13; 1864, Apr. 1, July; 1865, Mar. 9, Apr. 12.
GRASS LICK, 1862, Apr. 23.
GRAVELLY RUN, 1865, Mar. 29.

## BATTLES, ENGAGEMENTS, COLLISIONS, ETC. 669

GRAYSON, 1862, Sept. 30.
GREASY CREEK, 1863, May 11.
GREAT BETHEL, 1861, June 10.
GREAT FALLS, and G. RUN, 1861, July 7, Sept. 4; 1862, Aug. 23.
GREEN HILL, 1863, Apr. 6.
GREEN RIVER, 1861, Oct. 15, Dec. 12, 16; 1862, Feb. 1, Sept. 12; 1863, July 4; —.
GREEN'S CHAPEL, 1862, Dec. 25.
GREENBRIER, 1861, Oct. 3; 1863, Dec. 31.
GREENCASTLE, 1863, June 15, 20, July 1, 7.
GREENLAND GAP, 1863, Apr. 26.
GREENSBORO', 1864, Nov. 20.
GREENTOWN, 1864, June 1.
GREENUPSBURG, 1862, Oct. 3.
GREENVILLE, 1863, Feb. 23, July 19, Oct. 28; 1864, Sept. 4.
GREENWICH, 1863, May 30.
GREENWOOD, 1863, Mar. 11–13.
GREGG'S CREEK, 1863, July 20.
GREGORY'S LANDING, 1864, Dec. 6.
GRENADA, 1862, Dec. 2; 1863, Aug. 17.
GREYSVILLE, 1863, Nov. 26.
GRIDER'S HILL.
GRIEGER'S LAKE, 1862, Sept. 3.
GRIMBALL'S, 1865, Feb. 15.
GRISWOLDVILLE, 1864, Nov. 23.
GROVETON, 1862, Aug. 29.
GUM SWAMP, 1863, May 22.
GUNTOWN, 1864, June 10.
GUY'S GAP, 1863, June 24.
GUYANDOTTE, 1861, Nov. 10, 11.

### H.

HACKETT'S POINT, 1862, Dec. 6.
HAGERSTOWN, 1862, Sept. 10–14, Oct. 10; 1863, June 14, 29, July 6–12; 1864, July 5–9.
HAINES' BLUFF, 1862, Aug. 16–18, Dec. 27; 1863, May 18.
HALIFAX ROAD, 1865, Mar. 29.
HALL'S HILL.
HALLTOWN, 1862, Nov. 9, 22, Dec. 20.
HAMILTON, 1862, July 9, Oct. 2, Nov. 4.
HAMPTON, H. BRIDGE, and H. CREEK, 1861, May 23, Aug. 7, 8, Nov. 19.
HAMPTON ROADS.
HANCOCK, 1862, Jan. 6, Oct. 10.
HANGING ROCK,
HANNIBAL, 1861, July 10.
HANOVER, Ala., Aug. 27.
HANOVER, Pa., 1863, June 30.
HANOVER, H. COURT HOUSE, H. GAP, and H. JUNCTION, Va., 1862, May 29; 1863, June 24, 29; 1864, May 26; —.
HANOVERTOWN, 1864, May 27–31.
HARDEEVILLE, 1864, Dec. 19.
HARE'S HILL, 1865, Mar. 25.
HARPER'S FERRY, 1861, Apr. 21, June 29, July 4, Oct. 16, 18; 1862, Feb. 7, 24, May 30, Sept. 12–18; 1863, June 16, July 3, Oct. 5–7; 1864, Jan. 4, July 3, 7; —.
HARPETH SHOALS, 1863, Jan. 13, 16; 1864, Oct. 11.
HARRISBURG, 1863, June 16, 28.
HARRISON, and H. ISLAND, 1861, Oct. 21; 1863, July 13; —.
HARRISON'S LANDING, 1861, Oct. 21; 1862, July 30, Aug. 4.
HARRISONBURG, 1862, Apr. 22, May 6, June 6; 1864, May 2.
HARRISONVILLE, 1861, July 18; 1862, Nov. 8.
HARRODSBURG, 1862, Oct. 10.
HART'S ISLAND.
HARTFORD, Ky., 1863, May 25.
HARTSVILLE, 1862, Dec. 7; 1863, Jan. 10, 11.
HARTWOOD CHURCH, 1863, Feb. 25, Aug. 27.
HATCHER'S RUN, 1864, Oct. 27, Dec. 9; 1865, Feb. 5, 6, Mar. 25, 30.
HATCHIE (The), 1862, July 24, Oct. 5.
HATTERAS, 1861, Aug. 29, Sept. 8, 9; Oct. 5; —.
HAWES' STORE, 1864, May 28.
HAWESVILLE, 1862, Oct. 10; 1865, Jan. 6.
HAWK'S NEST, 1861, Aug. 20.
HAXALL'S LANDING, 1864, July 26.
HAYMARKET, 1862, Oct. 18; 1863, Oct. 20.
HAYNESBOROUGH, 1864, Dec. 3.
HAYNESVILLE, 1861, July 1.
HAZEL GREEN, 1863, Feb. 23.
HEDGESVILLE, 1862, Oct. 22; 1863, Oct. 15.
HELENA, Ark., 1862, Aug. 11, 14, Oct. 11, 18, 22, Dec. 5, 14; 1863, Feb. 17, July 4, 9; —.
HELENA, Ky., 1863, Apr. 20.
HENDERSON, and H. HILL, 1862, Nov. 25; 1864, Mar. 14, 21, July 21; 1865, Jan. 6.
HERNANDO, 1862, Aug. 28.
HERTFORD, 1863, Aug. 15.
HICKMAN, 1861, Sept. 4; 1863, July 15.
HICKORY HILL.
HIGH BRIDGE, 1865, Apr. 7.
HILLSBORO', and H. RIVER, 1861, Oct. 8; 1863, Mar. 8, June 28; 1864, Feb. 14, 21, July 31.
HILTON HEAD, 1861, Nov. 7; —.
HODGESVILLE, 1861, Oct. 23.
HOLLY GAP, 1863, July 4.
HOLLY RIVER, 1862, Apr. 18, May 13.
HOLLY SPRINGS, 1862, June 17, Nov. 13, Dec. 19, 20; 1863, Jan. 12, July 18.
HOLSTON RIVER, 1863, Nov. 15, Dec. 3; 1864, Jan. 19.
HONEY SPRINGS, and H. HILL, 1863, July 17; 1864, Nov. 29, 30; 1865, Feb. 11.
HOOVER'S GAP, 1863, July 3.
HOPEFIELD, 1863, Feb. 19.
HOPKINSVILLE, 1862, Aug. 16; 1864, Oct. 8, Dec. 13, 18.
HORSE SHOE, 1863, May 9.

## BATTLES, ENGAGEMENTS, COLLISIONS, ETC.

HORTON'S MILLS, 1862, Apr. 27.
HOUSTON, 1861, Nov. 4.
HOWE CROSS ROADS, 1865, Apr. 5.
HOWLETT'S HOUSE.
HUDSON, 1861, Dec. 20.
HUDSONVILLE, 1862, Nov. 8.
HUMBOLDT, 1861, Sept.; 1862, July 29, Dec. 20.
HUMONVILLE, 1862, Mar. 26.
HUNNEWELL, 1862, Jan. 3.
HUNTER, 1861, Sept. 22.
HUNTER'S CHAPEL, and H. FORD, 1861, Dec. 2; 1863, Oct. 17.
HUNTERSTOWN, 1863, July 2.
HUNTERSVILLE, 1861, Dec. 31; 1862, Jan. 4; 1864, Sept. 30.
HUNTOON'S MILLS, 1863, Jan. 8.
HUNTSVILLE, 1861, Dec. 1; 1862, Apr. 11, Aug. 31, Nov. 11, Dec. 7; 1863, July 17; 1864, Sept. 30, Oct. 2.
HURRICANE BRIDGE, and H. CREEK, 1861, Oct. 12; 1864, Aug. 13.
HUTTONSVILLE.
HYATTSTOWN, 1862, Oct. 12.

### I.

IATON, 1861, June 3.
INDEPENDENCE, 1862, Feb. 18, Mar. 22, Aug. 11, 13.
INDIAN RIVER, 1862, Oct. 23, 28, Dec. 10.
INDIAN VILLAGE, 1863, Jan. 27.
INDIANOLA, 1861, Apr. 17; 1862, Oct. 26; 1863, Dec. 2; 1864, Mar. 13.
INGHAM'S MILLS, 1863, Oct. 12.
IRON BANKS and MOUNT, 1861, Oct. 7.
IRONTON, 1861, Sept. 12, Oct. 15; 1864, Sept. 29.
IRVINE, 1863, July 16.
IRWINSVILLE, 1865, May 10, 11.
ISLAND FORD, 1864, July 18–20.
ISLAND NUMBER TEN, 1862, Mar. 16, —; Apr. 1–8, Oct. 17; 1863, Feb. 1; —.
ISLE OF WIGHT COURT HOUSE, 1862, Dec. 22.
IUKA, 1862, Sept. 19, 20.
IVY MOUNTAINS.

### J.

JACKSON, Miss., 1863, May 14, June 16, July 11–16; 1864, Feb. 5, July 5, Nov. 24.
JACKSON, Mo., 1863, Apr. 28.
JACKSON, N. C., 1863, Aug. 3; 1865, Mar. 8.
JACKSON, Tenn., 1862, Dec. 20; 1863, July 19.
JACKSON'S RIVER, 1863, Dec. 17.
JACKSONVILLE, 1862, Mar. 12, Apr. 9, Oct. 5; 1863, Mar. 10, 27, 28; 1864, Feb. 5–9.
JAMES BAYOU, 1861, Sept. 29.
JAMES ISLAND, 1862, June 5–16; 1863, June 1, July 16; 1864, July 1; 1865, Feb. 10–15; —.
JAMES RIVER, 1861, Dec. 2; 1862, Mar. 9, July 3, Aug. 1; 1864, June 1; —.

JARRATT'S STATION, 1864, May 4.
JASPER, 1864, June 4.
JEFFERSON CITY, 1861, June 14–17; 1864, Oct. 7, 8.
JENKINS'S FERRY, Ark.
JENNIE CREEK, 1862, Jan. 7.
JERICHO FORD, 1864, May.
JERUSALEM PLANK ROAD, 1864, June 22, Aug. 5, Sept. 9, 28, Nov. 5.
JETTERSVILLE, 1865, Apr. 3, 5.
JOHN'S ISLAND, 1864, July 1, 2, 9.
JOHNSON'S ISLAND.
JOHNSONVILLE, 1864, Nov. 2–5.
JOINER'S BRIDGE, 1862, Dec. 24.
JONES'S FORD, 1864, May 5.
JONESBORO', 1864, Sept. 1, Nov. 14, 17.
JONESVILLE, 1862, Dec.; 1864, Jan. 3.
JORDAN'S ROAD.
JOY'S FARM, 1864, Feb. 22.
JUPITER INLET, 1863, Jan. 5, 8.

### K.

KANAWHA, 1861. Aug. 20; —.
KANSAS CITY, 1861, Sept. 14, Nov. 20.
KEAWAH ISLAND, 1862, May 21, —.
KEITTSVILLE, 1862, Feb. 26, Mar. 8.
KELLEY'S FORD, 1862, Aug. 21; 1863, Mar. 17, Nov. 7.
KENANSVILLE, 1863, July 1, 7.
KENESAW MOUNTAIN, 1864, June 4–29, July 3, Oct. 5; —.
KERNSTOWN, 1864, Nov. 11.
KETTLE RUN, 1862, Aug. 27; 1863, May 30.
KEY WEST; —.
KINDERHOOK, 1862, Aug. 11.
KING GEORGE COURT HOUSE, 1862, Dec. 2, 7.
KING'S BAY, 1862, Nov. 4.
KINGSPORT, 1861, Dec. 13.
KINGSTON, Ga., 1864, May 18, 20, Nov. 22; 1865, May 12.
KINGSTON, Tenn., 1863, Sept. 2, Nov. 18.
KINSTON, 1862, Nov. 17, Dec. 12–14; 1863, Dec. 14; 1864, June 21, Dec. 12; 1865, Mar. 8, 11, 16; —.
KIRKSVILLE, 1862, Aug. 7.
KITTOCHIN MOUNTAINS, —.
KNOB NOSTER.
KNOXVILLE, 1863, Sept. 1, 4, 10, Nov. 14, 15, 17, Dec. 3, 4; 1864, Jan. 20, 21; —.

### L

LABADIEVILLE, 1862, Oct. 27.
LABONE PASS, 1865, May 25.
LAFAYETTE, 1863, Sept. 19, 20, Dec. 2, 4, 12, 28; 1864, June 23–26.
LAFOURCHE, 1862, Oct. 27; 1863, June 20, 21, July 14.
LAGRANGE, Ark., 1863, Jan. 3, May 1.

## BATTLES, ENGAGEMENTS, COLLISIONS, ETC. 671

LAGRANGE, Miss., 1862, Nov. 4.
LAGRANGE, Tenn., 1862, Nov. 9, 11; 1864, Aug. 31.
LAKE CITY, and L. STATION, 1864, Feb. 14, 21.
LAKE ERIE, 1864, Sept. 19.
LAKE GEORGE, 1864, Mar. 18.
LAKE HARNEY, 1864, Mar. 18.
LAKE PROVIDENCE, 1863, Feb. 4, June 10.
LAMAR, Kan., 1862, Aug. 24.
LAMAR, Miss., 1862, Nov. 11.
LAMAR, Mo., 1862, Nov. 5, 7.
LANCASTER, 1861, Nov. 24.
LANES', 1861, July 26; 1864, Aug. 21.
LANGVILLE.
LATONIA SPRINGS, 1862, Sept. 11.
LAUDERDALE SPRINGS, 1864, Feb. 14, 21.
LAUREL HILL, 1861, July 10, 11; 1865, Mar. 8.
LAVACCA, 1862, Nov. 1.
LAVERGNE, 1862, Oct. 6, 7, Nov. 27, Dec. 9; 1863, Nov. 16.
LAWRENCE, 1863, Aug. 20, 21.
LAWRENCEBURG, 1862, Apr. 7, Oct. 9; 1863, Nov. 3, 4.
LEATHERWOOD, 1862, Nov. 6.
LEAVENWORTH, 1861, Nov. 2.
LEBANON, Ala., 1864, Feb. 3.
LEBANON, Ky., 1862, July 12; 1863, Jan. 1, July 5.
LEBANON, Mo., 1861, Oct. 13; 1862, Mar. 12.
LEBANON, Tenn., 1862, May 5, Nov. 11, Dec. 6; 1863, Feb. 8, July 5.
LEE'S MILLS, 1862, Apr. 16, 22.
LEESBURG, 1861, Oct. 21, 22; 1862, Mar. 7, May 23, Sept. 17, Oct. 5, 13, 30, Nov. 20, Dec. 11; —.
LEESTOWN, 1863, Aug. 21; 1864, Aug. 25.
LEESVILLE, 1862, Mar. 7.
LEGAREVILLE, 1863, Dec. 24.
LEIPER'S FERRY, 1863, Oct. 30.
LENNOX, 1863, June 19.
LENOIR, 1863, Nov. 14, 15.
LEWINSVILLE, 1861, Sept. 11, 25; 1863, Oct. 4.
LEWISBURG, 1862, May 23; 1863, Nov. 5, 7.
LEXINGTON, Ky., and Va., 1862, July 15, Sept. 1, Oct. 2, 7, 17, 18, Dec. 17; 1864, June 10.
LEXINGTON, Mo., 1861, Aug. 29, Sept. 10-29, Oct. 16; 1864, Oct. 17, 19.
LEXINGTON, S. C., 1865, Feb. 15.
LEXINGTON, Tenn., 1863, July 27.
LIBERTY, La., 1864, Nov. 21.
LIBERTY, Mo., 1861, Apr. 20, June 19.
LIBERTY, Tenn., and L. GAP, 1863, Feb. 3, June 24, 25.
LIBERTY, and L. MILLS, Va., 1863, Oct. 22; 1864, Dec. 22.
LICKTOWN, 1863, Feb. 25.
LIMESTONE STATION, 1863, Sept. 9.
LINDEN, Tenn., 1863, May 12.
LINDEN, Va., 1862, May 15.
LINN CREEK, 1861, Oct. 14; 1862, Feb. 8.
LITHINGTON'S MILLS.
LITTLE BETHEL, 1861, June 10.
LITTLE BLACK RIVER, 1863, May 28; —.
LITTLE BLUE, 1861, Nov. 11, 27; 1862, Apr. 12; 1864, Oct. 22; —.
LITTLE OSAGE, —.
LITTLE RIVER, 1863, Jan. 5, Aug. 24; 1865, Feb. 4, Apr. 9.
LITTLE ROCK, 1862, May 31; 1863, Sept. 10.
LITTLE RUN, 1862, Nov. 18.
LITTLE SALKAHATCHIE, 1865, Feb. 5.
LITTLE SANTA FE, 1861, Nov. 6; 1862, Apr. 21.
LITTLE TENNESSEE RIVER, —.
LITTLE WASHINGTON, 1864, Apr. 28-30.
LITTLETOWN, 1863, June 16.
LIVERPOOL HEIGHTS, 1864, Mar. 5.
LOCKWOOD, 1864, Jan. 11.
LOCUST HILL, and GROVE.
LOGAN'S CROSS ROADS, 1862, Jan. 19.
LONDON, 1863, Oct. 30, Nov. 14, 17.
LONE JACK, 1862, Aug. 16.
LONG BRIDGE, 1862, July 1.
LONGVIEW, 1864, Mar. 26.
LOOKOUT MOUNTAIN, and VALLEY, 1863, July 7, Sept. 8, Oct. 27, 29, Nov. 3, 23-27; —.
LOST MOUNTAIN, 1864, June 8
LOUDON, Tenn., 1863, Nov. 1, 14, 20.
LOUDON, Va., 1861, Sept. 13, Oct. 18; 1864, Jan. 10.
LOUISVILLE, 1862, Sept. 22-26; 1863, Nov. 28.
LOVEJOY'S STATION, 1864, Aug. 20, Nov. 14, 16.
LOVETTSVILLE, 1861, Aug. 8; 1862, Oct. 21.
LOWRY'S POINT, 1862, Apr. 14.
LUCAS BEND, 1861, Sept. 10, 26.
LURAY, 1862, June 30, July 29; 1863, Dec. 23, 24; 1864, Sept. 21, 24.
LYNCHBURG, 1864, June 16, 18; 1865, Apr. 11.
LYNN HAVEN, 1861, June 24, Oct. 9.

## M.

MACKEY'S POINT, 1862, Oct. 28.
MACKINTOSH CREEK.
MACON, 1864, July 31, Nov. 20-22; 1865, Apr. 20, 21.
MADISON, and M. COURT HOUSE, 1862, July 24; 1863, Sept. 22; 1864, Apr. 20, Nov. 19, Dec. 21; —.
MADISONVILLE, 1862, Aug. 26, Nov. 5.
MAGNOLIA, 1863, May 1; 1864, Mar. 21, July 11.
MAIRGE'S HEIGHTS, 1863, May 2-4; 1864, May 3-8.
MALVERN HILLS, 1862, July 1, 24, Aug. 5, 7.
MAMMOTH CAVE.
MANASSAS—(Bull Run), 1861, July 21; 1862, Mar. 10, Aug. 26, 30, Oct. 24; 1863, July 23.

MANCHAC, 1862, June 18.
MANCHESTER, 1862, Aug. 29; 1863, Jan. 5, June 26, July 3.
MANSFIELD, 1864, Apr. 8.
MARIANNA, 1862, Nov. 8; 1864, Sept. 27.
MARIAS DES CYGNES, 1864, Oct. 27.
MARIATOWN, 1861, Sept. 17.
MARIETTA, 1864, June 2, 27, July 3, Nov. 9.
MARION, 1864, Feb. 14, 21, Dec. 16; 1865, Mar. 21.
MARKHAM'S STATION.
MARRIOTTSVILLE, 1863, June 29.
MARSH RUN, 1863, July.
MARSHFIELD, 1862, Oct. 20,
MARTIN'S CREEK, 1864, Feb. 8.
MARTINSBURG, 1861, July 2, 15; 1862, Mar. 3, May 25, 31, Sept. 6, Oct. 1; 1863, June 14, Oct. 16; 1864, July 3, 20-28, Aug. 19, Sept. 18; —.
MATTOX CREEK, 1865, Mar. 16.
MARYLAND HEIGHTS, 1862, Sept. 13, 15; 1833, June 30, —; 1864, July 4.
MARYE'S HILL, 1863, May 3.
MARYSVILLE, and MARY'S HEIGHTS, 1863, Nov. 12.
MASON'S HILL, and MASONIC HILL.
MASONBORO' INLET, 1863, Jan. 16.
MATAGORDA BAY, and ISLAND, 1863, Nov. 27-30, Dec. 1.
MATAMORAS, 1864, Sept. 6.
MATTAPONY, 1862, Aug. 6; 1864, May 22; —.
MATTHIAS POINT, 1861, June 24, 27, Nov. 11, —.
MAYFIELD, 1861, Sept. 20; 1863, Nov. 2; 1864, Jan. 17.
MAYNARDSVILLE, 1863, Dec. 1, 2.
MAYSVILLE, Ark., 1862, Oct. 22.
MAYSVILLE, Ky., 1862, Sept. 11, 14.
MAYSVILLE, Va., 1862, Oct. 31.
MCCONNELLSBURG, 1863, June 19, 24-29.
MCCORMICK'S GAP.
MCCOY'S CREEK, and MILLS, 1861, Nov. 14; 1862, Oct. 10.
MCDONOUGH, 1864, Nov. 17.
MCDOWELL, 1862, May 7, 8.
MCLEAN'S FORD, 1863, Oct. 13.
MCMINNSVILLE, 1862, Mar. 26, Aug. 30; 1863, Apr. 22, May 24, Sept. 28, Oct. 3.
MCNEIL'S FORD, 1864, Feb. 4.
MECHANICSBURG, 1861, Sept. 23; 1863, June 28.
MECHANICSTOWN, 1863, July 5.
MECHANICSVILLE, 1862, May 24, June 25, 26.
MEADOW BRIDGE, 1864, May 12.
MEDON, 1862, Aug. 31.
MEMPHIS, Mo., 1862, July 13, 18.
MEMPHIS, Tenn., 1862, June 6, 7, Aug. 3; 1864, Feb. 21, Aug. 21; —.
MERCERSBURG, 1862, Oct. 10.
MERIDIAN, 1864, Feb. 14.

MERRILL'S CROSSING, 1863, Oct. 12, 13.
MERRIWETHER'S FERRY, 1862, Aug. 15.
MESILLA, 1861, Aug. 3.
MIDDLE CREEK, and M. FORK, 1861, July 6; 1862, Jan. 10.
MIDDLEBURG, Miss., 1863, Dec. 21.
MIDDLEBURG, Va., 1862, Mar. 29; 1863, Jan. 26, Feb. 6, Apr. 29, June 18-21.
MIDDLEBURY, 1863, Dec. 21.
MIDDLETON, 1863, Feb. 1, 2, May 21, 22.
MIDDLETOWN, Md., and Va., 1862, Sept. 9, 10, 11; 1863, June 12, July 4; 1864, July 7, Oct. 19.
MIDDLETOWN, N. C., 1862, Nov. 1.
MIDWAY, 1865, Feb. 2.
MILFORD, 1861, Dec. 18; 1864, May 21.
MILL CREEK HILL, 1861, Oct. 26; 1862, May 25.
MILL POINT, 1863, Nov. 5.
MILL SPRING, 1862, Jan. 19, 20.
MILLEDGEVILLE, 1864, Nov. 20, 23.
MILLEN, 1864, Nov. (Prison.)
MILLIKEN'S BEND, 1862, Aug. 18; 1863, June 6, 8; —.
MILLVILLE, 1861, July 16.
MILLWOOD, 1863, Feb. 6.
MILTON, 1863, Mar. 20.
MINE CREEK, and M. RUN, 1863, Nov. 27, 30; 1864, May 5, Oct. 26.
MINGO, and M. SWAMP, 1862, Nov. 29; 1863, Feb. 3.
MINOR'S HILL, 1861, Oct. 14.
MISSIONARY RIDGE, and MOUNTAINS, 1863, Nov. 23-27; —.
MISSISSIPPI CITY, 1862, Mar. 8.
MISSISSIPPI RIVER, SOUND, and PASSES, 1861, Oct. 12, Nov. 12, Dec. 7; 1862, Apr. 4, —.
MISSOURI RIVER, —.
MITCHELL'S FORK, and CREEK, 1865, Mar. 26.
MOBILE, and M. BAY, and HARBOR, 1861, May 27, Dec. 25; 1863, July 18; 1864, Aug. 5; 1865, Mar. 17, Apr. 14, —.
MOBJACK BAY, 1863, Apr. 25.
MONET'S BLUFF.
MONOCACY, 1864, May, July 9; —.
MONROE, 1861, July 10, 11.
MONTAUK, 1864, Aug. 12.
MONTEITH, 1864, Dec. 9.
MONTEREY, Tenn., 1862, Apr. 28, 29, May 13.
MONTEREY, Va., 1862, Apr. 8, 12; 1863, July 4.
MONTEVALLE, 1865, Mar. 29.
MONTGOMERY, 1862, June 11; 1865, Apr. 11, 14.
MONTICELLO, Ky., 1863, May 1, 31, June 9.
MONTICELLO, Mo., 1862, Aug. 6; 1864, Mar. 30.
MOORE'S BLUFF, and M. MILL, 1862, July 28; 1863, Sept. 29.
MOORE'S CROSS ROADS, 1865, Mar. 15.
MOOREFIELD, 1862, June 29, Nov. 9; 1863, Jan. 3, Sept. 5, 11; 1864, Jan. 2, Feb. 4, Aug. 7; 1865, Feb. 5; —.

## BATTLES, ENGAGEMENTS, COLLISIONS, ETC. 673

Morehead City, 1862, Mar. 23.
Morgan's Bend, 1863, Sept. 7.
Morganfield, 1862, Aug. 31.
Morgantown, 1861, Oct. 31; 1862, Oct. 24; 1863, Apr. 27; 1865, Apr. 20.
Morganzia, 1863, Sept. 29, Oct. 4.
Morris Ferry, and M. Farm, 1863, July 3; 1865, Mar. 19.
Morris Island, 1861, Jan. 9; 1862—, ; 1863, July 10, 18, Aug. 26, Sept. 6; —.
Morristown, 1861, Sept. 17; 1863, Dec. 10, 12; 1864, Nov. 13.
Morton's Ford, 1863, Nov. 15; 1864, Feb. 6.
Moscow, 1863, Dec. 2, 4.
Mosquito Inlet, 1862, Mar ; —.
Mossy Creek, 1863, Dec. 29; 1864, Jan. 11, Oct. 15.
Motley's Ford, 1863, Nov. 5.
Mound City, 1863, Jan. 14, 15.
Mount Airy, 1864, Dec. 14.
Mount Crawford, 1864, June 5.
Mount Elba, 1864, Mar. 30.
Mount Jackson, 1862, Apr. 17, June 12; 1863, Nov. 18.
Mount Olive, 1865, Mar. 21.
Mount Pleasant, 1861, July 28; 1863, Mar. 30.
Mount Sterling, 1862, July 29; 1863, Feb. 23, Mar. 22, June 11, Dec. 2; 1864, June 9, 10; 1865, May 1.
Mount Vernon, 1863, Apr. 11.
Mount Washington, 1862, Oct. 2.
Mount Zion, 1861, Dec. 28.
Mountain Store, 1862, July 26.
Mud Town, 1862, Feb. 24.
Mulberry Fork, and M. Island, 1861, Dec. 2; 1865, Mar. 29.
Muldraugh's Hills, 1862, Dec. 28.
Munfordsville, 1861, Dec. 17; 1862, Sept. 14–21, Dec. 24, 25; —.
Munson's Hill, 1861, Aug. 31, Sept. 28; —.
Murfreesboro', 1862, July 13, Dec. 23–31; 1863, Jan. 1–4, 21, Mar. 2, June 4; 1864, Sept. 1–3, Dec. 5–7, 13–15; —.
Murray Hill
Musquito Inlet, 1862, Mar.; —.

### N.

Nanna Hubba Bluff, 1865, May 9.
Nansemond River, 1863, Apr. 14, 15, 30, May 2; —.
Napoleon, 1861, Apr. 23.
Nashville, 1862, Feb. 23–25, Oct. 6, 22, Nov. 5, Dec. 12, 21; 1864, Nov. 30, Dec. 10–19; —.
Natchez, 1862, May 13, Sept. 1, 10; 1863, July 7–12, 29; 1864, Jan. 23; —.
Natchitoches, 1864, Mar. 13–30.
Needham's Cut-off, 1862, Apr. 13.
Nelson's Farm, 1862, June 30.

Neosho, 1862, Apr. 26, May 29–31.
Neuse River, —.
New Albany, 1863, Oct. 5.
New Baltimore, 1862, Nov. 3, 5.
New Bridge, 1862, May 22, June 5, 28.
New Creek, 1861, June 19; 1864, Feb. 1, Aug. 4, Nov. 28.
New Haven, 1862, Dec. 16.
New Hope, and N. H. Church, 1862, July 11; 1863, Oct. 8; 1864, May 28, 31.
New Iberia, 1863, Apr. 13.
New Inlet, —.
New Kent, 1862, May 10; 1863, June 15.
New Lawrence, 1863, Nov. 3.
New Lisbon, 1863, July 26.
New Madrid, 1862, Mar. 3, 13, Dec. 28.
New Market, Ala., 1862, Aug. 5.
New Orleans, 1862, Apr. 14–28, May, Dec. 14; —
New River, N. C., —.
New River, Va., 1861, Nov. 7; 1864, May 10.
New Ulm, 1862, Aug.
New Windsor, 1863, June 29.
Newark, 1862, Aug. 1.
Newbern, 1862, Mar. 14, Nov. 11; 1863, Feb. 27, Mar. 8, 14; 1864, Feb. 1, 4, 7, 29, May 10; 1865, Apr. 2; —.
Newburg, 1862, July 18.
Newmarket, 1861, July 19, Nov. 11, 12, 29, Dec. 22; 1862, Apr. 17, June 30, Sept. 11; 1863, Nov. 18; 1864, Jan. 18, May 15, Sept. 28–30, Oct. 7, Dec. 21; —.
Newman, 1864, July 30.
Newport News, 1861, June 5, July 5, Dec. 2; 1862, Mar. 9.
Newport, Ky., 1862, Sept. 30.
Newtonia, 1862, Sept. 30; 1864, Oct. 28.
Newtown, 1863, Oct. 4.
Nickajack Trace, 1864, Apr. 23.
Nineveh, 1864, Nov. 12.
Nolensville, 1863, Feb. 15.
Nonconnor, 1863, Apr. 19.
Norfolk, Mo., 1861, Sept. 10.
Norfolk, Va., 1861, Apr. 20, May 20; 1862, May 10; —.
Norristown, 1864, Oct. 28.
North Anna, 1862, July 23; 1864, May 19–24; —.
North Branch, 1864, Feb. 2.
North Fork, 1862, Nov. 9.
North River Mills, 1862, Aug. 18.
Nottoway, 1864, June 22, Dec. 8.

### O.

Oak Grove, Hill and Woods, 1861, Aug. 10; 1862, June 25; 1863, Nov. 25.
Occoquan, 1861, Nov. 12; 1862, Jan. 28, Feb. 4, 20, Mar. 8, Dec. 19, 20, 27; —.
Ocean Pond, 1864, Feb. 20.
Ocmulgee, —.

OCRACOKE, 1861, Sept. 16; —.
OHIO RIVER, —.
OKOLONA, 1864, Feb. 15, 22, Apr. 3, Dec. 21.
OLATHE, 1861, Dec. 7; 1862, Sept. 6.
OLD CHURCH.
OLD FORT WAYNE, 1862, Oct. 22.
OLD RIVER, 1863, Feb. 10.
OLD TOWN, 1864, Aug. 8.
OLIVE HILL, 1862, Oct. 2.
OLUSTEE, 1864, Feb. 20, 21.
ONSLOW, 1862, Nov. 23.
OPELOUSAS, 1863, Apr. 20, Oct. 21.
OPEQUAN, 1864, Sept. 19.
ORANGE COURT HOUSE, 1862, July 20, 25, Aug. 1, 2; 1863, Nov. 27, 30; 1864, Feb. 6, May 4; 1865, Feb. 5; —.
ORANGEBURG, 1865, Feb. 11.
ORIZABA, 1862, Nov. 3.
ORLEANS, 1863, June 11, 17.
OSAGE RIVER, 1862, Oct. 29; —.
OSCEOLA, 1861, Sept. 25.
OSSABAW SOUND, 1861, Dec. 11; 1863, Jan. 21; 1864, June 2;—.
OVERALL'S CREEK, 1864, Dec. 4.
OVERTON'S HILL, 1864, Dec. 16.
OWENSBORO', 1862, Sept. 20; 1865, Jan. 6.
OXFORD, 1862, Dec. 3.
OYSTER POINT, 1863, June 28.
OZARK, 1862, Aug. 2.

## P.

PADUCAH, 1861, Sept. 6; 1864, Mar. 25, 26, Apr. 14; 1865, Mar. 22.
PAINE'S CROSS ROADS, 1865, Apr. 5.
PAINESVILLE, 1864, Apr. 13.
PAINTSVILLE, 1862, Jan. 7, 10; 1864, Apr. 12.
PALMETTO BRANCH, and P. STATION, 1864, July 28; 1865, May 11.
PALMYRA, 1861, Nov. 17; 1862, Sept. 13; 1863, Apr. 4, Nov. 13.
PAMLICO SOUND, 1862, Feb. 7, 8; —.
PAMUNKEY RIVER, 1862, May 18, June 11; 1863, July 1; 1864, May 29; —.
PANOLA, 1863, June 24.
PANTHER GAP, and SPRINGS, 1864, Mar. 5, Nov. 13.
PAOLI, 1863, June 17.
PAPINSVILLE, 1861, Sept. 21, Dec. 13.
PARATA, 1862, Apr. 23.
PARIS, Ky., 1862, July 30, Sept. 1, 15; 1863, Mar. 11, July 29, 31; 1864, June 8.
PARIS, Tenn., 1862, Feb. 12, Mar. 12; 1863, Sept. 13.
PARIS, Va., 1862, Oct. 13; 1863, July 29, 31.
PARKER'S CROSS ROADS, 1862, Dec. 30, 31.
PARKERSBURG, 1861, May.
PARKSVILLE, 1864, July 8.
PASCAGOULA, 1863, Apr. 9; 1864, Dec. 15.

PASQUOTONK RIVER, 1863, Aug. 15, Sept. 29.
PASS A L'OUTRE, 1863, Apr. 6.
PASS CABELLO, 1863, Nov. 30, Dec. 1.
PASS CHRISTIAN, 1862, Apr. 4.
PATTEN, 1862, July 26.
PATTERSON, and P.'s CREEK, 1861, June 26; 1863, Apr. 20; 1864, Jan. 2, Feb. 2.
PATTERSONVILLE, 1863, Jan. 14, Apr. 1.
PAW PAW, 1862, Oct. 4.
PAXTON'S CUT.
PEA RIDGE, 1862, Mar. 5–9, Apr. 24.
PEA VINE CREEK, 1863, Nov. 26.
PEACH ORCHARD, and P. HILL, 1862, June 29; 1864, Apr. 8.
PEACH TREE CREEK, 1864, July 18–20.
PEEBLE'S FARM, 1864, Sept. 30.
PELHAM, 1863, July 1.
PENINSULA (The), —.
PENSACOLA, 1861, Jan. 12, Sept. 14, Nov. 22, 23; 1862, Jan. 1, May 9, 12, Oct. 28; —.
PERRYVILLE, 1862, Oct. 7, 8; 1863, Aug. 25, Sept. 19; 1864, Sept. 3.
PETERSBURG, Tenn., 1863, Mar. 2.
PETERSBURG, Va., 1861, Sept. 12; 1864, Jan. 30, May 9, June 10, 15–July 30; 1865, Mar. 29, 30–Apr. 3; —.
PETTIE'S MILLS, 1863, May 5.
PHILADELPHIA, Tenn., 1863, Oct. 21, 24–26.
PHILIPPI, 1861, June 3, 19.
PHILLIP'S CREEK, 1862, May 21.
PHILOMONT, 1862, Nov. 1, 2; 1863, June 18; 1864, Feb. 20.
PIANKATANK RIVER, 1864, Mar. 7.
PIEDMONT, 1861, June 19; 1862, Nov. 3; 1863, May 16; 1864, June 5, Oct. 13.
PIG POINT, 1861, June 5; 1862, June 1.
PIKETON, 1861, Nov. 8, 9; 1862, Nov. 5; 1863, July 16.
PIKEVILLE, 1862, Sept. 6; 1863, Apr. 15.
PILATKA, 1864, Mar. 10.
PILOT KNOB, 1864, Sept. 26.
PINCKNEY ISLAND, 1862, Aug. 21; —.
PINE BARREN RIDGE, 1864, Nov. 10.
PINE BLUFF, and P. MOUNTAIN, 1863, Sept. 11, Oct. 25; 1864, Apr. 25, June 15, 21; 1865, May 10.
PINE HOOK, 1864, Dec. 26.
PINESVILLE, 1862, Mar. 5; 1863, Aug. 15.
PINEY FACTORY, and P. WOODS, 1863, Oct. 30; 1864, Mar. 31.
PINOLA, 1863, June 28.
PITTMAN'S FERRY, 1862, Oct. 28, Nov. 2.
PITTSBURG LANDING, 1862, Mar. 2, 16, Apr. 4–9; —.
PLANTERSVILLE, 1865, Mar. 21.
PLAQUEMINE, 1862, Nov. 29; 1863, Jan. 27.
PLATTE CITY, 1861, Dec. 15.
PLATTSBURG, 1861, Oct. 27; 1863, May 21.

BATTLES, ENGAGEMENTS, COLLISIONS, ETC. 675

PLEASANT GROVE, HILL, and VALLEY, 1861, Nov. 17; 1862, July 11, Sept. 9; 1864, Apr. 1, 7, 9.
PLYMOUTH, 1862, Sept. 2, Dec. 10; 1864, Apr. 14–20, Oct. 31.
PO.
POCAHONTAS, Ark., 1862, Apr. 12; 1863, Aug. 18, 25.
POCAHONTAS, Miss., 1863, June 18, Dec. 2.
POCATALIGO, 1862, May 29, Oct. 22; 1864, Dec. 6; 1865, Jan. 14.
POCOMAKE.
POHICK CHURCH, 1861, Oct. 4.
POINT ISABEL, 1863, Nov. 5.
POINT LICK, 1862, Oct. 23.
POINT LOOKOUT, 1861, June 28.
POINT OF ROCKS, 1861, Aug. 5, Sept. 24, Nov. 14, Dec. 19; 1863, June 17; 1864, July 4; —.
POINT PLEASANT, 1862, Mar. 9, 14; 1863, Mar. 25.
POINT ROCK RIVER, 1863, Aug. 12.
POLLARD, 1864, Dec. 16; 1865, Mar. 25.
POLLOCKSVILLE, 1863, Jan. 17.
POMEROY, 1863, July 20.
PONCHATOULA, 1862, Sept. 15; 1863, Mar. 24, May 13.
PONTOTOC, 1864, Feb. 13, July 11, 13.
POOLESVILLE, 1862, Sept. 4, 8, Oct. 12, Nov. 25, Dec. 14; 1863, June 11, Aug. 14; 1864, Oct. 14.
POPLAR SPRINGS CHURCH, 1864, Sept. 30.
POQUOSIN BAY.
PORALTO, 1862, Apr. 15.
PORT CONWAY, 1863, Sept. 2.
PORT GIBSON, 1863, May 1.
PORT HUDSON, 1862, Dec. 12; 1863, Mar. 9, 14, May 8, 10–27, June 11, 14, July 8; 1864, July 5; —.
PORT REPUBLIC, 1862, June 8, 9.
PORT ROYAL, 1861, Nov. 7, Dec. 8; 1862, Jan. 1, 5, Dec. 4, 10; 1863, Apr. 22, Sept. 1; 1864, Mar. 19; —.
PORT WALTHAL JUNCTION, 1864, May 16.
PORTLAND, Mo., 1862, Aug. 8.
PORTLAND HARBOR, Me., 1863, June 27.
PORTSMOUTH, Va., 1861, Apr. 20.
POTOMAC RIVER and SHORES, —.
POTOSI, 1861, May 15, Oct. 15.
POUND GAP, 1862, Mar. 16.
POWDER MILL, 1864, Sept. 19.
POWELL'S VALLEY.
POWHATAN, 1862, June 27.
PRAIRIE DE ANNA, and PRAIRIE GROVE, 1862, Dec. 7; 1864, Apr. 17.
PREBLE'S FARM, 1864, Sept. 30.
PRENTISS, 1862, Sept. 20.
PRESTONBURG, 1861, Nov. 5; 1862, Jan. 11.
PRICE'S HILL, and LANDING, 1861, Nov. 18.
PRINCETON, Ark., 1863, Dec. 9.
PRINCETON, Ky., 1862, Dec. 3; 1864, June 10.
PRINCETON, Va., 1862, May 18.

PRITCHARD'S MILLS, 1861, Sept. 15.
PROCTOR'S BRIDGE, and CREEK.
PROVIDENCE CHURCH, 1863, Jan. 9.
PULASKI, 1862, May 1; 1863, Dec. 25; 1864, Sept. 26, Dec. 18.
PUMPKINVINE CREEK, 1864, May 25, 28.
PUNGO CREEK, and RIVER, 1862, Nov. 1; 1863, July 5; —.
PURDY, 1862, Apr. 27–30.
PUTNAM'S FERRY, 1862, Apr. 1, Oct. 27.

Q.

QUAKER BRIDGE, Q. CHURCH, and Q. ROAD, 1863, July 6; 1864, June 17; 1865, Mar. 29
QUALLATOWN, 1864, Feb. 7.
QUANTICO, 1861, Oct. 11.
QUITMAN, 1864, Feb. 14, 21.

R.

RACCOON FORD, 1863, Oct. 8, Nov. 15.
RAINBOW BLUFF.
RALEIGH, 1865, Apr. 13, 26.
RANDOLPH, 1862, Sept. 23.
RAPIDAN BLUFFS, RIVER, and STATION, 1862, July 13; 1863, Sept. 14, Nov. 26, Dec. 1; —.
RAPPAHANNOCK RIVER, and STATION, 1861, June 24; 1862, Aug. 21–23, Nov. 8; 1863, Jan. 22, June 5, Oct. 24, Aug. 1, 4, Nov. 7; —.
RATTLESNAKE MOUNTAIN.
RAVENNA, 1864, Feb. 28.
RAVENSWOOD, 1862, Sept. 4.
RAWLE'S MILLS.
RAYMOND, 1863, May 12.
READY CREEK, 1862, May 13.
READYVILLE, 1862, Aug. 28; 1864, Sept. 7.
REAM'S STATION, 1864, June 28, 29, Aug. 18, 19, 25; 1865, Mar. 22.
RED MOUND, 1863, Jan. 1.
RED RIVER, 1863, Feb. 8, July 14, Oct. 7, Dec. 23; 1864, Apr. 12; 1865, June 3; —.
REELSVILLE, 1862, Aug. 11.
REEVES' POINT, and R. STATION, 1863, Apr. 20; 1865, Jan. 16.
REISTERSTOWN, 1863, June 29; 1864, July 10.
RELAY HOUSE, 1861, May 6.
RENICK, 1861, Nov. 1.
RESACA, 1864, May 13–15, Oct. 12.
REYNOLDS' FORD, 1862, Sept. 23.
RICE'S STATION.
RICH INLET, and R. MOUNTAIN, 1861, July 11; 1863, Sept. 23.
RICHMOND, Ky., 1862, July 27, Aug. 29, 30; 1863, July 28.
RICHMOND, La., 1863, June 15.
RICHMOND, Miss., 1863, Mar. 30, June 16.
RICHMOND, Mo., 1863, May 19.
RICHMOND, Va., siege and investment, 1861–1865, Apr. 3; —.

42

RIDGEVILLE, Va., 1862, Sept. 11, Oct. 29.
RIENZI, 1862, Aug. 19, Nov. 27; 1863, July 11; 1864, June 7.
RIKER'S ISLAND.
RINGGOLD, 1862, Dec. 14; 1863, Sept. 10, Nov. 27, 30; 1864, Jan. 31, Feb. 21, 22, Oct. 15.
RIO GRANDE, —.
RIP RAPS, —.
RIPLEY, Miss., 1862, Nov. 3, Dec. 2; 1864, July 7.
RIPLEY, Tenn., 1863, Jan. 8, June 18.
RIPLEY, Va., 1861, Dec. 19; 1862, Sept. 14.
ROANOKE ISLAND, and RIVER, 1862, Feb. 7, 8; 1864, May 5; —.
ROBERTSON'S FORD, and RIVER, 1863, Oct. 10, 11.
ROCHEFORT, 1863, May 30, June 1, 2.
ROCK CREEK, and SPRINGS, 1863, July 2.
ROCKFORD, 1863, Nov. 14.
ROCKVILLE, 1863, June 28, Sept. 22; 1864, July 10.
ROCKY-FACED RIDGE, 1864, Feb. 24; May 8, 14.
ROCKY CROSSING, and R. GAP, 1863, June 18, Aug. 26, 30.
ROCKY HILL, 1863, July 4.
ROCKY MOUNT, 1863, July 22.
RODMAN'S POINT, 1863, Apr. 4.
ROGERSVILLE, Ala., 1862, May 13.
ROGERSVILLE, Ky., 1862, Aug. 29, 30.
ROGERSVILLE, Tenn., 1863, Nov. 6; 1864, Aug. 22.
ROLLA, 1864, Sept. 27.
ROLLING FORK.
ROME, Ga., 1864, Feb. 8, May 18, 20, Oct. 12.
ROME, Tenn., 1863, Mar. 26.
ROMNEY, 1861, June 11, 26, Sept. 23, Oct. 26; 1862, Jan. 8, Feb. 7; 1863, Feb. 16; —.
ROOD'S HILL, 1864, Nov. 22.
ROSE HILL.
ROSEWELL, 1864, July 10.
ROSSVILLE, 1863, Sept. 19–21, Nov. 23–25; 1864, Apr. 6.
ROUGH AND READY, 1864, Aug., Nov. 16.
ROUND TOP MOUNTAIN, 1864, Oct. 9.
ROVER, 1863, Jan. 31, June 28.
ROWANTY, 1865, Feb. 5, Mar. 30.
RUMSEY, 1861, Nov. 17.
RURAL HILLS, 1862, Nov. 18.
RUSSELLVILLE, and RUSSELL'S HOUSE, 1862, Feb. 20, May 17, July 29, Sept. 30.
RUTHERFORD'S CREEK, 1863, Mar. 10.
RUTLEDGE, 1864, Nov. 18, 19.

S.

SABINE CITY, and CROSS ROADS, 1862, Oct. 17; 1864, Apr. 8.
SABINE PASS, 1862, Sept. 25; 1863, Jan. 21, Apr. 3, 18, Sept. 8, 12; 1864, May 24; 1865, May 25–27; —.
SACRAMENTO, 1861, Dec. 28.
SAILOR'S CREEK, 1865, Apr. 6.

SAINT ALBAN'S.
SAINT ANDREW'S BAY, and SOUND; —.
SAINT AUGUSTINE, 1862, Mar. 12, 21.
SAINT CATHERINE'S, 1863, July 29; 1864, Jan. 15.
SAINT CHARLES, Ark., 1862, June 13, 17.
SAINT CHARLES, Mo., 1864, June 27.
SAINT CLOUD.
SAINT FRANCIS'S RIVER, 1862, Nov. 29.
SAINT GEORGE.
SAINT JOHN'S, Fla., and ST. J.'S RIVER, 1862, Sept. 17, Oct. 3; 1864, Apr. 16, May 23; —.
SAINT JOHN'S, N. B., 1863, Dec. 6.
SAINT JOSEPH'S, 1861, Sept. 13; 1862, May 5.
SAINT LOUIS, 1861, Apr. 25, May 11.
SAINT MARK'S, 1864, Jan. 18, Feb. 20, 27, Mar. 1.
SAINT MARY'S, and ST. M. RIVER, 1862, Mar. 6, Oct. 26, Nov. 9; 1864, June 22; —.
SALATIA, 1864, Feb. 5.
SALEM, Ark., 1862, Mar. 16, 18.
SALEM, Ind., 1863, July 10.
SALEM, Miss., 1863, Oct. 8.
SALEM, Mo., 1861, Dec. 3; 1863, Sept. 12, 13.
SALEM, Tenn., 1863, Mar. 2; 1865, Mar. 13.
SALEM, Va., 1862, Nov. 5, 21; 1863, Apr. 29, Dec. 15–18; 1865, Mar. 12.
SALINEVILLE, 1863, July.
SALISBURY, N. C., 1865, Apr. 12; —. (Prison.)
SALISBURY, Tenn., 1862, Aug. 11.
SALKAHATCHIE, 1865, Jan. 24, Feb. 3.
SALT FORK, and S. LICK, 1863, Oct. 12, 13.
SALTPETRE CAVE, 1864, Feb. 3.
SALTVILLE, 1864, Oct. 2, Dec. 20.
SALURIA, 1861, Apr. 25.
SAMBRO HARBOR, N. S., 1863, Dec. 17.
SANDERSON, 1864, Feb. 20, 21.
SANDERSVILLE, 1864, Nov. 26.
SANDY HOOK, and RIVER, 1864, Aug. 11–13.
SANGSTER'S, 1863, Dec. 17.
SANTA FE, 1861, Nov. 6; 1862, Apr. 21.
SANTA ROSA ISLAND, 1861, Oct. 9.
SANTEE.
SARATOGA, 1861, Oct. 26.
SARTATIA.
SARTORIA, 1863, June 4.
SAULSBURY, 1863, Dec. 2.
SAVAGE'S STATION, 1862, June 29.
SAVANNAH, Ga., 1861, May 28; 1864, Dec. 10–21; —.
SAVANNAH, Tenn., 1862, Apr. 16.
SAVANNAH RIVER, 1862, Jan. 28; —.
SCAREY CREEK, HILL, and TOWN, 1861, July 17.
SCATTERSVILLE, 1862, July 10.
SCOTLAND, 1863, June 11.
SCOTTSVILLE, 1864, Jan. 28.
SEABROOK, and S. ISLAND, 1862, June, 1; 1864, July 1; —.
SEARCEY, 1862, May 17.
SEARED MOUNTAIN.

## BATTLES, ENGAGEMENTS, COLLISIONS, ETC. 677

SECESSIONVILLE, 1862, June 16.
SEDALIA, 1864, Oct. 15.
SELINA, 1863, Apr. 18.
SELMA, 1865, Apr. 2.
SEMMESPORT, 1864, Mar. 13, 14.
SENATOBIA, 1863, May 25.
SENECA, and S. MILLS, and STATION, and CREEK, 1861, June 14, Sept. 20; 1863, Mar. 21, June 11, Sept. 15.
SEVEN PINES, 1862, May 29–31.
SEVIERVILLE, 1864, Jan. 15, 27.
SEWALL'S POINT, 1861, May 19, Dec. 29; 1862, May 8; —.
SHADY GROVE, and S. SPRINGS, 1862, Aug. 28; 1864, May 5.
SHALLOTTE, and S. INLET, 1862, Oct. 22; 1865, Feb. 8.
SHANGHAI, 1861, Sept. 27.
SHANNONDALE.
SHARPSBURG, Ky., 1863, Oct. 18.
SHARPSBURG, Md., 1861, Dec. 11; 1862, Sept. 14, 15, 17, 29; 1863, July 10.
SHAWNEE MOUND, and TOWN, 1861, Dec. 17; 1862, Oct. 18; 1863, June 6; 1864, Aug. 13.
SHEFF'S MOUNTAIN, 1862, May 24.
SHELBINA, 1861, Sept. 4.
SHELBURNE, 1862, Sept. 15.
SHELBY FARM, 1862, Aug. 25, Oct. 23.
SHELBYVILLE, Ky., 1862, Oct. 1.
SHELBYVILLE, Tenn., 1863, Jan. 31, June 4, 24, 26, Oct. 6.
SHELL MOUND, 1863, Aug. 23.
SHENANDOAH, (The,) —.
SHEPHERDSTOWN, 1861, Sept. 13; 1862, Sept. 23, Oct. 1, 16, Nov. 25; 1863, July 16, 17.
SHEPHERDSVILLE, 1862, Sept. 7, 21.
SHERWOOD, 1863, May 18.
SHILOH, 1862, Mar. 2, 16, Apr. 6, 7; —.
SHIP ISLAND, 1861, May 22, Sept. 16, Dec. 4; —.
SHIP'S GAP, 1864, Oct. 16.
SHIPPENSBURG, 1863, June 24.
SHIPPING POINT, 1861, Dec. 9; 1862, Mar. 24, 28, Apr. 6, Sept. 30.
SHIRLEY'S FORD, 1862, Sept. 20.
SHORTER HILL.
SHREVEPORT, 1864, Mar. 16, Apr. 7–9.
SHUTER'S HILL.
SIBLEY'S LANDING, 1862, Oct. 7; 1863, Mar. 28.
SIKESTON, 1862, Feb. 28.
SILVER CREEK, 1862, Jan. 8.
SIMMSPORT, 1863, June 3, 4; 1864, Mar. 14.
SIMON'S BLUFF, 1862, June 21.
SINKING CREEK, 1862, Nov. 25.
SISTER'S FERRY, 1864, Dec. 7; 1865, Jan. 30.
SIX-MILE STATION, 1864, Aug. 18, 19.
SKEET, 1863, Mar. 4.
SKIDAWAY ISLAND, 1862, Mar. 25.
SKIPWITH LANDING, 1865, Jan. 8.

SLATE CREEK, 1863, June 11.
SLATER'S MILLS, and SLATERVILLE, 1862, May 7, 9.
SLAUGHTERSVILLE, and SLAUGHTER'S MOUNTAIN, 1862, Aug. 9, Sept. 3.
SMITH'S ISLAND, 1863, Aug. 3; 1865, Jan. 16.
SMITHFIELD, 1862, Mar. 6; 1863, Feb. 13, Sept. 15; 1864, Feb. 1, Apr. 12, Aug. 26–28; 1865, Mar. 19; —.
SMITHLAND, 1861, Sept. 25; 1864, Jan. 21.
SMITHSBURG, 1863, July 4.
SMITHVILLE, 1862, June 18; 1865, Jan. 16.
SMYRNA, 1863, July 26.
SNAKE CREEK GAP, 1864, May 9, Oct. 15.
SNICKER'S FERRY, and S. GAP, 1862, Oct. 13, 27, Nov. 2, 29; 1864, July 17–20, Aug. 13; —.
SNOWHILL, 1863, Apr. 2.
SNYDER'S BLUFF, 1863, May 21.
SOCIAL CIRCLE, 1864, Nov. 18.
SOMERSET, 1862, Jan. 19; 1863, Mar. 30, May 28.
SOMERVILLE, 1862, May 7; 1863, Mar. 29.
SOUTH ANNA, 1863, June 28; 1864, May 19–26; —.
SOUTH FORK, 1862, Nov. 9; 1864, Feb. 4, 13.
SOUTH MILLS, 1862, Apr. 15, 19, Sept. 4.
SOUTH MOUNTAIN, 1862, Sept. 14; 1863, June 21; —.
SOUTH QUAY, and S. SHOAL, 1863, Apr. 17, May 1, June 20.
SOUTHSIDE RAILROAD, —.
SOUTHWEST CREEK, and So. W. MOUNTAIN, 1862, Aug. 9, Dec. 13; —.
SOUTHWEST PASS, 1861, Oct. 11; 1862, Jan. 23;—.
SPANISH WELLS, and S. FORT, 1863, Mar. 13; 1865, Mar. 27, Apr. 8.
SPARTA, 1862, Apr. 19, Aug. 4; 1863, July 19, Nov. 26.
SPOONVILLE, 1864, Apr. 2.
SPORTING HILL, 1863, June 28, 30.
SPOTTSYLVANIA, 1863, Apr. 30; 1864, Feb. 28, May 7–13, 18; —.
SPRING HILL, 1863, Mar. 5; 1864, Nov. 29.
SPRINGFIELD, 1861, Aug. 5, 10, Oct. 25; 1862, Feb. 12, 13; 1863, Jan. 7, 8, Mar. 4; 1864, Feb. 2; —.
STAFFORD COURT HOUSE, 1862, Apr. 2.
STALEY'S CREEK, 1864, Dec. 17.
STANFORD, 1862, Oct. 14; 1863, July 31.
STANNARDSVILLE, 1864, Feb. 29.
STATISBOROUGH, 1864, Dec. 4.
STAUNTON, 1862, Apr. 26, May 9, June 21; 1864, June 6–10, 24, Sept. 26; 1865, Mar. 2; —.
STEUBENVILLE, 1863, Apr. 28.
STEVENS, and S. GAP, 1862, Apr. 12; 1863, Sept. 8.
STEVENSBURG, 1863, Nov. 8.
STEVENSON, 1862, Sept. 1; 1863, Aug. 30.
STEWART'S CREEK, and S. LANDING, 1862, Dec. 29, 30; 1864, Aug. 20.
STOCKTON, 1862, Aug. 9.

678   BATTLES, ENGAGEMENTS, COLLISIONS, ETC.

STONE BRIDGE, and RIVER, 1861, July 21; 1862, Dec. 30, 31; 1863, Jan. 1, 2, 30, May 9; —.
STONO RIVER, and INLET, 1863, Dec. 25; —.
STONE MOUNTAIN, 1864, Oct. 26.
STONY CREEK, and POINT, 1862, Apr. 2; 1864, May 5, June 28, Dec. 1; —.
STRASBURG, 1862, Mar. 13, 27, May 21, June 2; 1863, Feb. 26, Apr. 22; 1864, Oct. 9, 12, 19; —.
STRAW HILL, 1863, Feb. 23.
STRAWBERRY PLAINS, 1864, Jan. 10–18, Feb. 20, Aug. 14.
STURGEON, 1862, Sept. 22.
SUFFOLK, 1862, May 13, 18, Dec. 28; 1863, Jan. 30, Apr. 13–24, May 15, 16, July 3. 1864, Mar. 10; —.
SUGAR CREEK, 1862, Feb. 17, Mar. 6.
SUGAR LOAF MOUNTAIN, and S. VALLEY, 1864, May 13; 1862, Sept. 10; —.
SULLIVAN'S ISLAND, —.
SULPHUR SPRINGS, 1862, Aug. 23, 24; 1863, Nov. 8; 1864, Aug. 11.
SUMMERSET KNOB.
SUMMERSVILLE, Va., 1861, Aug. 10, 26, Sept. 10; 1862, July 24; 1863, Feb. 9, Nov. 15; 1864, Apr. 2.
SUMMERVILLE, Miss., 1862, Nov. 26; 1863, Dec. 21.
SUMMERVILLE, Tenn., 1863, Dec. 25.
SUMMIT POINT, 1864, Aug. 21.
SUMTER, 1865, Apr. 9.
SURREY COURT HOUSE, 1864, Sept. 24.
SUTHERLAND'S STATION, 1865, Apr. 3.
SUTTON, 1862, Jan. 9, Sept. 23.
SUWANEE RIVER, —.
SWALLOW'S BLUFF, 1863, Sept. 13.
SWANQUARTER, 1862, Nov. 1; 1863, Nov. 4.
SWANSBORO', 1862, Aug. 13.
SWIFT CREEK.
SYCAMORE CHURCH, 1864, Sept. 16.
SYKESVILLE, 1863, June 29.

T.

TAH-KAH-O-KUTY MOUNTAIN, 1864, Aug. 7.
TALLAHATCHIE, 1862, Dec. 1; 1863, Mar. 13;—.
TAMPA BAY, 1862, June 30, Nov. 3; 1863, May 8, Oct. 16; —.
TANGIPAHO, 1864, Dec. 1.
TAPPAHANNOCK, 1863, Feb. 25, May 30.
TARBORO', 1862, Nov. 4.
TARKEYTOWN, 1864, Oct. 28.
TAYLOR'S FORD, and T. RIDGE, and BAYOU, and CREEK, 1861, Nov. 10; 1862, Oct. 15; 1864, Feb. 23; 1865, Mar. 16.
TAYLORSVILLE, 1864, May 24.
TAZEWELL, 1862, Aug. 5, 6, 9; 1864, Jan. 26, May 7.
TECHE, 1863, Nov. 3.
TEBB'S BEND, 1863, July 4.

TELFORD, (see Tilford.)
TENALLYTOWN, 1864, July 11.
TENNESSEE RIVER, —.
TENSAS RIVER, —.
THE HATCHIE, —.
THE WILDERNESS, 1863, May 1–5; 1864, May 3–10; 1865, —.
THIBODEAUX, 1862, Oct. 28; 1863, June 23, 24.
THOMAS'S STATION, 1864, Nov. 28, Dec. 3.
THOMPSON'S HILL, and STATION, 1863, Mar. 4, May 1.
THORNTON'S GAP.
THOROUGHFARE GAP, and MOUNTAIN, 1862, Apr. 2, Oct. 17, 30, Nov. 3; 1863, May 29, Sept. 22; —.
THREE-MILE STATION, 1864, Jan. 14.
TICKFAU 1863, May 10.
TIGER CREEK, 1864, Apr. 29.
TILFORD, 1863, Sept. 9.
TILTON, 1861, July; 1864, Oct. 12.
TIPTONSVILLE, 1864, Feb. 17.
TODD'S TAVERN, 1864, May 7, 8.
TOLANDA, 1863, Oct. 29.
TOLOPOTOMY, 1864, May 31.
TOM BROOK, 1864, Oct. 9.
TOM CREEK, 1865, Feb. 20.
TOMBIGBEE RIVER, —.
TOMPKINSVILLE, 1862, July 7; 1863, Apr. 22.
TONEY'S CREEK.
TORTUGAS.
TRACY CITY, 1864, Jan. 20.
TRANTER'S CREEK, 1862, June 5.
TRENT RIVER, 1863, July 6.
TRENTON, N. C., 1862, May 14.
TRENTON, Tenn., 1862, Aug. 7, Dec. 20; 1863, Jan. 30, Sept. 8.
TREVILLIAN, 1864, June 11, 12.
TRINITY, 1862, July 24.
TRIPLETT'S BRIDGE, 1863, June 16.
TRIUNE, 1863, June 4, 9, 11; 1864, Sept. 3.
TULLAHOMA, 1863, June 25, July 1, Oct. 23.
TUNICA BEND, 1864, June 15.
TUNISVILLE, 1864, Jan. 14.
TUNNEL HILL, 1863, Nov. 23–25; 1864, Jan. 28, Feb. 8, 26, May 7; —.
TUPELO, 1863, May 6; 1864, July 13.
TURKEY BEND, and T. ISLAND, and T. ROOST, 1862, July 1, 20; 1864, May 6, Dec. 5.
TUSCALOOSA, 1865, Apr. 4.
TUSCON, 1862, June 7.
TUSCUMBIA, 1862, Dec. 4, 13; 1863, Feb. 22, Apr. 24, Oct. 26.
TYBEE ISLAND, 1861, Nov. 24; —.

U.

UNION, and U. CHURCH, 1862, June 8, Nov. 2.
UNION CITY, 1862, Mar. 30; 1864, Mar. 24.
UNION MILLS, 1861, July 21; 1862, Aug. 20.

BATTLES, ENGAGEMENTS, COLLISIONS, ETC.     679

UNIONVILLE, 1863, Mar. 7.
UPPERVILLE, 1863, June 21, Sept. 25, Nov. 3; 1864, Feb. 26.
UPTON'S HILL, 1861, Sept. 28, Oct. 12.
URBANA, 1861, Nov.; 1862, Apr. 14, Nov. 26.

V.

VALVERDE, 1862, Feb. 21.
VAN BUREN, 1862, Oct. 22, Dec. 28; 1863, Jan. 28.
VANDALIA, 1863, Aug. 31.
VAUGHAN ROAD, 1865, Mar. 29, 31.
VAUGHT'S HILL, 1863, Mar. 20.
VENICE, 1863, July 13.
VENUS POINT, 1862, Feb. 15.
VERMILLIONVILLE, 1863, Apr. 17, Oct. 4, 8, 9, 21, Nov. 20.
VERNON, 1863, July 11.
VERONA, 1864, Dec. 25.
VERSAILLES, 1862, Sept. 2, Oct. 11.
VICKSBURG, 1862, May 12, June 26–29, July 1–22, Dec. 27–Jan. 2, 1863; 1863, Jan. 20, 22, Feb. 18, Mar. 25, Apr. 16, May 12–27, June 1–July 4; —.
VIDALIA, 1863, Sept. 15; 1864, Feb. 7
VIENNA, 1861, June 17, Nov. 26, Dec. 3; 1863, July 11.
VILLAGE CREEK, 1862, June 12, 27.
VIOLET STATION.

W.

WACHITA, 1863, Feb. 10.
WADDELL FARM, 1862, June 12.
WADE'S POINT, 1863, July 5.
WALDRON, 1864, Jan. 29.
WALKER'S FORD, 1863, Dec. 2.
WALKERTOWN, 1863, June 4; 1864, Mar. 1.
WALLEN CREEK, 1862, Nov. 19.
WALNUT CREEK, and W. HILLS, 1863, May 21; 1864, Nov. 19.
WAPPING HEIGHTS, (see Manassas,) 1863, July 24.
WARDENSVILLE, 1862, May 20, 29.
WARE'S BOTTOM CHURCH.
WARM SPRINGS.
WARRENSBURG, 1861, Nov. 18; 1862, Mar. 26, 28, Dec. 11.
WARRENTON, Miss., 1863, Mar. 21–27, May 7.
WARRENTON, Va., 1862, Apr. 1, July 29, Aug. 23, Sept. 26, 28, Oct. 24, Nov. 5–20, Dec. 1; 1863, Feb. 1, May 3, 14, Oct. 21, 31; 1864, Feb. 22; —.
WARRINGTON, 1861, Nov. 22, 23; 1862, Jan. 1.
WARSAW, 1861, Sept. 24, Oct. 16, Nov. 19; 1832, Feb. 16.
WARSAW SOUND, 1863, June 17; —.
WARTRACE, 1863, June 25.
WARWICK, and W. RIVER, 1861, Nov. 22; 1862, Apr. 16; 1863, June 5; —.
WASH CHANNEL, 1863, Jan. 19.

WASHINGTON, D. C., 1864, July 11, 12.
WASHINGTON, La., 1863, May 4.
WASHINGTON, N. C., 1862, Mar. 21, May 9, Sept. 6; 1863, Mar. 30, Apr. 5, 15, Nov. 1, 28, Dec. 31; —.
WASHINGTON, O., 1863, July 24.
WASHITA RIVER, —.
WASSAU, —.
WATAUGA, 1861, Nov. 10; 1862, Dec.
WATER LICK CREEK, 1865, Feb. 15.
WATERFORD, 1862, Mar. 8, Aug. 27.
WATERLOO BRIDGE, 1862, Aug. 24.
WATERPROOF, 1864, Feb. 14.
WATERVALLEY, 1862, Dec. 4.
WATSON'S FORD, 1863, Dec. 2.
WATT'S CREEK, 1862, Apr. 1.
WAUHATCHIE, 1863, Oct. 29; —.
WAVERLEY, 1862, Oct. 23; 1863, Apr. 10.
WAYNE COURT HOUSE, 1861, Aug. 25, 27; 1864, Feb. 14, Apr. 14.
WAYNESBORO', 1864, Nov. 27, Dec. 4; 1865, Mar. 3.
WAYNESVILLE, 1863, Nov. 2.
WEBB'S CROSS ROADS.
WEBER FALLS, 1863, Apr. 24.
WELDON, and W. ROAD, 1864, June 22, 23, Aug. 21, 23; —.
WEST BAY, 1863, Dec. 11, 19; 1864, Feb. 17.
WEST BRANCH, 1863, Apr. 19.
WEST GULF, —.
WEST LIBERTY, 1861, Oct. 23.
WEST LICKING RIVER, 1862, Sept. 11.
WEST POINT, 1862, May 7; 1863, June 24; 1864, Feb. 20, 21, Aug. 14, 15; 1865, Apr. 16; —.
WESTMINSTER, 1862, Sept. 11; 1863, June 29; 1864, July 9.
WESTPORT, 1863, June 17; 1864, Oct. 23.
WET GLAZE, 1861, Oct. 13.
WHEATLAND, 1862, Mar. 8.
WHEDON.
WHEELING, 1861, May.
WHIP-POOR-WILL BRIDGE, 1861, Dec. 4.
WHIPPY SWAMP, 1865, Feb. 2.
WHITAKER'S MILL, 1863, Oct. 11.
WHITE HOUSE, 1862, May 10, June 27; 1863, Jan. 8, May 7, July 9; 1864, June 20, 24; —.
WHITE OAK CREEK, BRIDGE, ROAD, and SWAMP, 1862, June 28, 30, July 1, Aug. 19; 1863, Aug. 5; 1865, Mar. 31.
WHITE PLAINS, 1863, Sept. 16.
WHITE POINT, 1864, July 2
WHITE RIVER, 1862, May 22, June 17, Aug. 4; 1863, Dec. 9; 1864, Apr. 1, June 22, 24, Sept. 4, 14; —.
WHITE STONE HILL, 1863, Sept. 3, 5.
WHITE SULPHUR SPRINGS, 1863, Aug. 26, 30.
WHITE TAVERN, 1864, Aug. 16.

BATTLES, ENGAGEMENTS, COLLISIONS, ETC.

WHITE'S FORD, 1862, Oct. 12.
WHITEHALL, 1862, Dec. 16.
WHITEMARSH ISLAND, 1862, Apr. 9.
WIGGINSTON'S MILLS, 1863, Feb. 5.
WILCOX'S LANDING, 1864, June 13; —.
WILD CAT, 1861, Oct. 21.
WILDERNESS, 1863, May 1-5; 1864, May 3-10; 1865; —.
WILKINSON'S PIKE, 1864, Dec. 7.
WILLIAM'S BRIDGE, 1862, June 27.
WILLIAMSBURG, 1862, May 5, 6, July 11, Sept. 9, Nov. 10; 1863, Feb. 7, Apr. 12, July 7, 13, 14;—.
WILLIAMSPORT, 1861, June 1, July 2, Dec. 8; 1862, Mar. 13, May 26, July 4, Aug. 11; 1863, July 6, 13, 14, Dec. 29; 1864, Jan. 28; —.
WILLIAMSTOWN, 1862, Nov. 2; 1863, July 13.
WILLIS' CHURCH.
WILLOUGHBY POINT, 1862, May 10.
WILMINGTON, and ISLAND, and RIVER, 1861, Dec. 5; 1862, Mar. 25, Apr. 16; 1865, Jan. 20-22, Feb. 11-22; —.
WILSON'S CREEK, 1861, Aug. 10; 1863, June 13.
WILSON'S FARM, and MILL, 1861, Sept. 27.
WINCHESTER, KY., 1863, Feb. 23, July 30.
WINCHESTER, VA., 1861, July 21; 1862, Mar. 12, 23, May 25, Sept. 3, Nov. 24, Dec. 4, 23; 1863, May 19, June 14, Oct. 13; 1864, Jan. 6, July 3, 18-24, Sept. 13, 19; —.
WINDSOR, 1864, Jan. 29.
WINFIELD, 1861, Oct. 12; 1864, Oct. 26.
WINSBURG, 1863, Mar. 29.
WINSTON'S GAP, 1863, Sept. 8.
WINTON, 1862, Feb. 20.
WIREMAN'S SHOALS, 1862, Dec. 14.
WISE'S FORD, and FORK, 1865, Mar. 9, 10.
WOLF RIVER BRIDGE, 1863, Jan. 11, Dec. 2, 5.

WOLFTOWN, 1862, Aug. 7.
WOOD'S FORK, 1862, Jan. 11.
WOODBRIDGE HILL.
WOODBURN, 1863, Feb. 26, May 12.
WOODBURY, 1861, Oct. 29; 1863, Jan. 26, Apr. 2, May 26.
WOODSONVILLE, 1861, Dec. 17; 1862, Dec. 14.
WOODSTOCK, 1862, Apr. 1.
WOODVILLE, 1862, Oct. 21; 1863, Aug. 9; 1864, Oct. 8.
WORTHINGTON, 1861, Sept. 2.
WRIGHTSVILLE, 1863, June 27-29.
WYATT'S, 1863, Oct. 13.
WYTHEVILLE, 1863, July 18, 24; 1864, May 10, Dec. 14, 16; 1865, Mar. 14.

Y.

YAZOO CITY, and PASS, 1863, Feb. 20, May 13, 24, July 13; 1864, Feb. 5, 9, 28, Mar. 5, 6, Apr. 23, May 10; —.
YELLOW BAYOU, Y. BLUFF, Y. CREEK, and Y. TAVERN, 1862, Aug. 13; 1864, May 11, 18.
YELLOW MEDICINE RIVER, 1862, Sept. 23.
YELLVILLE, 1862, Nov. 30.
YORK, PA., 1863, June 27, 30.
YORK RIVER, —.
YORKTOWN, 1862, Apr. 5, 11, 16, 18, 24, 26, May 4; —.
YOUNG SQUIRREL CHURCH.
YOUNG'S CROSS ROADS, and MILLS, 1862, Apr. 7, July 26.
YOUNG'S ISLAND, 1865, Feb. 1.

Z.

ZOLLICOFFER'S HEIGHTS, 1863, Oct. 11.
ZUNI, 1862, Nov. 25, Dec. 12.

# LIST OF THE PUBLIC VESSELS
## TO WHICH THE NAVAL AND SIMILAR ANECDOTES IN THIS WORK RELATE.

### A.
A. Houghton,
A. C. Powell,
A. O. Tyler,
Abraham,
Acacia,
Adela,
Adirondack,
Adolph Hugel,
Agamenticus,
Agawam,
Aiken,
Alabama,
Albatross,
Albemarle,
Alert,
Alexandria,
Alfred Robb,
Algonquin,
Alice Dean,
Alleghany,
Amanda,
America,
Ammonoosuc,
Anacostia,
Anderson,
Anna,
Annie,
Antietam,
Antona,
Arago,
Arapoho,
Argosy,
Ariel,
Aries,
Arizona,
Arkansas,
Arletta,
Aroostook,
Arthur,
Ascutney,
Ashuelot,
Atlanta,
Atlantic,
Augusta,
Augusta Dinsmore.

### B.
Bainbridge,
Baltic,
Baltimore,
Banshee,
Baron de Kalb,
Barrataria,
Bat,
Beauregard,
Belvidere,
Ben Deford,
Ben Morgan,
Benton,
Bermuda,
Bienville,
Blackbird,
Black Hawk,
Bloomer,
Bohio,
Bombshell,
Boston,
Brandywine,
Braziliera,
Brilliant,
Britannia,
Brooklyn.

### C.
C. P. Williams,
Cahawba,
Cairo,
Caleb Cushing,
Calhoun,
Calypso,
Camanche,
Cambridge,
Camellia,
Canada,
Canandaigua,
Canonicus,
Carmita,
Carnation,
Carondelet,
Casco,
Catawba,
Catskill,
Cayuga,
Ceres,
Champion,
Charles Phelps,
Charlotte,
Chattanooga,
Chenango,
Chickasaw,
Chicopee,
Chicora,
Chillicothe,
Chimo,
Chippewa,
Choctaw,
Chocura,
Chotank,
Cimmarron,
Cincinnati,
Circassian,
Clara Dolsen,
Clifton,
Clover,
Clyde,
Cœur de Lion,
Cohasset,
Cohoes,
Colorado,
Columbia,
Columbine,
Commodore,
Commodore Barney,
Commodore Hull,
Commodore Jones,
Commodore McDonough,
Commodore Morris,
Commodore Perry,
Commodore Read,
Conemaugh,
Conestoga,
Congress,
Connecticut,
Constellation,
Constitution,
Contoocook,
Corwin,
Corypheus,
Courier,
Covington,
Cowslip,
Cricket,
Crocus,
Crusader,
Cumberland,
Curlew,
Currituck,
Cyane.

### D.
Dacotah,
Daffodil,
Dahlia,
Dai-Ching,
Daisy,
Dale,
Dan,
Dan Smith,
Dandelion,
Darlington,
Dart,
Dawn,
Daylight,
Decatur,
Delaware,
De Soto,
Diana,
Dictator,
Dolphin,
Don,
Dragon,
Dunderberg.

### E.
E. B. Hale,
Eastport,
Ella,
Ellen,
Ellis,
Emma,
Empire City,
Eolus,
Era,
Essex,

682 LIST OF PUBLIC VESSELS.

ESTRELLA,
ETHAN ALLEN,
ETLAH,
EUGENIE,
EUREKA,
EUTAW,
EXCHANGE.

**F.**

FAHKEES,
FAIR PLAY,
FALMOUTH,
FANNY,
FARALLONES,
FAWN,
FEAR NOT,
FERN,
FERNANDINA,
FLAG,
FLAMBEAU,
FLORIDA,
FOREST ROSE,
FORT DONELSON,
FORT HENRY,
FORT HINDMAN,
FORT JACKSON,
FORT MORGAN,
FOX,
FRANKLIN,
FREDONIA,
FUCHSIA,
FULTON.

**G.**

G. L. BROCKENBOROUGH,
G. W. BLUNT.
GALATEA,
GALENA,
GEM OF THE SEA,
GEMSBOK,
GENERAL BRAGG,
GENERAL HOWARD,
GENERAL LYON,
GENERAL PILLOW,
GENERAL PUTNAM,
GENERAL STERLING
GENESEE,            [PRICE,
GEORGE MANGHAM,
GEORGE PEABODY,
GERANIUM,
GERMANTOWN,
GERTRUDE,
GETTYSBURG,
GLAUCUS,
GLIDE,
GORDON,
GOVERNOR,
GOVERNOR BUCKINGHAM,

GRAND DUKE,
GRAND GULF,
GRANITE,
GRANITE CITY,
GREAT WESTERN,
GUERRIERE.

**H.**

HARRIET LANE,
HARTFORD,
HARVEST MOON,
HASSALA,
HASTINGS,
HATTERAS,
HELIOTROPE,
HENDRIK HUDSON,
HENRIETTA,
HENRY ANDREW,
HENRY BRINKER,
HENRY CLAY,
HENRY JAMES,
HETZEL,
HIBISCUS,
HIGHLANDER,
HOLLYHOCK,
HOME,
HOMER,
HONDURAS,
HONEYSUCKLE,
HOPE,
HORACE BEALS,
HOUQUA,
HOUSATONIC,
HUNCHBACK,
HUNTSVILLE,
HURON,
HUZZAR,
HYACINTH,
HYDRANGEA.

**I.**

I. N. SEYMOUR,
IDA,
IDAHO,
ILLINOIS,
INDEPENDENCE,
INDIANOLA.
INO,
ION,
IOSCO,
IRIS,
IRON AGE,
IROQUOIS,
ISAAC SMITH,
ISABEL,
ISLAND BELLE,
ITUSCA,
IVY,

IZILDA.

**J.**

J. C. KUHN,
J. S. MACOMB,
JACOB BELL,
JAMES ADGER,
JAMES L. DAVIS,
JAMES S. CHAMBERS,
JAMESTOWN,
JASMINE,
JAVA,
JEFF. DAVIS,
JOHN ADAMS,
JOHN GRIFFITH,
JOHN HANCOCK,
JOHN L. LOCKWOOD,
JOHN P. JACKSON,
JONQUIL,
JOSIAH BELL,
JUDAH,
JUDGE TORRENCE,
JULIA,
JULIET,
JUNIATA,
JUNIPER.

**K.**

KAKA,
KANAWHA,
KANSAS,
KATAHDIN,
KAWANEE,
KEARSARGE,
KENNEBEC,
KENSINGTON,
KENTUCKY,
KENWOOD,
KEOKUK,
KEOSAUQUA,
KEWANEE,
KEWAYDIN,
KEY WEST,
KEYSTONE STATE,
KICKAPOO,
KINEO,
KING PHILIP,
KINGFISHER,
KINSMAN,
KITTATINNY,
KLAMATH,
KOSCIUSCO,
KUHN.

**L.**

LACKAWANNA,
LADONA,
LAFAYETTE,

LANCASTER,
LARKSPUR,
LAUREL,
LEHIGH,
LENAPEE,
LESLIE,
LEVIATHAN,
LEWIS CASS,
LEXINGTON,
LILAC,
LILLIAN,
LILY,
LINDEN,
LIONESS,
LITTLE ADA,
LITTLE REBEL,
LOCKWOOD,
LODONA,
LOUISIANA,
LOUISVILLE,
LUPIN.

**M.**

M. J. CARLTON,
MACEDONIAN,
MACKINAW,
MADAWASKA,
MADGIE,
MAGNOLIA,
MAHASKA,
MAHOPAC,
MANAYUNK,
MANHATTAN,
MANITTO,
MAPLE LEAF,
MARATANZA,
MARBLEHEAD,
MARCELLA,
MARIA A. WOOD,
MARIETTA,
MARIGOLD,
MARINER,
MARION,
MARMORA,
MARY SANFORD,
MASSACHUSETTS,
MASSASOIT,
MATTABESETT,
MATTHEW VASSAR,
MAUMEE,
McCLELLAN,
MEMPHIS,
MENDOTA,
MERCEDITA,
MERCURY,
MERRIMAC,
METACOMET,
MIAMI,

# LIST OF PUBLIC VESSELS. 683

Miantonomah,
Michigan,
Midnight,
Mignonette,
Milwaukee,
Mingoe,
Minnesota,
Mississippi,
Mistletoe,
Mobile,
Moduc,
Mohawk,
Mohican,
Mohongo,
Molly Martin,
Monadnock,
Monarch,
Mondamin,
Monitor,
Monocacy,
Monongahela,
Montauk,
Monterey,
Montgomery,
Monticello,
Moose,
Morning Light,
Morse,
Mosholu,
Mound City,
Mount Vernon,
Mount Washington,
Muscoota,
Myrtle,
Mystic.

## N.

Nahant,
Nansemond,
Nantucket,
Napa,
Narcissus,
Narragansett,
Nashville,
National Guard,
Naumkeag,
Nausett,
Nemaha,
Neosho,
Neptune,
Nereus,
Neshaminy,
Nettle,
New Era,
New Ironsides,
New London,
New National,
New Orleans,

New York,
Newbern,
Niagara,
Nightingale,
Niphon,
Nipsic,
Nita,
Norfolk Packet,
North Carolina,
Norwich,
Nyack,
Nyanza.

## O.

O. M. Pettit,
Octorara,
Ohio,
Oleander,
Oliver H. Lee,
Oneida,
Oneota,
Onondaga,
Ontario,
Onward,
Orvetta,
Osage,
Osceola,
Ossipee,
Otsego,
Ottawa,
Ouachita,
Owasco,
Ozark.

## P.

Pacific,
Pampero,
Panola,
Pansy,
Para,
Passaconaway,
Passaic,
Patapsco,
Patroon,
Paul Jones,
Paw Paw,
Pawnee,
Pawtuxet,
Peerless,
Pembina,
Pembroke,
Penguin,
Pennsylvania,
Penobscot,
Pensacola,
Peoria,
Pequot,
Periwinkle,

Perry,
Peterhoff,
Petrel,
Philadelphia,
Pinola,
Pinta,
Piscataqua,
Pittsburg,
Planter,
Plymouth,
Pocahontas,
Pompanoosuc,
Pontiac,
Pontoosuc,
Poppy,
Port Royal,
Portsmouth,
Potomac,
Potomska,
Powhatan,
Prairie Bird,
Preble,
Primrose,
Princess Royal,
Princeton,
Proteus,
Pulaski,
Puritan,
Pursuit,
Pushmataha.

## Q.

Quaker City,
Queen,
Queen City,
Queen of the West,
Quinsigamond.

## R.

R. B. Forbes,
R. R. Cuyler,
Racer,
Rachel Seaman,
Raritan,
Rattler,
Red Rover,
Reindeer,
Release,
Reliance,
Relief,
Remington,
Renshaw,
Republic,
Rescue,
Resolute,
Restless,
Retribution,
Rettimar,

Rhode Island,
Richmond,
River Queen,
Roanoke,
Robert McLelland,
Rocket,
Roebuck,
Roman,
Romeo,
Rosalie,
Royal Yacht.

## S.

S. R. Spaulding,
Sabine,
Sachem,
Saco,
Sacramento,
Sagamore,
Saginaw,
Saint Clair,
Saint Lawrence,
Saint Louis,
Saint Mary's,
Sam Houston,
Samson,
Samuel Rotan,
San Jacinto,
Sandusky,
Sangamon,
Santee,
Santiago de Cuba,
Sarah Bruen,
Saranac,
Saratoga,
Sassacus,
Satellite,
Saugus,
Savannah,
Sciota,
Sea Bird,
Sea Foam,
Sebago,
Seminole,
Seneca,
Shakamaxon,
Shamokin,
Shamrock,
Shark,
Shawmut,
Shawnee,
Shawseen,
Shenandoah,
Shepherd Knapp,
Shiloh,
Shokokon,
Sidney C. Jones,
Signal,

## LIST OF PUBLIC VESSELS.

SILVER CLOUD,
SILVER LAKE,
SLIDELL,
SMITH BRIGGS,
SNOWDROP,
SOMERSET,
SONOMA,
SOPHRONIA,
SOUTH CAROLINA,
SOUTHFIELD,
SOVEREIGN,
SPIREA,
SPRINGFIELD,
SQUANDO,
STAR,
STAR OF THE SOUTH,
STAR OF THE WEST,
STARS AND STRIPES,
STATE OF GEORGIA,
STEPPING STONES,
STETTIN,
STONEWALL,
SULTANA,
SUMTER,
SUNCOOK,
SUNFLOWER,
SUPPLY,
SUSQUEHANNA,
SUWANEE,
SWEET BRIER,
SWITZERLAND.

**T.**

T. A. WARD,
TACONY,
TAHGAYUTA,
TAHOMA,
TALLAHOMA,
TALLAPOOSA,
TAWAH,
TEASER,
TECUMSEH,
TENNESSEE,
TENSAS,
THISTLE,
THOMAS COLYER,
THOMAS FREEBORN,
TICONDEROGA,
TIME,
TIOGA,
TIPPECANOE,
TONAWANDA,
TREFOIL,
TRISTRAM SHANDY,
TRITONIA,
TUSCARORA,
TUSCUMBIA,
TWO SISTERS,
TYLER.

**U.**

UMPQUA,
UNADILLA,
UNCAS,
UNCLE BEN,
UNDERWRITER,
UNION,
UNITED STATES.

**V.**

VALLEY CITY,
VALPARAISO,
VANDALIA,
VANDERBILT,
VARUNA,
VERMONT,
VICKSBURG,
VICTORIA,
VICTORY,
VINCENNES,
VIOLET,
VIRGINIA,
VIXEN.

**W.**

W. G. PUTNAM,
W. H. BROWN,
W. W. COIT,
WABASH,
WACHUSETT,
WAMPONOAG,
WAMSUTTA,
WANALOSET,
WANDERER,
WANDO,
WAPPING HEIGHTS,
WARREN,
WASHINGTON,
WASSUC,
WATAUGE,
WATER WITCH,
WATEREE,
WAXSAW,
WEEHAWKEN,
WE-NO-SHEPOKES-SLOW,
WEST POINT,
WESTERN WORLD,
WESTFIELD,
WHITEHALL,
WHITEHEAD,
WILDERNESS,
WILLIAM BACON,
WILLIAM BADGER,
WILLIAM G. ANDERSON.
WILLIAM H. WEBB,
WILLIAMETTE,
WINNEBAGO,
WINNIPEC,
WINONA,
WINOOSKI,
WISSAHICKON,
WYALUSING,
WYANDANK,
WYANDOTTE,
WYOMING.

**Y.**

YANKEE,
YANTIC,
YAZOO,
YORK,
YOUNG AMERICA,
YOUNG ROVER,
YUMA.

**Z.**

ZOUAVE.

# NAMES OF THE CHIEF LAND AND NAVAL OFFICERS,

## NORTH AND SOUTH,

UNDER WHOSE COMMAND, OR IN WHOSE DEPARTMENTS, THE ANECDOTICAL INCIDENTS, &c., HERE GIVEN, OCCURRED.

**A.**

Abbott,
Abercrombie,
Adams,
Albright,
Alden,
Allen,
Almy,
Alvord,
Ames,
Ammen,
Anderson,
Andrews,
Archer,
Armistead,
Armstrong,
Arnold,
Asboth,
Atchison,
Atkins,
Augur,
Aulick,
Averell,
Ayres.

**B.**

Bailey,
Baily,
Baird,
Baker,
Balch,
Baldwin,
Ball,
Ballier,
Bankhead,
Banks,
Barlow,
Barnard,
Barnes,
Barnett,
Barnum,
Barron,
Barry,
Bartlett,
Barton,
Bartow,
Bassett,
Bate,
Bates,
Battle,
Baxter,
Bayard,
Beal,
Beatty,
Beaumont,
Beauregard,
Beaver,
Beckwith,
Bee,
Belknap,
Bell,
Benham,
Bennett,
Benning,
Benton,
Berrien,
Berry,
Beveridge,
Biddle,
Bidwell,
Birge,
Birney,
Bissell,
Blackman,
Blair,
Blake,
Blenker,
Blunt,
Boarman,
Boggs,
Bohlen,
Boss,
Bowen,
Bowers,
Bowl,
Boyle,
Bradley,
Bragg,
Braine,
Branch,
Branson,
Brasher,
Brattan,
Brayman,
Breckinridge,
Breese,
Brewster,
Brice,
Briggs,
Brisbin,
Brook,
Brooks,
Broome,
Brown,
Bryan,
Bryant,
Bryson,
Buchanan,
Buckingham,
Buckland,
Buckner,
Buel,
Buford,
Bullin,
Burbridge,
Burns,
Burnside,
Burr,
Bussey,
Busteed,
Butler,
Butterfield.

**C.**

Cabell,
Cadwallader,
Caldwell,
Cameron,
Campbell,
Canby,
Carleton,
Carlin,
Carr,
Carrington,
Carroll,
Carson,
Carter,
Case,
Casement,
Casey,
Chalmers,
Chamberlain,
Chambers,
Chambliss,
Champlin,
Chapin,
Chapman,
Chauncey,
Cheatham,
Chetlain,
Christ,
Chrysler,
Churchill,
Clanter,
Clanton,
Clark,
Clary,
Clay,
Clayton,
Cleburne,
Clingman,
Clitz,
Cluseret,
Cobb,
Cochrane,
Cocke,
Cockerill,
Cogswell,
Cohen,
Coleman,
Colgrave,
Colhoun,

# NAMES OF GENERALS AND NAVAL COMMANDERS.

COLLIER,
COLLINS,
COLLIS,
COLOOCOREOSIS,
COLSTON,
COMMAGER,
COMSTOCK,
CONNOR,
CONOVER,
COOK,
COOKE,
COOPER,
COPELAND,
CORBIN,
CORBY,
CORCORAN,
CORSE,
COUCH,
COULTER,
COWDIN,
COX,
CRABBE,
CRAFT,
CRAIG,
CRAVEN,
CRAWFORD,
CREIGHTON,
CRITTENDEN,
CROCKER,
CROFTON,
CROOK,
CROSBY,
CROXTON,
CRUFT,
CULLUM,
CUMMING,
CURTIN,
CURTIS,
CUSHING,
CUSTAR,
CUTLER.

## D.

DAGGETT,
DAHLGREN,
DANA,
DAVENPORT,
DAVIDSON,
DAVIES,
DAVIS,
DAWSON,
DEARING,
DEAS,
DEBRAY,
DE CAMP,
DE COURCEY,
DEITZLER,
DENISON,

DENNIS,
DENVIR,
DETROBRIAND,
DEVENS,
DEVINE,
DIVEN,
DIX,
DODGE,
DONALDSON,
DOOLITTLE,
DORNIX,
DORUBLEZER,
DOUBLEDAY,
DOVE,
DOW,
DOWNES,
DRAKE,
DRAPER,
DRAYTON,
DRESSY,
DUDLEY,
DUFFIE,
DUFFIELD,
DUKE,
DUMONT,
DUNCAN,
DUNNOVAN,
DUPONT,
DURYEE,
DUVAL,
DWIGHT.

## E.

EAGAN,
EAGLE,
EARLY,
EASTON,
EATON,
EDWARDS
EKIN,
ELLET,
ELLIOTT,
ELLSWORTH,
ELZEY,
EMMONS,
EMORY,
ENGLE,
EUSTIS,
EVANS,
EWELL,
EWING.

## F.

FAGAN,
FAIRFAX,
FARNSWORTH,
FARRAGUT,
FARRAN,

FEARING,
FEBIGER,
FENDALL,
FERGUSON,
FERRERO,
FERRY,
FESSENDEN,
FIELD,
FINNEGAN,
FISK,
FITCH,
FLOYD,
FONTANE,
FOOTE,
FORCE,
FORD,
FORREST,
FORSYTH,
FOSTER,
FRAILEY,
FRANKLIN,
FREMONT,
FRENCH,
FRONEN,
FROST,
FRY,
FULLER,
FURGUSON.

## G.

GAINES,
GAMBLE,
GANSEVOORT,
GANTT,
GARDNER,
GARFIELD,
GARNETT,
GARRARD,
GARTRELL,
GARY,
GEARY,
GERSHAM,
GETTY,
GHOLSON,
GIBBON,
GIBBS,
GIBSON,
GILBERT,
GILLEM,
GILLESPIE,
GILLIS,
GILLMORE,
GIST,
GLASGOW,
GLASSON,
GLENDY,
GLISSON,
GLYNN,

GODON,
GOLDSBOROUGH,
GOODING,
GORDON,
GORMAN,
GOVAN,
GRAHAM,
GRANBURY,
GRANGER,
GRANT,
GRAYSON,
GREENE,
GREER,
GREGG,
GREGORY,
GRESHAM,
GRIERSON,
GRIFFIN,
GROSE,
GROVER,
GUEST,
GWYN.

## H.

HACKELMAN,
HAGGERTY,
HAGOOD,
HALL,
HALLECK,
HAMBLIN,
HAMILTON,
HAMLIN,
HAMMOND,
HAMPTON,
HANCOCK,
HANDY,
HARDEE,
HARDIE,
HARDIN,
HARKER,
HARLAND,
HARNEY,
HARRELL,
HARRIS,
HARRISON,
HARROW,
HART,
HARTRANFT,
HARTSUFF,
HARTWELL,
HARWOOD,
HASCALL,
HASKIN,
HATCH,
HAUPT,
HAWKINS,
HAWLEY,
HAYES,

## NAMES OF GENERALS AND NAVAL COMMANDERS.

Haywood,
Hazard,
Hazen,
Heath,
Hebb,
Hebert,
Heckman,
Heintzelman,
Henderson,
Henry,
Herbert,
Herron,
Heth,
Higgen,
Hill,
Hindman,
Hinks,
Hitchcock,
Hobart,
Hobson,
Hodge,
Hoff,
Hoffan,
Hoffman,
Hoke,
Hollins,
Holmes,
Holtzelaw,
Hood,
Hooker,
Hopkins,
Horn,
Hovey,
Howard,
Howe,
Howell,
Hubbard,
Huger,
Hughes,
Hull,
Hume,
Humphreys,
Hunt,
Hunter,
Hunton,
Hurlbut.

### I.
Imboden,
Ingalls,
Ingraham,
Inman,
Innes,
Iverson.

### J.
Jackman,
Jackson,
Jameson,
Jamesson,
Jarvis,
Jenkins,
Johnson,
Johnston,
Jones,
Jourdan,
Judah.

### K.
Kæmerlino,
Kane,
Kautz,
Kearny,
Keifer,
Keim,
Kelley,
Kemper,
Kenly,
Kershaw,
Ketchum,
Keyes,
Kilpatrick,
Kilty,
Kimball,
King,
Kingsbury,
Kintzing,
Kirby,
Kirk,
Kirkland,
Kitching,
Knipe,
Koltes,
Krzyzanowski.

### L.
Lander
Lane,
Lanier,
Laman,
Lardner,
Latimer,
Lauman,
Lavellette,
Lawler,
Ledlie,
Lee,
Leggett,
Leroy,
Lewis,
Liddell,
Lightburn,
Lincoln,
Linch,
Littlefield,
Livingstone,

Lippincott,
Littell,
Lockwood,
Logan,
Lomax,
Long,
Longstreet,
Loring,
Love,
Lovell,
Lowe,
Lowell,
Lowndes,
Lucas,
Ludlow,
Lynch,
Lyon,
Lytle.

### M.
Macey,
Madill,
Macomb,
Maffitt,
Maggi,
Magruder,
Mahone,
Maltby,
Maney,
Manigalt,
Mansfield,
Manson,
Marchand,
Marcy,
Marin,
Marmaduke,
Martindale,
Marshall,
Marston,
Mason,
Matthias,
Maury,
Maxcy,
McAllister,
McArthur,
McBride,
McCall,
McCauley,
McCausland,
McClellan,
McClernand,
McCluney,
McCook,
McCraig,
McCrellis,
McCulloch,
McDougall,
McDowell,

McGinnis,
McGowan,
McIntosh,
McKean,
McKenzie,
McKibben,
McKinstry,
McLaughlin.
McLaws,
McLean,
McMillan,
McMullen,
McNeil,
McPherson,
McRae,
Meade,
Meagher,
Meigs,
Mercer,
Meredith,
Merrill,
Merritt,
Mervine,
Middleton,
Miles,
Miller,
Milligan,
Milroy,
Missroon,
Mitchel,
Mitchell,
Mitchie,
Molineux,
Monigel,
Monroe,
Montgomery,
Moody,
Moore,
Morell,
Morgan,
Morris,
Morse,
Morton,
Mosby,
Mott,
Mouton,
Mower,
Mulford,
Mullany,
Mulligan,
Murray,
Myers.

### N.
Nagler,
Negley,
Neill,
Nelson,

NEWCOMB,
NEWTON,
NICHOLAS,
NICHOLS,
NICHOLSON,
NICKERSON

**O.**

OGDEN,
OGLESBY,
OLIVER,
OPDYKE,
ORD,
ORME,
OSBAND,
OSTERHAUS,
OWENS.

**P.**

PAINE,
PALMER,
PARDEE,
PARKER,
PARKES,
PARROTT,
PARSONS,
PATRICK,
PATTERSON,
PATTON,
PAUL,
PAULDING,
PAXTON,
PAYNE,
PEABODY,
PEARCE,
PEARSON,
PECK,
PEERCE,
PEGRAM,
PEMBERTON,
PENDER,
PENDERGRAST,
PENNOCK,
PENNYPACKER,
PENROSE,
PERING,
PERRY,
PETTIGREW,
PHELPS,
PHILLIPS,
PIATT,
PICKERING,
PIERCE,
PIKE,
PILE,
PILLOW,
PITCHER,
PLAISTED,

PLEASANTON,
PLUMMER,
POE,
POLK,
POOR,
POPE,
PORTER,
POTTER,
POTTS,
POWELL,
PRATT,
PREBLE,
PRENTISS,
PRESTON,
PRICE,
PRINCE,
PRITCHARD,
PRYOR,
PURVIANCE,
PUTNAM,
PYLE.

**Q.**

QUANTRILL,
QUARLES,
QUINBY.

**R.**

RADFORD,
RAINS,
RAMSAY,
RANSOM,
RAUM,
RAWLINGS,
READ,
REED,
REID,
REILLY,
RENO,
REVERE,
REYNOLDS,
RHIND,
RHODDY,
RHODES,
RICE,
RICHARDSON,
RICKETTS,
RIDGELEY,
RING,
RINGGOLD
RIPLEY,
RITCHIE,
RIVES,
ROBBINS,
ROBERTS,
ROBERTSON,
ROBINSON,
RODGERS,

RODMAN,
ROLANDO,
RONCKENDORFF,
ROSECRANS,
ROSS,
ROSSEAU,
ROSSER,
ROWAN,
ROWLEY,
RUCKER,
RUDD,
RUGER,
RUNYON,
RUSSELL,
RUST.

**S.**

SALOMON,
SALSMON,
SALTER,
SANBORN,
SANDERS,
SANFORD,
SARGEANT,
SARTORI,
SATTERLEE,
SAUNDERS,
SAXTON,
SCAMMON,
SCHEMMELFENNING,
SCHENCK,
SCHERMERHORN,
SCHOEPF,
SCHOFIELD,
SCRIBER,
SCHURZ,
SCOTT,
SCRIVER,
SEARS,
SEDGWICK,
SELFRIDGE,
SEMMES,
SEWARD,
SEYMOUR,
SHACKELFORD,
SHALER,
SHANKS,
SHARP,
SHAW,
SHELBY,
SHEPARD,
SHEPLEY,
SHERIDAN,
SHERMAN,
SHERWOOD,
SHIELDS,
SHIRAS,
SHIRLEY,

SHUBRICK,
SHUFELDT,
SHUNK,
SHUTTLEWORTH,
SIBLEY,
SICKLES,
SIGEL,
SIGFRIED,
SILL,
SIMONDS,
SINGLETON,
SLACK,
SLAUGHTER,
SLEMMER,
SLOAT,
SLOCUM,
SLOUGH,
SMITH,
SMYTH,
SORRELL,
SPEARS,
SPICER,
SPINOLA,
SPOTTS,
SPRAGUE,
STOCK,
STAHEL,
STANLEY,
STANNARD,
STARKWEATHER,
STEDMAN,
STEEDMAN,
STEELE,
STEIN,
STEINWEHR,
STELLWAGEN,
STEMBEL,
STEMMEN,
STEVENS,
STEPHENSON,
STEWART,
STILES,
STOLBRAUD,
STONE,
STONEMAN,
STORER,
STOUGHTON,
STOVALL,
STRAHL,
STRALBRAND,
STRIBLING,
STRINGHAM,
STRONG,
STROPHEL,
STUART,
STURGIS,
SULLIVAN,
SULLY,

SUMNER,
SWAIN,
SWAYNE,
SWARTWOUT,
SWEENY,
SWEET,
SYKES.

**T.**

TALIAFERRO,
TATNALL,
TAYLOR,
TEBBETTS,
TERRILL,
TERRY,
THATCHER,
THAYER,
THOMAS,
THOMPSON,
THURSTON,
TIBBITTS,
TIDBALL,
TILGHMAN,
TILLSON,
TILTON,
THOMPKINS,
TOOMBS,
TORBERT,
TOWER,
TOWNSEND,
TRACY,
TRENCHARD,
TROBRIAND,
TRUE,
TUCKER,
TURCHIN,
TURNER,
TUTTLE,
TWIGGS,
TYLER,
TYNDALE.

**U.**

UHMAN,
UNDERWOOD.

**V.**

VAN ALEN,
VAN BRUNT,
VAN CLEVE,
VAN DORN,
VAN VLEIT,
VAN WYCK,
VANDERVER,
VAUGHN,
VEATCH,
VIELE,
VILLEPIGUE,
VINCENT,
VINTON,
VOGDES,
VON STEINWEHR,
VORIS.

**W.**

WADE,
WADSWORTH,
WAGNER,
WAINWRIGHT,
WALCUTT,
WALKE,
WALKER,
WALLACE,
WALLEN,
WALTHALL,
WARD,
WARNER,
WASHBURNE,
WARREN,
WEAVER,
WEBB,
WEBER,
WEBSTER,
WEED,
WEISIGNER,
WEITZEL,
WELLES,
WELLS,
WELSH,
WERDEN,
WESSELLS,
WEST,
WHARTON,
WHEATON,
WHEELER,
WHEELOCK,
WHIPPLE,
WHITE,
WHITING,
WHITTAKER,
WIGFALL,
WILDE,
WILKES,
WILCOX,
WILLIAMS,
WILLIAMSON,
WILLICH,
WINSLOW,
WINTHROP,
WISTAR,
WOHER,
WOLCOT,
WOOD,
WOODBURY,
WOODHULL,
WOODS,
WOODWORTH,
WOOL,
WORDEN,
WRIGHT,
WYMAN.

**Y.**

YOUNG.

**Z.**

ZOLLICOFFER,
ZOOK.

# INDEX

## TO THE LEADING ANECDOTES, INCIDENTS, ETC.

☞ Those in *Italics* relate to WOMAN'S RECORD in the Scenes and Events of the War.

### A.

| | PAGE. |
|---|---|
| A "Long" Portrait | 146 |
| A Pass that would'nt Pass | 434 |
| *Abe and Andy* | 422 |
| Absence of Col. J. from C't M.,—and Why | 436 |
| Accidents will Happen | 61 |
| Accommodating himself to Circumstances | 152 |
| Admiral Farragut, Tete-a-Tete with | 390 |
| Admiral Farragut's Final Answer to the Emissaries of Treason | 354 |
| *Admiral Farragut's Gallantry to Miss Victor* | 379 |
| " Foote—Farewell Scene | 378 |
| " Foote's Terms to Gen. Tilghman | 367 |
| " Porter's Big Scare | 361 |
| Advantage of Military Firmness | 439 |
| Advice from the Disbanded Volunteer | 33 |
| Advised to Stick to his Business | 46 |
| *Affecting Appeal to a Union Commissary* | 473 |
| *Affecting Mementoes of Gettysburg* | 627 |
| *Afraid of the Girl's Eye!* | 26 |
| After the Firing on Old Sumter | 176 |
| Agreeable Inducements to Travelers | 462 |
| *Agreeable Reciprocity of Union Sentiment* | 566 |
| *Ah, Mother, Mother! I knew you would come!* | 534 |
| Ahead of his Troops | 346 |
| "Aint no business wid a gun," | 490 |
| Alabama and Kearsarge, Combat between | 365 |
| Alabama Planter and the Anti-Slavery Leaders together | 37 |
| Albemarle Ram, Sinking the | 371 |
| Alas! the Poor Soldier | 608 |
| Albert, the Drummer Boy of the Mass. 23d. | 267 |
| All a Mother Can Do | 161 |
| *All for her Lover* | 577 |
| All for Nothing | 614 |
| All for the Whiskey | 479 |
| All through a Mistake | 298 |
| American Soldiers Then and Now | 142 |
| Ammunition sent by the Enemy Just in Time | 511 |
| *Amours and Fancies of the Camp* | 536 |
| " *of a New Orleans Judge* | 552 |
| An Hibernian's Tustle with a Miss. "Tiger" | 333 |
| *An Honor to her Sex* | 473 |
| "And a little child shall lead them." | 587 |
| "And the brother shall deliver up the brother to death" | 59 |
| Anderson and his brave little Company leaving Fort Sumter | 254 |
| Andrew Jackson's Famous "Union" Toast | 23 |
| Andy Johnson and the Clerical Secessionist | 89 |
| " " 's (Gov.) Supplement to one of Lorenzo Dow's Stories | 48 |
| *Anglo-African Daughter of the Regiment* | 193 |
| *Anna Manley, the Baltimore Heroine* | 528 |
| *Annie Lillybridge and Lieutenant W* | 621 |
| Another Cassabianca | 373 |
| " *of the Uncle Toms* | 104 |
| Answering the Secretary and the General | 647 |
| Anxious for a Trade | 468 |

NOTE.—It has been made a point to present, in this Index, the names of noted *persons* and *places* as fully as possible in the headings, in order to facilitate the reader's reference, through that means, to anecdotes pertaining to particular scenes and their actors. In the nature of the case, however, this mode of specific designation was practicable only to a very limited extent, without enlarging the list almost indefinitely; and, therefore, the names of the multitude of localities, commanders, divisions, corps, regiments, vessels, etc., to which these anecdotes relate, are, in the great majority of instances, to be found embodied in the reading matter itself, rather than in the indexed titles or textual captions. It may also be remarked, that nearly *five-sixths* of the anecdotes which came under notice in the preparation of this work, were rejected as *worthless for preservation*; only the best were retained,—thus enabling the volume to appear in convenient size and handsome and readable type.

## INDEX TO THE LEADING ANECDOTES AND INCIDENTS.

Appeal for a Furlough—with an Appendage...435
Application of the term "Contraband" by Gen. Butler............102
Appointment of Burnside as a Cadet........565
" of Mrs. Reynolds as a Major in the Army............268
Arkansas, Front-Door Confabulations in......43
Armstrong, the Rebel Dominie, before Gen'l Butler............145
Army Matrimonial Advertisements—Hint to Romantic Young Ladies............575
Arrest of Joe Guild by Col. Myers..........64
" of one of Gen. Grant's Aids by a Colored Guard............429
As good as a Captured Gun............343
Astonishing Ignorance on board a Gunboat..391
Atlanta Young Lady, Conversation with an...607
Attending to Business in Regular Order......643
Aunt Charlotte, the old Cook at Newbern......507
Availing himself of a Joke............58

**B.**

Backing the Commander-in-Chief..........150
Bad Atmosphere for a Patriot's Lungs......140
" for the Cow............46
" Habit amongst Mules............458
Badge of Treason in a New York Ball Room.111
Bailey's Dam for saving the Miss. Squadron..376
Baker, Ellsworth, Lyon—a Brave Trio......520
Balance of Power Maintained between Turkeys and Chickens............475
Baltimore Heroine—Anna Manley..........528
Baltimore Unconquerables, Examin'g one of the.135
Bankhead (Com.), Expensive Joke on, by a Southern Dame............384
Banking Operations of Gen. Schoepf in Ky..469
Banks' (Gen.) Morning Call at Marshal Kane's Door............53
Banks' (Gen.) Reply to a Boston Lady......143
Baptism for the Dead............588
Bates, Reception of the Rebel Commissioners in London by Mr............25
Battle with Snow-balls at Chattanooga......275
Bearing the Standard through Baltimore.....309
Beauties of Rebel Conscripting............181
Beautiful but Dead on the Field of Honor...518
Beauty of Nullification and of the Guillotine.149
Became a Soldier after all............606
Beecher's Case of Muskets for the South....405
Beef Steak and Hot Rolls every Morning....483
Behind the Trees : Maine and Georgia......244
Bell's (John) Tennessee Iron Works........103
Ben Butler in Council with the Secession Conspirators............32
Ben McCulloch and Joe Baxter............590
Ben Phillips, the Hoary Old Bloodhound....265
Benefit of Clergy............71
Beware of a Soldier's Wife !............629
Bibles on Shipboard—Touching Scene......393

Big Job in Prospect............150
Billiards on board the Ironsides............371
Billy Shelton, the Martyr Patriot Boy......148
Billy Wilson's Zouaves : Extraordin'y Scene.184
Birney (Gen.), Startling Adventure of......234
Births of Boys and Girls in War Times.....566
Bishops Meade and Polk in Consultation....260
Black, the Scotch Deserter at Leesburg......177
Bleeding, but had his Colors with him......287
" to Death, but Sound as a Trout....302
Blenker scorning to Retreat............310
Blondin's Art serving a Good Figure..........69
Bloody Sabre Charge by Col. Minty........304
Bloody (The) Flag of Fort Pillow..........570
Blue-Jacket on the Quarter-Deck of his Mule.368
Bob, the Spunky Drummer Boy............339
Bogus Yankee Legislature in Georgia......117
Bold Female Smuggler and Highwayman.....487
Bounty-Jumper Captured by a Dog..........200
Bowie Knife Conflict at Battle of Pea Ridge.318
Boy Soldiers at the Old One's Trade........316
Boy (The)Father to the Man............80
"Boys, I'm for the Union still !"............281
Branding Deserters at Castle Thunder......203
Brandy at Fort Sumter: Poor Pryor..........491
" for a Sick Lieutenant............451
" " All Hands............514
Brave and Good but must be Shot............409
Bravo for Pea Ridge............328
Bread Cast upon the Waters............555
Breckinridge's Son............327
Bridegroom and Volunteer the Same Night....23
Brief but Eventful History............153
Bright Girls in Missouri............604
Brilliant Strategy of Gen. Smith at Red River.312
Brondbrim's Method with Secessionists......110
Brownell (Mrs.), the Heroine of Newbern.....268
Brownlow, a Point for· Helping a Soldier....469
" expressing his Sentiments in Jail..67
" prefers the 'Direct' Route to Hell.125
Buchanan's Cabinet. Dramatic Scene in......26
Buchanan's (Admiral) Sword Yielded with a Bad Grace............380
Buckner hung his Head............415
Buford's Method of Stirring-up Teamsters...509
Bull Run Battlefield, Horrors of............323
" " , Horse Incidents at............499
Buried with his Sister's Picture............628
Burlesque on Peace Propositions............47
Burnside, Appointment of, as a Cadet.......565
" Directing a Retreat............336
" , Mose Bryan ,aying his Respects to.578
Bushwhackers Kept at Bay by a Brave Girl...619
Butler (Gen.) as a Young Lawyer..........607
" in Council with the Secessionist Conspirators............32
Butler's Laconic Hint to a Pilot............374
" 's "Shameful Tyranny" in N. Orleans..495
" 's Style of Clearing off a Table......482

INDEX TO THE LEADING ANECDOTES AND INCIDENTS. 693

Buzzard's Roost, Reading the Amnesty Proclamation at..............................124
By-Scene at the Battle of Leesburg.........286

C.

Cabinet Pictures Before and After the Election.69
Calhoun, Garrison at the Grave of..........151
" John Quincy Adams foretelling the Future to...............................123
Calhoun's Escape from the Gallows..........128
California Joe and his Telescopic Rifle......236
Calumnious Charge of Loyalty against John Hawkins..................................28
Canadian Editor's Interview with President Lincoln................................489
Canine Patriotism, Sufferings, and Honors...504
Capital Ruse to save Springfield...........267
Capt. Dickson's Ride with the Pretty Secesh...524
" Strong delivering his Revolvers......259
" Tilden's Lucky Escape..............342
" ———'s Trade for a Kiss............605
Career of Frank Henderson..................173
Carolinian Unionist Showing the Track......52
Carter's Polite Mode of giving Information..259
Carving his own Headboard..................595
Cass's Backbone............................139
Castle Thunder, Branding Deserters at......233
Caught in his Own Trap.....................424
Cause for Rejecting a Recruit..............194
Cavender, the Martyr Preacher..............139
Challenging the Sentinel...................401
Chance for a "Lady of Character"..........548
Change of Tune and Position................261
Changed his Mind...........................199
Characteristic Lady's Joke.................593
" Pluck of a Western Soldier....296
"Charge! Chester, Charge!"................356
Charleston Women under Fire................585
Chase, Joke of the President on Secretary...465
Chase of the "Sovereign"...................388
Chattanooga, Battle with Snow-balls at.....275
Cheers and a "Tiger" for Harry Bumm.....192
" instead of a Speech..................56
Chickamauga and Chattanooga................503
Childhood's Prayer in the Last Hour........548
Chronicles of a Railway Trip...............147
Circulation of Union Proclamations in South Carolina..............................109
Circumstances Alter Principles.............108
Cities Built and in Embryo: Schaeffer and Ould at a Joke..........................69
Clerical Prisoners of State................130
Clerks of the President....................135
Clever Dogs, but both Sucked Eggs..........620
" Use of the Countersign...............212
Clinging to the Guns.......................365
Close of McPherson's Noble Career..........253
Cluster of little Courtesies...............484
Coffee for Jack............................383

Colonel Farrar Winding-up a Dance.........517
Colonel Gazley doing a little Guard-Duty....418
" Owen's Squad Drill...............407
" Polk, and Sanders the Refugee.....100
Combat between the Kearsarge and Alabama.365
"Come from 'Ginny, sure,"................116
Comedy of Cabinet Errors...................54
Coming Events cast their Shadows before....143
Command of the Virginia Forces tendered to Gen. Scott............................71
Comment on Mr. Sloanaker's "Beautiful Portrait."............................643
Commission of Major conferred on a Lady....558
Commissioner deciding a Question of Age...184
Complimentary Responses of a Soldier to his General...............................432
Complimentary Salutations to his General...195
Compliments of the Season..................330
Compromising the Capitol Flag..............73
Conciliatory Mesmerism.....................108
Conditional Offer of his Autograph by General Grant................................564
Confederate Brooches not to Gen. Viele's Taste.620
" Notes in Maryland.................68
Confession of a Rebel Officer to Gen. Grant....60
Congressman Ely at the Confederate Passport Office...................................424
Connecticut Tenth, Corporal of the.........205
" Twelfth, Weitzel satisfied with the.415
Constructive Parole Rights..................94
Consul and General matched against each other in Savannah......................511
Contempt for Confederate Lines, Paroles, etc...536
"Contraband," Application of the Term by Gen. Butler............................102
Contra'd News: an Editor before the Cabinet.492
Contrast between the Two...................641
Conundrums at the Wrong Time...............502
Conversation with an Atlanta Young Lady....607
" on his Threatened Assassination.640
Converting Lady Rebels.....................595
Cord for Cord—Secession Currency..........474
Corinth, Gould the Hero of.................103
Cost of a Canteen of Water.................317
Cotton Burners in Louisiana................453
Could not Wait for Death...................510
Could'nt Pass with his Cigar...............406
Courage of Woman during Battle.............594
Court-Martialing a Whole Division..........312
Crossing Fox River..........................85
Culpepper, Maiden Loveliness at............571
Cumberland, Last Gun of the Ship...........352
Curiosity of Rebel Soldiers to hear President Lincoln's Message......................131
Customer for Grant's Biography.............511

D.

Dalliance and Treachery—Lt. H. and Mrs. C.531
Dam (Bailey's) for saving the Miss. Squad'n.376

694    INDEX TO THE LEADING ANECDOTES AND INCIDENTS.

Danger of Freedmen Voting................69
Daring Attack upon a Paymaster's Boat.....397
Davis (Gen. J. C.), Tragical Encounter between Gen. Nelson and..................413
Davis, Jefferson, and Elizabeth Self..........134
Davis's Chairs in Readiness for Ulysses.....114
Davis's Trap for Grant....................274
Deaf and Dumb Soldier..................196
Dealing with a Rebel Trader..............504
Death Preferred to the Southern Oath......127
"   Smiling in Victory's Embrace........370
Death-bed Scene of the Murdered President..635
Deathly Encounter between Hunt and Loughborough...............................227
Delirious Bravery of a Southern Hotspur....334
Delivered at the Eleventh Hour..............580
Delivering up their Swords at Fort Pulaski..334
Delivery of their Ammunition before Surrendering...................................294
Dem Rotten Shell........................370
Description of So. Carolina by Judge Pettigru.74
Deserting a Bad Cause....................192
Determined Capture of a Texan Battle Flag..342
Devotion of a Private to Gen. McPherson...330
"   of Farragut's Men to their Admiral.374
"   to the Stars and Stripes............64
Dick Bowles parting with his Revolver......231
Dick, the Four-footed Orderly...............559
Dickson's (Capt.) Ride with the Pretty Secesh.524
Didn't like Vallandigham's Defeat............70
Disappointed Expectations................642
Discussion between Major Downing and Mr. Linkin...................................44
Diseases of the Brain and Heart..............92
Disguised as a Bell-Wether.................260
Dissensions in "the Happy Family,"........659
Distribution of his Bounty..................216
Disturbing an Orator........................61
Divide is the Word, or you are a Dead Johnny.484
"Divil a Macarthy drawn at-all-at-all".......203
Dixie, On the Road to....................105
"Do they miss me at Home?"..............324
Doctor ———'s Dismissal for Drunkenness and Kissing.................................437
Doctor ———'s Loyalty rather Coppery......63
Donelson, Frankie Bragg the little Patriot at..613
Donning the Breeches.....................196
'Don't shoot there any more—that's Father!'.241
Doubtful Loyalty, Political and Matrimonial..570
"Doughnation" from the Maine Ladies.......492
Douglas (Senator) and Gen. Stewart on "the Situation,"...............................57
Douglas's last Message to his Sons...........127
Douglas's (Mrs.) Noble Resistance to Southern Persuasion..............................536
Down upon the Table Waiters..............421
Dr. Cottman in Butler's Hands..............60
Dr. Rucker—his Case and Escape...........75
Dramatic Scene in Mr. Buchanan's Cabinet...26

Duel on Horseback in one of the Peninsula Battles..................................224
Dutch Landlord's use of Grayback Twenties.445

E.

Eager to be a Soldier: Handsome Lizzie.....204
Eagle at the Mast Head...................390
Easy Way of Cutting Red Tape, by Grant..428
Eating up the Stars and Bars..............623
Effect of Crinoline on "Union" Sentiments...182
Eighth Ohio Blazing Away.................294
Eleven-Year-Old Warrior Picking-off the Enemy..................................241
Elizabeth Comstock and the Dying Soldier....526
Ellsworth, Baker, Lyon—a Brave Trio......520
Ellsworth's Assassination..................321
Ely (Congressman) at the Confederate Passport Office..............................424
Emphatically a Bootless Undertaking.........281
Emptying a Hawk's Nest..................344
Encounter of Picket Wits..................271
Enlistment of "Stonewall Jackson" in the Union Army.............................183
Entombment of a Virginia Loyalist.........106
Equal to the Emergency...................192
Escape from Libby Prison through a Young Lady's Intervention.......................585
Escape of Gen. Tyler and his Staff.........251
Estimate of Confederate "Promises to Pay," Down South............................481
Examining one of the Baltim'e Unconquerables.135
Executive Favor well Bestowed.............548
Expensive Joke on Commander Bankhead by a Southern Dame.........................384
Explaining the Initials "O. V. M.".........224
Exploits of "the French Lady."............367

F.

Failed to Hold his Position: Gen. Palmer to Gen. Pope..............................270
Faith and its Reward.....................546
Falling Back at the Wrong Moment.........605
Falstaff in the Cavalry Service.............313
Familiar Chat about Generals..............112
"   Talk with Mr. Lincoln on the Emancipation Proclamation...................651
Family Quarrel settled on the Battle-field....245
Family Swords not to be Exempted..........550
Fanny and Nellie of the 24th New Jersey.....170
Farewell Scene among the Tars............378
Farragut, Gallantry of, to Miss Victor.......379
"   when a Midshipman..............369
Farragut's Final Answer to the Emissaries of Treason................................354
Farragut's Men, Devotion of, to their Adm'l..374
Farrar (Col.) Winding up a Dance.........527
Fatal Fulfillment of a Jest.................586
Fate of a Coward........................168

INDEX TO THE LEADING ANECDOTES AND INCIDENTS.   695

Fate of two German Brothers............309
"Father, I will never Surrender to a Rebel!".239
Fearful Ordeal for a Deserter............174
Female Government Contractor...........483
  "    Loveliness at Fort Henry...........545
  "    Traitors making Ashes of the Glorious Flag..................................59
Fiction left in the Shade : the Corporal o. the Tenth Connecticut......................205
Field Carriages and Millinery Dispensed with.485
Fiendish Deeds of a Western Amazon........296
Fierce Artillery Duel.....................278
Fight for the Flag at Petersburg............330
  "    with the Iron Monster " Tennessee,"...385
Fightin' ober a Bone......................194
Fighting, Dying, and Buried "with his Niggers."..................................249
Final Answer of Farragut to the Emissaries of Treason.............................354
Final Scene on board of the " Mississippi,"..357
Fine Trap but no Game....................571
Firing 22 Rounds with a Ball in his Thigh...261
Firm Devotion of a Loyal Southern Woman to the Colors...........................40
First Oath and Testimony of a Slave in Va....90
First "Union Demonstration" in Old Virginia.602
Five Hundred Dollars for a Plate of Cream..527
Flight, Capture, and Death of Booth........637
Flight from the Shenandoah................505
Florence Nightingale's Contribution..........601
Flowers from Lovely Hands for the Fallen Brave530
Following their Leader....................294
Foote's Terms to Gen. Tilghman............367
"For Life, if the Nation will take me,"......163
Foreshadowings of their Fate—Ellsworth, Baker, Lyon............................520
Forgetting his Usual Courtesy...............55
Fort Donelson, Western Regiments at.......266
  "      "    Young America at.........227
Fort Henry, Woman's Tongue betraying the Rebel Torpedoes at....................589
Fort McAllister, Sherman watching the Capture of.................................295
Fort Pickens Reinforced...................395
  "    Pillow, Remember...................305
  "    Pillow's Bloody Flag................570
  "    Pulaski,—Delivery of Swords at......334
  "    Sumter, Anderson and his brave little Company leaving......................254
Fort Sumter, Brandy at : Poor Pryor.......491
  "     "    Hail Columbia and the Star Spangled Banner at...................68
Fort Sumter, Unfortunate Absence at the Seige of..............................101
Fort Warren—Exit of Mason and Slidell....133
"Forward! March!"—Last Words of a Federal Lieutenant at Newbern..............257
Four-Legged Messenger proving Disloyal....510
Four-Legged Pets in the Army.............583

Four Confederates bagged by a Union Soldier.256
Fox River, Crossing.......................85
Frank, the Pretty Bugler of the Eighth Mich..622
Frank Henderson, Career of................173
Frankie Bragg, the little Patriot at Donelson..613
Fredericksb'g, Humphrey's Deadly Charge at.288
  "      Incident in the Battle of........547
Fremont's whole Body-Guard charged upon by one Rebel.........................239
French Sensibility........................86
Fresh Pork for the Eighth Illinois...........466
Friendly Advice to a Doubtful Unionist......62
From a Palace to the Attic.................474
From Deck to Camp........................174
Front-Door Confabulations in Arkansas......43
Fruit in Old Age..........................251
Fulfillment of the Sergeant's Prophecy......547

G.

Gallant Vindication of the Flag Abroad......30
Gallantry of Farragut to Miss Victor........379
Garrison at the Grave of Calhoun...........151
Gathering Violets on the Battle-field........236
Gazley (Col.) doing a little Guard Duty.....418
General Baker, Foreshadowing of his Fate...520
  "    Baker's Tragical Death.............319
  "    Banks, No Passes to Official Speculators by.........................425
General Banks's Morning Call at Marshal Kane's Door..........................53
General Banks's Reply to a Boston Lady.....143
  "    Birney's Startling Adventure.......234
  "    Blenker scorning to Retreat........310
  "    Bragg and his Supposed Army......232
  "    Bragg's Prompt Settlement of a Claim482
  "    Burnside Directing a Retreat.......336
  "    Butler as a Young Lawyer.........607
  "    Butler's application of the term "Contraband,"...........................102
General Butler's Glorious Success in saving the "Old Ironsides,"..................360
General Carter's Polite Mode of Giving Information............................259
General Cheatham whipped by Peggie McHue.426
  "    Dumont's Rebuke of a Secessionist.....60
  "    Grant and the Pumpkin Pie Story....463
  "    Grant, Confess'n of a Reb. Officer to.60
  "      "    Jeff. Davis's Trap for........274
  "      "    No Calculation of that sort by321
  "      "    Unacquainted with Politics....97
  "    Grant's Biography, Customer for....511
  "      "    Conditional Offer of his Autograph...............................564
General Grant's Easy Way of cut'g Red Tape428
  "      "    Idea—Worse to Lose Five than One.............................411
General Grant's Shotted Salute at Midnight..324
  "    Halleck and the Teamster..........420
  "    Halleck's use of a Bad Report......457

# 696　INDEX TO THE LEADING ANECDOTES AND INCIDENTS.

General Holt's Dinner....................470
" Hooker and the Newspaper Correspondents...................477
General Hooker's Battle above the Clouds...311
"　　" Magnificent War Horse "Lookout,"...........................465
General Hovey's Brilliant Charge..........346
General Howard on the Wrong Side of the Battle-field...........................338
General Howard, the Havelock of the War..629
General Humphreys' Deadly Charge at Fredericksburg...............................288
*General Hunter's Special Aid*..............567
"　Jenkins's Mode of Parolling Deserters.159
"　　" Visit at a Penn. Editor's....461
"　Johnston, Last Talk of, with his Generals.............................300
General Johnston's Whipping at Resaca.....326
"　Kearny, the "One-arm Devil,".......318
"　Kilpatrick's Battle-Flag at Hagerst'n.247
"　Lander and the Bible..............557
"　Lee's Great Army Surrendered......346
"　Longstreet's Instant Detect'n of a Spy283
"　Lyon leading his Charge at Springfi'd.585
"　Lyon's Bravery and Sacrifice........224
"　Magruder's Table..................478
"　McClellan and Darkey John........439
"　　" Dismounting to the Guard.410
"　McCook's Pass for Old Buz........417
"　McCulloch and Joe Baxter.........590
"　McPherson, Devotion of a Private to.330
"　McPherson's Noble Career, Close of..253
"　Meade and " Ale,"................594
General Mower's Successful Trick upon the Rebel Dispatch Bearer...................325
General Nelson in a Fix..................402
"　Nelson's Half-Hour with a Pedler....459
"　　" Tragical Encounter with Gen. Davis................................413
*General O.'s Stern Particularity as to his Night Wardrobe*............................523
*General Paine's Conversation with the Wife of a Secessionist*...........................122
General Palmer to Gen. Pope..............270
"　Palmer's Spy Glass................591
"　Pemberton's Question about Grant answered.............................344
General Phelps's Insanity Investigated by Gen. Butler.............................142
General Polk in the Tightest Place.........345
"　Price, and Van Dorn, pitted against Rosecrans.............................289
"　　Rice to his Mother.................615
"　　Rosecrans and Pat's Furlo'.........411
"　　" and Vallandigham coming to an Understanding.....................138
*General Rosecrans' Orderly Sergeant Delivered of a Baby in Camp*......................554
General Rosseau's First Step towards making Loyal Men of Rebels.....................63

General Schoepf's Banking Operations in Ky.469
"　Scott, Comm'd of the Virginia Rebel Forces tendered to.......................71
General Scott, Official Farewell to..........124
"　Scott's Plan of the War............232
"　*Sedgwick's Present of a Turkey*......474
"　Sheridan and the Moonlight Picture.280
"　　" at Stone River..............293
"　　" riding to the Front.........315
"　Sherman, Signaling for: Meeting of the Warriors..........................392
General Sherman's Absence of Mind........589
"　Sherman's Courage before the Enemy.274
"　　" Heroism on the Battle-field of Shiloh..............................253
General Smith's Brill't Strategy at Red River312
"　Steedman taking the Flag..........317
"　Stewart and Senator Douglas on "the Situation,"............................57
General Stewart Too Late to Dinner........464
"　Terry's Colored Cook and his Shell..456
"　Tilghman, Adm'l Foote's Terms to..367
"　　' and his Loyal Mother.....556
"　Tyler's Escape with his Staff.......251
"　Wadsworth—Refusal to Receive Pay for Fighting for his Country..............468
General Wadsworth's Shoe Raid...........458
"　Weitzel Satisfied with the 12th Conn.415
"　Zollicoffer's Death at the Hands of Col. Fry...............................237
Generals among the Bullets................331
Generals Grant and Meade in Consultation before Richmond.......................256
Gens. Nelson and Davis's Tragical Encounter413
Generosity of Poor Jack...................360
George Peabody Repudiating the Rebel Commissioners..............................126
*Georgia Girls and Federal Lieutenants*.......496
*Georgia, Northern Schoolma'ams in*..........611
*Gettysburg, Affecting Mementos of*..........627
Gettysburg, Mrs. Wade the Loyal Bread Baker at..................................568
Girl-Boy Drummer........................206
*Girl-Boy Soldier in the Ninetieth Illinois*....567
*Girl Recruit for the Cavalry*................168
Giving 'em Fits...........................407
Glad for Burnside.........................318
Glorious Effect of National Music upon the Troops................................287
Glorious Success of Gen. Butler in saving "Old Ironsides,".........................360
Glorious to Die for One's Country..........272
" God bless the old fla—,"................243
*God's Flag*...............................140
Going in Quest of Satisfaction.............241
Going over his Battles Again...............479
*Going to see the Rebel Ram*..................353
Good Charlie, the Union Guide............105
Good Humor towards a Journalist.........655
"　Luck for an Iowan Soldier..........469

INDEX TO THE LEADING ANECDOTES AND INCIDENTS. 697

Good Samaritan in an Unexpected Hour and Place........................250
Good-Natured Jerry......................386
Got the Point twisted around Wrong.........162
Gottlieb Klobberyoss on the Draft..........189
Gould, the Hero of Corinth................103
Governor Andy Johnson's Supplement to one of Lorenzo Dow's Stories..................48
Gov. Todd and the Applicant for Exemption..185
Gov. Yates giving Grant a Desk in his Office.405
Grant and Meade in Consultation before Richmond..................................256
Grant, Confession of a Rebel Officer to.......60
Grant's Biography, Customer for...........511
Grant's Easy Way of Cutting Red Tape....428
" Objection to having any Trade Partnership..................................475
Great Act for a little Girl..................584
Great Day's Work for a Scout: the Misses Scott.....................................563
Grim War and the Innocents...............626

H.

Had no White Flag on Board..............382
Had to Acknowledge the Breed............204
Hail Columbia and the Star Spangled-Banner at Fort Sumter............................68
Hail Columbia in a New Version...........418
Half-Hour's Experience of a Pedler with Gen. Nelson...................................459
Halleck and the Teamster.................420
Halleck's Use of a Bad Report.............457
Halting Effect of "the Ardent,"............404
Hamlin (Vice-President), a Private in Co. A.100
Handsome Rebuke from an Alabamian......132
Happy Ending to a Sad Mistake...........185
Happy to make Gen. Gordon's Acquaintance.203
Hard on Negley...........................431
Hard-Shell Brethren dealing with a Contumacious Member..........................65
Hard Tack for the Fifth Excelsior..........575
Hard to tell Pork from Tomatoes...........468
Hard-up for a Blacksmith..................123
Hard Work for a Drafting Col. in Savannah.165
Hardee's Tactics with a Point left out......427
Harp and Shamrock, Stars and Stripes.....322
Harper's Ferry Flag, Quite a Safe Place for the588
Harry Bumm, Cheers and a "Tiger" for....192
Hatred of Southern Unionists to Southern Rebels....................................93
He was Too Big not to be a Soldier.........258
Heart-Rending Scene......................579
Hearts and Swords.......................599
Heavy Firing—No Casualties; and Why?...340
Helping a Soldier: a Point for Brownlow....469
Hercules-Africanus going to the War........202
Heroism of a Naval Engineer..............387
" of Sherman, on the Battlefield of Shiloh..................................253

Hiding their Infant Moses..................538
Hiding the Flag: Female Artifice............36
His Discharge Confirmed by Heaven........482
His Favorite Flag for a Winding Sheet......378
His Knapsack told the Tale.................223
History of a Sword........................509
Hoax upon Rebel Sharpshooters............255
Hoisting the Flag on Independence Hall, by President Lincoln..........................37
Holding the Hill—Valor of Burnside........290
Homage to the Flag by an Eagle............39
Home and the Battle-field..................577
Home Scene in the Cradle of Rebellion.......555
Honesty on the Battle-field.................480
Honorable Commendation instead of Ignominious Death..............................425
Hooker and the Newspaper Correspondents..477
Hooker's Battle above the Clouds...........311
" Magnificent War-Horse "Lookout,".465
Hoosier Straightforwardness...............271
Hopeful Tackett—his Mark.................177
Hopeless Cases............................612
Horrors of the Bull Run Battle-field........323
Horse Incidents at Bull Run................499
Hostage Wanted for his Wife and Family....623
Hovey's brill't Charge—the Preacher's Regt.346
"How are you, Conscript?".................211
"How does he grow 'em?"..................157
How the Flag was planted at Vicksburg.....306
How to Spike a Gun.......................470
How to take the Oath......................615
Howard (Gen.) on the Wrong Side of the Battle-field...............................338
Howard (Gen.), the Havelock of the War...629
Howe, the little Drummer-Boy in the Fifty-ninth Illinois............................235
Humphrey's Deadly Charge at Fredericksb'g.288
Hurrah for the Gunspiker..................314
Hurrahs for Jeff. Davis in the Wrong Place...34

I.

"I am proud to Die for my Country."........540
"I likes de Job."...........................169
"I told you I would do it,".................288
Ignoble end of a Washington...............341
"I'll do it, tell Gen. Grant!"..............248
Illinois Eighth Regiment, Fresh Pork for the.466
" Fifty-ninth's little Drummer Boy.....235
" Ninetieth, Girl-Boy Soldier in the.....567
" Sixteenth's Regim'tal Clothes-Washer.205
" Twenty-seventh's Happy Burial Occas'n506
Important Witness on the Stand............153
Impositions upon Furloughed Men.........432
Impressive Sight aboard Ship on Sunday...381
Improving on Acquaintance................554
Impromptu Enforcement of Discipline......423
In and out of the Vicksburg Caves..........606
In Bed with a Shell—Lively Times.........499
Inability to furnish Supplies to both Armies..477

698  INDEX TO THE LEADING ANECDOTES AND INCIDENTS.

Incident of the Battle of Fredericksburg......547
Incident of the 119th New York Regiment...280
Independent Southern Girls..................567
Indiana 16th—Capture of the Texas Flag...312
Indiana Volunteer Ninety-two Years Old....196
Ingenuity of a Yankee Wife in getting a Pass.419
Instance of Loyalty in Virginia..............551
Interceding for her Father: Elizabeth Self and
 Jeff. Davis..............................134
Interesting Contribution to a Sanitary Fair...620
" Historical Episode, Civil and Military....79
Interesting Scrap of History................144
Interview at the Libby, between Morgan and
 Neal Dow................................551
Interview of a Canadian Editor with President Lincoln..............................489
Intrepid Conduct of Two Drummer Boys....338
Investigation by General Butler into General
 Phelps's Insanity........................142
Iowa and Texas—Terrible Encounter.......239
Iowa Cavalry: Swearing-in a Cook.........447
Iowan Soldier's Good Luck.................469
Ira's Wife and his Breeches.................165
Irish Logic concerning "Shmall Arms.".....430
Irish Military Imagination..................125
"Ironsides," Billiards on board the.........371
Island No. 10, Roberts's Half-Hour at.......358
Is the Colonel at Home?....................230
It was the baby that did it!.................217
I've Enlisted, Sir..........................191

J.

Jackson's Famous "Union" Toast...........23
Jeb Stuart playing Orderly to Gen. Buford...543
Jeff. Davis's Fellow Citizens in Mississippi,
 Loyalty of one of........................82
Jeff. Davis's Northern Present...............133
" " Trap for Grant.................274
Jenkins's (Gen.) Mode of Parolling Deserters.159
" " Visit at a Penn. Editor's....461
Jerry the Genius looking through General
 Palmer's Spy-Glass.......................591
Jim Morgan and the New Recruit......:...169
Joe Guild, Arrest of, by Col. Myers..........64
Joe Johnston's Whipping at Resaca..........326
Joe Parsons's "little favor" from a Rebel ...242
John Bell's Tennessee Iron Works...........103
John Letcher's Views on a Personal Subject..138
John Minor Botts between Two Fires........132
John Morgan and Mr. Clay's Horses.........488
John Quincy Adams Foretelling the Future to
 Mr. Calhoun.............................123
John Wells's "Idee" as to Splitt'g the Union115
Johnnie and Yank at a Trade.................485
Johnson (Andy) and the Clerical Secessionist..89
" (Gov.) and his Supplement to one of
 Lorenzo Dow's Stories....................48
Joke of Pres. Lincoln on Secretary Chase...465

Judge Baldwin Soliciting a Pass.............431
" G.'s Idea of the Rebellion............64
Just like Jack..............................368
Just the kind of Arms a Quaker could bear....206
Justice surviving Clemency..................646
Juvenile Political Sentiments...............137

K.

Kane's Door, Banks's Morn. Call at Marshal..53
Kearny, the "One-Arm Devil,"..............318
Kearsarge and Alabama Combat............365
Kentucky, Gen. Schoepf's Bank'g Operat's in.469
Kentucky Girl's Spirit......................538
" Provisional Gov't on an Excursion..41
Kentucky's Joan d' Arc.....................525
Kilpatrick's Battle-Flag at Hagerstown......247
Kind o' wanted to be in the Front...........332
Knotty Argument for Secession Ladies........116

L.

Laconic Hint to a Pilot by Gen. Butler.....374
Lander (Gen.) and the Bible................557
Lane (Senator) and the Stage Driver.......111
Last Day's Incidents in the President's Life..633
Last Gun of the Cumberland................352
Last Message to his Father.................444
Last Thoughts of the Dying Boy-Soldier.....562
Laughable Arrest of Colonel H. by two Young
 Ladies..................................538
"Leatherbreeches" in the Federal Service...322
Leave of Absence for a Novel Reason........436
Leave-Taking at the Station.................604
Lee's Great Army Surrendered and the Rebellion in its Final Gasp...................346
"Lee's Miserables,".........................561
Leesburg, Black—the Scotch Deserter at....177
Leesburg, By-Scene at the Battle of.........286
Left to Dine Alone..........................108
Legislative Scene for a Painter.............125
Lending to the Government..................462
Length of the War according to Floridan
 Chronology..............................143
Letcher's (John) Views on a Personal Subject138
Letter of Sympathy from a Union Soldier to a
 Confederate Officer's Betrothed............626
Letter to Eight Young Ladies from a Soldier..503
Letting them judge by the Tunes............109
Libby Prison, Escape from, through a Young
 Lady's Intervention......................585
Lieutenant Davis's Delicate Little Task.....263
" ———'s Perfumed Breath.......478
Life of Lincoln written by himself..........654
Lillybridge (Annie) and Lieut. W...........621
Lincoln, Conversation with, on his Threatened
 Assassination...........................640
Lincoln, Deathbed Scene of.................635
Lincoln's Message, Curiosity of Reb. Soldiers
 to hear..................................131
Lincoln's Moderate Ideas of a Competency..513

INDEX TO THE LEADING ANECDOTES AND INCIDENTS. 699

Literal Interpretation of North'n Sympathy by a Rebel General...........................32
Literal " Stump" Speech of a Soldier.......116
Little overweighted with Cold Lead.........546
Lizzie's Mark on the Handkerchief..........566
Logic of Sugar and Coffee..................501
Long Table-Cloths for Southern Cavalrymen.308
Longstreet's Instant Detection of a Spy.....283
Looking after a Soldier's Wife..............603
Looking out for Hospital Accommodations....556
Lost Mountain, Waving the Stars and Stripes from the Summit of......................303
Louisiana Cotton Burners...................453
Love and Treason...........................529
Love-Greetings to the Soldiers..............567
Loved the Old Flag still....................296
Loyal Breeze from Port Hudson..............112
" Demonstration with a Crutch..........90
Loyalty and Abolitionism supposed Synonymous 579
Loyalty of one of Jeff. Davis's Fellow Citizens in Mississippi............................82
Lucky Moment on board the Pirate Sumter..373
Lyon, Baker, Ellsworth—a Brave Trio......520
Lyon (Gen.) leading his Charge at Springfi'd585
Lyon's Bravery and Sacrifice................224

M.

Magic of Washington's Name...............120
Magruder Sharing his Liquor...............449
Maiden Loveliness at Culpepper............571
Maiden, Wife, Volunteer, and Widow—Love and Patriotism..........................161
Maine and Georgia: Behind the Trees......244
Maine and Maryland: Nuptials in Camp.....535
Maine Ladies' " Doughnation."..............492
Major Downing on the "Merrymac,"........355
Major Anderson and his Brave Little Company leaving Fort Sumter.....................254
Major B. en route with the Spanish Widow..623
Making a Family Matter of it...............164
Man of Experience—Sure...................363
Manley (Anna), the Baltimore Heroine......528
Marian and her Brave Boy in Blue..........159
"Mark Time !"—Gen. Nelson in a Fix......402
Marriage Scene in the Army of the Potomac..592
Married Applicants for Exemption..........183
Marshall's Demijohn Drill..................424
Mary Birkitt and her 2,000,000 Percuss'n Caps497
Maryland, Confederate Notes in............68
" Queer Drafting Scene in..........195
Maryland Slaveholder driving his Slaves to the Recruiting Officer...................206
Massachusetts and So. Carolina pitted against each other in Battle....................322
Massachusetts Minute Men..................72
" 23d Regiment's Drummer Boy267
Master and Servant meeting in a Strange Place149
Material for the Novelist's Pen..............524
Material of which " Mudsill " Regiments are made up...............................466

Maternal Love and Patriotic Duty...........215
Matrimonial Army Advertisements: Hint to Romantic Young Ladies..................575
Matronly Opinion of " Corduroy,"..........420
McClellan and Darkey John................439
" Dismounting to the Guard.......410
McCook's Pass for Old Buz.................417
McCulloch and Joe Baxter..................590
McPherson(Gen.), Devotion of a Private to..330
McPherson's Noble Career, Close of.........253
Meade and " Ale,".........................594
Meade and Grant in Consultation before Richmond..............................256
Meade and Polk (Bishops) in Consultation..260
Medicinal Properties of Blankets gloriously Illustrated.............................530
Melancholy End of Johnson the Deserter....214
Memorable Interview at the White House...148
Mending a Faulty Pass.....................437
Merited Rebuke of a Secessionist by General Dumont................................60
Merriment in the Wrong Place.............544
Michigan 8th—Frank, the Pretty Bugler of the522
Midnight Charge of the Mule Brigade.......279
Mighty Big Risk............................333
Milesian's (A) Plucky Defence of the Flag..343
Military Etiquette..........................435
Military Monomania of a Brooklyn Girl.....520
Military Notation according to Pres. Lincoln.258
Milk with Accompaniments.................450
Minister Cameron and his German-Africanus..42
" Faulkner and the Emperor Napoleon on Secession..........................129
Minnesota Regiment, Wilkinson's Veteran....58
Minty's Bloody Sabre Charge...............304
Minute Men of Mass.; 1775 and 1861.......72
Misfortunes of a Cotton Speculator.........471
Miss Captain Taylor of the First Tennessee...544
Miss Clemmie's Album......................630
Miss Lee and the Yankee Corporal..........582
Miss Major Cushman among her Captors....549
Miss ——'s copy of Byron, and the Reb. Serjt.519
Missing their Booty........................254
Mission Ridge Crest, Planting the Flag at....221
" Mississippi," Scenes on board the Steamer.357
Mississippi, Witnessing and Dying for the Truth in..............................120
Miss. Squadron saved by Bailey's Dam......376
Missouri, Bright Girls in....................604
Missouri, One of Bill Myers's Capers in......306
Mistook the Genus.........................561
Mistook his Man............................83
Moderate Ideas of a Competency...........513
Mohican, Sailing into the Jaws of the......370
Money Could Not Buy his Vote.............132
Montgomery's Ride into the Hampton Legion's Nest...........................262
" More Brains, Lord !"......................31
More than a Match against Six..............284
Morgan, John, and Mr. Clay's Horses........488

# 700 INDEX TO THE LEADING ANECDOTES AND INCIDENTS.

Morgan! Morgan!........................244
Morning Call at Marshal Kane's Door........53
Morris Island—Very Obliging Picket.......280
Mose Bryan paying his Respects to General Burnside............................578
*Mother (A) puts out the eyes of her own son, to keep him from the War*...................188
*Mother-Corporal on a Ten Days' Furlough*....411
Mower's Successful Trick upon the Rebel Despatch-Bearer........................325
"*Mr. and Mrs. Grant.*"...................554
Mr. Beecher's Case of Muskets for the South.405
Mr. Cass's Backbone....................139
"Mr. Lincoln Forgot It"..................135
Mr. Lincoln, Original Cons'acy to Assassinate.95
Mr. Richardson Initiating his Escape........584
Mr. S., the Countryman, and his Substitute...193
*Mrs. Belmont's Concert for the Sanitary Com.*.587
*Mrs. Brownell, the Heroine of Newbern*......268
*Mrs. Douglas's Noble Resistance to Southern Persuasion*............................536
*Mrs. Partington on the New Military Crop*...461
*Mrs. Polk defining her Political Position*.....144
*Mrs. Reynolds' App't as a Major in the Army*.268
*Mrs. Smith's Husband to be Exchanged*.......187
*Mrs. Wade, the Loyal Bread-Baker at Gettysb.*568
"Mudsills" on the Sacred Soil..............114
*Music in the Hospital*....................527
"Mustered In,"..........................71
*Mutability of Public Reputation: Banks's Reply to a Boston Lady*...................143
*My Bold Soldier Boy*....................597
*My Gift to my Country*..................188
*My Mary Ann*..........................604
*My Mother's Hand*......................627
*My Son! Has he Come?*..................539

### N.

Napoleon on "French Youngsters" in the Federal Army............................49
Nasby's Reasons why he should not be Draft'd211
*Nashville Ladies working the Card*..........557
National Oath of Allegiance according to Southern Honor..........................74
Nature in Council upon the Union..........127
Negley (Gen.), Hard on....................431
Negro Rifleman brought down at Yorktown..319
"Nellie," the brave Battle-Horse...........500
Nelson's (Gen.) Half-Hour's Experience with a Pedler..............................459
Nelson's (Gen.) Tragical Encounter with Gen. Davis................................413
Nerving his Hand One Instant More........243
Nervous Customer in the Red-Tape Dep't....172
Neutral Cornfield before Petersburg.........325
*New Jersey Twenty-fourth: Fannie and Nellie.*170
*New Orleans Flag Presentation*.............94
*New Orleans Judge, Amours of a*...........552
New Orleans, Shameful Tyranny of Butler in495

*New York Ball-room Badge of Treason*......111
" " 119th Regt., Incident of the.....280
*New York Scene in the Park Barracks*......596
*Newbern, "Aunt Charlotte"—the Old Cook at* 507
*Newbern, Mrs. Brownell—the Heroine of*.....268
New-comer into Camp.....................408
"Newport News,"........................102
Newspaporial Forestalling of Dying Sentiments, etc.............................467
*No Appeal Left*..........................183
No Calculation of that Sort by Grant........321
No Dead Cavalry Men....................280
*No Fancy for Salt Pork, Hard Tack and Minie Bullets*..........................162
No Heart in the Cause....................154
*No Letter from his Sweetheart for nearly a Year*495
No Passes to Official Speculators...........425
*No Quarter—the Black Flag*...............293
*No Respect for the Tender Passion*..........278
No Title of "Soldier" given to the Devil....209
*No Wickedn's like the Wickedn's of a Woman*597
Noble Greeting by a Loyal Southerner to a Green Mountain Boy....................67
Noble Words and Actions of a Slavemaster...175
Non-Combatant—but a Tough One..........78
*Northern Instructors of Southern Teachers*.....81
" Muscle and Southern Chivalry....283
" Present to Jefferson Davis.......133
" Schoolma'ms in Georgia..........611
Not a single General on the Battle-field......223
Not a Star Obscured......................352
Not "Jeff." but "Geoffrey" Davis..........24
Not Yankees but Wolford's Cavalry.........308
Nothing agin the Old Flag.................128
" lost by True Courage.............248
*Nuptials in Camp: Maine and Maryland*....535

### O.

Oath-Taking in St. Louis..................115
Obeying Orders in his Own Way...........412
Object of the War on the Rebel Side........141
Object of the War on the Union Side.......141
Official Farewell to Gen. Scott.............124
Official Likeness of President Lincoln......514
*Off-hand Eloquence of a Rough Cavalryman*..598
"Oh, for Four Regiments!"..............265
Ohio Battle-Flag in the hands of a Bishop....81
Ohio Eighth Blazing Away.................294
Ohio Toll-gate Keeper's Talk with Val'dig'm.48
Old Abe fixing the Responsibility..........592
Old Abe hand-up for a Joke for once........43
*Old "Cotton Beard" and his Girls*..........108
*Old Hannah and the Restored Soldier*........574
Old Hickory's Three Swords and Three Injunctions............................110
"Old Ironsides," Glorious Success of General Butler in Saving........................360
Old Magruder Sharing his Liquor..........449
Old Men Turning-out when Eng. Pitches-in..158

## INDEX TO THE LEADING ANECDOTES AND INCIDENTS. 701

Old Rosy, and not Old Pap................333
"Old Sortie," the Rebel General.........502
Old Zack and his Son-in-Law.............119
"O'Meara is Dead!".......................298
On the Road to Dixie.....................105
One Day before the Battle: Last Talk of Johnston with his Generals..............300
One Man's Service to his Country........486
One Obscure Patriot Baffling a Whole Rebel Army................................231
One of Bill Myers's Capers in Missouri..306
One of the Best..........................443
One of the Most Brilliant Achievements..269
One of the Things to be Done..............62
Orders on the Battle-field...............438
Original Conspiracy to Assassinate Lincoln...95
Other Side of the Case...................104
Our dear old Flag never touched the Ground.240
Our Generals among the Bullets...........331
Out of Ammunition for a Time.............243
Outflanked for Once......................438
Overtaken at Last........................494
Owen's (Col.) Squad Drill................407
Owning-up................................314

### P.

Paid his Assessment on the Spot..........456
Paine's (Gen.) Conversation with the Wife of a Secessionist............................122
Palmer to Pope: Failed to Hold his Position.270
Pamphlet of Jokes in the corner of Mr. Lincoln's Desk.............................645
Parson Brownlow Expressing his Sentiments in Jail.................................67
Parson Brownlow prefers the 'Direct' Route to Hell..................................125
Parting and Singular Meeting of Two War Correspondents..........................499
Password as unders'd by the German Guard.423
Pat's Compliments to "Desarters,".......197
Patience of Mr. Lincoln tried too Far....640
Pathetic Offering of Genius to the Dead..629
Patriotism of the Rarest Kind.............72
Pay-Day in the Future....................498
Paying his Penalty—Cash Down............404
Paying to have a hand in the Fight......341
Pea-Ridge, Bowie-Knife Conflict at Battle of..318
Pea Ridge, Bravo for.....................328
Peculiar Question of Bounty..............201
Peabody, George, Repudiating the Rebel Commissioner...........................126
Peggie McHue who whipped Gen. Cheatham426
Pelicans vs. Eagles.......................88
Pemberton's Question about Grant answered.344
Pen with which the Emancipation Proclamation was Signed..........................113
Peninsula Battles—Duel on Horseback....224
Penn. Editor's, Visit of Gen. Jenkins at a..461
Pensacola Wedding-Table Flag............566

Perils of Correspondents.................488
Petersburg, Fight for the Flag at........330
      "      Neutral Cornfield...........325
Pettigru's Description of South Carolina..74
Phil. Sheridan at Stone River............293
Phillips, the Hoary Old Bloodhound......265
"Physical Disability" exempting from the Draft and Something Else....................593
Picket Repartee at Vicksburg.............335
Pickets, Shaken down among the..........412
Pictorial Humors of the War..............375
Pictures of Mrs. Major P. and her Boy....610
Pittsburg Landing—Skulking and Fourth of July Speeches.........................250
Place for the Watch in Battle............384
Planting the Flag on Mission Ridge Crest..221
Pleasant little Trade....................369
Pleasant Hoax all Round..................363
Pocket-full of Coin ready for Delivery...646
Pointed Rebuke from a Soldier's Death-bed.568
Political Courtesies at the White House...55
Political Dialogue in Camp...............132
Political Rendering of Hamlet.............56
Polk (Col.), and Sanders the Refugee....100
Polk (Mrs.) Defining her Political Position..144
Polk, the Rev. Gen., in the Tightest Place..345
Polly's Baby.............................646
Poor Bragg and his Supposed Army........232
Poor Pat's Idea of the Thing.............137
Poorer Pay but Better Business...........175
Port Hudson—Loyal Breeze................112
Port Royal Welcome to the Troops.........94
Portable Iron-Clad Breastworks...........236
Porter's Big Scare.......................361
Potomac Army Marriage-Scene..............592
Power of the Tender Passion on a Union Lieut.602
Prayer-Books and Scalping Knives.........494
Prayers for the Pres. by a Dying Soldier.257
Preaching the Sword and Using It.........124
Predict'n of Beckerdite, the South'n 'Prophet,'83
Preferred to Die in the Field............292
Present of a Turkey to Gen. Sedgwick....474
Presentation to a Brave Woman............373
Pres. Lincoln at the Play of Macbeth....134
Pres. Lincoln Forgetting his Usual Courtesy..55
Pres. Lincoln Hoisting the American Flag at Independence Hall......................37
President Lincoln, Last Day's Incidents in the Life of...............................633
Pres. Lincoln Mending a Faulty Pass.....437
President Lincoln treating the Richmond Commissioners to a little Story.........25
Pres. Lincoln, Widow Shultz's Appeal to..434
Pres. Lincoln's Conversation on his Threatened Assassination.......................640
President Lincoln's Deathbed Scene......635
President Lincoln's First Dollar........653
President Lincoln's Interview with a Canadian Editor................................489

## 702  INDEX TO THE LEADING ANECDOTES AND INCIDENTS.

President Lincoln's Joke on See'y Chase.....465
Pres. Lincoln's Life, written by himself......654
Pres. Lincoln's Message, Curiosity of Rebel Soldiers to hear..........................131
President Lincoln's Military Notation.......258
President Lincoln's Official Likeness........514
President Lincoln's Presidential Prospects....42
President Lincoln's Representative Recruit...191
President Washington's Summary Dealing with Rebellion..........................118
Presidential Favor at last for Everybody......85
Pretty Widows and Imprisoned Lovers.......628
Price and Van Dorn pitted against Rosecrans289
Price of Chivalry in Hard Cash..............50
Private Notions and Public Laws...........202
Private W. in Love and Luck...............610
"Pro Patria" Pictures at the Soldiers' Fair..548
Pro-Southern Dominie Delineated...........65
Promises of Bravery in Advance............264
Prompt Administration of the Law..........71
Prompt Settlement of a Claim...............482
Proof Against Federal Gallantry............569
Prospective Value of the War................54
Protection under the Constitution............96
Provisional Gov't of Ky. on an Excursion....41
Public Opinion Baths......................644
Pumpkin Pie Story of Lieut. Wickfield and Gen. Grant..............................463
Purging the Prayer Book...................121
Putting 'em through a Course of Sprouts.....52
Putting him through the Discipline.........403
Putting his Hand to the Roll................181
Puzzling a Draft Commissioner.............194

### Q.

Quality of Secessionist Oaths...............150
Queer Drafting Scene in Maryland..........195
Question in Infantry Practice...............488
Questions and Replies : "Nothing agin the Old Flag,"...............................76
Quid Pro Quo..............................190
Quite a Safe Place for the Harper's Ferry Flag588
Quite the Youngest Recruit for Uncle Sam....185

### R.

Racy Conversation between Mrs. Polk and Gen. Mitchell on "the Situation,"..............544
Ragged Texans : Boots and Booty..........302
Raising the Flag.............................63
Rallying again for the Battle................247
Rare Page in Woman's History.............543
Rare Trick upon a War Correspondent......476
Rather be a Soldier's Widow than a Coward's Wife...................................620
Rather Doubtful Allegiance.................154
Rather too Spunky for them................390
Ratifying the Ordinance—Startling Scene....78
Raw Captains..............................408
Raw Recruits on Camp Guard..............273

Reading the Amnesty Proclamation at Buzzard's Roost............................124
Ready Mode of meeting Difficulties by Gen. Butler..................................429
Real and Artificial Cock-Tails..............486
Rebuff to a Trafficker in Exemption Papers..194
Reception of the Rebel Commissioner in London by Mr. Bates......................25
Record of a Loyal Family: Five Martyr Sons576
Recruiting Extraordinary....................196
Red River, Brilliant Strategy of General Smith at.................................312
Red, White and Blue,—God's Flag.........545
Redfield's Stolen March....................233
Re-enlisting, but on a Different Side........201
Refusal to Receive Pay for Fighting for his Country.................................468
Refusing to Volunteer in the Rebel Army......106
Regimental Clothes-Washer for the 16th Illin's.205
Reinforcement of Fort Pickens—How it was Done...................................395
Reliable Information.......................465
Relieved through the Mercy of Death.......581
Remember Fort Pillow !....................305
Reporters on a Bender.....................480
Reporting at the Front.....................300
Representative Recruit for Pres. Lincoln,....191
Resaca, Joe Johnston's Whipping at........326
Retort Courteous from an American in Paris to M. Thouvenel..........................73
Revenge upon a Goose for Hissing at the National Air..............................447
Reward of a Speech after Fifteen Years from its Delivery.............................643
Reynolds' (Mrs.) Ap't as a Major in the Army268
Rice (Gen.) to his Mother..................615
Rich by Shoddy Contracts..................490
Richardson Initiating his Escape............584
Richmond, Gen'ls. Grant and Meade in Consultation before..........................256
Richmond War News Wanted..............465
Rigging up a ' Long Tom' out of Billy Luly.386
Right kind of Gov't to be established Down South....................................87
Right Word in the Right Place.............539
River Devils for carrying on the War.......383
River Steamers and Yankee Pilots..........369
Robbery by Mistake........................594
Roberts's Half-Hour's Visit at Island No. 10.358
Rockafellow's Right Arm left still..........285
Roiled because he could not Fight..........187
Romantic Adventure of a Tenn. Loyalist.....98
"Root Hog or Die"—Music hath Charms....242
Rosecrans, and Pat's Furlo'................411
Rosecrans and Vallandigham coming to an Understanding...........................138
Rosecrans—Price and Van Dorn pitted ag'st.289
Rosecrans's Orderly Sergeant Delivered of a Baby in Camp...........................554

INDEX TO THE LEADING ANECDOTES AND INCIDENTS. 703

Rosseau's First Step towards making Loyal Men of Rebels........................63
*Rubbing it in—Scene in the Park Barr'ks, N.Y.*596
Running an Engine in the Confed. Service...454
*Ruse to obtain a Furlough*..................406

**S.**

Sad Result of Patriotic Courage in a Youth.169
Saddling to Suit the Route................513
Safe Across the River.....................255
Sailing into the Jaws of the Mohican......370
*Sailors and Sweethearts on the Ohio*........387
Samaritanism of the Genuine Type.........534
Same old Planter's Crochet................119
Saved a Comrade's Life but Lost his Own...297
*Scarcely Seventeen Years but a Heroine*.....582
Scared before being Hurt..................364
Scene at Fort Warren: Exit of Mason and Slidell.................................133
Scene in the President's Room, the Evening preceding the First Proclamation for Troops.29
*Scene of Domestic Sadn's: Woman's Firmn's*.200
Schaeffer and Ould at a Joke—Cities Built and in Embryo.........................69
Schoepf's (Gen.) Banking Operations in Ky.469
Scott (General), Command of the Virginia Forces Tendered to.....................71
Scott's Plan of the War...................232
Scouting the Doctrine that Majorities are to Rule..................................84
Secesh Taming............................97
*Secession Damsels and Federal Foragers*.....460
Second Reflection in the Looking Glass.....648
Secret of the Unanimous Vote in the Senate..49
Sec'y Stanton and Gen. Butler on an Official Point.................................436
*Sedgwick's Present of a Turkey*.............474
Seeking a Naval Appointment..............375
Semmes outwitting the Vanderbilt..........379
Senator Douglas's Last Message to his Sons..127
Senator Lane and the Stage Driver.........111
*Senor B. and the Confed. Brigadier's Daughter*609
Sentiments of a Dying Soldier..............53
Sentry Encounter with a "Regular,".......402
Sergeant Davis's Tender Beef..............453
*Serious Indisposition of Two Uncles*........431
*Settling an Irish Volunteer Case*............166
Seven Rebels captured by One Fed.........314
"Shackasses" just at the Right Moment....244
Shaken-Down among the Pickets............412
Shaking Hands in the Middle of the River...283
Shaky Abutments...........................74
"Shameful Tyranny" of Butler in N. Orleans.495
Sharing Gen. Magruder's Table.............478
Sharp Practice among Volunteers......... 210
Sharp Practice of Confederate Cruisers in English Waters........................381
*She Loved a Soldier Lad*...................580
*Shenandoah, Flight from the*...............505

Sheridan and the Moonlight Picture.........280
Sheridan at Stone River............ .....289
Sheridan Riding to the Front..............315
Sherman Outflanked for Once..............438
Sherman Watching the Capture of Fort McAllister....... ...........................295
Sherman's Absence of Mind................589
Sherman's Courage before the Enemy.......274
Sherman's Heroism on Battle-field of Shiloh..253
Shoe-Raid by Gen. Wadsworth.............458
Shotted Salute at Midnight from Grant to Lee324
Shultz's Timely Discovery.................512
Sickness after Furlough....................427
Signaling for Sherman....................392
Silence of a Drummer-Boy before the Flag..240
*Silk-Petticoats—Southern Fashion*..........497
Simple but Effective Point taken by Mr. Lincoln in a Capital Case....................654
Sinking the Albemarle Ram in the bottom of the Roanoke.............................371
Sir Frederick's Question Answered.........651
Six Generals waiting to Receive Battle......335
Sixteen Brothers in One Regiment..........205
*Sixth Massachusetts Regiment's Daughter*.....535
*Skull-bone Memento kept by a Lady*..........619
Slave Insurrection Foiled by Union Generals...76
Sleeper's Saucy Battery....................311
Slidell's Consolation......................131
Smith's Brilliant Strategy at Red River.....312
Smuggling "the critter" into Camp.........483
Snake-Hunter's Style of Drill..............406
Snaked Away and Drummed In..............213
Sold !...................................404
Sold by his Intended Victim...............218
Soldier Mechanics.........................509
Soldiers' Offering at the Grave of Washington Irving................................556
Sole Condition for Re-enlisting............176
Solemn Scene at Midnight..................31
Solitary and Alone in Favor of Grant.......655
*Solution of a Problem Peculiarly Southern*....569
Some Mistake in the Card..................24
Something to Cogitate Upon................164
Song of Patriotism in the Forest...........268
Sources of Merriment .....................269
South Carolina, Circulation of Union Proclamations in............................109
South Carolina Described by Judge Pettigru...74
South Carolina Union Men Safe in Jackson's Day..................................121
Southern Black-Horse Guards and Yankee Fire-Zouaves..........................238
*Southern Female Chivalry*..................571
*Southern War Widows*......................603
*Special Aid to General Hunter*..............567
Specimen of Ninth Corps Discipline........470
*Speedy Realization of an Angry Wish*.......525
*Spirit of a Kentucky Girl*..................538
Spirited Fight between Two Girls at Church...593

# 704 INDEX TO THE LEADING ANECDOTES AND INCIDENTS.

'Spiritual' Revelations on the Conduct of the War .................................................. 50
Splendid Service in a Bad Cause ........... 276
Springfield, Capital Ruse to Save ........... 267
Sprinkling Blood in the Face of the Nation ... 88
St. Louis Oath-Taking ............................ 115
Stanton and the "Old General," ............ 149
Stanton's First Meeting with Cabinet Traitors 34
Startling Adventure of Gen. Birney ......... 234
Stating it Just Right ........................... 286
Stating the Exact Alternative ............... 126
Steedman taking the Flag ..................... 317
Stewart (Gen.) too Late to Dinner .......... 464
Sticking to the Original Order .............. 426
Stone River, Phil. Sheridan at .............. 293
Stonewall Jackson's Enl't in the Union Army 183
Strange Blotch on Calhoun's Right Hand ..... 39
Stray Leaf in the Vicksburg Campaign ..... 225
"Strictly Confidential," ....................... 502
Strong (Capt.) Delivering his Revolvers .... 259
*Strong Case of Conscience* .................. 175
Strong Professional Illustration ........... 271
Style of Clearing off a Table by Gen. Butler.482
Substit'e Broker Sold: Indians for the Army 180
Such a Sight as Thrills the Nerves ......... 130
*Sue Munday, the Female Guerrilla* ......... 596
Sumter, Unfortunate Absence at the Siege of. 101
Sumter (Pirate), Lucky Moment on board the 373
Sunk with the Stars and Stripes still Waving 362
*Supper for All—Woman's Goodness* ........ 578
"Swamp Angel" Incident ..................... 480
Swear him in and let him go! ............... 114
Swearing-in a Cook for the 1st Iowa Cavalry.447
*Sweet Seventeen Overhauling the Secessionists*..541
*Sweet Sixteen on the Mule side, and a 'Darling' too* ......................................... 209
*Sweetness of Secession Female Temper* ..... 599

## T.

Table-Turning at the Recruiting Office ..... 171
*Tableau Political* ............................ 117
Taken in and done for ........................ 160
Taking a Hint .................................. 380
Taking his Choice ............................. 140
*Talk with a Pretty Secession Miss* ........ 522
Tapping the Telegraph Wires ................. 477
Tarpaulin Raking a Traitor Fore and Aft... 351
*Tender Burial of a Union Drummer-Boy by Two Girls* ................................... 522
Tender in Years but strong in Devotion to his Country ..................................... 207
*Tenderness of the President towards the Lowly*.217
Tennessee, Fight with the Iron Monster ..... 385
Tennessee Loyalist's Romantic Adventure ... 98
*Tenth of May at Irwinville* .................. 648
Terrible Encounter—Texas and Iowa ........ 239
Terry's Colored Cook and his Shell ......... 456
*Tete-a-Tete with the Old Admiral* .......... 390
*Texas Flag captured by the 16th Indiana* ... 312
That Card from Willard's Hotel .............. 49

That Dinner at Gen. Holt's .................. 470
*That Flag is Doubly Dear to me this Morning!*588
*That Flag Presentation in New Orleans* .... 94
That is my Brother! .......................... 519
The Day and the Event ........................ 394
The Last Battery in Lee's Army .............. 659
Them and Theirs—not Us ...................... 99
They had heard of him ........................ 73
Thirteen Battles and Three Flags ........... 246
Thirty Tremendous Minutes ................... 357
"Thpit on It," ................................ 228
Three German Flank Movements ............... 486
*Three Hundred Ladies with their Union Flags*.85
*Three Noble Union Girls* .................... 626
Three Soldiers captured by a Boy with a Coffee Pot ..................................... 337
Tigers and Treason ........................... 103
Tilden's Lucky Escape ........................ 342
*Tilghman, the Rebel General, and his Mother*..556
To the Manor Born ............................. 93
*Tod (Gov.), and the Applicant for Exempt'n*..185
Told the Truth at the Right Time ........... 331
Tom Taylor's Flag of Truce .................. 416
Too Brave a Man to Disarm ................... 264
Too Fond of Chestnuts ........................ 320
Toombs's Idea of Passports .................. 426
Tough Time with a Mule ...................... 452
Tracing his Political Pedigree .............. 87
*Tracts vs. Pound Cake* ...................... 521
Tragedy of Ellsworth's Assassination ....... 321
Tragical Death of General Baker ............ 319
Tragical Encounter between Generals Nelson and Davis .................................. 413
Traitor Generals conferring over the "Last Ditch," .................................... 229
Transfer of 'President Davis's' Table Service 657
Treason in an Unexpected Quarter ........... 92
*Treason's Badge in a New York Ball Room*...111
Treating his Guests to a Good Drink ........ 659
Treating them according to their Sympathies..27
Tricks and Tactics in the Ranks ............. 433
Tricks to Avoid Duty ......................... 428
*Troubles of a Feminine "Secesh"* ........... 431
Two College-Mates Cols. in Opposing Armies 229
*Two Desertions—a Double Tragedy* .......... 158
Two Kings at the South ....................... 91
*Two Made One: the Sergeant and the Daughter of the Regiment* ........................ 527
*Two Noble Women Saving a Regiment* ....... 245
Two Things that Sounded Alike ............... 387
Tyler (Gen.), and his Staff, Escape of ..... 251

## U.

*Umbrellas in Military Service* .............. 368
Unacquainted with Politics .................. 97
Uncle Sam's Mule Cleaners ................... 445
Uncomfortably Warm Place for a Soldier .... 286
Unconsciously a Hero ......................... 496
Under Lock and Key ........................... 655
*Under the Star Spangled Banner* ............ 73

# INDEX TO THE LEADING ANECDOTES AND INCIDENTS. 705

Unexpected Rebuff......................142
Unfortunate Absence at the Siege of Fort Sumter................................101
Unintentional Trick taught by an Examining Physician............................186
Union Men safe in South Carolina in General Jackson's Day........................121
Unknown Lady Visitor at the N. O. Fleet.....354
Unquestionably a Hard Case...............204
Unrequited Gallantry in a N. O. Street Car...564
Unsuccessful Search for Information at Headquarters................................471
Unuttered Thought of a Dying Soldier.......537
Unwilling to Forfeit his Right to Escape.....107
Up the Cumberland—Grit of the Old Major...394

## V.

Vallandigham's Talk with the Ohio Toll-Gate Keeper................................48
Vanderbilt (Steamer) Outwitted by Semmes.379
Van Dorn and Price pitted against Rosecrans289
Vanity of Patriotism and Honor............70
Verbal Sharpshooting.....................537
Very Obliging Picket at Morris Island......280
Very Pleasant Surprise for Two............580
Vice President Breckinridge's Son..........327
Vice President Hamlin a Private in Co. A...100
Vicksburg Campaign, Stray Leaf in the.....225
Vicksburg Caves, In and Out of the..........606
Vicksburg, How the Flag was Planted at....306
Vicksburg Picket Repartee.................335
Virginia, Entombment of a Loyalist in......106
Virginia, First Oath and Testim'y of a Slave in90
Virginia, First "Union" Demonstration in Old602
Virginia Forces, Command Tendered to General Scott..............................71
Virginia—Instance of Loyalty..............551
Visit of Gen. Jenkins at a Penn. Editor's....461
Voting for a Candidate on Principle.........28

## W.

Wadsworth's (Gen.) Shoe Raid.............458
Wanted a Furlough........................429
Wanted to draw on the Blue Clothes........170
War Dispatches in Church.................151
War News from Richmond Wanted.........465
War's Doings to One Family................202
Wash. Litchtiter, one of Morgan's Converts..154
Washington's (John A.), Ignoble End......341
Watch kept by a Dog over Lieut. Pfieff's Grave587
Waving the Stars and Stripes from the Summit of Lost Mountain...................303
Wedding-Table Flag at Pensacola...........566
Weitzel Satisfied with the Twelfth Conn.....415
Welcome to the Troops at Port Royal.......94
Well Done for a Youth....................246

Western Regiments on a Charge at Fort Donelson...................................266
Western Soldier's Characteristic Pluck......296
Western Steamboat Saved by a Woman......359
Western Zeal in Volunteering..............186
"Where's dat Nigger ?"....................430
What Mr. Lincoln said to a N. Orleans Editor449
What One Noble Woman Did..............450
When Gen. Buckner hung his Head........415
When will the War end ?..................113
Where are they ?..........................138
Where is your Heart ?.....................75
Which Side ?..............................92
Whisper Good-Night, Love!................559
Whiz-z-z and Whist........................266
Why John Rawley became a Substitute......197
Widow Shultz's Appeal to the President......434
Wigs on Rebel Majors.....................258
Wilkinson's Veteran Minnesota Regiment....58
Willing to part with his other Leg..........397
Wilson's (Billy) Zouaves — Extraordinary Scene..................................184
Wine and Sentiment for the Hospital Soldiers.598
Wisconsin Body-Guard for the President....187
Witnessing and Dying for the Truth in Miss.120
Wolford's Cavalry—not Yankees...........308
Woman as a Dernier Resort.................616
Woman's Tongue betraying the Rebel Torpedoes at Fort Henry......................589
Woman's Trials and Triumph...............472
Won his Wager............................279
Wood and Wedded—with Embellishments....600
Work of a Second..........................301
Working the Monster Parrott Gun..........508
Worse than being Drafted..................198
Worse to lose Five than One—Gen. Grant's Philosophy............................411

## Y.

Yankee Doodle in the Storm of Shot.......356
Yankee Forever !..........................193
Yankee Pris'ner 'scaped from Richmon'.....612
Yates (Gov.) Giving Grant a Desk in his Office.................................405
Yielding only when he Lost his Head.......261
Yorktown Negro Rifleman brought down....319
Young America at Fort Donelson..........227
Young Feminine Spoiling for a Fight........605
Young Woman (A) Shoots a Guerrilla to Avenge the Murder of her Lover..........617

## Z.

Zealous for the Cause but not for the Scrip...460
Zollicoffer's Death at the Hands of Col. Fry.237
"Zou ! Zou ! Zou !".......................310
Zouaves on Picket Duty....................237

Milton Keynes UK
Ingram Content Group UK Ltd.
UKHW020846030424
440506UK00008B/1051